Footprint South India

Annie Dare
3rd edition

It has been my long-standing conviction that India is like a donkey carrying a sack of gold … The load of gold is the fantastic treasure – in arts, literature, culture, and some sciences like Ayurvedic medicine – which we have inherited from the days of the splendor that was India.

Nani Ardeshir Palkhiwala (Indian lawyer & philanthropist)

❶ Thieves' bazar
Browse Bollywood memorabilia and Indian antiques at this Mumbai market, page 449.

❷ Football match
Goans are fanatical about football; catch a match in Mapusa or Margao, pages 381 and 406.

❸ Anjuna Flea
Hippies, gypsies, snake charmers and charter tourists rub shoulders at this eye-popping jamboree on Goa's most legendary beach, page 390.

❹ Old Goa
The Portuguese Empire's eastern answer to Rome crumbles elegantly under the thick forest canopy, page 371.

❺ Gokarna
Unspoilt secluded beaches, including an Om-shaped stretch of sand, tempt backpackers away from Goa, page 295.

❻ Bijapur
Atmospheric, tomb-strewn landscape of the Deccani sultans, page 304.

❼ Hampi
Dawn breaks over the boulders of the Hindu kingdom capital of Hampi, page 300.

❽ Hyderabad
Shop for pearls in the bedlam of Muslim souks in this dotcom capital, page 326.

❾ Backwaters
Soak up Keralite waterfront life on a boat trip along endlessly intersecting rivers, page 196.

❿ Mysore
Don't miss the colourful 10-day Dasara celebrations, page 269.

South India Highlights
See colour maps at back of book

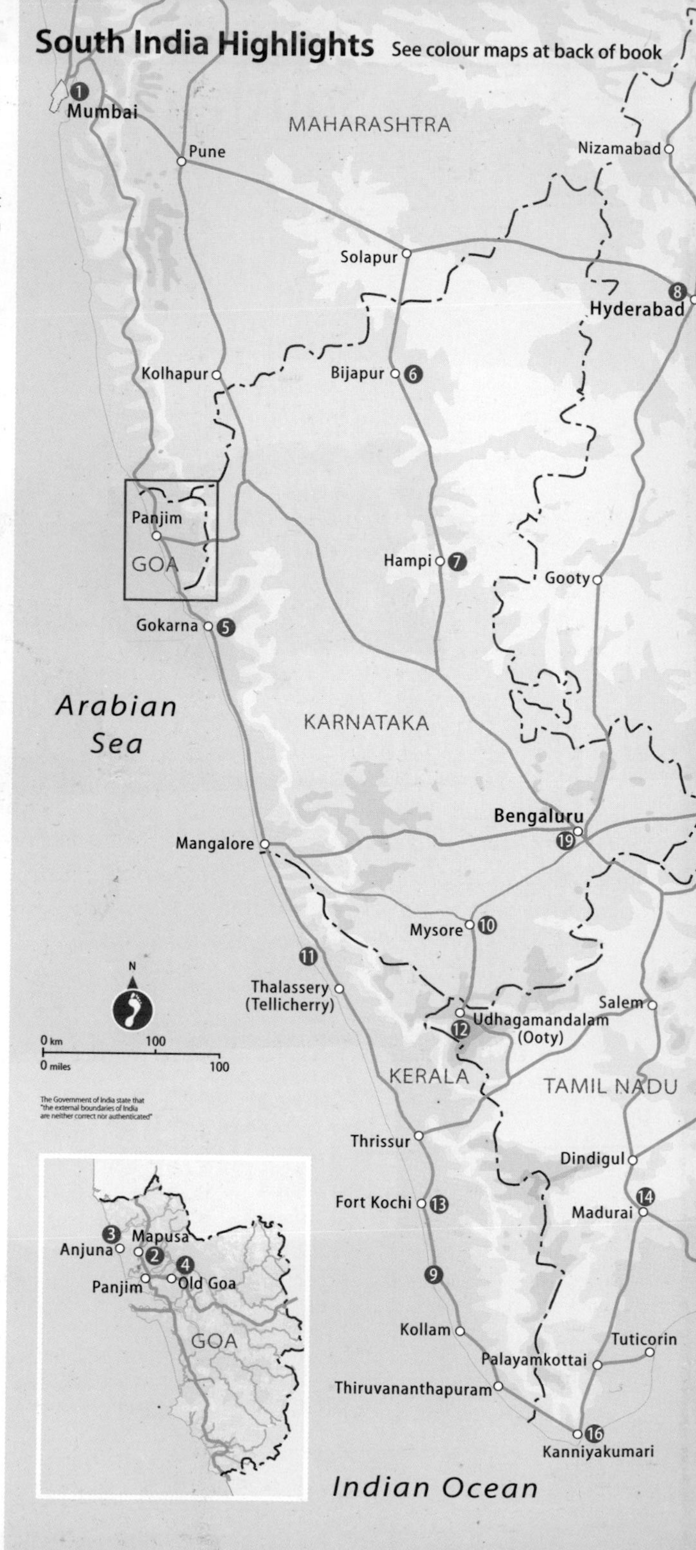

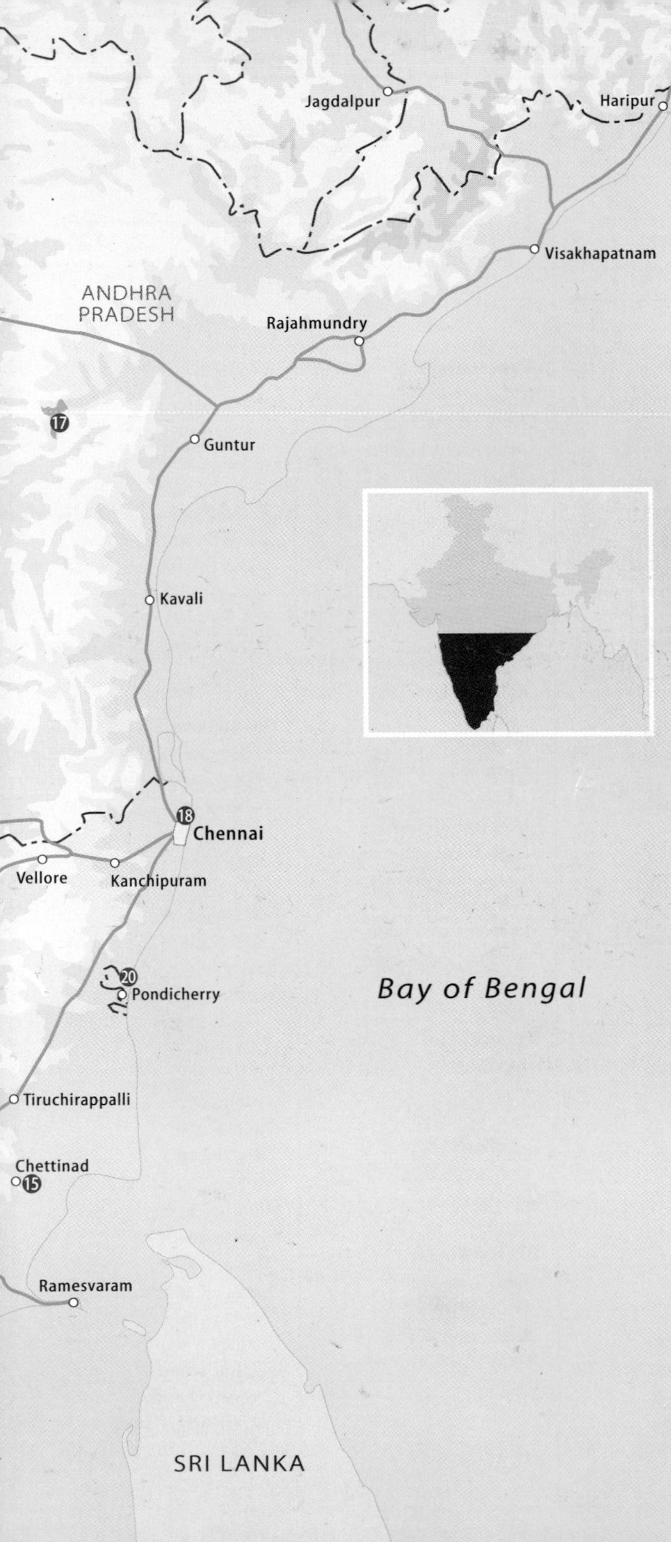

⑪ Malabar Coast
Clashing swords of martial artists and temple dances of the possessed, page 237.

⑫ Ooty
Puff up the rack-and-pinion railway on the steam train to this 'Queen of Hill Stations', page 133.

⑬ Fort Kochi
Watch dusk fall over Fort Kochi harbour, lined with Chinese fishing nets, page 208.

⑭ Madurai
Lose yourself in the heady swirl of the temple of the fish-eyed goddess, page 153.

⑮ Chettinad
Wander the palace-filled ghost towns of the Chettiar caste, page 159.

⑯ Kanniyakumari
India's holy toe-tip: here the moon sets and sun rises in the waters where three seas meet, page 166.

⑰ Nagarjunakonda Island
Board a boat to reach one of India's oldest Buddhist sites, page 338.

⑱ Chennai
Explore the Shiva Kapaleeshwarar temple, Chennai's oldest, in Mylapore, page 77.

⑲ Bengaluru (Bangalore)
The cool and cosmopolitan heart of India's silicon valley, page 257.

⑳ Pondicherry
The old French enclave still retains a gallic flavour, page 107.

Contents

Life in the slow lane on National Highway 47 in Kerala.

Karnataka 251

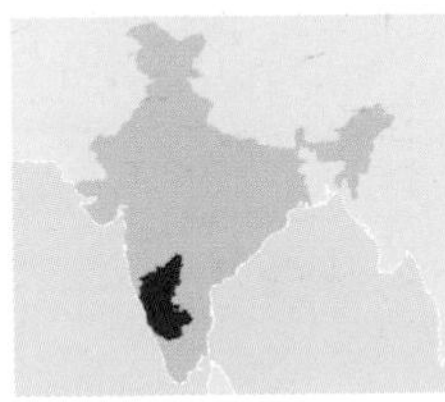

Andhra Pradesh 321

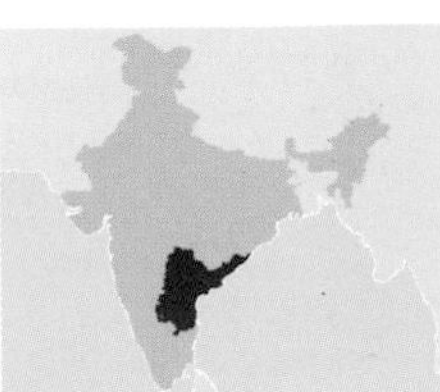

Coasting it

Coco-huts to rent for a song, hammocks strung under coconut trees and pristine sand are just a few features attracting young and hip European travellers to Palolem Beach, Goa.

Channel hopping

Breathtaking vistas of mangrove swamp, lotus flowers and water hyacinth open up along the canals criss-crossing Kerala's famously lyrical Backwaters.

A foot in the door

South India is a spellbinding intersection of old and new, and is the best place to grasp the nature of the colossus that is modern day India. A quick-changing place that clings hard to its past, it stands at the very apex of those paradoxical forces that make the subcontinent today so fascinating and dynamic.

The thriving southern cities, where fast-talking graduate professionals ride the crest of the globalization wave against a backdrop of wide British-built boulevards and Gothic architecture, are prime engines of India's recent economic growth. But beyond these cities of software chips, biotech booms and shopping malls lies a land singularly unmoved by the upheaval of burgeoning business. There is the tropical calm of Kerala's bucolic backwaters, the splendid insouciance of Goa's Portuguese-steeped villages and the riotous exuberance of Hindu temples teeming with gaudy gods and braying demons. Streaming bazars bustle and dusty markets are crammed with marigold garlands and spice sacks. Sacked Hindu empires exude their bewitching beauty while all that remains of spent Muslim dynasties are brooding tombs.

From paddy fields, coconut groves and mangrove thickets come enchanting glimpses of meringue-white churches and blue-tiled synagogues. Between spice plantations and hill stations lies parkland overrun with elephants and monkeys, while giddying waterfalls crash to the floor of forests packed with precious flora and fauna. Along the spectacular coastline beaches are lapped by the warm waters of the Andaman Sea and Indian Ocean.

As with the whole subcontinent, expect excess in everything. Come prepared for a colour palette running riot in its vibrancy, a lush and relaxed kaleidoscope of what India has been and what India is bracing herself to become.

Contemporary India

In the 60 years since Independence, India has gone through nothing short of a revolution. The prospect of bankruptcy in 1991 forced the country to adopt a programme of dramatic economic reform that has turned India into the world's fourth largest economy, with political ambitions to match: an enthusiastic campaigner for a permanent seat on the UN Security Council, with its first moon probe slated for 2008.

Manmohan Singh, the architect of the policy shift when he was finance minister, has been India's prime minister since 2004. His reforms – slashing taxes and lifting trade restrictions to knit India into the global economy while restructuring the public sector and breaking up monopolies – have let India harvest the fruits of globalization and have recently propelled the country to the top of the Forbes Asian rich list for the first time. Nowhere is the change as visible as in the south: Mumbai, seat of the famous film industry, leads the charge with its booming stock market and financial services centre, while Bengaluru (Bangalore) and Hyderabad boast the

Cyber city

India's dramatic leap in technological and software services has transformed the once sleepy state capital of Bengaluru (Bangalore) into the country's answer to Silicon Valley – a dynamic, cosmopolitan Mecca.

futuristic campuses of homegrown software giants Infosys and Wipro. Chennai's automotive industry could well outpace Detroit's, while Fort Kochi, long synonymous with the romantic silhouettes of its medieval Chinese fishing nets and famous as the jumping-off point for lyrical Backwater tours, is to be remade, with Dubai development money, into a major modern international container port.

India's middle class has ballooned – at last count 250 million people, representing a quarter of India's population – but not everyone has shared in India's new success; the disparities between India's new rich and its legion poor are alarmingly pronounced. India's population is 70% rural, 40% of the world's poor are reckoned to live here and half of India's children are malnourished. And, while the south is generally more enlightened than the north and there's less fanatical religious politics, dogma has not diminished with all India's economic development. The subcontinent holds 165 million Dalits or 'untouchables' and social and gender hierarchy remains a key fault line for discrimination and violence.

Holy cow!
The Jallikattu festival, a twist on the Spanish bull run, sees hundreds of bulls sent bucking down a seething human corridor of tens of thousands of Tamil men.

1

2

4

5

7

8

10

11

3

6

9

12

1 *Mumbai's Gateway of India was the ceremonial departure point for the last British regiment at the end of the colonial rule.* ▸▸ *See page 434.*

2 *Huge cantilevered fishing nets stand in silhouette against the deep-water harbour off Fort Kochi.* ▸▸ *See page 208.*

3 *The Qutb Shahi Tombs in Hyderabad, Andhra Pradesh.* ▸▸ *See page 335.*

4 *Huge, mono-crop tea plantations still cover much of the misty Western Ghat mountains.* ▸▸ *See page 219.*

5 *Krishna's Butterball, an immoveable boulder balanced above lifelike bas reliefs at Mahabalipuram.* ▸▸ *See page 89.*

6 *Colourful Lambada and Banjara gypsy women from Karnataka and Andhra Pradesh hawk their wares at Goa's famous flea market in Anjuna.* ▸▸ *See page 390.*

7 *In theyyam, a flamboyant pre-dawn ritual of North Kerala, divine spirits possess temple dancers' bodies to re-enact local legends and bless families.* ▸▸ *See page 237.*

8 *Tens of thousands clatter daily under the brightly painted stucco gateways of Madurai's grand, medieval Meenakshi Temple compound.* ▸▸ *See page 153.*

9 *The beautiful grassland and dense forests in Eravikulam National Park, Kerala.* ▸▸ *See page 226.*

10 *The Indo-Saracenic city palace lends a little fairytale magic to the felicitous jumble that is Mysore: a city of flower stalls, silks and sandalwood in Karnataka.* ▸▸ *See page 269.*

11 *For 200 years the seat of a Hindu empire covering South India, Hampi's wondrous relics are now home to gypsies, backpackers and monkeys.* ▸▸ *See page 300.*

12 *Ganesh, the elephant god, is revered across India, but in Kerala elephants have special significance. Many temples have their own and here, one elephant is bejewelled for a festival.* ▸▸ *See page 171.*

Temple trailers

South India is considered the heartland of pure Hinduism and no state more so than Tamil Nadu: 90% Hindu, worship is omnipresent: roadside shrines are daubed with potash and hung with marigolds and gods are balanced on dashboards. You could spend weeks on the dizzying temple trail alone, with the smell of sacrificial burning camphor in your nostrils and the memory of sculptures black with gingelly smeared over centuries of devotion, a place with endless gods awash with sandal powder, bathed in buttermilk and wreathed with jasmine garlands. But Tamil also yields the crumbling old homes of Gallic Pondicherry and the regal palace ghost towns of Chettinad.

Spice coast

Neighbouring Kerala, a narrow, lush slip of a state by comparison, is where you'll tread a more self-indulgent path to heaven: the life science of Ayurveda, practised at every corner here, can redress imbalanced 'dosha' and ease weary limbs. There are other languid treats too: tarrying through the backwaters on rice boats for a snail's-pace window on waterfront village life, walking round one of South India's most charming towns in the spice sack-littered Fort Kochi and the pleasures of sampling the unsung tastes from Kerala's kitchens. Stews and sweets come laden with the juice and cream of the bumper crop of coconut whose trees cover almost the entire state in a thick blanket of green. Here, too, there are the fabled literacy rates and intellectualism of the enlightened Malayalis themselves – the Keralites are avid consumers of current affairs and you'll find them every bit as ready to discuss politics in the Balkans as the problems in their own backyard.

Pilgrims trace Siva's trident in vermilion and turmeric powder around the extraordinary shrine to Sri Meenakshi, his wife, deep in the heart of the doggedly devout state of Tamil Nadu.

Desolate romance and the remains of inordinate architectural sophistry, as seen at Vittala Temple, are all that's left of the desolate, sacked capital of the Vijayanagar empire at Hampi.

Cool, calm and collected

Sandwiched between Tamil Nadu and Kerala are the hill stations, alpine landscapes packed with pine trees and covered with the stubble of tea shrubs. These are the former summer playgrounds of the imperial Madras Presidency. In their wake the British left planters with 1950s manners and the English language, grand colonial houses and fossilized clubhouses whose walls still drip with sepia photographs of the colonizers' hunts. The natural beauty of the mountains – the spine of the ghats – run north into Karnataka, to the home of the unique and proud warrior Coorg clan. Here, the primary forests yield to coffee plantations whose flowers bloom in a wave of honeysuckle scent.

Roads to ruins

Where Tamil has temples, and Kerala nature, Karnataka, outside cosmopolitan Bengaluru (Bangalore), excels in ruins. Every one of India's major religions is represented – sacked, dog-eared, and half-drowned in dust, but here nonetheless – in the free-standing giant Jain sculpture, in the site of Tipu Sultan's last stand against the British near Mysore and in the ancient Hindu kingdom capital of Vijayanagar at Hampi. Others include the less-visited carvings at Aihole and Badami – as delicate as lace and dainty as doilies – and the onion-dome tombs of the Muslim rulers of the Deccan at Bijapur.

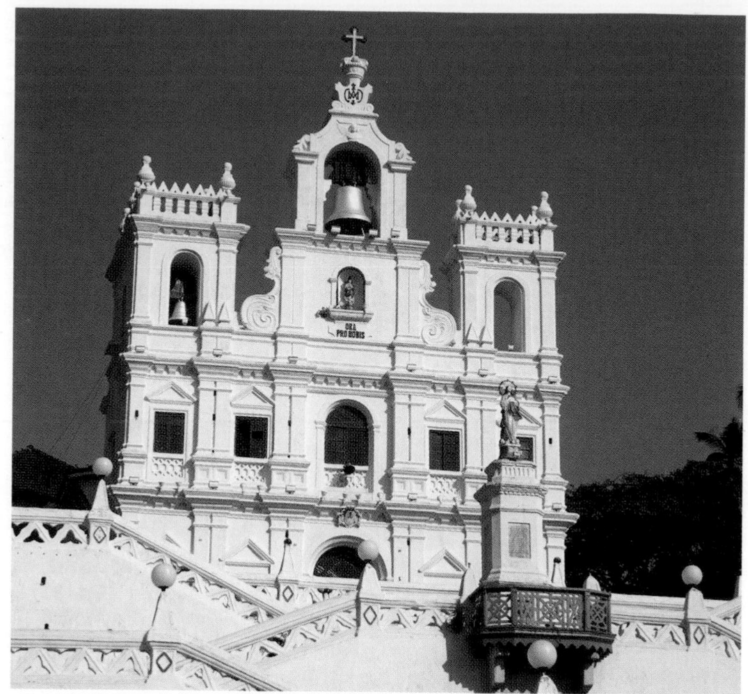

After 400 years of Portuguese rule, Goa was left with a large Catholic population, who still worship at beautiful whitewashed churches like Our Lady of the Immaculate Conception, Panaji.

The Latin quarter

The biggest anomaly of them all comes in the bite-sized chunk of land that is Goa: India's Latin Quarter and the subcontinent's smallest state. Its sights, such as the rococo and baroque marvels in Old Goa, are no match for the giant landmarks of broader India and seldom feature on tourist T-shirts. It's a humbler beauty you'll find here in the homes of the old elite that stand crumbling in the shade of jackfruit trees, in the curious hybrid temples built by the Hindus fleeing Portuguese missionary zeal, in the easy living of a people steeped in the lazy outlook of their Lisbon-based imperial opposite numbers with their gift for wine, food and song. This state is your best bet for seaside hedonism and for swimming in beautiful wide-sweeping bays and tiny, tucked-away coves. Come evening you can choose from jazz-inflected local music to the infamous Freak-inspired dance marathons of Goa Trance, nurse cashew moonshine in any number of poky bars or knock back liquor on a floating casino. Lime-white churches gleam against bright green paddy and skies of unbroken bright blue. More than anywhere else in India – where you can go for weeks, even on the routes of better-established sights, without seeing a foreigner – it's in Goa that you'll be aware of your fellow tourist.

Essentials

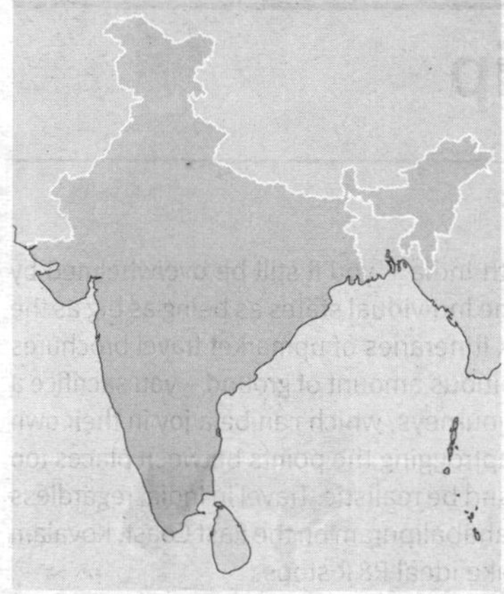

Footprint features

Planning your trip

Where to go

The trick is to not be too ambitious in South India – you'll still be overwhelmed by what you see. Distances are huge (think of the individual states as being as big as the countries of Western Europe). The two-week itineraries of upmarket travel brochures promise enormous variety but cover an ambitious amount of ground – you sacrifice a lot by packing too much in. Ditto long train journeys, which can be a joy in their own right, but you do yourself a disservice by leapfrogging the points between places too much. Instead, think of less as being more, and be realistic. Travel in India, regardless of budget, is tiring. Allow yourself breaks: Mahabalipuram on the East Coast, Kovalam on the West, the hill stations, or Goa, all make ideal R&R stops.

The possibilities for how you invest your time are daunting: there's everything from the cool climates of the lush Western Ghats mountain ranges running like a spine inland of the west coast, to the steamy heat and rich culture of the east coast lowlands. You could travel for weeks without seeing it all. Prioritize what you want from any one trip, and, perhaps the best advice of all, come back.

Three weeks is just enough to skate through some of the South's highlights. To get the most out of this type of time frame you could consider internal flights – India has a low-cost airline industry as competitive as Europe's – but to curb carbon emissions pursue routes along the networks of road and rail, and see much more of the landscape. Your best bet is to limit yourself and properly explore one region in depth rather than trying to notch up the sights against an exhaustive inventory.

Unless you have a fetish for bureaucracy you'd do well to use the travel agents listed throughout the book to make your transport bookings for you. Their fees are negligible, and the time they can save you is immense. Trains, though, can now be booked online which cuts down queuing immeasurably.

Goa and the Deccan

One month For Goa and the Deccan the easiest entry point is either Goa's Dabolim airport (via charter flights) or via the subcontinent's economic capital, Mumbai. The metros of Hyderabad and Bengaluru (Bangalore) are within realistic striking distance and both should have direct flight connections with the UK soon. The Konkan railway has brought Mumbai within comfortable reach of Goa which, after a night on the tiles in the big smoke, is the ideal antidote. Acclimatize in this, India's Latin quarter, with easy living, relaxed dress codes, excellent food and experienced tourist infrastructure. There's still plenty here that unimaginative tourism has left unexplored, but once you've had a swim, shopped at the flea, and had a good look at the Portuguese churches of Old Goa, Chandor, you can push on into Karnataka – south to Gokarna for a beautiful beach-cum-seething pilgrim centre, or east for prize culture in the ruins of a homegrown vanquished empire at Hampi, stone-masonry cut like lace at Badami, Pattadakal and Aihole and the onion tombs of the Deccan's Islamic rulers at Bijapur. Keep east to pursue the Muslim trail: Gulbarga and Bidar make fascinating stops on the road to the old fort of Golconda, the Qutb Shahi tombs, taking you to the one-time capital of the Nizam's princely state, in the hi tech city of Hyderabad. From here fly to Chennai and the British Fort Area, then catch your breath at Mahabalipuram's shore temple before stopping at Pondicherry for a slice of Gallic India. Great Hindu temples are scattered across Tamil Nadu's central plains, and Srirangam near Trichy and Madurai offer access to some of the most spectacular. From Madurai it is possible to experience a

Packing for India

Travel light. It's possible to get most essentials in larger cities and shops in five-star hotels. Here are some items you might find helpful: loose-fitting, light cotton clothes including a sarong. Remember that women should dress modestly at all times; brief shorts and tight vest tops are best avoided, though on the beach modest swimwear is fine. Locally bought inexpensive and cool *kurta pyjama* for men, and *shalwar kameez* for women are excellent options on the plains but it can be cold in the north December to February and also everywhere over 1500 m, where some heavier clothing is essential. Comfortable shoes, sandals or trainers are essential. Take high-factor sun screen and a sun hat. It's almost impossible to buy film outside the 100 to 400 ASA range.

Indian pharmacies can be very cheap but aren't always reliable, so take a supply of medicines from home, including inhalers and anti-malarial drugs (Proguanil is not available). For protection against mosquitoes, take Mosiguard repellent. See also Health, page 52.

Photocopies of documents, passport ID and visa pages, and spare photos are useful when applying for permits or in case of loss or theft.

For budget travellers: nets aren't always provided in cheap hotels so take an impregnated mosquito net. Earplugs are handy. Take a good padlock to secure your budget room too, though these are cheaply bought in India hardware stores too. A cotton or silk sheet sleeping bag are useful when you can't be sure of clean linen.

complete change of climate and scenery by climbing the Western Ghats to the tiger reserve at Periyar. From Periyar, a day's journey takes you to Kerala's west coast port of Kochi where the pre-British Jewish and Dutch connections can be traced. From here you can sample the idyllic backwaters in a rice boat before returning by plane to Mumbai.

Karnataka and Malabar

Two to three weeks It makes sense to combine Bengaluru (Bangalore) and Mysore – and Tipu Sultan's palace at Srirangapatnam – with a trip to Hassan and the wonderful Hindu temples at Belur and Halebid and the monolithic freestanding Jain sculpture at Sravanabelagola. From here head for the old Kodagu (Coorg) capital Madikeri, south of Hassan, an excellent place to relax and get a feel of the unspoilt hill country. Stay in the mountains for Sultan's Battery and the Waynad, Kerala's little explored jungly coffee plantation country, crossing over to Tamil Nadu for Ooty and Coonoor and clipped tea trees, or, if you've already had your fill of the high country, slip straight down into North Kerala – 'Malabar'. Telicherry, Kannur and Calicut all offer a fascinating insight into the Moplah community and a side of Kerala very distinct from the God of Small Things script. Don't skip Fort Kochi and the backwaters country that begins on the city's fringes – the Christian belt of Kottayam and its environs.

Temple trail

Two to three weeks You can really overdose on temples in Tamil Nadu: start off at Chennai for nearby seaside Mahabalipuram with its rock-cut and structural temples. If you are feeling energetic you can take a day trip to see either the great temples of Kanchipuram, also famous as a silk making town, or the fort at Gingee and the magnificent temple at Tiruvannamalai. Continue to the centres of ancient Tamil culture with remarkable temples at Chidambaram, and stop at Swamimalai, where exquisite deities are still cast in solid bronze, to visit Darasuram, Kumbakonam and Gangaikondacholapuram en route to Thanjavur and Madurai. Return via Trichy and Srirangam to Chennai.

Making more of a Kerala beach package

Two to three weeks Fly to Thiruvananthapuram on a charter and take advantage of the good value package holiday on the beach at **Kovalam** for 14-21 days. From there you can visit the museums in the Kerala capital and venture further south along the coast. A long day allows you to visit the atmospheric old wooden palace at Padmanabhapuramand to go to the very tip of the peninsula at **Kanniyakumari** with the Vivekananda Rock out at sea. Take a few days away from your beach hotel and explore the interior, travelling by car or bus through rubber plantations beyond Kottayam, the heart of Christian Kerala, up to the tea gardens on the high hills at **Munnar**. Go and see the rich mixture of East and West in **Kochi** and sample the backwaters on a riceboat, before driving back to Kovalam.

Wildlife tours

South India's distinctive habitats are home to some outstanding reserves which offer many opportunities for seeing wildlife. The suggested tours take you to the most popular of these and also allow excursions to cultural sites. Most national parks charge foreigners Rs 100-350 per head for entry. Bear in mind though that camera fees, vehicle charges and guides (usually compulsory), can add a lot to the cost.

20 days Start in **Chennai** (2) to visit the bird sanctuary of **Vedanthangal** and **Mahabalipuram**(2), by the sea, with its ancient temples. Then travel down to **Trichy** (2) to climb up the rock fort and see the great temple of Srirangam on the banks of the Kaveri. From there the route continues to the hill station of **Coonoor** (2) going up to **Udhagamandalam** (Ooty) (1) on the Blue Mountain railway (if it is running), then on to the rich wildlife sanctuary of **Mudumalai-Bandipur** (3). Travelling north into Karnataka, you can visit the beautiful national park of **Nagarhole** (3). A stop in **Mysore** (3) gives a chance to visit and stay in palaces, and to see Tipu Sultan's **Srirangapatnam** before ending the tour at **Bengaluru (Bangalore)** (2).

The numbers in brackets after the place names indicate suggested number of nights' stay.

Sampling the south

Three weeks From **Chennai** (2) drive to **Swamimalai** (2) known for traditional bronze casting and continue south to the ancient Tamil temples at **Thanjavur** (2) and **Madurai** (2). A morning start allows a stop at **Padmanabhapuram Palace** on the way across to Kerala on the west coast to relax by the beach at **Kovalam** (3), which is near Thiruvananthapuram. Take a boat along the backwaters as you move to **Kochi** (3), a fascinating meeting point of Eastern and European cultures. Then drive across to the tea estates of **Munnar** (2), high in the Western Ghats before dropping to the Tamil plains to visit the ancient fort and temples at **Trichy** (2) and **Srirangam**. Before returning home from Chennai, stop by the sea for the rock-cut cave temples at **Mahabalipuram** (3).

Longer trips

With six weeks, allow yourself longer rest breaks, stop in between the more landmark sites, so for example from Chennai and Mahabalipuram you can explore Gingee's historic fort and the temple town of Tiruvannamalai, then head for the active religious centres like Chidambaram, Kumbakonum and Trichy, or more deserted temples at Thanjavur, Gangakondaicholapuram or Darasuram. From the former French colonial

town of Pondicherry you can venture into the Aurobindo Ashram and the utopian planned city of Auroville nearby.

With more time, too, you could travel through the Chettiar country from Thanjavur and Trichy to Madurai, with its vibrantly active Meenakshi Temple. A wonderfully scenic road climbs the Western Ghats to one of South India's best known national parks at Thekkady/Periyar. Then allow a day's travel to the coast at Kovalam, before wending your way up to Fort Kochi's Jewish synagogue, spice markets and palaces.

After exploring Kerala, you can take the Konkan railway up the coast all the way to Mumbai, stopping off at Canacona for the lovely Palolem beach in southern Goa, or Margao for one of the splendid central Goa beaches such as Benaulim (or get there by road). There are other interesting places on the route, including the important Hindu pilgrimage centre of Udupi, famous for its vegetarian cuisine, and Jog Falls, the highest in India. In Goa there is plenty to see away from the beaches, and it's a good place for a final week in South India before flying back from Goa to Mumbai or Chennai.

A much longer tour of, say, three months gives you the chance to see something of all the strands that give richness to peninsular India, including getting right off the beaten track. You might choose to combine elements of the routes described above. For example, from Kannur travel to Madikeri and then explore Karnataka, and Andhra Pradesh at leisure. From Mangalore it is easy to get to Hassan for a trip around Karnataka before returning to Chennai. Or from Goa venture out to Hampi and then north to Bijapur and Hyderabad, before returning south to Bengaluru (Bangalore) to see the rest of Karnataka.

When to go

South India is very warm or hot throughout the year. Coastal regions are generally humid. In Kerala and Karnataka the main rainy season is June to September, but in Tamil Nadu and central Andhra the rains come later, between October-December. The hill stations in the Western Ghats are beautiful in the drier months from January to early June though they can be quite cold from January to March.

Some of India's great festivals such as *Dasara* and *Diwali* are celebrated in autumn and winter. In Tamil Nadu *Pongal* is a January harvest festival, which in Kerala is known as *Onam*, a great rainy season festival.

Activities and tours

Adventure sports familiar in Europe of the US are still rare in South India. Despite the great lengths of sandy beach, surfing is unheard of outside Kovalam in Kerala, though there are some good swimming beaches. The hills of the Western Ghats offer excellent walking and treks. For a list of tour operators, see page 63.

Biking

For those keen on moving faster along the road, by travelling on the two wheels of a motorbike (preferably a 'Bullet'), see page 38.

Birdwatching

South India is wonderfully rich in birdlife – in towns and cities as well as the countryside or even more abundantly in the national parks and sanctuaries. There are spectacular sanctuaries for migrating birds (see below), but every village water tank is home to a wide variety of local and migratory birds.

A Birdwatcher's Guide to India by Krys Kazmierczak and Raj Singh (Prion Ltd, 1998), is well researched and comprehensive and has helpful practical information and maps.

★ Head for ...
Pulicat Lake, Andhra Pradesh, page 354
Ranganathittu Bird Sanctuary, Karnataka, page 274
Vedanthangal Bird Sanctuary, Tamil Nadu, page 94

Contact
www.delhibird.net
www.orientalbirdclub.org
www.sacon.org
Bird Link, biks@giasdl01.vsnl.net.in, is concerned with conservation of birds and their habitat.

Cricket

This has become one of India's greatest and most popular entertainment. Cricket has an almost fanatical following across South India. Reinforced by satellite TV and radio and a national side that enjoys high world rankings and outstanding individual talent, cricket has become a national obsession. Stars have cult status and children model themselves on their game on every open space.

Contact
India's cricket board (BCCI), www.bcci.cricket.deepthi.com.
abcofcricket.com, focricinfo.com, a good section to keep up to date with all the latest in Indian cricket.r information and tickets.

Cycling

Cycling offers a peaceful and healthy alternative to cars, buses or trains. Touring on locally hired bicycles is possible along country roads – ideal if you want to see village life in South India and the lesser known wildlife parks. Consult a good Indian agent for advice. See also page 38.

Football

Football is played from professional level to kickabout in any open space. The season is Oct-Mar and details of matches are published in the local papers. Top class game tickets are Rs 25, but they are sold for much more on the black market. The crowds generate tremendous fervour for big matches, and standards are improving. African players are now featuring more frequently with Indian teams and monthly salaries have risen to over Rs 40,000 per month, an excellent wage by Indian standards.

★ Head for ...
Goa, page 359
Kerala, page 171

Contact
www.indianfootball.com, for the latest news.

Trekking

The Hill Stations of the Western Ghats where the Nilgiri hills, the 'blue mountains', rise to 2500 m are ideal for walking and 'trekking'. At the same time the wide range of habitat from dense cover of *shola* forests to scrub and meadow grassland, offer a rich variety of birdlife, some wildlife. The May to Nov monsoon months can be too wet and overcast to make trekking worthwhile.

The easily accessible parts of the national parks and reserved forests provide ample opportunity for walking but if you want to venture deeper you'll need to take a local guide as paths can soon become indistinct and confusing. Some areas (such as Silent Valley in Kerala) require a permit to visit since the authorities wish to keep disturbance to wildlife and tribal communities to a minimum.
The government wildlife and forestry departments and private tour operators will be able to set you on the right path but you need to ask, sometimes as much as a month, in advance. There are simple lodges and guest houses in most areas including tribal villages, but comfortable jungle camps and luxury safari lodges also exist in national parks, which can be used as a base for day treks.

★ Head for ...
Anamalai (Indira Gandhi) National Park, Tamil Nadu, page 141
Bandipur National Park, Karnataka, page 276
Biligiri Rangaswamy Wildlife Sanctuary, Karnataka, page 275
Madikeri, Karnataka, page 278
Mudumalai Wildlife Sanctuary, Tamil Nadu, page 137
Munnar, Kerala, page 223

Nagarhole (Rajiv Gandhi) National Park, Karnataka, page 278
Nilgiri Hills Around Udhagamandalam (Ooty): Chanduvarai, Coonoor, Grass Hills, Kilavarai, Kodaikkanal, Monamboli, Pollachi, Topslip, Vaguvarai, Valparai. The hills can be damp during Nov-Dec and are best Jan-May.
Periyar National Park, Kerala, page 220
Western Ghats: Igutappa, Ponnampet, Srimangala, Tadiandamole, Tala Cauvery.

Contact

Chalukya Vadayakadu, Kunnukzhy, Thiruvananthapuram, Kerala, T0471-244 4618.
Clipper Holidays, 4 Magrath Rd, Bengaluru (Bangalore), Karnataka, T080-2559 2023, clipper@bangalore.wipro.net.in.
Indian Adventures, T022-2640 8742, www.indianadventures.com.
Jungle Lodges and Resorts, T080-2559 7025, www.junglelodges.com.
Jungle Retreat, Bokkapuram, Mudumalai, Tamil Nadu, T0423-256469, www.jungleretreat.com.
Seagull, by 8 Ramanashree Complex, Hardinge Circle, Mysore, Karnataka, T0821-252 9732, www.seagulltravels.net.

Watersports

Sun, sand and warm waters for safe swimming are not the only attractions along the long stretches of unspoilt coastal South India. Select beaches in Goa and the crystal clear waters around the Laccadive islands are excellent for diving. Snorkelling is possible more widely, as well as parasailing, wind surfing and waterskiing. Scuba diving centres offer well-run courses that cost around US$85 for an introductory dive, US$400 for 4 days, or US$600 plus for a 2-week Dive Master course. Coastal resorts in Kerala and Goa also offer fishing trips and dolphin viewing during the season, sometimes with a beach barbecue.

★ Head for ...

Lakshadweep, Minicoy and Amindivi Islands, page 247
Bogmalo beach, Goa, page 410

Contact

PADI Europe, Oberwilerstrasse 3, CH-8442, Hettlingen, Switzerland, T52-304 1414, admin@padi.ch.
PADI International Head Office, Unit 6, Unicorn Park, Whitby Rd, Bristol BS4 4EX, T0117-971 1717, www.padi.co.uk.

Yoga and meditation

There has been a growing Western interest in the ancient life disciplines in search of physical and spiritual wellbeing, as practised in ancient India. Yoga is supposed to regulate the nervous system and aims to attain the union of body, mind and spirit through the practice of *asanas* (body postures), breath control, discipline, cleansing, contemplation and awareness. It seeks to achieve moral purification through abstinence and restraint (dietary and sexual). Meditation which complements yoga to relieve stress, increase awareness and bring inner peace prescribes the practice of *dhyana* (purposeful concentration) by withdrawing oneself from external distractions and focusing ones attention to consciousness itself. This leads ultimately to *samadhi* (release from worldly bonds). Hatha yoga has captured the Western imagination as it promises good health through postural exercises, while the search for inner peace leads others to learn meditation techniques.

Centres, especially in Kerala, offer courses for beginners and practitioners. Some are at special resort hotels which offer all-inclusive packages in idyllic locations, some advocate simple communal living in an ashram while others may require rigorous discipline in austere monastic surroundings. Whether you wish to embark on a serious study of yoga or sample an hour's introductory meditation session, South India offers opportunities for all, though you may need to apply in advance for some popular courses. Popular centres in places frequented by travellers are listed thoughout the book.

Taking a tour

You may choose to try an inclusive package holiday or let a specialist operator quote for a tailor-made tour. Out of season these can be worth exploring. The lowest prices quoted from the UK vary from about US$550 (£274) for a week (including flights, hotel and breakfast) in the low season to over US$3000 (£1500) for 3 weeks during the peak season. Most will chalk out individual itineraries and cover the major sights with small groups. A list of specialist tour operators, who arrange anything from general tours to wildlife safaris to ashram retreats, can be found on page 63.

Local customs and laws

Customs

Most travellers experience great warmth and hospitality. With it comes an open curiosity about personal matters. You should not be surprised if total strangers ask for details of your job, income and family circumstances or discuss politics and religion.

Conduct

Respect for the foreign visitor should be reciprocated by a sensitivity towards local customs and culture. How you dress is how people will judge you; cleanliness, modest clothes and a smile go a long way. Scanty, tight clothing draws unwanted attention. Nudity is not permitted on beaches in India and although there are some places where this ban is ignored, it causes much offence. Public displays of intimacy are inappropriate in public. You may at times be frustrated by delays, bureaucracy and inefficiency, but displays of anger and rudeness will not achieve anything positive, and often make things worse. People's concept of time and punctuality is also often rather vague so be prepared to be kept waiting.

Courtesy

It takes little effort to learn common gestures of courtesy and they are greatly appreciated. The greeting when meeting or parting, used universally among the Hindus across India, is the palms joined together as in prayer, sometimes accompanied with the word *vanakkam* in Tamil. Muslims use the greeting *assalãm aleikum*, with the response *waleikum assalãm*, meaning 'peace be with you'; 'please' is *mehrbani-se*; 'thank you' Is often expressed by a smile, or with the somewhat formal *dhannyabad*, *shukriya* (Urdu), and *nandri* in Tamil.

Hands and eating

Traditionally, Indians use the right hand for giving, receiving, shaking hands and eating, as the left is considered to be unclean since it is associated with washing after using the toilet. In much of rural India cutlery is alien at the table except for serving spoons, and at humble restaurants you will be offered only small spoons to eat with. If you visit an ashram or are lucky enough to be invited to a temple feast day, you will be expected to eat with your hands. Watch and copy others until the technique becomes familiar.

Women → *See also page 68.*

Indian women in urban and rural areas differ in their social interactions with men. To the Westerner, Indian women may seem to remain in the background and appear shy when approached. Yet you will see them working in public, often in jobs traditionally associated with men in the West, in the fields or on construction sites. It is not considered polite for men to photograph women without their consent, so ask before you start snapping.

Women do not usually shake hands with men as physical contact between the sexes is not acceptable. A westernized city woman, however, may feel free to shake hands with a foreign visitor. In certain, very traditional rural circles, it is still the custom for men to be offered food first, separately, so don't be surprised if you, as foreign guest (man or woman), are awarded this special status when invited to an Indian home.

Visiting religious sites

Visitors to all religious places should be dressed in clean, modest clothes; shorts and vests are inappropriate. Always remove shoes before entering (and all leather items in Jain temples). Take thick socks for protection when walking on sun-baked stone floors. Menstruating women are considered 'unclean' and should not enter places of worship. It is discourteous to sit with one's back to a temple or shrine. You will be expected to sit cross-legged on the floor – avoid pointing your feet at others when attending prayers at a temple. Walk clockwise around a shrine (keeping it to your right).

Non-Hindus are sometimes excluded from the inner sanctum of Hindu temples and occasionally even from the temple itself. Look for signs or ask. In certain temples and on special occasions you may enter only if you wear unstitched clothing such as a dhoti.

In Buddhist shrines, turn prayer wheels in a clockwise direction.

In mosques, visitors should only have their face, hands and feet exposed; women should also cover their heads. Mosques may be closed to non-Muslims shortly before formal prayers.

Some temples have a register or a receipt book for **donations** which works like an obligatory entry fee. The money is normally used for the upkeep and services of the temple or monastery. In some pilgrimage centres, priests can become unpleasantly persistent. If you wish to leave a donation, put money in the donation box; priests and Buddhist monks often do not handle money. It is also not customary to shake hands with a priest or monk. *Sanyasis* (holy men) and some pilgrims depend on donations.

Guide fees

Guides at tourist sites vary considerably in their knowledge and ability. Government trained and licensed guides are covered by specified fees. Local temple and site guides should charge less. Approximate charges for four people for half a day are Rs 280, for a full day Rs 400; for five to 15 people for half a day Rs 400, for a full day Rs 530. Rs 125 for a language other than English

Begging

Beggars are often found in busy street corners in large Indian cities, as well as at bus and train stations where they often target foreigners. Visitors can find this distressing, especially the sight of severely undernourished children or those with physical deformity. You may be affected when some persist in making physical contact. You may see Indian worshippers giving freely to those less fortunate than themselves near religious sites since this is tied up with gaining 'merit'. Dealing with begging is a personal choice but it can be better to give to a recognized charity than to make mostly ineffectual handouts to individuals. Children offer to do 'jobs' such as call a taxi, carry shopping or pose for a photo. You may want to give a coin in exchange. While travelling, some prefer to hand out fruit to the many open-palmed children they encounter.

Charitable giving

A pledge to donate a part of one's holiday budget to a local charity could be an effective formula for 'giving'. Some visitors like to support self-help cooperatives, orphanages, refugee centres, disabled or disadvantaged groups, or international charities like Oxfam, Save the Children or Christian Aid which work with local partners, by either making a donation or by buying their products. Some of these charities are listed under the appropriate towns. A few (which also welcome volunteers) are listed here.

Leave a small footprint

As well as respecting local cultural sensitivities, travellers can take a number of simple steps to reduce, or even improve, their impact on the local environment. Environmental concern is relatively new in India, but don't be afraid to pressurize businesses by asking about their policies.

Litter Many travellers think that there is little point in disposing of rubbish properly when the tossing of water bottles, plastic cups and other non-biodegradeable items out of train windows is already so widespread. Don't follow an example you feel to be wrong. You can immediately reduce your impact by refusing plastic bags and other excess packaging when shopping – use a small backpack or cloth bag instead – and if you do collect a few, keep them with you to store other rubbish until you get to a litter bin.

Filtered water vs bottled water Plastic mineral water bottles, an inevitable corollary to poor water hygiene standards, are a major contributor to India's litter mountain. However, many hotels, including nearly all of the upmarket ones, most restaurants and bus and train stations, provide drinking water purified using a combination of ceramic and carbon filters, chlorine and sometimes UV irradiation. Ask for 'filter paani'; if the water tastes at all like a swimming pool it is probably quite safe to drink, though it's worth introducing your body gradually to the new water.

Bucket baths vs showers The biggest issue relating to responsible and sustainable tourism is water. The traditional Indian 'bucket bath', in which you wet, soap then rinse off using a small hand-held plastic jug dipped into a large bucket, uses on average around 15 litres of water, as compared to 30-45 for a shower. These are commonly offered except in four- and five-star hotels.

Support responsible tourism Spending your money carefully can have a positive impact. Sleeping, eating and shopping at small, locally owned businesses directly supports communities, while specific community tourism concerns, such as those operated by The Blue Yonder in Kerala, www.theblueyonder.com, provides an economic motivation for people to stay in remote communities, protect natural areas and revive traditional cultures, rather than exploit the environment or move to the cities for work. People who are keen to minimize the impact of tourism include Bhakti Kutir in Palolem (see page 417) and Yogamagic, Anjuna (see page 395).

Transport Choose walking, cycling or public transport over fuel-guzzling cars and motorbikes.

Concern India Foundation, 6K Dubash Marg, Mumbai, T022-2202 9708, www.concernindia.org. An umbrella organization working with local charities.
Oxfam, Sushil Bhawan, 210 Shahpur Jat, New Delhi 110049, T011-2649 1774; 274 Banbury Rd, Oxford OX2 7D2, UK, www.oxfam.org (400 grassroots projects).
SOS Children's Villages, A-7 Nizamuddin West, New Delhi 110013, T011-2435 9450, www.soscvindia.org. Over 30 children's projects in India, eg opposite Pital Factory, Jhotwara Rd, Jaipur 302016, T0141-228 0787.
Save the Children India, 4C Swapnalok, 47 LJ Mard, Mumbai 400036, www.savethechildrenindia.org.

Photography

Many monuments and national parks charge a camera fee ranging from Rs 20-100 for still cameras, and as much as Rs 500 for video cameras (more for professionals). Special permits are needed from the Archaeological Survey of India, New Delhi, for using tripods and artificial lights. When photographing people, it is polite to first ask – they will usually respond warmly with smiles. Visitors often promise to send copies of the photos – don't unless you really mean to do so. Photography of airports, military installations, bridges and in tribal and 'sensitive border areas', is not permitted.

Drugs

Certain areas, such as Goa's beaches, Kovalam (Kerala), Gokarna and Hampi (Karnataka), have become associated with foreigners who take drugs. These are likely to attract local and foreign drug dealers but be aware that the government takes the misuse of drugs very seriously. Anyone charged with the illegal possession of drugs risks facing a fine of Rs 100,000 and a minimum 10 years' imprisonment. Several foreigners have been imprisoned for drugs-related offences in the last decade.

Getting there

Air

South India is accessible from virtually every continent. There are some direct flights from Europe and elsewhere in Asia to cities such as Chennai, Bengaluru (Bangalore) and Tiruvananthapuram, but it can be much cheaper to fly in via Mumbai or Delhi, which have far more international flights.

Alternatively you can fly to numerous destinations across India with Jet Airways at very competitive prices if any domestic flights are booked in conjunction with Jet on the international legs. In 2007 the cheapest return flights to Chennai from London started from as little as £370, but leapt to £800 plus as you approached high season of Christmas, New Year and Easter. The cheapest flights to Mumbai start at £350 or so, from where you can get internal flights from around £50 to reach the far south. It is easy to fly to Chennai, Trichy or Tiruvananthapuram from Colombo, in Sri Lanka and it costs £55-£65 including tax. Singapore also has direct flights to Chennai and Bengaluru. Some carriers permit 'open-jaw' travel, arriving in, and departing from, different cities in India.

Some (eg **Air India, British Airways, Lufthansa** and **Virgin Atlantic**) have convenient non-stop flights from London to Delhi or Mumbai taking only nine hours, and to Chennai between 11 and 12 hours. Virgin Atlantic flies to Delhi in 8½ hours or Mumbai in 9½ hours. Bear in mind that the cheapest fares from Europe are often with Central European, Central Asian or Middle Eastern airlines. There are no direct flights between Goa and North America or Australasia. Again, flights to Mumbai, Delhi and Chennai are your best bets: **Air India** and **Continental Airlines** have direct flights from New York. Continental Airlines says it plans to launch daily direct flights from New York to Mumbai from October 2007, subject government approval. **Delta Airlines** flies from New York and Atlanta to Mumbai and **American Airlines** also flies to Mumbai and Delhi. The American west coast route is run by **Cathay Pacific, Singapore Airlines** or **Malaysia Airlines**. Some west coast old hands recommend booking a cheap flight to Bangkok then getting a connecting ticket, which can work out cheaper, although more fraught. **Air Canada** operates between Vancouver and Delhi. **Qantas, Air India, Thai Airlines, Cathay Pacific, Singapore Airlines** and **Malaysia Airlines** are the operators for Australia, although Qantas is the only one that flies direct.

There are many low-cost domestic airlines within India: **Jet, Sahara, Spice Jet, Go Air, Kingfisher** and **Indian Airlines** all fly between Mumbai Santa Cruz and Goa's Dabolim for less than US$100 in around an hour, but there are also connections with Bengaluru (Bangalore), Calicut, Fort Kochi, Delhi and Trivandrum.

Charter flights Several tour operators from the UK, the Netherlands, Switzerland, Russia to Goa (especially from Britain, eg **JMC, Jewel in the Crown, Manos, Somak, Tropical Places**) flying from Gatwick and Manchester, offer package holidays between October and April to Kerala and Goa (**NB** they are not available to Indian nationals). Check Charter Flight Centre, T0845-0450153, www.charterflights.co.uk, which shows flights from Manchester to Goa and Trivandrum. They are often exceptional value (especially in November and from mid-January to mid-March). Government rules protect Air India's monopoly on flight-only deals to Goa, but you can sidestep these by searching for holiday deals, rather than just flight-only deals, which work out cheaper than flights-only. Including accommodation these can cost as little as £199 for a week (including basic dormitory or one- or two-star accommodation which you can forfeit on arrival – you're under no obligation to stay), whereas flight-only deals cost £280 or so. You will need to book through a tour operator (see above). During high season it's sometimes cheaper to book a scheduled flight; most often Mumbai, but it's worth looking at Hyderabad and Bengaluru (Bangalore) as less hectic entry points.

NB Officially, charter passengers can only stay for a maximum of 45 days, although this restriction can be bent somewhat if you have a valid visa to cover the duration of your proposed extension.

Stopovers and Round-the-World tickets

You can arrange several stopovers in India on Round-the-World and long distance tickets. RTW tickets allow you to fly in to one and out from another international aiport. You may be able to arrange some internal flights using international carriers eg **Air India** sometimes allows stopovers within India for a small extra charge.

If you plan to visit two or more South Asian countries within three weeks, you may qualify for a 30% discount on your international tickets. Ask your national tourist office. International air tickets can be bought in India though payment must be made in foreign currency.

Ticket agents and airlines

Agents

Abercrombie & Kent, www.abercrombie kent.com, www.abercrombiekent.com.au.
Adventure Company, T0870-794 1009, www .adventurecompany.co.uk. Competitive fares.
Adventure World, www.adventureworld.com.au.
Bridge the world, T020-7911 0900, www.b-t-w.co.uk.
Council Travel, www.counciltravel.com.
Ebookers, T020-7757 3000, www.ebookers.com.
Flight Centres, www.flightcentre.com.
Goa Way & Czech-It-Out, 111 Bell St, London, NW1 6TL, T0870-890 7800, www.goaway.co.uk.
Hari World Travels, www.hariworld.com.
Jet Airways, 188 Hammersmith Rd, London W6 7DJ, T020-8970 1500, for Gulf Air, Kuwait Airways, etc.
North South Travel, T01245-492882, www .northsouthtravel.co.uk. Profits go to charity.
Orient International (Travels) Ltd, 91 Charlotte St, London W1P 1LB, T020-7637 1330.
Peregrine, www.peregrine.net.au.
STA, London, T0871-230 0040, www.statravel.co.uk. Over 100 offices worldwide, offers special deals for under 26s.
Trailfinders, London, T0845-058 5858, www.trailfinders.com. Worldwide agencies.
Travel Corporation of India, www.tcindia.com.

Travel Cuts, www.travelcuts.com. US and Canadian agent.
Welcome Travels, 58 Wells St, London W1P 3RA, T020-7436 3011, www.welcome travels.com. For Air India.
www.lastminute.com.
www.expedia.co.uk.
www.bargainholidays.com.
www.travelocity.com.
www.opodo.com.

Airlines
Air India, www.airindia.com.
British Airways, www.ba.com.
Cathay Pacific, www.cathaypacific.com.
Emirates, www.emirates.com.
Go Air, www.goair.in.
Gulf Air, www.gulfairco.com.
Indian Airlines, indian-airlines.nic.in.
Jet, www.jetairways.com.
Kingfisher, www.flykingfisher.com.
KLM, www.klm.com.
Kuwait Airways, www.kuwait-airways.com.
Lufthansa, www.lufthansa.com.
Malaysian Airlines, www.malaysiaairlines.com.
Qantas, www.qantas.com.au.
Royal Jordanian, www.rja.com.jo.
Sahara, www.airsahara.net.
Singapore Airlines, www.singaporeair.com.
Spice Jet, www.spicejet.com.
Thai Airways, www.thaiair.com.
Virgin Atlantic, www.virgin-atlantic.com.

From the UK, Continental Europe and the Middle East

The best deals are offered from the UK. You can pick up attractive deals on **Air India** which flies direct to Delhi and Mumbai throughout the year with direct connections to Chennai, Hyderabad, Bengaluru (Bangalore), Thiruvananthapuram and other South Indian cities. (Direct flights between the UK and Mumbai start at £370, while flights-only between the UK and Goa can be almost double that at £700.) **Jet Airways** flies direct to Mumbai and Delhi throughout the year with direct connections to Goa, Chennai, Trivandrum, Hyderabad.

A few European airlines (eg Lufthansa, KLM) and several from the Middle East (eg Emirates, Gulf Air, Kuwait Airways, Royal Jordanian) offer good discounts to Mumbai and some state capitals from London, but fly via their hub cities, so adding to the journey time. Good deals can be offered by General Sales Agents (GSAs).

From Australasia via the Far East

Qantas, Singapore Airlines, Thai Airways, Malaysian Airlines, Cathay Pacific and **Indian Airlines** are the principal airlines connecting the continents. They all fly to one of the Indian regional capitals. STA and Flight Centres offer discounted tickets from their branches in major cities in Australia and New Zealand. Abercrombie & Kent, Adventure World, Peregrine and Travel Corporation of India organize tours.

From North America

From the east coast, it is best to fly direct to India from New York via London by **Air India** (18 hours), or pick up a direct charter from UK to Goa or Thiruvananthapuram but this will usually involve a stopover in London. Discounted tickets on British Airways, KLM, Lufthansa, Gulf Air and Kuwait Airways are sold through agents although they will invariably fly via their country's capital cities. From the west coast, it is best to fly via Hong Kong, Singapore or Bangkok to Mumbai using one of those countries' national carriers. Hari World Travels and STA have offices in New York, Toronto and Ontario. Student fares are available from Council Travel, with offices in the USA and Travel Cuts in Canada.

Airport information

Documentation and tax

The formalities on arrival in India have been increasingly streamlined during the last five years and facilities at the major international airports greatly improved. However, arrival can still be a slow process. Disembarkation cards, with an attached customs declaration, are handed out to passengers during the inward flight. The immigration form should be handed in at the immigration counter on arrival. The customs slip will be returned, for handing over to the customs on leaving the baggage collection hall. You may well find that there are delays of over an hour at immigration in processing passengers passing through immigration who need help with filling in forms.

Transport from airports

Pre-paid taxis to the city are available at all major airports. Some airports have up to three categories, 'limousine', 'luxury' and 'ordinary'. The first two usually have prominent counters, so you may have to insist if you want to use the standard service. Insist on being taken to your chosen destination even if the driver claims the city is unsafe or the hotel has closed down. For further information about getting from the airport into the city centres of Mumbai, Chennai, Thiruvananthapuram, Bengaluru (Bangalore) and Hyderabad, see pages 432, 77, 178, 257 and 326, respectively.

Rail

There are two trains a day between Mumbai and Goa (Madgaon). You can book tickets in advance via local agents or within 10 days via the website: www.konkanrailway.com. Prices range from Rs 293 for sleeper (ie non a/c) class to Rs 1111 for a/c 2-tier for the eight-hour (ish) journey or Rs 1900 for first class. The creakingly slow 12-16 hour bus marathon is only just cheaper than the train (Rs 300-700). These are run by state bus companies as well as private companies such as Paulo Tours and Travel. It will take you 10 hours to reach Panjim by taxi from Mumbai and it'll cost you Rs 6000 return.

Sea

No regular passenger liners operate to India. A few cruise ships stop at some ports like Mumbai, Margao, Kochi and Chennai. Operators include **Swan Hellenic** 77 New Oxford St, London WC1A 1PP, T020-7800 2200, www.swanhellenic.com.

From Sri Lanka amd Maldives

It is very unusual for foreign tourists to arrive by sea but shipping agents in Colombo (Sri Lanka) or Male (Maldives), may, in exceptional circumstances, allow passengers on their cargo boats to Tuticorin in Tamil Nadu.

Getting around

Air

India has a comprehensive air network linking the major cities of the different states. In addition to **Indian Airlines** (the nationalized carrier), and its subsidiary **Alliance Air**, there are several airlines such as **Jet Airways**. Domestic low cost carriers are plentiful, including: **Go Air**, **Kingfisher** and **Spice Jet**. Competition from the efficiently run private sector has, in general, improved the quality of services provided by the nationalized airlines. The Airports Authorities too have made efforts to improve handling on the ground.

For a list of relevant airline websites, see page 30.

Although flying is expensive, for covering vast distances or awkward links on a route, it is an option worth considering, although delays and re-routing can be irritating. However, for short distances, and on some routes – eg Chennai to Trichy or Bengaluru (Bangalore) – it makes more sense to travel by train.

NB If you don't want to take a connecting flight down to Goa the Konkan railway makes a pretty, and increasingly speedy, alternative. Don't be tempted to take the bus.

Tickets

All the major airlines are connected to the central reservation system and there are local travel agents who will book your tickets for a fee if you don't want to spend precious time waiting in a queue. Remember that tickets are in great demand in the peak season on some sectors so it is essential to get them months ahead.

Foreign passport holders buying air tickets in India must pay the 'US dollar rate' and pay in foreign exchange (major credit cards and travellers' cheques are accepted), or in rupees against an encashment certificate which will be endorsed accordingly.

The best way to get an idea of the current routes, carriers and fares is to use a third-party booking website such as **www.flightraja.com, www.cleartrip.com** or **www.yatra.com**; the latter also deals with international flights. Booking with these is a different matter: some refuse foreign credit cards outright, while others have to be persuaded to give your card special clearance. Tickets booked on these sites are typically issued as an email ticket or an SMS text message – the simplest option if you have an Indian mobile phone, though it must be converted to a paper ticket at the relevant carrier's airport offices before you will be allowed into the terminal.

Special fares

Indian Airlines and **Jet Airways** offer special 7, 15 and 21 day unlimited travel deals (some are limited to one sector) from around US$300 to US$800. A 25% discount is given on US dollar fares for anyone aged 12-30 years and 25% discount fares exist on some late night flights (between 2000 and 0800) between metropolitan cities. **Air India** has relaunched the companion free scheme for routes between USA/Canada and UK/Europe. Valid until 31 March 2008.

Rail

Trains can still be the cheapest and most comfortable means of travelling long distances whilst saving you hotel expenses on overnight journeys into the bargain. It gives access to booking station Retiring Rooms, which can be useful from time to time (see page 42). Above all, you have an ideal opportunity to meet local travellers and catch a glimpse of life on the ground although the dark glass fitted on air-conditioned coaches does restrict vision.

High-speed trains

There are several air-conditioned 'high-speed' **Shatabdi** (or 'Century') **Expresses** for day travel, and **Rajdhani Expresses** ('Capital City') for overnight journeys which connect major South Indian cities. As these are in high demand you need to book them well in advance (up to 90 days). Meals and drinks are usually included.

Steam

For rail enthusiasts, the steam-hauled narrow-gauge trains between Mettupalayam and Coonoor, and the special one between Ooty and Runneymede in the Nilgiris, are an attraction. See the IRCTC and Indian Railways website www.irctc.co.in. **Williams Travel** ⓘ *18/20 Howard St, Belfast BT1 6FQ, Northern Ireland, T01232-329477*, and **SD Enterprises** (see under Indrail passes below) are recommended for tailor-made trips.

Classes

A/c First Class, available only on main routes and cheaper than flying, is very comfortable (bedding provided). It will also be possible for tourists to reserve special coaches (some air conditioned) which are normally allocated to senior railway officials only. **A/c Sleeper** two and three-tier, are clean and comfortable and good value. **A/c Executive Class**, with wide reclining seats are available on many *Shatabdi* trains at double the price of the ordinary **A/c Chair Cars** which are equally comfortable. **2nd Class** (non-a/c) two and three-tier, provides exceptionally cheap travel but can be crowded and uncomfortable, and toilet facilities can be unpleasant. It is nearly always better to use the Indian-style squat loos rather than the Western-style ones as they are better maintained.

Indrail passes

These allow travel across the network without having to pay extra reservation fees and sleeper charges but you have to spend a high proportion of your time on the train to make it worthwhile. However, the advantages of pre-arranged reservations and automatic access to 'Tourist Quotas' can tip the balance in their favour for some travellers.

Tourists (foreigners and Indians resident abroad) may buy these passes for periods ranging from half a day to 90 days from the tourist sections of principal railway booking offices, and pay in foreign currency, major credit cards, travellers' cheques or rupees with encashment certificates. Fares range from US$57 to US$1060 for adults or around half that for children. Rail-cum-air tickets are also to be made available.

Indrail passes can also conveniently be bought abroad from special agents. For most people contemplating a single long journey soon after arriving in India, the Half- or One-day Pass with a confirmed reservation is worth the peace of mind; Two- or Four-Day Passes are also sold. The UK agent is **SD Enterprises Ltd**, 103 Wembley Park Drive, Wembley, Middlesex HA9 8HG, UK, T020-8903 3411, www.indiarail.co.uk. They make all necessary reservations and offer excellent advice. They can also book Indian Airlines and Jet Airways internal flights.

Other **international agents** are: **Australia: Adventure World** ⓘ *PO Box 480, North Sydney NSW 2060, T9587766, www.adventureworld.com.au*. **Canada: Hari World Travels** ⓘ *1 Financial Pl, 1 Adelaide St East, Concou Level, Toronto, T366 2000, www.hariworld.com*. **South Africa: MK Bobby Naidoo** ⓘ *PO Box 2878, Durban, T21-3094710*. **USA: Hari World Travels** ⓘ *25W 45th St, 1003, New York, NY 10036, T212-9573000, www.hariworld.com.*

A White Pass allows A/c Class Travel (the top rung); a Green a/c two-tier, a/c three-tier Sleepers and Chair Cars, the Yellow, only second class travel.

The cost of the Indrail pass is dependent on the class and duration of travel. Details are given below:-

Period	US$ A/c 2-tier	Period	US$ A/c 2-tier
½ day*	34.50	21 days	229
1 day*	53	30 days	280
7 days	156	60 days	462
15 days	215	90 days	614

*Special half and one day passes are only sold abroad.

Fares for individual journeys are based on distance covered and reflect both the class and the type of train. Higher rates apply on the Mail and Express trains and the air-conditioned *Shatabdi* and *Rajdhani Expresses*.

Rail travel tips

Bedding: It can get cold in air-conditioned coaches when travelling at night. Bedding is provide on second class air-conditioned sleepers. On others it can be hired for Rs 30 from the Station Baggage Office for second class.

Berths: It is worth asking for upper berths, especially in second class three-tier sleepers, as they can also be used during the day when the lower berths are used as seats. Once the middle berth is lowered for sleeping the lower berth becomes too cramped to sit on. Passengers with valid tickets but no berth reservations are sometimes allowed to travel overnight, causing discomfort to travellers occupying lower berths.

Credit cards: Some main stations now have separate credit card booking queues – even shorter than women's queues!

Delays: Allow lots of time for booking and for making connections. Delays are common on all transport. The special **Shatabdi** and **Rajdhani Express** are generally quite reliable. Ordinary Express and Mail trains have priority over local services and occasionally surprise by being punctual, but generally the longer the journey time, the greater the delay. Delays on the rail network are cumulative, so arrivals and departures from mid-stations are often several hours behind schedule. Allow at least two hours for connections, more if the first part of the journey is long distance.

Food and drink: It is best to carry some though tea, bottled water and snacks are sold on the platforms (through the windows). Carry plenty of small notes and coins on long journeys. Rs 50 and Rs 100 notes can be difficult to change when purchasing small food items. On long-distance trains, the restaurant car is often near the upper class carriages (bogies).

Getting a seat: It is usually impossible to make seat reservations at small 'intermediate' stations as they don't have an allocation. You can sometimes use a porter to get you a seat in a 2nd class carriage. For about Rs 20 he will take the luggage and ensure that you get a seat!

Internet services: Much information is now available online via the websites www.railtourismindia.com, www.indianrail.gov.in and www.trainenquiry.com, where you can check timetables (which change frequently), numbers, seat availability and even the running status of your train. The third party site, www.indiagroove.com, can also help plan complex itineraries with various changes of train. Internet tickets can theoretically be bought on www.irctc.co.in, though a credit card is required; foreign cards may not be accepted. An alternative is to seek out a local agent who can sell e-tickets, which can cost as little as Rs 5-10 (plus Rs 20 reservation fee), and can save hours of hassle; simply present the printout to the ticket collector.

Left luggage: Bags can be left for up to 30 days in station cloakrooms. These are especially useful when there is time to go sightseeing before an evening train. The bags must be lockable and you are advised not to leave any food in them.

Ladies' compartments: A woman travelling alone, overnight, on an unreserved second class train can ask if there is one of these. Lone female travellers may feel more comfortable in air-conditioned sleeper coaches, which require reservations and are used extensively by Indian families.

Ladies' and seniors' queues: Separate (much shorter) ticket queues may be available for women and senior citizens. Travellers over 60 can ask for a 30% discount on the ticket price.

Overbooking: Passengers with valid tickets but no berth reservations are sometimes permitted to travel overnight, causing great discomfort to travellers occupying lower berths. Wait-listed passengers should confirm the status of their ticket in advance by calling enquiries at the nearest computerised reservation office. At the station, check the reservation charts (usually on the relevant platform) and contact the Station Manager or Ticket Collector.

Porters: These can carry prodigious amounts of luggage. Rates vary from station to station (sometimes listed on a board on the platform) but are usually around Rs 10-25 per item of luggage.

Pre-paid taxis: Many main stations have a pre-paid taxi (or auto-rickshaw) service which offers a reliable service at a fair price.

Quotas: A large number of seats are technically reserved as quotas for various groups of travellers (civil servants, military personnel, foreign tourists, etc). Tourist quota is available at main stations. As a tourist you are not obliged to use it, but it can get you on an otherwise 'full' train; you will need your passport, and either pay in US dollars or pounds sterling or in rupees with a currency encashment certificate/ATM receipt. In addition, many stations have their own quota for particular trains so that a train may be 'fully booked' when there are still some tickets available from the special quota of other stations. These are only sold on the day of departure so wait-listed passengers are often able to travel at the last minute. Ask the superintendent on duty to try the 'Special' or 'VIP Quota'. The 'Tatkal' system releases a small percentage of seats at 0800 on the day before a train departs; you pay an extra Rs 75-200 (depending on class and season) to get on an otherwise heavily booked train.

Reservations: Ask for the separate Tourist Quota counter at main stations, and while queuing fill up the reservation form which requires the number and name of the train, preferred class of travel, and the passenger's name, age and sex (for Tourist Quota you may need to mention the passport number and nationality); you can use one form for up to six passengers. If you don't have a reservation for a particular train but carry an Indrail Pass, you may get one by arriving about three hours early. Tourist Quota tickets must be paid for in foreign exchange, so have an exchange certificate handy if you use rupees. It is possible to buy tickets for trains on most routes countrywide at many of the 520 computerized reservation centres across India. A short cut is to buy an ordinary second-class ticket and try upgrading to air conditioning by paying the conductor.

Security: Keep valuables close to you, securely locked, and away from windows. For security, carry a good lock and chain to attach your luggage.

Tickets and reservations: Unreserved tickets are available at any station by queueing at the window – a skill in itself – and represent the quickest way to get on a train that is about to depart. On most trains (not *Rajdhani* or *Shatabdi Express*) you can attempt to upgrade an unreserved ticket by seeking out the station manager's office, or the black-suited TTE (Travelling Ticket Examiner) if the train is at the platform, and asking if a seat is available; an upgrade fee is payable. This can save time waiting in the slower line for reservations.

It is now possible to reserve tickets for virtually any train on the network from one of the 520 computerized reservation centres across India. It is always best to book as far in advance as possible (usually up to 60 days). To reserve a seat on a particular train, note down the train's name, number and departure time and fill in a reservation form while you line up at the ticket window; you can use one form for up to four passengers. At busy stations the wait can take an hour or more. You can save a lot of time and effort by asking a travel agent to get your tickets for a fee of Rs 50-100. If the class you want is full, ask if special 'quotas' are available (see above). If not, consider buying a 'wait list' ticket, as seats often become available close to the train's departure time; phone the station on the day of departure to check your ticket's status. If you don't have a reservation for a particular train but carry an Indrail Pass, you may get one by arriving three hours early. Be wary of touts at the station offering tickets, hotels or exchange.

Timetables: Regional timetables are available cheaply from station bookstalls; the monthly 'Indian Bradshaw' is sold in principal stations. The handy 'Trains at a Glance' (Rs 30) lists popular trains likely to be used by most foreign travellers and is available in the UK from SD Enterprises Ltd (see above under Indrail passes, page 33).

Road

Road travel is often the only choice for reaching many of the places of outstanding interest. But for the uninitiated, travel by road can also be a worrying experience because of the apparent absence of conventional traffic regulations. Vehicles drive on the left – in theory. Routes around the major cities are usually crowded with lorry traffic, and the main roads are often poor and slow. There are no motorways, and many main roads are single track. Some district roads are quiet, and although they are not fast they can be a good way of seeing the country and village life if you have the time.

Bus

Buses now reach virtually every part of South India, offering a cheap, if often uncomfortable, means of visiting places off the rail network. Very few villages are now more than 2-3 km from a bus stop. Services are run by the State Corporation from the State Bus Stand (and private companies which often have offices nearby). The latter allow advance reservation and though tickets prices are a little higher, they have fewer stops and are a bit more comfortable.

There are three categories. **A/c luxury coaches**: though comfortable for sightseeing trips, apart from the very best 'sleeper coaches', even these can be very uncomfortable for really long journeys. Journeys over 10 hours can be extremely tiring so it is better to go by train if there is a choice. **Express buses**: run over long distances (frequently overnight), these are often called 'video coaches' and can be an appalling experience unless you appreciate loud film music blasting through the night. Ear plugs and eye masks may ease the pain. They rarely average more than 45 km per hour. **Local buses**: these are often very crowded, quite bumpy and slow and usually poorly maintained. However, over short distances, they can be a very cheap, friendly and easy way of getting about. Even where signs are not in English someone will usually give you directions. Many larger towns have **minibus** services which charge a little more than the buses and pick up and drop passengers on request. Again very crowded, and with restricted headroom, they are the fastest way of getting about many of the larger towns.

Bus travel tips Some towns have different bus stations for different destinations. Booking on major long-distance routes is now computerized. Book in advance and avoid the back of the bus where it can be very bumpy. If your destination is only served by a local bus you may do better to take the Express bus and 'persuade' the driver, with a tip in advance, to stop where you want to get off. You will have to pay the full fare to the first stop beyond your destination but you will get there faster and more comfortably.

Car

A car provides a chance to travel off the beaten track, and gives unrivalled opportunities for seeing something of India's great variety of villages and small towns. The most widely used hire car, the Hindustan Ambassador is often very unreliable, and although they still have their devotees, many find them uncomfortable for long journeys. For a similar price, Maruti cars and vans (Omni) are much more reliable. Gypsy four-wheel drives and jeeps are also available, especially in the hills, where a few Sumos have made an appearance. Maruti Esteems are comfortable and have optional reliable air conditioning. A specialist operator can be very helpful in arranging itineraries and car hire in advance.

Car hire, with a driver, is often cheaper than in the West. A car shared by three or four can be very good value. Two- or three-day trips from main towns can also give excellent opportunities for sightseeing off the beaten track in reasonable comfort. Local drivers often know their way much better than drivers from other states, so where possible it is a good idea to get a local driver who speaks the state language. Drivers may sleep in the car overnight, though hotels sometimes provide a bed for them. They are responsible for all their expenses, including their meals. A tip at the end of the tour of Rs 100 per day in addition to their daily allowance is perfectly acceptable. Check beforehand if fuel and inter-state taxes are included in the hire charge.

When booking emphasize the importance of good tyres and general roadworthiness.

Cars can be hired through private companies. International companies such as **Hertz, Europcar** and **Budget** operate in some major cities and offer reliable cars; their rates are generally higher than those of local firms (eg **Sai Service, Wheels**). The price of an imported car can be three times that of the Ambassador.

Car with driver	Economy Maruti 800 Ambassador	Regular A/C Maruti 800 Contessa	Premium A/C Maruti 1000 Opel etc	Luxury A/C Esteem Qualis
8 hrs/80 km	Rs 800	Rs 1000	Rs 1400	Rs 1800+
Extra km	Rs 4-7	Rs 9	Rs 13	Rs 18
Extra hour	Rs 40	Rs 50	Rs 70	Rs 100
Out of town				
Per km	Rs 7	Rs 9	Rs 13	Rs 18
Night halt	Rs 100	Rs 200	Rs 250	Rs 250

Importing a car Tourists may import their own vehicles into India with a Carnet de Passage (Triptyques) issued by any recognized automobile association or club.

Self-drive car hire is still in its infancy and many visitors may find the road conditions difficult and sometimes dangerous. If you drive yourself it is essential to take great care. Pedestrians, cattle and a wide range of other animals roam at will. This can be particularly dangerous when driving after dark especially as even other vehicles often carry no lights.

Car travel tips Fuel: on main roads across India petrol stations are reasonably frequent, but some areas are poorly served. Some service stations only have diesel pumps though they may have small reserves of petrol. Always carry a spare can. Diesel is widely available and normally much cheaper than petrol. Petrol is rarely above 92 octane. **Insurance**: drivers must have third party insurance. This may have to be with an Indian insurer, or with a foreign insurer who has a national guarantor. **Asking the way**: can be very frustrating as you are likely to get widely conflicting advice each time you stop to ask. On the main roads, 'mile' posts periodically appear in English and can help. Elsewhere, it is best to ask directions often. **Accidents**: often produce large and angry crowds very quickly. It is best to leave the scene of the accident and report it to the police as quickly as possible. **Provisions**: ensure that you have adequate food and drink, and a basic tool set in the car.

India's space agency is busy developing the Indian Regional Navigational Satellite System (IRNSS) to provide the country with a regional satellite navigation system. The US's GPS and the Russian GLONASS systems are currently in use. It tends to be the larger westernised car hire firms that can offer GPS. Europcar has installed GPS in certain fleets of cars in a tie up with Jet Air, although these are mainly aimed at business travellers. In Mumbai, Meru taxis have GPS installed and plans are afoot to roll the technology out in Hyderabad and Chennai.

The **Automobile Association (AA)** offers a range of services to members. Chennai: AA of Southern India, AASI Centre, 187 Anna Salai, T044-2852 1162, www.aasindia.in.

Mumbai: Western India AA, Lalji Narainji Memorial Building, 76 Vir Nariman Rd, Churchgate, T022-2204 1085.

Cycling

Cycling is an excellent way of seeing the quiet by ways of India. It is easy to hire bikes in most small towns for about Rs 20-30 per day. Indian bikes are heavy and without gears, but on the flat they offer a good way of exploring comparatively short distances outside towns. It is also quite possible to tour more extensively and you may then want to buy a bicycle.

Buying a bicycle There are shops in every town and the local Raleighs are considered the best, with Atlas and BSA good alternatives; expect to pay around Rs 1500-2000 for a second-hand Indian bike but remember to bargain. At the end of your trip you can usually sell it quite easily at half that price. Imported bikes have the advantage of lighter weight and gears, but are more difficult to get repaired, and carry the much greater risk of being stolen or damaged. If you wish to take your own, it is quite easy if you dismantle it and pack it in its original shipping carton; be sure to take all essential spares including a pump. All cyclists should take bungy cords (to strap down a backpack) and good lights from home; take care not to leave your machine parked anywhere with your belongings though. Bike repair shops are universal and charges are nominal.

It is possible to cover 50-80 km a day quite comfortably – "the national highways are manic but country roads, especially along the coast, can be idyllic, if rather dusty and bumpy", one traveller writes. You can even put your bike on a boat for the backwater trip or on top of a bus. Should you wish to take your bike on the train, allow plenty of time for booking it in at the parcels office.

It is best to start a journey early in the morning, stop at midday and resume cycling in the late afternoon. Night riding, though cooler, can be hazardous because of lack of lighting and poor road surfaces. Try to avoid the major highways as far as possible. Fortunately foreign cyclists are usually greeted with cheers, waves and smiles and truck drivers are sometimes happy to give lifts to cyclists (and their bikes). This is also a good way of taking some of the hardship out of cycling round India.

Hitchhiking

Hitchhiking is uncommon in India, partly because public transport is so cheap. If you try, you are likely to spend a very long time on the roadside. However, getting a lift on motorbikes or scooters and on trucks in areas with little public transport can be worthwhile. It is not recommended for women on their own.

Motorcycling

→ *See also under Car and Cycling above for general advice.*

Motorcycling is a particularly attractive way of getting around. It is easy to buy new Indian-made motorcycles such as the Enfield Bullet and several 100 cc Japanese models, including Suzukis and Hondas made in collaboration with Indian firms. Buying new also ensures greater reliability and a fixed price; Indian Rajdoots are less expensive but have a poor reputation for reliability. Buying secondhand in rupees takes more time but is quite possible (and expect to get a 30-40% discount) and repairs are usually easy to arrange and relatively cheap. You can get a broker to help with the paperwork involved (certificate of ownership, insurance, etc) for a fee (see also Insurance on page 55). They charge about Rs 5000 for a No Objection Certificate (NOC), which is essential for reselling; it is easier to have the bike in your name. Remember to bring your own helmet and an International Driving Permit.

When selling a motorbike, don't be in a hurry, and only negotiate with "ready cash" buyers and be aware that black bikes are easier to sell than a coloured ones.

Peter and Friends Classic Adventures, see page 66, runs organized motorbike tours in South India ranging from four days to three weeks. They also hire out Enfield motorbikes in Goa (US$120-US$165 per week). Tours with full back-up are also offered by **Royal Enfield Motors** ⓘ *Chennai, T0445-43300, F543253* (about US$1200-1600 for 14 days). For expert advice contact **Cyclists' Touring Club** ⓘ *UK, T0870-873 0060.*

Rickshaws

Auto-rickshaws ('autos') These are almost universally available in towns across India and are the cheapest convenient way of getting about. In addition to using them for short journeys it is often possible to hire them by the hour, or for a half or full day's sightseeing. In some areas younger drivers who speak some English and know their local area well, may want to show you around. However, rickshaw drivers are often paid a commission by hotels, restaurants and gift shops, so advice is not always impartial. Drivers sometimes refuse to use a meter, quote a ridiculous price or attempt to stop short of your destination. If you have real problems it can help to threaten to go to the police.

It is best to walk a short distance away from a hotel gate before picking up an auto to avoid paying an inflated rate.

Cycle-rickshaws and horse-drawn tongas These are more common in the more rustic setting of a small town or the outskirts of a large one. You will need to fix a price by bargaining. The animal attached to a tonga usually looks too undernourished to have the strength to pull the driver, let alone passengers.

Taxis

'Yellow-top' taxis in cities and large towns are metered, although tariffs change frequently. These changes are shown on a fare chart which should be read in conjunction with the meter reading. Increased night time rates apply in some cities, and there is a small charge for luggage. Insist on the taxi meter being 'flagged' in your presence. If the driver refuses, the official advice is to call the police. This may not work, but it is worth trying. When a taxi doesn't have a meter, you will need to fix the fare before starting the journey. Ask at your hotel for a guide price.

Taxi tips At stations and airports it is often possible to share taxis to a central point. It is worth looking for fellow passengers who may be travelling in your direction and get a pre-paid taxi. At night, always have a clear idea of where you want to go and insist on being taken there. Taxi drivers may try to convince you that the hotel you have chosen 'closed three years ago', is 'completely full' or is an 'unsafe den'. You may have to say that you have an advance reservation. See individual city entries for more details.

Sleeping

South India has an enormously wide range of accommodation and, generally speaking, away from the metropolitan cities, room rates tend to be lower than the North, while the standard of cleanliness is higher. You can stay safely and very cheaply by Western standards in all four states. In all the major cities there are also high quality hotels, offering a full range of personal and business facilities. Expect to pay more in Mumbai, and to a lesser extent in Chennai and Bengaluru (Bangalore) for all types of accommodation. In small centres even the best hotels are far more variable. Prices tend to be lower there for comparable hotels. In the peak season (December to April for most of South India, May for the hill resorts) bookings can be extremely heavy in popular destinations. It is sometimes possible to book in advance by phone, fax or email either from abroad or in India itself. However, double check your reservation, and always try to arrive as early as possible in the day.

I-Escape.com is a useful online hotel resource with pictures of all of the accommodation options that it describes.

Hotels

Unmarried couples sharing hotel rooms usually cause no difficulty. Some cheaper hotels in India attracting tourists don't allow Indian guests in order to avoid 'unwanted harassment'.

Price categories

The category codes used in this book are based on prices of double rooms excluding taxes. They are **not** star ratings and individual facilities vary considerably. Modest hotels may not have their own restaurant but will often offer 'room service', bringing in food from outside. Many hotels operate a 24-hour check-out system. Make sure that this means that you can stay 24 hours from the time of check-in.

Off-season rates

Large reductions are made by hotels in all categories out of season in many resort centres. Always ask if any are available. You may also request the 10% agent's commission to be deducted from your bill if you book direct. Clarify whether the agreed figure includes all taxes.

Taxes

In general most hotel rooms rated at Rs 1200 or above are subject to a tax of 10%. Many states levy an additional luxury tax of 10-25% and some hotels add a service charge of 10% on top of this. Taxes are not necessarily payable on meals, so it is worth settling your meals bill separately. Most hotels in the **C** category and above accept payment by credit card. Check your final bill carefully. Visitors have complained of **incorrect bills**, even in the most expensive hotels. The problem particularly afflicts groups, when last-minute extras appear mysteriously on some guests' bills. Check the evening before departure, and keep all receipts.

Hotel facilities

You have to be prepared for difficulties which are uncommon in the West. It is best to inspect the room and check that all equipment (air conditioning, TV, water heater, toilet flush) works before checking in at a modest hotel.

Sleeping and eating price guides

Sleeping

LL	Over US$200	B	US$46-65	E	US$12-20
L	US$151-200	C	US$31-45	F	US$7-11
AL	US$101-150	D	US$21-30	G	US$6 and under
A	US$66-100				

Price of a double room in high season, excluding taxes.

Eating

TTT	Over US$12	TT	US$7-12	T	Under US$6

For a two-course meal for one person, excluding drinks and taxes.

Air conditioning (A/c) Usually, only category **C** and above have central air conditioning. Elsewhere air-conditioned rooms are cooled by individual units and occasionally by large 'air-coolers' which can be noisy and unreliable. When they fail to operate tell the management as it is often possible to get a rapid repair done, or to transfer to a room where the unit is working. During power cuts generators may not be able to cope with providing air conditioning. Fans are provided in all but the cheapest of hotels.

Heating Hotels in hill stations often supply wood fires in rooms. Usually there is plenty of ventilation, but ensure that there is always good air circulation, especially when charcoal fires are provided in a basket.

Insects At some times of the year and in some places mosquitoes can be a real problem, and not all hotels have mosquito-proof rooms or mosquito nets. If you have any doubts check before confirming your room booking. In cheap hotels you need to be prepared for a wider range of insect life, including flies, cockroaches, spiders, ants and geckos (harmless house lizards). Poisonous insects, including scorpions, are extremely rare in towns. Hotel managements are nearly always prepared with insecticide sprays. Many small hotels in mosquito-prone areas supply nets. Remember to shut windows and doors at dusk. Electrical mats and pellets are now widely available, as are mosquito coils that burn slowly. Dusk and early evening are the worst times for mosquitoes so trousers and long-sleeved shirts are advisable, especially out of doors. At night, fans can be very effective in keeping mosquitoes off. A traveler recommends Dettol soap to discourage mosquitoes.

Noise Hotels close to temples can be very noisy, especially during festivals. Music blares from loudspeakers late at night and from very early in the morning, often making sleep impossible. Mosques call the faithful to prayer at dawn. Some travellers find ear plugs helpful.

Power supply In some states power cuts are common, or hot water may be restricted to certain times of day. The largest hotels have their own generators but it is best to carry a good torch.

Service Where staff training is lacking, the person who brings up your cases may proceed to show you light switches, room facilities, TV tuning, and hang around waiting for a tip. Room boys may enter your room without knocking or waiting for a response to a knock. Both for security and privacy, it is a good idea to lock your door when you are in the room. At the higher end, you should expect to tip bellboys a little for every favour. Don't be surprised that staff don't always wait for a response to knocking before entering: lock your door when you are in your room if this is a problem.

Toilets Apart from those in the **A** category and above, 'attached bath' does not necessarily refer to a bathroom with a bathtub. Most will provide a bathroom with a toilet, basin and a shower. In the lower priced hotels and outside large towns, a bucket and tap may replace the shower, and an Indian 'squat' toilet instead of a Western WC (squat toilets are very often the cleaner). Even mid-price hotels, which are clean and pleasant, don't always provide towels, soap and toilet paper.

Water supply In some regions water supply is rationed periodically. Keep a bucket filled to use for flushing the toilet during water cuts. Occasionally, tap water may be discoloured due to rusty tanks. During the cold weather and in hill stations, **hot water** will be available at certain times of the day, sometimes in buckets, but is usually very restricted in quantity. Electric water heaters may provide enough for a shower but not enough to fill a bath tub! For details on drinking water see page 43.

Tourist bungalows

The different state tourism development corporations run their own hotels and hostels which are often in places of special interest. These are very reasonably priced, though they may be rather dated, restaurant menus may be limited and service is often slow.

Railway and airport retiring rooms

Railway stations often have Retiring Rooms or Rest Rooms which may be hired for periods of between one and 24 hours by anyone holding an onward train ticket. They are cheap and simple though often heavily booked. Some major airports (eg Mumbai) have similar facilities.

Hostels

The Department of Tourism runs 16 youth hostels, each with about 50 beds, usually organized into dormitory accommodation. The YHA also have a few sites all over India. Travellers may also stay in religious hostels (*dharamshalas*) for up to three days. These are primarily intended for pilgrims and are sometimes free, though voluntary offerings are welcome. Usually only vegetarian food is permitted; smoking and alcohol are not.

Camping

Mid-price hotels with large grounds are sometimes willing to allow camping. Regional tourist offices have details of new developments. For information on YMCA camping facilities contact: **YMCA**, National General Secretary, National Council of YMCAs of India, PB No 14, Massey Hall, Jai Singh Rd, New Delhi 1.

Eating

Food

→ *See also box on restaurant price codes, page 41 and food glossary in Footnotes, page 543.*

You find just as much variety in dishes and presentation crossing South India as you would on an equivalent journey across Europe. Combinations of spices give each region its distinctive flavour.

The larger hotels, open to non-residents, often offer buffet lunches with Indian, Western and sometimes Chinese dishes. These can be good value (Rs 250-300; but around Rs 450 in the top grades), and can provide a welcome, comfortable break in the cool. The health risks, however, of food kept warm for long periods in metal containers are considerable, especially if turnover at the buffet is slow. We have received several complaints of stomach trouble following a buffet meal, even in five-star hotels.

It is essential to be very careful since food hygiene may be poor, flies abound and refrigeration in the hot weather may be inadequate and intermittent because of power cuts. It is best to eat only freshly prepared food by ordering from the menu (especially meat and fish dishes). Avoid salads and cut fruit.

If you are unused to spicy food, go slow! Stick to Western or mild Chinese meals in good restaurants and try the odd Indian dish to test your reaction. Popular local restaurants are obvious from the number of people eating in them. Try a traditional thali, which is a complete meal served on a large stainless steel plate (or very occasionally on a banana leaf). Several preparations, placed in small bowls, surround the central serving of wholewheat chapati and rice. A vegetarian thali would include dhal (lentils), two or three curries (which can be quite hot), and crisp poppadums, although there are regional variations. A variety of pickles are offered – mango and lime are two of the most popular. These can be exceptionally hot, and are designed to be taken in minute quantities alongside the main dishes. Plain *dahi* (yoghurt) usually acts as a bland 'cooler'.

Vegetarian food The South excels in the vegetarian cuisine arena, with a diet that reflects what grows in abundance in the region – particularly coconut, chillies, tamarind and bananas. Many Tamilians are vegetarian and the strict Brahmins among them avoid the use of garlic and onion, and in some cases even tomatoes. Favourites for breakfast or tiffin (snack) include dosa (thin crisp pancakes, plain or masala when stuffed with mildly spiced potato and onion), iddli (steamed, fermented rice cakes), delicious rice-based *pongal* (worth searching out) and *vadai* (savoury lentil doughnuts), all served with a coconut chutney and *sambar* (a spicy lentil and vegetable broth). A thali here centres around boiled rice with a selection of vegetable preparations served in small steel containers, as well as pickles, papadum, *rasam* (a clear, peppery lentil 'soup'), and plain curd. The food from Chettinad tends to be particularly hot and spicy. The dessert is usually *payasam* (similar to creamy rice pudding) to round off the meal. South Indian coffee is a treat. It is freshly ground and filtered, mixed with hot milk and sugar, and traditionally served frothed up in small stainless steel tumblers.

Western food Many city restaurants offer some so-called European options such as toasted sandwiches, stuffed pancakes, apple pies, crumbles and cheese cakes. Italian favourites (pizzas, pastas) can be very different from what you are used to. Western confectionery, in general, is disappointing. Ice creams, on the other hand, can be exceptionally good (there are excellent Indian ones as well as international brands.

Fruit India has many delicious tropical fruits. Some are highly seasonal (eg mangoes, pineapples and lychees), while others (eg bananas, grapes, oranges) are available throughout the year. It is safe to eat the ones you can wash and peel.

Drink

Drinking water used to be regarded as one of India's biggest hazards. It is still true that water from the tap or a well should never be considered safe to drink since public water supplies are often polluted. Bottled water is now widely available although not all bottled water is mineral water; some is simply purified water from an urban supply.

Buy from a shop or stall, check the seal carefully (some companies now add a second clear plastic seal around the bottle top) and avoid street hawkers; when disposing bottles puncture the neck which prevents misuse but allows recycling for storage. There is growing concern over the mountains of plastic bottles that are collecting and the waste of resources needed to produce them, so travellers are being encouraged to use alternative methods of getting safe drinking water. In some towns purified water is now sold for refilling your own container. You may wish to purify water yourself. A portable water filter is a good idea, carrying the drinking water in a plastic bottle in an insulated carrier. Always carry enough drinking water with you when travelling. It is important to use pure water for cleaning teeth.

Hot drinks Tea and coffee are safe and widely available. Both are normally served sweet, and with milk. If you wish, say 'no sugar' (*chini nahin*), 'no milk' (*dudh nahin*) when ordering. Alternatively, ask for 'Set Tea' for a pot of tea, milk and sugar brought separately; a 'Full Set' with four cups, a 'Half Set' with two. Freshly brewed coffee is a common drink in South India. Even in aspiring smart cafés *espresso* or *cappuccino* may not turn out quite as one would expect in the West.

Soft drinks Bottled carbonated drinks such as Coke, Pepsi, Teem and Gold Spot are universally available but always check the seal when you buy from a street stall. There are now also several brands of fruit juice sold in cartons, including mango, pineapple and apple. Don't add ice cubes as the water source may be contaminated.

Alcohol Indians rarely drink alcohol with a meal, water being on hand. In the past wines and spirits were generally either imported and extremely expensive, or local and of poor quality. Now, the best Indian whisky, rum and brandy (IMFL or 'Indian Made Foreign Liquor') are widely accepted, as are good Champagnoise and other wines from Maharashtra. If you hanker after a bottle of imported wine, you will only find it in the top restaurants and have to pay Rs 800-1000 at least.

For the urban elite, cooling Indian beers are popular when eating out and so are widely available. Pubs have sprung up in the major cities. Elsewhere, seedy, all-male drinking dens in the larger cities are best avoided for women travellers, but can make quite an experience otherwise; you will sometimes be locked into cubicles for clandestine drinking. If that sounds unsavoury head for the better hotel bar instead; prices aren't that steep. In rural India, local rice, palm, cashew or date juice *toddy* and *arak* is deceptively potent.

Most states have alcohol free 'dry' days, or enforce degrees of Prohibition. Some upmarket restaurants may serve beer even if it's not listed, so it's worth asking.

Eating out

Eating out is still frowned on in the upper echelons of more conservative Hindu society, so in many towns there is little deviation from the most basic and cheap foodstuffs. You will get very used to the *iddli sambar* and *masala dosa* on the less touristed routes – they're on almost every hotel menu in the South.

Entertainment

Despite an economic boom in cities like Chennai, Hyderabad and Bengaluru (Bangalore) and the rapid growth of a young business class, India's nightlife remains meagre, and mainly focused on discos in the biggest hotels. In Goa beach trance

Entertainment

Indian films are exported to the USA, UK, Canada, Eastern Europe, Middle East, East Africa and South East Asia, and to a lesser extent South Africa and Japan. In revenue terms, the US, the UK and Indonesia are the three largest markets. Of the 1000 films made in India each year the most are made in the Telegu language followed by Hindi and Tamil.

parties usually take place in makeshift venues and continue to attract large groups of young foreigners particularly during Christmas and the New Year. However, the government has threatened to close down these venues. More traditional popular entertainment is widespread across Indian villages in the form of folk drama, dance and music, each region having its own styles and open-air village performance being common. The hugely popular local film industry comes largely out of this tradition. It's easy to find a cinema, but prepare for a long sitting with a standard story line and set of characters and lots of action. For cricket and football, see page 23.

Festivals and events

Festivals for all seasons

Every month is brightened by the riot of colour, sound and feasting that mark religious or seasonal festivals. These usually follow the lunar calendar. They offer you a chance to experience the region's rich heritage of traditional customs, music, dance and folk theatre.

In **Tamil Nadu**, *Pongal*, celebrated at Makar Sankranti (**14 January**), is a thanksgiving for a good harvest. A sweet milk and 'first rice' dish is prepared and the cattle are specially honoured. Decorated with brightly painted horns, they are festooned with balloons and garlands of flowers and paraded along town and village roads accompanied by bands of rustic musicians and cheering children.

In **Kerala**, the magnificent eight-day *Pooram* at Thrissur in **April-May**, is a grand spectacle staged by rival temples with elaborately ornamented elephants carrying glittering parasols which are accompanied by skilled drummers and horn players and magnificent displays of fireworks. The summer harvest festival is *Thiruvonam* (*Onam*) in **August-September** which is marked with grand elephant processions, elaborate mime performances of the *Kathakali* dance-dramas, fireworks and the famous Snake Boat races in some coastal towns along the backwaters.

In addition to the major Hindu, Christian and Muslim festivals, **Goa** celebrates its own special ones. Check dates with the tourist office.

January 6th *Feast of the Three Kings*, celebrated in Cansaulim (Cuelim), Chandor and Reis Magos.

February/March The *Carnival* is a non-religious festival celebrated all over Goa. On the first day (*Fat Saturday*), 'King Momo' leads a colourful procession of floats with competing 'teams' dressed in flamboyant costumes as they wind through the towns' main streets.

March *Shigmotsav* Similar to *Holi*, at full moon, particularly in Panaji, Mapusa, Vasco da Gama and Margao, is accompanied with plenty of music on drums and cymbals. *Procession of all Saints* in Goa Velha, on the Monday of Holy Week.

April *Feast of Our Lady of Miracles*, Mapusa, on the nearest Sunday, 16 days after Easter.

May 30th *Goa Statehood Day*, when all Government offices and many shops close.

June 13th *Feast of St Anthony*, with songs requesting the gift of rain. *Feast of St John the Baptist* (*Sao Joao*) (24th). *Festival of St Peter* (29th), Fort Aguada, with a pageant on a floating raft.

August *Janmashtami* (birth of Lord *Krishna*) marked with mass bathing in the Mandovi River off Divar Island. *Harvest Festival of Novidade* (different dates from 21st to 27th). The first sheaves of rice are offered to the priests, the Governor and Archbishop, and placed in the Cathedral on the 24th. The festival includes a re-enactment of one of the battles between Albuquerque and the Adil Shah on the lawns of the Lieutenant Governor's Palace.

October *Narkasur* On the eve of *Diwali*, Goan Hindus remember the victory of Lord Krishna over the demon Narkasur. In Panaji there are processions. *Fama of Menino Jesus* at Colva.

December *Feast of St Francis Xavier* (3rd) at Old Goa. *Liberation Day* (17 December) marking the end of Portuguese colonial rule (public holiday). *Food Festival, Christmas* (25 December). *Midnight Mass.*

Major Hindu and Muslim festivals celebrated in India often have a different edge in the South. Particularly spectacular are *Dasara* in **October** which celebrates the triumph of Good over Evil, and *Diwali*, the striking festival of lights which follows soon after on the dark night of the new moon, when the night sky bursts out with spectacular displays of fireworks. In Karnataka, *Mahanavami* in **October** is marked with great pomp during its impressive *Dasara* celebrations at the Mysore palace and at Chamundi Hill.

The Hindu Calendar

→ *For Hindu and corresponding Gregorian calendar months, see page 514.*

Hindus follow two distinct eras: The *Vikrama Samvat* which began in 57 BC and the *Salivahan Saka* which dates from 78 AD and has been the official Indian calendar since 1957. The *Saka* new year starts on 22 March and has the same length as the Gregorian calendar. In most of South India, the New Year is celebrated in the first month, *Chaitra* (corresponding to March-April). However, in Tamil Nadu it is celebrated in the second month of *Vaishakh*. The 29½ day lunar month with its 'dark' and 'bright' halves based on the new and full moons, are named after 12 constellations, and total a 354 day year. The calendar cleverly has an extra month (*adhik maas*) every two and a half to three years, to bring it in line with the solar year of 365 days coinciding with the Gregorian calendar of the West. The year is divided into six seasons: *Vasant* (spring), *Grishha* (summer), *Varsha* (rains), *Sharat* (early autumn), *Hemanta* (late autumn) and *Shishir* (winter).

National holidays

26 Jan Republic Day
15 Aug Independence Day
2 Oct Mahatma Gandhi's Birthday
25 Dec Christmas Day.

Other festivals and fairs

1 Jan **New Year's Day** is accepted officially when following the Gregorian calendar but there are regional variations which fall on different dates, often coinciding with spring/harvest time in Mar and Apr: **Ugadi** in Andhra and **Vishu** in Kerala.

14 Jan **Makar Sankranti** marks the end of winter and is celebrated with kite flying.

Feb **Vasant Panchami**, the Spring (Vasant) festival when people wear bright yellow clothes and mark the advent of the season with singing, dancing and feasting.

Feb-Mar **Maha sivaratri** marks the night when Siva danced his celestial dance of destruction (*Tunduva*) celebrated with feasting and fairs at Siva temples, but preceded by a night of devotional readings and hymn singing. Orthodox Shaivites fast during the day and offer prayers every 3 hrs; devotees who remain awake through the night believe they will win the Puranic promise of prosperity and salvation.

Carnival (Goa): Spectacular costumes, music and dance, float processions and feasting mark the 3-day event.

Mar Holi, the festival of colours, marks the climax of spring. Although this festival is celebrated more widely in North India it is also commonly enjoyed in parts of the South. The night before, bonfires are lit symbolizing the end of winter (and conquering of evil). People have fun throwing coloured powder and water at each other and in the evening some gamble with friends. If you don't mind getting covered in colours, you can risk going out but celebrations can sometimes get rowdy. Some link the festival to worship of Kama the god of pleasure; some worship Krishna who defeated the demon Putana.

Apr/May Buddha Jayanti, the first full moon night in Apr/May marks the birth of the Buddha. Celebrations are held in several parts of the country. **International Spice Festival** – Fort Kochi (Cochin), Kerala.

Pooram – Thrissur, Kerala.

Jul/Aug Raksha (or Rakhi) Bandhan (literally 'protection bond') commemorates the wars between Indra (the King of the Heavens) and the demons, when his wife tied a silk amulet around his wrist to protect him from harm. The festival symbolizes the bond between brother and sister, celebrated mainly at full moon. A sister says special prayers for her brother and ties coloured (silk) threads around his wrist to remind him of the special bond. He in turn gives a gift and promises to protect and care for her. Sometimes *rakshas* are exchanged as a mark of friendship. **Narial Purnima** on the same full moon. Hindus particularly in coastal areas of South India make offerings of *narial* (coconuts) to the Vedic god Varuna (Lord of the waters) by throwing them into the sea.

15 Aug Independence Day, a national secular holiday. In cities it is marked by special events. **Ganesh Chaturthi**, unlike most Hindu festivals, was established just over 100 years ago by the Indian nationalist leader Tilak. The elephant-headed god of good omen is shown special reverence. On the last of the 5-day festival after harvest, clay images of Ganesh (Ganpati) are taken in procession with dancers and musicians, and are immersed in the sea, river or pond.

Aug/Sep Janmashtami, the birth of Krishna, is celebrated at midnight at Krishna temples.

Sep/Oct Dasara has many local variations. In parts of South India, celebrations for the 9 nights (*navaratri*) are marked with **Ramlila**. Various episodes of the Ramayana story (see section on Hinduism, page 505) are enacted and recited, with particular reference to the battle between the forces of good and evil. In some parts of India it celebrates Rama's victory over the Demon king Ravana of Lanka with the help of loyal Hanuman (Monkey). Huge effigies of Ravana made of bamboo and paper are burnt on the 10th day (**Vijaya dasami**) in public open spaces. In other regions the focus is on Durga's victory over the demon Mahishasura.

Onam – Kerala.

Oct/Nov 2 Oct Gandhi Jayanti, Mahatma Gandhi's birthday is remembered with prayer meetings and devotional singing.

Diwali/Deepavali (from the Sanskrit *Dipa* lamp), the festival of lights, is celebrated in Karnataka and other parts of South India. Some Hindus celebrate Krishna's victory over the demon Narakasura, some Rama's return after his 14 years' exile in the forest when citizens lit his way with earthen oil lamps. If the festival is properly celebrated it is believed that gods may visit the earth. It falls on the dark *chaturdasi* (14th) night (the one preceding the new moon), when rows of lamps or candles are lit in remembrance, and *rangolis* are painted on the floor as a sign of welcome. Fireworks have become an integral part of the celebration which are often set off days before *Diwali*. Equally, Lakshmi, the Goddess of Wealth (as well as Ganesh) is worshipped by merchants and the business community, who open the new year's account on the day. Most people wear new clothes; some play games of chance.

25 Dec Christmas Day, Indian Christians celebrate the birth of Christ in much the same way as in the West; many churches hold services at midnight. There is an air of festivity in city markets, which are specially decorated and illuminated.

31 Dec **New Year's Eve** In Kerala specially designed and brightly lit paper stars decorate homes for a month before the festival. Some churches mark the night with a midnight mass. **Hampi-Vijaynagar** festival – Karnataka.

Muslim holy days

These are fixed according to the lunar calendar, see page 516. According to the Gregorian calendar, they tend to fall 11 days earlier each year, depending on the sighting of the new moon.

Ramadan Start of the month of fasting when all Muslims (except young children, the very elderly, the sick, pregnant women and travellers) must abstain from food and drink from sunrise to sunset.

Id ul Fitr 3-day festival marking the end of *Ramadan*.

Id ul Zuha/Bakr Id Commemoration of Ibrahim's sacrifice of his son according to God's commandment; the main time of pilgrimage to Mecca (the Hajj). It is marked by the sacrifice of a goat, feasting and alms giving.

Muharram When the killing of the Prophet's grandson, Hussain, is commemorated by Shi'a Muslims. Decorated *tazias* (replicas of the martyr's tomb) are carried in procession by devout wailing followers who beat their chests to express their grief. Hyderabad is famous for their grand *tazias*. Shi'as fast for the 10 days.

Shopping

India excels in producing fine crafts at affordable prices through the tradition of passing down of ancestral skills. You can get handicrafts of different states from the government emporia in the major cities which guarantee quality at fixed prices (no bargaining), but many are poorly displayed, a fact not helped by reluctant and unenthusiastic staff. Private upmarket shops and top hotel arcades offer better quality, choice and service but at a price. Vibrant and colourful local bazaars are often a great experience but you must be prepared to bargain.

Bargaining

Bargaining can be fun and quite satisfying but it is important to get an idea of prices being asked by different stalls for items you are interested in, before taking the plunge. Some shopkeepers will happily quote twice the actual price to a foreigner showing interest, so you might well start by halving the asking price. On the other hand it would be inappropriate to do the same in an established shop with price tags, though a plea for the "best price" or a "special discount" might reap results even here. Remain good humoured throughout. Walking away slowly might be the test to ascertain whether your custom is sought and you are called back.

The country is a vast market place but there are regional specializations. If you are planning to travel widely, wait to find the best places to buy specific items. Export of certain items is controlled or banned (see page 50).

Carpets and dhurries

The handicrafts of India are widely available across the four southern states. The superb hand-knotted carpets of Kashmir, using old Persian designs woven in wool or silk or both, are hard to beat for their beauty and quality. Kashmiri traders can now be found throughout India, wherever there is a hint of foreign tourism. Tibetan refugees in Karnataka produce excellent less expensive carpets of very high quality.

Jewellery

Whether it is chunky tribal necklaces from the Himalaya, heavy 'silver' bangles from Rajasthan, fine Orissan filigree, legendary pearls from Hyderabad, Jaipuri uncut gems set in gold or semi-precious stones in silver, or glass bangles from Varanasi, you'll be drawn to the arcade shop window as much as the wayside stall. It's best to buy from reputable shops as street stalls often pass off fake ivory, silver, gems and stones as real.

Metal work

The choice is vast, from brass, copper and white-metal plates and bowls from the North, exquisite Jaipuri enamelled silver pill boxes, tribal lost-wax *dhokra* toys from Orissa, Bihar and Bengal, Nawabi silver-on-gunmetal Bidri pieces from around Hyderabad, to exceptional copies of Chola bronzes cast near Thanjavur.

Stoneware

Artisans inspired by the Taj Mahal continue the tradition of inlaying tiny pieces of gem stones on fine white marble, to produce something for every pocket, from a small coaster to a large table top. Softer soapstone is cheaper. Stone temple carvings are produced for sale in Tamil Nadu (try Mahabalipuram).

Textiles

Handlooms produce rich shot silk from Kanchipuram, skilful *ikat* from Gujarat, Orissa and Andhra, brocades from Varanasi, golden *muga* from Assam, printed silks and batiks from Bengal or opulent *Himroo* shawls from Aurangabad. Sober handspun *khadi*, colourful Rajasthani block-printed cottons using vegetable dyes, tribal weaving from remote Himalayan villages, and tie-dyed Gujarati *bandhni* are easier on the pocket. Unique pieces also from Kashmiri embroidery on wool, Lucknowi *chickan* shadow-work on fine voil or *zari* (gold/silver thread) work on silk.

Wood craft

Each region has its special wood – rosewood in particular in the South. Carving, inlay and lacquer work are specialities.

Pitfalls

Taxi/rickshaw drivers and tour guides get a commission when they deliver tourists to certain shops, but prices are invariably inflated. Small private shops can't always be trusted to pack and post your purchases: unless you have a specific recommendation from a person you know only make such arrangements in government emporia or a large store. Don't enter into any arrangement to help 'export' marble items, jewellery, etc no matter how lucrative your 'cut' of the profits may sound. Make sure, too, that credit cards are run off just once when making a purchase.

Essentials A to Z

Accident and emergency

Contact the relevant emergency service (police T100, fire T101, ambulance T102) and your embassy (see under Directory in major cities such as Chennai, Mumbai, etc). Make sure you obtain police/medical reports required for insurance claims.

Children

Children of all ages are widely welcomed. However, care should be taken when travelling to remote areas where health services are primitive. It's best to visit in the cooler months since you need to protect children from the sun, heat, dehydration and mosquito bites. Cool showers or baths help; avoid being out during the hottest part of the day. Diarrhoea and vomiting are the most common problems, so take the usual precautions. Breastfeeding is best and most convenient for babies. In the big cities you can get safe baby foods and formula milk. It doesn't harm a baby to eat an unvaried and limited diet of familiar food carried in packets for a few weeks if local dishes are not acceptable, but it may be an idea to give vitamin and mineral supplements. Wet wipes and disposable nappies are difficult to find. The biggest hotels provide babysitting. Many European families have permanently relocated to Goa and the facilities here are accordingly good. See also Health, page 52.

Customs and duty free

Duty free

Tourists are allowed to bring in all personal effects 'which may reasonably be required', without charge. The official customs allowance includes 200 cigarettes or 50 cigars, 0.95 litres of alcohol, a camera with 5 rolls of film and a pair of binoculars. Valuable personal effects and professional equipment including jewellery, special camera equipment and lenses, laptop computers and sound and video recorders must be declared on a Tourist Baggage Re-Export Form (TBRE) in order for them to be taken out of the country. These forms require the equipment's serial numbers. It saves considerable frustration if you know the numbers in advance and are ready to show them on the equipment. In addition to the forms, details of imported equipment may be entered into your passport. Save time by completing the formalities while waiting for your baggage. It is essential to keep these forms for showing to the customs when leaving India, otherwise considerable delays are very likely at the time of departure.

Currency regulations

There are no restrictions on the amount of foreign currency or TCs a tourist may bring into India. If you are carrying more than US$5000 in cash or US$10,000 or its equivalent in cash and TCs you need to fill in a currency declaration form. This could change with a relaxation in the currency regulations.

Prohibited items

The import of dangerous drugs, live plants, gold coins, gold and silver bullion and silver coins not in current use are either banned or subject to strict regulation. It is illegal to import firearms into India without special permission. Enquire at consular offices abroad for details.

Export restrictions

Export of gold jewellery purchased in India is allowed up to a value of Rs 2000 and other jewellery (including settings with precious stones) up to a value of Rs 10,000. Export of antiquities and art objects over 100 years old is restricted. Ivory, musk, skins of all animals, *toosh* and *pashmina* wool, snakeskin and articles made from them are banned, unless you get permission for export. For further information, contact the Indian High Commission or consulate, or access the Central Board of Excise and Customs website, www.cbec.gov.in/travellers.htm.

Disabled travellers

India is not specially geared up for making provisions for the physically handicapped or wheelchair-bound traveller. Access to buildings, toilets (sometimes squat type), pavements, kerbs and public transport can prove frustrating, but it is easy to find people to give a hand to help with lifting and carrying. Provided there is an able-bodied companion to help and you are prepared to pay for at least mid-price accommodation, car hire and taxis, India should be rewarding, even if in a somewhat limited way.

Some travel companies are now specializing in exciting holidays tailor-made for individuals depending on their level of disability:

Accessible Journeys Inc, 35 West Sellers Av, Ridley Park, PA 19078, T610-521 0339, www.disability travel.com, runs some packages to India.

Global Access, Disabled Travel Network, www.globalaccessnews.com, is dedicated to providing travel information for 'disabled adventurers' and includes a number of reviews and tips from members of the public.

Responsible Travel.com, 3rd floor, Pavillion House, 6 Old Steine, Brighton, BN1 1EJ, UK, T01273-600030, www.responsibletravel.com, backed by Body Shop founder Anita Roddick, specializes in eco-friendly holidays and has some tailored to the needs of disabled travellers.

Nothing Ventured, edited by Alison Walsh (HarperCollins), gives personal accounts of worldwide journeys by disabled travellers, plus advice and listings.

Electricity

India supply is 220-240 volts AC. Some top hotels have transformers. There may be pronounced variations in the voltage, and power cuts are common. Power back-up by generator or inverter is becoming more widespread, even in humble hotels, though it may not cover a/c. Socket sizes vary so you are advised to take a universal adaptor; low quality versions are available locally. Many hotels, even in the higher categories, don't have electric razor sockets.

Embassies and consulates

For information on visas and immigration, see page 67. For a complete list of embassies and consulates, see http://meaindia.nic.in/onmouse/mission.htm.

Indian embassies abroad

Australia 3-5 Moonah Place, Yarralumla, Canberra, T02-6273 3999, www.hcindia-au.org; Level 2, 210 Pitt St, Sydney, T02-9223 9500; 15 Munro St, Coburg, Melbourne, T03-9384 0141.

Canada 10 Springfield Rd, Ottawa, Ontario K1M 1C9, T613-744 3751, www.hciottawa.ca; Toronto, T416-960 0751;, Vancouver, T604-662 8811.

France 15 rue Alfred Dehodencq, Paris, T01-4050 7070, www.amb-inde.fr.

Germany Tiergartenstrasse 17, 10785 Berlin, T030-257950. Consulates: Bonn, T0228-540132; Frankfurt, T069-153 0050, Hamburg, T040-338036, Munich, T089-210 2390, Stuttgart, T0711-153 0050.

Ireland 6 Leeson Park, Dublin 6, T01-497 0843, www.indianembassy.ie.

Nepal 336 Kapurdhara Marg, Kathmandu, T+9771-441 0900, www.south-asia.com/embassy-india.

Netherlands Buitenrustweg-2, 2517 KD, The Hague, T070-346 9771, www.indianembassy.nl.

New Zealand 180 Molesworth St, Wellington, T+64-4473 6390, www.hicomind.org.nz.

Singapore India House, 31 Grange Rd, T6737 6777, www.embassyofindia.com.

South Africa 852 Schoeman St, Arcadia, Pretoria 0083, T012-342 5392, www.india.org.za.

Sri Lanka 36-38 Galle Rd, PO Box No 882, Colombo 3, T+94-1-232 7587, www.indiahcsl.org.

Switzerland 9 rue de Valais, CH-1202, Geneva, T022-906 8686.

UK India House, Aldwych, London WC2B 4NA, T020-7836 8484 (open 0930-1300, 1400-1730; visas 0800-1200), www.hcilondon.net. Consulates: 20 Augusta St, Jewellery Quarter, Hockley, Birmingham, B18 6JL, T0121-212 2782, www.cgibirmingham.org; 17 Rutland Square, Edinburgh, EH1 2BB, T0131-229 2144, www.cgiedinburgh.org.

USA 2107 Massachusetts Av, Washington DC 20008, T202-939 7000. Consulates: New York, T212-774 8600; San Francisco, T415-668 0662; Chicago, T312-595 0405.

Gay and lesbian travellers

Indian law forbids homosexual acts for men (but not women) and carries a maximum sentence of life imprisonment. Although it is common to see young males holding hands in public, this very rarely indicates a gay relationship and is usually an expression of friendship. Overt displays of affection between homosexuals (and heterosexuals) give offence and should be avoided.

Health

Local populations in South India are exposed to a range of health risks not encountered in the Western world. Many of the diseases are major problems for the local poor and destitute and, although the risk to travellers is more remote, they cannot be ignored. Obviously 5-star travel is going to carry less risk than backpacking on a budget.

Health care in the region is varied. There are many excellent private and government clinics/hospitals. As with all medical care, first impressions count. It's worth contacting your embassy or consulate on arrival and asking where the recommended (ie those used by diplomats) clinics are. You can also ask them about locally recommended medical do's and don'ts. If you do get ill, and you have the opportunity, you should also ask your medical insurer whether they are satisfied that the medical centre or hospital that you have been referred to is of a suitable standard.

Before you go

Ideally, you should see your GP or travel clinic at least 6 weeks before your departure for general advice on travel risks, malaria and vaccinations; see page 67 for a list of recommended vaccinations. Make sure you have travel insurance, get a dental check (especially if you are going to be away for more than a month), know your own blood group and if you suffer a long-term condition such as diabetes or epilepsy make sure someone knows or that you have a Medic Alert bracelet/necklace with this information on it. Remember that it is risky to buy medicinal tablets abroad because the doses may differ and India has a huge trade in false drugs.

A-Z of health risks

If you are unlucky (or careless) enough to receive a venomous **bite or sting** by a snake, spider, scorpion or sea creature, try to identify the creature, without putting yourself in further danger (do not try to catch a live snake). Snake bites in particular are very frightening, but in fact rarely poisonous – even venomous snakes bite without injecting venom. Victims should be taken to a hospital or a doctor without delay. Commercial snake bite and scorpion kits are available, but are usually only useful for the specific types of snake or scorpion. Most serum has to be given intravenously so it is not much good equipping yourself with it unless you are used to making injections into veins. It is best to rely on local practice in these cases, because the particular creatures will be known about locally and appropriate treatment can be given. To prevent bites, do not walk in snake territory in bare feet or sandals – wear proper shoes or boots. For scorpians and spiders, keep beds away from the walls and look inside your shoes and under the toilet seat every morning. Certain tropical sea fish when trodden upon inject venom into bathers' feet. This can be exceptionally painful. Wear plastic shoes if such creatures are reported. The pain can be relieved by immersing the foot in hot water (as hot as you can bear) for as long as the pain persists. Citric acid juices in fruits such as lemon are reported as being useful.

Chikungunya is a relatively rare mosquito-borne disease has become prevalent in several parts of India, including Kerala and Goa, particularly during the monsoon when flooded areas encourage the carrier mosquitoes to breed. The disease manifests within 12 days of infection and symptoms resemble a severe fever, with headaches, joint pain, arthritis and exhaustion lasting from several days to several weeks; in vulnerable sections of the population it can be fatal. Neither vaccine nor treatment are available, so rest is the best cure.

Unfortunately there is no vaccine against **dengue fever** and the mosquitoes that carry it bite during the day. You will be ill for

2-3 days, then get better for a few days and then feel ill again. It should all be over in 7-10 days. Heed all the anti-mosquito measures that you can.

The standard advice for **diarrhoea** prevention is to be careful with water and ice for drinking. If you have any doubts about where the water came from then boil it or filter and treat it. There are many filter/treatment devices now available on the market. Food can also transmit disease. Be wary of salads (what were they washed in, who handled them), re-heated foods or food that has been left out in the sun having been cooked earlier in the day. There is a simple adage that says wash it, peel it, boil it or forget it. Also be wary of unpasteurized dairy products, these can transmit a range of diseases from brucellosis (fevers and constipation), to listeria (meningitis) and tuberculosis of the gut (constipation, fevers and weight loss).

The key treatment with all diarrhoea is rehydration. Try to keep hydrated by taking the right mixture of salt and water. This is available as Oral Rehydration Salts (ORS) in ready-made sachets or can be made up by adding a teaspoon of sugar and a half teaspoon of salt to a litre of clean water. Drink at least 1 large cup of this drink for each loose stool. You can also use flat carbonated drinks as an alternative. Alternatively, Immodium (or Pepto-Bismol, used a lot by Americans) is good if you have a long coach/train journey or on a trek, although is not a cure. Antibiotics like Ciproxin (Ciprofloaxcin) – obtained by private prescription in the UK – can be a useful antibiotic for some forms of travellers' diarrhoea. If it persists beyond 2 weeks, with blood or pain, seek medical attention.

If you go **diving** make sure that you are fit to do so. The British Sub-Aqua Club (BSAC), Telford's Quay, South Pier Rd, Ellesmere Port, Cheshire CH65 4FL, UK, T01513-506200, www.bsac.com, can put you in touch with doctors who do medical examinations. Protect your feet from cuts, beach dog parasites (larva migrans) and sea urchins. The latter are almost impossible to remove but can be dissolved with lime or vinegar. Keep an eye out for secondary infection. Check that the dive company know what they are doing, have appropriate certification from BSAC or PADI, Unit 7, St Philips Central, Albert Rd, St Philips, Bristol BS2 OTD, T0117-300 7234, www.padi.com, and that the equipment is well maintained.

Hepatitis means inflammation of the liver. The most obvious symptom is a yellowing of your skin or the whites of your eyes. However, prior to this all that you may notice is itching and tiredness. Early on, depending on the type of hepatitis, a vaccine or immunoglobulin may reduce the duration of the illness. There are vaccines for hepatitis A and B; the latter spread through blood and unprotected sexual intercourse, both of these can be avoided. Unfortunately there is no vaccine for hepatitis C or the increasing alphabetical list of other hepatitis viruses.

If infected with **leishmaniasis**, you may notice a raised lump, which leads to a purplish discoloration on white skin and a possible ulcer. The parasite is transmitted by the bite of a sandfly. Sandflies do not fly very far and the greatest risk is at ground levels, so if you can avoid sleeping on the jungle floor do so, under a permethrin treated net and use insect repellent. Seek advice for any persistent skin lesion or nasal symptom. Several weeks of treatment is required under specialist supervision.

Various forms of **leptospirosis** occur throughout the world, transmitted by a bacterium which is excreted in rodent urine. Fresh water and moist soil harbour the organisms, which enter the body through cuts and scratches. If you suffer from any form of prolonged fever consult a doctor.

Malaria has some seasonality but it is too unpredictable to not take malaria prophylaxis. In the UK we still believe that Chloroquine and Paludrine are sufficient for most parts of India, but the US disagree and recommend either Malarone, Mefloquine or Doxycycline.

For **mosquito repellents**, remember that DEET (Di-ethyltoluamide) is the gold standard. Apply the repellent 4-6 hrs but more often if you are sweating heavily. If a non-DEET product is used check who tested it. Validated products (tested at the London School of Hygiene and Tropical Medicine) include Mosiguard, Non-DEET Jungle formula and non-DEET Autan. If you want to use citronella remember that it must be applied very frequently (hourly) to be effective. If you are a target for insect bites or develop lumps quite soon after being bitten, carry an Aspivenin kit.

Prickly heat is a common intensely itchy rash, avoided by frequent washing and by wearing loose clothing. It is cured by allowing skin to dry off through use of powder – and spending a few nights in an a/c hotel!

Remember that **rabies** is endemic throughout certain parts of India, so avoid dogs that are behaving strangely and cover your toes at night from the vampire bats, which also carry the disease. If you are bitten by a domestic or wild animal, do not leave things to chance: scrub the wound with soap and water and/or disinfectant, try to at least determine the animal's ownership, where possible and seek medical assistance at once. The course of treatment depends on whether you have already been satisfactorily vaccinated against rabies. If you have (and this is worthwhile if you are spending lengths of time in developing countries) then some further doses of vaccine are all that is required. If you are not already vaccinated then anti-rabies serum (immunoglobulin) may be required in addition. It is important to finish the course of treatment.

The range of visible and invisible **sexually transmitted diseases** is awesome. Unprotected sex can spread HIV, hepatitis B and C, gonorrhea (green discharge), chlamydia (nothing to see but may cause painful urination and later female infertility), painful recurrent herpes, syphilis and warts, just to name a few. You can cut down the risk by using condoms, a femidom or avoiding sex altogether.

Make sure you protect yourself from the **sun** with high-factor sun screen and don't forget to wear a hat.

Ticks usually attach themselves to the lower parts of the body often after walking in areas where cattle have grazed. They swell up as they start to suck blood. The important thing is to remove them gently, so that they do not leave their head parts in your skin, because this can cause a nasty allergic reaction later. Do not use petrol, Vaseline, lighted cigarettes, etc to remove the tick, but, with a pair of tweezers remove the beast gently by gripping it at the attached (head) end and rock it out in very much the same way that a tooth is extracted.

Certain **tropical flies** which lay their eggs under the skin of sheep and cattle also occasionally do the same thing to humans with the unpleasant result that a maggot grows under the skin and pops up as a boil or pimple. The best way to remove these is to cover the boil with oil, Vaseline or nail varnish to stop the maggot breathing, then to squeeze it out gently the next day.

There are a number of ways of purifying **water**. Dirty water should first be strained through a filter bag and then boiled or treated. Bringing water to a rolling boil at sea level is sufficient to make the water safe for drinking, but at higher altitudes you have to boil the water for a few minutes longer to ensure all microbes are killed. There are sterilising methods that can be used and there are proprietary preparations containing chlorine (eg *Puritabs*) or iodine (eg *Pota Aqua*) compounds. Chlorine compounds generally do not kill protozoa (eg Giardia). There are now a number of water filters on the market available in personal and expedition size. They work either on mechanical or chemical principles, or may do both. Make sure you take the spare parts or spare chemicals with you and do not believe everything the manufacturers say.

Further information

Websites

Blood Care Foundation (UK), www.bloodcare.org.uk The Blood Care Foundation is a Kent-based charity 'dedicated to the provision of screened blood and resuscitation fluids in countries where these are not readily available'. They will dispatch certified non-infected blood of the right type to your hospital/clinic. The blood is flown in from various centres around the world.

British Travel Health Association (UK), www.btha.org This is the official website of an organization of travel health professionals.

Department of Health Travel Advice (UK), www.doh.gov.uk/traveladvice This excellent site is also available as a free booklet, T6, from post offices. It lists vaccine requirements for each country.

Fit for Travel, www.fitfortravel.scot.nhs.uk This site from Scotland provides a quick A-Z of vaccine and travel health advice requirements for each country.

Foreign and Commonwealth Office (FCO) (UK), www.fco.gov.uk This is a key travel advice site, with useful information on the country, climate and lists UK embassies/ consulates. The site also promotes the concept of 'know before you go' and encourages travel insurance and travel health advice. It has links to the Department of Health travel advice site, see above.

The Health Protection Agency www.hpa.org.uk This site has up-to-date malaria advice guidelines for travel around the world. It gives specific advice about the right drugs for each location. It also has useful information for those who are pregnant, suffering from epilepsy or planning to travel with children.

Medic Alert (UK), www.medicalalert.co.uk This is the website of the foundation that produces bracelets and necklaces for those with existing medical problems. Once you have ordered your bracelet/necklace you write your key medical details on paper inside it, so that if you collapse, a medical person can identify you as someone with epilepsy or allergy to peanuts, etc.

Travel Screening Services (UK), www.travelscreening.co.uk A private clinic dedicated to integrated travel health. The clinic gives vaccine, travel health advice, email and SMS text vaccine reminders and screens returned travellers for tropical diseases.

World Health Organisation, www.who.int The WHO site has links to the WHO Blue Book on travel advice. This lists the diseases in different regions of the world. It describes vaccination schedules and makes clear which countries have yellow fever vaccination certificate requirements and malarial risk.

Books

International Travel and Health World Health Organisation Geneva, ISBN 92 4 158026 7.

Lankester, T, *The Travellers Good Health Guide*, ISBN 0-85969-827-0.

Warrell, D and Anderson, A (eds), *Expedition Medicine (The Royal Geographic Society)*, ISBN 1 86197 040-4.

Young Pelton, R, Aral, C and Dulles, W, *The World's Most Dangerous Places*, ISBN 1-566952-140-9.

Insurance

Buying insurance with your air ticket is the most costly way of doing things: better go to an independent. Ask your bank too; some now offer travel insurance for current account holders. See also the website www.dh.gov.uk/policyandguidance/ healthadvicefortravellers.

If you are carrying specialist equipment – expensive cameras, VCRs, laptops – you will probably need to get separate cover for these items (otherwise you risk claims for individual items being limited to £250, not a good return on a digital SLR) unless they are covered by existing home contents insurance. It is always best to dig out all the receipts for these expensive personal effects. Take photos of the items and note down all serial numbers.

Also check exactly what your medical cover includes, eg ambulance, helicopter rescue or emergency flights back home. Most importantly check for exclusions in the policy before you travel. You may find that even activities such as mountain biking are not covered and travellers would do well to note that drinking alcohol is likely to invalidate a claim in the event of an accident. Also check the payment protocol. You may have to pay first – known as an excess charge – before the insurance company reimburses you.

Always carry with you the telephone number of your insurer's 24-hr emergency helpline and your insurance policy number (and details).

Most annual policies have a trip limit of around a month. If you plan to be abroad for longer insurers including **Columbus**, **Direct Travel Insurance**, **Flexicover** and **Insure and Go** offer suitable cover. If travelling abroad several times in a year, an annual, worldwide insurance policy will save you money. A 45-year-old buying no-frills annual, worldwide cover can expect to pay between £55-110. A family of 4 should expect to pay £100-200. Prices vary widely so it is best to get several quotes before you buy.

Senior travellers should note that some companies will not cover people over 65 years old, or they may charge higher premiums.

Insurance companies

In North America

Young travellers from North America can try the International Student Insurance Service (ISIS), which is available through **STA Travel**, T1-800-777 0112, www.sta-travel.com. Other recommended travel insurance companies include: **Access America**, T1-800-284 8300; **Council Travel**, T1-888-COUNCIL, www.counciltravel.com; **Travel Assistance International**, T1-800-821 2828; **Travel Guard**, T1-800-826 1300, www.noel group.com; **Travel Insurance Services**, T1-800-937 1387.

In the UK

STA Travel and other reputable student travel organizations offer good value policies for students. There are also several companies who specialise in gap year travel insurance such as **Columbus Direct**, www.columbusdirect.com, **Down Under Travel Insurance**, www.duinsure.com, and **Endsleigh**, www.endsleigh.co.uk. Other companies include: **American Express**, T0800-028 7573, www.americanexpress .co.uk/travel; **Biba**, T0870-950 1790, www.biba.org.uk; **Churchill**, T0800-026 4050, www.churchill.com; **Direct Line**, T0845-246 8704, www.directline.com; **Esure**, T0845-600 3950, www.esure.com; **Flexicover**, www .flexicover.com; **Moneysupermarket.com**, www.moneysupermarket.com; **MRL**, T0870-876 7677, www.mrlinsurance.co.uk; **Medici Travel**, www.medicitravel.com, **MIA Online**, www.miaonline.co.uk; **Preferential**, T0870-600 7766, www.preferential.co.uk; **World Nomads**, www.worldnomads.com.

The best policies for senior travellers in the UK are offered by **Age Concern**, T01883-346964, www.ageconcern.org.uk, and **Saga**, T0800-056 5464, www.saga.co.uk.

Internet

India is at the forefront of the technology revolution and raced to embrace the internet. In 2007, 21.1 million Indians were online, making it the third largest user in the world, behind only the USA and China. And you're never far from an internet café or PCO (public call office), which also offers the service. The Indian communications ministry declared 2007 the year of broadband, which will include a major focus on providing Wi-Fi. Cyber capitals of the software sector savvy states of Kamataka and Andhra Pradesh already have lightning fast computers for dial connection to the internet and the even quicker broadband.

In small towns there is less internet access and it is recommended to take precautions: write lengthy emails in word, saving frequently, then paste them into your web-based email server rather than risking the loss of sweated-over missives home when the power fails or the connection goes down. Browsing costs vary dramatically depending on the location: these can be anything from Rs 20-100, with most charging somewhere in between. As a general rule, avoid emailing from upmarket hotels as their prices can be exorbitant unless you are a guest, in which case it's often free. If you intend to stay in India for a while it is worth signing up for membership with the internet chain **I-way**.

Language

Hindi, spoken as a mother tongue by over 400 million people, is India's official language. The use of English is also enshrined in the Constitution and used for a wide range of official purposes, notably communication between Hindi and non-Hindi speaking states. However, South India is the region of the Dravidian languages, a quite different language family from that of the Indo-European languages of North India. Each of the 4 states has its own dominant language, with its own distinctive script. Tamil, the oldest living language of India, reaches back over 2000 years and is spoken by 7% of India's population. Telugu (8.2%), the language of Andhra Pradesh, Kannada (4.2%), spoken in Karnataka, and Malayalam (3.5%) the seemingly unpronounceable language (to anyone other than a native Malayali speaker) of Kerala, each contribute to a rich cultural tradition of literature, poetry, song and film. In this book many town names are written in the appropriate script as many place names on sign boards, buses and stations are only given in the regional script. It is possible to study a number of Indian languages at language centres. See also individual area directories.

See also Culture, page 486. For Hindi words and phrases, a food and drink glossary and a glossary of terms, see pages 540-553.

Laundry

Laundry services are generally speedy. Laundry can be arranged very cheaply (eg a shirt washed and pressed for Rs 15-20 in **C-D** category; but Rs 50 or more in **LL-AL** hotels) and quickly (in 12-24 hours). It is best not to risk delicate fibres, though luxury hotels can usually handle these and also dry clean items.

Media

International **newspapers** (mainly English language) are sold in the bookshops of top hotels in major cities and occasionally by booksellers elsewhere. India has a large and lively English language press. They all have extensive analysis of contemporary Indian and some international issues. The major papers now have websites, excellent for keeping daily track on events, news and weather.

The best known are the traditionalist *The Hindu*, www.hinduonline.com/today/. *The Hindustan Times*, www.hindustantimes.com, the slightly more tabloid-establishment *Times of India*, www.timesofindia.com/ and *The Statesman*, www.thestatesman.org. *The Economic Times* is good for world coverage. *The Telegraph*, www.telegraphindia.com, has good foreign coverage. *The Indian Express*, www.express india.com, stands out as being consistently critical of the Congress Party and the government. *The Asian Age* is now published in the UK and India simultaneously and gives good coverage of Indian and international affairs. Of the news weeklies, some of the most widely read are current affairs *India Today*, *Frontline* and *The Week*, which are journals in the *Time* or *Newsweek* mould. *Business Today* is of course economy-based, while *Outlook* has a broader remit and has good general interest features. There is also *Outlook Traveller*, probably the best of the domestic travel titles.

India's national **radio** and **television** network, *Doordarshan*, broadcasts in national and regional languages but things have moved on. The advent of satellite TV has hit even remote rural areas and there are over 500 local broadcast television stations – each state has its own local-language current affairs broadcaster plus normally at least one other channel for entertainment. The 'Dish' can help travellers keep in touch through Star TV from Hong Kong, accessing BBC World, CNN etc, VTV (music) and Sport, is now available even in modest hotels in the smallest of towns.

Money

Indian currency is the Indian rupee (Re/Rs). It is **not** possible to purchase these before you arrive. If you want cash on arrival it is best to get it at the airport bank (see page 30 for details of international airport facilities). Rupee notes are printed in denominations of Rs 1000, 500, 100, 50, 20, 10. The rupee is divided into 100 paise. Coins are minted in denominations of Rs 5, Rs 2, Rs 1 and 50 paise. **NB** Carry money, mostly as TCs, in a money belt worn under clothing. Have a small amount ready in an easily accessible place.

Exchange rates (August 2007)
US$1 = Rs 40; UK £1 = Rs 82; AUS$1 = Rs 34; NZ$1 = Rs 31; €1 = Rs 56

Travellers' cheques (TCs)

TCs issued by reputable companies (eg Thomas Cook, American Express) are widely accepted. They can be easily exchanged at small local travel agents and tourist internet cafés but are rarely used directly for payment. Try to avoid changing at banks, where the process can be time consuming; opt for hotels and agents instead, take large denomination cheques and change enough to last for some days. Most banks, but not all, will accept US dollars, pounds sterling and euro TCs so it is a good idea to carry some of each. Other major currency TCs are also accepted in some larger cities. One traveller warns that replacement of lost Amex TCs may take weeks. If travelling to remote areas it can be worth buying Indian rupee TCs from a major bank, as these are more widely accepted than foreign currency ones.

Credit cards

Major credit cards are increasingly acceptable in the main centres, though in smaller cities and towns it is still rare to be able to pay by credit card. Payment by credit card can sometimes be more expensive than payment by cash, whilst some credit card companies charge a premium on cash withdrawals. **Visa** and **Mastercard** have a growing number of ATMs in major cities and several banks offer withdrawal facilities for Cirrus and Maestro cardholders. It is however easy to obtain a cash advance against a credit card. Railway reservation centres in 17 major cities are now taking payment for train tickets by Visa card which can be very quick as the queue is short, although they cannot be used for Tourist Quota tickets.

ATMs

By far the most convenient method of accessing money, ATMs are appearing all over India, usually attended by security guards, with most banks offering some services to holders of overseas cards. Banks whose ATMs will issue cash against Cirrus and Maestro cards, as well as Visa and Mastercard, include **Bank of Baroda, Citibank, HDFC, HSBC, ICICI, IDBI, Punjab National Bank, State Bank of India** (SBI), **Standard Chartered** and **UTI**. A withdrawal fee is usually charged by the issuing bank on top of the various conversion charges applied by your own bank. Fraud prevention measures quite often result in travellers having their cards blocked by the bank when unexpected overseas transactions occur; it may be worth advising your bank of your travel plans before leaving.

Changing money

The **State Bank of India** and several others in major towns are authorized to deal in foreign exchange. Some give cash against Visa/Mastercard (eg **ANZ**, **Bank of Baroda** who print a list of their participating branches, **Andhra Bank**). American Express cardholders can use their cards to get either cash or TCs in Mumbai and Chennai. They also have offices in Coimbatore, Goa, Hyderabad and Thiruvananthapuram. The larger cities have licensed money changers with offices usually in the commercial sector. Changing money through unauthorized dealers is illegal. Premiums on the currency black market are very small and highly risky. Large hotels change money 24 hours a day for guests, but banks often give a substantially better rate of exchange. It is best to exchange money on arrival at the airport bank or the Thomas Cook counter. Many international flights arrive during the night and it is generally far easier and less time consuming to change money at the airport than in the city. If you cash sterling, always make certain that you have been given rupees at the sterling and not at the dollar rate. You should be given a foreign currency encashment certificate when you change money through a bank or authorized dealer; ask for one if it is not automatically given. It allows you to change Indian rupees back to your own currency on departure. It also enables you to use rupees to pay hotel bills or buy air tickets for which payment in foreign exchange may be required. The certificates are only valid for 3 months.

Transferring money to India

HSBC, **Barclays** and **ANZGrindlays** and others can make 'instant' transfers to their offices in India but charge a high fee (about US$30). **Standard Chartered Bank** issues US$ TCs. Sending a bank draft (up to US$1000) by post (4-7 days by Speedpost) is the cheapest option.

Cost of living

The cost of living in India remains well below that in the West. The average wage per capita is about Rs 34,000 per year (US$800). Manual, unskilled labourers (women are often paid less than men), farmers and others in rural areas earn considerably less. However, thanks to booming global demand for workers who can provide cheaper IT and technology support functions and many Western firms transferring office functions or call centres to India, salaries in certain sectors have sky rocketed. An IT specialist can earn an average Rs 500,000 per year (US$12,000) and upwards, a rate that is rising by around 15% a year.

Cost of travelling

Most food, accommodation and public transport, especially rail and bus, are exceptionally cheap. There is a widening

Money matters

→ It can be difficult to use torn or very worn currency notes. Check notes when you are given them and refuse any that are damaged.
→ Request some Rs 100 and 50 notes. Rs 500 (can be mistaken for Rs 100) notes reduce 'wallet bulge' but can be difficult to change.
→ A good supply of small denomination notes always comes in handy for bus tickets, cheap meals and tipping. Remember that if offered a large note, the recipient will never have any change!
→ It can be worth carrying a few clean, new sterling or dollar notes for use where travellers' cheques and credit cards are not accepted. It is likely to be quite a while before euro notes are widely accepted.

range of moderately priced but clean hotels and restaurants outside the big cities, making it possible to get a great deal for your money. Budget travellers sharing a room, taking public transport, avoiding those pesky, pretty souvenir stalls, and eating nothing but rice and dhal can get away with a budget of Rs 350-400 (about US$8 or £4) a day. This sum leaps up if you drink booze (still cheap by European standards at about US$2, £1 or Rs 80 for a pint), smoke fags or want to have your own wheels (you can expect to spend Rs 100 to hire a Honda Kinetic per day). Those planning to stay in fairly comfortable hotels and use taxis sightseeing should budget at US$30 (£15) a day. Then again you could always check into somewhere like the Nilaya for Christmas and notch up an impressive $450 (£225) bill on your B&B alone. India can be a great place to pick and choose, save a little on basic accommodation and then treat yourself to the type of meal you could only dream of affording back home. Also, be prepared to spend a fair amount more in Mumbai, Hyderabad, Bengaluru (Bangalore) and Chennai, where not only is the cost of living significantly higher but when it's worth coughing up extra for a half-decent room: penny-pinch by the beach when you'll be spending precious little time indoors anyway. A newspaper costs Rs 5 and breakfast for two with coffee can come to as little as Rs 15 in a South Indian 'hotel', but if you intend to eat along the beach areas you won't get much change from Rs 100 per person – still only just over a pound sterling.

Opening hours

Banks are open Mon-Fri 1030-1430, Sat 1030-1230. Top hotels sometimes have a 24-hour money changing service. Post offices are usually open Mon-Fri 1000-1700 and Sat mornings. Government offices open Mon-Fri 0930-1700, Sat 0930-1300 (some open on alternate Sat only). Shops open Mon-Sat 0930-1800. Bazars keep longer hours.

Post

The post is frequently unreliable, and delays are common. It is best to use a post office where you can hand over mail for franking across the counter, or a top hotel post box. Valuable items should only be sent by registered mail. Government emporia or shops in the larger hotels will send purchases home if the items are difficult to carry.

Airmail services to Europe, Africa and Australia take at least a week and a little longer for the Americas. Speed post (which takes about 4 days to the UK) is available from major towns. Speed post to the UK from Tamil Nadu costs Rs 675 for the first 250g sent and an extra Rs 75 for each 250g thereafter. Specialist shippers deal with larger items, normally around US$150 per cubic metre. Courier services (eg **DHL**) are available in the larger towns. At some main post offices you can send small packages under 2 kg as **letter post** (rather than parcel post), which is much cheaper at Rs 220. **Book post** (for printed paper only, sent by sea mail) is cheaper still, approximately Rs 170 for 5 kg. Book parcels must be sewn in cloth (best over transparent plastic) with a small open 'window' slit for contents to be seen; larger post offices often have their own parcel stitcher, or you can take the package to a tailor. The parcel must be marked on the front with the words 'Sea Mail – Book Post' and 'Printed Matter Only'; in some post offices the process can take up to 2 hrs, while delivery takes no less than 3 months. Check that the post office holds necessary customs declaration forms (2-3 copies needed). Write 'No commercial value' if returning used clothes, books etc. **Sea mail** costs Rs 800 for 10 kg. 'Packers' do necessary cloth covering, sealing etc for Rs 20-50; you address the parcel, obtain stamps from a separate counter; stick stamps and a customs form to the parcel with glue available (the other form/s must be partially sewn on). Post at the Parcels Counter and obtain a registration slip. Maximum dimensions: height 1 m, width 0.8 m, circumference 1.8 m. Cost varies by destination and is normally displayed on a board beside the counter.

Poste restante facilities are widely available in even quite small towns at the GPO where mail is held for 1 month. Ask for mail to be addressed to you with your surname in capitals and underlined. When asking for mail at Poste Restante check under surname as well as Christian name.

Any special issue **foreign stamps** are likely to be stolen from envelopes in the Indian postal service and letters may be thrown away. Advise people who are sending you mail to India to use only definitive stamps (without pictures).

Public holidays

See page 45 for details of national holidays.

Safety

Personal security

In general the threats to personal security for travellers in India are remarkably small. However, incidents of petty theft and violence directed specifically at tourists have been on the increase so care is necessary in some places, and basic common sense needs to be used with respect to looking after valuables. Follow the same precautions you would when at home. There have been incidents of sexual assault in and around the main tourist beach centres, particularly after full moon parties. Avoid wandering alone outdoors late at night in these places. During daylight hours be careful in remote places, especially when alone. If you are under threat, scream loudly. Never accept food or drink from casual acquaintances, it may be drugged.

Some parts of South India are subject to political violence, particularly the Naxalite-controlled areas of Andhra Pradesh. They have a long history of conflict with state and national authorities, including attacks on police and government officials. The Naxalites have not specifically targeted Westerners, but have attacked symbolic targets including Western companies. The Naxalite party is officially banned in Andhra Pradesh. As a general rule, travellers are advised to be vigilant in the lead up to and on days of national significance, such as Republic Day (26 Jan) and Independence Day (15 Aug) as militants have in the past used such occasions to mount attacks.

Following a major explosion on the Delhi to Lahore (Pakistan) train in Feb 2007, increased security has been implemented on many trains and stations. Similar measures at airports may cause delays for passengers so factor this into your timing. Also check your airline's website for up-to-date information on luggage restrictions. In Mumbai, the UK's Foreign and Commonwealth Office warns of a risk of armed robbers holding up taxis travelling along the main highway from the airport to the city in the early hours of the morning (0200-0600) when there is little traffic on the roads. If you are using the route during these times, you should, if possible, arrange to travel by coach or seek advice at the airport on arrival.

That said, in the great majority of places visited by tourists, violent crime and personal attacks are extremely rare.

Travel advice

It is better to seek advice from your own consulate than from travel agencies. Before you travel you can contact: British Foreign & Commonwealth Office Travel Advice Unit, T0845-850 2829 (Pakistan desk T020-7270 2385), www.fco.gov.uk. US State Department's Bureau of Consular Affairs, Overseas Citizens Services, Room 4800, Department of State, Washington, DC 20520-4818, USA, T202-6471488, http://travel.state.gov. Australian Department of Foreign Affairs Canberra, Australia, T02-6261 3305, www.smartraveller .gov.au. Canadian official advice is on www.voyage.gc.ca.

Theft

Theft is not uncommon. It is best to keep TCs, passports and valuables with you at all times. Don't regard hotel rooms as being automatically safe; even hotel safes don't guarantee secure storage. Avoid leaving valuables near open windows even when you are in the room. Use your own padlock in a budget hotel when you go out. Pickpockets and other thieves operate in the big cities. Crowded areas are particularly high risk. Take special care of your belongings when getting on or off public transport.

If you have items stolen, they should be reported to the police as soon as possible. Keep a separate record of vital documents, including passport details and numbers of TCs. Larger hotels will be able to assist in contacting and dealing with the police. Dealings with the police can be very difficult and in the worst regions such as Bihar even dangerous. The paperwork involved in reporting losses can be time consuming and irritating and your own documentation (eg passport and visas) may be demanded.

In some states the police themselves sometimes demand bribes, though you should not assume that if procedures move slowly you are automatically being expected to offer a bribe. The traffic police are tightening up very hard on traffic offences in some places. They have the right to make on-the-spot fines for speeding and illegal parking. If you face a demand for a fine, insist on a receipt. If you have to go to a police station, try to take someone with you.

If you face really serious problems, for example in connection with a driving accident, you should contact your consular office as quickly as possible. You should ensure you always have your international driving licence and motorbike or car documentation with you.

Confidence tricksters are particularly common where people are on the move, notably around railway stations or places where budget tourists gather. A common plea is some sudden and desperate calamity; sometimes a letter will be produced in English to back up the claim. The demands are likely to increase sharply if sympathy is shown. See also Shopping, page 48.

Travel safety

Motorcycles don't come fitted with helmets and accidents are commonplace so exercise caution, the horn and the brake. Horns carry their own code: pip to make pedestrians, stray dogs and other bikers (you hear little over your own engine) aware you're about to overtake or hold a screaming continuous note to communicate urgent alarm to anything fast bearing down on you – even then be prepared to dive from the tarmac.

First-class compartments on **trains** are self-contained and normally completely secure, although nothing of value should be left close to open train windows. Two-tier a/c compartments are larger, allowing more movement of passengers and are therefore not so secure. Most thefts occur in non-a/c sleeper class carriages. Attendants may take little notice of what is going on, and thefts – particularly on the Goa to Hampi train route – are on the rise, so luggage should be chained to a seat for security overnight and care taken in daylight. Locks and chains are easily available at main stations and bazars. Travelling bags and cases should be made of tough material, and external pockets (both on bags and on clothing) should never be used for carrying either money or important documents. Strong locks for travelling cases are invaluable. Use a leather strap around a case for extra security. Some travellers prefer to reserve upper berths, which offer some added protection against theft and also have the benefit of allowing daytime sleeping. If you put your bags on the upper berth during the day, beware of fellow passengers climbing up for a 'sleep'. Be guarded with new friends on trains who show interest in the contents of your bag and be extra wary of accepting food or drink from casual acquaintances; travellers have reported being drugged and then robbed. Pickpockets and other thieves operate in crowded areas.

Senior travellers

Travellers over the age of 60 can take advantage of several discounts on travel, including 30% on train fares and up to 50% on some air tickets. Ask at the time of booking, since these will not be offered automatically.

Smoking

Several state governments have passed a law banning smoking in all public buildings and transport but exempting open spaces. To avoid fines, check for notices.

Student travellers

Full-time students qualify for an ISIC (International Student Identity Card) which is issued by student travel and specialist agencies (eg Usit, Campus, STA) at home. The card allows certain travel benefits such as reduced prices and concessions into certain sites. For details see www.isic.org or contact STIC in Imperial Hotel, Janpath, New Delhi, T011-2334 3302. Those intending to study in India may get a year's student visa (see page 67). For details of student travel insurance, see page 55.

Telephone

The international code for India is 0091. International Direct Dialling is now widely available in privately run call booths, usually labelled on yellow boards with the letters 'PCO-STD-ISD'. You dial the call yourself, and the time and cost are displayed on a computer screen. Cheap rate (2100-0600) means long queues may form outside booths. Telephone calls from hotels are usually much more expensive (check price before calling), though some will allow local calls free of charge. Internet phone booths, usually associated with cyber cafés, are the cheapest way of calling overseas.

A double ring repeated regularly means it is ringing. Equal tones with equal pauses means engaged. Both are similar to UK ringing and engaged tones.

One disadvantage of the tremendous pace of the telecommunications revolution is the fact that millions of telephone numbers go out of date every year. Current telephone directories themselves are often out of date and some of the numbers given in this book will have been changed even as we go to press. The answer is to put an additional 2 on the front of existing numbers. Unfortunately only some states have implemented this while others have reverted to the existing number. **Our best advice is if the number in the text does not work, add a 2**. Directory enquiries, T197, can be helpful but works only for the local area code.

Mobile phones are for sale everywhere, as are local SIM cards that allow you to make calls within India and overseas at much lower rates than using a 'roaming' service from your normal provider at home – sometimes for as little as Rs 0.5 per minute. Arguably the best service is provided by the government carrier BSNL/MTNL but security provisions make connecting to the service virtually impossible for foreigners. Private companies such as Airtel, Hutch, Reliance and Tata Indicom are easier to sign up with, but the deals they offer can be befuddling and are frequently changed. To connect you'll need to complete a form, have a local address or know a friendly hotel owner who'll vouch for you, and present photocopies of your passport and visa plus 2 passport photos to an authorised reseller – most phone dealers will be able to help, and can also sell top-up vouchers. India is divided into a number of 'calling circles' or regions, and if you travel outside the region where your connection is based you will pay higher charges for making and receiving calls, and any problems that may occur – with 'unverified' documents, for example – can be much harder to resolve.

Fax services are available from many PCOs and larger hotels, who charge either by the minute or per page.

Time

India doesn't change its clocks, so from the last Sun in Oct to the last Sun in Mar the time is GMT +5½ hrs, and the rest of the year it's +4½ hrs (USA, EST +10½ and +9½ hrs; Australia, EST -5½ and -4½ hrs).

Tipping

A tip of Rs 10 to a bellboy carrying luggage in a modest hotel (Rs 20 in a higher category) would be appropriate. In upmarket restaurants, a 10% tip is acceptable when service is not already included, while in places serving very cheap meals, round off the bill with small change. Indians don't normally tip taxi drivers but a small extra amount over the fare is welcomed. Porters at airports and railway stations often have a fixed rate displayed but will usually press for more. Ask fellow passengers what a fair rate is.

Tourist information

There are Government of India tourist offices in the state capitals, as well as state tourist offices (sometimes Tourism Development Corporations) in the major cities and a few important sites. They produce their own tourist literature, either free or sold at a nominal price, and some also have lists of city hotels and paying guest options. The quality of material is improving though maps are often poor. Many offer tours of the city, neighbouring sights and overnight and regional packages. Some run modest hotels and midway motels with restaurants and may also arrange car hire and guides. The staff in the regional and local offices are usually helpful.

Tourist offices overseas

Australia Level 5, Glasshouse,135 King St, Sydney, NSW 2000, T02-9221 9555, info@indiatourism.com.au.
Canada 60 Bloor St West, Suite No 1003, Toronto, Ontario, T416-962 3787, indiatourism@bellnet.ca.
Dubai 6 Post Box 12856, NASA Building, Al Maktoum Road, Deira, T04-227 4848, goirto@emirates.net.ae.
France 11-13 Bis Boulevard Hausmann, 75009, Paris T01-4523 3045.
Germany Baserler St 48, 60329, Frankfurt AM-Main 1, T069-242 9490, www.india-tourism.de.
Italy Via Albricci 9, Milan 20122, T02-805 3506, info@indiatourismmilan.com.
Japan B9F Chiyoda Building, 6-5-12 Ginza, Chuo-Ku, Tokyo 104-0061, T03-3571 5062, indiatourt@smile.ocn.ne.jp.
The Netherlands Rokin 9-15, 1012 KK Amsterdam, T020-620 8991, info@indiatourismamsterdam.com.
Singapore 20 Kramat Lane, 01-01A United House, 228773, Singapore, T6235-3800, indtour.sing@pacific.net.sg.
South Africa P.O. Box 412452, Craig Hall 2024, 2000 Johannesburg, T011-325 0880, goito@global.co.za.
UK 7 Cork St, London WIS 3LH, T020- 7437 3677, T08700-102183, info@indiatouristoffice.org.
USA 3550 Wilshire Boulevard, Room 204, Los Angeles, California 90010, T213-380 8855, goitola@aol.com; Suite 1808, 1270 Av of Americas, New York, NY 10020-1700, T212-586 4901, ny@itony.com.

Tour operators

UK

Andrew Brock, 29a Main St, Lyddington, Oakham, Rutland LE15 9LR, T01572-821330, www.coromandelabt.com. Tailor-made tours (some by car) in South India including Kerala and the Coromandel Coast.

Colours Of India, Marlborough House, 298 Regents Park Rd, London, N3 2TJ, T020-8343 3446, www.colours-of-india.co.uk. Tailor-made cultural, adventure, spa and cooking tours.

Discovery Initiatives, The Travel House, 51 Castle St, Cirencester, Gloucestershire GL7 1QD, T01285-643333, www.discoveryinitiatives.com. Wildlife safaris, tiger study tours and cultural tours.

Dragoman, Camp Green, Debenham, Stowmarket, Suffolk IP14 6LA, T01728-861133, www.dragoman.com. Overland adventure travel company, including camping.

Greaves Tours, 53 Welbeck St, London, T020-7487 9111, www.greavesindia.com. Luxury, tailor-made tours, scheduled flights only. Traditional travel such as road and rail preferred to flights between major cities.

Indian Explorations, Afex House, Holwell, Burford, Oxfordshire, OX18 4JS, T01993-822443, www.explorationcompany.com. Bespoke holidays.

Kerala Connections, School House Lane, Horsmonden, Kent TN12 8BP, T01892-722440, www.keralaconnect.co.uk. Specializes in tailor-made tours of South India, including Lakshadweep, with great homestays.

Kerala Vacations, Roper Rd, Canterbury, CT7 7EX, T07931-104010, www.Kerala Vacations.com. Individually designed holidays to South India.

Kuoni, Kuoni House, Dorking, Surrey RH5 4AZ, T01306-747002, www.kuoni.co.uk. Runs week-long tours on culture and relaxation.

STA Travel, T020-7361 6100 (head office), T0870-160 6070 (general enquiries), www.sta travel.co.uk. Student and young persons' travel agent.

Steppes Travel, 51 Castle St, Gloucester-shire, GL7 1QD, T01285-651010, www.steppestravel.co.uk.

Trans Indus, Northumberland House, 11 The Pavement, Popes Lane, Ealing, London W5 4NG, T020-8566 2729, www.transindus.com. Tailor-made and group tours and holidays.

India

Ibex Expeditions, G 66 East of Kailash, New Delhi 110065, T91-11-2691 2641, www.ibexexpeditions.com. Award-winning tour operator for tours, safaris and treks.

Paradise Holidays, 312-Ansal Cassique Tower, Rajouri Garden, New Delhi 11027, T981-105 2376 (Rajnish), www.paradise holidays.com. Wide range of tailor-made tours, from cultural to adventure to religious.

Pyramid Tours, 'Deccan Dreams', B-3, Jyothi Complex, 134/1, Infantry Rd, Bangalore, T91-80-2286 7589/90/91/92, www.pyramidsdeccan.com. Academics as guides, conservationists on heritage, nature, culture and rejuvenation packages.

Royal Expeditions, R-184, Greater Kailash, New Delhi, T91-11-2623 8545, www.royal expeditions.com. Tailor-made independent tours including wildlife, adventure and culture.

North America

Absolute Asia, 180 Varick St, 16th Floor, New York, T212-627 1950, www.absoluteasia.com. Luxury custom-designed tours: culinary, pilgrimage of the south, honeymoon, 'Jewish India' tour plus Tamil tour bundling Tamil Nadu with Sri Lanka.

General Tours, 53 Summer St, Keene, New Hampshire, T1-800-221-2216, www.generaltours.com. Packages include Kerala spas, houseboats and wildlife, South India and Karnataka, South India and Tamil Nadu, Goa add-ons.

Greaves Tours, 304 Randolph St, Chicago, T1-800-3187801, www.greavesindia.com. Luxury, tailor-made tours only using scheduled flights.

Sita World Travel, 350 Fifth Av, Suite 1421, New York, T212-279 6865, www.sitatours.com. Top-end set packages including 7-day ayurveda programmes, Trails of South India tour and Goa add-ons.

Spirit of India, USA T888-367 6147, www.spirit-of-india.com. General and spirituality focused tours. Local experts.

Australia and New Zealand

Abercrombie & Kent, 19-29 Martin Pl, Sydney, T02-9238 2356, www.abercrombie&kent.com.au.

Adventure World, 73 Walkers St, North Sydney, T02-8913 0755, www.adventureworld.com.au. Independent tour operator with packages from 7 nights in Kerala. Also at 101 Great South Rd, Remuera, Auckland, T64-9-524 5118, www.adventureworld.co.nz.

Classic Oriental Tours, 35 Grafton St, Woollahara, T02-9657 2020, www.classicoriental.com.au. Travel arrangements in groups and for independent travellers, at all standards ranging from budget to deluxe.

Intrepid Travel, 11-13 Spring St, Fitzroy, Victoria 3065, T1300-360 887, www.intrepidtravel.com. Everything from cookery courses to village stays.

Europe

Academische Reizen, World Travel Holland, Academische Reizen BV, Prinsengracht 783-785, 1017 JZ Amsterdam, T020-589 2940, www.academischereizen.nl. All-India group culture tours.

Chola Voyages, 190, rue du Fbg St Denis, 75010 Paris, T01-4034 5564, delamanche@hotmail.com.

La Maison Des Indes, 7 Place St Sulpice, 75006 Paris, T01-5681 3838, www.maisondes indes.com. Bespoke or group cultural tours.

Neckermann/Thomas Cook, NL Scorpius 1, 2132 LH Hoofddorp, T023-513 5960, Noortje.aarts@neckermann.nl. Charters to Goa and South India.

The Shoestring Company, Meidoornweg 2, 1031 GG Amsterdam, T020-685 0203, info@shoestring.nl. Group leisure and adventure tours.

Activity holidays

Peter and Friends Classic Adventures, Casa Tres Amigos Assagao 403 507, Goa, India. www.classic-bike-india.com. An Indo-German company which arranges high-octane tours around South India on Enfield motorbikes.

Purple Valley Yoga Center, Assagao, www.yogagoa.com. Retreats and drop-in yoga classes with peerless international ashtanga yoga teachers like John and Lucy Scott.

Royal Enfield, www.royalenfield.com. Indian website has information on pilgrim tours by motorbike and how to buy a new Bullet, and www.indax.com has useful stuff on motorbike touring hazards.

Specialists in homestays

At the upmarket end, more and more people are looking to stay in private homes and guesthouses when in India, opting out of the hotel chains that keep you at arm's length from a culture and instead getting into home-cooked meals in heritage houses and learning about a country through talking to your often fascinating hosts. Kerala leads the field in this type of set-up. The following are a few of the operators who specialize in arranging this sort of accommodation. Tourist offices have lists of families with more modest homestays.

Kerala Connections, see under UK, page 65.

MAHout, 36a Kensington Mansions, Trebovir Rd, London SW5 9TQ, T020-7373 7121, www.mahoutuk.com. Boutique hotels representation specialist.

Pyramid Tours, see India tour operators, page 65.

Sundale Vacations, 39/5955A, Atlantis Jn, MG Rd, Cochin-682015, Kerala, T0484-235 9127, www.sundale.com. A mix of unusual accommodation, cultural activities and sightseeing tours in Kerala.

Unusual Places, 40/7382, Ist floor, Meenakshi Estate, Rajaji Rd, Ernakulam-682035, T0484-237 1066, www.unusualplaces.info. The largest off-beat accommodation company in South India. Promotes a network of independent bungalows, plantation villas and farmhouses across Kerala and Tamil Nadu.

Vaccinations

If you need vaccinations, see your doctor well in advance of your travel. Most courses must be completed by a minimum of 4 weeks. Travel clinics may provide rapid courses of vaccination, but are likely to be more pricey. The following vaccinations are recommended: typhoid, polio, tetanus, infectious hepatitis and diptheria. For details of malaria prevention, see page 53.

The following vaccinations may also be considered: rabies, possibly BCG (since tuberculosis is still common) and in some cases meningitis and diphtheria (if you're staying in the country for a long time). Yellow fever is not required in India but you may be asked to show a certificate if you have travelled from Africa or South America. Japanese encephalitis may be required for rural travel at certain times of the year (mainly rainy seasons). A new and effective oral cholera vaccine (Dukoral) is now available as 2 doses (1 week apart) providing 3 months' protection.

Visas and immigration

For embassies and consulates, see page 51. Virtually all foreign nationals, including children, require a visa to enter India. Nationals of Bhutan and Nepal only require a suitable means of identification. The rules regarding visas change frequently and arrangements for application and collection also vary from town to town so it is essential to check details and costs with the relevant embassy or consulate. These remain closed on Indian national holidays. In London, applications are processed in a couple of hours (0800-1200) if you appear at the office in person. At other offices, it can be much easier to apply in advance by post, to avoid queues and frustratingly low visa quotas. Postal applications can take up to 15 working days to process.

Visitors from countries with no Indian representation may apply to the resident British representative, or enquire at the **Air India** office. An application on the prescribed form should be accompanied by 2 passport photographs and your passport which should be valid 6 months beyond the period of your visit. Note that visas are valid from the date granted, not from the date of entry. For the most up-to-date information on visa requirements see www.india-visa.com.

No foreigner needs to register within the 180-day period of their tourist visa. All foreign visitors who stay in India for more than 180 days need to get an income tax clearance exemption certificate from the Foreign Section of the Income Tax Department in Delhi, Mumbai, Kolkata or Chennai.

Currently the following visa rules apply:

Transit For passengers en route to another country (no more than 72 hours in India).

Tourist 3-6 month visa from the date of issue with multiple entry.

Business 3-6 months or up to 2 years with multiple entry. A letter from the company giving the nature of business is required.

5 year For those of Indian origin only, who have held Indian passports.

Student Valid up to 1 year from the date of issue. Attach a letter of acceptance from Indian institution and an AIDS test certificate. Allow up to 3 months for approval.

Visa extensions Applications should be made to the Foreigners' Regional Registration Offices at New Delhi, Mumbai, Kolkata or Chennai, or an office of the Superintendent of Police in the District Headquarters. After 6 months, you must leave India and apply for a new visa – the Nepal office is known to be difficult. Anyone staying in India for a period of more than 180 days (6 months) must register at a convenient Foreigners' Registration Office, see Registration below.

Permits and restricted and protected areas

Some areas are politically sensitive and special permits may be needed to visit though the government is relaxing regulations. Currently you need a special permit to visit the Lakshadweep Islands. Foreigners may visit Bangaram and Suheli Islands only; permits from the Lakshadweep Administration, Willingdon Island, Harbour Rd, Fort Kochi.

Work permits

Foreigners should apply to the Indian representative in their country of origin for the latest information about work permits.

Weights and measures

Metric system has come into universal use in the cities. In remote areas local measures are sometimes used. One lakh is 100,000 and 1 core is 10 million.

Women travellers

Independent travel is still largely unheard of for Indian women: if you travel alone outside Goa expect plenty of questions, but it can be fun too. Goa is easy enough on solitary female travellers and friends are easy to meet along the way. Cautious solo women travellers recommend dying blonde hair black and wearing wedding rings, but the most important measure is to dress appropriately, in loose-fitting, non-see-through clothes, covering shoulders, arms and legs (a salwaar kameez, say). Take advantage, too, of the gender segregation on public transport, both to duck hassle and talk with local women.

In mosques women should be covered from head to ankle. Unaccompanied women are most vulnerable in major cities, crowded bazaars, beach resorts and tourist centres where men may follow them and touch them. ('Eve teasing' is the euphemism for physical harassment.) If you are harassed, it's normally useful to make a scene, on which the average Indian Joe will tend to rally round to defend your modesty. Be firm and clear if you don't wish to speak to someone. Most railway booking offices have separate women's ticket queues or ask women to go to the head of the general queue. It is best to be accompanied at night, especially when travelling by rickshaw or taxi in towns. Some women complain they have been 'felt up' while being measured for clothing in tailors' shops. If possible, take a friend with you. See also page 25.

Working in India

See also Visas and immigration, page 67.
It is best to arrange voluntary work well in advance with organizations in India (addresses are given in some towns, eg Delhi, Darjeeling, Dharamshala, Kolkata and Leh); alternatively, contact an organization abroad.

Students may spend part of their year off helping in a school or teaching English.

Voluntary work

In the UK

1 to 1, Woodside House, 261 Low Lane, Leeds, LS18 5NY, T0800-011 1156, www.i-to-i.com.
International Voluntary Service (IVS), Old Hall, East Bergholt, Colchester, CO7 6TQ, T01206-298215; Oxford Place Centre, Oxford Place, Leeds, LS1 3AX, T0113-246 9900; St John's Centre, Edinburgh EH2 4BJ, www.ivs-gb.org.uk.
VSO, 317 Putney Bridge Rd, London SW15 2PN, www.sci.ivs.org.
Volunteer Work Information Service, PO Box 2759, Lewes, BN7 1WU, UK, T01273-470015, www.workingabroad.com.

In the USA

Council for International Programs, 1700 East 13th St, Suite 4ME, Cleveland, Ohio, T216-566-108, www.cipusa.org.

In Australia

The website www.ampersand.org.au has links to a variety of volunteer organisations, of which the biggest is:
Australian Volunteers International, 71 Argyle St, Fitzroy, VIC 3065, T03-9279 1788, www.australianvolunteers.com.

Goa

A growing number of foreigners are making their homes in Goa and working as small-time entrepreneurs, from making clothes to running restaurants and accommodation. Some canny locals have looked to these businesses for inspiration, so ecotourism concerns, say, have grown by imitation, but others resent success of outsiders. This envy has caused some unrest in the past, especially as many foreign-owned businesses employ remittance workers from outside Goa, so the local economy doesn't benefit. Ask the more high-profile foreign entrepreneurs for ways on reducing problems with the local community.

Tamil Nadu

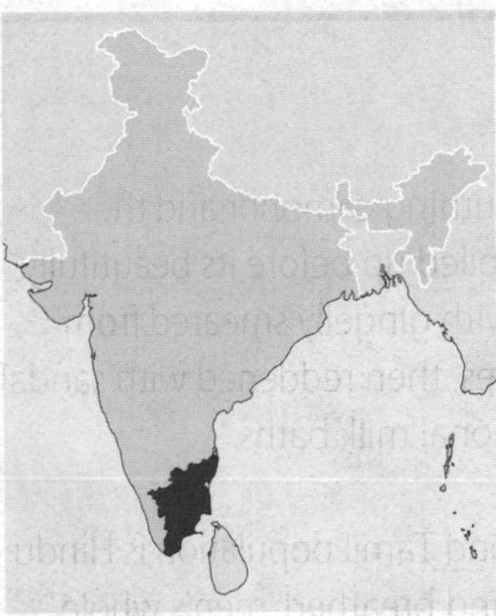

Footprint features

Introduction

Tamil Nadu smells of sacrificial burning camphor and the perfume from jasmine garlands piled up before its beautifully carved granite gods, well oiled with gingelly smeared from the palms of centuries of devotees, then reddened with sandal powder and washed with devotional milk baths.

About 90% of the 60 million-strong Tamil population is Hindu and religious ritual here is lived and breathed: men's whole foreheads are daubed with potash, huge horizontal sweeps or fingernail-thin red edges drawn from the hair's centre-parting sideways, while women sprinkle intricate geometric designs of ground rice powder on their hearths every dawn. It's rare to find a temple that has outlived its religious purpose – seldom the shrine that is mere monument. But nor is worship confined to the feats of architecture that dot Tamil Nadu. Banyan trees are festooned with dangling sacred talismen; tridents are slammed into the ground to create makeshift mounds of worship; village gods in life-size stucco renderings bare their teeth and brandish knives at every roadside, and files of nomads pick their way along baked dirt tracks.

Here, then, is the heady temple trail: Kancheepuram, Mahabalipuram, Chidambaram, Tanjore, Madurai, the second Varanasi of Rameswaram, and the holy toe-tip of India in Kanniyakumari; the contrasting ashram atmospheres at the traditionalist Tiruvannamalai and the futuristic utopia of Auroville.

Welcome antidotes to temple fatigue come in the form of the charming domestic architecture in French Pondicherry and the palatial homes in Chettinad, or in big breaths of nature in the Nilgiri blue mountains around the celebrated tea-planters' hill stations of Ooty and Kodai.

★ Don't miss …

1 **Descent of the Ganga** A ninth-century bas relief that outclasses the Renaissance masters, in seaside Mahabalipuram, page 89.

2 **Pondicherry belly** A fine showcase for Gallic gastronomic art, page 106.

3 **Thanjavur** The fortnightly bathing of the beautiful Big Temple's Nandi with milk and gingelly draws a spellbound hoard of devotees, page 122.

4 **Chidambaram** Explore this unique Brahmin temple society, page 126.

5 **Snooty Ooty** Puff up the ghats on the rack-and-pinion railway to reach this hill station bolt hole of the Madras Presidency, page 133.

6 **Temple of the fish-eyed goddess Madurai** A heady swirling temple to female fecundity, in the divine form of Meenakshi Devi, page 153.

7 **Chettinad** Gaudy palaces standing empty in little-visited arid ghost towns, and India's hottest cuisine, page 159.

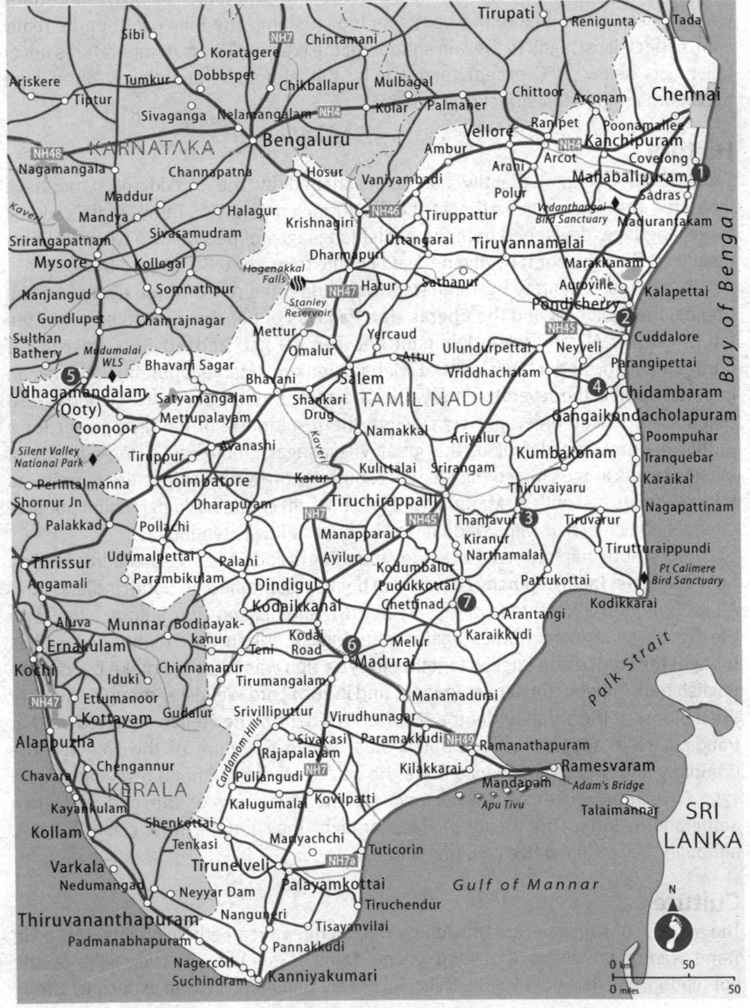

Background → *Population: 62.1 mn. Area: 130,000 sq km.*

The land

Geography Tamil Nadu rises from the flat coastal plains in the east to the Western Ghats – the Nilgiris in the north and the Palani, Cardamom and Anamalai hills in the south. The Nilgiris – 'blue mountains' – rise like a wall above the haze of the plains to heights of over 2500 m. The plains are hot, dry and dusty, with isolated blocks of granite forming bizarre shapes on the ancient eroded surface. The coast itself is a flat alluvial plain, with deltas at the mouths of major rivers. The occasional medieval water tanks add beauty to the landscape.

Tamil Nadu's coast bore the brunt of India's casualties of the 2004 tsunami. Along 1000 km of shoreline, at least 8000 people died, and 470,000 were displaced. As well as loved ones, the wave washed away infrastructure: communities, homes, livelihoods, schools, and health clinics. See box opposite.

Climate Most rain falls between October and December and is the worst time to travel. The best time to visit is from mid-December to early March when the dry sunny weather sets in and before the heat gets too crushing. The hills can then be really cold, especially at night. In the rain shadow of the Western Ghats, temperatures never fall much below 21°C except in the hills, but although humidity is often high maximum temperatures rarely exceed 42°C.

History

Tamil Nadu's cultural identity has been shaped by the Dravidians, who have inhabited the south since at least the fourth millennium BC. Tamil, India's oldest living language, developed from the earlier languages of people who were probably displaced from the north by Aryan-based culture from 2000 BC to 1500 BC.

By the fourth century BC Tamil Nadu was under the rule of three dynasties: the **Cholas**, the **Pandiyas** and the **Cheras**. The **Pallavas** of Kanchi came to power in the fourth century AD and were dominant between AD 550 and AD 869. Possibly of northern origin, under their control Mahabalipuram (Mamallapuram) became an important port in the seventh century. The **Cholas** returned to power in 850 and were a dominant political force until 1173 before the resumption of Pandiya power for a further century. The defeat of the great Vijayanagar Empire by a confederacy of Muslim states in 1565 forced their leaders south. As the Nayaka kings they continued to rule from as far south as Madurai well into the 17th century. When Muslim political control finally reached Tamil Nadu it was as brief as it was tenuous.

It was more than 150 years after their founding of Fort St George at Madras in 1639 before the **East India Company** could claim political supremacy in South India. Haidar Ali, who mounted the throne of Mysore in 1761, and his son Tipu Sultan, allied with the French, won many battles against the English. When the Treaty of Versailles brought the French and English together in 1783 Tipu was forced to make peace. The English took Malabar (in Kerala) in 1792, and in 1801 Lord Wellesley brought together the majority of the south under the Madras Presidency. **The French** acquired land at Pondicherry in 1673. In 1742, Dupleix was named Governor of the French India Company and took up residence there. He seized Madras within a few years but in 1751 Clive attacked Arcot. His victory was the beginning of the end of French ambitions in India. The Treaty of Paris brought their Empire to a close in 1763, although they retained five counting houses.

Culture

The majority of Tamilians are Dravidians with Mediterranean ethnic origins, settled in Tamil Nadu for several thousand years. Tamil is spoken by over 85% of the population, which is 90% Hindu. Five per cent are Christian, a group especially strong

The continuing effects of the tsunami

The tsunami waves triggered by the Bay of Bengal earthquakes on 26 December 2004 struck over 2000 km of India's coastline, penetrating as far as 3 km inland with waves of up to 10 m. Twelve tremors measured over six on the Richter scale, with a further 103 registering over five. It was a natural disaster of huge humanitarian scale throughout the Indian Ocean; on the Indian mainland alone, according to a UN, World Bank and Asian Development Bank joint assessment, nearly 11,000 people died, nearly 8000 of these in the South Indian state of Tamil Nadu. The death toll was highest in Nagapattinam, but tourist centres of Chennai, Mahabalipuram, Kanyukumari and Pondicherry were all badly affected.

The waves touched all areas of Tamil life: 54,620 homes were hit, 68,000 boats destroyed and 252 schools wiped out. Where seawater washed inland over farmland it left a thick layer of saline deposits. Agricultural observers estimated it would take three monsoons before the land can be used again.

Relief was swift, and the government response in particular praised, but with a reconstruction effort of this scale (the total cost to India is put at US$1.2 billion), involving the rebuilding of homes, schools, health centres, roads and power lines, the work goes on. Of the 44,200 displaced people, three quarters should have been permanently rehoused by the summer of 2007, under the 'build back better mantra'.

It hasn't all been good news, however. The relief effort broke against society already fragmented by caste and gender inequality, and efforts to help dalits, for example, were in some cases fiercely opposed by village panchayats. Human trafficking among women and children was already relatively high in Tamil Nadu, and the chaos and economic problems following the tsunami provided an extra window of opportunity for exploitation; rates of organ harvesting, for example, have increased. In other areas the relief effort has been a victim of its own success, diminishing the self-sufficiency of fishing communities. Oversupply of resources such as boats has led some boys to skip school to go fishing, and handouts has allowed others to turn to the bottle. The stampede of relief agencies to the Andaman and the Nicobar islands has damaged the delicate social fabric of these formerly isolated communities.

Key tourist sites such as Mahabalipuram's Shore Temple escaped damage, and the government was swift in its rebuilding efforts to allow tourism to support local businesses and people. Of the natural attractions, while the Point Calimere Sanctuary is saltier than before, and the flamingoes have flown inland, ecologists believe the tsunami's effects to be glancing. The Gulf of Mannar Marine National Park was sheltered by Sri Lanka. Only 2% of India's coral reef appears to have been damaged.

in the south where Roman Catholic and Protestant missions have been active for over 500 years. There are small but significant minorities of Muslims, Jains and Parsis. There are isolated groups of as many as 18 different types of **tribal people** in the Nilgiri Hills. Some of them are of aboriginal stock although local archaeological discoveries suggest that an extinct race preceded them. The **Todas'** life and religion revolve around their long-horned buffalo which are a measure of wealth. Their small villages

The new organ grinders

While Karnataka, with its glut of world-class cardiac surgeons, pitches itself as the hot new health tourism destination, neighbouring Tamil Nadu has drummed up its own less enviable reputation on the operating table. The state is at the centre of the Indian organs racket as its poor harvest their own kidneys as a lucrative cash crop. Around 60 to 70 transplants take place in the state each month.

A *Journal of the American Medical Association* investigation revealed that in 96% of cases those going under the knife did so to pay off debts. The fee? Not steep, by international standards; Indian donors typically receive around US$1070 (although most are initially promised more than double). Still, not bad for a state where the poverty line is US$538 a year per family.

Transplant tourism began in the subcontinent in the 1980s, but has since boomed, even though the success rate is pitifully low; as many as half of those kidneys bought abroad fail, and a third of patients die. But with almost a third of the 40,000 awaiting transplant in Europe dying in the queue for a legal donor, it's clearly a risk many feel is worth taking.

India outlawed the trade in 1995, when individual states set up medical authorization committees to determine the authenticity of relationships between donor and recipient – or to uncover evidence of financial inducements – but name changes and speedy weddings between Gulf men and Indian women (followed by equally swift post-operative divorces), make these committees easy to hoodwink. An investigation by *The Hindu* newspaper found that the Tamil Nadu committee had cleared 1936 kidney donors between 2004 and 2007 – and rejected just 127.

Nor has South India's burgeoning medical industry done much to impede the trade; transplant operations bring in cash and confer prestige on institutions and surgeons.

And while the lure of short-term cash prizes will replenish the numbers in the donor queues, evidence shows that most quickly sink back to earlier levels of indebtedness, only now with the added handicap of one less kidney.

There has been little political will to end the trade, except for the storm triggered in early 2007 when local NGO Karunalaya unearthed a high number of kidney donations among a small fishing community devastated by the 2004 tsunami. In one village just north of Chennai 150 women had sold a kidney. But Tamil Nadu's vulnerable are desperate to fight their common enemy, poverty, even at the cost of their health, with the only tool they have: their own organs.

are called *munds* with around six igloo-like windowless bamboo and dried grass huts. Their chief goddess Tiekirzi, the creator of the indispensable buffalo, and her brother On rule the world of the dead and the living. There are only about 1000 Todas left. The **Badagas** are the main tribal group and probably came from Karnataka. They speak a mixture of Kannada and Tamil and their oral tradition is rich in folk tales, poetry, songs and chants. As agriculturalists their villages are mainly in the upper plateau, with rows of three-roomed houses. They worship Siva and observe special tribal festivals. Progressive and adaptable, they are being absorbed into the local community faster than others.

Cuisine Many Tamilians are vegetarian and the strict Brahmins among them avoid the use of garlic and onion and in some cases even tomatoes. Favourites for breakfast or *tiffin* (snacks) include dosa (thin crisp pancakes, plain or stuffed with mildly spiced

Screen gods

Tamil Nadu's lively temple society also keeps aflame sculpture and the arts, and makes for a people singularly receptive to iconography. Tamil film-making is every bit as prolific and profitable as its closest rival, Hindi-language Bollywood. The state's industry is famous for its dancing and choreography and the super-saturated colour of its film stock. Film stars too, are massive here; heroes worshipped like demigods, their careers often offering them a fast track into politics, where they are singularly well placed to establish personality cults. Two such figures who have hopped from the screen into the state's political driving seat as chief minister are the cherished MGR – MG Ramachandran, the film star and charismatic chief minister during the 1980s – and Jayalalitha, his one-time girlfriend and contentious successor, three times chief minister since 1991 despite being the figure of multiple corruption scandals.

potato and onion as *masala dosa*), iddli (steamed, fermented rice cakes), delicious rice-based *pongal* (worth searching out) and *vadai* (savoury lentil doughnuts), all served with coconut chutney and *sambar* (a spicy lentil and vegetable broth). A thali here will come as boiled rice with small steel containers of a variety of vegetables, pickles, papadum, *rasam* (a clear, peppery lentil 'soup') and plain curd. The food from Chettinad is famously spicy. Dessert is usually the creamy rice pudding *payasam*. South Indian coffee comes freshly ground, filtered and frothy, with hot milk and sugar.

Literature As the oldest living Indian language, Tamil has a literature stretching back to the early centuries before Christ. A second century AD poets' academy, the **Sangam** in Madurai, suggests that sages sat at the top of the Tamil social order, followed by peasants, hunters, artisans, soldiers, fishermen and scavengers – in marked contrast to the rest of the subcontinent's caste system. From the beginning of the Christian era Tamil religious thinkers began to transform the image of Krishna from the remote and heroic figure of the epics into the focus of a new and passionate devotional worship – *bhakti*. From the seventh to the 10th century there was a surge of writing new hymns of praise, sometimes referred to as the Tamil *Veda*.

Music Changes constantly occurred in different schools of music within the basic structure of **raga-tala-prabandha** which was well established by the seventh century. Differences between the *Hindustani* or the northern system (which included the western and eastern regions) and the *Carnatic* or the southern system became noticable in the 13th century. The southern school has a more scale-based structure of *raga* whereas the northern school has greater flexibility and thus continued to develop through the centuries. The *tala* too is much more precise. It is nearly always devotional or didactic whereas the northern system also includes non-religious, every day themes and is occasionally sensuous. Telugu naturally lends itself to the southern system. The violin accompanies the vocal music – imported from the West but played rather differently.

Dance and drama **Bharata Natyam** may be India's oldest classical dance form: a highly stylized solo for a woman of movement, music, mime, *nritta* (pure dance) and *nritya* (expression). Its theme is usually spiritual love.

Modern Tamil Nadu

Tamil Nadu took its present form as a result of the States Reorganization Act of 1956. Until 1967 the Assembly was dominated by the Indian National Congress, but after an attempt by the central government to impose Hindi as the national language the Congress Party was routed in 1967 by a regional party, the Dravida Munnetra

Tamil stats in words

Tamil Nadu's state's wealth and literacy rates are far lower here than in neighbouring Kerala: Tamil Nadu's infant mortality rate is more than double Kerala's and its literacy levels is 20% less. Tamil is deeply agricultural: Keralites, whose higher level of education have made them tire of tending fields, import most of their vegetables from here. The bullock cart continues to square up against the goods truck on the state's roads and housing is often basic: mud thatch with woven banana roofs. Migrant workers in the steel industry, cotton, or road building cross the countryside for jobs, while for those at the higher end of society, the metro lifestyles of Chennai and preferably Bengaluru (Bangalore) beckon.

Kazhagam (the DMK) under its leader CN Annadurai. After his death the party split and since then either the DMK, or the splinter party, the All India Anna DMK, has been in power in the state. Neither party has any constituency beyond Tamil Nadu and thus at the all India level each has been forced to seek alliances with national parties. From the late 1960s the AIADMK, which controlled the State Assembly for most of the time, has been led by two film stars. The first, MG Ramachandran, remained the chief minister until his death (even after suffering a stroke which left him paralysed). The record of Jayalalitha, his successor, one-time lover and fellow film star, has been less consistent, and her rule dogged by scandal. She and her party were ousted by the DMK in the May 1996 elections and she was temporarily jailed until, cleared of a wide range of criminal charges, she re-entered the Legislative Assembly in March 2002, taking over once more as Chief Minister after winning the state elections with an 80% margin (her administration then arrested the previous chief minister, senescent 83-year-old Karunanidhi, in a corruption case that some say was motivated by revenge). In the May 2004 national elections, though, the party, allied to the BJP and vocal in its opposition to Sonia Gandhi's foreign origin, failed to win a single seat. A coalition of opposition parties, arguing that she had lost her political mandate, demanded Jayalalitha's resignation, but she hung on to office, albeit swiftly reversing a raft of controversial policies – such as scrapping free electricity schemes, reducing rice rations, banning animal sacrifices – introduced during the earlier years of power. Karunanidhi, though, DMK co-founder in 1949, got the last laugh and became CM for the fifth time in the elections of May 2006.

The situation of the Tamil population, and the activities of the liberation movement the LTTE, in neighbouring Sri Lanka play a role in the politics of the state. While Karunanidhi has been a vocal advocate for Tamil rights, Jayalalitha suggests that the LTTE have been using Tamil Nadu as a sanctuary for their continuing struggle against the Sinhalese majority rule on the island.

Economy Since Independence in 1947 Tamil Nadu has become India's second largest industrial state. With a quarter of India's spinning capacity, textiles are tremendously important and the state is famous both for handloom cottons and silks and for factory-made textiles. Leather and fabrics have also long been a vital export industry, but new industries exploiting abundant raw materials like iron ore, bauxite and magnesite have also developed. Chennai, home to the Ford and Hyundai car factories and manufacturer of lorries, buses and trains, has been dubbed India's Detroit. Software is strong too, thanks to the creation of Special Economic Zones of guaranteed 'flexibility' and autonomy in working hours. Tamil Nadu is the fifth largest economy and the seventh most populous state in India, but remains deeply agricultural.

Chennai and the Pallava country

Chennai (Madras), South India's sprawling chief metropolis and India's fourth largest city, is dubbed India's Detroit thanks to its chiefly automotive industrial revolution. Polluted, congested, tricky to negotiate and with 40% of its population living in slums, it has little of the with-it dynamism of cosmopolitan Bengaluru (Bangalore) or the sleepy charm of Cochi and Trivandrum, but as the first capital to the British Raj the city holds stunning early examples of Indo-Saracenic architecture; and is the capital of South Indian high culture.

The nearby former Pallava capital of Kancheepuram, one of India's seven sacred cities, is chock-full of temples and silks, spun straight from the loom, while on the coast lies lovely Mahabalipuram, a charming town entirely given over to sculpture, ancient and modern, part open-air museum, part contemporary workshop. The seventh-century bas-reliefs are some of the world's largest and most intricate, telling the Indian flood myth, Descent of the Ganga. Nearby masons industriously pile their shacks and yards high with freshly chiselled, fantastical, beautiful deities. And beyond, an inviting curve of sand stretches towards the Bay of Bengal. » *For Sleeping, Eating and other listings, see pages 94-106 .*

Chennai (Madras) » *pp94-106.*

Colour map 3, grid A6.

➔ *Phone code: 044. Population: 5.36 mn.*

Apart from anomalous little pockets of expats, like Chetbet's Jamaican and South African communities, life in Chennai is led much as it always was; there are brahminical neighbourhoods that still demand strict vegetarianism of all tenants while flat sharing, a commonly accepted practice among the young in Bengaluru (Bangalore), is taboo. Superstition is big here too: rents are decided according to vasthu, India's equivalent of feng shui, and a wrong-facing front door can slash your payments.

You have to squint hard today to picture the half-empty grandeur that was the Madras of the East India Presidency. Triplicane has some of the finest architectural remains but the derelict district is better known today as 'bachelors' neighbourhood' due to its popularity with young men come to make their fortune in the city.

The long expanse of Marina Beach just seaward of Triplicane made Chennai's residents tragically vulnerable to the 2004 tsunami, which devastated this public land – the city's cricket court, picnic ground and fishing shore. There's no trace of the ferocity of the waves today, but here alone it took about 200 lives.

Ins and outs

Getting there Chennai's international and domestic air terminals are about 15 km from the city: allow 50 minutes, although it may take as little as half an hour. Airport buses run the circuit of the main hotels, and include Egmore station; otherwise it's best to get a pre-paid taxi: either yellow-topped government taxis or the more comfortable and expensive private cabs (note the number written on your charge slip). Trains from the north and west come into the Central Station behind the port. Lines from the south terminate at Egmore, which has hotels nearby. State-owned buses terminate at the Koyembedu Moffusil terminus, private buses at the nearby Omni terminus. Buses often drop passengers along the route, so it's worth asking whether the driver can drop you closer to your destination.

Getting around Chennai is very spread out and walking is usually uncomfortably hot so it's best to find an auto. Most, however, refuse to run their meter, so ask your hotel for an approximate rate to your destination. Taxis are comparatively rare and expensive. The bus network is extensive with frequent services, but it's often very crowded. ▸▸ *See Transport, page 101, for further details.*

Orientation and information Chennai is far from an organized city. The main harbour near the old British military zone of **George Town** is marked by cranes for the cargo business. Nearby is the **Fort**, the former headquarters of the British and now the Secretariat of the Tamil Nadu government and the High Court. The **Burma bazar**, a long line of pokey shops, runs between the two near Parry's Corner. The **Pondy bazar** is the 'common man's' bazar, **T Nagar** the main shopping area (Anna Salai's best for clothes). South of **Adya** are the headquarters of car companies like Hyundai and Ford. **Mylapore,** older than Chennai itself and the cultural heart of the city, is just south of the city centre.

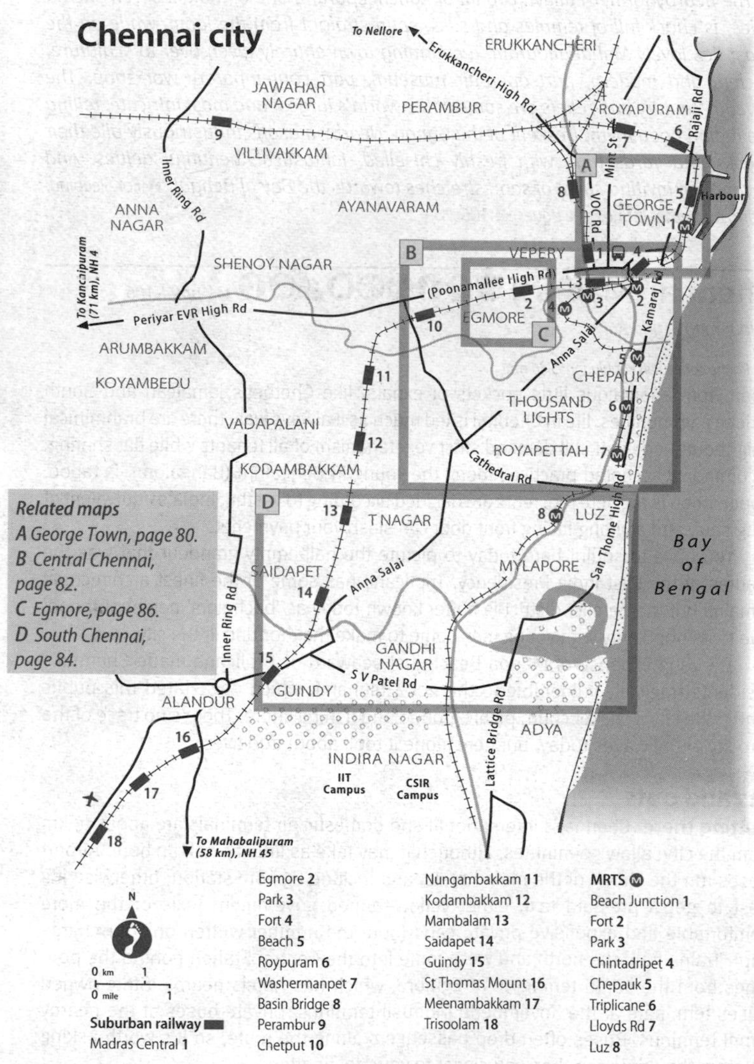

Tourist information **Tamil Nadu Tourism** ⓘ *Tourism Complex, Wallaja Rd, T044-2538 8785, www.tamilnadutourism.org*. See also www.chennaionline.com.

History

Armenian and Portuguese traders had settled the San Thome area before the arrival of the British. In 1639, **Francis Day**, a trader with the East India Company, negotiated the grant of a tiny plot of sandy land to the north of the Cooum River as the base for a warehouse or factory. The building was completed on 23 April 1640, St George's Day. The site was chosen partly because of local politics – Francis Day's friendship with Ayyappa Nayak, brother of the local ruler of the coast country from Pulicat to the Portuguese settlement of San Thome – but more importantly by the favourable local price of cotton goods.

By 1654 the patch of sand had grown into Fort St George, complete with a church and English residences – the 'White Town'. To its north was 'Black Town', referred to locally as Chennaipatnam, after Chennappa Nayak, Dharmala Ayyappa Nayak's father. The two towns merged and Madraspatnam grew with the acquisition of neighbouring villages of Tiru-alli-keni (Lily Tank) now Triplicane, in 1676. In 1693, Governor Yale (founder of Yale University in the USA) acquired Egmore, Purasawalkam and Tondiarpet from Emperor Aurangzeb, who had by then extended Mughal power to the far south. In 1746 Madras was captured by the French, to be returned to British control as a result of the Treaty of Aix-la-Chapelle in 1748. Villages like Nungambakkam, Ennore, Perambur, San Thome and Mylapore (the 'city of the peacock') were absorbed by the mid 18th century with the help of friendly Nawabs. In 1793, the British colonial administration moved to Calcutta, but Madras remained the centre of the East India Company's expanding power in South India.

It was more than 150 years after they had founded Fort St George at Madras (in 1639) before the East India Company could claim political supremacy in South India. Haidar Ali, who mounted the throne of Mysore in 1761, and his son Tipu Sultan, allied with the French, won many battles against the English. The 1783 Treaty of Versailles forced peace. The English took Malabar in 1792, and in 1801 Lord Wellesley brought together most of the south under the Madras Presidency.

The city continues to grow, although many services, including water and housing, are stretched beyond breaking point. Since Independence an increasing range of heavy and light goods industries, particularly automotive, has joined the long-established cotton textiles and leather industries.

The fort and port: St George and George Town

Madras began as nothing more than a huddle of fishing villages on the Bay of Bengal, re-christened Madras by British 17th-century traders after they built the Factory House fortifications on the beach. The present fort dates from 1666. The 24 black **Charnockite** pillars, see page 523, were reclaimed by the British in 1762 after the French had carried them off to Pondicherry in 1746. Now the site of state government, the **State Legislative Hall** has fine woodwork and black and white stone paving. You can also see the old barracks and officers' quarters including Lord Clive's house, which he rented from an Armenian merchant. One room, Clive's Corner, has small exhibits. The house of the future Duke of Wellington, Arthur Wellesley, is 100 m further along.

The Fort's governor Streynsham Master was responsible for the most interesting building in the compound, **St Mary's Church** ⓘ *T044-2538 2023*. Built between 1678 and 1680, it ranks as the first English church in India and the oldest British building to survive. It's unusually well fortified for a house of God – all solid masonry with semi-circular cannon-proof roofs and 1.3 m-thick walls – so that in times of siege it could function as a military dormitory and storehouse, and had to be almost entirely rebuilt in 1759 after military action in a siege. **Governor Elihu Yale** and **Robert Clive** were both married in the church. Yale, an American (born to English parents), who worked as a writer for the East India Company from the ages of 24 to 39, rose to become Governor; his son David is buried under the Hynmers Obelisk in the old burial ground. The famous missionary **Schwartz**, at one time the intermediary between the British and Haidar Ali, is also celebrated here for his role just "going about doing good." Job Charnock is commemorated for carrying a Hindu widow from the funeral pyre she was about to burn herself on and whereupon he took her as his wife. You can also learn the unhappy end of poor Malcolm McNeill, a colonel of the Madras Light Cavalry, who died at Rangoon in 1852 from neither battle nor disease but from a case of sunstroke. Nor is he alone: many Britishers appear to have fallen "a martyr to an ungenial climate."

The original black font, made from 3000-million-year-old Charnockite from Pallavaram, has been in continuous use since the church was consecrated. Outside the west entrance lies one of the oldest British inscriptions in India: the tombstone of Elizabeth Baker.

Also in the compound is an 18th-century building housing the **Fort Museum** ⓘ *Sat-Thu 1000-1700, US$2 (foreigners), photography prohibited*, with exhibits from 300 years of British Indian history including brilliant portraits of Madras governors. It includes prints, documents, paintings, sculpture, arms (medieval weapons with instructions on their use) and uniforms. The Indo-French gallery has some Louis XIV furniture and clocks. Clive Corner, which includes letters and photographs, is particularly interesting. The building itself was once an exchange for East India company merchants, becoming an officers' mess later.

Within walking distance of the compound north, is the city's long-standing commercial centre, **George Town**. The area was renamed after the future King George V when he visited India in 1905. You first reach the grand Indo-Saracenic

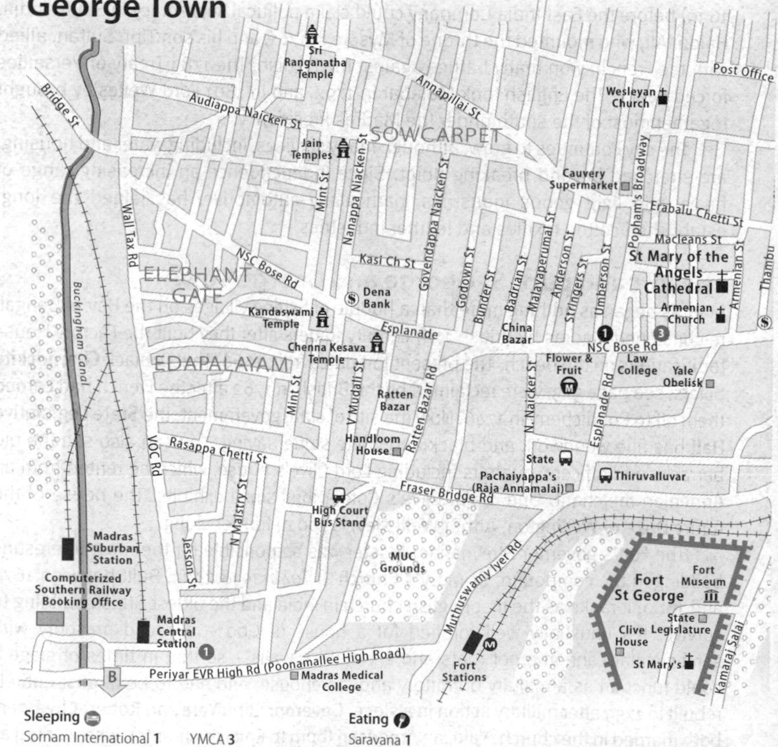

complex of the **High Court** ⓘ *Mon-Sat 1045-1345, 1430-1630, contact Registrar for visit and guide*, developed in the style of the late 19th-century architects like **Henry Irwin**, who was also responsible for the National Art Gallery. You are allowed to visit the courtrooms by using the entrance on the left. A fine example is Court No 13 which has stained glass, fretted woodwork, carved furniture, silvered panels and a painted ceiling. The huge red central tower, nearly 50 m tall (you can climb to the top), built like a domed minaret to serve as a lighthouse, can be seen 30 km out at sea. It was in use from 1894 until 1977. The original **Esplanade Lighthouse**, southeast of the High Court, is in the form of a large Doric pillar and took over from the Fort lighthouse in 1841.

Cross NSC Bose Road from the High Court's north gate to walk up Armenian Street for the beautiful **Armenian Church** of the Holy Virgin Mary (1772). Solid walls and massive 3 m-high wooden doors conceal the pretty open courtyard inside, where the oldest Armenian tombstone dates from 1663. The East India Company praised the Armenian community for their 'sober, frugal and wise' lifestyle and they were given the same rights as English settlers in 1688. Immediately north again is the Roman Catholic Cathedral, **St Mary of the Angels** (1675). The inscription above the entrance – 1642 – celebrates the date when the Capuchin monks built their first church in Madras.

Popham's Broadway, west from St. Mary's Cathedral, takes its name from a lawyer called Stephen, in Madras between 1778-1795, who was keen to improve the city's sanitation, laying out what was to become Madras's main commercial street. Just off Popham's Broadway in Prakasham Road is the **Wesleyan Church** (1820).

In the 18th century there was major expansion between what is now First Line Beach (North Beach Road) and **Mint Street** to the west of George Town. The Mint was first opened in 1640, and from the late 17th century minted gold coins under licence for the Mughals, but did not move to Mint Street until 1841-1842.

The 19th-century growth of Madras can be traced north from **Parry's Corner**. **First Line Beach**, built on reclaimed land in 1814 fronted the beach itself. The **GPO** (1844-1884) was designed by Chisholm. The completion of the harbour (1896), transformed the economy of the city.

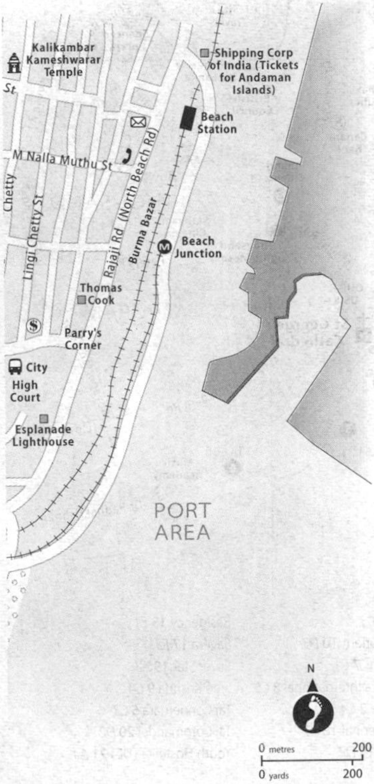

Central Chennai and the Marina

Triplicane and **Chepauk** contain some of the finest examples of late 19th-century Indo-Saracenic architecture in India, concentrated in the area around the University of Madras. The Governor of Madras, Mountstuart Elphinstone Grant-Duff (1881-1886), decided to develop the Marina as a promenade, since when it has been a favourite place for thousands of city inhabitants to walk on a Sunday evening, a custom which has continued in spite of the 2004 tsunami.

Until the harbour was built at the end of the 19th century the sea washed up close to the present road, but the north-drifting current has progressively widened the Marina beach. **Anna Park** is named after the founder of the political party the

Central Chennai

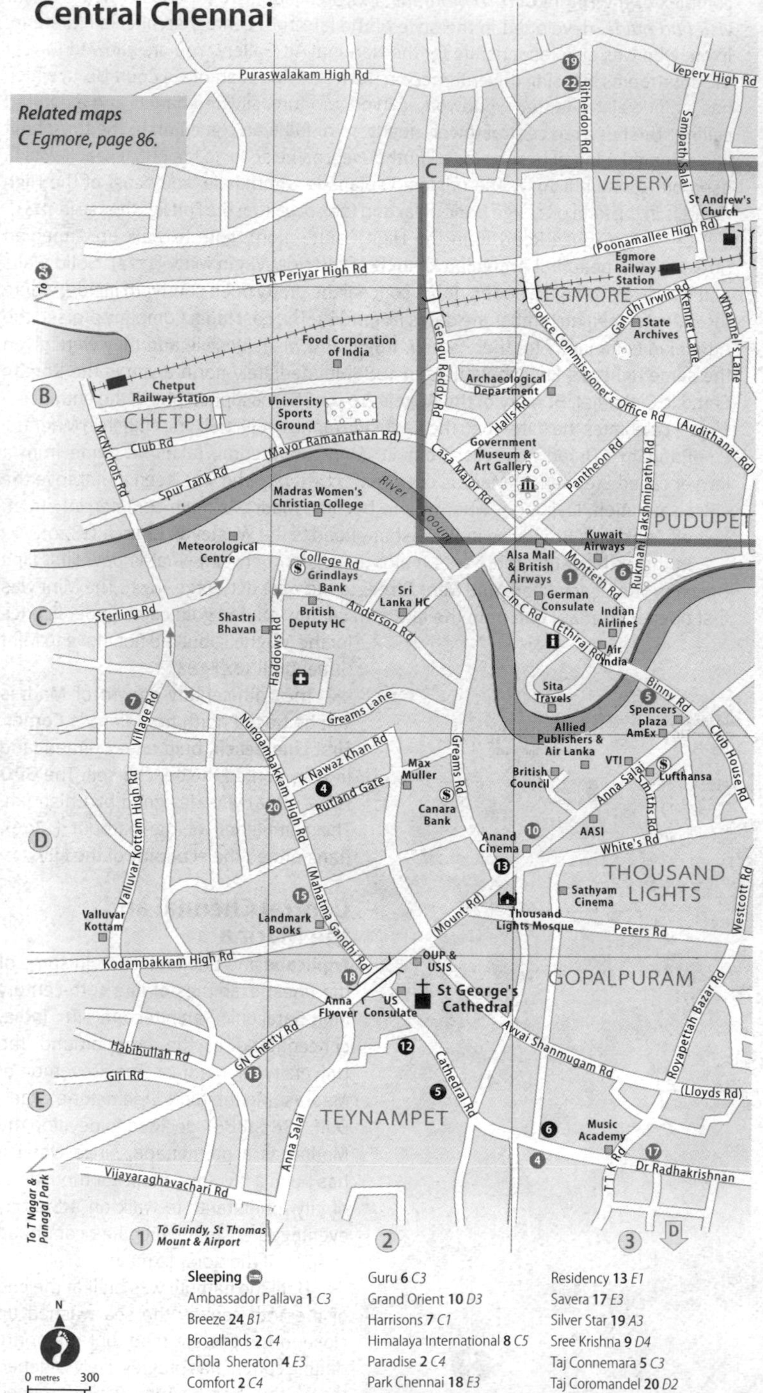

Sleeping

Ambassador Pallava **1** *C3*
Breeze **24** *B1*
Broadlands **2** *C4*
Chola Sheraton **4** *E3*
Comfort **2** *C4*
Cristal **3** *C5*
Guru **6** *C3*
Grand Orient **10** *D3*
Harrisons **7** *C1*
Himalaya International **8** *C5*
Paradise **2** *C4*
Park Chennai **18** *E3*
Ranjith **15** *D2*
Residency **13** *E1*
Savera **17** *E3*
Silver Star **19** *A3*
Sree Krishna **9** *D4*
Taj Connemara **5** *C3*
Taj Coromandel **20** *D2*
Youth Hostel (TTDC) **21** *A4*

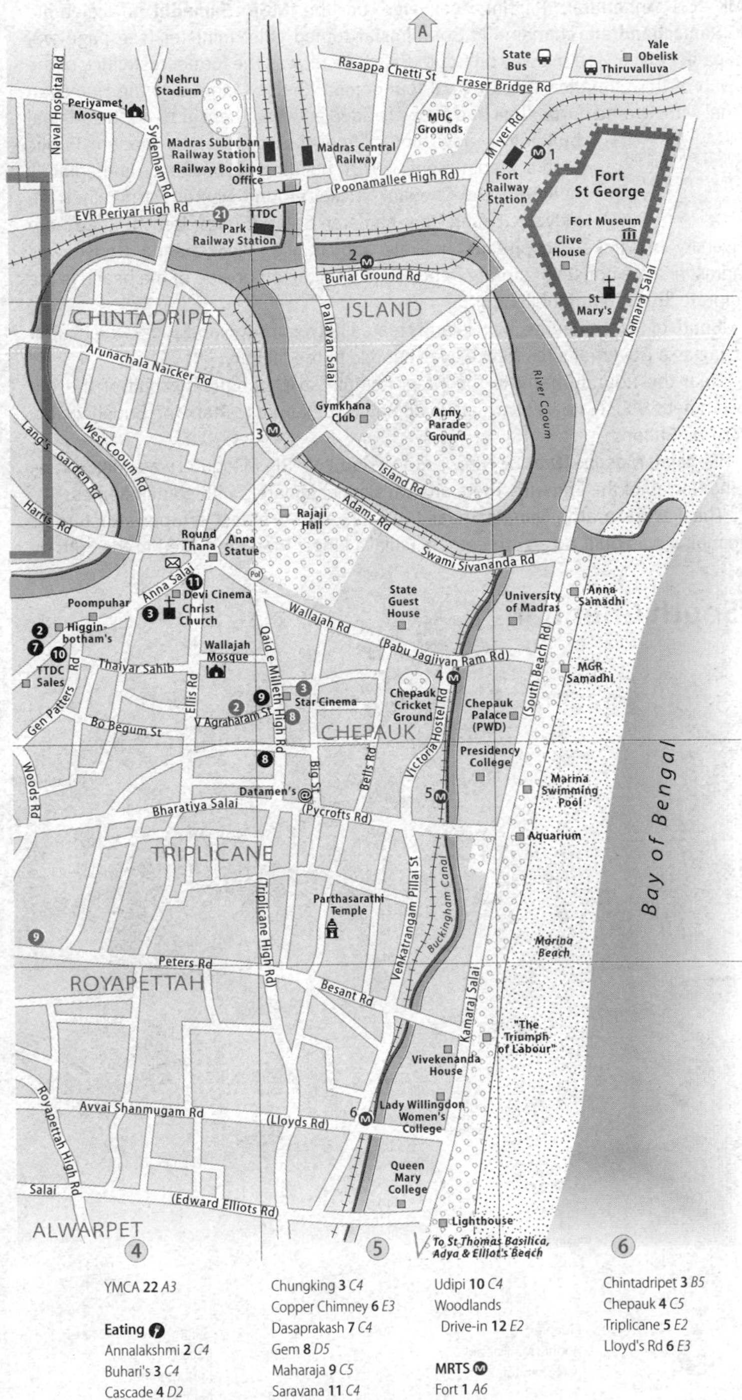

YMCA **22** *A3*

Eating
Annalakshmi **2** *C4*
Buhari's **3** *C4*
Cascade **4** *D2*
Chinatown **5** *E2*
Chungking **3** *C4*
Copper Chimney **6** *E3*
Dasaprakash **7** *C4*
Gem **8** *D5*
Maharaja **9** *C5*
Saravana **11** *C4*
Southern Chinese **13** *D2*
Udipi **10** *C4*
Woodlands Drive-in **12** *E2*

MRTS
Fort **1** *A6*
Park **2** *A5*
Chintadripet **3** *B5*
Chepauk **4** *C5*
Triplicane **5** *E2*
Lloyd's Rd **6** *E3*

DMK, CN Annadurai. Pilgrims converge on the **MGR Samadhi** to celebrate **MG Ramachandran**, charismatic 80s filmstar turned chief minister (see page 75). **Chepauk Palace**, 400 m away on South Beach Road, was the former residence of the Nawab of the Carnatica. The original four-domed Khalsa Mahal and the Humayun Mahal with a grand *durbar* hall had a tower added between them in 1855. The original building is now hidden from the road by the modern Public Works Department (PWD) building, Ezhilagam. Immediately behind is the Chepauk **cricket ground** where test matches are played. Lining the Kamaraj Salai (South Beach Road) are university buildings. Despite its unlikely appearance, **Vivekenanda House** was Madras' first ice house for storing imported ice. On the other side of the beach is the sculpture 'the Triumph of Labour'.

The Sunday afternoon market on the beach is worth visiting.

South of Fort St George is an island created between 1696 and 1705, which, after serving as a Governor's residence, was handed to the military.

Near the Round Thana is the Greek temple style banqueting hall of the old Government House, now known as **Rajaji Hall** (1802), built to mark the British victory over Tipu Sultan.

Wallajah Mosque ⓘ *0600-1200, 1600-2200*, the 'Big Mosque', was built in 1795 by the Nawab of the Carnatic. There are two slender minarets with golden domes.

The Parthasarathi Temple, near the tank, is the oldest temple structure in Chennai. It was built by eighth-century Pallava kings, then renovated in the 16th by

South Chennai

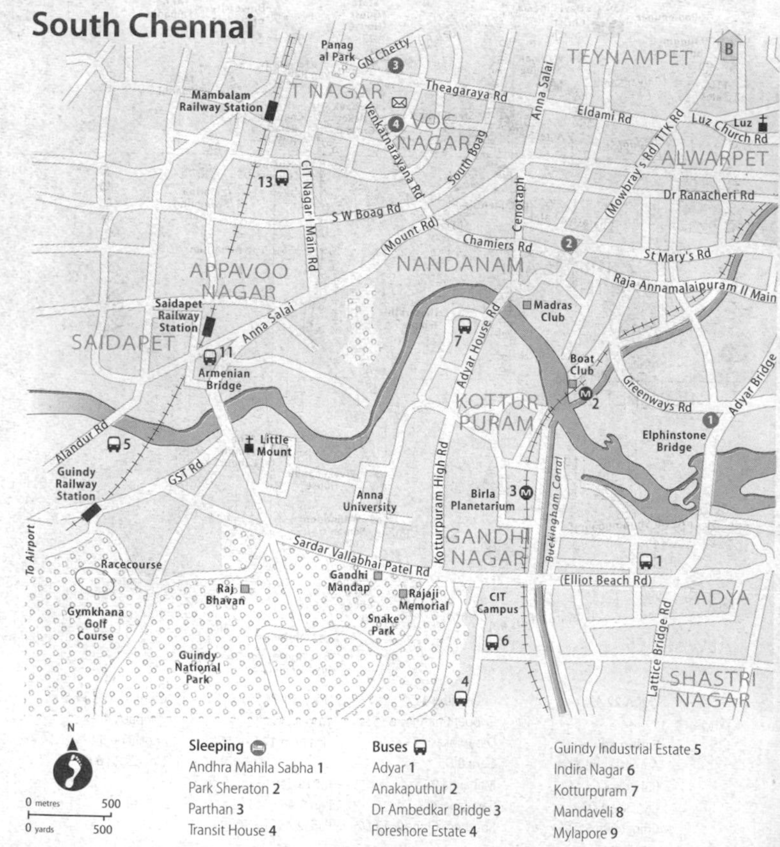

Vijayanagara rulers. Dedicated to Krishna as the royal charioteer, it shows five of Vishnu's 10 incarnations – and is the only temple dedicated to Parthasarathi.

Egmore

→ *See map, page 86.*

A bridge across the Cooum at Egmore was opened in 1700, and by the late 18th century, the area around Pantheon Road became the fulcrum of Madras's social and cultural life, a 'place of public entertainment and balls'. Egmore's development, which continued for a century, started with the building of Horden's garden house in 1715. The original pantheon (public assembly rooms) was completely replaced by one of India's National Libraries. The **Connemara Library** (built in 1896) began in 1662, when residents exchanged a bale of Madras calico for books from London. At the southwest corner of the site stands Irwin's Victoria Memorial Hall, now the **Government Museum and Art Gallery** ⓘ *486 Pantheon Rd, T044-2819 3238, Sat-Thu 0930-1700, closed bank holidays, US$5, US$2.50 children, US$1.50 students and teachers.* The red brick rotunda surrounded by an Italianate arcade was described by Tillotson as one of "the proudest expressions of the Indo-Saracenic movement". There are locally excavated Stone and Iron Age implements and striking bronzes including a 11th-century Nataraja from Tiruvengadu, seated images of Siva and Parvati from Kilaiyur, and large figures of Rama, Lakshmana and Sita from Vadakkuppanaiyur. Buddhist bronzes from Nagapattinam have been assigned to Chola and later periods. The beautiful Ardhanariswara statue here is one of the most prized of all Chola bronzes: Shiva in his rare incarnation as a hermaphrodite. There are also good Tanjore glass paintings, Rajput and Mughal miniatures and 17th-century Deccan paintings. Contemporary art is at the **Gallery of Modern Art** ⓘ *T044-2819 3035.*

Egmore has other reminders of the Indo-Saracenic period of the 19th and early 20th centuries, the station itself being one of the last to be built, in the 1930s. Located to the northeast of the station is the splendid **St Andrew's Church** ⓘ *Poonamalle High Rd, T044-2538 3508.* With a façade like London's St Martin-in-the-Fields, it has a magnificent shallow-domed ceiling. Consecrated in 1821, it has an active congregation.

Queen Mary Art College **10**
Saidapet **11**
Taramani **12**
T Nagar **13**

MRTS
Luz **1**
Mandavalli (Planned) **2**
Greenways Rd **3**

Mylapore and South Chennai

Mylapore, which is technically older than Chennai and is the seat of city's urban elite, is more charming than the city centre. The present **Basilica of San Thomas** ⓘ *24 San Thome High Rd, T044-2854 5444,* built in 1898, surrounded now by the tenement rehousing scheme of a fishermen's colony, is claimed as one of the very few churches to be built over an apostle's tomb. St Thomas Didymus (Doubting Thomas) is believed to have come to India in AD 52. According to one legend, he crossed the peninsula from his landing on the west coast to reach Mylapore – the 'town of peacocks' – where he proceeded to live and preach, taking shelter from persecution in Little Mount (see below). An alternative story argues King Gondophernes invited him to Taxila, where he converted the king and his court before moving to South India. Some claim that his body was ultimately buried in the Italian town of Ortona. The basilica is now subject to an ambitious US$164,400 restoration project. To stop the Mangalore tile roof leaking, concrete reparations are being peeled back and replaced with original lime mortar.

Kapaleeswarar Temple ⓘ *0600-1200, 1600-2200*, just to the west, is a 16th-century Siva temple with a 40-m *gopuram* (gateway), built after the original was destroyed by the Portuguese in 1566. Sacred to Tamil Shaivites, non-Hindus are only allowed in the outer courtyard where there are several bronze statues.

The diminutive Portuguese **Luz Church**, 1547-1582 (the 1516 date in the inscription is probably wrong), is possibly the oldest church in Chennai. Its Tamil name, *Kattu Kovil*, means jungle temple. Legend has it that Portuguese sailors lost at sea in a storm followed a light to the shore, where it disappeared. In gratitude they built the church. There are a number of 19th-century marble plaques to wives of the Madras civil service inside the church and an ornate crypt.

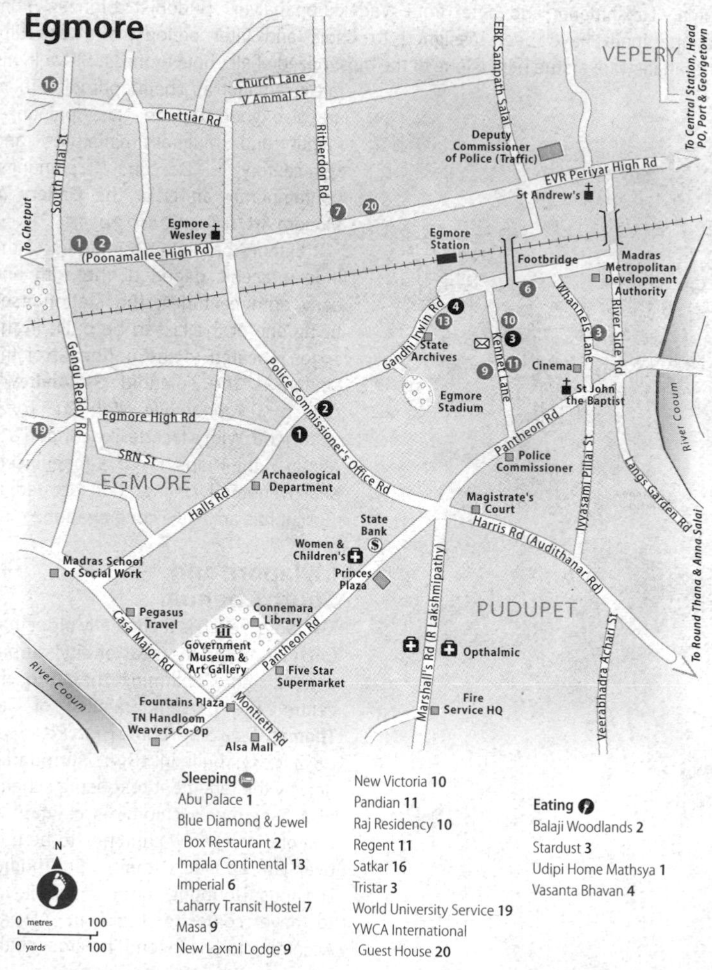

To the south of Elphinstone Bridge the **Theosophical Society** ⓘ *Mon-Fri 0830-1000, 1400-1600, Sat 0830-1000; bus 5 from Central Chennai, ask taxi for Ayappa Temple on San Thome High Rd,* is set in large and beautifully quiet gardens. There are several shrines of different faiths and a Serene Garden of Remembrance for Madame Blavatsky and Colonel Olcott who founded the society in New York in 1875 and moved its headquarters to Madras in 1882. There's a 400-year-old banyan past the kitchen garden, a library and a meditation hall. The brackish river attracts waders and seabirds.

Tucked away near Saidapet is the **Little Mount** area. The older of the two churches (1551), with its small vaulted chapel, was built by the Portuguese. The modern circular church was built in 1971. St Thomas is believed to have been martyred and bled to death in AD 52 on the **Great Mount**, though others believe he was accidentally killed by a hunter's arrow. On top of the 90 m high 'mount' is the **Church of Our Lady of Expectation**. The altar marks the spot where, according to legend, Thomas fell. Some legends suggest that after St Thomas had been martyred on the Little Mount, near Saidapet Bridge, his body was brought back to the beach which had been his home and was buried there. The **Armenian Christians** who came from Persia are believed to have found St Thomas' grave and built a tomb and a church over it in AD 530. The village was called San Thome. Marco Polo in his travels in 1293 recorded the chapel on the seashore and a Nestorian monastery on a hill to the west where the apostle was put to death. In 1523, when the Portuguese started to rebuild the church they discovered the tomb containing the relics consisting of a few bones, a lance head and an earthenware pot containing bloodstained earth. The church was replaced by the neo-Gothic structure which has two spires and was granted the status of a basilica in 1956. The relics are kept in the sacristy and can be seen on request. There are 13th-century wall plaques, a modern stained glass window, a 450-year-old Madonna brought from Portugal and a 16th-century stone sundial.

Mahabalipuram (Mamallapuram)

⏩ *pp97-106. Colour map 3, grid B6.*

→ *Phone code: 04114. Population: 12,050.*

Mahabalipuram's mix of magnificent historic rock temples, exquisite alfresco bas reliefs and inviting sandy beach bestows a formidable magnetism and it has matured into a mellow backpacker hamlet. The craftsmanship that built the temples continues today and the whole place echoes with the sound of chisels tapping industriously on stone, with hundreds of workshops' yards crowded with fantastical sculptures of deities.

If travelling from Chennai, there are two good breaks before Mahabalipuram. The first is 19 km from Chennai at **Cholamandal Artists' Village** ⓘ *East Coast Rd, Enjampakkam, T044-2449 0092, 0900-1900, free*. The artists' community, started in 1969, gives working and exhibition space for artists creating sculptures, pottery and batik. They hold dance performances in a small open-air theatre. The second stop is Madras Craft Foundation's model village of **Dakshinchitra** ⓘ *East Coast Rd, T044-2491 8943, Wed-Mon 1000-1800, Rs 50*, which presents the arts and crafts of the four southern states and performance of folk arts. There's also a restaurant.

Ins and outs

Getting there and around Buses from Chennai take around 1½ hours to the bus stand in the centre of the small village. They may stop at hotels north of Mahabalipuram, on the way, otherwise autos from anywhere in the village will ferry you there for Rs 50. Arriving by car, you may have to pay a Rs 20 toll at the booth near the post office on Covelong Rd.

Hiring a bike to get a bit further afield can be fun. ⏩ *See Transport, page 104, for further details.*

History

The coastal temple town Mahabalipuram is officially known as Mamallapuram after 'Mamalla' (great wrestler), the name given to Narasimhavarman I Pallavamalla (ruled AD 630-668). The Pallava ruler made the port famous in the seventh century and was largely responsible for the temples. There are 14 cave temples and nine monolithic *rathas* (shrines in the shape of temple chariots), three stone temples and four relief sculptured rock panels.

The **Dravida** or Dravidian style underwent several changes over the course of the different dynasties that ruled for about 1000 years from the time of the Pallavas who laid its foundations. In Mahabalipuram, rock-cut cave temples, *mandapas* (small excavated columned halls), and *rathas* were carved out by the early Pallavas. These were followed by structural temples and bas relief sculptures on giant rocks. The Ekambaresvara Temple in Kanchipuram (see page 92) shows the evolution of the Dravidian style; the shrine with its pyramidal tower and the separate *mandapa* (pillared portico) all within the courtyard with its high enclosure wall made up of cells. Some 600 years later the two structures were joined by the covered hall (*antarala*). A large subsidiary shrine, in place of an entrance gateway, also hinted at the later *gopuram*.

A characteristic feature of the temples here was the system of water channels and tanks, drawn from the **Palar River**, which made it particularly suitable as a site of

Mahabalipuram

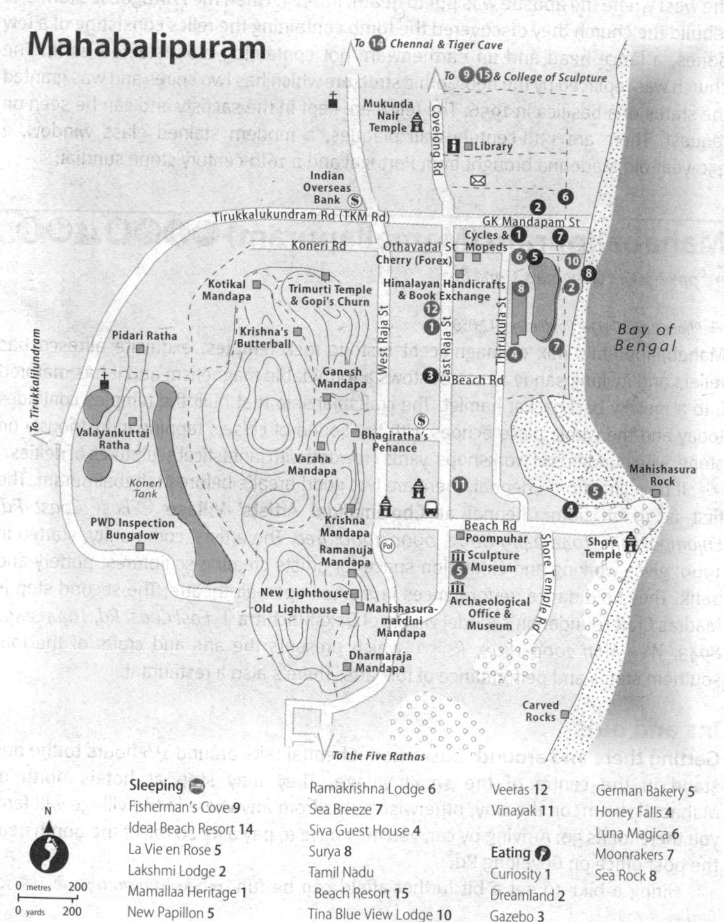

Go South

Early morning is an excellent time to travel in most places in India, but especially in the South. The air is fresh and cool, the light limpid. Southwards from Chennai on the road to Mahabalipuram, Pondicherry and Cuddalore there are groves of casuarina trees, many recently planted, alternating with coconut and palmyra palms. In January and February, at harvest time, there is also a delightful scent of fresh straw in the air. Paddy, groundnut and sugarcane grow in the fields and grain is often spread out across the road to dry or be threshed by passing traffic.

religious worship. The *naga*, or serpent cult associated with water worship, can be seen to be given prominence at Bhagiratha's Penance.

Carving in stone is still a living art; stone masons can be heard chipping away from dawn to dusk along the dusty roadsides, while students at the **Government School of Sculpture** ⓘ *Wed-Mon 0900-1300, 1400-1830*, near the bus stand, continue to practise the skills which flourished centuries ago.

Sights

Bhagiratha's Penance *Descent of the Ganga*, also called **Arjuna's Penance**, is a bas relief sculpted on the face of two enormous adjacent rocks, 29 m long and 7 m high. It shows realistic life-size figures of animals, gods and saints watching the descent of the river from the Himalaya. Bhagiratha, Rama's ancestor, is seen praying to Ganga. A man-made waterfall issues from the natural crack between the two rocks. Some see the figure of an ascetic (to the top left-hand side of the rock, near the cleft) as representing Arjuna's penance when praying for powers from Siva, though this is disputed. There are scenes from the fables in the *Panchatantra* and a small shrine to Vishnu.

The best time to visit is early morning, especially for the best light on Bhagiratha's Penance. Allow two hours for a circuit. The paths on the top of the rock are not always clear, but it is difficult to get really lost.

A path north goes to the double-decker rectangular **Ganesh** *ratha* with a highly decorative roof and two pillars with lions at their base – an architectural feature which was to become significant. The Ganesh image inside is mid-20th century. To the west are the **Valayankuttai** and twin **Pidari** *rathas*. The path continues past the precariously balanced **Krishna's Butterball** through some huge boulders at the north end of the hillock to the **Trimurti Temple** caves that hold three shrines to Brahma, Vishnu and Siva, the last with a lingam.

Mandapas ⓘ *US$5*. The 10 *mandapas* are shallow, pillared halls or porticos in the rocky hillside which hold superb sculptures from mythological tales, and illustrate the development of the Dravidian (South Indian) temple style.

On the south is a **Durga niche** (AD 630-660), while next door is the **Gopi's Churn**, a Pallava cistern. Walk back along the ridge, passing Krishna's Butterball on your left and boulders with evidence of incomplete work. The **Varaha Mandapa** (AD 640-674) on the left of the ridge shows two incarnations of Vishnu – Varaha (boar) and Vamana (dwarf) – among scenes with kings and queens. The base forms a narrow water pool for pilgrims to use before entering the temple. From here you can walk to the top of Bhagiratha's Penance.

'Temple cars' or 'rathas' are tall and often elaborately carved and painted temple-shaped chariots which carry temple deities through the streets during celebratory procession. They're commonly parked up in makeshift garages of corrugated iron canopies at the side of temples between festivals.

Stone temple pilot

When the British Council first sponsored the Bristol-born artist Stephen Cox to scout India for a place to make his huge-scale stone works for the national art prize the Indian Triennale, he chose not the city's best art schools, but a little fishing village on the Coromandel coast of Tamil Nadu. It may sound bloody minded, until you arrive in Mahabalipuram, where the whole air clatters with the sound of chisel on rock. It must be the most industrious seat of Hindu idol-making the world over; everywhere you look masons sit on their haunches hammering away at the local dolerite rock.

As Cox explains: "I didn't go to India to work with like-minded contemporary artists, I wanted people who could work with great big blocks of stone without fear. Mahabalipuram is totally unique in having this unbroken, living tradition of making idols for people to pray to, and that means that they are also used to working with huge monolithic stone so no-one's daunted by making my 14-tonne sculptures." Although he has kept a studio there from that first year, 1986, you won't find any of his sculpture in the town itself – these are mainly kept for cities: the British High Commission at Delhi, the British Council's office in Chennai and dotted about London's Square Mile. Indeed his work, too minimalist for Hindu temple carving purists, has been received with something less than gusto by some of the local craftsman, and journalist Mark Tully, branded Cox's use of Indian labour a form of 'neo-colonialism'. One sculpture alone can take up to a year to make and will have passed through, on average, 20 pairs of Indian hands before being shipped for exhibition. "At the end of the day of course, I wouldn't be working in India over Carrara in Italy if it wasn't economically viable," Cox concedes, but he also says "my raison d'être for working in India is because, in working amongst and with the temple carvers, I can immerse myself in a living antique tradition. It is not just the cost factor. The hand skills of the silpies have been lost to the rest of the world."

The town has changed dramatically since he arrived in 1986, but Cox spares the burgeoning tourist industry infrastructure to reserve his criticism for the Architectural Survey of India's maintenance of the monuments themselves. "Since it was declared a World Heritage Site, they've buggered the Shore Temple up; it's not a shore temple anymore, instead it sits in a bijou plot of grassland, while the five *rathas* are fenced off, destroying the whole beauty of these wonderful monuments in a natural environment."

And his favourite piece of sculpture in a town teeming with them? It's the Pallava's flair for observation that still gets him: "the naturalism that Giotto was supposed to have invented you find in a ninth-century relief carving here. It is amazing. I only hope fewer and fewer people come."

Krishna Mandapa (mid-seventh century) has a bas relief scene of Krishna lifting Mount Govardhana to protect a crowd of his kinsmen from the anger of the Rain God, Indra. The cow licking its calf during milking is remarkably realistic.

Kotikal Mandapa (early seventh century) may be the earliest of the *mandapas*, roughly carved with a small shrine with no image inside. **Ramanuja Mandapa** was originally a triple-cell Siva temple, converted later into a Vaishnava temple.

South of the new lighthouse the simple **Dharmaraja cave** (early seventh century) contains three empty shrines. To its west is **Isvara Temple** (or Old Lighthouse), a truncated Siva temple still standing like a beacon on the highest summit, with a view for miles around. (To the south, across the Five Rathas, is the nuclear power station of Kalpakkam; to the west is the flat lagoon and the original port of Mahabalipuram.)

Mahishasuramardini Mandapa (mid-seventh century) is immediately below. It has fine bas relief and carved columns with lion bases. The main sculpture shows the goddess Durga slaying the buffalo demon Mahishasura while another relief shows Vishnu lying under Adishesha, the seven-hooded serpent.

Rathas These mid-seventh-century monolithic temples, 1½ km south of the Old Lighthouse, were influenced by Buddhist architecture as they resemble the *vihara* (monastery) and *chaitya* (temple hall). They imitate in granite temple structures that were originally built of wood and are among the oldest examples of their type.

The five *rathas* to the south of the hill are named after the Pancha Pandava (five Pandava brothers) in the epic *Mahabharata* and their wife Draupadi. The largest is the domed **Dharmaraja** with many images including an interesting Ardhanarishvara (Siva-Parvati) at the rear. The barrel-vaulted **Bhima** nearby has a roof suggestive of a thatched hut, while next to it the dome-shaped ratha **Arjuna** imitates the Dharmaraja. **Draupadi ratha** is the smallest and simplest and is again in the form of a thatched hut. The base, now covered by sand, conceals a lion in front which appears to carry it, which suggests that it may be a replica of a portable shrine. Immediately east is a large unfinished *Nandi*. To its west is the apsidal **Nakula-Sahadeva ratha** with a freestanding elephant nearby. The Bhima and Nakula-Sahadeva follow the oblong plan of the Buddhist *chaitya* hall and are built to two or more storeys, a precursor to the *gopuram*, the elaborate entrance gateway of the Dravidian temple.

Shore Temple ⓘ *US$5, includes Five Rathas.* This beautiful sandstone World Heritage Site, built in the seventh century by King Rajasimha, is unusual for holding shrines to both Siva and Vishnu. Its gardens have been laid out to ape their ancient antecedents. Its base is granite and it has a basalt *kalasha* at its top. Its position on the water's edge, with an east-facing altar designed to catch the rising sun and a stone pillar to hold the beacon for sailors at night, meant that there was no space for a forecourt or entrance gateway, but two additional shrines were built to the west. The second smaller spire adds to the temple's unusual structure. The outer parapet wall has lines of *Nandi* (Siva's sacred bull) and lion pilasters.

Saluvankuppam Five kilometres north of Mahabalipuram, on the coast, is the temple at Saluvankuppam. It holds the **Tiger Cave** *mandapa* with carvings of tiger heads. The cave, not signposted from the beach, is secluded and peaceful – perfect for a picnic. On the way you will see the **Mukunda Nayar Temple**.

Beaches Check the safety of swimming in the sea. To sunbathe undisturbed pay Rs 100 to use the small pool at **Crystal Shore Palace** or **Sea Breeze**, or the bigger pool, 1 km north at **Tamil Nadu Beach Resort**. Be warned: the beach north of the temples towards the **Ashok** and the rocky area behind the Descent of the Ganga are open latrines for the village.

Around Mahabalipuram

Tirukkalukundram is a small Siva temple dedicated to Vedagirishvara on top of the 3000-million-year-old rock 14 km west of Mahabalipuram. About 400 steps take you to the top of the 160 m hill which has good views, plus money-conscious priests and 'guides'. Be prepared for a hot barefoot climb, 'donations' at several shrines and Rs 10 for your shoes. At midday, two Neophran vultures (Pharaoh's chickens) sometimes fly down to be fed by the priests. The Bhaktavatsleesvara in town with its *gopuram* (gateway) stands out like a beacon. The tank is considered holy and believed to produce a conch every 12 years. Small shops in the village sell cold drinks. Buses from Mahabalipuram take 30 minutes or you can hire a bike.

Sriperumbudur, 44km from Chennai on National Highway 4, is the birthplace of the 11th-century Hindu philosopher Ramanuja, and is where Rajiv Gandhi was assassinated on 21 May 1991. There is a memorial at the site in a well-kept garden.

Kanchipuram

▸▸ *pp97-106. Colour map 3, grid A5.*

➔ *Phone code: 04112. Population: 153,000.*

What Darjeeling is to tea, and Cheddar is to cheese, so Kanchipuram is to silk. One of Hinduism's seven most sacred cities (see page 502), 'the Golden City of a Thousand Temples', dates from the early Cholas in the second century. The main temple complexes are very spacious and only a few of the scattered 70 or so can be seen in a day's visit. The town itself relatively quiet except for crowds of pilgrims.

History

The **Pallavas** of Kanchi came to power in the fourth century AD and were dominant from AD 550 to 869. Possibly of northern origin, under their control Mahabalipuram became an important port in the seventh century. Buddhism is believed to have reached the Kanchipuram area in the third century BC. Successive dynasties made it their capital and built over 100 temples, the first as early as the fourth century. As well as being a pilgrimage site, it was a centre of learning, culture and philosophy. Sankaracharya and the Buddhist monk Bodhidharma lived and worked here.

Sights

Ekambaresvara Temple ⓘ *Small entry fee, cameras Rs 3, only Hindus are allowed into the inner sanctuary.* The temple has five enclosures and a 'Thousand-pillared Hall' (for the pedantic, the number is actually 'only' 540). Dedicated to **Siva** in his ascetic form it was begun by the Pallavas and developed by the Cholas. In the early 16th century the Vijayanagara king Krishna Deva Raya built the high stone wall which surrounds the temple and the 59-m-tall *rajagopuram* (main tower) on which are sculpted several figures of him and his consort.

The main sanctuary has a *lingam* made of earth (Siva as one of the elements) and the story of its origin is told on a carved panel. The teasing Parvati is believed to have unthinkingly covered her husband Siva's eyes for a moment with her hands which resulted in the earth being enveloped in darkness for years. The enraged Siva ordered Parvati to do severe penance during which time she worshipped her husband in the form of an earth *lingam* which she created. When Siva sent a flood to test her, she clung to the *lingam* with her hands until the waters subsided. Some believe they can see her fingerprints on the *lingam* here. On 18 April each year the sun's rays enter the sanctum through a small square hole. ▸▸ See Festivals, page 99.

Have change ready for 'donations' to each temple you visit. Temples are usually open from 0700 and closed 1200-1600.

Kailasanatha Built in the early seventh century, this is considered to be the most beautiful of the town's temples. It was built of sandstone by the Pallava king Narasimha Varman II with the front completed by his son Mahendra III. The outer structure has a dividing wall with a shrine and doorways, separating a large courtyard from a smaller one. The unusual enclosure wall has 58 small raised shrines with a *Nandi* in most pavilions and some frescoes have survived. The seven shrines in the temple complex have images of different Siva forms. The intricately carved panels on the walls depict legends about Siva with accompanying text in ancient Grantha script. It has been extensively restored. The festival **Mahashivaratri** is held here in February.

Vaikuntha Perumal Eighth century and dedicated to Vishnu, this temple was built by the Pallava king Nandivarman just after the Kailasanatha and illustrates the progress of Dravidian temple architecture. The sanctuary is separated from the *mandapa* by an open space. The cloisters are built from rows of lion pillars. Panels of bas relief accompanied by lines in old Tamil trace the history of the wars between the Pallavas and Chalukyas. There is an unusual *vimana* (tower) with shrines in three tiers with figures of Vishnu in each.

Varadaraja (Devarajasvami) ⓘ *Hindus only are allowed into the sanctum.* Built by the Vijayanagara kings (circa 16th century), 3 km southeast of town, it has superb sculpture in its marriage hall (with 96 pillars). Figures on horseback wear half North Indian/half South Indian costumes. Note the rings at each corner and the massive flexible chain supposedly carved out of one piece of granite, although it is no longer in one piece. The main shrine is on an elephant-shaped rock, Hastagiri. The **Float Festival** is in February and November, **Brahmotsavam** in May and **Garuda Sevai** in June.

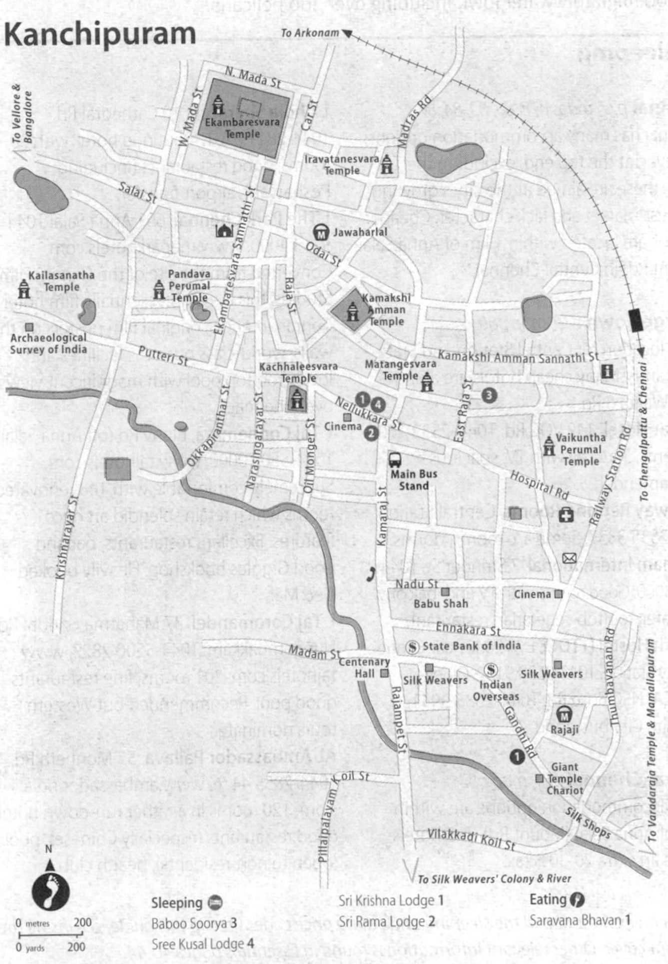

Chengalpattu (Chingleput) The fort here was built by the Vijayanagar king Thimmu Raya after his defeat at the Battle of Talikotta in 1565. After 1687 it was absorbed into the Mughal Empire. Then in 1750 it was taken by the French, who held it until it was captured by Clive in 1752; British control was only finally established after the defeat of Haidar Ali in 1781. Although the fort is now almost totally destroyed (the railway runs through the middle of it), the Raja Mahal ('King's Palace') remains.

Around Kanchipuram

On the Trichy Road, 87 km from Chennai and 60 km from Mahabalipuram, the **Vedanthangal Bird Sanctuary** and Karikili Tank are thought to have existed as a protected area for about 250 years. The marshy site attracts numerous water fowl and provides their main nesting place. Visitors and residents include crested cormorants, night herons, grey pelicans, sand pipers, grey wagtails, open-billed storks, white ibis, egrets, little grebe and purple moorhens. The best time to visit is November to February, at dawn and from 1500 to 1800; avoid weekends and holidays.

Marakkanam, mentioned in Roman records as an important port in the first century AD, has an ancient Siva temple with many inscriptions. Immediately inland is the Kaliveli Tank, an extremely important staging post and wintering area for about 40,000 migratory water fowl, including over 200 pelicans.

Sleeping

Chennai *p77, maps p78, 80, 82, 84, 86*
Chennai has many accommodation options; however, at the top end, excluding the Taj chain, these are aimed at the city's growing business market and lack character. Cheaper options are located within 1 km of Anna Salai (Mount Rd) in Central Chennai.

George Town *p79, map p80*
Good location for Central Station and State Bus Stands. Many cheap hotels are along VOC (Walltax) Rd.

E Great Hotel, 149 VOC Rd, T044-2533 1706. 44 rooms, 3 a/c, all with TV, spacious. Recommended.

E Railway Retiring Rooms, Central Station, T044-2535 3337. Some a/c rooms, dorms.

E Sornam International, 7 Stringer St, T044-2535 3060. Good rooms with TV and balcony, hot water, rooftop vegetarian restaurant.

E Youth Hostel (TTDC), EVR Park, near Central Railway Station, T044-2538 9132. Quiet.

F YMCA, NSC Bose Rd, T044-2538 3941, opposite City bus stand.

Central Chennai *p81, map p82*
Many accommodation options are within 1 km of Anna Salai (Mount Rd). **A-E** hotels charge an extra 20-30% tax.

L Chola Sheraton, 10 Cathedral Rd, T044-2811 0101. 'Boutique hotel' with 80 rooms, good restaurants (including Peshawari), airport transfer.

L The Park Chennai, 601 Anna Salai T044-5214 4000, www.theparkhotels.com. Converted from the site of the Gemini Film Studios, this is a quintessentially film hotel. Conran interiors, original film posters on the walls, world-class business facilities and lovely rooftop pool with magnificent views over Chennai.

L Taj Connemara, Binny Rd (off Anna Salai), T044-5500 0000, www.tajhotels.com. Supremely comfortable with 148 renovated rooms which retain splendid art deco features. Excellent restaurants, bar and good **Giggles** bookshop. Heavily booked Dec-Mar.

L Taj Coromandel, 37 Mahatma Gandhi Rd, Nungambakkam, T044-5500 2827, www.tajhotels.com. 201 rooms, fine restaurants, good pool. Recommended but Western tours dominate.

AL Ambassador Pallava, 53 Montieth Rd, T044-2855 4476, www.ambassadorindia.com. 120 rooms in a rather run-down hotel, good restaurants (especially Chinese), pool (open to non-residents), health club.

For an explanation of the sleeping and eating price codes used in this guide, see inside the front cover. Other relevant information is found in Essentials pages 40-44.

A-B Grand Orient, 693 Anna Salai, T044-2852 3411, F2852 3412. Half of the 66 rooms have been renovated but others are very worn, clean (usual hazard of cockroaches), helpful staff, good location.
B Residency, 49 GN Chetty Rd (convenient for airport), T044-2825 3434, www.theresidency.com. 112 very comfortable spacious rooms, 4th floor upwards have good views (9th floor, plush **A** suites). Excellent **Ahaar** restaurant (good buffet lunches), exchange, good car hire with knowledgeable drivers. Better rooms and service than some higher priced hotels. Highly recommended, reserve ahead.
B Savera, 69 Dr Radhakrishnan Rd, T044-2811 4700, hotsave@md2.vsnl.net.in. 260 comfortable rooms (standard rooms identical to superior), good pool (non-residents, Rs 150), older hotel but smart and clean, disaster-prone travel desk.
D Comfort, 22 Vallabha Agraharam St, T044-2858 7661. 40 rooms, some a/c, friendly, clean Indian hotel 5 mins from Marina Beach.
D Guru, 69 Marshall's Rd, relatively near Egmore railway station, T/F044-2855 4067. Large hotel, fairly clean rooms, some a/c good vegetarian restaurant, no credit cards.
D Harrisons, 154/5 Village Rd, T044-2827 5271. Some a/c rooms, restaurant (South Indian/Chinese), bar.
D Himalaya International, 54 Triplicane High Rd, T044-2854 7522. Modern, bright, welcoming, 45 rooms with nice bath, some a/c, clean. No food but available from **Hotel Gandhi** next door.
D Paradise, 17/1 Vallabha Agraharam St, T044-2854 7542, F853 0052. Spacious clean rooms with fans (some with 2), shower, good value, very friendly and helpful owners.
D Ranjith, 9 Nungambakkam High Rd, T044-2827 0521, F827 7688. Cool, pleasant and relaxing, 51 rooms, some a/c, restaurant (good non-vegetarian continental), excellent and reasonable bar, travel desk.
E Sree Krishna, 159 Peters Rd, T044-2852 2897. 15 rooms, some a/c with bath.
E YMCA, 14 Westcott Rd, Royapettah, T044-2853 2158.

Egmore *p85, map p86*

Many hotels (including several good budget options) are around the station and EVR Periyar (Poonamallee) High Rd, an auto-rickshaw ride away to the north of the railway line. Kennet Lane budget hotels are often full.
A-B New Victoria, 3 Kennet Lane (200 m from station), T044-2819 3638, F2819 0070. 51 a/c rooms, restaurant (excellent breakfast), bar, spacious, quiet, ideal business hotel. Recommended.
B Tristar, 29 Whannels Rd, T044-2855 0006, F855 0561. New hotel with good a/c rooms, all facilities.
C Abu Palace, 926 EVR Periyar High Rd, T044-2643 1010, F2642 8091. Plush, well insulated rooms, restaurant, bar, smart business hotel, concrete fortress-like exterior, huge enclosed lobby.
C Breeze, 850 EVR Periyar High Rd, T044-2641 3334, F2641 3301. Modern, popular, 94 rooms, fridges, satellite TV, internet.
C-D Raj Residency, 2 Kennet Lane, T044-2821 2214. Spacious, 72 rooms with balcony, vegetarian restaurant, bar.
D Blue Diamond, 934 EVR Periyar High Rd, T044-2641 2244, F642 8903. 33 rooms, some a/c, quieter at rear, good a/c restaurant (busy at peak times), exchange.
D Pandian, 15 Kennet Lane, T044-2819 1010, www.hotelpandian.com. Decent budget choice close to Egmore train station, 90 small but quiet rooms, some a/c, restaurant with a/c, bar, clean but spartan, helpful staff and good travel desk, expensive room service. Branch of i-way internet. Near the mosque so noisy at prayer times.
D YWCA International Guest House, 1086 EVR Periyar High Rd, T044-2532 4234. Restaurant (rate includes breakfast), 60 rooms, with bath, few a/c, for men and women, popular so book early, excellent value, also campsite.
D-E Imperial, 6 Gandhi Irwin Rd, T044-2825 0376, F2825 2030. Friendly, 80 good size average rooms, some a/c, best at rear, good food, 4 restaurants, reasonable price, bar.
E Impala Continental, opposite station, T044-2825 0564. Near **Vasanta Bhavan** restaurant, 50 excellent clean rooms with TV, good service.
E Masa, 15/1 Kennet Lane, T044-2825 2966, F825 1261. 88 clean functional a/c rooms, hot water.
E New Laxmi Lodge, 16 Kennet Lane, T044-2825 4576. Old building, set back in garden, with 50 rooms around courtyard.

E Regent, 8 Kennet Lane, T044-2825 3347. 45 renovated clean rooms set around courtyard, friendly. Recommended.
E Satkar, 65 Ormes Rd (Flowers and Millers Rd junction), T044-2642 6304. Spotless rooms with bath, some a/c, good vegetarian **Suryaprakash** restaurant, helpful staff, good value but very noisy.
E Silver Star, 5 Purasawalkam High Rd, T044-2642 4414. Set back from the road, 38 simple clean rooms, open-air restaurant in courtyard, helpful and friendly staff.
E YMCA (1), 14 Westcott Rd, Royapettah, and **(2)**, 17 Ritherdon Rd, Vepery, T044-2532 2831, where there are **D** rooms with bath.
F Laharry Transit Hostel, for women under 30 only, very cheap and good value.
F Railway Retiring Rooms, T044-2825 2527.
F World University Service, East Spur Tank Rd, T044-2826 3991. Some rooms with bath, dorm, international student cards needed, couples not allowed to share, cheap canteen for Indian snacks, good value, well situated for Egmore and south central Chennai.
F-G Cristal, 34 CNK Rd, Triplicane, T044-2857 2721. Clean basic rooms with tiled bath, very helpful service, better and cheaper than some others in the area.

South Chennai *p85, map p84*
L-AL Park Sheraton, 132 TTK Rd, T044-2499 4101, F499 7201. Good pool, 160 rooms, **Dakshin Chettinad** restaurant.
C Parthan, 75 GN Chetty Rd (near Panagal Park), T044-2815 8792. Restaurant (Chinese), 29 clean, large, comfortable and quiet rooms, exchange. Recommended.
C Shelter, 19-21 Venkatesa Agraharam St, T0411-2495 1919, www.hotelshelter.com. Business hotel located in Mylapore. Clean rooms with hot water, central a/c, very helpful staff, internet café, exchange, restaurant.
D Transit House, 26 Venkataraman St, T Nagar, T044-2434 1346. Some a/c rooms, dorm (Rs 60), snack bar and pleasant garden, no credit cards.
E Andhra Mahila Sabha, 12 D Deshmukh Rd, T044-2493 8311. Some **D** a/c rooms, vegetarian restaurant.

Airport *p77*
These hotels offer free airport transfers. Other hotels are 12-15 km from the airport.
L Trident, 1/24 GST Rd, T044-2234 4747. 166 rooms in characterless but functional hotel. Pleasant swimming pool in the garden.
AL Le Royal Meridien, T044-2231 4343, www.leroyalmeridien-chennai.com. Plush new hotel with all facilities including good restaurants and bars.
B-C Mount Heera, 287 MKN, Alandur, T044-2233 5656, hotelmountheera@yahoo.com. New hotel with modern facilities and free airport transfers.

Mahabalipuram *p87, map p88*
Even modest hotels charge 20% luxury tax. Several new places in the Othavadai St area. It's busy during the Jan dance festival.
L-AL Fisherman's Cove (Taj), Covelong Rd, 8 km north, T04114-272304, www.tajhotels.com. Beautiful site, 80 rooms, some a/c cottages with sea view, excellent seafood restaurant on the beach ("very special"), excellent facilities, ask reception about seasonal turtle walks.
B-C Ideal Beach Resort, Covelong Rd (3½ km north), T04114-242240, www.idealresort.com. 30 rooms in cottages, some a/c (limited hours), good restaurant, exchange, pool and gardens, clean, comfortable. Poor service reported though.
C-D Sea Breeze, East Raja St, T04114-243035, seabreeze hotel@hotmail.com. Clean, spacious, well- furnished rooms (some a/c with fridge, Rs 700), good position, direct beach access (dubious swimming), pool (non-residents Rs 100), good food, Chennai airport pick-up Rs 600. Iffy 'hot water', mediocre upkeep. Next door annexe is cheaper, see below.
D Mamallaa Heritage (previously Mamalla Bhavan Annexe), 104 East Raja St, T04114-242260. Spotless, friendly and reasonable value, 43 clean spacious rooms, 17 a/c, nice balconies, excellent vegetarian restaurant, exchange, travel, 24 hr hot water, and complimentary toiletries. Recommended.
D Sea Breeze Annexe, see above, clean doubles with fan and deck. Tariff includes access to the hotel pool.
D Tamil Nadu Beach Resort, T04114-242361, F42268. Beautiful setting, 48 cottages, some a/c but neglected, damp, restaurants, bar (limited hours), exchange, good pool (gets deep suddenly!) (non-residents Rs 75).

D-E Surya, 1 Thirukula St, T04114-242292, F42992. Set in quiet shaded gardens, 12 cottages overlooking small lake (1st floor with balcony more expensive), some a/c, camping, a/c restaurant, knowledgeable, friendly/overbearing manager. Complaints about mosquitos and cleanliness.

D-E Veeras, East Raja St, T04114-242288. 16 rooms (10 a/c), clean, well kept, good restaurant, bar.

D-E Vinayak, 68 East Raja St, next to bus stand, T04114-242445. Comfortable, 14 rooms with balcony overlooking garden in new hotel, TV, phone.

E Lakshmi Lodge, Othavadai St, T04114-242463. riendly, popular with backpackers, 26 clean rooms, upstairs small but light, downstairs dark and poor, restaurant with beach view, notice "prohibits drugs but staff try to sell you hemp".

E-F Siva Guest House, 2 Othavadai Cross St, T04114-243234, F243534, sivaguesthouse@hotmail.com. 11 very clean rooms, taxi hire, internet, friendly. Highly recommended.

E-F Tina Blue View Lodge, 1 Othavadai St, T04114-242319, F242511. Friendly, 25 rooms with bath and balcony (No 9 best), cottages for long-term stays, garden. Recommended.

F La Vie en Rose, 9 Old College Rd, near bus stand, T04114-242522, Lavieenrose45@hotmail.com. 7 rooms overlooking garden, friendly, internet, interesting backpacker restaurant with balcony, French spoken.

F New Papillon, off Beach Rd, towards Sunrise. Clean but simple rooms, shower (Rs 70), good restaurant upstairs (try muesli).

F Ramakrishna Lodge, 8A Othavadai St, T04114-242431. Friendly, good value, 31 well-kept, clean rooms with fan, shower, Western toilets, no nets (Rs 125), courtyard, good rooftop restaurant with travellers' menu and music; contact Vijay for informal yoga classes. Recommended.

Kanchipuram *p92, map p93*

C-D Baboo Soorya, 85 East Raja St, T04112-222555, set back off main road down palm fringed lane. 38 clean, spacious rooms, some a/c, restaurant, snack bar, glass 'bubble' lift, friendly staff, quiet.

E Sri Rama Lodge, 20 Nellukkara St, near Bus Stand, T04112-222435. Fairly basic rooms, some a/c and TV, a/c restaurant, relatively quiet, helpful staff.

F Sree Kusal Lodge, 68C Nellukkara St, T04112-223356. 25 clean and good value rooms, TV, vegetarian restaurant.

F Sri Krishna Lodge, 68A Nellukkara St, T04112-222831. Helpful, friendly manager, 28 good, clean rooms, some with bath.

Eating

Central Chennai *p81, map p82*

Most restaurants are in Central Chennai and are open 1200-1500, 1900-2400. Those serving non-vegetarian dishes are often more expensive.

TTT Chola Sheraton, see page 94. Chinese in the hotel (chef from Beijing) and good rooftop restaurant, superb views.

TTT Copper Chimney, opposite Chola Sheraton. International, a/c, good tandoori, very clean, pleasant seating.

TTT Patio, at the **Taj Coromandel**, see page 94, is exquisite Continental but pricey. Also at the **Golden Dragon**; excellent Chinese. **Southern Spice** offers very good South Indian, along with evening dance recitals and freezing a/c.

TTT Raintree, at **Taj Connemara**, see page 94, is a romantic outdoor restaurant with good food, atmosphere and ethnic entertainment but cavalier service. Very good buffet dinner on Sat night.

TTT Savera, see page 95, has an excellent Indian, very friendly, helpful service, live Indian music in the evenings.

TT Annalakshmi, Anna Salai (near Higginbotham's bookshop). Wholesome, health-restoring offerings, Southeast Asian specialities (profits to charity, run by volunteers). Recommended.

TT Buhari's, 83 Anna Salai. Good Indian. Dimly lit a/c restaurant, with terrace and unusual decor. Try crab curry, egg *rotis* and Muslim dishes; also in Park Town near Central Station.

TT Cascade, 15 Khaderi Nawaz Khan Rd. Chinese, Thai, Japanese and Malay.

TT Chinatown, 74 Cathedral Rd (a/c), Chinese.

TT Chungking, 67 Anna Salai (opposite PO) (1030-2200), Chinese; lack of atmosphere (dim lighting) compensated for by good food.

TT Dasaprakash, Anna Salai (next to Higginbotham's bookshop). 1200-1445, 1900-2345. South Indian (buffets Rs 120), also excellent milk shakes.

ΨΨ **Dynasty**, at **Harrisons**, see Sleeping, is a recommended Chinese restaurant.
ΨΨ **Gem**, Triplicane High Rd (200 m south of **Broadlands**). Non-vegetarian. Tiny Muslim restaurant.
ΨΨ **Southern Chinese**, 683 Anna Salai, Thousand Lights (next to Anand Theatre). Recommended.
Ψ **Maharaja**, Triplicane High Rd, 100 m from **Broadlands** hotel. Indian vegetarian.
Ψ **Saravana**, 209 NSC Bose Rd. Spotlessly clean, excellent snacks, fruit juices (try pomegranate!), sweetmeats, all freshly made.
Ψ **Udipi**, 8/9 Anna Salai (near Higginbotham's), good range of snacks.
Ψ **Woodlands Drive-In Restaurant**, 30 Cathedral Rd. 0600-2100. Rows of tables, simple, busy, go for breakfast.

Chennai: Egmore *p85, map p86*
ΨΨ **Jewel Box**, at **Blue Diamond**, see Sleeping. Cool a/c, good for breakfasts, snacks and main courses (also Chinese).
ΨΨ **Stardust**, 5 Kennet Lane. Multi-cuisine and pizzas, dimly lit.
Ψ **Balaji Woodlands**, **Vee Yes Hotel**, Egmore. Indian vegetarian.
Ψ **Udipi Home Mathsya**, 1 Hall's Rd (corner of Police Commissioner's Rd). A/c, excellent, wide range of food. Recommended.
Ψ **Vasanta Bhavan**, 10 Gandhi Irwin Rd, opposite Egmore station, 1st floor. Very clean, excellent food, friendly staff, downstairs bakery does delicious sweets.

Mahabalipuram *p87, map p88*
Beachside cafés are pleasant for a drink: Sea Rock and Luna Magica in particular. In top hotels waterfront cafés are especially attractive in the evening.
ΨΨ **Curiosity**, Othavadai St. Wide range, excellent food, very willing to please.
ΨΨ **Gazebo**, East Raja St. Charcoal-grilled fish, pleasant seating.
ΨΨ **German Bakery**, selling good bread, great cakes, tasty pastas (try yak cheese lasagne) and Chinese dishes, very friendly, relaxed atmosphere, Nepali-run, open Dec-Apr. Recommended.
ΨΨ **Honey Falls**, Shore Temple Rd. Few tables, served with delicious fish.
ΨΨ **La Vie en Rose** hotel, upstairs near the Archaeological Office. French. Very good food, 'special teas' (in absence of licence), friendly French manager.
ΨΨ **Moonrakers**, Othavadai St, www.moonrakersrestaurant.com. Pleasant and friendly. Recommended.
ΨΨ **Temple View**, GRT Temple Bay Kovalam Rd, T4114-242251. Multi-cuisine restaurant overlooking shore temple, breakfast lunch and dinner, plus less formal, open-air Beach Comber and High Tide bars (1000-2200).
ΨΨ **Tina Blue View Lodge**, breezy restaurant, mixed reports (slow, unfriendly service).
ΨΨ **Village**, near **Surya**. Some outdoor seating in pleasant lakeside position, rustic design, average food, chilled beers.
Ψ **Dreamland**, Othavadai St. Western favourites, very friendly, relaxed.
Ψ **Mamalla Bhavan Annexe** hotel. Good South Indian vegetarian restaurant. Try paper dosa and outstanding *palak* dishes. Indoors a/c, or outdoors evenings.

Kanchipuram *p92, map p93*
Ψ **Baboo Soorya** hotel, a/c, cheap Indian vegetarian restaurant, good thalis.
Ψ **Bakery Park Place**, Odai St, cakes and sweets.
Ψ **Saravana Bhavan**, next to Jaybala International 504 Gandhi Rd (50 m off the road). "Best in town".
Ψ **Sri Rama Lodge**, a/c, and **Sri Vela**, Station Rd, good breakfasts.

Bars and clubs

Chennai *p77, maps p78, 80, 82, 84, 86*
You can buy booze without difficulty despite local restrictions. Regulations change periodically, however, and All India Liquor Permits are available from either an Indian mission or a Government of India tourist office abroad or in one of the regional capitals.
Bikes and Barrels, Sri Thyagaraya Rd, T Nagar, T044-2815 6363. Restaurant and bar, playing rock, trance and house.
Dublin, Park Sheraton hotel, TTK Rd, T044-2499 4101. Irish pub-cum-nightclub.
The Leather Bar, The Park, 601 Anna Salai, T044-5214 4100. A dark womb of a bar with black leather floors and olive suede walls.
Oakshott Bar, Taj Connemara Hotel, Binny Rd, is a large, bright bar, offering huge tankards of beer, "exceptional 'side-snacks', huge TV; casual clothes accepted".

Entertainment

Chennai *p77, maps p78, 80, 82, 84, 86*
Although Chennai is revered for its strong cultural roots, much of it is difficult for the common tourist to access. Events are often publicized only after they have passed.

Cinemas

Those which show foreign (usually English language) films are mostly in the centre of town on Anna Salai.

Music, dance and art galleries

Chennai Music Academy, TTK Rd, is the scene of numerous performances of Indian music, dance and theatre, not only during the prestigious 3-week Music Festival from mid-Dec but right through the year; **Sabhas** are membership societies that offer cultural programmes 4 times a month to its members, but occasionally tickets are available at the door.
Kalakshetra, Tiruvanmiyur, T044-2446 1943. 1000-1800 daily. A temple of arts founded by Rukmani Devi Arundale in 1936 to train young artists to revive Bharat Natyam.
Shree Bharatalaya, in Mylapore. One of the key dance fine arts institutes run by respected guru Sudharani Raghupathy, Sura Siddha, 119 Luz Church Rd, T044-2499 4460.

Festivals and events

Chennai *p77, maps p78, 80, 82, 84, 86*
Jan 14: **Pongal Makara Sankranti**, the harvest thanksgiving, is celebrated all over Tamil Nadu for 3 days (public holiday). After ritually discarding old clothes and clay pots, festivities begin with cooking the first harvest rice in a special way symbolizing good fortune, and offering it to the Sun god. The second day is devoted to honouring the valuable cattle; cows and bulls are offered special new-rice dishes prepared with jaggery or nuts and green lentils. You will see them decorated with garlands, bells and balloons, their long horns painted in bright colours, before being taken out in procession around villages. Often they will pull carts decorated with flowers and carrying children, accompanied by noisy bands of musicians. On the last day of feasting, it is the turn of the 'workers' to receive thanks (and bonuses) from their employers.

Mahabalipuram *p87, map p88*
Dec-early Feb: 6-week **Dance Festival** starting on 25 Dec; at Bhagiratha's (Arjuna's) Penance, Classical 1800-2030, Folk 2030-2100, every Sat, Sun and holidays. Long speeches in Tamil on opening (full moon) night. **Mar**: **Masi Magam** attracts large crowds of pilgrims. **Apr-May**: **Brahmotsava** lasts for 10 days. **Oct-Nov**: The **Palanquin Festival** is held at the Stalasayana Perumal Temple.

Kanchipuram *p92, map p93*
Mar-Apr: The **Panguni Uthiram Festival** is the largest and possibly the most atmospheric of Kanchipuram's festivals, also celebrated all over Tamil Nadu.

Shopping

Chennai *p77, maps p78, 80, 82, 84, 86*
Parry's Corner and **Anna Salai** are the main centres. Most shops open Mon-Sat 0900-2000, some close for lunch 1300-1500. Weekly holidays may differ for shops in the same locality. Bear in mind that drivers – even those from reputable agents and companies – see little wrong in collecting a sweetening kickback from Kashmiris staffing huge shopping emporia, in exchange for dumping you on their doorstep. These are expert salesmen and they do have some beautiful items, but will ask at least double. The commission is from whatever you buy, so exercise restraint. There are often discount sales during the festival seasons of Pongal, *Diwali* and Christmas. The weekly *Free Ads* (Rs 5, Thu) has listings for second-hand cameras, binoculars etc which travellers might want to buy or sell.

Books

Most bookshops open 0900-1900. Also in hotels.
Higginbotham's, 814 Anna Salai and F39 Anna Nagar East, near Chintamani Market.
Side Effects, G17 Eldorado, 112 NH Rd, closes 1430-1600.

Clothes and crafts

Atmosphere, K Nawaz Khan Rd. Beautiful modern furniture fabrics and curtains – mostly silks – which can be shipped anywhere within India within 72 hrs.

Cane & Bamboo, 26 C-in-C Rd.
Central Cottage Industries, opposite Taj Coromandel hotel, is recommended.
Cinnamon, 27 Shafee Mohammed Rd. Designer clothes and modern items by Indian designers.
Habitat, K Nawaz Khan Rd nearby, good for special, unusual gifts.
Jamal's, 44 Devraja Mudali St.
Kalakshetra at Thiruvanmiyur excels in *kalamkari* and traditional weaving, also good household linen.
Kalpa Druma, 61 Cathedral Rd (opposite Chola Sheraton), has attractive selection of wooden toys and panels.
Khazana at Taj Coromandel, good for special, unusual gifts.
New Kashmir Arts, 111 Anna Salai, for good carpets.
Poompuhar, 818 Anna Salai, specializes in first-class bronzes.
Tiffany's, 2nd floor, Spencer's Plaza (antiques, bric-a-brac).
Vatika, 5 Spur Tank Rd, good for special, unusual gifts.
Victoria Technical Institute, Anna Salai near **Taj Connemara** hotel and opposite the Life Insurance Corporation of India. This fixed-rate, government-backed operation is the best for South Indian handicrafts (wood carving, inlaid work, sandalwood). Other Govt Emporia are along Anna Salai.

Department stores

Most open 0900-2000.
Burma Bazar, Rajaji Salai, for imports, especially electronic goods. Bargain hard.
Five Stars, 60 Pantheon Rd, Egmore.
Harringtons, 99 Harrington Rd, Chetput.
Isapahani Centre, 123/4 Nungambakkam High Rd. This is where the hip Madrasis hang out. It has some very snazzy designer 'ethnic' clothes shops.
Spencer's Plaza, Anna Salai near **Taj** Connemara, is a dizzyingly huge mall with excellent choice for shopping in comfort.
Supermarket, 112 Davidson St and TNHB Building, Annanagar (closed Fri).

Fabrics

Chennai was founded because of the excellence and cheap prices of the local cotton.
Co-optex (government run) shops stock handloom silks and cottons.
Khadi stores specialize in handspun and handwoven cotton.
Shilpi; **Urvashi**, TTK Rd, good for cottons.

Jewellery

Radha Gold Jewellers, 43 North Mada St, T044-2491923. You can also get 'antique' finished things and dance jewels 0930-1300 1600-2100. Next door, at 42, is
Sri Sukra Jewels, , Mylapore, T044-2464 0699, www.sukra.com. Brilliant temple – ie costume – jewellery. Fixed price.

Silk and saris

Look out for excellent Kanchipuram silk and saris. Recommended for quality and value: **Handloom House**, 7 Rattan Bazar.
Nalli (opposite Panagal Park) with excellent selection, both in T Nagar.
Rupkala, 191 Anna Salai, good prices, helpful staff.

Mahabalipuram *p87, map p88*

Handicrafts shops sell small figures in soapstone and metal.
Hidesign, 138 East Raja St. Excellent Western-style leather goods, very reasonable. Recommended.
Himalayan Handicrafts, 21 East Raja St, also has 900 books for exchange.
JK Books, off the beach on Othavadai St. Books and newspapers.
Silver Star, 51 East Raja St, good tailor.

Kanchipuram *p92, map p93*

Silk and cotton fabrics with designs of birds, animals and temples or in plain beautiful colours, sometimes 'shot', are sold by the metre in addition to saris. It is best to buy from government shops or Co-operative Society stores.
AS Babu Shah, along Gandhi Rd, has high quality silks.
BM Silks, 23G Yadothagari, Sannathi St. Worth a look.
Sreenivas, 135 Thirukatchi Nambi St (Gandhi Rd).

▲ Activities and tours

Chennai *p77, maps p78, 80, 82, 84, 86*

Body and soul

Krishnamacharya Yoga Mandiram, New No 31 (Old #13), Fourth Cross St, R K Nagar,

T044-2493 7998, www.kym.org. Runs 2- and 4-week intensive courses in yoga.

Golf

At Guindy Race Course.

Sports clubs

Temporary membership is available at most clubs, sometimes for sports only. Facilities in clubs are for members only, but you may be allowed in on the recommendation by a member. Some hotel facilities may be used on payment of a fee.
Chennai Cricket Club, Chepauk. Tennis, swimming, cricket, billiards, bar.
Chennai Gymkhana Club, Anna Salai. Tennis, swimming, cricket, billiards, library, bar.
Chennai Riders' Club, Race View, Race Course, Velachery Rd. Riding (including lessons) throughout the year except Jun.
Cosmopolitan Club, Anna Salai. Tennis, billiards, golf, library, bar.

Swimming

Hotel pools are open to non-residents at Ambassador Pallava and Savera (see page 95). Chennai Cricket Club has an excellent pool (less crowded before noon); you need an introduction. Others open to the public are at Marina Beach and the YMCA pool at Saidapet. Sea bathing is safe at Elliot's Beach, though no longer attractive.

Tennis

Clubs allowing members' guests and temporary members to use courts are: Chennai Club, Gymkhana Club, Cricket Club, Cosmopolitan Club, Presidency Club and Lady Willingdon Club. YMCA at Saidapet also has courts.

Tours

The following are on deluxe coaches and accompanied by a guide:
Tamil Nadu Tourism (TTDC). Departure points and reservations: Sales Counters at 4 EVR Periyar High Rd (opposite Central Station), T044-2536 0294; Express Bus Stand near High Ct compound, T044-2534 1982 (0600-2100).
Welcome Tours, 150 Anna Sali (Agarchand Mansions), T044-2852 0908. Sales agents. Open 24 hrs.
City sightseeing half-day Daily 0800-1300, 1330-1830. Fort St George, Government Museum (closed Fri), Valluvar Kottam, Snake Park, Kapaleeswarar Temple, Elliot's Beach, Marina Beach. Rs 105, a/c Rs 150.
Full-day Daily 0800-1900. Drive along Marina Beach, Kapaleeswarar Temple, Snake Park, Vallavur Kottam, Museum, Fort St George (US$2 entry), St Mary's Church, Birla Planetarium, Muttukadu Boat House and VGP Golden Beach. Rs 160 (a/c Rs 240). Visitors have found the tours disappointing.
Excursions Mahabalipuram and Kanchipuram, 0730-1900, Rs 200 (a/c Rs 350) and Tirupati, 0630-2200, Rs 375 (a/c Rs 600).

Tour operators

Cox & Kings, A15 Eldorado Building, NH Rd.
Mercury, 191 Anna Salai, T044-28522993.
STIC, 142 NH Rd, T044-28271195
Sita, 26 C-in-C Rd, T044-28278861.
Southern Holidays, 19, Nageswara Rd, T044-28236029, www.southernholidays.com.
Surya, 1st fl, Spencer's Plaza, Anna Salai. Very efficient, friendly, personal service.
Thomas Cook, 45 Montieth Rd, opposite Ambassador Pallava hotel.
Welcome Tours, See under Tours opposite.

Mahabalipuram *p87, map p88*

Hi Tours, 123 East Raja St, T04114-243260, travexs@vsnl.com. Train/air tickets, tours, foreign exchange, Kerala house boats.
Tamil Nadu Tourism (TTDC), to Kanchipuram and Mahabalipuram. 0500-1900. Tiring, but good value if you don't mind being rushed. It also includes a stop at the appallingly garish Indian kitsch, VGP Beach Resort.

Kanchipuram *p92, map p93*

Tourist information at **Hotel Tamil Nadu**, T04112-222461, 1000-1700.

Transport

Chennai *p77, maps p78, 80, 82, 84, 86*

Air
The **Aringar Anna International Airport** (named after CN Annadurai) with 2 terminals and the **Kamaraj Domestic Airport** are on one site at Trisoolam in Meenambakkam, 12 km from the centre. Enquiries, T140, arrivals and departures, T142. Pre-paid taxis from both; to Chennai Central or Egmore, Rs 150-180 (yellow taxis

are cheaper than private), 30 mins; Rs 450 to Mahabalipuram. Buses to centre Rs 75 (day), Rs 100 (night). Airport, T044-2234 6013. Auto-rickshaws to Chennai Central, Rs 100. The Suburban Railway is the cheapest way into town, from Trisoolam suburban line station to Egmore and Fort, but trains are often packed. Free Fone in the main concourse, after collecting baggage in the international airport, you can use this phone to ring hotels. Railway Bookings 1000-1700. Watch out for international prices for food and drink.

Indian Airlines, 19 Marshalls Rd, T044-2855 5200 (daily, 0800-2000). Reservations, all 24 hrs: T044-2855 5209. Mini Booking Offices: 57 Dr Radhakrishnan Rd, T044-2827 9799; Umpherson St (near Broadway); 9 South Bagh Rd, T Nagar, T044-2434 7555; Airport T044-2234 3131. Check-in T044-2234 8483. To **Bengaluru (Bangalore)**, **Bhubaneswar**, **Coimbatore**, **Delhi**, **Goa**, **Hyderabad**, **Kochi**, **Kolkata**, **Madurai**, via Tiruchirappalli; **Mumbai**, **Port Blair** and **Pune**, **Puttaparthy**, **Thiruvananthapuram**, **Visakhapatnam**. International flights include: **Bangkok**, **Kuala Lumpur**, **Kuwait**, **London**, **New York**, **Paris,** and **Singapore.**

Airlines Air France, 43 Montieth Rd, T044-2855 4916. **Air India**, 19 Marshalls Rd, T044-2855 4477 (0930-1730, avoid 1300-1400), airport T044-2234 4927. **British Airways**, Khalili Centre, Montieth Rd, T044-2855 4680, Airport T044-2234 8282. **Cathay Pacific**, Spencer's Plaza, 769 Anna Salai, T044-2852 2418. **Gulf Air**, 52 Montieth Rd, T044-2855 3091. **Jet Airways**, 43 Montieth Rd, Egmore, T044-28414141, airport T044-2256 1818. **KLM**, Taj Connemara, T044-2852 4437. **Kuwait Airways**, 43 Montieth Rd, T044-2855 3797. **Lufthansa**, 167 Anna Salai, T044-2852 5095. **Malaysian Airlines**, 498 Anna Salai, T044-2434 9651. **Qantas**, 112 NH Rd, T044-2827 8680. T044-2852 2871. **Sabena**, 47 White's Rd, T044-2851 4337. **Saudia**, 560 Anna Salai, T044-2434 9666. **Singapore Airlines**, 108 Dr Radhakrishna Rd, T044-2852 2871. **Sri Lankan**, 73 Cathedral Rd, T044-2826 1535. **Swissair**, 47 Whites Rd, T044-2852 6560.

General Sales Agents (GSA): **Air Kenya**, **Garuda Airways**, **Japan Airlines**, Global Travels, 703 Anna Salai, T044-285 23957. **Alitalia**, 548 Anna Salai, T044-2434 9822. **American Airways, Air Canada, Bangladesh Biman, Royal Jordanian** and **TWA**, Thapar House, 43 Montieth Rd, T044-2856 9232. **Delta**, at Aviation Travels, 47 Whites Rd, T044-2825 9655. **Egypt Air** and **Yemen Air**, at BAP Travels, 135 Anna Salai, T044-284 9913. **Iberian and Royal Nepal Airlines**, at STIC Travels, 142 NH Rd, T044-2827 1195. **Maldive Airways**, at Crossworld Tours, 7 Rosy Tower, NH Rd. **Sahara**, T044-2826 3661. **Thai International**, at Inter Globe, 144 Kodambakkam High Rd, T044-2826 2294.

Bus

Local The cheap and convenient local bus service is not overcrowded and offers a realistic alternative to auto-rickshaws and taxis outside the rush hour (0800-1000, 1700-1900). Make sure you know route numbers as most bus signs are in Tamil (timetables from major bookshops). **Pallavan Transport Corp (PTC)**, Anna Salai, runs an excellent network of buses from 0500-2300 and a skeleton service through the night. '**M**' service on mini-buses are good for the route between Central and Egmore stations and journeys to the suburban railway stations. The 'V' service operates fast buses with fewer stops and have a yellow board with the route number and LSS (Limited Stop Service). PTC has a ½ hourly 'luxury' mini-bus service between **Egmore Station, Indian Airlines**, Marshall's Rd office and the airports at **Meenambakkam** picking up passengers from certain hotels (inform time keeper at Egmore in advance, T044-2536 1284). The fare is about Rs 20.

Long-distance For long-distance journeys, the state highways are reasonably well maintained but the condition of other roads varies. The new East Coast Rd (ECR) for Express buses and cars only has helped to cut some journey times. Fast long-distance Korean air buses now run on some routes, giving a comfortable ride on air-cushioned suspension.

Chennai is amazingly proud of its new bus station, **Mofussil Bus Terminus** on Jawaharlal Nehru Rd, near Coimbedu Market, T044-2479 4705. Asia's biggest, it has 30 arrival and 150 departure terminals.

Tamil Nadu Govt Express Parry's, T044-2534 1835, offers good connections within the whole region and the service is efficient and inexpensive. Best to take a/c coaches or super deluxe a/c. Bookings 0700-2100. Other state and private companies cover the region but you may wish to avoid their video coaches which make listening, if not viewing, compulsory as there are no headphones. **Interstate Bus Depot**, Broadway Bus Stand, handles enquiries and reservations. Computer reservations are now made on long distance routes.

Beware of children who 'help' you to find your bus in the expectation of a tip; they may not have a clue! There have also been reports of men in company uniforms selling tickets which turn out to be invalid; it is best to buy on the bus. The listings given are for route number, distance. **Coimbatore** *No 460*, 500 km; **Chidambaram** and **Nagapattinam** *326*; **Kanchipuram** *76B*; **Kanniyakumari** *282 and 284*, 700 km; **Kumbakonum** *303F*, 289 km, 6½ hrs; **Madurai** *137*, 447 km, 10 hrs; **Mahabalipuram** *109*, Rs 19, 1½ hrs (*108B* goes via Meenambakkam airport, 2½ hrs) can be very crowded; **Nagercoil** *198*, 682 km, 14 hrs; **Ooty** *468*, 565 km, 13 hrs; **Pondicherry** *803*, 106 km, 3 hrs; **Thanjavur** *323*, 320 km, 8 hrs; Tiruchirappalli *123*, 320 km and Route *124*, 7 hrs; **Tiruvannamalai** 180 km, 5 hrs; **Yercaud** *434*, 360 km, 8 hrs; **Bengaluru (Bangalore) via Vellore and Krishnagiri** *831*, 360 km, 8 hrs; **Bengaluru (via Kolar)** 350 km, 7½ hrs; **Mysore via Bengaluru** *863*, 497 km, 11 hrs; **Tirupati via Kalahasti** *802*, 150 km, 3½ hrs. Also several **Andhra Pradesh STC** buses to Tirupati daily. APSTC runs daily buses to many other towns in the state, as does **Karnataka State Express Bus Service** to Karnataka.

Car

A/c or ordinary cars with drivers are good value and convenient for sightseeing, especially for short journeys out of the city shared between 3-5 people. Large hotels can arrange, eg Regency (Rs 600 per 8 hrs; Rs 750 for Mahabalipuram). **Ganesh Travels**, 36 PCO Rd, T044-825 0066; **Window to the World** (Trichy), T0431-243 6052, faithpandian@sify.com, for tours from Chennai (and other towns); **Hertz**, 426 Anna Salai, T044-2433 0684; **TTDC**, 4 EVR Periyar Rd, T044-2536 0294.

Ferry

Visas are now also issued on arrival at Port Blair. Regular passenger ships to the Andaman and Nicobar Islands take 3 days. The **Shipping Corporation of India**, Jawahar Building, Rajaji Salai, T044-2523 1401. Also, **Deputy Directorate of Shipping Services**, A & N, 6 Rajaji Salai, T044-2522 6873.

Tickets to the Andaman Islands

At 0900 pick a 'letter of intent' to visit the Andamans, and collect details of sailings from the **Shipping Corporation of India** office. Go to the Foreigners' Registration Office at Shastri Bhavan, 26 Haddows Rd, and complete an application form for a permit and submit it with 2 photos before 1230; pick up at 1700 on the same day (or a day later if the application is submitted after 1230). Next day, take photocopies of your passport identification/Indian Visa pages and also of the Andamans permit, to the SCI office. Pick up a Ticket "Order Form", fill it in and queue for a ticket, 1000-1300. Women have an advantage when queuing!

Motorbike hire or purchase

Southern Motors, 282 TTH Rd, T044-2499 0784, is a good modern garage with efficient service. The **YWCA**, EVR Periyar Rd, is a good hotel for bikers and has a big shaded garden to park bikes securely.

MRTS

The Mass Rapid Transit System (raised, above-ground railway) covers the Beach-Chepauk and Chepauk-Mylapore sections.

Rickshaws

Three-wheeler scooter taxis, taking 2 adults and 1 child or more for a negotiable fee will hike charges by 25% between 2100-0500. In theory Rs 7 should be the minimum charge for the first kilometre, after which it should be metered. You can insist on using the meter, but these can be rigged and will often result in your driving around in circles to rack up the rate. Locally, most people agree a fare to a fixed destination; Rs 30 gets you between most neighbourhoods. As always, drivers get kickbacks from emporium owners to encourage detours via shops. Cycle-rickshaws are often no cheaper.

Taxi

Bharati Call Taxi, T044-28142233. **Chennai Call Taxi**, T044-25384455. **Fast Tack**, T044-24732020. Tourist cabs are the best choice in case you want to tour the city all day or visit nearby places like Mahabalipuram etc. It costs about Rs 4 per kilometre and Rs 30 per hour as hire charges. The minimum hire is for 5 hrs or 50 km. **Tiruvalluvar Travels**, T044-2474 5807.

Train

Suburban railway Inexpensive and handy, but very crowded at peak times. Stops between Beach Railway Station and Tambaram (every 5 mins in rush hour) include Fort, Park, Egmore, Chetpet, Nungambakkam, Kodambakkam, Mambalam, Saidapet, Guindy, St Thomas Mt. Also serves suburbs of Perambur and Villivakkam. Convenient stop at Trisoolam for the airports, 500 m walk from the terminals.

Long distance Smoking is banned on trains, stations and in railway offices. There is a penalty of Rs 100. Chennai has 2 main stations, **Chennai Central (MC)** for broad gauge trains to all parts of India and **Egmore (ME)** for metre gauge (and some sections converted to broad gauge). The 2 have a mini-bus link; taxis take 5 mins. Beach Station is for suburban services. **Chennai Central** enquiry, T131, reservations, T132, arrivals and departures, T133, then dial train no. Advance Reservations Centre, Southern Railway, is in a separate building in front of suburban station, Mon-Sat 0800-1400, 1415-2000, Sun 0800-1400. You can also order bedding. Indrail Passes and booking facilities for foreigners and NRIs on the first floor. **Egmore** enquiry, T135, arrivals and departures, T134. There are also Southern Railway Booking Offices in Mambalam, T044-2483 3755, Tambaram and Chennai Beach. Meenambakkam Airport has a Rail Booking Counter. You may reserve 30 days in advance. From Chennai Central to **Bengaluru (Bangalore)** *Shatabdi Exp 2007* 0600, not Tue, 7 hrs; *Lalbagh Exp 2607*, 1545, 5¾ hrs; *Brindavan Exp 2639*, 0715, 6 hrs. **Coimbatore** *Kovai Exp 2675*, 0615, 7¾ hrs; *West Coast Exp 6627*, 1100, 8¾ hrs; *Cheran Exp 2673*, 2145, 8½ hrs. **Delhi (ND)** *Tamil Nadu Exp 2621*, 2200, 33½ hrs; *G.T. Exp 2615*, 1630, 37½ hrs. **Delhi (HN)** *Rajdhani Exp 2431*, 1915, Tue, Thu, 29½ hrs. **Guntakal** (for Hospet): *Chennai Dadar Exp 1064*, 0650, 8 hrs; *Chennai-Mumbai Mail 6010*, 2220, 10 hrs. **Hyderabad** *Charminar Exp 2759*, 1810, 14½ hrs; *Chennai-Hyderabad Exp 7053*, 1600, 15 hrs. **Kochi (Cochin)** *Chennai-Aleppey Exp 6041*, 1945, 13¾ hrs; *Guwahati Cochin Exp 5624*, 1210, Fri, 14¾ hrs. **Kolkata (H)** *Coromandel Exp 2842*, 0905, 29 hrs; *Howrah Mail 6004*, 2230, 32½ hrs. **Mettupalayam** *Nilgiri Exp 6605*, 2015, 10 hrs. **Mumbai (CST)** *Chennai-Mumbai Mail 6010*, 2155, 30 hrs; *Chennai-Mumbai Exp 6012*, 1145, 27 hrs. **Mysore** *Shatabdi Exp 2007*, 0600, daily not Tue, 7 hrs; *Chennai Mysore Exp 6222*, 2245, 9¼ hrs. **Thiruvananthapuram** *Guwahati Trivandrum Exp 5628*, 1210, Wed, 19¼ hrs; *Howrah Trivandrum Exp 6324*, 0440, Tue, Sun, 18½ hrs. From **Egmore Kanniyakumari** *Chennai-Kanniyakumari Exp 6121*, 1900, 15 hrs. **Madurai** *Chennai-Kanniyakumari Exp 6121*, 1815, 10 hrs; *Vaigai Exp 2635*, 1225, 8 hrs; *Pandyan Exp 6717*, 2100, 9½ hrs via Kodai Rd (this connects with the bus service at **Kodaikkanal** arriving at midday). **Tiruchirappalli** *Vaigai Exp 2635*, 1225, 5½ hrs; *Pallavan Exp 2606*, 1530, 5½ hrs.

Mahabalipuram *p87, map p88*

Bicycle hire from tourist office and shops in East Raja St and hotels, Rs 25 per day. Recommended for **Tirukkalukundram** – from Dec to Feb a comfortable and attractive ride. **VM Hire**, Othavadai St (opposite Uma Lodge). Bicycle Rs 25, moped Rs 100. Mopeds also at **Bala Lodge** and **Vinodhara**, Rs 125.

Car hire from the tourist office. **Buses** from Chennai also go to **Tirukkalukundram** and **Pondicherry**. *Nos 19C, 68, 119A*. **Taxis** charge Rs 700-1000 for 1-day excursion from Chennai; Rs 450 to airport. To **Pondicherry**, Rs 700 (bargain hard).

The nearest **train** station is Chengalpattu, 29 km away with buses taking an hour.

Kanchipuram *p92, map p93*

The town is flat and easy to negotiate so the best and cheapest way to get about is by hiring a bike from near the bus stand or off East Raja St. **Cycle** and **auto-rickshaws** are available for visiting temples.

The **bus** station in the middle of town with direct Govt Express to **Chennai** (*No 828*)

2½ hrs, **Bengaluru (Bangalore)** (*No 828*), **Kaniyakumari** (*No 193*), **Pondicherry** (*No 804*, 109 km) 3½ hrs, and **Tiruchirappalli** (*No 122*). For **Mahabalipuram** (65 km) 2 hrs, direct bus or take a bus to Chengalpattu (35 km) and catch one from there. Frequent buses to **Vellore**, other buses go to **Tirupati** and **Tiruttani**.

The **train** station, on a branch line, is under 1 km to the northeast of the bus stand. There is 1 direct train to **Chennai Egmore** and **Chennai Beach**: *Kanchipuram- Chennai Beach Pass 172 (S)*, 0705, 2 hrs **Egmore**; 2½ hrs **Chennai Beach**. Also trains to Arakkonam on the Chennai-Bengaluru (Bangalore) line.

Around Kanchipuram *p94*

Vedanthangal Sanctuary

From Chennai by car or bus from the Broadway Bus Stand, Chennai (only weekends) or one from Mahabalipuram. It is also included in some coach tours.

The train to **Chengalpattu** (28 km) and then bus or taxi, 30 km to sanctuary.

Directory

Chennai *p77, maps p78, 80, 82, 84, 86*

Banks

Most open either 0830-1230 or 1000-1400 on weekdays; morning only on Sat. Closed Sun, national holidays and 30 Jun and 31 Dec (foreign exchange dealing may close an hr early). A few big hotels have 24-hr banks. **State Bank of India, Thomas Cook, TT Travels** at International Airport, 24 hrs. **American Express**, G17, Spencer Plaza, Anna Salai, T044-285 23628, 0930-1930, offers all foreign exchange and TC services. **Thomas Cook** branches at: 45 Montieth Rd, Egmore. 20 Rajaji Salai. 112 NH Rd, T044-282 74941, Mon-Fri 0930-1830 (closed 1300-1400), Sat 0930-1200. Both recommended. **Madura Travels**, Kennet Lane (near corner of Gandhi Irwin Rd), Egmore, change TCs, good rate. Many banks have branches on Anna Salai, Cathedral, Dr Radhakrishnan and EVR Periyar Rds. Visa ATMs at **CitiBank**, Anna Salai (24 hrs). Alsa Promenade, Door 149, AA Block, 3rd Ave, Anna Nagar. Pushpa Shoppe, Adyar. **HSBC**, 30 Rajaji Salai. Pushpa Shoppe No 1, Adyar. **Standard Chartered Bank**, 37 Royapettah High Rd.

Embassies and consulates

Most open 0830-1330, Mon-Fri.
Austria 115 NH Rd, T044-2827 6036.
Belgium 97 Anna Salai, T044-2235 2336.
Denmark 8 Cathedral Rd, T044-2827 3399.
Finland 742 Anna Salai, T044-2852 4141.
France 16 Haddows Rd, T044-2826 6561.
Germany 22 C-in-C Rd, T044-2827 1747.
Greece 72 Harrington Rd, T044-2826 9194.
Italy 19 Rajaji Salai, T044-2534 2141.
Japan 60 Spur Tank Rd, T044-2826 5594.
Malaysia 6 Sri Ram Nagar, T044-2434 3048.
Mauritius 145 Starling Rd, T044-2827 1841.
Netherlands 64 Armenian St, T044-2538 4894. **Norway** 44-45 Rajaji Salai, T044-251 7950. **Singapore** 109 Habibulla Rd, T044-2827 6393. **Spain** 8 Nimmo Rd, San Thome. **Sri Lanka** 9D Nawab Habibulla Av, off Anderson Rd, T044-2827 6751. **Sweden** 6 Cathedral Rd, T044-2827 5792. **UK Deputy** High Commission, 24 Anderson Rd, Nungambakkam, T044-2827 5130.
USA 220 Anna Salai, T044-2827 3040.

Internet

Cybervision, off Anna Salai, 64 k ISDN; Datamen's, 273 Pycrofts Rd, good access, Rs 90 per hr; serves soft drinks. **SRIS**, 1st floor, F22-A, Spencer Plaza, 769 Anna Salai.

Language schools

Bharatiya Vidya Bhavan, 38/39 R E Mada St, T044-2494 3450, for Sanskrit. **Hindi Prachar Sabha**, T Nagar, T044-244 1824. **International Institute of Tamil Studies**, Central Polytechnic, T044-241 2992.

Some of the foreign cultural centres have libraries and arrange film shows. **Alliance Française**, 3/4A College Rd, Nungambakkam, T044-2827 2650. **American Center**, 561 Anna Salai, library 0930-1800, closed Sun, T044-2827 7825. **British Library**, 737 Anna Salai, 1000-1900, closed Mon, T044-2285 2002. **Max Müeller Bhawan**, Mon-Sat 0900-1900, 13 Khadar Nawaz Rd, T044-2826 1314. **Russian**, 27 Kasturi Rangan Rd, T044-2499 0050.

Medical services

Ambulance services Ambulance (Government), T102; **St John's Ambulance**, T044-2826 4630, 24-hr. **Dental hospital** (Government), T044-2534 0411; **All-in-One**, 34 Nowroji Rd, T044-2641 1911, 0400-2000,

0900-1200 Sun. **Chemists** SS Day & Night Chemists, 106D, 1st Main Rd, Anna Nagar. **Hospitals** Apollo Hospital, 21 Greams Rd, T044-2827 7447. CSI Rainey, GA Rd, T044-2595 1204. Deviki Hospital, 148 Luz Church Rd, Mylapore, T044-2499 2607. National Hospital, 2nd Line Beach Rd, T044-2251 1405.

Post

Poste restante at the GPO, Rajaji Salai, George Town; other major post offices which accept Speed Post Mail are in Anna Salai, Pondy Bazar, T Nagar, Meenambakkam, NH Rd, Flower Bazar and Adyar. CTO, Rajaji Salai (near Parry's Corner). Opening times vary, the first 3 are open 0800-2030. Computerized ISTD booths all over town, some open 24 hrs.

Telephone

Directory enquiry (national) T183, only from Chennai city itself.

Tourist offices

Govt of India (GITO), 154 Anna Salai, T044-2852 4785, Mon-Fri 0915-1745, Sat until 1300. Domestic Airport Counter, 24 hrs; International Airport Counter, at flight times. India Tourism Development Corporation (ITDC), 29 Victoria Crescent, C-in-C Rd, T044-2827 8884, 0600-2000, Sun 0600-1400. Tamil Nadu (TTDC), 4 EVR Periyar Rd (opposite Central Station), T044-2538 2916, www.tamilnadutourism.com, includes booking of TTDC hotels and tours; Express Bus Stand, T044-2534 1982. TTDC, 25 Radhakrishnan Rd, T044-854 7335; information centres at Central Railway, Gate 2 (Sales counter on Sun), Egmore stations, and domestic airport terminal, T044-2234 0569, 0700-2300. Govt of Tamil Nadu, Pangal Building, Saidapet. State tourist offices open Mon-Sat 1030-1700 (closed 2nd Sat). Andaman and Nicobar Islands, Andaman House, North Main Rd Ext, Anna Nagar West Ext, Padi Village, T044-2625 9295.

Useful addresses

Andaman and Nicobar Islands, Andaman House, North Main Rd Ext, Anna Nagar West Ext, Padi Village, T044-2625 9295. Foreigners' Registration Office, ground floor, Shastri Bhavan Annexe, 26 Haddows Rd. T044-2827 8210, for visa extensions, Mon-Fri 0930-1800. Govt of Tamil Nadu, Pangal Building, Saidapet. State tourist offices usually open from 1030-1700 on weekdays (closed Sun and 2nd Sat).

Mahabalipuram *p87, map p88*

Banks Cherry, Beach St, for exchange. LKP, 130 East Raja St. Good rate, speedy. Prithvi Securities, opposite Mamalla Bhavan Annexe, no commission, transfers money. **Libraries** English language dailies. Book exchange at Himalayan Handicrafts. **Post** Post office on a back street off Covelong Rd. **Tourist offices** Tamil Nadu, Covelong Rd (300 m north of Othavadai St), T04114-242232, Mon-Fri 0945-1745. 2 guides available here; others from Chennai. Car and cycle hire possible.

Kanchipuram *p92, map p93*

Banks State Bank of India, Gandhi Rd. Amex TCs not accepted; Indian Overseas Bank, Gandhi Rd. **Post** Head Post Office, 27 Gandhi Rd.

Pondicherry and Auroville

Pretty little Pondicherry, in pockets, has all the lazy charm of former French colonies; its stately whitewashed 18th-century homes froth with bright pink bougainvillea and its kitchens still smack gloriously of Gaul: excellent French breads, hard cheese and ratatouilles, accompanied by French wine. The primly residential French quarter contrasts wonderfully with the dog-eared heritage houses of the Tamil districts, whose streets were built to tilt towards Mecca, while scores of pristine grey mansions indicate the offices of the Sri Aurobindo Ashram. Up the road is the 60s westernized branch of Aurobindo's legacy, Auroville, the 'City Of Dawn', 'a place where human beings could live freely as citizens obeying one single authority, that of the supreme Truth.' This is the industrious fulcrum of people seeking an alternative lifestyle – a place of spirulina, incense, and white cotton weeds. ▸▸ *For Sleeping, Eating and other listings, see pages 110-114.*

Pondicherry (Puducherry)

» *pp110-114. Colour map 3, grid B5.*

→ *Phone code: 0413. Population: 220,700.*

Pondicherry is the archetypal ambling town: cleaved in two with the **French quarter** along the beach, boasting pretty high-ceilinged wood-slatted residential houses with walled gardens and bougainvillea, and with the markets, mess, businesses and 'talking streets' of the **Tamil** ('black') town to its west. While the French area, with 300 heritage buildings, is well maintained (the majority owned by the ashram), the Tamil area, despite its 1000 homes now classified as heritage, is dangerously dilapidated. The European Commission has funded the restoration of Calve Subraya Chetty (Vysial) street (between Mission and Gandhi streets). Muslim domestic architecture is clearly visible in the rues Kazy, Mulla and Tippu Sultan, in the south side of the Tamil quarter.

Many travel to Pondicherry for the Ashram of Sri Aurobindo Ghosh and his chief disciple Mirra Alfassa, 'The Mother'. Ghosh was an early 20th-century Bengali nationalist and philosopher who struggled for freedom from British colonial power (see page 513). In his aim to create an ashram utopia he found a lifelong compadre in the charismatic Frenchwoman Alfassa who continued as his spiritual successor after his death in 1950. She died in 1973 at the age of 93.

Ins and outs

Getting there Buses take under four hours from Chennai on the East Coast Road. Both the state and private bus stands are just west of the town, within walking distance, or a short auto-ride from the centre (expect the usual hassle from rickshaw-wallahs). The train station on a branch line from Villupuram, with trains to major destinations, is a few minutes' walk south of the centre.

Getting around Pondicherry is lovely to explore on foot, but hiring a bike or moped will give you the freedom to venture further along the coast independently. » *See Transport, page 113, for further details.*

Tourist information **Pondicherry Tourism** ⓘ *40 Goubert Salai, T0413-233 9497, http://tourismpon.nic.in, 0845-1300, 1400-1700*. Town maps, brochures, tours, sea cruises, fishing, car/bicycle hire, well run. The **Indian National Trust for Art and Cultural Heritage (INTACH)** ⓘ *14 Rue Labourdonnais, T0413-222 5991*, is particularly active in Pondicherry and runs heritage walks from its offices.

History

Ancient Vedapuri was where the sage **Agastya Muni** had his hermitage in 1500 BC and in the first century AD Romans traded from nearby Arikamedu. The **French** renamed it Puducherry in 1673. In 1742, Dupleix, newly named Governor of the French India Company, took up residence. In 1746 British lost Fort St George in Madras to Dupleix but in 1751 Clive counter-attacked by capturing Pondy in 1761. Puducherry was handed over to the Indian government in 1954 and became the Union Territory of Pondicherry.

Sri Aurobindo Ashram ⓘ *0800-1200, 1400-1800, free, meditation Mon-Wed, Fri 1925-1950; in the Playground: Thu, Sun 1940-2015*, has its main centre in rue de la Marine. The Ashram buildings can be recognized by the pale grey highlighted with white. The focus of reverence in the Main Building is the stone Samadhi (memorial) of the founders which is under a tree within the complex. Further information from the Bureau Central on Ambur Salai which has occasional films, lectures and other performances. There is also a **library** ⓘ *0730-1130, 1400-1645*.

The French Institute, rue St Louis, was set up in 1955 for the study of Indian culture and the Scientific and Technical Section for ecological studies. There's a French and English library looking over the sea, and the colonial building is an architectural treat in its own right.

Pondicherry

Sleeping
Balan Guest House 2 *C3*
Cottage Guest House 20 *A3*
de l'Orient 3 *E5*
de Pondicherry 4 *F5*
Excursion Centre 5 *F3*
Executive Inn 6 *B5*
Family Guest House 7 *E3*
Garden House 8 *A4*
International Guest House 9 *C5*
Mass 10 *D1*
Palm Beach Cottages 21 *A3*
Park Guest House 11 *F5*
Railway Retiring Rooms 17 *F3*
Ram Guest House 12 *D3*
Sea Side Guest House 13 *C5*
Suguru 14 *A3*
Tourist Bungalow 15 *F3*
Villa Helena 16 *E5*
Youth Hostel 19 *A3*

Eating
Ashram Dining Hall 1 *C5*
Au Feu de Bois 2 *E5*
Blue Dragon 3 *F5*
Hot Breads 4 *C4*
Indian Coffee House 5 *C4*

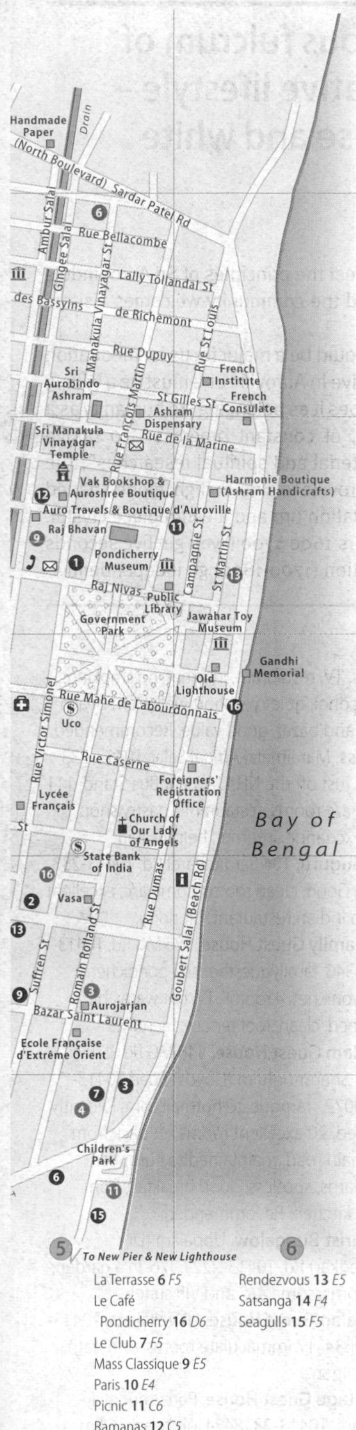

Pondicherry Museum ⓘ *next to the library, rue St Louis, Tue-Sun 1000-1700, closed public holidays, free,* has a good sculpture gallery and an archaeological section with finds discovered at the Roman settlement at Arikamedu. The French gallery charts the history of the colony and includes Dupleix's four-poster bed. Another place worth seeking out is the grand whitewashed **Lycée Français**, in rue Victor Simonel, with its lovely shady courtyard and balconies.

The French Catholic influence is evident in a number of churches, notably the **Jesuit Cathedral** (Notre Dame de la Conception, 1691-1765). The attractive amber and pink **Church of Our Lady of Angels** (1855) holds an oil painting of Our Lady of Assumption given to the Church by King Louis Napoleon III.

Opened in 1826, the **Botanical Gardens**, south of City Bus Stand, are pleasant. The **Government (Pondicherry) Park**, laid out with lawns, flower beds and fountains (one at the centre is of the Napoleon III period), lies in front of the Raj Niwas, the residence of the lieutenant governor. This was the original site of the first French garrison, Fort Louis, which was destroyed in Clive's raid of 1761.

Auroville » pp111-113.

Colour map 3, grid B5.

→ Phone code: 0413. Population 1700.

ⓘ *Visitors' centre, International Zone, T0413-262 3449, www.auroville.org.in, Mon-Sat 0945-1200 and 1345-1600, Sun 0945-1230. All visitors must come here first to park their cars. Passes for visits to Matrimandir Gardens and Amphitheatre will be issued only from here for same-day visits. Visits are Mon-Sat 1000-1230 and 1400-1630, Sun 1000-1300. It is only possible to visit the Inner Chamber of the Matrimandir if you have already visited the Gardens and the Amphitheatre, open Sun 1430-1730. Book in advance.*

Futuristic Auroville, 'City of Dawn', was set up in 1968 as a tribute to Sri Aurobindo, and draws more Europeans and Americans than the Pondicherry

“” This is the industrious fulcrum of people seeking an alternative lifestyle – a place of spirulina, incense and white cotton weeds …

Ashram. Its major buildings are supposed to reflect the principles of Sri Aurobindo's philosophy. It is a striking living experiment and the community welcomes visitors who have a genuine interest in its philosophy.

The Mother's aspiration was that Auroville would be a major focus for meditation and spiritual regeneration. The Charter says "To live in Auroville one must be a willing servitor of the Divine Consciousness" and describes it as belonging "to humanity as a whole ... the place of an unending education, of constant progress ... a bridge between the past and the future ... a site of material and spiritual researches". The Matrimandir (started in 1968) at the centre of Auroville is a 30-m high globe-shaped meditation room with a lotus bud shaped foundation urn and a centrepiece crystal, said to be the largest in the world. Open to visitors 1600-1700 ("you get five seconds to see the crystal"), but to spend time in meditation (1700-1800) go independently.

Sleeping

Pondicherry *p107, map p108*

A **The Dune**, T0413-265 5751, www.thedune.in/ welcome.htm. Funky beachside eco-hotel 15 km from Pondicherry with reflexology, yoga, ayurvedic massage, organic food and optional detox programmes. Colourful, clean and comfortable rooms. Pool, tennis, free bike hire.

A **Hotel de l'Orient**, 17 Romain Rolland St, T0413-234 3067, www.neemranahotels.com. Beautifully renovated 19th-century school now a small exclusive hotel, with 16 tastefully decorated rooms in colonial style with objets d'art. Mixed reviews of the restaurant (French/Creole) and service, but achingly lovely situation. Recommended.

B **Hotel de Pondicherry**, 38 rue Dumas, T0413-222 7409. Simple, clean, tastefully decorated 10 rooms (some with no windows but private courtyard), in the same colonial-style building as the popular French bistro Le Club (so can get noisy). Very friendly and efficient staff. A/c. Babysitting available.

B **Villa Helena**, 14 Suffren St, T0413-222 6789, galleryhotels@hotelstamilnadu.com. 5 comfortable rooms with antique furniture set around large shady courtyard (1 first-floor suite), includes breakfast.

C **Executive Inn**, 1a Perumal Koil St, T0413-233 0929, sumer@satyam.net.in. 11 a/c suites, TV, restaurant, internet, no smoking, no alcohol, quiet yet short walk from beach front and bazar, good value. Recommended.

C **Mass**, Maraimalai Adigal Salai, T0413-233 7221, just off the NH45A, near Bus Stand. 111 clean a/c rooms, restaurants, pastry shop, bar, exchange, internet, helpful staff.

C-D **Suguru**, 104 Sardar Patel Rd, T0413-233 9022. Good, clean rooms, some a/c, excellent South Indian restaurant, bit noisy.

D-E **Family Guest House**, 526 MG Rd, T0413-234 0346, familyguesthouse@pondicherry.everyone.net. 4 rooms, TV, hot water, bit cramped, clean, roof terrace, friendly.

D-E **Ram Guest House**, 546 MG Rd, 278 Avvai Shanmugham (Lloyds) Road T0413-222 0072, ramguest@hotmail.com. Recently opened, 20 excellent rooms set back from the main road, maintained to European standards, spotless, good breakfast from clean kitchen. Recommended.

E **Tourist Bungalow**, Uppalam (Dr Ambedkar) Rd, T0413-222 6376. In a garden, 12 rooms, some a/c, and VIP suites.

E-F **Balan Guest House**, 20 Vellaja St, T0413-233 0634. 17 immaculate rooms with bath, clean linen.

F **Cottage Guest House**, Periarmudaliar-chavadi, T0413-2338434, on beach, 6 km north of town. Rooms in cottages, French food, bike and motorcycle hire, peaceful, good beach under palm and casuarina trees, very popular.

F Excursion Centre, Uppalam (Dr Ambedkar) Rd. Very cheap bunk beds in dorm, suitable for groups, south of town, clean and quiet, very good value.

F Palm Beach Cottages, by Serenity Beach, 5 km north of town. Clean huts (Rs 150), concrete beds with mattress, small garden, 5-min walk from beach, friendly staff, excellent food, especially fish, good for bikers but noisy from the highway.

F Railway Retiring Rooms for passengers. Quieter than most stations. These are all about 20-30 mins' walk from the centre, so hire a bicycle.

F Youth Hostel, Solaithandavan Kuppam, T0413-222 3495, north of town. Dorm beds (Rs 30), close to the sea among fishermen's huts. Bicycle or transport essential.

Ashram guesthouses

Though these are mainly for official visitors, they are open to others (but 'not to hippies'); no alcohol or smoking. They close by 2230 (latecomers may be locked out). Book well in advance, with a day's rate.

D Park Guest House, near Children's Park, T0413-2237495, parkgh@auroville.org.in. 93 excellent sea-facing rooms (Rs 400), breakfasts, clean, quiet, great garden, reading room, ideal for long stays. Recommended.

D Sea Side Guest House, 14 Goubert Salai, T0413-2331713, seaside@sriaurobindo society.org.in. 25 excellent, large rooms, hot showers, breakfast, spotless, sea views. Recommended.

E-F International Guest House, Gingee Salai, T0413-2336699. 57 very clean and airy rooms, some a/c, huge for the price, very popular so often full.

F Garden House, 136 Akkasamy Madam St (north of town). Decent, clean rooms with bath (major bed bug problem and sewer nearby), quiet, gates locked at 2230.

Auroville *p109*

Food is available at most guesthouses and there are a number of restaurants and bakeries in Auroville. *Experience! Auroville* guide, e-india@webstudio6.com, available from Pondicherry Tourism, has an excellent breakdown of the accommodation options. Guests are accommodated in 5 settings (Central, Exurban, Beach, Farm and Forest, Pukka), each of which has its own characteristics (location, quietness, family-orientated, interaction with Aurovilians, language, etc). There are 39 guesthouses and 412 beds Costs vary from **C-F**, though some operate a kibbutz-type arrangement.

D-E Centre Guest House, T0413-262 2155. Most short-stay visitors are accommodated here ("welcomes those who wish to see and be in Auroville, but not to work there"), lovely setting, famous weekly pizza.

E-F New Creation, T0413-262 2125.

F Coco Beach Cottage, East Coast Main Rd, Kottakuppam, opposite turning for Auroville. 4 rooms, a very friendly, clean guest house with a popular restaurant.

Eating

Pondicherry *p107, map p108*

TTT Le Club, 38 rue Dumas, T0413-233 9745. Tue-Sun 0830-1830. French and Continental. Smart, excellent cuisine (Rs 400 for a splurge), French wine (Rs 1000), opinions differ, "we could have been in a French Bistro!" to "dearest but not the best".

TT Blue Dragon, 30 rue Dumas near New Pier (south end of Goubert Salai). Chinese. Excellent food, antique furniture.

TT La Terrasse, 5 Subbaiyah Salai. Thu-Tue 0830-2000. Excellent Continental. Good value, huge salads, no alcohol.

TT Paris, 104 Ambur Salai. Sat-Thu. Vietnamese.

TT Rendezvous, 30 Suffren St. French and Continental. Attractive, modern, reasonable food (dish Rs 100) but overpriced wine, nice roof terrace, pleasant atmosphere: the owner worked for a wealthy American family for 20 years and so his continental grub is first rate.

TT Satsanga, 30 rue Mahe de Labourdonnais, T0413-222 5867. Closed Thu. Continental (quite expensive wine Rs 200), friendly, French atmosphere with art 'gallery'. Garden setting and staff make up for mediocre food.

For an explanation of the sleeping and eating price codes used in this guide, see inside the front cover. Other relevant information is found in Essentials pages 40-44.

Seagulls, near Children's Park. Continental and others. Large first-floor terrace overlooking sea, bit overpriced, bar.
Ashram Dining Hall, north of Govt Pl. Indian vegetarian. Simple, filling, meals (Rs 20 per day) in an unusual setting, seating on cushions at low tables, farm grown produce, non-spicy and non-greasy. 'Ticket' from Ashram guesthouses or Central Bureau; then turn up at 0640, 1115, 1745 or 2000. Recommended though staff can be off-hand.
Au Feu de Bois, rue Bussy. Pizzas, salads, crêpes at lunchtime.
Hot Breads, Ambur Salai. Good burgers, chicken puffs (Rs 35) pizzas, pastries, great sandwiches, shakes (Rs 18), 0700-2100.
Indian Coffee House, 41 Nehru St. Real local vegetarian fare from 0700.
Le Café Pondicherry, Goubert Salai, by Gandhi statue. Pleasant spot, but ordinary snack fare (daytime).
Mass Classique, Bazar St Laurent, bakery.
Picnic, Kamaraj Salai. Very good vegetarian.
Ramanas, 25 Nehru St, excellent Indian, tasty fast food, a/c section.

Festivals and events

Pondicherry *p107, map p108*
4th-7th Jan: International Yoga Festival held at Kamban Kalairangam, contact Pondicherry Tourism for full details. **Jan**: Pongal is a 3-day harvest, earth and sun festival, popular in rural areas. **Feb/Mar**: Masi Magam on the full moon day of the Tamil month of Masi, pilgrims bathe in the sea when deities from about 40 temples from the surrounding area are taken in colourful procession for a ceremonial immersion. 'Fire walking' sometimes accompanies festivals here. **14th Jul**: Bastille Day. **Aug**: Fete de Pondicherry is a cultural programme.

Shopping

Pondicherry *p107, map p108*
The shopping areas are along Nehru St and Mahatma Gandhi Rd. *Experience! Pondicherry* booklet has a good shopping guide.

Dolls of papier-mâché, terracotta and plaster are made and sold at Kosapalayam. Local grass is woven into *Korai* mats. Craftsmen at the Ashram produce marbled silk, hand dyed cloths, perfumes and incense sticks.

Antiques **Heritage Art Gallery**, rue Romain Rolland.

Books Focus, 204 Cathedral St, good choice of Indian writing in English, cards, stationery, CDs, very helpful. **Kailash French Bookshop**, 87 Lal Bahadur Shastri St, large stock.

Clothes and crafts Several Ashram outlets on Nehru St. **Aurosarjan**, rue Bussy. Auroville clothes and crafts. **Cluny Centre**, 46 Romain Rolland St, T/F0413-2335668. Run by a French order in a lovely colonial house where nuns both design and oversee high-quality embroidery. **Curio Centre**, 40 Romain Rolland St, has some fine antiques and good reproduction colonial furniture. **Kalki**, 134 Cathedral St, T0413-239166. Exceptional printed and painted silk scarves, hangings etc. **Sri Aurobindo Handmade paper 'factory'**, 44 Sardar Patel Rd. Shop sells attractive products. **Vasa**, rue Mahe de Labourdonnais, next to Hotel Qualité, Smart ladies' clothes.

Activities and tours

Pondicherry *p107, map p108*
Body and soul **Ananda Ashram**, on Yoga Sadhana Beach, 16 Mettu St, Chinamudaliarchavadi, Kottakuppam. It runs 1-, 3- and 6-month courses starting in Jan, Apr, Jul and Oct; or book through Pondicherry Tourism, Rs 1500 for 10 lecture modules.

Fishing Deep-sea fishing trips booked through **Pondicherry Tourism (PTDC)** (see below), 6/12 hrs, Rs 1500/2500.

Swimming Pools in **Hotel Blue Star** and Calva Bungalow, Kamaraj Salai open to non-residents for a fee.

Tours and tour operators
Auro Travels, Karikar Building, Nehru St. Efficient, quick service.
PTDC Sightseeing, Rs 45, Ashram, 0815-1300: Ashram and related departments. Auroville (Matrimandir), 1430.
Sita, 124 Cathedral St, T0413-233 6860.

Auroville *p109*
With a guest pass to Auroville, www.miraura.org, you can participate in retreat activities from

Indian dance to ashtanga yoga. There's also a Quiet Healing Centre on the nearby beach, well known for its underwater body treatments. The hydrotherapy treatment tank is a little public so it may be best to stick to the ayurvedic massages.

Tours 0830-1100 from Ashram, Pondicherry, autocare@auroville.org.in. 1430-1745 from Cottage Complex, Ambur Salai, includes Auroville Visitors' Centre and Matrimandir. Visitors recommend going independently. For a 5-day residential introduction to Auroville contact Centre Guest House, T0413-262 2155 (Rs 1000).

Transport

Pondicherry *p107, map p108*

Bicycle/scooter hire

Super Snack, Nehru St opposite Information Centre. **Jaypal**, Gingee Salai. Also a hire shop just off Subbaiyah Salai (South Blvd). **Vijay Arya**, 9 Aurobindo St. Daily: cycle, Rs 25, scooter, Rs 120. Well worthwhile as the streets are broad, flat and quiet.

Motorbikes for travelling round South India, Rs 250 per day. **Pondicherry Tourism** (PTDC) and **Le Café Pondicherry**, Beach Rd, hire bicycles, Rs 5 per hr, Rs 40/400 per day/month.

Bus

Local Negotiate fare first; bus stands to centre, Rs 20. Also cycle-rickshaws and auto-rickshaws found here. **Local Bus Stand**: T0413-233 6919. 0430-1230, 1330-2130.

Long distance State Express Bus Stand, NH45A, just west of the traffic circle. T0413-233 7464. Computerized Reservations: 0700-2100 (helpful staff). **Mofussil (New) Bus Stand**, further west, serves all other bus companies. **Pondicherry Tourism Corporation** (PTC), T0413-233 7008, 0600-2200, also runs long distance services. Check times.

Bengaluru (Bangalore), 7½ hrs; **Chennai**, frequent Express buses, under 3 hrs; **Chidambaram**, frequent buses by all companies, 1½ hrs; **Coimbatore** via **Salem** and **Erode**, 8½-9½ hrs; **Gingee**, infrequent, 2 hrs; **Kanniyakumari**, overnight service; **Kannur** and **Mahé**, 15 hrs; **Karaikal**, 4 hrs; **Madurai** via **Tiruchirappalli**, 6½-8 hrs overnight; **Mahabalipuram**, several, 4 hrs; **Tirupati**, 6½-7 hrs; **Tiruvannamalai** (via **Villupuram**), 3-3½ hrs; **Kottakarai**, frequent service from Town Bus Stand.

Car hire

Round trips to many destinations can be arranged at reasonable rates, eg return to **Bengaluru (Bangalore)** (310 km) Rs 2000; **Chidambaram** (74 km), Rs 550; **Chennai** (166 km), Rs 1000; **Mahabalipuram** (130 km), Rs 800.

Taxi

Particularly along the canal; 4 hrs (50 km) Rs 250, 8 hrs (100 km) Rs 500. **Jupiter Travels**, 170A Anna Salai, has luxury taxis.

Train

Reservations, T0413-2336684, 0800-1400, 1500-1900, Mon-Sat; 0800-1400, Sun. 4-m gauge trains (1 hr) daily to **Villupuram** which offer prompt main line connections to **Chennai**, **Madurai**, **Tiruchirappalli**. No *652*, 0745 for Chennai and Madurai; *654*, 1920 for Chennai; *646*, 1655 for Chennai and Tiruchirappalli; *656*, 0500 for *Pandyan Exp 6717* to Tiruchirappalli, Kodai Rd and Madurai; *Quilon Mail 6105* to Tiruchirappalli and Kollam. From **Villupuram**: 4 trains daily for Pondy departs 0610, 0900, 1745, 2025. The half hourly bus to Villupuram stops 100 m from station and connects with trains. Railway station, enquiries: 0900-1200, 1500-1800. It's possible to make computerized reservations from Pondy station to any other station, and there is a quota on major trains leaving from Chennai Central.

Auroville *p109*

Bicycle

Rent a bicycle (Rs 15 per day, though at some guest houses they are free) and take advantage of the many cycle paths. **Centre Guest House** is one of several places renting bikes and mopeds.

Rickshaw/taxi

Mopeds and taxis cost Rs 60/100 per day.

Either of the 2 roads north from Pondicherry towards Chennai leads to Auroville. A rickshaw from Pondicherry will cost around Rs 100, a taxi not much more (or Rs 300 for a 3-hr wait-and-return).

Directory

Pondicherry *p107, map p108*
Banks Andhra Bank, Cathedral St, offers cash against Visa. State Bank of India, 5 Suffren St, changes cash and TCs (Amex, Thomas Cook), 24-hr ATM. UCO Bank, rue Mahé de Labour- donnais, opposite Government Park, quick and efficient. LKP, rue Mahé de Labourdonnais. No commission. **Cultural centres** French Institute, rue St Louis, close to the north end of Goubert Salai, and Alliance Française at the southern end of Goubert Salai for cultural programmes, Mon-Fri 0800-1230, 1500-1900, Sat 0830-1200. **Embassies and consulates** French Consulate, 2 Marine St. **Hospitals** General Hospital, rue Victor Simone, T0413-233 6389; Jipmer, T0413-237 2381. Ashram Dispensary, Depuis St, near seaside. **Internet** Café.com, Dolphin House, 236 Mission St, plays DVDs, serves great coffee and real Italian pasta besides. Ohm Infotech, 11 Nehru St. High speed. There are also several other options. **Post** Head Post Office, northwest corner of Govt Place. CTO, Rangapillai St. **Useful addresses** Foreigners' Regional Registration Office, Goubert Salai.

Palar Valley

Running between the steep-sided northern Tamilnad hill range is the broad, flat bed of the River Palar, an intensively irrigated, fertile and densely populated valley cutting through the much poorer and sometimes wooded high land on either side. The whole valley became the scene of an Anglo-French-Indian contest at the end of the 18th century. Today it is the centre of South India's vitally important leather industry and intensive agricultural development. ▸▸ *For Sleeping, Eating and other listings, see pages 117-119.*

Vellore → *Phone code: 0416. Colour map 3, grid A5. Population: 177,400.*

The once strategically important centre of Vellore, pleasantly ringed by hills, is now a dusty, though busy, market town; its fort and temple are reminders of its historic importance. The fort is a major attraction, but Vellore is now world famous for its **Christian Medical College Hospital**, founded by the American missionary Ida Scudder in 1900. Started as a one-room dispensary, it extended to a small hospital through American support. Today it is one of the country's largest hospitals with over 1200 beds and large out-patients' department which caters for over 2000 patients daily. The college has built a reputation for research in a wide range of tropical diseases. One of its earliest and most lasting programmes has been concerned with leprosy and there is a rehabilitation centre attached. In recent years it has undertaken a wide-ranging programme of social and development work in villages outside the town to back up its medical programmes.

Vijayanagar architecture is beautifully illustrated in the temple at **Vellore Fort**, a perfect example of military architecture and a *jala durga* or water fort. Believed to have been built by the Vijayanagara kings and dating from the 14th century, the fort has round towers and huge gateways along its double wall. The moat, still filled with water by a subterranean drain, followed ancient principles of defence: a colony of crocodiles. A wooden drawbridge crosses the moat to the southeast. In 1768 Vellore came under the control of the British, who defended it against Haidar Ali. After the victory in Seringapatnam in 1799, Tipu Sultan's family was imprisoned here and a mutiny of 1806, in which many British and Indian mutineers were killed, left many scars. In the fort is a parade ground, the CSI church, the Temple and two-storeyed mahals which are used as government offices.

Jalakantesvara Temple ⓘ *bathing Rs 2*, with a 30-m-high seven-storeyed granite *gopuram*, has undergone considerable restoration. Enter from the south and inside on the left, the *kalyana mandapa* (wedding hall), one of the most beautiful structures of its kind, has vivid sculptures of dragons and 'hippogryphs' on its pillars. The temple consists of a shrine to Nataraja in the north and a lingam shrine in the west.

Gingee → *Phone code: 04145. Colour map 3, grid B5.*

Gingee (pronounced *Senjee*), just off the NH45, situated between Chennai and Tiruvannamalai, has a remarkable 15th-century Vijayanagar fort with much to explore. It is well off the beaten track, very peaceful and in beautiful surroundings. Spend the night here if you can. Lovers come here at the weekends; it's on the domestic tourist map because it is often used as a film location. The landscape is made up of man-sized boulders, like Hampi, piled on top of each other to make mounds the texture of cottage cheese.

The fort ⓘ *0900-1700, allow 2½ hrs for Rajagiri, and 2 hrs for Krishnagiri (if you have time), Rs 100 includes both forts,* was intensely contested by successive powers before being captured by an East India Company force in 1762, by the end of the century however, it had lost its importance. Although it had Chola foundations, the 'most famous fort in the Carnatic' was almost entirely rebuilt in 1442. It is set on three strongly fortified Charnockite hills: Krishnagiri, Chakklidrug and Rajagiri. In places the hills on which the fort stands are sheer cliffs

> *It's a cooler climb with less hazy views in the morning. Only for the fit and healthy.*

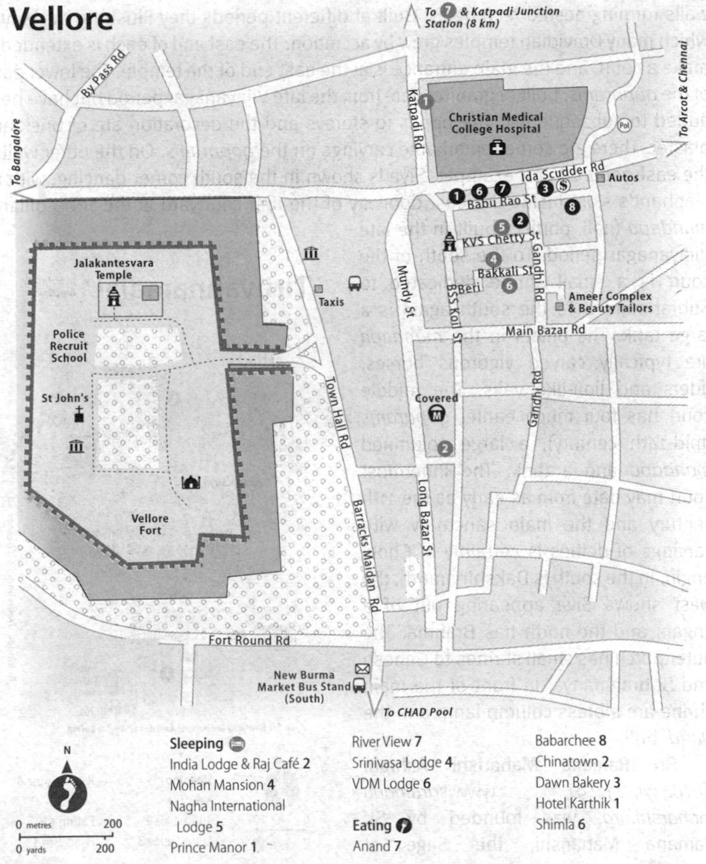

over 150 m high. The highest, Rajagiri ('King's Hill'), has a south-facing overhanging cliff face, on top of which is the citadel. The inner fort contains two temples and the Kalyana Mahal, a square court with a 27-m breezy tower topped by pyramidal roof, surrounded by apartments for the women of the Governor's household. On top of the citadel is a huge cannon and a smooth granite slab known as the Raja's bathing stone. An extraordinary stone about 7 m high and balanced precariously on a rock, surrounded by a low circular brick wall, it is referred to as the Prisoner's Well. There are fine Vijaynagara temples, granary, barracks and stables and an 'elephant tank'. A caretaker may unlock a temple and then expect a tip.

The Archaeological Survey of India Office is just off the main road towards the fort. They may have guides to accompany you to the fort. Carry provisions, especially plenty of drinks; a few refreshments are sold, but only at the bottom of the hill.

Tiruvannamalai → *Phone code: 04175. Colour map 3, grid B5. Population: 130,300.*

In a striking setting at the foot of the rocky Arunachala Hill, Tiruvannamalai is one of the holiest towns of Tamil Nadu, and locally considered the home of Siva and his consort Parvati. It is a major pilgrimage centre.

One of the largest temples in South India, **Arunachala Temple** ⓘ *may close 1230-1530*, (16th and 17th centuries) was built mainly under the patronage of the Vijayanagar kings and is dedicated to Siva as God incarnate of Fire. Its massive *gopurams*, the tallest of which is 66 m high, dominate the centre of the town. The temple has three sets of walls forming nested rectangles. Built at different periods they illustrate the way in which many Dravidian temples grew by accretion. The east end of each is extended to make a court, and the main entrance is at the east end of the temple. The lower parts of the *gopurams*, built of granite, date from the late Vijayanagar period but have been added to subsequently. The upper 10 storeys and the decoration are of brick and plaster. There are some remarkable carvings on the *gopurams*. On the outer wall of the east *gopuram*, for example, Siva is shown in the south corner dancing, with an elephant's skin. Inside the east doorway of the first courtyard is the 1000-pillared *mandapa* (hall, portico) built in the late Vijayanagar period. To the south of the court is a small shrine dedicated to Subrahmanya. To the south again is a large tank. The pillars in the *mandapa* are typically carved vigorous horses, riders and lion-like yalis. The middle court has four much earlier *gopurams* (mid-14th century), a large columned *mandapa* and a tank. The innermost court may date from as early as the 11th century and the main sanctuary with carvings of deities is certainly of Chola origin. In the south is Dakshinamurti, the west shows Siva appearing out of a lingam and the north has Brahma. The outer porch has small shrines to Ganesh and Subrahmanya. In front of the main shrine are a brass column lamp and the *Nandi* bull.

> ❢ *Priests insist on guiding visitors and expect payment.*

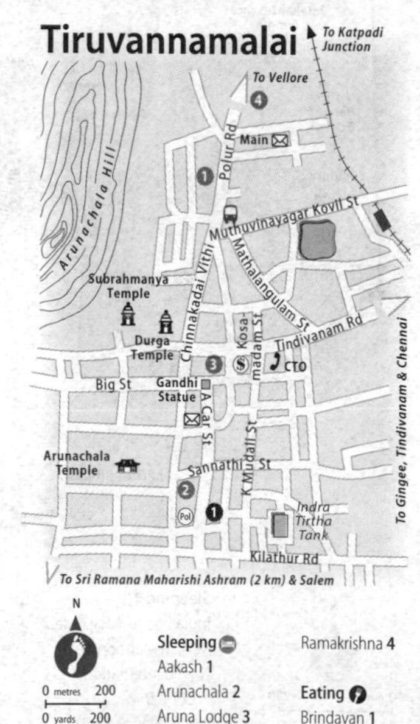

Sri Ramana Maharishi Ashram ⓘ *T04175-237491, www.sriramanamaharshi.org*, was founded by Sri Ramana Maharishi, the Sage of

Arunachala, born in 1879 and died in 1950, who apparently spoke little and wrote less; not for him the life of a globetrotting guru. Aged 16, he set out to seek enlightenment at the sacred mountain in Tiruvannamalai, which is revered as Siva in mountain form. He spent 20 years in caves, until his mother died at the base of the mountain in 1922 and he formed an ashram there. He was, albeit quietly, accessible by day or night, unlike the choreographed darshans held at the ashrams of Amma and Satya Sai Baba. There is a library (with 40,000 spiritual books), whose president is Maharishi's nephew's son, and which is popular with a sizeable community of Westerners (who, come April, have left the south for ashrams in Rishikesh, Dharamsala and the cooler northern mountains). Here are many photos of Maharishi, the last of which were taken by Henri Cartier-Bresson, who photographed him when he was alive and also the morning after his death in April 1950. Foreigners wishing to stay need to write to the ashram president with proposed dates of stay.

Sleeping

Vellore *p114, map p115*
D Prince Manor, 41 Katpadi Rd, T0416-227106, central. Comfortable rooms, very good restaurant.
D River View, New Katpadi Rd, T0416-225251, 1 km north of town. 31 rooms, some a/c (best on tank side), modern, pleasant courtyard with mature palms, 3 good restaurants.
F India Lodge, inexpensive rooms and **Raj Café**, good vegetarian restaurant downstairs.
F Mohan Mansion, 12 Beri Bakkali St, T0416-227083, 15 mins' walk from bus stand. Small hotel, basic and clean, quieter than others near hospital.
F Nagha International Lodge, 13/A KVS Chetty St, T0416-222 6731. Some **E** a/c de luxe rooms.
F Srinivasa Lodge, Beri Bakkali St, T0416-226389. Simple and clean.
G VDM Lodge, T0416-222 4008. Very cheap, pleasant, helpful staff.

Gingee *p115*
Avoid **Aruna Lodge**, near bus stand.
E Shivasand, M Gandhi Rd, opposite bus stand, T04145-222218. Good views of fort from roof, 21 clean, adequate rooms with bath, 1 more expensive a/c, vegetarian restaurant, a/c bar and non-vegetarian meals, helpful manager.

Tiruvannamalai *p116, map p116*
At full moon pilgrims arrive to walk around Arunachala Hill and hotels are overbooked.
D-E Arunachala, 5 Vadasannathi St, T04175-228300. Has 32 clean, rooms, 16 a/c, TV, hot water, best away from temple end, can get noisy during festivals, vegetarian meals.
D-E Ramakrishna, 34F Polur Rd, T04175-225004, info@hotelramakrishna.com. Modern, 42 rooms, 21 a/c, TV, hot water, excellent vegetarian tandoori restaurant, parking, helpful and friendly staff. Recommended.
F Aakash, 9 Polur Rd, T04175-222151. 22 rooms, friendly but rather noisy.
F Aruna Lodge, 82 Kosamadam St, T04175-223291. 24 clean, adequate rooms with bath.

Eating

Vellore *p114, map p115*
Anand, Ida Scudder Rd, for excellent breakfasts.
Babarchee, Babu Rao St. Good fast food and pizzas.
Best, Ida Scudder Rd. Some meals very spicy, nice parathas, 0600 for excellent breakfast.
Chinatown, Gandhi Rd. Small, friendly, a/c. Good food and service.
Dawn Bakery, Gandhi Rd. Fresh bread and biscuits, cakes, also sardines, fruit juices.
Geetha and **Susil**, Ida Scudder Rd, rooftop or inside, good service and food.
Hotel Karthik's, has a good veg restaurant.
Shimla, Ida Scudder Rd. Tandoori, naan very good.

Tiruvannamalai *p116, map p116*
Brindavan, 57 A Car St. This town is a thali lover's paradise with plenty of 'meals' restaurants including this one, Rs 15.
Auro Usha, varied menu, **German Bakery**, and **Manna**, salads and snacks.

Festivals and events

Tiruvannamalai *p116, map p116*
Nov-Dec: Karthikai Deepam is full moon day when a huge beacon is lit on top of the hill behind the temple. The flames, which can be seen for miles around, are thought of as Siva's lingam of fire, joining the immeasurable depths to the limitless skies. A cattle market is also held.

Shopping

Vellore *p114, map p115*
Most shops are along Main Bazar Rd and Long Bazar St. Vellore specializes in making 'Karigari' glazed pottery in a range of traditional and modern designs. Vases, water jugs, ashtrays and dishes are usually coloured blue, green and yellow.
Beauty, Ameer Complex, Gandhi Rd. Cheapest good quality tailoring.
Mr Kanappan, Gandhi Rd. Very friendly, good quality tailors, bit pricier.

Activities and tours

Vellore *p114, map p115*
Hillside Resort, CHAD (Community Health and Development), south of town. Excellent private pool, Rs 250 per day. Popular with CMC medical students. Open early morning to late evening, closed Mon and 1200-1500. Good snack bar.

Transport

Vellore *p114, map p115*
Bus
The Bus Station is off Long Bazar St, east of the Fort. Buses to **Tiruchirappalli**, **Tiruvannamalai** (from Burma Market Bus Stand), **Bengaluru (Bangalore)**, **Chennai**, **Ooty**, **Thanjavur** and **Tirupathi**. The regional state bus company PATC runs frequent services to **Kanchipuram** and **Bengaluru** from 0500 (2½ hrs) and **Chennai**.

Train
Katpadi Junction, the main station, 8 km north of town is on the broad gauge line between **Chennai** and **Bengaluru**. Buses and rickshaws (Rs 35) into Vellore. **Chennai (C)**: *Cheran Exp 2674*, 0505, 2¼ hrs; *West Coast Exp 6628*, 1303, 2½ hrs; *Kovai Exp 2676*, 1915, 2 hrs. **Bengaluru (C)**: *Brindavan Exp 2639*, 0903, 4¼ hrs; *Chennai-Bangalore Exp 6023*, 1515, 4½ hrs; it is also on the metre gauge line to **Villupuram** to the south, with daily passenger trains to **Tirupathi**, **Tiruvannamalai** and **Pondicherry**.
The Cantonment Station is about 1 km south of the GPO, and has a daily train to **Tiruchchirappalli**, *Tirupati Tiruchchi Exp 6801*, 1910, 10¾ hrs.

Gingee *p115*
Bus
Buses to/from **Pondicherry**, infrequent direct buses (2 hrs); better via Tindivanam (45 mins). To/from **Tiruvannamalai**, 39 km: several buses (1 hr), Rs 13; Express buses will not stop at the fort. TPTC bus 122 to/from **Chennai**.

Rickshaw
To visit the fort take a cycle-rickshaw from the bus stand to the hills; about Rs 30 for the round trip, including a 2-hr wait. There are bicycles for hire next to the bus station.

Tiruvannamalai *p116, map p116*
Bicycle
Bicycle hire near the Bus Stand is not recommended; cycling can be hazardous in this very busy small town.

Bus
Buses to major cities in **Tamil Nadu**, **Kerala** and **Karnataka**. Local people will point out your bus at the bus stand; you can usually get a seat although they do get crowded. To **Gingee**, frequent, 1 hr; **Chennai**, 5 hrs, Rs 30; **Pondicherry**, 3-3½ hrs.

Train
Train to **Tirupati** via Vellore Cantt, Katpadi and Chittor: *Tiruchchi Tirupati Exp 6802*, 2300, 6½ hrs. **Pondicherry**: *Tirupati-Pondicherry Fast Pass 641 (S)*, 0640, 3½ hrs.

Directory

Vellore *p114, map p115*
Banks Central Bank, Ida Scudder Rd, east of hospital exit, is at least 10 mins faster at

changing TCs than the State Bank of India. **Hospital** CMC, Ida Scudder Rd, T0416-232102. **Internet** Net Paradise, north of bus stand. **Post** CMC Hospital has PO, stamps, takes parcels.

Tiruvannamalai *p116, map p116*
Bank Vysya Bank, Sannathi St. Quick for cash and TCs. **Internet** TICS, 4 Kosamadam St. Also Western Union. **Post** A Car St.

Chola Heartland and the Kaveri Delta

Chidambaram, Trichy and Tanjore together represent the apotheosis of Tamilian temple architecture: the great temples here act as thirthas, or gateways, linking the profane to the sacred. This pilgrim's road boasts the bare granite Big Temple in the charming agricultural town of Tanjore, which was for 300 years the capital of the Cholas; Trichy's 21-gopuram, seven-walled island city of Sri Rangam, a patchwork quilt of a temple built by successive dynastic waves of Cholas, Cheras, Pandyas, Hoysalas, Vijayanagars and Madurai Nayaks; and the beautiful Nataraja Temple at Chidambaram, with its two towers given over to bas reliefs of the 108 mudras, or gestures, of classical dance. » *For Sleeping, Eating and other listings, see pages 128-133.*

Tiruchirappalli

» *pp128-132. Colour map 3, grid B5.*

→ *Phone code: 0431.*

Trichy, at the head of the fertile Kaveri delta, is an industrial city that is more spread out than Madurai although its population is smaller. Land prices are high here, and houses, as you'll see if you climb up to its 84 m-high rock fort, are densely packed, outside the elegant doctors' suburbs. If you are taking public transport you will want to break here to visit the sacred Srirangam temple but if you have your own wheels you may prefer to bypass the city, which has little else to offer by way of easily accessed charms. Allow at least half a day to tour Srirangam, then stay in the more laid-back agricultural centre of Tanjore to the north or the more atmospheric temple madness of Madurai further south.

Ins and outs

Getting there Trichy airport, 8 km from the centre, has flights to Madurai and Chennai. Well connected by train to major towns, the Junction Railway Station and the two bus stations are in the centre of the main hotel area, all within walking distance.

Getting around Much of Trichy is quite easy to see on foot, but plenty of autos and local buses run to the Rock Fort and Srirangam. » *See Transport, page 131, for further details.*

Background

Trichy was mentioned by Ptolemy in the second century BC. A Chola fortification from the second century, it came to prominence under the Nayakas from Madurai who built the fort and the town, capitalizing on its strategic position. In legend its name is traced to a three-headed demon, Trisiras, who terrorized both men and the gods until Siva overpowered him in the place called Tiruchi. Cigar making became important between the two world wars, while the indigenous *bidis* continue to be made, following a tradition started in the 18th century. Trichy is the country's largest artificial diamond manufacturing centre. Jaffersha Street is known as Diamond Bazar. The town is also noted for its high-quality string instruments, especially veenas and violins.

Sights

Rock Fort, 1660, stands on an 84 m-high rock. **Vinayaka Temple** (or Ucchi Pillayar Koil) ⓘ *Tue-Sun 0800-1300 then 1400-2000, camera Rs 10, video Rs 50*, approached from Chinna Bazar, is worth climbing for the stunning views but don't expect much from the temple. At the top of the first flight of steps lies the main 11th-century defence line and the remains of a thousand-pillared hall, destroyed in 1772. Further up is a hundred-pillared hall. At the end of the last flight is the **Tayumanasvami Temple**, dedicated to Siva, which has a golden *vimana* and a lingam carved from the rock itself. There are further seventh-century Pallava cave temples of beautiful carved pillars and panels.

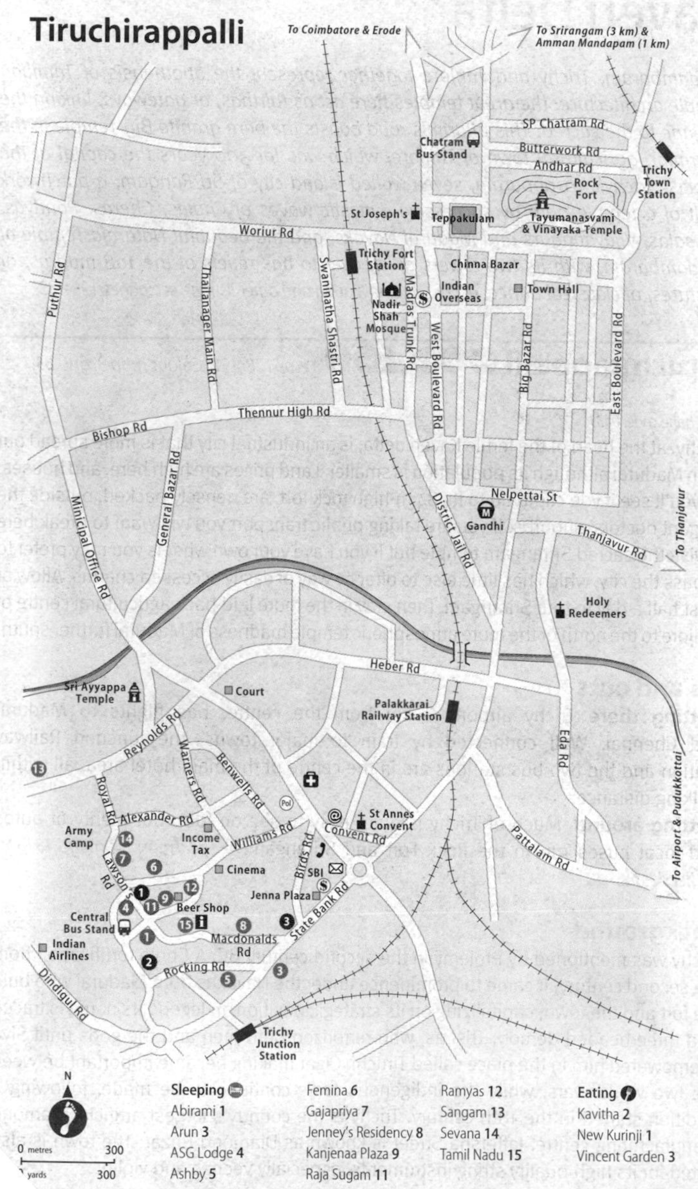

Try to make time to explore the atmospheric old city, particularly **Big Bazar Street** and **Chinna Bazar**. The Gandhi Market is a colourful vegetable and fruit market.

Among the dozen or so mosques in the town, the **Nadir Shah Mosque** near the city railway station stands out with its white dome and metal steeple, said to have been built with material taken from a Hindu temple. **St Joseph's College Church** (Church of our Lady of Lourdes), one of several Catholic churches here, was designed as a smaller version of the Basilica at Lourdes in France. It has an unusual sandalwood altar but is rather garish inside. The grounds are a peaceful spot. The 18th-century **Christ Church**, the first English church, is north of the Teppakulam, while the early 19th-century **St John's Church** has a memorial plaque to Bishop Heber, one of India's best known missionary bishops, who died in Trichy in 1826.

Around Trichy

▸▸ pp131-132.

Srirangam

The temple town on the Kaveri, just north of Trichy, is surrounded by seven concentric walled courtyards, with magnificent gateways and several shrines. On the way to Srirangam is an interesting river *ghat* where pilgrims take their ritual bath before entering the temple. The countryside to the west of the temple is an excellent place to sample rural Indian life and a good way to spend a couple of hours.

Sri Ranganathasvami Temple ⓘ *0615-1300, 1515-2045, camera, Rs 20, video Rs 70 (Rs 10 for the rooftop viewing tower), allow about 2 hrs, guides will greet you on arrival. Their abilities are highly variable; some tell you that the staircase to the viewpoint will close shortly, which is usually a scam to encourage you to use their services,* is one of the largest in India and dedicated to Vishnu. It has some fine carvings and a good atmosphere. The fact that it faces south, unlike most other Hindu temples, is explained by the legend that Rama intended to present the image of Ranganatha to a temple in Sri Lanka but this was impossible since the deity became fixed here, but it still honours the original destination. The temple, where the Vaishnava reformer **Ramanuja** settled and worshipped, is famous for its superb sculpture, the 21 impressive *gopurams* and its rich collection of temple jewellery. The 'thousand' pillared hall (904 columns) stands beyond the fourth wall, and in the fifth enclosure there is the unusual shrine to Tulukka Nachiyar, the God's Muslim consort. Non-Hindus are not allowed into the sanctuary but can enter the fourth courtyard where the famous sculptures of *gopis* (*Radha's* milk maids) in the Venugopala shrine can be seen.

Nearby, on the north bank of the Kaveri, **Amma Mandapam** is a hive of activity. The *ghats*, where devotees wash, bathe, commit cremated ashes and pray, are interesting to visit, although some may find the dirt and smell overpowering.

So named because a legendary elephant worshipped the lingam, **Tiruvanaikkaval** is located 3 km east of Srirangam. It has the architecturally finer **Jambukesvara Temple** ⓘ *officially 0600-1300, 1600-2130, camera Rs 10, non-Hindus are not allowed into the sanctuary*, with its five walls and seven splendid *gopurams* and one of the oldest and largest Siva temples in Tamil Nadu. The unusual lingam under a *jambu* tree always remains under water. It is 200 m east off the main Tiruchi-Chennai road, a short stroll from Srirangam or easily reached by bus.

Pudukkottai and around

Pudukkottai, 50 km south of Trichy, was the capital of the former princely state ruled by the Tondaiman Rajas, founded by Raghunatha Raya Tondaiman in 1686. At one entrance to the town is a ceremonial arch raised by the Raja in honour of Queen Victoria's jubilee celebrations. The town's broad streets suggest a planned history; the temple is at the centre, with the old palace and a tank. The new palace is now the District Collector's office.

The rock-cut **Sri Kokarnesvarar Temple** ⓘ *at Thirukokarnam, 5 km north of the railway station, closed 1200-1600,* dates from the Pallava period. The natural rock shelters, caves, stone circles, dolmens and Neolithic burial sites show that there was very early human occupation.

The **museum** ⓘ *Big St, Thirukokarnam 5 km away, except Fri, 2nd Sat, public holidays, 0930-1700, free, allow 40 mins, recommended,* has a wide range of exhibits including sections on geology, zoology and the economy as well as sculptures and the arts. The archaeology section has some excellent sculptures from nearby temples. There is a notable carving of Siva as *Dakshinamurti* and some fine bronzes from Pudukkottai itself.

Sittannavasal, 13 km away, has a Jain cave temple (circa eighth century) with sculptures, where monks took shelter when they fled from persecution in North India. In a shrine and verandah there are some fine frescoes in the Ajanta style and bas-relief carvings. You can also see rock-hewn beds of the monks. The *Brahmi* inscriptions date from the second century BC.

Thanjavur (Tanjore) » *pp129-132.*

Colour map 3, grid B5.

→ *Phone code: 04362. Population: 215,700.*

Thanjavur's mathematically perfect Brihadisvara Temple, a World Heritage Site, is one of the great monuments of South India, its huge Nandi bull washed each fortnight with water, milk, turmeric and gingelly in front of a rapt audience that packs out the whole temple compound. In the heart of the lush, rice growing delta of the Kaveri, the upper echelons of Tanjore life are landowners, rather than industrialists, and the city itself is mellow in comparison with Trichy.

Ins and outs

Getting there Most long-distance buses stop at the New bus stand 4 km southwest of the centre, but there are frequent buses and autos (Rs 25) to town and train station. **Getting around** It is less than a 15-minute walk from the hotels to the Brihadisvara Temple. » *See Transport, page 132, for further details.*

Sights

Brihadisvara Temple ⓘ *0600-2030; inner sanctum closed 1230-1600*, known as the Big Temple, was the achievement of the Chola king Rajaraja I (who ruled AD 985-1012). The magnificent main temple has a 62-m-high *vimana* (the tallest in India), topped by a dome carved from an 80-tonne block of granite, which needed a 6½-km-long ramp to raise it to the top. The attractive gardens, the clean surroundings and well-lit sanctuaries make a visit doubly rewarding, especially in the evening.

The entrance is from the east. After crossing the moat you enter through two *gopurams*, the second guarded by two *dvarapalas* typical of the early Chola period, when the *gopurams* on the outer enclosure walls were dwarfed by the scale of the *vimana* over the main shrine. An enormous Nandi, carved out of a single block of granite 6 m long, guards the entrance to the sanctuary. According to one of the many myths that revolve around the image of a wounded Nandi, the Thanjavur Nandi was growing larger and larger, threatening the temple, until a nail was driven into its back.

The temple, built mainly with large granite blocks, has superb inscriptions and sculptures of Siva, Vishnu and Durga on three sides of the massive plinth. Siva appears in three forms, the dancer with 10 arms, the seated figure with a sword and trident, and Siva bearing a spear. The carvings of dancers showing the 81 different Bharat Natyam poses are the first to record classical dance form in this manner.

The main shrine has a large lingam. In the inner courtyard are Chola frescoes on walls prepared with lime plaster, smoothed and polished, then painted while the surface was wet. These were hidden under later Nayaka paintings. Since music and dance were a vital part of temple life and dancing in the temple would accompany the chanting of the holy scriptures which the community attended, Rajaraja also built two housing colonies nearby to accommodate 400 *devadasis* (temple dancers). Subsidiary shrines were added to the main temple at different periods. The Vijayanagara kings built the Amman shrine, the Nayakas the Subrahmanya shrine and the Marathas the Ganesh shrine.

The Palace ⓘ *Thu-Sun 0900-1300, 1400-1700*, built by the Nayakas in the mid-16th century and later completed by the Marathas, is now partly in ruins, its walls used as makeshift hoardings for the latest Tamil movie release or political campaign. Still, there's evidence of its original splendour in the ornate Durbar Hall. The towers are worth climbing for a good view; one tower has a whale skeleton which was washed up in Chennai. The **art gallery** ⓘ *0900-1300, 1500-1800*, with bronze and granite sculptures, **Sangeeta Mahal** with excellent acoustics, and the **Tamil University Museum** are here, together with some government offices. The pokey **Saraswati Mahal Library** ⓘ *Thu-Tue 1000-1300, 1330-1730*, is brilliant: among its 40,000 rare books are texts from the medieval period, beautiful botanical pictures

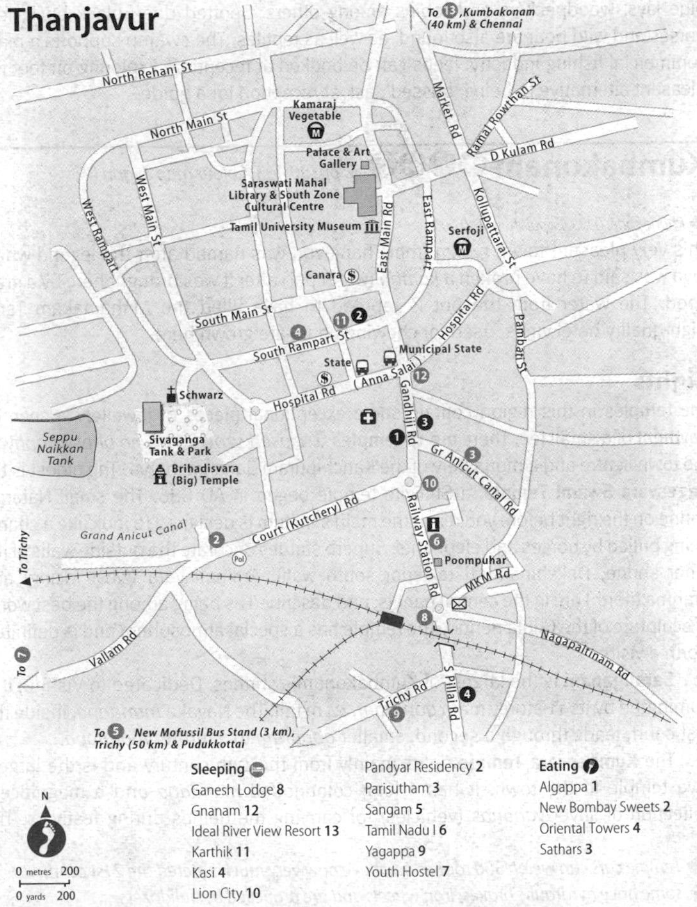

from the 18th century, palm leaf manuscripts of the Ramayana, intricate 250-year-old miniatures, and splendid examples of the gaudy Tanjore style of painting. It also has old samples of dhoti cloth design, and 22 engravings illustrating methods of torture from other oriental cultures in the 'Punishments of China'.

Around Thanjavur

A visit to **Thiruvaiyaru,** 13 km away, with the Panchanatheswara Siva temple, known for its **Thyagaraja Music Festival,** gives a glimpse of South Indian rural life. Hardly visited by tourists, music connoisseurs arrive in large numbers in January. Performances vary and the often subtle music is marred by loud amplification. The Car Festival is in March. Catch one of the frequent, crowded buses from the old bus station in Thanjavur, taking 30 minutes.

Point Calimere (Kodikkarai) Wildlife and Bird Sanctuary ⓘ *open throughout the year, best season mid-Dec to Feb, Rs 5, camera Rs 5, video Rs 50,* is 90 km southeast of Thanjavur. The coastal sanctuary, half of which is tidal swamp, is famous for its migratory water birds. The Great Vedaranayam Salt Swamp (or 'Great Swamp') attracts one of the largest colonies of flamingos in Asia (5000-10,000) especially in December and January. Some 243 different bird species have been spotted here. In the spring green pigeons, koels, mynahs and barbets can be seen. In the winter vegetables and insects attract paradise flycatchers, Indian pittas, shrikes, swallows, drongos, minivets, blue jays, woodpeckers and robins among others. Spotted deer, black buck, feral horses and wild boar are also found, as well as reptiles. The swamp supports a major commercial fishing industry. Jeeps can be booked at reception. Exploring on foot is a pleasant alternative to being 'bussed'; ask at reception for a guide.

Kumbakonam

» *pp130-133. Colour map 3, grid B5.*

→ *Phone code: 0435. Population: 140,000.*

This very pleasant town, 54 km from Thanjavur, was named after the legend where Siva was said to have broken a *kumbh* (water pot) after it was brought here by a great flood. The water from the pot is reputed to have filled the Mahamakam Tank. High-quality betel vines, used for chewing paan, are grown here.

Sights

The temples in this region contain some exceptional pieces of jewellery – seen on payment of a small fee. There are 18 **temples** ⓘ *closed 1200-1630, no photography,* in the town centre and a monastery of the Kanchipuram Sankaracharya. The oldest is the **Nagesvara Swami Temple,** a Shaivite temple begun in AD 886. The small Nataraja shrine on the right before you reach the main sanctum is designed to look like a chariot being pulled by horses and elephants. Superb statues decorate the outside walls of the inner shrine; Dakshinamurti (exterior south wall), Ardinarisvara (west facing) and Brahma (north) are in the central panels, and described as being among the best works of sculpture of the Chola period. The temple has a special atmosphere and is definitely worth a visit.

Sarangapani is the largest of Kumbakonam's shrines. Dedicated to Vishnu, it is dominated by its 11-storey main *gopuram*, 44 m tall. The Nayaka *mandapa*, inside the first court, leads through a second, smaller *gopuram* to a further *mandapa*.

The **Kumbesvara Temple** dates mainly from the 17th century and is the largest Siva temple in the town. It has a long colonnaded *mandapa* and a magnificent collection of silver *vahanas* (vehicles) for carrying the deities during festivals. The

Temple cars can weigh 300 tonnes and have now very much entered the 21st century: some have hyrdraulic brakes, iron wheels and are propelled by bulldozers.

Ramasvami Temple is another Nayaka period building, with beautiful carved rearing horses in its pillared *mandapa*. The frescoes on the walls depict events from the *Ramayana*. The Navaratri Festival is observed with great colour.

The **Mahamakam Tank** is visited for a bathe by huge numbers of pilgrims every 12 years, when 'Jupiter passes over the sign of Leo'. It is believed that on the day of the festival nine of India's holiest rivers manifest themselves in the tank, including the Ganga, Yamuna and Narmada.

Darasuram

ⓘ *Open sunrise to sunset. There is a small museum in the northeast corner.*

About 5 km south of Kumbakonam is Darasuram with the **Airavatesvara Temple** after Thanjavur and Gangaikondacholapuram, the third of the great Chola temples, built during the reign of **Rajaraja II** between 1146-1172. The entrance is through two gateways. A small inner gateway leads to a court where the mainly granite temple stands in the centre. The *gopuram* is supported by beautifully carved *apsaras*. Inside, there are friezes of dancing figures and musicians. The *mandapa* is best entered from the south. Note the elephant, ridden by dwarfs, whose trunk is lost down the jaws of a crocodile. The pillars illustrate mythological stories for example 'the penance of Parvati'. The five gods Agni, Indra, Brahma, Vishnu and Vayu in the niches are all shown paying homage to Siva. The **main mandapa**, completely enclosed and joined to the central shrine, has figures carved in black basalt on the outside. The ceilings are also richly decorated and the pillars have the same flower emblems as in the outer *mandapa*. The main shrine has some outstanding sculptures; the guardians on the north are particularly fine. Sculpted doorkeepers with massive clubs guard the entrance to the main shrine which has a *Nandi* at the entrance. Some of the niches inside contain superb early Chola sculptures of polished black basalt, including a unique sculpture of Ardhanarisvara with three faces and eight arms, a four-armed Nagaraja and a very unusual sculpture of Siva destroying Narasimha.

The **outer walls** are also highly decorative. Siva as Dakshinamurti on the south wall, Brahma on the north wall and Siva appearing out of the lingam on the west wall.

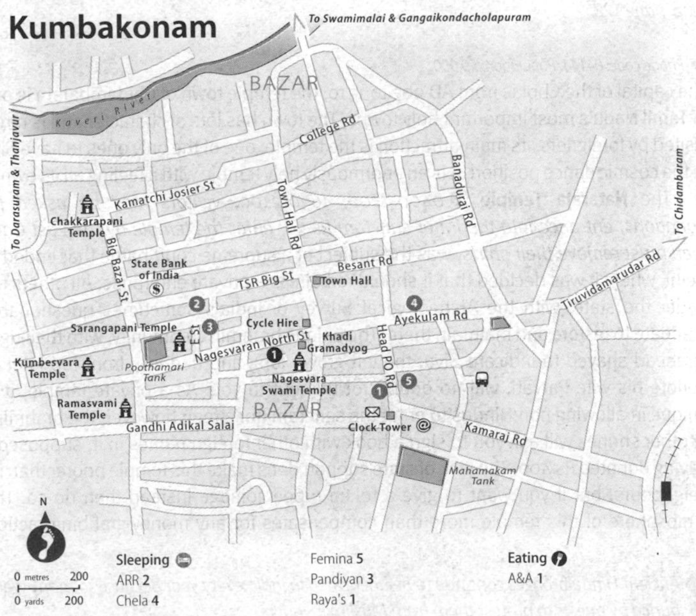

The inner wall of the encircling walkway (*prakara*) is divided into cells, each originally to house a deity. The corners of the courtyard have been enlarged to make four *mandapas*, again with beautiful decoration.

Gangaikondacholapuram

Once the capital of the Chola king Rajendra (1012-1044), this town (whose name means 'The city of the Chola who conquered the Ganga') has now all but disappeared. The temple and the 5-km-long 11th-century reservoir embankment survive.

The **temple** that Rajendra built was designed to rival the Brihadisvara temple built by Rajendra's father Rajaraja in Thanjavur. Unlike the *Nandi* in Thanjavur, the huge *Nandi* facing the *mandapa* and sanctuary inside the compound by the ruined east *gopuram* is not carved out of one block of stone. As in Thanjavur, the *mandapa* and sanctuary are raised on a high platform, orientated from west to east and climbed by steps. The whole building is over 100 m long and over 40 m wide. Two massive doorkeepers (*dvarapalas*) stand guard at the entrance to the long closed *mandapa* (the first of the many subsequent *mandapas* which expanded to 'halls of 1000 pillars'); the plinth is original. A narrow colonnaded hall (*mukha-mandapa*) links this hall to the shrine. On the east side of this hall are various carvings of Siva for example bestowing grace on Vishnu, who worships him with his lotus-eye. On the northeast is a large panel, a masterpiece of Chola art, showing Siva blessing Chandikesvara, the steward. At the centre of the shrine is a huge *lingam* on a round stand. As in Thanjavur there is a magnificent eighth-tiered, pyramidal *vimana* (tower) above the sanctuary, nearly 55 m high. Unlike the austere straight line of the Thanjavur temple, however, here gentle curves are introduced. Ask the custodian to allow you to look inside (best for light in the morning). Immediately to the north of the *mandapa* is an excellently carved shrine dedicated to Chandikesvara. To north and south are two shrines dedicated to Kailasanatha with excellent wall sculptures. The small shrine in the southwest corner is to Ganesh.

Chidambaram

» *pp-133. Colour map 3, grid B5. See also map, page 128.*

→ *Phone code: 04144. Population: 59,000.*

The capital of the Cholas from AD 907 to 1310, the temple town of Chidambaram is one of Tamil Nadu's most important holy towns. The town has lots of character and is rarely visited by foreigners. Its main attraction is the temple, one of the only ones to have Siva in the cosmic dance position. It is an enormously holy temple with a feeling all its own.

The **Nataraja Temple** ⓘ *0400-1200, 1630-2100, visitors may be asked for donations, entrance into the inner sanctum Rs 50, enter the temple by the East Gate, men must remove their shirts*, was the subject of a supreme court battle that ended in Delhi, where it was decided that it should remain as a private enterprise. All others fall under the state, with the Archeological Survey of India's sometimes questionable mandate to restore and maintain them. The unique brahmin community, with their right forehead shaved to indicate Siva, the left grown long and tied in a front top knot to denote his wife Parvati, will no doubt trot this out to you. As a private temple, it is unique in allowing non-Hindus to enter the sanctum (for a fee); however, the brahmins at other shrines will ask you to sign a book with other foreign names in it, supposedly having donated Rs 400. The lack of state support does make this temple poorer than its neighbours, but if you want to give a token rupee coinage instead then do so. The atmosphere of this temple more than compensates for any money-grabbing tactics,

Ancient Hindu bronzes continue to be unearthed in India every year because so many were buried by priests to protect them from Muslim invaders.

however. Temple lamps still hang from the hallways, the temple music is rousing and the *puja* has the statues coming alive in sudden illumination. The brahmins themselves have a unique, stately presence too. One legend surrounding its construction suggests that it was built by 'the golden-coloured Emperor', Hiranya Varna Chakravarti, who suffered from leprosy. He came to Chidambaram on a pilgrimage from Kashmir in about AD 500. After bathing in the temple tank he was reputed to have recovered from the disease and in gratitude offered to rebuild and enlarge the temple. The evening puja at 1800 is particularly interesting. At each shrine the visitor will be daubed with *vibhuti* (sacred ash) and paste. It is not easy to see some of the sculptures in the interior gloom. You may need patience and persuasive powers if you want to take your own time but it is worth the effort.

There are records of the temple's existence before the 10th century and inscriptions from the 11th century. On each side are four enormous *gopurams*, those on the north and south being about 45 m high. The east *gopuram* (AD 1250), through which you enter the temple, is the oldest. The north *gopuram* was built by the great Vijayanagar king **Krishna Deva Raya** (1509-1530). Immediately on entering the East Gate is the large **Sivaganga** tank, and the **Raja Sabha**, a 1000-columned *mandapa* (1595-1685). In the northwest of the compound are temples dedicated to Subrahmanya (late 13th century), and to its south the 12th century shrine to Sivakumasundari or Parvati (circa 14th century). The ceiling paintings are 17th century. At the southern end of this outer compound is what is said to be the largest shrine to **Ganesh** in India. The next inner compound has been filled with colonnades and passageways. In the innermost shrine are two images of Siva, the Nataraja and the lingam. A later Vishnu shrine to Govindaraja was added by the Vijayanagar kings. The **inner enclosure**, the most sacred, contains four important *Sabhas* (halls), the

Nataraja Temple, Chidambaram

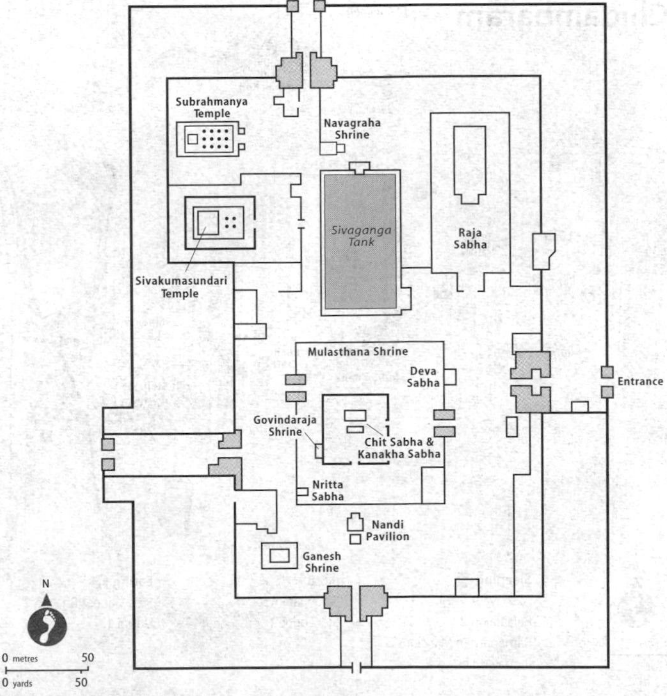

deva sabha, where the temple managers hold their meetings; the **chit sabha** or *chit ambalam* (from which the temple and the town get their names), meaning the hall of wisdom; the **kanakha sabha**, or golden hall; and the **nritta sabha**, or hall of dancing. Siva is worshipped in the *chit ambalam*, a plain wooden building standing on a stone base, in his form as Lord of the Dance, Nataraja. The area immediately over the deity's head is gold plated. Immediately behind the idol is the focus of the temple's power, the Akasa Lingam, representing the invisible element, 'space', and hence is itself invisible. It is known as the Chidambaram secret.

Around Chidambaram

The Danish king Christian IV received permission from Raghunath Nayak of Thanjavur to build a fort here at **Tranquebar** (Tharangampadi) in 1620. The Danish Tranquebar Mission was founded in 1706 and the Danesborg **fort** and the old **church** still survive. The Danes set up the first Tamil printing press, altering the script to make the casting of type easier and the Danish connection resulted in the National Museum of Copenhagen today possessing a remarkable collection of 17th-century Thanjavur paintings and Chola bronzes. There is a **museum** and a good beach. From Chidambaram most transport requires a change at Sirkazhi. From Thanjavur there are some direct buses; other buses involve a change at Mayiladuthurai (24 km)

Sleeping

Tiruchirappalli *p119, map p120*

A Jenney's Residency, 3/14 Macdonalds Rd, T0431-241 4414. Pool (non-residents Rs 100), 93 top quality a/c rooms, good restaurants, excellent travel desk, exchange, beauty salon.

B-D Femina, 14C Williams Rd, T0431-241 4501, try_femina@sancharnet.in. 157 clean rooms, 140 a/c, vegetarian restaurants, bar, pool in new block, good value, modern, comfortable 4-storey hotel.

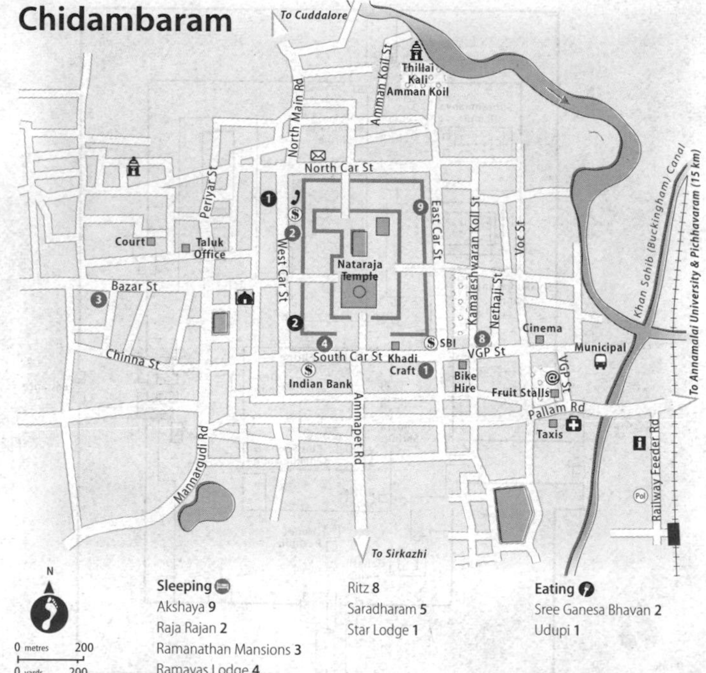

C Sangam, Collector's Office Rd, T0431-246 4480. Very friendly, 58 comfortable a/c rooms, restaurants (great tandoori), good breakfast in coffee shop, pleasant bar, exchange, pool, spacious lawns.

C-D Kanjenaa Plaza, 50 Williams Rd (2-min walk from bus stand), T0431-240 1501, kanjenaaplaza@rediffmail.com. 90 spacious, comfortable rooms with bath, 26 a/c, restaurant, bar, travel agent, very quiet, new and clean.

C-D Ramyas, 13D/2 Williams Rd, T0431-241 5128, vatnaa@eth.net. 78 spotless rooms, 24 a/c, restaurants, bar.

D Abirami, 10 Macdonalds Rd, T0431-241 5001. Old fashioned, noisy location, 55 rooms, some a/c with bath, good busy a/c restaurant (vegetarian), exchange.

D-E Ashby, 17A Junction Rd, T0431-246 0652. Set around courtyard, 20 large a/c rooms with bath, good restaurants, bar, oldest hotel in town, with Raj character, a bit noisy but excellent friendly staff, good value.

D-E Gajapriya, 5 Royal Rd, T0431-241 4411. 66 good-value rooms, 28 a/c (no twin beds), restaurant, bar, library, parking, spacious hotel, quieter than most.

D-E Tamil Nadu (TTDC), Macdonalds Rd, Cantt, T0431-2414346. Run down, 36 rooms , some a/c with bath, restaurant, bar and tourist office.

E-F Sevana, 5 Royal Rd, Cantt, T0431-241 5201. Quiet, friendly, 44 rooms, some a/c with bath, a/c restaurant (Indian), bar.

F Arun, 24 State Bank, Rd T0431-241 5021. 40 rooms in garden setting, restaurant, bar, TV, excellent value. Recommended.

G ASG Lodge opposite. Very noisy but quite clean (from Rs 75).

G Raja Sugam, 13b Royal Rd, T0431-246 0636.

Thanjavur *p122, map p123*

Even modest hotels charge 20% Luxury Tax. The last 3 listings are for Point Calimere (Kodikkarai) Wildlife Sanctuary, where Nov-Dec are busy; advance reservation is recommended, at Wildlife Warden, 3 Main St, Thanjavur.

A Parisutham, 55 GA Canal Rd, T04362-231801, www.hotelparisutham.com. 52 clean a/c rooms in 1980s building, passable restaurants, poorly maintained pool, exchange, good atmosphere (avoid smaller, noisy a/c ground floor rooms).

B Ideal River View Resort, Vennar Bank, Palli Agraharam, 6 km north of centre, T04326-250533, www.idealresort.com. Clean, comfortable cottages (some a/c) in large grounds, restaurant, boating, peaceful, big swimming pool, shuttle to town. Recommended.

C-D Hotel Gnanam, Anna Salai (Market Rd), T04362-278501, www.hotelgnanam.com. 30 rooms (some a/c) with hot water, vegetarian multi-cuisine restaurant, safety deposit lockers and travel desk. Mid-range sister hotel to Parasutham.

D Pandyar Residency, Kutchery Rd, near Big Temple, T04362-230574. Some of the 63 rooms overlook temple, some a/c, restaurant, bar.

D-E Lion City, 130 Gandhiji Rd, T04362-275650, hotellioncity@hotmail.com. 25 well-appointed rooms, TV, hot water, clean, spacious, good service. Recommended.

D-E Tamil Nadu I (TTDC), Gandhiji Rd, 5-min walk from railway, T04362-231421. Pleasant setting around a cool inner courtyard, 32 small rooms with bath, rather dark, some a/c, simple restaurant, bar, tourist office.

D-E Yagappa, off Trichy Rd, south of station, T04362-230421. Good size, comfortable rooms with bath, restaurant, bar, good value.

E-F Karthik, 73 S Rampart St, T04362-278662. Friendly, 43 adequate rooms, 3 a/c, popular vegetarian restaurant (eat off a banana leaf at lunch time).

E-F Kasi, 1494 S Rampart St, T04362-231908. 42 nice, clean rooms (from Rs 115), some with TV, hot showers, 3 a/c. Recommended.

F Calimere Rest House, Point Calimere (Kodikkarai) Sanctuary. 4 derelict rooms.

F Ganesh Lodge, next to train station, T04362-231113. Good vegetarian restaurant, 25 basic but clean rooms (de luxe overpriced).

F PV Thevar Lodge, 40 North Main St, Vedaranyam, 50 m from bus station (English sign high up only visible in daylight), T04362-250330. Good value, 37 basic rooms with bath and fan, can be mosquito-proofed, fairly clean, very friendly owners. Indian vegetarian meals in the bazar near bus stand.

For an explanation of the sleeping and eating price codes used in this guide, see inside the front cover. Other relevant information is found in Essentials pages 40-44.

G Poonarai Ilam, Point Calimere (Kodikkarai) Sanctuary, 14 simple rooms with bath and balcony (Rs 15 pp), caretaker may be able to arrange a meal with advance notice, intended for foreign visitors, rooms are often available.
G Youth Hostel, Medical College Rd, T04362-223597. Dorm (Rs 40).

Kumbakonam *p124, map p125*
20% Luxury Tax is always added.
D Chela, 9 Ayekulam Rd, T0435-243 0336. 30 rooms, 8 a/c, clean, restaurant, spacious. Recommended.
D Raya's, 18 Head PO Rd, near tank, T0435-243 2170. 43 clean rooms, some a/c with bath, TV, safes, mirrored VIP suite, good restaurant, bar, 24-hr check-out, exchanges cash.
E ARR, 21 TSR Big St, T0435-242 1234. 50 good-size, clean rooms, some a/c, with bath, TV, bar, room service meals.
E Femina, Head PO Rd (towards tank), T0435-242 0369. Clean and quiet rooms.
F Pandiyan, 52 Sarangapani East Sannadi St, T0435-243 0397. Good value, 20 clean rooms with bath (some dark), good restaurant.

Chidambaram *p126, map p128*
The choice of accommodation partly explains why most people visit the town on day trips only.
C-D Saradharam, 19 VGP St, T04144-221336. Noisy, with 46 basic, tired, grubby overpriced rooms, but highly recommended restaurants.
D Ritz, 2 VGP (Venugopal Pillai) St, T04144-223312. Very clean, modern hotel, with 18 excellent a/c rooms, rooftop restaurant. Highly recommended.
D-E Akshaya, 17-18 East Car St, T04144-220192. Comfortable small hotel right in the centre (can be noisy), 24 rooms, mostly non a/c, rooftop overlooks temple grounds.
F Raja Rajan, 162 West Car St, T04144-222690. Friendly, 14 pleasant rooms, 1 a/c.
F Ramanathan Mansions, 127 Bazar St, T04144-222411. Away from busy temple area, quieter than most, 28 rooms with bath, spacious and airy (no power sockets), friendly.
F Ramayas Lodge, 120 South Car St, T04144-223011. Good value, 24 clean rooms with bath, 2 a/c, TV, phone.
F Star Lodge, 101 South Car St, T04144-222743. Set around open central landings, 37 basic rooms, friendly.

Eating

Tiruchirappalli *p119, map p120*
TT Abirami's, T0431-246 0001. A/c, Vasantha Bhawan at the back, serves excellent vegetarian; front part is a meals-type eatery.
TT Jenney's Residency, T0431-246 1301. Good Chinese, extensive menu, attentive service but freezing a/c. Also Wild West bar.
TT Kavitha, Lawson's Rd. A/c. Excellent breakfasts and generous vegetarian thalis.
TT Sangam's, T0431-246 4480. Indian and continental.
TT Vincent Garden, Dindigul Rd. Pleasant garden restaurant and pastry shop, lots of coloured lights but on a busy road.

Good Indian vegetarian places in Chinna Bazar are **T New Kurinji**, below Hotel Guru, Lawson's Rd. A/c vegetarian. **T Ragunath** and **Vasantha Bhawan**, thalis, good service.

Thanjavur *p122, map p123*
TT Oriental Towers, for quality food.
TT Parisutham, good North Indian meat dishes, excellent vegetarian thalis ("best of 72 curries"), service can be slow.
T Algappa, Gandhiji Rd. A/c, non-vegetarian.
T New Bombay Sweets, tasty Indian snacks.
T Sathars, Tandoori. Recommended.
T Vasantha Vihar on west side of Railway Station Rd between station and **Tamil Nadu** hotel. Good thalis and snacks.

Kumbakonam *p124, map p125*
T A&A, Ayekulam Rd. Excellent vegetarian restaurant. Good, clean.

Chidambaram *p126, map p128*
TT Hotel Saradharam, 10 VGP St. Popular, a/c. Excellent range of meals, pizzas and European dishes. Good variety and value.
T Sree Ganesa Bhavan, West Car St. South Indian vegetarian. Friendly, helpful staff.
T Udupi, West Car St. Good vegetarian, clean.

Entertainment

Thanjavur *p122, map p123*
Bharat Natyam, 1/2378 Krishanayar Lane, Ellaiyamman Koil St, T04362-233759. Shows by Guru Herambanathan from a family of dancers.
South Zone Cultural Centre Palace, T04362-231272. Organizes programmes in the Big Temple, 2nd and 4th Sat; free.

Festivals and events

Tiruchirappalli *p119, map p120*
Mar: Festival of Floats on the Teppakulam when the temple deities are taken out onto the sacred lake on rafts.

Around Trichy *p121*
In **Srirangam** Vaikunta Ekadasi (bus No 1 (C or D) from Trichy or hire a rickshaw), and associated temple car festival, in **Dec/Jan** draws thousands of pilgrims who witness the transfer of the image of the deity from the inner sanctum under the golden *vimana* to the *mandapa*.

In **Tiruvanaikkaval**, there are special festivals in **Jan** and the **spring**. In **Aug** Pancha Piraharam is celebrated and in the month of **Panguni** the images of Siva and his consort Akhilandesvari exchange their dress.

In **Pudukkottai**, in **Jan** and **Feb** bullock races (*manju virattu*) are held in the area.

Chidambaram *p126, map p128*
Feb/Mar: Natyanjali dance festival for 5 days starting with Maha Sivaratri. **Jun/Jul**: Ani Tirumanjanam Festival. **Dec/Jan**: Markazhi Tiruvathirai Festival.

Shopping

Thanjavur *p122, map p123*
You may not export any object over 100 years old. Thanjavur is known for its decorative copper plates with silver and brass relief (*repoussé*) work, raised glass painting, wood carving and bronze and brass casting. Granite carving is being revived by the government through centres which produce superbly sculpted images. Craft shops abound in Gandhiji Rd Bazar.
Govindarajan's, 31 Kuthirai Katti St, Karandhai (a few kilometres from town), T04362-230282, is a treasure house of pricey old, and affordable new, pieces; artists and craftspeople at work.

Activities and tours

Tiruchirappalli *p119, map p120*
Tour operators
Galaxy, Williams Rd (Kanjenaa Plaza). For air and train tickets.
Window to the World, 33 Chandra Nagar, Srirangam, T0431-243 5219, www.tourism-southindia.com. Tours from Chennai, Bengaluru (Bangalore), Kochi, Madurai and Thiruvananthapuram. Recommended for tours (good cars with drivers), ticketing, general advice.

Thanjavur *p122, map p123*
Tour operators
TTDC, Temple tour of Thanjavur and surroundings by a/c coach. Enquire at Tourist Office. Mon-Fri, 1000-1745.

Transport

Tiruchirappalli *p119, map p120*
Air
The airport is 8 km from the centre (taxi Rs 75). **Indian Airlines**, Dindigul Rd, 2 km from Express Bus Stand, T0431-248 1433, airport T0431-242 0563; flies to **Chennai** daily except Mon and Fri. **Sri Lankan**, 14 Williams Rd, T0431-241 4076 (0900-1730) to **Colombo**.

Bus
Local Good City Bus service. From airport, Nos 7, 63, 122, 128, take 30 mins. The Central State Bus Stand is across from the tourist office (No 1 Bus passes all the sights); 20 mins to Chatram Bus Stand.
Long distance The bus stands are 1 km from the railway station and are chaotic; TN Govt Express, T0431-246 0992, Central, T0431-246 0425. Frequent buses to **Chennai** (6 hrs), **Coimbatore** 205 km (5½ hrs), **Kumbakonam** 92 km, **Madurai** 161 km (3 hrs), **Palani** 152 km (3½ hrs), **Thanjavur** (1½ hrs). Also 2 to **Kanniyakumari** (9 hrs), **Kodai** (5½ hrs) and **Tirupati** (9½ hrs).

Taxi
Unmetered taxis, and tourist taxis from **Kavria Travels**, Hotel Sangam, Collector's Office Rd, T0431-246 4480. **Note** Cycle-rickshaws and auto-rickshaws are best avoided.

Train
Enquiries, T131. **Bengaluru (Bangalore)**: *Thanjavur Mysore Exp 6231*, 2040, 9½ hrs, continues to **Mysore**, 3¼ hrs. **Chennai**: *Pallavan Exp 2606*, 0630, 5½ hrs; *Vaigai Exp*

2636, 0910, 5¼ hrs. **Kollam**: *Nagore-Quilon Exp 6361*, 1615, 12½ hrs. **Madurai**: *Vaigai Exp 2635*, 1745, 2¾ hrs. **Villupuram (for Pondicherry)**: *Tiruchi Tirupati Exp 6802*, 1400, 7 hrs; *Cholan Exp 6854*, 0800, 6½ hrs, plus frequent bus to Pondicherry (1 hr) or another train (4 daily).

Pudukkottai and around *p121*
Bus to **Tiruchirappalli**, **Thanjavur**, **Madurai**, **Ramnad**, **Ramesvaram**, and to **Sittanavasal** (see above).

The **train** station is 2 km southwest of the bus stand. Trains for Egmore, change at Tambaram. **Trichy** 1¼ hrs. **Ramesvaram** *Tambaram Ramesvaram Exp 6701*, 0833, 5¼ hrs.

Thanjavur *p122, map p123*
Air
Tiruchirappalli airport is about 1 hr by car.

Bus
Old State and Municipal Bus Stand, south of the fort, for local services. Buses from Kumbakonam stop at the corner before going out to the New Bus Stand, T04362-233455. CRC (Cholan), T04362-232455. New (Mofussil) Bus Stand is on Trichy Rd. Daily service to **Chennai** (8 hrs), **Chidambaram** (4 hrs), **Kumbakonam** (1 hr), **Madurai** (3½ hrs), **Pondicherry** (6 hrs), **Tirupathi**, **Tiruchirappalli** (1½ hrs). Also to **Vedaranyam** (100 km) for Point Calimere, about hourly, 4-4½ hrs.

Train
Reservations, T04362-231131, Mon-Sat 0800-1400, 1500-1700; Sun 0800-1400. **Bengaluru (Bangalore)**: *Thanjavur Mysore Exp 6231*, 1845, 11½ hrs, continues to **Mysore**, 3¼ hrs. **Chennai (ME)**: *Rockfort Exp 6878*, 2000, 9 hrs. **Tiruchirappalli**: *Tambaram Rameswaram Exp 6701*, 0520, 2 hrs; *Fast Passenger Exp 6761*, 1300, 3 hrs; *Cholan Exp 6853*, 1700, 1¾ hrs.

Around Thanjavur *p124*
Buses via Vedaranyam which has services to/from **Thanjavur**, **Tiruchirappalli**, **Nagapattinam**, **Chennai** etc. From Thanjavur buses leave the New Bus Stand for **Vedaranyam** (100 km) about hourly (4-4½ hrs); buses and vans from there to **Kodikkarai** (11 km) which take about 30 mins. Avoid being dropped at 'Sri Rama's Feet' on the way, near a shrine that is of no special interest.

Kumbakonam *p124, map p125*
Car hire for half day for excursions, Rs 400. TN Govt Express **buses** to **Chennai**, No 305, several daily (7½ hrs); half hourly to **Thanjavur**. The railway station is 2 km from town centre. **Trains** to **Chennai** (Egmore), 1010-2110, change at Tambaram (8½-9 hrs), **Chidambaram** (2 hrs), **Thanjavur** (50 mins) and **Tiruchirappalli**, 0600-1555 (2½ hrs).

Chidambaram *p126, map p128*
The **bus** station is chaotic with daily services to **Chennai**, **Madurai**, **Thanjavur**, and to **Karaikal** (2 hrs), **Nagapattinam** and **Pondicherry** (2 hrs).

Train reservations T04144-222298, Mon-Sat 0800-1200, 1400-1700; Sun 0800-1400. **Chennai (E)** (change at Tambaram): *Rameswaram Tambaram Exp 6702*, 2307, 6¾ hrs; *Cholan Exp 6854*, 1153, 6 hrs. **Kumbakonam**: *Sethu Exp 6713*, 1832, 2 hrs, continues to **Thanjavur**, 3 hrs and **Tiruchirappalli**, 5 hrs; *Cholan Exp 6853*, 1410, 2 hrs, continues to **Thanjavur**, 3 hrs, and **Tiruchirappalli**, 4¾ hrs.

Directory

Tiruchirappalli *p119, map p120*
Banks Exchange is available at Western Union money transfer in Jenne Plaza, Cantonment. Mon-Sat 0900-1730. Quick; good rates. **Internet** Mas Media, Main Rd, 6 terminals; Central Telegraph Office, Permanent Rd.

Pudukkottai and around *p121*
Banks State Bank of India, East Main St.

Thanjavur *p122, map p123*
Banks Canara Bank, South Main St, changes TCs. **Hospitals** Govt Hospital, Hospital Rd, south of the old town.
Post Head Post and Telegraph Office are off the Railway Station Rd.
Useful addresses Police, south of the Big Temple between the canal and the railway, T04362-232200.

Kumbakonam *p124, map p125*
Banks Changing money is difficult. State Bank of India, TSR Big St. **Internet** End of Kamaraj Rd, close to clock tower. **Post** Near Mahamakam Tank.

Chidambaram *p126, map p128*
Banks Changing money can be difficult. City Union Bank, West Car St has exchange. Indian Bank, 64 South Car St, changes cash.
Post Head Post Office, North Car St.

Tamil's hill stations

The Tamil ghats were once shared between shola forest and tribal peoples. But the British, limp from the heat of the plains, invested in expeditions up the mountains and before long had planted eucalyptus, established elite members' clubs and substituted jackals for foxes in their pursuit of the hunt. Don't expect to find the sheer awe-inspiring grandeur of the Himalaya, but there is a charm to these hills where neatly pleated, green tea plantations run like contour lines about the ghats' girth, bringing the promise of a restorative chill and walking tracks where the air comes cut with the smell of eucalyptus. ▸▸ *For Sleeping, Eating and other listings, see pages 142-150.*

Ins and outs

The northern Nilgiris or the more southerly Palani hills offer rival opportunities for high-altitude stopovers on the route between Tamil Nadu, Karnataka and Kerala. The most visited towns of Ooty and Kodai both have their staunch fan bases – Ooty tends to attract nostalgic British and rail enthusiasts, while Kody gets the American vote, thanks in part to its international schools. Both are well connected by road; Kody is best approached from Madurai and Ooty makes a good bridge to Kerala from Mysore or Tamil's more Northern temple towns. The famous narrow gauge rack-and-pinion railway is most dramatic between Mettupalayam and Coonoor, which in turn has trains from Coimbatore and Chennai. ▸▸ *See Transport, page 148, for further details.*

The roads worsen dramatically when you cross the Tamil border from Kerala, reflecting the different levels of affluence between the two states.

Udhagamandalam (Ooty)

▸▸ *pp142-150. Colour map 3, grid B3.*

→ *Phone code: 0423. Population 93,900. Altitude: 2286 m.*

Ooty has been celebrated for rolling hills covered in pine and eucalyptus forests and coffee and tea plantations since the first British planters arrived in 1818. A Government House was built and the British lifestyle developed with cottages and clubs – tennis, golf, riding – and teas on the lawn. But the town is no longer the haven it once was; the centre is heavily built up and can be unpleasant in the holiday months of April to June, and again around October. Either stay in the grand ruins of colonial quarters on the quiet outskirts where it's still possible to steal some serenity or opt instead for the far smaller tea garden town of Coonoor, see page 136, just 19 km down mountain.

Sights

The **Botanical Gardens** ⓘ *0800-1800, Rs 25, camera, Rs 50, video Rs 500, 3 km northeast of railway station,* hold over 1000 varieties of plant, shrub and tree including orchids, ferns, alpines and medicinal plants, but is most fun for watching giant family groups picnicking and gambolling together among beautiful lawns and glass houses. To the east of the garden in a Toda *mund* is the Wood House made of logs. The Annual Flower Show is held in the third week of May. The **Rose Garden** ⓘ *0800-1800, 750 m from Charing Cross,* has over 1500 varieties of roses.

The Blue Mountain Railway

Ever since 15 June 1899, the narrow gauge steam Mountain Railway, in its blue and cream livery, has chugged from Mettupalayam to Ooty via Coonoor, negotiating 16 tunnels and 31 major bridges and climbing from 326 m to 2193 m. It's a charming 4½-hour (46 km) journey through tea plantations and forest, but – outside first class – come ready for an amiable Indian holidaymakers' scrum. There are rest stops at Hillgrove (17 km) and Coonoor (27 km).

This was the location for the railway scenes of the Marabar Express in the film *A Passage to India*.

For enthusiasts, the pricier and more spacious Heritage Steam Chariot runs between Ooty and Runneymede picnic area, 23 km away, at weekends (more often in high season). The drawback is that you can be stranded for hours when the engine breaks down; some decide to scramble to the nearest road to flag down a bus.

Ooty Lake ⓘ *0800-1800, Rs 3, camera Rs 10, video Rs 100*, 2½ km long, was built in 1825 as a vast irrigation tank and is now more than half overgrown with water hyacinth, though it is still used enthusiastically for boating and pedalo hire.

Kandal Cross ⓘ *3 km west of the railway station*, is a Roman Catholic shrine considered the 'Jerusalem of the East'. During the clearing of the area to make way for

Udhagamandalam (Ooty)

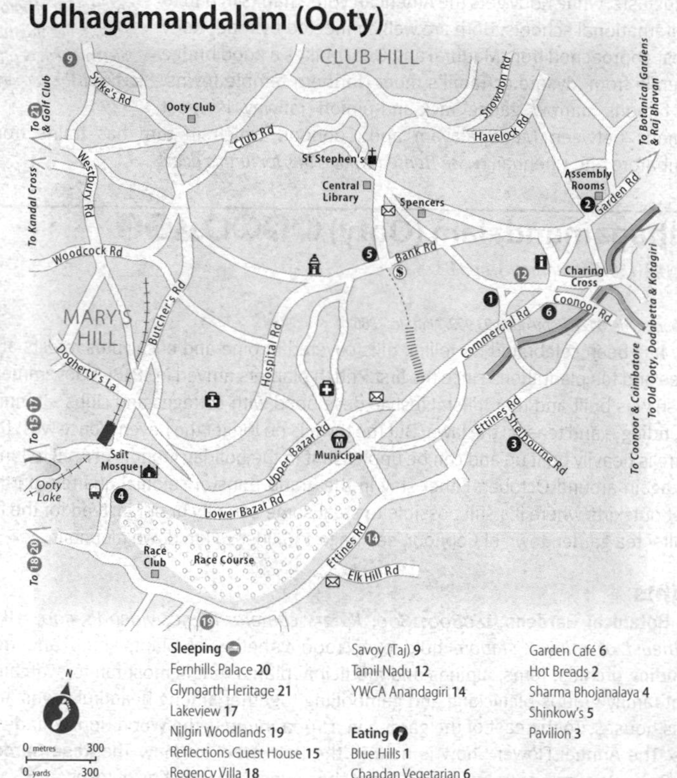

Snooty Ooty

Ooty was once considered the queen of hill stations: old maps and aquatints indeed show a gem of a hill station: a smattering of colonnaded houses, a golf course, the private members' club where billiards was invented.

Ooty may no longer be quite the queen she was (the 'no to plastics' slogans painted on every bus shelter are addressing a very real problem), but there are some hotels that reek of the Raj era and there is still the hangover of better days in the form of the club: a place of Mappin & Webb cutlery, beautiful old paintings, photographs of the hunt, and entry only in shirts with collars. A member, dressed in a cravat and gilet, claims, with some reason, that they are"the only true Englishman left in India".

Stories of the Britishers' excesses abound: one hall still bears the marks of the soles of a particular lady's feet as, borne aloft by her compatriots, she danced upside down on the ceiling. The Queen still hangs in the meeting room in her coronation finery. Queen Victoria, meanwhile, has been left to hang inside the kids' room to scare the children. You can judge for yourself how Ooty has aged; the club's walls also feature a series of panoramic photos of Ooty taken at 25 year intervals from 1875.

a graveyard in 1927, an enormous 4-m-high boulder was found and a cross was erected. Now a relic of the True Cross brought to India by an Apostolic delegate is shown to pilgrims every day. The annual feast is in May.

St Stephen's Church was Ooty's first church, built in the 1820s. Much of the wood is said to be from Tipu Sultan's Lal Bagh Palace in Srirangapatnam. The inside of the church and the graveyard at the rear are worth seeing.

Dodabetta ⓘ *buses from Ooty, 1000-1500, autos and taxis (Rs 200 round trip) go to the summit*, is 10 km east of the railway station off the Kotagiri road. Reaching 2638 m, the 'big mountain' is the second highest in the Western Ghats, sheltering Coonoor from the southwest monsoons when Ooty gets heavy rains. The top is often shrouded in mist. There is a viewing platform at the summit. The telescope isn't worth even the nominal Rs 2 fee.

Walks and hikes around Ooty

Hiking or simply walking is excellent in the Nilgiris. It is undisturbed, quiet and interesting. Climbing Dodabetta or Mukurti is hardly a challenge but the longer walks through the *sholas* are best undertaken with a guide. It is possible to see characteristic features of Toda settlements such as *munds* and *boas*, see page 72.

Dodabetta-Snowdon-Ooty walk starts at Dodabetta Junction directly opposite the 3 km road to the summit. It is a pleasant path which curves gently downhill through a variety of woodland (mainly eucalyptus and conifers) back to Ooty and doesn't take more than a couple of hours. For longer treks, contact **Nilgiris Trekking Association** ⓘ *Kavitha Nilayam, 31-D Bank Rd, or R Seniappan, 137 Upper Bazar, T0423-244 4449, sehi appan@yahoo.com.*

There are isolated groups of up to 18 different types of tribal people who live in the Nilgiri Hills, see page 72.

Mukurti Peak ⓘ *buses from Ooty every 30 mins from 0630 or you can take a tour (see page 147), book early as they are popular*, is 36 km away, off the Gudalur road. After 26 km you reach the 6-km-long Mukurti Lake. Mukurti Peak (the name suggests that someone thought it resembled a severed nose), not an easy climb, is to the west. The Todas believe that the souls of the dead and the sacrificed buffaloes leap to the next world from this sacred peak. It is an excellent place to escape for walking, to view the occasional wildlife, to go fishing at the lake or to go boating.

Avalanche ⓘ *buses from Ooty, 1110,* a valley, is a beautiful part of the *shola*, 24 km from town, with plenty of rhododendrons, magnolias and orchids and a trout stream running through it, and is excellent for walking. The Forestry Department Guest House is clean and has good food.

The **River Pykara** ⓘ *several buses from 0630-2030, or take a car or bicycle,* 19 km from Ooty, has a dam and power plant. There is breathtaking scenery. The Falls, about 6 km from the bridge on the main road, are best in July though it is very wet then, but they are also worth visiting from August to December.

Coonoor

» pp142-150. Colour map 3, grid B3.

→ *Phone code: 0423. Population: 50,100. Altitude: 1800 m.*

Smaller and much less developed than Ooty, Coonoor is an ideal starting point for nature walks and rambles through villages. There's no pollution, no noise and very few people. The covered market, as with many towns and cities in South India, is almost medieval and cobblers, jewellers, tailors, pawn brokers and merchants sell everything from jasmine to beetroot. The picturesque hills around the town are covered in coffee and tea plantations.

When you arrive by train or bus (which doesn't always stop at the main bus stand if going on to Ooty), the main town of Lower Coonoor will be to the east, across the river. Upper Coonoor, with the better hotels 2-3 km away, is further east.

The real attraction here is the hiking, though there are a couple of sights in town. The large **Sim's Park** ⓘ *0800-1830, Rs 5,* named after a secretary to the Madras Club, is a well-maintained botanical garden on the slopes of a ravine with over 330 varieties of rose but is only really worth the journey for passionate botanists. Contact the United Planters' Association of South India (UPASI), Glenview, to visit tea and coffee plantations. The **Wellington Barracks**, 3 km northeast of Lower Coonoor, which are the raison d'être for the town, were built in 1852. They are now the Headquarters of the Indian Defence Services Staff College and also of the Madras Regiment, which is over 250 years old, the oldest in the Indian Army.

Around Coonor

Lamb's Rock, on a high precipice, 9 km away, has good views over the Coimbatore plains and coffee and tea estates on the slopes. At **Dolphin's Nose** ⓘ *several buses 0700-1615,* 12 km away, you can see Catherine Falls, a further 10 km away. It's best seen in the early morning. **Droog** ⓘ *buses 0900, 1345,* 13 km away, has ruins of a 16th-century fort used by Tipu Sultan, and requires a 3-km walk. **Kotagiri** ⓘ *frequent services from Coonoor, Mettupalayam Railway Station and Ooty,* has an altitude of 1980 m and is 29 km from Ooty. It sits on the northeast crest of the plateau overlooking the plains. It has a milder climate than Ooty. The name comes from Kotar-Keri, the street of the *Kotas* who were one of the original hill tribes and who have a village to the west of the town. You can visit some scenic spots from here: **St Catherine Falls** (8 km) and **Elk Falls** (7 km), or one of the peaks, **Kodanad Viewpoint** (16 km) – reached through the tea estates or by taking one of the several buses that run from 0610 onwards – or **Rangaswamy Pillar**, an isolated rock, and the conical Rangaswamy Peak.

Mettupalayam and the Nilgiri Ghat Road

» pp143-149.

The journey up to Coonoor from Mettupalayam is one of the most scenic in South India, giving superb views over the plains below. Between Mettupalayam and the start of the Ghat road, there are magnificent groves of tall, slender areca nut palms. Mettupalayam has become the centre for the areca nut trade as well as producing synthetic gems. The palms are immensely valuable trees: the nut is used across India wrapped in betel vine leaves – two of the essential ingredients of India's universal after-meal digestive, *paan*.

The town is the starting point of the ghat railway line up to Ooty, see box page 134. If you take the early morning train you can continue to Mysore by bus from Ooty on the same day, making a very pleasant trip.

Mudumalai Wildlife Sanctuary

» *pp143-149.*

Colour map 3, grid B3.

ⓘ *0630-0900, 1600-1800, Rs 150; still camera Rs 10. There is a Ranger Office at Kargudi and a Reception Centre, 0630-1800, at Theppakadu where buses between Mysore anld Ooty stop.*

The sanctuary adjoins Bandipur National Park (see page 276) beyond the Moyar River, its hills (885 m-1000 m), ravines, flats and valleys being an extension of the same environment. The park is one of the more popular and is now trying to limit numbers of visitors to reduce disturbance to the elephants.

There are large herds of elephant, sambar, barking deer, wild dog, Nilgiri langur, bonnet monkey, wild boar, four-horned antelope and the rarer tiger and leopard, as well as smaller mammals and many birds and reptiles. Elephant Camp, south of Theppakadu, tames wild elephants. Some are bred in captivity and trained to work for the timber industry. You can watch the elephants being fed in the late afternoon, learn about each individual elephant's diet and the specially prepared 'cakes' of food.

You can hire a jeep for about Rs 6 per km but must be accompanied by a guide. Most night safaris are best avoided. Elephant rides at 0630 (Rs 100 per elephant for four for 45 minutes); check timing and book in advance at the Wildlife Office, Mahalingam Building, Coonoor Road, Ooty. They can be fun even though you may not see much wildlife. The 46-seater coach, first come, first served, Rs 25 each, can be noisy with shrieking children. There are *machans* near waterholes and salt licks and along the Moyar River. With patience you can see a lot, especially rare and beautiful birds. Trekking in the remoter parts of the forest with guides can be arranged from some lodges. You can spend a day climbing the hill and bathe at the impressive waterfalls. The core area is not open to visitors.

Best time to visit is September-October and March-May when the undergrowth dies down and it's easier to see animals, especially at dawn when they're on the move.

Coimbatore and the Nilgiri Hills

» *pp148-150.* *Colour map 3, grid B3.*

Coimbatore → *Phone code: 0422. Population: 923,000.*

As one of South India's most important industrial cities since the 1930s development of hydroelectricity from the Pykara Falls, Coimbatore holds scant charm to warrant more than a pit stop. It was once the fulcrum of tussles between Tamilian, Mysorean and Keralite coastal rulers (the word *palayam* crops up tellingly often in Coimbatore – its translation being 'encampment') and sadly violence continues today. You are likely to stay here only if fascinated by the cotton trade or stuck for an onward bus or train.

Coimbatore's nickname is 'India's Manchester', because it is the subcontinent's capital of cotton weaving – skyscrapers called things like 'Viscose Towers' aren't uncommon.

Salem → *Phone code: 0427. Colour map 3, grid B4. Population: 693,200.*

Salem, an important transport junction, is surrounded by hills: the Shevaroy and Nagaramalai Hills to the north and the Jarugumalai Hills to the southeast. It is a busy, rapidly growing industrial town – particularly for textiles and metal-based industries – with modern shopping centres.

The old town is on the east bank of the River Manimutheru. Each evening around Bazar Street you can see cotton carpets being made. The **cemetery**, next to the Collector's office, has some interesting tombstones. To the southeast of the town on a ridge of the Jarugumalai Hills is a highly visible *Naman* painted in *chunam* and ochre. On the nearby hill the temple (1919) is particularly sacred to the weavers' community. Some 600 steps lead up to excellent views over the town.

Yercaud and the Shevaroy Hills → *Phone code: 04281. Altitude: 1515 m.*

The beautiful drive up the steep and sharply winding ghat road from Salem quickly brings a sharp freshness to the air as it climbs to over 1500 m. The minor resort has a small artificial **lake** and Anna Park nearby. Some attractive though unmarked walks start here. In May there is a special festival focused on the **Shevaroyan Temple**, on top of the third highest peak in the hill range. Many tribal people take part but access is only possible on foot. Ask for details in the **Tamil Nadu Tourist Office** in Chennai, see page 79. There's also a tourist information office in the **Tamil Nadu** hotel in town, see page 144.

Just outside town is **Lady's Seat**, overlooking the ghat road, which has wonderful views across the Salem plains. Near the old Norton Bungalow on the Shevaroyan Temple Road is another well-known local spot, **Bear's Cave**. Formed by two huge boulders, it is occupied by huge colonies of bats. The whole area is full of botanical interest. There is an **orchidarium-cum-nursery** and a **horticultural research station**.

Kodaikkanal (Kodai) and the Palani Hills

» pp144-150. Colour map 3, grid C4.

→ *Phone code: 04542. Population: 32,900. Altitude: 2343 m.*

The climb up the Palanis starts 47 km before Kodaikkanal (Kodai) and is one of the most rapid ascents anywhere across the ghats. The views are stunning. In the lower reaches of the climb you look down over the Kambam Valley, the Vaigai Lake and across to the Varushanad Hills beyond. Set high in the Palani Hills around a small artificial lake, the town has crisply fresh air, even at the height of summer, and the beautiful scent of pine and eucalyptus make it a popular retreat from the southern plains. Today Kodai is a fast growing resort and many believe it superior to Ooty. Created in 1910 by building a dam just below the International School (established in 1901), the lake acts as a focus for the town. The 5-km walk around its perimeter offers some beautiful and contrasting views across the water and into the surrounding woods.

Ins and outs

Buses make the long climb from Madurai and other cities to the central bus stand, which is within easy walking distance from most hotels. The nearest train station is Kodai Rd. Kodai is small enough to walk around, though for some of the sights it is worth getting an unmetered taxi. » *See Transport, page 150, for further details.*

History

The **Palani Hills** were first surveyed by British administrators in 1821, but the surveyor's report was not published until 1837, 10 years after Ooty had become the official sanitorium for the British in South India. A proposal to build a sanitorium was made in 1861-1862 by Colonel Hamilton, who noted the extremely healthy climate and the lack of disease. Despite the warmth of that recommendation the sanitorium was never built because the site was so inaccessible. Freedom from malaria was the greatest incentive for opening a hill station here. The American Mission in Madurai, established in 1834, had lost six of their early missionaries within a decade. It looked as if the Sirumalai Hills, at around 1300 m, might provide a respite from the plains, but it was soon discovered that they were not high enough to eliminate malaria. The first two bungalows were built by June 1845.

The major transformation came at the turn of the 20th century with the arrival of the car and the bus. In 1905 it was possible to do the whole journey from Kodai Road station to Kodai within the hours of daylight. The present road, up Law's Ghat, was opened to traffic in 1916.

Sights

Kodaikkanal Lake ⓘ *Rs 5, toilets at south entrance*, covers 24 ha in a star shape surrounded by wooded slopes. The walk around the lake takes about one hour, boating is popular and you can fish (with permission), although the water is polluted. The view over the plains from **Coaker's Walk**, built by Lieutenant Coaker in the 1870s, can be magnificent; on a clear day you can see Madurai. It is reached from a signposted path just above the bazar, 1 km from the Bus Stand.

Kurinji Andavar Temple, northeast of the town, past Chettiar Park, is dedicated to Murugan associated with the *kurinji* flower that blossoms once in 12 years. There

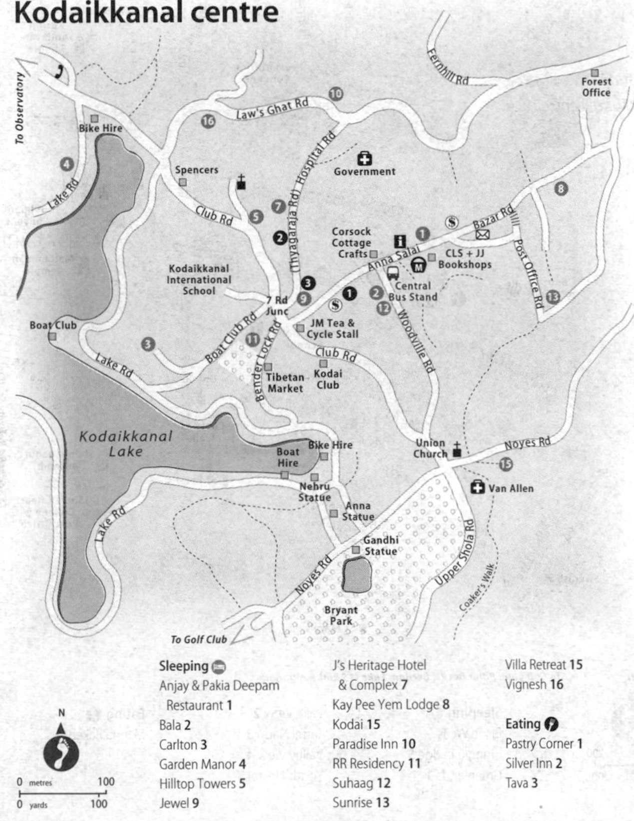

are excellent views of the north and southern plains, including Palani and Vagai Dams. **St Peter's Church** (Church of South India), built in 1884, has a stained glass window dedicated to Bishop Caldwell. **The International School** has a commanding position on the lakeside, and provides education for children from India and abroad between the ages of five and 18. There is also the Highclere School for Girls and the Bhavan's Gandhi Vidyasram School, founded in 1983, which are on the way to Pillar Rocks.

Bear Shola Falls, named because it once attracted bears, is a favourite picnic spot about 2 km from the Bus Stand. These falls and others around Kodai have been reduced to a trickle. **Solar Physical Observatory** ⓘ *4 km to the west from the Bus Stand, T04542-240588, during the season, Fri 1000-1230, 1900-2100*, was established in 1899 at a height of 2347 m. **Pillar Rocks**, 7 km from the lake, is another striking viewpoint. There are three granite formations over 120 m high. There have been over 100 dolmens and other megalithic remains discovered in the Palanis, all datable to around the second century AD.

The small but interesting **Shenbaganur Museum** ⓘ *1000-1130, 1500-1700*, is the local flora and fauna museum including 300 orchid species at the Sacred Heart College, a theological seminary founded in 1895. It also has some archaeological remains. There is an attractive walk downhill from the town passing waterfalls.

Kodaikkanal

Related map
A Kodaikkanal centre, page 139.

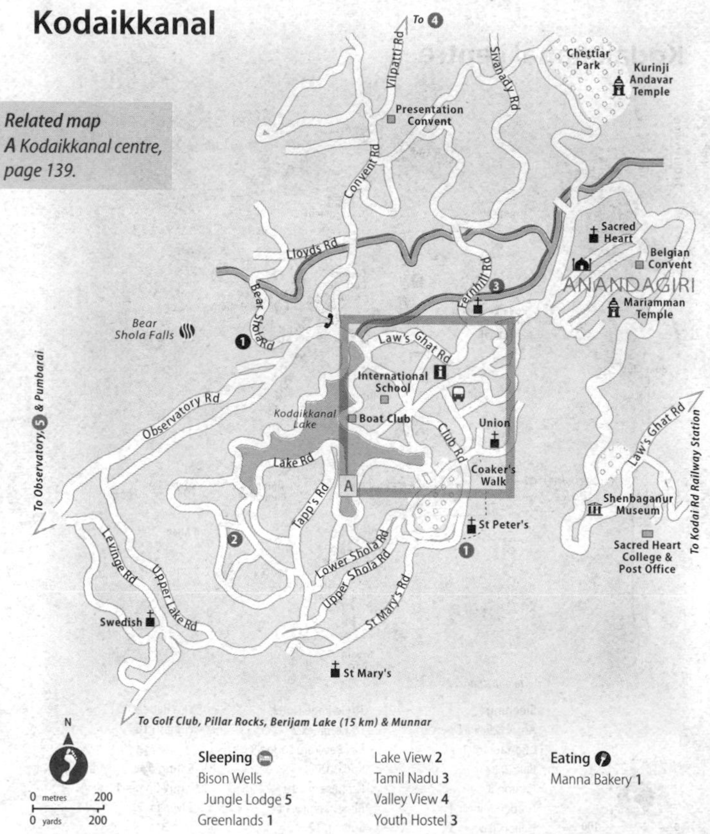

Around Kodaikkanal

A road runs west past the golf course and Pillar Rocks to **Berijam Lake**, 15 km away, which has beautiful views over the lake before running down to it. Apart from timber lorries the road is little used. You can walk to Berijam in about four hours and stay at the adequate **Forest Rest House**, Rs 50. There is a restaurant but no shop here.

You can continue the next day, by a short cut to **Top Station** in Kerala in five to six hours, where there is Forest Hut and shops and tea stalls selling snacks. There are then buses to **Munnar** 41 km away.

The ghat road to **Palani** passes through smallholdings of coffee, oranges and bananas. Interplanting of crops such as pepper is further increasing the yields from what can be highly productive land, even on steep slopes. The hilltop shrine to **Murugan** (Subrahmanya) is a very important site of pilgrimage. At full moon in January to February pilgrims walk from up to 80 km around and climb the 659 steps up to the shrine. Many carry shoulder poles with elaborate bamboo or wooden structures on each end, living out the myth that surrounds the origin of the shrine. There are buses to Kodai and Madurai (three hours).

Pollachi has a population of 88,300 and is 61 km from Madurai. It has been an important trading centre for over 2000 years, as is witnessed by the finds of Roman silver coins bearing the heads of the emperors Augustus and Tiberias. Today it still occupies an important position on the route from east to west through the Palakkad Gap. It is also the gateway to the small but very attractive sanctuary.

Anamalai (Indira Gandhi) National Park ⓘ *Reception and Information Centre is at Top Slip, written permission is needed from District Forest Officer, Pollachi, T04259-225356 (1½ km out of town on road towards Top Slip), best time to visit Dec-Jun, avoid Sun, 0630-1830*, near Pollachi, covers an area of 960 sq km in the western ghats. It is a beautiful, unspoilt forest, rarely visited, except by Indian day trippers. Wildlife includes Nilgiri langur, lion-tailed macaque, elephant, *gaur*, tiger, panther, sloth, wild boar, birds – including pied hornbill, drongo, red whiskered bulbul, black-headed oriole – and a large number of crocodiles in the Amaravathi reservoir. There is an elephant camp reached by a minibus ride through the forest, but rides can be disappointing. To view there are Forest Department vans (for eight), Rs 80. Restricted zone viewing, 0630-1900, 1700-1830. Birdwatching from Kariam Shola watch tower, 2 km from Topslip.

There are some **trekking** routes that vary from easy treks to Pandaravara (8 km), Kozhikamuthi (12 km) and Perunkundru peak (32 km), which is demanding. Permits from Range Officer, Topslip. Private guides charge Rs 50 for two.

Dindigul » *pp145-150.*

Now a large market town, Dindigul, north of Madurai, commands a strategic gap between the **Sirumalai Hills** to its east and the **Palani Hills** to the west. The market handles the produce of the Sirumalai Hills, including a renowned local variety of banana. Dindigul is particularly known for its cheroots.

The massive granite rock and **fort** ⓘ *2 km west of the bus stand, 0730-1730, Rs 5, foreigners Rs 100, autos Rs 20*, towers over 90 m above the plain. The Mysore army captured it in 1745 and Haidar Ali was appointed governor in 1755. It was ceded to the British under the Treaty of Seringapatam. There are magnificent views of the town, the valley and the hills on either side from the top of the rock fort. **Our Lady of Dolours Church**, one of several churches in the town, is over 250 years old and was rebuilt in 1970. The Old City is interesting to walk around; you can walk up to the fort from there. The station is 2 km south of the bus stand that has cheap lodges nearby.

Sleeping

Ooty *p133, map p134*
Rates quoted are for the 'Season'. Good discounts Jul-Mar except during Puja and Christmas. Add 30% tax in upper categories. Winter nights can be bitterly cold and hotel fireplaces are often inadequate. Avoid the budget accommodation round Commercial Rd and Ettines Rd, particularly if you are a woman travelling alone.

LL-L Fernhills Palace, Fernhill Post, T0423-244 3910, www.fernhillspalace.com. After years of stop-start renovation, Wadiyar, the current Mysore Maharaja has opened his ancestral palace as a luxury heritage hotel. It offers 30 suites, with teak furniture, wooden panelling, fireplaces and jacuzzis. Spa, gym, plus correspondingly high price tags.

AL Savoy (Taj), 77 Sylkes Rd, T0423-244 4142, www.tajhotels.com. Worth visiting for its interesting history and lovely gardens. 40 well-maintained rooms with huge wooden doors and separate dressing areas.

B-C Hotel Regency Villa, Fernhill Post, T0423-244 2555, regency@sancharnet.in. The Maharaja of Mysore's staff had some of the best sunset views of the blue hills from their bungalows. Today it has mismatched carpets, peeling paint and the cheaper rooms are small and musty, but despite that the hotel, with its rows of colonial photographs, reeks of character too. Log fire fuel costs extra.

C Glyngarth Heritage, Golf Club Rd, Fingerpost (2 km from centre), T0423-244 5754, www.glyngarthvilla.com. Just 5 huge double rooms with period furniture plus original fittings including all-teak floors and fireplaces in a Raj building – complete with metal roof – dating from 1853. Modern bathrooms, meals made from fresh garden produce, large grounds, clean, excellent service, tremendously characterful (too much for some) good value. Walking distance to golf course. Recommended.

C-D Hotel Lakeview, West Lake Rd, T0423-244 3580, lakeview@md3.vsnl.net.in. A little bit of an Indian hill station Butlins. 115 big rooms in rows of pink bungalows with fireplaces, TV and matching furniture. Lawns to sit on with busloads of domestic tourists.

C-D The Nilgiri Woodlands, Race Course Rd, T0423-244 2551, nilgiris_woodlands@yahoo.com. 22 rooms ranging from paint-peeling doubles to spacious cottages. Shared veranda outside racecourse-facing rooms that give onto a garden and the pink/green/blue bungalows of Ooty central. Quiet and spacious rooms tucked round the back (without views) are best value.

D Tamil Nadu (TTDC), Charing Cross, up steps by Tourist Office, T0423-244 4378. Spotless rooms and penthouse with good views, restaurant, bar, exchange, pleasant hotel tucked away. Avoid the food.

D YWCA Anandagiri, Ettines Rd, T0423-244 2218. Basic, a little institutional, 32 rooms set around large complex screened from town by pine trees, with nice sitting rooms and dining hall, potted geraniums dotted around. Pleasant, large cottages, dorm beds Rs 99.

D-E Reflections Guest House, North Lake Rd, T0423-244 3834. Clean, homely, quiet, with good views of the lake, 9 rooms (cheaper dorm beds), pleasant dining and sitting room serving good food, friendly owners. Rs 50 for wood for the fire or to use the stove for your own cooking, dodgy plumbing, can get chilly, restricted hot water.

Coonoor *p136*
Most hotels are 3-5 km from the station and bus stand.

AL-A Taj Garden Retreat, Church Rd, Upper Coonoor, T0423-223 0021, www.tajhotels.com. 32 rooms, spacious cottage style and homely (**A** off season), many with open fires, very well kept, good dining room though service can be slow, beautiful gardens, yoga studio, treadmill, table tennis, tennis, ayurvedic centre, but no pool. Wood-panelled high-ceilinged bar, **The Hampton**, 1130-1500, 1830-2200. Lunch 1230-1500, dinner 1930-2230.

A The Tryst, Carolina Tea Estate, Coonoor, T0423-220 7057, www.trystindia.com. The shelves at this homestay groan under years of hoarding, the playlist is strictly jazz or country and western. 5 double rooms in this deceptively large house with well-stocked

For an explanation of the sleeping and eating price codes used in this guide, see inside the front cover. Other relevant information is found in Essentials pages 40-44.

library, snooker table, games galore and gym. Unexpected and in an outstanding location away from all other accommodation cradled in the nape of a rolling tea estate. Excellent walking. Book in advance.

E Tamil Nadu (TTDC), Ooty Rd, Mt Pleasant (1 km north of station), T0423-223 2813. Simple rooms, TV, restaurant, bar and youth hostel dorm.

E 'Wyoming' Holiday Home (YWCA), near Hospital, Upper Coonoor (auto from bus stand Rs 25), T0423-223 4426. In house with character and idyllic views, 8 large rooms and 2 dorms (8-bedded), excellent food (no alcohol) but some warn you should check bill and watch out for the neurotic Labrador who is known to bark through the night. Garden, friendly, helpful, popular. Manager qualified in alternative therapies (runs clinic and courses). Book ahead.

E Top Hill Lodge, near police station, Kotagiri. With rooms, restaurant and bar.

F Blue Star, Kotagiri, next to bus station. Rooms with shower and toilet in modern building.

Mettupalayam *p136*

D Saravana Bhavan, out of town on Ooty road near gates to Black Thunder Water theme park. Newish and finding its feet.

E-F Bharath Bharan, 200 m from railway station. Very basic, some with bath and a/c, could be cleaner, quiet surroundings.

F Surya International, town centre, fairly clean rooms (Rs 150), rooftop restaurant, often empty, quiet, but characterless.

Karna Hotel in the bus station is good for dosas.

Mudumalai Wildlife Sanctuary *p137*

Advance booking is essential especially during the season and at weekends. Accommodation is better near Masinagudi which also has restaurants and shops but there is some in Bokkapuram, 3 km further south. Ask private lodges for pick-up if arriving by bus at Theppakadu.

B Bamboo Banks Farm Guest House, Masinagudi, T0423-252 6222, bambanks@hotmail.com. 6 clean rooms, 4 in cottages in a fine setting, attractive garden, good food, birdwatching, riding, jeep.

C Jungle Retreat, Bokkapuram, T0423-252 6469, www.jungleretreat.com. 5 large rooms and 7 cottages with modern baths, private terrace, superb views, "wonderful quiet place", friendly relaxed owners (Mr and Mrs Mathias), high standards, TV, hot water etc, good treks with local guides, elephant rides, excellent swimming pool, somewhat pricey food (choice of Indian and Western). TCs accepted. Highly recommended.

C Monarch Safari Park, Bokkapuram, on a hill side, T0423-252 6326. Large grounds, with 14 rooms in twin *machan* huts on stilts with bath (but rats enter at night), open-sided restaurant, cycles, birdwatching, good riding (Rs 150 per hr), some sports facilities, meditation centre, "lovely spot", management a bit slack but friendly, if slow, service.

C-D Blue Valley Resorts, Bokkapuram, T0423-252 6244. Scenic location, 8 comfortable huts (**C** suites), restaurants, wildlife tours.

C-D Jungle Hut, near Bokkapuram, T0423-252 6240. In valley, 12 clean, simple rooms with bath in 3 stone cottages, good food ("lovely home cooking"), pool, jeep hire, game viewing and treks, very friendly welcome. Recommended.

D Forest Hills Farm, 300 m from **Jungle Hut**, T0423-252 6216. Friendly, 6 modern rooms with bath and views, good food, game viewing. Recommended.

D Jungle Trails, 2 km off Sighur Ghat Rd (23 km from Ooty, ask bus to stop; flat walk, well marked), T0423-252 6256. 3 clean rooms in a bungalow, rustic ("bamboo shutters propped open with poles"), dorm beds (Rs 100), and *machan* hut good for viewing the moving tapestry (4 trails and a waterhole are visible). Meals Rs 200. The place is dedicated to animal watching: be quiet after dark, no candles on verandah, and no sitting in the garden by moonlight. Read *Cheetal Walk*, 1997, by A Davidas, the owner's father. Recommended.

D-E Mountania, Masinagudi (500 m from bus stand), T0423-252 6337. Rooms in cottages (prices vary), "nice but a bit overpriced", restaurant, jeep tour to waterfalls, easy animal spotting (evening better than morning).

E Tamil Nadu (TTDC Youth Hostel), Theppakadu, T0423-252 6249. 3 rooms, 24 beds in dorm (Rs 45), restaurant, van for viewing.

Several Government Forest Department huts charge Rs 80 for double rooms; reserve in

advance through the Wildlife Warden, Mudumalai WLS, 1st floor, Mahalingam Building, Coonoor Rd, Ooty, T0423-244098 or Wildlife Warden, Kargudi.
F Peacock, Kargudi, 50-bed dorm, excellent food.
Abhayaranyam Rest House, Kargudi, 2 rooms.
Annexe, Kargudi, 2 rooms. Recommended.
Minivet and **Morgan**, Kargudi, dorm, 8 and 12 beds. All Rs 5 per bed.
Rest House and **Annexe**, Kargudi, ask for de luxe rooms.
Log House, Masinagudi, 5 rooms.
Rest House, Masinagudi, 3 rooms.

Coimbatore *p137*

B Heritage Inn, 38 Sivaswamy Rd, T0422-223 1451. Good restaurants, internet, excellent service, 63 modern, a/c rooms ('standard' good value).
B Nilgiris Nest, 739-A Avanashi Rd, T0422-221 7247, nilgiris@md3.vsnl.net.in, 2 km railway. 38 a/c rooms, some small, restaurant, bar, amazing supermarket downstairs (for Western snacks and last stop for supplies like tampons), business facilities, roof garden. Recommended.
B-C City Tower, Sivaswamy Rd (just off Dr Nanjappa Rd), Gandhipuram, near bus stand, T0422-223 0641, hotelcitytower@sify.com. 91 excellent redecorated rooms, some a/c, small balconies, 2 restaurants (rooftop tandoori), no alcohol, superb service. Recommended.
D-F Channma International, 18/109 Big Bazar St, T0422-239 6631. Oldish art deco-style hotel, 36 spacious clean rooms, tiny windows, restaurant, internet, health club and pool next door.
E-F KK Residency, 7 Shastri Rd, by Central Bus Stand, Ramnagar, T0422-223 2433. 42 smallish but clean rooms, 6 a/c, good condition, restaurant, friendly service. Recommended.
E-F Meena, 109 Kalingarayar St, T0422-223 5420. Small family hotel with 30 clean and pleasant rooms, vegetarian restaurant.

Salem *p138*

It is advisable to choose rooms away from the side of the road.
C Salem Castle, A-4 Bharati St, Swarnapuri, 4 km railway, T0427-244 8702. Rather brash modern hotel with 64 comfortable, very clean a/c rooms. Restaurants (good Chinese but expensive, the rest are Indian-style), coffee shop, bar, exchange, pool.
D-E City View, Omalur Main Rd, T0427-244 9715. Rooms with bath, some clean, strong a/c, meals, travel. **Shree Saravanabhavan** in the same block does good south Indian vegetarian.
D-E Ganesh Mahal, 323 Omalur Rd, T0427-233 2820. Modern and comfortable, 45 pleasant rooms, TV, good restaurant, bar.
D-E Raj Castle, 320 Omalur Rd, T0427-233 3532. 21 nicely fitted rooms, 4 a/c, some with balcony, TV, hot water mornings, tourist car.
D-E Selvam, T0427-244 9331. Clean rooms with bath, some a/c, good restaurant.
F Railway Retiring Rooms, battered but with olde-worlde feel.

Yercaud *p138*

Most hotels offer off-season discounts Jan-Mar, Aug-Dec.
C Sterling Resort, near Lady's Seat, T04281-222700. 59 rooms (few **B** suites), modern, excellent views.
D Shevaroys, Main (Hospital) Rd, near lake, T04281-222288. 32 rooms, 11 **C** cottages with baths, restaurant, bar, good views.
D Tamil Nadu (TTDC), Salem-Yercaud Ghat Rd, near lake, behind Panchayat Office, T04281-222273. 12 rooms, restaurant, garden.
E Kapilaksa, Arthur Seat Rd (10-min walk from bus stand). Clean rooms, good views from balcony and roof, quiet, no discount.
G Youth Hostel, dorm bed (Rs 125), simple, reservations T04281-283 0390.

Kodaikkanal *p138, maps p139 and p140*

More expensive hotels are some distance from the centre. Off-season rates are given. Prices rise by 30-50% Apr-Jun; 20% tax and service charges apply. On Anna Salai cheap basic lodges, mostly with shared bathroom, can charge Rs 400 in season.
A Carlton, Boat Club Rd, T04542-240056, carlton@krahejahospitality.com. Fully modernized but colonial-style hotel with 91 excellent rooms. Excellent restaurant, billiards, tennis, golf and boating, superb position on lake, often full in season. Recommended.
A-B Lake View (Sterling), 44 Gymkhana Rd, T04542-240313. Cottages, modern hotel/ apartment complex.

A-C Elephant Valley, T0413-265 5751, www.elephantvalley.com. The sister retreat to The Dune in Pondicherry, a 40-ha organic farm 20 km from Kodaikanal, and a great base for trekking, horse riding or just chilling out.
B Valley View (Sterling), Pallangi Rd, Vilpatti, T04542-240635. A bit overpriced, 39 modern rooms but most without valley view, half-board in season.
C Green Acres, 11/213 Lake Rd, T04542-242384. Well-appointed, clean rooms in pleasant colonial-style home, quiet, peaceful.
C RR Residency, Boathouse Rd, T04542-244300, rrresidency@rediffmail.com. 7 well-furnished, top-quality rooms in newish hotel, vegetarian restaurant next door.
C-D Bala, 11/49 Woodville Rd, opposite the bus station (entrance tucked away in private courtyard), T04542-241214, www.balacares.com. Classy hotel, 57 rooms, good vegetarian restaurant, friendly staff.
C-D Bison Wells Jungle Lodge, Camp George Observatory, T04542-224 0566, www.wilderness-explorer.com. This is cottage is for the nature purist, with no electricity and space for only 3, a whole mountain range away from the rest of the hill station. Jeep transport from Kody arranged on request at extra cost.
C-D Garden Manor, Lake Rd (10-min walk from bus), T04542-240461. Good location in pleasant gardens overlooking lake, with 7 rooms (including a 4-bed), restaurant with outdoor tables.
C-D J's Heritage, PT Rd, T04542-241323, jaherit@md5.vsnl.net.in. 14 clean, comfortably furnished rooms, quiet. Friendly and helpful management but expensive for what it is.
C-D Tamil Nadu (TTDC), 47 Fernhill Rd, T04542-241336. 15 mins' walk from Bus Station (away from most interesting walks), restaurant and bar.
C-D Villa Retreat, Coaker's Walk, T04542-240940, www.villaretreat.com. 8 de luxe rooms in an old house, 3 cottages (open fireplace), rustic, good service. Garden setting, excellent views, clean but overpriced.
D Hilltop Towers, Club Rd, T04542-240413, httowers@md3.vsnl.net in. 26 modern comfortable rooms, can be noisy but very friendly management, good restaurant, bakery. Recommended.
D Kodai, north end of Coaker's Walk, T04542-240632, krh@pronet.net.in. 50 well-furnished 'cottages' with balcony, great views, restaurant. Clean, spacious, quiet setting.
D-E Suhaag, opposite bus stand, T04542-241143. Good value, 20 comfortable rooms, TV, hot water; buses silent at night.
E Jewel, 7 Rd Junction, T04542-240518. 9 clean, adequate rooms, 24-hr hot water, friendly, good value.
E Kay Pee Yem Lodge, Anna Salai, T04542-240555. With 16 rooms.
E Paradise Inn, Laws Ghat Rd, T04542-241075. Now rather faded, but good views, 40 comfortable spacious rooms, restaurant.
E Vignesh, Laws Ghat Rd, near lake, T04542-244348. Old period-style house, 6 spacious rooms (can interconnect), good views, garden setting. Recommended.
E-F Anjay, Anna Salai, T04542-241080. 24 adequate rooms with balcony, popular.
E-F Sunrise, PO Rd. Basic but clean rooms with bath, front rooms best with excellent views, good value.
F Railway Station, cheap rooms and dorm.

Youth hostels

F Youth Hostel (TTDC), Fernhill Rd, T04542-241336. **D** rooms, dorm beds (Rs 60-1255).
G Greenlands, St Mary's Rd, Coaker's Walk end, T04542-240899. Clean, small and friendly budget traveller choice. 15 very basic, clean rooms (jug and bucket of hot water 0700-0900), amazing views. A few newish rooms are less atmospheric but have hot water on tap. Pleasant gardens, 62-bed dorm (Rs 55-65).

Around Kodaikkanal *p141*

E Sakti, Pollachi. Newish, large and smart, rooms, vegetarian restaurant.
F Forest Rest Houses, Top Slip, Mt Stuart, Varagaliar, Sethumadai and Amaravathinagar. May allow only 1 night's stay. Reservations: District Forest Officer, Coimbatore S Div, Mahalingam Nagar, Pollachi, T04259-22508. The friendly canteen serves good dosa and thalis for lunch.

Dindigul *p141*

B Cardamom House, Athoor village, Kamarajar Lakeside, T0451-262 4710. This pretty home of a retired British doctor from Southsea introduces you to Tamil village life in Athoor and is a good bridge for journeys between either Kerala and Tamil Nadu or

Trichy and Madurai. Tucked out of the way at the foothills of the Palani hills overlooking the birdlife-rich lake, 7 rooms spread across three buildings all with lake views.

C-D Maha Jyothi, Spencer Compound, T0451-243 4313, hotelmahajyothi@rediffmail.com. Range of rooms, a/c, clean, modern.

D Sukanya Lodge, by bus stand. Small, rather dark a/c rooms, but very clean, friendly staff, good value.

F Prakash, 9 Thiruvalluvar Salai, T0451-242 3577. 42 clean, spacious rooms. Recommended.

G Venkateshwar Lodge, near bus stand, T0451-242 5881. Very cheap, 50 rooms, basic, clean, vegetarian restaurant next door.

Eating

Ooty *p133, map p134*

There are usually bars in larger hotels. Southern Star is recommended, but pricey.

TTT Savoy, olde-worlde wood-panelled dining hall serving up and good food. Also has bar, café, snooker and table tennis halls.

TT Chandan Vegetarian, Nahar Nilgiris, Charing Cross, T0423-244 2173. Open 1230-1530, 1900-2230. Roomy restaurant inside the Nahar hotel complex serving up vegetarian North Indian and Chinese food.

TT The Pavilion, **Fortune Hotel**, 500 m from town, Sullivan Court, 123 Shelbourne Rd, T0423-244 1415. In modern hotel, good multi-cuisine plus separate bar.

T Blue Hills, Charing Cross. Good value Indian and Continental, non-vegetarian.

T Garden Café, Nahar Nilgiris, Charing Cross. 0730-2130. Lawn-side coffee shop and snack bar with South Indian menu: iddli, dosa and *chats* from Rs 30.

T Hot Breads, Charing Cross. Tasty hot dogs, pizzas etc.

T Hotel Ooty Saravanaa's, 302 Commercial Rd. 0730-1000, 1130-2230. The place for super-cheap south Indian breakfast: large mint green place that does a fast trade in iddli, dosa and meals.

T Sharma Bhojanalaya 12C Lower Bazar Rd. Gujarati and North Indian food served upstairs in comfortable (padded banquettes) but not aesthetically pleasing venue, overlooks race course, good vegetarian lunch thali (Rs 40).

T Shinkow's, 38/83 Commissioner's Rd (near Collector's Office) T0423-244 2811. 1200-1545, 1830-2145. Authentic Chinese, popular, especially late evening. Chicken chilli Rs 120. Tartan tablecloths and fish tank. Highly recommended.

Cafés

Try the local institutions **Sugar Daddy** and **King Star** (established in 1942), 1130-2030, for brilliant homemade chocolates like fruit'n'nut and fudges. **Nilgiri Dairy Farms** outlets sell quality milk products.

Coonoor *p136*

TT Velan Hotel Ritz, Bedford, T0423-223 0632. Open 0730-1030, 1230-1530, 1930-2230. Good multi-cusine restaurant overlooking the Ritz's lawns – don't expect speedy service though.

T The Only Place, Sim's Park Rd. Simple, homely, good food.

T Sri Lakshmi, next to bus station. Freshly cooked, quality vegetarian; try paneer butter masala and Kashmiri naan.

Coimbatore *p137*

TTT Cloud Nine, **City Tower Hotel**. Excellent views from rooftop of one of city's tallest buildings, good international food (try asparagus soup), buzzy atmosphere especially when it's full of families on Sun evening, pleasant service but slightly puzzling menu.

TT Dakshin in **Shree Annapoorna Hotel** Complex, 47 East Arokiasamy Rd, RS Puram. International. Very smart, serving good food.

TT Dasa, vegetarian. A/c, good ice creams.

TT Solai Drive-in, Nehru Stadium, near VOC Park. Chinese, Indian food and good ice creams.

T Indian Coffee House, Ramar Koil St. South Indian snacks.

T Royal Hindu, opposite Junction station. Indian vegetarian.

Kodaikkanal *p138, maps p139 and p140*

TTT Carlton Hotel, set in very pleasant grounds overlooking lake and Garden Manor, good for tea and snacks.

TTT Tava, Hospital Rd, very good Indian.

TT Royal Tibet Hotel, J's Heritage Complex, "try noodle soup and beef momos".

₹₹ Silver Inn, Hospital Rd. Indian and travellers' breakfasts. Popular, slow service.
₹₹ Tibetan Brothers Hotel, J's Heritage Complex. 1200-2200 (closed 1600-1730) serves excellent Tibetan, homely atmosphere, good value. Highly recommended.
₹ Apna Punjab in 7 Rd (Indian).

Bakery and fast food
Eco-Nut, J's Heritage Complex, good whole foods, brown bread, jams, peanut butter etc (cheese, yoghurts, better and cheaper in Dairy across the road).
Hot Breads, J's Heritage Complex. For very good pastries.
Manna Bakery on Bear Shola Rd. Also serves pizzas and western vegetarian.
Pastry Corner Anna Salai Bazar, has brown bread and some pastries.
Philco's Cold Storage, opposite Kodai International School, J's Heritage Complex. For homemade chocolate, cakes, frozen foods, delicatessen. Also internet.
Spencer's Supermarket, Club Rd. Wide range of local and foreign products (cheeses).

Dindigul *p141*
Cascade Roof Garden, at Sree Arya Bhavan, 19 KHF Building, near the bus stand, which serves very good vegetarian. West of the bus stand, Main Road is the shopping area.
Janakikarm, near new Roman Catholic Church. Don't miss their pizzas, sweets and snacks, surprisingly good value, "*channa samosa* to die for".

Festivals and events

Ooty *p133, map p134*
Jan: Pongal. **May**: the **Annual Flower and Dog Shows** in the Botanical Gardens. **Summer Festival** of cultural programmes with stars from all over India.

Kodaikkanal *p138, maps p139 and p140*
May: Summer Tourist Festival: Boat race, flower show, dog show etc.

Shopping

Ooty *p133, map p134*
Most shops open 0900-1200, 1500-2000. The smaller shops keep longer hours.
Higginbotham's, Commercial Rd, Ooty, T0423-244 3736. 0930-1300, 1550-1930, closed Wed. Bookseller.
Toda Showroom, Charing Cross, sells silver and tribal shawls.
Variety Hall, Silver Market, old family firm (1890s) for good range of silk, helpful, accepts credit cards.

Kodaikkanal *p138, maps p139 and p140*
Belgian Convent shop, east of town. Hand embroidered linen.
Cottage Crafts Shop, Anna Salai (Council for Social Concerns in Kodai). Volunteer run, Mon-Sat 0900-1230, 1400-1830.
Govt Sales Emporium near Township Bus Stand. Only open in season.
Kashmir Handicrafts Centre, 2 North Shopping Complex, Anna Salai. Jewellery, brass, shawls, walnut wood crafts and Numdah rugs.
Khadi Emporium, Handloom Co-op, Travancore Craft Works, Post Office Rd.

Activities and tours

Ooty *p133, map p134*
Horse riding
Gymkhana Club, T0423-244 2254. Big bar open 1130-1530 or 1830-2300. Temporary membership; beautifully situated amidst superbly maintained 18-hole golf course. Riding from Regency Villa: Rs 500 for 2 hrs with 'guide'; good fun but no helmets.

Tours
TTDC, Reservations, **Hotel Tamil Nadu**, T0423-244 4370. Ooty and Mudumalai: Ooty Lake, Dodabetta Peak, Botanical Gardens, Mudumalai Wildlife Sanctuary. 0830-2000. Rs 150. Kotagiri and Coonoor: Kotagiri, Kodanad View Point, Lamb's Rock, Dolphin's Nose, Sim's Park. 0830-1830. Rs 130.
Woodlands Tourism, Race Course Rd, T0423-244 2551. Offers Ooty and Coonoor: 0930-1730. Rs 130. Stunning views.

Tour operators
Blue Mountain, Nahar Complex, Charing Cross, T0423-244 3650. Luxury coach bookings to neighbouring states.
George Hawkes, 52C Nahar Complex, T0423-244 2756. For tourist taxis.
Sangeetha Travels, 13 Bharathiyar Complex, Charing Cross, T0432-244 4782. Steam train.

Yoga

Rajayoga Meditation Centre, 88 Victoria Hall, Ettines Rd.

Coonoor *p136*

TTDC from Ooty (reserve in Ooty Tourist Office). Coonoor-Kotagiri Rs 120, 6 hrs; visiting Valley View, Sim's Park, Lamb's Rock, Dolphin's Nose, Kodadu view point.

Yercaud *p138*

Tourist information at **Hotel Tamil Nadu**, T04281-22273.

Kodaikkanal *p138, maps p139 and p140*

Boating

Boat Club, T04542-241315. Allows daily membership with club facilities. 0900-1730.
TTDC Boathouse, next door. 0900-1730.

Golf

Club, T04542-240323.

Riding

Ponies near the Boat House; officially Rs 100 per hr, doubled to include 'guide' (bargaining essential).

Tour operators

Sugam, PO Rd, Upper Coonoor, Railway Out Agency.
Vijay Tours, near Tourist Information Centre, Anna Salai, T04542-241137. Local sights, Rs 70-80 per person.

Transport

Ooty *p133, map p134*

Arrive early for buses to ensure a seat. They often leave early if full. Ghat roads have numerous hairpin bends which can have fairly heavy traffic and very bad surfaces at times. The Gudalur road passes through Mudumalai and Bandipur sanctuaries (see page 137). You might see an elephant herd and other wildlife, especially at night.

Air

Nearest airport, Coimbatore, 105 km.

Bus

Cheran, T04223-244 3970. Frequent buses to **Coimbatore** (every 20 mins, 0530-2000, 3½ hrs), **Coonoor** (every 10 mins, 0530-2045), and **Mettupalayam** (0530-2100, 2 hrs). Also to **Bengaluru (Bangalore)** (0630-2000), **Mysore** (0800-1530, 3½-5 hrs) and **Kozhikode** (0630-1515), **Chennai** (1630-1830), **Palakkad** (0715-1515), **Palani** (0800-1800). Daily buses to **Hassan** (1130, 1500), **Kannur** (0915, 2000), **Kanniyakumari** (1745), **Kodaikkanal** (0630, 9½ hrs via magnificent route through Palani, Madikere (0700, 1100), **Pondicherry** (1700), **Salem** (1300). Check timings. Several on the short route (36 km) to **Masinagudi/Mudumalai**, Rs 7, 1½ hrs; a steep and windy but interesting road.

Train

Railway station, T0423-244 2246. From **Mettupalayam** *Blue Mountain* (steam to **Coonoor**; then diesel to Ooty), 2 return trains daily, see Mettupalayam transport, below. The *Heritage Steam Chariot* to **Runneymede** runs at weekends (more frequent in season). It departs Ooty 1000, returns 1600 (delayed when engine runs out of steam!). Highly recommended. Tickets include Indian packed lunch: Rs 280, or Rs 550 in Maharaja coach, from Sangeetha (listed above) or Ooty railway station.

Coonoor *p136*

Bus

Frequent buses to **Ooty** (every 10 mins from 0530) some via Sim's Park and many via Wellington. Also regular services to **Kotagiri** and **Coimbatore** (every 30 mins) through **Mettupalayam**. Direct bus to **Mysore** (or change at Ooty).

Train

The *Blue Mountain Railway* runs from **Mettupalayam** to Coonoor (steam), 3 hrs; continues to **Ooty** (diesel), 1½ hrs. See Mettupalayam transport, below. The *Heritage Steam Chariot* runs from Ooty to **Runneymede** beyond Coonoor. See Ooty transport, above.

Mettupalayam *p136*

The *Nilgiri Exp* from Chennai via Coimbatore, connects with the *Blue Mountain Railway*. (This line is subject to landslides and washouts that can close the route for some months. Check before travelling.) From **Chennai** *6605*, 2015, 10 hrs; to Chennai,

6606, 1925, 10½ hrs. For those coming from Coimbatore, it is better to arrive in advance at Mettupalayam by bus; this avoids a mad dash at the station from Platform 2 to 1 to catch the connecting train.

The first part of the *Blue Mountain Railway* from Mettupalayam to Coonoor is by steam when not disrupted by landslides (great to look around the engine sheds!); from there to Ooty by diesel. To **Coonoor** and **Ooty** 2 return trains daily; *562(S)*, 0710, arrive Coonoor, 1030, Ooty, 1200 (5½ hrs); return from Ooty, *561(S)*, 1500, arrive Coonoor, 1605, Mettupalayam 1835, 3½ hrs. Also *564(S)*, 1315, arrive Coonoor, 1610, Ooty, 1745; return from Ooty next day *567(S)*, 0915, arrive Coonoor, 1025, Mettupalayam 1245. The *Heritage Steam Chariot* runs from Ooty to Runneymede. See Ooty above.

Mudumalai Wildlife Sanctuary *p137*
Theppakadu is on the Mysore-Ooty bus route. From **Mysore**, services from 0615 (1½-2 hrs); last bus to Mysore around 2000. From **Ooty** via **Gudalur** on a very winding road (about 2½ hrs); direct 20 km steep road used by buses, under 1 hr. Few buses between Theppakadu and Masinagudi.

Jeeps are available at bus stands and from lodges.

Coimbatore *p137*
Air Peelamedu Airport, 12 km centre, runs airport coach into town, Rs 25; taxis Rs 150-200; auto-rickshaw Rs 85. On Trichy Rd: **Indian Airlines**, T0422-239 9833, airport T0422-257 4623, 1000-1300, 1345-1730. To **Bengaluru (Bangalore)**, **Chennai**, **Delhi**, **Kochi**, **Kozhikode**, **Mumbai**. Jet Airways: 1055/1 Gowtham Centre, Avinashi Rd, T0422-221 2034, airport T0422-257 5375 to **Bengaluru (Bangalore)**, **Chennai**, **Mumbai**.

Bus City buses run a good service: several connect the bus stations in Gandhipuram with the Junction Railway Station 2 km south. No 20 goes to the airport (Rs 20).

There are 4 long-distance bus stations, off Dr Nanjappa Rd. **City or 'Town' Bus Stand** in Gandhipuram. **Thiruvallur Bus Stand**, Cross Cut Rd. Computerized reservations 0700-2100, T0422-226700. Frequent Government Express buses to **Madurai** (5 hrs), **Chennai** (12 hrs), **Mysore** (6 hrs), **Ooty** (3 hrs), **Tiruchirappalli** (5½ hrs). 'Central' Bus Stand is further south, on corner of Shastri Rd. State buses to **Bengaluru (Bangalore)** and **Mysore**; **Ooty** via **Mettupalayam** (see below for train connection) and **Coonoor** every 20 mins, 0400-2400, 5 hrs. **Ukkadam Bus Stand**, south of the city, serves towns within the state (**Pollachi**, **Madurai**) and in north Kerala (**Pallakad**, **Thrissur**, **Munnar**).

Taxi Tourist taxis and yellow top taxis are available at the bus stations, railway station and taxi stands. Rs 2.50 per km; for out-station hill journeys, Rs 3 per km; minimum Rs 30.

Train Junction Station, enquiries, T132, reservations, T131, 0700-1300, 1400-2030. **Bengalore (Bangalore)**: *Tilak Exp 1014*, 0515, 7¼ hrs; *Intercity Exp 2678*, 1425, 7 hrs; **Kanniyakumari**: *Bangalore Exp 6525*, 1955, 9 hrs. **Chennai**: *West Coast Exp 6628*, 0630, 9 hrs; *Kovai Exp 2676*, 1340, 7½ hrs; *Nilgiri Exp 6606*, 2040, 9¼ hrs. **Kochi** (HT): *Tiruchirappalli- Kochi Exp 6865*, 0045, 5½ hrs; *Hyderabad-Kochi Exp 7030*, 0935, daily, 5½ hrs. Other trains: *W Coast Exp* (Chennai-Coimbatore-Kozhikode -Bengaluru), daily to Kozhikode (4½ hrs) and Bengaluru (9 hrs). For **Ooty**, train departing 0625 connects with narrow gauge steam train from Mettupalayam. Line to Coonoor is subject to landslides. Narrow gauge diesel from Coonoor to Ooty. There are two connecting trains daily: *Nilgiri Exp 6605*, 0525, change to train *562* (S), 0710, arrive Ooty 1200; *Trichur-Mettypalayam Pass 534 (S)*, 1100, change to train *564* (S), 1315 arrive Ooty 1745.

Salem *p138*
Bus The new bus stand (T0427-2265917), north of the Hospital, off Omalur Rd, has buses to **Namakkal**, 1¼ hrs. Salem is well connected by bus with all major towns in Tamil Nadu, Kerala and South Karnataka. TN Government Express buses, to **Dindigul**, 4 hrs.
Train Junction is the main train station. Enquiries, T132. Reservations, T131, 0700-1300, 1400-2030. **Bengaluru (Bangalore)**: *Tilak Exp 1014*, 0750, 4½ hrs; *Intercity Exp 2678*, 1705, 4 hrs. **Chennai (C)**: *Coimbatore-Chennai Exp 2680*, 0835, 5 hrs. **Kochi (HT) (Cochin)**: *Hyderabad Cochin Exp 7030*, 0615, not Tue, 9 hrs; *Raptisagar Exp 5012/5222*,

0830, Mon, Thu, Fri, Sun, 9¾ hrs. **Madurai**: *Mumbai-Nagercoil Exp 6339,* not Tue, Wed, Sun, 1735, 6 hrs. **Ramesvaram**: no direct trains, change at Dindigul. For **Ooty**, *Nilgiri Exp 6605,* 0135, connects with narrow gauge steam train from Mettupalayam; departs **Mettupalayam** at 0745, arrives Ooty at 1200.

Yercaud *p138*
Bus No local buses. Some from Salem (1 hr) go through town, connecting with villages.

Kodaikkanal *p138, maps p139 and p140*
Bicycle Hire bikes at the top of the bazar. JM Tea shop and cycle hire, at Junction of Club Rd and Anna Salai, good bikes Rs 5 per hr, Rs 50 per day.

Bus Check timings; reservations possible. To **Bengaluru (Bangalore)**, overnight, 12 hrs; **Chennai** (497 km) 12 hrs, **Coimbatore** 6 hrs; **Dindigul** (90 km) 3½ hrs, Kodai Rd, **Madurai** (120 km), 0730-1830, 4 hrs, about Rs 25; **Kumily** (Periyar), 1415, 5½ hrs, Rs 35 (very busy) change buses at Vatigundu; **Palani** 3 hrs; **Tiruchirappalli** (197 km) 5 hrs, during the season.

Taxi Unmetered taxis available. Tourist taxis only from Madurai.

Train Reservations, Jayaraj Hall, Coaker's Walk Rd. **Kodai Road**, 80 km away, is the nearest station.

Around Kodaikkanal *p141*
From chaotic bus station at Pollachi (for Parambikulam) 0600, 1130, 1500 (check times); ask for Top Slip, from Perambikulam, 0700, 1300.

Dindigul *p141*
Bus Good and frequent bus service to **Tiruchirappalli**, **Chennai**, **Salem** and **Coimbatore** and long-distance connections.
Train Service to **Chennai (ME)** *Vaigai Exp 2636* (AC/CC), 0745, 6¾ hrs via **Tiruchirappalli** 1½ hrs. **Madurai** *Vaigai Exp 2635* (AC/CC), 1905, 1¼ hrs. Broad gauge to **Karur** 2240, 1½ hrs.

Directory

Ooty *p133, map p134*
Banks State Bank of India, on Bank Rd, deals in foreign exchange. **Internet** Gateways, 8/9 Moosa Sait Complex, Commercial Rd. Excellent, fast, ISDN lines, Rs 30 per hr. **Hospital** Govt Hospital, Hospital Rd, T0423-244 2212. **Post** Head Post Office, Collectorate and Telegraph Office, Town W Circle. **Tourist offices** Tamil Nadu, 7/72 Commercial Rd, Super Market, Charing Cross, T0423-244 3977, lacks efficiency. **Useful addresses** Police, T100. Wildlife Warden, 1st floor, Mahalingam Building, T0423-244098, 1000-1730. Closed 1300-1400.

Coonoor *p136*
Banks Travancore Bank, Upper Coonoor, (Bedford Circle) changes cash. South Indian Bank, Mount Rd, 1000-1400 changes cash and TCs. **Hospital** Lawley Hospital, Mt Rd, T0423-223 1050.

Coimbatore *p137*
Banks Several on Oppankara St. State Bank of India (exchange upstairs), and Bank of Baroda are on Bank Rd. **Hospital** Government Hospital, Trichy Rd. **Post** Near flyover, Railway Feeder Rd, fax. **Travel agents** Alooha, corner near Heritage Inn, helpful. **Useful addresses** Automobile Association, 42 Trichy Rd, T0422-222 2994.

Yercaud *p138*
Banks Banks with foreign exchange are on Main Rd. **Hospitals** Govt Hospital, 1 km from Bus Stand; Providence Hospital, on road to Lady's Seat. **Post** On the Main Rd.

Kodaikkanal *p138, maps p139 and p140*
Banks Several on Anna Salai, Mon-Fri 1000-1400, Sat 1000-1200. Indian Bank, for 15-min service. Hotel Tamil Nadu, has an exchange counter. **Hospitals** Van Allan Hospital, T04542-241273, is recommended. Consultations (non-emergency): Mon-Fri 0930-1200, 1530-1630. Sat 1000-1200. Clean and efficient, good doctors (not keen to prescribe antibiotics unnecessarily). Government Hospital, T04542-241292. **Post** Head Post Office on Post Office Rd. Others in Main Bazar, Observatory, Lake View, Anantha Giri, Pambapuram and Shenbaganur. **Tourist offices** Tamil Nadu, Rest House, near bus stand, T04542-241675. Open 1000-1745, except holidays. Helpful staff, maps available.

Madurai and around

→ *Phone code: 0452. Colour map 3, grid C4. Population: 922,900.*

Madurai is a maddening whirl of a temple town: the red-and-white striped sanctuary of the 'fish-eyed goddess' is a towering edifice crested by elaborate gaudy stucco-work gopurams, soundtracked by tinny religious songs, peopled by 10,000 devoted pilgrims prostrating themselves at shrines, lighting candles and presenting flower garlands to idols, seeking blessings from the temple elephant, or secure palmistry on the shores of the Golden Lotus tank. Even the city's town planning reflects the sanctity of the spot: surrounding streets radiate like bicycle spokes from the temple in the mandala architectural style, a sacred form of geometry. There is the usual combination of messy crumbling buildings harking back to times of greater architectural aspirations, modern glass-and-chrome palaces, internet cafés, flower sellers, tailors and tinkers and Kashmiri antique and shawl dealers. The centre seems all dust and cycle-rickshaws, but Madurai, as the second biggest city in Tamil Nadu, is also a modern industrial place that never sleeps. Around the city the area of fertile agricultural land is dotted with exotically shaped granite mountain ranges such as Nagamalai (snake hills) and Yanaimalai (elephant hills). ▸▸ *For Sleeping, Eating and other listings, see pages 160-165.*

Madurai ▸▸ *pp160-165.*

Ins and outs

Getting there The airport is 12 km from town and is linked by buses to the city centre, but there are also taxis and autos. The railway station is within easy walking distance of many budget hotels (predatory rickshaw drivers/hotel touts may tell you otherwise). Hire an auto to reach the few north of the river. The main express bus stand is next to the station though there are two others 3-6 km away, with bus links between them. ▸▸ *See Transport, page 163, for further details.*

Getting around The city centre is compact and the temple is within easy walking distance of most budget hotels. Prepare for hordes of touts. To visit the sights around the city, buses and taxis are available.

Tourist information ⓘ *W Veli St, T0452-233 7471, Mon-Fri 1000-1745*, has useful maps, tours arranged through agents, guides for hire. Also at Madurai Junction Railway Station ⓘ *Main Hall, 0630-2030*, and airport counter, during flight times.

History

According to legend, drops of nectar fell from Siva's locks on this site, so it was named Madhuram or Madurai, the nectar city. The city's history goes back to the sixth century BC. Ancient Madurai, which traded with Greece and Rome, was a centre of Tamil culture, famous for its writers and poets during the last period of the three *Sangam* (Tamil 'Academies') nearly 2000 years ago. The Pandiyans, a major power from the sixth to the early 10th century, made Madurai their capital. For the following 300 years, they remained here, although they were subservient to the Cholas who gained control over the area, after which the Pandiyans returned to power. For a short period it became a Sultanate after Malik Kafur completely destroyed the city in 1310.

William Dalrymple explains in The Age of Kali *that the Vaigai River, along whose banks Madurai is laid out, "was created by Lord Sundareshvara, the husband of Minakshi, to quench the thirst of one of his wedding guests, a dwarf named Pot Belly who had developed an unbearable thirst after eating 300 pounds of rice."*

In 1364 it was captured by Hindu Vijayanagar kings, who remained until 1565, after which the local governors the Nayakas asserted their independence.

After the defeat of Vijayanagar by the Muslim sultans of the Deccan, the Hindu rulers were pushed further south. The **Nayakas** emerged in the 17th century with their capital at Madurai and continued to build temple complexes with tall *gopurams*. These increased in height to become dominating structures covered profusely with plaster decorations. The tall *gopurams*of Vijayanagar and Nayaka periods may have served a strategic purpose, but they moved away from the earlier *Chola* practice of giving the central shrine the tallest tower. The *kalyana mandapa* or marriage hall with a 'hundred' or 'thousand' pillars, and the temple tank with steps on all four sides, were introduced in some southern temples, along with the *Nandi* bull, Siva's vehicle, which occupies a prominent position at the entrance to the main Shaivite shrine.

By the fourth century, Madurai, Tirunelveli and a part of southern Kerala were under the **Pandiyas**. Their power rose after the decline of the Cholas and they ruled from 1175 to 1300. In the 13th century, international trade flourished under their control and was only superseded by the rise of Vijayanagar (see Hampi, page 300).

The defeat of the great Vijayanagar Empire by a confederacy of Muslim states in 1565 forced their leaders south. As the Nayaka kings they continued to rule from as far

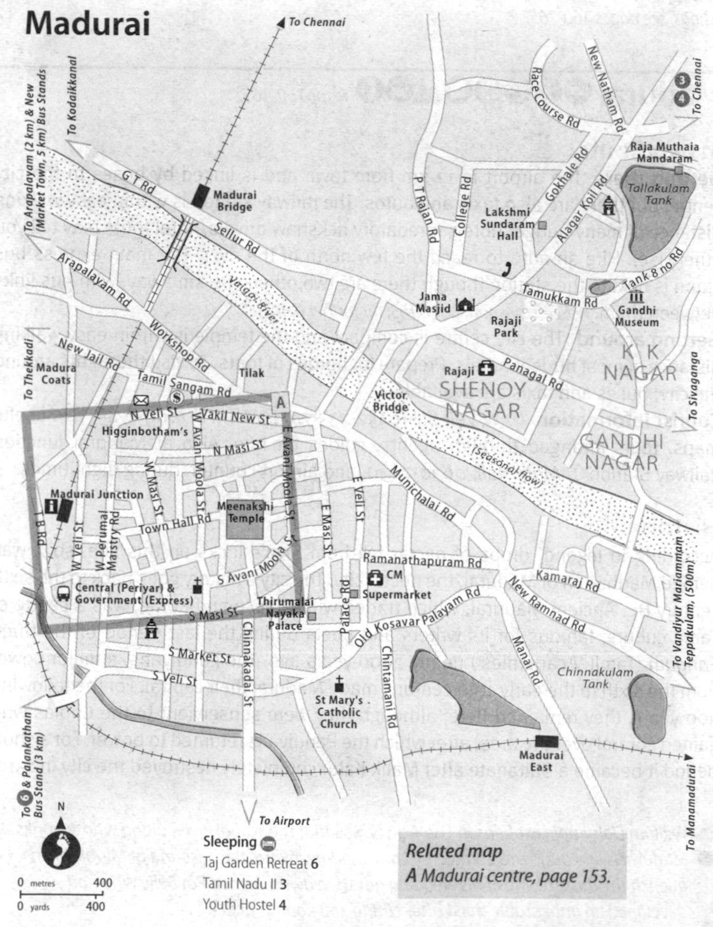

Related map
A Madurai centre, page 153.

south as Madurai well into the 17th century. Ultimately when Muslim political control finally reached Tamil Nadu it was as brief as it was tenuous.

The Nayakas have been seen essentially as warriors, given an official position by the Vijayanagar rulers; though in Sanskrit, the term applied to someone of prominence and leadership. Burton Stein comments, "the history of the Vijayanagara is essentially the history of the great Telugu Nayakas" from Madurai.

The Vijayanagar kings were great builders and preserved and enriched the architectural heritage of the town. The Nayakas laid out the old town in the pattern of a lotus with narrow streets surrounding the Minakshi Temple at the centre. The streets on the four sides of the central temple are named after the festivals which take place in them and give their relative direction, for example South 'Masi' Street, East 'Avanimoola' Street and East 'Chitrai' Street. The greatest of the Nayaka rulers, Thirumalai (ruled 1623-1655), built the *gopurams* of the temple. In 1840, after the Carnatic Wars, the British destroyed the fort, filling in the surrounding moat (its original site now followed by the four Veli streets).

Sights

Meenakshi Temple ⓘ *Inner Temple 0500-1230, 1600-2130, camera fee Rs 30, video not allowed, tickets at South Entrance (valid for multiple entry), the sanctuary is open only to Hindus, art museum 0600-2000, Rs 2, camera fee Rs 30 at the temple office near the South Tower, good views from the top of the South Gate when open.* This is an outstanding example of Vijayanagar temple architecture and an exact contemporary of the Taj Mahal in Agra. Meenakshi, the 'fish-eyed goddess' and the consort of Siva, has a temple to the south, and Sundareswarar (Siva), a temple to the west. Since she is the presiding deity the daily ceremonies are first performed in her shrine and, unlike the practice at other temples, Sundareswarar plays a secondary role. The temple's nine towering *gopurams* stand out with their colourful stucco images of gods, goddesses and animals which are renewed and painted every 12 years. There are about 4000 granite sculptures on the lower levels. In addition to the

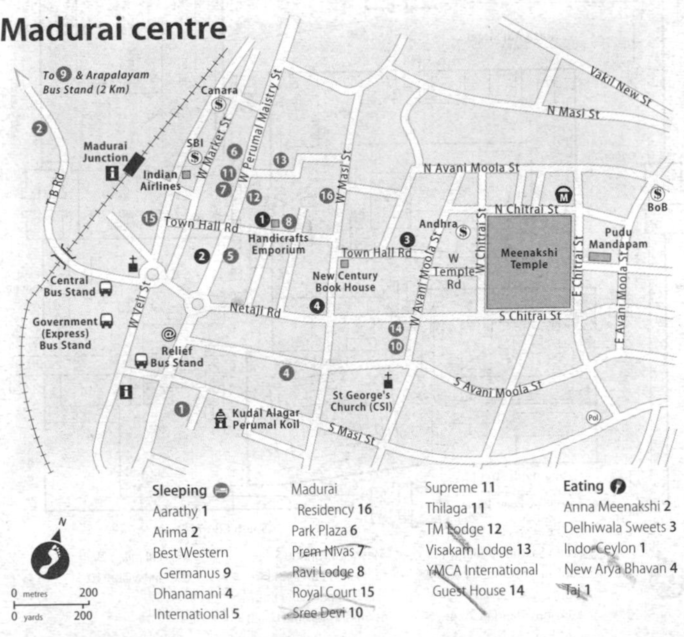

 Golden Lotus tank and various pillared halls there are five *vimanas* over the sanctuaries.

The temple is a hive of activity, with a colourful temple elephant, flower sellers and performances by **musicians** ⓘ *1800-1930, 2100-2200*. There is an evening ceremony in Madurai at 2040 and 2115, when an image of Sundareswarar is carried in procession (worth attending) from the shrine near the east *gopuram* to Meenakshi, to 'sleep' by her side, and is returned the next morning. The procession around the temple is occasionally led by the elephant and a cow. During the day the elephant is on continual duty, 'blessing' visitors with its trunk and then collecting a small offering. The flower and vegetable market, north end of East Chitrai Street, is a profusion of floral colour. Beware: offers of good viewpoints made by helpful bystanders will invariably turn out to be from the roofs of nearby shops.

The main entrance is through a small door of the **Ashta Sakthi Mandapa (1)** (Porch of the Eight Goddesses) which projects from the wall, south of the eastern *gopuram*. Inside to the left is the sacred **Tank of the Golden Lotus (2)**, with a lamp in the centre, surrounded by pillared cloisters and steps down to the waters. The Sangam legend speaks of the test that ancient manuscripts had to undergo; they were thrown into the sacred tank and if they sank they were worthless, if they floated they were considered worthy! The north gallery has 17th-century murals, relating 64 miracles said to have been performed by Siva, and the southern has marble inscriptions of the 1330 couplets of the *Tamil Book of Ethics*. To the west of the tank is the **Oonjal Mandapa (3)**, the pavilion leading to the Meenakshi shrine. Here the pillars are carved in the form of the mythical beast *yali* which recurs in temples throughout the region. Golden images of Meenakshi and Sundareswarar are brought to the *oonjal* or swing each Friday evening where they are worshipped. Cages with parrots, Meenakshi's green bird which brings luck, hang from the ceiling of the

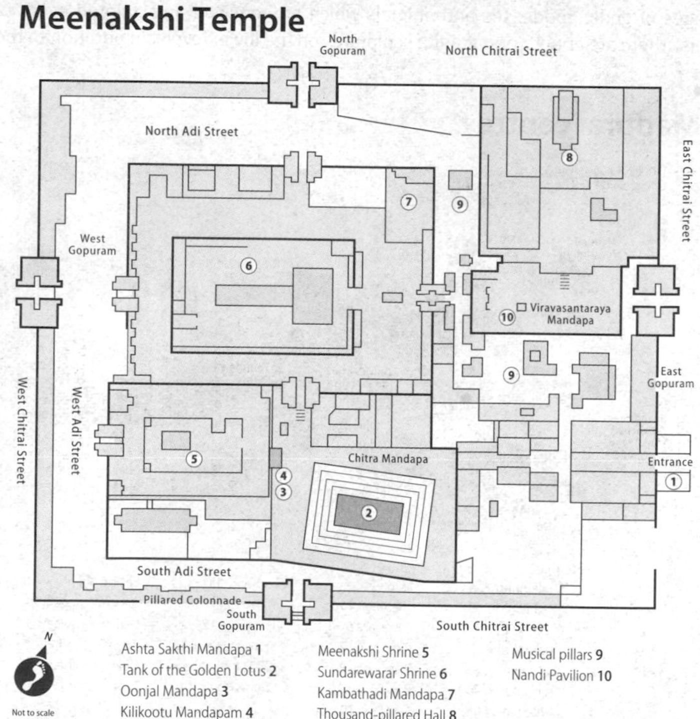

neighbouring **Kilikootu Mandapam (4)** which is flanked by finely carved columns. The **Meenakshi shrine (5)** with the principal image of the goddess, stands in its own enclosure with smaller shrines around it.

To the north of the tank is another enclosure with smaller *gopurams* on four sides within which is the **Sundareswarar shrine (6)** guarded by two tall *dwarapalas*. In the northeast corner, the superb sculptures of the divine marriage of Meenakshi and Sundareswarar being blessed by Vishnu and Brahma, and Siva in his 24 forms are in the 19th-century **Kambathadi Mandapa (7)**, around the golden flagstaff.

The mid-16th century **Thousand-pillared Hall (8)** is situated in the northeast corner of the complex. The 985 exquisitely carved columns include a lady playing the *vina*, a dancing Ganesh, and a gypsy leading a monkey. The art museum here exhibits temple art and architecture, fine brass and stone images, friezes and photos (the labelling could be improved). Just inside the museum to the right is a cluster of five **musical pillars (9)** carved out of a single stone. Each pillar produces a different note which vibrates when tapped. Nayaka musicians could play these as an instrument.

The **Nandi pavilion (10)** is to the east and is often occupied by flower sellers. The long *Pudu Mandapa* (New Mandapa), with its beautiful sculptures of *yalis* and Nayaka rulers and their ministers, is outside the enclosure wall, between the east tower and the base of the unfinished *Raya Gopuram* which was planned to be the tallest in the country.

Northeast of the Meenakshi Temple, off N Avani Moola Street, is the **flower market**, at its best 0500-0730. It is a two-storey hall with piles of jasmine of all colours, lotuses, and huge jumbles of floral prettiness in a sea of decomposing mulch of flowers trampled underfoot.

Thirumalai Nayaka Palace ⓘ *0900-1300, 1400-1700, bus 17, 17A, 11, 11A*. Built in 1636 in the Indo-Mughal style, its 15 domes and arches are adorned with stucco work while some of its 240 columns rise to 12 m. Its *Swarga Vilasam* (Celestial Pavilion), an arcaded octagonal structure, is curiously constructed in brick and mortar without any supporting rafters. Special artisans skilled in the use of traditional lime plaster and powdered seashell and quartz have renovated parts. The original complex had a shrine, an armoury, a theatre, royal quarters, a royal bandstand, a harem, a pond and a garden but only about a quarter survives since Thirumalai's grandson removed sections to build another palace in Tiruchirappalli, and the original *Ranga* Vilasam was destroyed by Muslim invaders. It is a bit run down.

Vandiyur Mariammam Teppakulam ⓘ *Buses 4 and 4A take 10 mins from the bus stand and railway station*. To the southeast of town, this has a small shrine in its centre where the annual **Float Festival** takes place in January/February.

Located in the 300-year-old Rani Mangammal Palace is Madurai's best museum, the **Gandhi Museum** ⓘ *1000-1300, 1400-1730, free, excellent bookshop*, which is informative, interesting and well laid out. It contains an art gallery, memorabilia (Gandhi's *dhoti* when he was shot) and traces the history of the Independence struggle from 1800 and the Quit India movement. It also has sections for Khadi and Village Industries and South Indian handicrafts. Yoga classes daily (in Tamil only) at 0630.

Thirumalai Nayaka Palace Museum This museum concentrates on the history of Madurai and has galleries on the famous Nayaka king as well as exhibits on the art and architecture of Tamil Nadu. There's also a Sound and Light show, see Entertainment, page 162.

Ramesvaram and around

» pp161-164.

Colour map 3, grid C5.

→ *Phone code: 04573. Population: 38,000.*

The conch-shaped island of Ramesvaram is usually lapped by limpid blue Gulf of Mannar waters, which turn into ferocious stormy waves during cyclones. Rama is believed to have worshipped Siva here, making it sacred to both Shaivites and Vaishnavites, and so a pilgrim to Varanasi is expected to visit Ramesvaram next, if he is to reach salvation.

Ins and outs

Getting there Ramesvaram is connected to Madurai and other centres by regular bus and train services. The bus stand is 2 km from the centre, the railway station 1 km further in and about 1 km southwest of the great temple.

Getting around Local buses go to the temple where there are a few places to stay. Avoid visiting on Monday when it's crowded with pilgrims. » *See Transport, page 164, for further details.*

Tourist information Offices ⓘ *14 East Car St, T04573-221371, 1000-1700.* Railway Station ⓘ *T04573-221373, open (with some breaks) 0700-2030.* The Temple Information is east side of the temple.

History

The *Ramayana* tells how the monkey king Hanuman built the bridges linking Ramnad to Pamban and Danushkodi (a spot where Rama is believed to have bathed) to help rescue Sita from the demon king Ravana. When he returned he was told by the *rishis* that he must purify himself after committing the sin of murdering a Brahmin, for *Ravana* was the son of a Brahmin. To do this he was advised to set up a *lingam* and worship Siva. The red image of Hanuman north of the main East Gate illustrates this story.

The original shrine long predates the present great Ramesvaram temple. It is one of India's most sacred shrines and is visited by pilgrims from all over India. The temple benefited from huge donations from the 17th-century *Setupatis* (the so-called guardians of the causeway), who derived their wealth from the right to levy taxes on crossings to the island. The temple stands on slightly higher ground, surrounded by a freshwater lake.

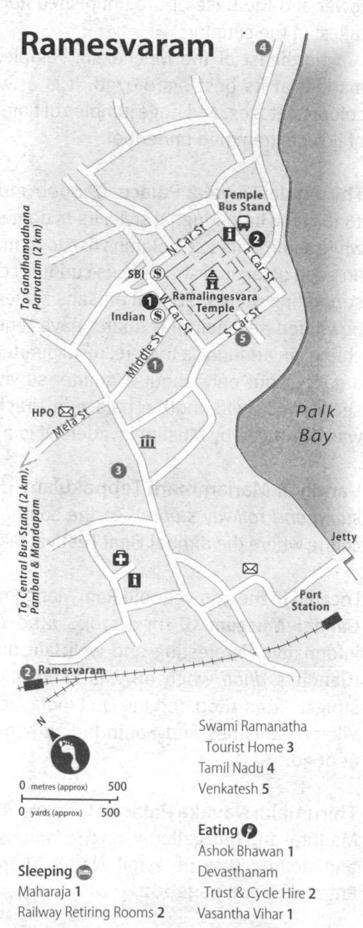

To Ramesvaram and Adam's Bridge

Seen from the air the plains of the Vaigai River form one of India's most remarkable landscapes, for there are over 5000 tanks and irrigation has been so developed that barely a drop of water is wasted. The

Holy dips

Pilgrims, once they've travelled the two days from North India and Varanasi, will part with any money to attain the sanctity they came for. It's a seller's market for the priests at the temple here: unlike Madurai where the Meenakshi temple has clear tariffs for *pujas*, the brahmins here (there are supposed to be 420 employees of the temple) make an assessment from your clothes, speech and skin. If you want to experience the *theertham* (dunking) – the emptying of 22 buckets drawn from holy wells, ponds, and the sea – you shouldn't pay more than Rs 100, but it seems somehow churlish to bargain with holy men, and most pilgrims don't. Also, take care: despite the best efforts of the *natrajs* (the temple guardians) local guides will of course do the decent thing and hold on to your belongings when you are being doused. Thefts do occur. Leave valuables outside the temple if you are bathing, and best bring a change of clothes (there are changing rooms inside the temple).

coastal districts of Ramnad have their own highly distinct economy and society. For the Hindus the sandbanks barely concealed in the Palk Strait are like giant stepping stones linking India and Sri Lanka: Adam's Bridge. Both Hindu and Muslim communities have long-established trading links across the Bay of Bengal, to Malaysia and Southeast Asia and to Sri Lanka. Small settlements along the coast like Kilakkarai have long been associated with smuggling. The civil war in Sri Lanka has made it a sensitive region.

Ramesvaram

The **Ramalingesvara (or Ramanathasvami) Temple** was founded by the Cholas but most of the temple was built in the Nayaka period (16th-17th centuries). It is a massive structure, enclosed by a huge rectangular wall with *gopurams* in the middle of three sides. Entrances through the east wall are approached through columned *mandapas* and the east *gopuram* is on the wall of the inner enclosure rather than the outer wall. Over 45 m high, it was begun in 1640 but left incomplete until recently. The west *gopuram* is comparatively new. In contrast the north and south *gopurams* were built by Keerana Rayar of the Deccan in about AD 1420. The most remarkable feature of the temple is its pillared *mandapas*. The longest corridor is over 200 m long. The pillars, nearly 4 m tall, are raised on moulded bases and the shafts decorated with scrollwork and lotus motifs. They give an impression of almost unending perspective, those on the north and south being particularly striking. There are two gateways on the east side which give access to the Parvati and Ramalinga shrines at the centre. The masonry shrine is probably the oldest building on the site, going back to 1173. On entering the East Gate you see the statue of Hanuman, then the *Nandi* flanked by statues of the Nayaka kings of Madurai, Visvanatha and Krishnama. The *Sphatikalinga Puja* is performed daily at 0500. Worshippers take a holy bath in a calm bay 25 km away, where waters are believed to wash away their sins. Fishermen take visitors for a boat ride. The fishing village has good views, but is very pungent.

Open courtyards, trefoil arches and chariot forms are the hallmarks of Rameswarem's distinctive style of temple architecture.

Gandhamadana Parvatam

Gandhamadana Parvatam, 2 km north of Ramesvaram, takes its name from the Sanskrit words *gandha* (fragrance) and *mad* (intoxicate), 'highly fragrant hill'. Dedicated to Rama's feet, this is where Hanuman is believed to have surveyed the area before taking his leap across the narrow Palk strait to Sri Lanka. There is a great view from the top of the *mandapa*.

Troubled waters

Fishermen working along the maritime boundary between India and Sri Lanka have long found themselves caught up in a military no man's land. The tactics of the Sri Lankan suicide rebel group – the Tamil Tigers – include sequestering Indian fishing vessels under whose disguise they launch stealth attacks on the Sri Lankan navy. The Navy has taken to shooting down Indian fishing junks on sight, just to be on the safe side, reports the news magazine *Frontline*.

Dhanuskodi

Dhanuskodi, – 'the end of the bow' – is the island's toe-tip where the Bay of Bengal meets the Indian Ocean, so named because Rama, at the request of Vibishana, his friend, destroyed the bridge to Sri Lanka with the end of his bow. Some 20 km to the east of Ramesvaram island, it is considered particularly holy. There is a good beach, on which pilgrims will be making *puja*, and beautiful flat turquoise waters in which they take their holy bath, not to mention excellent views. A trip across the scrappy sand dunes is only recommended for the really hardy – get a local person to go with you. Travel by bus, and then join a pilgrim group on a jeep or lorry for the last desolate few miles (this should cost Rs 50 round trip but establish the price up front). Alternatively, take an auto to Adam's Bridge; insist on going as far as the radio mast for beach and fishing shack photos.

Cardamom Hills » *p164. Colour map 3, grid C3/4.*

To the south of Madurai is a series of modest towns situated in the lee of the southern ranges of the Western Ghats. From Madurai to Thiruvanathapuram it is a comfortable day's drive either via Tirunelveli or over the ghats, but there are several interesting places on the way if you wish to take your time. » *For Transport see page 164.*

Rajapalayam

ⓘ *To Sankaracoil, Rs 5, 30 mins; from there to Kalugumalai, Rs 3, 30 mins, buses to and from Tenkasi, Rs 10, 2 hrs.*

The town originated on the dispersal of the Vijayanagar families after 1565, see page 254. The Sankarankovil temple is worth visiting. The Western Ghats rise to heights of over 1200 m immediately behind the town. Wild elephants still come down through the forests, devastating farmland.

Tenkasi

ⓘ *To Courtallam Falls frequent buses, Rs 3, to Courtallam Bus Stand, then walk through the grey arch to the 'Main Falls'. See Rajapalayam for transport to Tenkasi.*

Literally the Kashi (Varanasi) of the South, Tenkasi is the nearest town to the Kuttalam (Courtallam) Falls, 6 km away. The impressive 16th-century Visvanatha Temple dedicated to Siva has some fine carvings inside. The temple flagstaff is believed to be 400 years old. From Tenkasi the road goes through a low pass into the densely forested hills of Kerala.

Courtallam (Kuttalam)

With average temperatures of 22-23°C, Courtallam is a very popular health resort, especially during the monsoon. The most impressive, and busiest, Main Falls is in town where the river Chittar cascades over 92 m. The approach is lined with spice, banana chips and knick-knack stalls and at the Falls you'll find pilgrims washing themselves and their clothes. There is massage, toilets, special postal and other facilities available there. The waters, widely believed to have great curative powers, draw big crowds at the **Saral Festival** in July. The **Thirukutralanathar Temple** holds old inscriptions while the small **Chitra Sabha Temple** nearby has religious murals.

Virudhunagar

The name Virudhupatti (Hamlet of Banners) was changed to Virudhunagar (City of Banners) in 1915, and was upgraded to a full municipality in 1957, reflecting the upwardly mobile social status of the town's dominant local caste, the Nadars. Originally low caste toddy tappers, they have established a wide reputation as a dynamic and enterprising group. The powerful Congress leader, Kamaraj Nadar, was chiefly responsible for Mrs Gandhi's selection as prime minister.

Kalugumalai

Some 6 km south of Kovilpatti, Kalugumalai (Kazhugumalai) has a profusion of magnificent fifth-century bas-relief Jain figures on a huge rock which are well worth the detour. The Jain temple is to the north of the rock and is easily missed. There is also an unfinished monolithic cave temple to Siva (circa AD 950).

Chettinad

» *pp 161-165. Colour map 3, grid B5/C5.*

The magnificent palaces of South India's old merchant and banking classes rise from the hot and dusty plains to stand as strong as fortresses and as gaudy as a packet of French Fancies. As the merchants, bankers and moneylenders of the British Empire, the Nattukottai Chettiars raked in enormous riches on their postings to places such as Burma, Sri Lanka, Indochina and South Africa, wealth they ploughed into these glorious architectural pastiches that explode in a profusion of colour in the arid desertscape.

But now their monumental arches and long processional corridors open onto empty halls, the bats are more at home here than princes and shafts of light break on empty cobwebbed dining rooms. The Nattukottai Chettiars saw their riches contract with World War Two and the wanton palaces they built they turned into tombstones, the series of south Indian villages they stand in left empty as ghost towns. Architectural salvage merchants in the main town of Karaikudi sell off the family portraits and granite pillars of this proud caste, which are surrendered to stave off financial hardship.

Karaikkudi

Karaikkudi is in the heart of Chettinad, and has several typical mansions, as well as antique and textile shops. You can visit the local *santhat* (market), see craftsmen working in wood and metal, and gold and silversmiths in their workshops. At **Avudayarkoil**, 30 km northeast of Karaikkudi, the **Athmanathar temple** has one of the most renowned sites in Tamil cultural history. A legend tells that Manickavaskar, a Pandyan prime minister, redirected money meant for the purchase of horses to build the temple. However, his real fame is as author of the *Thiruvasakam* ('Holy Outpourings'), one of the most revered Tamil poetic texts. Off the beaten track, the temple has superb sculptures and is noted for the absence of images of Siva or Parvati, the main deities, whose empty pedestals are worshipped. The wood carvings on the temple car are notable too.

Even the roofs of Chettiar buildings are symbols of their wealth; look up to see the wanton use of tiles, layered many times over, on top of each other.

Spice of life

Chettinad food is famous as South India's spiciest: its hallmarks are fresh ground ginger and garlic pastes plus heaps of pepper, cloves, saffron and cinnamon. Chettinad's pepper chickens are recommended anywhere, but while in Chettinad itself go looking for *nandu* (crab) and *yerra* (prawn) in *varuvals* (fries), *puttus* (minces) or curries.

Paal Paniharam is a special *kheer* (milk and rice pudding).

Kanadukathan, 5 km north of Karaikkudi, has a number of formerly magnificent mansions, some of them empty except for bats, monkeys – and antique dealers. You can visit the **Raja of Chettinad's Palace**, an amazing place overlooking the town's pond and full of sepia, larger-than-life-size portraits of stern family members, the frames garlanded with heavy yellow flowers. Next door is **Visalakshi Ramaswamy's house**, with a museum of local crafts, artefacts and handlooms upstairs. The Raja's waiting room at the railway station is also pretty special.

It has been estimated that the Burma teak and satinwood pillars in just one of the village's Chettiar houses weighed 300 tonnes, often superbly carved. The plaster on the walls is made from a mixture of lime, egg white, powdered shells and myrobalan fruit (the astringent fruit of the tree *Phyllantles emblica*), mixed into a paste which, when dried, gave a gleaming finish. Most houses have the goddess of wealth, Lakshmi, made of stucco over the main arch.

Devakottai, 18 km away, is Chettinad's second largest town and offers similarly rich pickings in the way of old mansions and palaces: look out for the particularly grand Periya Minor's *veedu*. **Athangudi**, 8 km from Kairakudi, has factories making the town's famous eponymous hand-made terracotta tiles.

Sleeping

Madurai *p151, maps p152 and p153*
20% tax is added by even modest hotels. Although there are slick hotels across the Vaigai these have neither character, easy access to the town's atmosphere, nor are they good value. Either visit Madurai from the charming remove of the Taj, on its hilltop, or abandon yourself to the throng and take a room near the temple.

AL Taj Garden Retreat, Pasumalai Hills, 7 TPK Rd, 5 km southwest of centre on NH7, T0452-260 1020, www.tajhotels.com. A real oasis, great views over surrounding country, 30 rooms (some in old colonial house) sheltered by the shade of trees, gardens full of peacocks, outdoor dining, good bookshop, lovely pool.

B Best Western Germanus, 28 By-Pass Rd, T0452-238 2001. Quiet, bright rooms, functional, fridge, bath, take rooms at the rear to save you from the busy roundabout in front, excellent food and service. Standards assured through the chain's quarterly inspections. Rooftop restaurant 1900-2300 for Chettinad specials.

B Royal Court, 4 West Veli St, T0452-535 6666, www.royalcourtindia.com. 70 extremely clean a/c rooms with bath, satellite TV and great views from rooftop (open 1900-2300), good value.

B-C Park Plaza, 114 W Perumal Maistry St, T0452-234 2112. Some of the 55 smart, 60s-print, stylish a/c rooms offer temple views, breakfast included, excellent rooftop restaurant (1800-2300), bar, all facilities. Extremely helpful. Free pick-up from airport/ railway station. Highly recommended.

B-C Supreme, 110 W Perumal Maistry St, T0452-234 3151, www.supremehotels.com. 69 slightly tatty but adequately clean rooms

For an explanation of the sleeping and eating price codes used in this guide, see inside the front cover. Other relevant information is found in Essentials pages 40-44.

with marble and plastic furniture, 31 a/c, good rooftop restaurant (temple views **Surya** 1600-0000), bar, 24-hr travel desk, exchange, internet, a bit noisy, a mite overpriced. Security and service both wanting. **D** single non a/c rooms, **B** for suites sleeping up to 3.

C-E The Madurai Residency, 14-15 West Marret St, T0452-234 3140, www.madurairesidency.com. Rather grand for Madurai: 75 rooms over 7 floors, glass lift. Economy rooms better than a/c due to musty smell.

D Aarathy, 9 Perumalkoil, west of Kundalalagar Temple, T0452-273 1571. Well-appointed rooms if a bit dingy, some a/c with balcony, vegetarian restaurant, quiet, friendly.

D Tamil Nadu II (Star), Alagar Koil Rd, T0452-253 7462. 51 rooms, some a/c, good restaurant, bar, exchange, quiet.

D YMCA International Guest House, Main Guard Sq, near temple, T0452-274 6649, ymca@maduraionline.com. Simple a/c double rooms, profits to worthwhile projects.

D-E International, 46 W Perumal Maistry St, T0452-2341552. Friendly, 34 clean and tidy rooms with views from upper floors, TV.

D-E Prem Nivas, 102 W Perumal Maistry St, T0452-234 2532, premnivas@eth.net. Shabby rooms with bath, 15 **D** a/c, 25 non a/c, basic but good value. Single rooms too small for comfort. A/c vegetarian restaurant (ultra hot).

D-F Elements Boutique Hostel, No 642, KK Nagar, opposite Hindu Office, T0452 439 1116, www.elementshostel.com. Alcohol and drug free, all a/c, 2 doubles, 4 dorms, lockers, washing machine and drier, free Wi-Fi, 24-hr check in and hot water, mini library. Friendly. 10% discount with student card.

E Arima, 4 TB Rd, T0452-260 3261. 37 rooms, some a/c, modern, simple, clean.

E Sree Devi, W Avani Moola St, T0452-274 7431. Rooms with bath, some **D** a/c, (avoid noisy ground floor), good value, cleanish, modern tower block with views of temple gateway from rooftop, changes TCs, friendly.

E TM Lodge, 50 W Perumal Maistry St, T0452-234 1651, http://maduraitmlodge.com. 57 rooms (hot water), some a/c, some with TV, balcony, very clean, bookings for rail/bus journeys. Glowing reports.

E Hotel Tamil Nadu, West Veli St, T0452-233 7471. A very friendly tourist office, mint-coloured guest house dating from 1968 set around courtyard. In bad need of a new lick of paint – it's pretty grubby – but there are TVs, huge rooms and the staff are very charming.

E-F Dhanamani, 20-22 Sunnamukara St, T0452-234 2703. Nice rooms (some with bath, fan, TV), good roof terrace with temple views, sitting area (8th floor).

E-F Ravi Lodge, 12 Mandayan Asari Lane, Town Hall Rd, T0452-234 3493. Good value, 30 clean rooms with shower, fan, very quiet.

F Thilaga, 111 W Perumal Maistry St, T0452-274 9762. Www.elementshostel.com. Friendly, 15 double clean rooms with TV, hot water. Recommended.

F Tower View Lodge, nice clean rooms with toilet, shared clean hot shower, excellent food, friendly and helpful family, internet.

F Visakam Lodge, 9 Kakathope St, T0452-274 1241. 18 very clean rooms. Excellent value. Recommended.

F Youth Hostel, MGR Stadium, Race Course, dorm (Rs 40-50).

Ramesvaram *p156, map p156*

D-E Maharaja, 7 Middle St, west of the Temple, T04573-221271. 30 rooms, some a/c with bath, exchange, temple music broadcast on loudspeakers, otherwise recommended.

D-E Hotel Tamil Nadu (TTDC), 14 East Car St, T04573-221066. Sea-facing balconies, 53 rooms (2-6 beds), some a/c, clean, grubby restaurant (breakfast from 0700), bar, sea bathing nearby (when calm), exchange. Very popular; book well in advance.

D-E Venkatesh, West Car St, T04573-221296. Some a/c rooms, modern.

F Railway Retiring Rooms, T04573-221226, 9 rooms and dorm.

F Swami Ramanatha Tourist Home, between station and temple, opposite museum, T04573-221217. Good clean rooms with bath, best budget option.

Chettinad *p159*

There are very few suitable places to stay in the area. The below are in Karaikkudi unless stated otherwise.

AL The Bangala, Senjai, T04565-220221, bangala@vsnl.com. 8 bright and spacious a/c rooms with period colonial furniture, in restored 1916 bungalow, a heritage guest house of character set amidst orchards and palms, authentic Chettinad meals (or continental), serves full-on feasts for a fair whack at Rs 800 per meal and must be booked in advance, rest stop facilities for day visitors (lunch US$15-20) and a full-board option. The family here wrote the (coffee table) book on Chettinad architecture.

A-B Chettinadu Mansion, Kanadukathan, book through **Deshadan Tours and Travels**, 4th Floor South Sq, Av Rd, Cochin, T0484-231 7052, www.deshadan.com. A 105-year-old house with 7 rooms, bright coloured hand-painted tiles and old phones. Meals cost Rs 300 and must be booked in advance.

C Hotel Subalakshmi, T04565-235202, and **C-D Hotel Udayam**, T04565-233142. Both cheap options, but they do not have the guides on hand to gain access to the old private homes (without whose help the Chettinad Palace may be the only house you look inside).

F Nivaas, in Devakottai, first left from bus station coming from the north, (no sign in English), is basic (no electric sockets), no English spoken.

Eating

Madurai *p151, maps p152 and p153*

TTT Temple View, at **Park Plaza Hotel**. Excellent rooftop venue.

TT Surya, **Hotel Supreme**, 1700-2400. Seventh-floor rooftop restaurant with international as well as Indian menu. Excellent Andhra thalis, very busy Sun evenings.

T Anna Meenakshi, W Perumal Maistry St. Popular South Indian.

T Delhiwala Sweets, W Tower St. Delicious Indian sweets and snacks.

T Muniyandi Vilas, at **Indo-Ceylon Restaurant**, and other outlets. Non-vegetarian. Try paratha and mutton curry.

T New Arya Bhavan, North and South Indian choices, ice cream.

T Taj, Town Hall Rd. Good value thalis (Rs 35), friendly.

T Tamil Nadu II hotel restaurant. Good Indian/Chinese.

Ramesvaram *p156, map p156*

Don't expect anything other than thalis here. **Ashok Bhawan** and **Vasantha Vihar** on West Car St and also at the Central Bus Stand, Indian vegetarian including Gujarati, but even poorer than **Hotel Tamil Nadu**. **Devasthanam Trust**, has a canteen opposite the east gate of the temple.

Entertainment

Madurai *p151, maps p152 and p153*

Meenakshi Temple, 'Bedtime of the God' 2110, is not to be missed (see page 153).

Thirumalai Nayaka Palace, Sound and Light show: English 1845-1930; Rs 5 (take mosquito repellent), sadly, "poor, faded tape". During the day, dance drama and concerts are held in the courtyard.

Festivals and events

Madurai *p151, maps p152 and p153*

Jan: **Jallikattu Festival** (Taming the Bull).

Jan/Feb: The annual **Float Festival** marks the birth anniversary of Thirumalai Nayaka. Many temple deities in silks and jewels, including Meenakshi and Sundareswarar, are taken out on a full moon night on floats colourfully decorated with hundreds of oil lamps and flowers. The floats carry them to the central shrine to the accompaniment of music and chanting.

Apr/May: The 10-day **Chitrai Festival** is the most important at the Meenakshi Temple, celebrating the marriage of Siva and Meenakshi.

Aug/Sep: The **Avanimoolam** is the Coronation Festival of Siva when the image of Lord Sundareswarar is taken out to the river bank dressed as a worker.

Shopping

Madurai *p151, maps p152 and p153*

Kashmiri emporia pay 40-50% commission to touts. Best buys are textiles, wood and stone carvings, brass images, jewellery and appliqué work for temple chariots. Most shops are on South Avani Moola St (for jewellery), Town Hall Rd, Masi St and around the Temple.

Books

Higginbotham's Book Exchange, near the temple. **New Century Book House**, Town Hall Rd. Recommended.

Handicrafts

Handicrafts Emporium, 39-41 Town Hall Rd. **Khadi Gramodyog Bhandar** and **Surabhi** on W Veli St.

Textiles and tailors

Femina, 10 W Chitrai St. Similar to the market (you can take photos of the Meenakshi Temple from their rooftop).
Hajee Moosa, 18 E Chitrai St. Tailoring in 8 hrs; 'ready-mades' at **Shabnam**, at No 17.
Market near Pudu Mandapam, next to Meenakshi East Gate. Sells fabric and is a brilliant place to get clothes made.

Chettinad *p159*

Muneesvaran Kovil St in Karaikkudi is lined with antiques shops selling old sepia photographs, temple lamps, old advertising posters, scrap book matter, religious paintings and Czech pewter jars (from Rs 50).
Kattu Raja's, Palaniappa Chettiar St.
Old Chettinad Crafters, Murugen Complex, 37/6 Muneesvaran Kovil St, Karaikkudi, T098428-223060, chettinaduantiques@yahoo.co.in. One of the best.
VJ Murugesan, sells old wooden furniture, household articles, wooden pillars, glass.
Venkateswara Furniture and Timber Merchant, No 8 Keela Oorani West, Karaikkudi, T098424-232112. If you're in the market for bigger objects and weight is no object, this architectural salvage yard is a good starting point. Bargain hard: a granite pillar shouldn't cost more than Rs 1500.

MM Street and The Weavers' Lane beside the Bangala have Chettinad cotton for sale straight off the loom. Ask locally for the next *sandais*, the colourful local weekly markets.

Activities and tours

Madurai *p151, maps p152 and p153*

Body and soul

Yoga classes at Gandhi Museum, T0452-248 1060. 0630, daily.

Swimming

Rs 300 gets you unlimited use of the pool at the **Taj Garden Retreat**, page 160.

Tour operators

Meraj, 46B Perumal Koil South Mada St.
Pleasant Tours and Travels, Mr Ian Fernandez, Plot No 6, St Joseph St, (opposite Ellis Nagar Telephone Exchange T0452-261 0614, ptt@sancharnet.in.
Siraj, 19A TPK Rd, opposite Malai Murasu, T0452-273 9666, mshersha@md4.vsnl.net.in. Ticketing, good multilingual guides, cars.
Trade Wings, 279 North Masi St, T0452-273 0271.
Window to the World (Trichy), T0431-436052, faithpandian@sify.com. Tours from Madurai (and other towns). The Pandians are very helpful, efficient, South India tours, car with excellent driver. Highly recommended.

Tours

Ex-Serviceman Travels, 1 Koodalalagar, Perumal Kovil St, T0452-273 0571, **City** half day, 0700, 1500, Rs 140; **Kodaikkanal** or **Ramesvaram** 0700-1900, Rs 2750; overnight to **Kanniyakumari** 2200-1900, Rs 350.
TTDC, book at **Hotel Tamil Nadu**, West Veli St, T0452-233 7471. **Temple tour** of Madurai and attractive surroundings by a/c coach; half day, 0700-1200, 1500-2000. Rs 125. Recommended for an overview. Apr-Jun: **Courtallam** Rs 300. **Kodaikkanal** 0700-2100, Rs 250. **Rameswaram** Rs 275.

Transport

Madurai *p151, maps p152 and p153*

Air

Airport to city centre (12 km) by Pandiyan coach (calls at top hotels); taxi (Rs 375) or auto-rickshaw (Rs 80). **Indian Airlines**, 7A W Veli St, T0452-274 1234. 1000-1300, 1400-1700; Airport, T0452-267 0433. Flights to **Chennai** and **Mumbai**. **Air India**, opposite train station, W Veli St. **Jet Airways**, T0452-252 6969; airport T0452-269 0771. To **Chennai**.

Bus

Local There is a good network within the city and the suburbs.
Long distance Approaching on a long-distance bus from the south, to get to the centre, change to a city bus at Tirumangalam (15 km south). State and private companies (MPTC, PRC, but check bus details carefully) run services to other cities. Most intercity buses use the **New Central Bus Stand** (or Muttuthavani Bus Terminal), 6 km northeast of town, in open countryside, continuation of Alagar Koil Rd, on the toll ring road

(25 mins, Rs 40 by rickshaw, or city bus from town centre). Buses for **Bengaluru (Bangalore)** (11 hrs), **Ernakulam** (**Kochi**), **Chennai** (10 hrs), **Pondicherry** (9 hrs), **Thiruvananthapuram** (8 hrs), **Kumbakonum**, **Ramesvaram** (under 4 hrs, every 15 mins), **Thanjavur** (4 hrs), **Tiruchirappalli** (2½ hrs), **Tirunelveli** (4 hrs, Rs 40). Arapalayam Bus Stand, 3 km northwest of centre (Bus route No 7A, auto-rickshaws Rs 20), T0452-260 3740, for destinations to the north and northwest, including **Kodaikkanal**, buses (crowded in peak season, Apr-Jul); 3½ hrs (longer via Palani), Rs 150. Also buses to **Coimbatore** (5 hrs, change there for Mysore or Ooty), **Periyar/ Kumili** (4 hrs), **Salem** (5½ hrs), **Dindigul**. Central (Periyar) Bus Stands, near W Veli St, are now used for buses around town and destinations nearby.

Car

To **Kodaikkanal**, Rs 950 (Rs 1600 a/c), see local transport above.

Rickshaw

Autos Rs 25, cycle Rs 20 for trips around town. Bargain hard first.

Taxi/car hire

Unmetered; 10 hrs/225 km, Rs 450, Rs 675 (a/c); 6 hrs sightseeing, Rs 490 (Rs 750 a/c); 1 hr/10 km, Rs 65, Rs 100 (a/c). Janakiraman, 184 North Veli St; Supreme, 110 Perumal Maistry St, T0452-274 3151.

Train

Madurai Junction is the main station: enquiries, T0452-237597; reservations: 1st Class T0452-223535, 2nd Class T0452-233535. 0700-1300, 1330-2000. New Computer Reservation Centre to south of main entrance. Left luggage facilities. Pre-paid auto-rickshaw kiosk outside. **Chennai (ME)** via Villupuram for **Pondicherry**: *Vaigai Exp 2636*, 0645, 8 hrs; *Pandiyan Exp 6718*, 2020, 10 hrs. **Coimbatore**: *Fast Pass Exp 6716*, 2135, 7 hrs; *Quillon Coimbatore Exp 6782*, 0640, 5 hrs. **Kollam**: connect with trains from Virudhunagar (see page 159). **Kanniyakumari**: *Chennai Egmore Kanniyakumari Exp 6121*, 0415, 5¾ hrs. **Ramesvaram**: *Coimbatore-Ramesvaram Exp 6715*, 0600, 4¾ hrs. **Thiruvananthapuram**: see Virudhunagar on page 159. **Tiruchirappalli**: several, *Vaigai Exp 2636*, 0645, 2½ hrs (beautiful countryside); *Pandiyan Exp 6718*, 1925, 3½hrs.

Ramesvaram *p156, map p156*

Bicycle

Bike hire from West Car or East Car St.

Bus

Local Marudhu Pandiyan Transport Corporation (MPTC) covers the town and the area around. The bus station is 2 km west of town. Take a bus from the train station to the Ramalingesvara Temple, to Pamban or to Dhanuskodi (both via the temple). From the temple's east gate to Dhanuskodi roadhead and to Gandhamadana Parvatam, every 2 hrs.

Long distance State, MPTC and private bus companies run regular services via **Mandapam** to several towns nearby. The central bus stand is 2 km from the main temple gate. Govt Express Bus Reservations, North Car St, 0700-2100. There are frequent buses to **Madurai**, 173 km (4½ hrs); tourist coaches (hotel-to-hotel) are better.

Taxi

A few cars and jeeps are available from the train station and hotels.

Train

Ramesvaram Railway Station, enquiries and reservations, T226. 0800-1300, 1330-1730. **Chennai**: *Sethu Exp 6714*, 1510, 17¾ hrs via **Chengalpattu**, 16½ hrs. **Coimbatore**: *Coimbatore Fast Pass 6716*, 1610, 12¼ hrs. **Madurai**: *Coimbatore Fast Pass 6716*, 1610, 5 hrs. **Tiruchirappalli**: *Ramesvaram Tambaram Exp 6702*, 1200, 5½ hrs; *Sethu Exp 6714*, 1510, 6¼ hrs.

Virudhunagar *p158*

Bus Leave Madurai early morning for Kollam train; get off at police station and go to the end of the road opposite and turn left; the railway station is about 1 km on the right (take a rickshaw if carrying heavy luggage).

Train To **Kollam** and **Thiruvananthapuram**, Platform 3 across the bridge. **Kollam**: *Fast Pass Exp 6761*, 2150, 7 hrs.

Chettinad *p159*
Bus Routes link Karaikkudi with every part of the state. The trains *The Ramesvaram* and *Sethu Exp* connect Tambaram and Ramesvaram with Karaikkudi.

Directory

Madurai *p151, maps p152 and p153*
Banks Several on East Avani Moola St. Alagendran Finance, 182D N Veli St, good rate for cash US$ but not for TCs. Andhra Bank, W Chitrai St, accepts credit cards; Canara Bank, W Veli St, cashes Amex and sterling TCs. **Internet** Dolphin, Madurai Junction station. Many west of the temple and in the budget hotel area charge Rs 20 per hr. **Hospitals** Christian Mission Hospital, East Veli St; Grace Kennet Hospital, 34 Kennet Rd. **Post** The town GPO is at the north end of W Veli St (Scott Rd). In Tallakulam: Head Post Office and Central Telegraph Office, on Gokhale Rd.

The far south

The southernmost tip of mainland India is a focus of pilgrimage that captures the imagination of millions of Hindus on a daily basis. Kanniyakumari occupies a beautiful rocky headland site, where the Bay of Bengal, the Indian Ocean and the Arabian Sea meet to give spectacular backdrop to the sunrise, sunset and moonrise. An hour further towards Kerala is Padmanabhapuram Palace, the painstakingly maintained ancient seat of the Travancore rulers. Tirunelveli, one-time capital of the Pandyas, is now a market and educational centre that is often passed over on the trail towards Madurai. » *For Sleeping, Eating and other listings, see pages 169-170.*

Tirunelveli and Palayamkottai » *pp169-170.*

Colour map 3, grid C4.

→ *Phone code: 0462. Population: 411,300.*

On the banks of the Tamraparni, the only perennial river of the south, Tirunelveli is an attractive town surrounded by a belt of rice fields ('nelveli' means 'paddy-hedge') irrigated from the river's waters. Rising only 60 km to the east at an altitude of over 1700 m, the river benefits from both the southwest and southeast

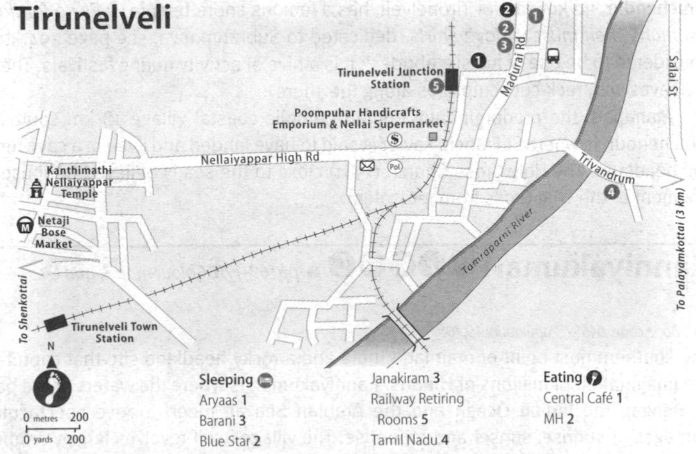

The terrifying guardian deities

Many Hindu villagers in Tamil Nadu believe in guardian deities of the village – Ayyanar, Muneeswaram, Kaliamman, Mariamman and many more. Groups of larger-than-life images built of brick, wood or stone and covered in brightly painted lime plaster (*chunam*) guard the outskirts of several villages. They are deliberately terrifying, designed to frighten away evil spirits from village homes, but villagers themselves are also very frightened of these gods and try to keep away from them.

The deities are supposed to prevent epidemics, but if an epidemic does strike special sacrifices are offered, mainly of rice. Firewalking, often undertaken in fulfilment of a vow, is a feature of the special festivals at these shrines. Disease is also believed to be held at bay by other ceremonies, including piercing the cheeks and tongue with wire and the carrying of *kavadis* (special carriages or boxes, sometimes designed like a coffin).

monsoons. It tumbles down to the plains where it is bordered by a narrow strip of rich paddy land.

Tirunelveli is now joined with the twin settlement of Palayamkottai. It is a market town and one of the oldest Christian centres in Tamil Nadu. St Francis Xavier settled here to begin his ministry in India in the early 16th century, but it has also been a centre of Protestant missionary activity. In 1896 it became the head of an Anglican diocese, now Church of South India.

Kanthimathi Nellaiyappar Temple ⓘ *closed 1230-1600, no photography*, is worth visiting; it is a twin temple, with the north dedicated to Siva (Nellaiyappar) and the south to Parvati (Kanthi). Each section has an enclosure over 150 m by 120 m. The temples have sculptures, musical pillars, valuable jewels, a golden lily tank and a 1000-pillared *mandapa*. There is a large white Nandi at the entrance. There is a **car festival** in June/July. The old town area around the temple is well worth a few hours of anyone's time, with the blue-painted houses reminiscent of Jodhpur (but without the tourist crowds). **Palayamkottai** has **St John's Church** (Church Missionary Society) with a spire 35 m high, a landmark for miles around. The town produces palm-leaf items.

Around Tirunelveli

Tiruchendur, 50 km east of Tirunelveli, has a famous shore **temple** ⓘ *Rs 50 for 'fast darshan', men must remove shirts*, dedicated to Subrahmanya, see page 294. It is considered to be one of his six 'abodes'. It is a hive of activity during festivals. There are caves with rock-cut sculptures along the shore.

Manapad, the predominantly Roman Catholic coastal village 18 km south of Tiruchendur, is where St Francis Xavier is said to have landed and lived in a cave near the headland. The Holy Cross Church (1581) close to the sea is believed to house a fragment of the True Cross from Jerusalem.

Kanniyakumari

» *pp169-170. Colour map 3, grid C4.*

→ *Phone code: 04652. Population: 19,700.*

The southernmost point of mainland India and a rocky headland site that captures the imagination of millions of Hindus. Kanniyakumari is where the waters of the bay of Bengal, the Indian Ocean and the Arabian Sea all meet, to give spectacular vantages of sunrise, sunset and moonrise. The village itself revolves largely around the pilgrim market that sells tacky plastic knick-knacks linked with the Goddess Kumari, the virgin, Kanniyakumari (Cape Comorin). The memorial to Swami Vivekananda, on a rocky promontory just over 400 m offshore, now dominates the view and the town heaves with pilgrims who assemble in the pre-dawn light to see the day break over it. The Bay of Bengal, the Indian Ocean and the Arabian Sea meet here, giving a magnificent sunrise, sunset and moonrise. In April the sun and the moon appear on the same horizon. The beach sands here are of different colours (black monazite and red garnet), having been deposited from different directions.

Sights

The **Kanniyakumari Temple** ⓘ *0400-1200, 1700-2000, non-Hindus are not allowed into the sanctuary, shoes must be left outside and men must wear a dhoti to enter,* overlooks the shoreline. The legend tells of the Devi Kanya, one of Parvati's incarnations, who sought to marry Siva by doing penance. When she was unsuccessful she vowed to remain an unmarried virgin. The deity who is the 'protector of India's shores' has an exceptionally brilliant diamond on her nose ring which is supposed to shine out to sea. The East Gate is opened only on special occasions.

Some of Mahatma Gandhi's ashes were on public view before immersion in the sea and **Gandhi Mandapam** was built so that the sun at midday on his birthday, 2 October, shines on the spot where the ashes were placed. The **Lighthouse** is closed to visitors.

Vivekananda Memorial ⓘ *Wed-Mon 0700-1100, 1400-1700, Rs 10, ferry Rs 20, 15 mins (see transport below), allow 1 hr for the visit, smoking and eating prohibited, take off shoes before entering, can be hot underfoot,* stands on one of two rocks separated by about 70 m, about 500 m from the mainland. The Bengali religious leader and philosopher Swami Vivekananda who came here as a simple monk and devotee of the Devi, swam out and sat in long and deep meditation on one of the rocks in 1892. He left inspired to speak on Hinduism at the Parliament of Religions in Chicago, preaching that "the Lord is one, but the sages describe Him differently". He looked on religion as the most powerful instrument of social regeneration and individual development. On his return, he founded the Ramakrishna Mission in Chennai, which now has spread across the world. The rock was renamed Vivekananda Rock and a memorial was built in 1970. The design of the *mandapa* incorporates different styles of temple architecture from all over India and now also houses a statue of Vivekananda. People also come to see Sri Pada Parai, the 'footprint' of the Devi where she did her penance on the rock – divine footprints are believed to be raised when enshrined on rock. A giant

Kanniyakumari

To Trivandrum (NH 47) & Madurai (NH 7)
Vivekanandapuram
Guganathan Temple
Church of Our Lady of Ransom
Main Rd
N Car St
E Car St
S Car St
Kovalam Rd
Lighthouse
Jetty
Toilet
Beach Rd
Tamil Nadu Sales Emporium
Gandhi Mandapam
Shops
Vinayaka Temple
Kanniyakumari Temple & Kumari Ghat
Vivekananda Memorial

N

0 metres 200
0 yards 200

Sleeping
Lakshmi **1**
Maadhini **2**
Manickam **3**
Parvathi Nivas **4**
Sankar Guest House **7**
Shivas Residency **8**
Singaar **9**
Tamil Nadu Guest House **10**

Eating
Sangam **6**
Sravanas **2**

40-m statue of the poet Thiruvalluvar is now installed on the rock nearby and work is progressing to allow visitors to land.

An informative photo exhibition, in **Vivekanandapuram**, 1 km north, can be reached by an easy walk along the beach though there is no access from the north side. The Yoga Kendra there runs courses from June to December. Further north there is a pleasant sandy beach, 3½ km along Kovalam Road.

Around Kanniyakumari

Suchindram temple ⓘ *open to non-Hindus, priests acting as guides may expect donations*, was founded during the Pandiyan period but was expanded under Thirumalai Nayaka in the 17th century. It was also used later as a sanctuary for the rulers of Travancore to the west and so contains treasures from many kingdoms. One of the few temples dedicated to the Hindu Trinity, Brahma, Vishnu and Siva, it is in a rectangular enclosure that you enter through the massive ornate seven-storeyed *gopuram*. North of the temple is a large tank with a small shelter in the middle while round the walls is the typically broad street used for car festivals. Leading to the entrance is a long colonnade with musical pillars and sculptures of Siva, Parvati, Ganesh and Subrahmanya on the front and a huge Hanuman statue inside. The main sanctuary, with a *lingam*, dates from the ninth century but many of the other structures and sculptures date from the 13th century and after. There are special temple ceremonies at sunset on Friday.

Nagercoil is 19 km from Kanniyakumari and is set with a stunning backcloth of the Western Ghats, reflected from place to place in the broad tanks dotted with lotuses. The landscape begins to feel more like Kerala than Tamil Nadu. It is an important railway junction and bus terminal. It is often a bottleneck filled with lorries so be prepared for delays. The old town of **Kottar**, now a suburb, was a centre of art, culture and pilgrimage. The **temple** ⓘ *0630-0900, 1730-2000,* to Nagaraja, after which the town is named, is unique in that although the presiding deity is the Serpent God *Naga*, there are also shrines to Siva and Vishnu as well as images of Jain *Tirthankaras*, Mahavira and Parsvanatha on the pillars. The temple is alive with snakes during some festivals. Christian missionaries played an important part in the town's development and left their mark in schools, colleges, hospitals and churches of different denominations. There is also a prominent Muslim community in Kottar, reflected in the shops closing on Fridays and remaining open on Sunday.

Padmanabhapuram » p170.

ⓘ *Tue-Sun 0900-1700 (last tickets 1630), Rs 5 (accredited guide is included, but expects a 'donation' after the tour), still camera Rs 5, video Rs 500. Best at 0900 before coach parties arrive.*

Padmanabhapuram, the old palace of the Rajas of Travancore, contains some fascinating architecture and paintings but some of the methods employed during its restoration have been criticized. Although decaying somewhat, the Kuthiramalika Palace in Trivandrum – if you are venturing into Kerala – might be better worth looking round. The name Padmanabhapuram (*Padma*, lotus; *nabha*, navel; *puram*, town) refers to the lotus emerging from the navel of Vishnu. From the ninth century this part of Tamil Nadu and neighbouring Kerala were governed by the Ay Dynasty, patrons both of Jainism and Hinduism. However, the land was always contested by the Cholas, the Pandiyas and the Cheras. By the late 11th century the new Venadu Dynasty emerged from the Chera rulers of Kerala and took control of Kanniyakumari District in AD 1125 under Raja Kodai Kerala Varman. Never a stable kingdom and with varying degrees of territorial control, Travancore State was governed from Padmanabhapuram between 1590-1790, when the capital was shifted to Thiruvananthapuram.

Although the Rajas of Travancore were Vaishnavite kings, they did not neglect Siva, as can be seen from various sculptures and paintings in the palace. The King never officially married and the heir to the throne was his eldest sister's oldest son. This form of matrilineal descent was characteristic of the earlier Chera Empire (who ruled for 200 years from the early 12th century). The palace shows the fine craftsmanship, especially in woodworking, characteristic of Kerala's art and architecture. There are also some superb frescoes and excellent stone-sculpted figures. The outer cyclopean stone wall is fitted together without mortar. It encloses a total area of 75 ha and the palace buildings 2 ha.

Sleeping

Tirunelveli *p165, map p165*
Hotels are often full during the wedding season (Apr-Jun). Book ahead or arrive early.
B-D Janakiram, 30 Madurai Rd, near Bus Stand, T0462-233 1941. 70 clean rooms, with hot shower, some a/c, lift, smart, brightly lit, outstanding vegetarian rooftop restaurant. Highly recommended.
C-E Aryaas, 67 Madurai Rd, T0462-233 9001. 69 rooms, 25 a/c, in dark bordello style, non a/c better value, restaurants (separate vegetarian one, but it's also a mosquito's heaven), bar. Excellent internet café opposite. Several budget hotels are clustered near Junction Railway Station. Rooms usually with Western toilet and shower.
C-E Barani, 29 Madurai Rd, T0462-233 3234. 43 rooms, with hot shower, 10 a/c, clean, well maintained, vegetarian restaurant, in large modern block, lift, ample parking.
E Tamil Nadu, T0462-232 4268. Some dull rooms, bath, restaurant, poorly maintained.
F Blue Star, 36 Madurai Rd, T0462-233 4495. 50 rooms with cold shower, 10 a/c, good vegetarian restaurant, Indian style, modern. Good value.
F Railway Retiring Rooms. Clean, secure rooms and dorm. Excellent value.

Kanniyakumari *p166, map p167*
Hotels are in heavy demand; book well in advance. Better hotels have rooms with en suite facilities (cold showers, hot tap and Western toilets)
B Hotel Singaar, 2 km from attractions, T04652-247992. Smart, popular large hotel with big rooms, many with balcony. Nice pool, decent restaurant. Breakfast included.
B-C Maadhini, East Car St, T04652-234 6787. Comfortable rooms with bath and fan (mosquito-proof), best with sea views (tell reception if you don't want be woken early to watch the sunrise!). 'Garden' restaurant in courtyard (evenings). Recommended.
B-C Seaview, East Car St, T04652-234 7841. 61 excellent, large rooms, 30 a/c, in newish hotel, all facilities, roof terrace. Highly recommended.
B-C Singaar, 5 Main Rd, T04652-234 7992, singaar@sancharnet.in. 76 spacious, clean rooms, most a/c with balconies in modern hotel with well-maintained pool (non-residents Rs 100, 2 hrs), restaurant, extensive grounds, away from temple noise and crowds. Bit overpriced.
C-D Tamil Nadu Guest House, Beach Rd, T04652-234 6257. Good location, beautiful sunset views, 45 rooms, some with bath, 15 a/c, **B** twin cottages, but very slow service.
D Lakshmi, East Car St, T04652-234 6333. 40 spotless rooms, some a/c with views, Indian toilet, restaurant, 24-hr coffee shop, friendly and helpful staff, but noisy because guests arrive at 0400-0500 to see sunrise from the roof. Otherwise excellent value.
D Shivas Residency, South Car St, T04652-234 6150. Fairly new hotel, 18 rooms, 3 a/c. Spacious, quiet, very clean. Recommended.
D-E Manickam, North Car St, T04652-234 6387. Some of the 55 pleasant rooms have sea view and balcony, restaurant. Recommended.
E Sankar Guest House, Main Rd, T04652-234 6260. Some of the 36 large rooms de luxe with TV, sea view.
F Arunagiri, 59 Madurai Rd, T04652-233 4553. Excellent value, 62 rooms with TV, some have balconies, spacious, shady courtyard.
F Parvathi Nivas, West Car St, T04652-234 6352. Old-style, interesting lodge offering 22 basic, cool rooms with character.

Around Kanniyakumari *p168*
D Parvathi, Nagarcoil, T04652-233020. Similar to **Rajam**.
D Rajam, MS Rd, Vadasery, Nagarcoil, T04652-232581. Good value, 32 rooms, some a/c, restaurant, roof garden, exchange.

Eating

Tirunelveli *p165, map p165*
Central Café, near station, good vegetarian.
MH Restaurant, opposite **Aryaas**. Western fast food, pizzas. Modern.

Kanniyakumari *p166, map p167*
Sangam, good thalis.
Sravanas, 2 near Jetty and on Sannathi St. Vegetarian. Recommended.
TTDC Restaurant, looks like a barracks, but excellent non-vegetarian Indian meals.

Festivals and events

Kanniyakumari *p166, map p167*
Chitra Purnima is a special full moon celebration at the temple usually held in the 2nd week of **Apr**. Sunset and moonrise can be seen together. In 1st week of **Oct** Special Navarathri celebrations.

Transport

Tirunelveli *p165, map p165*
Bus Good connections to **Kanniyakumari**, **Thiruvananthapuram**, and to **Madurai** (faster to change buses at Tirumangalam), **Tiruchirappalli** and **Chennai**. For **Courtallam**, go to Tenkasi (Rs 12, 1½ hrs) and take bus to Courtallam (Rs 2, 20 mins).

Train To **Chennai (ME)**: *Nellai Exp 6120* (AC/CC), 1900, 13¾ hrs. Broad gauge to **Chennai (MC)**: *Kanniyakumari Exp 6020*, 1740, 15 hrs. Also to Madurai and Kanniyakumari.

Kanniyakumari *p166, map p167*
Bus Central bus station, west of town, 15 mins' walk from centre, T04652-271285, with restaurant, waiting room and **Retiring** Rooms upstairs. Frequent services to **Nagercoil** (½ hr), **Kovalam** and **Thiruvananthapuram** (2½ hrs) but the journey can be tiring and uncomfortable. Govt Express buses go to major towns including **Chennai** (16 hrs), **Madurai** (6 hrs), **Ramesvaram** (8½ hrs).

Ferry To **Vivekananda Rock**, at least every 30 mins, 0700-1100, 1400-1700; sometimes 2 run simultaneously. Rs 10. Expect long queues during festivals.

Train The station to the north, off the Trivandrum Rd, is large and well organized, T71247. **Chennai (ME)** (via Madurai): *Kanniyakumari Chennai Egmore Exp 6122*, 1550, 15¾ hrs. **Delhi (ND)**: *Him Sagar Exp 6317/6787*, Fri, 1245 (it does not stop in Chennai; it stops at **Katpadi** and then **Gudur**. If you take this train to its ultimate destination of **Jammu** the journey lasts 3 days 1½ hrs, the longest in India!). **Madurai**: *Kanniyakumari Chennai Egmore Exp 6122*, 1550, 5¼ hrs. **Mumbai (CST)**: *Kanniyakumari Mumbai Exp 1082* (AC/II), 0445, 48 hrs. **Thiruvananthapuram**: *Kanniyakumari Mumbai Exp 1082* (AC/II), 0445, 2¼ hrs.

Around Kanniyakumari *p168*
At **Nagarcoil**, the railway station is 3 km from the bus station. **Mumbai** (CST): *Nagercoil-Mumbai Exp 6340*, Mon, Tue, Wed, Sat, 0545, 39½ hrs; *Kanniyakumari Mumbai Exp 1082*, 0520, 47 hrs. Frequent bus connections to **Thiruvananthapuram**, **Kanniyakumari** and **Madurai**.

Padmanabhapuram *p168*
Bus Regular services to **Thiruvananthapuram** and **Kanniyakumari**. Less frequent buses to and from **Kovalam**. From Kovalam, depart around 0940 to **Thuckalai**. Return buses from Thuckalai depart 1445, 1530.

Taxi From Kovalam and Thiruvananthapuram including Padmanabhapuram, Suchindram and Kanniyakumari costs Rs 800.

Directory

Tirunelveli *p165, map p165*
Banks On Trivandrum High Rd.
Hosptials In High Ground, Palayamkottai.
Post GPO, Trivandrum High Rd.

Kanniyakumari *p166, map p167*
Banks Branches of Canara Bank, Main Rd; State Bank of India; State Bank of Travancore, Beach Rd. **Post** Head Post Office, Main Rd. Branches at Vivekandandapuram, 1100-1600 and Sannathi St, 1000-1400.

Kerala

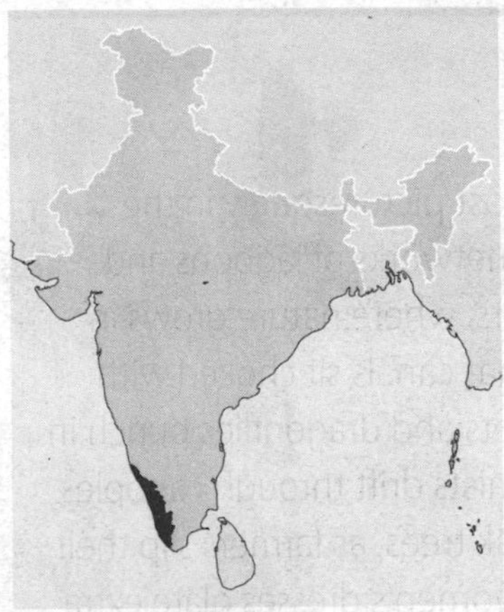

Footprint features

Introduction

Kerala ebbs by at snail's pace: most picturesquely in the slow-flowing calm found in the networks of lagoons and rivers that make up its backwaters, where nature grows in such overwhelming profusion that canals sit choked with tangles of pretty water-lily thickets and dragonflies bunch in clouds over lotus leaves. Dawn mists drift through canopies made by antique mango and teak trees, as farmers slip their oars into the silent waters, and women's dresses glare extra bright in the reflections of the still glass waters.

In the ramshackle port city of Fort Kochi, it's as if the clocks stopped a few centuries back: wizened traders sift spice in the shadows of derelict go-downs, the churches glow lime white, at the harbour's edge lines of cantilevered Chinese fishing nets swoop for their next catch of silvery sprats, and medieval streets and antique shops thread the route between the tiny blue-tiled synagogue and grand Dutch wooden palace of Mattancherry.

Unwind with ayurvedic massages on the southern beaches of Kovalam and Varkala, but Malabar, in the north, is the real unsung jewel of the state, an outpost of staunch Hindu religiosity and capital of the Muslim Moplah community. Here, hushed families gather at dawn in leafy temple gardens to watch spectacles of the unique, hypnotic temple dance-form *Theyyam*, and come nightfall the precision athletes of the swashbuckling martial art *Kalarippayattu* draw their swords.

Switchback turns bear you from the lush green paddy fields of the plains through spindly rubber plantations and blooming coffee tree forests up to the thick tea shrub territory of the high mountain villages of Thekaddy and Munnar; Julie Andrews territory whose nature reserves hide herds of tigers and elephants.

★ Don't miss ...

1 **Keraleeyam** Kerala is the centre for ayurvedic medicine. Take part in a rejuvenation programme in this lakeside therapy centre in a remote corner of Allepey, page 193.

2 **The Backwaters** Thread through canals and drift on lakes as still as mirrors to see coir making, toddy tapping and fishing from the quiet of a traditional dugout or a luxury houseboat, page 196.

3 **Alappuzha** This backwaters town is the base for spectacular August snake boat races, page 200.

4 **Fort Kochi** The historic harbour town is at its romantic best when its iconic Chinese fishing nets stand silhouetted against the tropical dusk, page 208.

5 **Periyar** The high mountain national park teems with monkeys and macaques swooping between prehistoric jackfruit trees, page 220.

6 **Thrissur** The Pooram, held at the end of April, is an unmissable grand festival with elephants, parasols, drums and fireworks, page 236.

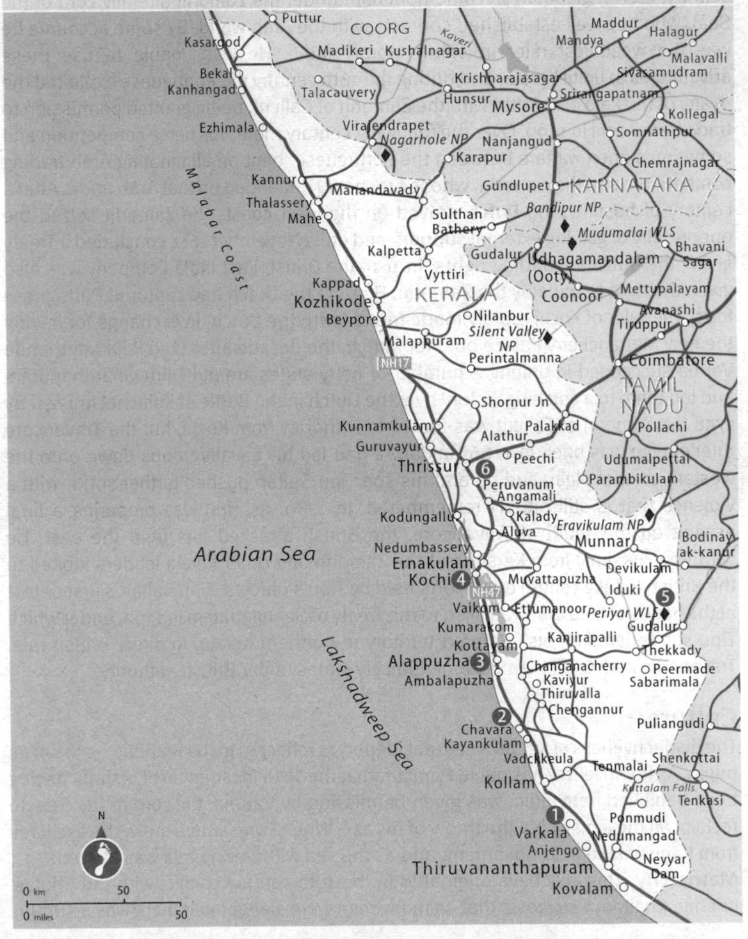

Background → *Population: 32 mn. Area: 39,000 sq km.*

The land

Geography Stretching from some of the highest mountains of the Western Ghats to the lush coastal plain, Kerala encapsulates the rich diversity of western India's coastal landscapes. Its narrow coastal fringe has been raised from the sea in the last million years. Immediately inland are low, rolling hills of laterite, succeeded by the ancient rocks that form the backbone of the Western Ghats.

Climate Kerala does not have an extended totally dry season characteristic of the rest of India, but is particularly wet from June to September. Maximum temperatures rarely rise above 32°C while minimum temperatures at sea level are never below 20°C.

History

The **Cheras**, who established themselves in the Kuttanad region around Alappuzha as the first Kerala power, developed a wide network of trade links in which both the long-established Christian community and the Jewish community participated fully. However, the neighbouring Cholas launched several successful attacks against Chera power from AD 985. When Chola power disintegrated at the end of the 11th century, Calicut gradually became dominant under the **Zamorin** (literally Lord of the Sea), who had well-established contacts with the Arab world. By some accounts he was the wealthiest ruler in contemporary India. He was unable to use these advantages to unite Kerala, and during the 16th century the Portuguese exploited the rivalry of the Raja of Kolattiri with the Zamorin of Calicut, being granted permission to trade from Kochi in 1499. Over the following century there was fierce competition and sometimes open warfare between the Portuguese, bent on eliminating Arab trading competition, and the Zamorin, whose prosperity depended on that Arab trade. After a century of hostility, the **Dutch** arrived on the west coast. The Zamorin seized the opportunity of gaining external support, and on 11 November 1614 concluded a Treaty giving the Dutch full trading rights. In 1615 the British East India Company was also given the right to trade by the Zamorin. By 1633 the Dutch had captured Portuguese forts. The ruler of Kochi rapidly made friends with the Dutch, in exchange for having the new Mattancherry Palace built for him. In the decade after 1740 Raja Marthanda Varma succeeded in uniting a number of petty states around Thiruvananthapuram and led them to a crushing victory over the Dutch in the Battle of Kolachel in 1741. By 1758 the Zamorin of Calicut was forced to withdraw from Kochi, but the **Travancore** ruler's reign was brief. In 1766 Haidar Ali had led his cavalry troops down onto the western coastal plain, and he and his son Tipu Sultan pushed further south with a violence that is still bitterly remembered. In 1789, as Tipu was preparing a final assault on the south of Travancore, the British attacked him from the east. He withdrew his army from Kerala and the Zamorin and other Kerala leaders looked to the British to take control of the forts held by Tipu's officers. Tipu Sultan's first defeat at the hands of Lord Cornwallis led to the Treaty of Seringapatam in 1792, under which Tipu surrendered all his captured territory in northern Kerala, to direct British rule. Travancore and Kochi then became Princely states under British authority.

Culture

The distinctiveness of Kerala's cultural identity is reflected in the Brahmin myths of its origin. As Robin Jeffrey has put it, Parasurama, the sixth incarnation of Vishnu, having been banished from India, was given permission by Varuna, the Lord of the Sea, to reclaim all the land within the throw of his axe. When Parasaruma threw the axe it fell from Kanniyakumari to Gokarnam, and as the sea withdrew Kerala was formed.

Matriarchy This may have originated in the 10th-century conflict with the Cholas. Krishna Chaitanya suggests that as many men were slaughtered there was a surplus

Kerala's social underbelly

The Communist Party of India has dominated Kerala's state politics since the 1960s. However, the outwards signs of Marxist ideology's impact is scant. This is despite robust labour laws to enervate entrepreneurs, a relatively high minimum wage by Indian standards, weekly strikes, and the state's rejection of plants owned by Coca-Cola, that quintessential symbol of global capitalism, after a well-organized public protest mobilized against the company's use of groundwater.

The state scores exceptionally well in quality of life indicators, but Kerala's relative prosperity is dictated less by government policy and proletarian consciousness than by the individual labours of the huge preponderance of Malayalis who work in the Middle East and send their substantial wages back home. Large sums of these wages are spent in building houses, meaning that the Kerala construction sector far outstrips local industrial and manufacturing sectors, creating an anomalous economic model. And relative affluence harvests social problems: Kerala has both the highest suicide rate and one of the highest rates of alcohol consumption per capita on the subcontinent.

of women, encouraging the development of a matrilineal system in which women controlled family property. Kerala is the first state in India to claim 100% **literacy** in some districts and women enjoy a high social status. The 2001 Census shows that overall literacy has reached 91%, and uniquely in India there are more women than men in the population.

Religion The majority of the population is Hindu, but as much as a quarter of the population is Christian and there is also a large Muslim population. Religious communities have often lived amicably together. There is no conflict between the varying Hindu sects, and most temples have shrines to each of the major Hindu divinities. Christianity, which is thought to have been brought by St Thomas the Apostle to the coast of Kerala at Kodungallur in AD 52, has its own very long tradition. The equally large Muslim community traces its origins back to the spread of Islam across the Indian Ocean with Arab traders from the seventh century.

Cuisine Kerala's cuisine reflects its diverse religious traditions, its location on the seaboard and the ubiquitous presence of the coconut. For example, uniquely in India, beef is widely eaten, although seafood is far more common. *Fish Moilee* is prepared with coconut milk and spices while for *pollichathu* the fish is baked with chilli paste, curry leaves and spices. Coconut-based dishes such as *thoran*, a dry dish of mixed vegetables chopped very small, herbs and curry leaves, with *avial*, similar to *thoran* but cooked in a sauce, are widely eaten. *Erisseri* is a thick curry of banana or yam and *kichadi* is beetroot or cucumber in coconut-curd paste. You can try these with the soft centred, lacy pancake *appam* or the soft noodle rice cakes *iddiappam*. Jack fruit, pineapples, custard apples and a endless variety of bananas also play a vital part in many dishes. For dessert, you might get milk *payasam*, made with rice or vermicelli.

Language Malayalam, the state language, is the most recent of the Dravidian languages, developing from the 13th century with its origin in Sanskrit.

Dance The special dance form of Kerala, *Kathakali*, has its origins in the *Theyyam*, a ritual tribal dance of North Kerala, and *Kalaripayattu*, the martial arts practised by the high-caste Nayars, going back 1000 years. In its present form of dance-drama, *Kathakali* has evolved over the last 400 years. The performance is usually outdoors, the stage bare but for a large bronze oil lamp, with the drummers on one side and the singers with cymbal and gong, who act as narrators, on the other. The art of mime

Body language

Ayurveda, a Sanskrit word meaning 'the knowledge (veda) of life (ayur)', is an Indian holistic system of health dating back over 5000 years. Indians see it as a divine gift from Lord Brahma, their Hindu creator God, which has been developed by sages and holy men over the centuries. In contrast to the Western system of medicine, which is geared to treating an already diseased body or mind, ayurveda seeks to help the individual strengthen and control both mind and body in order to prolong life and prevent illness. In today's world, it's a brilliant complement to Western medicine and, as well as detoxing the body and mind and relieving stress, has been used to treat ME, high blood pressure, allergies, asthma, back pain, rheumatism, skin diseases, migraines and insomnia, and is used as an effective follow-up treatment to chemotherapy.

How it works In essence, ayurveda combines body treatments and detoxification therapies with a balanced diet, gentle exercise and meditation to promote wellbeing. The type of treatments and therapies are dictated by an individual's constitution, defined by a balance of three bodily energies or doshas: vata, pitta and kapha. Composed of the five elements – earth, water, fire, air and ether (or space) – these doshas govern our bodily processes: vata controls circulation and the nervous system, for example, pitta the metabolism and digestion, kapha bodily strength and energy. When we feel out of kilter, our doshas are likely to be out of balance, which a course of ayurvedic treatments will seek to remedy. If we're uptight and prone to multi task, it will calm us down and help us focus. If we're sluggish and suffer from bad digestion, it will energize us and get our bowels moving again.

An experienced ayurvedic doctor will diagnose your dosha type by taking your pulse, and observing such things as how quickly you speak and move, your build, the colour of your eyes and the quality of your skin. You'll also be asked

reaches its peak in these highly stylized performances which used to last through the night; now they often take just three to four hours. The costume is comprised of a large billowing skirt, a padded jacket, some heavy ornaments and headgear. The make-up is all-important: *Pacha* (green) characterizing the Good and *Kathi* (knife, shape of a painted 'moustache'), the Villain; *Thadi* (bearded), white for superhuman *hanumans*, black for the hunter and red for evil and fierce demons; *Kari* (black) signifying demonesses; *Minukku* (shining) 'simple' make-up representing the Gentle and Spiritual. The paints are natural pigments while the stiff 'mask' is created with rice paste and lime. The final application of a flower seed in the lower eyelid results in the red eyes you will see on stage. This classical dance requires lengthy, hard training to make the body supple, the eyes expressive. The 24 *mudras* express the nine emotions of serenity, wonder, kindness, love, valour, fear, contempt, loathing and anger. The gods and mortals play out their roles amid the chaos brought about by human ambition, but the dance ends in peace and harmony restored by the gods.

Modern Kerala

Government Kerala politics have often been unstable – even turbulent – since the first elections were held, after the reorganization of the Indian States, in March 1957, when Kerala became the first state in the world to democratically elect a Communist government. Between then and the mid-80s, President's Rule was imposed seven times. The debate has always been dominated by the struggle between the Marxist Communist Party, the Congress, and various minor parties: and the state government lots of questions about your preferences – on anything from climate to the spiciness of food. The more open and honest you are, the more accurate a judgement will be, though it's uncanny how the best doctors will read you just right, whatever you tell them.

What you do Any programme of ayurveda will include preparation treatments and elimination (or detox) therapies. The former include soothing, synchronized oil applications and massages, and swedana (purifying steam and herbal baths), while the latter involve ingesting or retaining herbal medicines, medicated oils and ghee (or clarified butter), inhalations, bastis (or oil enemas), therapeutic vomiting and bloodletting. Preparation treatments often include sleep-inducing shirodara, when a wonderful continuous stream of warm oil is poured across your forehead; choornaswedana, where hot herbal or lemon poultices are massaged all over you to induce sweating; and the supremely nourishing four-handed abhyanga and marma massage. Pizzichilli is often regarded as the 'Marmite' of ayurveda. Gallons of cleansing sesame oil are poured continuously over your body and massaged in by two therapists as the oil increases in heat. You'll slip about like a sardine in a tin, but this treatment is very effective. Look at the oil afterwards, and you'll be shocked at just how dirty you were. If you're a smoker, it's likely to be black.

Any hotel or retreat venue that offers only ayurvedic massages is offering only a part of what ayurveda is all about. You need time for ayurveda treatments to have any real effect. A proper course of ayurveda needs at least two weeks to be effective and offer any real lasting benefit, and rest between treatments is vital. Most people who undertake a course of ayurveda have a 'panchakarma' – which literally translates as five therapies, and which also refers to a general ayurveda detox lasting two weeks or more.

has often been formed by coalitions. Although some say their support has grown slightly, the Hindu nationalist BJP does not sit at the top table of politics in the left-leaning state; politics here are resolutely secular. The incumbent Congress party in the state though, whose term was defined by internecine fighting, fared little better, and failed to win a single seat for the Lok Sabha for the first time since Independence. The state in 2004, spurred on by the ruling Congress government's poor handling of one of the state's worst droughts in the run-up to the elections, voted instead to be represented at the Center by the Communist Party of India (Marxist) and the Left Democratic Front.

Economy Traditionally Kerala's economy has depended heavily on agriculture. Estate crops, especially tea and rubber, make a major contribution to exports, while coconut and coconut products like coir, the coarse fibre used for matting and string and rope production, or copra, the oil-rich flesh of the coconut, continue to be vital to the state. Newer cash crops like pineapples have also begun to establish a national and international market. Rice production has been in long-term decline, and between 1990 and 2000 production fell by 25% as farmers converted paddy land to other more profitable uses, stimulated by the rise of Kerala as a remittance economy, with large flows of money being repatriated by Malayali workers in the Gulf to invest in land, housing and small-scale industries. Business leaders bemoan the leftist culture of the state and the stranglehold the trade unions have on its workforce, which makes for a working week dominated by strikes, thus barring the way for the high levels of foreign investment that characterize Bengaluru (Bangalore), Hyderbad and Chennai's urban economies.

Thiruvananthapuram and the far south

The state capital, a pleasant city built over gently rolling coastal land, is very much a village as soon as you step away from the crowded centre: there's none of the throb, bustle and boom-time of Ernakulam, its opposite city up north, and no-one could accuse it of being cosmopolitan: you'll be pushed to find a club or bar or even any traffic on the roads after midnight. It is, however, a stone's throw from here to the white sands of Kovalam, still a working fishing village, albeit one that survives under the lengthening shadow cast by unchecked tourist development. The backpackers who first populated Kovalam have left it to the package holidaymakers and those staying in luxury resorts to head instead to Varkala, a pilgrimage village and beach marked out by its sheer red rock face. Inland are the little visited forests of Ponmudi and just over the southern border lies Kanniyakumari: the sacred toe-tip of India where three seas converge. ▸▸ *For Sleeping, Eating and other listings, see pages 183-195.*

Ins and outs

Getting there Outside rush hour, the international airport is 15 minutes' drive (6km) from the centre, half an hour to Kovalam. It has 30 air links, including direct flights to Colombo, the Maldives, Singapore and the Middle East. **Indian Airlines** and **Jet Airways** operate domestic flights within India. You can hire a pre-paid taxi or auto into town or wait for a local bus. There are direct trains to all Kerala's main towns and India's main cities; for rail enquires T131. At the southern end of town are the central (long-distance) bus station – KSRTC (Kerala State Railway Transport Co) Thampanoor Bus Stand, T0471-232 3886 – and railway station. Short-distance buses, including those bound for Kovalam, leave from the City stand (T0471-246 3029), opposite the fort entrance southwest of the station.

Buses to Kovalam stop at Waller Junction, before Kovalam, five minutes' walk from the Samudra beach hotels. A further 1½ km on they turn off for the main bus stand at Ashok Hotel gate, five minutes from most southern hotels and cafés. Autos and taxis can get to the steep, narrow, Lighthouse Road. ▸▸ *See Transport, page 193, for further details.*

Getting around Thiruvanathapuram is relatively strung out, though the centre is compact. Autos or taxis are more convenient than the packed buses but bargain hard: businesses have fast acclimatized to the price naïvety that goes hand in hand with package tourism. Minimum charges start at Rs 75 for taxis, Rs 7 for autos; thereafter the rate per running kilometre for cars is Rs 4.50 (non a/c), Rs 6.50 (a/c), rickshaws Rs 3. Drivers may be reluctant to accept the going rate.

Tourist information Tourist offices have plenty of leaflets and information sheets and are very helpful. Thiruvanathapuram's main tourist office is at the **Department of Tourism** ⓘ *Park View, T0471-232 1132, www.keralatourism.org, Mon-Sat 1000-1700* (runs day and half-day tours around the city (Rs 110 and Rs 70 respectively). There are also offices at Thampanoor Central Bus Station and the airport.

Climate Temperature: highs of 33°C in February-March, dipping to 20°C for rest of year. Rainfall: December-April, average 50 mm; May-November, average 200 mm. Best time to visit: December-March; even at the end of March it can get very hot around midday.

Kerala is known locally as the 'city state' because its levels of population density which, at 819 people per sq km is more than double the national average of 324. Only West Bengal (with 904) and Bihar (with 880) have more.

Thiruvananthapuram (Trivandrum)

Sleeping
Chaithram 1
Geeth 4
Greenland 2
Highland 3
Kukies Holiday Inn 4
Manacaud 6
Residency Tower 8
Thamburu International 9
Wild Palms Homestay 10
Youth Hostel 7

Eating
Arul Jyoti 2
Indian Coffee House 1
Kalavara 5
Kalpakavadi 6
Kerala House 7
Mascot 3
Queen's 4

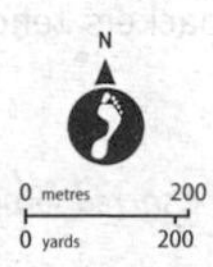

Thiruvananthapuram (Trivandrum)

» pp183-195. Colour map 3, C3.

Sights

→ *Phone code: 0471. Population: 744,739 of 3,234,356 in the Trivandrum District.*

Sri Padmanabhaswamy Temple ⓘ *East Fort, T0471-245 0233, 0415-0515, 0645-0715, 0830-1115, 1145-1200, 1700-1615, 1845-1930*. According to legend, the temple was built in stages to house the statue of Vishnu reclining on the sacred serpent *Ananta*, which was found in the forest. It was rebuilt in 1733 by Raja Marthanda Varma who dedicated the whole kingdom, including his rights and possessions, to the deity. Unusually for Kerala, it is in the Dravidian style with beautiful murals, sculptures and 368 carved granite pillars which support the main pavilion or *Kulashekhara Mandapa*. You can see the seven-storeyed *gopuram* with its sacred pool from outside; otherwise to get a closer look you first have to persuade the famously strict Kerala Brahmins to waive the Hindus-only entry restriction. It becomes easier to do so if men have donned a crisp white *dhoti*, women a sari and blouse.

The Travancore king, Maharajah Swathi Thirunal Balarama Varma, was a musician, poet and social reformer, and his palace, just next door to the temple, **Kuthiramalika (Puthenmalika) Palace** ⓘ *Temple Rd, East Fort, T0471-247 3952, Tue-Sun 0830-1230, 1530-1730, Rs 20, camera Rs 15*, is a fine reflection of his patronage of the arts. On the upper level a window gives an angle on scores of fine wood-carved horses that look like a huge cavalry charge, and among the portraits painted in the slightly unsettling Indian/European classical hybrid style is one from an artist who trumped his rivals by painting not just eyes that follow you around the room, but also feet. Sadly, it is ill maintained, but a gem nonetheless.

Napier Museum ⓘ *North Park Grounds, city north, T0471-231 8294, Tue-Sun 1000-1645, Wed morning only, closed public holidays*, is a spectacular landmark. The structure designed by RF Chisholm in traditional-Kerala-meets-Indo-Saracenic style, was completed in 1872. Today, it houses a famous collection of eighth to 18th-century South Indian bronzes, mostly from Chola, Vijayanagar and Nayaka periods, a few Jain and Buddhist sculptures and excellent wood carvings. **Sri Chitra Art Gallery** ⓘ *just north, closed Mon and Wed mornings, 1000-1645, Rs 5*, has a fine catalogue of Indian art from early to modern schools: works by Raja Ravi Varma, 20th-century pioneer of the radical post-colonial school of painting, sit among paintings from Java, Bali, China and Japan, Mughal and Rajput miniatures. The Tanjore paintings are studded with semi-precious stones. The **Zoological Park** ⓘ *Tue-Sun 0900-1845, Rs 5, cameras Rs 15, entrance at southwest corner of park*, is a hilly woodland of frangipani and jacaranda with a wide collection of animals and a well-labelled botanical garden.

Kovalam and surrounding resorts

» pp184-195. Colour map 3, C3.

→ *Phone code: 0471. Population: 25,400.*

The sleepy Lakshadweep seaside fishing village has now been almost completely swallowed up by package tourist infrastructure: ayurveda, trinkets, tailoring and tour operator shops line every inch of the narrow walkways behind the shore. In peak season it's something of an exotic god's waiting room, popular with pensioners, and it's safe and sedate enough for families. Backpackers tend to return off season.

Thiruvananthapuram is derived from Tiru Ananta Puram, the abode of the sacred serpent Ananta upon whose coils Vishnu lies in the main temple.

Kovalam

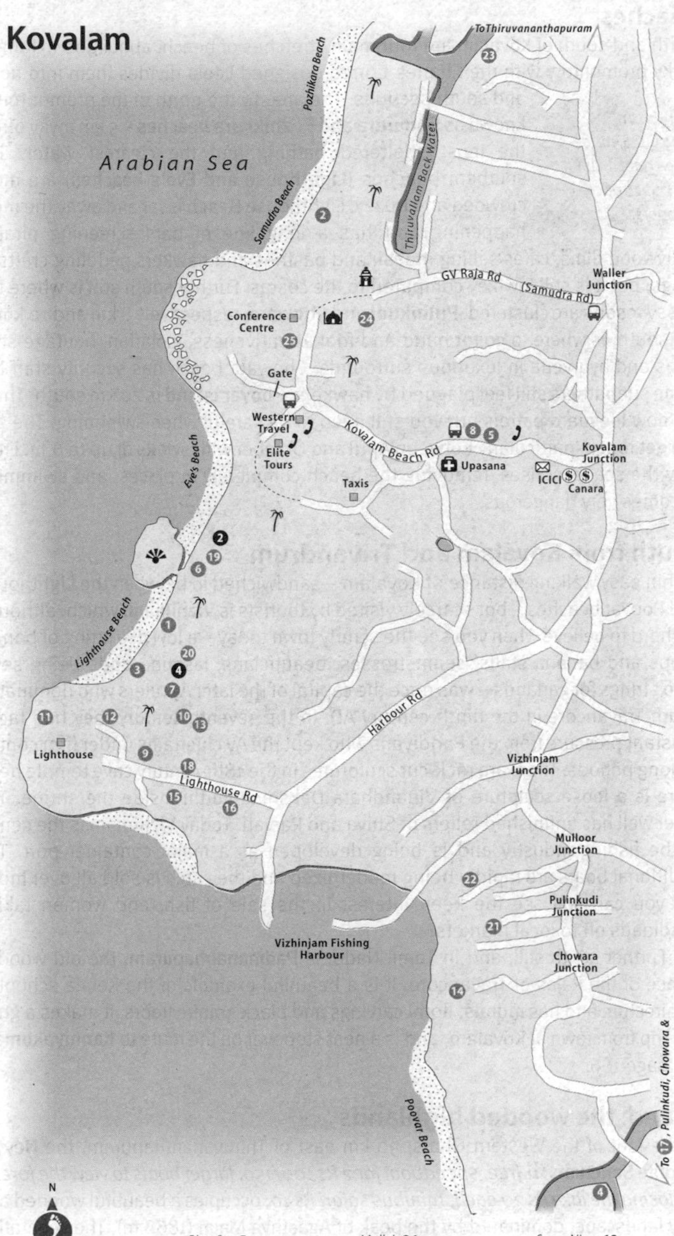

Sleeping
Abad Palm Shore 16
Achutha 1
Al Italia Beach Resort 2
Beach, Fusion Restaurant & German Bakery 3
Blue Sea 5
Coconut Bay Beach Resort 22
Dwaraka Lodge 6
Friday's Place Poovar 4
Green Valley Cottages 7
Holiday Home 8
Lagoona Davina 23
Leela 25
Maharaju Palace 10
Molly's 24
Nice Rest House 18
Paradise Rock 12
Pink Flowers 13
Poovar Island Resort 17
Rockholm 15
Sea Flower Home 11
Seaweed 9
Somatheeram & Manaltheeram 14
Surya Nivas 13
Surya Samudra Beach Garden 21
Swami Tourist Home 19
Wilson Beach Resort 20

Eating
Lonely Planet 4
Sea Face 2

Beaches

North and south of Kovalam are four main stretches of beach, about 400 m long. A rocky promontory with the Charles Correa-designed **Leela** divides them into north and south sections. The area to the north of the promontory – known as **Samudra and Pozhikkara beaches** – 5 km away offers the most sheltered bathing and the clearest water. The southern beaches (**Lighthouse and Eve's beaches**) are more crowded and buzzy. Lighthouse Beach is far and away the most happening and has a long line of bars screening pirated Hollywood films, cafés selling muesli and pastries and hawkers peddling crafts or drugs; but it is still low-key compared to the costas. Further south still is where the classy resorts are clustered. **Pulinkudi** and **Chowara**, respectively 8 km and 10 km to the south, is where to go for hand-and-foot attentiveness, isolation, heritage-style villas and ayurveda in luxurious surrounds. Chowara beach has security staff but some sunbathers still feel plagued by hawkers. **Poovar Island** is 20 km south. There are now lifeguard patrols but you still need to be careful when swimming. The sea can get rough, particularly between April and October with swells of up to 6 m. From May the sea level rises, removing the beach completely in places, and swimming becomes very dangerous.

Kerala Tourism, T0471-248 0085, inside Le Meridien gate, helpful manager but erratic opening hours.

South from Kovalam and Trivandrum

Within easy walking distance of Kovalam – sandwiched in between the Lighthouse and Poovar beaches – but scarcely visited by tourists is **Vizhinjam**, which, although it's hard to believe when you see the scruffy town today – a low rise string of bangle shops and banana stalls, seamstresses, beauticians, jasmine buds being sewn onto strings for garlands – was once the capital of the later Ay rulers who dominated South Travancore in the ninth century AD. In the seventh century they had faced constant pressure from the Pandiyans who kept the Ay chieftains under firm control for long periods. There are rock-cut sculptures in the 18th-century cave temple here: there is a loose sculpture of Vinandhara Dakshinamurthi inside the shrine. The outer wall has unfinished reliefs of Shiva and Parvati. Today Vizhinjam is the centre of the fishing industry and is being developed as a major container port. The traditional boats are rapidly being modernized and the catch is sold all over India, but you can still see the keen interest in the sale of fish, and women taking headloads off to local markets.

Further south still, and in Tamil Nadu, is **Padmanabhapuram**, the old wooden palace of the Rajas of Travancore. It is a beautiful example of the Kerala school of architecture and has murals, floral carvings and black granite floors. It makes a great day trip from town or Kovalam, and is a neat stopover on the route to **Kanniyakumari**, see page 166.

Inland: the wooded highlands

At the foot of the Western Ghats, 30 km east of Thiruvananthapuram, the **Neyyar Wildlife Sanctuary** ⓘ *free, speedboat for 2 Rs 100/150, larger boats to view the forests enclosing the lake Rs 20 each, minibus safari Rs 10*, occupies a beautiful wooded and hilly landscape, dominated by the peak of Agasthya Malai (1868 m). The vegetation ranges from grassland to tropical, wet evergreen. Wildlife includes gaur, sloth bear, Nilgiri tahr, jungle cat, sambar deer, elephants and Nilgiri langur; the most commonly seen animals are lion-tailed macaques and other monkeys. Tigers and leopards have also been reported. **Neyyar Dam** supports a large population of crocodiles and otters; a crocodile farm was set up in 1977 near the administrative complex.

Immediately to the northeast of the Neyyar Wildlife Sanctuary an area of dense forest, **Agasthya Vanam**, was set aside as a biological park in 1992 to recreate biodiversity on a wide scale. Nearby, the **Sivananda Yoga Vedanta Dhanwantari Ashram**

ⓘ *T0471-227-3093, www.sivananda.org/neyyardam, minimum stay 3 days*, runs meditation and yoga courses. It is quite an intensive schedule, with classes that start just after dawn and a strict timetable including karma yoga. It is only really suitable for the hardy; others may find it heavy on Hinduism and Indian diet.

Further north sits **Ponmudi** ⓘ *buses from Trivandrum, Thampanoor bus stand, 0530-1630; return from between 0615 and 1905 (2½ hrs)*, the nearest hill station to Thiruvananthapuram, 65 km away. In a spectacular and peaceful setting, the tourist complex, though basic, serves as a good base for trekking, birdwatching and visiting the nearby minimalist deer park.

Varkala

» *pp187-195. Colour map 3, C3. See also map, p188.*

→ *Phone code: 0472. Population: 42,300.*

Like Gokarna in Karnataka, Varkala is a pilgrimage centre for both backpackers and Hindus. The former come for the ruddy beach which lies at the bottom of the dramatic drop of a laterite cliff, the latter for the Vaishanvaite Janardhanaswamy temple and the Sivagiri Mutt of social reformer Sree Narayana Guru. The sea is far from calm (it has lifeguards for good reason), and the main beach – Papanasam, accessed by steep steps hacked in the cliffs – is shared between holidaymakers and fishermen. Along the cliff path, particularly along the North Cliff, is the tourist village high street; sizeable concrete hotels, travel agents, cyber cafés, tailors stitching out endless pairs of fisherman's trousers and a huge preponderance of Kashmiri and Tibetan sales people pushing their turquoise, silverware and carpets. Further north, the tourist shacks bleed into fishing village life around the Alimood Mosque (dress modestly).

! Watch your step around the cliff, particularly at night. Carry a torch.

The south, bordered by a golden beach, has a lovely village feel: traditional houses built around the 13th century temple dedicated to Vishnu (the Arratu festival in March-April draws thousands).

Opposite is the **Sri Rama Hanuman Temple**, whose large temple tank three wheeler drivers splash through in the morning, and women thwack their lungis clean on its steps. The main 'town' area (including the train station) is a further 2 km inland from Temple Junction.

A two-hour excursion takes you to **Golden Island** for a glimpse of local backwaters; there's a small temple here but it's the type of visit you'd make for the atmosphere more than anything else. A boat round the island should cost Rs 50 for the hour.

Lullaby@Varkala, www.lullabyatvarkala.in, runs tours to introduce tourists to anganwadis, childcare centres for underprivileged families. The project helps feed, clothe and educate its beneficiaries.

Sleeping

Thiruvananthapuram *p180, map p179*

A-C Residency Tower, Press Rd, T0471-233 1661, www.residencytower.com. 80 top-quality rooms in a predominantly business hotel, 60 a/c with full facilities, highly efficient, good restaurants, bar, rooftop pool (non-residents Rs 350). A bit swish.

C Wild Palms Homestay, Mathrubhoomi Rd, Vanchiyoor, 10-min walk Statue Junction or ask for pick-up, T0471-247 1175, wildpalm@md3.vsnl.net.in. 6 rooms in modern guesthouse set in pretty tropical garden in the leafy suburbs, some a/c, spacious, cool, welcoming. Price includes breakfast, credit cards accepted.

D-E Chaithram (KTDC), Station Rd, T0471-233 0977, www.ktdc.com. 80 rooms, 24 a/c, good a/c restaurant, bar, exchange, modern, very clean, next to railway and bus stand, noisy area but good value, often full.

D-F Geeth, off MG Rd, near GPO, Pulimudu, T0471-247 1987. 50 rooms, some a/c, rooftop restaurant recommended.

D-F Highland, Manjalikulam Rd, T0471-233 3200. 85 clean, comfortable rooms, some a/c in a tall block, satellite TV. Spotless.

D-F Thamburu International, Aristo Junction, opposite railway station, T0471-232 1974 www.thamburu.com. Quiet, well-run hotel with 35 comfortable, wood-panelled rooms (some a/c, suites have balcony, TV, bath, hot water 24 hrs), excellent value, alarmingly blue elevator, central, with great views. Sometimes full.

F Kukies Holiday Inn, Luke's Lane, T0471-247 8530. Small, quiet, big clean rooms that are a bit decrepit, with a pleasant flower-filled courtyard, good value.

F Manacaud, Manjalikulam Rd, T0471-233 0360. 46 basic rooms, some with bath, very friendly.

F Youth Hostel (KTDC), Veli (10 km from centre). Rooms and dorm (Rs 10), very cheap vegetarian lunches, pretty lagoon separated from the sea by a sandbar, surrounded by coconut groves, clean beach, boating, some watersports, good views.

G Greenland, near Aristo Junction, T0471-232 3485, short walk from station and bus. Double rooms with bath, not wildly friendly but very safe, good value. 24-hr checkout.

Airport

E Asha, 200 m from airport, T0471-250 1050. Very handy for early departures, decent rooms with bath.

Kovalam and surrounding resorts

p180, map p181

Long power cuts are common here, so a/c often doesn't work. Look for rooms with windows on two walls to get a good through-breeze. The area behind the Lighthouse Beach is full of hotels with a range of rooms from Rs 100-1000. There are numerous budget cottages and rooms to let. Scouts greet arrivals at the bus stand but you may pay considerably more if you use their services. You will find rooms to let, behind bars and restaurants, by walking from the Sea Rock hotel towards the lighthouse, and on the Samudra Beach and GV Raja Rd (Samudra Rd). Rates shown here are for the high season. Prices skyrocket in all hotels for the 2-week peak period (20 Dec-10 Jan), though it still pays to bargain. High season is 1-19 Dec, 11 Jan-28 Feb; in the low season, especially May-Jul, expect 40-75% discounts.

LL The Leela, Samudra Beach, Kovalam, www.theleela.com. Uber-snazzy chain hotel built on the most lovely crest of a hill above Kovalam where every bright room has a sea view. The grounds are brilliant, and you can even zip about in golf buggies. 2 huge infinity pools boast some of the world's best coastal views. A brand spanking new ayurvedic spa, the Divya, has one of the prettiest yoga shalas in the world. Down-to-earth American teacher, Bridget Shields (www.bridgetshields.com) runs retreat packages here. 70 beach view rooms, 16 deluxe, 2 suites, 20 garden view pavilion rooms, 22 sea view pavilion rooms. And if this isn't luxurious enough for you, splash out on a stay at The Club, the hotel's discreet and de luxe clubhouse that is strictly heads of state and filmstars territory, with a matching price tag. Each suite has unfathomably beautiful views over the Arabian Sea, there's a 24-hr butler service, your own spa and living room. 60 rooms, 3 suites, 1 maharaja suite.

L Friday's Place Poovar, T0142-874 1510, www.fridaysplace.biz. Remote, watery eco-hideaway with 4 teak and mahogany cottages on an isolated sandbank amid rows of palms and hibiscus, frangipani and bougainvillea, run by British couple Mark and Sujeewa, the latter a sivananda yoga teacher and reiki healer. There's kayaking and temple tours. Food is fresh, with fruit for breakfast, thali lunches, fish and chicken suppers. Shared bathroom and solar powered.

L Taj Green Cove Resort, GV Raja Vattapara Rd, Kovalam, T0471-248 7733, www.tajhotels.com. Set in 10 acres of tropical grounds with superb views of the sea, 57 rooms, 9 suites, infinity pool, spa, gym and Wi-Fi.

A-D Abad Palm Shore, T0471-248 1481, www.abadhotels.com. 35 a/c rooms, popular with groups, holiday camp atmosphere but lovely pool and beach access. Money change and ayurvedic health centre.

A-D The Beach Hotel, T0471-248 1937, the_beach_hotel_kovalam@yahoo.co.in. 8 airy rooms with big bathrooms facing the

For an explanation of the sleeping and eating price codes used in this guide, see inside the front cover. Other relevant information is found in Essentials pages 40-44.

beach, modern terracotta tiles and antique furniture. As it's under the same scrupulous management as **Fusion Restaurant** and the **German Bakery** (upstairs) you get breakfast thrown in at the latter free. Recommended.

A-D Rockholm, Lighthouse Rd, T0471-248 0406, www.rockholm.com. Very pleasant hotel owned by an Anglo-Indian family with immaculately mannered staff, charmingly old-fashioned. 22 very good rooms and penthouse in a wonderful position just above the lighthouse. Good terrace restaurant (see page 190), clean and spacious..

B Kailasam Yoga and Ayurveda Holidays, Kovalam, T0471-248 4018, www.yogaindia.co.uk. A peaceful oasis set up by UK yoga teacher Diana Shipp and her ayurvedic physician partner Mohan. 5 singles, 3 twins/doubles. Yoga classes held in tiled areas under coconut-leaf roofs, surrounded by trees and open-sided to catch the sea breezes. From US$711 per person for 2 weeks, including yoga classes.

B Molly's, Samudra Beach Road, Kovalam, T0471-326 2099, mollyskovalam@rediffmail.com. 2-storey hotel set around a pool opposite the Taj. Each room has a terrace overlooking a jungly thicket of coconuts. The restaurant, which serves Mexican, European, Indian and tandoor food, is very popular. Heather, who's English, and her Malayalam husband Dama both cook.

B-C Wilson Beach Resort, up path behind Neelkantha, T0471-221 0019, wilson6@md4.vsnl.net.in. 24 pleasant and quiet rooms with bath, 14 a/c, open-air restaurant, garden, balconies with fan, exchange, clean, safe, friendly and helpful service. Recommended.

B-D Hotel Seaweed, Lighthouse Rd, Kovalam, T0471-480391, seeweed@md3.vsnl.net.in. Green and white complex with huge sea-facing sit-outs from 12 of the 38 rooms. Money change, airport pick-up.

C-D Al Italia Beach Resort, Samudra Beach, T0471-248 0042. 4 simple but modern rooms, secluded beachfront (with fishermen early morning), quiet, breezy, shady restaurant, delicious food.

C-E Blue Sea, near Telegraph office, T0471-248 1401, homerest@md3.vsnl.net.in. An unusual, calm hotel, 15 a/c rooms, in a converted Kerala-style mansion with curious circular towers, large garden with good pool (non-residents Rs 150), great restaurant area.

D-F Maharaju Palace, near the lighthouse, T0471-248 5320, martienweber@hotmail.com. 6 lovely rooms with balconies in a beautiful, shady garden setting, very peaceful. Recommended.

E Achutha, Lighthouse Beach. Restaurant, good clean rooms and good food.

E Dwaraka Lodge, Lighthouse Beach, T0471-248 0411, marytambini@hotmail.com. 8 basic but clean rooms, some with bath, restaurant, quiet beachfront location, art gallery, boat trips.

E Green Valley Cottages, T0471-248 0636, indira_ravi@hotmail.com. 21 clean, fresh and quiet rooms with bath in lovely surroundings, restaurant. Recommended.

E Paradise Rock, Lighthouse Rd, T0471-248 0658. 4 large rooms, hot showers, close to beach, good views and breeze.

E White House, Lighthouse Beach, T0471-248 3388, whitehouse@vsnl.com. 12 clean and airy rooms, nets, use of common fridge and kitchen, close to beach, very good value. Recommended.

E-F Nice Rest House, Lighthouse, T0471-248 0684, abayadhara@yahoo.com. 10 clean rooms across 2 wings, 1st floor has amazing views of the beach.

E-F Sea Flower Home, Lighthouse Beach, T0471-248 0554, visitindia@eth.net. Right on the beach with 9 rooms over 3 storeys and own rooftop restaurant. Nice doubles with basins built inside the rooms themselves and clean bathrooms.

F Pink Flowers, Lighthouse Beach, behind Neptune hotel. 4 immaculate rooms with bath, good location, friendly.

F Surya Nivas, Lighthouse Beach. 4 very clean rooms with bath, quiet, friendly.

F Swami Tourist Home, with good clean rooms, good food and friendly service.

F-D Hotel Holiday Home, Beach Rd (10 mins' walk from sea), T0471-248 0497. Clean, pleasant rooms and cottages, some a/c, dorm (Rs 150), good food, beautiful flower garden, internet, quiet, friendly, excellent service. Recommended.

Beaches *p182*

Pozhikkara Beach (5 km north) *p182*

AL-B Lagoona Davina, Pozhikkara beach, near Trivandrum, T0471-238 0049, www.lagoonadavina.com. A modest fiefdom on the backwaters between

Trivandrum and Kovalam established by dynamic Londoner Davina. An island of sand separates the river bank from the wider sea. Small library, plenty of cushion-strewn seats cut into the seawall to read the books in, and a small shop selling Davina's hybrid Indian-Western clothes, part-saree, part-Kings Road. Tasty and healthy scran, orthopaedic beds, your own 'houseboy', excellent yoga and massage and jasmine piles fragrance your room at night. But iffy water pressure and internet connectivity, a fan rather than a/c and only a small swimming pool may put some off. Popular with independent female travellers. Breakfasts US$8, lunch US$12, dinner US$18. Yoga, massage, meditation all US$18 an hour for private sessions or US$8 for shared. Reiki for US$36 (and 15% tax throughout).

C-D Backwater House, Pozhikkara beach, T0471-259 0155, bwhouse2001@hotmail .com. Simple but comfortable rooms.

Mulloor (6 km south)

B Coconut Bay Beach Resort, Mulloor, T0471-248 0566, www.coconutbay.com. 13 spacious brick/stone cottages on beach, good restaurant, friendly, secluded location in traditional fishing village, next to Siddharth Ayurvedic and Yoga Centre. Recommended.

Pulinkudi and Chowara

LL Karikkathi Beach House, near Nagar Bhagavathy Temple at Mulloor Thottam, Pulinkudi, T0471-240 0956, www.karikkathi beachhouse.com. 2 doubles with linked lounge, palm thatch roof, no a/c or TV, perfect for honeymooners or those used to being kept; the house comes with private beach, chef, waiter and servants. There's a cottage should families or groups need extra beds. Full board an extra US$18 per day.

L Surya Samudra Beach Garden, Pulinkudi, near Kovalam, T0471-226 7333, www.surya samudra.com. Sitting high on a rocky bluff between Kovalam and Kannyukamari, this elite resort has just added a world-class, immaculate spa. There are just 21 traditional Keralan cottages, with four-posters, big plantation chairs and open-air bathrooms, spread over its 23 acres of jackfruit, bamboo, cinnamon, mango, frangipani, palm and hibiscus trees. It offers ayurveda from its beautifully designed complex, splashing fountains and lawns. Clients are flush Europeans. The Octopus restaurant serves great North and South Indian specials and Western food and the kitchen will rustle up bespoke sattvic stuff for those embarking on ayurvedic treatments. Excellent Sivananda school yoga on a one-on-one basis at an open-air pavilion overlooking the sea.

AL-A Somatheeram & Manaltheeram, Chowara Beach, south of Kovalam, T0471-226 8101 (central reservations), www.somatheeram.org, www.manal theeram.com. Kerala's first ayurvedic resort, Somatheeram is also the repeated winner of the state's competition to find the best. Its cottages and traditional Kerala a/c houses set in coconut groves are dotted over a steep hill above the beach. If you want more peace on level ground and the use of an oyster-shaped pool with whirlpool, stay at the sister resort of Manaltheeram. Choose from Kerala-style a/c houses and brick and coconut palm thatch cottages. 15 doctors and 90 therapists work in 48 treatment rooms at the shared ayurvedic facilities. British-based holistic health and beauty therapist, Bharti Vyas (T+44 (0)20-7935 5312, www.bharti-vyas.com), leads 10-day retreats here, or join a yoga retreat with uplifting American vinyasa flow teacher, Shiva Rea (www.yogaadventures.com).

A-C Bethsaida Hermitage, Pulinkudi, T0471-226 7554 www.kerala.com. 33 rooms in eco-friendly stone and bamboo beach *cabanas* in coconut groves built for single or double occupancy. Profits support 2600 children at the orphanage next door. Family friendly, informal and unpretentious.

Poovar Island

This is 20 km south and accessible only by boat. Taxis Rs 200

LL Poovar Island Resort, Poovar Island, T0471-221 2068, www.poovarisland resort.com. Award-winning boutique hotel with 16 'floating' cottages where the backwaters meet the sea. 64 land cottages. Pool, handicrafts, ayurveda, watersports.

Inland: the wooded highlands *p182*

Agasthya

E Agasthya House (KTDC), opposite viewing tower, near Forest Information Centre,

Kattakada, T0471-227 2160. On the edge of the reservoir, 6 rooms, built like a concrete bunker, disappointing restaurant, lunch Rs 20-50, beer, views, very helpful staff.

Ponmudi

L Duke's Forest Lodge, Anappara, near Ponmudi, T0471-226 8822, www.dukesforest.com. 5 luxury villas, each with its own plunge pool, set on organic estate. Great trekking.

F Ponmudi Tourist Resort, T0471-289 0230. 24 rooms and 10 cottages, in attractive gardens surrounded by wooded hills, spartan facilities but spacious rooms, restaurant serves limited but reasonable vegetarian meals, beer available, also a post office and general stores.

Varkala *p183, map p188*

There are at least 50 guesthouses, plus rooms in private houses. The North Cliff area is compact, so look around until you find what you want: the northernmost area is where the most laid-back, budget options are and have the most character, while the far south side has a few fancier places. None, however, is actually on the beach. Outside the high season of Nov-Mar, prices drop by up to 50%. During the monsoon (Jun-Jul) many close.

AL Taj Garden Retreat, near Government Guest House, 500 m from the beach, T0470-260 3000, www.tajhotels.com. 30 slightly musty rooms in the old palace of the Maharaja of Travancore. Far from the beach, with partial sea views, a/c, lovely garden, pool, good if slightly pricey restaurant, questionable-looking ayurveda facility. The 2 suites have baths, but each room has a small terrace balcony, of which 11 are seafacing, 17 garden facing. TV. Free bike hire, tennis court, badminton, volleyball, table tennis, and swings and slides for kids.

A Hindustan Beach Retreat, Papanasam Beach, Janardhanapuram, T0470-260 4254 www.hindustanbeachretreat.com. Not much to look at from outside, but inside are 27 very well-appointed rooms with amazing sea views, plunge pool set in small lawn and rooftop restaurant. Executive rooms have balconies, suites have chaise lounges. All a/c. Easily the smartest place to stay in Varkala if you need all mod cons.

A Varkala Deshadan, Kurakkanni Cliff, T0472- 320 4242, www.deshadan.com. 12 rooms all with TV, bath and a/c in new Chettinadu-style bungalow complex set around a pool. Hot water. Spotlessly clean. Breakfast included.

A-E Marine Palace, Papanasam Beach, on path down from cliff, T0471-248 1428, www.hotelmarinepalace.com. 12 rooms, some a/c in small bungalows (not a palace), good Tandoori restaurant very close to beach (but very slow service), simple, friendly, comfortable, popular with older people.

B Villa Jacaranda, Temple Rd West, South Cliff, T0470-261 0296, www.villa-jacaranda.biz.

Varkala

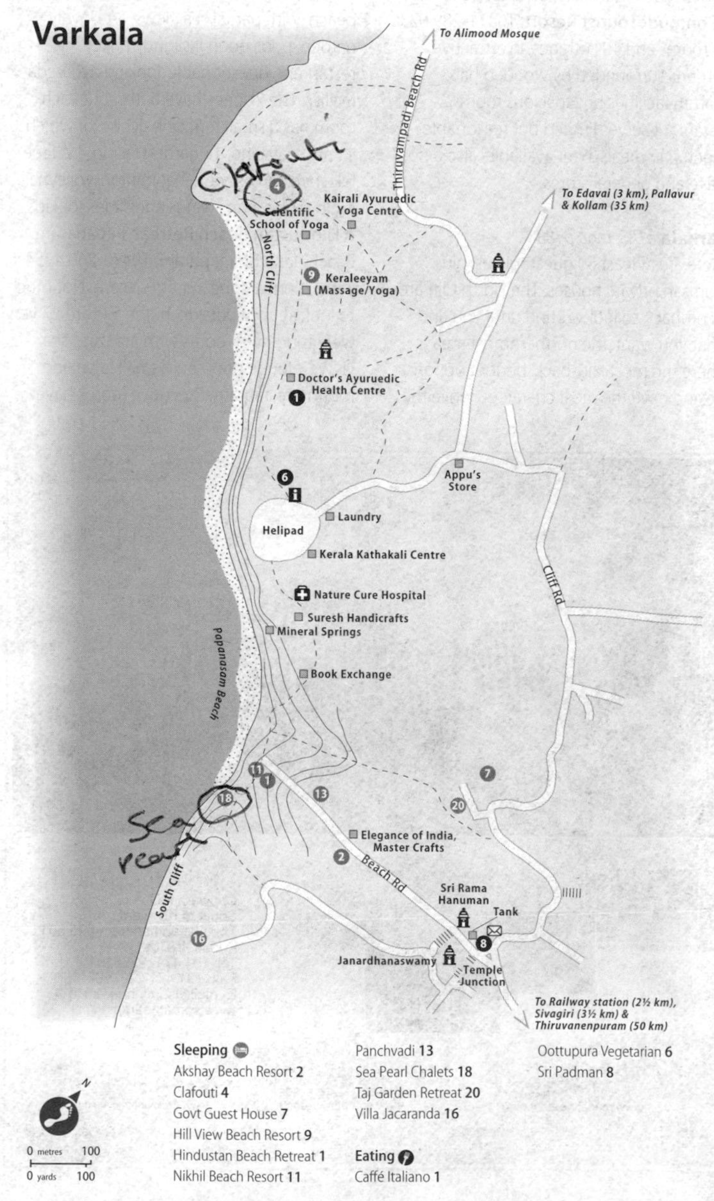

Sleeping
Akshay Beach Resort 2
Clafouti 4
Govt Guest House 7
Hill View Beach Resort 9
Hindustan Beach Retreat 1
Nikhil Beach Resort 11
Panchvadi 13
Sea Pearl Chalets 18
Taj Garden Retreat 20
Villa Jacaranda 16

Eating
Caffé Italiano 1
Oottupura Vegetarian 6
Sri Padman 8

A delightful guesthouse home to Londoners Ajay and Wesley, with 5 huge rooms elegantly but sparely decorated. Jasmine, birds of paradise and magnolia blossoms are tucked into alcoves, there's a lotus-filled pond and tropical garden and everything is immaculately maintained. Guests have their own keys and entrance. Really special.

B-D Akshay Beach Resort, Beach Rd (about 200 m from beach), T0470-260 2668. 17 rooms, 4 spacious doubles with a/c, bathtub and TV, but singles very small, standard good value, bright, clean and smart, TV lounge, good restaurant.

B-E Nikhil Beach Resort, Beach Rd, T0470-260 5191, www.nikhil-resort.com. 11 rooms, 4 a/c, exchange and money transfer. Clean, pleasant, good value.

C Hill View Beach Resort, North Cliff, T0470-260 0566, www.hillviewbeachresort.com. 20 rooms: self-contained cottages, budget rooms with bathroom attached and de luxe room with bathtub. Fast onsite internet, pick-up from airport, hot water. Efficient.

D Panchvadi, Beach Rd, T0470-260 0200. 8 clean rooms (2 luxury) with bath (excellent showers), 24-hr check-in, laundry, Kerala- style restaurant, good security, friendly helpful staff, close to beach. Recommended.

E Clafouti, North Cliff, T0470-260 1414, clafouti@rediffmail.com. 8 lovely rooms in new house (Rs 750), old house (Rs 200), all tiled baths, very clean, French-run bakery for excellent pastries (see page 190).

E Sea Pearl Chalets, Beach Rd, T0470-260 5875, seapearlvarkala@hotmail.com. 10 circular thatched huts in breezy location on south cliff, great views, breakfast.

E-G Sunshine Home/Johnny Cool & Soulfood Café, North Cliff, Varkala Beach, T0934-120 1295. 4 rooms in a private-walled rasta house, lots of conscious reggae around, bongo drums and Marley posters, plus a little standalone thatched cottage out the back. The 2 top rooms have bathrooms and balcony, there's a 'family apartment' and downstairs 2 single rooms. The café does pastas, noodles, fish and chips – but in its own sweet time.

F Govt Guest House, towards **Taj Garden Retreat**, T0470-260 2227. 8 rooms in the leafy former summer residence of the Maharaja, with huge high ceilings. Individual buildings are better than rooms in the main house. Generally idyllic and quiet, marble floors, big baths, shaded porches. All the prettiness and isolation of the **Taj** site without the facilities and price tag. Book in advance. Recommended.

F Sea Splendour, North Cliff end, Odayam Beach, T0470-266 2120, seasplendour1@hotmail.com. Rooms with bath in retired teacher's guesthouse, excellent home cooking (unlimited and spoilt for choice), very quiet.

F-G RubyBleu House, Varkala cliff side, behind Ootupura restaurant (ask for Akash), T999-504 0495, katalin@rubybleu.org. RubyBleu is Leon, Katalin and baby Yoko's flamboyant home, fluttering with prayer flags and covered with passion fruit vines. These are much-lived people (Leon's been in India 27 years), and you stay here for the atmosphere, because there are no frills. Katalin teaches yoga and is a reiki practitioner. There's a good esoteric and beat generation library, and lots of rock'n'roll. No food, but they'll make proper coffee. 4 rooms with attached bath and there are 7 campbeds on the roof if you want to sleep under the stars.

Eating

Thiruvananthapuram *p180, map p179*

The first 4 options are in hotels, see Sleeping.

TTT-TT Mascot, excellent lunchtime buffet, pleasant, 24-hr coffee shop for all types of snacks, good value, a cool haven at midday.

TT Kalavara, Press Rd, T0471-232 2195, Indian, Continental, Chinese fast food (burgers, shakes) takeaway. Food average, slow service but good value buffets in upstairs thatched section with a patch of garden – good ambience, limited views.

TT Kalpakavadi, Press Rd. Mixed menu. Modern and smart. Recommended.

TT Kerala House, near Statue Junction, T0471-247 6144. Kerala cuisine in the basement of shopping complex. Clean, slow for breakfast but newspapers available, outside seating in the evening in roadside car park area is cheaper. Colourful and fun place to pass some time, even if the food arrives cold. Try *neem, kappa* and rice (delicious fish with tapioca), or inexpensive chicken dishes with coconut; bakery in the complex does excellent samosas and puffs.

TT Queen's, Aristo Junction. Indian non-vegetarian. Chilli chicken recommended.

Ɏ **Arul Jyoti**, MG Rd, opposite Secretariat. South Indian vegetarian. With a/c family room, clean, wide choice of good value dishes, try jumbo dosas. Great Tamil Nadu thalis.

Ɏ **Indian Coffee House**, 2 on MG Rd (1 near YWCA, north of the Secretariat, and 1 near KSRTC bus stand (the latter designed by the English architect Laurie Baker). Worth seeing, excellent value coffee and snacks.

Kovalam and surrounding resorts *p180, map p181*

There are hundreds of restaurants here. Service can be slow, and quality hit-and-miss since management often changes hands. Below is a very short list of those that have proved consistent. The restaurants at the **Leela** and the **Taj** are good, if predictable; the **Leela**'s Sunday brunch has a giant salad counter and loud live music. **Ashok** and **Samudra** are licensed and open to non-residents. Avoid 'catch of the day' on Sundays – it's unlikely to be fresh. Some restaurants will screen pirated DVDs, sometimes to compensate for underwhelming cuisine.

ƔƔ **Fusion**, Hawa/Lighthouse Beach, near sunset view rocks, T0471-248 4153, fusion_in_kovalam@yahoo.co.in. Swish restaurant and coffee bar from owner of **The German Bakery**, stone banquettes, varied menu (Indian food, continental; the middle panel is reserved for the food 'where east meets west', everything from baked potatoes to dhal and curry to Italian fried prawn) plus good juices, herbal teas.

ƔƔ **The German Bakery**, has a justly evangelical following: mains include seer fish, biryani, pizza, pasta and Thai, cinnamon danish pastries, apple crumble but also delicious fresh herbal teas and fish dishes in new premises above the **Beach Hotel**, with a huge terrace half open to the heavens.

ƔƔ **Rockholm Hotel**, Lighthouse Rd. Very good international food served on a pleasant terrace with beautiful views, especially early morning. Staid, great setting, tandooris.

ƔƔ **Sea Face**, breezy raised terrace on the beach by a pleasant pool. Varied choice including versatile fish and seafood. Friendly and attentive.

Ɏ **Lonely Planet**, wholesome, mildly spiced ayurvedic vegetarian food. Set inland around a pond with ducks – and mosquitoes. Sells recipe books and runs cookery courses.

Varkala *p183, map p188*

Many restaurants close out of season. Take extra care with drinking water. There are numerous restaurants along North Cliff, most with facsimile menus, slow service and questionable kitchens. 'Catch of the day' splayed out for you to inspect, usually costs Rs 100-150 depending upon the type/size of fish, but make sure you don't get 'catch of yesterday' (fresh fish keep their glassy eyes and bright silvery scales).

ƔƔƔ **Taj Garden Retreat** hotel, see page 187, (Rs 300, includes pool use), on Sun 1230-1530, good eat-all-you-want buffet, delicious rich vegetarian Indian.

ƔƔ **Caffé Italiano**, North Cliff, T984-605 3194. Good Italian food, but quite pricey.

ƔƔ **Clafouti**, Clafouti hotel (page 189). Fresh pastries and cakes, but standards seem to drop when the French-Keralan owners are away.

ƔƔ **Oottupura Vegetarian Restaurant**, Helipad Cliffside Varkala, near helipad, T0472-260 6994, jickys2002@yahoo.co.in. Excellent 100% vegetarian (*masala dosa* Rs 20, dishes Rs 30-40). 60 vegetarian curries, then everything from Chinese to macaroni cheese. Breakfast can be Kerala iddlies, or toasted sandwiches, all served under a giant pistachio tree covered in fairy lights.

ƔƔ **Sri Padman**, Sreepadmam T0472-260 5422. With the best position in town, come here for South India vegetarian breakfast served in big stainless steel thali trays, oily parathas to sop up spicy curries and coconut chutneys on terrace overlooking the temple tank.

Entertainment

Thiruvananthapuram *p180, map p179*

Performances of *Kalarippayattu*, Kerala's martial art, can be seen through:
CVN Kalari, East Fort, T0471-247 4182 (0400-0700, 1700-2000); and **Balachandran Nair Kalari Martial Arts Gymnasium**, Cotton Hill (0600-0800 and 1800-1930).

Kovalam and surrounding resorts *p180, map p181*

Kalakeli Kathakali Troupe, T0471-248 1818. Daily at hotels **Ashok** and **Neptune**, Rs 100.

Varkala *p183, map p188*
Varkala is a good place to hang out, chill and do yoga but there's no organized nightlife to speak of, only impromptu campfire parties. **Kerala Kathakali Centre**, by the helipad, holds a daily *Kathakali* demonstration (Rs 150, make-up 1700-1800, performance 1830-2000). The participants are generally students of the art rather than masters.

Festivals and events

Thiruvananthapuram *p180, map p179*
Mar: **Chandanakuda**, at Beemapalli, a shrine on Beach Rd 5 km southwest of the railway station. 10-day festival when local Muslims go to the mosque, holding incense sticks and pots. Marked by sword play, singing, dancing, elephant procession and fireworks.
Mar-Apr (Meenam) and **Oct-Nov** (Thulam): **Arattu** is the closing festival of the 10-day celebrations of the Padmanabhaswamy Temple, in which the deity is paraded around the temple inside the fort and then down to the sea (see also page 183).
Sep/Oct: **Navaratri** at the special *mandapa* in Padmanabhaswamy Temple. Several concerts are held which draw famous musicians. **Thiruvonam week** in **Sep**.
Oct: **Soorya Dance Festival** is held 1-10 Oct.
Nov-Mar: A similar **Nishangandhi Dance Festival** is held at weekends when all-important classical Indian dance forms are performed by leading artistes at Nishagandhi open-air auditorium, Kanakakkunnu Palace.

Shopping

Thiruvananthapuram *p180, map p179*
Shopping areas include the Chalai Bazar, the Connemara market and the Main Rd from Palayam to the East Fort. Usually open 0900-2000 (some take a long lunch break). Although ivory goods have now been banned, inlay on wood carving and marquetry using other materials (bone, plastic) continue to flourish. *Kathakali* masks and traditional fabrics can be bought at a number of shops.

The shopping centre opposite East Fort bus stand has a large a/c shop with a good selection of silks and saris but is not cheap. *Khadi* recommended from shops on both sides of MG Rd, south of Pulimudu Junction. **Co-optex**, Temple Rd, good for fabrics and lungis; **Handloom House**, diagonally across from Partha's, has an excellent range of fabrics, clothes and export quality dhurries; **Partha's**, towards East Fort, recommended; **Premier Stationers**, MG Rd, opposite Post Office Rd, are best in town; **Raymonds**, Karal Kada, East Fort, has good men's clothing.

Handicrafts

For handicrafts: **Gram Sree**, excellent village crafts; **Kairali**, items of banana fibre, coconut, screw pine, mainly utilitarian, also excellent sandalwood carvings and bell-metal lamps, utensils; **Kalanjali**, Palace Garden, across from the museum, is recommended; **Natesan Antique Arts and Gift Corner**, MG Rd, high quality goods including old dowry boxes, carved wooden panels from old temple 'cars', miniature paintings and bronzes; **SMSM Handicrafts Emporium**, behind the Secretariat, government-run, literally heaps of items reasonably priced.

Kovalam and surrounding resorts *p180, map p181*
Numerous craft shops, including Kashmiri and Tibetan shops, sell a wide range of goods. Most are clustered around the bus stand at the gate of the **Ashok** with another group to the south around the lighthouse. Good quality paintings, metalwork, woodwork and carpets at reasonable prices. Gems and jewellery are widely available but it is notoriously difficult to be sure of quality.

Tailoring is available at short notice and is very good value with the fabrics available. Charges vary, about Rs 50-80 per piece. **Brother Tailors**, 2nd Beach Rd; **Raja**, near hotel Surya; **Suresh**, next to Garzia restaurant.

Zangsty Gems, Lighthouse Rd, sells jewellery and silver and has a good reputation for helpfulness and reliability.

Varkala *p183, map p188*
Most of the handicraft shops are run by Kashmiris, who will tell you that everything (including the tie-dye t-shirts) is an antique from Ladakh.

If shopping, bear in mind that prices are relatively high here: traders seldom honour the standard rates for 92.5 silver, charging by piece not weight.

Elegance of India and **Mushtaq**, Beach Rd. Sell Kashmiri handicrafts, carpets, jewellery, etc, reported as honest, will safely air-freight carpets etc.

Satori, T9387-653 261. Clifftop boutique, selling pretty Western clothes made with local fabric and jewelled Rajasthani slippers.

Suresh, on the path south from helipad to Marine Palace, has handicrafts from Karnataka.

Activities and tours

Thiruvananthapuram *p180, map p179*

Body and soul

Institute of Yogic Culture, Vazhuthacaud.

Sivananda Ashram, T0471-229 0493, Neyyar Dam, see page 182.

Swimming

Mascot Hotel, small rooftop pool at the Residency Tower (0700-1900, Rs 250), with great views.

Waterworks, pool near museum, T0471-231 8990. Entry Rs 2, 0830-1200, 1400-1530, 1815-2000, closed Mon.

Tour operators

IATA-approved agencies include:

Aries Travel, Press Rd, T0471-233 0964, ariestravel@satyam.net.in.

Gt India Tour Co, Mullassery Towers, Vanross Junction, T0471-233 1516, gitctrv@vsnl.net.in. Reliable but pricey.

Jayasree, PO Box 5236 Pettah, T0471-247 6603, www.jayasreetravels.com. One-stop travel service, good coaches.

TourIndia, MG Rd, T0471-233 0437, tourindia@vsnl.com. Runs unique tours, eco-friendly treehouse, backwater cruises, Periyar trek, sport fishing off Kochi.

Trekking and birdwatching

Trekking is best done Dec-Apr. Obtain permission first from the Chief Conservator of Forests (Wildlife), Forest HQ, Thiruvananthapuram, T0471-232 2217, or the Assistant Wildlife Warden at Neyyar Dam, T0471-227 2182.

Tours

Kerala Tourism, from Hotel Chaithram, T0471-233 0031, www.keralatourism.org.

1 City tour: 0800-1900, including Kovalam (125 km), Rs 130 including lunch, boating; half day, 1400-1900 including boating, Rs 90.

2 Kanniyakumari: 0730-2100, including Kovalam, Padmanabhapuram and Kanniyakumari (200 km), Rs 250 daily (Padmanabhapuram closed Mon);

3 Ponmudi: 0830-1900, daily, Golden Valley and Ponmudi (125 km), Rs 210. Long tours can be very exhausting, the stops at sites of interest are often very brief.

Great India Tour Co, Mullassery Towers, Vanross Square, T0471-233 1516, offers afternoon city tours, among others.

Kovalam and surrounding resorts *p180, map p181*

Body and soul

Ayurvedic treatment are also offered by most upmarket resorts (massage about Rs 700).

Dr Franklin's Panchakarma Institute and Research Centre, Chowara, T0471-248 0870, www.dr-franklin.com. The good doctor's family have been in ayurveda for 4 centuries, and he himself is the former district medical officer of Kerala government. Programmes include treatment for infertility, sluggishness, paralysis and obesity. 15-day body purification therapy (*panchakarma* and *swetakarma*) costs US$714, 21-day *Born To Win* programme US$968. Others include *You and your spine*, *Body Mind Soul*, and there are age-reducing treatments including body immunization and longevity treatments (28 days, US$1290). The slimming programme takes 28 days, US$1200. 51-day *panchakarma*, US$2390. Cheaper treatments include: face pack US$7, 1-hr massage US$17. Also training courses in massage, ayurveda and *panchakarma*.

Medicus, Lighthouse Rd, T0471-248 0596, where Dr Babu and his wife have clients returning year after year.

Padma Nair, book at 'Karma', TC6/2291 Kundamankadavu, Trivandrum 695013, T0471-363038, www.yogaonashoestring. One of *Kalaripayattu* master Balachandran Nair's students, Padma Nair has 10-day massage programmes at her village home from US$180. Yoga on a Shoestring also organizes holidays to Kerala at Oceano Cliff Ayurvedic Resort (www.oceanocliff.com).

Vasudeva, T0471-222 2510, behind **Neptune Hotel**, is simple but with experienced professionals.

Fishing

Can readily be arranged through the hotels, as can excursions on traditional catamarans or motor boats. Some near **Ashok** hotel beach promise corals and beautiful fish just offshore (don't expect to see very much).

Indian martial arts

Guru Balachandran Nair is the master of the Indian School of Martial Arts, Parasuvykal, 20km from Trivandrum, T0471-272 5140, www.kalari.in. This is a college teaching *Kalaripayattu*, India's traditional martial art. *Kalari* warriors were healers as well as fighters with an intricate knowledge of the body. Stay here at Dharmikam ashram, to learn *Kalaripayattu* as well as *Kalarichikitsa*, an ancient Indian healing tradition combining ayurveda with marma therapy, which manipulates the vital pressure points of the body to ease pain. A fighter would have had an intimate knowledge of these points to know what to harm or how to heal. A fascinating place to stay.

Tour operators

East India Premier Tours, behind Neelkantha Hotel, T0471-248 3246. Can suggest unusual hotels.
Great Indian Travel, Lighthouse Rd, T0471-248 1110, www.keralatours.com. Wide range, exchange, eco-friendly beach resort.
Visit India, Lighthouse Rd, T0471-248 1069. Friendly and helpful, exchange, short backwater tours from Thiruvallam.

Varkala *p183, map p188*

Body and soul

Keraleeyam, North Cliff. One of the best of the many yoga/ayurvedic massage centres.
Lakshmi Herbal Beauty Parlour, Clafouti Beach Resort, North End Cliff, 0900-1800, T0470-260 6833. Individual attention, amazing massages plus waxing, henna etc.
Nature Cure Hospital, opened in 1983, treats patients entirely by diet and natural cures including hydrotherapy, chromotherapy (natural sunbath with different filters) and mud therapy, each treatment normally lasting 30 mins.
Naturomission Yoga Ashram, near the Helipad. Runs 1-, 2- and 7-day courses in yoga, massage, meditation, and healing techniques. Payment by donation.
Scientific School of Yoga and Massage, Altharamoodu, Janardhana Temple. 10-day yoga and massage course (2 classes daily), Rs 500, professionally run by English-speaking doctor, T0470-269 5141. Also shop selling ayurvedic oils, soaps, etc.

Tour operators

Most hotels offer tours, air tickets, backwater trips, houseboats etc, as do the many agents along North Cliff.
JK Tours & Travels, Temple Junction Varkala, T0802-668 3334. Money change, 0900-2100, 7 days.

Transport

Thiruvananthapuram *p180, map p179*

Air

The airport, T0471-250 1269, is closed at night so you can't wait there overnight, see Sleeping page 184. The airport is 6 km away from the beach. International flights via the Gulf states are very good value. **Transport to town**: by local bus no 14, pre-paid taxi (Rs 85) or auto (about Rs 30, 20 mins). Confirm international bookings and arrive in good time. Inflated prices at refreshments counter though cheap tea and coffee in the final lounge after 'Security' check. Banks at the airport are outside arrivals. **Johnson & Co** travel agent opposite Domestic Terminal, T0471-250 3555.

Airlines Maldive Airways, Sri Lankan, Spencer Building, MG Rd, T0471-232 2309, and T0471-247 5541. **Gulf Air**, T0471-250 1205, and **Kuwait Airways**, National Travel Service, Panavila Junction, T0471-232 1295 (airport T0471-250 0437). **Saudi Airways**, Arafath Travels, Pattom. **Indian Airlines**, Mascot Sq, T0471-231 8288 (and **Sri Lanka**, T0471-250 1140). **Air India**, Museum Rd, Velayambalam, T0471-231 0310.
Indian Airlines flies to **Bengaluru (Bangalore)**, **Chennai**, **Delhi**, **Mumbai**. Air India flies to **Mumbai**. Jet Airways flies to **Chennai**, **Mumbai**. Indian Airlines flies to **Colombo** and **Male**. Air India flies to **London, New York, Frankfurt, Paris** and **the Gulf**.

Bus

Local City Bus Stand, T0471-246 3029. To **Kovalam** from East Fort, No 888, 30 mins, Rs 7.

Long distance Long-distance journeys through heavy traffic can be very uncomfortable and tiring. KSRTC (Kerala State Railway Transport Co) Thampanoor Bus Stand, near railway station, T0471-232 3886. Buses to **Kanniyakumari via Nagercoil** or direct, frequent departures, 2½ hrs; **Kozhikode**, 10 hrs (Exp); **Madurai**, 1230, 6½ hrs; **Thrissur**, 7 hrs (Exp). Buses to **Ernakulam/Kochi** via Alappuzha and Kollam, start early, 5 hrs (Exp) or 6½ hrs. You can include a section of the backwaters on the way to Kochi by getting a boat from Kollam (shared taxis there cost Rs 60 each, see below). **TNSTC** to **Chennai, Coimbatore**, **Cuddalore, Erode, Kanniyakumari**, **Madurai** from opposite the Central Railway station.

Motorcycle

Asian Trailblazers, MG Rd, T0471-247 8211, asiantrailblazers@yahoo.com, for Enfields.

Rickshaw

Tell auto-rickshaw drivers which Kovalam beach you want to get to in advance, otherwise they will charge much more when you get there. Minimum Rs 6.50 (will use meter if pressed); you may need to bargain for Kovalam, especially in the evening (Rs 70 is fair).

Taxi

From outside Mascot Hotel charge about Rs 7 per km; to **Kovalam**, Rs 175, return Rs 225 (waiting: extra Rs 50 per hr). Outside train station, Rs5 per km. Kanniyakumari with stop at Padmanabhapuram charge Rs 850/900.

Train

Central Station, after 1800. Reservations in building adjoining station, T132. Advance, upstairs, open 0700-1300, 1330-1930, Sun 0900-1700; ask to see Chief Reservations Supervisor, Counter 8; surprisingly no 'Foreigners' quota'. To **Alappuzha**: *Intercity 6342*, 1630, 3 hrs. **Bengaluru (Bangalore)**: *Kanniyakumari-Bangalore Exp 6525*, 0920, 19½ hrs; *Trivandrum Bangalore Exp 6322*, 1505, Wed, 18¾ hrs. **Chennai**: *Trivandrum-Guwahati Exp 6321* (AC/II), Thu, 1245, 18¼ hrs; *Trivandrum Chennai Mail 6320* (AC/II), 1400, 18 hrs. **Delhi (HN)**, *Rajdhani Exp 2431*, 1915, Tue, Thu, 31 hrs. **Ernakulam (Kochi)**: 10 trains daily between 0500-2145. *Trivandrum Ernakulam Exp 6342*, 1630, 4¼ hrs; *Kerala Exp 2625* (AC/II), 1110, 4¼ hrs, are two. **Kolkata (H)**: *Trivandrum-Guwahati Exp 5627* (AC/II), 1245, Sun, 49 hrs; *Trivandrum- Howrah Exp 6323*, 1245, Thu, Sat, 49 hrs. **Kanniyakumari**: *Bangalore Kanniyakumari Exp 6526*, 1515, 2¼ hrs. **Kollam via Varkala**: 12 trains 0725-2035, 1¼ hrs.

Kovalam and surrounding resorts

p180, map p181

There are 3 main points of access to Kovalam's beaches. Remember to specify which when hiring an auto or taxi.

Bus

Local Frequent buses (0540-2100) into East Fort, **Thiruvananthapuram**, from bus stand outside Ashok Hotel gate (Kovalam beach), fast Rs 4.50, slow 3.30 (30 mins), also picks up from Waller Junction (Main Rd/Samudra beach). From East Fort bus station, auto-rickshaw to town centre, Rs 6, or walk. Green buses have limited stops; yellow/red buses continue through town up to museum.

Long distance To **Kanniyakumari**, **Kochi** via **Kollam (Quilon)** and via **Kottayam**, **Nagercoil**, **Padmanabhapuram**, **Varkala**, **Thodopuzha** via **Kottayam**.

Rickshaw

Auto-rickshaw to **Thiruvananthapuram**, Rs 70-80, but you need to bargain hard.

Taxi

From taxi stand or through Ashok or Samudra hotels. One-way to Thiruvananthapuram or airport, Rs 200; station Rs 175; city sights Rs 600; Kanniyakumari, Padmanabhapuram Rs 1750 (8 hrs); Kochi Rs 2250 (5 hrs); Kollam Rs 1100; Thekkady Rs 2650 (6 hrs).

Varkala *p183, map p188*

Bus

To/from Temple Junction (not beach) for **Alappuzha** and **Kollam**, but often quicker to go to Paripally on NH47 and catch onward buses from there.

Motorcycle
Kovalam Motorcycle hire, Voyager Travels, Eye's Beach Rd, T0471-248 1993. Next door to **JA Tourist Home**, Temple Junction; and **Mamma Chompo**, Beach Rd.

Rickshaw/Taxi
Catch them from Beach Rd and Helipad. Both charge Rs 25 to train station. A taxi to **Thiruvananthapuram**, Rs 350 (1¼ hrs).

Train
Several daily to coastal towns including **Thiruvananthapuram**: 0435, 0810, 0940, 1752 and 2103 (50 mins). Also to **Kanniyakumari**:1107, 1400 (3½ hrs); **Kollam**: 0550, 0640, 1710, 1834, 2150, 2232 (35 mins); **Mangalore**: 0640, 1834 (14 hrs).

Directory

Thiruvananthapuram *p180, map p179*
Banks Mon-Fri 1000-1400, Sat 1000-1200. **Andhra Bank**, near Canara Bank, on opposite side of road, cash against Visa, ICICI and IDBI. **Canara Bank**, near Spencer Junction, no-hassle cash against Visa, friendly staff. Both on MG Road with ATMs. **State Bank of India**, near Secretariat, with 24-hr ATM. The airport has banks, including **Thomas Cook**, T0471-250 2470. **Chemists** Many chemists, near hospitals; a few near Statue Junction. **Opticians: Lens & Frames**, Pulimudu Junc, T0471-247 1354. **Hospitals** General **Hospital**, Vanchiyoor, T0471-244 3874. **Ramakrishna Ashrama Hospital**, Sasthamangalam, T0471-232 2123. **Ayurveda Hospital**, T0471-234 0938. **Homeopathy Hospital**, T0471-232 2125. **Internet** Central Telegraph office: Statue Rd, 200 m to its north; open 24 hrs, best value internet. **Megabyte**, CSI Building, 3rd and 4th floors, MG Rd, email: send Rs 15, receive Rs 10, friendly. **Tandem Communications**, Statue Rd (MG Rd end), good telephone and fax centre; colour photocopying, laser printing. **Post** **Poste Restante**, Pulimudu Junction, T0471-247 3071, 0830-1800, efficient. **PO**: north of Secretariat, off MG Rd, is better; **Speed Post** (computerized; affected by power failures), **DHL** T0471-232 7161; PO at Thampanoor, opposite Manjalikulam Rd.

Useful address Foreigners' Regional **Registration Office**, City Police Commissioner, Residency Rd, Thycaud, T0471-232 0486; allow up to a week for visas, though it can take less. Mon-Sat 1000-1700. **Wildlife Warden**, PTP Nagar, Vattiyoorkavu, T0471-236 0762.

Kovalam and surrounding resorts
p180, map p181
Banks 3 ATMs: **Canara Bank**, T0471-248 1950; **ICICI Bank**, both at Kovalam Junction; and **HDFC Bank**, Vazhuthakadu T0471-233 7615. **Central Bank**, branch in Kovalam Hotel (around the corner near the bookshop) changes money and TCs for non-residents after 1045, T0471-248 0101. Exchange at **Pournami Handicrafts; Wilson's**, T0471-248 1647, changes money, any time, no hassle. Best rates (up to 3% higher), however, are at the airport. Or try **Phroze Framroze & Co** near Kovalam Bus Station T0471-248 7450. **Hospitals** Emergency assistance either through your hotel or from **Govt Hospital** in Thiruvananthapuram. **Upasana Hospital**, near *Le Meridien* gate, T0471-248 0632, has experienced English-speaking doctor; prompt, personal attention. **Internet** Several on Lighthouse Beach. **Post** Inside Le Meridien gate. **Telephone** Check printed prices before paying for calls. Some ISD booths near the bus stand. **Western Travel**, opposite Bus Stand, until 2200. **Elite Tours**, T0471-248 1405, 2nd Beach Rd (30 m below bus stand), 24-hr ISD from the **Batik House**, Lighthouse Beach.

Varkala *p183, map p188*
Banks **State Bank of Travancore** changes TCs, but will not change cash or accept Visa; **Bank of Baroda**, next door, does. **Canara**, near train station, gives advances on Visa cards (1% commission). There are several **money changers**: along the north cliff and around Temple Junction (lower than US$/£ rate at Trivandrum airport), and most will give cash advances on credit cards (at a hefty 5% commission).
Internet Several places along north cliff, helipad and Temple Junction (Rs 60 per hr).
Post Next to Sree Padman, Temple Junction, Mon-Sat 1000-1400; ISD phones opposite; also at Maithalam and along North Cliff.

The Backwaters

Kerala is synomymous with its lyrical Backwaters: a watery cat's cradle of endlessly intersecting rivers, streams, lagoons and tanks that flood the alluvial plain between the Indian Ocean and Western Ghats. They run all the way from Kollam via Alleppey and Kottayam to Kochi to open up a charming slow-tempo window onto Keralite waterfront life: this is the state's lush and fertile Christian belt, Arundhati Roy country, with lakes fringed by bird sanctuaries, idyllic little hamlets, beside huge paddy ponds rustling in the breeze.

The silent daybreak is best, as boats cut through mists, geese and ducks start to stir along banks, plumes from breakfast fires drift out across the lagoons. As the hamlets and villages wake, Kerala's domestic scene comes to life: clothes are pounded and smashed clean, teeth brushed, and smartly turned out primary school children swing their ways to class.

Luxury houseboats are the quintessential way of seeing the waterfront, but they are pollutants and if your budget or attention span won't stretch that far, the state-operated ferries will give you much the same access for a fraction of the fee. Alternatively, borrow a bicycle or move around by car; the roads and canals are interchangeable. Both thread their way through flood plains the size of football pitches, brown lakes with new shoots prodding out, pools of paddy nurseries, or netted over prawns and fish, snooped over by white egrets.

At dusk the young men sit about on bridges, near fishermen selling catch, or congregate by teashops made of corrugated iron, as men shimmy up coconut palms to tap a fresh supply of sour moonshine toddy, and kids catch fish with poles, beside paddy grown golden and thick like straw. ▸▸ *For Sleeping, Eating and other listings, see pages 201-207.*

Ins and outs

Getting there and around Kollam is 70 km north of Trivandrum and linked to Alappuzha, Kottayam and Kochi by road and rail. Alappuzha is 64 km south of Kochi. The largest backwater body is the Vembanad Lake, which flows through Alappuzha and Kottayam districts to open into the sea at Kochi Port. This has made Alappuzha the principal departure point for houseboat operators. Kollam sits on Ashtamudi Lake, the second largest after Vembanad. Starting here gives you the longest ride (eight hours); the ferry for Alappuzha leaves at 1030. ▸▸ *See Transport, page 206, for further details.*

Tourist information **Kollam** ⓘ *DTPC, Govt Guest House Complex, T0474-274 2558, dtpcqln@md3.vsnl.net.in*, can provide details of cruises, coach tours and *Kathakali* performances; ⓘ *KSRTC bus station, T0474-274 5625*; and at the train station and also at the ferry jetty; ⓘ *KTDC, Yatri Nivas, Ashramam, T0474- 274 8638.* **Alappuzha** ⓘ *KTDC, Motel Araam, T0477-224 4460*; ⓘ *ATDC, Komala Rd, T0477-224 3462, info@atdca alleppey.com*; **DTPC** ⓘ *KSRTC bus station near jetty, T0477-225 3308, 0830-2000*, is helpful and offers good backwaters trips. **Kottayam** ⓘ *Kerala Tourist office, Govt Guest House, Nattakom, T0481-256 2219.*

Kollam (Quilon)

▸▸ *pp-207. Colour map 3, C3.*

→ *Phone code: 0474. Population: 361,400.*

Kollam is a busy shaded market town on the side of the Ashtamudi Lake and the headquarters of India's cashew nut trading and processing industry. It is congested and there's little reason to linger, but its position at the south end of Kerala's backwaters

Kerala backwaters

Sleeping
Anthraper Home Stay **1**
Ashram **10**
Ashtamudi Resorts **11**
Coconut Lagoon **12**
Kayaloram Lake Resort **2**
Keraleeyam Lake Side Ayurvedic Health Resort **3**
Marari Beach **4**
Marari Beach Home **4**
Olavipe **5**
Palm Lagoon **13**
Pooppally's Heritage Homestay **6**
Taj Garden Retreat **9**
Thanneermukkom Ayurvedic Lake Resort **7**
Vembanad House Home Stay **8**

makes it one of the main centres for boat trips up the canals; see page 205.

Known to Marco Polo (as *Koilum*), its port traded with Phoenicians, Persians, Greeks, Romans and Arabs as well as the Chinese. Kollam became the capital of the Venad Kingdom in the ninth century. The educated and accomplished king Raja Udaya Marthanda Varma convened a special council at Kollam to introduce a new era. After extensive astronomical calculations the new era was found to start on 15 August AD 825. The town was also associated with the early history of Christianity.

Roughly a third of the town is covered in the waters of the **Ashtamudi Lake** ⓘ *boats for hire from the Kollam Boat Club or DTPC, for 2 or 4, Rs 20 per hr each.* The lake, with coconut palms on its banks and picturesque promontories, extends north from the town. You might see some 'Chinese' fishing nets and in wider sections large-sailed dugouts carrying the local coir, copra and cashew.

Kollam to Alappuzha

➔ *Backwater tours: A ferry leaves for Alappuzha at 1030 (8 hrs).*

Mata Amritanandamayi Ashram ⓘ *www.amrita puri.org, Vallikkavu, 10 km north of Kollam, accessible by boat or road (via Kayambkulam or Karungappally), Rs 150 per day*, a giant, pink skyscraper that is sandwiched on the backwaters between the sea and the river, is the ashram of 'Amma' (the hugging 'Mother'). Thousands of Western and Indian alike attend *Darshan* in hope of a hug. The ashram feels a bit lacklustre when Amma is on tour. She reckons that she has hugged 30 million people so far. In the early days, these used to last for minutes; now she averages one hug every 1½ seconds, so she can happily hug 30,000 in a day. The ashram has shops, a bank, library and internet. Smoking, sex and alcohol are forbidden. See also box, page 198.

Mannarsala, located 32 km before Alappuzha, has an extremely atmospheric **Nagaraja temple** buried deep in a dense jungle forest. Traditionally *naga* (serpent) worshippers had temples in serpent

Amma

India's spiritual gurus have a history of philanthropy, but that of Sri Mata Amritanandamayi Devi – 'Amma' or 'The Hugging Mother' – is hard to beat. Her trademark pink palaces of medicine – the free or subsidized care offered at the Amrita Institute of Medical Sciences in Kochi was inaugurated by no less than the then prime minister Vajpayee – and other charitable projects are scattered the length of India. And not just in her home state of Kerala – there's even a Mother's Kitchen in the US that doles out about 40,000 meals a year. She has funded 50,000 pensions to Indian women, particularly widows, since 1998, has built 25,000 pink homes for homeless and slum-dwellers since the mid-90s, runs schools, and is embracing new technology by running eight computer institutes, and has even set up Coimbatore-based institutions of engineering and management to turn out 'excellent managers with compassionate hearts'. The Amrithapuri ashram, in Kollam district, is the centre of Amma's worldwide organization. She already has a tremendous fan base: for Amma's 50th birthday in September 2003 a whopping two million people flocked to Kochi over four days. Amma's support means time has had to be shaved off the length of her famous hugs.

She was born abnormally dark – the dark blue of Krishna and Goddess Kali, they now say – into a pale-skinned Keralite fishing family in 1953. Although legend has it that she skipped the ordinary phases of child development: crawling, toddling et al, by jumping, up age six months, and immediately walking; her divine complexion was nonetheless read as a dishonour to her family. Accordingly, she was treated as a servant and her innate compassion – begging for gruel to feed the cows, or stealing food to give to the poor or elderly – punished.

She began to embrace people spontaneously from her 20s. As word spread, people began to arrive in their hundreds. Her first monastic disciples set up home in 1979. These grew into an ashram, now peopled by 1800 devotees, that was officially founded in 1981. It wasn't till 1987 that she made her first world tour, but her good deeds are increasingly recognized on the world stage: her humanitarian works have been awarded at the United Nations.

The ashram is a surreal pink skyscraper but has none of the rock'n'roll connotations of the Osho ashram at Pune. There's a 1800-0600 curfew, fasting takes place once a week, and there are admonishments not to leave children unattended, after all, 'the ashram is not a playground,' notices read.

Online newsletter amritavani: ammachi.org and amma-europe.org. Outside India: amritapuri.org is the main site. Foreigners' office: inform@amritapuri.org, T0476-289 6278.

groves. Mannarsala is the largest of these in Kerala with '30,000 images' of snake gods lined up along the path and among the trees, and many snakes living around the temple.

Childless women come for special blessing and also return for a 'thanksgiving' ceremony afterwards when the child born to the couple is placed on special scales and gifts in kind equalling the weight are donated. The temple is unusual for its chief priestess.

The backwaters

The backwaters are lagoons fed by a network of perennial rivers with only two permanent outlets to the sea: one at Kodungallur in the north and the other at Kochi, with a third opening during the southwest monsoon at Thottappally. The salts are flushed out between May and September, but seawaters rush inland by up to 20 km at the end of the monsoon and the waters become increasingly brackish through the dry season. This alternation between fresh and saltwater has been essential to the backwaters' aquatic life.

But as land value has rocketed in the state, reclamation for agriculture has reduced the surface water area, and the building of a barrier across the Vembanad Lake, north of Kumarakom, and other changes have altered the backwaters' ecology. Few problems are immediately visible during one of the unquestionably idyllic backwaters tours. But however picturesque the experience, most of the original mangrove swamps have now been destroyed; just one small residual patch at Kumarakom has limited protection, while the reclaimed areas (plots known as *pokkali*) are now used alternately for paddy and for fish and shrimp farming.

Bunds, cement and granite embankments – which you can see throughout the backwaters – fence areas off from the main lake so these can then be drained with electric pumps. This leaves the lake suffering from excessive saline flooding and the reduced exchange between the lakes and the sea severely worsens pollution, causing mass fish kills, while excessive use of fertilizers on agricultural land results in sharp increases in water weed infestation.

Most people find that the typical eight-hour journey on a motor boat between Kollam and Alappuzha drags a little. Opt instead for a shorter round trip from Kollam, Alappuzha (between Changanacherry or Kottayam) or close to Kochi. If you'd rather not cough up for the contrivance of an upmarket rice boat, go local and hop aboard a ferry bus: the views are the same.

Haripad has one of Kerala's oldest and most important **Subrahmanya temples**. The four-armed idol is believed to have been found in a river, and in August the three-day **Snake Boat Race** at Payipad, 3 km by bus, commemorates its rescue and the subsequent building of the temple. There are boat processions on the first two days followed by competitive races on the third day. There is a guest house on **Mankotta Island** on the backwaters; the large comfortable rooms with bath are well kept.

Squeezed between the backwaters and the sea, and 12 km from Haripad station, **Thottapally** makes a good stop on a backwaters trip and is situated about two hours from Alappuzha.

About 10 km from Chengannur, **Aranmula** has the **Parthasarathi Temple** and is well known for its unique metal mirrors. The **Vallamkali (or Utthrittathi) festival** on the last day of Onam (August-September) is celebrated with the Boat Race. The festival celebrates the crossing of the river by Krishna, who is believed to be in all the boats simultaneously, so the challenge is to arrive at the same time, rather than race.

Alappuzha (Alleppey) and around

▸▸ *pp205-207. Colour map 3, C3.*

➔ *Phone code: 0477. Population: 177,100.*

Alappuzha (pronounced *Alappoorra*) has a large network of canals choked with the blue flowers of water hyacinth passing through the town. It's the chief depot for backwater cruises and also the venue for the spectacular snake boat races; see page 205 for details. There may not be many tourist sites as such, although St Thomas's Church is worth a look, but it's a pleasant, bustling town to walk around and explore.

Mararikulam, 15 km north of Alappuzha on the coast, is a quiet, secluded beach which, until recently, was only known to the adjoining fishing village. The main village has a thriving cottage industry of coir and jute weaving.

Some 16 km southeast of Alappuzha is the hushed backwaters village of **Champakulam** where the only noise pollution is the odd squeak of a bicycle and the slush of a canoe paddle. The Syrian Christian church of **St Mary's Forane** was built in 1870 on the site of a previous church dating from AD 427. The English-speaking priest is happy to show visitors round.

Nearby the **St Thomas Statuary** makes wooden statues of Christ for export round the world: a 2-m tall Jesus will set you back US$450. To get there, take the Alappuzha-Changanacherry bus (every 30 minutes) to Moncombu (Rs 4), then rickshaw to Champakulam (4 km, Rs 12). Alternatively the Alappuzha-Edathna ferry leaves at 0615 and 1715 and stops at Champakulam. In the Backwaters village of **Edathna,** you can visit the early Syrian **St George's Church.**

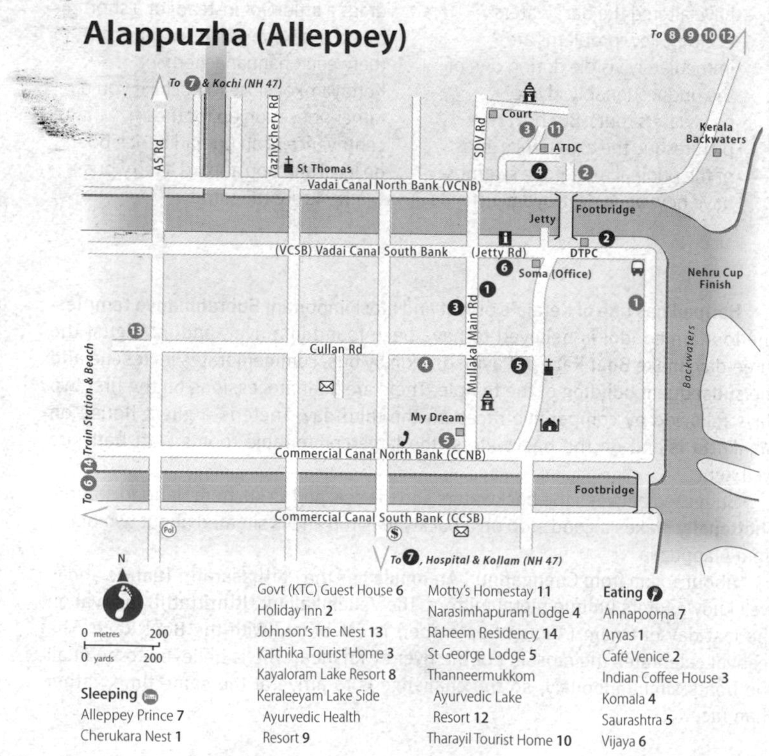

Kottayam and Kumarakom » pp204-207.

Colour map 3, C3.

→ *Phone code: 0481. Population: 60,700.*

Around Kottayam lies some of the lushest and most beautiful scenery in the state, with hills to its east and backwaters to its west, but avoid the congested town itself and instead stick to the pretty outskirts.

Kottayam is the capital of Kerala's Christian community, who belonged to the Orthodox Syrian tradition up till the Portuguese arrival; two churches of the era survive 2 km north of town. One of these is the 450-year-old **Cheria Palli** ('Small' St Mary's Church) which has beautiful vegetable dye mural paintings over its altar.

The **Valia Palli** ('Big' St Mary's Church), from 1550, has two Nestorian crosses carved on plaques behind two side altars. One has a Pallavi inscription on it, the other a Syriac. The cross on the left of the altar is the original and may be the oldest Christian artefact in India; the one to the right is a copy. By the altar there is an unusual small triptych of an Indian St George slaying a dragon. Note the interesting Visitors' Book 1898-1935 – a paper cutting reports that "the church has attracted many European and native gentlemen of high position". Mass at Valia Palli at 0900 on Sunday, and Cheria Palli at 0730 on Sunday and Wednesday. The Malankara Syrian Church has its headquarters at Devalokam.

Tucked among the waterways of Vembanad Lake, in mangrove, paddy and coconut groves with lily-studded shores, is **Kumarakom**, 16 km from Kottayam. Here are stacks of exclusive hotels where you can be buffed and ayurvedically preened, stretched into yoga postures, peacefully sunbathe or take to the water: perfect honeymoon territory.

The Tourism Department has developed an old rubber plantation set around the Vembanad Lake into a **bird sanctuary** ⓘ *1000-1800*. A path goes through the swamp to the main bird nesting area, while the island in the middle of the lake (**Pathiramanal**, or midnight sands) can be reached by boat. The best season for birdlife is June to August; early mornings are best.

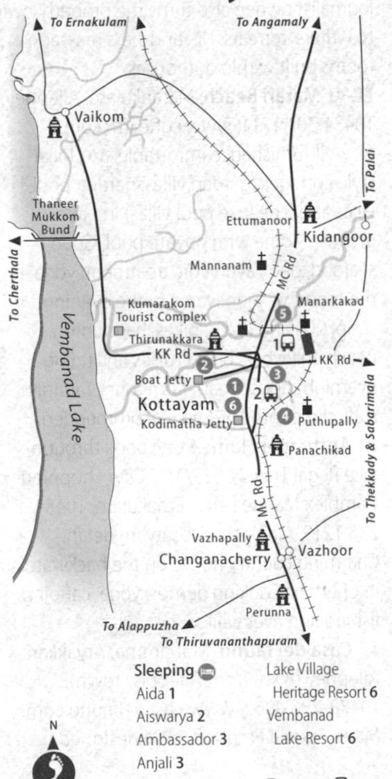

Sleeping

Kollam *p196, map p197*

AL-A Ashtamudi Resorts, Chavara South (north of town), T0476-288 2288, www .ashtamudiresort.com/codes/location.htm. 30 mins by car, 10 mins by speed boat. Ayurvedic resort with 20 rooms in 5 traditional chalets (Queen's Cottages and King's Palace more expensive), all a/c with good views. Catamaran trips.

A-B Aquaserene, Paravoor, 15 mins from town by road or boat, T0474-251 2410, aqserene@md3.vsnl.net.in. Splendid backwaters location, well-furnished chalets

(some reassembled Kerala houses) with TV, restaurant, ayurvedic treatment, boat rides.
C Palm Lagoon, Vellimon West, T0474-254 7214, www.palmlagoon.com. Delightful setting 18 km from town centre on north side of Ashtamudi Lake, can be reached from backwater cruise. Attractive thatched cottages, including full board.
C-F Sudarsan, Hospital Rd, Parameswar Nagar, 5 mins from jetty, T0474-274 4322, www.hotelsudarsan.com. 28 rooms in cheap Indian business hotel, some a/c with bath, rear quieter, dim a/c restaurant, bar, exchange, backwater trips. Close to the boat jetty. Money change, coffee shop 1000-2300.
E Shah International, TB Rd, Chinnakkada, T0474-272 4362. Good value, 72 rooms, some **D** with a/c, adequate restaurant, quiet.
E Valiyavila Family Estate , Thoppikadavu, T0474-2794669, www.kollamlakeview resort.com. Near Thevally Bridge (5 km from station; 10-min walk from small post office northwest of town). Beautiful position along lakeside. 4 clean, renovated rooms (2 have large balcony), lovely garden, good waterside restaurant, bar (occasionally noisy), friendly staff. Recommended.
F Mahalaxmi Lodge, opposite bus station near Ashtamudi Lake, T0474-749440. 7 tiny rooms, shared outside toilet, adequate.
G Govt Guest House, Ashramam, T0474-274 3620. Fine 200-year-old building – former British Residency – with garden on edge of lagoon. 8 large rooms, simple meals, Boating, small pool and park by the lake. Loads of character but therefore often full.
G-F Yatri Nivas, Guest House Compound by Ashtamudi Lake, Ashramam, T0474-274 5538. A wide choice of rooms overlooking the canal, including family rooms that sleep 6 and great views from balconies. Ugly block building but clean and good value, with helpful staff, bike hire, restaurant, beer, boating and free boat service from town jetty. Book at tourist office in Alappuzha, see page 196.

Kollam to Alappuzha *p197, map p197*
C-D Coconut Palms, Eco Heritage Resort, Kumarakodi, Thottapally, T0477-229 8057. Idyllic 200-year-old traditional house in shaded compound, on backwaters and 100 m from sea. Yoga and ayurveda also offered, and package deals available, including transport from **Aries Travel**, Trivandrum, T0471-233 1165, ariestravel@gmail.com. Daily tourist boat from Kollam and Alappuzha (5 and 2 hrs respectively) drops you at Kumarakody boat jetty, about 200 m from the resort.
E Ashram, Vallikkavu. Spartan but spacious accommodation is offered in a multi-storey block here; Rs 150 includes very basic South Indian food. Western canteen (at extra cost) has a range of American-choice meals.

Alappuzha and around *p200, maps p197 and p200*
Book ahead to avoid the scramble off the ferry. Hotels north of Vadai Canal are quieter.
LL Raheem Residency, Beach Rd, Alleppey, T0477-223 9767, www.raheemresidency.com. Special luxury heritage hotel housed in a beautifully restored Mughal/colonial 19th-century bungalow on a pristine piece of Kerala's coast with 6 en suite a/c rooms, palatial living room and lovely pool under a velvet apple tree. Bibi Baskin, Raheem's Irish journalist owner, also turns the property over to writers' retreats. His-and-hers massage rooms built within outhouses.
LL-AL Marari Beach, Mararikulam, Alleppey, T0484-301 1711, www.cghearth.com. 62 well-furnished, comfortable, a/c, local style cottages (garden villas, garden pool villas and 3 de luxe pool villas) in palm groves – some with private pool. Good seafood, pool, ayurvedic treatment, yoga in the morning, pranayama in the evening, shop, CDs and DVDs, bikes, badminton, beach volleyball, boat cruises (including overnight houseboat), farm tours, friendly staff, discounts Apr-Sep. Recommended.
AL Anthraper Home Stay, book through Vice Regal Travels, S17/18 GCDA Shopping Complex Marine Drive, Ernakulam, T0484-235 1219, ranibachani@satyam.net.in. Charming country house on the backwaters in Chertala. Cooking demos, yoga, canoing, fishing and river walks.
AL Casa del fauno, Muhamma, Aryakkara, Alleppey (8 km from Alleppey town), T0478-286 0862, www.casadelfauno.com. Maria Angela Fernhoff, who designed

For an explanation of the sleeping and eating price codes used in this guide, see inside the front cover. Other relevant information is found in Essentials pages 40-44.

the Shalimar Spice Garden in Thekkady, has inched a step further to paradise with her gracious home on the Vembanad Lake, with pool, yoga, massage, private sandy beach, ayurveda, internet and wholefood dishes.

AL Olavipe, Thekanatt Parayil, Olavipe, 25 km from Cochin, T0484-240 2410, www.olavipe .com. Century-old mansion belonging to family of Syrian Christan notables Parayil Tharakans, on a 40-acre organic farm on the lush island of Olavipe. 5 rooms: 3 in the main house and 2 in a cottage.

AL Vembanad House Home Stay, Puthankayal, Alappuzha, T0478-286 8696, www.vembanadhouse.com. 4 spacious self-contained rooms in stately century-old house surrounded by the lake in the pretty Muhamma area, opposite Kumarakam and Pathiramanal. Fresh food from the family farm cooked to Kerala recipes. Traditional architecture with modern bathrooms (no a/c). The house is managed by the delightful Balakrishnan family.

AL-A Marari Beach Home, Mararikulam Cherthala, T0477-224 3535, www.marari beachhomes.com. 4 self-catering cottages right on Marari Beach in converted fishermen's shacks.

A Emerald Isle Heritage Villa, Alleppey, T0477-270 3899, www.emeraldislekerala .com. From Utopian ancestral home to the Job family: 4 doubles on shores of a floating island of lush jungle, surrounded by sunken paddy field. Toddy on tap, cookery courses, boat trips, ayurveda. The magic of the place begins on the 10 km journey from Alleppey.

A Motty's Homestay, Kidangamparambu Rd, T0477-226 0573, motty1@satyam.net.in. Just 2 double rooms – old furniture and 4-poster beds – in private house on Alleppey's outskirts. Excellent home cooking.

A-B Kayaloram Lake Resort, Punmamada, on Vembanad Lake, 4 km; 15 mins by boat from jetty then 300 m walk or at 'Punchiri', Jetty Rd, T0477-223 2040, www.kayaloram .com. 12 Kerala-style wood and tile cottages around small inner 'courtyard' with 'open-to-sky' showers. Comfortable, very quiet and peaceful. Pool, restaurant (typical Kerala cuisine, continental), ayurveda. Backwaters or lake trips. Recommended.

A-B Pooppally's Heritage Homestay, Alleppey, T0477-276 2034, www.pooppallys .com Traditional wooden cottage (water bungalow) and rooms in 19th-century family farmhouse, shaded by a mango tree, set in a garden stretching down to the River Pampa. Great home-cooked food, open-air bathrooms. Catch the ferry to Alleppey for 90 mins of free houseboat.

A-C Thanneermukkom Ayurvedic Lake Resort, Cherthala, Alleppey, T0478-258 3218, www.ktdc.com. Spartan Kerala Tourism Development Corporation take on ayurveda retreat beside the Thanneermukkom Watergate to Kumarakom lake. Shady gardens and 37 clean rooms with ayurvedic packages led by respected Keraleeyam Ayurveda Samajam, including breakfast and dinner.

B Keraleeyam Lake Side Ayurvedic Health Resort, off Thathampally main road, Alleppey, T0477-223 7161, www.keraleeyam .com. Keraleeyam sits on one of the prettiest nubs of the backwaters – it's hard to find a prettier place to sit. It's like a slow-moving painting, and does Arundhati Roy and the Kerala Tourist Board proud. One of the most reasonable places to embark on a proper Ayurvedic programme. Doctors attend daily and the resort is a division of SD Pharmacy medicinal factories. No alcohol, diet according to ayurvedic type. Rooms, all on the lake, are a bit ethnic. Bring your own books. Tour packages from US$170 for 2 nights; a month's ayurvedic massage package costs from US$2220. Prices include accommodation, treatments, meals, sightseeing and transfers. Recommended.

B-D Alleppey Prince, AS Rd (NH47), 2 km north of centre, T0477-224 3752. 30 good, clean rooms, central a/c, very dark bar, pool, luxury boats for backwaters.

B-E Green Palace Health Resort, Champakulam, T0477-273 6262, www.greenpalacekerala.com. With Kerala meals and ayurvedic massage.

D Cherukara Nest, just round the corner from bus station, T0477-225 1509, lakeslagoon@satyam.net.in. Pleasant traditional home, clean rooms with bath, very helpful staff. Kerala meals on request.

D Johnson's The Nest, Lal Bagh Factory Ward (West of Convent Sq), T0477-224 5825, mobile T984-646639, johnsongilbertlk1@ hotmail.com. Friendly family-run guesthouse with 5 rooms, each with balcony in a garden of orchids in a quiet area between town and the beach. Johnson is something of a Jim'll Fix lt. A home from home. Free pick-up, 3 mins from town centre houseboat facility.

E-F Tharayil Tourist Home, 750 m from boat jetty near lake, Thotampally, T0477-223 6475, tharayiltouristhome@yahoo.co.in. Some a/c rooms, clean, local furniture in a family home.

E-G Govt (KTC) Guest House, Beach Rd, 4 km bus stand, T0477-225 4275. Excellent value, reasonable food (order in advance) but indifferent service. Reservations: Dist Collector, Collectorate, Dist HQ, Alappuzha.

F Holiday Inn, Vadai Canal North Bank, T0477-225 1961. Good location, 3 adequate rooms, but with no food.

F Karthika Tourist Home, near Zilla Court, SDV Rd, north of canal, opposite Jetty, T0477-224 5524. Good value, 39 clean, pleasant rooms, some large with baths (cockroaches), best No 31. Helpful, friendly staff.

F Narasimhapuram Lodge, Cullen Rd, T0477-226 2662. Some a/c rooms, occasional weight-lifting competition with live commentary over loudspeakers!

F St George Lodge, CCNB Rd, A-5, T0477-225 1620. Good value, 80 basic rooms, some with bath, popular with backpackers, exchange, book ahead.

Kottayam and Kumarakom *p201, map p197*

In Kumarakom 26% taxes are added to bills.

LL Philipkutty's Farm, Pallivathukal, Ambika Market, Vechoor, Kottayam, T0482-927 6529, www.philipkuttysfarm.com. 5 immaculate waterfront villas sharing an island in Vembanad Lake with the delightful and genteel Anu Mathew's family farmhouse. The working farm boasts coconut, banana, nutmeg and vanilla groves. Delicious home cooking and personal attention from all the family. No a/c or TV. Cooking and painting holidays.

LL-AL Coconut Lagoon Vembanad Lake Kumarakom (CGH Earth), T0484-301 1711, www.cghearth.com. 28 comfortable heritage *tharavads* (traditional Kerala wooden cottages), some a/c, 14 heritage mansions and 8 pool villas. Outdoor restaurant facing lagoon, good dinner buffet, good pool, yoga, very friendly, ayurvedic treatments, attractive waterside location, spectacular approach by boat (10 mins from road). Vechoor cows mow the lawns. Recommended. Discounts Apr to Sep.

L Privacy at Sanctuary Bay, Kannamkara, Chertala, opposite Kumarakom, T0478-258 2794, www.malabarhouse.com. 2-bedroom bungalow for beautiful lakeside isolation owned by Malabar House designers and with same mixture of modern interiors and old Keralite building. Fully staffed, stunning verandas, ultimate luxury.

L-AL Taj Garden Retreat, 1/404, 14 km west of Kottayam, Kumarakom, T0481-252 4377, www.tajhotels.com. 19 a/c rooms, in attractive 120-year-old 'Bakers' House', as featured in *The God of Small Things*. Sympathetically renovated, newer cottages and a moored houseboat, good meals, an intimate hotel but packed.

AL Houseboat (KTDC), Kumarakom, contact Kumarakom Tourist Village, T0481-2252 4258. Unique, idyllic experience on the backwaters at a price. Kerala meals included, Rs 7500 (day only), Rs 8750 (1 night, 2 days). Highly recommended.

AL Lake Village Heritage Resort, near Kodimatha Jetty (next to **Vembanad Resort**), 3 km south Kottayam, T0481-236 3739, wcastle@satyam.net.in. Comfortable bungalows with 'inside-outside' baths, excellent huge open-sided restaurant, very friendly.

AL-A Kumarakom Lake Resort, Kumarakom, T0481-252 4900, www.klresort.com. 22 heritage-style villas and 26 pool villas with open-roofed showers set in landscaped grounds. Lovely lakeshore pool and yoga and ayurveda packages. 2 presidential suites have own pools. A touch contrived, but good for families. DVDs, gym, library, indoor games, watersports and floorshows. Recommended. Also small dug-outs for exploring the canals and luxury houseboats (www.kumarakom house boat.com), plus daily sunset cruises.

B Vallikappen Home Stay, XIII/179B Manganam, T0481-257 2530, simtom@satyam.net.in. A special alternative just outside Kottayam, 2 comfortable, clean rooms, interesting, cultured hosts, good Kerala/Western meals included. Boats, heritage and wildlife visits.

C-E Anjali, KK Rd, 4 km from railway, Kottayam, T0481-256 3661. Central a/c, 27 rooms with bath, good restaurants, exchange (limited).

D-F Green Park, Kurian Uthup Rd, Nagampadam, T0481-256 3331, greenparkhotel@yahoo.co.in. 33 rooms with bath, 11 with noisy a/c, non-a/c at back too hot, restaurant.

E Vembanad Lake Resort, near Kodimatha Jetty, 5 km from centre, 2 km from bus stand, T0481-236 0866, www.vembanad lakeresort .com. Simple rooms in 10 cottages (5 a/c), waterside garden, good house-boat restaurant.

E-F Aida, MC Rd, 2 km railway in Kottayam, T0481-256 8391, aida@sancharnet.in. 40 rooms with bath, some a/c, back quieter, restaurant, bar, clean and pleasant.

E-G Aiswarya (KTDC), near Thirunakkara Temple, 500 m from jetty, 2 km the bus stand, Kottayam, T0481-258 1440, aiswarya_int@ yahoo.com. 30 rooms, some a/c, food, beer.

E-G Ambassador Hotel, KK Rd (set back), T0481-256 3293, www.fhrai.com. 18 rooms, some a/c, pleasant Indian-style hotel and good restaurant, bar, exchange, friendly and helpful staff, very good value.

F Govt Rest House, on hill 2 km south of Kottayam overlooking flat paddy land. Remarkable late 19th-century building, superb furniture and original cutlery and tableware. Reservations: District Collector, Kottayam or Executive Engineer, PWD Kottayam.

F Kaycees Lodge, off YMCA Rd, Kottayam, T0481-256 3440. Good value, clean.

F Venad Tourist Complex, Ancheril Building, near State bus stand, Kottayam, T0481-256 1383. Modern building, clean, restaurant. Recommended.

Eating

Kollam *p196, map p197*

Eat N Pack, near Taluk Office, Main St. Excellent value, clean, good choice of dishes, friendly. Recommended.

Indian Coffee House, Main Rd. 0800-2030. For good coffee and vegetarian and non-vegetarian South Indian food. Nice waiter service and good atmosphere.

Suprabhatam, opposite Clock Tower, Main St. Adequate, vegetarian.

Alappuzha and around *p200, map p200*

ΨΨ **Vemanad**, Alleppey Prince Hotel, International, comfortable a/c restaurant, reasonable food, alcohol in bar only.

Ψ **Annapoorna**, does excellent vegetarian food – served by waitresses!

Ψ **Aryas**, south of Jetty. Good for iddli, dosa, *vadai* etc.

Ψ **Café Venice**, just by the DTPC office.

Ψ **Indian Coffee House**, does good value, tasty non-vegetarian snacks.

Ψ **Komala**, excellent South Indian thalis and some Chinese (poor rooms).

Ψ **Saurashtra**, vegetarian, ample helpings on banana leaf, locally popular.

Ψ **Vijaya**, good South Indian vegetarian and Chinese.

Kottayam and Kumarakom *p201, map p197*

Listed below are eateries in Kottayam. For Kumarakom, see Sleeping.

ΨΨ **Aida**, large, uninspired menu, pleasantly cool ('chilled' drinks may arrive warm).

ΨΨ **Green Park**, international. Reasonable but slow service. Serves beers, dinner in mosquito-ridden garden (or in own room for guests).

On TB Rd near the State bus station:

Ψ **Black Stone**, good vegetarian.

Ψ **Milkshake Bar**, opposite Blackstone Hotel. Does 20 flavours, with or without ice cream.

Festivals and events

Kollam *p196, map p197*

Jan: Kerala Tourism boat race on 19th. **Apr**: vibrant 10-day **Vishnu festival** in Asram Temple with procession. **Aug-Sep**: Avadayattukotta Temple holds 5-day **Ashtami Rohani** festival. **Muharram** has processions at town mosque.

Alappuzha and around *p200, maps p197 and p200*

For more details: www.keralatourism.org.

9-12 Jan: Cheruppu is celebrated in Mullakkal Devi Temple with elephant procession, music and fireworks. **17-19 Jan**: Tourism Boat Race. **Jul/Aug**: DTPC Boat Race (third Sat) in the backwaters. **Champa- kulam Boat Race**, Kerala's oldest, takes place 16-km ferry ride away on 'Moolam' day. The Nehru Trophy, from 1952, is the state's largest **Snake Boat Race**. Up to 40 decorated 'snake boats' with carved prows are rowed before huge crowds. Naval helicopters do mock rescue operations and stunt flying. Tickets Rs 125 (Rs 60/ 75 for access to overcrowded and dangerous areas). Other snake boat races are held all year.

Activities and tours

Kollam *p196, map p197*

Tours

You will be spoilt for choice where back-water trips are concerned. There are trips for groups of 10, or a 'cruise' for 20 to Alappuzha with a guide. Be aware that timings do alter. The gentle pace and quiet make this very worthwhile, but the heat and humidity may sometimes make overnight stays on houseboats uncomfortable (no fans).

DTPC (District Tourism Promotion Council), Ashramam, T0474-274 2558, dtpcqln@md3 .vsnl.net, daily 1030-1830, Rs 300 (ISIC Rs 250), halfway to Alumkadavu, Rs 150, runs an 8-hr 'Luxury' cruise from the jetty near abattoir in season. En route, stops may include the world's longest snake boat, Champakulam, an 11th-century granite Buddha statue at Karumadi, and a coir processing village at Thrikkunnapuzha. But some say that the only stops are for meals, so check in advance. Some find the trip too long and samey. Or take the DTPC canal trip to Munroe Island village, 0900-1300, Rs 300.

DTPC also has a more expensive alternative, the luxury *kettuvallam*, with 1-3 rooms, a bath and a kitchen hired out for Rs 3500-5000 (full day or from afternoon till early the following morning), including traditional Kerala meals. The 24-hr trips start at Rs 8200, or packages combine day house- boat cruises with overnight stays at back- water resorts from Rs 5500. The 25-hp outboard engine does 10 km per hr. Or hire a motor boat 'safari cruise' for 8 people, Rs 400-500 per hr. Contact **DTPC**, **Soma**, T0471-226 8101, or **TourIndia** T0471-233 1507. See www.dtpckollam.com.

Independent operators include:

Southern Backwaters Tour Operators, Kollam Alappuzha cruise, T0474-746037, www.southernbackwaters.com. 8-hr cruises depart 1030-1830, report 30 mins before at Jetty Rd/Boat Jetty near KSRTC bus stand. Ferry Rs 300 one way. Village boat tours, Rs 300.

Tourindia pioneered these houseboat trips; contact at Karukapparambil, near Nehru Trophy Finishing Point, T0474-226 4961.

Visit Kerala, opposite KRSTC Bus Station, Jetty Rd, Kollam, T0474-274 0416. 8-hr cruise between Kollam and Alappuzha, departs 1030, arrives 1830. Also offers houseboats between 1 and 2 nights. Backwater village tours: 1-hr motorboat, 2 hrs on small cruise, departs 0900-1300 or 1400-1800.

Alappuzha and around *p200, map p200*

Tours

This is a starting point of backwater boat trips to Kollam, Changanacherry, Kottayam and Kochi. For information ask at **DTPC**, KSRTC Bus Station, Alappuzha, T0477-225 3308.

Alleppey Tourism Development Cooperative Society, A837 Komala Rd, Alappuzha, T0477-224 3462, www.atd calleppey .com. From Aug-May, 8-hr cruises depart at 1030, Mon, Wed, Fri, Rs 150, with stops for lunch and tea. Halfway cruise to Alamkadavu, Rs 100 (ISIC gets reduction) on a local ferry, one-way (29 km) costs Rs 10, from 0500-2100, 2½ hrs. Some visitors feel that this trip is so different from the Kollam-Alappuzha trip that it is worth doing both. Ferry to Kottayam, 1130, takes 2½ hrs, Rs 8. Towards Kochi on a large canal is less interesting. The journeys in the daytime are more interesting for watching unspoilt village life of Kerala.

Private operators offer similar trips, sometimes shorter (sometimes only stopping for a swim and lunch):

CGHEarth, Kochi, T0484-301 1711, casino@vsnl.com. US$325, runs a Spice Boat Cruise in modified *kettuvallams*, which are idyllic if not luxurious: shaded sit-outs, modern facilities including solar panels for electricity, 2 double rooms, limited menu.

Discovery 1, see **Malabar House**, page 214. Malabar Escapes' take on the houseboat is silent and pollutant free. As it's nimble and trips are for a minimum of 3 nights, it takes you far from the wider watery motorways bigger rice boats ply. 1 bedroom, large bathroom and sitting room plus sun deck. Food is to the Malabar House's high standard.

Rainbow Cruises, VCNB Rd, opposite Boat Jetty, Alappuzha, T0477-224 1375, www.backwaterkerala.com. 10 boats a/c, non-a/c, solar powered with high safety standards and speedboat support for emergency (houseboats have been known to sink).

Soma, opposite the boat jetty, 212 Raiban Annex, T0477-26 1017, soma@md2.vsnl.net.in.

Transport

Kollam *p196, map p197*

Local auto-rickshaws are plentiful and bikes are available for hire.

Bus

Local buses are plentiful. Long distance from KSRTC, T0474-275 2008. Buses every 30 mins to **Alappuzha** (85 km, 2 hrs) and **Kochi** (140 km, 3½ hrs) and other coastal towns. Daily bus to **Kumily** for **Periyar National Park** (change at Kottayam), 1000, 7 hrs. Also buses to **Kanniyakumari**. Frequent buses start at 0600: services to **Kochi**, 3 hrs; **Thiruvananthapuram**, 'super-fast' bus takes under 4 hrs. **Varkala** is difficult by bus; go to Kollambalam and change. Southbound trains stop at Varkala.

Taxi
To Alappuzha, Rs 750, from the bus station.

Train
Junction railway station, T131, is 3 km east of the boat jetty and bus station. **Chennai (MC)**: *Trivandrum Chennai Mail 6320* (AC/II), 1520, 16¾ hrs. **Mumbai (CST)**: *Kanniyakumari Mumbai Exp 1082*, 0845, 44 hrs. **Thiruvananthapuram**: *Vanchinad Exp 6303*, 0853, 1½ hrs; *Parasuram Exp 6350*, 1725, 1½ hrs; *Bangalore Kanniyakumari Exp 6526*, 1335, 1¾ hrs, continues to **Kanniyakumari**, 2¼ hrs.

Alappuzha and around *p200, map p200*
Rickshaw drivers board incoming ferries and help you with luggage and offer to transport you to the Kochi/Ernakulam bus stand, but it's only a 5-min walk away.

Bus
Bus station, T0477-225 2501. Frequent buses to **Champakulam**; **Kochi**, 0630-2330, 1½ hrs; **Kollam** 2½ hrs; **Kottayam** 1½ hrs; **Thiruvananthapuram** 3½ hrs. **Coimbatore**, 0615, 7 hrs.

Car
A car with driver from Alappuzha to Fort Kochi (65 km) costs Rs500-600.

Ferry
For ferries, T0477-225 2015. They sail to **Champakulam**, 9 trips 0430-2300, 1½ hrs; **Changanacherry**, 3½ hrs; **Chengannur**, 5 hrs; **Kollam**, 8 hrs.

Train
The train station, T0477-225 3965, is 3 km from the jetty with occasional buses from there. Trains to **Ernakulam (Junction)** depart 0600-1925. To **Chennai**: *Alleppey Chennai Exp 6042*, 1500, 15¾ hrs. **Thiruvananthapuram**: *Ernakulam Trivandrum Exp 6341*, 0615, 3½ hrs.

Kottayam and Kumarakom *p201, map p197*
Bus
The New Private Bus Station is near the railway station. Buses from Kottayam, 30 mins, go to **Kumarakom** Tourist Village. Frequent, fast buses to **Kochi**, **Thekkady**, **Thiruvananthapuram**; also 4 daily to **Madurai**, 7 hrs; 5 to **Munnar**, 5 hrs. State Bus Station, 2 km south, is chaotic, especially to get on the **Thekkady/Periyar** bus. Direct bus at 0900, 4 hrs; or every 2 hrs to **Kumily** 0900-2250, change at Kumily. Thekkady to Kottayam (7 hrs) via Thekkady pass.

Car
Car with driver to **Thekkady**, Rs 850, 4 hrs

Ferry
All year (in summer, backwater boats leave from Kodimatha Jetty; during the monsoons, use the Town Jetty, 3 km southwest of the train station). Ferries to **Alappuzha**, 0715- 1730, 3 hrs; interesting trip but very busy in peak season. **Champakulam**, 1530, 4 hrs; **Mannar**, 1430, 3 hrs. To **Champakulam**, 1600, 4 hrs. Alternatively, take ferry from Kumarakom to **Muhama** village (½-hourly from 0630-2100), 40 mins, and then go to **Alappuzha** by bus.

Train
Kollam: *Chennai Trivandrum Mail 6319*, 0805, 2 hrs; *Bangalore Kanniyakumari Exp 6526*, 1110, 2¼ hrs; *Vanchinad Exp 6303*, 0655, 2 hrs (and on to **Thiruvananthapuram**, 3¼ hrs); also *Venad Exp 6301* (AC/II), 1825, 3½ hrs.

Directory

Kollam *p196, map p197*
Hospitals District Hospital, T0474-279 3409. **Post** Head Post Office, Parameswara Nagar. Mon-Sat to 2000, Sun to 1800.

Alappuzha and around *p200, map p200*
Bank Bank of Baroda, Mullakal Rd, Visa/Mastercard advances. Canara, opposite DTPC; changes TCs, not cash. **Hospitals** District Hospital, T0477-225 3324. **Internet** Several on Mullakal Rd. **Post** Office off Mullakal Rd.

Kottayam and Kumarakom *p201*
Bank Kottayam: Bank of India and Hotel Anjali change currency and Amex TCs. **Post** MC Rd, 0800-2000, 1400-1730 on holidays.

Fort Kochi and Ernakulam

➔ *Phone code: 0484. Colour map 3, C3. Population: 1.15 mn (Kochi 596,500, Ernakulam 558,000).*

Charming Fort Kochi (Cochin) and its twin town Mattancherry is an island of slowly disintegrating stone walls, crumbling shopfronts and well-tended churches, where every turn takes you down some new gloriously picturesque, narrow winding street.

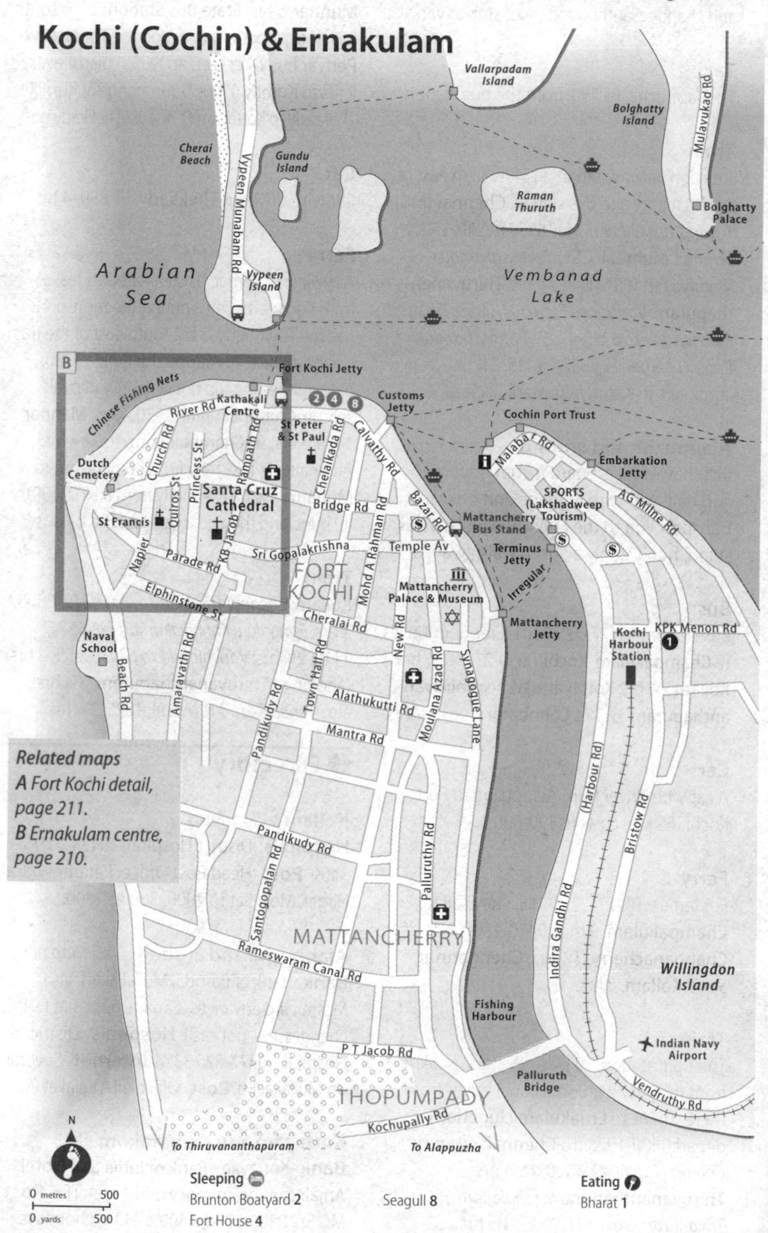

New building was only actually banned in 1976 – but most of the ramshackle island still feels frozen way back in the 15th and 16th centuries, and the huge trees here are so old their parasitic afids are tall as trees themselves. The iconic batwing Chinese fishing nets, first used in the 14th century, stand on the shores of the north, Fort, area, silhouetted against the lapping waters of one of the world's finest natural harbours, a wide bay interrupted by narrow spits of land and coconut-covered islands. The southern quarter of Mattancherry is just as romantically fossilized: row upon row of wood-fronted doors give glimpses of rice and spice merchants sitting sifting their produce into small 'tasting' bowls. A ferry journey east across the Vembanad Lake will land you in Ernakulam, a grubby but dynamic city, which is like the uncouth Mr Hyde to Cochi's cultured Dr Jekyl. ▸▸ *For Sleeping, Eating and other listings, see pages 213-219.*

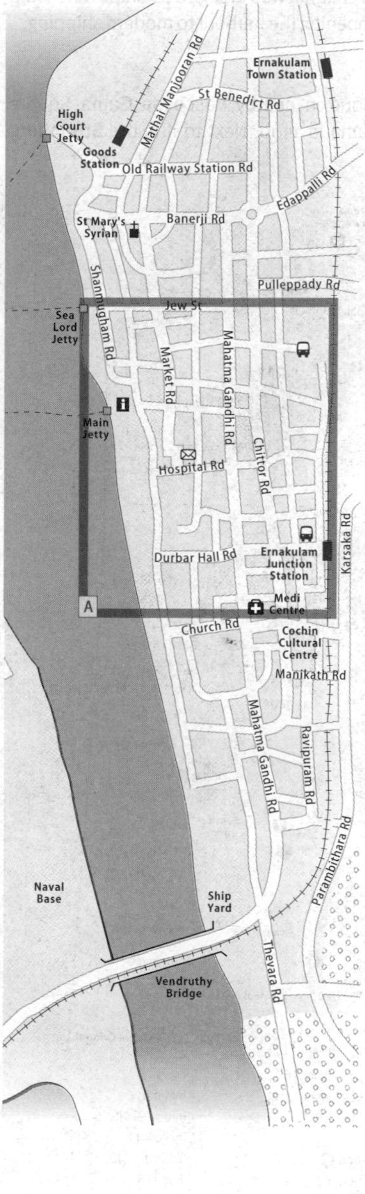

Ins and outs

Getting there The Kochi International Airport is at Nedumbassery, 36 km away. Both the main railway station, Ernakulam Junction and the main long-distance bus station are within easy walking distance of Ernakulam hotels, but Fort Kochi is a bus or ferry ride away. ▸▸ *See Transport, page 217, for further details.*

Getting around There are three main places to stay, but everything to see is in Fort Kochi, on the southern promontory. Willingdon Island, with a naval airport, Kochi harbour station and little charm, is awkwardly placed if you don't have your own transport. Located across the causeway from Willingdon Island is Ernakulam. Immediately opposite the jetty at Ernakulam is Bolghatty Island, and beyond it Vypeen Island.

During the day, a fun and quick ferry service stops at major points around the bay. Once in Fort Kochi, the palace and the synagogue in Jew Town are close to a jetty but you'll need to rent a rickshaw or bicycle to get to St Francis' Church.

Tourist information **KTDC** ⓘ *Shanmugham Rd, Ernakulam, T0484-235 3234, 0800-1800,* **Tourist Desk** ⓘ *Main Boat Jetty, Ernakulam, T0484-237 1761, touristdesk@satyam.net.in, 0900-1800*. A travel agent with good maps, runs country boat backwater tour, 0900, 1400, three hours, Rs 300, and sells tickets between Allepuzha and Kollam. They also have details of over 2000 temple festivals in Kerala and they run the Costa Malabari guest house.

History

"If China is where you make your money," declared Italian traveller Nicolas Conti in the Middle Ages, "then Kochi surely is the place to spend it." Kochi has acted as a trading port since at least Roman times, and was a link in the main trade route between Europe and China. From 1795 until India's Independence the long outer sand spit, with its narrow beach leading to the wide bay inland, was under British political control. The inner harbour was in Kochi State, while most of the hinterland was in the separate state of Travancore. The division of political authority delayed development of the harbour facilities until 1920-1923, when the approach channel was dredged so ships that could get through the Suez Canal could dock here, opening the harbour to modern shipping.

Sights

If you get off at the Customs Jetty, a plaque in nearby Vasco da Gama Square commemorates the landing of Vasco da Gama in 1500. Next to it is the **Stromberg**

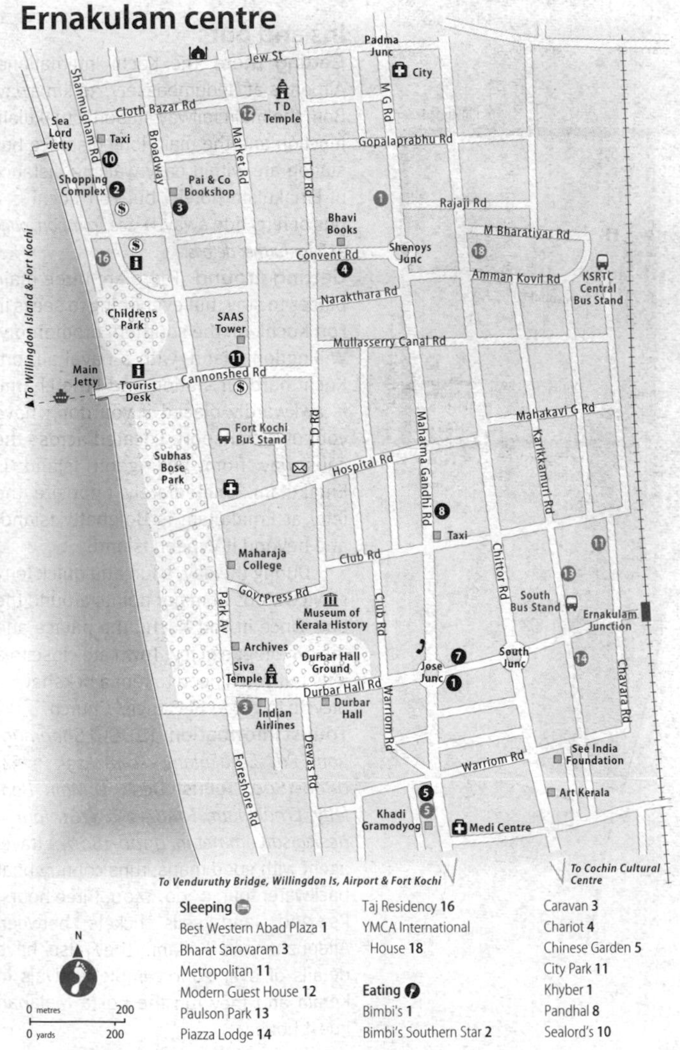

Bastion, "one of the seven bastions of Fort Emanuel built in 1767", named after the Portuguese King. Little is left of the 1503 Portuguese fort except ruins. Along the seafront, between the Fort Kochi bus stand, the boat jetty and the Dutch cemetery, run the cantilevered Chinese fishing nets. These are not unique to Kochi, but are perhaps uniquely accessible to the short-stay visitor.

Mattancherry Palace and Parikshith Thampuran Museum ⓘ *Mattancherry, daily 1000-1700 except Fri and national holidays, Rs 2, photography not allowed*, was first built by the Portuguese around 1557 as a sweetener for the Raja Veera Kerala Varma of Kochi bestowing them trading rights. In 1663, it was largely rebuilt by the new trading power, the Dutch. The layout follows the traditional Kerala pattern known as *nalukettus*, meaning four buildings, which are set around a quadrangle with a temple. There are display cases of the Rajas of Kochi's clothes, palanquins etc but these are no match for the amazing murals. The royal bedroom's low wooden walls squeezes the whole narrative of the *Ramayana* into about 45 late 16th-century panels. Every inch is covered with rich red, yellow, black and white. To the south of the Coronation Hall, the *kovinithilam* (staircase room) has six large 18th-century murals including the coronation of Rama. Vishnu is in a room to the north. Two of the women's bedrooms downstairs have 19th-century murals with greater detail. They relate Kalidasa's *Kumarasambava* and themes from the *Puranas*. This stuff is triple x-rated. If you are of a sensitive disposition avert your eyes from panel 27 and 29, whose deer, birds and other animals are captioned as giving themselves up to 'merry enjoyment', a coy way of describing the furious copulation and multiple penetration in plain view. Krishna, meanwhile, finally works out why he was given so many limbs, much to the evident satisfaction of the gopis who are looking on.

Fort Kochi detail

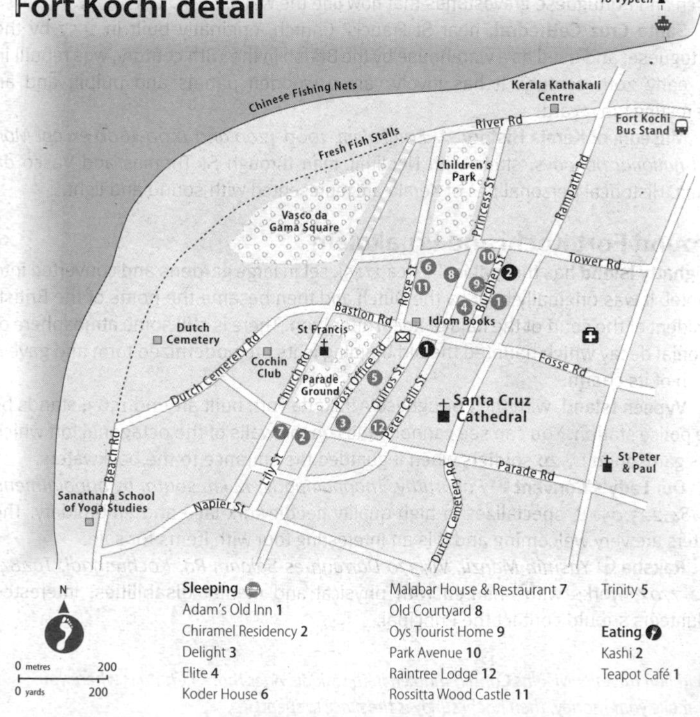

The **synagogue** ⓘ *Mattancherry, Sun-Thu 1000-1200, 1500-1700, no video cameras, shoes must be removed*, dating from 1568 (rebuilt in 1662), is near Mattancherry Palace at the heart of what is known as Jew Town. It is a fascinating mixture of shops (some selling antiques), warehouses and spice auction rooms. Stepping inside is an extraordinary experience of light and airiness, partly due to the 18th-century blue Cantonese ceramic tiles, hand painted and each one different, covering the floor. There are original glass oil lamps. For several centuries there were two Jewish communities. The earlier group (often referred to as 'black' Jews), according to one source, settled here as early as 587 BC. The earliest evidence of their presence is a copper inscription dated AD 388 by the Prince of Malabar. Those referred to as 'white' Jews came much later, when, with Dutch and then British patronage, they played a major role as trading agents. Speaking fluent Malayalam, they made excellent go-betweens for foreigners seeking to establish contacts. The community has shrunk to six families, with many now settled at Moshav Nevatim in Israel's Negev desert. The second Jewish synagogue (in Ernakulam) is deserted.

St Francis' Church ⓘ *Fort Kochi, Mon-Sat 0930-1730, Sun afternoon, Sun services in English 0800 (except for the third Sun each month)*, was originally dedicated to Santo Antonio, the patron saint of Portugal and is the first church to reflect the new and European-influenced tradition. The original wooden structure (circa 1510) was replaced by the present stone building (there is no authority for the widely quoted date of 1546). Vasco da Gama died on the site in 1524 and was originally buried in the cemetery. Fourteen years later his body was removed to Portugal. The church was renamed St Francis in 1663, and the Dutch both converted it to a Protestant church and substantially modified it. They retained control until 1795, adding the impressive gable façade at the entrance. In 1804, it became an Anglican church. In 1949 the congregation joined the Church of South India. Note the old string-pulled *punkahs* (fans) and the Dutch and Portuguese gravestones that now line the walls.

Santa Cruz Cathedral, near St Francis' Church, originally built in 1557 by the Portuguese, and used as a warehouse by the British in the 18th century, was rebuilt in the early 20th century. It has lovely carved wooden panels and pulpit, and an interesting graveyard.

Museum of Kerala History ⓘ *Ernakulam, 1000-1200 and 1400-1600 except Mon and national holidays*, starts with Neolithic man through St Thomas and Vasco da Gama. Historical personalities of Kerala are represented with sound and light.

Around Fort Kochi and Ernakulam

Bolghatty Island has the 'palace' (circa 1745), set in large gardens and converted into a hotel. It was originally built by the Dutch and then became the home of the British Resident at the court of the Raja of Kochi after 1799. There is still some atmosphere of colonial decay which haunted the old building in its premodernized form and gave it much of its charm.

Vypeen Island, with the Portuguese Azhikotta Fort, built around 1503, stands by the police station. You can see cannon holes on the walls of the octagonal fort which was garrisoned by 20 soldiers when it guarded the entrance to the backwaters.

Our Lady's Convent ⓘ *Palluruthy, Thoppampady, 14 km south, by appointment, T0484-223 0508*, specializes in high-quality needlework lace and embroidery. The sisters are very welcoming and it is an interesting tour with items for sale.

Raksha ⓘ *Yasmin Manzil, VII/370 Darragh-es-Salaam Rd, Kochangadi, T0484-222 7707*, works with children with physical and mental disabilities. Interested volunteers should contact the Principal.

Italian traveller Nicolas Conti remarked in the Middle Ages that "If China is where you make your money, then Kochi surely is the place to spend it."

Hill Palace Archaeological Museum ⓘ *Thirpunithura, 12 km east of Ernakulam, Tue-Sun 0900-1230, 1400-1700, Rs11.* Huge historical records and artefacts of the old royal state of Cochin, with portraits, ornaments, porcelain, palm leaf records and ancient musical instruments.

Sleeping

Fort Kochi has bags more character than the busy commercial centre of Ernakulam; book well in advance for the Christmas period.

Ernakulam *p208, maps p208 and p210*
AL-B Taj Residency, Marine Drive, T0484-237 1471, www.tajhotels.com. 109 rooms, good restaurants, pastry shop, all business facilities, commanding views over bay, immaculate, friendly, good value.
A-D Best Western Abad Plaza, MG Rd, T0484-238 1122, abadhotels.com. 80 a/c rooms, fridge (free soft drinks), on busy street, best rooms quieter on 5th floor (free breakfast and fitness club), restaurants recommended (no alcohol), good rooftop pool and jacuzzi, good value. Recommended.
C-D Bharat Hotel Sarovaram (BTH), Gandhi Sq, Durbar Hall Rd, T0484–230 5519, www.bharathotel.com. 91 clean rooms, some spacious, a/c, best sea-facing, pleasant a/c restaurant, also excellent lunch thalis (South Indian and North Indian), exchange, efficient, excellent service, popular, good value.
C-D Dwaraka, MG Rd, T0484-238 3238. 39 good-sized rooms with TV, some a/c (non-a/c **D**), in established family-run hotel, fab South Indian vegetarian restaurant, good value.
C-E Metropolitan, Chavara Rd, near Junction Station, T0484-2376931, www.metropolitancochin.com. 39 spotlessly clean modern a/c rooms, excellent restaurants and service, superb value. "Best railway station hotel in South India". Recommended.
D Paulson Park, Carrier Station Rd, T0484-2382179, paulsonpark@satyam.net.in. 55 clean, comfortable rooms in modern building, some good value a/c, restaurant, friendly staff. Recommended.
D-E SAAS Tower Hotel, Canon Shed Rd, T0484-236 5322, www.saastower.com. 72 good rooms (some a/c) with fitted wardrobes in modern hotel (beds rather short), tasty Indian meals, good value.
D-E YMCA International House, 100 m from Central Bus Station, T0484-235 3479, www.ymcaernakulam.org. Simple rooms (some a/c), restaurant, welcoming.
E Piazza Lodge, Kalathiparambu Rd, near south railway station, T0484-236 7408. 33 good rooms (some a/c), clean, quiet, friendly, excellent value.
F Modern Guest House, Market Rd, T0848-235 2130. Rooms with bath, clean, well-maintained, friendly staff. Recommended.

Fort Kochi *p208, maps p208 and p211*
LL Koder House, Tower Road, T0484-221 8485, www.koderhouse.com. Boutique hotel built in striking heritage town house formerly owned by prominent Jewish family and sometime home to ambassadors and heads of state. 6 luxury suites, all with huge bedroom, sitting room, bathroom and jacuzzi. Indoor pool and Serena Spa, with massage and facials, plus valet, business centre.
LL Trinity, 1/658 Ridsdale Road, Parade Ground, T0484-221 6669, www.malabarhouse.com. Ultra-modern, minimalist and modish 3-bedroom apartment with airy bathrooms, spacious sitting/dining room, mezzanine, tiny swimming pool. Service is immaculate, food is at **Malabar House** (see below) on the other side of the parade ground.
LL-AL Old Harbour Hotel, T984-7029 0000 www.oldharbourhotel.com. Newly renovated 300-year-old Portuguese and Dutch building slap on the harbour front, opposite **Brunton Boatyard** (see below). Impeccably restored with 13 rooms, private balconies, harbour views, large garden plus swimming pool. Wi-Fi, ayurveda, jacuzzi.
L Casino Hotel, Willingdon Island, T0484-301 1711, www.cghearth.com. Pool, ayurveda centre, great seafood restaurant.

For an explanation of the sleeping and eating price codes used in this guide, see inside the front cover. Other relevant information is found in Essentials pages 40-44.

L Taj Malabar, Willingdon Island, T0484-266 8010, www.tajhotels.com. Overlooking the harbour, 96 rooms and 9 suites, pool, spa, gym and 5 bars and restaurants.

L-AL Brunton Boatyard (Casino), T0484-221 5461, www.cghearth.com. Easily the best address in Fort Kochi, adjacent to the Chinese fishing nets on the edge of the Arabian Sea. 18 characterful rooms and 4 de luxe suites, each of which overlooks the harbour in an elegantly restored original boatyard and merchant's house built around a courtyard with a giant raintree. Charming details: air perfumed with lemongrass, jasmine on pillows, generous swimming pool, discounts Apr-Sep.

L-AL Malabar House, 1/268 Parade Rd, near St Francis' Church, T0484-221 6666, www.malabarhouse.com. Old meets new in 17 comfortable, a/c rooms in characterful, stylish 18th-century colonial house, period furniture, dining pavilion (good Italian, South Indian), tandoori on terrace, plunge pool in shaded grassy courtyard. German/Indian owners.

A-C Rossitta Wood Castle, Rose Street, T0484-221 5671, www.rossittawoodcastle.com. 300-year-old Dutch mansion, set around an open-air restaurant courtyard with art gallery, library internet café, spa, hot water, yoga.

A-D Old Courtyard, 1/371, Princess St, T0484-221 6302, www.oldcourtyard.com. 8 beautiful, comfortable rooms, superbly styled with old wooden furniture, some shared balconies, modern baths, a/c (musty) or charming non a/c, no TV, overlooking large, breezy courtyard of pretty pot plants and sit-outs. The suite is easily the most romantic with a 4-poster bed and white cotton. Attentive liveried staff, breakfast included, average food but excellent cakes and Turkish coffee, and lovely calm atmosphere. Recommended.

B Caza Maria Hotel, 6/125 Jew Town Rd, Mattancherry, T989-529 0758, cazamaria@rediffmail.com. Just 2 huge and wonderful rooms in beautiful converted house, with tiled floors, huge wooden furniture and antiques: isolated (the only hotel in Jew Town), romantic and shabbily elegant. Fan only. Breakfast is included, at French/Indian restaurant of same name (on the opposite side of the street). Highly recommended.

B-D Ballard Bungalow, Ballard Rd, T0484–221 5854, www.cochinballard.com. Adequate a/c and non a/c rooms in the charming former residence to the British collector of Cochin, Mr Ballard, with restaurant, satellite TV, foreign exchange and travel desk.

D Fort House, 2/6A Calvathy Rd, T0484-221 7103, fort_hs@yahoo.com. A few simple rooms within a walled courtyard with its own little jetty, lovely outlook. Extremely mixed reports on service and rooms, some of which are charmingly old fashioned, others made from bamboo. New block built in 2007. Good restaurant overlooking the water.

D Raintree Lodge, T0484-395 1489. No-frills but clean lodge in the Fort area, with pretty balcony and really helpful staff.

D Vintage Inn, Ridsdale Branch Rd, near Jaliparambu Junction, T0484-221 5064, vintageinn@hotmail.com. New in 2003, this small, homely and well-run place has maid service to clean rooms, washing line, TV, a/c and hot water on request, all for very reasonable rates. Owners arrange 6-hr waterway cruise for Rs 400.

D-E Delight, Post Office Rd, opposite 'village green', T0484-221 7658. Spotless and stylish, 8 large rooms, breakfast served, very friendly, family run, in a lovely private house complete with lawn and white picket fence. Highly recommended.

D-F Park Avenue, Princess St , T0484-221 6671, hotel_parkavenue@bplnet.com. Marble-faced hotel with 25 rooms with bath, some a/c, pleasant and airy, roof restaurant, quiet location. Good value but little charm.

E Chiramel Residency, 1/296 Lily St opposite Parade Ground, T0484-221 7310. Characterful house, 5 clean rooms, some with bath, friendly family.

E Elite, Princess St, T0484-222 5733. Cheaper rooms long way from toilets, rooms at rear quieter, cheap restaurant.

E-F Adam's Old Inn, CC1/430 Burgher St, T0484-221 7595. Restored old building, 10 rooms with bath (1 a/c), dorm beds, meals, helpful hosts.

E-G Seagull, Calvathy Rd, between ferry stops, T0484-222 8128. Converted old warehouses on the waterside, 8 rooms, some a/c (some damp and dark), good restaurant, exchange.

G Oys Tourist Home, Burgher St, T0484-221 5475. 6 pleasant rooms in lamp-lit old building, lots of plants, good value but little privacy.

Eating

Ernakulam *p208, maps p208 and p210*

ŦŦ **Avenue Regent**, excellent buffet lunch Rs 200.

ŦŦ **Bimbi's Southern Star**, Shanmugam Rd. Excellent food, generous portions.

ŦŦ **Canopy**, coffee shop for snacks, good food, buffet breakfast and service but no alcohol.

ŦŦ **Chinese Garden**, off MG Rd. A/c, authentic Chinese cuisine.

ŦŦ **Khyber**, North Indian meals upstairs.

ŦŦ **Pandhal**, MG Rd. Keralan, Chinese, Continental, a/c, clean, serving tasty meals, excellent value. Recommended.

ŦŦ **Sealord's**, rooftop for good fish dishes and Chinese.

Ŧ **Bharat**, very good vegetarian thalis and Indian specialities in clean surroundings.

Ŧ **City Park**, opposite *New Colombo*. Excellent Keralan meals.

Ŧ **Malabar**, Market Rd. Excellent South Indian but rather gloomy.

Ŧ **New Colombo**, Canon Shed Rd (next to Maple). Good snacks, fruit juices.

Cafés

Bimbi's, near Durbar Hall/MG Rd corner. Good fast food.

Caravan, Broadway (south). For ice creams and shakes.

Chariot, Convent Rd. Good café-style meals.

Coffee Beanz, Shanmugan Rd. Daily 0900-2300. Cold coffees, *appam*, *dosa*, popular, poky a/c coffee bar with just 6 tables.

Oven, Shanmugham Rd. Good pizzas and snacks (savoury and sweet).

Fort Kochi *p208, maps p208 and p211*

ŦŦŦ **Malabar House Residency**, excellent seafood platter (Rs 180) and chef's salad, the latter of huge dimensions. Authentic Mediterranean and local dishes.

ŦŦ **Teapot Café**, Peter Celli St, T0484-221 8035, tpleaz@hotmail.com. Bare terracotta roof tiles dangle with teapots and fans, walls – a tea-stained shade of white – are hung with antique tea-related paraphernalia and tea crates are tables. Try a brew of Darjeeling, Assam, Nilgiris or mint-flavoured teas, with death by chocolate, orange and banana cake or Indian rarebit. Chicken sandwiches and Kerala favourites like prawn *moilee* and mustard fish and *appam* with vegetable stew also served. Lovely.

Ŧ **Caza Maria**, Jew Town Rd (opposite hotel). 1200-2130. 2 large rooms with wooden chairs, frescoes and old framed prints on the wall. Small menu includes fish *moilee* and lime rice, *palak paneer* and *chapatti* and apple pie and ice cream. Lovely atmosphere.

Ŧ **Kashi**, Burgher Street, Kochi, T0484-221 5769, www.kashiartgallery.com. If you've been away a while, Kashi is the type of place you'll fall on in wonder. The first 2 rooms are the art gallery, the rest is a restaurant with a simple, brilliantly well-edited menu – drink filter coffee fresh from your own Bodum cafetière, perfect cappuccinos or masala chai from big beakers. There's a handful of excellently made sweets and a choice of 1-2 dishes they make for breakfast or lunch.

Ŧ **Kayikka's**, Rahmathulla Hotel, Kayees, New Road, Near Aanavaadal, Fort Kochi, T0484-222 6080, kayees@sify.com. 1200-1430, 1830-2030. Named after its owner, this family concern is the busiest biryani restaurant in Kochi and a local institution. Mutton biryani Rs 30, with date chutney on the side. You can get good fish biryanis on Fri and prawn on Tue, but chicken is served all week. Arrive early to avoid disappointment.

Ŧ **Seagull**, Calvathy Rd. Good value (Rs 80 buffet lunch), pleasant verandah for drinks and dining overlooking harbour. For really original fast food buy your own fresh fish when brought in by boat or from the nets, take it over to **Europa**, 'you buy, we cook' stalls on the seafront where they'll be grilled or masala-fried with chips (Rs 120). Delicious!

Entertainment

Kochi-Ernakulam *p208, map p208, p210, p211*

There are daily *Kathakali* performances. Arrive early to watch the extraordinary make-up being applied.

Cochin Cultural Centre, Manikath Rd, off Ravipuram Rd, Ernakulam, T0484-236 8153. A/c 'theatre', authentic, English explanations; 1830-1930, make-up 1630, Rs 125.

ENS Kalari, Nettoor, Fort Kochi, T0484-280 9810. *Kalarippayattu* , 0400-0700, 1700-2000.

Kerala Kathakali Centre, River Rd, New Bus Stand, Fort Kochi, T0484-222 1827. Rustic surroundings but lively performance, enjoyable; 1830-1930 (make-up 1700); check times, Rs 100.

See India Foundation, Kalathil Parampil Lane (enter Chittoor Rd south) near Junction station, Ernakulam, T0484-236 9471. Dr Devan's 'interpreted' taste of *Kathakali* with esoteric English commentary; 1845-2000 (make-up from 1800), Rs 125.

Festivals and events

Kochi-Ernakulam *p208, map p208, p210, p211*

Jan/Feb: Ulsavam at the Siva Temple in Ernakulam for 8 days and at Tripunithura Temple in **Nov/Dec**. There are elephant processions each day and folk dance and music performances. **Aug/Sep**: Onam.

Shopping

Kochi-Ernakulam *p208, map p208, p210, p211*

Coir products (eg mats), carvings on rosewood and buffalo horn and antiques may catch your eye here. Several narrow streets in Jew Town, towards the Synagogue, have become popular for 'antique' hunters in the last 25 years. All these shops sport a similar range of old (some faux) and new curios. There are several Government Emporia on MG Rd, Ernakulam, including **National Textiles** (another in Banerji Rd). Other shopping areas are in Broadway, Super Bazar, Anand Bazar, Prince St and New Rd.

Cinnamon, Stuba Hall, 1/658 Ridsdale Rd, Parade Ground, Fort Kochi, T0484-221 7124. Posh clothing, fabrics and interiors shop.

Dhamdhere, Pandithan Temple Rd, Mattanchery, T0484-222 4481. Interesting perfume manufacturers. Many scents are synthetic (Rs 12), but sandalwood oil is real (Rs 100).

Idiom Books, VI/183 Synagogue Lane, Jew Town, T0484-224028 and behind St. Francis Church in the Fort. Very good range on India, travel, fiction, religion, philosophy etc.

Activities and tours

Kochi-Ernakulam *p208, map p208, p210, p211*

Body and soul

Be Beautiful, 1/605 PeterCelli St, Fort Kochi, T0484-221 5398. 0900-2030. Good, cheap beauty salon with massage, hairdressers, pedicure and manicure in new premises.

Sanathana School of Yoga Studies, XV/2188-D Beach Road Junction, Cochin, T0484-394 4150 sanathanam@yahoo.com. Daily classes 0730-0930 and 1630-1830 pranayama, and asanas plus 28 day-long teacher training programmes in a pretty residence in downtown Fort Cochi.

Sree Narayana Holistic Clinic, Vypeen Island, Fort Kochi, T0484-250 2362, ayurdara@sancharnet.in. Ayurveda, 1-hr massage plus a Keralan thali on a rooftop with harbour views, Rs 500.

Tour operators

CGH Earth, Casino Building, Willingdon Island, T0484-266 8221. Recommended.

Clipper, 40/6531 Convent Rd, T0484-236 4443, clipcol@md2.vsnl.net.in.

Olympus, south end of MG Rd, near Little Kingdom shop, T0484-237 3630. Very competent and helpful.

Paradise Tours & Travel, Calvetty, Cochin, T918-4221 5331, www.aspinwall group.com. Experienced, slick Kerala package company and surface travel agent with networks across India. A/c and non-a/c cars available.

Pioneer Personalized Holidays, Pioneer House, 5th Cross, Willingdon Island, T0484-266 6148, www.pner.com. Fleet of cars with tailor-made tour packages from a well-established and highly competent tour company. Efficient and knowledgeable, they offer unusual homestays and guest houses.

Sundale Vacations, 39/5955 Atlantis Junction, MG Rd, T0484-238 0127, www.sundale.com. Surface and hotel arrangements in Kerala, specializes in homestays catering to 'foreign independent tourists', promoting insight into Kerala's customs. Programmes from US$467.

Unusual Places, 639 1st floor, Santo Complex, RS Rd, Aluva, Ernakulam, www.unusualplaces.info. Will matchmake you with properties in Kerala (generally rooms without a/c and TV – old bedrooms but new bathrooms) divided into city, wildlife or beach categories.

Viceregal Travels and Resorts, S17/18 GCDA Shopping Complex, Marine Drive, Fort Cochi, T0484-235 1219, viceregal@md3.vsnl

.net.in, runs a 9-day homestay package to charming properties, including a/c Ambassador cab, from Cochin to Peermade, Chertala for the backwaters and Kovalam for Kannyukamari. Rs 21,000 per person.

Tours

Backwaters KTDC Backwater Village tours, T0484-237 1761. Daily from Kuthiathode, 0830-1300, afternoon 1430-1900 (40-min road transfer), country boat for 8-10, Rs 275. Moonlight cruise on full moon nights.

An alternative 'backwater' trip is to get a boat from High Court jetty to Mulavukadu Jetty, then ask for the Varapuzha boat. Get off at the last stop, Chetty Bhagam. Boat every 30 mins, 2-hr journey, Rs 5.

Tourindia, T0477-264961. Also has *kettuvallams*; Ernakulam to Kuttanad backwaters and return. Rs 3000 per head.

Tourist Desk, www.indiatouristdesk.com. One of the best budget tour operators. Tours include overnight houseboat, Rs 4000 for 2. 7-hr backwater cruise from Kochi starts main boat jetty 0830-0700: 4 hrs on a houseboat through wide canals then 3 hrs village cruise on country boat with thali meals, Rs 425.

Visit India, Mr A Edassery, Island Club House, 1st Main Rd, Willingdon Island, T0484-266 8819, www.visitindiatravel.com. Organizes a delightful boat tour along Kochi's backwaters in a dugout, punted and engineless, through very peaceful shady waterways passing unspoilt villages with toddy tappers, coir making, fishing etc; led by an excellent guide. Rs 350 for 4 hrs, depart 0830, 1430, 40-min drive to jetty. Highly recommended. They also have traditional *kettuvallams*; Rs 5000 (for couple) or Rs 8000 (2 bedroom); for 24 hrs, includes all meals.

Sightseeing KTDC (see above), boat tours daily to Dutch Palace, Jewish Synagogue, St Francis' Church, Chinese Fishing Nets, Bolghatty Island. Depart from Sea Lord Jetty, Ernakulam. 0900-1230, 1400-1730; mornings cooler. Rs 70. Highly recommended.

Visit India, 35/871 North Janatha Rd, Palarivattom, T0484-233 6483, tours@visitindiatravel.com. Also has fleet of 10 house- boats and transport division with excellent drivers of standard, premium and luxury cars.

Transport

Kochi-Ernakulam *p208, map p208, p210, p211*

Air

New international airport, 36 km northeast, T0484-261 0113. Pre-paid taxis to Fort Kochi, Rs 350-400. **Indian Airlines**, T0484-236 0796, airport T0484-261 0041 (domestic), T0484-261 0101 (international): **Bengaluru (Bangalore)**, **Chennai**, **Mumbai**, **Delhi** via Goa, **Thiruvananthapuram**: daily; **Coimbatore**, **Hyderabad**, **Kozhikode** and **Tiruchirapalli**, several flights per week. Flights to **Doha**, **Kuwait**, **Muscat**, **Sharjah**. **Jet Airways**, T0484-236 9212, airport T0484-261 0037: **Mumbai**, **Chennai**, **Bengaluru**, daily.

Airline offices On MG Rd unless stated otherwise. International: **Air India**: T0484-235 1260. **British Airways**, T0484-236 4867. **Cathay Pacific** and **KLM**, T0484-236 2064. **Lufthansa**, T0484-237 0776. **Japan Airlines**, T0484-235 0544. **Maldive Airlines**, T0484-235 1051. **Singapore Airlines** and **Swissair**, T0484-236 7911. Domestic: **Indian Airlines** and **Alliance Air**, Durbar Hall Rd, near Bharat Hotel, T0484-237 0242. **Jet Airways**, Elmar Sq Bldg, MG Rd, T0484-236 9212.

Bus

Local Journeys between Ernakulam, Willingdon and Fort Kochi are useful and fairly frequent after ferries stop running.

Long distance KSRTC, T0484-236 0531, run 'Express' and 'Fast' services from Ernakulam Terminus near Junction Railway station to major cities in the south; computerized reservations not always available. To **Alappuzha**, every 20 mins, 1½ hrs, Rs 30; **Devikulam**, 6 hrs, Rs 42; **Kannur**, 7 hrs (Exp), 8½ hrs, Rs 85; **Kottayam**, 2½ hrs, Rs 38; **Kozhikode**, 5 hrs (Exp), Rs 72, 6½ hrs, Rs 65; **Munnar**, via **Aluva**, 4 hr, 0630; **Thekkady** (Kumily) for **Periyar**, 0630, 6¾ hrs, Rs 80, or take later bus to Kottayam (frequent) which has several daily to Thekkady; **Thiruvananthapuram**, 5 hrs (Exp), Rs 75, 6½ hrs, Rs 60; **Thrissur**, 1½ hrs (Exp), Rs 25. Interstate buses to: **Bengaluru (Bangalore)** via **Kozhikode**, **Sulthan Bathery** and **Mysore**, 0600-2100, night 12 hrs, day 15 hrs, Rs 175-210. **Mysore**, 2000, 10 hrs, Rs 190. **TNSTC**,

T0484-2372616. To **Coimbatore** via **Thrissur** and **Palakkad**, 4¾ hrs (Exp), Rs 75; Kanniyakumari Exp, 8 hrs, Rs 110; **Chennai** via **Coimbatore**, **Erode**, **Salem**, 1530, 15 hrs, Rs 185; **Madurai**, via **Kottayam**, **Kumly**, **Thekkady** 9 hrs (Exp), Rs 115; **Mysore**, 11 hrs, Rs 145. Private operators from Kalloor and Ernakulam South bus stands including Indira Travels, DH Rd, T0484-236 0693 and SB Travels, MG Rd, opposite Jos Annexe, T0484-235 3080, Princey Tours, opposite Sealord Hotel, T0484- 235 4712. Overnight coaches to **Bengaluru (Bangalore)**, 12 hrs, and **Mysore** 10 hrs. To **Kottayam**, every 30 mins, 2 hrs, **Munnar**, 4 hrs. Also to **Chennai** and **Coimbatore**.

Ferry

Ferries are faster, cheaper and much more comfortable than buses or autos.

Ernakulam Main Boat Jetty is 200 m from Junction railway station; High Court Jetty for ferries to Bolghatty.

Fort Kochi 'Customs' (main stop) with a separate one for Vypeen Island.

Willingdon Island 'Embarkation' (north) and 'Terminus' (west). From Ernakulam, to **Bolghatty** public ferry every 20 min, from High Court Jetty, 0600-2200. Ferries do not operate on Sun. Some take bikes/motor bikes. To **Fort Kochi** Customs 0600-2110 (30 mins). To **Willingdon**: ½-hourly from 0630 to 2110. To **Vypeen Island** via Willingdon Embark- ation: ½-hourly, from 0530-2230, 30 mins. To **Mattancherry**: 6 from 0710-1740, 30 mins. From Bolghatty to Ernakulam and Fort Kochi, 1745-2000, Rs 50; speed boat hire from Bolghatty Palace, Rs 200 to Fort Kochi. From **Fort Kochi**: customers to Malabar Hotel, ½-hourly to Vypeen Island, about 2 car ferries per hour. To **Varapusha**, 6 boats, 0740-1500, 2 hrs. **Ferry hire**: motor boat for up to 20, from Sea Lord jetty, book at KTDC office, Rs 200 per hr. 3-hr harbour tour and Fort Kochi sights; most people will want longer. KTDC Fort Kochi tour, 0900, 1400, 3½ hrs, Rs 60. **Taxi boats** are faster and more convenient – jetty closer to Bolghatty Palace, Rs 20 per head.

Rickshaw

Auto-rickshaw drivers have a reasonably good reputation here. But, if you are likely to arrive late at night, insist on being taken directly to your hotel. Beware: antique and jeweller shops work on commission basis here. Fares within Fort Kochi: Rs 20.

Taxi

Ernakulam Junction to Fort Kochi, Rs 150. On MG Rd, Ernakulam: Corp Taxi Stand, T0484-236 1444.

Train

Ernakulam/Kochi is on the broad gauge line joining Thiruvananthapuram to Mangalore, Bengaluru (Bangalore) and Chennai. Most trains from major cities stop at Ernakulam Junction (the main station) although a few stop at Ernakulam town, T0484-239 0920. Enquiries: Ernakulam Junction, T131. From Ernakulam Junction to: **Alappuzha**: several, including *Ernakulam Trivandrum Exp 6341*, 0615, 1 hr; *Cannanore Ernakulam Alleppey Exp 6308*, 1130, not Thu or Sat, 1¼ hrs; *Guruvayur Madurai Exp 6726*, 2350, 1 hr. **Chennai (MC)**: *Alleppey Chennai Exp 6042* (AC/II), 1500, 15¾ hrs; *Trivandrum Chennai Mail 6320*, 1900, 13 hrs. **Delhi (HN)**: *Ernakulam Nizamuddin Mangala Lakshadweep Exp 2617*, 1155, 40 hrs. **Thiruvananthapuram**: *Vanchinad Exp 6303*, 0550, 4½ hrs; *Venad Exp 6301* (AC/CC), 1715, 5 hrs. From Ernakulam Town to: **Mangalore**: *Parasuram Exp 6349* (AC/CC), 1055, 10 hrs; *Malabar Exp 6329*, 2305, 11¾ hrs. **Mumbai (CST)**: *Kanniyakumari Mumbai Exp 1082* (AC/II), 1230, 40½ hrs. **Thiruvananthapuram**: *Parasuram Exp 6350*, 1355, 5 hrs; *Cannanore Trivandrum Exp 6348*, 0040, 5¼ hrs.

Directory

Kochi-Ernakulam *p208, map p208, p210, p211*

Banks Most open till 1500. Several on MG Rd, Shanmugham Rd and on Broadway, Ernakulam, and on Mattancherry Palace Rd, Fort Kochi. Ernakulam Head PO does Western Union money transfer. Thomas Cook, Palal Towers, 1st floor, Right Wing, MG Rd, T0484-236 9729, Mon-Sat, 0930-1800, exchange, TCs, very quick service. ICICI has an ATM in Fort Cochi on Chelaikada Road, HDFC has an ATM in Thopumpaday on Pallurthy Road, south of Palluruth Bridge.

Union Bank, Panampilly Nagar, opens Sun. **Dentist** City Dental Clinic, T0484-236 8164. **Internet** Café De Net, Princess St, Fort Kochi, 0930-2230. Very fast internet, coffee shop. **Net Point**, near Junction Station. Fast connection Rs 30 per hr. **Satyam i-way**, Esplanade Building, close to the main jetty. Broadband and net phone (cheap calls to Europe). **Hospitals** General Hospital, Hospital Rd, Ernakulam, T0484-236 0002. **Govt Hospital**, Fort Kochi, T0484-222 4444. On MG Rd: **City**, T0484-236 1809, and **Medical Trust Hospital**, T0484-237 1852, have 24-hr pharmacies. **Post** CTO: (24 hrs) Jos Junction Building, 2nd floor, MG Rd, Ernakulam. **Ernakulam Head PO**, Hospital Rd, 0830-2000, Sat 0930-1430, Sun 1000-1600, other holidays 1400-1700. **Kochi Main PO**, Mattancherry (for **Poste Restante**), 0800-2000, Sun 0930-1700; often empty. North End PO, Willingdon Island.

Useful addresses AA: South India, MG Rd (opposite Hotel Dwaraka), T0484-235 1369. **Tourist Police**: T0484-266 6076, help with information of all kinds. **Visa extension**: City Police Commissioner, High Court Ferry Station, Ernakulam, T0484-236 0700. Foreigners' Regional Registration Office, T0484-235 2454.

Munnar and Idukki's high ranges

Inland from the plains around Kottayam and Kochi lie first tropical evergreen forests, then plantations of rubber and of spice. These give way to pepper then cardamom, until your climb up the ghats takes you to high hills rolling with tea and the thin clean air of the well-kept estates of Munnar in the north of landlocked Idukki district. To the south sit the evergreen forests and jungles of Periyar and Thekkady, home to tiger and elephant. These make perfect high-mountain pauses before crossing the border into Tamil Nadu. Thekkady comes covered in rubber and fruits and is chiefly peopled by tribals converted to Christianity: long lines of crucifixes litter some of the most beautiful mountain ridges. Periyar is famous for its tigers and its elephants but you are unlikely to see either; instead, outsized butterflies beat wings as big as bats under the canopies of prehistoric jack trees and teak trees hanging with bee sacks. Spiders webs are spun to human proportions. Mynah birds and parakeets gossip in the enormous branches of ficus trees. And the thud and thwack of leaves and branches up above is the signpost of a swooping gang of Nilgiri Langur swinging through the upper reaches of the nature park. You can track macaques, glad-eye brownbush butterflies, wander among trees with roots at head height and peer at a tiger's fresh paw prints. At 1600 m, Munnar is much higher and, once one of the summer boltholes for the British Government of South India, is now almost wholly owned by Tata's tea company. Three mountain streams meet at Munnar: Mudrapuzha, Nallathanni and Kundala, and it has one of the highest populations worldwide of the endangered ibex, or Nilgiri tahr. » *For Sleeping, Eating and other listings, see pages 226-230.*

Ins and outs

Getting there and around Munnar is closest to Kochi-Ernakulam while Thekkady (Periyar reserve/Kumily town) is best accessed from Kottayam. There are no train links to the high ranges; buses take a minimum of four hours to climb the hills to both hill stations, and roads linking the two take the same length of time. » *See Transport page 230, for further details.*

Tourist information District tourism offices are at **Kumily** ⓘ *T0486-232 2620*, and **Old Munnar** ⓘ *T04865-253 1516*.

The first rubber plantation was cultivated in 1902. India is now within the top three rubber producers worldwide, and most of that comes from Kerala.

The Midlands (Kottayam to Thekkady)

An interesting drive to the hills, this route follows the Ghat road which has superb views down the east side of the Ghats onto the Tamil Nadu plains. You may meet herds of Zebu cattle, buffalo and donkeys being driven from Tamil Nadu to market in Kerala. Above 1000 m the air freshens and it can be cold. Be prepared for a rapid change in temperature.

Pala, off the Kottayam-Thekkady road, is a town famous for its learned citizens – graduates of the European-style Gothic university, which was built, along with the Gothic church, by one of its affluent sons. Nehru visited in the 1950s and said that Pala was full of "people of vision". The town was the most literate place in India long before Kerala achieved 100% literacy, and Meenachil *Taluka* has the maximum number of educated women in the country. It is also famous for its tamarind and pepper as well as its rubber estates belonging to the Dominic family, whose beautiful 100-year-old traditional Kerala plantation bungalow and a 50-year-old estate mansion is where hot Syrian-Catholic lunches are served. Plantation tours to watch latex collection and packing can be arranged through **CGH Earth**, see page 216. Further east lies **Erattupetta**, whose grey St George's Church holds naïve wood-painted doves and disembodied cherubims and hosts the **High Range Festival** every April. Carry on for **Vagamon**, a village set on a chain of three hills: Thangal, Murugal and Kurisumala, in a mark of religious harmony. A dairy farm here is managed by Kurisumala monks.

Some 25 km south from Vagamon is **Peermade** (regular buses between Kottayam and Kumily, three hours, Rs 45, several per day to/from Ernakulam) considerably lower than Thekkady. It is surrounded by tea, rubber and cardamom plantations and there are a number of picturesque spots around the town, which was named after Peer Mohammed, a Sufi saint and crony of the royal family of Travancore. **Abraham's Spice Garden** ⓘ *Kottayam-Kumily Rd (bus route), Rs 50 expected,* offers excellent tours with a family member.

Sabarimala Many Hindu pilgrims make the journey to the forest shrine dedicated to Sri Aiyappan at Sabarimala, 191 km north of Thiruvananthapuram, see box opposite. Aiyappan is a particularly favoured deity in Kerala and there are growing numbers of devotees. It is only open on specific occasions: **Mandalam**, mid-November to the end of December; **Makaravilakku**, mid-January; **Vishu**, mid-April; **Prathistha** one day in May-June; and during the **Onam** festival in August-September.

Thekkady (Periyar National Park, Kumily Town)

» *pp227-230. Colour map 3, C3.*

→ *Phone code: 0486.*

Set on an attractive Periyar lakeside, major wildlife sightings in the **Periyar National Park** ⓘ *T0486-922 4571, www.periyartigerreserve.org, Rs 50 (foreigners) for 5 days, video camera fee Rs 100, for more information visit the Eco Tourism Information Centre, Ambady Junction, 0800-1800,* are uncommon, but the beautiful setting attracts over 300,000 visitors a year. In 1895 the lake was created by building a dam that covered 55 sq km of rich forest. A 180 m-long tunnel led the water which had flowed into the Arabian Sea east into the Suruli and Vaigai rivers, irrigating extensive areas of Ramanathapuram and Madurai districts. The 780 sq km sanctuary was created by the old Travancore State government in 1934. The small Kumily village with most of the guest houses and eating places is 3 km above the lake.

Ideal times are dawn and dusk so stay overnight (winter nights can get quite cold). Avoid weekends and holidays.

A modern mass pilgrimage

Sabarimala pilgrims are readily visible in many parts of South India as they wear black dhotis as a symbol of the penance they must undergo for 41 days before they make the pilgrimage. In addition to the black dress, pilgrims must take two baths daily and only eat food at home during this period. The pilgrimage, which begins at Deepavali, is only for males and prepubescent and post-menstrual females, to avoid the defilement believed to be associated with menstruation.

The pilgrimage in January is deliberately hard, writes Vaidyanathan, because "the pilgrimage to the shrine symbolizes the struggle of the individual soul in its onward journey to the abode of bliss and beautitude. The path of the spiritual aspirant is always long, arduous and hazardous. And so is the pilgrimage to Sabarimala, what with the observance of severe austerities and trekking up forested mountains, risking attacks from wild animals". See below.

Ins and outs

Getting there Long-distance buses reach Thekkady lakeside via Kumily Town. » *See Transport, page 230, for further details.*

Getting around Buses run between Kumily and the lake jetty, or you can hire a bike, share a jeep or take the pleasant walk. 'Cruises' at 0700, 0930, 1130, 1400, 1600.

Tourist information District Tourism Information Office ⓘ *T0486-232 2620*, runs plantation tours to Murikkady (5 km), Vandiperiyer (18 km) and Vandanmedu (25 km).

Sights

Some visitors are disappointed, due to the small number of wildlife sightings, but for others the beautiful setting compensates. It was designated a part of Project Tiger in 1973 though **tigers** are very rarely seen and it is better known for its **elephants**, which you are very likely to see until March/April. Most bull elephants here are tuskless

Periyar National Park

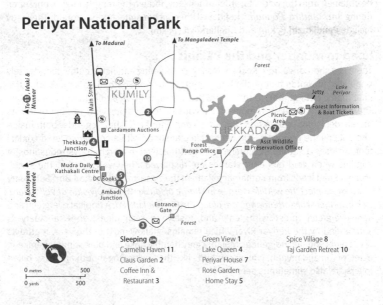

Sleeping
Carmelia Haven 11
Claus Garden 2
Coffee Inn & Restaurant 3
Green View 1
Lake Queen 4
Periyar House 7
Rose Garden Home Stay 5
Spice Village 8
Taj Garden Retreat 10

 (*makhnas*). **Bison**, **sambar**, **wild boar** and **barking deer** are also fairly common. In addition to 246 species of **bird**, there are 112 species of **butterfly**. Smaller animals include black Nilgiri **langur**, **bonnet** and **lion-tailed macaque**, **giant** and **flying squirrels** and **otter**; look out for a flight of flying foxes (fruit bats) over the Spice Village each evening at about 1830.

The forests have special viewing platforms which you can use if you prefer to walk with a game ranger who can act as a guide. The three-hour trek is for five people only, 0700, Rs 60, and you need to queue for about an hour outside the office. Much depends on your guide and your luck but not everybody comes face to face with a herd of elephants; some return very disappointed. Carry water and beware of leeches. An overnight stay in a watchtower (24-hour trek) for two, Rs 100, gives you more chance of seeing deer, bears, bisons and elephants. Guides arrange unofficial walking tours privately in the park periphery in the afternoon (not the best time for spotting wildlife); try to assess the guide before signing up. A motor launch trip on the lake is recommended. Ask the wildlife preservation officer.

Two-hour boat trips depart 0700, 0930, 1130, 1400 and 1600 (Rs15-100). Two-hour tribal heritage tours 0800-1600 (Rs100), while three-hour nature treks depart 0700, 1100 and 1400 (Rs100, up to five people). No advance reservation is required. Book at the boat jetty Information Centre/Tribal Heritage Office in the park. You need to book the day before for all other activities: tiger trails for two or three days, one or two nights, depart 0900 twice a week (Rs 3000/5000, including food and tent, up to five people); border hiking 0800-1700 (Rs 1000, including food, up to 10 people); bamboo rafting (Rs 1000, up to 20 people); coracle and bullock cart rides depart 0600 and 1430 (Rs 1000, up to nine people); 24-hour jungle camp (Rs 1000, up to 30 people); and 'jungle patrol' night trekking (1900-2200, 2200-0100, 0100-0400, Rs 500, up to five people). Up to two people can stay in a cottage overnight (1500-0900) at the Jungle Inn; the price includes dinner and trekking.

Around Thekkady

There are a number of attractions within easy reach of Thekkady. These include the traditional Keralan-style **Mangaladevi Temple**, set amongst dense woodland on the peak of a 1337 m hill, 15 km northeast of Thekkady. Permission to visit the area must be obtained from the wildlife warden, Thekkady, though the temple itself is only open during the *Chithra Pounami* holiday. Other picturesque spots around Thekkady include **Pandikuzhi** (5 km) and **Chellarkovil** (15 km).

Road to Munnar and the Palanis

There is a short drive from Kochi across the undulating and richly cultivated, densely populated lowlands before climbing rapidly up one of South India's most attractive ghat roads. **Ettumanoor**, to the south, has possibly the wealthiest temple in Kerala. The present Mahadeva Temple was reconstructed in 1542, and is famous for its murals depicting scenes from the *Ramayana* and the Krishna legends, both inside and outside the *gopuram*. The typical circular shrine with a copper-covered conical roof encloses a square sanctuary. The **Arattu festival** in March draws thousands of pilgrims when gold elephant statues are displayed. They weigh 13 kg. The Kochi-Munnar Road leads from Kothamangalam, to the 25 sq km **Thattekkad Bird Sanctuary** ⓘ *20 km, contact the wildlife warden in charge of Idukki Wildlife Division at Vellappara, 13 km northeast of Kothamangalam along the Pooyamkutti Rd.* A tropical evergreen and semi-evergreen forest with teak and rosewood plantations, the sanctuary is surrounded by the Periyar River which remains shallow most of the year. It attracts water birds and the indigenous Malabar grey hornbill, rose and blue-winged parakeet, egret, heron and mynah, while rarer birds like the Ceylon frog-mouth and rose-billed rollers are also sometimes seen here.

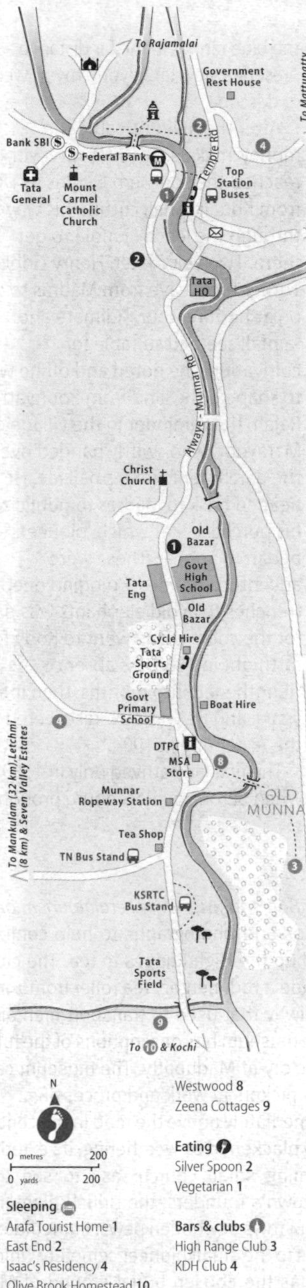

Munnar

» pp226-230. Colour map 3, C3.

→ *Phone code: 04865. Altitude: 1520 m.*

A major centre of Kerala's tea industry, close to Anaimudi, and at 2695 m the highest peak in South India, Munnar is the nearest Kerala comes to a genuine hill station. The landscape is European Alpine minus the snow. It is surrounded by about 30 tea estates, which are among the highest in the world, and forest that is still rich in wildlife, including the reclusive Nilgiri tahr, despite the increasingly commercial use of the hills. The workers on the tea estates are mostly Tamilians who moved here around eight or nine generations ago. The surrounding hills are also home to the rare Neelakurunji orchid (*Strobilanthes*), which covers the hills in colour for a month once every 12 years (next one due 2018). Cotton wool swabs of cloud shift and eddy across hillsides sodden as a sponge with fresh rains, and springs burst their banks and surge across the pathways where villagers, dark-skinned tribals in their ski jackets and woollen noddy hats, swing past on Enfields on their way home from a day on the tea plantations.

Ins and outs

Getting there The easiest access is by bus or taxi from Kochi, but there are also daily buses to major towns in Kerala and Tamil Nadu. » *See Transport, page 230, for further details.*

Getting around The town is small and pleasant for exploring on foot, although there are autos. It is worth hiring a bike or a jeep for trips out of town.

Tourist information DTPC ⓘ *T04865-231516, www.munnar.com*, run tours of plantations and rents cycles. Try also the free tourist information service, which is in the Main Bazar, opposite the bus stop. Joseph Iype is also a mine of information.

Crops are determined by height: tea grows above 1500 m, cardamom, coffee and other spices between 1500 m and 600 m, coconut and rubber below 600 m.

The lone high ranges

"Unexplored regions covered by thick, fever-haunted forests, the abode of elephants, tigers, bisons and leopards, having no means of communication," stated the State Manual of Travancore of Munnar in 1880. Today, the High Range is "totally explored, every possible acre of land is cultivated with tea, eucalyptus, and… there is a population of over 60,000."

The first European to visit the Kanan Devan hills was the Duke of Wellington in his 1790 hunt for Tipu Sultan. He thought it a "capital place", but had to press on to try to track down the Muslim ruler. The next outsider was General Douglas Hamilton who came in 1862 in search of an R&R station for his troops: "Surpassingly grand and incomparably beautiful," he judged it. "The views from this mountain are the grandest and most extensive I have ever beheld; some of the precipices are of stupendous magnitude, and the charming variety of the scenery, comprising undulating grassy hills, wooded valleys, rocky crags, overhanging precipices, the green fields in the valley of Unganaad with the grand mass of the Pulnees beyond, and the blue ranges in the far distance, present a view far beyond my power to describe."

After the military, came the money-makers. The first surveyor reached the Southern Nilgiris in 1877 from Kodaikkanal, cutting his way through the leechy jungle to get there. Two years later, Henry Gribble Turner took leave from Madras to go on a shooting tour. "Climate and rainfall seemed suitable for cultivation," he noted and off he went to snap up the land from Poonyattu Rajah, the zaminder in the village of Marayoor, who swiftly handed over the parchments for a small fee. He headed back to Madras to publicize his purchase – at which 'pioneers' began to appear. These were adventurous types – digging deep trenches to avoid elephants was par for the course. One went to Kody for a fortnight in 1883, his absence "lengthened into months, then into years; and he was next discovered in the Argentine in 1904."

The first lady arrived only in 1889 when Baron von Rosenburg brought

Sights

Tata Tea Museum ① *Nullatanni Estate, T04865-230561, www.keralatourism.org, 1000-1600, Rs 50*, has a heap of artefacts, curios and photographs to help conjure something of the lives of the men who opened up the High Ranges to tea. The crop has grown here for over a century so relics include a rudimentary tea roller from 1905 and a wheel from the Kundale Valley Light Railway that used to transport men and materials between Munnar and Top Station. The museum has descriptions of the fully automated technology of today from the tea factory at Madupatty. The museum can also arrange a visit to this factory, watching tea pickers at work and processing.

In the centre of Old Munnar, set on a hill immediately above the road in the centre of town, is **Christ Church**. Rather squat and now blackened by weathering, its exterior is unprepossessing, but inside it is a charming small church: ask to see the diminutive record of births and deaths of the town's founders, the British planters. Consecrated in 1910, it still contains its original 14 rows of wooden pews. Immediately behind the church a zigzag path up the hill leads to the small pioneer cemetery which was established long before the church itself as the chosen burial ground of Mrs Eleanor Knight, General Manager Knight's 24-year-old bride who caught cholera after arriving in the High Range in 1894. Built to serve tea estate managers and workers of the High Ranges, the last English language service was held in 1981. Its origins are suggested in memorial plaques on the wall and it is now shared between protestant up his bride, daughter of the aforementioned Henry Gribble. A post office followed in 1892 (only granted after pioneers arranged for their friends to send them post cards to justify its opening). Gradually, coffee and rubber were phased out to make Kanan Devan Hills Produce a solely tea-producing company. The jungle was pushed back and the town developed: an estate bazar sprang up to trade in the weekly shipment of rice and fresh bread carried up by ponies, donkeys and bullocks. The company agreed to the "present opium and ganja contractor of Devikolam conducting sales… on the premises of Munnar Town," to supply the workers who had moved in families from drought-starved Madras state to secure minimum wages, free housing, piped water, and medical care. A High Range currency was minted to prevent them from bolting after getting their pay cheque.

The first party was in 1900: a social scene of amateur dramatics, blood sports and gymkhanas added to financial success and pleasant, cool climes to make the planters' lot content.

All the jollity was interrupted by the Second World War in 1939. 18 High Rangers departed for service in that year alone. Air Force personnel passed through on R&R. Tea markets slumped, prices falling below the cost of production. A road was cut between Munnar and Kody to allow for evacuation from Japanese attack.

Nor did problems halt with the end of hostilities: returning menfolk found the Quit India movement had gained momentum in their absence. After Independence, a few Britishers hung about, but Kerala communism bred a culture of strikes and the pickings weren't so rich for the opportunistic expats. The Company, James Finlay and Co, struck a joint venture with Tatas of India. Finally, in 1967, the rupee was devalued: expat labour became too expensive and, although some were second or third generation High Rangers, they were sent home, leaving an Alpine landscape littered with club houses peopled by cravat-wearing members with a fondness for polo.

Tamil and Malayalam worshippers. Sunday services are in Tamil (0800) and Malayalam (1000).

Mount Carmel Roman Catholic church, the first Catholic church in the High Ranges, is in Old Munnar on the road up to the Tata General Hospital. The first chapel on the site was founded in 1898 by Friar Alphonse who arrived in Munnar from Spain in 1854. The present church was built by the then Bishop of Vijayapuram in 1938.

High Range Club ① *T04865-230253*, is a private members' club more relaxed than the famously 'Snooty' Ooty Club (see page 133). A tradition allowed members to hang their hats on the wall of the bar after 30 years of belonging to the club – the last was hung in 1989 to make 51 hats in all. Saturday is strictly jacket and tie only and backpackers will need to scrub up well to get in any day of the week. "We like scholars and researchers, professionals and club people," says the club secretary. "They know how to move in a club." It's a wonderful place with teak floors, squash courts, library and fascinating planters to chat to if you're interested in the planters' social history.

Around Munnar

Mattupatty Lake ① *T04865-230389, visits between 0900-1100, 1400-1530, Rs 5*, located 13 km from Munnar at an altitude of 1700 m, is flanked by steep hills and woods. It was created by the small hydro-electricity dam. To its south is the Kerala Livestock Development Board's research and cattle breeding centre, formerly the

Indo-Swiss dairy project. In a beautiful semi-Alpine setting surrounded for much of the year by lush green fields, the centre offers interesting insights into the practical realities and achievements of cattle breeding in India today.

Top Station On the Tamil Nadu border, 41 km from Munnar at an altitude of 2200 m, Top Station has some of the highest tea estates in India. It is an idyllic spot, with superb views over the Tamil Nadu plains and the edge of the Western Ghats. There are tea and soft drinks stalls. Top Station took its name from a ropeway that connected it via Middle Station to Lower Station at the valley bottom. The small town of **Bodinayakkanur**, which can be reached on the Devikulam road, lies in the valley. Buses leave from the shelter north of Munnar post office at 0715, 0915 and 1115, to Kovilor, passes Mattupetty Lake and Kundala Dam. Get off at Top Station, return bus after about one hour.

Eravikulam/Rajamalai National Park ⓘ *closed during the monsoons, Rs 50, plus Rs 10 for vehicles taken into the park, visitors are allowed in the Rajamala section of the park only*, 14 km northeast of Munnar, was set up in 1978 to preserve the endangered Nilgiri tahr (Nilgiri ibex). The conservation programme has resulted in the park now supporting the largest population of the species in the world, of nearly 2000. The sure-footed wild goats live in herds on the steep black rocky slopes of the Anaimudi mountains. They are brownish, have short, flat horns with the male carrying a thick mane, and can be easily seen around the park entrance. There are also elephants, sambars, gaurs, macaques and the occasional leopard and tiger. The scenery is magnificent, though the walks into the forest are steep and strenuous. There is an easier well-made, paved path from the park entrance following the road immediately below the bare granite outcrop of the Naikundi Hill to the Rajamalai Gap.

Cycling There are some excellent cycle rides around Munnar, not all of them steep. One ride goes up a gentle slope through a beautiful valley 8 km to the Letchmi Estate. There is a *chai* stall at the estate and the road continues to the head of the valley for views down to the forest. A second ride (or walk) leaves Munnar by the south road for 3 km, turning left at Head Works Dam, taking a right turn past Copper Castle, then left to a tea stall, viewpoint, tea and cardamom plantations, again with superb views. Continue to the next tea pickers' village for a tea stall. A shorter option for this route is to cross the dam and turn left, taking the quiet road north to the High Range Club and Munnar.

Sleeping

The Midlands (Kottayam to Thekkady) *p220*

AL Kottukapally Nazarani Tharavad, Palai, T04822-212438, www.nazarani tharavad.com. An opportunity to stay with the Kottukapally family, Kerala political royalty. There are grand Byzantine icons, Persian carpets and Travancore brass lamps. The roomy 250-year-old Kerala/Dutch/Spanish-style house of teak, rosewood and Basel tiles has 3 roomy doubles. Advance booking essential.

AL Vanilla County, Mavady Estate, Teekoy, Vagamon, T0482-228 1225, www.vanilla county.in. At the source of the Meenachil river. A charming, family-friendly place with 3 rooms within 60-year-old estate house that you share with your hosts. Coffee is from the plantation around you and you can walk to swim in natural ponds. Internet access.

A The Pimenta, Haritha Farms, the Pimenta, Kadalikad Post, T0485-226 0216, T0944-730 2347, www.harithafarms.com. Eco-tourism concern in the pepper growing north of Kerala run by Mrs Mathew, son Jacob and

For an explanation of the sleeping and eating price codes used in this guide, see inside the front cover. Other relevant information is found in Essentials pages 40-44.

grandson Ranjeet. Guest numbers are limited to minimize impact on the village. 4 newly built simple cottages close to the family farmhouse. Advocates of the return to traditional methods of agriculture, Haritha is a spice and coconut garden, growing bio-organic spices, medicinal herbs and tropical fruit and replanting crops lost to monoculture tea and rubber plantations. The pimenta lies in the Kerala 'Midlands', a lesser explored area of the Travancore kingdom called Vadakkumkur (today's Muvattupuzha, Thodupuzha, Meenachil).

B Grandma's Mansion, Plassnal, near Palai, T0482-227 2080. 3 rooms in a charming homestay built in the traditional Christian style with a genteel, elderly hostess, Thankamma Joseph. An immaculately maintained house with fans, narrow beds and swinging daybeds and set in a garden with pond. Advance booking essential.

B Heron's Pool, Kallivayalil House, Mundakayam East, Idukki, T0486-928 0982, homestay@heronspool.com. Traditional planter Kallivayalil family throw open the doors of their laid-back home, set in groves of rubber, vanilla, cardamom, coffee, pepper, cocoa and banana. Rosewood and teak floors and furniture, private sit-outs overlooking the plantation, gardens, bar and library. Dining under the stars, *naalu kuttu*, cobbled courtyard. Classic Kerala cuisine with fresh ingredients. Fish, swimming, tennis, badminton, billiards, golf.

Thekkady *p220*

Check www.thekkady.com

LL Paradisa Plantation Retreat, Murinjapuzha, Kottayam-Kumily Rd, T0469-270 1311, www.paradisaretreat.com. 10 traditionally built new cottages with beautiful antique granite pillars, Kerala door frames and walls from old rice godowns on an organic plantation estate with stunning valley views and a pool. Yoga recommended but booking essential, the Swarmy jets in from Chennai.

L Serenity Payikad, T0481-245 6353, www.malabarhouse.com. 5 stylish bedrooms looking out to the Blue Mountains in a 2-storey 1920s rubber estate, set in tropical spice gardens on a small hilltop on the way to Periyar. Activities include plantation walk, cycling tours and day with the elephants. Butler, chef, resident yoga teacher and pool.

L-AL Lake Palace, T0486-223 9701, www.lakepalacekerala.com. 6 rooms in interesting building, restaurant (adequate, uninspired), access by free ferry (20 mins) from jetty (last trip 1600), idyllic island setting, superb views, wildlife spotting, relaxed and informal.

L-B Hotel Treetop, Thekkady Road, Idukki, T0486-922 3286, www.hoteltreetop.com. Clean and efficient resort of gabled cottages just on the fringes of the Periyar National Park with all mod cons. Good facilities, especially for families who can opt for the bungalow with kitchen and living area. Each cottage has a private sits-out, TV, phone and hot water.

AL Spice Village (CGH Earth), Thekkady-Kumily Rd, T0484-301 1711, www.cghearth.com. 52 rooms in cottages with elephant grass thatch (cool and dark with wide eaves), spice garden, badminton, tennis, good pool, excellent restaurant, lunch and dinner buffets (Rs 500), chilled beer. Good cookery demonstrations. Yoga centre, great ayurvedic massage and forest walks to see smaller wildlife. Luxurious, quiet, restful, friendly, with superb service. Discounts Apr-Sep.

AL Taj Garden Retreat, Amalambika Rd, Via Kumily, T0486-922 2401, www.tajhotels.com. 32 well-appointed rooms in thatched, a/c cottages, large windows with good views, attractive pool, excellent facilities, attentive.

AL-A Cardamom County, between Kumily and Thekkady, T0486-222 2816, www.cardamomcounty.com. Spacious, comfortable cottages, good restaurant, nice pool, friendly (request off-season discount). Recommended.

A-C Carmelia Haven, Vandanmedu (20 km north on Puliyanmala Rd), on a tea, spice and coconut plantation, T0486-827 0272, www.nivalink.com/carmeliahaven/. Exclusive and private, with a real tree house 6 m above ground, a cave house 3 m below, and a few discreetly spaced cottages in a local style using lots of thatch. An excellent open-air restaurant serves delicious Malabari food. Tours of tea factory, cardamom plantations, treks and boating. Tea and cardamom are for sale.

B-C Periyar House (KTDC), 5-min walk from lake, T0486-232 2026, periyar@sancharnet.in. 48 rooms, some with bath (price includes meals), simple, very pleasant, clean and comfortable, dorm is reasonable if slightly dingy. Buffet meals and strong Goan beer available. Pleasant place, good service.

E Mickky Farm House, Kumily, T0486-223 3696. Pleasant rooms, best with balcony, friendly family, excellent value. Highly recommended.

E-F Hill Park, Main St, T0486-268 5509. 17 rooms with bath, fan, net, friendly, helpful.

E-F Lake Queen, T0486-222 2084, www.lakequeen.com. Basic rooms, fan, nets, small bath, pleasant upper floors (Rs 150-300), fairly clean, functional, run by Catholic Diocese (profits to charity).

E-G Green View, Hotel Ambadi Junction, Thekkady Bypass Road, T0486-922 4617, www.sureshgreenview.com. 13 'deluxe', 4 budget and 3 single rooms in 2 buildings, hammocks and hanging wicker chairs slung out in the big garden. Owner a previous tour guide in the park so you get excellent guidance thrown in. Parking, hot and cold water, TV, cookery classes and roof garden.

F Claus Garden, Rosapukandam, 10 mins uphill from bus stand behind PO, 3rd turn right. Clean, simple rooms, shared toilet/shower, kitchenette, quiet, friendly.

F Manakala Forest Rest House, 7 km in the forest, T0954-8632 2027. 3 rooms (sleep on wooden floor, bring sleeping bag, soft mat, net, mosquito repellant, food and plenty of water), cook/guide accompanies, well placed for walks and watching animals close by at night, Rs 300 including boat transfer. Book ahead. Recommended.

F-G Coffee Inn, 5-min walk from entrance gate and 3 km from information centre, coffeeinn@satyam.net.in. 12 rooms in basic cottages, fan, nets (Rs 150-400), clean shared baths, lockers, lovely garden with hammocks, popular budget traveller hang-out. No reservations – first come first served.

F-G Rose Garden Home Stay, Hotel Ambadi Junction, Thekkady Bypass Rd, T0486-922 3146, rosegardenhomestay@yahoo.co.in. Simply furnished rooms in the back garden of a flowered house near the **Taj Spice Village**. Mosquito proof, hanging wicker chairs in porches, TV in rooms and hot and cold water. Towels, loo roll and soap provided. Lovely family provide Kerala breakfasts and suppers. Discounts for long stays.

Road to Munnar and the Palanis *p222*

AL Plantation Homestay, Mundackal Estate, Pindimana, Kothamangalam Junction, T0485-570717, nestholidays@hotmail.com. 3 rooms in George and Daisy Jose's homestay that lies deep inside their rubber, pepper and coconut plantations. Daisy is a mean cook and offers lessons (US$20), while George arranges boat trips to the bird sanctuary.

A Periyar River Lodge, Anakkayam, Kothamanagalam, T0485-258 8315, www.periyarriverlodge.com. 2-bedroom cottage in a rubber plantation on the banks of Periyar River right next to Thattekad Bird Sanctuary. Bamboo rafting, fishing, forest treks, jeep safaris to 30 m-high waterfalls for swimming, boat and bike tours. Lounge, en suite, river views. Keralan food.

Munnar *p223, map p223*

L-A Tea Country (KTDC), out of town, T04865-230460, www.ktdc.com. 43 rooms, good facilities, beautiful views, great walking, own transport essential.

AL The Tea Sanctuary, KDHP House, T04865-230561, www.theteasanctuary.com. 6 quaint old-fashioned bungalows on the working Kanan Devan tea estate, pukka colonial-style atmosphere plus activities like mountain biking, trekking, horse riding, golf and angling, and everything clubbable at the High Range and Kundale Clubs.

AL The Windermere Estate, Pothamedu, T04865-230512, www.windermeremunnar.com. 2 stand-alone cottages, an alpine farmhouse with 5 rooms and a planters' bungalow with 3 rooms. Off-season discounts 25%. Charming but spartan place with sweeping views from the aptly named Observatory Hill across the tops of clouds.

AL-L Tall Trees, PO Box 40, Bison Valley Rd, (out of town), T04865-230593 www.ttr.in. Very clean new cottages in beautiful location, excellent food, charming staff.

A-B Copper Castle, Kannan Devan Hills (out of town), T0486-523 0633, coppercastle@vsnl.com. Perched on hillside with beautiful views, good-sized comfortable rooms with baths (hot showers) and restaurant (good sizzlers). Friendly staff but slow service.

B East End, Temple Rd, T04865-230452. 18 pleasant rooms and some cottages (solar heated water), good but pricey restaurant, attractively designed, quiet garden location.

B Olive Brook Homestead, Pothamedu, 3 km south of Munnar, T04865-230588, www.olivebrookmunnar.com. 5 well-appointed double rooms in beautiful lush location, excellent alfresco barbecues on request.

B Westwood, T04865-230884. Modern wood-panelled hotel, 40 spacious clean rooms, lovely design, restaurant, quiet, friendly.

B-C Isaac's Residency, Top Station Rd, T04865-230501. Excellent quality, 32 lovely rooms with contemporary furnishings, Executive rooms with great views, 2 restaurants, bar. Recommended.

C-D Royal Retreat, Kanan Devan Hills, T04865-230240, www.royalretreat .co.in. Nice clean doubles with TV and hot water.

D John's Cottage, MSA Rd, near Munnar Supply Association, T04865-231823. Small bungalow home in a well-tended lawn running down to the river, with 8 clean rooms. Indian/Chinese food or use of kitchen.

E Arafa Tourist Home, Upper Bazar, T04865-230302. 14 rooms with TV, phone in newly renovated lodge. Clean and excellent value.

E Homestay Kochery, T04865-231147, kocheryhomestay@sancharnet.in. Some of the best rooms in town at Kochery, chez Babu Peter and wife Mary. 4 rooms have balconies, with beautiful hilltop views across tea plantations. Charming garden, 24-hr hot water and only 2 mins from town.

E Zeena Cottages, near **Hill View Hotel** in Tata tea plantation, T04865-230560, www.hillviewhotel.com. Rooms in colonial house, good views, friendly people. Ask at Tourist Information Service.

G Sisiram Cottage Homestay, IX/18A MSA Road, T04865-231908, www.sisiram.com. 3-storey cottage on the riverbank.

Eating

Thekkady *p220*

₸₸₸ Spice Village, international, excellent food and service, rustic decor, fresh garden vegetables and chef's show cooking nightly.

₸₸ Coffee Inn. 0700-2200. International dishes served at tables outside under the palms, bonfire in the evening, relaxed and peaceful. Friendly, but very slow.

₸₸ German Bakery, Lake Rd. Delicious food, pleasant atmosphere, big set breakfast Rs 40.

₸ Edassery's Farm Yard, NH 49 Chattupara Adimali Idukki, T04864-224210. 0600-2200. Makes a good break on the Kottayam-Kumily road with tasty soups and meals, dosa and vegetable stews.

Munnar *p223, map p223*

₸₸ East End's, The Greens. Pleasant, glassed-in verandah serving good food, smart. Or cheap simple meals, in the eatery below.

₸₸ Royal Retreat, international. Very pleasant, wide choice.

₸ Silver Spoon, near Munnar Inn, for good breakfast choices.

₸ Vegetarian Restaurant (next to Misha), Old Bazar. Serves very good meals.

Bars and clubs

Munnar *p223, map p223*

High Range Club, T04865-230253. Charming colonial-style planters' club, members only (or with reciprocal arrangements), visit by asking a planter to introduce you.

KDH Club, for Tata staff, also old-world, visit with permission, excellent pool table.

Entertainment

Thekkady *p220*

Mudra Daily Kathakali Centre, Thekkady Rd, Kumily, T0944-715 7636, www.mudrakathakali.com. Classical dance theatre show by performers from Kalamandalam school of dance. Make-up 1600 and 1830, showtimes 1630 and 1700. Rs125, video charge Rs 200.

Shopping

Munnar *p223, map p223*

Good for tea, cardamom and pepper.

Munnar Supply Assoc (MSA), next to tourist information. Established 1900, a bit of the old world, where you can get everything. Tailors in the bazar can copy your garments in 24 hrs. The newer Main Bazar is to the north.

Red Frog, T0486-922 4560. Wildly overpriced antiques in carefully understated shop. Go for the organic spices and teas, elegantly packaged in 100 g and 200 g weights, and local Wayanad products. Fixed price – with the bar codes to prove it.

Uravu, near Ambady Junction, Idukki, T0938-746 9369, www.uravu.org. Fair trade outfit supporting local producers of agrihorticultural products, bamboo products, processed foods, handicrafts, forest honey, spices tea and coffee.

Activities and tours

Munnar *p223, map p223*

DTPC, Old Munnar Bazar, runs tours. Tea Valley, 1000-1800, Rs 250; Sandal Valley and Wildlife, 0900-1900, Rs 300. Idukki will escort you on excellent mountain walks.

Sibi Thomas at Toby's Trails, PB No 49 Kannan Devan Hills. For treks.

Transport

Thekkady *p220*

Beware 3-wheelers and guides at the bus station, who'll try to take commission. 3-wheelers run on a fixed charge in Kerala, starting with a minimum of Rs 10.

Bus

Local Minibuses hourly from Kumily go down to **Aranya Nivas** on the lakeside, Rs 2. At Kumily jeep drivers tell you there is no bus to Thekkady and charge Rs 50 for the trip; autos charge Rs 25 plus.

Long distance Regular state and private buses run between from Kumily: to **Alappuzha** 1115, 1345; **Kochi/Ernakulam** (6 hrs), 6 per day; **Kodaikkanal** (cancelled occasionally), 0630 (5½ hrs), or go to **Vathalakundu** and change; **Thiruvananthapuram**, 285 km (8 hrs), 3 per day. Buses also go from Thekkady itself (behind *Aranya Nivas*): to **Kottayam** (0600, 1430); several per hr to **Madurai**; late afternoon **Kollam** (4½ hrs). KTDC 2-day tours from Ernakulam, Sat depart 0730, return 2000, Rs 120.

Motor launches

On the lake 2-hr motor launch trips are inexpensive, scheduled every 2 hrs from 0700-1500; tickets sell out in peak season, Rs 50 (top deck Rs 90).

Munnar *p223, map p223*

Bike hire Raja, Rs 40 per day, Rs 20 per half day; from tourist information, Rs 50 per day.

Bus

Frequent services to **Mattupetty** (30 mins), **Devikulam** (30 mins), **Adimali** (1 hr) and **Top Station** (1 hr). Daily to **Coimbatore** (6 hrs); **Ernakulam/ Kochi** (4½ hrs); **Kodaikkanal** 0700 via Udumalpettai, change for Palani and Kodai. If the Palani-Kodai Rd is closed a further bus goes to Vatalakundu and then Kodai; **Kottayam** (5 hrs); **Madurai** via Theni (5 hrs); **Palani** (4½ hrs); **Thekkady** (4½ hrs); **Thiruvanantha puram** (9 hrs), **Thrissur via Perumbavoor** (5 hrs).

Jeeps/taxis

Go to the Eravikulam National Park.

Directory

Munnar *p223, map p223*

Banks Federal Bank, near Tata Hospital Rd, very helpful; State Bank of India, 1000-1400, Sat 1000-1200. **Internet** Next to Misha Hotel, Rs 40 per hr. Phone connections from Munnar are unreliable; alternative nearest ISD phone is in Kothamangalam. **Hospital** Excellent Tata General Hospital, T04865-530270, on the north edge of town on the Rajamalai Rd. **Post** New Town centre.

Thrissur and Palakkad

Busy Thrissur, the state's cultural capital, is unmissable in April and May when it holds its annual fireworks display, or Pooram. Millions pack into the city's central square, sardine-style, to watch the elephant procession and gunpowder display. Coastal Guruvayur, meanwhile, is among Kerala's most sacred Hindu pilgrimage spots, has one of India's wealthiest temples as well as an elephant yard filled with huge tuskers and their mahouts relaxing before they hit the road on the way to the next festival. Inland, the rich agricultural yields of nearby Palakkad make it Kerala's granary, and a good stopover point on the route to or from Tamil Nadu. *» For Sleeping, Eating and other listings, see pages 234-237.*

To Thrissur and Palakkad via Kalady

One of South India's most important historically strategic routes, the road rises gently to the lowest pass through the Western Ghats along their entire length.

Kalady ⓘ *0530-1230, 1530-2000*, on the bank of the Periyar River, 45 km from Kochi, is the birthplace of one of India's most influential philosophers, **Sankaracharya**. Living in the eighth century, Sankaracharya founded the school of *advaita* philosophy, see page 501, which spread widely across South India. There are now two shrines in his memory, one as Dakshinamurti and the other to the Goddess Sarada. The management of the shrines is in the hands of the Math at Sringeri in Karnataka, see page 294. The **Adi Sankara Kirti Stambha Mandapam** ⓘ *0700-1900, small entry fee, Kalady can easily be visited in an afternoon from Kochi or from Aluva by bus (40 mins)*, is a nine-storeyed octagonal tower, 46 m high, and details Sri Sankara's life and works and the Shan Maths, or six ways to worship. There are a couple of basic places to stay.

Thrissur (Trichur) and around

→ *Phone code: 0487. Colour map 3, B2. Population: 317,500.*

Thrissur is on the west end of the Palakkad gap which runs through the low pass between the Nilgiri and the Palani Hills. The route through the Ghats is not scenic but it has been the most important link to the peninsula interior since Roman times. Thrissur is built round a hill on which stand the Vadakkunnathan Temple and an open green. The town's bearings are given in cardinal directions from this raised 'Round'.

The **Vadakkunnathan Temple** ⓘ *0400-1030, 1700-2030, non-Hindus are not permitted inside except during the Pooram festival*, a predominantly Siva temple, is also known as the Rishabhadri or Thenkailasam ('Kailash of the South'). At the shrine to the Jain Tirthankara Vrishabha, worshippers offer a thread from their clothing, symbolically to cover the saint's nakedness. The shrine to Sankara Narayana has superb murals depicting stories from the *Mahabharata*. It is a classic example of the Kerala style of architecture with its special pagoda-like roof richly decorated with fine wood carving. The temple plays a pivotal role in the *Pooram* celebrations, see page 236. In September and October, there are live performances of Chakyarkothu, a classical art form. There is a small elephant compound attached to the temple. The **Town Hall** is a striking building housing an art gallery with murals from other parts of the state. In the **Archaeological Museum** ⓘ *Town Hall Rd, Tue-Sun 0900-1500*, ask to see the royal chariot. Next door, the **Art Museum** has wood carvings, sculptures, an excellent collection of traditional lamps and old jewellery. Nearby, **Thrissur Zoo** ⓘ *Tue-Sun 1000-1700, small fee*, is well known for its snake collection. The impressive **Lourdes Church** contains an interesting underground shrine.

The **Kerala Kalamandalam Vallathol Nagar** ⓘ *29 km north of Thrissur near Shornur Junction, T0488-426 2305, www.kalamandalam.com, closed Sat, Sun, public holidays and in Apr and May*, is Kerala's answer to the dance academy campus from *Fame*. On the banks of the Nila river it is dedicated to preserving the state's unique forms of performance art and the college's foundation led to a revival of *Kathakali* dancing. It is a centre for teaching music, drama, *Mohiniyattam* and *Ottam Thullal* in addition to *Kathakali*. The school and the state tourism department runs a tour, A Day With the Masters (US$25), which is a three-hour programme with in-depth explanations of the significance and background of the art forms, the academy and its architecture, but you can still just walk in to look around the campus at the open-air *kalaris* (classrooms) where classes start at 0400 and watch training sessions. There are all-night *Kathakali* performances on 26 January, 15 August, and 9 November. The college was built in 1930 after patronage for the arts from provincial rulers and rajas dwindled in line with their own plummeting wealth and influence. *Koodiyattam*, the oldest surviving form of Sanskrit theatre, is enshrined by UNESCO as an 'oral and intangible heritage of humanity'. Frequent private buses from Thrissur northern bus stand (Vadakkechira bus stand) go straight to Kalamandalam, taking about one hour.

Palakkad (Palghat)

» pp235-237. Colour map 3, B3.

➔ *Phone code: 0491. Population: 130,700.*

Kerala's rice cellar, prosperous Palakkad has long been of strategic import for its gap – the only break in the mountain ranges that otherwise block the state from Tamil Nadu and the rest of India. Whereas once this brought military incursions, today the gap bears tourist buses from Chennai and tractors for the rich agricultural fields here that few educated modern Keralites care to plough using the old bullock carts (although memories of the tradition are kept alive in January when yoked oxes are raced in *kaalapoottu* through deep mud-churned paddy fields).

The whole of Palakkad is like a thick paddy forest, its iridescent blue old mansions, many ruined by the Land Reform Act, crumbling into paddy ponds. There are village idylls like a Constable painting. Harvest hands loll idly on pillows of straw during lunch hours, chewing ruminatively on chapatis.

The annual festival of **Chinakathoor Pooram** (late February to early March) held at the Sri Chinakathoor Bhagavathy Temple, Palappuram, features a 33-tusker procession, plus remarkable evening puppet shows. Bejewelled tuskers can also be seen at the 20-day **Nenmara-Vallangi Vela**, held at the Sri Nellikulangara Bhagavathy temple, Kodakara (early April): an amazing festival with grander firework displays than Trichur's Pooram but set in fields rather than across the city.

Sights

The region is filled with old architecture of *illams* and *tharavadus* belonging to wealthy landowners making a visit worthwhile in itself – but chief among the actual sights is **Palakkad Fort**, a granite structure in Palakkad town itself, built by Haider Ali in 1766, and taken over by the British in 1790. It now has a Hanuman temple inside.

Also, ask directions locally to the 500-year-old Jain temple of **Jainimedu** in the town's western suburbs, a 10 m-long granite temple with Jain *Thirthankaras* and *Yakshinis* built for the Jain sage Chandranathaswami. Only one Jain family is left in the

Pala is a type of tree and Kadu means forest: the area was once thickly covered in forests of this tree.

region, but the area around this temple is one of the only places in Kerala where remnants of the religion have survived.

Also well worth visiting in the region are the many traditional Brahmin villages: **Kalpathy**, 10 km outside Palakkad, holds the oldest Siva temple in Malabar, dating from 1425 AD and built by Kombi Achan, then Raja of Palakkad. But the village itself, an 800 year-old settlement by a self-contained Tamil community, is full of beautiful houses with wooden shutters and metal grills and is now a World Heritage Site that gives you a glimpse of village life that has been held half-frozen in time for nearly 1000 years. The temple here is called **Kasiyil Pakuthi Kalpathy** meaning Half Banares because its situation on the river is reminiscent of the Banares temple on the Ganges. A 10-day **car festival** in November centres on this temple and features teak chariots tugged by people and pushed by elephants.

Another unique feature of Palakkad is the **Ramassery Iddli** made at the **Sarswathy tea stall** ⓘ *daily 0500-1830, iddli Rs 1.50, chai Rs 2.50.* If you spend any time on the street in South India, your morning meal will inevitably feature many of these tasty steamed fermented rice cakes. Palakkad is home to a peculiar take on the dumpling, one that has been developed to last for days rather than having to be cooked from fresh. The four families in this poky teashop churn out 5000 iddlis a day. Originally settlers from somewhere near Coimbatore, in Tamil Nadu, over 100 years ago, they turned to making this variety of iddli when there wasn't enough weaving work to sustain their families. They started out selling them door to door, but pretty soon started to get orders for weddings. The furthest the iddlis have travelled so far is to Delhi by plane in a shipment of 300. Manufacturers have lately been arriving to buy the secret recipe of the longlife iddli.

Nelliyampathy, 56 km from Palakkad town, is a hill station with a tiny community of planters. It is famous for its oranges, but there are also orchids, bison, elephant and butterflies in abundance. You get an amazing bird's eye view across the Keralite plains from Seethakundu; a third of the district lies spread out under you. Good trekking too.

Kodungallur

At one time Kodungallur, just over the border into Trichur from Ernakulam district, was the west coast's major port, and the capital of the Chera king Cheraman Perumal. Nearby **Kottapuram** is where St Thomas is believed to have landed in AD 52. The commemorative shrine was built in 1952. Kodungallur is also associated by tradition with the arrival of the first Muslims to reach India by sea. Malik-ibn-Dinar is reputed to have built India's first **Juma Masjid**, 2 km from town. **Tiruvanchikulam Temple** and the **Portuguese fort** are worth visiting.

The Syrian orthodox church in **Azikode** blends early Christian architecture in Kerala with surrounding Hindu traditions. Thus the images of Peter and Paul are placed where the *dvarapalas* (doorkeepers) of Hindu temples would be found, and the portico in front of the church is for pilgrims.

Guruvayur

As one of the holiest sites in Kerala, Guruvayur, 29 km west of Trichur, is a heaving pilgrimage centre, filled with stalls and thronged from 0300 to 2200 with people wanting to take *darshan* of Guruvayurappan.

It is one of the richest temples in India: there is a waiting list for the auspicious duty of lighting its oil lamps that stretches to 2025. On well-augured marriage days there is a scrum in which couples are literally shunted from the podium by new pairs

Devotees to Guruvayur's Sri Krishna temple aren't afraid to put their money where their mouths are, and in one month alone the temple can earn as much as nearly Rs11 million along with just short of 4 kg of gold and almost 14 kg of silver.

 urgently pressing behind them in the queue, and the whole town is geared towards the wedding industry; most hotels here have huge marriage halls and expect guests to stay a maximum of two nights. The ceremony of children's first rice feed falls on the first of every *Malayali* month.The **Sri Krishna Temple** which probably dates from at least the 16th century has an outer enclosure where there is a tall gold-plated flagpost and a pillar of lamps. The sanctum sanctorum is in the two-storeyed *srikoil*, with the image of the four-armed Krishna garlanded with pearls and marigolds. Photography of the tank is not allowed. Non-Hindus are not allowed inside and are not made to feel welcome.

On the left as you walk towards the temple is the **Guruvayur Devaswom Institute of Mural Painting** ⓘ *Mon-Fri 1000-1600*, a tiny educational institute where you can see the training of, and buy finished works from, the next generation of mural painters. In a similar vein to *Kathakali*, with the weakening structure of feudalism and opposition to the caste system, the age-old decorative arts of temple culture steadily declined during the 20th century. When Guruvayur lost three walls to a fire in 1970 there were hardly any artists left to carry out renovation, prompting authorities to build the school in 1989. Today the small institute runs a five-year course on a scholarship basis for just 10 students. Paintings sell from Rs 500-15,000 depending on size, canvas, wood, etc. Humans are stylized – facial expressions and gestures can be traced back to *Kathakali* and *Koodiyattom* – and have wide-open eyes, elongated lips, over-ornamentation and exaggerated eyebrows and hand gestures.

There are some pleasant beaches nearby which you can get to by rickshaw but none have facilities.

Punnathur Kotta Elephant Yard ⓘ *0900-1700, bathing 0900-0930, Rs 25, take care as elephants can be dangerous, buses from Thrissur (45 mins)*, is situated within a fort 4 km out of town. Temple elephants (68 at the last count) are looked after here and wild ones are trained. There are some interesting insights into traditional animal training but this is not everyone's cup of tea. Though captive, the elephants are dedicated to Krishna and appear to be well cared for by their attendants. The elephants are donated by pious Hindus but religious virtue doesn't come cheap: elephants go for Rs 500,000 a pop.

Megalith trail: Guruvayur to Kunnamkulam

The Palakkad gap has been one of the few relatively easy routes through the Ghats for 3000 years and this area is noted for its wide range of megalithic monuments. Megalithic cultures spread from the Tamil Nadu plains down into Kerala, but developed their own local forms. The small villages of Eyyal, Chowanur, Kakkad, Porkalam, Kattakampala and Kadamsseri, between Guruvayur and Kunnamkulam, have hoodstones, hatstones, dolmens, burial urns and menhirs.

Sleeping

Thrissur *p231*

Reserve ahead during Pooram, prices rocket.

A **Kadappuram Beach Resort**, Nattika Beach, Trichur, T+44 (0)1647-433950, www.kadappurambeachresorts.com. Self-contained complex of bungalows and cottages in traditional Kerala design, but the emphasis here is on the ayurveda and most come for the 14-day *panchakarma* (€560). The ayurveda centre is functional and not luxurious, but massage and medical attention are excellent. After treatments, cross the pretty river to a huge garden of coconut trees and hammocks that separates the hotel from the sea.

B **Surya Ayurvedics**, 15 km from town, 8 km from beach, T0487-263 0326, www.ayurveda resorts.com. 10 rooms

For an explanation of the sleeping and eating price codes used in this guide, see inside the front cover. Other relevant information is found in Essentials pages 40-44.

(some a/c) in impressive old buildings, vegetarian meals, ayurvedic treatments, yoga, exchange, lawn.

C-D Cheruthuruthy River Retreat, 1½ km from train station, Cheruthuruthy, T0488-246 2244, riverretreat@zyberway.com. The summer palace to the maharajas of Cochin with splendid views of Bharatpuza river, has been modernized to make 24 spacious a/c rooms with TV, traditional furniture and modern baths. **Riviera Restaurant** is good for a chilled beer and snacks.

D-F Luciya Palace, Marar Rd, T0487-242 4731, luciyapalace@hotmail.com. 35 rooms, 15 a/c, 2 suites, Large, clean and quiet rooms, TV, garden restaurant, internet next door, good service, very pleasant hotel.

E-F Bini Tourist Home, Round North, T0487-233 5703. 24 rooms, TV, shower, 10 a/c, rather spartan but clean and spacious rooms, restaurant, bar.

F Railway Retiring Rooms. Well looked after and very good value.

Palakkad *p232*

LL Kalari Kovilakom, Kollengode, T0492-326 3155, www.kalarikovilakom.com. Ayurveda for purists. Far from the routine ayurveda tourist traps, the Maharani of Palakkad's 1890 palace has been restored to make this very elite retreat. It's extremely disciplined yet very luxurious: the indulgence of a palace meets the austerity of an ashram. Offers anti ageing, weight detoxing, stress management and ailment healing. Lessons include yoga, meditation, ayurvedic cookery. Strictly no exertion: that means no sunbathing, no swimming. Nothing is diluted, no mod cons (TV etc), bar, internet. US$414 per day all-inclusive. Minimum stay 14, 21 or 28 days.

AL Kandath Tharavad, Thenkurussi, T0492-228 4124, www.tharavad.info. A magical place tucked away in Palakkad's fields, 6 rooms in a 200-year-old mud and teak ancestral home with natural dyed floor tiles of ochre, terracotta and blue. Nadumuttams open out onto the stars and doors are thick wedges of teak and brass. Bagwaldas, your gracious host, will guide you through local customs and culture as engagingly as he steers you through the physical landscape. Highly recommended.

AL-A Olappamanna Mana, Vellinezhi, T0466-228 5797, www.olappamanna mana.com. Majestic old manor house – in rosewood, teak and jackfruit trees – to the highest Keralite Hindu caste of namboodris, parts of which date back 3 centuries. Pure vegetarian cuisine, no alcohol, 6 bedrooms, with bathroom and fan, no a/c.

C-E Indraprastha, English Church Rd, T0491-253 4641, www.hotelindraprastha.com. Kitsch and cool: 30 rooms in 1960s block, dark wood, leather banquettes and bronze lettering. Dark bar permanently packed, lawn service, 24-hr vegetarian coffee shop, exchange, internet, bookshop. Restaurant serving multi-cuisine dishes.

C-F Fort Palace, West Fort Rd, T0491-253 4621. Groovy old-style hotel, some good a/c, 19 rooms, restaurant, brash mock turrets. Satellite TV and hot water. Continental and Indian food in restaurant, and bar, both gloomy and packed (lawn service). Nice shared sit-out on 1st floor, spotless, large double beds. Chandeliers, wood panelling.

D-F Green Land Farmhouses, Palagapandy, Nelliyampathy, T0492-324 6266. A complex of farmhouses perched on top of the hillside of Nelliyampathy set in large lawns. Lovely views from the Vantage cottage.

E-F Garden House (KTDC), Malampuzha, T0491-281 5217. A 1-star government restaurant on hilltop overlooking popular domestic picnic spot (Malampuzha gardens with lotus pond) with 17 somewhat chintzy rooms, mostly non a/c, pleasant.

Guruvayur *p233*

A Kairali Ayurvedic Health Resort, Kodumbu, T0492-322 2553, www.kairali.com. Excellent resort, beautifully landscaped grounds, own dairy and farm, pool, tennis, extensive choice of treatments (packages of ayurveda, trekking, astrology, golf, pilgrimage), competent and helpful staff. Recommended.

A-C Mayura Residency, West Nada, T0487-255 7174, www.mayuraresidency.com. 65 good value, well-appointed rooms in high-rise hotel with excellent views from its rooftop. 24-hr coffee shop, **Amrutham** vegetarian (continental, South or North Indian) restaurant.

C Krishna Inn, East Nada, T0487-255 1723, www.krishnainn.com. Another glossy hotel:

white marble floors and spacious. 24-hr coffee shop, pure vegetarian, multi-cuisine Thulasi restaurant.

C-D Sree Hari Guest House, Samuham Rd, West Nada, T0487-255 6837. Guest house stuffed with Krishnas and 1960s-style curtains, 8 big rooms, some a/c, with hot water, draped with purple crushed velvet.

D-E Hotel Vanamala, Kusumam South Nada, T0487-255 5213. Popular with domestic tourists, 2-star hotel, very clean rooms with big beds and TV, telephone and hot water. A/c, ¥ vegetarian restaurant (Keralan food, 0600-2300), laundry.

Eating

Thrissur *p231*

Most **D** hotels have good restaurants, particularly **Siddhartha Regency's Golden Fork**. In general, though, eating out is still somewhat frowned on by the traditional Brahmin families of Kerala, so most eating options are down-at-heel *dhabas*.

¥¥ **City Centre**, next to **Priya Tourist Home**. Serves Western snacks and has a bakery and good supermarket.

¥¥ **Navaratna**, Naduvilal, Round West, T0487-242 1994. 1000-2300. Pure vegetarian North Indian restaurant divided into booths, diner-style.

¥ **Elite Bharat**, Chembottil Lane. For good South Indian breakfast and lunch.

¥ **Sapphire**, 0630-2200. "For best chicken biriyani". Excellent lime green and stone eatery dishing up thalis with chappati, Rs 50.

Palakkad *p232*

¥ **Ashok Bhavan**. Modest vegetarian South Indian snacks.

¥ **Hotel Noor Jehan**, GB Rd, T0491-252 2717. Non vegetarian a/c restaurant that specializes in *moplah biryani* and *pathiri*, chappatis made from rice.

¥ **KR Bakes**, 0900-2300. a castle to cake: puffs, ice creams, *halva* plus juice bar and savoury meals after 1600.

Festivals and events

Thrissur *p231*

Jan-Feb: Several temple festivals involving elephants are held in the surrounding villages which can be as rewarding as *Pooram* (eg **Koorkancherry Thaippoya Mahotsavam**, or **Thaipooya Kavadiyattam**, held at Sri Maheswara Temple, Koorkancherry, 2 km from Thrissur). Also held at the end of Feb is the **Uthralikavu Pooram**, at its most colourful at the Sri Ruthura Mahakalikavu Temple, Parithipra, Vodakancherry, en route to Shornur Junction. **End Mar**: 7-day **Arratupuzha Festival** at the Ayappa temple, 14 km from Thrissur. On the 5th day the deity parades with 9 decorated elephants, while on the 6th day **Pooram** is celebrated on a grand scale with 61 elephants in the temple grounds.

Apr-May: the magnificent 8-day **Pooram**, a grand festival with elephants, parasols, drums and fireworks, should not be missed. Several temples in town participate but particularly the Thiruvambady and Paramekkavu. It is marked by very noisy, colourful processions, joined by people from all religious groups, irrespective of caste. The festivities are held 1300-1700 and again at night from around 2000. Elaborately bedecked elephants (each temple allowed up to 15) specially decorated with lamps and palm leaves, march to the Vadakkunnathan Temple carrying priests and deities to the accompaniment of extraordinary drumming. On the final day temple teams meet on the Tekkinkadu *maidan* for the drumming and *Kudumattam* competition; the festival terminates with a huge display of fireworks. **Aug/Sep**: the district also celebrates **Kamdassamkadavu Boat Races** at *Onam*. Also performances of **Pulikali**, unique to Thrissur, when mimers dressed as tigers dance to drumbeats.

Guruvayur *p234*

Punnathur Kotta

Feb/Mar: Utsavam, 10 days of festivities start with an elephant race and continue with colourful elephant processions and performances of *Krishnanattom* dances. Details from Kerala tourist offices.

Nov-Dec: 5-day **Ekadasi** with performances of *Krishnanattom*, a forerunner of *Kathakali* – an 8-day drama cycle.

Transport

Thrissur *p231*

Bus

There are yellow-top local buses. For long distance, there are 3 bus stands. **KSRTC**, near railway station, southwest of 'Round' including to **Alappuzha** (3½ hrs), **Bengaluru (Bangalore)** (10 hrs), **Coimbatore** (3 hrs), **Guruvayur** (1 hr), **Kochi** (2 hrs), **Kozhikode**, **Chennai** (13 hrs), **Palakkad**, **Thiruvananthapuram** (7 hrs). North (Priyadarshini), just north of 'Round', buses to **Cheruthuruthy**, **Ottapalam**, **Palakkad**. Sakthan Thampuran, 2 km south of 'Round', for frequent private buses to **Guruvayur**, **Kannur**, **Kozhikode**.

Rickshaw
Yellow-top local auto-rickshaws available.

Train
Kochi (Cochin): *Tiruchchirappalli Cochin Exp 6865*, 0335, 2¾ hrs; *Hyderabad Cochin Exp 7030*, 1245, not Tue, 2¼ hrs; *Raptisagar Exp 5012/5222*, 1530, Mon, Thu, Fri, Sun, 2¾ hrs. **Chennai (MC)**: *Alleppey-Chennai Exp 6042* (AC/II), 1810, 12½ hrs; *Trivandrum Chennai Mail 6320*, 2045, 11¼ hrs; *Raptisagar Exp 5011* (AC/II), 1110, Tue, Wed, Fri, Sat, 12¼ hrs.

Palakkad *p232*
Long distance bus
KSRTC, from Municipal Bus Stand: **Kozhikode**, **Mannarghat** (Silent Valley), **Pollachi**.

Train
The main Junction station is 5 km northeast of town. Also Town Station. **Coimbatore**: *West Coast Exp 6628*, 0500, 1½ hrs; *Cochin Hyderabad Exp 7029*, 1405, 1¼ hrs; *Kerala Exp 2625*, 1905, 1¼ hrs. **Chennai**: *West Coast Exp 6628*, 0500, 10½ hrs; *Alleppey Chennai Exp 6042*, 2025, 10¼ hrs.
Ernakulam Junction: *Kerala Exp 2626* (AC/II), 0720, 3 hrs; *Hyderabad Cochin Exp 7030*, 1045, not Tue, 3½ hrs. **Kochi** (Cochin): *Hyderabad Cochin Exp 7030*, 1045, not Tue, 4¼ hrs.

Directory

Thrissur *p231*
Banks State Bank of India, Town Hall Rd, Round East, near Paramekkavu Temple; State Bank of Travancore (upstairs), located opposite.
Internet Sruthy, north of the temple ring. Offers good connections, Rs 30 per hr.
Hospital Amala Cancer Hospital, Amalanagar (9 km away, along the Guruvayur Rd), T0487-221 1950. Recommended for medicine and surgery.

Malabar Coast

The Malabar region is the unsung jewel of Kerala: the combination of the state's political administration down south plus the pious Muslim community and orthodoxy of the Hindu population have made it more resistant to tourist development than the more easygoing, Catholic-influenced stretch south from Kochi. Any cohesion between north and south Kerala is political, not cultural: Malabar was under the Madras Presidency before Independence, lumped together with the Travancore south only in 1956. The atmosphere couldn't be more different. The coastal towns of Calicut, Telicherry and Cannur are the strongholds of the Muslim Moplah community, whose long-standing trading links with the Middle East have also bred a deep-seated cultural affinity.

Not catering to the tourist rupee means that beaches are often strewn with litter. Also, swimming togs can cause alarming levels of attention even outright hostility.

The Waynad district inland from Kozhikode experiences some of the heaviest levels of rainfall in the world and is covered in the familiar stubble of tea plantations. Malabar is also one of the best places to see Kerala's unique religious and cultural traditions in their proper context: Theyyam, the Hindu ritual temple dance that spawned Kathakali *and* Kalari, *the stunning martial art, are both practised here.*

▸▸ *For Sleeping, Eating and other listings, see pages 243-246.*

Kozhikode (Calicut)

» pp243-246. Colour map 3, B2.

→ *Phone code: 0495. Population: 436,500.*

Kozhikode is a major commercial centre for northern Kerala and the centre for Kerala's timber industry; it is also dependent on the petrodollar, as testified by the scores of direct flights to the Gulf each day. The city itself is engaged in mostly small-scale retail. Off the ugly brash main boulevard, tiny roads thread through high laterite walls with everything happening on the street. Remnants of the spice trade remain and the markets are great – Court Road is home to pepper, the black gold that lured Vasco, as well as copra and coconut oil. There are beautiful wooden mosques built like temples, and in nearby Beypore, where the Chaliyar river meets the Arabian Sea, you can see the engineering of *urus*: massive deep-sea hauler-sized wooden boats built by Khalasis in much the same way as they've done since Cheraman Perumal first ordered one for a visit to Arabia in the sixth century.

Ins and outs

Getting there and around Karipur airport, 25 km south, has connections with several major Indian cities. The station and main bus stand are near the town centre within easy reach of several hotels. Autos are widely available and surprisingly cheap. **Tourist information Kerala Tourism**, Govt Guest House and Railway Station.

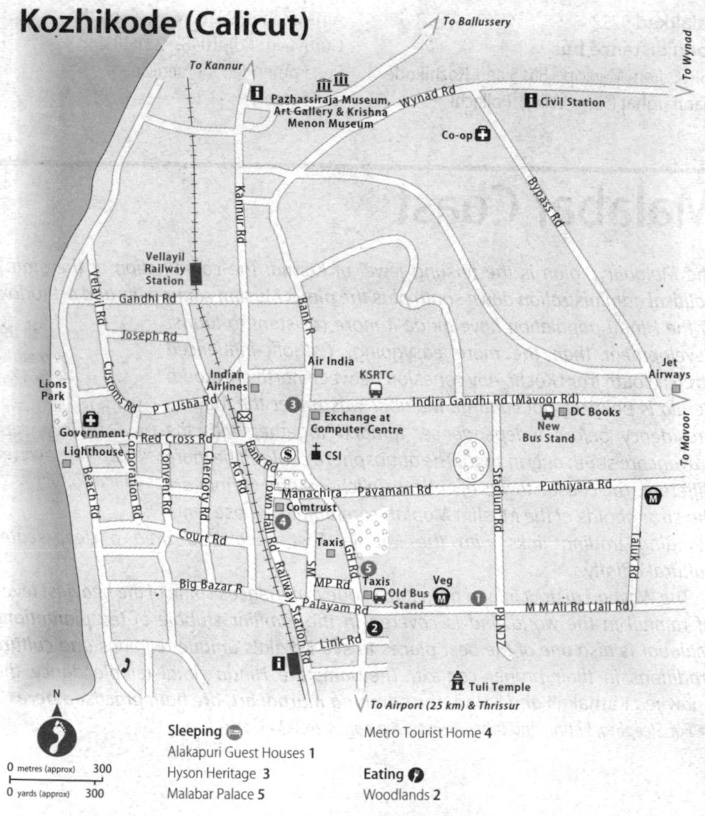

The petro dollar versus the yankee dollar

Figures suggest that 30 million jobs, from banks, hotels, financial institutions and airlines, will be 'business process outsourced' from the Western, developed world by 2020 chiefly to India, China and the Philippines. These jobs are the sweat shops of corporations: graduate employees work night shifts to duck time zones cold calling and inputting data entry. The leading companies – with names in India like Spectramind and Intellinet – command salaries as small as Rs 6000 (US$148). Nothing to sniff at in India (in Tamil Nadu the average per capita monthly income is US$36), although a trainee at the Barista coffee chain starts at Rs 7000. Call centre staff, mostly based in Bengaluru (Bangalore) and Chennai, will be trained to speak in plummy English, sat down in front of soaps like Eastenders and British weather forecasts to give them a crash course in an alien popular culture – they're even given anglicized names. As academic Harish Trivedi of Delhi University told Indian news magazine *The Week*: "It's the ultimate humiliation. We are being asked to pretend to be foreigners. No one wants to know us as Indians; our identity is not good enough."

Outsourcing is projected to become a US$ 680 million business by 2008 – small wonder when offshore workers cost less than 20% of their domestic equivalents. Trivedi scoffs: "These companies are here because we are cheap. What will happen when they find a poorer country and cheaper labour?" It may seem like neocolonialism to him, but it's a world that Keralite entrepreneurs feel excluded from. There are no Wipros or Infosys home-grown success stories here, nor multinationals – the state is dependent on tourism and agriculture – and Keralites still head to the Gulf in droves as economic migrants. A few get good jobs, the rest of the Malayalis work like dogs – their passports confiscated by their employers, having to sleep in shifts, and going without holiday for two years at a time, in order to save up a nest egg big enough to build their own house and educate their children when they get home. And while the Gulf states may prefer employing Keralite Muslims, the market for cheap blue collar labour in Gulf countries is likely to shift to ever lower cost centres: in Nepal, the Philippines and Sri Lanka.

Sights

The Sunni Muslim quarter of **Kuttichira**, behind the railway station towards the sea, to the west of town, holds several fascinating multi-tiered mosques made of wood that date from the 15th century. Women should cover their head, shoulders and limbs in this area particularly. The mosques bear a puzzlingly close resemblance to Hindu temple structures, complete with pillars, ventilation and huge green pond around which flocks of white-capped elders range up in the late afternoon (legend has it that a ghost within the pond seizes a human sacrifice each year: the body surfaces after three days). **Mishkal Masjid** is one of the oldest, and was named for the wealthy trader who built it, but also look for **Jami Mosque** and **Munchunthi Palli.** The latter has a 13th-century *vattezhuthu* (inscribed slab of stone) that proclaims the donation of the land to the mosque by a Zamorin.

The Calicut passport office is for six districts: the Waynad, Kannur, Kozhikode, Mallapuram, Kasaragod and Pallakad. It processes 1300 fresh passport applications daily. Around 1.2 million Keralites work in the Gulf, generating revenue of about US$12 billon for Kerala.

Look too at the size of the houses around here: known to accommodate over 150 family members each because the *puyappala* tradition (literally translates as 'fresh husband') means that each marrying daughter takes the husband back into her parents' house. One house is supposed to have 300 people living under the same roof: each building has an average of three kitchens. From here you can walk along the Beach Road: the old buildings here that were trading centres are now being busily demolished. The beach itself is more of a town latrine than a place for swimming.

Pazhassiraja Museum ⓘ *5 km on East Hill, Tue-Sun 1000-1230, 1430-1700*, has copies of original murals plus bronzes, old coins and models of the some of the area's megalithic monuments. The **Art Gallery** and **Krishna Menon Museum** ⓘ *Mon, Wed afternoon only, 1000-1230, 1430-1700, free,* named after the Kerala politician who became a leading left-wing figure in India's post-Independence Congress government, is next door. There's an excellent collection of paintings by Indian artists; as well as wood and ivory carvings. A section of the museum is dedicated to VK Krishna Menon.

Around Kozhikode (Calicut)

Kappad, 16 km north, and now the site of a small, poor, mainly Muslim fishing village, is where Vasco da Gama landed on 27 May 1498 with 170 men and has an old plaque by the approach road to the beach commemorating the event. Although it is a pleasant spot, the sea is unsuitable for swimming since pollution from Kozhikode filters down this far and the beach itself is used as a toilet by the fishermen.

Beypore, half an hour south of Calicut, was once a significant port, but is now famous only for its shipbuilding trade. You can visit the boatyard here, where families of Khalasis have used traditional methods to make *urus* – huge wooden vessels – for 1500 years. These men craft the ships using ancient techniques, but their popularity is dwindling. They used to work 365 days a year, but now they'll have two or three months without work in between commissions from Arab clients.

Mahé → *Colour map 3, B2.*

The borders of the 9 sq km that make up French Kerala are marked, not by baguette bakeries or pavement cafés, but by shops screaming 'Foreign Liquor'. By night, Mahé, the 35,000 members of the union territory of Pondicherry colony, disappear to make way for the truckers who rush through to stock up on half-price whiskies and brandies, taking advantage of the colony's special tax status. By day, Mahé is pretty enough: policemen wear French hats and the town is beautifully positioned on a slight hill overlooking the river; it was named after M Mahé de Labourdonnais, when he captured it for the French in 1725. Many still speak French and the very French **Church of St Theresa** celebrates her feast day on 14-15 October. The beaches to the south and north of town are dirty and are not safe for swimming due to the undercurrents.

Thalassery (Tellicherry) » *pp243-246. Colour map 3, B2.*

→ *Phone code: 0490.*

Like everywhere along the Malabar's increasingly gold coast, banks here have queues for gold loans where your branch manager doubles as pawnbroker. Despite an obsession with wealth, at the wide, tree-covered street level you'll find a town that's friendly, brilliantly walkable and lined with 19th-century shops complete with original wooden cupboards and cobwebs. Author Herman Hesse's mother was born here.

Sights

Thalassery was set up by the British East India Company in 1683 to export pepper and cardamom. In 1708 they obtained permission to build a **fort** which, having survived a siege laid by Haidar Ali, is still standing today on a rocky promontory about 15 m above sea level. Its proud little gateway, raised on a flight of steps, is flanked by colourful mustachioed figures. There are some attractive old buildings. The **Armenian church** is rather shabby now but the Catholic church still thrives though the population is largely *Moplah* (Kerala Muslims). The **Odathil Mosque**, believed to be 400 years old, is in the traditional Kerala style with a gabled roof and copper sheeting.

If its booze you're after, head south over the flyover to queue at the Kerala State Beverages outlet where locals line the street waiting for Indian Made Foreign Liquor.

Mambally's Royal Biscuit Factory ⓘ *near Old Police Station, T0490-232 1207, 0900-2030,* established in 1880, claims to be where cake was first baked in Kerala. Nowadays you'll find jam rolls, ketchup, Nestlé milky bars and lime pickle along with the fresh bakes. The downstairs of double-decker shops is crowded with hessian sacks full of cinnamon from China, cloves from Madagascar, Ceylon and Hyderabad, raisins from Afghanistan and star anise from China and Vietnam. Some of the owners are third generation traders.

The **fish market** ⓘ *0600-1800*, is one of the liveliest in Kerala. Men with cleavers stand tall over barracudas and manta, stacks of clams, mussels, shrimps and mackerel are constantly replenished with new loads. Fish are then sped along the state highway to reach markets in Cochin or even Mangalore.

Thalassery is also a centre for training in gymnastics and circus acts, so street performers and acrobats are not uncommon; 90% of India's circus companies originate here. You can see martial arts in local *kalaris*: one of the best being the tricky-to-find *kalari* of **K Viswanathan Gurukkal** ⓘ *MKG Kalari Sangham, Kuzhippangad, PO Chirakkara, T0490-237110, call in advance.*

Muzhapilangad Beach, 8 km from Telicherry, is nicknamed Drive In Beach. It is an unspoilt, beautifully picturesque 4 km-long stretch of golden sand edged by palm trees at the northern end. Amazingly empty most of the time, it earned its nickname from the local custom of ragging trucks or ambassadors up and down its firm sands.

Kannur (Cannanore)

» pp243-246. Colour map 3, B2.

→ *Phone code: 0497.*

Standing on raised ground with cliffs at the sea face, this town boasts a coconut-fringed coastline with some attractive beaches. Weavers' co-operatives and *beedi* factories provide employment but this is also a good place to watch *Theyyam* dances.

Sights

Kannur, the centre of the Moplah community, a group of Arab descent, was also the capital of the North Kolathiri Rajas for several hundred years. **Fort St Angelo** was built out of laterite blocks by the Portuguese in 1505 and taken over by the British in 1790 as their most important military base in the south. The highly picturesque **Moplah town** is round the bay to the south of the fort. The attractive **Payyambalam Beach** is just 2 km away.

Handloom weavers produce silk and cotton saris, shirts and lungis, as well as soft furnishings, sold through local cooperatives. **Kanhirode Weavers' Cooperative Society**

Thalassery is the home to Doctor V. Bharathan who is famous for freezing off piles (discharged patients are given a picture of the good doctor in his orchid garden to meditate on should symptoms persist after treatment).

 ⓘ *Koodali Kannur, T0497-285 7259, 0900-1700, free*, was founded in 1952 on Gandhian principle, has a yearly turnover of Rs 150 million (US$3.7 million) and exports 95% of its pure handloom fabric to the UK for the Futon Bed Company. Spun cotton is shipped in from Coimbatore, and dyed in huge vats after which the cooperative's 450 staff are expected to feed bobbins through the high wooden looms fast enough to make 42 m within 3½ days for women, or three for men. While some weave, others feed the raw heaps of cotton from wire frames onto wheels to make thread – in the silk section they use bicycle wheels. The rooms, chock-full with the Chettiar caste for whom this is hereditary occupation, clatter with activity. The daily wage is Rs 100 (US$2.45), and apparently the co-op is having trouble recruiting more of the caste, who, as caste rules relax, are going for higher paid jobs elsewhere. A visit here is well worth the journey.

Bekal and Kasaragod → *Phone code: 0499.*

Bekal, 16 km south of Kasaragod, has an ancient fort on the sea, the largest and best preserved in Kerala, which gives superb views of the coastline. Originally built by the Kadamba kings, the fort passed under the control of Vijayanagar and of Tipu Sultan before being brought into the hands of the East India Company. Excavations have exposed some interesting structures. Just outside the fort is the **Sri Mukhyaprana Temple**. Bekal also has a beautiful and undeveloped beach that Kerala Tourism talks of turning into a major resort. For *Theyyam* and *Yakshagana* performances contact the **Bekal Tourist Office** ⓘ *T0499-273 6937*. En route to Bekal the road passes **Ezhimala**, with a beach and a hill famous for its ayurvedic herbs and **Neeleshwar**, a tranquil spot on a good beach and the nearby backwaters.

Kasaragod is the northernmost town in Kerala. From the bus stand, the walk to the sea through a sprawling residential area – mainly Moplah – takes about 30 minutes. The beach is magnificent and deserted. You can walk a long way before scrambling back to the main road, crossing paddy fields, backwaters, and the Konkan railway line.

The Waynad » p244.

→ *Phone code: 0493. Colour map 3, B2.*

The Waynad occupies some of Kerala's untouched, forest-clad hills and is in part pure virgin rainforest and part cardamom, coffee, pepper tree and vanilla plantations. The route from Kozhikode on the coast, across the Western Ghats to Mysore (214 km, 5½ hours) or Ooty, is one of Kerala's most picturesque journeys. Many of the tea and coffee plantations now take in paying guests, and a number of imaginative accommodation options have recently opened.

The road to Mysore passes through **Vyittiri** (65 km), and **Kalpetta** (9 km) before dividing. The more northerly route passes through Mananthavady (30 km), whilst the more southerly route to Mysore is via Sulthan Bathery (25 km) and Waynad Wildlife Sanctuary. The route to Ooty via Gudalur is marginally less scenic than the road to Mysore.

Kalpetta lies at the heart of one of Kerala's most scenic regions, and provides a good base from which to explore the area. The rugged, wild **Chembra Peak** (2100 m), 14 km west, the highest point in Waynad, is ideal for trekking. The hike south to **Pookot Lake** (10 km) is particularly rewarding. It is a popular destination for domestic tourists, making accommodation hard to come by during holiday periods. (The State Bank of Travancore offers foreign exchange.)

Sulthan Bathery (Sultan's Battery) ⓘ *the road from Sulthan's Bathery to Gudalur (Tamil Nadu) is very rough, especially across the border, and can take 2½ hrs by bus*, to the east of Kalpetta was formerly known as Ganapathivattom, or 'the fields of Ganapathi'. In the 18th century, Tipu Sultan built a fort here in the heart of the Waynad coffee and cardamom growing region, but not much of it remains. Some 6 km east of the fort is a natural deep crack in the rock on which four inscriptions have been carved and there are some rough drawings.

Waynad Wildlife Sanctuary is contiguous with Karnataka's Bandipur National Park and Tamil Nadu's Mudumalai National Park, although the latter two are far more developed in terms of accommodation and tours on offer. If you wish to visit the sanctuary, noted for its elephants, from the Kerala side, contact the Chief Conservator of Forests, Thiruvananthapuram, T0471-322217.

Sleeping

Kozhikode *p238, map p238*

AL Harivihar Ayurvedic Heritage Home, T0495-276 5865, www.harivihar.com. In Calicut's pretty Brahminical suburbs, an immaculate former royal home surrounded by lawns with giant mango and jackfruit trees and a beautiful green water tank where you can undertake pukka ayurveda or study Indian philosophy, Sanskrit, vasthu and yoga in a small guest house setting run by conventional medics. You can also stay on a B&B basis, in one of 5 doubles and 3 singles. Gentle sivananda yoga, ayurveda from Coimbatore Arya Vaidya Pharmacy, no alcohol.

B-D Malabar Palace, GH Rd, Manuelsons' Junction, T0495-272 1511, www.malabar palacecalicut.com. 52 a/c rooms (Koran in every room), excellent a/c restaurant, bar, very helpful reception. Recommended.

B-G Hyson Heritage, 114 Bank Rd, T0495-276 6423, www.nivalink.com/hysonheritage. 89 spotless, smallish rooms with phone, TV, bath, 47 a/c, set around a large courtyard. A breezy business hotel, peaceful, efficient. Well-maintained. Benhur restaurant. Cable TV.

C Tasara, North Beypore, T0495-241 4233, www.tasaraindia.com. 6 rooms in homestay-cum-textile-weaving factory. Weaving courses available: 5-day 4-night package –

tie-dyeing, batik printing, and weaving on silk, cotton, or wool, costs US$240.

D-F Hotel Asma Tower, Mavoor Rd, T0495-272 3560, www.asmatower.com. 44 a/c and non a/c rooms in gleaming new tower. Inside, expect two-tone mint green decor, frosty a/c system, perfumed air, muzak and TV and telephone in every room. Good value.

D-G Alakapuri Guest Houses, Moulana Mohammed Ali Rd, T0495-272 3451. 40 rooms set around a charming garden brimming with plants and trees and lotus pond. Simple, spacious, with old furniture, phone, tubs and TV. Dates from 1958, and easily Calicut's most characterful mid-range option. Bar 1000-2200, dining hall 0700-2200.

E Gayathri International, T0495-235 5367. 10 small cottage-like rooms with modern facilities, bar, restaurant.

E-F Metro Tourist Home, Mavoor Rd Junction, T0495-276 6029. Bustling hotel with 42 pleasing rooms, some with TV, a bit noisy, South Indian restaurant. Gloomy with grubby paintwork but clean sheets, big mirrors and good fans, TV and blaring Hindi film music.

F Railway Retiring Rooms, very spacious, clean, good service.

Thalassery *p240*

LL Ayisha Manzil, Court Rd, T0490-234 1590, www.ayishamanzil.uniquehomestays.com. A delightful mid-19th century, colonial-style heritage home overlooking the sea. 6 huge a/c rooms with carved teak and rosewood furniture, massive baths, lots of British and Malabari memorabilia, amazing fresh seafood and cookery courses, temple pond pool, superb panoramic views, excursions.

C-E Pranam Tourist Home, AVK Nair Rd, Narangapuram, T0490-232634. 14 cleanish rooms with bath – 4 with a/c, a little grubby. A/c de luxe has an extraordinary green carpeted sitting room attached.

D-G Paris Presidency, New Paris Complex, Logan's Rd, T0490-234 2666, www.paris presidency.com. 24 clean and comfortable rooms with baths, TV, phone, restaurant, wood furniture, bright white walls in busy shopping area. Multi-cuisine restaurant.

Kannur *p241*

C Costa Malabari, near Adykadalaya Temple, 6 km south of town (on buses ask to get out at Thazhe Chowwa), T0484-237 1761, www.costamalabari.com. An unpretentious guest house converted from a warehouse with 5 rooms off a main hall. The two-man partnership also authored a book on Kerala's festivals which gives them encyclopaedic knowledge of the local *Theyyam* scene. There are 5 idyllic, wholly empty, beaches, within walking distance. Difficult to get to and far from the centre. Tariff includes meals.

C-D Royal Omars Thavakkara Kannur, T0497-276 9091. Spanking new, very close to the railway station and colourful market area, has spacious standard non a/c doubles at bargain rates. 65 rooms, TV, credit cards.

C-E Mascot Beach Resort, near Baby Beach, Burnassery, 2 km from centre, T0497-270 8445, www.mascotresort.com. Good rooms in high-rise business hotel overlooking the sea, residents-only pool, located in the quietcantonment area (ayurvedic centre attached).

D-E Hotel Savoy, Beach Rd, T0497-276 0074. Bags of character in this super-clean, old-fashioned complex of bungalow cottages set around a lawn. A/c cottages are wonderfully spacious and cool. Bar attached.

Bekal and Kasaragod *p242*

LL Neeleshwar Hermitage, 30 km south of Bekal, Neeleshwar, T0467-228 7510, www.neeleshwarhermitage.com. The first beach and spa resort in Northern Kerala. Opens February 2008.

The Waynad *p242*

LL Green Magic Nature Resort, T0471-233 1507, www.tourindiakerala.com. Tree house in the rainforest canopy, 26 m above ground open plan accessible only by a hand-winched wicker cage, has showers and flush toilets, solar energy. From Kozhikode by 4WD.

A-C Green Gates, 2 km north of Kalpetta, T04936-202001, www.greengates hotel.com. Scenically located on a hillside amid woods within walking distance from town. Modern rooms with a/c, TV and baths

For an explanation of the sleeping and eating price codes used in this guide, see inside the front cover. Other relevant information is found in Essentials pages 40-44.

(hot showers), disappointing restaurant, sit-outs with views and ayurvedic spa. Helpful travel desk arranges trips to caves, wildlife sanctuaries and tribal colonies of Wayanad, and fishing.

B-F Haritagiri, Padmaprabha Rd, T04936-203145, www.hotelharitagiri.com. A modern building in the heart of Kalpetta just off the highway, some a/c rooms, clean and comfortable, restaurant 'reasonable', good value but rather noisy.

D-E Pankaj, just off highway at south end of Kalpetta. Has a range of reasonable rooms, good cheap restaurant.

In Sulthan Bathery there are **E-F** guest houses. Ask for Dwaraka (T04936-220358) or Isaac's, (T04936-220510) or stay at **A Edakkal Hermitage**, www.edakkal.com, a sustainable tourism initiative with 5 cottages built round the local rocks, tree house and cottages near the site of Neolithic cave art. The hermitage was established to promote the cave art.

Eating

Kozhikode *p238, map p238*

🍴🍴 **Malabar Palace**, International, a/c, excellent food, efficient service.

🍴 **Dakshin**, 17/43 Mavoor Rd, T0495-272 2648. 0630-2230. Dead cheap place for dosa, pizza, cutlet and curd rice (meals from Rs 15).

🍴 **Hotel Sagar**, 5/3305 IG Rd, T0495-272 0152, abdul@sagarhotels.com. 0530 onwards. So popular they've launched their own hotel, and another restaurant (the original is already multi-storey). Sagar is famous for its biriyanis. Upstairs is for families and a/c rooms; downstairs is the cheaper scrum of cattle class.

🍴 **Woodlands**, GH Rd (near Old Bus Stand). South Indian vegetarian.

🍴 **Zain's Hotel**, Convent Cross Rd, T0495-276 1482. A simple place run by a Muslim husband and wife. Mussels, biriyanis for Rs 30 and fish curries for Rs 15.

Thalassery *p240*

🍴🍴 **Ayisha Manzil**, Court Rd, T0490-234 1590. Peerless homestay, serving food unlike you'll get anywhere outside a home. Phone for meals in advance.

🍴 **Royal Visitors' Family Restaurant**, Pranam Tourist Home, T0490-234 4292. Open 0630-2300. Grilled mussels etc.

Kannur *p241*

🍴🍴 **Chakara Drive in Restaurant**, Cliff Exotel International, Payyabalam, T0497-271 2197. Specials are sizzlers plus spicy fried Kallumakais mussels and Malabar biriyani.

🍴 **Indian Coffee House**, Fort Rd. For snacks.

🍴 **Mascot Beach Resort's Restaurants**, near Baby Beach, Burnasseri, T0497-270 8445, www.mascotresort.com. Some of the best top-end eating in town.

🍴 **MVK Restaurant**, SM Rd, T0497-276 7192. A local institution which has been packed from its opening 50 years ago, 1000-2200, thanks to its commitment to fresh, home-ground spice mixes for its biriyanis, their rice grains steeped in ghee. Serves beautiful, potent lime tea too.

🍴 **Regency Snacks and Fast Food**, opposite Sangeetha Theatre, SN Park Rd, T0497-276 8676. Popular café with locals.

🍴 **Your Choice Restaurant**, Fort Rd. Authentic Malabari food.

Entertainment

Kannur (Cannanore) *p241*

Theyyam dance

At Parssinikadavu temple, 20 km north of Kannur, reached by bus. Performances (Dec-Mar) of ritual dance theatre at dawn (taxi essential) and often late afternoon to dusk. Pilgrims sometimes seek blessing from the principal dancer who may go into a trance after taking on the role of Mutthapan, a manifestation of Siva as Hunter.

Activities and tours

Kannur (Cannanore) *p241*

Ayurveda

PVA Ayurvedic Multi Speciality Nursing Home, Onden Rd, T0497-276 0609, www.pvaayurvedic.com. The down-at-heel PVA provides training courses in ayurveda as well as rejuvenation, purification packages and direct treatments for ailments like disc prolapse, psoriasis and obesity. The 3 doctors here are highly regarded.

Houseboats

Malabar floatels and cruises, House Boats, T0497-311 5551. Tourism-starved North wants a piece of the action. Happily it has amazingly pristine mangrove.

Transport

Kozhikode (Calicut) *p238, map p238*

Air

Airport, T0495-712762. Transport to town: pre-paid taxi Rs 250; but from town Rs 35. Indian Airlines, Eroth Centre, Bank Rd, T0495-766243, Airport T0495-766056, flies to **Mumbai**, **Coimbatore**, **Goa** (Mon, Fri), **Chennai**, **Tiruchirapalli** (Wed, Sun) and **Bahrain**, **Doha**, **Fujairah**, **Kuwait**, **Ras-Al-Khaimah** and **Sharjah**. Air India, Bank Rd. **Mumbai** and Middle East (**Abu Dhabi**, **Dubai**, **Muscat**). Jet Airways, 29 Mavoor Rd, T0495-740518, Airport T0495-712375, to Mumbai.

Bus

KSRTC, T0495-722771, from Mavoor Rd (near Bank Rd junction) to **Bengaluru (Bangalore)**, **Thiruvanantha puram** (via Thrissur, Ernakulam, Alappuzha, Kollam), 0630-2200 (10 hrs), **Ooty** (see Waynad below), etc. The New Bus Stand is further east on Mavoor Rd for private buses to the north including **Kannur**. Buses to the south go from the Old Bus Stand (Palayam).

Train

Trains to **Mangalore** (5 hrs), **Ernakulam** (4½ hrs), **Thiruvananthapuram** (9½-10 hrs). Also to **Chennai** and **Coimbatore**, and **Goa** and **Mumbai** up the Konkan Railway line.

Kannur (Cannanore) *p241*

Bus

T0497-707777. To **Kozhikode** (2½ hrs), **Mangalore** (4½ hrs), **Mercara** (6 hrs), **Mysore** (6 hrs).

Train

T0497-705555. To **Mangalore**: *Chennai Mangalore Mail 6601* (AC/II), 1045, 3¼ hrs; *Parasuram Exp 6349* (AC/CC), 1820, 3¾ hrs. **Palakkad**: *Mangalore Tiruchchirappalli Exp 6684*, 0920, 5½ hrs (continues to **Coimbatore**, add 1¼ hrs); *West Coast Exp 6628*, 2315, 5¾ hrs (continues to **Chennai (MC)**, add 10½ hrs); *Mangalore Chennai Mail 6602*, 1420, 5 hrs (continues to **Chennai (MC)**, add 10 hrs).

Directory

Kozhikode (Calicut) *p238, map p238*

Banks Exchange at SBI, Bank Rd. Good rates, no commission, friendly. Also Thomas Cook. **Internet** Nidhi, near New Bus Stand or behind *Malabar Mansion*, SM St. Fast, Rs 30 per hr. Sreeram Travels, shop 3, opposite district hospital. T0495-253 4807. **Hospitals** Govt Hospital, T0495-236 5367. Medical College Hospital, T0495-242 1050. **Post** Near Mananchira.

Thalassery *p240*

Banks Federal Bank, MM Rd, 1000-1530 (Sat 1000-1230 Sun closed) for speedy transactions. **Internet** Telynet Internet Café, Masjid Building Near Municipal Office, MG Rd, T0490-234 4390, telynet@rediffmail .com. 0900-2100.

Kannur *p241*

Internet Search World, near Railway Station, MA Rd, T0497-270 4735. Very fast connection, Rs 30 per hr.

Lakshadweep, Minicoy and Amindivi Islands

→ *Population: 60,600. 225-450 km west of Kerala. Area: 39,000 sq km. Total land area: 32 sq km.*

The islands, which make up the Lakshadweep ('100,000 islands'), have superb beaches and beautiful lagoons. There are, despite the name, only 11 inhabited and 11 uninhabited islands making up the group. Minicoy, the southernmost island, is 183 km from Kalpeni, its nearest neighbour. Geologically they are the northernmost extensions of the chain of coral islands that extends from the far south of the Maldives. The atolls are formed of belts of coral rocks almost surrounding semi-circular lagoons, with none more than 4 m above sea level. They are rich in guano, deposits of centuries of bird droppings. The wealth of coral formations (including black coral) attracts a variety of tropical fish – angel, clown, butterfly, surgeon, sweetlip, snappers and groupers. There are also manta and sting rays, harmless sharks and green and hawksbill turtles. At the right time of the year you may be able to watch them laying eggs, arriving on the beach at night, each laying 100 to 200 eggs in the holes they make in the sand. »» *For Sleeping, Eating and other listings, see pages 249-250.*

Ins and outs

Getting there You can only visit the islands on a package tour – individuals may not book independently. Lakshadweep Tourism's Society for Promotion of Recreational Tourism and Sports (SPORTS) and other tour operators organize package tours. »» *See Tour operators, Tours and Transport, page 249, for further details.*

Tourist information Everyone needs a permit, for which you need to provide details of the place and date of birth, passport number, date and place of issue, expiry date, four photos; apply two months ahead. If you plan to go diving, get a doctor's certificate. Foreign tourists may only visit Bangaram and Kadmat Islands; Indians, Kadmat, Kavaratti, Kalpeni and Minicoy. Thinakkara and Cheriyam are being developed.

Lakshadweep Islands

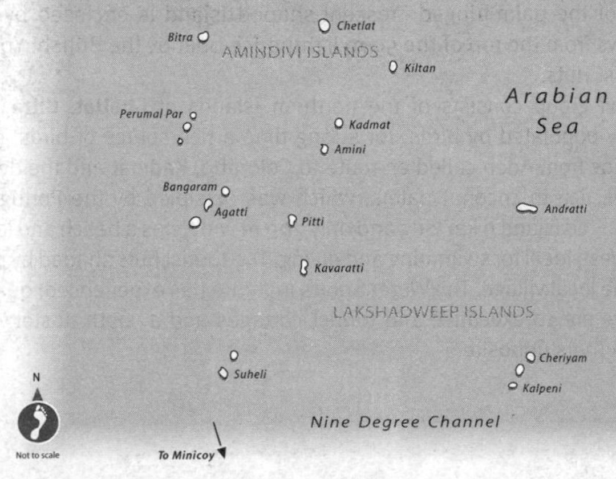

Kavaratti, the administrative capital, is in the centre of the archipelago. The Ajjara and Jamath mosques (of the 52 on the island) have the best woodcarvings and the former has a particularly good ceiling carved out of driftwood; a well inside is believed to have medicinal water. The aquarium with tropical fish and corals, the lake nearby and the tombs are the other sights. The woodcarving in the Ajjara is by superb local craftsmen and masons. **Dak Bungalow**, basic, with two rooms and a **Rest House** with four rooms may be reserved through the Administrator, Union Territory of Lakshadweep, Kozhikode 1. Local food from *dhabas*. There is a bank here.

Some of the other islands in the group are **Andratti**, one of the largest which was first to be converted to Islam, and **Agatti** (the only one with an airport which neighbours Bangaram) and also has a beautiful lagoon and 20-bed **Tourist Complex**.

Barren, desolate and tiny, **Pitti** Island comprises a square reef and sand bank at its south end. It is a crucially important nesting place for terns and has now been listed as a wildlife sanctuary. Conservation groups are pressing for a ban on the planting of trees and the mining of coral, but the main risk to the birds is from local fishermen who collect shells and the terns' eggs for food. Nearby **Cheriyam** and **Kalpeni** have suffered most from storm damage.

Bangaram is an uninhabited island where CGH Earth runs the **Bangaram Island Resort** (see Sleeping opposite).

Kalpeni, with its group of three smaller uninhabited satellite islands, is surrounded by a lagoon rich in corals, which offers excellent snorkelling and diving. The raised coral banks on the southeast and eastern shores are remains of a violent storm in 1847; the Moidin Mosque to the south has walls made of coral. The islands are reputedly free from crime – the women dress in wrap-around lungis (sarongs), wearing heavy gold ornaments here without any fear. Villagers entertain tourists with traditional dances, *Kolkali* and *Parichakkali*, illustrating themes drawn from folk and religious legends and accompanied by music and singing. On Koomel Bay overlooking Pitti and Tilakam islands, the **Dak Bungalow** and **Tourist Huts** provide accommodation.

Minicoy (Maliku), the southernmost and largest, is interesting because of its unique Maldivian character, having become a part of the archipelago more recently. The people speak Mahl similar to Dhivehi (the script is written right to left) and follow many of their customs; a few speak Hindi. The ancient seafaring people have been sailing long distances for centuries and the consequential dominance by women may have led Marco Polo to call this a 'female island'. Each of the nine closely knit matrilineal communities lives in an *athir* (village) and is headed by a *Moopan*. The village houses are colourfully furnished with carved wooden furniture. Tuna fishing is a major activity and the island has a cannery and ice storage. The superb lagoon of the palm-fringed crescent-shaped island is enclosed by coral reefs. Good views from the top of the 50-m lighthouse built by the British. You can stay at the **Tourist Huts**.

The **Amindivi** group consists of the northern islands of **Chetlat**, **Bitra** – the smallest (heavily populated by birds, for a long time a rich source of birds' eggs), **Kiltan** where ships from Aden called en route to Colombo, **Kadmat** and the densely populated **Amini**, rich in coconut palms, which was occupied by the Portuguese. **Kadmat**, an inhabited island 9 km long and only 200 m wide, has a beach and lagoon to the east and west, ideal for swimming and diving. The tourist huts shaded by palms are away from the local village. The Water Sports Institute has experienced, qualified instructors. There are 10 executive and tourist cottages and a youth hostel with a dorm for 40, see Tours opposite.

Sleeping

Accommodation varies on the islands. Kavaratti and Kadmat have basic tourist cottages resembling local huts. Each hut has 1 or 2 bedrooms, mosquito nets, fans and attached baths; electricity is wind or diesel. Meals are served on the beach and are similar to Keralan cuisine, with plenty of coconut. Breakfast might be iddlis or puris with vegetables. Lunch and dinner might be rice and vegetable curry, sambhar, meat or fish curry. Vegetarian meals available on request. Alcohol is available on board ship and on Bangaram Island (tourists requested not to carry it though).

L Bangaram Island Resort, T0484-301 1711, www.cghearth.com. 26 standard huts on the beach with fan, fridge and bathrooms or 3 de luxe beach huts which sleep 4. Scuba, diving, snorkelling, deep sea fishing, kayaking. International cuisine served.

Activites and tours

Tour operators

Book at least 2 months ahead (see Ins and outs, page 247).

Ashok Travels, Everest Building, 46 JL Nehru Rd, Kolkata, T033-2242 3254.

CGH Earth, Kochi, see page 216.

Clipper Holidays, 4 Magrath Rd, Bengaluru (Bangalore), T080-2559 9032, clipper@bangalore.wipro.net.in.

ITDC, Kanishka Plaza, 19 Ashok Rd, New Delhi, T011-2332 5035.

Lakshadweep Foundation, KSRM Building, Lighthouse Hill, Mangalore, T0824-221969.

Lakshadweep Travelinks, Jermahal 1st floor, Dhobitalo, Mangalore, T022-2205 4231.

Lakshadweep Travels, 1 Gandhi Rd, Kozhikode, T0495-276 7596.

Mercury, Everest Building, 46 JL Nehru Rd, Kolkata, T033-2242 3555, and 191 Mount Rd, Chennai, T044-2852 2993.

SITA, F-12 Connaught Pl, New Delhi, T011-2331 1133.

SPORTS (Lakshadweep Tourism), Indira Gandhi Rd, Willingdon Island, Kochi T0484-286 8387, T0484-266 8141.

Tours

Tourism is still in its infancy and facilities are limited on the islands you will be allowed to visit. The relatively expensive package tours (the only way to visit) operate Oct-May. Schedules may change, so allow for extra days when booking onward travel. Most tours are monthly from late Jan to mid-May.

CGH Earth, for the resort only, US$250-350 (for 2), US$500-700 for 4, US$70 extra person (discounts Apr-Sep). **Bangaram** Kayaks, catamarans and sailing boats are free. For an extra charge each time: scuba diving for beginners and the experienced (equipment for hire); deep sea big game fishing from 1 Oct-15 May – only minimal fishing equipment and boat crew; excursion to 3 neighbouring islands or snorkelling at shipwreck (for 8); glass-bottomed boat. Snorkelling in the lagoon can be disappointing due to poor visibility and dead corals. **Katmad Island Scuba Diving**: US$800, 1 Star CMAS Certificate US$30, Certified diver US$25 per dive; accompanying adult US$350, child (under 10) US$165. Travel by ship from Kochi (deck class) included; return air from Kochi or Goa to Agatti, US$300; return helicopter (Agatti-Kadmat), 15 mins, US$60, or local *pablo* boat.

SPORTS (Lakshadweep Tourism), see Tour operators above. 3 packages costing Rs 6000-10,000 per person (student discounts), including transport from Kochi. **Coral Reef**: 5 days to Kavaratti, Kalpeni and Minicoy Islands. **Kadmat Water Sports**: 6 days (including 2-day sailing, stay in *Kadmat Cottages* or *hostel*). **Paradise Island Huts**: 6 days to Kavaratti.

Watersports

Windsurfing, scuba diving (**Poseidon Neptune School**), parasailing, waterskiing and snorkelling. Deep sea fishing (barracuda, sailfish, yellow-fin, travelly) is possible on local boats with crew; serious anglers bring their own equipment; no diving or deep sea fishing Apr-Sep. The satellite islands of Tamakara, Parali I and II can be visited for the day.

For an explanation of the sleeping and eating price codes used in this guide, see inside the front cover. Other relevant information is found in Essentials pages 40-44.

Package Rs 3500-9500 per head, ordinary and de luxe and depending on season. Reservation: **TCI**, MG Rd, Ernakulam, Kochi (opposite Kavitha Theatre), or in Mumbai office Chander Mukhi, Nariman Point, or **Casino Hotel**, see page 213.

Transport

Air

Agatti has a basic airport. **Indian Airlines** by 15-seater Dorniers (baggage allowance 10 kg), unreliable service, "plane broke down": to/from **Kochi**, daily except Tue and Sun; to/from **Goa**: Tue, Sat. 1¼ hrs, US$300 return; transfer by *pablo* boat; helicopter May-Sep. **Casino/Taneja** by 5-seater P68C, 2 a week.

Ferry

MV *Tipu Sultan* sails from Kochi. 26 passengers in 1st and executive class have 2- and 4-berth a/c cabins with washbasins, shared toilets, Rs 5000; 120 passengers in 2nd class in reclining seats in a/c halls, Rs 3500. Ship anchors 30-45 mins away from each island; passengers are ferried from there. Total travel time from Kochi can take up to 30 hrs. **Inter-island transfers** are by helicopter (when available) during monsoons, 15 May-15 Sep (return US$60), or by *pablo* boats for 8.

Directory

Agatti has a medical centre; emergencies on the islands have helicopter back-up.

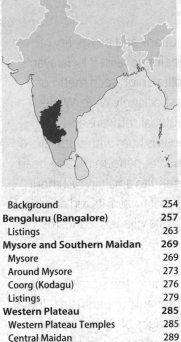

Karnataka

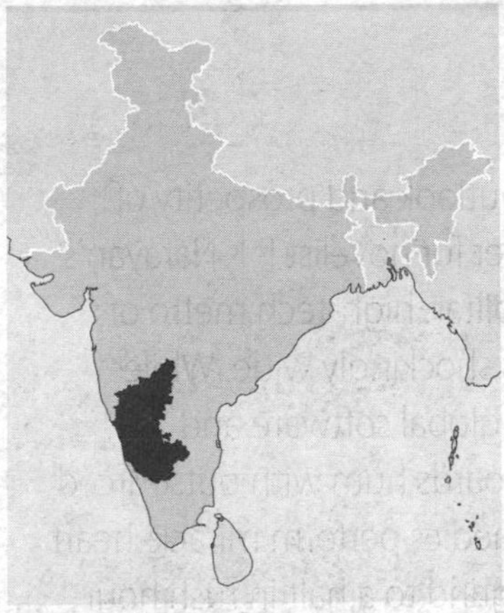

Footprint features

Introduction

The chasm between the values, outlook and prosperity of rural Karnataka – the source matter for novelist R K Narayan's *Malgudi Tales* – and the cosmopolitan high-tech metro of Bengaluru (Bangalore), is at times shockingly wide. While the city takes huge strides on the global software and biotechnology stages, its switchboards hum with outsourced call centre traffic, its world-class medics perform miracle heart and brain surgeries and its roads grind to a halt in rush hour traffic, much of Karnataka remains as if frozen: its red and black earth rocky and covered with scrub, its villagers' concerns wholly agrarian.

Wealth has always come and gone here: the state's interior, home to some of the earliest settlements in peninsular India, bears chastening witness to the ravages of time. The state has been seat to a roll-call of dynasties, both alien and homegrown, Hindu, Muslim, Jain, British, whose once-great cities and civilizations now stand largely in dusty ruins. This means that it is brimming with architectural and archaeological riches: the still-emerging Vijayanagara kingdom capital Hampi in the north; Chalukyan and Hoysala temples throughout Pattadakal, Belur and Halebid; the Islamic palaces of Tipu Sultan in the south; the onion-dome tombs of his Turkish and Persian antecedents in the far northeast; the British boulevards of Bengaluru and the wondrous palaces of the Hindu Maharajas at Mysore.

Karnataka's three great rivers, the Kaveri, Tungabhadra and Krishna, originate in the beautiful, forested hill country of the Western Ghats, the state's natural and hugely biodiverse border. Here awesome waterfalls – Jog Falls being one of the world's highest – stud the Malnad's wildlife parks. The little-visited coastline is emerald lush with river estuaries feeding unique mangrove swamps that rival Kerala's famous backwaters.

★ Don't miss ...

1 **Bengaluru (Bangalore)** The famously cosmopolitan city has India's liveliest nightlife, and India's best shopping, page 257.

2 **Mysore** Sunday night at the fairytale Amba Vilas sees the Maharaja's palace kitschly aglow with 97,000 light bulbs, page 270.

3 **Coorg** For low-key rambling in a lush, virgin rainforest kingdom, page 276.

4 **Western plateau temples** Admire 12th-century Hoysala intricacies at Belur and Halebid and the freestanding behemoth of Jain ascetic, page 285.

5 **Gokarna** Hippies and devout Hindus collide in this stunning pilgrimage town with its sacred Om-shaped beach, page 295.

6 **Hampi** The ancient Vijayanagar empire, page 300.

7 **Bijapur to Badami** Brooding 17th-century Turkish Muslim ruler's tomb and transcendentally fine Hindu temples and caves, pages 304-310.

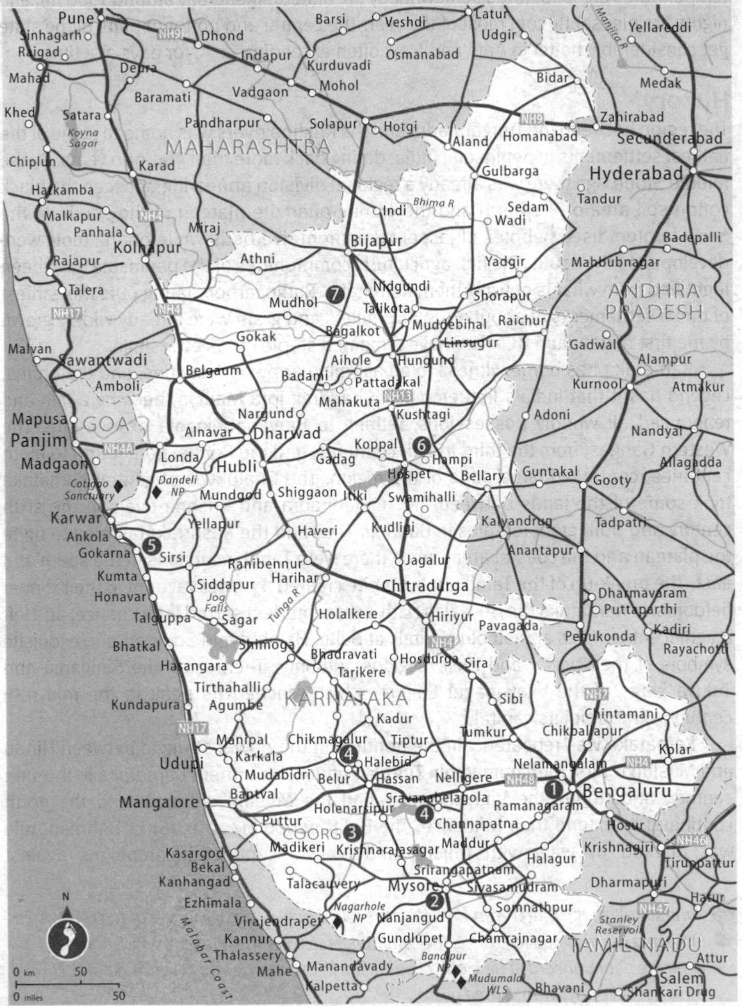

Background → *Population: 52.7 mn. Area: 192,000 sq km.*

The land

Geography The Western Ghats, called the Malnad or hill country, have beautiful forests with waterfalls and wildlife parks. To the east stretches the Mysore Plateau. Parts of northern Karnataka are barren, rocky and covered with scrub, but the state in other places is richly fertile (particularly around the 'sugar bowl' region of Mandya) and it has a lush coastline. From Coondapur to Karwar, the estuaries of the short fast-running rivers flowing west from the Ghats still have mangroves, some in uniquely good condition, although commercial exploitation seriously threatens their survival.

Climate The whole of the west coast is extremely wet from June to September, with 1500 mm falling in June and July alone. However, immediately to the east of the Western Ghats rainfall decreases dramatically. Temperatures rise to the low 30°C between February and June but fall slightly during and after the monsoon. On the plateaus of the south, especially around Bengaluru (Bangalore) and Mysore, temperatures are moderated somewhat by the altitude (generally around 1000 m), and nights are pleasantly cool most of the year. The central and northern parts of the state get considerably hotter in April and May, often exceeding 40°C for days at a time.

History

The region between the Tungabhadra and the Krishna rivers was home to some of the earliest settlements in peninsular India, dating back more than 500,000 years. By the Middle Stone Age there was already a regional division appearing between the black cotton soil area of the north and the granite-quartzite plateau of the south. In the north hunters used pebbles of jasper taken from riverbeds while quartz tools were developed to the south. The first agricultural communities of the peninsula have been identified from what is now northern Karnataka. Radiocarbon dating puts the earliest of these settlements at about 3000 BC; millets and gram were already widely grown by the first millennium BC. They have remained staple crops ever since.

Karnataka has borne witness to an alarming array of dynasties, and their ruins. Legend has it that India's first emperor, Chandragupta Maurya, became a Jain and renounced all worldly possessions, retiring to Sravanabelagola to meditate. The Western Gangas, from the third to 11th centuries, and the Banas, from fourth to ninth centuries, controlled large parts of the region. The Chalukyas of central Karnataka took some of the lands between the Tungabhadra and Krishna rivers in the sixth century and built great temples in Badami. They and the Rashtrakutas tried to unite the plateau and the coastal areas while there were Tamil incursions in the south and east. The break-up of the Tamil Chola Empire created a power vacuum in their former fiefdoms. In Karnataka the Hoysalas (11th-14th centuries) seized their chance, and left magnificent temples at their old capitals at Belur, Halebid and Somnathpur, exquisite symbols of their power and their religious authority. Then came the Sangama and Tuluva kings of the Vijayanagar Empire, which reached its peak in the mid-16th century with Hampi its capital.

Karnataka was repeatedly in the frontline in the power struggle between Hindu and Muslim rulers. **Muhammad bin Tughlaq** attacked northern Karnataka in the 13th century, and during the Vijayanagar period the **Muslim sultanates** to the north continued to extend their influence. The Bidar period (1422-1526) of Bahmani rule was marked by wars with Gujarat and Malwa, continued campaigns against

Kannadigas argue that the unanimous benevolence of successive waves of rulers has bred in them a deep-rooted tolerance; the communal tensions so endemic in post-partition India are near unheard of here and people of all faiths charge into celebration of each other's festive days with shared gusto.

Vijayanagar, and expeditions against Orissa. **Mahmud Gawan**, the Wazir of the Bahmani sultanate, seized Karnataka between 1466 and 1481, and also took Goa, formerly guarded by Vijayanagar kings. By 1530 the kingdom had split into five independent sultanates. At times they came together to defend common interests, and in 1565 they co-operated to oust the Vijayanagar Raja. But two of the sultanates, Bijapur and Golconda, gathered the lion's share of the spoils until the Mughals and British supplanted them.

South Karnataka saw a different succession of powers. While the Mughals were preoccupied fighting off the Marathas, the Hindu **Wodeyar** rulers of Mysore took Srirangapatnam and then Bengaluru (Bangalore). They lost control to **Haidar Ali** in 1761, the opportunist commander-in-chief who joined forces with the French to extend his control west to make Srirangapatnam his capital. The fierce Mysore Wars followed and with Haidar Ali's and then his son Tipu Sultan's death, the **British** restored the Wodeyars' rule in 1799. The Hindu royal family was still administering Mysore up to the reorganization of the states in the 1950s when the Maharaja was appointed State Governor.

Culture

A fault line runs through mainstream Kannada culture and politics, cleaving society into the northern Karantaka peasant caste, the **Lingayats** and the **Vokkaligas**, of the south. Lingayats follow the egalitarian and keen educationalist 12th-century saint Basavanna. The name Vokkaligas comes from 'okkalu', meaning to thresh, and these people are mostly farmers. The Kodavas from the south-west are a culture apart, physically fair and tall, worshippers of the goddess Cauvery and Lord Iguthappa. Karnataka has its share of tribal people. The nomadic Lambanis in the north and west are among several tribal peoples in the hill regions. The Siddis are of African origin, Navayats Arab. The state has a significant Muslim minority of nearly seven million, and Mangalore particularly has a notable Catholic community.

Cuisine The Kannada temple town of Udupi has spawned its own fabled brand of pure vegetarian meal such as iddli and dosa – traditionally served on a plantain leaf or stainless steel plate – variations of which you can taste all over the state and South India.

Language Most people speak the Dravidian language *Kannada* (Kanarese), although this has fused to form Indo-Aryan dialects in the north. Kannada has the second oldest Dravidian literary tradition. The earliest known classic is the ninth-century *Kavirajamarga*.

Art and architecture Karnataka's role as a border territory was illustrated in the magnificent architecture of the Chalukyan Dynasty from AD 450 to 650. Here, notably in Aihole, were the first stirrings of *Brahman* temple design. Relics show the parallel development of Dravidian and North Indian temple architecture: in Pattadakal alone there are four temples built on North Indian *Nagari* principles and six built on South Indian *Dravida* lines. Belur, Halebid and Somnathpur's star-shaped bases, bell-towered shrines and exquisite carvings represent a distinctive combination of both traditions. The Vijayanagara kings advanced temple architecture to blend in with the rocky, boulder-ridden landscape at Hampi. Bijapur has some of the finest Muslim monuments on the Deccan from the austere style of the Turkish rulers to the refinement in some of the pavilions and the world's second largest dome at the Gol Gumbaz.

Dance, drama and music Open-air folk theatre or *Bayalata* grew from religious ritual and is performed in honour of the local deity. Actors improvise their plays on an informal stage. Performances usually start at night and often last into the early hours. The famous *Yakshagana* or *Parijata* tends to have just one narrator while other forms

Karnataka is the origin of 70% of India's raw silk, 70% of its flower exports and is also by far India's largest coffee producer. The first beans were supposed to have been smuggled back to the subcontinent by a Haj pilgrim, Baba Budan, in the 17th century.

Indian tiger

The economic transformation of India is one of the greatest business stories of modern times. So powerful has the economy become that after 60 years of independence the colonized have turned colonizers.

Nowhere was this more evident than in the April 2007 takeover of Anglo-Dutch steel giant Corus, whose ancestry can be traced through British Steel to many of the companies that once symbolized Britain's industrial pre-eminence. Tata Steel, part of an Indian conglomerate that is one of the country's first, family owned, capitalist enterprises, gobbled up the business for US$13.2 billion, dwarfing all previous Indian acquisitions abroad.

India's commerce and industry minister, Kamal Nath, said the acquisition showed that "It is a two-way street now. Not only is India seeking foreign investment, but Indian companies are emerging investors in other countries."

Tata Chairman Ratan Tata proudly boasted that the takeover "is the first step in showing that Indian industry can step outside its shores into an international market place as a global player".

As stifling regulations have been lifted, entrepreneurship has flourished such that for the first time in 20 years India beat Japan to the top slot for the Asian country with the most billionaires.

Forbes' latest figures show that in 2006-7 India was behind only Russia for the number of new billionaires added to its annual rich list. Russia had 19 and India 14. Brothers Mukesh and Anil Ambani, who split up their family's conglomerate in 2005, joined Lakshmi Mittal, head of the world's biggest steel company, Arcelor Mittal, among the world's 20 wealthiest.

India is also considered to be at the forefront of the global information technology market and a major player in pharmaceuticals.

In what came as a ringing endorsement of India's world player status, Cisco, the world's largest maker of computer network equipment, announced at the start of 2007 that it will invest US$1.1 billion in India over the next five years and plans to have 20 per cent of its top executive based there within the next three years. IBM is among a number of Western firms that have major research facilities in India, employing thousands of workers, and HSBC, Aviva and Prudential are among the global and UK institutions that have transferred call centres to the country in the last five years.

India is producing a healthy flow of talented, young engineers and scientists at a time when Western universities are struggling to attract students to the professions. With young, able Indians able to offer developed world skills at developing world wages, many say India's workers pose a serious threat to US and UK jobs. Provided the steady flow of skilled workers can keep pace with burgeoning demand for their services the Indian Tiger's roar is sure to be heard reverberating around the globe for many decades to come.

have four or five, assisted by a jester. The plots of the *Dasarata* which enacts several stories and *Sannata* which elaborates one theme, are drawn from mythology but sometimes highlight real-life incidents. The *Doddata* is less refined than the *Yakshagana* but they have much in common, beginning with a prayer to the god Ganesh, using verse, and drawing from the stories of the epics *Ramayana* and *Mahabharata*. The costumes are elaborate with fantastic stage effects, loud noises and war cries and vigorous dances.

Modern Karnataka

Government The 19 districts are grouped into four divisions: Bengaluru (Bangalore), Mysore, Belgaum and Gulbarga. Caste rivalry between Vokkaligas and Lingayats remains a powerful factor and faction fighting within parties is a recurrent theme. In 2004, Congress suffered a swingeing backlash against its liberal economic policies that had fuelled Bengaluru's rise to become the darling of the IT and biotechnology industries. The BJP became the largest single party in the Assembly with 79 seats, the Congress's 65 and the Janata Dal's 58, producing a coalition government, first with Dharam Singh of the BJP as chief minister, followed by HD Kumaraswamy of the Janata Dal (Secular). Opponents have seized on the apparent opportunism of a party with 'secular' in its title joining forces with the avowedly Hindu nationalist BJP. The coalition has witnessed major tensions and some question whether it will last the full term.

Economy Karnataka is one of India's most rapidly modernizing states, and an undisputed leader in IT skills, biotech and industrial activity. Based on its early development of aeronautics and high precision machine tools, Bengaluru has become a world centre for the computer industry, receiving a much-quoted seal of approval from Bill Gates. Outside the cities agriculture and forestry remain important. Demand for irrigation is growing rapidly against a backdrop of frequent droughts. The water issue is the cause of escalating tension with neighbouring Tamil Nadu, a conflict that plays out at the top political level, with a verdict reached by the Indian Supreme Court to allocate resources in 2007, and as a trigger for mass demonstrations, rallies have led to violent clashes against Tamilian interests, property and people within Karnataka's borders.

Bengaluru (Bangalore)

→ *Phone code: 080. Colour map 3, A4. Population: 6.2 mn.*

IT capital Bengaluru (Bangalore), the subcontinent's fastest growing city, is the poster boy of India's economic ascendance. Its buoyant economy has cost the so-called 'garden city' and 'pensioner's paradise' its famously cool climate and sedate pace, while its wealthy retirees are long gone. In their place is a cosmopolitan café culture, lively music scene and dynamic, liberal-minded people, making the city a vibrant and relaxed entry metro, with more in common with San Francisco than the red baked earth of the surrounding state of Karnataka.

And there's more to Bengaluru than Wipro, Infosys and call centres. Bengaluru rivals Kancheepuram for silks, is India's aeronautical defence industry's head-quarters, boasts a mammoth monolithic Nandi Bull temple, has boulevards shaded by rain and flame trees and the great green lungs of Lal Bagh Gardens and Cubbon Park and holds a number of fine administrative buildings left over from the British. For all its outward-looking globalism, to walk around the jumbles of rope and silk shops, flower garland-sewers, tailors, temples and mosques in the ramshackle old city and the unruly bazars of Gandhi Nagar, Sivaji Nagar, Chickpet and City Market, is to forget the computer chip had ever been invented. ▸▸ *For Sleeping, Eating and other listings, see pages 263-269.*

Ins and outs

Getting there The airport at Bengaluru (Bangalore), with direct flights from Frankfurt, the Middle and Far East, Sri Lanka and Nepal, is 9 km east of the Mahatma Gandhi (MG)/Brigade Rd area (which has the bigger hotels). There are airport buses, autos and pre-paid taxis into town. Only use rickshaws on the meter; they charge 50% extra after 2200. About 5 km west of MG Rd, the main City Station and bus stations are

24 hours in Bengaluru

Firstly, make sure your 24 hours fall on a weekend - otherwise they'll be spent choking on exhaust fumes as you try to negotiate Bengaluru's impossibly oversubscribed roads.

Make your first stop coincides with the morning rush of flowers at the **City Market**, then stroll past the fort up Avenue Road to reach **Tipu's Summer Palace**, pausing for a healthy, hygienic dosa or iddly breakfast at one of the big Indian vegetarian chain restaurants over the road. Keep on through the markets around **Gandhi Bazar** to reach the **Bull Temple**, outside which you can pick up a coconut and sit in the shade of the fruit trees in **Bugle Park**.

To see how the big biotech cheeses live you could tee off on one of Bengaluru's golf courses, or go for a dip in one of the municipal swimming pools, pound the pavement around **MG Road** to be dazzled by some shimmering silks in one of the fabric emporia, pick up international fashion brands, browse book stores or people watch over an iced coffee.

Come dusk, try to catch one of the folk performances in **Lal Bagh Gardens**, after which you should pop over to the vegetarian Bangalorean institution, the **MTR** or **Mavalli Tiffin Rooms**, some of whose clientele look like they've been coming here since the place was set up in the 1920s. Walk off your supper around the bustling markets of **Chikpete**, then head back to MG Road area to knock back a beer at one of Bengaluru's many pubs or clubs – try **13th Floor** for the excellent views, or **Athena** and **Fuga** to rub shoulders with the city's beautiful people.

in Gandhi Nagar (along with most of the budget accommodation). For hotels in Sivaji Nagar and the MG Road area, get off at the Cantonment Station. A new airport 35 km north in Devanahalli is under construction and is scheduled to open in April 2008. ▸▸ *See Transport, page 267, for further details.*

Getting around Bengaluru (Bangalore) is very spread out and you need transport to get around. City buses run a frequent and inexpensive service throughout the city.

Tourist Information Karnataka State Tourism Development Corporation head office ⓘ *No 49, Khanija Bhavan, West Gate, Race Course Rd, T080-2235 2901*; Booking Counter ⓘ *Badami House, NR Square, T080-2227 5869, http://kstdc.nic.in*. Pick up the fortnightly listings magazine *City Info* (www.explocity.com) for events and clubs.

History

The 16th-century Magadi chieftain Kempe Gowda built a mud fort and four watchtowers in 1537 and named it Bengalaru (you can see his statue in front of the City Corporation buildings). Muslim king Haidar Ali strengthened those fortifications before his death at the hands of the British, leaving his son Tipu Sultan to pick up where he left off. When the British gained control after 1799 they installed the Wodeyar of Mysore as the ruler and the Rajas developed it into a major city. In 1831 the British took over the administration for a period of 50 years, making it a spacious garrison town, planting impressive avenues and creating parks, building comfortable bungalows surrounded by beautiful lawns with tennis courts, as well as churches and museums.

In 2006 Bengaluru (Bangalore) became the fourth metro, after Mumbai (Bombay), Kolkotta (Calcutta) and Chennai (Madras), to ditch its anglicized moniker. It reverted to Bengaluru, a name possibly derived from the phrase 'benda kalu', or 'boiling bean' in reference to the meal fed to a lost Prince Hoysala by an old peasant woman who took him in.

Bengaluru: India's hi-tech centre

The contemporary hi-tech and biotech blossoming in Bengaluru (Bangalore) has deep roots: the city was consciously developed into India's research capital after Independence, with public sector units in electronics, aeronautical industry and telecoms established in the city, and educational institutions to match. National programmes of space research and aircraft design continue to be concentrated here, and it is home to the Indian Institute of Science.

Sights

The 1200 ha of **Cubbon Park** in the Cantonment area was named after the 19th-century British representative in Bangalore. The leafy grounds with bandstand, fountains and statues are also home to the Greco-Colonial High Court, State Library and museums, now overshadowed by the post-Independence granite of Vidhana Soudha, the state's legislature and secretariat buildings across the street.

Government Museum ① *Kasturba Rd, Cubbon Park, T080-2286 4563, Tue-Sun 1000-1800, Rs 4*, is idiosyncratic and slightly dog eared; opened in 1886, it is one of the oldest in the country. There are 18 galleries: downstairs teems with sculptures, huge-breasted Durga and a 12th-century figure of Ganesh from Halebid sit alongside intricate relief carvings of Rama giving his ring to Hanuman, and there are Buddhas from as far afield as Bihar. An upstairs gallery holds beautiful miniatures in both Mysore and Deccan styles, including a painting of Krishnaraj Wodeyar looking wonderfully surly. There are also Neolithic finds from the Chandravalli excavations, and from the Indus Valley, especially Mohenjo Daro antiquities. In the same complex, the **K Venkatappa Art Gallery** ① *Kasturba Rd, Cubbon Park, T080-2286 4483, Tue-Sun 1000-1700*, shows a small cross-section of work by the late painter (born 1887). His paintings of the southern hill stations give an insight into the Indian fetishization of all things pastoral, woody and above all cold. There is also the story and blueprints of his truncated design for the Amba Vilas Durbar Hall in Mysore and miniatures of revered painter Abanindranath Tajore (1871-1951), alongside a second portrait of Krishnaraj Wodeyar.

Visveswaraya Industrial and Technological Museum ① *Kasturba Rd, next to the Government Museum, Tue-Sun 1000-1800, Rs 15*, will please engineering enthusiasts, especially the basement which includes a 1917 steam wagon and India's oldest compact aircraft. Others might be left cold by exhibits on the 'hydrostatic paradox' or 'the invention of the hook and eye and zip fastener technology'. Upstairs is a wing devoted to educating the inhabitants of Bengaluru (Bangalore) on genetic engineering. You might find the debate a little one-sided: "agricultural biotechnology is a process ... for the benefit of mankind," it states in upper case. A small corner (next to the placard thanking AstraZeneca, Novo Nordisk Education Foundation, Novozymes and Glaxo-SmithKline), is dubbed Concerns, but you can see how cloning and genetically strengthened 'golden' rice might seem more attractive when put in the context of the growling Indian belly.

To the southwest lies the summer palace that Tipu Sultan, the perennial thorn in the side of the British, boasted was 'the envy of heaven'. **Tipu's Summer Palace** ① *City Fort, 0830-1530, Rs 100, video camera Rs 25*, was begun by his father Haidar Ali and was completed by Tipu in 1789. Based on the Daria Daulat Bagh in

Despite a subway under construction and flyovers already in place, infrastructure in Bengaluru (Bangalore) has failed to keep up with the transport explosion. City traffic is so bad that weekdays are best avoided; aim instead for a weekend.

Bengaluru

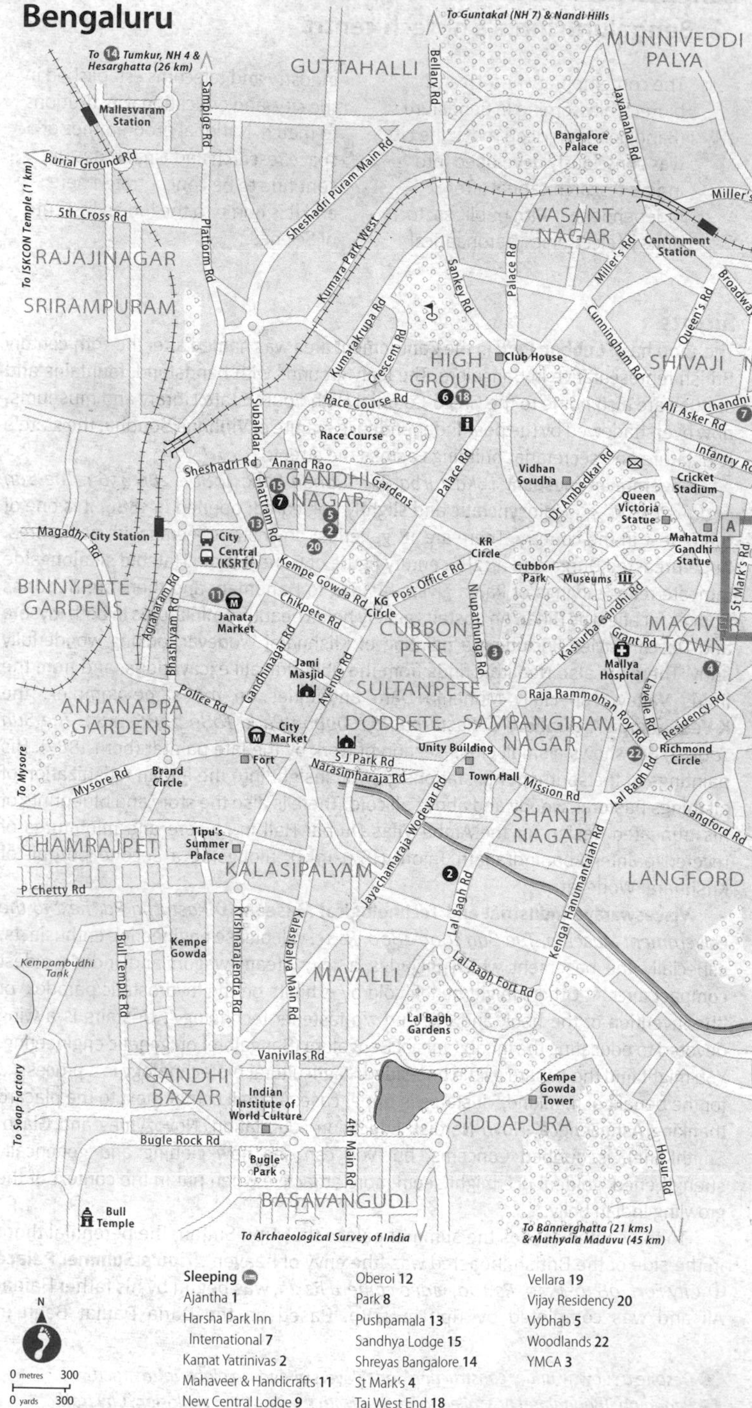
To Guntakal (NH 7) & Nandi Hills
To 14 Tumkur, NH 4 & Hesarghatta (26 km)
MUNNIVEDDI PALYA
GUTTAHALLI
Bellary Rd
Sampige Rd
Mallesvaram Station
Jayamahal Rd
Bangalore Palace
Burial Ground Rd
To ISKCON Temple (1 km)
Sheshadri Puram Main Rd
Miller's
5th Cross Rd
VASANT NAGAR
Cantonment Station
Kumara Park West
Platform Rd
Miller's Rd
RAJAJINAGAR
Sankey Rd
Palace Rd
Broadway
SRIRAMPURAM
Queen's Rd
Kumarakrupa Rd
Crescent Rd
Cunningham Rd
HIGH GROUND
Club House
SHIVAJI N
Race Course Rd
Chandni
Ali Asker Rd
Subahdar
Race Course
Infantry Rd
Sheshadri Rd
Anand Rao
Chattram Rd
GANDHI NAGAR
Gardens
Palace Rd
Vidhan Soudha
Dr Ambedkar Rd
Cricket Stadium
Queen Victoria Statue
Mahatma Gandhi Statue
Magadhi Rd
City Station
City Central (KSRTC)
KR Circle
Cubbon Park
Museums
BINNYPETE GARDENS
Kempe Gowda Rd
Post Office Rd
KG Circle
Nrupathunga Rd
Kasturba Gandhi Rd
St Mark's Rd
Agraharam Rd
Janata Market
Chikpete Rd
CUBBON PETE
Grant Rd
MACIVER TOWN
Bhashiyam Rd
Gandhinagar Rd
Avenue Rd
Mallya Hospital
Jami Masjid
SULTANPETE
Police Rd
Raja Rammohan Roy Rd
Lavelle Rd
Residency Rd
ANJANAPPA GARDENS
DODPETE
SAMPANGIRAM NAGAR
City Market
Fort
Unity Building
S J Park Rd
Richmond Circle
To Mysore
Mysore Rd
Brand Circle
Narasimharaja Rd
Town Hall
Mission Rd
Lal Bagh Rd
Jayachamaraja Wodeyar Rd
SHANTI NAGAR
Langford Rd
CHAMRAJPET
Tipu's Summer Palace
KALASIPALYAM
Kengal Hanumantaiah Rd
LANGFORD
P Chetty Rd
Lal Bagh Rd
Bull Temple Rd
Kempe Gowda
Krishnarajendra Rd
Kalasipalya Main Rd
MAVALLI
Lal Bagh Fort Rd
Kempambudhi Tank
Lal Bagh Gardens
Vanivilas Rd
Kempe Gowda Tower
GANDHI BAZAR
Indian Institute of World Culture
To Soap Factory
4th Main Rd
SIDDAPURA
Bugle Rock Rd
Bugle Park
Hosur Rd
BASAVANGUDI
Bull Temple
To Archaeological Survey of India
To Bannerghatta (21 kms) & Muthyala Maduvu (45 km)
N
0 metres 300
0 yards 300
Sleeping
Ajantha 1
Harsha Park Inn International 7
Kamat Yatrinivas 2
Mahaveer & Handicrafts 11
New Central Lodge 9
Oberoi 12
Park 8
Pushpamala 13
Sandhya Lodge 15
Shreyas Bangalore 14
St Mark's 4
Taj West End 18
Vellara 19
Vijay Residency 20
Vybhab 5
Woodlands 22
YMCA 3

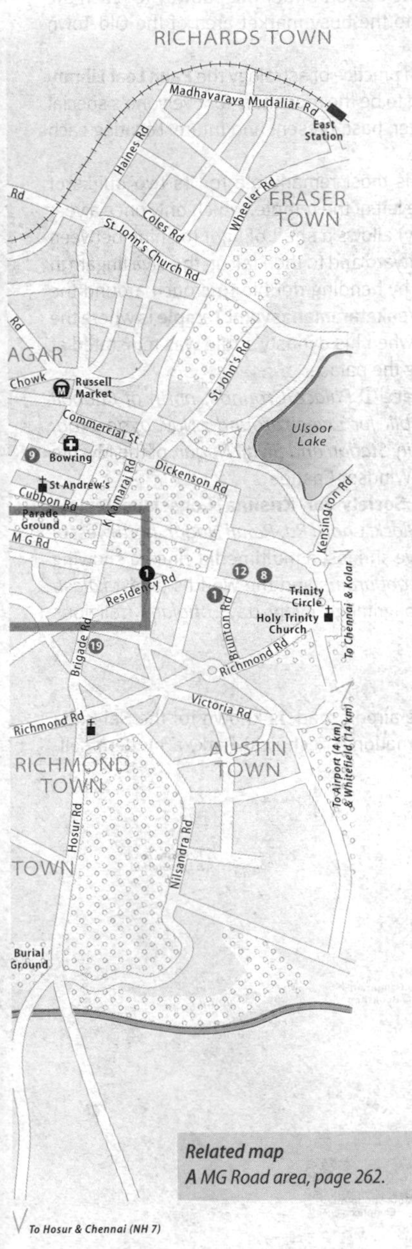

Related map
A MG Road area, page 262.

Eating
Amarvathi **1**
Chalukya **6**
MTR **2**
Sukh Sagar **7**

Srirangapatnam, the understated two-storey structure is largely made of teak with walls and ceilings painted in brilliant colours with beautiful carvings. A room downstairs is given over to documenting Haidar and Tipu's reigns and struggles against the British.

Lal Bagh Gardens ⓘ *southeast of the Summer Palace, 0900-1830, Rs 7,* were laid out across 240 acres by Haidar Ali in 1760 and are second only to Kolkatta's in size. Tipu added a wealth of plants and trees from many countries (there are over 1800 species of tropical, subtropical and medicinal plants) and the British brought a bandstand. Sadly, the Indian affection for botanical beauty means that the rose gardens are kept behind bars. At dusk, Lal Bagh is popular with businessmen speed walking off their paunches and courting couples and newlyweds who sit on the banks of the lotus pond eating ice cream. The rocky knoll around the Kempe Gowda tower has great city views, and is popular at sunset. There are fortnightly Sunday evening performances of Kannada folk theatre, song and dance; go on for supper at MTR for a pukka Bengaluru evening. The Glass House, with echoes of London's Crystal Palace and Kew Gardens, holds flower shows in January and August to mark Republic and Independence days.

Further south, the hefty **Nandi Bull at Bull Temple** ⓘ *Bull Temple Rd, Basavanagudi,* was carved at the behest of Kempe Gowda, making it one of the city's oldest temples. The monolithic Nandi was believed to be growing until a trident was slammed into his forehead: he now towers nearly 5 m high and is 6 m in length. His huge proportions, draped imperiously in jasmine garlands, are made of grey granite polished with a mixture of groundnut oil and charcoal. Under his hooves you can make out the *veena* or south Indian sitar on which he's resting. Behind him is a yoni-lingam. Just outside the temple are two bodhi trees, with serpent statues draped with sacred strands in offering for children. To your right as you exit the temple lies Bugle Park, a pretty little patch of wood whose trees are packed with fruit bats. It also holds one of Kempe Gowda's four 16th-century watchtowers. You can walk past the old fort under the subway to reach the atmospheric City Market, and from there to the busy market area of the Old Town around Avenue Road and Chikpet.

For those interested in an ancient Indian practice of astrology the **Palm Leaf Library** ⓘ *33 V Main Rd, Chamarajpet*, is supposed to be the repository for everyone's special leaf, which gives accurate details of character, past, present and future. Locating each leaf is not guaranteed.

Sri Gavi Gangadhareshwara Temple is most remarkable for its two quirks of architecture. First, the 'open window' to the left of the temple, which only once a year (on Makara Sankrati day, 14th/15th January) allows a shaft of light to shine between the horns of the stone Nandi bull in the courtyard and to then fall on the Siva lingam in the inner sanctum. The second you reach by bending double to crouch around the back of the cave shrine. The Dravida-style **Venkataramanasvami Temple** is where the Wodeyar Maharaja chose to worship first, when his dynasty's rule was reinstated at the end of the 18th century, before entering the palace.

The grand, Tudor-style **Bangalore Palace** ⓘ *Palace Grounds, north of Cubbon Park, T080-2334 1778, only open to the public for 1 week around 1 Nov, 0700-1300, 1600-2030, free, frequent buses from the City Station and Sivaji Nagar*, of the Mysore Maharajas, was incongruously inspired by Windsor Castle.

The sprawling modern **International Society for Krishna Conscious temple complex (ISKCON)** ⓘ *Hare Krishna Hill, 1R Block, Chord Rd, Rajaji Nagar, northwest of the centre, 0700-1300, 1615-2030*, holds five shrines, a multimedia cinema showing films on the Hare Krishna movement, lofty *gopurams* and the world's tallest *kalash shikara*. Around 9000 visitors make the pilgrimage every day; *bhajans* (religious songs) are sung daily.

Around Bengaluru

Whitefield, 16 km east of Bengaluru on the airport road, is known for the **Sai Baba Ashram** at Brindavan. It also has the International Technical Park, a modern self-contained community of high tech workers.

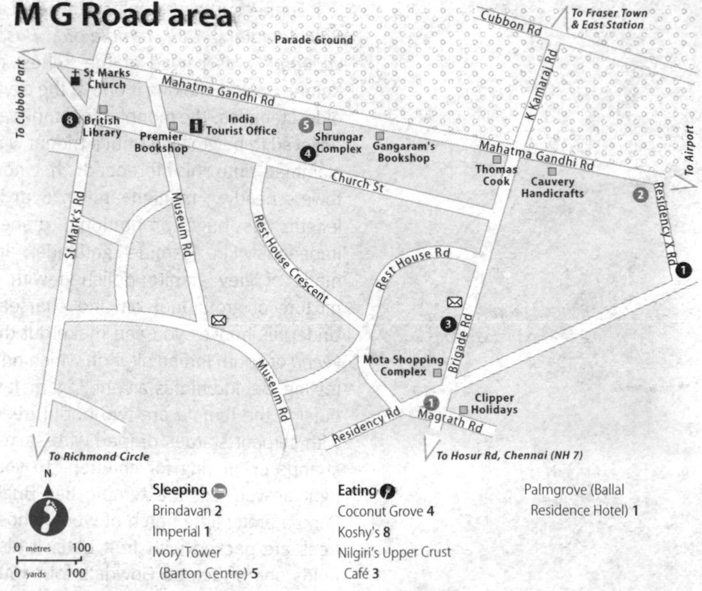

Health tourism

For decades, Western travel to India was synonymous with emaciated hippies, and backpackers' conversations invariably veered towards the scatological as everyone, at some stage, was sure to catch the dread 'Delhi belly'. It's a sign of a times that, although the British National Health Service failed to award India its whole back-up project in 2004, the country has become a very real alternative to private health care, representing huge cost reductions on surgery.

The centrepiece for this emerging industry is arguably Bengaluru (Bangalore), which has the largest number of systems of medicine approved by the World Health Organization in a single city: cardiac, neurology, cancer care and dentistry are just a few of the areas of specialization, and clients include the NHS and America's largest insurance company. Open-heart surgery will set you back US$4500 in Bengaluru, for example, as opposed to US$18,000 abroad. And, afterwards of course, you can recuperate at an ayurveda resort. Lately Bengaluru has knitted its medical specialists with its IT cred to pioneer virtual medicine too, whereby cardiac experts in the city hold teleconferences with outposts up and down the subcontinent to treat emergencies, examine and monitor patients via phone, text and video, a method specialists at Narayana Hrudayalaya confidently predict will one day become the norm.

Nandidurg, a fortified summer retreat for Tipu with sheer cliffs on three sides, lies on top of granite hills 10 km from Chikballapur to the north of Bengaluru. Literally 'the fort of Nandi', the place, today a minor hill resort with great views from the 60-m-high 'Tipu's drop', was named after Siva's bull in the Nandi Hills. The ninth-century **Bhoganandisvara Temple** at the foot of the hill is a good example of the Nolamba style; its walls are quite plain but the stone windows feature carvings of Nataraja and Durga. The 16th century brought typical Vijayanagar period extensions such as the *gopuram* at the entrance. At the Central Bus Stand ask for Nandi Hill bus (not Nandidurga). They leave at 0730, 0830, 0930, returning at 1400, 1630, 1830.

Nrityagram, 30 km from Bengaluru, is a dance village where young dancers learn all disciplines of traditional Indian dance. It was founded by the late Odissi dancer Protima Gauri. Guided tours include lunch, dance demonstrations and a short lecture.

Sleeping

Bengaluru *p257, maps p260 and p262*
Luxury hotels can add 25% in taxes. Power cuts are still routine so carry a torch.

LL Oberoi, 39 MG Rd, T080-2558 5858, www.oberoihotels.com. 160 superb rooms and suites with private sit-outs, all with views across lush tropical gardens and decent-sized swimming pool. Good restaurants, bar, spa and fitness centre, beauty salon.

LL The Park, 14/7 MG Road, T080-2559 4666, www.theparkhotels.com. Global minimalist chic, 109 plush rooms in achingly hip business hotel. Each room has a balcony, there's a lovely long pool surrounded by gazebos, cool black and white photographs on the walls, DVDs, library, Wi-Fi and 24-hr room service. Some suites have jacuzzi.

LL Shreyas Bangalore, T+91 (0)80-2773 7183 www.shreyasretreat.com. The place for

For an explanation of the sleeping and eating price codes used in this guide, see inside the front cover. Other relevant information is found in Essentials pages 40-44.

peace and yoga in 5-star luxury, with twice-daily classes and silent meditations, Vedanta consultants, life coaching. Pampering includes Balinese massage and exotic fruit body scrubs, and the vegetarian cuisine is exceptional. Alcohol is forbidden, but there's a gym, book and DVD library. 6-night packages cost from US$2000.

LL Soukya International Holistic Health Centre, 17km from Bengaluru, T080-2531 8405, www.soukya.com. This healing centre offers restorative, personalized programmes: detox, de-stress and weight loss, or relax with naturopathy and ayurveda suited to asthma, diabetes, hypertension and addictions. Accommodation is in individual cottages around lawns, flowers and trees. Programmes cost from US$80-600 a day.

LL The Taj West End, No 23 Race Course Rd, near railway, T080-2225 5055, www.tajhotels.com. Charming 1887 colonial property set in beautiful gardens; much more than a business hotel. 117 immaculately appointed suites and rooms with balconies and verandahs, Wi-Fi, flat screen TV. There's also a splendidly restored Heritage Wing, dating from 1907. George Soros, Gordon Brown and Sting are some of its former guests. Pool (non-residents, Rs 500), good restaurant and Blue Bar, with house/lounge music, (until 2330).

LL-L Royal Orchid Central, Manipal Centre 47/1 Dickenson Rd, off MG Rd, T080-2558 4242, www.royalorchidhotels.com. 130 rooms, plush but sparely designed interiors, doubles to executive. Chiefly business, with Wi-Fi connectivity.

AL St Mark's Hotel, 4/1 St. Mark's road, T080-2227 9090, www.stmarkshotel.com. Nice carpeted rooms in very quiet and capable business hotel. All rooms have Wi-Fi and bath. Good views, questionable decorative taste. Price includes breakfast.

AL Villa Serena, No 6A, Vinutha Reddy Layout, Basavanagar, T080-2522 6338, www.villaserena.in. Excellently maintained spic-and-span giant rooms with wooden floors in private house set in large gardens just around the corner from the airport. Wi-Fi. Complimentary breakfast.

AL-A Ivory Tower, Penthouse (12th) floor of Barton Centre, 84 MG Rd, T080-2558 9333, www.hotelivorytower.com. 22 comfortable, spacious rooms (huge beds) in slightly ragged venue, stunning views over city, old fashioned but spotless, good value, friendly. Wi-Fi, a/c, fridge, phone. Good terrace bar and restaurant onsite (see page 265).

AL-A Vijay Residency (Comfort Inn), 18, III Main Rd, near railway and City Bus Station, Gandhinagar, T080-2220 3024, www.vijayresidency.net. 47 safe, comfortable and well maintained rooms, good vegetarian and multi-cuisine restaurant, 24-hr room service (no alcohol), tea and coffee makers in room, very friendly and efficient. Central a/c, Wi-Fi, lockers, teamaker in room.

A Villa Pottipati, 142 8th Cross, 4th Main Rd, Mallesaram, T080-2336 0777, www.neemranahotels.com. 8 rooms in historic townhouse furnished with rosewood 4-posters and sepia Indian portrait photography. Set in garden in the charming quiet tree-lined avenues of Bengaluru's Brahminical suburbs. A/c and internet facilities, small plunge pool. Atmospheric, but a bit lacklustre. Thin mattresses.

B Harsha Park Inn International, 11 Venkataswamy Naidu Rd (Park Rd), Shivajinagar, T080-2286 5566, harshahotel@yahoo.com. 80 clean rooms, 40 a/c, restaurants, bar, exchange, pool.

B-D Woodlands Hotel, 5 Raja Ram Mohan Roy Rd, T080-2222 5111, info@woodlands.in. Large but charming old-fashioned hotel with 240 rooms, some a/c and cottages, with attached baths and fridge, good a/c restaurant, bar, coffee shop, exchange, safe, good location but calm, good value. Phone, satellite TV, lockers.

C-D Kamat Yatrinivas, 1st Cross, Gandhinagar, T080-2226 0088, www.kamatyatri.in. 57 decent rooms set around a central courtyard. Thin mattress spring beds, but it's clean and well maintained. 2 dining rooms, North Karnataka and South Indian meals. Satellite TV, direct dial phone, lockers.

C-E Vellara, 283 Brigade Rd, T080-2536 9116. 36 immaculate and spacious rooms with TV (top floor best), excellent value and location. TV and phone in each room. Recommended.

C-F Brindavan, 40 MG Rd, T080-2558 4000. Giant old school budget hotel in an excellent location.113 very basic rooms with shower, some **C** a/c, superb thali restaurant, fairly quiet, non a/c good value, suites are quite nice, Recommended.

D-F Ajantha, 22A MG Rd (7 km, City railway), T080-2558 4321. Bungalow in compound filled with bougainvillea and pot plants. 62 basic rooms with campbed-style beds, some a/c and cottages, with WC, showers, restaurant (South Indian vegetarian), very helpful. Calm location.

E Imperial, 93-94 Residency Rd, T080-2558 8391. Decent value place in good location with 20 clean rooms with bath.

E Mahaveer, 8/9 Tank Bund Rd, opposite bus station, near City railway station, T080-2287 3670. Modern 5-storey hotel with 44 smallish rooms, 5 a/c. Clean and basic, front rooms can be very noisy, larger (**D**) de luxe rooms at back quieter.

E New Central Lodge, 56 Infantry Rd, at the Central St end, T080-2559 2395. 35 simple, clean enough rooms, some with bath, hot water (0500-1000).

E Pushpamala, 9, 2nd Cross, SC Rd (neon sign stands out above others), T080-2287 4010, opposite Bus Station, travel agent. Clean, good value and surprisingly quiet, cheap and cheerful.

E Railway Retiring Rooms, 23 rooms cheaper dorm for passengers in transit.

E Sandhya Lodge, 70 SC Rd, T080-2287 4065. 100 good rooms with bath, train reservations.

E Vybhab, 60 SC Rd, T080-2287 3997. 29 clean rooms with bath (cold water), TV, down a passage, opposite cinema, great value.

E-F YMCA (City), Nrupathunga Rd, near Cubbon Park, T080-221 1848. None too clean, but great atmosphere, excellent café.

F YHA Guest House and Programme Centre. Contact Mr Sridhara, KFC Building, 48 Church St, T080-2558 5417.

Eating

Look out for Grover wine, which is the product of the first French grape grown in Indian soil, sown 40 km from Bengaluru at the foot of the Nandi hills. Veuve Clicquot has a stake in the company, which is now exporting to France.

Bengaluru *p257, maps p260 and p262*

For excellent fresh, cheap, south Indian staples like iddli, dosa and vada look for branches of **Darshini**, **Shiv Sagar**, **Shanthi Sagar**, **Sukh Sagar** and **Kamat** all of which are hygienic and efficient. At the other end of the price scale, The Taj West End hotel has the Vietnamese restaurant **Blue Ginger**, the Oberoi has **Thai Rim Naam**, The Park the Italian **i-t.ALIA**, all of which are pricey but excellent if you yearn for Western fare. The Sunday all you-can-eat brunch at the Leela is popular with expats and the city's business elite. If you're missing international fast food head for Brigade and MG Road and the food court at the Forum shopping mall, with branches of **McDonald's**, **KFC**, **Pizza Hut**, **Domino's** and **Subways**. Chains of **Barista** and **Cafe Coffee Day** are also ubiquitous.

TT Amarvathi, 45/3 Residency Rd. T080-2558 0440. Excellent traditional spicy South Indian, Andhra and Chettinad dishes. A local favourite.

TT Ebony Restaurant, **Hotel Ivory Tower**, T080-4178 3344. 1300-1530 and 1900-2330. Parsee dishes like mutton dhansak and curry chawal, along with Muglai, Tandoor and French food, but come for the views from this penthouse terrace restaurant, which are the best in Bengaluru.

TT Koshy's, 39 St Mark's Rd, T080-2221 3793. 0900-2330. Pleasant, old fashioned, atmospheric, licensed. Good grills and roasts, Syrian Christian fish curries and Sunday South Indian brunch. Also does Western breakfasts like baked beans on toast, eggy bread, cutlets and eggs any way. Local institution.

TT Tandoor, MG Rd, T080-2558 4620. 1230-1500 and 1900-2330. Possibly the city's best non-vegetarian restaurant serving North Indian food: Punjabi, Muglai and Tandoor.

T Coconut Grove, 86 Spencer Building, Church St, T080-2559 6149. Varied and good Southern Indian menu (Chettinad, Keralan and Kodagan), beers, buzzy place with sit-outs under shades.

T Palmgrove, Ballal Residence Hotel, 74/4 III Cross, Residency Rd, T080-2559 7277. Atmospheric Indian, a/c serves excellent giant lunch thalis Rs 75.

Vegetarian

T Chalukya, Race Course Rd, by the **Taj West End Hotel**. Excellent vegetarian.

T MTR (**Mavalli Tiffin Rooms**), 11 Lalbagh Rd, T080-222 0022. Tiffin 0600-1100 and 1530-1930, lunch 1230-1430 and 2000-2100. Closed Mon lunch. The quintessential Bengaluru restaurant: a classic old-era Kannadiga Brahmin vegetarian oozing 1920s atmosphere, full of Bengaluru elders, at the edge of Lalbagh gardens. A 14-course lunch lasts 2 hrs, but you'll be lucky to get a table. If you're in a hurry it does parcels but, though the simple vegetarian food is superb, the interiors and people watching is half the fun.

Vidyarthi Bhavan, 32 Gandhi Bazaar, T080-2667 7588. Sat-Thu 0630-1130 and 1400-2000. Unassuming joint in the Basavanagudi district (near Nandi Bull and Gandhi Bazaar) whose Mysore Masala Dosa is justly famous, served with a side order of butter, coconut chutney and potato and onion curry. Since 1938.

Cafés, bakeries and ice cream

Nilgiri's Upper Crust Café, Brigade Rd, is primarily a supermarket.

Bars and clubs

Bengaluru *p257, maps p260 and p262*

Bengaluru has what is possibly India's coolest party scenes, with bars playing everything from hiphop and house to rock (although new regulations to try to stamp out a rise in crime mean everything must close by 2330). New venues come up all the time, while others fall out of fashion, so ask around, but **The Blue Bar** (T080-6660 5660) at the Taj West End hotel and **Athena** (T080-4126 5411) at the Leela are the swankiest; **Fuga** (1 Castle St, Ashok Nagar, T080-4147 8625) and **Taika** (the Pavilion, 62,3, entry in Church St, MC Gorad T080-4151 2828) the newest.

13th Floor, Hotel Ivory Tower, 84 MG Rd, T080-2558 9333, is the least pretentious bar and has the best view.

F-Bar and Lounge and **Insomnia**, joint ventures between **Le Meridien** and **Fashion TV**

i-Bar, at **The Park Hotel**, 14/7 MG Rd, T080-2559 4666. Sleek, pared down.

Spinn, 80 3rd Cross, Residency Rd, T080-2558 1555, is in the coolest old colonial building.

Shopping

Bengaluru *p257, maps p260 and p262*

Bengaluru is a byword for shopping in India. **Commercial St**, **MG Rd** and **Brigade Rd** remain favourite hangouts for the city's youth, but 21st-century Americana in the form of shopping malls like **The Forum**, Hosur Rd, Kaoramangala have sprung up, with an estimated 50,000 city inhabitants passing through the Forum's electric doors every weekend. The food court here has international food like burritos too, if you have a hankering for un-Indian cuisine. Unless you want Western goods, though, the best shopping is to be had at the **City Market** in Chickpet for silver, gold and silk saris; it's supposed to be the country's biggest silk wholesale/retail district and makes for seriously fun people watching when it comes alive at dusk. **Russel Market**, meanwhile, in Shivajinagar is stuffed with vegetables, meat and antiques.

Shops and markets open early and close late (about 2000) but are closed 1300-1600.

Local specialities

Most gold and jewellery is on Jewellers St, but also look along MG Rd, Brigade Rd, Residency Rd and Commercial St. Bargains from KG Rd, Melleshwaram and Shivajinagar include brass, copper, soap- stone statues and sandalwood and rosewood carvings. Also sandalwood oils, incense, ceramics, carpets, fabrics (silk, cotton, georgette), watches and silver jewellery.

Cauvery, MG Rd. **Khadi Gramudyog**, Silver Jubilee Park Rd, near City Market. **Manjusha**, MG Rd. **Mota Shopping Complex**, Brigade Rd. **Raga**, A-13, Devatha Plaza, 131 Residency Rd, for attractive gifts. **Shrungar**, MG Rd. **UP Handlooms**, 8 Mahaveer Shopping Complex, Kempe Gowda Rd.

Books

Gangarams, 72 MG Rd. Has a wide-ranging and expanding collection.

Higginbotham's, No. 68, MG Rd.

Premier, 46/1 Church St (and Museum Rd). Small, with a good selection of specialist and academic books (as well as an impressive PG Wodehouse collection), helpful owner.

Silk and saris

Silk is, to many, what shopping in Bengaluru is really all about. There's a vast range at:

Deepam, MG Rd. Fixed prices, great service, ready 24 hrs from placing an order.

Janardhana, Unity Building, JC Rd.

Karnataka Silks Industries, Gupta Market, Kempe Gowda Rd.

Mysore Silk Showroom, Leo Complex, MG Rd.

Vijayalakshmi, Kempe Gowda Rd. Also make shirts.

Activities and tours

Bengaluru *p257, maps p260 and p262*

Golf

Bangalore Golf Club, Sankey Rd. Foreign visitors pay US$35. New International Championship Golf Course, near the airport. Tue-Sun 0600-1800.

KGA Golf Club, Rs 200 Mon-Fri, Rs 400 Sat-Sun.

Horse racing

Bengaluru is famous for racing and stud farms. **Bangalore Turf Club**, Race Course Rd. Season May-Jul and Nov-Mar.

Swimming

Expect to pay through the nose for pools in hotels; pools at the Leela and the Grand Ashok both cost Rs 1200, with most others now following suit. However, there are great municipal pools, with swimming times segregated by gender. Try Corp Office, near Square, Kensington Park Rd, near Ulsoor Lake, Sankey Tank, Sadhiv Nagar, Jayanagar 3rd Block. Rs 40, closes at 1600.

Tour operators

Clipper Holidays, 4 Magrath Rd, T080-2559 9032, www.clipperholidays.com. Tours, treks (everything provided), Kerala backwaters etc. Very helpful and efficient.

Greenwood Adventures, 2080, 12th B Main, MIG 3rd Phase, Newtown, Yelhalanka, T080-2846 2354, greenwood_adventures@hotmail.com. Specializes in treks in Karnataka and Kerala.

Pioneer Holidays, Mahesh Complex, 1st floor, New Thippasandra Rd, HAL 3rd Stage, T080-2521 0832, www.pioneertravels.com.

Regal Holidays, 105/17 8th Cross, RMV Extn, T080-2331 4566, regal@giasbg01.vsnl.net.in. Royal connections, culture, wildlife, horse safaris (Rs 4000 a day).

Sita, St Mark's Rd, T080-221 2826.

Thomas Cook, 55 MG Rd, T080-2559 4168, (foreign exchange and TCs), and 70 MG Rd (all services), T080-2558 6439.

Tours

Karnataka State Tourism, tours from Badami House, opposite Corporation Office NR Square, T080-2227 5883. **Bangalore Walks**, T984-552 3660, guided tour of the city's cultural and historic landmarks. **Bangalore City Sightseeing**: Tipu's Palace, Bull Temple, Lal Bagh, Ulsoor Lake, Vidhan Soudha, Museums, also stops at Government Emporia. Half-day, 0700-1330 and 1400-1930. Rs 90. Recommended. **India Tourism tour**, departing from Swiss Complex, No 33 Race Course Rd, T080-2256 0001, same schedule but lasts whole day and includes ISKCON. 0900-1700. Rs 130. **1-day Sravanabelagola, Belur and Halebid**, Fri, Sun (except monsoons), 0715-2200, Rs 340; **Mysore** daily, 0715-2300, Rs 240-300 including meals.

Transport

Bengaluru *p257, maps p260 and p262*

Air

Transport to town: (9-14 km) taxi takes 20 mins but leave an extra 30 mins in case of roadworks, Rs 150-200; auto-rickshaw, Rs 80. KSRTC coach from airport to major hotels, MG Rd and bus station, Rs 40. To airport: special bus leaves from Sivajinagar Stop (near **Hotel Harsha**). **Indian Airlines** and **Alliance Air**, Cauvery Bhavan, Kempe Gowda Rd, T080-2221 1914, airport T080-2526 6233, Reservations T141: **Chennai**, **Coimbatore**, **Delhi**, **Goa**, **Hyderabad**, **Kochi**, **Kolkata**, **Manga lore**, **Mumbai**, **Pune**, **Thiruvananthapuram**. Jet Airways, 1-4 M Block, Unity Bldg, JC Rd, T080-2227 6617, airport T080-2522 0688: **Chennai**, **Coimbatore**, **Delhi**, **Goa**, **Hyderabad**, **Kochi**, **Kolkata**, **Mumbai**. Sahara: Church St, T080-2558 6976, airport T080-2526 2531. Twice daily to **Delhi** and **Mumbai**. Air India flies weekly to **Jakarta**.

Airline offices Air India, Unity Building, JC Rd, T080-2227 7747. Alltalia, G17 Gem Plaza, 66 Infantry Rd, T080-2559 1936. **Nippon/Virgin Atlantic/Iberia/Thai/Emirates/Royal Nepal**, all at G 5, Imperial Court, Cunningham Rd, T080-2225 6194. At Sunrise Chambers, 22 Ulsoor Rd: **Air France**, T080-2558 9397, **Gulf Air**, T080-2558 4702. **Indian Airlines**, (City Office) T141 or T080-2522 6233. **Kuwait**, T080-2559 4243, **Royal Jordanian, American Airlines, TWA, Austrian, Bangladesh, Air Seychelles**, all on: T080-2559 4240, **British Airways**, 7 Sophia's Choice, St Marks Rd, T080-2227 1205. **Cathay Pacific**, Taj West End, Race Course Rd, T080-2225 5055. **El Al**, 131/132 1st Fl Devatha

Plaza Residency Rd T080-2227 2575. **KLM**, Taj West End, T080-2226 5562. **Lufthansa**, 44/42 Dickenson Rd, T080-2558 8791. **Qantas**, Westminster Cunningham Rd, T080-2226 4719. **Royal Nepal Airlines**, 205 Barton Center, MG Rd, T080-2559 7878. **Singapore**, Park View, 17 Curve Rd, Tasker, T080-2286 7868. **South African Airways/Air New Zealand/Anset Australia/Varig/ Canadian Pacific**, 17-20 Richmond Towers, 12 Richmond Rd, T080-2224 4625. **Sri Lankan Airlines**, CS Plaza Residency Rd, T080-2207 5020. **SwissAir/Sabena/Delta**, Park View, 17 Curve Rd, Tasker, T080-2286 7873. **United Airlines**, 17-20 Richmond Towers, 12 Richmond Rd, T080-2224 4620.

Bus

Long-distance video coaches can be noisy and very tiring. City Bus Station, opposite the City Railway Station, is very busy but well organized. Central (KSRTC) Bus Station is just to the south, T080-2287 1261. **Karnataka (KSRTC), Andhra (APSRTC)** and **Tamil Nadu (TTC)** run efficient, frequent and inexpensive services to all major cities in South and Central India. Frequent service to **Mysore** (3 hrs); several to **Hassan** (4 hrs), **Hyderabad**, **Madikeri** (6 hrs), **Madurai** (9 hrs), **Mangalore** (9 hrs), **Ooty** (7 hrs), **Puttaparthi** (4-5 hrs, Rs 65), **Tirupati** (6½ hrs). Private operators' De luxe or Ordinary coaches are usually more comfortable though a bit more expensive. They operate from the City and Kalasipalyam bus stations.

Car

Firms for city and out-of-town sightseeing include **Cab Service**, Sabari Complex, Residency Rd, T080-558 6121. **City Taxi**, T080-2553 9999. Use meters (min charge Rs 30), or Rs 400 for 4 hrs (40 km free then Rs 8 per km), call out service, reliable. **Europcar**, T080-2221 9502. **Hertz**, T080-2559 9408. **Karnataka STDC** (see page 258). About Rs 600-800 for 8 hrs or 80 km; extra km Rs 4-7. Out-of-town, Rs 1200 (Rs 2000 a/c).

Taxi

Taxis at railway stations.

Train

Pre-paid taxi service available at City Station. Pre-paid auto-rickshaw to MG Rd, Rs 25-30. Enquiries and reservations, T132; arrival and departure, T133. City Railway Station, computerized advance reservations in newer building on right of entrance; No 14 is Foreigners' Counter (also for disabled); the Chief Reservations Officer is on the ground floor. For Tourist Quota you need your passport and a "wait-listed" ticket number (Ticket Office is to the left of the station). If you are booking a ticket for a journey out of the Southern Region go to 1st floor booking office and join the queue for your region; no special queue for foreigners on the 1st floor. Buying tickets here can be a complicated business. Cantt Station, T135. Disembark at Cantt Station for some hotels. **Bhopal**: *Rajdhani Exp 2429*, Mon, Wed, Thu, Sun, 1835, 27 hrs (reaches **Delhi (HN)** in 35 hrs). **Chennai**: *Shatabdi Exp, 2008*, daily except Tue, 1625, 5 hrs; *Lalbagh Exp 2608*, 0630, 5½ hrs; *Brindavan Exp 2640*, 1430, 5¼ hrs; *Bangalore-Chennai Exp 6024* (AC/II), 0800, 6 hrs. **Delhi (ND)**: see Bhopal. **Goa** (Londa): *Chalukya Exp 1018*, Mon, Tue, Fri, 0600, 10½ hrs; *Ranichennamma Express 6589*, 2030, 11 hrs. **Hospet**: *Hampi Exp 6592*, 2200, 10 hrs. **Kolkata (H)**: *Bangalore Guwahati Exp 5625*, Wed, Fri, 2330, 38¼ hrs. **Mumbai (CST)**: *Udyan Exp 6530*, 2030, 24 hrs; *Chalukya Exp 1018*, Mon, Tue, Fri, 0600, 26 hrs. **Maddur** and **Mysore**: *Chamundi Exp 6216*,1815, 2½ hrs; *Tipu Express 6206*, 1415, 2½ hrs; or **Mysore**: *Tipu Express 6206*, 1415, 2½ hrs; *Shatabdi Exp 2007*, daily except Tue, 1100, 2 hrs (for a/c, Rs 280). **Secunderabad**: *Bangalore Secunderabad Exp 7086* (AC/II), 1705, 13½ hrs. **Thiruvananthapuram**: *Kanniyakumari Exp 6526* (AC/II), 2100, 18¼ hrs.

Directory

Bengaluru *p257, maps p260 and p262*

Banks Usually open 1000-1400, Mon-Fri. There are hundreds of 24-hr ATMs that are compatible with cards bearing the Visa Mastercard, Maestro, Cirrus or Plus logos. **Citibank, Hongkong** and **Shanghai Banks**, HDFC are reliable. In the MG Rd area try HSBC, 7 MG Rd, Citibank Nilgiris Complex, Brigade Rd. For counter services: **Bank of Nova Scotia**, MG Rd, T080-2558 1415, **Citibank**, MG Rd, T080-2559 9855, **HDFC**, Kasturba Rd, T080-2222 3223, **Standard Chartered**, MG Rd, T080-2559 7777, **State Bank of India**, St

Mark's Rd, T080-2227 4701. **Chemists** At hospitals and Cure, 137 GF2, Business Point, Brigade Rd T080-2227 4246. **Cultural centres** Alliance Française, Millers Tank Bund Rd, off Thimmaiah Rd, opposite station. British Library, St Mark's Rd/Church St corner (Koshy's Bldg), 1030-1830, Tue-Sat. Max Mueller Bhavan, 3 Lavalle Rd. **Dentist** Grace, 1 Dinnur Main Rd, RT Nagar, T080-2333 4638. Excellent. **Hospitals** Bowring and Lady Curzon Hospital, Hospital Rd, T080-2559 1362, north of Cubbon Park. Mallya Hospital, Vittal Mallya Rd, south of Cubbon Park, T080-2227 7979/7991, one of the best. **Internet** Computer Planet, 1st floor, 5th Avenue shopping plaza, Brigade Rd, T080-2559 7116, superfast with USB ports and software/ hardware retailer. Cyber Café on Brigade Rd (near Church St); very good, safe cold coffee. Cyber Q, Brigade Rd, near Vellara, with pool tables; St Mark's Business Centre, 8 St Mark's Plaza, 14 St Mark's Rd T080-5112 1032. Mon-Sat 0830-1930. Internet and scanning, lamination, colour zerox and CD writing. Trans World, 2 Magrath Rd, with coffee shop. **Mobile phone shops** Ericsson, T080- 2299 4088, Nokia, T080-2558 2439, Philips, T080-2331 2184, Siemens, T080-2526 3312. **Post** GPO, Cubbon Rd near Raj Bhawan, 1000-1800. Poste Restante, Mon-Sat, 1030-1600. DHL, Jubilee Building, 43 Museum Rd, T080-2558 8855. UPS, 4 1st Cross 10th Main Indiranagar, T080- 2525 3445. **Useful addresses** Ambulance: T102. Visa extensions: Commissioner of Police, Infantry Rd. Police 100 Fire 101 Chief Wildlife Warden, Aranya Bhavan, 18th Cross, Malleswaram, T080-2334 1993.

Mysore and Southern Maidan

The charming, unruly city of Mysore, the former capital of the princely state, does a brisk trade in its eponymous shimmering silks, sandalwood and jasmine against a backdrop of its stunning, borderline gaudy Indo-Saracenic palace. On the outskirts of the city is the empty ruin of Srirangapatnam, the island fortress of Britain's nemesis Tipu Sultan, and the bird-crammed Ranganathittu Sanctuary.

Further on is the Chennakesava Temple of Somnathpur, a spellbinding example of Hoysala architecture. Leopards and tigers stalk the two parklands, Bandipur and Nagarhole, that spill over Karnataka's borders with neighbouring Tamil Nadu and Kerala, and closer to the coast you can climb the Ghats to the tiny Kodagu district for forests of wild elephants and coffee plantations nursed by a unique warrior people. Also in Kodagu lies Sera, the university at the centre of one of India's biggest Tibetan Buddhist refugee settlements. » *For Sleeping, Eating and other listings, see pages 279-285.*

Mysore » *pp279-285. Colour map 3, B3.*

→ *Phone code: 0821. Population: 742,300.*

Mysore centre is a crowded jumble presided over by the gaudy, wondrous kitsch of the Maharaja's Palace, a profusion of turquoise-pink and layered with mirrors. But for some Mysore's world renown is centred less on the palace, its silk production or sandalwood than on the person of Sri Pattabhi Jois and his Mysore-style ashtanga yoga practice (see box, page 272). This all happens outside the chaotic centre, in the city's beautiful Brahmin suburbs, wide boulevard-like streets overhung with bougainvillea.

Ins and outs

Getting there The railway station is about 1 km to the northwest of the town centre while the three bus stands are all central within easy reach of hotels. » *See Transport, page 284, for further details.*

Getting around Karnataka's second biggest town, Mysore is still comfortably compact enough to walk around, though there are plenty of autos and buses as well.

Tourist information **Department of Tourism** ⓘ *Old Exhibition Building, Irwin Rd, T0821-242 2096, www.mysore.nic.in, 1000-1730*. See also www.karnataka.com/tourism/mysore. Counters at train station and bus stand. **KSTDC** ⓘ *Yatri Nivas, 2 JLB Rd, T0821-242 3652*, efficient.

Sights

Maharaja's Palace ⓘ *T0821-243 4425, enter by south gate, 1030-1730, Rs 15, cameras must be left in lockers (free, you take the key), allow 1 hr, 2 hrs if you wish to see everything (worth taking a guide), guidebook Rs 10. Go early to avoid the crowds. Downstairs is fairly accessible for the disabled.*

The City Palace (Amba Vilas) was designed by Henry Irwin and built in 1897 after a fire burnt down the old wooden incarnation. It is in the Indo-Saracenic style in grand proportions, with domes, arches and colonnades of carved pillars and shiny marble floor. The stained glass, wall paintings, ivory inlaid doors and the ornate golden throne (now displayed during *Dasara*) are remarkable. The fabulous collection of jewels is seldom displayed. Try to visit on a Sunday night, public holiday or festival when the palace is lit up with 50,000 fairy lights.

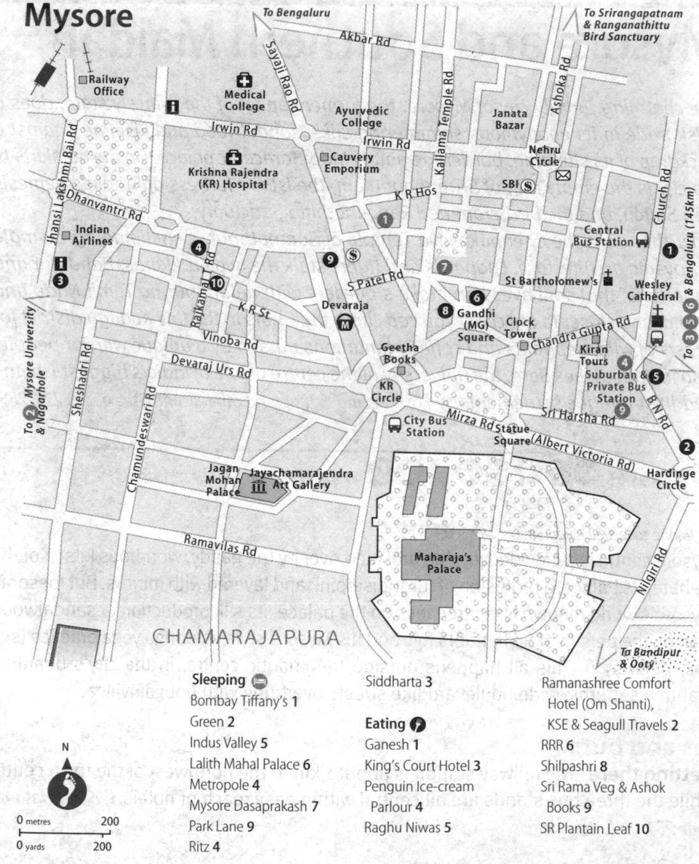

Medieval pageantry at Mysore

The brilliantly colourful festival of *Dasara* is celebrated with medieval pageantry for 10 days. Although the *Dasara* festival can be traced back to the Puranas and is widely observed across India, in the south it achieved its special prominence under the Vijayanagar kings. As the Mahanavami festival it has been celebrated every year since it was sponsored by Raja Wodeyar in September 1610 at Srirangapatnam. It symbolizes the victory of goddess Chamundeswari (Durga) over the demon Mahishasura. On the last day a bedecked elephant with a golden howdah carrying the statue of the goddess processes from the palace through the city to Banni Mantap, about 5 km away, where the Banni tree is worshipped. The temple float festival takes place at a tank at the foot of Chamundi Hill and a car festival on top. In the evening there is a torchlight parade by the mounted guards who demonstrate their keen horsemanship and the night ends with a display of fireworks and all the public buildings are ablaze with fairy lights.

Ground Floor Visitors are led through the 'Car Passage' with cannons and carriages to the *Gombe thotti* (Dolls' pavilion). This originally displayed dolls during *Dasara* and today houses a model of the old palace, European marble statues and the golden *howdah* (the Maharaja used the battery-operated red and green bulbs on top of the canopy as stop and go signals to the *mahout*). The last is still used during *Dasara* but goddess Chamundeshwari rides on the elephant. The octagonal *Kalyana Mandap* (marriage hall), or Peacock Pavilion, south of the courtyard, has a beautiful stained glass ceiling and excellent paintings of scenes from the *Dasara* and other festivities on 26 canvas panels. Note the exquisite details, especially of No 19. The Portrait Gallery and the Period Furniture Room lead off this pavilion.

First Floor A marble staircase leads to the magnificent Durbar Hall, a grand colonnaded hall measuring 47 m by 13 m with lavishly framed paintings by famous Indian artists. The asbestos-lined ceiling has paintings of Vishnu incarnations. A passage takes you past the beautifully ivory-on-wood inlaid door of the Ganesh Temple, to the Amba Vilas where private audiences (*Diwan-i-Khas*) were held. This exquisitely decorated hall has three doors. The central silver door depicts Vishnu's 10 incarnations and the eight *dikpalas* (directional guardians), with Krishna figures on the reverse (see the tiny Krishna on a leaf, kissing his toes), all done in *repoussé* on teak and rosewood. The room sports art nouveau style, possibly Belgian stained glass, cast iron pillars from Glasgow, carved wood ceiling, chandeliers, etched glass windows and the *pietra dura* on the floors.

The jewel-encrusted Golden Throne with its ornate steps, which some like to attribute to ancient Vedic times, was originally made of figwood decorated with ivory before it was padded out with gold, silver and jewels. Others trace its history to 1336 when the Vijayanagar kings 'found' it before passing it on to the Wodeyars who continue to use it during *Dasara*.

The **Maharaja's Residence** ⓘ *1000-1830, Rs 15*, is a slightly underwhelming museum. The ground floor, with a courtyard, displays costumes, musical instruments, children's toys and numerous portraits. The upper floor has a small weapon collection.

Visit the **market in Devaraja** at noon when it's injected with fresh pickings of marigolds and jasmines. The bigger flowers are stitched onto a thread and wrapped into rolls which arrived heaped in hessian sacks stacked on the heads of farmers.

Immediately to the southeast of the town is **Chamundi Hill** ⓘ *vehicle toll Rs 10, City Bus No 185*, with a temple to Durga (Chamundeswari), guardian deity to the

Power yoga

If you know the primary series, speak fluent ujayyi breath and know about the mulla bandha odds are that you have heard the name of Sri Pattabhi Jois, too. His is the version of yoga that has most percolated contemporary Western practice (it's competitive enough for the type-A modern societies we live in, some argue), and although for most of the years of his teaching he had just a handful of students, things have certainly changed.

A steady flow of international students make the pilgrimage to his town of Mysore all year, peaking at Christmas when at least 200 lithe disciples of his type of teaching descend on Mysore to wake up before dawn and take his uncompromising instruction at his yogashala.

Studying with Jois is not for dilettante yogis; the Westerners here are extremely ardent about their practice – mostly teachers themselves – and there is a strict pecking order which first-timers could find alienating. Classes start from first light at 0400, and the day's teaching is over by 0700, leaving you free for the rest of the day. The schooling costs US$500 a month. At a push you can pop in for a week but it'll set you back US$200. There's no rule that says you must know the series, but it might be better, and cheaper, to dip a toe in somewhere less hardcore, such as **Purple Valley** in Goa (see page 391).

Jois, who is in his 90s, now shares the burden of teaching with his grandson Sharath and his daughter Saraswati. There are times when it's ridiculously busy: just mat space. Some yogis advocate heading for Sharath's shala over Gurujis – it's marginally cheaper too.

Alternatively, in Mysore, for Hatha yoga practice, there's Vankatesh. His own practice is formidably advanced: his are pretzel poses bordering on contortionism, and he's always picking up awards at the international yoga competitions. Students are evangelical about his backbend workshops. See www.atmavikasa.com and the **Ashtanga Yoga Research Institute**, Mysore: www.ayri.com.

Wodeyars, celebrating her victory over the buffalo god. There are lovely views, and a giant Nandi, carved in 1659, on the road down. Walk to it along the trail from the top and be picked up by a car later or catch a return bus from the road. If you continue along the trail you will end up having to get a rickshaw back, instead of a bus.

The **Sandalwood Oil Factory** ⓘ *T0821-248 3651, Mon-Sat 0900-1100, 1400-1600 (prior permission required), no photography inside*, is where the oil is extracted and incense is made. The shop sells soap, incense sticks and other sandalwood items.

At the **Silk Factory** ⓘ *Manathavadi Rd, T0821-481803, Mon-Sat, 0930-1630, no photography*, weavers produce Mysore silk saris, often with gold *zari* work. Staff will often show you the process from thread winding to jacquard weaving, but they speak little English. The shop sells saris from Rs 3000. Good walks are possible in the Government House if the guard at the gate allows you in.

Jayachamarajendra Art Gallery ⓘ *0830-1730, Rs 10, no photography*, at Jagan Mohan Palace (1861). Priceless collections of Mysore's erstwhile rulers, including Indian miniature paintings and others, such as Ravi Varma and Nicholas Roerich. There's also an exhibition of ceramics, stone, ivory, sandalwood, antique furniture and old musical instruments. Sadly, there are no descriptions or guidebooks and many items are randomly displayed.

Passage to Mysore

The southern route to Mysore through Kanakapura and Malvalli is longer than the more northerly rail and road route. This way crosses the open parkland of the Maidan, rising to over 1200 m. The ancient rocks of some of the oldest granites in India which give reddish or brown soils, often with extraordinary hilly outcrops and boulders, provided David Lean and Richard Goodwin with the ideal filming location to capture the atmosphere of E M Forster's Barabar Cave for their film of *A Passage to India* without the hazards of working in Bihar. The lower cave sequences were filmed at **Savandurga**. Get BTS bus from Bengaluru City bus stand 0700, 0900, or to Magadi, then auto-rickshaw, Rs 50, ask at the Lakshmi store for directions or a guide. It's a stunning climb up Kempi Gowda hill.

There is also a small Forest Park and the upper caves at **Rama Dhavara**, 2 km from Ramanagaram. The caves are visible from the road and easy to find, though only false entrances were made for the film, with interior shots filmed in a studio.

Sri Mahalingeshwara Temple ⓘ *12 km from Mysore, 1 km off the Bhogadi road (right turn after K Hemmanahalli, beyond Mysore University Campus), taxi or auto-rickshaw,* is a 800-year-old Hoysala Temple that has been carefully restored by local villagers under the supervision of the Archaeological Survey of India. The structure is an authentic replica of the old temple: here, too, the low ceiling encourages humility by forcing the worshipper to bow before the shrine. The surrounding garden has been planted with herbs and saplings, including some rare medicinal trees, and provides a tranquil spot away from the city.

Around Mysore » *pp280-284.*

Srirangapatnam

Phone code: 08236. Colour map 3, B3. Population: 21,900.

Srirangapatnam, 12 km from Mysore, has played a crucial role in the region since its origins in the 10th century. Occupying an easily fortified island site in the Kaveri River, it has been home to religious reformers and military conquerors. It makes a fascinating day trip from Mysore; Daria Daulat Bagh and the Gumbaz are wonderful.

The name comes from the temple of Vishnu Sri Ranganathasvami, which is far older than the fort or the town. The site was frequently a focal point in South India's political development. The fort was built under the Vijayanagar kings in 1454. Some 150 years later the last Vijayanagar king handed over authority to the Hindu Wodeyars of Mysore, who made it their capital. In the second half of the 18th century it became the capital of Haidar Ali, who defended it against the Marathas in 1759, laying the foundations of his expanding power. He was succeeded by his son Tipu Sultan, who also used the town as his headquarters. Colonel Wellesley, the future Duke of Wellington, established his military reputation in the battle in which Tipu Sultan was finally killed on 4 May 1799, see page 468, though victory should be more correctly attributed to his brother, the Governor General. Tipu died in exceptionally fierce fighting near the north gate of the fort; the place is marked by a simple monument.

The island is over 3 km long and 1 km wide so it's best to hire a cycle from a shop on the main road to get around.

The fort had triple fortifications, but the British destroyed most of it. The **Jama Masjid** ⓘ *0800-1300, 1600-2000*, which Tipu had built, has delicate minarets, and there are two Hindu **temples**, Narasimha (17th century) and Gangadharesvara (16th century). **Daria Daulat Bagh** (Splendour of the Sea) ⓘ *Sat-Thu 0900-1700, US$2, 1 km to the east of the fort*, is Tipu's beautiful summer palace set in a lovely garden and dates from 1784. This social historical jewel has colourful frescoes of battle scenes between the French, British and Mysore armies, ornamental arches and gilded paintings on the teak walls and ceilings crammed with interesting detail. The west wall shows Haidar Ali and Tipu Sultan leading their elephant forces at the battle of Polilur (1780), inflicting a massive defeat on the British. As a result of the battle Colonel Baillie, the defeated British commander, was held prisoner in Srirangapatnam for many years. The murals on the east walls show Tipu offering hospitality to neighbouring princes at various palace durbars. The small museum upstairs has 19th-century European paintings and Tipu's belongings.

The **Gumbaz** ⓘ *Sat-Thu 0900-1700, donation collected*, is the family mausoleum approached through an avenue fo cypresses 3 km away and was built by Tipu in memory of his father. The ornate white dome protects beautiful ivory-on-wood inlay and Tipu's tiger-stripe emblem, some swords and shields. Haider Ali's tomb is in the centre, his wife to the east and Tipu's own to the west.

On the banks of the Cauvery, just north of the Lal Bagh Palace (Rs 2), is a jetty where six-seater **coracles** are available for river rides.

Ranganathittu Bird Sanctuary

ⓘ *0600-0900, 1600-1800, Rs 150, camera Rs 10. Boats (0830-1330, 1430-1830), Rs 10 each, minimum Rs 20. Jun-Oct best. Mysore City Bus 126, or auto from Srirangapatnam.*

The riverine site of this sanctuary, 5 km upstream of Srirangapatnam, was established

in 1975. Several rocky islands, some bare while the larger are well wooded, provide excellent habitat for waterbirds, including the black- crowned night heron, Eurasian spoonbill and cormorants. Fourteen species of waterbirds use the sanctuary as a breeding ground from June onwards. There is a large colony of fruit bats in trees on the edge of the river and a number of marsh crocodiles between the small islands. Boat and guide from the jetty for 15-20 minute rides.

Somnathpur → *Phone code: 08227.*

This tiny village boasts the only complete Hoysala temple in the Mysore region. The drive east from Srirangapatnam via Bannur is particularly lovely, passing a couple of lakes through beautiful country and pretty, clean villages.

The small but exquisite **Kesava Temple** (1268) ⓘ *0900-1700, US$2, allow 1 hr, canteen, buses from Mysore take 1-1½ hrs; via Bannur (25 km, 45 mins) then to Somnathpur (3 km, 15 min by bus or lovely walk or bike ride through countryside)*, is one of the best preserved of 80 Hoysala temples in this area. Excellent ceilings show the distinctive features of the late Hoysala style, and here the roof is intact where other famous temples have lost theirs. The temple has three sanctuaries with the *trikutachala* (triple roof) and stands in the middle of its rectangular courtyard (70 m long, 55 m wide) with cloisters containing 64 cells around it. From the east gateway is a superb view of the temple with an ambulatory standing on its raised platform, in the form of a 16-pointed star. The pillared hall in the centre with the three shrines to the west give it the form of a cross in plan. Walk around the temple to see the fine bands of sculptured figures. The lowest of the six shows a line of elephants, symbolizing strength and stability, then horsemen for speed, followed by a floral scroll. The next band of beautifully carved figures (at eye level) is the most fascinating and tells stories from the epics. Above is the *yali* frieze, the monsters and foliage possibly depicting the river Ganga and uppermost is a line of *hamsa*, the legendary geese.

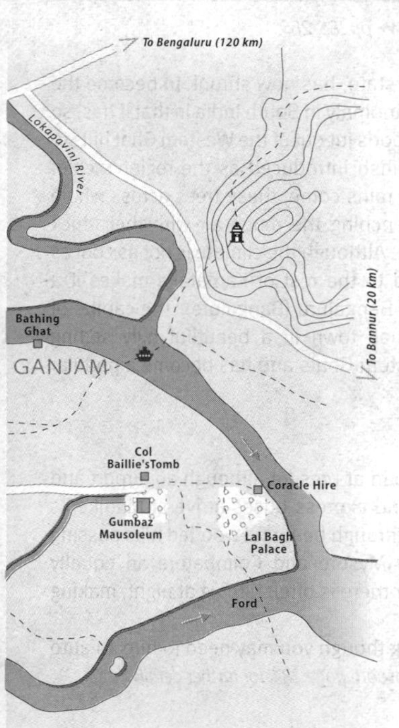

Sivasamudram

Here, the Kaveri plunges over 100 m into a series of wild and inaccessible gorges. At the top of the falls the river divides around the island of Sivasamudram, the Barachukki channel on the east and the Gaganchukki on the west. The hydro-electricity project was completed in 1902, the first HEP scheme of any size in India. It's best visited during the wet season, when the falls are an impressive sight, as water cascades over a wide area in a series of leaps.

Biligiri Rangaswamy Wildlife Sanctuary → *Altitude: 1000-1600 m.*

ⓘ *From Mysore, via Nanjangud (23 km) and Chamrajnagar, Nagavalli and Nellore villages. The Ghat Rd starts at the Forest Check Post after passing 2 lakes. The camp (90 km from Mysore) is beyond the second check post.*

A hilly area with moist deciduous and semi-evergreen forests interspersed with grassland southeast of Mysore. The best time for wildlife sighting is November to May. Soliga tribals pay special respect to an ancient champak tree (*Dodda sampige mara*) believed to be 1000 years old. Wildlife includes panther, sloth bear (better sightings here than at other southern sanctuaries), elephant, deer, gaur and tiger (infrequent) as well as 270 species of birds.

Bandipur National Park → *Colour map 3, B3. Altitude: 780-1455 m. Area: 874 sq km.*

ⓘ 0600-0900, 1600-1800, Rs 150, still camera Rs 10, best time Nov-Feb to avoid the hot, dry months, buses stop at the main entrance.

Bandipur was set up by the Mysore Maharaja in 1931. It has a mixture of subtropical moist and dry deciduous forests (principally teak and anogeissus) and scrubland in the Nilgiri foothills. The wetter areas support rosewood, silk cotton, sandalwood and *jamun*. You should easily spot gaur, chital (spotted deer), elephant, sambar, flying squirrel and four-horned antelope, but tigers and leopards are rare. Also good variety of birdlife including crested hawk, serpent eagles and tiny-eared owls.

Private cars are not allowed. Jeeps and vans are available through the Forestry Department; one-hour coach rides (morning and afternoon, 0630-1630) cost Rs 10 each but other noisy visitors scare away wildlife. Viewing is best from *machans* (raised platforms) near watering places; ask to reserve ahead. Dull-coloured clothes are recommended. There are no extended elephant rides in the park now, only 30-minute 'joy rides' at 0930.

Coorg (Kodagu) » pp285-285.

Coorg, once a proud warrior kingdom, then a state, has now shrunk to become the smallest district in Karnataka. It is a beautiful anomaly in South India in that it has, so far, retained its original forests. Ancient rosewoods jut out of the Western Ghat hills to shade the squat coffee shrubs which the British introduced as the region's chief commodity. Like clockwork, 10 days after the rains come, these trees across whole valleys burst as one into white blossom drenching the moist air with their thick perfume, a hybrid of honeysuckle and jasmine. Although the climate is not as cool as other hill stations, Coorg's proximity by road to the rest of Karnataka makes it a popular weekend bolt hole for inhabitants of Bengaluru (Bangalore). The capital of Coorg District, Madikeri, is an attractive small town in a beautiful hilly setting surrounded by the forested slopes of the Western Ghats and has become a popular trekking destination.

Ins and outs

Getting there Coorg is only accessible by road at present although an airport and railway station are planned. Frequent local and express buses arrive at Madikeri's bus stand from the west coast after a journey through beautiful wooded hills passing small towns and a wildlife sanctuary. From Mysore and Coimbatore an equally pleasant route traverses the Maidan. In winter there is often hill fog at night, making driving after dark dangerous.

Getting around Madikeri is ideal for walking though you may need to hire an auto on arrival to reach the better hotels. » *See Transport, page 284, for further details.*

Background

Although there were references to the Kodaga people in the Tamil Sangam literature of the second century AD, the earliest Kodaga inscriptions date from the eighth century. After the Vjiayanagar Empire was defeated in 1565, many of their courtiers moved south, establishing regional kingdoms. One of these groups were the Haleri

Like clockwork, 10 days after the rains come, rosewood trees across valleys burst as one into white blossom, drenching the moist air with their thick perfume, a hybrid of honeysuckle and jasmine ...

Rajas, members of the Lingayat caste whose leader Virarajendra set up the first Kodaga dynasty at Haleri, 10 km from the present district capital of Madikeri.

The later Kodagu Rajas were noted for some bizarre behaviour. Dodda Vira (1780-1809) was reputed to have put most of his relatives to death, a pattern followed by the last king, Vira Raja, before he was forced to abdicate by the British in 1834. In 1852 the last Lingayat ruler of Kodagu, Chikkavirarajendra Wodeyar, became the first Indian prince to sail to England, and the economic character of the state was quickly transformed. Coffee was introduced, becoming the staple crop of the region.

The forests of Kodagu are still home to wild elephants, who often crash into plantations on jackfruit raids, and other wildlife. The Kodaga, a tall, fair and proud landowning people who flourished under the British, are renowned for their martial prowess; almost every family has one member in the military. They also make incredibly warm and generous hosts, a characteristic you can discover thanks to the number of plantation homestays in inaccessible estates of dramatic beauty pioneered here following the crash in coffee prices. Kodagu also has a highly distinctive cuisine, in which pork curry *(pandi curry)* and rice dumplings *(kadumbuttu)* are particular favourites.

Madikeri (Mercara)

➔ *Phone code: 08272. Colour map 3, B2. Population: 32,300. Altitude: 1150 m.* *See also map, page 278.*

The **Omkareshwara Temple**, dedicated to both Vishnu and Siva, was built in 1820. The tiled roofs are typical of Kerala Hindu architecture, while the domes show Muslim influence. On high ground dominating the town is the **fort** with its three stone gateways, built between 1812-1814 by Lingarajendra Wodeyar II. It has a small **museum** ⓘ *Tue-Sun 0900-1700, closed holidays*, in St Mark's Church as well as the town prison, a temple and a chapel while the palace houses government offices. The **Rajas' Tombs** (*Gaddige*), built in 1820 to the north of the town, are the memorials of Virarajendra and his wife and of Lingarajendra. Although the rajas were Hindu, their commemorative monuments are Muslim in style; Kodagas both bury and cremate their dead. The Friday **Market** near the bus stand is very colourful as all the local tribal people come to town to sell their produce. It is known locally as shandy, a British bastardization of the Coorg word *shante*, meaning market. On Mahadevped Road, which leads to the Rajas' tombs, is a 250-year-old **Siva temple** which has an interesting stone façade. Madikeri also has an attractive nine-hole golf course.

Around Madikeri

Madikeri and the surrounding area makes for beautiful walking but if you want to venture further you'll need to take a guide as paths can soon become indistinct and confusing. **Abbi Falls** is a 30-minute rickshaw ride (9 km, Rs 150 round trip) through forests and coffee plantations. It is also an enjoyable walk along a fairly quiet road. The falls themselves are beautiful and well worth the visit. You can do a beautiful short **trek** down the valley and then up and around above the falls before rejoining the main road. Do not attempt it alone since there are no trails and you must depend on your sense of direction along forest paths. Honey Valley Estate (see page 281) has a book of walks around the guest house.

Bhagamandala ⓘ *half-hourly service from Madikeri's private bus stand from 0630-2000, Rama Motors tour bus departs 0830, with 30-min stop*, is 36 km southwest. The Triveni bathing ghat can be visited at the confluence of the three rivers: Kaveri, Kanike and Suiyothi. Among many small shrines the **Bhandeshwara temple**, standing in a large stone courtyard surrounded by Keralan-style buildings on all four sides, is particularly striking. You can stay at the temple for a very small charge.

Kakkabe ⓘ *From Madikeri to Kakkabe, bus at 0630; jeep 1 hr*. This small town, 35 km from Madikeri, gives access to the highest peak in Coorg, **Thandiandamole** (1800 m). Padi Iggutappa nearby is the most important temple in Coorg.

Nisargadhama ⓘ *0900-1800, Rs 150, still camera Rs 10*. This small island reserve is in the Kaveri River, 2 km from Kushalnagar, and is accessed over a hanging bridge. Completely untouched by tourism, it consists mostly of bamboo thickets and trees, including sandalwood, and is very good for seeing parakeets, bee eaters, woodpeckers and a variety of butterflies. There is a deer park, pedalo boating, a resident elephant and tall bamboo tree houses for wildlife viewing.

Nagarhole (Rajiv Gandhi) National Park → *Colour map 3, B2.*

ⓘ *Main entrance is near Hunsur on the northern side of the Park. Buses run between Hunsur and Kote-Hand Post (35 km). Indians Rs 15, foreigners Rs 150, camera Rs 10. The southern entrance is 5 km from Kabini River Lodge at Karapur.*

Nagarhole – meaning snake streams – was once the Maharajas' reserved forest and became a national park in 1955. Covering gentle hills bordering Kerala, it includes swampland, streams, moist deciduous forest, stands of bamboo and valuable timber in teak and rosewood trees. The Kabini River, which is a tributary of the Kaveri, flows through the forest where the upper canopy reaches 30 m. The park is accessible both

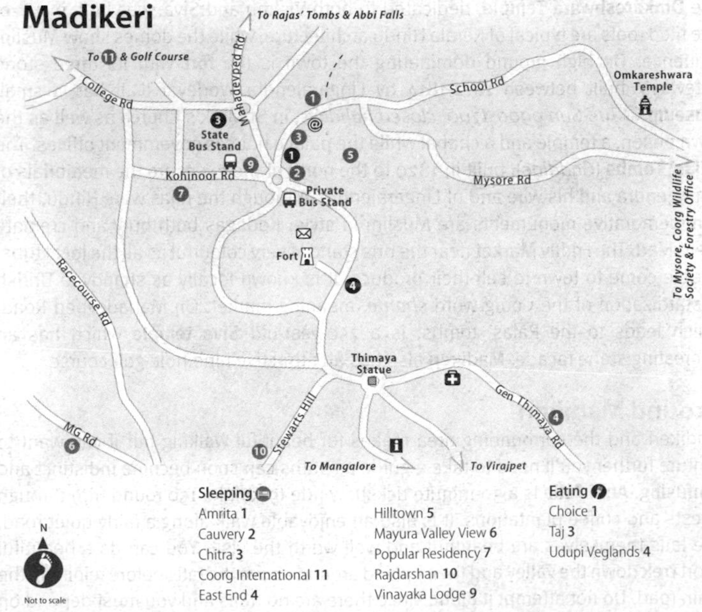

by road and river. A number of tribesmen, particularly Kurumbas (honey gatherers) who still practise ancient skills, live amongst, and care for, the elephants.

In addition to elephants, the park also has gaur (Indian bison), dhole (Indian wild dogs), wild cats, four-horned antelopes, flying squirrels, sloth bears, monkeys and sambar deer ("better sightings than at Mudumalai"). Tigers and leopards are sighted very rarely. Many varieties of birds include the rare Malabar trogon, great black woodpecker, Indian pitta, pied hornbill, whistling thrush, green imperial pigeon and also waterfowl and reptiles.

The edge of the dam between March to June during the dry period makes viewing easier. Jeeps, vans and guides are available through the Forest Department; there's a one-hour tour at 1715 with viewing from *machans* near the waterholes. Trekking is possible with permission (enquire at Hunsur office, T80-2222 52041 well in advance). You can also visit the Government's Elephant Training Camp at Haballa. Organized one-hour tours are available on 15 and 26 seater coaches, which are not very suitable for the purpose. Four-seater jeeps are far quieter.

Sleeping

Mysore *p269, map p270*
May is the most important wedding month and so hotels get booked in advance. In the expensive hotels sales tax on food, luxury tax on rooms and a service charge can increase the bill significantly. The Gandhi Square area has some Indian-style hotels which are clean and good value. JLB Rd is Jhansi Lakshmi Bai Rd, B-N Rd is Bengaluru-Nilgiri Rd.

LL-A Lalith Mahal Palace (ITDC), Narasipur Rd, Siddartha Nagar T0821-224 7047. 54 rooms (**A**) and suites (US$230-740) in the palace built in 1931 for the Maharaja's non- vegetarian, foreign guests. Regal setting near Chamundi Hill, old fashioned (some original baths with extraordinary spraying system), for nostalgia stay in the old wing, attractive pool, but avoid the below par restaurant.

B Indus Valley, near Lalith Mahal, T0821-247 3437, www.ayurindus.com. Health resort in a splendid location, halfway up a hill, 22 rooms (in main building or in cottage), hot showers and Western toilets, TV in lounge, ayurvedic massages, pleasant walks, vegetarian ayurvedic restaurant, herbal wines, friendly staff, family run.

B Kaynes Hotel, off Hunsur Rd, T0821-240 2931. 22 rooms with bath, reasonable restaurant, pool, tennis, gym.

B-C Green Hotel (Chittaranjan Palace), 2270 Vinoba Rd, Jayalakshmipuram (near Mysore University), T0821-251 2536, www.greenhotelindia.com. Princess's beautiful palace lovingly converted with strong sustainable tourism ethos: hot water from solar panels, profits to charity and staff recruited from less advantaged groups. The best of the 31 rooms are in the palace but if you stay in the cheaper, newer block you can still loll about in the huge upper lounges: excellent library, chess tables and day beds. Unique, but beyond walking distance from Mysore centre.

B-C Royal Orchid Metropole, 5 JLB Rd, T0821-252 0681, www.baljeehotels.com. After languishing in disrepair for years, the Karnataka government has resuscitated the glorious colonial Metropole building. Hopefully it will be lovely; it's also central and pristine. Prices still to be confirmed. Call to check.

C-D Mayura Hoysala (KSTDC), 2 JLB Rd, T0821-242 5349. Lovely, ochre- painted, ramshackle Raj-style hotel: full of chintzy soft furnishings, overspilling with plant pots. 20 rooms, en suite bathrooms have both Western and squat loos, tiny whitewashed cane stools are propped up on terracing along with mismatched 1970s furniture. 3 restaurants, bar, tourist desk.

C-E Bombay Tiffany's, 313 Sayyaji Rao Rd, T0821-243 5255, bombaytiffanys@yahoo.co.in. Affable owner in hotel with 54 rooms, 12 a/c in new hotel, clean and in mint condition, if a little plasticky and gilt. The regular rooms are spartan, but the de luxe and a/c ones are very good value.

For an explanation of the sleeping and eating price codes used in this guide, see inside the front cover. Other relevant information is found in Essentials pages 40-44.

D Hotel Ritz, Bengaluru-Nilgiri Rd near Central Bus Station, T0821-242 2668, hotelritz@rediffmail.com. Bags of character in this 60-year-old house and garden set back from the busy road. 4 rooms with wooden furniture off cool communal area with TV, dining table and chairs. Pleasant open shaded courtyard. A legendary budget option of backpacker folklore so book ahead.
D-E Mysore Dasaprakash, Gandhi Sq, T0821-244 3456, www.hoteldasaprakash@sancharnet.in. Holds 144 rooms in its labyrinthine blue-white complex set around an attractive, large courtyard. Milk coffee-coloured rooms are stocked with wood furniture and scrupulously clean white sheets. Peaceful and quiet despite being slap bang in the centre.
D-E Siddharta, 73/1 Guest House Rd, Nazarabad, T0821-252 2888, www.siddhartagroup.com. 105 rooms, some a/c, huge with baths, good restaurant (Indian vegetarian), exchange, immaculate, well run.
F Greens' Boarding and Lodging, 2722/2 Curzon Park Rd, T0821-242 2415. Dark hallways give onto these green gloss-painted rooms with dark wood furniture. Cool, spacious, central and darn cheap, but bathrooms are not the best.
F Park Lane, 2720 Sri Harsha Rd, T0821-243 0400, parklanemysore@yahoo.com. 8 quirky, higgledy-piggledy rooms packed with shelving units, shared corridor/terrace area with wicker chairs. The noise, including nightly classical Indian performances, from popular downstairs restaurant does travel; closing time is 2330. Restaurant opens 1030.

Srirangapatnam *p273, map p274*
C Fort View Resort, T08236-252777. 12 upmarket rooms (4 with corner tub), Rajasthani architecture, huge beds, shady landscaped gardens, gloomy restaurant (pricey), organic kitchen garden, pool, boating, fishing, efficient.
D Mayura River View, Mysore Rd, T08236-252114. Beautifully situated on the river (has crocs!) with 8 comfortable rooms, sit-outs, 2 a/c, good vegetarian restaurant (Indian, Chinese), most relaxing, really quiet.
D-E Balaji Garden Resort, Mysore Rd (1 km from Piriyapatna Bridge), T08236-253297. 12 good-value cottages and 28 smallish rooms built with some style around a central courtyard, well furnished, tiled and comfy, cottages are good value, swimming pool, restaurant.
F PWD Rest House, charming former residence of George Harris. Basic rooms (Rs 50), but clean and quiet. Book ahead at PWD office near Ranganathaswami Temple, T08236-252051.

Biligiri Rangaswamy Wildlife Sanctuary *p275*
B K Gudi Camp, Kyathadevara, book via Jungle Lodges, T080-2559 7025, www.junglelodges.com. 8 twin-bedded quality tents with modern toilets, simple meals in the open air or 4 rooms with 4 beds at royal hunting lodge, elephant ride, birding, trekking, comfortable experience despite remoteness.

Bandipur National Park *p276*
Reserve rooms in advance; avoid weekends.
LL Bush Betta Wildlife Resort, 5 km from entrance. 2 dirty jungle huts, lacks staff, highly overpriced (foreigners pay double, US$200).
B-C Tusker Trails, Mangla Village, 3 km from Bandipur campus. 6 rustic cottages with verandahs around pool with good views, bamboo hut on stilts, nearby 'dam' attracts wildlife, includes meals, entry and park rides. Foreigners pay double.
D Jungle Trails, outside the park. A small guest house owned by wildlife enthusiast, simple meals, wildlife viewing from netted porch and *machans* on riverside.
E Mayura Prakruti (KSTDC), at Melkamanahalli nearby, T08229-233001. Simple rooms in cottages and restaurant under shady trees.
F Venuvihar Lodge, in beautiful Gopalaswamy Hills (20 km). Meals available but take provisions. Book in advance through Forest Department, Woodyard, Mysore, T0821-248 0110.

Madikeri *p277, map p278*
Power cuts are common. Carry a torch, keep candles handy. Book early during holidays.
B Coorg International, Convent Rd, T08272-228071. Overpriced, 27 large, comfortable rooms, poor restaurant, pool, tours, trekking.
C Capitol Village, 5 km from town. 13 large, airy rooms, dorm (Rs 150), traditional Keralan building (tiled roof, wooden beams) set in a coffee, cardamom and pepper estate, very

quiet, outdoor eating under shady trees (Rs 75-150), rickshaw from centre Rs 40. Book 10 days in advance through **Hotel Cauvery**.

C-D Rajdarshan,116/2 MG Rd, T08272-229142, hrdij@vsnl.net. 25 well laid-out, clean rooms (need renovating), excellent restaurant, friendly staff, modern, with views over town.

D-E Cauvery, School Rd, T08272-225492. 26 clean, pleasant but basic rooms with fans, Indian meals, bar, away from main road. Helpful management, information on trekking (stores luggage).

D-E Hilltown, Daswal Rd, T08272-223801, hilltown@rediffmail.com. 38 modern, pleasant and airy rooms with TV in new hotel, marble-floored throughout, restaurant, great value. Highly recommended.

D-E Popular Residency, Kohinoor Rd. 10 clean and pleasant rooms in new hotel, well fitted out, North Indian vegetarian restaurant, good value.

E Amrita, T08272-223607. Resembling something out of a Spanish soap opera, clean rooms with bath, restaurant and eager to please staff.

E Chitra, School Rd, near bus stand, T08272-225372. Simple but clean, 31 nondescript rooms with Western toilets, hot shower, North Indian vegetarian restaurant, bar, helpful and knowledgeable English-speaking trekking guide (Mr Muktar).

E East End, Gen Thimaya Rd, T08272-229996. Darkish rooms but good restaurant, serves excellent dosas.

E Mayura Valley View (KSTDC), Raja's Seat, T08272-228387, or book at Karnataka Tourism, Bengaluru (Bangalore), T080-2221 2901. Perched on clifftop, stunning views over town especially at sunset and across rolling forests, 25 rooms but sadly very run down and half deserted.

E-F Vinayaka Lodge, 25 m from bus stand, T08272-229830. Good value 50 rooms with bath, hot water buckets, friendly staff, clean, quiet (bus stand can be noisy early morning).

Around Madikeri *p277*

D-E Cauvery Nisargadhama, Nisargadhama, contact Forestry Office, Madikeri, T08272-26308. Built largely of bamboo/teak, 8 simple cottages, some with balconies on stilts over the water, electricity (no fan), hot water, peaceful (despite nocturnal rats), but poor food.

D-E Palace Estate, 2 km south of Kakkabe along Palace Rd, T08272-238446 (rickshaw from Kakkabe Rs 35). A small, traditional farm growing coffee, pepper, cardamom and bananas lying just above the late 18th-century Nalnad Palace, a summer hunting lodge of the kings of Coorg. 6 basic rooms with shared veranda looking across 180° of forested hills all the way to Madikeri. Isolated and an excellent base for walking; Coorg's highest peak is 6 km from the homestay. Home-cooked local food, English-speaking guide Rs 150.

D-F Honey Valley Estate, Yavakapadi, Kakkabe, 3 km up a track only a jeep can manage, T08272-38339, honeyvalley_2001 @yahoo.com. This place has less stunning views than **Palace Estate** (the house is screened by tall trees) but equally good access by foot to trekking trails. Facilities are mostly better and it can fit over 30 guests, charming host family too. Also has a hut 2 km into the forest for those wanting more isolation.

Nagarhole *p278*

From Sep-Jun:

AL-A Kabini River Lodges (Karnataka Tourism), at Karapur on reservoir bank. 14 rooms in Mysore Maharajas' 18th-century hunting lodge and bungalow, 6 newer cabins overlooking lake, 5 tents, simple but acceptable, good restaurant, bar, exchange, package includes meals, sailing, rides in buffalo-hide coracles on the Kaveri, jeep/minibus at Nagarhole and Murkal complex, park tour with naturalist, very friendly and well run. Foreigners pay double. Book via **Jungle Lodges**, T080-2559 7025, www.junglelodges.com, or **Clipper Holidays**, T080-2559 2043, clipper@bangalore.wipro.net.in.

AL-A Waterwoods, 500 m away, surrounded by the Kabini river, T08228-244421. Exquisitely furnished ranch-style house, 6 luxury rooms with sit-outs, beautiful gardens on water's edge, delicious home cooking, solar power, friendly staff, boating, jeep, ayurvedic massage, gym, swimming, walking, charming, informal atmosphere, peaceful, secluded. Highly recommended.

A Jungle Inn, Veeranahosahalli, T08222-246 022, contact via **Hammock Leisure Holidays**, Bengaluru (Bangalore), T080-2530 7963.

Colonial-style lodge, 7 well-appointed rooms, 3 dorms, meals, boating, elephant rides. Forest Department Rest Houses in the Park: **B Gangotri**, book at least 15 days in advance on T0821-248 0901. 3 rooms with bath, simple but comfortable, dorm beds (Rs 40), services of cook.

Eating

Mysore *p269, map p270*

TTT Green, atmospheric, with food served in the palace itself, on a veranda, or under the stars in the hotel's immaculate garden. But not the best food.

TTT Ramanashree Comfort's Om Shanti, in hotel. Pure vegetarian either with/without a/c, thronged with domestic tourists, which is a fair reflection of its culinary prowess.

TT King's Court hotel, MG Sq, Mysore Memories and outdoor Raintree BBQ restaurants are popular.

TT Park Lane hotel. Red lights hang from the creeper-covered trellis over this courtyard restaurant: turn them on for service. Superb classical music played every evening 1900-2130, good food, including barbecue nights. Popular, lively and idiosyncratic.

TT Shanghai, Vinoba Rd. Superb Chinese despite shabby interior. 1100-1500, 1830-2300.

TT Shilpashri, Gandhi Sq. Comfortable rooftop, reasonably priced, tourist orientated, chilled beers, friendly but service can be slow.

TT Siddharta hotel, great South Indian but in crowded non-a/c room facing car park.

T Amaravathi (Roopa's), Hardinge Circle. Excellent, spicy hot Andhra meals served on banana leaves.

T Dasaprakash Hotel, good breakfast, huge southern thali (Rs 25).

T Ganesh opposite central bus stand. Great dosas, sweets.

T Jewel Rock, **Maurya Palace**, Sri Harsha Rd. Dark interior, great chicken tikka, spicy cashew nut chicken, go early to avoid queues.

T Mylari, **Hotel Mahadeshwara**, Nazarbad Main Rd (ask rickshaw driver). The best dosas in town served on a palm leaf, mornings until 1100, basic surroundings, may have to queue. Biriyanis also legendary.

T RRR, Gandhi Sq. Part a/c, tasty non-vegetarian on plantain leaves, good for lunch.

T SR Plantain Leaf (Chalukya's), Rajkamal Talkies Rd. Decent vegetarian thalis on banana leaf; also tandoori chicken.

T Samrat, next to Indra Bhavan, Dhanvantri Rd. Range of tasty North Indian vegetarian.

T Santosh, near bus station. Excellent value thalis (Rs 16).

Cafés and fast food

Bombay Tiffany's, Devraja Market Building. Try the *Mysore Pak*, a ghee-laden sweet.

Indra Café, Sayaji Rd, on fringes of market. Excellent *bhel puri*, *sev puri*, *channa puri*.

Penguin Ice-cream Parlour, comfortable sofas shared with local teens listening to Hindi pop.

Raghu Niwas, B-N Rd, opposite **Ritz**. Does very good breakfasts.

Sri Rama Veg, 397 Dhanvantri Rd. Serves fast food, good juices.

Madikeri *p277, map p278*

Capitol, near private bus stand. Despite its unpromising exterior, serves excellent vegetarian fare.

Choice, School Rd. Wide menu, very good food, choice of ground floor or rooftop.

Taj, College Rd. 'Cheap and best', clean and friendly.

Udupi Veglands, opposite fort. Lovely, clean, spacious wooden eatery, delicious and cheap vegetarian thalis.

Bars and clubs

Mysore *p269, map p270*

The best bars are in hotels: **Lalitha Mahal Palace** and **Lokranjan Mahal Palace**.

Festivals and events

Mysore *p269, map p270*

Mar-Apr: **Temple car festival** with a 15-day fair, at the picturesque town of Nanjangud, 23 km south (Erode road); **Vairamudi** festival which lasts 6 days when deities are adorned with 3 diamond crowns, at Melkote Temple, 52 km. **11 Aug**: **Feast of St Philomena**, 0800-1800, the statue of the saint is taken out in procession through the city streets ending with a service at the gothic, stained glass-laden cathedral. **End Sep-early-Oct**: **Dasara**, see box, page 271.

Shopping

Mysore *p269, map p270*

Books

Ashok, Dhanvantri Rd, T0821-243 5533. Excellent selection.

Clothing

Badshah's, 20 Devraj Urs Rd, T0821-242 9799. Beautifully finished salwar kameez. Mr Yasin speaks good English.

Craft Emporium and cloth shops in the middle part of Vinoba Rd are recommended for good selection and quality but beware those pretending to be government emporia. Competent tailors will make up and deliver within a few hours. For silks at good prices, try Sayaji Rao Rd. You can watch machine weaving at the factory shop at **Karnataka Silk Industry** on Mananthody Rd, T0821-248 1803. Mon-Sat 1030-1200, 1500-1630.

Handicrafts

Superb carved figures, sandalwood and rosewood items, silks, incense sticks, handicrafts. The main shopping area is Sayaji Rao Rd.

Cauvery Arts & Crafts Emporium, for sandalwood and rosewood items, closed Thu (non-receipt of parcel reported by traveller).

Devaraja Market, lanes of stalls selling spices, perfumes and much more; good 'antique' shop (fixed price) has excellent sandalwood and rosewood items. Worth visiting.

Ganesh, 532 Dhanvantri Rd.

Shankar, 12 Dhanvantri Rd.

Sri Lakshmi Fine Arts & Crafts (opposite the zoo) also has a factory shop at 2226 Sawday Rd, Mandi Mohalla.

Activities and tours

Mysore *p269, map p270*

Body and soul

Jois Ashtanga Yoga Research Institute, www.ayri.org. Not for dilettante yogis at Rs 8000 a month, the minimum period offered.

Sri Patanjali Yogashala, Parakala Mutt, next to Jaganmohan Palace. Ashtanga Vinyasa yoga; daily instruction in English from BNS Iyengar, 0600-0900, 1600-1900, US$100 per month: some say the conditions here are slapdash, although teaching is good.

Swimming

Mysore University, Olympic-sized pool, hourly sessions 0630-0830 then 1500-1600, women only 1600-1700.

Southern Star Mysore, 13-14 Vinoba Rd, T0821-242 1689, www.ushalexushotels.com. More of a pool to relax by and sunbathe.

Tour operators

Seagull Travels, 8 Hotel Ramanashree Complex, BN Rd, T0821-252 9732, seagulltravels@yahoo.com. Good for cars, drivers, flights, wildlife tours, etc, helpful.

Skyway International Travels, No. 370/4, Jansi Laxmibai Rd, T0821-244 4444, www.skywaytour.com.

TCI, Gandhi Sq, T0821-2443023. Very pleasant and helpful.

Tours

KSTDC, **Yatri Nivas**, 2 JLB Rd, T0821-242 3492. Mysore, daily 0715-2030, Rs115, local sights and Chamundi Hill, Kukkara Halli Lake, Somanathapura, Srirangapatnam and Brindavan Gardens. Belur, Halebid, Sravanabelagola: Tue, Wed, Fri, Sun, 0715-2200, Rs 210 (long and tiring but worth it if you are not travelling to Hassan).

Madikeri *p277, map p278*

Fishing

Coorg Wildlife Society, see page 285, arranges a licence for fishing on the Kaveri river (Rs 500 per day, Rs 1000 weekend). The highlight is the prospect of pulling in a mahseer up to 45 kg in weight; all fish to be returned to the river. At Trust Land Estate, Valnoor, near Kushalnagar, with a lodge but you'll need food. Mr Ponappa has keys to the lodge and can issue the licence. Contact Professor MB Madaiah, T0827-676443.

Trekking

Friends' Tours and Travel, below Bank of India, College Rd. Recommended for their knowledge and enthusiasm. Tailor-made treks Rs 275 per person per day including guide, food and accommodation in temples, schools, etc. A base camp is at Thalathmane, 4 km from Madikeri, which people can also stay at even if not trekking. Basic huts for Rs 50 each, home cooking nearby at little extra cost. Contact Mr Raja Shekar on T08272-29974 (1000-1930) or T08272-25672 (2100-0900). **Hotel Cauvery**, see page 281, will also arrange treks.

Transport

Mysore *p269, map p270*

Bus

Local City bus station, southeast of KR Circle, T0821-242 5819. To **Silk Weaving Centre**, Nos 1, 2, 4 and 8; **Brindavan Gardens**, No 303; **Chamundi Hill**, No 201; **Srirangapatnam**, No 313. Central Bus Station, T0821-2529853. **Bandipur**, Platform 9, **Ooty** etc, Platform 11.

Long distance There are 3 bus stations: Central, mainly for long distance SRTC, T0821-252 0853, City for local buses, and B3 Suburban and Private including Somnathpur. SRTC buses of Karnataka, Tamil Nadu and Kerala run regular daily services between Mysore and other major cities. Check timings. Many private companies near Gandhi Sq operate overnight sleepers and interstate buses which may be faster and marginally less uncomfortable. Book ahead for busy routes (eg Hassan). The bus station has a list of buses with reserved places. **Somnathpur**: few from Surburban station, which take around 1 hr direct, or longer via Bannur or via Narasipur. Several buses daily to many towns from Central bus station. **Bengaluru (Bangalore)**: every 15 mins from non-stop platform. Semi-de luxe, every 15 mins. **Coimbatore**: 0845; **Hospet**: 1930 (10 hrs), very tiring; **Salem**: 1030 (7 hrs); **Thiruvananthapuram**: Super de luxe, 14 hrs. Several to **Satyamangalam** where you can connect with buses to Tamil Nadu. The journey is through wilderness and forests with spectacular scenery as the road finally plunges from the plateau down to the plains.

Car

Travel companies and KSTDC, about Rs 500 (4 hrs/40 km) for city sightseeing; Rs 850 to include Srirangapatnam and Brindavan. KSE charges Rs 700 for Somnathpur, Srirangapatnam and Bird Sanctuary.

Train

Advance Computerized Reservations in separate section; ask for foreigners' counter. T131. Enquiries T0821-252 0103, 0800-2000 (closed 1330-1400); Sun 0800-1400. Left luggage 0600-2200, Rs 3-6 per day. Tourist Information, telephone and toilets on Platform 1. Taxi counter at entrance. To **Bengaluru (Bangalore)** (non-stop): *Tipu Exp, 6205*, 1120, 2½ hrs; *Shatabdi Exp, 2008*, daily except Tue, 1410, 2 hrs (continues to **Chennai** another 5 hrs). **Bengaluru (Bangalore)** via **Srirangapatnam**, **Mandya** and **Maddur**: *Chamundi Exp 6215*, 0645, 3 hrs; *Kaveri Chennai Exp 6221*, 1805, 2¾ hrs. **Chennai**: *Chennai Exp 6221*, 1805, 10½ hrs; *Shatabdi Exp, 2008*, not Tue, 1410, 7 hrs. **Madurai**: change at Bengaluru (Bangalore). **Mumbai**: *Sharavathi Exp, 1036*, Sat only, 0600, 26 hrs.

Srirangapatnam *p273, map p274*

Trains and buses between **Bengaluru (Bangalore)** and **Mysore** stop here but arrival can be tiresome with hassle from rickshaw drivers, traders and beggars. Buses 313 and 316 from Mysore City Bus Stand (half-hourly) take 50 mins.

Bandipur National Park *p276*

Bus

Bandipur is in Karnataka while the neighbouring park, Mudumalai, is in Tamil Nadu, but they are extensions of the same forest reserve which also stretches west to include the undeveloped Kerala reserve of Waynad. They are on the Mysore to Ooty bus route, about 2½ hrs south from Mysore and 2½ hrs from Ooty. Buses go to and from **Mysore** (80 km) between 0615-1530.

Madikeri *p277, map p278*

Auto-rickshaw

From Hotel Chitra to **Abbi Falls**, Rs 150 including 1 hr wait there.

Bus

Frequent express buses to **Bengaluru (Bangalore)** Plat 4, from 0615 (6 hrs); **Chikmagalur**; **Hassan** (3½ hrs); **Kannur**; **Mangalore**, Plat 2, 0530-2400 (3½ hrs); **Mysore** Plat 3, half-hourly 0600-2300 (3 hrs) via **Kushalnagar** (for Tibetan settlements) are very crowded during the rush hour; **Thalassery**. Daily to **Coimbatore**, **Kannur**, **Madurai** 1900, **Mumbai** 0930, **Ooty** 0730, 2030, **Virajpet**. Private Bus Stand: Kamadenu Travels above Bus Stand, T27024, for Purnima Travels bus to **Bengaluru (Bangalore)**. Shakti Motor Service to **Nagarhole** (4½ hrs); **Virajpet** .

Nisargadhama *p278*
The bus from Madikeri passes park gates 2 km before Kushalnagar. A rickshaw from Kushalnagar Rs 10.

Nagarhole *p278*
Bus
From **Mysore**, *Exp*, 3 hrs, Rs 35; **Madikeri**, 4½ hrs. **Bengaluru (Bangalore)**, 6 hrs. For **Kabini River Lodge** and **Waterworlds**, be sure to get the Karapur (not the Nagarhole) bus; Jungle lodges bus leaves Bengaluru at 0730, stops in Mysore (around 0930), reaching Kabini around 1230; return bus departs 1315. State bus from Mysore to Karapur.

Train
Nearest, Mysore (96 km). See **Bandipur**, page 276.

Directory

Mysore *p269, map p270*
Banks State Bank of Mysore, corner of Sayaji Rao Rd and Sardar Patel Rd and opposite GPO in city centre. **LKP Forex**, near Clock Tower. **Internet** Coca Cola Cyber Space, 2 Madvesha Complex, Nazarabad, near Sri Harsha Rd. **Cyber Net Corner**, 2/3B Indira Bhavan, Dhanvantri Rd. **Mysore I-Way**, has a branch near Green Hotel and the Jois yoga shala at 2996/1A 1st Floor, Kalidasa Rd, VV Mohalla, T0821-251 0467. **Pal Net**, Nehru Circle. Avoid **Internet World** near Ritz. **Hospitals** KR Hospital, T0821-244 3300; **Medical College**, corner of Irwin and Sayaji Rao Rd; **Mission Hospital** (Mary Holdsworth), Tilaknagar, in a striking building dating from 1906. **Post** GPO, on corner of Ashoka and Irwin roads; Poste Restante here. **Useful addresses** Forest Office, and **Project Tiger**, Forest Department, Woodyard, Ashokpuram, T0821-480110 (City Bus No 61).

Madikeri *p277, map p278*
Banks Canara Bank, Main Rd, accepts some TCs and Visa. **Internet** Cyber Zone, next to Chitra Hotel. Rs 30 per hr, excellent. **Post** Behind Private Bus Stand. **Useful addresses** Community Centre, south of Fort, Main Rd, holds occasional shows. **Coorg Wildlife Society**, 2 km from GT Circle along Mysore Rd, then 1 km to left, T08272-223505. **Forestry Office**, Aranya Bhavan, Mysore Rd, 3 km from town, T08272-225708.

Western Plateau

The world's tallest monolith, of the Jain saint Gommateshwara, has stood majestic, 'skyclad' and lost in meditation high on Sravanabelagola's Indragiri hill since the 10th century. It is a profoundly spiritual spot, encircled by long sweeps of paddy and sugar cane plains, and is one of the most popular pilgrimage points for practitioners of the austere Jain religion. Some male Jain followers of the Digambar or skyclad sect of the faith climb the rock naked to denote their freedom from material bonds. Nearby lie the 11th and 12th century capital cities of Halebid and Belur, the apex of Hoysala temple architecture whose walls are cut into friezes of the most intricate soapstone. These villages of the Central Maiden sit in the path of one of the main routes for trade and military movement for centuries. ▸▸ *For Sleeping, Eating and other listings, see pages 289-292.*

Western Plateau Temples ▸▸ *pp289-292.*

Sravanabelagola, Belur and Halebid can all be seen in a very long day from Bengaluru (Bangalore), but it's far better to stay overnight in one of the cities or Hassan. There are direct buses from Mysore and Bengaluru.

Hassan → *Phone code: 08172. Colour map 3, A2. Population: 117,400.*

This pleasant, busy and fast-developing little town is the obvious overnight base for visits to Belur and Halebid. Buses pull in at the centre and most hotels are within a short walking distance. The railway station is 2 km to the east.

In the town itself is the **Bhandari basti** (1159 and added to later), about 200 m to the left from the path leading up to the Gommateshwara statue. Inside are 24 images of Tirthankaras in a spacious sanctuary. There are 500 rock-cut steps to the top of the hill that take half an hour to climb. It is safe to leave luggage at the tourist office branch at the entrance, which closes 1300-1415. The **tourist office** ⓘ *Vartha Bhavan, BM Rd, T08172-268862*, is very helpful.

There are 14 shrines on **Chandragiri** and the Mauryan emperor **Chandragupta**, who is believed by some to have become a Jain and left his empire to fast and meditate, is buried here. The temples are all in the Dravidian style, the Chamundaraya Basti, built in AD 982 being one of the most remarkable. There is a good example of a free-standing pillar or *mana-stambha* in front of the *Parsvanathasvami Basti*. These pillars, sometimes as high as 15 m, were placed at the temple entrance. Here, the stepped base with a square cross-section transforms to a circular section and the column is then topped by a capital.

Belur → *Phone code: 08177. Colour map 3, A2.*

Belur, on the banks of the Yagachi River, was the Hoysala dynasty's first capital and continues to be a significant town that is fascinating to explore. The gloriously elaborate Krishna Chennakesavara temple was built over the course of a century from 1116 as a fitting celebration of the victory over the Cholas at Talakad.

The temples ⓘ *close at 2030, searchlight for interiors Rs 10; carry a torch, ASI trained guides onsite (often excellent), Rs 60-75 for 4 visitors, though official rate is higher.*

At first glance **Chennakesava Temple** (see also Somnathpur page 275) appears unimpressive because the superstructure has been lost. However, exquisite sculptures cover the exterior with friezes. A line of 644 elephants (each different) surrounds the base, with rows of figures and foliage above. The detail of the 38 female figures is perfect. Look at the young musicians and dancers on either side of

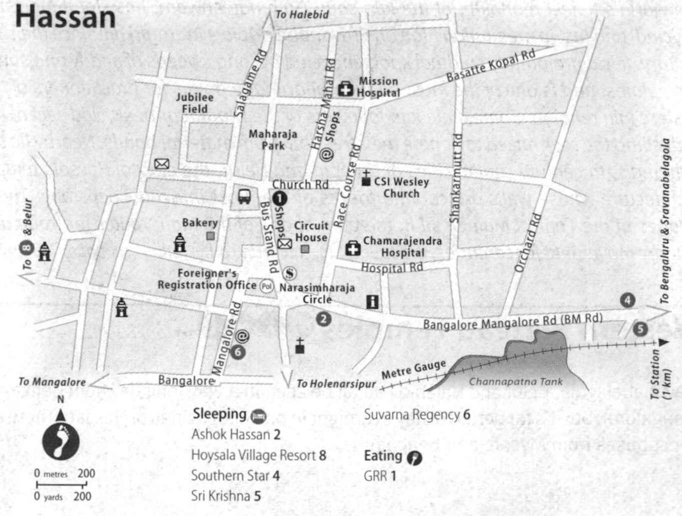

Small is beautiful: the temples of Belur and Halebid

The Hoysalas, whose kingdom stretched between the Krishna and Kaveri rivers, encouraged competition among their artisans; their works even bear 12th-century autographs. Steatite meant that sculptors could fashion doily-like detail from solid rock since it is relatively soft when fresh from the quarry but hardens on exposure to air. The temples, built as prayers for victory in battle, are small but superbly conceived.

the main door and the unusual perforated screens between the columns. Ten have typical bold geometrical patterns while the other 10 depict scenes from the *Puranas* in their tracery. Inside superb carving decorates the hand lathe-turned pillars and the bracket-figures on the ceiling. Each stunning filigree pillar is startlingly different in design, a symptom of the intensely competitive climate the sculptors of the day were working in. The **Narasimha pillar** at the centre of the hall is particularly fine and originally could be rotated. The detail is astounding. The jewellery on the figures is hollow and movable and the droplets of water seem to hang at the ends of the dancer's wet hair on a bracket above you. On the platform in front of the shrine is Santalesvara dancing in homage to Lord Krishna. The shrine holds a 3-m-high black polished deity, occasionally opened for *darshan*. The annual **Car Festival** is held in March-April. To the west is the **Viranarayana Temple** with some fine sculpture and smaller shrines around it. The complex is walled with an ambulatory. The entrance is guarded by the winged figure of Garuda, Vishnu's carrier, who faces the temple with joined palms.

Halebid

The ancient capital of the Hoysala Empire was founded in the early 11th century as *Dvarasamudra*. It was destroyed by the armies of the Delhi Sultanate in 1311 and 1327. The great Hoysalesvara Temple, still incomplete after the best part of a century's toil, survived but the capital lay deserted and came to be called Halebid (ruined village), a name it continues to live up to.

Detour 1 km south to walk around the Basthalli garden filled with remarkably simple 12th-century Jain Bastis. These have lathe-turned and multi-faceted columns, dark interiors and carved ceilings. The smaller **Kedaresvara Temple** with some highly polished columns is on a road going south. There are cycles for hourly hire to visit these quieter sites.

The **Hoysalesvara Temple** set in lawns has two shrines dedicated to *Siva* with a *Nandi* bull facing each. The largest of the Hoysala temples, it was started in 1121 but remains unfinished. It is similar in structure to Belur's, but its superstructure was never completed. Belur's real treats are in its interiors, while Halebid's are found on the outside reliefs. Six bands circle the star-shaped temple, elephants, lions, horsemen, a floral scroll and stories from the epics and the Bhagavata Purana. This frieze relates incidents from the *Ramayana* and *Mahabharata*; among them Krishna lifting Mount Govardhana and Rama defeating the demon god Ravana. The friezes above show *yalis* and *hamsa* or geese. There are exceptional half life-size deities with minute details at intervals. Of the original 84 female figures (like the ones at Belur) only 14 remain; thieves have made off with 70 down the centuries.

India's 11th prime minister, Haradanahalli Dodde Deve Gowda, hailed from Hassan district, a factor, some say, in the levels of development funnelled into the town after his brief tenure of office in 1996-1997.

The **Archaeological Museum** ⓘ *Sat-Thu 1000-1700, Rs 2, no photography*, is on the lawn near the south entrance where the Archaeological Survey of India maintains a gallery of 12th-13th-century sculptures, wood carvings, idols, coins and inscriptions. Some sculptures are displayed outside. To the west is a small lake.

Sravanabelagola (Shravanabelgola) → *Phone code: 08176*

The ancient Jain statue of Gommateshwara stands on Vindhyagiri hill (sometimes known as Indrabetta or Indragiri) which is 150 m above the plain; Chandragiri to the north (also known as Chikka Betta) is just under half that height. The 17-m-high Gommateshwara statue, erected somewhere between AD 980 and 983, is of the enlightened prince Bahubali, son of the first Tirthankara (or holy Jain teacher). The prince won a fierce war of succession over his brother, Bharata, only to surrender his rights to the kingdom to take up a life of meditation.

You'll have to clamber barefoot up over 700 hot steep granite steps that carve up the hill to reach the statue from the village tank (socks – sold onsite – offer good insulation from the boiling stone; carry your own water), or charter a *dhooli*, a cane chair tied between two poles and carried, to let four bearers do the work for you. The small, intricately-carved shrines you pass on the way up are the **Odeagal Basti**, the **Brahmadeva Mandapa**, the **Akhanda Bagilu** and the **Siddhara Basti**, all 12th-century except the Brahmadeva Mandapa which is 200 years older.

The carved statue is nude (possibly as he is a *Digambara* or 'sky-clad' Jain) and captures the tranquillity typical of much Buddhist and Jain art. The depth of the saint's meditation and withdrawal from the world is suggested by the spiralling creepers shown growing up his legs and arms, and by the ant hills and snakes at his feet. Although the features are finely carved, the overall proportions are odd: he has huge shoulders and elongated arms but stumpy legs.

The 'magnificent anointment' – or *Mastakabhisheka* – falls every 12th year when Jain pilgrims flock from across India to bid for 1008 pots – or *kalashas* – of holy water that are left overnight at the saint's feet. The next morning their contents, followed with ghee, milk, coconut water, turmeric paste, honey, vermilion powder and even a dusting of gold, are poured over the saint's head from specially erected scaffolding. Unusually for India, the thousands of devotees watching the event do so in complete silence. The next celebration is in 2012.

Chikmagalur

Situated northeast of Belur, Chikmagalur means younger daughter's town and according to legend it was the dowry for the younger daughter of a local chieftain. In addition to the Hoysala-style **Kodandarama Temple** there are mosques, the moated fort and the St Joseph's Roman Catholic Cathedral. The town is at the centre of one of India's major coffee growing areas. Coffee was first grown in the Baba Budan Hills, just to the north, in 1670. The Central Coffee Research Institute was set up in 1925.

Jog Falls → *Colour map 3, A2.*

These falls are a spectacular sight in the wet season and the best time to visit is late November to early January. The 50 km-long **Hirebhasgar Reservoir** now regulates the flow of the Sharavati River in order to generate hydroelectricity. The Mysore Power Corporation releases water to the falls every second Sunday from 1000 to 1800. Often during the monsoon the falls are shrouded in mist. Leeches are a hazard if you walk down to the base of the falls. In the dry season the water is often reduced to a trickle.

There are four falls. The highest is the **Raja**, with a fall of 250 m and a pool below 40 m deep. Next is the **Roarer**, while a short distance to the south is the **Rocket**, which spurts great shafts of water out into the air. In contrast the **Rani** (once called the White Lady) cascades over the rocks. The walk to the bottom of the falls is well worthwhile for the fit. A walk to the top (not in the monsoons) offering breathtaking views of the cascading river and the valley, is highly recommended. The Inspection Bungalow has excellent views.

Central Maidan » *pp290-291. Colour map 3, A3.*

Chitradurga

At the foot of a group of granite hills rising to 1175 m in the south, is Chitradurga, 202 km northwest of Bengaluru (Bangalore). The **Fort of Seven Rounds** ⓘ *open sunrise to sunset, closed public holidays, Rs 100, allow 2 hrs, 2 km from bus stand, 4 km from railway station*, was built in the 17th century by Nayak Poligars, semi- independent landlords who fled south after the collapse of the Vijayanagar Empire in 1565. They were crushed by Haidar Ali in 1779 who replaced the Nayaka's mud fort with stone and Tipu Sultan built a palace, mosque, granaries and oil pits in it. There are four secret entrances in addition to the 19 gateways and ingenious water tanks which collected rainwater. There are also 14 temples, including a cave temple to the west of the wall. They are placed in an extraordinary jumble of granite outcrops, a similar setting to that of Hampi 300 km to the north. The Hidimbeshwara temple is the oldest temple on the site.

Belgaum → *Phone code: 0831. Colour map 1, C4. Population: 399,600.*

An important border town, Belgaum makes an interesting stop on the Mumbai-Bengaluru (Bangalore) road or as a trip from Goa. The crowded market in the centre gives a glimpse of India untouched by tourism. With its strategic position in the Deccan plateau, the town had been ruled by many dynasties including the Chalukyas, Rattas, Vijaynagaras, Bahmanis and the Marathas. Most of the monuments date from the early 13th century. The **fort**, immediately east of the town centre, though originally pre-Muslim, was rebuilt by Yusuf Adil Shah, the Sultan of Bijapur, in 1481. Inside the **Masjid-i-Sata** (1519), the best of the numerous mosques in Belgaum, was built by a captain in the Bijapur army, Azad Khan. Belgaum is also noted for its Jain architecture and sculpture. The late Chalukyan **Kamala Basti**, with typical beautifully lathe-turned pillars and a black stone Neminatha sculpture, stands within the fort walls. To the south of the fort and about 800 m north of the **Hotel Sanman** on the Mumbai-Bengaluru (Bangalore) bypass, is a beautifully sculpted Jain temple which, according to an inscription, was built by Malikaryuna.

Sleeping

All hotels in Belur, Halebid and Sravanabelagola have only basic facilities, but compensate by allowing you to see these rural towns and villages and their stunning sites before or after the tour groups. Due to the height of the climb, Sravanabelagola particularly benefits from an early start. Hassan and Chikmagalur are the alternatives if you don't want to compromise on comfort.

Hassan *p286, map p286*

A Hoysala Village Resort, Belur Rd, T08172-256764, www.trailsindia.com. 33 big cottage rooms with hot water, TV, tea and coffee maker and fan spread out across landscaped resort 6 km from Hassan. Rustic, with small handicraft shops, good restaurant, very attentive service, good swimming pool.

A-B The Ashhok Hassan (ITDC), BM Rd, 500 m from bus stand, T08172-268731, www.hassanashok.com. Dramatic renovation creating 36 lovely rooms in immaculate, soundproofed central Hassan hotel. It's all been done on clean lines, with modern art. Charming suites have big rattan armchairs. Excellent service. Tidy garden

For an explanation of the sleeping and eating price codes used in this guide, see inside the front cover. Other relevant information is found in Essentials pages 40-44.

grounds, where construction of a pool was underway in 2007. Wi-Fi, a/c, TV. The Hoysaleshara suite has its own dining room, bar and steam bath (**AL**).

B Hotel Southern Star, BM Rd, T08172-251816, www.ushalexushotels. Large modern hotel with 48 excellent a/c rooms, newly renovated in 2007, hot water, phone, satellite TV, great views across town and countryside, excellent service.

C-E Hotel Suvarna Regency, 97 BM Rd (500 m south of bus stand) T08172-264006, www.hotelsuvarnaregency.com. 70 clean and big rooms, some with bath, a/c a bit musty but de luxe and suite rooms are spic and span, good vegetarian restaurant, car hire. Very helpful, efficient, excellent value. Also has 6 bed, 4 bed and triples.

E Hotel Sri Krishna, BM Rd, T08172-263240. 40 rooms with hot water 0600-1000, TV, some with a/c, also double bed twin suites for 4 and dorm for 10. Busy South Indian restaurant with plaintain leaf service, car hire. Good value.

Belur *p286*

E Mayura Velapuri (KSTDC), Temple Rd, T08177-222209. Reasonably clean and spacious 6 doubles, 4 triples and 2 dorms sleeping 20 (Rs 75 per person), hot water, with fan, TV and sitting areas. Friendly staff. Good South Indian meals in restaurant.

F Vishnu Regency, Main Rd, T08177-223011, vishnuregency_belur@yahoo.co.in. 20 adequate clean rooms opening onto an enclosed courtyard, some with TV, fan, hot water in the morning, in a welcoming hotel with shop and good vegetarian restaurant serving tandoor, curries and thalis.

Halebid *p287*

G Mayura Shantala (KSTDC), T08177-273224. Inspection Bungalow compound in nice garden overlooking temple. 4 twin-bed tiled rooms with fan, nets and bath, limited kitchen.

Sravanabelagola *p288*

E Karnataka Bhavan, reserve at Karnataka Tourism, 9 St Mark's Rd, Bengaluru (Bangalore), T08176-257 9139. 50 rooms.

G Vidyananda Nilaya Dharamshala, closest to the bus stand, reserve through SDJMI Committee. Rooms with toilet and fan, bucket shower, blanket but no sheets, courtyard, good value at Rs 60.

G Yatri Niwas (SDJMI), large rooms, good attached baths, clean (Rs 160).

Chikmagalur *p288*

A-B Taj Garden Retreat, outside town, on a hillside, T08262-220202, www.tajhotels.com. 29 luxury a/c rooms lined along the pool, good for visiting Belur and Halebid (40 km).

Jog Falls *p288*

Hotels are very basic and there are no eating facilities available at night. Local families take in guests. Stalls near the falls serve reasonable breakfast and meals during the day.

F-G Mayura Gerusoppa (KSTDC), Sagar Taluk, T08186-244732. 10 rooms.

G Youth Hostel, Shimoga Rd. T08186-244251 Empty rooms (no beds), some dorm beds with dirty bedding.

Chitradurga *p289*

C-D Amogha International, Santhe Honda Rd, T08194-220762. Clean, spacious, modern rooms, some a/c suites, 2 restaurants, good vegetarian but service slow. Best in town.

F Maurya, Santhe Bagilu (within city walls), T08194-224448. 12 acceptable rooms, bit noisy.

Belgaum *p289*

C-D Adarsha Palace, College Rd, T0831-243 5777. Small, modern and personal, some a/c rooms, excellent **Angaan** vegetarian restaurant (rooftop non-vegetarian), good value, pleasant atmosphere, friendly staff. Recommended.

C-D Sanman Deluxe, College St, T0831-243 0777. Similar to **Adarsha Palace**, in a new building (much cheaper in old **Sanman**), 2 restaurants.

D Milan, Club Rd (4 km railway), T0831-247 0555. Good value, 45 rooms with bath (hot shower), some a/c, vegetarian restaurant.

D-E Keerthi, Poona-Bengaluru Rd, short walk from Central Bus Stand, T0831-246699. Large modern hotel, some a/c rooms, restaurant.

E-F Sheetal, Khade Bazar near bus station, T0831-247 0222. Clean-ish rooms with bath (prices vary), vegetarian restaurant, Indian style, noisy hotel in busy and quite entertaining bazar street.

F Mayura Malaprabha (KSTDC), Ashok Nagar, T0831-247 0781. 6 simple clean rooms in modern cottages, dorm (Rs 40), restaurant, bar, tourist office.

Eating

Hassan *p286, map p286*
There's not much here. The vegetarian restaurant and multicuisine **Suvarna Gate** at **Hotel Suvarna Regency** are the best in town, but the restaurant at **Hotel Sri Krisha** is popular, while the restaurants attached to **Hassan Ashhok, Hoysala Village** and **Southern Star** are best for those worried about hygiene.
GRR, opposite bus stand. For non vegetarian food and friendly staff.

Belur *p286*
This sizeable town has numerous tea shops and vegetarian stands, and **Vishnu Hotel** has the best tourist restaurant.

Transport

Hassan *p286, map p286*
Bus
For local buses, T08172-268418. Long-distance buses at least hourly to **Belur** from about 0700 (35 km, 1 hr) and **Halebid** from about 0800 (31 km, 1 hr); all crowded. Few direct to **Sravanabelagola** in the morning (1 hr); alternatively, travel to Channarayapatna and change to bus for Sravanabelagola. Also to **Bengaluru (Bangalore)** every 30 mins (4½ hrs), **Goa** (14 hrs), **Hampi, Mangalore** (5 hrs), **Mysore** hourly (3 hrs). You can reserve seats for the 0730 depart to **Hospet** (9 hrs).

Taxi
Cauvery Tourist Centre, Race Course Rd, T08172-268026. Private Tourist Taxis and tongas available.

Train
Railway Station is 2 km east of centre. New broad gauge line is now running. **Arsikere**: 1050, 2100, 1 hr. **Mysore**: 0605, 1830, 3 hrs.

Belur *p286*
Bus
The bus stand is about 1 km from the temples. Half-hourly to **Hassan** (1 hr; last at 2030); to **Halebid** (30 mins). To **Shimoga** for **Hampi** and **Jog Falls** (4 hrs), 0800, 0845 (check at bus stand); to **Mysore** (1½ hrs).

Halebid *p287*
Bus
The bus stand is near the temples. KSRTC buses, half-hourly to Hassan (45 mins) and on to **Bengaluru, Mangalore, Mysore**. Also direct to **Belur** (12 km, 1 hr) and on to Hassan.

Sravanabelagola *p288*
Bus
Direct buses to/from **Mysore** and **Bengaluru (Bangalore)** run in the morning; in the afternoon, change at Channarayapatna. The morning express buses to/from Mysore serve small villages travelling over dusty, though interesting, roads up to Krishnarajapet; very few stops between there and Mysore.

Jog Falls *p288*
Bus
Buses to/from **Karwar** daily, arriving evening, and leaving Jog in the morning. Also to: **Sagar, Shimoga** for **Belur** or **Hassan** (4 hrs), **Sirsi** (2 hrs). A new road connects Honavar with Jog. **Goa**: (8 hrs) 1100 bus to **Colva** is very crowded, on the 2300 bus it's easier to get a seat.

Taxi
To **Panaji**, Rs 1500 (6 hrs).

Train
Jog is 16 km from the railway at **Talguppa**. For **Bengaluru** change at **Shimoga**.

Chitradurga *p289*
Bus
Buses to/from **Bengaluru (Bangalore), Davangere, Hospet, Hubli** and **Mysore**. Train from **Arsikere, Bengaluru, Guntakal, Hubli**.

Belgaum *p289*
Bus
Central Bus Stand for long-distance services. **Panaji** (0600-1715), **Margao** (0545- 1500), **Mapusa** (0715-1715) take 5 hrs, Rs 45.

Train
The station is near the bus stand, 4 km south of centre; autos available. **Bengaluru**: *Ranichennamma Exp, 6590*, 1810, 13 hrs. **Mumbai (CST) and Pune**: change at Pune for Mumbai *Chalukya/Sharavathi Exp, 1018/1036*, Mon, Tue, Fri, Sat, 1805, 14 hrs. **Goa via Londa**: 8 trains daily, 0135-2030, 1 hr.

Directory

Hassan *p286, map p286*
Banks State Bank of Mysore and State Bank of India, Narasimharaja Circle, change US dollars, pounds sterling and TCs. **Internet** next to Suvarna and Vaishnavi hotels. **Hospitals** General Hospital, Hospital Rd, **Mission Hospital**, Race Course Rd. **Post** 100 m from bus stand.

West coast

Poor transport has made Karnataka's sapphire coast to Goa one of the least travelled scenic routes in India. This is now changing and the state government is trying to draw tourists to its sands. The Western Ghats are never far away, while the road and the Konkan railway frequently skirt the Arabian Sea in the north passing some magnificent beaches. The hilly port town of Mangalore makes a pleasant, relaxing stop between Goa and Kerala but the jewel in the Sapphire Coast's crown, thus far, is undoubtedly Gokarna: a hippy stronghold, mass pilgrimage site and tremendously sacred Hindu centre. It's little more than one narrow street lined with traditional wooden houses and temples, but it is packed with pilgrims and has been adopted, along with Hampi, by the Goa overspill: people lured by spirituality and the beautiful, auspicious-shaped Om beach. No-frills hammocks and beach huts of yore have now been joined by the snazzy, eco-conscious Keralite hotel group CGH Earth's well-regarded boutique yoga hotel, based on the Bihar school. » *For Sleeping, Eating and other listings, see pages 297-299.*

Mangalore » *pp297-299. Colour map 3, A2.*

→ *Phone code: 0824. Population: 328,700.*

Capital of South Kanara District, and rarely visited by Western tourists, Mangalore does in fact offer some interesting churches and decent accommodation and so is worth bearing in mind, if only as a stopping point. Once a shipbuilding centre (during Hyder Ali's time) it is now a major port for export of coffee spices and cashew nuts.

Ins and outs

Getting there Bajpe airport is 22 km from town. The Konkan railway has trains from Goa and Mumbai while the old broad gauge goes down the coast to Kozhikode and then inland to Coimbatore. The new Kankanadi station is 6 km northeast of the City station that is just south of the centre at Hampankatta. The KSRTC Bus Station is 3 km north of the private bus stand in the busy town centre.
Getting around Although the centre is compact enough to be covered on foot, autos are handy but may refuse to use their meters. » *See Transport, page 298, f or further details.*
Tourist information ⓘ *Hotel Nalapauds, Lighthouse Rd, Hampankatta, T0824-244 2926*. Helpful, friendly, if limited, tourist information.

Sights

St Aloysius College Chapel ⓘ *Lighthouse Hill, 0830-1000, 1200-1430, 1530-1800*, has remarkable 19th-century frescoes painted by the Italian-trained Jesuit priest Moscheni, which cover the walls and ceilings in a profusion of scenes. The town has a sizeable Roman Catholic population (about 20%).

The tile-roofed low structure of the 10th-century **Mangaladevi Temple** is named after a Malabar Princess, Mangala Devi, who may have given her name to Mangalore. The 11th-century **Sri Manjunatha Temple** (with the Kadri Caves), 3 km from the centre – a cycle rickshaw ride away – has a rough lingam; its central image is a bronze

Lokeshwara (AD 968). **Shremmanti Bai Memorial Museum** ⓘ *0900-1700, free*, has a collection including archaeology, ethnology, porcelain and wood carvings. **Mahatma Gandhi Museum** ⓘ *Canara High School, Mon-Sat 0930-1230 and 1400-1730, closed holidays, free*, includes zoology, anthropology, sculpture, art and manuscripts.

There are also lakes containing water with medicinal properties, and the 18th-century Old Lighthouse. It is generally believed to have been built by Haider Ali, who built a naval dockyard in Mangalore. You can take a trip out to the sand bar at the river mouth to watch fascinating boat building and river traffic on the Netravathi River.

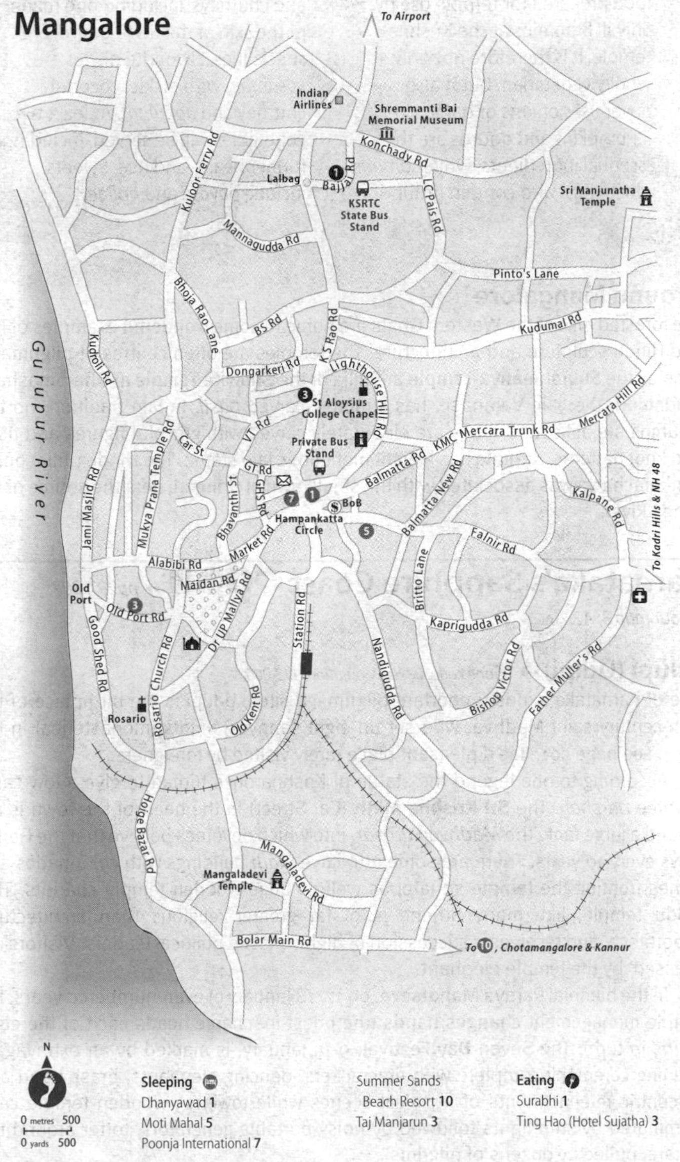

Vegetarian victuals

The name of Udupi is associated across South India with authentic Brahmin cooking, which means vegetarian food at its best. But what is authentic Udupi cuisine? Pamela Philipose, writing in the *Indian Express*, suggests that strictly it is food prepared for temple use by Shivali Brahmins at the Krishna temple. It is therefore not only wholly vegetarian, but it also never uses onions or garlic.

Pumpkins and gourds are the essential ingredients, while *sambar*, which must also contain ground coconut and coconut oil, is its base. The spicy pepper water, *rasam*, is compulsory, as are the ingredients jackfruit, heart-shaped colocasia leaves, raw green bananas, mango pickle, red chilli and salt. *Adyes* (dumplings), *ajadinas* (dry curries) and chutneys, including one made of the skin of the ridge gourd, are specialities. Favourite dishes are *kosambiri* with pickle, coconut chutney and *appalam*. At least two vegetables will be served, including runner beans, and rice. Sweets include *payasa* and *holige*.

Around Mangalore

The forested hills of the Western Ghats are home to some wonderful examples of Jain and Hindu sculpture and architecture. The temples are often centres of pilgrimage, such as the **Subrahmanya Temple** at Sullia or the **Shaivite Temple** at Dharamashala. **Mudabidri**, the 'Jain Varanasi', has superbly carved *basti*. In Jain tradition, no two columns are alike, and many are elaborately carved with graceful figures and floral and knot patterns. **Karkala** has a giant monolithic Jain statue. The Hindu philosopher Sankaracharya was associated with the small town of **Sringeri**, near the source of the Tunga River.

Karnataka's Sapphire Coast » pp297-299.

Colour map 3, A2.

Udupi (Udipi) → *Phone code: 0820. Population: 113,000.*

One of Karnataka's most important pilgrimage sites, Udupi is the birthplace of the 12th-century saint Madhva, who set up eight sannyasi *maths* (monasteries) in the town, see page 501. It is a pleasant place rarely visited by foreigners.

According to one legend the statue of Krishna once turned to give a low caste devotee *darshan*. The **Sri Krishna Math** (Car Street) in the heart of the town is set around a large tank, the *Madhva Sarovar*, into which devotees believe that the Ganga flows every 10 years. There are some attractive *math* buildings with colonnades and arches fronting the temple square, as well as huge wooden temple chariots. This Hindu temple, like many others, is of far greater religious than architectural importance, and receives a succession of highly placed political leaders. Visitors are 'blessed' by the temple elephant.

In the biennial **Paraya Mahotsava**, on 17/18 January of even-numbered years, the temple management changes hands (the priest-in- charge heads each of the eight *maths* in turn). The **Seven Day Festival**, 9-15 January, is marked by an extravagant opening ceremony complete with firecrackers, dancing elephants, brass band and "eccentric re-enactments of mythical scenes while towering wooden temple cars, illuminated by strip lights followed by noisy portable generators, totter around the square, pulled by dozens of pilgrims".

Sri Ananthasana Temple, where Madhva is believed to have dematerialized while teaching his followers, is in the centre of the temple square. The eight important *maths* are around Car Street: Sode, Puthige and Adamar (south); Pejawar and Palamar (west); Krishna and Shirur (north); and Kaniyur (east). Udupi is almost as well known today as the home of a family of Kanarese Brahmins who have established a chain of coffee houses and hotels across South India.

Manipal

Some 5 km inland from Udupi, Manipal is famous throughout Karnataka as the centre of **Yakshagana** dance drama, which like *Kathakali* in Kerala is an all-night spectacle. **Rashtrakavi Govind Pai Museum** ⓘ *MGM College*, has a collection of sculpture, bronze, inscriptions and coins.

Malpe

Five kilometres west of Udupi, Malpe is one of the best port sites in southern Karnataka. Across the bay is the island of Darya Bahadurgarh and 5 km to the southwest is **St Mary's Isle**, which is composed of dramatic hexagonal basalt, where Vasco da Gama landed in 1498 and set up a cross.

The fishing village at one end of the beach and the fish market on the docks are very smelly; the beach too is used as a public toilet in places. If you are prepared for an unpleasant walk or cycle ride, you can reach a deserted sandy beach but there are no facilities so take your own food and water.

Bhatkal

One of the many bullock cart tracks that used to be the chief means of access over the Western Ghats started from Bhatkal. Now only a small town with a principally Muslim population, in the 16th century it was the most important port of the *Vijayanagar* Empire.

It also has two interesting small temples. From the north, the 17th-century Jain *Chandranatha Basti* with two buildings linked by a porch, is approached first. The use of stone tiling is a particularly striking reflection of local climatic conditions, and is a feature of the Hindu temple to its south, a 17th-century Vijayanagar temple with typical animal carvings. In the old cemetery of the church is possibly the oldest British memorial in India, inscribed: "Here lyeth the body of George Wye merchant dec. XXXI March Anno Dom NRT Christi Sal Mundi MDCXXXVII, 1637".

Gokarna → *Phone code: 08386. Colour map 3, A1.*

The narrow streets, traditional houses and temples together with its long wide expanse of beach have long lured backpackers moving on from Goa who search for an alternative hideaway on the five unspoilt beaches (besides Om these are Gokarna, Kudle, Half Moon and Paradise) to the south. This makes for a curious hybrid of Hindu pilgrims and hippy castaways, who would do well to dress modestly in town. Gokarna's name, meaning cow's ear, possibly comes from the legend in which Shiva emerged from the ear of a cow – but also perhaps from the ear-shaped confluence of the two rivers here. Today Gokarna is also a centre of Sanskrit learning.

Ganesh is believed to have tricked **Ravana** into putting down the famous Atmalinga on the spot now sanctified in the **Mahabalesvara temple**. As Ravana was unable to lift the lingam up again, it is called *Mahabala* (the strong one). **Tambraparni Teertha** stream is considered a particularly sacred spot for casting the ashes of the dead.

Most travellers head for the beaches to the south. The path from town passing **Kudle** (pronounced *Koodlee*) **Beach** is well signposted but quite rugged, especially south of the **Om Beach** (about 3 km), and should not be attempted with a full backpack during the middle of the day. Also, though parts are lit at night, stretches are isolated; single women especially should take a companion. Boats from Gokarna to Om charge around Rs 200 single. Om Beach can now also be reached by a motorable track which can be accessed from near Mayura Samudra hotel. It is no longer quite the secluded paradise it once was. As with Kudle, in season it can get extremely busy and the combination of too many people, shortage of fresh water and poor hygiene results in dirty beaches. **Half Moon** and **Paradise Beaches**, popular with long-stayers, can be reached by continuing to walk over the headlands and are another 2 km or so apart.

Project Seabird, Karwar and Anjedives

→ *Colour map 3, A1.*

Karwar, on the banks of the Kalinadi River, is the administrative headquarters of North Kanara District. **Devbagh Beach**, off the coast, has a deep-water naval port protected by five islands. One of these was 'Anjedive' of old, known to seafarers centuries before Vasco da Gama called at the island in 1498, and the Portuguese built a fort there. It was later used as a Goan penal colony. From 1638 to 1752 there was an English settlement here, surviving on the pepper trade. The Portuguese held it for the next 50 years until the old town was destroyed in 1801. Today Karwar, strung out between the port and the estuary, has an unpleasant beach. However, the beaches south rival those of Goa but are still deserted. Of interest is the hill fort, an octagonal church, and a 300-year old temple.

India's Western Naval Command, which controls the 'sword arm' of the subcontinent's powerful Western fleet, has since the 1960s planned to move here from Mumbai – a principally commercial port and one that is worryingly close to Pakistani missiles – but work on the immense **Project Seabird** only began in October 1999. When complete it will be the largest naval base this side of the Suez Canal and will hold over 140 warships, aircraft and dockyards, while the hillsides will be put to use concealing submarines. Karwar, crucially, is 900 nautical miles from Karachi versus Mumbai's 580. Since the area is under the control of the Navy it is off-limits to foreigners but driving past it gives a striking portrait of the subcontinent's military might and ambition.

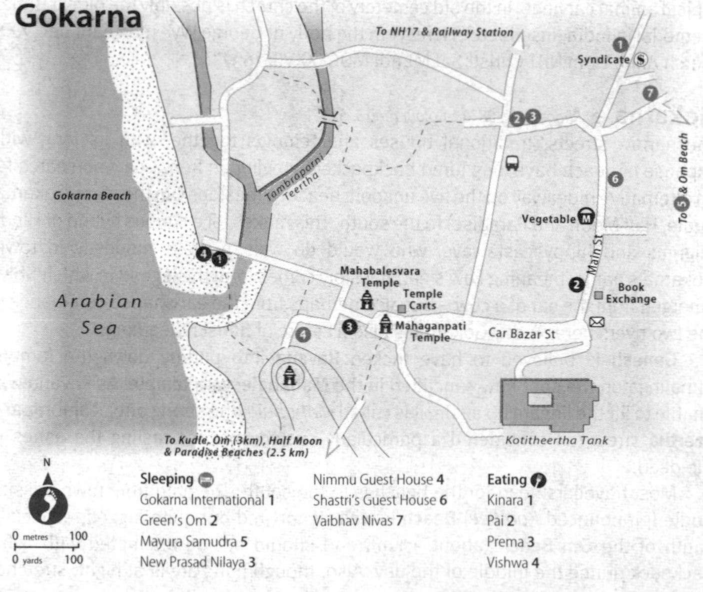

Sleeping

Mangalore *p292, map p293*

A-B Taj Manjarun, Old Port Rd, T0824-242 0420, www.tajhotels.com. 101 excellent rooms with tubs ('budget' rooms perfectly adequate), some with sea/river view, restaurant, all facilities, swimming pool (non-residents half-day Rs 200), friendly service.

B-C Moti Mahal, Falnir Rd, T0824-244 1411. 90 a/c rooms, restaurant and bar, coffee shop, pool and poolside barbecue.

C-D Hotel Mangalore International, KS Rao Rd, T0824-244 4860. Modern, airy, 45 clean, well-appointed rooms, 30 a/c, vegetarian restaurant (no alcohol), excellent service.

C-D Poonja International, KS Rao Rd, T0824-244 0171, www.hotelpoonja international.com. 154 rooms, central a/c, wide range of facilities including exchange, spotlessly clean, excellent complimentary buffet breakfast, great value.

C-D Summer Sands Beach Resort, Ullal Beach, 10 km south of town, T0824-246 7690, www.summer-sands.com. 85 rooms, 30 a/c, in simple but comfortable local-style bungalows, superb Konkani meals, bar, good pool, ayurvedic treatments, yoga, local trips.

D-E Dhanyawad, Hampankatta Circle, T0824-244 0066. 44 spacious rooms, good value, convenient (open late).

F Adarsh Lodge, Market Rd, T0824-244 0878. 60 basic rooms, some with TV, well kept and friendly, excellent service, good value.

F Surya, Greens Compound, Balmatta Rd, T0824-242 5736. 18 rooms with bath, excellent vegetarian restaurant, internet (Rs 30) with good connection, set back from road, uninspiring exterior but tranquil.

Udupi and around *p294*

B-C Valley View International, on campus, Manipal. Has 70 good a/c rooms with upmarket facilities, pool. Recommended.

C-D Srirama Residency, opposite Post Office, Udupi, T0820-253 0761. Top- quality new hotel with 30 excellent rooms, bar, 2 restaurants, travel desk, good service.

C-E Swadesh Heritage, MV Rd, Udupi, T0820-252 9605, www.hotelswadesh.com. 34 spotlessly clean rooms, 14 a/c, in newish hotel (even basic rooms very good value), bar, 2 restaurants. Highly recommended.

D Green Park, Manipal. 38 rooms, some a/c, has a restaurant.

D-E Udupi Residency, near Service Bus Stand, Udupi, T0820-253 0005. New hotel with 33 excellent rooms, 11 a/c, clean, well maintained, restaurant. Highly recommended.

E Silver Sands, T0820-222223, Thotham Beach, 1 km north of Malpe, hard to find. 8 pleasant cottages, limited menu restaurant, friendly. Recommended.

E Tourist Home, half way to Thotham Beach, Malpe. 4 pleasant, seaside rooms. Indian breakfast at the top of the road.

Gokarna *p295, map p296*

LL SwaSwara, Om beach, Gokarna, T08386-257131, www.swaswara.com. Elite retreat with 'yoga for the soul' on 12 ha complex 15 mins from town along the curve of gorgeous Om beach, taught by Indian swamis: ashtanga, hasya, kundalini, yoga nidra (psychic sleep) and meditation. Thatched Konkan stone villas with private gardens. Beds are strewn with flowers in the day and philosophical quotes in the evening. Also offers ayurveda, archery, kayaking, trekking, butterfly and birdwatching, and jungle walks. Mud and palm leaf huts with shared facilites Rs 30-60 (extra for a mattress). The lack of security in beach huts has prompted the guest houses in town to offer to store luggage for a small charge. The 3 beach options below are secure.

D-E Gokarna International, Main Rd, Kumta Taluk, T08386-265 6848. 43 modern rooms (3 a/c) with bath and tubs, back quieter and have balconies, restaurant, bar, friendly staff, and the first lift in Gokarna! Recommended.

E-F Green's Om, Ganjigadde, 2-min walk from bus stand, T08386-265 6445. Great value, 20 clean, airy, well-maintained rooms with bath, 2 a/c, restaurant (Nepali, Indian, Western) and bar operates in peak season.

For an explanation of the sleeping and eating price codes used in this guide, see inside the front cover. Other relevant information is found in Essentials pages 40-44.

E-F New Prasad Nilaya, near New Bus Stand, Gangigadde T08386-265 7135. Spacious but very run-down rooms with shower, some balconies, upstairs slightly better, friendly staff.
E-F Shri Laxmi, Bus Stand Rd, T08386-256 0365. Clean, spacious rooms in converted family house. Small scale, friendly, good value.
F Mayura Samudra (KSTDC), 2 km north on hilltop facing the sea, T08386-256236. Quite a trek, 3 rooms, garden, helpful staff.
F Nimmu Guest House, near Temple, Mani Bhadra Rd, T08386-265 6730. 15 clean rooms with shared Indian toilets, 5 newest are better value as they are big, bright and catch the breeze, limited roof space for overspill, garden, laid-back and friendly, safe luggage storage. Recommended.
F Shastri's Guest House, Dasanamath, T08386-256220. 24 rooms with bath, some 3-4 bedded, set back from road, quiet.
F Vaibhav Nivas, Ganjigadde off Main St (5 mins walk from bazar), T08386-256714. Family guest house, small rooms, annexe with 10 rooms, some with bath (Indian and Western WC), meals, luggage store.

On beaches

F Shiva Prasad, Kudle Beach, with decent brick-built rooms with fan.
F Namaste, Om Beach, adequate rooms, though far from the best swimming areas.
G Nirvana, Om Beach, Rs 40 for no bed. Hammock or inflatable mattress recommended, shower, restaurant.

Eating

Mangalore *p292, map p293*

TTT Embers, for open-air dinners by the pool at Taj Manjarun Hotel.
T Hao Hao and **T Hao Ming**, in Balmatta, good Chinese, a/c.
T Lalith, Balmatta Rd, T0824-242 6793. Basement restaurant with excellent food, cold beer and friendly service.
T Surabhi, Tandoori and cold beer, handy if waiting for a night bus.
T Ting Hao at **Hotel Sujatha**, KS Rao Rd. Dark, a/c, large portions of Chinese/Indian (opens 1800).

Udupi and around *p294*

Dwarike, Car St, facing Temple Sq, Udupi. Immaculately clean, modern, good service, comfortable, Western and South Indian food, excellent snacks, ice creams.
Gokul, opposite **Swadeshi Heritage hotel**, Udupi. Excellent vegetarian, good value.
JJ's Fast Food, **Hotel Bhavani**, Parkala Rd, Manipal. For Western snacks.

Gokarna *p295, map p296*

Soft drinks can be wildly overpriced; check before ordering. Cheap vegetarian thalis are available near the bus stand and along Main St while shacks at the entrance to the town beach serve up the usual array of travellers' favourites. Standards are improving on the southern beaches with traveller food, drinks and internet access becoming available, though often only in the peak season. **Spanish Chai** shop, Kudle, and **Hotel Look Sea** are popular.
T Kinara, near Gokarna Beach. Ice creams, Indian and some Western food. Basic but clean and well run.
T Pai, near Vegetable Market, does good *masala dosa*.
T Prema, opposite Mahabalesvar temple. With a large room upstairs, does great fruit salads, ices, *gudbad* and its own delicious soft garlic cheese. Popularity has resulted in slow and surly service. Ice cream parlours abound; try *gudbad* with nuts and fruit.
T Vishwa, on the beach. Nepali-run, varied menu including Tibetan, large helpings.

Karwar *p296*

Fish Restaurant, in the **Sidvha Hotel**. Excellent bistro-type place.

Transport

Mangalore *p292, map p293*

Air

Bajpe airport is 22 km out of town. Transport from town: taxi, Rs 200; shared Rs 50 each; coach from **Indian Airlines**, Hathill Complex, Lalbag, T0824-245 5259. Airport, T0824-275 2433. **Chennai** via Bengaluru (Bangalore), **Mumbai**. **Jet Airways**: Ram Bhavan Complex, Kodaibail, T0824-244 1181, airport, T0824-275 2709. **Bengaluru (Bangalore)** and **Mumbai**.

Bus

Numerous private long distance bus companies around **Taj Mahal Restaurant**,

Falnir Rd (and a few opposite KSRTC) serve **Bengaluru (Bangalore)**, **Bijapur**, **Goa**, **Ernakulam**, **Hampi**, **Gokarna**, **Kochi**, **Mumbai**, **Udupi** etc. KSRTC State bus stand, Bajjai Rd, is well organized. Booking hall at entrance has a computer printout of timetable in English; main indicator board shows different bus categories: red ordinary; blue semi-de luxe; green super-de luxe. (*Exp* buses may be reserved 7 days ahead). For town centre and railway, leave bus stand, turn left 50 m to private bus shelter for bus 19 or 33. **Mysore** and **Bengaluru (Bangalore)**: 296 km, 7 hrs and 405 km, 9 hrs, every 30 mins from 0600 (route via Madikeri is the best); trains take 20 hrs. **Chennai** 717 km; **Madurai** 691 km, 16 hrs. **Mumbai**; **Panaji**, 10 hrs.

Car
Hire for Rs 4 per km, Rs 7 for a/c.

Rickshaw
Auto minimum charge Rs 8. Rs 35 to Kankanadi station from centre and Rs 25 from KSRTC Lalbag, Bus Station (higher than the meter charge because of the 'locality').

Train
Central Station has a computerized booking office. **Chennai**: *Mangalore Mail 6602* (AC/II), 1115, 19 hrs; *West Coast Exp 6628*, 2010, 19 hrs. **Kollam**: *Malabar Express 6330*, dep 1630, 15 hrs, and **Thiruvananthapuram**, 17 hrs: also *Parasuram Exp 6350*, 0345. **Madgaon (Margao)**: *Matsyagandha Exp 2620*, 1450, 4½ hrs (on to Thane and LT for Mumbai). **Palakkad**: *Mangalore-Tiruchirappalli Exp 6684*, 0600, 8 hrs; *W Coast Exp 6628*, 2010, 8½ hrs. From **Kankanadi Station**: **Mumbai** (Lokman- ya Tilak) via Madgaon: *Nethravati Exp 6346*, 1450, 17½ hrs. **Madgaon**: *Lakshadeep Exp 2617*, 2310, 4 hrs.

Udupi and around *p294*

Bicycle
Bikes available for hire in Udupi.

Bus
From Udupi, frequent service to **Mangalore** (1½ hrs). Mornings and evenings to **Bengaluru (Bangalore)** and **Mysore** from 0600; **Hubli** from 0900; **Dharmashala**, from 0600-0945, 1400-1830; **Mumbai** at 1120, 1520, 1700, 1920.

Train
The station is 5 km from the town centre; auto, Rs 35. **Madgaon**: *Netravati Exp 6636*, 1608, 4 hrs, and on to **Mumbai** (LT).

Gokarna *p295, map p296*

Bus
KSRTC buses provide a good service: **Chaudi** 2 hrs; **Karwar** (via Ankola) frequent (1 hr); **Hospet** 0700, 1425 (10 hrs); **Jog Falls** 0700, 1130 (6 hrs); **Margao**, 0814 (4 hrs); **Mangalore** via **Udipi** 0645 (7 hrs); **Panaji** 0800 (5 hrs).

Train
Gokarna Road Station is 10 km from town, 2 km from the NH17; most trains are met by auto-rickshaws and private bus. Rs 10 to Gokarna bus stand. State buses can be flagged down on the NH17. **Madgaon (Margao)**: *Mangalore-Madgaon Pass KR2 (K)*, 1110, 2¼ hrs; **Mangalore**: *Madgaon-Mangalore Pass KR1 (K)*, 1532, 5 hrs.

Karwar *p296*

Bus
To **Jog Falls**, 0730 and 1500 (6 hrs). Frequent buses to **Palolem**, **Margao** (Madgaon) and **Panaji**, also direct buses to Colva. Buses often full; you may have to fight to get on. The road crosses the Kali River (car toll Rs 5) then reaches the Goa border and check post (8 km north).

Directory

Mangalore *p292, map p293*

Bank Bank of Baroda, Balmatta Rd, exchange on credit cards.
Internet Frontline, Ayesha Towers, KS Rao Rd, T0824-244 1537, charges Rs 40 per hr. **Internet World**, City Light Building, Falnir Rd. Cheap, helpful.
Post Panje Mangesh Rd (1st left after Poonja Arcade, by petrol station) has Speed Post.

Gokarna *p295, map p296*

Exchange Pai STD, opposite Ramdev Lodge, and **Kiran's Internet**, change money. **Internet** Several in town and on Kudle and Om beaches. **Sriram**, near post office, is best.

Northern Karnataka

Down the centuries, northeast Karnataka has been host to a profusion of Deccani rulers: Hampi, site of the capital city of the Vijayanagar Hindu empire that rose to conquer the entire south in the 14th century, is the region's most famous, and is an extraordinary site of desolate temples, compounds, stables and pleasure baths, surrounded by a stunning boulder-strewn landscape. The cluster of temple relics in the villages of Aihole, Pattadakal and Badami dates from the sixth century, when the Chalukyans first started experimenting with what went on to become the distinct Indian temple design. Nearby are the Islamic relics of Bijapur and Bidar, sudden plots of calm tomb domes with their Persian inscriptions ghosted into lime, and archways into empty harems; all the more striking for being less visited. ➡ *For Sleeping, Eating and other listings, see pages 315-320.*

Hampi-Vijayanagar ➡ *pp315-320.*

Colour map 1, C5.

→ *Phone code: 08394.*

Climb any boulder-toppled mountain around the ruins of the Vijayanagar Empire and you can see the dizzying scale of the Hindu conquerors' glory; Hampi was the capital of a kingdom that covered the whole of Southern India. Little of the kingdom's riches remain; now the mud huts of gypsies squat under the boulders where noblemen once stood, and the double decker shopfronts of the bazar where diamonds were once traded by the kilo is now geared solely towards profiting from Western tourists and domestic pilgrims. Away from the bazar, there is a unique romantic desolation. You'll need at least a full day to do it justice.

Ins and outs

Getting there and around Apart from the hugely expensive five-seater aircraft, buses and trains arrive in Hospet, from where it is a 30-minute rickshaw (around Rs 200) or bus ride away. The site is spread out, so hiring a bicycle is a good idea though some paths are too rough to ride on. ➡ *See Transport, page 318, for further details.*

Tourist information You enter the area from the west at Hampi Bazar or from the south at Kamalapuram. The **tourist office** ⓘ *0800-1230, 1500-1830, is on the approach to Virupaksha Temple.* Before entering the precinct, foreigners are expected to register at the police office on the left. It's US$5 to enter the Vitthala temple, with its amazing stone pillars. This includes the Lotus Mahal, same day only. The rest is free. A four-hour guided tour of the site (without going into the temples) costs Rs 250.

History

Hampi was founded on the banks of the Tungabhadra river by two brothers, Harihara and Bukka, in 1336 and rose to become the seat of the mighty Vijayanagar Empire and a major centre of Hindu rule and civilization for 200 years. The city, which held a monopoly on the trade of spices and cotton, was enormously wealthy – some say greater than Rome – and the now-sorry bazar was packed with diamonds and pearls, the crumbled palaces plated with gold. Although it was well fortified and defended by a large army, the city fell to a coalition of Northern Muslim rulers, the Deccan Sultans, at Talikota in 1565. The invading armies didn't crave the city for themselves, and instead sacked it, smiting symbolic blows to Hindu deities and taking huge chunks out of many of the remaining white granite carvings. Today, the craggy

Today Hampi has a population of 3000 across its 62 sq km. Once that figure was closer to 1½ million.

26 sq km site holds the ghost of a capital with aquaducts, elephant stables and baths as big as palaces. The dry arable land is slowly being peeled back by the archaeologists to expose more and more of the kingdom's ruins; 80 have been found so far.

The site for the capital was chosen for strategic reasons but the craftsmen adopted an ingenious style to blend in their architectural masterpieces with the barren and rocky landscape. Most of the site is early 16th century, built during the 20-year reign of Krishna Deva Raya (1509-1529) with the citadel standing on the bank of the river. Excavations undertaken by the Archaeological Survey of India are still in progress.

Sacred Centre

The road from the west comes over Hemakuta Hill, overlooking the sacred centre of Vijayanagar (the 'Town of Victory', 13 km northeast of Hospet town), the Virupaksha Temple and the Tungabhadra River to its north. On the hill are two large monolithic Ganesh sculptures: and some small temples. The road runs down to the village and the once world-famous market place. You can now only see the wide pathway running

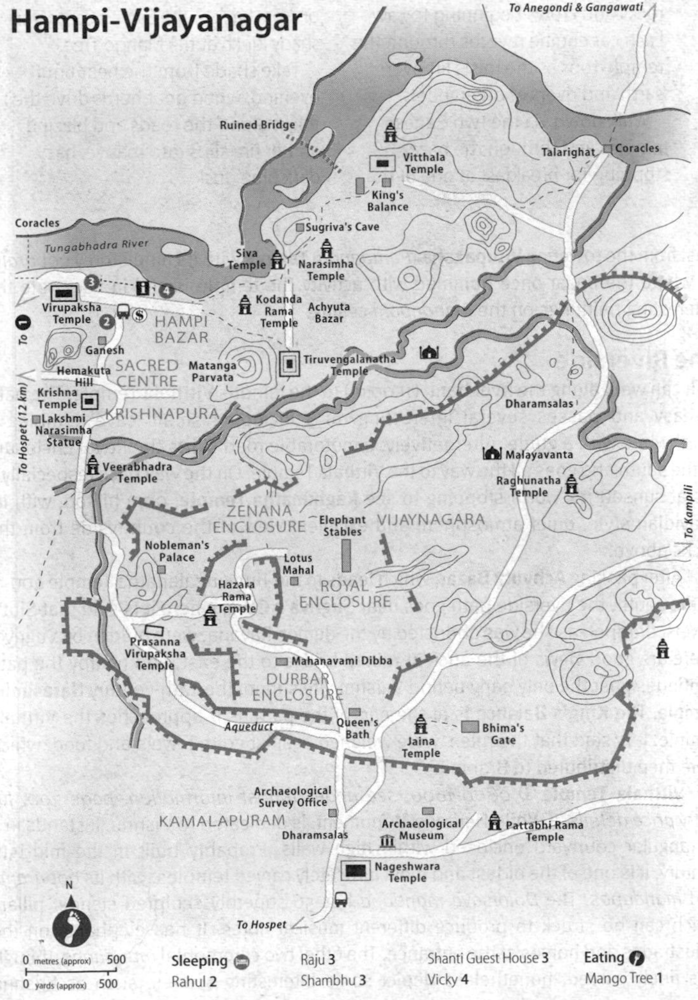

A day in the life of Hampi

Climb the giant piano key steps leading up Matanga Parvat, over the road from Hemakuta Hill, at 0530 for a spectacular dawn (take a torch and, if alone, a guide: there have been muggings). Devotional songs blow across a land emptied of humans in the one-time empire capital that is now a horizon of great big cleft cliffs, boulder piles that make up the mountain ranges. The dawn rush hour consists of bullock carts wheeling along with sugar cane loads, squirrels scamping about the rocks and crows beginning to caw. Each car engine reverbs through the temple tops as the mists lift over earth and rivers of green pools.

Walk down via the two Ganesh temples and through the bazar stopping for breakfast at one of the budget cafés that once peddled pearls not dosas.

Go into the living temple of Virupaksha – women do their washing and slap their wet saris on the granite ground to dry. Make sure you see the inverted *gopuram*, a 15th-century pinhole camera.

By coracle, cross the river to hire bicycles for pedalling round paddy-filled Anegundi: to the east is the Hanuman temple, to the west a swimming lake.

Lunch can be either at **Boulder Hotel** or cross back to the Sacred Centre for shady lunch at the Mango Tree.

Take shade from the heat until evening, when goat herds drive their flocks along the roads and blazing amber fire slips into mauve, hazy dark blue dusk.

east from the towering **Virupaksha** (*Pampapati*) **Temple** with its nine-storey *gopuram*, to where the bazar once hummed with activity.The temple is still in use; note the interesting paintings on the *mandapam* ceiling.

The Riverside

You can walk along the river bank (1500 m) to the famous Vitthala Temple. The path is easy and passes several interesting ruins including small 'cave' temples – worthwhile with a guide. Alternatively, a motorable road skirts the Royal Enclosure to the south and goes all the way to the Vitthala Temple. On the way back (especially if it's at sunset) it's worth stopping to see **Raghunatha Temple**, on a hilltop, with its Dravidian style, quiet atmosphere and excellent view of the countryside from the rocks above.

After passing **Achyuta Bazar,** which leads to the Tiruvengalanatha Temple 400 m to the south, the riverside path goes near **Sugriva's Cave**, where it is said that Sita's jewels, dropped as she was abducted by the demon Ravana, were hidden by Sugriva. There are good views of the ancient ruined bridge to the east, and nearby the path continues past the only early period Vaishnavite shrine, the 14th-century **Narasimha Temple**. The **King's Balance** is at the end of the path as it approaches the Vitthala Temple. It is said that the rulers were weighed against gold, jewels and food, which were then distributed to Brahmins.

Vitthala Temple ⓘ *0800-1600, see under Tourist information, page 300, for entry price details*, a World Heritage Monument, is dedicated to Vishnu. It stands in a rectangular courtyard enclosed within high walls. Probably built in the mid-15th century, it is one of the oldest and most intricately carved temples, with its *gopurams* and *mandapas*. The *Dolotsava mandapa* has 56 superbly sculpted slender pillars which can be struck to produce different musical notes. It has elephants on the balustrades and horses at the entrance. The other two ceremonial *mandapas*, though less finely carved, nonetheless depict some interesting scenes, such as Krishna hiding in a tree from the *gopis* and a woman using a serpent twisted around a stick to churn a pot of buttermilk. In the courtyard is a superb chariot carved out of granite, the wheels raised off the ground so that they could be revolved!

Krishnapura

On the road between the Virupaksha Bazar and the Citadel you pass Krishnapura, Hampi's earliest Vaishnava township with a Chariot Street 50 m wide and 600 m long, which is now a cultivated field. **Krishna temple** has a very impressive gateway to the east. Just southwest of the Krishna temple is the colossal monolithic **statue of Lakshmi Narasimha** in the form of a four-armed man-lion with fearsome bulging eyes sheltered under a seven-headed serpent, Ananta. It is over 6 m high but sadly damaged.

The road south, from the Sacred Centre towards the Royal Enclosure, passes the excavated **Prasanna Virupaksha** (misleadingly named 'underground') **Temple** and interesting watchtowers.

Royal Enclosure

At the heart of the Metropolis is the small **Hazara Rama Temple**, the Vaishanava 'chapel royal'. The outer enclosure wall to the north has five rows of carved friezes while the outer walls of the *mandapa* has three. The episodes from the epic *Ramayana* are told in great detail, starting with the bottom row of the north end of the west *mandapa* wall. The two-storey **Lotus Mahal**ⓘ *0600-1800, US$5, allows entry to Vitthala Temple on the same day*, is in the **Zenana** or ladies' quarter, screened off by its high walls. The watchtower is in ruins but you can see the domed **stables** for 10 elephants with a pavilion in the centre and the guardhouse. Each stable had a wooden beamed ceiling from which chains were attached to the elephants' backs and necks. In the **Durbar Enclosure** is the specially built decorated platform of the **Mahanavami Dibba**, from which the royal family watched the pageants and tournaments during the nine nights of *navaratri* festivities. The 8-m-high square platform originally had a covering of bricks, timber and metal but what remains still shows superb carvings of hunting and battle scenes, as well as dancers and musicians.

The exceptional skill of water engineering is displayed in the excavated system of aqueducts, tanks, sluices and canals, which could function today. The 22 m square **Pushkarini** is the attractive stepped tank at the centre of the enclosure. The road towards Kamalapuram passes the **Queen's Bath**, in the open air, surrounded by a narrow moat, where scented water filled the bath from lotus-shaped fountains. It measures about 15 m by 2 m and has interesting stucco work around it.

Hospet » *pp320-320. Colour map 1, C5.*

➔ *Phone code: 08394. Population: 163,300.*

Hospet is famous for its sugar cane; the town exports sugar across India, villagers boil the milk to make jaggery and a frothing freshly wrung cup costs you just Rs 4. Other industries include iron ore, biscuit making and the brewing of Royal Standard rum. The main bazar, with its characterful old houses, is interesting to walk around.

Muharram, the Muslim festival that marks the death of Mohammed's grandson Imam Hussein, is celebrated with a violent vigour both here and in the surrounding villages and with equal enthusiasm by both the area's significant Muslim population and Hindus. Ten days of fasting is broken with fierce drum pounding, drink and frequent arguments, sometimes accompanied by physical violence. Each village clusters around icons of Hussein, whose decapitation is represented by a golden crown on top of a face covered with long strings of jasmine flowers held aloft on wooden sticks. Come evening, fires are lit. When the embers are dying villagers race through the ashes, a custom that may predate Islam's arrival. The beginnings or ends of livestock migrations to seasonal feeding grounds are marked with huge bonfires. Cattle are driven through the fires to protect them from disease. Some archaeologists suggest that Neolithic ash mounds around Hospet were the result of similar celebrations over 5000 years ago.

Tungabhadra Dam ⓘ *Rs 5, local bus takes 15 mins,* 6 km away, is 49 m high and offers panoramic views. One of the largest masonry dams in the country, it was completed in 1953 to provide electricity for irrigation in the surrounding districts.

Bijapur

» *pp316-320. Colour map 1, C5. See also map, page 306.*

→ *Phone code: 08352. Population: 245,900.*

Mohammed Adil Shah was not a man to be ignored; the tomb he built from the first day of his rule in anticipation of his own death hovers with dark magnificence over Bijapur and is so large it can be seen from over 20 km away. His brooding macabre legacy threw down the gauntlet to his immediate successor. Ali Adil Shah II, who took over from Mohammed in 1656, began his own tomb, which would surely have been double in size and architectural wonder had he not died too soon, 26 years into his reign, with only archways complete. His Bara Kamaan is nearby, while to the north of the city lies Begum's equally thwarted attempt to match Mohammed's strength in death. Bijapur has the air of a northern Muslim city with its mausolea, mosques and palaces. It has some of the finest mosques in the Deccan and retains real character. The chowk between the bus station and MG Road is quite atmospheric in the evening. Overall it is a provincial, grubby but unhurried town.

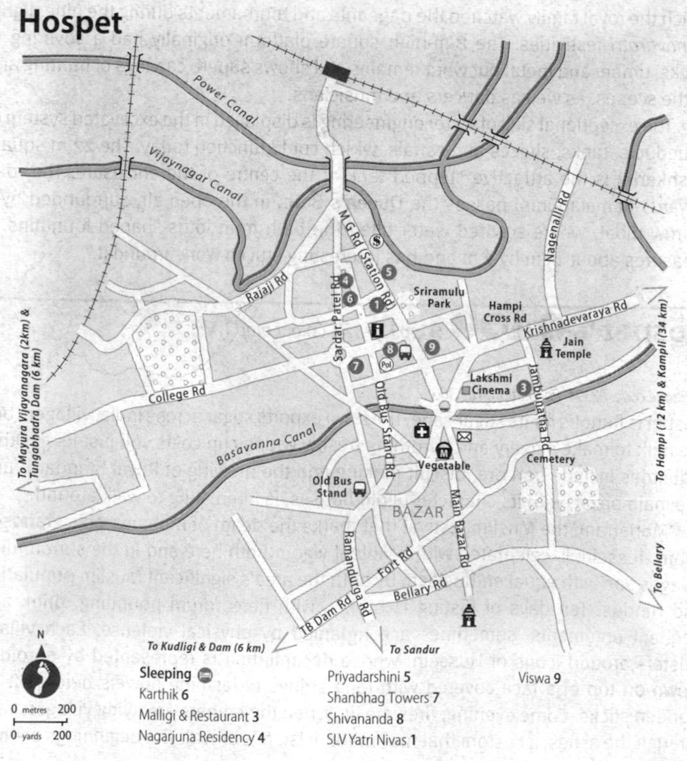

Ins and outs

Getting there The railway station is just outside the east wall of the fort less than 1 km from the Gol Gumbaz while long distance buses draw in just west of the citadel. Both arrival points are close enough to several hotels.

Getting around It is easy to walk or cycle round the town. There are also autos and tongas; negotiate for 'eight-sight tour price'. » *See Transport, page 319, for further details.*

Tourist information There's an office opposite the stadium ⓘ *T08352-250 3592, Mon-Sat 1030-1330 and 1415-1730*, but it's pretty useless.

History

The Chalukyas who ruled over Bijapur were overthrown in the late 12th century. In the early years of the 14th century the Delhi Sultans took it for a time until the Bahmanis, with their capital in Gulbarga, ruled through a governor in Bijapur who declared Independence in 1489 and founded the Adil Shahi Dynasty. Of Turkish origin, they held power until 1686.

The canon, which weighs 55 tons, was employed against Vijayanagar. Ali Adil Shah I, whose war it was, was at least somewhat chastened at the destruction his marauding Muslim armies had wreaked on the Hindu empire at Hampi. By way of atonement, and in a show of the inordinate riches that had fallen into his lap by supplanting Vijayanagar, he did his communal civic duty and built the exquisite Jama Masjid. It was his nephew Mohammed, he of the giant Gol Gumbaz, who later commissioned the rich Quaranic calligraphy that so sumptuously gilds the western wall.

Sights

The **Jama Masjid**, one of the finest in the Deccan, has a large shallow, onion-shaped dome and arcaded court. Built by Ali Adil Shah I (ruled 1557-1579) during Bijapur's rise to power it displays a classic restraint. The Emperor Aurangzeb added a grand entrance to the Masjid and also had a square painted for each of the 2250 worshippers that it can accommodate. The **Citadel** with its own wall has few of its grand buildings intact. One is the Durbar Hall, **Gagan Mahal** (Sky Palace), open to the north so that the citizens outside were not excluded. It had royal residential quarters on either side with screened balconies for the women to remain unseen while they watched the court below. Another worth visiting is the **Jal Manzil,** or the water pavilion, a cool sanctuary.

Ibrahim Rauza ⓘ *0600-1800, US$2, video camera Rs 25, visit early morning to avoid crowds*, the palatial 17th-century tomb west of the city wall, is well proportioned. It has slender minarets and carved decorative panels with lotus, wheel and cross patterns as well as bold Arabic calligraphy, bearing witness to the tolerance of the Adil Shahi Dynasty towards other religions. Built during the dynasty's most prosperous period (after the sacking of Vijayanagar) when the arts and culture flourished, it also holds the tomb of Ibrahim Adil Shah II (ruled 1580-1626) who had it built for his wife but died first. Near the Rauza is a huge tank, the Taj Bauri, built by Ibrahim II in memory of his wife. The approach is through a giant gateway flanked by two octagonal towers.

Gol Gumbaz ⓘ *0630-1730, US$2, video camera Rs 25, some choose to just view it from the gate*, the vast whitewashed tomb of Mohammad Adil Shah buried here with his wife, daughter and favourite court dancer, has the world's second largest dome (unsupported by pillars) and one of its least attractive. Its extraordinary **whispering gallery** carries a message across 38 m which is repeated 11 times. However, noisy crowds make hearing a whisper quite impossible; it's quietest in the early morning. Numerous narrow steps in one of the corner towers lead to the 3-m-wide gallery. The plaster here was made out of eggs, cow dung, grass and jaggery. There is an excellent view of the city with its walls from the base of the dome.

The **Nakkar Khana**, the gatehouse, is now a museum. The **Asar Mahal** (circa 1646) was built with a tank watered by the old conduit system. It was used as a court house and has teak pillars and interesting frescoes in the upper floor. The **Mehtar Mahal** (1620) with its delicate minarets and carved stone trellises and brackets supporting the balconies which form a decorative gateway, was supposed to have been built for the palace sweepers.

To the west, **Sherza Burj** (Lion Gate) in the 10-km-long fort wall, has the enormous 55 tonne, 4.3-m-long, 1½-m-diameter cannon *Malik-i-Maidan* (Ruler of the Plains) on the west. (To avoid being deafened the gunner is believed to have dived into the tank off the platform!) It was cast in the mid-16th century in Ahmadnagar, and was brought back as a prize of war pulled by "400 bullocks, 10 elephants and hundreds of soldiers". Note the muzzle, which is a lion's head with open jaws and an elephant being crushed to death inside. Inside the city wall nearby is **Upli Burj**, the 24-m-high watchtower on high ground with its long guns and water tanks.

The **Bara Kaman** was possibly a 17th-century construction by Adil Shah III. Planned as a huge 12-storey building with the shadow of the uppermost storey designed to fall onto the tomb of the Gol Gumbaz, construction was ended after two storeys with the death of the ruler. An impressive series of arches on a raised platform is all that remains.

The **Archaeological Museum** ⓘ *1000-1700, Rs 2*, in the gatehouse of the Gol Gumbaz has an excellent collection of Chinese porcelain, parchments, paintings, armoury, miniatures, stone sculpture and old Bijapur carpets.

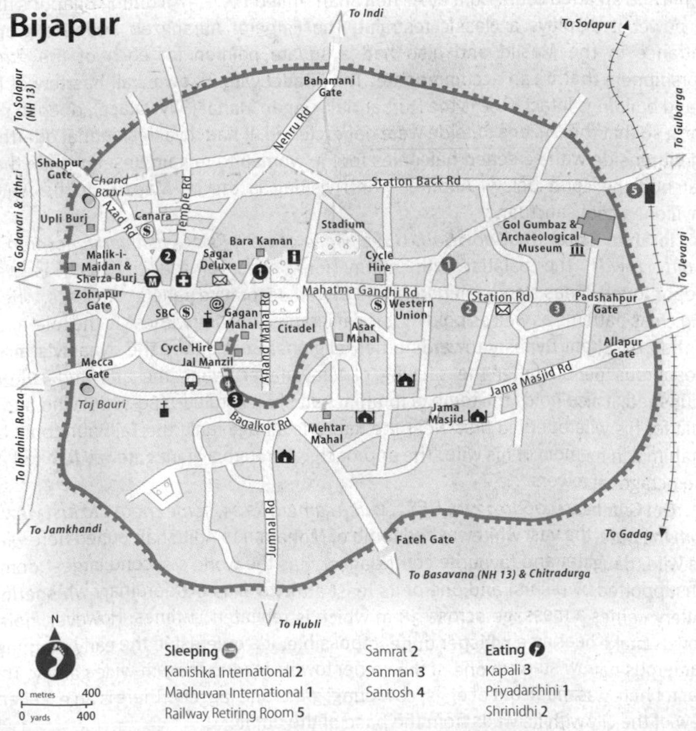

Sleeping
Kanishka International 2
Madhuvan International 1
Railway Retiring Room 5
Samrat 2
Sanman 3
Santosh 4

Eating
Kapali 3
Priyadarshini 1
Shrinidhi 2

Cradle of Hindu Temple architecture

» pp317-320.

Although Bijapur became an important Muslim regional capital, its surrounding region has several villages which, nearly 1500 years ago, were centres of Chalukyan power and the heart of new traditions in Indian temple building. At a major Indian crossroads, the temples at Aihole represent the first finely worked experiments in what were to become the distinct styles of North and South India.

Ins and outs

Since it takes a half day to see Badami, visiting the sites by bus doesn't allow time for Mahakuta. It is well worth hiring a car in Bijapur which allows you to see all the sites quite comfortably in a day. If travelling by bus it is best to visit Badami first, followed by Pattadakal and Aihole. By car it is best to start at Aihole and end at Badami. » *See Transport, page 319, for further details.*

Aihole → *Phone code: 0831. Colour map 1, C5.*

ⓘ *The main temples are now enclosed in a park, open sunrise to sunset, US$2, flash photography prohibited.*

Aihole was the first Chalukyan capital, but the site was developed over a period of more than 600 years from the sixth century AD and includes important Rashtrakuta and late Chalukyan temples, some dedicated to Jain divinities. It is regarded as the birthplace of Indian temple architectural styles and the site of the first built temples, as distinct from those carved out of solid rock. Most of the temples were dedicated to Vishnu, though a number were subsequently converted into Shaivite shrines.

There are about 140 temples – half within the fort walls – illustrating a range of developing styles from Hoysala, Dravida, Jain, Buddhist, Nagara and Rekhanagara. There is little else. All the roads entering Aihole pass numerous temple ruins, but the road into the village from Pattadakal and Bagalkot passes the most important group of temples which would be the normal starting point for a visit. Some prefer to wander around the dozens of deserted (free) temples around town instead of joining the crowds in the park.

Durgigudi Temple is named not after the Goddess Durga but because it is close to the *durga* (fort). Dating from the late seventh century, it has an early *gopuram* structure and semi-circular apse which imitates early Buddhist *chaitya* halls. It has numerous superb sculptures, a series contained in niches around the ambulatory: walking clockwise they represent Siva and *Nandi*, Narasimha, Vishnu with *Garuda*, Varaha, Durga and Harihara.

According to recent research **Lad Khan Temple** has been dated from around AD 700, not from AD 450 as suggested by the first Archaeological Survey of India reports in 1907. This is indicated by the similarity of some of its sculptures to those of the Jambulinga temple at Badami, which has been dated precisely at AD 699. Originally an assembly hall and *kalyana mandapa* (marriage hall), it was named after Lad Khan, a pious Muslim who stayed in the temple at the end of the 19th century. A stone ladder through the roof leads to a shrine with damaged images of Surya, Vishnu and Siva carved on its walls. It bears a striking resemblance to the megalithic caves that were still being excavated in this part of the Deccan at the beginning of the period. The roof gives an excellent view of the village.

Gaudar Gudi Temple, near the Lad Khan temple, is a small, rectangular Hindu temple, probably dating from the seventh century. It has a rectangular columned *mandapa*, surrounded on three sides by a corridor for circumambulation. Its roof of stone slabs is an excellent example of North Indian architecture. Beyond the Gaudar Gudi Temple is a small temple decorated with a frieze of pots, followed by a deep well. There are others in various states of repair. To see the most important of the remaining temples you leave the main park. Excavations are in progress, and the boundaries of the park may sometimes be fenced. Turning right out of the main park, the Bagalkot road leads to the **Chikki Temple**. Similar in plan to the Gaudar Gudi, this temple has particularly fine carved pillars. The beams which support the platform are also well worth seeing.

Ravan Phadi Cave Temple is reached from the main park entrance on the left, about 300 m from the village. The cave (formerly known as the Brahman) itself is artificial, and the sixth-century temple has a variety of carvings of Siva both outside and inside. One is in the *Ardhanarisvara* form (half Siva, half Parvati), another depicts Parvati and Ganesh dancing. There is a huge lotus carved in the centre of the hall platform; and two small eighth-century temples at the entrance, the one to the northwest dedicated to Vishnu and that to the south, badly weathered, may have been based on an older Dravidian-style temple.

The **Buddhist Temple** is a plain two-storey Buddhist temple on a hill beyond the end of the village on the way to the Meguti Temple. It has a serene smiling Buddha with the Bodhi Tree emerging from his head, on the ceiling of the upper floor. Further uphill is the **Jain temple**, a plain structure lacking the decorations on the plinth, columns and *gopuram* of many Hindu temples. It has a statue of Mahavira in the shrine within. Climb up through the roof for a good view of Aihole.

The **Meguti Temple** (AD 634) is reached from the Buddhist Temple down a path leading to a terrace. A left-hand route takes you to the foot of some stairs leading to the top of a hill which overlooks the town. This is the site of what is almost certainly the oldest building in Aihole and one of the oldest dated temples in India. Its 634 date is indicated by an inscription by the court poet to the king Ravikirtti. A Dravidian-style temple, it is richly decorated on the outside, and although it has elements which suggest Shaivite origins, it has an extremely impressive seated Jain figure, possibly Neminath, in the sanctuary which comprises a hall of 16 pillars.

The **Kunti Group** is a group of four Hindu temples (dating from seventh to ninth centuries). To find them you have to return down to the village. The oldest is in the southeast. The external columns of its *mandapa* are decorated with *mithuna*, or erotic couples. The temple to the northwest has beautifully carved ceiling panels of Siva and Parvati, Vishnu and Brahma. The other two date from the Rashtrakuta period.

Beyond these temples is the **Hucchappayya Math**, dating from the seventh century, which has sculptures of amorous couples and their servants, while the beams inside are beautifully decorated. There is a tourist resthouse close to the temples should you wish to stay.

Pattadakal

On the banks of the Malaprabha River, Pattadakal, a World Heritage Site, was the second capital of the Chalukyan kings between the seventh and eighth centuries and the city where the kings were crowned. Ptolemy referred to it as 'Petrigal' in the first century AD. Two of their queens imported sculptors from Kanchipuram. Most of the **temples** ⓘ *sunrise to sunset, US$2*, cluster at the foot of a hill, built out of the pink-tinged gold sandstone, and display a succession of styles of the southern Dravida temple architecture of the Pallavas (even miniature scaled-down models) as well as the North Indian Nagara style, vividly illustrating the region's position at the crossroads of North and South Indian traditions. With one exception the temples are dedicated to Siva. Most of the site is included in the archaeological park. Megalithic monuments dating from the third to fourth centuries BC have also been found in the area.

Immediately inside the entrance are the small eighth-century **Jambulinga** and **Kadasiddheshvara Temples**. Now partly ruined, the curved towers survive and the shrine of the Jambulinga Temple houses a figure of the dancing Siva next to Parvati. The gateways are guarded by *dvarapalas*.

Just to the east is the eighth-century **Galaganatha Temple**, again partly damaged, though its curved tower characteristic of North Indian temples is well preserved, including its *amalaka* on top. A relief of Siva killing the demon Andhaka is on the south wall in one of three original porches.

The **Sangamesvara Temple** dating from the reign of Vijayaditya (696-733) is the earliest temple. Although it was never completed it has all the hallmarks of a purely Dravidian style. Beautifully proportioned, the mouldings on the basement and pilasters divide the wall. The main shrine, into which barely any light is allowed to pass, has a corridor for circumambulation and a *lingam* inside. Above the sanctuary is a superbly proportioned tower of several storeys.

To the southwest is the late eighth-century North Indian-style **Kashi Vishveshvara Temple**, readily distinguishable by the *Nandi* in front of the porch. The interior of the pillared hall is richly sculpted, particularly with scenes of Krishna.

The largest temples, the **Virupaksha** (740-744) with its three-storey *vimana* and the **Mallikarjuna** (745), typify the Dravida style, and were built in celebration of the victory of the Chalukyan king Vikramaditya II over the Pallavas at Kanchipuram by his wife, Queen Trailokyamahadevi. The king's death probably accounted for the fact that the Mallikarjuna temple was unfinished, and you can only mark out some of the sculptures. However, the king's victory over the Pallavas enabled him to express his admiration for Pallava architecture by bringing back to Pattadakal one of the chief Pallava architects. The Virupaksha, a Shaivite temple, has a sanctuary surrounded by passageways and houses a black polished stone Siva *lingam*. A further Shaivite symbol is the huge 2.6-m-high chlorite stone *Nandi* at the entrance, contrasting with the pinkish sandstone surrounding it. The three-storey tower rises strikingly above the shrine, the outside walls of which, particularly those on the south side, are richly carved. Many show different forms of Vishnu and Siva, including some particularly striking panels which show Siva appearing out of a *lingam*. Note also the beautifully carved columns inside. They are very delicate, depicting episodes from the *Ramayana*, *Mahabharata* and the *Puranas*, as well as giving an insight into the social life of the Chalukyas. Note the ingenuity of the sculptor in making an elephant appear as a buffalo when viewed from a different side.

In the ninth century the Rashtrakutas arrived and built a Jain temple with its two stone elephants a short distance from the centre. The carvings on the temples, particularly on the **Papanatha** near the village which has interesting sculpture on the ceiling and pillars, synthesizes Northern and Southern Indian architectural styles.

Mahakuta

Once reached by early pilgrims over rocky hills from Badami 5 km away, Mahakuta is a beautiful complex of Chalukyan temples dating from the late seventh century and worth a detour. The superstructures reflect both Northern and Southern influences and one has an Orissan *deul*.

The restored temple complex of two dozen shrines dedicated to Siva is built around a large spring-fed tank within an enclosure wall. The old gateway to the southeast has fasting figures of Bhairava and Chamunda. On entering the complex, you pass the *Nandi* in front of the older **Mahakutesvara Temple** which has fine scrollwork and figures from the epics carved on the base. Larger Siva figures appear in wall niches, including an *Ardhanarisvara*. The temple is significant in tracing the development of the superstructure which began to externally identify the position of the shrine in Dravidian temples. Here the tower is dome-like and octagonal, the tiers supported by tiny 'shrines'. The **Mallikarjuna Temple** on the other side of the tank is similar in structure with fine carvings at the entrance and on the ceiling of the columned *mandapa* inside, depicting Hindu deities and *mithuna* couples. The enclosure has many smaller shrines, some carrying fine wall carvings. Also worth visiting is the **Naganatha** Temple 2 km away.

Badami → *Phone code: 08357. Colour map 1, C5. Population: 25,900.*

Badami occupies a dramatic site squeezed in a gorge between two high red sandstone hills. Once called Vatapi, after a demon, Badami was the Chalukyan capital from AD 543-757. The ancient city has several Hindu and Jain temples and a Buddhist cave and remains peaceful and charming. The transcendent beauty of the Hindu cave temples in their spectacular setting warrants a visit. The village with its busy bazar and a large lake has whitewashed houses clustered together along narrow winding lanes up the hillside. There are also scattered remains of 18 stone inscriptions (dating from the sixth to the 16th century). The sites are best visited early in the morning. They are very popular with monkeys, which can be aggressive, especially if they see food. End the day by watching the sun set from the eastern end of the tank.

The **South Fort** ⓘ *US$2*, is famous for its cave temples, four of which were cut out of the hillside in the second half of the sixth century. There are 40 steps to **Cave 1**, the oldest. There are several sculpted figures, including Harihara, Siva and Parvati, and Siva as Nataraja with 18 arms seen in 81 dancing poses. **Cave 2**, a little higher than Cave 1, is guarded by *dvarapalas* (door keepers). Reliefs of Varaha and Vamana decorate the porch. **Cave 3**, higher still, is dedicated to Vishnu. According to a Kannada inscription (unique in Badami) it was excavated in AD 578. It has numerous sculptures including Narasimha (man-lion), Hari-Hara (Siva-Vishnu), a huge seated Vishnu and interesting friezes. Frescoes executed in the tempera technique are similar to that used in the Ajanta paintings, and so are the carved ceilings and brackets. **Cave 4**, probably about 100 years later than the three earlier caves, is the only Jain cave. It has a statue of the seated Parsvanatha with two *dvarapalas* at the entrance. The fort itself above the caves is closed to the public.

The area is well worth exploring by bicycle.

Badami

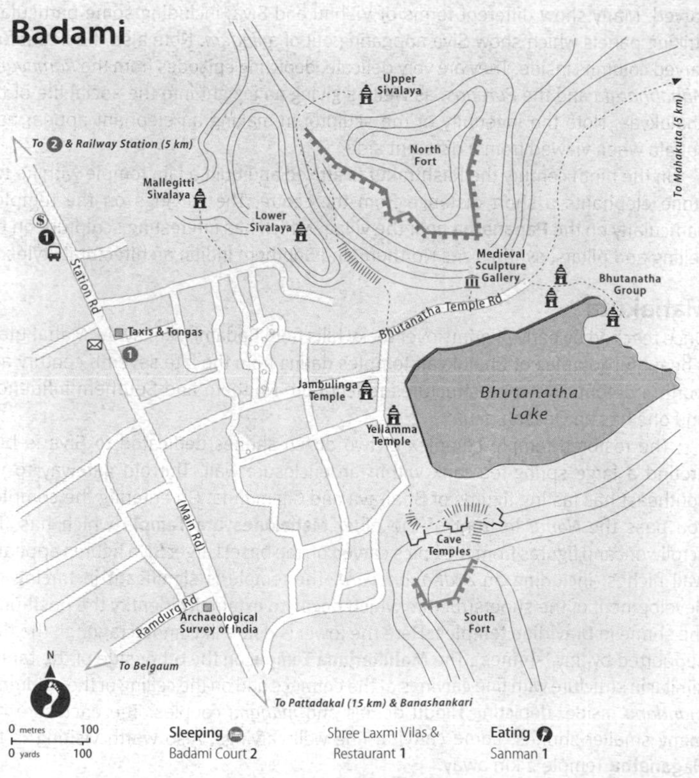

The **Buddhist Temple** is in the natural cave close to the ancient artificial Bhutanatha Lake (Agasthya Lake), where the mossy green water is considered to cure illnesses. The Yellamma Temple has a female deity, while one of the two Shaivite temples is to Bhutanatha (God of souls); in this form, Siva appears angry in the dark inner sanctuary.

The seventh-century **Mallegitti Sivalaya Temple**, which is one of the finest examples of the early Southern style, has a small porch, a *mandapa* (hall) and a narrower *vimana* (shrine), which Harle points out is typical of all early Western Chalukya temples. The slim pilasters on the outer walls are reminders of the period when wooden pillars were essential features of the construction. Statues of Vishnu and Siva decorate the outer walls, while animal friezes appear along the plinth and above the eaves. These are marked by a moulding with a series of ornamental small solid pavilions.

Jambulinga Temple is an early temple in the centre of the town near the rickshaw stand. Dating from 699 as attested by an inscription and now almost hidden by houses, the visible brick tower is a late addition from the Vijayanagar period. Its three chapels, dedicated to Brahma, Vishnu and Siva, contain some fine carving, although the deities are missing and according to Harle the ceiling decoration already shows signs of deteriorating style. The carvings here, especially that of the Nagaraja in the outside porch, have helped to accurately date the Lad Khan temple in Aihole (see page 307). Opposite the Jambulinga temple is the 10th-century Virupaksha Temple.

The mainly seventh-century **North Fort temples** ⓘ *Rs 2, carry water*, give an insight into Badami's history. Steep steps, almost 1 m high, take you to 'gun point' at the top of the fort which has remains of large granaries, a treasury and a watchtower. The **Upper Sivalaya Temple**, though damaged, still has some friezes and sculptures depicting Krishna legends. The North Fort was taken in a day by Colonel Munro in 1918, when he broke in through the east side.

An ancient **dolmen** site can be reached by an easy hike through interesting countryside; allow three and a half hours. A local English-speaking guide, Dilawar Badesha at Tipu Nagar, charges about Rs 2.

The Archaeological Survey's **Medieval Sculpture Gallery** ⓘ *Sat-Thu 1000-1700, free*, north of the tank, has fine specimens from Badami, Aihole and Pattadakal and a model of the natural bridge at Sidilinapadi, 5 km away.

Gulbarga

» *pp317-320. Colour map 1, B5. See also map, page 317.*

→ *Phone code: 08472. Population: 427,900.*

The dry and undulating plains from Hospet to Bidar are broken by rocky outcrops giving superb sites for commanding fortresses such as Gulbarga (and Bidar, see page 312). Gulbarga was the first capital of the Bahmanis (from 1347-1525). It is also widely known among South Indian Muslims as the home of Saiyid Muhammad Gesu Daraz Chisti (1320-1422) who was instrumental in spreading pious Islamic faith in the Deccan. The annual Urs festival in his memory can attract up to 100,000 people.

Sights

The town's sights and hotels are quite spread out so it is worth hiring an auto for half a day. The most striking remains in the town are the fort, with its citadel and mosque, the Jami Masjid, and the great tombs in its eastern quarter – massive, fortress-like buildings with their distinctive domes over 30 m high.

The **fort** is just 1 km west of the centre of the present town. Originally built by Ala-ud-din Bahmani in the 14th century, most of the outer structures and many of the buildings are in ruins. The outer door of the west gate and the *Bala Hissar* (citadel), a massive structure, however, remain almost intact although the whole place is very overgrown. A flight of ruined steps leads up to the entrance in the north wall. Beware of dogs. It's easy to see why the Bahamis were so keen to upgrade their fortress. The fat fort walls at Gulbarga – romantically named as the 'bouquet of lovers' – may sit proud above the more modern artificial lake, and the Bala Hissar (citadel) itself stands high with its plump rotund columns, but the whole is all too pregnable and too modest. And there's no commanding hilltop to provide the natural impenetrability which the plateaus around Bidar bequeathed the dynasty's subsequent rulers here.

All that remains of the palace structures are solitary walls stamped with arches, but the **Jami Masjid**, with its incongruous, uncanny likeness to the mosque at Córdoba in southern Spain, is both active and well maintained (similarities with the mosque at Córdoba have contributed to the legend that it was designed by a North African architect from the Moorish court). Beautiful geometrical angles of archways form as you walk under the 75 small roof domes zagging between the four corner domes. The whole area of 3500 sq m is covered by a dome over the *mihrab*, four corner domes and 75 minor domes, making it unique among Indian mosques. It was built by Firoz Shah Bahmani (1397-1432).

The **tombs** of the Bahmani sultans are in two groups. One lies 600 m to the west of the fort, the other on the east of the town. The latter have no remaining exterior decoration though the interiors show some evidence of ornamentation. The Dargah of the Chisti saint, **Hazrat Gesu Nawaz** – also known as Khwaja Bande Nawaz – who came to Gulbarga in 1413 during the reign of Firoz Shah Tughlaq, is open to visitors, see page 467. The two-storey tomb with a highly decorated painted dome had a mother-of-pearl canopy added over the grave. Please note that women are not allowed to enter the tombs. The **Dargah library**, which has 10,000 books in Urdu, Persian and Arabic, is open to visitors.

The most striking of all the tombs near **Haft Gumbaz**, the eastern group, is that of **Taj-ud-Din Firuz** (1422). Unlike the other tombs it is highly ornamented, with geometrical patterns developed in the masonry.

Bidar

» *pp317-320. Colour map 1, B6.*

→ *Phone code: 08357. Population: 172,300.*

The scruffy bungalow town that is modern day Bidar spreads out in a thin layer of buildings both within and without the imposing rust-red walls of the 15th-century fort that once played capital to two Deccan-ruling Muslim dynasties. The buildings may be new but there's still something of a medieval undercurrent to life here. Islam still grows sturdily: apart from the storehouses of government-subsidized industries to counter 'backwardness', the outskirts are littered with long white prayer walls to mop up the human overflow from over-burdened mosques during Id. A few lone tiles, tucked into high corners, still cling to the laterite brick structures that stand in for the succession of immaculately made palaces which must once have glowed incandescent with bright blue, green and yellow designs. Elsewhere you can only see the outline of the designs. The old fort commands grand vistas across the empty cultivated land below. Each successive palace was ruined by invasions then built anew a little further east.

History

The walled fort town, on a red laterite plateau in North Karnataka, once the capital of the **Bahmanis** and the **Barid Shahis**, remained an important centre until it fell to Aurangzeb in 1656. The Bahmani Empire fragmented into four kingdoms, and the ninth Bahmani

Bidar has a nearby Indian airforce base to which childless couples will voluntarily transfer in the hope that the legendarily virility-enhancing waters of Bidar will help them breed.

ruler, **Ahmad Shah I**, shifted his capital from Gulbarga to Bidar in 1424, rebuilding the old Hindu fort to withstand cannon attacks, and enriching the town with beautiful palaces and gardens. With the decline of the Bahmanis, the Barid Shahi Dynasty founded here ruled from 1487 until Bidar was annexed to Bijapur in 1619.

Sights

The intermingling of Hindu and Islamic architectural styles in the town has been ascribed to the use of Hindu craftsmen, skilled in temple carving in stone (particularly hornblende), who would have been employed by the succeeding Muslim rulers. They transferred their skill to Muslim monuments, no longer carving human figures, forbidden by Islam, but using the same technique to decorate with geometric patterns, arabesques and calligraphy, wall friezes, niches and borders. The pillars, often of wood, were intricately carved and then painted and burnished with gold to harmonize with the encaustic tiles.

The **Inner Fort** built by Muhammad Shah out of the red laterite and dark trapstone was later embellished by Ali Barid. The steep hill to the north and east provided natural

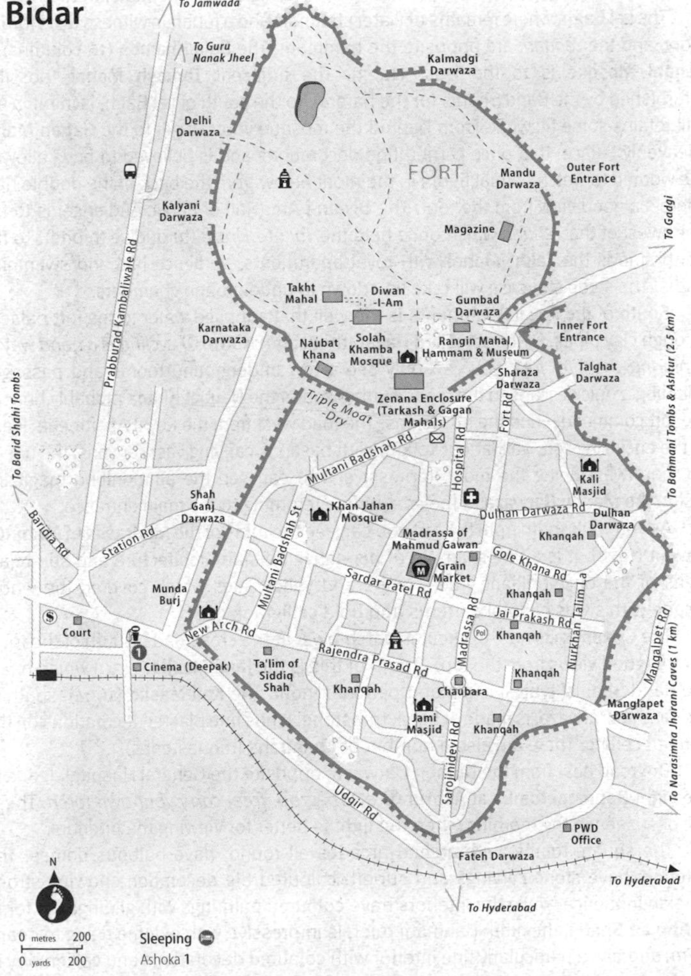

defence. It was protected to the south and west by a triple moat (now filled in). A series of gates and a drawbridge over the moat to the south formed the main entrance from the town. The second gate, the **Sharaza Darwaza** (1503) has tigers carved in bas relief on either side (Shia symbols of Ali as protector), the tile decorations on the walls and the *Nakkar Khana* (Drum gallery) above. Beyond this is a large fortified area which brings you to the third gate, the huge **Gumbad Darwaza**, probably built by Ahmad Shah Wali in the 1420s, with Persian influence. Note the decorated *gumbad* (dome).

You will see the triple moat to the right and after passing through the gateway, to your left are steps leading to the **Rangin Mahal** (Coloured Palace) where Muhammad Shah moved to, after finding the nearby Shah Burj a safe refuge in 1487 when the Abyssinians attacked. This small palace (an indication of the Bahmanis' declining years) was built by him, elaborately decorated with coloured tiles, later enhanced by Ali Barid with mother-of-pearl inlay on polished black granite walls as well as intricate wood carvings. If locked, ask at the museum (see below) for a key.

The old banyan tree and the **Shahi Matbak** (once a palace, but served as the Royal Kitchens) are to the west, with the **Shahi Hammam** (Royal Baths) next to it, which now houses a small **museum** ⓘ *0800-1700*. Exhibits include Hindu religious sculptures, Stone Age implements and cannon balls filled with bits of iron.

The **Lal Bagh**, where remains of water channels and a fountain witness to its former glory, and the *zenana*, are opposite the hammam. The **Sola Khamba** (16 columns) or **Zanani Mosque** is to the west (1423). The adjacent **Tarkash Mahal** (possibly refurbished by the Barid Shahis for the harem), to the south of Lal Bagh, is in ruins but still retains some tilework. From behind the mosque you can get to the **Gagan Mahal** (Heavenly Palace) that once carried fine decorations and is believed to have allowed the women to watch animal fights in the moat below from the back of the double hall. There's a good view from the roof. The **Diwan-i-Am** (Hall of Public Audience) is to the northwest of the *Zenana* which once held the *Takht-i-Firoza* (turquoise throne). To the north stands the **Takht Mahal** with royal apartments, audience hall and swimming baths. The steep staircase will take you down to underground chambers.

South of the Royal Apartments is the well that supplied water to the fort palaces through clay pipes. Of the so-called **Hazar** (thousand) **Kothri** ⓘ *cycling is a good way of exploring the site, free,* you can only see a few underground rooms and passages enabling a quick escape to the moat. Further south, the **Naubat Khana** probably housed the fort commander and the musicians. The road west from the Royal Apartments leads to the encircling Fort Wall (about 10 km) with bastions carrying vast canyons, the one to the northwest being the most impressive. You can see the ammunition magazine inside the **Mandu Darwaza** to the east before returning to the main entrance.

As you walk south from the fort you can see the ruins of the **Madrassa of Mahmud Gawan** (1472). It is a fine example of his native Persian architecture and still bears signs of the once-brilliant green, white and yellow tiles which covered the whole façade with swirls of floral patterns and bold calligraphy.

The **Chaubara** is a 23-m circular watchtower at the crossroads, south of the town centre (good views from the top). South of this is the **Jami Masjid** (1430) which bears the Barid Shahis' typical chain and pendant motif. The **Kali Masjid** (1694), south of the Talghat Darwaza, is made of black trapstone. It has fine plaster decorations on the vaulted ceiling. There are also a number of **khanqahs** (monasteries).

The road east from the Dulhan Darwaza, opposite the General Hospital, leads to the eight **Bahmani tombs** at **Ashtur** ⓘ *0800-1700, free, carry your own torch*. These are best seen in the morning when the light is better for viewing the interiors.

The square tombs, with arched arcades all round, have bulbous domes. The exteriors have stone carvings and superb coloured tile decoration showing strong Persian influence, while the interiors have coloured paintings with gilding. The tomb of **Ahmad Shah I**, the ninth Bahmani ruler, is impressive with a dome rising to nearly 35 m, and has a particularly fine interior with coloured decorations and calligraphy in the Persian style, highlighted with white borders. To the east and south are minor tombs of his wife and son. The tomb of **Alauddin Shah II** (1458) is possibly the finest. Similar in size to his father's, this has lost its fine painting inside but enough remains of the outer tilework to give an impression of its original magnificence.

On the way back is the **Chaukhandi of Hazrat Khalil-Ullah** which is approached by a flight of steps. Most of the tilework has disappeared but you can see the fine carvings at the entrance and on the granite pillars.

The **Barid Shahi tombs**, each of which once stood in its own garden, are on the Nanded Road to the west of the old town. That of **Ali Barid** is the most impressive, with the dome rising to over 25 m, with granite carvings, decorative plasterwork and calligraphy and floral patterns on the coloured tiles, which sadly can no longer be seen on the exterior. Here, abandoning the customary *mihrab* on the west wall, Ali Barid chose to have his tomb left open to the elements. It includes a prayer hall, music rooms, a combined tomb for his concubines and a pool fed by an aqueduct are nearby. There are fine carvings on the incomplete tomb to his son **Ibrahim Barid**, to the west. You can also see two sets of granite *ranakhambas* (lit battleposts) which may have been boundary markers. Other tombs show the typical arched niches employed to lighten the heavy walls which have decorative parapets.

The road north from Ali Barid's tomb descends to **Nanak Jhera**, where a *gurdwara* marks the holy place where Sikhs believe a miracle was performed by Guru Nanak (see page 521) and the *jhera* (spring) rose.

Raichur

» *p318. Colour map 1, C6.*

→ *Phone code: 08532. Population: 205,600.*

The main road from Hospet to Hyderabad passes through the important medieval centre of Raichur, once dominant in the Tungabhadra-Krishna *doab*, now an important but dusty market town, in the middle of a cotton-growing area.

The site of the **fort's citadel** at Raichur gives magnificent views over the vast open spaces of the Deccan plateau nearly 100 m below. Built in the mid-14th century Raichur became the first capital of the Bijapur Kingdom when it broke away from the Bahmani Sultans in 1489. Much of the fort itself is now in ruins, but there are some interesting remains. The north gate is flanked by towers, a carved elephant standing about 40 m away. On the inner walls are some carvings, and a tunnel reputedly built to enable soldiers access to barricade the gate in emergency. Near the west gate is the old palace. The climb to the citadel begins from near the north gate. In the citadel is a shrine with a row of cells with the Jami Masjid in the east. Its eastern gateway has three domes. The top of the citadel is barely 20 sq m.

There are some other interesting buildings in the fort below the hill, including the **Daftar ki Masjid** (Office Mosque), built around 1510 out of masonry removed from Hindu temples. It is one of the earliest mosques in the Deccan to be built in this way, with the bizarre result of producing flat ceilings with pillars carved for Chalukyan temples. The **Ek Minar ki Masjid** ('one-minaret mosque') is in the southeast corner of the courtyard. It has a distinctively Bahmani-style dome.

Sleeping

Hampi *p300, map p301*

Some use Hospet as a base for visiting Hampi; it has plusher accommodation and the nearest railway station. However, it means a commute to Hampi. Hampi is quieter and more atmospheric. Across the river (by coracle, Rs 15) you can reach the hamlet of Anegundi, a beautiful paddy planted village with budget guest houses, coco-huts and cottages to stay in. Power cuts are common; a supply of candles and a torch are essential. Mosquitos can be a real problem. A small selection from many guest houses are listed here. All are similar and mostly **E** or **F**; prices rise 30% at the height of the season, Nov-Jan.

D Ranjana Guest House, behind Govt school, T08394-244 1696. A friendly guest house with 5 rooms, plus hot water, cheaper rooms have a cooler, rather than a/c.

D-E Mayura Bhuvaneswari, 2 km from site, Kamalapuram, T08394-241574. 32 rooms (8 a/c, Rs 450), fairly clean, decent food, chilled beer, poor cycle hire.

E Archana, T08394-244 1547. 8 rooms, very clean, quiet, with nets and roof area, shop.

E Aum Guest House, T08394-244 1431. 4 rooms.

E Gopi, T08394-244 1695. 10 rooms with bath, nets, board games.

E Padma Guest House, T08394-244 1331. Family guest house, 4 doubles, exchange.

E Rahul, south of the bus stand but quite quiet. Basic sleeping under nets, clean. Good simple vegetarian food, views from rooftop.

E Raju, T08394-244 1349. 2 old characterful buildings by the river, with 2 and 14 rooms respectively. Clean, with a rooftop restaurant.

E Shakti Guest House, T08394-244 1953. 1 double room in a quiet family house.

E Shambhu, T08394-244 1383. 5 rooms with bath and nets, plenty of plants, rooftop restaurants (egg dishes), friendly.

E Shanti Guest House, down path to the right of the temple (signed), T08394-241568. 23 rooms with fans around pleasant courtyard with plenty of plants, common shower, roof for overspill, very clean, well run and friendly, cycle hire, good cakes (see page 318).

E Vicky, 200 m north of main road (turn off at tourist office), T08394-244 1694, vickyhampi@yahoo.co.in. 7 rooms (4 with bath), bucket hot water, Indian toilet, good rooftop restaurant, internet Rs 60 per hr.

Hospet *p303, map p304*

Station Rd is now Mahatma Gandhi Rd (MG Rd).

B-D Shanbhag Towers, College Rd, T08394-242 5910, shanbhagtowers@yahoo.com. 64 spacious rooms, 32 a/c with tub, TV, fridge, in new hotel, breathtaking Hampi theme, restaurants (one rooftop with great views), bar.

B-F Malligi, 6/143 Jambunatha Rd, T08394-242 8101. Generally pleasant, 140 rooms, 65 a/c, newer **D** are large with bath (4 **B** suites), always inspect first as standard varies a lot, restaurant and bar by pool (economy guests and non- residents pay Rs 25 per hr for pool), health club, exchange, travel (good Hampi tour Rs 80), creakingly slow internet and overpriced STD/ISD service.

C-E Priyadarshini, V/45 Station Rd, T08394-242 8838. Rather bare and bit overpriced, though friendly service, 82 fairly good rooms, 25 a/c, good restaurants, internet, parking.

D-E Karthik, 252 Sardar Patel Rd, T08394-242 6643. Quiet, modern hotel, 40 good sized, clean rooms, 10 a/c, garden dining, friendly and good value.

D-E Nagarjuna Residency, Sardar Patel Rd, opposite Karthik, T08394-242 9009. Spotless, modern, excellent value rooms, some a/c, extra bed Rs 30-50, very helpful. Recommended.

E SLV Yatri Nivas, Station Rd, T08394-242 1525. Clean, well-run hotel, 15 bright, airy rooms. Good vegetarian restaurant and bar. Recommended.

E Shivananda, next to bus stand, T08394-242 0700. 23 rooms, 4 a/c, simple but clean, and complete with resident astrologer!

F Viswa, MG Rd, opposite bus station, away from the road, T08394-242 7171. No frills but good value, 42 clean rooms (some 4-bed) with bath, adjacent **Shanthi** restaurant.

Bijapur *p304, map p306*

There has been a sudden spurt in decent hotels and restaurants.

B Madhuvan International, off Station Rd, T08352-255571. Very pleasant, 35 rooms, 10 a/c, good vegetarian garden restaurant and rooftop terrace, beer in rooms only, travel desk, but a bit overpriced. Quite noisy till 2330 because of restaurant.

B-D Hotel Kanishka International, Station Rd, T08352-223788. Decidedly garish decor (giant mirrors) in the 24 rooms (10 a/c), with cable TV, telephone, en suite, laundry and excellent **Kamat Restaurant** downstairs.

C-D Hotel Pearl, Opposite Gol Gumbaz, Station Rd, T08352-256002. Modern, modest mint pastel-coloured hotel set round a central courtyard , 32 rooms (17 a/c), scrupulously clean. Vegetarian basement restaurant (booze

For an explanation of the sleeping and eating price codes used in this guide, see inside the front cover. Other relevant information is found in Essentials pages 40-44.

and non-vegetarian food through room service). Telephones, cable TV in all rooms, laundry and parking.

D-E Hotel Navaratna International, Station Rd, T08352-222771. The grand colonnaded drive belies the modest price tag of the 34 rooms here (12 a/c). Communal areas scream with huge modernist paintings and rooms are done up with colour-coded care. TV, phone and smaller rooms have sit-outs. Very popular non-vegetarian courtyard restaurant, bar and pure vegetarian restaurant. They also have rooms and baths for drivers – a giant leap in the humane direction for an Indian hotel.

D-F Godavari, Athni Rd, T08352-253105. 48 good rooms, friendly staff, good vegetarian and non-vegetarian food.

D-F Samrat, Station Rd, T08352-251620. 30 basic rooms, 6 with a/c are passable, but the rest are battered. Good vegetarian garden restaurant but mosquitos like to dine here as well.

D-F Sanman, opposite Gol Gumbaz, Station Rd, T08352-251866. 24 clean, pleasant rooms with shower, nets, 6 a/c. Very good value. Separate vegetarian restaurant and a non-vegetarian restaurant with bar. Recommended.

E-F Santosh, T08352-52179. Convenient, good value, 70 good, clean rooms including some **D** a/c, quieter at back.

F Railway Retiring Room and dorm, exceptionally clean, contact ticket collector on duty. Recommended.

Badami *p310, map p310*

There is no formal money exchange but the Mukambika hotel may be persuaded to change small value TCs.

B Badami Court, Station Rd, T08357-220230. 2 km from town (pleasant stroll or frequent buses). 26 clean, modern, though cramped rooms (with bath), some a/c, good restaurant, pool (but small and only knee-deep, non-residents Rs 80 per hr) gym, garden. Rates sometimes negotiable, only accepts rupees, has the monopoly on accommodation and service; maintenance reflects the absence of competition.

F Shree Laxmi Vilas, simple rooms, 3 with balconies with great views back to the temples. Right in the thick of it, so it's interesting but noisy.

Gulbarga *p311, map below*

D Pariwar, Humnabad Rd, near station, T08472-221522. Some a/c rooms, some good value (**E**). Old but clean and tidy, friendly staff and tasty vegetarian meals (no beer).

D Santosh, University Rd (east of town), T08472-222661. Some a/c rooms, good non-vegetarian restaurant (beer). Best in town.

D-E Aditya, Humnabad Rd, T08472-202040. Reasonable rooms, some a/c with bath, clean vegetarian restaurant, very good value.

Bidar *p312, map p313*

E Ashoka, off Udgir Rd, near Deepak Cinema, T08482-226249. A bit of a dive, but the best Bidar has to offer, friendly, with 21 clean, good-sized rooms, hot water, some a/c. 'Restaurant' is more of a drinking den.

F Mayura Barid Shahi (KSTDC), Udgir Rd. Several very basic hotels near Old Bus Station. A roadside Punjabi *dhaba* near the

junction of NH9 and the Bidar Rd serves very good meals, clean (including toilet at back).

Raichur *p315*
F Laxmi Lodge at Koppal.
F Railway Retiring Rooms and dorm.

Eating

Hampi *p300, map p301*
All restaurants are vegetarian, eggs are sometimes available.
Boomshankar, on path to Vittahla temple. Well-prepared, fresh river fish.
Gopi, for good simple, cheap thalis.
Mango Tree, river bank, 500 m west of Temple. Relaxed and pleasant, slightly pricey riverside restaurant popular with backpackers.
Manju family run, simple but enticing food (apple *parathas*), takeaways for tiffin boxes (will even lend boxes).
Mayura Bhuvaneswari, Kamalapuram, does cheap adequate meals.
New Shanti, does good carrot/apple/banana/chocolate cakes to order.
Shambhu, opposite Shanti. For fresh pasta/noodles and espresso plus all the usual; also bus/train tickets for small commission.
Suresh, 30 m from Shanti, down a small alley. Very friendly family, made to order so takes a while, but worth the wait.

Hospet *p303, map p304*
The hotels serve chilled beer.
Waves, Malligi hotel, by pool. Multi cuisine. Good food, bar.
Iceland, Station Rd, behind the bus station, good South Indian meals.
Shanbhag, near the bus station, good South Indian meals.

Bijapur *p304, map p306*
Kapali, opposite bus stand. Decent South Indian food.
Priyadarshini. Vegetarian snacks.
Shrinidhi. Quality vegetarian meals.

Badami *p310*
Dhabas near the Tonga Stand sells snacks.
Laxmi Vilas, near taxi stand. Vegetarian meals.
Parimala and **Geeta Darshini**, South Indian breakfasts.
Sanman, near bus stand. Non vegetarian.

Festivals and events

Hampi *p300, map p301*
Jan-Feb: Virupaksha Temple Car festival.
3-5 Nov: **Hampi Music festival** at Vitthala Temple when hotels get packed.

Bijapur *p304, map p306*
Jan: **Siddhesvara Temple festival**. Music festival accompanied by Craft Mela.

Pattadakal *p308*
In **Jan Nrutytsava** draws many famous dancers and is accompanied by a Craft Mela. In **Mar-Apr Temple car** festivals at Virupaksha and Mallikarjuna temples.

Shopping

Bidar *p312, map p313*
Excellent bidriwork (see page 325) here, where it is said to have originated, especially shops near Ta'lim of Siddiq Shah. You can see craftsmen at work in the narrow lanes.

Activities and tours

Hospet *p303, map p304*
Tours from **KSTDC**, T08394-21008, and **SRK Tours and Travels** at Malligi hotel, to Hampi, Rs 75 (lunch extra); 0930-1630. Daytrips to Aihole, Badami, Pattadakal 0830-1930, Rs 275 per person with trip. Long drive. Local sightseeing Rs 700 per day. Bijapur 1 day trip by public bus Rs 175, taxi Rs 2100. English-speaking guide but rather rushed.

Transport

Hampi *p300*
Bicycle hire from Hampi Bazar (try stall behind the temple, Rs 30 per day), and Kamalapuram.
Coracles From the jetty west of Virupaksha Temple, Rs 5 (Rs 10 with luggage).
Air KSTDC has introduced an air route to Hampi from **Bengaluru**; US$1700 for a 5-seater plane or US$3990 for a 6-seater helicopter. Contact the state tourism office, Badami House, opposite City Corporation Office, NR Square T080-2227 5869.

Hospet *p303, map p304*
From Hospet to/from **Hampi**, travel via Kamalapuram, especially in the rainy season when the slower road to Hampi Bazar which winds through villages is barely passable. Auto-rickshaw to Hampi, Rs 200.

Bus
Frequent buses to **Hampi**'s 2 entry points (via Kamalapuram and museum, Rs 4 and via Hampi Bazar, 30 mins, Rs 3.50), from 0530; last return around 2000. Express bus to/from **Bengaluru (Bangalore)** (road now upgraded), several from 0700, 10 hrs; **Mysore**, 1830, 10½ hrs (Express buses to Belur/Halebid from both). Services to other sites, eg **Badami** (6 hrs), **Bijapur** (6 hrs), **Chitradurga** 0530 (3 hrs). Overnight **Karnataka Tourism luxury** coaches to various towns. Direct buses to **Panaji** (Goa); the road is being improved: *Luxury*, 0630 (10½ hrs), State bus, 0830 (reserve a seat in advance); others involve a change in Hubli (4½ hrs). **Paulo Travels Luxury Sleeper** coach from Hotel Priyadarshini, at 1845, Rs 350, daily; **West Coast Sleeper**, from Hotel Shanbhag, 1830, Rs 350; daily (Oct-Mar only); strangers may be expected to share a bunk. It's better to take a train to Londa (under 5 hrs) and get a bus to Madgaon or Panaji (3 hrs).

Rickshaw
From train station to bus stand about Rs 20.

Taxi
KSTDC, T08394-21008, T08394-28537 or from Malligi Hotel; about Rs 700 per day.

Train
Bengaluru (Bangalore), *Hampi Exp 6591*, 2010 (via Guntakal, 2½ hrs) 10½ hrs. **Guntakal**: *Amaravati Exp 7226*, 1610, 2½ hrs. For **Belur/ Halebid**: *Amaravati Exp 7225*, 1050 to **Hubli**; then *Hubli-Arsikere Pass 884 (S)*, 1440, arrive 2120. To **Badami**: via **Gadag**, 4 hrs. **Hyderabad** (via **Guntakal**): *Hampi/Rayalaseema Exp 6591/7430*, 2010, 14 hrs. **Madgaon**, *7227*, Tue, Fri, depart Hospet 1050, 9 hrs.

From nearby **Gadag**, train to **Bijapur**: *Golgumbaz Exp 7842*, 0715, 4½ hrs. **Guntakal** via **Hospet** (2 hrs): at 0037, 1412, 1802 and 2101, 4 hrs; **Hubli**: 8 daily 0322-2030, 1¾ hrs.

Bijapur *p304, map p306*
Bus
A service runs between the station (2 km east) to west end of town. Horse drawn carriages ply up and down MG Rd; a fine change from autos but bargain hard.

Buses are frequent between Bijapur and **Bidar**, **Hubli**, **Belgaum** and **Solapur** (2-2½ hrs). Buses to **Badami** 3½ hrs. For **Hospet**, travel via Gadag or Ikal. Reservations can be made on the following daily services to **Aurangabad**: 0600, 1830 (Rs 180), **Hospet**, **Bengaluru (Bangalore)**: 1700, 1800, 1930, 2130 (Rs 193, 12 hrs); Ultra fast at 1900, 2000 (Rs 252), **Belgaum**: 0630 (Rs 71), **Hubli**: 0900, 1400, 1600 (Rs 84), **Hyderabad**: 0600, 1800 (Rs 141); Deluxe at 2130 (Rs 203), **Mumbai (CT)** : 0800, 1600, 1700, 2030 (Rs 215), **Mumbai (Kurla)**: 1900, 2000, 2100 (Rs 210), **Mysore**: 1700 (Rs 230), **Panaji**: 1900 (Rs 126) and **Vasco de Gama**: 0715 (Rs 131). Several private agents also run services to **Bengaluru** (Rs 220, 12 hrs), **Mumbai** (Rs 250, 11 hrs) and **Pune** (Rs 200, 7 hrs).

Train
Computerized Reservation Office open 0800-2000, Sun 0800-1400. **Solapur**: 0945, 1635 (2½ hrs). **Gadag**: 5 trains daily for long distance connections. Otherwise, buses are more convenient.

Badami *p310, map p310*
Bicycle
Bike hire from stalls located along the main road, Rs 4 per hr; it's pleasant to visit Banashankari, Mahakuta and Pattadakal.

Bus
Few daily to **Hospet** (6 hrs), very slow and crowded but quite a pleasant journey with lots of stops; **Belgaum** via **Bagalkot**, 4 hrs; **Bijapur**, 0645-0930 (4 hrs). Several to **Pattadakal** and **Aihole** from 0730. **Aihole** (2 hrs), from there to **Pattadakal** (1600). Last return bus from Aihole 1715, via Pattadakal.

Car
Hire a car from Badami with driver for Mahakuta, Aihole and Pattadakal, about Rs 650.

Train

The station is 5 km north on the **Bijapur-Gadag** line; 6 trains daily in each direction (ask about times); frequent buses to town.

Gulbarga *p311, map p317*

Bus

There are bus connections to **Hyderabad** (190 km) and **Solapur**.

Train

Mumbai (CST): 8 trains daily, 13 hrs. **Bengaluru**: *Udayan Exp 6529*, 1900, 13½ hrs; *Lokmanya Tilak 1013*, 0905, 13 hrs. **Chennai (MC)**: *Chennai Exp 6011* (AC/II), 0130, 15 hrs; *Mumbai Chennai Mail 6009*, 1140, 18 hrs; *Dadar Chennai Exp1063*, 0605, 14 hrs. **Hyderabad**: *Mumbai-Hyderabad Exp 7031* (AC/II), 0020, 5¾ hrs; *Hussainsagar Exp 7001*, 0740, 5 hrs.

Bidar *p312, map p313*

Auto-rickshaw

Easily available, Rs 15 being the going rate for most short hops across town.

Bicycle

Cycling is the best way to get around and see the sights. 'Cycle taxis' can be hired for Rs 20 per day from several outlets all over town and near the New Bus Station. You may have to ask a few before you find a shop that will rent to you, but persevere. Don't waste time with Ganesh Cycle Taxi near New Bus Station.

Bus

Services from New Bus Station, 1 km west of centre, to most regional destinations, but check timings since the last bus is often quite early. From **Hyderabad** or **Gulbarga** (under 4 hrs), or **Bijapur** (8 hrs). Private buses to **Mumbai**: 1700, 5 hrs, Rs 260. **Pune**: 1530, 3½ hrs, Rs 220. Taxi to **Gulbarga** Rs 800.

Train

Bidar is on a branch line from Vikarabad to Parbhani Junction. Too slow to be of much use. **Aurangabad**: *Kacheguda-Manmad Exp 7664*, 2140, 8½ hrs. **Bengaluru (Bangalore)**: *Hampi Link Exp 6593*, 1237, 18 hrs. **Secunderabad**: *Manmad-Kacheguda Exp 7663*, 0352, 5 hrs.

Directory

Hampi *p300, map p301*

Exchange Several agents on main street. Modi Enterprises, Main road, near Tourist Office, changes TCs and cash. Also Neha Travels. **Internet, money change and tour agent** On main street and some lodges (eg *Shanti, Sree Rama*), Rs 60 per hr; but frequent power cuts.

Hospet *p303, map p304*

Banks State Bank of India, next to Tourist Office, only changes cash (US$ and £). Monica Travel, near Bus Station, changes TCs (3% charge). **Internet** Cybernet, College Rd, next to Shivananda. **Post** Opposite veg market.

Bijapur *p304, map p306*

Banks State Bank of India in the citadel, Canara Bank, north of market, best for exchange. **Internet** Cyber Park, first floor, Royal Complex, opposite GPO, 0930-2300 fast connections.

Andhra Pradesh

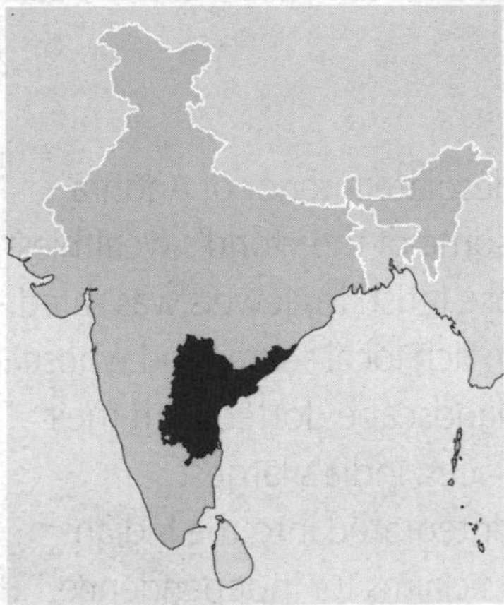

Footprint features

Introduction

The thin red soil of the hot and desolate interior of Andhra Pradesh was once the stage for some of the world's wealthiest men. The Deccani Sultans – whose fetish for jewels was sated with the diamonds quarried from rich local seams and whose ears dripped with pearls – left a landscape dotted with their courtly pleasure gardens and palaces. India's largest Muslim-ruled princely state was integrated into the Indian union when the army quashed its claims for independence, but much of the splendour of their architecture remains, particularly in Hyderabad and its nearby fortress city of Golconda. And the city's fortunes have revived along with the success of the software industries who have their headquarters at the glass-and-chrome satellite town of 'Cyberabad'.

The watersheds of Andhra Pradesh's rivers, the Krishna and Godavari, are second only to the Ganga and are vital in supporting the meagre agricultural subsistence of the bullock-and-cart paddy economy. Rural Andhra also holds the ancient Buddhist centres of Nagarjunakonda and Amaravati and one of India's most important modern Hindu pilgrimage centres, Tirumalai. Large areas of the northwest also hide the secretive Maoist Naxalite movement, a rebel army whose often violent opposition to aid and development has lead to the blocking of road-building efforts and several attempts on the state's former chief minister's life.

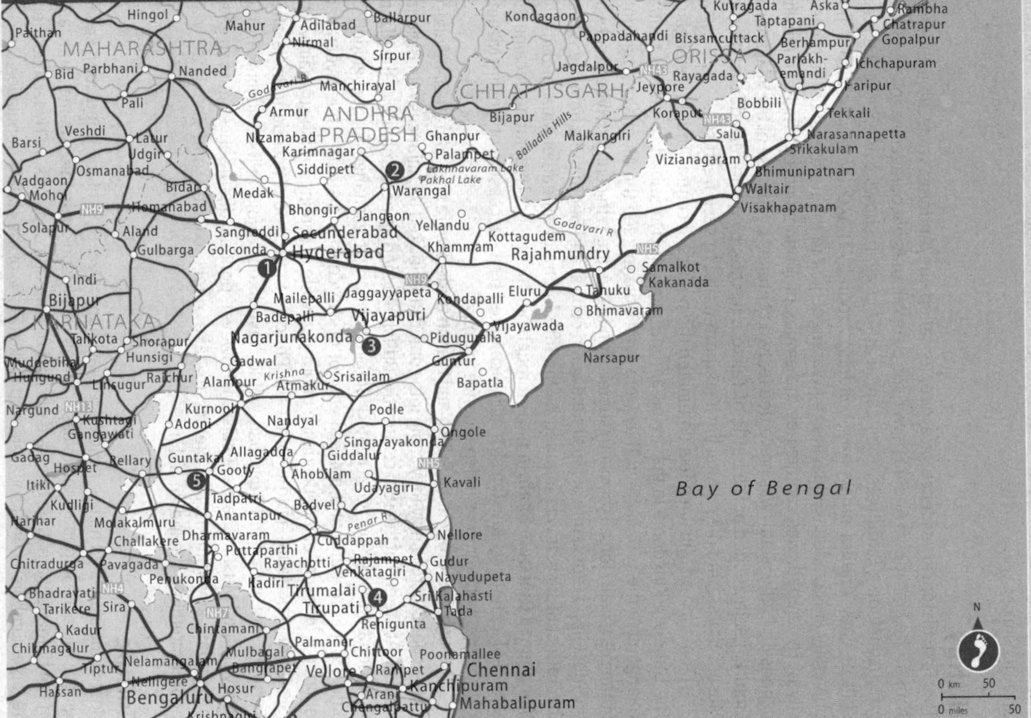

★ Don't miss ...

1 **Hyderabad** View the riches that once belonged to the Nizams at the Salar Jung Museum and visit the Mecca Masjid, especially during the quaranic call to prayer on Sunday afternoons when 40 people from ages 12 to 60 act as muezzin for the adhan, page 326.

2 **Warangal** Walk through the ruins of the medieval city, page 337.

3 **Nagarjunakonda Island** Take a boat ride across the lake to reach one of India's oldest Buddhist sites, page 338.

4 **Tirupati temple** Attend at *darshan* (special viewing) along with 10,000 other pilgrims, page 351.

5 **Vijayanagar Fort, Gooty** Climb to the top for spectacular views over the plains, page 356.

Background → *Population: 75.7 million. Area: 275,000 sq km.*

The land

Geography For much of the year the interior looks dry and desolate although the great delta of the Krishna and Godavari rivers retains its lush greenness by virtue of their irrigation water. Water is the state's lifeblood, and the great peninsular rivers have a sanctity that reflects their importance. The Godavari, rising less than 200 km north of Mumbai, is the largest of the peninsular rivers. The Krishna rises near Mahabaleshwar at an altitude of 1360 m. After the Ganga these two rivers have the largest watersheds in India, and between them irrigate nearly 60,000 sq km of farmland.

Climate Andhra Pradesh is hot throughout the year. The interior is in the rain shadow of the Western Ghats and receives less rainfall than much of the coast. The heaviest rainfall is between June and October, but the south gets the benefit of the retreating monsoon between October and December. Cyclones sweeping across the Bay of Bengal can wreak havoc in the flat coastal districts in November and December.

History

The first historical evidence of a people called the Andhras came from Emperor Asoka. The first known Andhra power, the **Satavahanas** encouraged various religious groups including Buddhists. Their capital at Amaravati shows evidence of the great skill of early Andhra artists and builders. Around AD 150 there was also a fine university at Nagarjunakonda. In 1323 Warangal, just to the northeast of the present city of Hyderabad, was captured by the armies of Muhammad bin Tughlaq. Muslim expansion further south was prevented for two centuries by the rise of the **Vijayanagar Empire**, itself crushed at the Battle of Talikota in 1565 by a short-lived federation of Muslim States, and the cultural life it supported had to seek fresh soil.

From then on **Muslim rulers** dominated the politics of central Andhra, Telangana. The Bahmani Kingdoms in the region around modern Hyderabad controlled central Telangana in the 16th century. They were even able to keep the Mughals at bay until Aurangzeb finally forced them into submission in the late 17th century. **Hyderabad** was the most important centre of Muslim power in central and South India from the 17th to the 19th centuries. It was founded by the fifth in line of an earlier Muslim dynasty, **Mohammad Quli Qutb Shah**, in 1591. Through his successors Hyderabad became the capital of a Princely State the size of France, ruled by a succession of Muslim Nizams from 1724 till after India's Independence in 1947.

Through the 18th century **British and French traders** were spreading their influence up the coast. Increasingly they came into conflict and looked for alliances with regional powers. At the end of the 18th century the British reached an agreement with the **Nizam of Hyderabad** whereby he accepted British support in exchange for recognition of British rights to trade and political control of the coastal districts. Thus Hyderabad retained a measure of independence until 1947 while accepting British suzerainty.

There was doubt as to whether the Princely State would accede to India after Partition. The Nizam of Hyderabad would have liked to join fellow Muslims in the newly created Muslim State of Pakistan. However, political disturbances in 1949 gave the Indian government the pretext to take direct control, and the state was incorporated into the Indian Union.

Culture

Most of the state's 78 million people are Dravidians. Over 85% of the population speak Telugu. There are important minorities. Tamil is widely spoken in the extreme south, and on the border of Karnataka there are pockets of Kannada speakers. In Hyderabad there are large numbers of Urdu speakers who make up 7% of the state's population.

Hyderabad, the capital of modern Andhra Pradesh, was the seat of government of the Muslim Nizams. Under their rule many Muslims came to work in the court, from North India and abroad. The Nizam's capital was a highly cosmopolitan centre, drawing extensively on Islamic contacts in North India and in west Asia, notably Persia.

Andhra **food** stands out as distinct because of its northern influence and larger number of non-vegetarians. The rule of the Muslim Nawabs for centuries is reflected in the rich, spicy local dishes, especially in the area around the capital. Try *haleem* (spiced pounded wheat with mutton), *paya* (soup) or *baghara baigan* (stuffed aubergines). Rice and meat biryani, *nahari*, *kulcha,* egg *paratha,* and *kababs* have a lot in common with the northern Mughlai cuisine. The abundance of locally grown hot chillies has led to a fiery traditional cuisine, for which 'Andhra-style' is a byword. Also grown locally, good quality grapes (especially *anab-e-shahi*) or *khobani* (puréed apricots) provide a welcome neutralizing effect.

Craft industries

Andhra's **bidriware** uses dark matt gunmetal (a zinc and copper alloy) with silver damascening in beautiful flowing floral and arabesque patterns and illustrates the Persian influence on Indian motifs. The articles vary from large vases and boxes, jewellery and plates to tiny buttons and cuff links. The name is derived from Bidar in Karnataka and dates back to the Bahmani rulers.

Miniature wooden figures, animals, fruit, vegetables and birds are common subjects of *Kondapalli* **toys** which are known for their bright colours. *Nirmal* toys look more natural and are finished with a herbal extract which gives them a golden sheen. *Tirupati* toys are in a red wood while *Ethikoppaka* toys are finished in coloured lacquer. Andhra also produces fine figurines of deities in sandalwood.

Hyderabadi **jewellers** work in gold and precious stones which are often uncut. The craftspeople can often be seen working in the lanes around the Char Minar – shops selling the typical local bangles set with glass lie to the west. Hyderabadi cultured pearls and silver filigree ware from Karimnagar are another speciality.

The state is famous for **himru shawls** and **fabrics** produced in cotton/silk mixes with rich woven patterns on a special handloom. Silver or gold threads produce an even richer brocade cloth. A boy often sits with the weavers 'calling out' the intricate pattern. The All India Handicrafts Board has revived the art of weaving special **ikat** fabrics. Interestingly, oil is used in the process of dyeing the warp and weft threads before weaving in to produce a pattern, hence the fabric's name teli rumal (literally oil kerchief).

Kalahasti, in Andhra's extreme south, produces distinctive **Kalamkari cloth paintings** (*kalam* refers to the pen used); the dyes come from indigo, turmeric and pomegranate. The blues stand out from the otherwise dullish ochre colours. Designed from mythology tales (*Mahabharata* and *Ramayana*), they make excellent wall hangings.

Modern Andhra Pradesh

Government In 1953 Andhra Pradesh was created on the basis of the Telugu-speaking districts of Madras Presidency. This was not enough for those who were demanding statehood for a united Telugu-speaking region. One political leader, Potti Sreeramulu, starved himself to death in protest at the government's refusal to grant the demand. In 1956, Andhra Pradesh took its present form; all Telugu-speaking areas were grouped together in the new state of Andhra Pradesh.

Andhra Pradesh was regarded as a stronghold of the Congress Party until 1983 when a regional party, the Telugu Desam, won a crushing victory in the State Assembly elections. The Assembly elections on 5 October 1999 saw a repeat performance, with the highly regarded modernizing Chief Minister N Chandrababu Naidu being swept back to power with nearly a two-thirds majority. Allied with the BJP in the governing coalition in New Delhi, the Telugu Desam had a reputation for pushing ahead with rapid economic modernization, particularly visible in Hyderabad, but Naidu, who borrowed heavily from the World Bank and took China, Singapore and Malaysia as his business models, won only 47 of the 295 seats in the State Assembly elections in 2004. The Congress and its newly formed regional party ally, the Telangana Rashtra Samiti, with 226 seats, reclaimed power. The Congress Chief Minister YS Rajasekhara Reddy (known as YSR) took charge of a state with high debts to the World Bank, where rural poverty was endemic and where suicide had become a major problem among poor farmers. The Congress-led government offered to resolve the long-standing terrorist activities of the Peoples War Group and the Naxalites by offering a peace settlement. However, talks broke down in 2004, and operating in some of the remotest areas of northwestern Andhra Pradesh, they continue to carry out murder, bombing and kidnapping and the execution of summary penalties through 'people's courts'.

North central Andhra Pradesh

Hyderabad and Secunderabad

» pp340-344. Colour map 2, B1.

→ *Phone code: 040. Population: 5.5 mn.*

The Twin Cities, founded by the rulers of two separate Muslim dynasties, have long since bled into one conglomerate metropolis. The southern (Hyderabadi) half holds the dusty and congested old city, with its beautiful but faded palaces of Islamic architecture, where the atmospheric lanes around Char Minar throb with a contemporary Muslim mania.

N Chandrababu Naidu, Andhra's chief minister from the late 1990s until 2004, had development dreams as lofty as the legendarily eccentric Nizam. The result is a city with town planning unequalled in India, huge theme resorts where you can stand at minus temperatures, a tribute to the famous heat of Andhra, and a Hi-Tech City to rival Silicon Valley, the brilliantly named Cyberabad, home to Microsoft's first overseas base. The success of these hi-tech and biotech industries has spawned a new elite to keep the old pearl peddlers in business since trade from the jewel-draped Nizams dried up. A splendid medieval fort, Golconda, and tranquil onion-dome tombs of the 16th-century Qutb Shahi rulers sit just on the modern city's outskirts.

Ins and outs

Getting there Begumpet airport is just 6 km from Secunderabad station and 15 km from Hyderabad Old City (which has most of the sights). Out of rush hour it takes 15 minutes to get there. Construction of a new airport, GMR Hyderabad International Airport, is underway 22 km from the city. Scheduled to open in 2008, it aims to cater for 50 million passengers a year, making Hyderabad India's airport hub, and will also allow for direct flights to and from most European cities. Secunderabad station, with trains to major cities, is in the Cantonment area, while the Hyderabad City station at Nampally is close to the Abids shopping district, with the majority of budget accommodation. The large Imbli-Ban Bus terminal for long-distance buses is on an island in the Musi River, south of Abids. The Jubilee Bus Terminal is in Secunderabad.

Getting around Autos (or taxis) are the best means of getting about the city north of the Musi and in Secunderabad, but in the congested old quarter you are best off walking, though there are cycle-rickshaws. » *See Transport, page 342, for further details.*

Tourist offices **Govt of AP** ⓘ *A Block, 3rd floor, Secretariat, T040-2345 6717; Tank Bund Rd, near Secretariat, T040-2345 3036.* **APTDC** ⓘ *3rd floor, FDC Complex, AC Guards, T040-2339 9416, apttdc@satyam.net.in, 0630-1830.*

History

In 1323 Warangal, just to the northeast of the present city of Hyderabad, was captured by the armies of Muhammad bin Tughlaq. Muslim expansion further south was prevented for two centuries by the rise of the **Vijayanagar Empire**, itself crushed at the Battle of Talikota in 1565 by a short-lived federation of Muslim States, and the cultural life it supported had to seek fresh soil.

From then on **Muslim rulers** dominated the politics of central Andhra, which was then called Telangana. The Shiite Bahmani Kingdoms in the region around modern Hyderabad controlled central Telangana in the 16th century. They were even able to keep the Sunni rivals, the Mughals, at bay until Aurangzeb finally forced them into submission at the end of the 17th century. Hyderabad was the most important centre of Muslim power in central and South India from the 17th to the 19th centuries. The city was founded by the fifth in line of an earlier Muslim Dynasty, **Mohammad Quli Qutb Shah**, under the original name of Bhagnagar, in 1591. Through his successors Hyderabad became the capital of a Princely State the size of France, ruled by a succession of Muslim Nizams from 1724 till after India's Independence in 1947. The Nizams were a dynasty that included some of the world's richest men, famous for their beautiful 'monuments, mosques and mistresses' and also for their diamond markets.

Through the 18th century **British and French traders** were scrambling to win allies with regional rulers as their influence spread up the coast and the fight for supremacy in India became more embittered. In the late 18th century the British reached an agreement with the **Nizam of Hyderabad** whereby he would accept British support in exchange for recognition of British rights to trade and political control of the coastal districts. Thus Hyderabad retained a measure of independence until 1947 while accepting British suzerainty.

It was doubted whether the Princely State would accede to India after Partition. The Nizam of Hyderabad wanted to join fellow Muslims in the newly created Muslim State of Pakistan. However, political disturbances in 1949 gave the Indian Government the excuse to take direct control, and the state was incorporated into the Indian Union.

Sayyid Abul A'la Maududi was born in the princely state of Hyderabad in 1903, and went on to become a fierce opponent of British rule. Although he initially opposed the foundation of the separate Pakistani state, instead calling for Muslim rule across the whole of India, he went on to found Jamaat-e-Islami, one of the most influential parties in Pakistan, which lobbied tirelessly for the Islamization of the state and society. He still remains an icon of fundamentalist Islamic political thought today.

Hyderabad has a large Muslim minority, even though the population was always predominantly composed of Telugu-speaking Hindus. Occasionally the political situation can become tense and parts of the city put under curfew. Fridays in the old city often see armed Indian paramilitary on the streets.

Old City and Char Minar

Sultan Mohammed Quli Qutb Shah built the lofty archway of **Char Minar** at the entrance to his palace complex. The structure, built of huge slabs of black granite quarried nearby, holds 10,000 at prayers. It has remained the showpiece and symbol of the city since it was built between 1591 and 1612, although today it stands at the centre of a busy crossroads, surrounded by the sprawling Old City bazar. The monument is lit up every evening and there is a Thursday market.

Devastating floods and outbreaks of plague at the beginning of the 19th century were followed by programmes of urban renewal initiated by Nizam Osman Ali Khan. A series of new public buildings date from this period including those from 1914 to 1921, under the supervision of British architect Vincent Esch, who attempted to build in an Indian style.

Hyderabad-Secunderabad

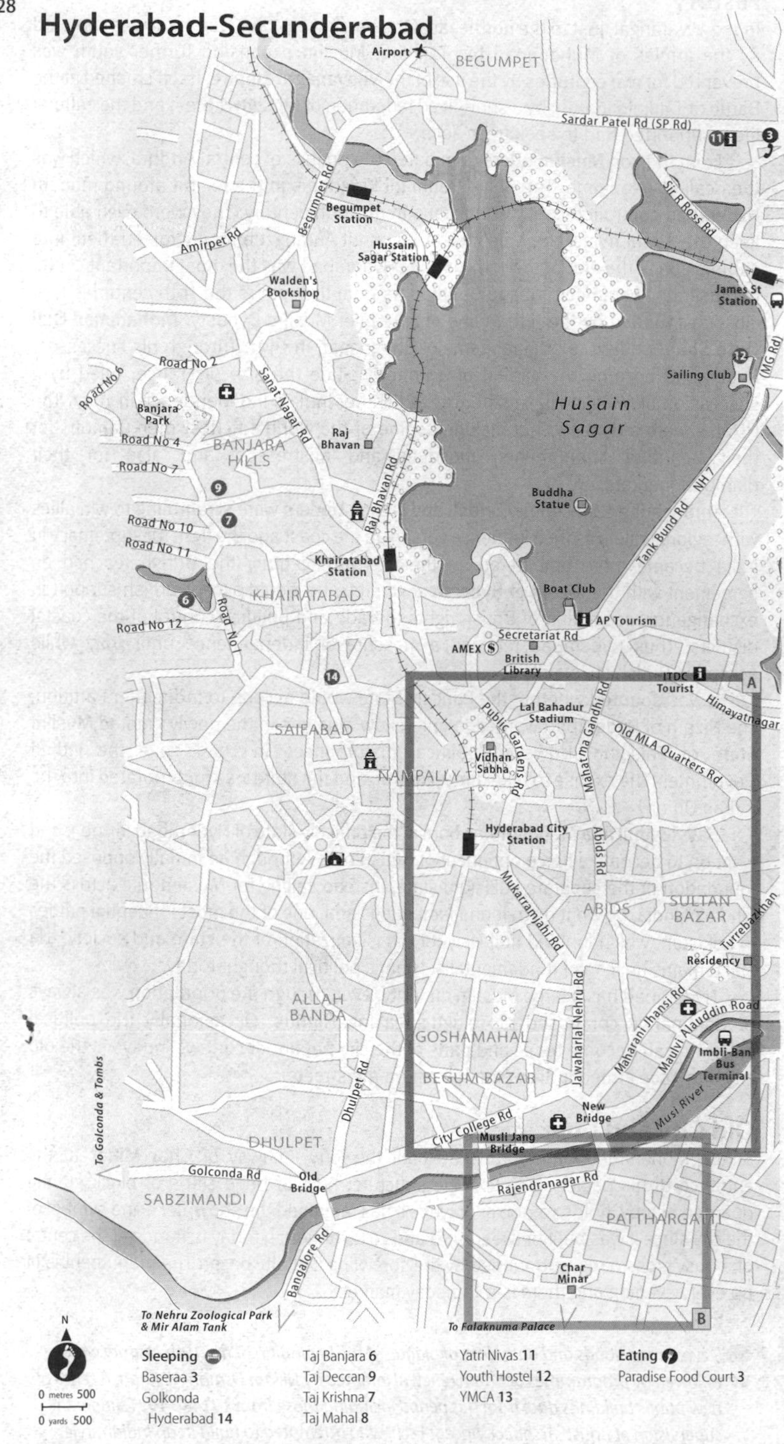
Airport
BEGUMPET
Sardar Patel Rd (SP Rd)
Begumpet Rd
Begumpet Station
Amirpet Rd
Hussain Sagar Station
Sir R Ross Rd
James St Station
Walden's Bookshop
Road No 2
Road No 6
Banjara Park
Sanat Nagar Rd
Sailing Club
(MG Rd)
Husain Sagar
Road No 4
BANJARA HILLS
Raj Bhavan
Road No 7
Raj Bhavan Rd
Buddha Statue
Tank Bund Rd
NH 7
Road No 10
Road No 11
Khairatabad Station
KHAIRATABAD
Road No 1
Road No 12
Boat Club
AP Tourism
Secretariat Rd
AMEX
British Library
ITDC Tourist
Himayatnagar
Lal Bahadur Stadium
Public Gardens Rd
Mahatma Gandhi Rd
Old MLA Quarters Rd
SAIFABAD
Vidhan Sabha
NAMPALLY
Hyderabad City Station
Abids Rd
Mukarramjahi Rd
ABIDS
SULTAN BAZAR
Turrebazkhan
Residency
ALLAH BANDA
Jawaharlal Nehru Rd
Maharani Jhansi Rd
Maulvi Alauddin Road
Imbli-Ban Bus Terminal
GOSHAMAHAL
BEGUM BAZAR
Musi River
New Bridge
City College Rd
Dhulpet Rd
To Golconda & Tombs
DHULPET
Musli Jang Bridge
Golconda Rd
Old Bridge
SABZIMANDI
Rajendranagar Rd
PATTHARGATTI
Bangalore Rd
Char Minar
To Nehru Zoological Park & Mir Alam Tank
To Falaknuma Palace
A
B
N
0 metres 500
0 yards 500
Sleeping
Baseraa 3
Golkonda Hyderabad 14
Taj Banjara 6
Taj Deccan 9
Taj Krishna 7
Taj Mahal 8
Yatri Nivas 11
Youth Hostel 12
YMCA 13
Eating
Paradise Food Court 3

Andhra Pradesh North central Andhra Pradesh

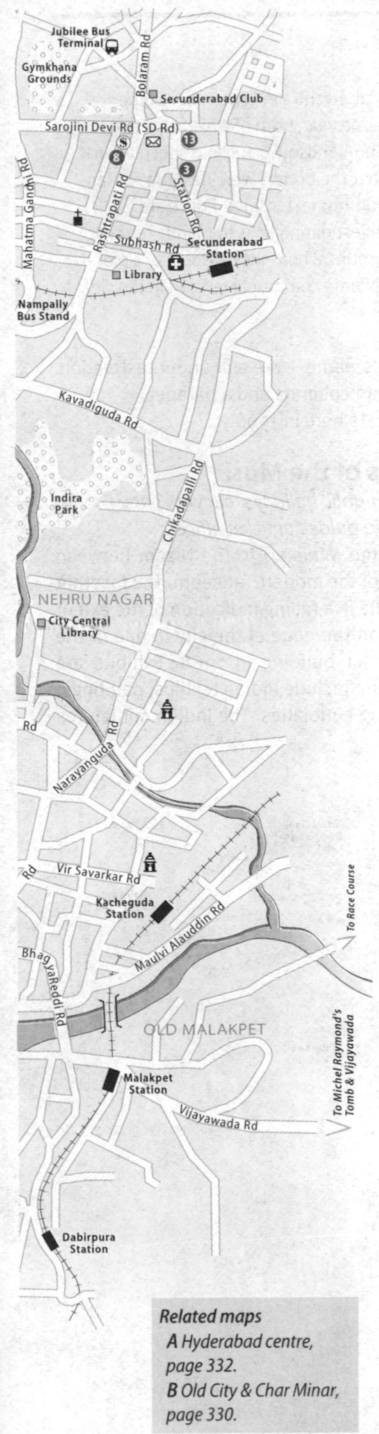

Related maps
A Hyderabad centre, page 332.
B Old City & Char Minar, page 330.

Mecca Masjid Immediately southwest of Char Minar, this vast mosque was started in 1614 by the sixth **Sultan Abdulla Qutb Shah** and completed by Aurangzeb when he annexed Golconda in 1692. Its structure, comprising huge slabs of black granite quarried nearby, was made hold 10,000 at prayers. Builders combined clay from Mecca with red colouring to make the entrance bricks. The tombs of the Asaf Jahi rulers, the Nizams of Hyderabad, are in an enclosure with a roof, to the left of the courtyard.

Jama Masjid Towards the river, the Jama Masjid is the second mosque built in the old city at the end of the 16th century, beyond which on Sadar Patel Road are the four arches of **Charkaman**. The eastern Black Arch was for the drums, while the western led to the palaces; the northern was the Fish Arch and the southern one was for the Char Minar.

Lad Bazar area The heart of the Muslim part of the city, the area around the Mecca Masjid and the Char Minar is a fascinating hive of bazars, made up of beautiful wooden buildings with stone carvings and pink elephant gates, packed with people. You arrive at the **Chowk**, with a mosque and a Victorian Clock Tower.

Southeast of the Lad Bazar is the enormous complex of the palaces which were built by the different Nizams, including the grand **Chowmahalla Palace** ⓘ *Sat-Thu 1000-1700, closed holidays, Rs 150*, a facsimile of the Shah's Palace in Tehran, whose stuccoed, domed Durbar Hall, courtyards and gardens have been carefully restored at the behest of Princess Esra, who is the eighth Nizam's wife. In the Durbar Hall is a platform of pure marble on which the Takht-e-Nishan (royal seat) was placed. Nizam Salabhat Jung began the splendid palace complex in 1750, but it was only completed more than 100 years later by Nizam Afzar-ud-Dawla Bahadur. The Khilwat, or Durbar Hall, Afzal Mahal, Mahtab Mahal, Tahniyat Mahal and Aftab Mahal – the

Attacks on mosques

A crude bomb detonated near the marble *wuzukhana* (ablution tank) in Mecca Masjid during Friday afternoon prayers on 18 May 2007 killed 11 people, with six more killed by police. The circumstances were similar to the bombing of Delhi's Jama Masjid in April 2006 and Malegaon in Maharashtra in September of the same year, both of which also targeted Sunni mosques, fuelling speculation that the bombs were designed to fan communal tensions. Police are investigating links to Islamic terrorist groups whom they suspect of a plot to inflame communal tension in the city.

four ('chow') palaces ('mahal') of the complex's name – are still under restoration. Aftab Mahal has a European façade of Corinthian columns and a parapet.

The Prince and Princess of Wales were guests here in 1906.

Salar Jung Museum and the banks of the Musi

ⓘ *Salar Jung Marg. Sat-Thu 1030-1700, closed public holidays, allow 1½ hrs. Rs 150, cameras and bags must be left at counter, audio guides at ticket office.*

Sir Yusuf Ali Salar Jung III was the Wazir (Prime Minister) to the Nizam between 1899-1949, and his collection forms the basis of the modern museum. The fact that it is one of only three national museums in India is a telling indication of the extent of the riches he amassed. Originally housed on the edge of the city in one of the palaces, it was rehoused in this purpose-built building in 1968. Exhibits are described in English, Urdu, Hindi and Telugu and include Indian textiles, paintings, armoury, Far Eastern porcelain and entertaining curiosities. The Indian miniatures are stunning.

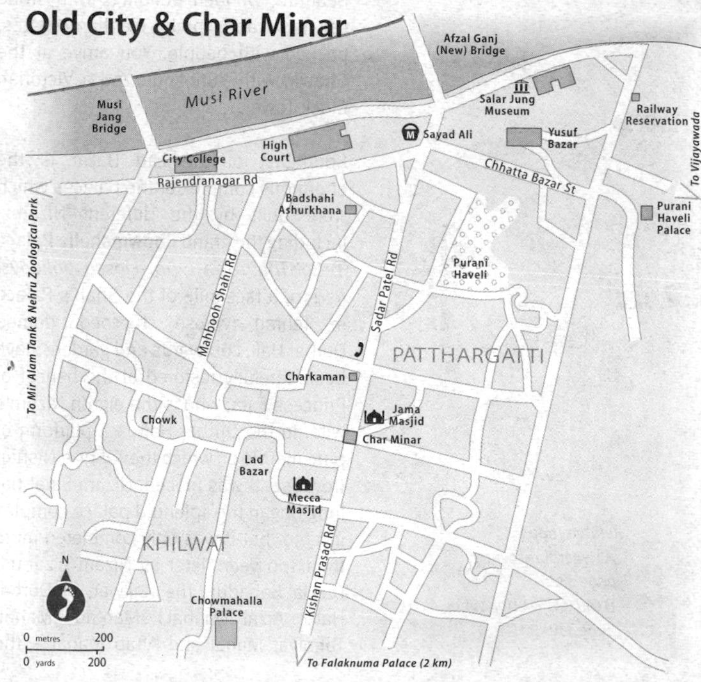

The **High Court**, built on the new roads laid out along the Musi's embankments after the great flood, is a splendid Mughal-style building in the old Qutb Shahi gardens, **Amin Bagh**, near the Afzal Ganj Bridge (New Bridge). This was Vincent Esch's most striking work. It was built in 1916 of local pink granite, with red sandstone carved panels and columns, a large archway and domes, but is now painted pink. A further recent change is the enclosure of the verandahs. The detail is Mughal, but some argue that the structure and internal form are Western.

Next door to the High Court is Esch's **City College** (1917-1920), originally the City High School for boys. Built largely of undressed granite, there are some distinctive Indian decorative features including some marble *jalis*. Esch deliberately incorporated Gothic features, calling his style Perpendicular Mogul Saracenic.

In the opposite direction along the riverbank from the Salar Jung Museum is one of the oldest *imambaras* in the country, the **Badshahi** (Royal) **Ashurkhana**, or house of mourning, built in the Qutb Shahi style in the late 16th century. It has excellent tile mosaics and wooden columns in the outer chamber, both later additions.

Over the river is the **Osmania Women's College**, the former British residency built by James Achilles Kirkpatrick – the central character of William Dalrymple's history, *White Mughals* – in 1803. This imposing colonial structure, whose grounds run down to the river bank, was the first symbol of British presence in the city. It was deliberately built to the same proportions as the Char Minar in order to be the only equal to its minarets on the city skyline. After decades of decline, the World Monuments Fund is carrying out structural conservation as well as fundraising for further restoration on the building, while it continues to function as an educational institute for 4000 girl students (whose modesty visitors are urged to respect), but the ornate separate palace Kirkpatrick built for his Muslim bride was razed in 1861 as a symbol of Kirkpatrick's perceived immorality. Dalrymple's book was launched from the stately, ochre-painted stately building's Durbar Hall. This is a room of giant chandeliers, French windows, mirrors shipped in from Brighton palaces, tatty fans and glorious floral tracings on its ceiling – which, although Moghul in form were probably imported from British papièr-mâche moldings. The Palladian-villa style central complex, the entrance porch with Corinthian columns, the Durbar hall, oval offices, billiard rooms and bedrooms were initially independent of the flanking wings, separated by draw- bridges, whose pulleys are still in place. Outlying buildings hold printing presses dating from the 1900s. Turn out of the Kings gate then left down a pathway towards the pigeon rook to see the model of the Residency that Kirkpatrick commissioned so his Hyderabadi princess Khairunnissa could see the main house without breaking her purda.

Hyderabad Centre: the New City

The **Osmania General Hospital** (1918-1921) is the third of Vincent Esch's impressive buildings in Hyderabad. It stands across the river, opposite the High Court. The 200 m-long building was one of the world's largest and best equipped hospitals when it was opened. Its Indian context is indicated by decorative detail rather than structure. To its east, also on the river, is the imposing **Asafia State Central Library** (1929-1934) with its priceless collection of Arabic, Persian and Urdu books and manuscripts. The Library was designed by anonymous architects of the Public Works Department (PWD).

The **Public Gardens** ⓘ *closed public holidays,* in Nampally, north of Hyderabad Station, contain some important buildings including the Archaeological Museum and Art Galleries and the State Legislative Assembly (Vidhan Sabha).

Andhra Pradesh State Museum ⓘ *near the Lal Bahadur Shastri Stadium, 10 mins by car from Banjara Hills area, 1030-1700, closed public holidays, nominal entrance fee, photography Rs 10, guidebook, Rs 15*, is a small museum with sections on prehistoric implements, sculptures, paintings, inscriptions, illuminated manuscripts, coins, arms, bidri ware, china, textiles and a crowd-drawing 4000-year-old Egyptian mummy. Behind the museum in Ajanta Pavilion are life-size copies of Ajanta frescoes while the Nizam's collection of rare artefacts is housed in the Jubilee Hall.

The **City Railway Station** (1914) was intended by Esch to be pure Mughal in style but built entirely of the most modern material then available – pre-cast, reinforced concrete. It has a wide range of distinctively Indian features – the *chhattris* of royalty, wide eaves (*chajjas*), and onion domes.

Naubat Pahad (Kala Pahad or Neeladri) are two hills situated north of the Public Gardens. The Qutb Shahis are believed to have had their proclamations read from the

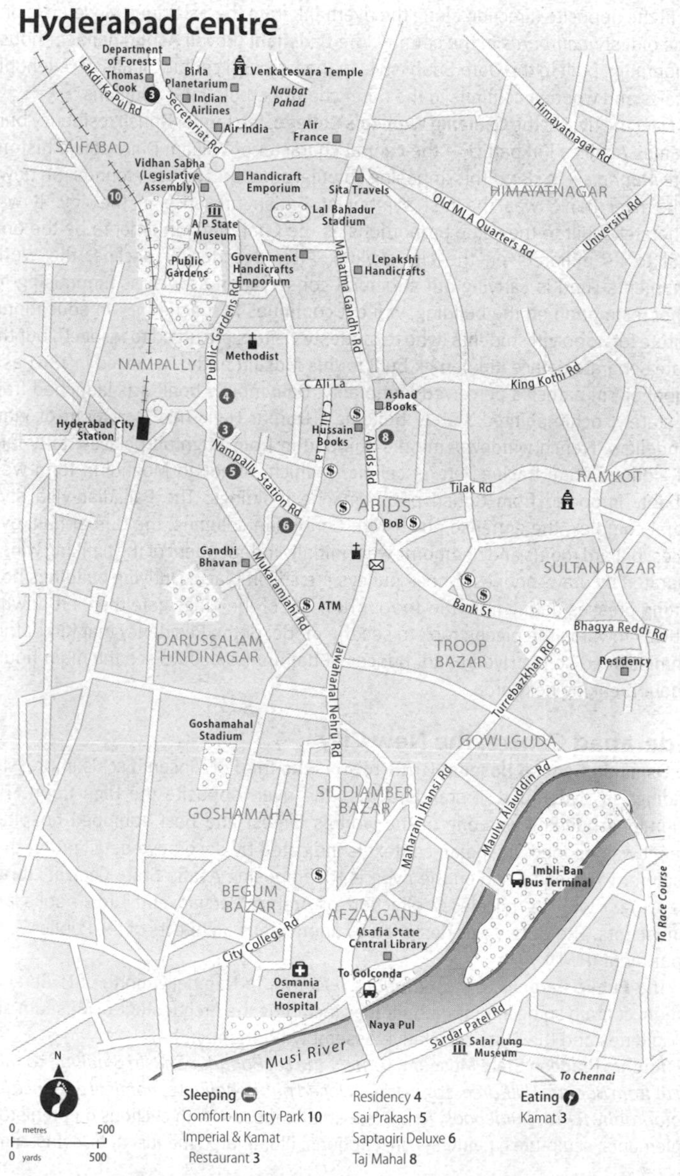

hill tops accompanied by drums. In 1940 pavilions were built and a hanging garden was laid out on top of one (now the Birla Planetarium and Science Centre).

Venkatesvara Temple (Birla Mandir) ⓘ *0700-1200, 1400-2100, photography of inner sanctum prohibited, reached by a stall-lined path opposite Thomas Cook on Secretariat Rd*, is a modern, stunning white marble temple with an intricately carved ceiling which overlooks Husain Sagar. It was built by the Birlas, the Marwari business family who were responsible for building important new Hindu temples in several major cities, including Laxmi Narayan Temple in New Delhi. Completed in 1976, the images of the deities are South Indian, although the building itself drew craftsmen from the north as well, among them some who claimed to have ancestors who built the Taj Mahal.

The massive State Legislative Assembly building, **Vidhan Sabha**, originally the Town Hall, was built by the PWD in 1922. Although Esch had nothing to do with its design, he reportedly admired it for its lightness and coolness, which the building maintained even on the hottest day. **Jubilee Hall** (1936), behind the Vidhan Sabha, is another remarkable PWD building, with clear simple lines.

Husain Sagar ⓘ *boat trips organized by APTDC leave from Lumbini Park, near the APTDC office on Secretariat Rd*, is 16 m deep and was created in the mid-16th century by building a *bund* linking Hyderabad and Secunderabad, and was named to mark the gratitude of Ibrahim Quli Qutb Shah to Hussain Shah Wali, who helped him recover from a illness. The *bund* is a favourite promenade for the city dwellers. At the far end of the lake is the **Nizamia Observatory**. The 17½-m-high, 350-tonne granite **statue of the Buddha** was erected in the lake after years of successive disasters and finally inaugurated by the Dalai Lama in 1993. The tank, fed by streams originating from the Musi River, supplies drinking water to Hyderabad. Although it supports a rich birdlife and is used for fish culturing it also receives huge amounts of industrial effluent, agricultural waste and town sewage.

Outside the city centre

Originally a rich nobleman's house, **Falaknuma Palace** was built in 1873 in a mixture of classical and Mughal styles. Bought by the Nizam in 1897, it has a superb interior (particularly the state reception room) with marble, chandeliers and paintings. The palace houses Eastern and European treasures, including a collection of jade, crystal and precious stones and a superb library. The Taj Hotel Group has converted the spectacular building and its interiors, but visits are restricted.

Osmania University, built by the Nizam in 1939, is just outside the city, towards the east. Inaugurated in 1917 in temporary buildings, its sprawling campus with its black granite Arts College combines Moorish and Hindu Kakatiya architectural styles. There is a botanical garden and the **State Archives**.

The **tomb of Michel Raymond** is off the Vijayawada Road, about 3 km from the Oliphant Bridge. The Frenchman joined the second Nizam's army in 1786 as a common soldier and rose to command 15,000 troops. His popularity with the people earned him the combined Muslim-Hindu name Moosa Ram, and even today they remember him by holding a commemorative *Urs* fair at his grey granite tomb, which is 7 m high and bears the initials JR.

Mir Alam Tank, to the southwest of the old city, is a large artificial lake. It was built by French engineers under instructions of the grandfather of Salar Jung III and is a popular picnic spot. It is now part of the Nehru Zoological Park which is to its north.

Nehru Zoological Park ⓘ *Tue-Sun 0900-1700, Rs 50, camera Rs 10, video Rs 75, bus 7Z from Secunderabad Station and Public Garden Rd*, occupies 13 ha of a low hilly area with remarkable boulders. The extensive grounds offer a welcome relief from the bustle of the city, and birdwatching here provides a good introduction to Indian avifauna; this is one of India's best zoos (the animals are kept in natural surroundings) and well worth a visit. There's also a lion safari park and a nocturnal house. The Natural History Museum, Ancient Life Museum and Prehistoric Animals Park are here as well.

Ramoji Film City ⓘ *T0841-524 6201, 0900-1800, weekdays Rs 150 (RS 100 under 12s), weekends and public holidays Rs 200 (Rs 150 under 12s)*, 25 km from Hyderabad on the Vijayawada Road, is a sherbet-dipped shrine to the many uses of plaster of Paris. Bus tours take visitors around the 'city'. Conducted mainly in Hindi, you'll still gather that everywhere from Mumbai's Chor Bazar to Mysore's Brindavan Gardens have been re-created since media baron Ramoji Rao founded his film lot in 1991. Over 3000 films have been shot here since then. It's oddly compelling to see an audience sit in rapt thrall to a show of aspiring film dancers gyrating in spandex hot pants, while their male opposite numbers inexplicably morris dance; this is only for the committed Indian film buff. It doesn't have the diversionary value of Universal Studios, but there is a theme park **Fundustan** for kids. There are regular bus services from Hyderabad.

Golconda

→ *Colour map 1, B6.*

ⓘ *11 km west of Hyderabad, 0700-2000, US$2. Official guides wait at the entrance (Rs 250), unofficial ones greet you with a hand clap under the Fateh Darwaza. Allow 2-3 hours. Both the fort and the tombs are popular sites and can get crowded and very noisy after 1000; if you arrive early it's worth asking to be allowed in. Excellent Sound and Light show in English, 1 hr, Nov-Feb 1830; Mar-Oct 1900 (see also Entertainment, page 341. Tickets at Golconda 1 hr before start, Rs 25, or at Yatri Nivas, 1000-1200. A coach trip from there (minimum number needed) departs at 1615 and returns 2115; Rs 100 includes show ticket and a couple of other sites. Some buy Sound and Light ticket as soon as the office opens and take a quick tour (45 mins) of the fort before sunset in time for the show. For details of getting here, see Qutb Shahi tombs, page 335.*

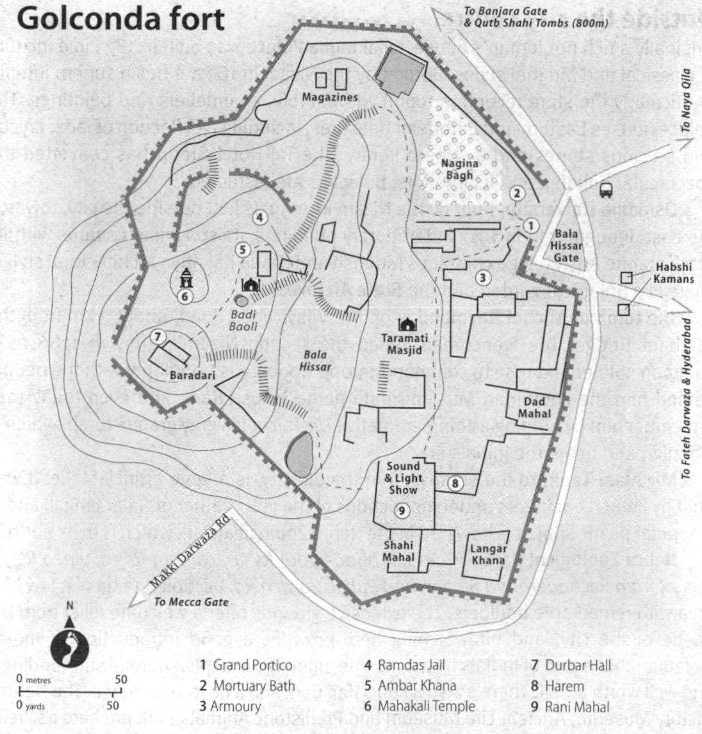

Golconda, one of the most accessible of great medieval fortresses in India, was the capital of the Qutb Shahi kings who ruled over the area from 1507 to 1687. Nizam-ul-Mulk repossessed it in 1724 and restored it to its former glory for a time. Modern day restorations are being carried out by the Archaeological Survey of India.

The fort

Originally built of mud in the 12th century by the **Hindu Kakatiyas**, the fort was reinforced by masonry by the Bahmanis who occupied it from 1363. The massive fort, built on a granite hill, was surrounded by three walls. One encircled the town, another the hill on which the citadel stood and the last joined huge boulders on the high ridge with parts of masonry wall. The citadel's 5 km double wall had 87 bastions with cannons and eight huge gates with outer and inner doors and guardrooms between. Some of the guns of the Qutb Shahis are still there with fortifications at various levels on the way up. Another of India's supposed underground tunnels is believed by some to run for about 8 km from a corner of the summit to Gosha Mahal. The fort had an ingenious system of laminated clay pipes and huge Persian Wheels to carry water to cool the palace chambers up to the height of 61 m where there were hanging gardens. The famous diamond vault once held the *Koh-i-noor* and *Hope* diamonds. The fort fell to Emperor Aurangzeb after two attempts, an eight-month siege and the help of a Qutb general-turned-traitor. English traveller Walter Hamilton described it as being almost deserted in 1820: "the dungeons being used by the Nizam of Hyderabad as a prison for his worst enemies, among whom were several of his sons and two of his wives".

The Fateh Darwaza or Victory Gate at the **Grand Portico (1)** entrance, made of teak, with a Hindu deity engraved, is studded with iron spikes as a defence against war elephants. The superb acoustics enabled a drum beat, bugle call or even a clap under the canopy of this gate to be heard by someone at the very top of the palace; it is put to the test by the crowds today. Glass cases display a map and some excavated finds.

Beyond the gate the **Mortuary Bath (2)** on the right has beautiful arches and a crypt-like ceiling; you see the remains of the three-storey **armoury (3)** and the women's palaces on the left. About halfway up is a large water tank or well and to the north is what was once the most densely populated part of the city. Nearby, the domed storehouse turned into the **Ramdas Jail (4)** and has steps inside that lead up to a platform where there are relief sculptures of deities on the wall, dominated by Hanuman. The **Ambar Khana (5)** (granary) has a Persian inscription on black basalt stating that it was built between 1626 and 1672. The steps turn around an enormous boulder with a bastion and lead to the top passing the Hindu **Mahakali Temple (6)** on the way. The breezy **Durbar Hall (7)** is on the summit. It is well worth climbing the stairs to the roof here for good views. The path down is clearly signposted to take you on a circular route through the **harem (8)** and **Rani Mahal (9)** with its royal baths, back to the main gate. A welcome chilled drink and snack is available at several cafés opposite the gate.

Qutb Shahi tombs

ⓘ *Sat-Thu 0900-1630, Rs 5, camera fee Rs 10, car Rs 10, bicycle Rs 1. Allow 2 hrs, or half a day for a leisurely exploration. Inexpensive guidebook available. Getting there: bus (Nos 119 or 142M from Nampally or 66G from Char Minar) takes 1 hr to the fort. Nos 123 and 142S go direct from Char Minar to the Qutb Shahi Tombs, Rs 5. Autos take 30 mins, Rs 150. Cycling in the early morning is a good option as it's an easy journey.*

About 800 m north-northwest of Golconda fort on a low plateau (a road leaves the fort through the Banjara Gate) are the Qutb Shahi Tombs. Each tomb of black granite or greenstone with plaster decoration is built on a square or octagonal base with a large onion dome and arches with fine sculptures, inscriptions and remains of glazed decoration. The larger tombs have their own mosque attached which usually comprises an eastward opening hall with a *mihrab* to the west. The sides have inscriptions in beautiful Naksh script, and remnants of the glazed tiles that used to cover them can still be seen in places. The tombs of the rulers were built under their own supervision but fell into disrepair and the gardens ran wild until the end of the 19th century when Sir Salar Jang restored them and replanted the gardens. It is now managed and kept in an excellent state of repair by the Archaeological Survey of India. The gardens are being further improved.

The road north from Golconda fort passes the tomb of **Abdullah Qutb Shah (1)** (1626-1672) as it approaches the entrance to the tombs, which is at the east gate of the compound. On the left side of the road just outside the compound is the tomb of **Abul Hasan Tana Qutb Shahi (2)** (ruled 1672-1687). He was the last of the kings to be buried here as the final king in the line of the Qutb Shahi Dynasty, Abul Hasan, died in the fort at Daulatabad in 1704. To the right of the entrance are the tomb of Princess **Hayat Baksh Begum (3)** (died 1677), the daughter of Ibrahim Qutb Shah, and a smaller mosque, while about 100 m directly ahead is the granite tomb of **Muhammad Qutb Shah (4)** (ruled 1612-1626). Tucked away due north of this tomb is that of **Pemamati (5)**, one of the mistresses of Muhammad Qutb Shah, dating from 1663. The path turns south and west around the tomb of Muhammad Qutb Shah. About 100 m to the south is a tank which is still open. The **Badshahi Hammam (11)**, the oldest structure in the compound, is the bath where the body of the king was washed before burial. You can still see the channels for the water and the special platforms for washing the body. The Badshahi kings were Shi'a Muslims, and the 12 small baths in the Hammam stand symbolically for the two *imams* revered by the Shi'a community. Next door, a small **Archaeological Museum** ⓘ *1000-1300, 1400-1630,* has some interesting items.

To the south of the hammam is a series of major tombs. The most striking lies due south, the 54 m-high mausoleum of **Muhammad Quli Qutb Shah (6)** (ruled 1581-1612), the poet king founder of Baghnagar (Hyderabad). It is apt that the man responsible for creating beautiful buildings in Hyderabad should be commemorated by such a remarkable tomb. The underground excavations here have been turned into a Summer House. You can walk right through the tomb and on to the tomb of the fourth king of the dynasty, **Ibrahim Qutb Shah (7)** (ruled 1550-1580), another 100 m to the south. At the

Qutb Shahi tombs

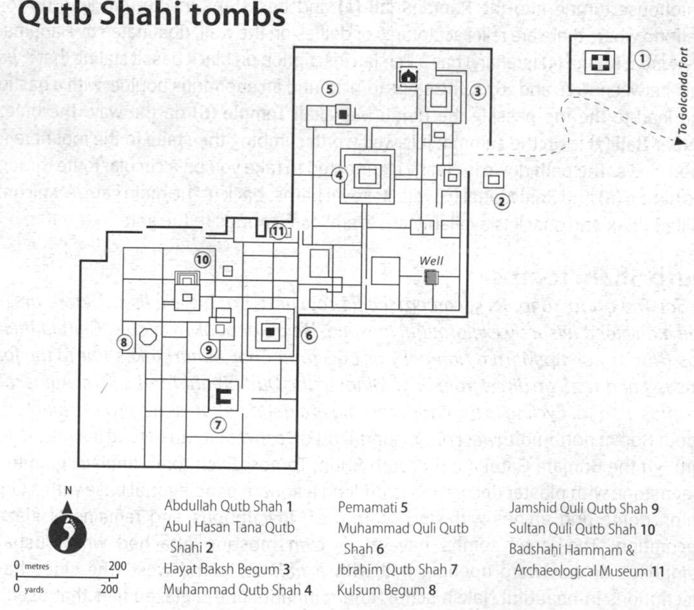

west edge of the compound is the octagonal tomb of **Kulsum Begum (8)** (died 1608), granddaughter of Mohammad Quli Qutb Shah. To its east is the tomb of **Jamshid Quli Qutb Shah (9)** (ruled 1543-1550), who was responsible for the murder of his 90-year-old father and founder of the dynasty, **Sultan Quli Qutb Shah (10)** (ruled 1518-1543). This has the appearance of a two-storey building though it is in fact a single-storey structure with no inscription. There are some other small tombs here.

Warangal

» *p343. Colour map 2, B1.*

→ *Phone code: 08712. Population: 528,600.*

The capital of the Kakatiya Empire in the 12th and 13th centuries, Warangal's name is derived from the Orugallu (one stone) Hill, a massive boulder with ancient religious significance that stands where the modern town is situated.

Ins and outs

Warangal is 156 km northeast of Hyderabad and most express trains between Chennai and Delhi stop here. **Warangal Tourist Office** ⓘ *1st floor, Talwar Hyndai Show Room, Chaitanyapuri, opposite REC Petrol Pump, Kazipet, T0870-244 6606.*

History

The city was probably laid out during the reigns of King Ganapatideva (1199-1262) and his daughter Rudrammadevi (until 1294). Warangal was captured by armies from Delhi in 1323, enforcing the payment of tribute. Control of Warangal fluctuated between Hindus and Muslims but between the 14th and 15th centuries it remained in Bahmani hands. Thereafter it repeatedly changed hands, and some argue that although the military fortifications were repeatedly strengthened, the religious buildings were largely destroyed, including the great Siva temple in the middle of the city. Marco Polo was highly impressed by Warangal's riches, and it is still famous for the remains of its temples, its lakes and wildlife, and for its three circuits of fortifications. The modern town itself, however, is not very interesting.

Sights

At the centre of the **'fort'** ⓘ *US$2*, is a circular area about 1.2 km in diameter. Most of it is now farmland with houses along the road. Near the centre are the ruins of the original **Siva temple**. Remains include the large beautifully carved stone entrance gateways to the almost square enclosure, aligned along the cardinal directions and beyond are overturned slabs, smashed columns, brackets and ceiling panels.

Nearby Siva temples are still in use, and to the west is the **Khush Mahal**, a massive royal hall used by the Muslim Shitab Khan in the early 16th century for state functions. It may well have been built on the site of earlier palaces, near its geometric centre, while some structures in the central area may have been granaries.

From the centre, four routes radiate along the cardinal directions, passing through gateways in the three successive rings of fortification. The innermost ring is made of massive granite blocks, and is up to 6 m high with bastions regularly spaced along the wall. The middle wall is of unfaced packed earth, now eroded, while the outermost circuit, up to 5 m high, is also of earth. The four main roads pass through massive gateways in the inner wall, and there are also incomplete gateways in the second ring of fortifications. Some of the original roads that crossed the city have disappeared.

Some have suggested that the plan of Warangal conforms to early Hindu principles of town planning. **'Swastika towns'**, especially suited to royalty, were achieved following the pattern of concentric circles and swastika of the *yantras* and *mandalas*. They were a miniature representation of the universe, the power of god and king recognized symbolically, and in reality, at the centre.

The Chalukya-style '1000-pillar' **Siva Rudresvar temple** on the slopes of the Hanamakonda Hill, 4 km to the north, has beautiful carvings. It is a low, compact temple, built on several stepped platforms with subsidiary shrines to Vishnu and Surya, rock-cut elephants, a large superbly carved *Nandi* in the courtyard and an ancient well where villagers have drawn water for 800 years.

Pakhal, Ethurnagaram and Lakhnavaram

ⓘ *Take a bus from Warangal Bus Station to Narsampet. Regular bus service from Narsampet to Pakhal Lake or take a taxi.*

The great artificial lakes 40 km northeast of Warangal – from the south, Pakhal, Lakhnavaram, Ramappa and Ghanpur – were created as part of the Kakatiya rulers' water management and irrigation schemes in the 12th and 13th centuries and are still in use. The lakes are fringed with an emerging marsh vegetation and surrounded by extensive grasslands, tropical deciduous forests and evergreens. The park was set up in 1952 and has problems of the grazing of domestic livestock and illegal burning.

This is the richest area for wildlife in the state with tiger, panther, hyena, wild dogs, wild boars, gaur, foxes, spotted deer, jackals, sloth bears and pythons. There are also otters and alligators and a variety of waterbirds and fish in the lakes. Pakhal Lake is especially important as an undisturbed site well within the sanctuary; Laknavaram Lake is 20 km to the north. They are superb for birdwatching (numerous migratory birds in winter) and occasional crocodile spottings. Tigers and panthers live deep in the forest but are rarely seen. Forest rangers might show you plaster casts of tiger pug marks.

Palampet → *Colour map 2, B2.*

Palampet lies close to the Ramappa Lake. The **Ramappa Temple**, dedicated to Siva as Rudreswara, was built in 1234 and is one of the finest medieval Deccan temples. The black basalt sculpture is excellent (even richer than that at the 1000-pillar temple) with famous Mandakini figures of female dancers which appear on brackets at the four entrances. The base of the temple has the typical bands of sculpture, the lowest of elephants, the second, a lotus scroll, the third which is the most interesting depicting figures opening a window on the life of the times and finally another floral scroll. There are more fine sculptures inside, some displaying a subtle sense of humour in common with some of the figures outside, and paintings of scenes from the epics on the ceiling. Note that no bottled water is available.

Nagarjunakonda » *pp342-344. Colour map 2, C1.*

→ *Phone code: 08680.*

Some 150 km southeast of Hyderabad is one of India's richest Buddhist sites, now almost under the lake created by the Nagarjunasagar Dam, completed in 1960. The remains of a highly cultured Buddhist civilization had remained undisturbed for 1600 years until their discovery by AR Saraswati in March 1926. The reconstructed small-scale buildings are in a peaceful setting on the hilltop fort, now an island with low trees.

Ins and outs

Getting there The island is 11 km from Vijayapuri. There are two ferries daily from the jetty, 0930 and 1330. Other ferries serve APTDC tours organized locally or from Hyderabad. **Tourist information AP State Tourist Office** ⓘ *Project House, Hill Colony, T08680-276333*. A guide is available; others from Hyderabad Tourist Office.

The Nagarjunasagar Dam project, completed in 1966, is one of the largest in India. The 124 m-high, 1 km-long dam is constructed across the Krishna River out of stone masonry. Two of the irrigation tunnels are said to be among the longest in the world.

History

Rising from the middle of the artificial lake is the Nagarjuna Hill which was once nearly 200 m above the floor of the secluded valley in the northern ranges of the **Nallamalais** (black hills) which surround the lake on three sides. On the fourth side was the great river **Krishna**, superimposed on the hills as it flows towards the Bay of Bengal.

Early archaeological work showed the remnants of Buddhist monasteries, many limestone sculptures and other remains. The Archaeological Survey carried out a full excavation of the sites before they were covered by the rising waters of the lake. More than 100 distinct sites ranging from the prehistoric early Stone Age period to the late medieval were discovered. Some of the most important remains have been moved and reconstructed on the hilltop fort. These include nine monuments, rebuilt in their original form, and 14 large replicas of the ruins.

The **Ikshvakus** made Nagarjunakonda the centre of extraordinary artistic activity from the third century AD. In the mid-fourth century AD the Pallavas pushed north from Tamil Nadu and eclipsed the Ikshvaku Kingdom, reducing Nagarjunakonda to a deserted village. However, during the Chalukya period between the seventh and 12th centuries a Saiva centre was built at Yellaswaram, on the other bank of the Krishna. In the 15th and 16th centuries the hill became a fortress in the contest for supremacy between the Vijayanagar, Bahmani and Gajapati kings. After the fall of the Vijayanagar Empire both the hill and the valley below lost all importance.

Sights

The Ikshvaku's capital was a planned city on the right bank of the Krishna – **Vijayapuri** (city of victory). The citadel had rampart walls on three sides with the river on the fourth. The buildings inside including houses, barracks, baths and wells were probably destroyed by a great fire. The nine temples show the earliest developments of Brahmanical temple architecture in South India. The Vishnu temple (AD 278) had two beautifully carved pillars which were recovered from its site. Five temples were dedicated to Siva or Karttikeya. The river bank was dotted with **Brahmanical shrines**.

Nagarjunakonda excavations also revealed some of India's finest early **sculptures** and **memorial pillars**. Over 20 pillars were raised in the memory not just of rulers and nobles but also of artisans and religious leaders. The sculptures represent the final phase of artistic development begun at Amaravati in the second century BC.

The **hill fort** (early 14th-century) has remnants of the Vijayanagar culture though the present layout of the fort probably dates from as recently as 1565. The main entrance was from the northeast, near where the ferry now lands on the island. In places the walls are still over 6 m high, with regular bastions and six gateways. There are two temples in the east, where the museum now stands.

The **Museum** ⓘ *Sat-Thu 0900-1600*, has a collection of coins and ornaments, but most importantly sculptures (including a 3-m-high standing Buddha). Also prehistoric and protohistoric remains and several panels and friezes depicting Buddhist scenes.

Srisailam Wildlife Sanctuary → *Colour map 2, C1. Altitude: 200-900 m.*

ⓘ *It's worth visiting AP Dept of Forests (see Useful addresses, page 344). Cars are not permitted in the tiger reserve 2100-0600. Temperature: 12-42°C. Rainfall: 1500 mm.*

The largest of the state's wildlife sanctuaries is at Srisailam (201 km from Hyderabad), near Nagarjunasagar. The park, named after the reservoir, is India's largest tiger reserve covering 3560 sq km in five neighbouring districts. At times the sanctuary is disturbed by political activists and can be very difficult to get permission to visit. Check the latest position with the Forest Officer.

The sanctuary, in an area deeply incised by gorges of the Nallamalai hills, has deciduous and bamboo forest and semi-desert scrubland. Besides tigers, there are leopards, Indian pangolins, panthers, wild dogs, civets, hyenas, jackals, wolves, giant squirrels, crocodiles, lizards, pythons, vipers, kraits and over 150 species of birds. Project Tiger was started here in 1973. Srisailam also attracts visitors to its **fort** and **temple** (originally circa second century AD) with one of 12 *jyotirlingas* in the country. It is a small pilgrimage town in the heart of the vast reserve of hilly dry forest. The ancient **Mahakali Temple** on a hill in the Nallamalai forest contains a rare *lingam* attracting large crowds of pilgrims daily and especially at *Sivaratri*, see page 356. There is a nature trail signposted 1 km short of Srisailam. Otherwise, you can walk the access road and explore from there. A guide is available. The best time to visit is from October to March.

Sleeping

Secundarabad is closer to the airport, interstate train station and business district, but Hyderabad is better placed for sightseeing. High demand from business travellers has meant soaring room rates at the middle and top end. Power cuts, also affecting street lighting, are routine. Larger hotels have generators, but a/c, lifts, etc in smaller hotels can fail.

Hyderabad *p326, maps p328 and p332*

LL Taj Banjara, T040-6666 9999, www.tajhotels.com. Technically a business hotel, the Banjara boasts faultless Taj service, 255 rooms, small swimming pool, tennis and boating and overlooks the hotel's landmark lake. Tennis and boating. Good open-air barbeque restaurant for evening kebabs and tandoor.

LL Taj Deccan, T040-6666 3939, www.tajhotels.com. Previously the Taj Residency, this hotel has 151 rooms, and similarly good facilities, similarly small swimming pool.

LL Taj Krishna, Road No 1, Banjara Hills, T040-6666 2323, www.tajhotels.com. The flagship luxury Taj hotel in the city's elite district has 2 restaurants (Indian, Chinese), 260 rooms, 24-hr gym, the city's best pool and nightclub, **Ahala**, beautiful gardens, immaculate service. The Presidential suite has its own private pool.

L The Golkonda Hyderabad, Masab Tank, Mahavir Marg, T040-6611 0101, www.thegolkondahyderabad.com. Completely renovated with new, minimalist decor and 5-star status, the Golkonda has 150 rooms, a/c, phone, TV, excellent showers. Breakfast included. Complimentary airport transfers.

A Residency (Quality Inn), Public Garden Rd, T040-3061 6161. Efficient business hotel, 95 a/c rooms, polite service, popular with Indians, good vegetarian restaurant and basement pub, One Flight Down (see page 341).

B Comfort Inn City Park, Chirag Ali Rd T040-6610 5510, www.cityparkhyd.com. 54 bright prefab rooms with phone, en suite and writing tables, car park, internet, but stale a/c smell. Well placed just at the edge of Abid shopping district. Breakfast included. Rooftop multi-cuisine restaurant Degh has panoramic views over city.

C-D Taj Mahal, 4-1-999 Abid Rd, T040-2475 8250, sundartaj@satyam.net.in. 20 good-sized simple a/c rooms in 1940s building. Busy South Indian vegetarian restaurant, meals, laundry, good value, friendly and the most characterful of the budget options. Recommended.

D Sai Prakash, Nampally Station Rd, T040-2461 1726, www.hotelsaiprakash.com. Business hotel with 102 clean, comfortable a/c rooms and a good restaurant.

E-F Hotel Saptagiri Deluxe, off Nampally Station Rd, T040-2461 0333, www.hotelsaptagirindeluxe.com. 36 scrupulously clean rooms in peaceful hotel in interesting area. Choice of a/c and non a/c. Western toilet, shower. Good. Gets busy; book in advance.

E-F Hotel Sri Brindavan, Nampally Station Rd, near the Circle, T040-2320 3970. 70 good, clean rooms in custard-colour compound set back from road. Mostly male guests; unsuitable for lone female travellers. Otherwise good value, good restaurants, good budget choice.

For an explanation of the sleeping and eating price codes used in this guide, see inside the front cover. Other relevant information is found in Essentials pages 40-44.

F Imperial, corner of Nampally Station and Public Gardens roads (5 mins from Hyderabad station), T040-2320 2220. Large Indian hotel with 48 clean rooms, some with bath, avoid roadside rooms, bucket hot water, helpful, excellent service.

Secunderabad *p326, map p328*
SD Rd is Sarojinidevi Rd.
LL-L Hyderabad Marriot Hotel, Tank Bund Rd, T040-2752 2999, www.marriott.com. Plush business hotel with charming pool, set on the shores of Hussain Sagar Lake. New spa in 2007. Rates fluctuate according to city conference schedule; it's worth phoning. Low categories exclude breakfast.
AL Green Park, Begumpet, T040-6651 5151, www.hotelgreenpark.com. A sedate and large Indian business and family hotel with 146 rooms. Rooms come with bath, a/c and TV. Complimentary Wi-Fi.
A Hotel Baseraa, 9-1, 167/168 SD Rd, T040-2770 3200, www.baseraa.com. 75 tatty but comfortable a/c rooms in busy friendly, family hotel with great service and good restaurants.
D Yatri Nivas (AP Tourism), SP Rd, T040-2781 6881. Clean, airy, well kept, 32 rooms, mostly a/c, 3 restaurants, bar.
D-F Taj Mahal, 88 SD Rd, T040-2781 2106, nadimane_taj@yahoo.com. 40-year-old characterful building with 4 faded but good rooms (a/c suite, a/c double, non-a/c double and non-a/c single). Popular South Indian vegetarian restaurant.
F Retiring Rooms, at Railway Station.
F YMCA, SD Rd, T040-2780 6049. This place has 15 rooms (mostly singles, but big enough to take an extra bed), shared bath, clean, roomy, friendly, 'treated as family', Extra charge for temporary membership.
F Youth Hostel, near Sailing Club, T040-2754 0763. Total of 90 beds in dorms. Extra charge for temporary membership.

Eating

Hyderabad *p326, maps p328 and p332*
There are branches of **Subway**, **KFC**, **Pizza Hut**, **McDonalds** and **Domino's** in the city, as well as South Indian pure vegetarian chain **Kamat**. The shopping malls **Lifestyle** and **Hyderabad Central** have good food courts. Madina crossroad in Char Minar has good authentic Hyderabadi street food.

TTT The Water Front, Eat St, Necklace Rd, T040-2330 8899. Lunch and dinner. Open-air restaurant right on the Hussain Sagar lake.
TTT-TT Firdaus, Taj Krishna hotel (see page 340), T040-2339 2323. Excellent Mughlai cuisine and one of the only places in the city where you can get the special Hyderabadi treat, Haleem. Meaning 'patience', this meat, wholewheat and gram dish is slowcooked for hours and is traditionally only made to break the Ramadan fast.
TT Hyderabad House, opposite Jntu College, Masab Tank, T040-2332 7861, and branches including opposite Mosque Rd, No 3, Banjara Hills, T040-2355 4747. Very good biryanis.
TT Southern Spice, 8-2-350/3/2, Rd No 3, Banjara Hills, T040-2335 3802. Breakfast, lunch and dinner. Good Andhra, Chettinad, Tandoor and Chinese cuisine.
TT-T Paradise Food Court, 38 Sarojini Devi Rd/MG Rd. T040-6631 3721. Open 1100-2400. Utterly synonymous with biryani, and such an institution that the surrounding area is now named Paradise. You can get parcels from downstairs, eat standing up at the fast food section, or go upmarket at Persis Gold.

Bars and clubs

Hyderabad-Secunderabad
p326, maps p328 and p332
These are mostly in the top-end hotels; night-life doesn't compare to Bengaluru (Bangalore).
Ahala at the **Taj Krishna** hotel (see page 340) is the most modish.
One Flight Down, below **The Residency**, opposite Hyderabad Railway Station, Public Garden Rd. Modern, British-style pub (with same opening hours, 1100-2300), snooker tables and TVs. Dark but popular.

Entertainment

Hyderabad-Secunderabad
p326, maps p328 and p332
Some cinemas show English language films.
Lalit Kala Thoranam, Public Gardens. Hosts art exhibitions and free film shows daily.
Ravindra Bharati, regularly stages dance, theatre and music programmes, a/c.
Sound and Light, Golconda Fort (page 334), spectacularly voiced over by Bollywood legend Amitabh Bachan. See also Tours below.

Shopping

Hyderabad-Secunderabad

p326, maps p328 and p332

Most shops open 1000-1900. Some close on Fri. When shopping for pearls, look for shape, smoothness and shine to determine quality. Size is the last criteria in deciding a pearl's price. Bargain for at least 10% off asking prices. Also look out for bidri ware, crochetwork, Kalamkari paintings, himroo and silk saris. For more on Andhra Pradesh's craft tradition, see page 325.

Visit **Lad bazar** around the Char Minar for bangles. At the other end of the scale, every second shop pedals pearls, but for quality try **Mangatrai Pearl and Jewellers**, 6-3-883 Punjagutta, T040-2341 1816, www.mangatrai.com. Jewellers to Indian nobility, with everything from Basra pearls to black Tahitian pearls. Also recommended is **Sri Jangadamba Pearls**, MG Rd, Secunderabad.

Antiques

Govind Mukandas, Bank St.
Humayana, Taj Banjara hotel.

Books

Akshara, 8-2-273 Pavani Estates, Rd No 2, Banjara Hills, T040-221 3906. Excellent collection on all aspects of India in English.
Haziq and Mohi, Lal Chowk. Good antiquarian bookshop, especially for Arabic and Persian.

Handicrafts

Govt Emporia: **Nirmal Industries**, Raj Bhavan Rd; **Lepakshi**, and **Coircraft**, Mayur Complex, Gun Foundry.
Co-optex, and several others in Abids.
Fancy Cloth Store, the silk people, 21-2-28 Pathergatti, Hyderabad, T040-2452 3983. Exports cloth to Selfridges in the UK.
Khadi, Sultan Bazar and Municipal Complex, Rashtrapati Rd, Secunderabad.
Others may charge a bit more but may have more attractive items.
Bidri Crafts, Abids.
Kalanjali, Hill Fort Rd, opposite Public Gardens. Large selection of regional crafts.

In **Secunderabad**: Baba Handicrafts, MG Rd, and **Jewelbox**, SD Rd.

Activities and tours

Hyderabad-Secunderabad

p326, maps p328 and p332

Swimming

BV Gurumoorthy Pool, Sardar Patel Rd.

Tours

APTTDC City sightseeing: full day, 0800-1745, from offices at Yatri Nivas and Secretariat Rd, Rs 150; unsatisfactory as it allows only 1 hr at the Fort and includes unimportant sights.
Golconda: Shilparamam craft village, Golconda (Sound & Light). 1600-2100, Rs 120.
Nagarjunasagar: daily to Dam, Nagarjunakonda Museum, Right Canal and Ethipothala Falls. 0700-2130, Rs 250.
Ramoji Film City: 0745-1800, Rs 400 (entry fee included). Allows 4-5 hrs at the studios, plus Sanghi Temple and shopping time!

Tour operators

Mercury, Public Gardens Rd, T040-223 4441, SD Rd, Secunderabad, T040-283 0670.
Sita, 3-5-874 Hyderguda, T040-223 3628, and 1-2-281 Tirumala, SD Rd, Secunderabad, T040-284 9155.
TCI, 680 Somajiguda, Greenlands Rd, T040-221 2722.
Thomas Cook, Saifabad, T040-222689.

Nagarjunakonda *p338*

AP Tourism's day trip from Hyderabad can be very tiring with 4 hrs on a coach each way, but is convenient and cheap. 0645-2145, Rs 225 including lunch. Nagarjunasagar is the village beside the dam from which boats ferry visitors to the temples and museum on the island (at 0800, 1200, 1500, trip takes 1 hr). If you take the second boat you still have time to visit the sights and return on the next boat. You can leave your luggage for a few hours at this pier provided someone is on duty.

Transport

Hyderabad-Secunderabad

p326, maps p328 and p332

Air

Transport to town: pre-paid taxi Rs 120-150; metered auto-rickshaw, Rs 65 to Banjara Hills, 30 mins. Airport, T140. **Bengaluru**

(Bangalore): 2 daily except Sun; **Kolkata**: some via Bhubaneswar and Nagpur; **Chennai**: 2 or 3 daily; **Delhi**: 2 daily; **Mumbai**: 3 daily; **Visakhapatnam**. **Bengaluru**, **Chennai**, **Delhi**, **Kolkata**, **Mumbai**, **Tirupati**, **Visakhapatnam**, all daily. **Sahara**, opposite Secretariat, Secretariat Rd, T040-2321 2767: **Mumbai**.

Airline offices Air India, Samrat Complex, Secretariat Rd, T040-223 7243. **Air France**, Nasir Arcade, Secretariat Rd, T040-223 6947. **British Airways**, Chapel Rd, T040-223 4927. **Cathay Pacific**, 89 SD Rd, Secunderabad, T040-284 0234. **Egypt Air**, Safina International, Public Garden Rd, T040-223 0778. **Indian Airlines**: opposite Ravindra Bharati, Saifabad, T040-2329 9333. **Jet Airways**, 6-3-1109 Nav Bharat Chambers, Raj Bhavan Rd, T040-340 1222; 201 Gupta Estates, Basheerbagh; airport T040-2790 0118. **KLM**, *Gemini Travels*, Chapel Rd, T040-223 6042. **Lufthansa**, 86 Shantinagar, T040-222 0352. **Saudia**, *Arafath Travels*, Basheerbagh, T040-223 8175. **Singapore Airlines** and **Swissair**, Regency Building, Begumpet. **Thai**, Chapel Rd, T040-223 6042.

Bicycle

Hire is easily available (ask for 'bicycle taxi' shop), Rs 20 per day but may ask for a large deposit. Good for visiting Golconda, but the city is only for cyclists who are experienced with heavy, fast-flowing traffic.

Bus

Local City buses are crowded in rush hour. No 119, 142M: Nampally to **Golconda Fort**.

Long distance APSRTC, T040-2461 3955. The vast **Imbli-Ban Bus Station**, T040-2461 3955, is for long-distance buses including **Srisailam** and **Nagarjunasagar Dam**. Private coaches run services to **Aurangabad**, **Bengaluru (Bangalore)**, **Mumbai**, **Chennai** and **Tirupati**. Reservations: Royal Lodge, entrance to Hyderabad Railway Station. Secunderabad has the **Jubilee Bus Station**, T040-2780 2203. **Nampally**: buses to **Golconda**. **Venus Travel**, opposite Residency Hotel, runs a bus to **Gulbarga**, 0730, 5 hrs.

Car

Tourist taxis and luxury cars from **AP Tourism**, Tank Bund Rd, T040-2345 3036, **Ashok Travels**, Lal Bahadur Stadium, T040-223 0766, Travel Express, Saifabad, T040-223 4035. Rs 550 per 8 hrs or 80 km, Rs 300 per 4 hrs.

Rickshaw

Auto-rickshaws charge Rs 6 for 2 km; will use meter after mild insistence and cheaper cycle rickshaws. Local taxis are expensive.

Train

Hyderabad (H); Secunderabad (S). South-Central Enquiries: T131. Reservations: T135. Bus No 20 links Hyderabad (Nampally) and Secunderabad stations, Rs 5. From Hyderabad/Secunderabad To: **Aurangabad**: Manmad Exp 7664 (AC/II), 1800 (S), 12½ hrs. **Bengaluru** (Bangalore): *Secunderabad Bangalore Exp 7085* (AC/II), 1740 (S), 13½ hrs; *Rajdhani Exp 2430*, 1910 (Tue, Wed, Thu, Sun) (S), 12 hrs. **Chennai (MC)**: Charminar Exp 2760 (AC/II), 1900 (H), 1930 (S), 14½ hrs; *Hyderabad Chennai Exp 7054*, 1550, 1625 (S), 14½ hrs. **Delhi (HN)**: Rajdhani Exp 2429, 0645 (Mon, Tue, Thu, Fri) (S), 22½ hrs; *Dakshin Exp 7021*, 2130 (H), 2200 (S), 32 hrs. **Delhi (ND)**: New Delhi AP Exp 2723, 0640 (H), 0700 (S), 26 hrs. All Delhi trains go via Nagpur and Bhopal. **Guntakal**: (for Hospet and Hampi), *Secunderabad Bangalore Exp 7085*, 1740, 6 hrs. **Kolkata (Howrah)**: *E Coast Exp 7046*, 32½ hrs. **Mumbai (CST)**: *Hyderabad-Mumbai Exp 7032*, 2040, 17 hrs; *Hussainsagar Exp 7002*, 1430 (H), 15¾ hrs; *Konark Exp 1020*, 1050 (S), 17½ hrs. **Tirupati**: *Krishna Exp 7406*, 0530 (H), 0600 (S), 16 hrs; *Rayalaseema Exp 7429 (AC/II)*, 1730 (H), 15½ hrs; *Narayanadri Exp 7424*, 1800 (S), 13½ hrs.

Warangal *p337*

Many Express trains stop here. **Nagpur**: Several, 7½-8½ hrs. **Delhi (ND)**: *Tamil Nadu Exp 2621*, 0724, 24 hrs; *Kerala Exp 2625*, 1417, 25½ hrs. **Vijayawada**: *Kerala Exp 2626*, 1140, 3¼ hrs; *GT Exp 2616*, 1951, 3½ hrs. **Chennai (MC)**: *Tamil Nadu Exp 2622*, 2101, 10 hrs; *GT Exp 2616*, 1951, 10½ hrs. **Secunderabad**: *Vijaywada Secunderabad Intercity Exp 2713*, 0902, 2½ hrs; *Konark Exp 1020*, 0735, 3½ hrs; *Golconda Exp 7201*, 1012, 3½ hrs; *Krishna Exp 7405*, 1704, 3½ hrs.

Srisailam Wildlife Sanctuary *p339*

Buses from Imbli-Ban Bus Station, Hyderabad, about 6 hrs. The nearest train station is Marchelna (13 km). Hire jeep beforehand.

Directory

Hyderabad-Secunderabad
p326, maps p328 and p332

Banks Mon-Fri 1000-1400, Sat 1000-1200. In Hyderabad, several banks on Bank St, Mahipatram Rd and Mukaramjahi Market and in Secunderabad on Rashtrapati Rd. Amex, Samrat Complex, 5-9-12, Saifabad, T040-2323 4591. Thomas Cook, Nasir Arcade, 6-1-57, Saifabad, T040-259 6521. Travel Club Forex, next door, carries Western Union transfers. **Cultural centres and libraries** Alliance Française, near Planetrium, Naubat Pahad, T040-222 0296. British Library, Secretariat Rd. Tue-Sat 1100-1900. Max Müller Bhavan, Eden Bagh, Ramkote. Bharatiya Vidya Bhavan, King Kothi Rd, T040-223 7825. **Hospitals** Outpatients usually from 0900-1400. Casualty 24 hrs. General Hospital in Nampally, T040-223 4344. Newcity (Secunderabad), T040-2780 5961. **Internet** Several in Abids and Charag Ali Lane (Rs 30-40 per hr). Good coverage throughout the twin cities. **Post** In Hyderabad: GPO (with Poste Restante) and CTO, Abids. In Secunderabad: Head PO in RP Rd and CTO on MG Rd. **Useful addresses** AP Dept of Forests, Public Garden Rd, near Secretariat (opposite Reserve Bank), T040-2406 7551. Provides excellent advice, may help with arrangements to visit wildlife reserves. The Assistant Conservator of Forests is very helpful. Foreigners' Regional Registration Office: Commissioner of Police, Purani Haveli, Hyderabad, T040-223 0191.

Nagarjunakonda *p338*
Banks and post offices at Hill Colony and Pylon (4 km).

Krishna-Godavari Delta

The rice-growing delta of the Krishna and Godavari rivers is one of Andhra Pradesh's most prosperous and densely populated regions, and the core region of Andhra culture. The flat coastal plains are fringed with palmyra palms and occasional coconut palms, rice and tobacco. Inland, barely 40% of the land is cultivated. About 120 km to the west of the road south to Chennai run the Vellikonda Ranges, only visible in very clear weather. To the north the ranges of the Eastern Ghats can often be clearly seen.

▸▸ *For Sleeping, Eating and other listings, see pages 346-347.*

Vijayawada → *Phone code: 0866. Colour map 2, C2. Population: 825,400.*

At the head of the Krishna delta, 70 km from the sea, the city is surrounded by bare granite hills. During the hot dry season these radiate heat, and temperatures of over 45°C are not uncommon in April and May. In winter they can be as low as 20°C. The Krishna delta canal scheme, one of the earliest major irrigation developments of the British period in South India completed in 1855, now irrigates nearly 10,000 sq km, banishing famine from the delta and converting it into one of the richest granaries of the country. The Prakasam Barrage, over 1000 m long, carries the road and railways. The name of this city, which is over 2000 years old, is derived from the goddess Kanakdurga or Vijaya, the presiding deity. There is a temple to her on a hill along the river.

There are several sites with caves and temples with inscriptions from the first century AD. The **Mogalarajapuram Temple** has an Ardhanarisvara statue which is thought to be the earliest in South India. There are two 1000-year-old **Jain temples** and the **Hazratbal Mosque** which has a relic of the Prophet Mohammed. The **Qutb Shahi** rulers made Vijayawada an important inland port. It is still a major commercial town and has capitalized on its position as the link between the interior and the main north-south route between Chennai and Kolkata. A colossal granite Buddha statue (now in Guntur) shows that the site was an important Buddhist religious centre even before the seventh century AD, when it was visited by Hiuen Tsang. **Victoria Jubilee Museum** ① *MG Rd, Sat-Thu 1030-1700, free, camera Rs 5,* has sculpture and paintings. **AP Tourist Office** ① *Hotel Ilapuram Complex, Gandhi Nagar, T0886-257*

Toddy tappers

In many villages of South India palm toddy is a common drink. Known in Andhra as *karloo*, this white, fizzy alcoholic drink is made by collecting sap from the palmyra palm. The tapper climbs the tree and cuts the main fronds of the palm, from which the sap is collected in small earthenware pots. This is poured into a larger pot carried by the toddy tapper on his waistband. If left, the juice ferments, but it may also be drunk fresh. It is drunk by holding a folded palm leaf to your mouth in both hands while the juice is poured in. Nod vigorously when you have had enough!

0255, 0600-2000, also has a counter at RTC Bus Stand, Machilipatnam Road and the train station.

Amaravati

Located 30 km west of Vijaywada, Amaravati was the capital of the medieval Reddi kings of Andhra. Some 1500 years before they wielded power Amaravati was a great Mahayana Buddhist centre (see page 518). Initially the shrine was dedicated to the Hinayana sect but under Nagarjuna was changed into a Mahayana sanctuary where the Buddha was revered as Amareswara. Its origins go back to the third and second centuries BC, though it was enlarged between the first and fourth centuries AD. Very little remains. Colonel Colin Mackenzie started excavations in 1797. Subsequently most of the magnificent sculpted friezes, medallions and railings were removed, the majority to Chennai and Kolkata museums. The rest went to London's British Museum. The onsite **Archaeological Museum** ⓘ *Sat-Thu 0900-1700, free, buses via Guntur or by ferry from Krishneveni Hotel*, contains mainly broken panels, as well as railings and sculptures of the Bodhi Tree (some exquisitely carved), *chakras* and caskets holding relics. There are also pottery, coins and terracotta. Apart from items excavated since 1905, some exhibits relate to other sites in the Krishna and Visakhapatnam districts.

Guntur → *Colour map 2, C2.*

From Vijayawada the NH5 southwest crosses the barrage – giving magnificent views over the Krishna at sunset – to Guntur, a major town dealing in rice, cotton and tobacco where the ancient charnockite rocks of the Peninsula meet the alluvium of the coastal plain. In the 18th century it was capital of the region Northern Circars and was under Muslim rule from 1766 under the Nizam of Hyderabad. The Archaeological Museum exhibits local finds including fourth-century Buddhist stone sculptures.

Rajahmundry → *Phone code: 0883. Colour map 2, C3. Population: 313,300.*

The capital of the Eastern Chalukyas, Rajahmundry was captured by the Muslims from the Vengi kings in 1471, then returned to the Orissan Kingdom in 1512. The Deccan Muslims retook it in 1571 and it was repeatedly the scene of bitter hostilities until being granted to the French in 1753. It is remembered for the poet Nannayya who wrote the first Telugu classic *Andhra Mahabharathamu*. Every 12 years the Pushkaram celebration (last held in 2003) is held by the river bank. The **Markandaya** and **Kotilingeswara Temples** draw pilgrims. Rajahmundry is noted for its carpets and sandalwood products and as a convenient base from which to visit the coastal districts. There are simple budget hotels in the town. Rajahmundry is one of two places where you can divert towards the hills of the Eastern Ghats. The Godavari, 80 km northwest of the town, cuts through a gorge and there is a succession of stunningly beautiful lakes, reminiscent of Scottish lochs, where you can take boat trips.

Sleeping

Vijayawada *p344*

Bundar Rd is now MG Rd.

D Ilapuram, Besant Rd, T0866-257 1282. 81 large clean rooms, some a/c, restaurants.

D Kandhari International, MG Rd, Labbipet, T0866-247 1311. Some a/c in the 73 rooms, also restaurants with a/c.

D-E Mamata, Eluru Rd (1 km centre), T0866 257 1251. Good a/c restaurants (1 rooftop), bar, 59 rooms, most a/c with bath.

E Krishnaveni (AP Tourism), Gopal Reddy Rd (opposite Old Bus Stand), T0866-242 6382. Clean rooms, restaurant, tourist office, car hire.

E Santhi, Eluru Rd, T0866-257 7355. Clean rooms with bath (hot water), good vegetarian restaurant.

F Railway Retiring Rooms, the reasonable restaurant opens at 0600.

There are some **F** hotels near the bus stand on MG Rd and near the railway station.

Guntar *p345*

D Vijayakrinshna International, Collectorate Rd, Nagarampalem, T0863-222 2221. Some a/c in 42 rooms, restaurant.

D-E Annapurna Lodge, opposite APSRTC bus stand. A/c and non-a/c rooms, quality meals for Rs 22, helpful and obliging.

D-E Sudarsan, Kothapet, Main Rd, T0863-222 2681. Some a/c in its 28 rooms. Indian vegetarian restaurant.

Eating

Vijayawada *p344*

The restaurants in the **Kandhari** and **Mamata** hotel are recommended.

Greenlands, Bhavani Gardens, Labbipet. Food served in 7 huts on the garden lawns.

Shopping

Vijayawada *p344*

Some shops close 1300-1600. Local Kondapalli toys and Machilipatnam Kalamkari paintings are popular. The emporia are in MG Rd, Eluru Rd, and Governorpet.

Recommended are: **Apco**, Besant Rd; **Ashok**, opposite Maris Stella College, T0866-247 6966; **Handicrafts Shop**, Krishnaveni Motel; **Lepakshi**, Gandhi Nagar.

Activities and tours

Vijayawada *p344*

KL Rao Vihara Kendram, Bhavani Island on Prakasham Barrage Lake, offers rowing, canoeing, water scooters, pedal boats.

Transport

Vijayawada *p344*

Bus

Good local network in city but overcrowded. SRTC buses to neighbouring states including **Chennai** (9 hrs). **New Bus Stand**, MG Rd, near Krishna River, T0866-247 3333. Bookings 24 hrs.

Car hire

From AP Tourism, see page 344.

Ferry

To **Bhavani Islands**, 0930-1730. Also services between Krishnaveni Hotel and **Amaravati**. Daily 0800. Rs 50 return. Book at hotel or at RTC Bus Station.

Rickshaw and taxi

Very few metered yellow-top taxis. Tongas, auto- and cycle-rickshaws are available.

Train

Vijayawada is an important junction. Reservations, 0800-1300, 1300-2000; tokens issued 30 mins earlier. **Bhubaneswar**: *Coromandel Exp 2842* (AC/II), 1600, 11½ hrs; *Konark Exp 1019* (AC/II), 1440, 16 hrs. **Kolkata (H)**: *Coromandel Exp 2842* (AC/II), 1600, 22 hrs. **Chennai (MC)**: *Pinakini Exp 2711*, 0600, 7 hrs; *Coromandel Exp 2841* (AC/II), 1045, 6¾ hrs. **Delhi (ND)**: *GT Exp 2615*, 2315, 30 hrs; *Kerala Exp 2625*, 1125, 28½ hrs. **Hospet**: *Amaravati Exp 7225*, 2200, 13 hrs. **Secunderabad**: *Satavahana Exp 2713*, 0610, 5½ hrs. **Hyderabad**: *Godavari Exp 7007*, 2355, 7 hrs; *Krishna Exp 7405*, 1330, 8¼ hrs (7 hrs to Secunderabad).

Guntar *p345*

Bus

APSRTC bus stand is well organized and clean.

Train

Kolkata: *Faluknama Exp 7201*, 2255, 23½ hrs. **Chennai**: *Hyderabad Chennai Exp 7054*, 2200, 8 hrs. **Hospet**: *Amravati Exp 7225*, 2310, 12 hrs. **Secunderabad**: *Palnad Exp 2747*, 0525, 5 hrs;

Nagarjuna Exp 7005, 3, 6¼ hrs; *Golconda Exp 7201*, 0530, 8 hrs.

Rajahmundry *p345*
Trains to **Kolkata (H)**: *Coromandel Exp 2842 (AC/II)*, 1830, 19½ hrs. **Vijayawada**: *Coromandel Exp 2841*, 0747, 2¾ hrs; *Chennai Mail 6003*, 1635, 3½ hrs; *Ratnachal Exp 2717, 1550*, 3 hrs. **Visakhapatnam**: *Coromandel Exp 2842* 1830, 3¾ hrs; *Chennai Howrah Mail 6004*, 0931, 4 hrs; *Ratnachal Exp 2718*, 0829, 3½ hrs.

Directory

Vijayawada *p344*
Banks State Bank of India, Babu Rajendra Prasad Rd. **Post** Kaleswara Rao Rd. **Useful addresses** Foreigners' Regional Registration Office, police superintendent, MG Rd.

Northeastern Andhra Pradesh

From Vijayawada the NH5 crosses the lush and fertile delta of the Krishna and Godavari to Rajahmundry and then travels over the narrowing coastal plain, the beautiful hills of the Eastern Ghats rising sharply inland. Check weather forecasts before travelling. The whole pattern of life here contrasts sharply with that further south. Higher rainfall and a longer wet season, alongside the greater fertility of the alluvial soils, contribute to an air of prosperity. Village houses, with their thatched roofed cottages and white painted walls, are quite different and distinctive, as are the bullock carts. » *For Sleeping, Eating and other listings, see pages 349-350.*

History

The area was brought under Muslim rule by the Golconda kings of the Bahmani Dynasty in 1575 and ceded to the French in 1753. In 1765 the Mughal Emperor granted the whole area to the East India Company, its first major territorial acquisition in India. The region is also the most urbanized part of Andhra Pradesh, with a dozen towns of more than 100,000 people. Most are commercial and administrative centres with neither the functions nor the appearance of industrial cities, but they serve as important regional centres for trade, especially in agricultural commodities, and they are the homes of some of Andhra's wealthiest and most powerful families.

Although the building of dams on both the Krishna and the Godavari rivers has eliminated the catastrophic flooding common until the mid-19th century, the area is still prone to cyclones; in 1864 one claimed over 34,000 lives. The totally flat delta, lying virtually at sea level, was completely engulfed by a tidal wave in 1883 when the volcano of Mount Krakatoa blew up 5000 km away. Further catastrophic cyclones in 1977 and 1996 caused massive damage and loss of life. You may notice the increasing number of small concrete buildings on raised platforms along the roadside designed to provide temporary shelter to villagers during cyclones.

Visakhapatnam »

pp349-350. Colour map 2, B4.

→ *Phone code: 0891. Population: 969,600.*

Set in a bay with rocky promontories, Visakhapatnam (Vizag) commands a spectacular position between the thickly wooded Eastern Ghats and the sea. It has become one of the country's most rapidly growing cities. Already India's fourth largest port, it has developed ship building, oil refining, fertilizer, petrochemical, sugar refinery and jute industries, as well as one of India's newest and largest steel mills. This is also the Navy's Eastern Fleet's home base. On the Dolphin's Nose, a cliff rising 174 m from the sea, is a lighthouse whose beam can be seen 64 km out to sea.

Its twin town of **Waltair** to the north used to be thought of as a health resort with fine beaches, though increasing atmospheric pollution is a problem. **Ramakrishna Beach**, along the 8 km Lawson's Bay and below the 300 m Mount Kailasa, 6 km away, is best. Don't swim at the harbour end of the beach.

Ins and outs

AP Tourism ⓘ *LIC Building, Daba Garden, T0891-271 3135, 1000-1700, closed Sun and 2nd Sat of the month*. Also at the railway station. **Transport Unit** ⓘ *8 RTC Complex, Dwarka Nagar, T0891-254646.*

Sights

Andhra University was founded in 1926 in the Uplands area of Waltair. The red stone buildings are built like a fortress and are well laid out on a large campus. The country's major **Ship Building Yard** at Gandhigram makes all types of ocean-going vessels: passenger liners, cargo vessels as well as naval ships. The **zoo** to the northeast is large and attempts to avoid cages, keeping its animals in enclosures which are close to their natural habitat.

Each of the three hills in Visakhapatnam is sacred to a different religion. The Hindu **Venkateswara Temple** on the Venkateswa Konda was built in 1866 by the European Captain Blackmoor. The Muslims have a **mausoleum of the saint Baba Ishaq Madina**

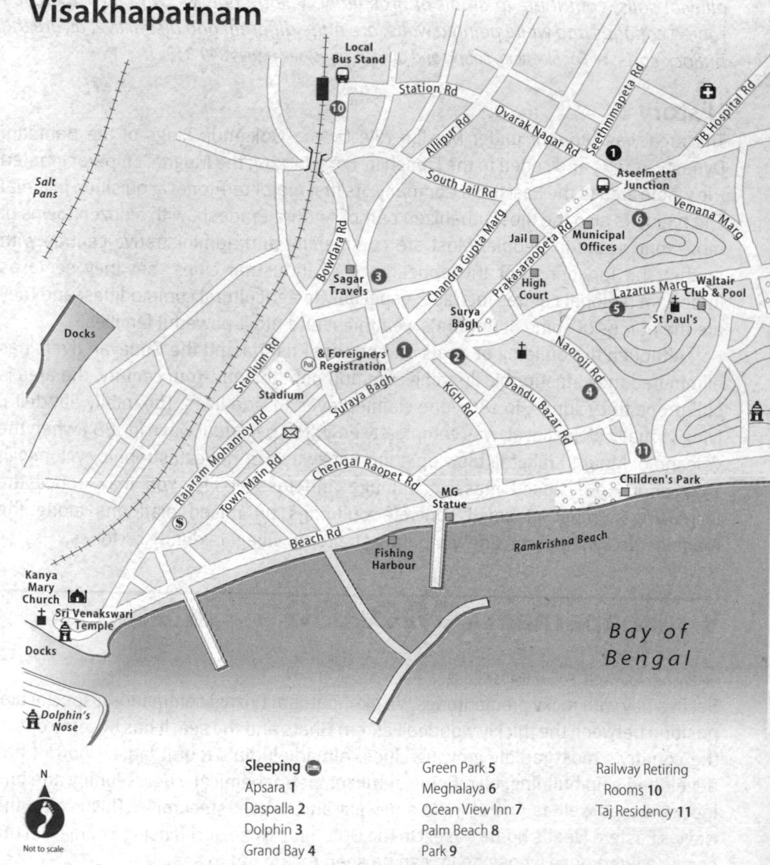

Sleeping
Apsara 1
Daspalla 2
Dolphin 3
Grand Bay 4
Green Park 5
Meghalaya 6
Ocean View Inn 7
Palm Beach 8
Park 9
Railway Retiring Rooms 10
Taj Residency 11

on the Darga Konda, while the highest Ross Hill has a **Roman Catholic Church**. A Buddhist relic was discovered at **Dhanipura** nearby.

Simhachalam, 16 km northwest, is noted for its 13th-century Varaha Narasimha Temple, set in the Kailasa Hills, which has some well-known hot springs.

Sleeping

Visakhapatnam *p347, map p348*
Late night arrivals are quoted high prices by auto-rickshaws to go to the beach. Stay overnight at a simple hotel near the bus station (walk right from railway station) and move next morning.

AL Park, Beach Rd, T0891-255 4488, www.theparkhotels.com. 64 rooms, pricey suites, spa with gym, clean pool, well-kept gardens, slick management, best for direct beach access (beware of rocks when swimming), popular with German and Czech expats.

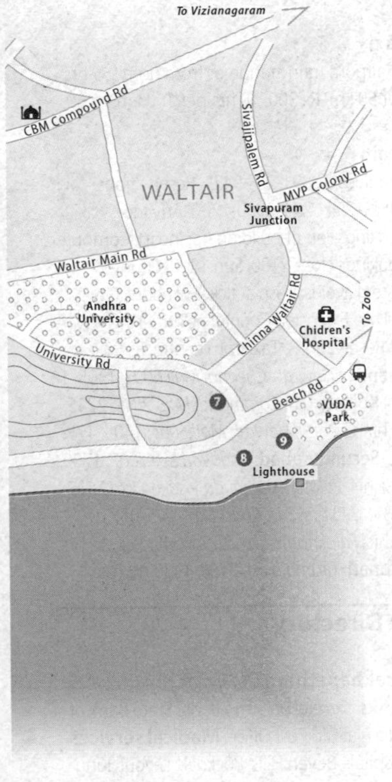

Eating
Blue Diamond **1**

AL-A Taj Residency, Beach Rd (2 km from centre), T0891-256 7756, www.tajhotels.com. 95 narrow sea-facing rooms, restaurant (pricey but generous), best in town, access to an unremarkable public beach across road.

A Grand Bay, Beach Rd, T0891-256 0101, www.itcwelcomgroup.in. 104 rooms, all business facilities, restaurants.

A Green Park, Waltair Main Rd, T0891-256 4444, www.hotelgreenpark.com. Modern business hotel, rooms vary.

B Dolphin, Daba Gardens, T0891-256 7000, www.dolphinhotelsvizag.com. Family-run hotel with 147 rooms, popular restaurants, rooftop has good views, live band, health club, exchange and pool (but quite a distance from the beach). Excellent service. Highly recommended but reserve ahead.

D Apsara, 12-1-17 Waltair Main Rd, T0891-256 4861. Central a/c, 130 rooms, restaurants, bar, exchange, very helpful and friendly staff.

D Daspalla, Surya Bagh, T0891-256 4825. 102 rooms, **C** suites, central a/c, 2 good restaurants (continental and thalis), exchange bar, set back from road, no late-night check-in.

D Punnai Punnami Beach Resort (AP Tourism), Bhimili Beach Rd, Rushikonda beach (15 km away), T0891-279 0734. New resort up the steps from clean beach, rooms with sea views, good food.

D-E Meghalaya, Asilametta Junction (5-min walk from bus, short rickshaw ride from station), T0891-255 5141. Popular with Indian tourists, good value, 65 rooms, some a/c, dull vegetarian restaurant (non-vegetarian available from room service), spacious lobby with murals, pleasant roof garden, friendly and helpful. Recommended.

D-E Ocean View Inn, Kirlampudi (north end of the beach), T0891-255 4828. Location spoilt by high-rise flats, quiet end of town. 48 rooms, some a/c, clean, comfortable. A/c restaurant.

D-E Palm Beach, Beach Rd (next to Park hotel), Waltair, T0891-255 4026. Pleasant, shady palm grove but run-down building. 34 rooms, 30 a/c, restaurant, beer garden, swimming pool.

E Lakshmi, next to St Joseph's Hospital, Maryland. 10 rooms a/c, some with bath, clean and welcoming, good Indian restaurant.
E Railway Retiring Rooms decent rooms, men's dorm.
E Saga Lodge, off Hospital Rd towards beach. Rooms with balcony, some with bath and sea view, no restaurant but excellent room service.
E Viraat, Indira Gandhi Stadium Rd, Old Bus Stand, T0891-256 4821. Some a/c in 42 rooms with bath, a/c restaurant and bar, exchange.

Eating

Visakhapatnam *p347, map p348*
Most eateries serve alcohol. Apart from hotels, there are restaurants on Station Rd.
Black Dog, Surya Bagh, close to the Jagdamba Theatre.
Blue Diamond, opposite RTC, Dabagardens.
Delight, 7-1-43 Kirlampudi, Beach Rd.

Festivals and events

Visakhapatnam *p347, map p348*
Dec: Navy Mela and Navy Day Parade along Beach Rd.

Activities and tours

Visakhapatnam *p347, map p348*
Swimming
Pools at **Park** and **Palm Beach** hotels are open to non-residents. **Waltair Club** has a pool.

Tours
AP Tourism, RTC Complex. Local sightseeing day trip, 0830, Rs 75. Araku Valley, 0700, Rs 80.
Taj Travels, Meghalaya Hotel, T0891-255 5141, ext 222.

Transport

Visakhapatnam *p347, map p348*
Air
Airport is 16 km from city centre; taxi (Rs 180) or auto-rickshaw. **Indian Airlines**, T0891-256 5018, **Airport**, T0891-255 8221 and Air India agent, **Sagar Travel**, 1000-1300, 1345-1700. Daily except Sun to **Hyderabad**; some to **Bhubaneswar**, **Kolkata**, **Chennai**, **Mumbai**. Jet Airways, VIP Rd, T0891-276 2180, airport T0891-262 2795, to **Hyderabad**.

Bus
Aseelmetta Junction Bus Station is well organized. APSRTC run services to main towns in the state. Enquiries, T0891-256 5038, reservations 0600-2000. **Araku Valley**, **Guntur** (0930, 1545, 2045), **Hyderabad** (638 km, 1630), **Kakinda**, **Puri** (0700), **Rajahmundry**, **Srikakulam**, **Vijayawada** (1945, 2015), **Vizianagram** (57 km, 0610-2130).

Ferry
Runs 0800-1700 between harbour and **Yarada Hills**. Also to Dolphin Lighthouse. Occasional service to **Port Blair**, Andaman Islands, at short notice: M/s AV Banojirow & Co, PO Box 17, opposite Port Main Gate.

Rickshaw
Offer Rs 2 over meter charge to make auto-rickshaws use a meter; night fares exorbitant. Only cycle rickshaws in centre.

Taxi
At airport, train station or from hotels: 5 hrs per 50 km, Rs 300; 10 hrs per 100 km, Rs 50.

Train
Enquiries, T0891-256 9421. Reservations T0891-254 6234. 0900-1700. Advance bookings, left of building (facing it). Computer bookings close 2100, Sun 1400. Counter system avoids crush at ticket window. City Railway Extension Counter at Turner's Chowltry for Reservations. Taxi from centre, Rs 50.
Chennai: *Howrah-Chennai Mail 6003*, 1305, 16 hrs. **Kolkata (H)**: *Coromandel Exp 2842*, 2235, 15 hrs; *Chennai Howrah Mail 6004*, 1405, 17¼ hrs; **Secunderabad**: *Godavari Exp 7007*, 1700, 13¾ hrs; *Palasa Kacheguda Visakha Exp 7615*, 1635, 15½ hrs; *East Coast Exp 7045*, 0525, 14 hrs; *Faluknama Exp 7027*, 0045, Tue, 12 hrs.
Tirupati: *Tirumala Exp 7488*, 1430, 16 hrs.

Directory

Visakhapatnam *p347, map p348*
Banks Several on Surya Bagh. **State Bank of India** is at Old Post Office. **Medical services** Hospitals: **Seven Hills**, Rockdale Layout; **King George**, Hospital Rd, Maharani Peta, T0891-256 4891. **Post office** Head Post Office, Vellum Peta; also at Waltair Railway Station. **Useful addresses** Foreigners' Regional Registration Office, SP Police, T0891-156 2709.

The Tamil borders

Tirupati and Tirumalai

» pp354-356.

Colour map 3, A5.

→ *Phone code: 08574 (Tirupati), 08577 (Tirumalai). Population: 245,500.*

The Tirumalai Hills provide a picture-book setting for the famous Sri Venkatesvara temple, at the top of the Ghat road, visited by 10,000 pilgrims daily. The main town of Tirupati lies at the bottom of the hill where there are several other temples, some also pilgrimage centres in their own right. The seven hills are compared to the seven-headed Serpent God Adisesha who protects the sleeping Vishnu under his hood.

Ins and outs

Getting there Flights from Chennai and Hyderabad arrive at the airport 15 km from Tirupati. The railway station in the town centre has several fast trains from Chennai and other southern towns while the main (central) bus stand is 500 m east of it with express buses from the region. To save time and hassle, buy a through Link ticket to Tirumalai. » *See Transport, page 355, for further details.*

Getting around Buses for Tirumalai leave from stands near the station, but there are also share taxis available. Some choose to join pilgrims for a four- to five-hour walk uphill, starting before dawn to avoid the heat though the path is covered most of the way. Luggage is transported free from the toll gate at the start of the 15 km path and may be collected from the reception office at in Tirumalai.

Tourist information **AP Regional ˈourist office** ⓘ *139 TP Area, near 3rd Choultry, T08574-255386*. **AP State tourist office** ⓘ *Govindraja Car St, T08574-124818*. **APTDC** ⓘ *Transport Unit, 12 APSRTC Complex, T08574-225602*. **Karnataka Tourism** ⓘ *Hotel Mayura* (see page 354). **TTD Information** ⓘ *1 New Choultry, T08574-222777* and at the railway station and airport.

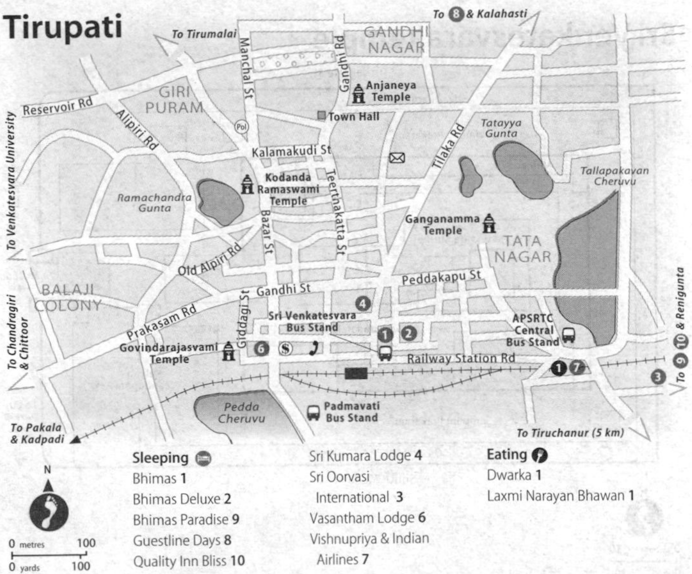

Sri Venkatesvara Temple Dating from the 10th century, this temple is believed to have been dedicated by the Vaishnava saint Ramanuja and is known as *Balaji* in the north and *Srinivasa Perumalai* in the south. Of all India's temples, this draws the largest number of pilgrims. The town of Tirupati, at the base of the hill, was established in approximately AD 1131 under the orders of Ramanuja that the temple functionaries who served in the sacred shrines must live nearby. Although a road runs all the way up the hill to a bus stand at the top, most pilgrims choose to walk up the wooded slope through mango groves and sandalwood forest chanting "*Om namo Venkatesaya*" or "*Govinda, Govinda*". Order is maintained by providing 'Q sheds' under which pilgrims assemble.

The atmosphere inside is unlike any other temple in India. Turnstiles control the flow of pilgrims into the **main temple complex**, which is through an intricately carved *gopuram*, much of which is rebuilt, on the east wall. There are three enclosures. The first, where there are portrait sculptures of the Vijayanagar patrons, include Krishnadeva Raya and his queen and a gold covered pillar. The outer colonnades are in the Vijayanagar style; the gateway leading to the inner enclosure may be of Chola origin. The second enclosure has more shrines, a sacred well and the kitchen. The inner enclosure is opened only once every year. The main temple and shrine is on the west side of the inner enclosure. The **sanctuary** (ninth to 10th centuries), known as *Ananda Nilayam*, has a domed *vimana* entirely covered with gold plate, and gold covered gates. The image in the shrine is a standing Vishnu, richly ornamented with gold and jewels. The 2 m-high image stands on a lotus, two of his four arms carry a conch shell and a *chakra* or discus and he wears a diamond crown which is said to be the most precious single ornament in the world. It is flanked by *Sridevi* and *Bhudevi*, Vishnu's consorts. There is a small **museum** ⓘ *0800-2000*, of temple art in the temple compound, with a collection of stone, metal and wooden images.

There are two types of queues for *darshan* or special viewing: Sarvadarsan is open to all, while those who pay for Special darshan (Rs 30) enter by a separate entrance and join a short queue. The actual *darshan* (from 0600-1100) itself lasts a precious second and a half even though the 'day' at the temple may last 21 hours. Suprabhatam 0300-0330 (awakening the deity) costs Rs 100; Tomala Seva

Sri Venkatesvara temple

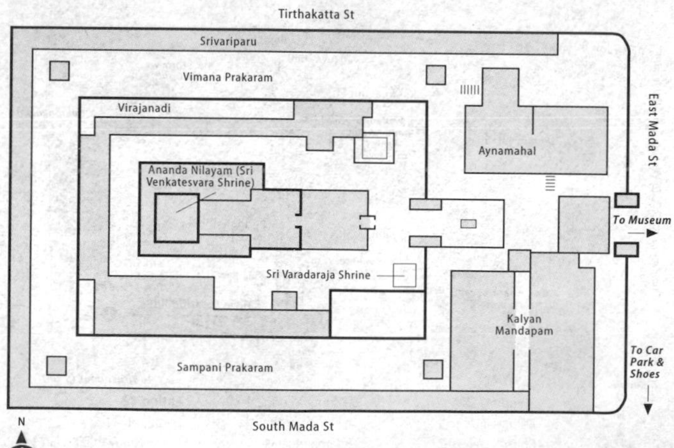

Tirupati haircuts

Architecturally Sri Venkatesvara Temple is unremarkable, but in other respects is extraordinary. It is probably the wealthiest in India, and the *devasthanam* (or temple trust) now sponsors a huge range of activities, from the Sri Venkatesvara University in Tirupati to hospitals, orphanages and schools. Its wealth comes largely from its pilgrims, numbering on average over 10,000 a day, but at major festivals many times that number may visit. All pilgrims make gifts, and the *hundi* (offering) box in front of the shrine is stuffed full with notes, gold ornaments and other offerings. Another important source of income is the haircutting service. Many pilgrims come to Tirupati to seek a special favour – to seek a suitable wife or husband, to have a child, to recover from illness – and it is regarded as auspicious to grow the hair long and then to offer the hair as a sacrifice. You may see many pilgrims fully shaven at the temple when appearing before the deity. Lines of barbers wait for the arriving pilgrims. Once, when coaches unloaded their pilgrims, one barber would line up customers and shave one strip of hair off as many heads as possible in order to maximize the number of customers committed to him before he returned and finished off the job! Now, a free numbered ticket and a razor blade can be collected from the public bath hall which pilgrims take to the barber with the same number to claim a free haircut. The hair is collected, washed and softened before being exported to the American and Japanese markets for wig making.

0330-0415 (flower offering), Rs 200. Mornings are particularly busy. Monday and Tuesday are less crowded. The temple is 18 km up the Ghat road; see Transport on page 355.

Every day is festival day with shops remaining open 24 hours. The image of Sri Venkatesvara (a form of Vishnu) is widely seen across South India, in private homes, cars and taxis and in public places, and is instantly recognizable from his black face and covered eyes, shielded so that the deity's piercing gaze may not blind any who look directly at him. In the temple the deity's body is anointed with camphor, saffron and musk. The holy *prasadam* or consecrated sweet is distributed to well over 50,000 pilgrims at special festivals.

Theoretically the inner shrines of the Tirumalai temple are open only to Hindus. However, foreigners are usually welcome. They are sometimes invited to sign a form to show they sympathize with Hindu beliefs. According to the tourist information leaflet: "The only criterion for admission is faith in God and respect for the temple's conventions and rituals".

Govindarajasvami Temple In Tirupati itself the Govindarajasvami Temple (16th-17th centuries), is the most widely visited. Built by the Nayakas, the successors to the Vijayanagar Empire, the temple has an impressive outer *gopuram*. Of the three *gopurams* the innermost is also the earliest, dating from the 14th to 15th centuries. The main sanctuaries are dedicated to Vishnu and Krishna. Another temple worth seeing is **Kapilesvarasvami**, in a beautiful setting with a sacred waterfall, **Kapila Theertham**.

About 1 km away are strange **rock formations** in a natural arch, resembling a hood of a serpent, a conch and a discus, thought to have been the source of the idol in the temple. There is a sacred waterfall **Akasa Ganga**, 3 km south of the temple. The **Papa Vinasanam Dam** is 5 km north.

Chandragiri, 11 km southwest, became the capital of the Vijayanagaras in 1600, after their defeat at the battle of Talikota 35 years earlier. The Palace of Sri Ranga Raya, built in 1639 witnessed the signing by Sri Ranga Raya of the original land grant to the East India Company of **Fort St George** ⓘ *state bus or taxi from Tirupati*, but seven years later the fort was captured by Qutb Shahi from Golconda. The fort was built on a 180 m-high rock where earlier fortifications may date from several hundred years before the Vijayanagar kings took over. You can still see the well-preserved defences and some of the palaces and temples. Visit the Rani Mahal and Raja Mahal with its pretty lily pond. The museum in Raja Mahal, contains Chola and Vijayanagar bronzes.

Sri Kalahasti or **Kalahasti** ⓘ *state buses run from Tirupati*, 36 km northeast of Tirupati, is very attractively sited on the banks of the Svarnamukhi River at the foot of the extreme southern end of the Vellikonda Ranges, known locally as the Kailasa Hills. The town and temple, built in the 16th and 17th centuries, developed largely as a result of the patronage of the Vijayanagar kings. The **Kalahastisvara Temple** dominates the town with its *gopuram* facing the river. It is built in the Dravida style like the famous temple of Tirumalai. The magnificent detached *gopuram* was built by the Vijayanagar Emperor Krishnadeva Raya. Set within high walls with a single entrance to the south, the temple is particularly revered for the white stone Siva *lingam* in the western shrine, believed to be worshipped by *sri* (spider), *kala* (king cobra) and *hasti* (elephant). The Nayaka style is typified by the columns carved into the shape of rearing animals and the riders. The temple to the Wind God *Vayudeva* is the only one of its kind in India. The bathing ghats of the Swarnamukhi (golden) River and the temple attract a steady flow of pilgrims. In addition to its function as a pilgrim centre, the town is known for its *kalamkaris*, brightly coloured **hand-painted textiles** used as temple decoration. There are fine examples in Salar Jung Museum, Hyderabad, see page 330.

Pulicat Lake, on the coast, 50 km north of Chennai, is the second largest saltwater lagoon in India and one of the most important wetlands for migratory shorebirds on the eastern seaboard of India. The northern area has large concentrations of greater flamingos near the islands of Vendadu and Irukkam. There are also many birds of prey. The shallow brackish waters are rich in crustaceans and **Sriharikotta Island** has patches of residual dry evergreen forest, although it is perhaps noted more today for its rocket launching site. About 20 km north of Suluru is the **Neelapattu Lake**, which was given protected status in 1976 to conserve a large breeding colony of spotbilled pelicans.

Sleeping

Tirupati and Tirumalai *p351, map p351*
Pilgrims are usually housed in well-maintained Temple Trust's *choultries* in Tirumalai which can accommodate about 20,000. They vary from luxury suites and well-furnished cottages to dorms and unfurnished rooms (some free). Contact PRO, TT Devasthanams, T08577-22753 or Reception Officer 1, T08577-22571. Those listed below are in Tirupati.

C Guestline Days, 14-37 Karakambadi Rd, 3 km from town, T08574-228366. 140 rooms, central a/c, restaurants (including non vegetarian), bar, pool.

C Quality Inn Bliss, Renigunta Rd near Overbridge, T08574-225793. 72 modern clean a/c rooms, restaurants.

D Bhimas, 42 Govindaraja Car St, T08574-220766. Near railway, 59 clean rooms with bath, some a/c, restaurant (South Indian vegetarian), roof garden.

D Bhimas Deluxe, 38 Govindaraja Car St, T08574-225521. Near **Bhimas**, 60 rooms, 40 a/c, restaurant (Indian, a/c), exchange.

D Bhimas Paradise, 33-37 Renigunta Rd, T08574-225747. This place has 3 clean rooms, some a/c, pool, garden, good restaurant.

D Mayura, 209 TP Area, T08574-225925. 65 rooms, half a/c, vegetarian restaurant, exchange. Pricier end of this price category.

D Sri Oorvasi International, Renigunta Rd, T08574-220202. Around 1 km from railway, 78 rooms, some a/c, restaurant (vegetarian).
D Vishnupriya, T08574-225060. 134 rooms, some a/c, restaurants, exchange, Indian Airlines office.
F Sri Kumara Lodge, near railway station. Decent rooms.
F Vasantham Lodge 141 G Car St, T08574-220460. Reasonable rooms with bath.

Eating

Tirupati and Tirumalai *p351, map p351*
In Tirumalai particularly, the Trust prohibits non-vegetarian food, alcohol and smoking. Outside hotels, vegetarian restaurants here include:
Laxmi Narayan Bhawan and **Dwarka**, opposite APSRTC Bus Stand; **Konark** Railway Station Rd; **New Triveni**, 139 TP Area; **Woodlands**, TP Area.
Tirupathi-Tirumalai Devasthanam Trust (TTD) provides free vegetarian meals at its guest houses.
Indian Coffee House and **Tea Board Restaurant** and both near the TTD Canteen and the APSRTC Bus Stand.

Festivals and events

Tirupati and Tirumalai *p351, map p351*
May/Jun: Govind Brahmotsavam.
Sep-Oct: Brahmotsavam is the most important, especially grand every 3rd year when it is called **Navarathri Brahmotsavam**. On the 3rd day the Temple Car Festival **Rathotsavam** is particularly popular. **Rayalseema Food and Dance** follows later in the month.

Shopping

Tirupati and Tirumalai *p351, map p351*
Copper and brass idols, produced at Perumallapalli village, 8 km away, and wooden toys are sold locally. Try **Poompuhar** on Gandhi Rd and **Lepakshi** in the TP Area.

Activities and tours

Tirupati and Tirumalai *p351, map p351*
AP Tourism, Room 15, Srinivasa Choultry, T08574-220602. Local tour starts at the APSRTC Central Bus Stand, 1000-1730. Rs 150. Tirupati (not Venkatesvara), Kalahasti, Tiruchanur, Chandragiri and Srinivasamangapuram. From Chennai to Tirumalai, Rs 300.

Transport

Tirupati and Tirumalai *p351, map p351*

Air
Transport to town by APSRTC coach to Tirupati (Rs 20) and Tirumalai (Rs 30); taxis Rs 150. **Indian Airlines**, Hotel Vishnupriya, opposite central bus stand, T08574-222349. 1000-1730. To **Chennai**: Tue, Thu, Sun and **Hyderabad**: Tue, Thu, Sat. **Jet Airways**, T08574-256916, airport T08574-271471, to **Hyderabad**.

Bus
Local Service between Tirupati and Tirumalai every 3 mins, 0330-2200.
In Tirupati: Sri Venkatesvara bus stand, opposite railway station for passengers with through tickets to Tirumalai; Enquiries: 3rd Choultry, T08574-220132. **Padmavati bus stand** in TP Area, T08574-220203; long queues for buses but buying a return ticket from Tirupati (past the railway footbridge) saves time at the ticket queue. The journey up the slow winding hill road – which some find worrying – takes about 45 mins. In **Tirumalai**, arrive at **Kesavanagar bus stand**, near central reception area, 500 m southeast of temple; walk past canteen and shop. Depart from **Rose Garden bus stand**, east of the temple.
Long distance Good service through SRTCs from the neighbouring southern states. **Chennai** 4 hrs, **Kanchipuram** 3 hrs, **Vellore** 2½ hrs. Central bus stand enquiries, T08574-222333. 24-hr left luggage.

Rickshaw
Auto-rickshaws: fixed point-to-point fares; cycle rickshaws: negotiable.

Taxi
Tourist taxis through AP Tourism from the Bus Stand and Railway Station to Tirumalai, Rs 600 return, for 5½ hrs. Share taxi between Tirupati and Tirumalai, about Rs 65 per person. **Balaji Travels**, 149 TP Area, T08574-224894.

Train

Trains are often delayed. Phone the station in advance if catching a night train as it could be delayed until next morning. **Chennai (C)**: *Intercity Exp 6204*, 0645, 3¼ hrs; *Saptagiri Exp 6058*, 1720, 3¼ hrs. **Mumbai (CST)**: bus to Renigunta (10 km) for *Chennai-Mumbai Exp 6012*, 1445, 24 hrs; or direct: *Tirupati-Mumbai CST Bi-Weekly Exp 6354*, Thu, Sun, 2140, 24 hrs. **Guntakal**: *Kacheguda Venkatadri Exp 7498*, 1750, 6¼ hrs; *Rayalaseema Exp 7430* (AC/II), 1850, 6½ hrs. **Mysore** (via Chennai): *Saptagiri Exp 6058*, 1720, 3¼ hrs, wait for 2¼ hrs, then take the*Chennai Mysore Exp 6222*, 2245, 11¼ hrs (total 16¾ hrs). **Hyderabad**: *Narayanadri Exp 7423*, 1830, 13¾ hrs (for Secunderabad).

Directory

Tirupati and Tirumalai *p351, map p351*
Banks Most are on Gandhi St. State Bank of India, opposite APSRTC. **Useful addresses** Foreigners' Regional Registration Office: 499 Reddy Colony, T08574-220503.

The arid western borders

For much of the way between Hyderabad and Bengaluru (Bangalore) the NH7 crosses the boulder covered plateau of the ancient peninsular granites and gneisses. On either side reddish or light brown soils are cultivated with millets or rice on the patches of irrigated land. ▸▸ *For Sleeping, Eating and other listings, see page 358.*

Kurnool → *Colour map 1, C6.*

Between 1950-1956 Kurnool, 214 km southwest of Hyderabad, was capital of the state of Andhra Desa before Hyderabad was chosen as the capital of the new state of Andhra Pradesh in 1956. At the junction of the Hindri and Tungabhadra rivers, it was an administrative centre for the Nawabs of Kurnool. Muslim influence is still evident in the ruined palace of the Nawabs on the steep bank of the Tungabhadra.

Srisailam → *Colour map 1, C1.*

A longer excursion, 170 km east of Kurnool on the route through Doranala, takes you to this popular site of Saivite pilgrimage on the banks of the Krishna, see page 340. The wooded Nallamalai Hills are home to the *Chenchu* tribes. The township has been built for workers on a massive dam construction project.

Srisailam's origins are obscure, and the **Mallikarjuna Temple** (14th century) on a hill, containing one of 12 *jyotirlingas*, has often been attacked and damaged. Some 300 m long (dated to 1456), the outer face is richly decorated with carved figures. These include a portrait of Krishna Deva Raya, the Vijayanagar Emperor who visited the site in 1514. The walls and gates have carvings depicting stories from the epics. Non-Hindus are allowed into the inner sanctuary to witness the daily puja ceremony. To avoid the long queue in the middle of the day, it is best to arrive early – first prayers at 0545. **Mahasivaratri Festival** draws large crowds. Srisailam can also be reached straight from Hyderabad (200 km) across the wide open Telangana Plateau.

Gooty → *Phone code: 08553. Colour map 1, C6.*

Gooty, south of Kurnool, has a dramatic **Vijayanagar Fort** with excellent views on a granite outcrop 300 m high. In the 18th century the fort fell into the hands of a Maratha chief but was captured in 1776 by Haidar Ali after a siege of nine months. Sir Thomas Munro (Governor of Madras), who died nearby in 1827, has his grave in the cemetery by the path leading up to the Fort though his body was moved to Fort St George in Madras.

The town, 4 km from the railway station, is a major crossroads and truck stop. A bypass has taken many of the hundreds of lorries that used to pass through it every day, leaving it once more as a typically pedestrian-dominated Indian market town.

Guntakal, 95 km west of Gooty, is an important railway junction with little to attract a tourist. It is en route to Bellary to visit Hampi and Hospet.

Bellary → *Colour map 1, C5.*

The first agricultural communities of the peninsula lived around Bellary. The black cotton soils are pierced by islands of granite hills, and the **Neolithic communities** here lived at roughly the same time as the early Indus Valley civilizations. Radio carbon datings puts the earliest of these settlements at about 3000 BC. **Ash mounds** have been discovered close to the confluence of the **Krishna** and **Tungabhadra**, and to the south of Bellary. The mounds are where cattle were herded together. Evidence from later sites in Karnataka shows that millets and grain were already widely grown by the first millennium BC. The unusual fort on a single 'pebble' dominates the town (402 steps to the top). The 1902 South African POW camp is 150 m north of the Cantonment Railway station, while the British cemetery is east of the rock.

Anantapur → *Colour map 3, A4.*

Rural Development Trust ⓘ *FVF Bangalore Highway, T08554-31503, fvfatp@hd2.dot.net.in*, is an NGO working with outcastes in over 1500 villages. The Director, a former Spanish Jesuit, Vincente Ferrer, started the project – which covers health, education, housing etc – over 30 years ago. If you are interested in seeing the work visitors can be accommodated for up to four days.

Puttaparthi → *Colour map 3, A4.*

Just southeast of Dharmavaram, **Puttaparthi** ⓘ *Bangalore bus takes 4-5 hrs*, has the principle Sai Baba Ashram, **Prasanthi Nilayam** ⓘ *0400-2100*, attracting followers from all over India and abroad. The present Sai Baba is widely believed to be a reincarnation of the Maharashtrian Sai Baba of Shirdi. The Ashram accommodation is good and open 0800-1900, but it is only for over-25s and to families. Flights from Chennai and Mumbai were introduced by the former prime minister Narasimha Rao, a Sai Baba follower.

Penukonda → *Colour map 3, A4.*

The second capital of the Vijaynagara Empire, the city grew in importance from the 14th to 17th century. You can climb Penukonda (literally 'big hill') by a steep path. At the base, east of the hill, are huge walls and gateways of the old fortifications. The **Jain Parsvanatha Temple** has an 11th-century sculpture of Parshvanatha, naked in front of an undulating serpent in late Chalukyan style. There are also two granite Hindu temples from the early Vijayanagar period dedicated to Rama and Siva, the mosque of Sher Ali (circa 1600), the Jama Masjid with a near spherical dome, and the **Gagan Mahal** palace.

Penukonda became the headquarters of the districts ceded to the East India Company by the Nizam of Hyderabad in 1800. There is a well carved 10-m-high column in the compound of the sub-collector's office.

Lepakshi

Approaching Lepakshi, 35 km south of Penukonda, from Chilamattur you see a massive sculpture of Siva's bull (*Nandi*), carved out of a granite boulder, 5 m high and 8 m long. This tiny village has a temple of outstanding interest for its murals. The **Virabhadra Temple**, built in 1538 under the Vijayanagar Emperor Achutyadeva Raya, has well-preserved sculptures, and striking mural paintings of popular legends from the *Puranas*, see page 492, and epics. On an outcrop of *gneiss*, the main temple has narrative reliefs on the south walls illustrate Siva legends, including Arjuna's penance. The principal sanctuary has a life-size Virabhadra, decked with skulls and carrying weapons, appropriate to this form of Siva, bent on revenge.

Sleeping

Kurnool *p356*
D Raja Vihar Deluxe, Bellary Rd, T0851-282 0702. Half of the 48 rooms have a/c, Indian restaurants with a/c.
D Raviprakash, Railway Station Rd (500 m from railway), T0851-282 1116. 46 rooms and bungalows, some a/c with baths, restaurants (Indian), lawns.

Gooty *p356*
A very basic hotel (with restaurant) is next to the bus stand.

Guntakal *p357*
An excellent value **F** hotel has a South Indian restaurant next door. Rickshaw drivers will take you there if you have to spend the night.

Bellary *p357*
C Hotel Pola Paradise, with comfortable a/c rooms, **B** suites, restaurant and pool.
D Ashoka, which is more modest.

Penukonda *p357*
F Sabina Lodge, near the bus stand, has simple clean rooms.

Lepakshi *p357*
F Rest House, opposite temple. 2 very basic rooms, and a simple restaurant nearby. Alternatively stay in **Hindupur**, where there are several hotels next to the state bus stand, near some good 'meals' restaurants.

Activities and tours

Penukonda *p357*
Stree Sangsheema Trust, on the main street north of the centre, organizes tours, promotes women's co-operative efforts and sells the *Penukonda* guidebook by Torsten Otto, 2001, Rs 25.

Transport

Kurnool *p356*
Train
Kurnool Town to **Chennai (MC)** via **Tirupati**: *Venkatadri/Tirupati-Chennai Exp 7497/6054*, 2237, 14 hrs. **Guntakal**: *Secunderabad-Bangalore Exp 7085*, 2125, 2 hrs. **Secunderabad**: *Tungabhadra Exp 7608*, 1510, 4½ hrs; *Bangalore Secunderabad Exp 7086*, 0230, 4 hrs.

Gooty *p356*
Train
Bengaluru (Bangalore): *Udyan Exp 6529*, 0120, 7¼ hrs. **Guntakal**: 14 Express/Mail trains daily including 0005, 0210, 0700, 0910, 1805, 1950 and 2310, ½ hr. **Chennai (MC)**: *Mumbai Chennai Exp 6011*, 0745, 9 hrs; *Mumbai Chennai Mail 6009*, 1935, 10 hrs. **Mumbai (CST)** : *Kanniyakumari Mumbai Exp 1082*, 0910, 29¾ hrs.

Gooty: Guntakal *p357*
Train
Chennai (MC): *Mumbai Chennai Exp 6011*, 0710, 8½ hrs; *Dadar Chennai Exp 1063*, 1130, 8½ hrs; *Mumbai Chennai Mail 6009*, 1835, 11 hrs. **Bengaluru (Bangalore)**: *Karnataka Exp 2628*, 0745, 6 hrs; *Hampi Exp/Nanded Bangalore Link Exp 6591*, 2300, 7½ hrs. **Kochi/Ernakulam**: *Mumbai CST-Trivandrum Exp 6331*, Tue, 0540, 20 hrs. **Hospet**: *Hampi Exp 6592*, 0510, 3 hrs; *Guntakal Hubli Pass 303*, 2120, 3¾ hrs; *Amaravati Exp 7225*, 0815, 2½ hrs; *Haripriya Exp 7315*, 0245, 2½ hrs. **Secunderabad**: *Bangalore Secunderabad Exp 7086*, 2345, 6¾ hrs. **Hyderabad**: *Rayalaseema Exp 7430*, 0130, 8½ hrs. **Mumbai (CST)**: *Udyan Exp 6530*, 0250, 17½ hrs; *Chennai Mumbai Mail 6010*, 0750, 20½ hrs. **Londa** (for Goa via Hubli): *Haripriya Exp 7315*, 0245, 7 hrs; *Amaravati Exp 7225*, 0815, 5½ hrs.

Bellary *p357*
Train
To **Gadag**: *Amravathi Exp 7225*, 0905 3 hrs.
To **Guntakal**: *Amravathi Exp 7226*, 1730, 1¼ hrs.

Goa

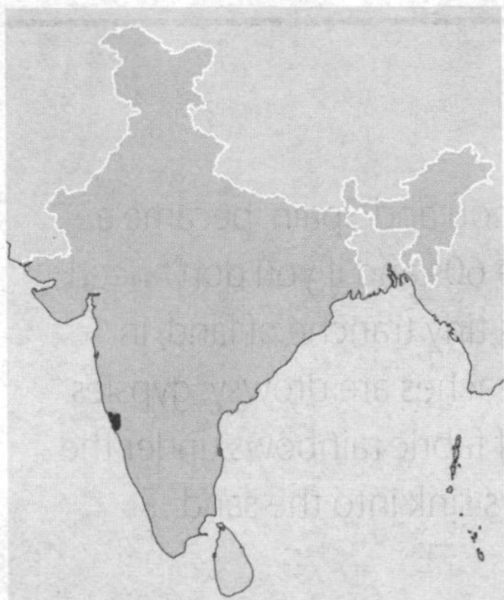

Footprint features

Introduction

Goa, like San Francisco, Kathmandu and Spain, became a Mecca of alternative living in the 60s and if you don't need your sand Mr Whippy white, this tiny tranche of land, in pockets, remains unmatched. Beaches are drowsy; gypsies unfurl sarongs to make shacks of fabric rainbows under the coconut canopy and sacred cows sink into the sand.

Meanwhile the relics of Goa's colonial past, though no match for the giant landmarks of broader India, are still rococo and baroque gems, half swallowed up by nature. Lush jungles twist their way around watchful ruined forts, and huge banyans shelter centuries-old church spires and lavish basilica.

There's humble, everyday beauty to be had elsewhere too: in village dawns where blue mists lie low and hazy across paddy and curl at the crumbling fronts of 18th-century Portuguese manors in pink, umber and blue, where exotic birds dive about sprawling raintrees and ravens caw as delivery boys push bicycles stacked with freshly baked breads. At sunset, as the amber hues blaze against the mottled green Arabian Sea, fire embers smoke at the feet of chickens and pigs, bullock carts dredge through muddy fields of paddy and boys in board shorts swing their cricket bats in the straw stubble. Then at velvet twilight Goa's fisherfolk steal out of quiet harbours in brightly coloured trawlers, whose torches twinkle like a thread of fairy lights along the night horizon as they fill their nets with silvery pomfret and snapper. These gentle-paced and easy living people also enjoy a shared flair for food, wine and song.

★ Don't miss …

1 **The Latin Quarter** Take an unhurried turn around the charming streets of San Thome and Fontainhas districts in Panjim, page 370.

2 **Old Goa** A ghost town of sprawling convents, churches and chapels in dense jungle, page 371.

3 **Ingo's and the Flea** Market days are vibrant social fixtures, page 390.

4 **Cabo da Rama** One of Goa's most dilapidated and ancient forts, page 413.

5 **Palolem** Charter a fishing boat and escape the mainland, page 413.

6 **Inland Goa** Explore by bicycle or motorbike and experience the unmanufactured life of the state, page 423.

7 **Spice plantations** Take a crash course in the medicinal values of plants, herbal Viagra and a slap-up Goan meal while you're at it, page 426.

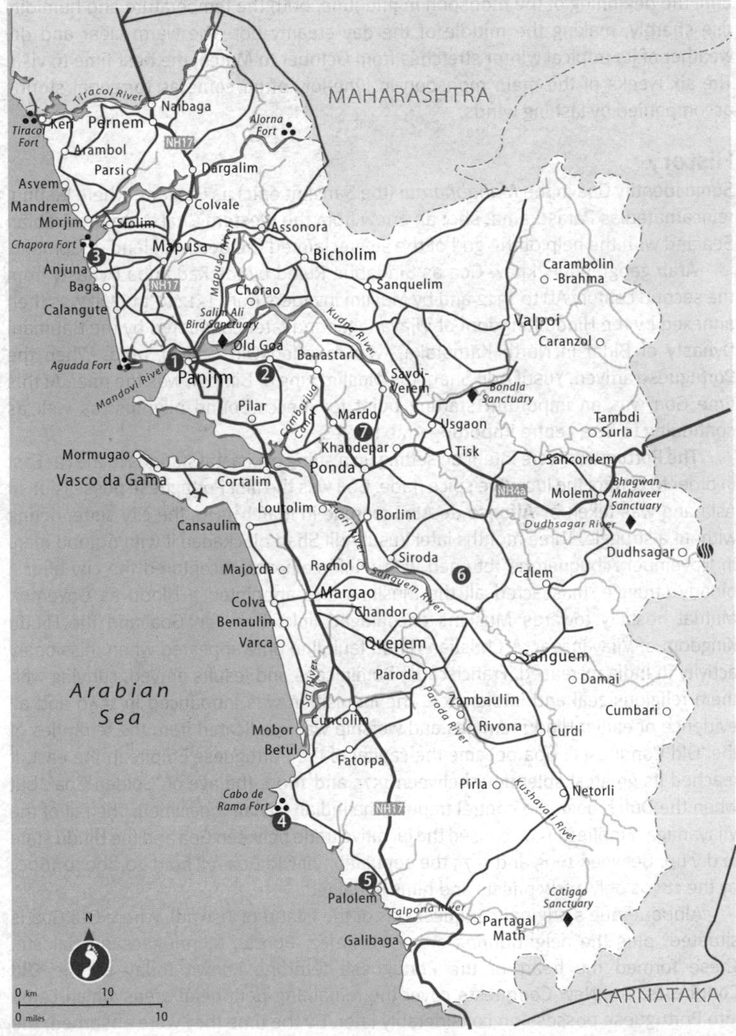

Background → *Population: 1.3 mn. Area: 3,800 sq km.*

The land

Geography By Indian standards Goa is a tiny state. The coastline on which much of its fame depends is only 97 km long. The north and south are separated by the broad estuaries of the Zuari and Mandovi rivers. Joined at high tide to create an island on which Panaji stands, these short rivers emerge from the high ranges of the Western Ghats less than 50 km from the coast. The 16th-century Portuguese naval general Alfonso de Albuquerque quickly grasped the advantages of this island site: large enough to give a secure food-producing base but with a defensible moat, at the same time well placed with respect to the important northwestern sector of the Arabian Sea.

Climate Goa is always warm, but its coastal position means it never suffers the sort of unbearable heat you experience elsewhere in India. Nonetheless, from mid-April until the beginning of the monsoon in mid-June, both the temperature and humidity rise sharply, making the middle of the day steamy hot. The warm clear and dry weather of its tropical winter stretches from October to March, the best time to visit. The six weeks of the main monsoon in June-July often come as torrential storms accompanied by lashing winds.

History

Some identify Goa in the *Mahabharata* (the Sanskrit epic) as Gomant, where Vishnu, reincarnated as Parasurama, shot an arrow from the Western Ghats into the Arabian Sea and with the help of the god of the sea reclaimed the beautiful land of Gomant.

Arab geographers knew Goa as Sindabur. Ruled by the Kadamba Dynasty from the second century AD to 1312 and by Muslim invaders from 1312 to 1367, it was then annexed by the Hindu Kingdom of Vijayanagar and later conquered by the Bahmani Dynasty of Bidar in North Karnataka, who founded Old Goa in 1440. When the Portuguese arrived, Yusuf Adil Shah, the Muslim King of Bijapur, was the ruler. At this time Goa was an important starting point for Mecca-bound pilgrims, as well as continuing to be a centre importing Arab horses.

The Portuguese were intent on setting up a string of coastal stations to the Far East in order to control the lucrative spice trade. Goa was the first Portuguese possession in Asia and was taken by **Alfonso de Albuquerque** in March 1510, the city surrendering without a struggle. Three months later Yusuf Adil Shah blockaded it with 60,000 men. In November Albuquerque returned with reinforcements, recaptured the city after a bloody struggle, massacred all the Muslims and appointed a Hindu as Governor. Mutual hostility towards Muslims encouraged links between Goa and the Hindu Kingdom of Vijayanagar. A Christian-Hindu fault-line only appeared when missionary activity in India increased. Franciscans, Dominicans and Jesuits arrived, carrying with them religious zeal and intolerance. The Inquisition was introduced in 1540 and all evidence of earlier Hindu temples and worship was eradicated from the territories of the 'Old Conquests'. Goa became the capital of the Portuguese Empire in the east. It reached its greatest splendour between 1575 and 1600, the age of 'Golden Goa', but when the Dutch began to control trade in the Indian Ocean it declined. The fall of the Vijayanagar Empire in 1565 caused the lucrative trade between Goa and the Hindu state to dry up. Between 1695 and 1775 the population of Old Goa fell from 20,000 to 1600; by the 1850s only a few priests and nuns remained.

Albuquerque's original conquest was of the island of Tiswadi, where Old Goa is situated, plus the neighbouring areas – Bardez, Ponda, Mormugao and Salcete. These formed the heart of the Portuguese territory, known today as the **Old Conquests**. The **New Conquests** cover the remaining peripheral areas which came into Portuguese possession considerably later. By the time they were absorbed, the full intolerant force of the Inquisition had passed. Consequently, the New Conquests did not suffer as much cultural and spiritual devastation.

The Portuguese came under increasing pressure in 1948 and 1949 to cede Goa, Daman and Diu to India. The problem festered until 1961 when the Indian Army, supported by a naval blockade, marched in and brought to an end 450 years of Portuguese rule. Goa became a Union Territory together with the enclaves of Daman and Diu, but on 30 May 1987 it became a full state of the Indian Union.

Culture

Religion While in the area of the Old Conquests tens of thousands of people were converted to Christianity, the Zuari River represents a great divide between Christian and predominantly Hindu Goa. Today about 70% of the state's population is Hindu, and there is also a small but significant Muslim minority.

Language Portuguese used to be much more widely spoken in Goa than was English in most of the rest of India, but local languages remained important. The two most significant were Marathi, the language of the politically dominant majority of the neighbouring state to the north, and Konkani, the language commonly spoken on the coastal districts further south and now the state's official language. English and Hindi are understood in parts visited by travellers but in rural areas, Konkani predominates.

Local cuisine The large seasonal expat community has brought regional kitchens with them to make for an amazingly cosmopolitan food scene. You can get excellent, authentic, cheap Thai spring rolls, fresh Italian egg pasta, wood-baked pizza, German schnitzel and German bread, Russian borscht, California wheatgrass shots and everything in between. Local food, though, is a treat, sharing much with the Portuguese palate, and building on the state's bounty in fresh fish and fruit. Unlike wider India, Christianity's heritage means beef is firmly on menu here, too. Generally, food is hot, making full use of the small bird's-eye chillies grown locally. Common ingredients include rice, coconut, cashew nuts, pork, beef and a wide variety of seafood. Spicy pork or beef *vindalho* marinated in garlic, vinegar and chillies is very popular, quite unlike the vindaloo you'll taste elsewhere. *Chourisso* is Goan sausage of pork pieces stuffed in tripe, boiled or fried with onions and chillies, eaten in bread. *Sorpotel*, a fiery dish of pickled pig's liver and heart seasoned with vinegar and tamarind, is perhaps the most famous of Goan meat dishes. *Xacutti* is a hot chicken or meat dish made with coconut, pepper and star anise. For *chicken cafrial,* the meat is marinated in pepper and garlic and braised over a fire.

'Fish curry rice', is the state staple, so everyday as to have entered the vernacular as the equivalent of England's fish'n'chips or ham and eggs. Most beach shacks offer a good choice of fish depending on the day's catch. *Apa de camarao* is a spicy prawn pie and *reichado* is usually a whole fish, cut in half, and served with a hot *masala* sauce. *Bangra* is Goa mackerel and *pomfret* a flat fish; fish *balchao* is a preparation of red masala and onions used as a sauce for prawns or kingfish. *Seet corri* (fish curry) uses the ubiquitous coconut. Spicy pickles and chutneys add to the rich variety of flavours.

Goan bread is good. *Undo* is a hard crust round bread, *kankonn*, hard and crispy and shaped like a bangle, is often dunked in tea. *Pole* is like chapatti, often stuffed with vegetables, and Goans prepare their own version of the South Indian iddli, the *sanaan*. The favourite dessert is *bebinca*, a layered coconut and jaggery treat of egg yolks and nutmeg. Other sweets include *dodol*, a mix of jaggery and coconut with rice flour and nuts, *doce*, which looks like the North Indian *barfi*, *mangada*, a mango jam, and *bolinhas*, small round semolina cakes. There are also delicious fruits: *alfonso* mangos in season, the rich jackfruit, papaya, watermelons and cashew nuts.

Drinks in Goa remain relatively cheap compared to elsewhere in India. The fermented juice of cashew apples is distilled for the local brew *caju feni* (*fen*, froth)

Pay back time

India's sizeable diaspora community banked US$24.6 bn for the country in 2006, making it the third largest remittance economy after Mexico and China. Of 25 million Indians abroad, an estimated three million are in North America, 2.5 million in the Gulf. The latter are mostly unskilled labour on short-term contracts in the oil-producing states of the Gulf.

which is strong and potent. Coconut or *palm feni* is made from the sap of the coconut palm. *Feni* is an acquired taste; it is often mixed with soda, salt and lime juice.

Modern Goa

The Goa Legislative Assembly has 40 elected members while the state elects three members to the Lok Sabha, India's central government. Political life is strongly influenced by the regional issue of the relationship with neighbouring Maharashtra, with the Congress Party's 2005 coalition partner the Maharashtrawadi Gomantak Party (which held office between 1963 and 1979) campaigning for Marathi to replace Konkani as the state language. Communal identity also plays a part in elections, with the Congress largely securing the Catholic vote and the BJP winning the support of a significant part of the Hindu population. There is also a strong environmental lobby, in which the Catholic Church plays a role. Goa has had a series of unstable governments with periods of governors imposed by the central government to try and override failures of the democratic process. The state assembly elections in 2007 saw the Congress win 16 and the BJP 14 of the total of 40 seats, and a Congress administration resumed office under the Chief Ministership of Digambar Kamat, who took office on the 8 June 2007.

In common with much of the west coast of India, Goa's rural economy depends on rice as the main food crop, cash crops being dominated by coconut, cashew and areca. Mangos, pineapples and bananas are also important, and forests still give some produce. Seasonal water shortages have prompted the development of irrigation projects, the latest of which was the interstate Tillari Project in Pernem *taluka*, completed with the Government of Maharashtra. Iron ore and bauxite have been two of the state's major exports but heavy industrial development has remained limited to pockets in the east of the state. Tourism – domestic and international – remains one of the state's biggest earners, and money also comes in the form of remittance cheques from overseas workers stationed in the Gulf or working on cruise ships (see box above).

Ins and outs

→ *For arrivals by train, see Panjim opposite.*

Vasco da Gama is the passenger railway terminus of the Central Goa branch line, and is the capital of the industrial heart of modern Goa. Dabolim airport is 3 km away and was developed by the Navy. It is currently shared between the needs of the military and the escalating demands of tourism. Vasco is 30 km from Panjim. Trains via Londa bring visitors from the north – Delhi and Agra – or the south – Hospet and Bengaluru (Bangalore).

Charter companies fly direct to Dabolim Airport between October and April from the UK, the Netherlands, Switzerland and Russia. There are several flights daily from various cities in India – including Mumbai, Thiruvananthapuram, Bengaluru (Bangalore), Delhi (some via Agra) and Chennai – to Goa with **Air India, Indian Airways, Sahara, Kingfisher** and **Jet Airways**. Package tour companies and luxury hotels usually arrange courtesy buses for hotel transfer. Arrivals is relaxed. A pre-paid taxi counter immediately outside the arrivals hall has rates clearly displayed (such as Panjim Rs 340, 40 minutes; north Goa beaches from Rs 450; Tiracol Rs 750; south Goa beaches from Rs 240; Palolem Rs 700). State your destination at the counter, pay and obtain a receipt that will give the registration number of your taxi. Keep hold of this receipt until you reach your destination. The public bus stop on the far side of the roundabout outside the airport gates has buses to Vasco da Gama, from where there are connections to all the major destinations in Goa (for rail reservations, call T0832-251 2833).

Panjim (Panaji) and Old Goa

➔ *Colour map 1a, B1.*

Sleepy, dusty Panjim was adopted as the Portuguese capital when the European empire was already on the wane, and the colonizers left little in the way of lofty architecture. A tiny city with a Riviera-style promenade along the Mandovi, it's also splendidly uncommercial: the biggest business seems to be in the sale of kaju *(cashews), gentlemen-shaves in the* barbieris *and* feni*-quaffing in the booths of pokey bars – and city folk still insist on sloping off for a siesta at lunch. The 18th- and 19th-century bungalows clustered in the neighbouring quarters of San Thome and Fontainhas stand as the victims of elegant architectural neglect. Further upriver, a thick swathe of jungle – wide fanning raintrees, the twists of banyan branches and coconut palms – has drawn a heavy, dusty blanket over the relics of the doomed Portuguese capital of Old Goa, a ghost town of splendid rococo and baroque ecclesiastical edifices.* ▸▸ *For Sleeping, Eating and other listings, see pages 375-379.*

Panaji is the official spelling of the capital city, replacing the older Portuguese spelling Panjim. It is still most commonly referred to as Panjim, so we have followed usage.

Ins and outs

Getting there Prepaid taxis or buses run the short distance from Dabolim airport across Mormugao Bay. The Konkan Railway's main terminus is at the headquarters of South Goa district, Margao, for trains from Mumbai and the north or from coastal Karnataka and Kerala to the south. Taxis and buses run to Panjim from there. Karmali station in Old Goa is the closest to Panjim, where taxis wait to transfer you. The state Kadamba buses and private coach terminals are in Patto to the east of town. From there it is a 10-minute walk across the footbridge over the Ourem Creek to reach the city's guesthouses. ▸▸ *See Transport, page 378, for further details.*

Getting around Panjim is very easy to negotiate on foot, but auto-rickshaws are handy and readily available. Motorcycle rickshaws are cheaper but are more risky. Local buses run along the waterfront from the city bus stand past the market and on to Miramar.

Tourist information Panjim holds the archbishop's palace, a modern port and government buildings and shops set around a number of plazas. It is laid out on a grid and the main roads run parallel with the seafront. **Department of Tourism Office of the Government of Goa** ⓘ *north bank of the Ourem Creek, beside the bus stand at Patto, T0832-243 8750, Mon-Sat 0900-1130, 1330-1700, Sun 0930-1400.*

When British explorer Richard Burton arrived in Goa in 1850, he described Old Goa, once the oriental capital of Portuguese empire-building ambition and rival to Lisbon in grandeur, as a place of "utter desolation" and its people "as sepulchral-looking as the spectacle around them."

History

The Portuguese first settled Panjim as a suburb of Old Goa, the original Indian capital of the sea-faring *conquistadores*, but its position on the left bank of the Mandovi River had already attracted Bijapur's Muslim king Yusuf Adil Shah in 1500, shortly before the Europeans arrived. He built and fortified what the Portuguese later renamed the Idalcao Palace, now the oldest and most impressive of downtown Panjim's official buildings. The palace's service to the Sultan was short-lived: Alfonso de Albuquerque seized it, and Old Goa upstream – which the Islamic rulers had been using as both a trading port and their main starting point for pilgrimages to Mecca – in March 1510. Albuquerque, like his Muslim predecessors, built his headquarters in Old Goa, and stationed a garrison at Panjim, making it the customs clearing point for all traffic entering the Mandovi.

The town remained little more than a military outpost and a staging post for incoming and outgoing viceroys on their way to Old Goa. The first Portuguese buildings, after the construction of a church on the site of the present Church of Our Lady of Immaculate Conception in 1541, were noblemen's houses built on the flat land bordering the sea. Panjim had to wait over two centuries – when the Portuguese Viceroy decided to move from Old Goa in 1759 – for settlement to begin in earnest. It then took the best part of a century for enough numbers to relocate from Old Goa to make Panjim the biggest settlement in the colony and to warrant its status as official capital in 1833.

Panjim

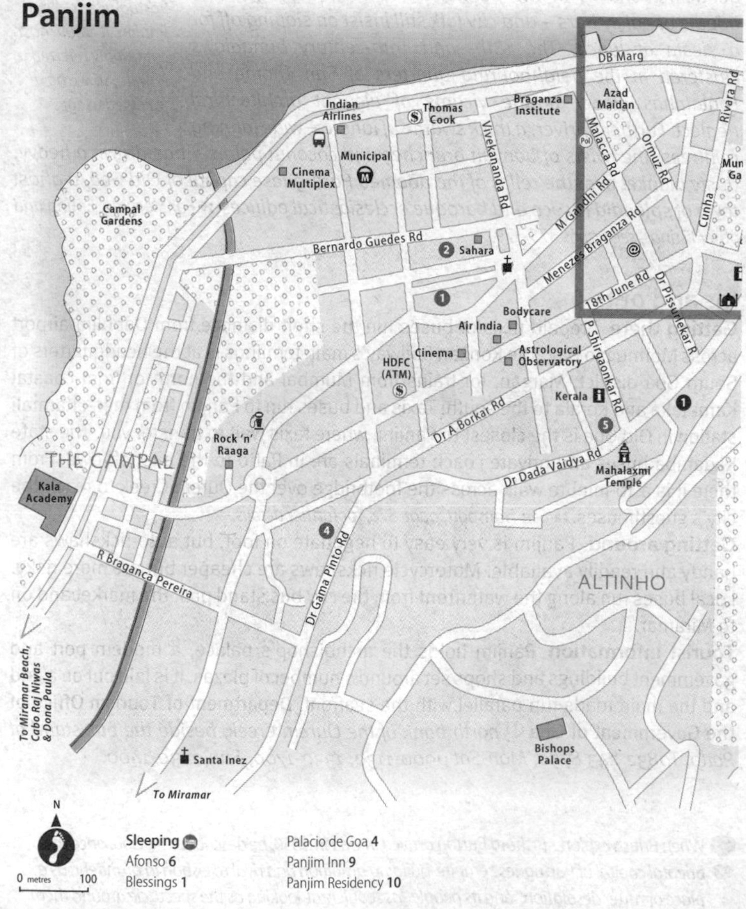

The waterfront

The leafy boulevard of Devanand Bandodkar (DB) Marg runs along the Mandovi from near the New Patto Bridge in the east to the Campal to the southwest. When Panjim's transport and communication system depended on boats, this was its busiest highway and it still holds the city's main administrative buildings and its colourful market.

Walking from the east, you first hit **Idalcao Palace** ⓘ *behind the main boat terminal, DB Marg*. Once the castle of the Adil Shahs, the palace was seized by the Portuguese when they first toppled the Muslim kings in 1510 and was rebuilt in 1615 to serve as the Europeans' Viceregal Palace. It was the official residence to Viceroys from 1759 right up until 1918 when the governor-general (the viceroy's 20th-century title) decided to move to the Cabo headland to the southwest – today's Cabo Raj Niwas – leaving the old palace to become government offices. After Independence it became Goa's secretariat building (the seat of the then Union Territory's parliament) until that in turn shifted across the river to Porvorim. It now houses the bureaucracy of the state passport office.

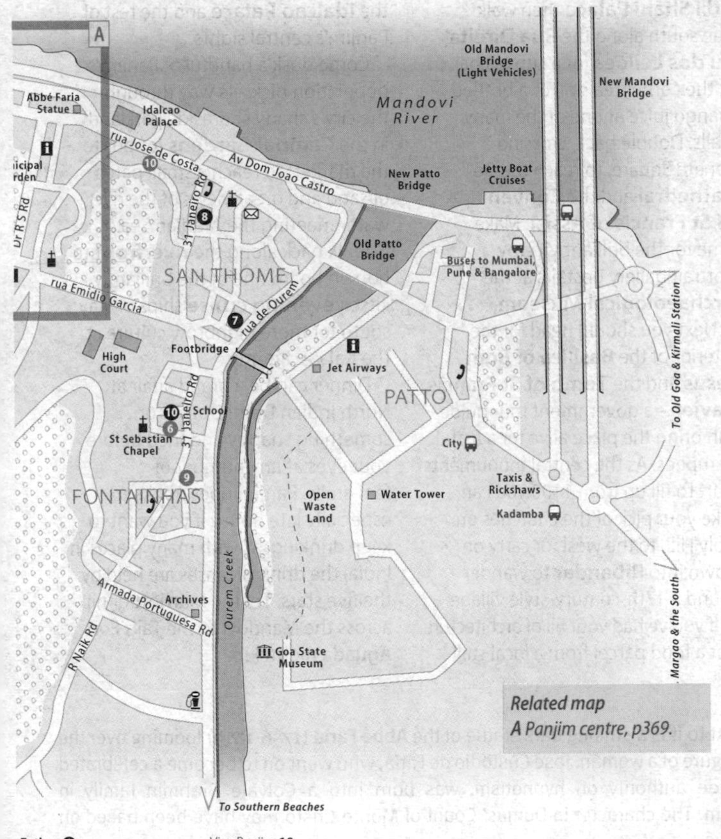

Related map
A Panjim centre, p369.

Eating
A Pastelaria **1**
Horseshoe **7**
Viva Panjim **10**

24 hours in Panjim and Old Goa

Once you're set up in a guesthouse or hotel in Panjim – plump for somewhere in Sao Thome or Fontainhas – cross the Ourem Creek for the 15-minute bus or taxi drive to Old Goa along the causeway road.

Head furthest east first and climb up to the beautifully-restored **Chapel of Our Lady of the Mount,** best at first light, for its 360-degree views over the former capital of the Portuguese. Back down the hill is the main complex (turn right for the stunning **Convent of St Cajetan**).

From here it's a gentle stroll down towards the river to take in the **Viceroy's Arch** and **Gate of Adil Shahi Palace** then walk due south along the **Rua Direita ou dos Leiloes** for a cup of chai at the corner tea stall or a bottled mango juice at one of the many stalls. Double back, crossing Senate Square, to reach the **Sé Cathedral** and the **Convent of St Francis of Assisi.** Make time for the brilliant Viceroy portrait gallery upstairs at the **Archaeological Museum**.

Next you should head for the interior of the **Basilica of Bom Jesus** and the **Tomb of St Francis Xavier** – a government tour guide can bring the place alive for a fistful of rupees. As the central monuments start to fill up from 1100 you can take your pick of the churches on Holy Hill, to the west, or carry on down into **Ribandar** to wander round a 17th-century-style village.

If you've had your fill of architecture, get a food parcel from a local stall and take the ferry crossing here to see some wildlife on **Chorao Island** at the **Salim Ali Bird Sanctuary**. Otherwise head straight on for a slap up lunch back in Panjim: **Venite** for atmosphere, the **Horseshoe** for a tasty, upmarket introduction to Goan Portuguese flavours or go for a more down-at-heel option like **Café Tato** for authentic Goan.

Slip into the Panjim way of life by taking a siesta, then, as the heat subsides around 1600, take a turn about the Sao Thome and Fontainhas districts, including the **San Sebastian Chapel**, following 31 Janiero Road to reach the **Church of the Immaculate Conception**, the **Idalcao Palace** and the rest of Panjim's central sights.

Come dusk a handful of Panjim's population picks its way through the city's shady shoreside parkland in the **Campal Gardens** (opposite the market) to reach a small patch of sand and great views of the river water meeting the Arabian Sea.

Walk back along the **riverfront** to hop on board one of the brilliantly kitsch **evening cruise** ships or stay south for more highbrow culture at the **Kala Academy**.

Dinner can be a grand affair at North Indian **Delhi Durbar** or something snappy and fried before your eyes at any number of feni-stalls. Panjim does not keep especially late hours: if you want to keep drinking, as with many places in India, the drinks licenses are held by the five stars. Try the **Marriott** or nip across the Mandovi to the Taj's **Fort Aguada** nightclub.

Next to it is a striking dark statue of the **Abbé Faria** (1756-1819) looming over the prone figure of a woman. José Custodio de Faria, who went on to become a celebrated worldwide authority on hypnotism, was born into a Colvale Brahmin family in Candolim. The character in Dumas' Count of Monte Cristo may have been based on this Abbé.

Further west, on Malacca Road, almost opposite the wharf, are the **central library** and public rooms of the **Braganza Institute** ⓘ *Mon-Fri 0930-1300, 1400-1745*. It was established as the Instituto Vasco da Gama in 1871, on the anniversary of the date that the Portuguese explorer da Gama sailed round the Cape of Good Hope, to stimulate an interest in culture, science and the arts. It was renamed for Luis Menezes de Braganza (1878-1938), an outstanding figure of social and political reform in early 20th-century Goa. The blue tile frieze in the entrance, hand painted by Jorge Colaco in 1935, is a mythical representation of the Portuguese colonization of Goa. An art gallery upstairs has paintings by European artists of the late 19th and early 20th centuries and Goan artists of the 20th century. The **central library** ⓘ *0930-1300, 1200-1700*, dating from 1832, has a rare collection of religious and other texts.

City centre

The giant whitewashed 16th-century **Church of the Immaculate Conception** ⓘ *Church Sq, Emidio Gracia Rd, Mon-Sat 0900-1230, 1530-1730, Sun 1100-1230, 1530-1700, free, English Mass Mon-Fri 0800, Sun 0830*, looms pristine and large up a broad sweep of steps off the main square, Largo Da Igreja, blue and white flags

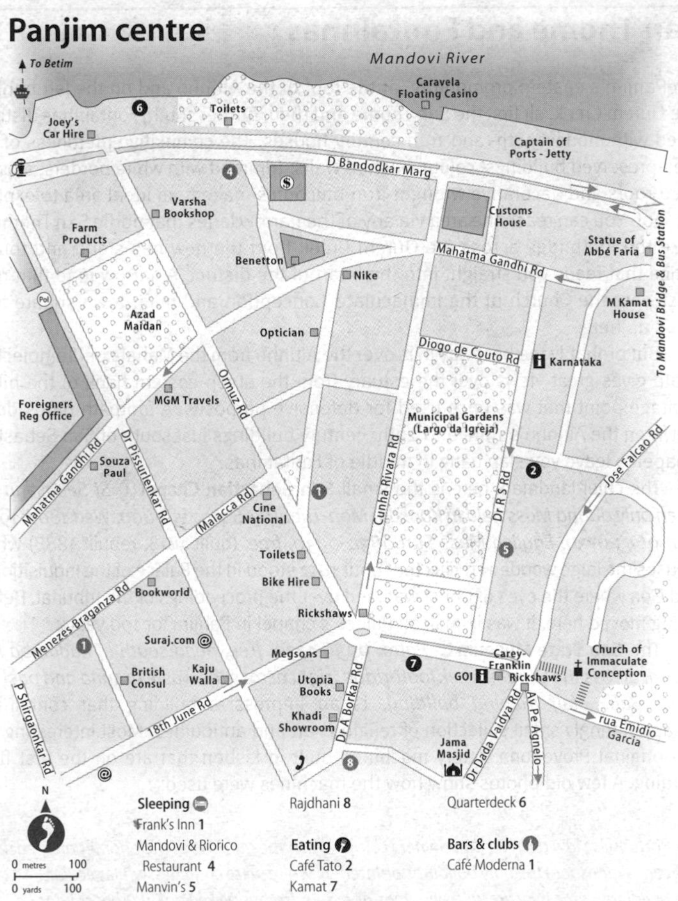

fluttering at its fringes. Its dimensions were unwarranted for the population of what was at the time of its construction in 1541, in Panjim, little more than a marshy fishing village; its tall, Portuguese baroque twin towers were instead built both to act as a landmark for and to tend to the spiritual needs of arriving Portuguese sailors, for whom the customs post just below the hill at Panjim marked their first step on Indian soil. The church was enlarged in 1600 to reflect its status as parish church of the capital and in 1619 was rebuilt to its present design. Inside is an ornate jewel in Goan Catholicism's trademark blue, white and gold, wood carved into gilt corkscrews, heavy chandeliers and chintz. The classic baroque main altar *reredos* (screens) are sandwiched between altars to Jesus the Crucified and to Our Lady of the Rosary, in turn flanked by marble statues of St Peter and St Paul. The panels in the Chapel of St Francis, in the south transept, came from the chapel in the Idalcao Palace in 1918. Parishioners bought the statue of Our Lady of Fatima her crown of gold and diamonds in 1950 (candlelight procession every 13 October). The church's feast day is on 8 December.

The Hindu **Mahalaxmi Temple** ⓘ *Dr Dada Vaidya Rd, free,* (originally 1818, but rebuilt and enlarged in 1983) is now hidden behind a newer building. It was the first Hindu place of worship to be allowed in the Old Conquests after the close of the Inquisition. The **Boca de Vaca** ('Cow's Mouth') spring, is nearby.

San Thome and Fontainhas

On Panjim's eastern promontory, at the foot of the Altinho and on the left bank of the Ourem Creek, sit first the San Thome and then, further south, Fontainhas districts filled with modest 18th- and 19th-century houses. The cumulative prettiness of the well-preserved buildings' colour-washed walls, trimmed with white borders, sloping tiled roofs and decorative wrought-iron balconies make it an ideal area to explore on foot. You can reach the area via any of the narrow lanes that riddle San Thome or take the footbridge across the Ourem Creek from the new bus stand and tourist office that feeds you straight into the heart of the district. A narrow road that runs east past the Church of the Immaculate Conception and main town square also ends up here.

But probably the best way in is over the Altinho from the Mahalaxmi Temple: this route gives great views over the estuary from the steep eastern flank of the hill, a vantage point that was once used for defensive purposes. A footpath drops down between the Altinho's 19th- and 20th- century buildings just south of San Sebastian Chapel to leave you slap bang in middle of Fontainhas.

The chief landmark here is the small **San Sebastian Chapel** ⓘ *St Sebastian Rd, open only during Mass held in Konkani Mon-Tue, Thu-Sat 0715-0800, Wed 1800-1900, Sun 0645-0730, English Mass Sun 0830-0930, free,* (built 1818, rebuilt 1888) which houses the large wooden crucifix that until 1812 stood in the Palace of the Inquisition in Old Goa where the eyes of Christ watched over the proceedings of the tribunal. Before being moved here, it was in Idalcao Palace's chapel in Panjim for 100 years.

The **Goa State Museum** ⓘ *Patto, 0930-1730, free, head south of Kadamba Bus Stand, across the Ourem Creek footbridge, right across the waste ground and past the State Bank staff training building,* is an impressive building that contains a disappointingly small collection of religious art and antiquities. Most interesting are the original Provedoria lottery machines built in Lisbon that are on the first floor landing. A few old photos show how the machines were used.

Portuguese law decreed that owners colour-wash the outsides of their homes after each year's monsoon; the only buildings painted all white were churches, while secular buildings came in ochre with windows and door frames picked out in other colours.

Old Goa and around

The white spires of Old Goa's glorious ecclesiastical buildings burst into the Indian sky from between the snarling depths of overgrown jungle that has sprawled where admirals and lieutenants and administrators of the Portuguese Empire once tended the oriental interests of their 16th-century King Manuel. The canopies of a hundred raintrees cast their shade across the desolate streets adding to the romantic melancholy beauty of the deserted capital. Tourists and pilgrims continue to flock to the remains of St Francis Xavier in the giddying baroque of Basilica of Bom Jesus, hawkers thrust spindly votive candles in their hands at the approach roads, and slake thirsts with the juice of fresh coconut, lime or sugarcane juice.

Ins and outs

Getting there Old Goa lies on the south bank of the Mandovi on the crest of a low hill 8 km from Panjim. The frequent bus service takes 15-20 minutes. Buses drop you off opposite the Basilica of Bom Jesus (Rs 5); pick up the return bus near the police station. Auto-rickshaws charge Rs 25, taxis Rs 150 return. Karmali station on the Konkan Railway, just east of the centre, has taxis for transfers.

Getting around The major monuments are within easy walking distance of the bus stop. All monuments are open daily all year, 0830-1730.

History

Old Goa is to Christians the spiritual heart of the territory. It owes its origin as a Portuguese capital to Afonso de Albuquerque and some of its early ecclesiastical development to St Francis Xavier who was here, albeit for only five months, in the mid-16th century. Before the Portuguese arrived it was the second capital of the Muslim Bijapur Kingdom. Today, all the mosques and fortifications of that period have disappeared and only a fragment of the Sultan's palace walls remain.

Under the Portuguese, Old Goa was grand enough to be dubbed the 'Rome of the East', but it was a flourishing port with an enviable trade even before the Portuguese arrived. The bustling walled city was peopled by merchants of many nationalities who came to buy and sell horses from Arabia and Hormuz, to trade

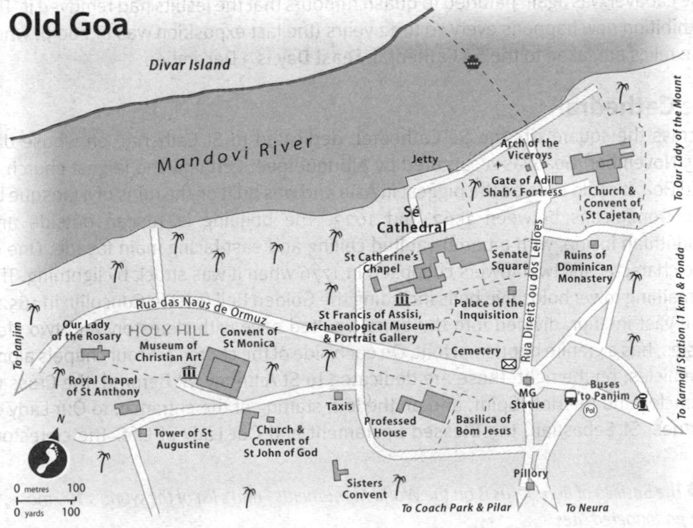

silk, muslin, calico, rice, spices and areca nuts from the interior and other ports along the west coast. It was a centre of shipbuilding and boasted fine residences and public buildings.

After the arrival of the Portuguese, Old Goa swelled still further in size and significance. In the west lay barracks, mint, foundry and arsenal, hospital and prison. The banks of the Mandovi held the shipyards of Ribeira des Gales and next door lay the administrative and commercial centre. Streets and areas of the city were set aside for different activities and merchandise, each with its own character. The most important, Rua Direita ou dos Leiloes (Straight Street), was lined with jewellers, bankers and artisans. It was also the venue for auctions of precious goods, held every morning except Sunday. To the east was the market and the old fortress of Adil Shah, while the true centre of the town was filled with magnificent churches built by the Franciscans, themselves joined by waves of successive religious orders: first the Dominicans in 1548, the Augustinians from 1572, the Carmelites from 1612 and finally the Theatines from 1655. By the mid-17th century, the city, plagued by cholera and malaria and crippled economically, was abandoned for Panjim.

The Basilica of Bom Jesus

The Renaissance façade of Goa's most famous church, the **Basilica of Bom (the Good) Jesus**, a UNESCO World Heritage Site, reflects the architectural transition to baroque then taking place in Europe. Apart from the elaborate gilded altars, wooden pulpit and the candy-twist Bernini columns, the interior is very simple.

The church has held the treasured remains of **St Francis Xavier**, a former pupil of soldier-turned-saint Ignatius Loyola, the founder of the Order of Jesuits since the 17th century. Francis's canonization was in 1622.

The tomb, which lies to the right of the main chancel (1698), was the gift of one of the last of the Medicis, Cosimo III, Grand Duke of Tuscany, and took the Florentine sculptor Giovanni Batista Foggini 10 years to complete. It is made of three tiers of marble and jasper; the upper tier holds scenes from the saint's life. The casket is silver and has three locks, the keys being held by the Governor, the Archbishop and the Convent Administrator. You can look down on to the tomb from a small window in the art gallery next to the church.

After his canonization, St Francis's body was shown on each anniversary of his death until 1707, when it was restricted to a few special private expositions. In 1752, the cadaver was again paraded to quash rumours that the Jesuits had removed it. The exhibition now happens every 10 to 12 years (the last exposition was in 2005), when the relics are taken to the Sé Cathedral. **Feast Day** is 3 December.

Sé Cathedral

Across the square sits the Sé Cathedral, dedicated to St Catherine on whose day (25 November) Goa was recaptured by Albuquerque. Certainly the largest church in Old Goa, it could even be the biggest in Asia and was built on the ruins of a mosque by the Dominicans between 1562 and 1623. The building is Tuscan outside and Corinthian inside, with a barrel-vaulted ceiling and east-facing main façade. One of the characteristic twin towers collapsed in 1776 when it was struck by lightning. The remaining tower holds five bells including the Golden Bell (cast in Cuncolim in 1652). The vast interior, divided into the barrel-vaulted nave with clerestory and two side aisles, has a granite baptismal font. On each side of the church are four chapels along the aisles; on the right, these are dedicated to St Anthony, St Bernard, the Cross of Miracles and the Holy Spirit, and on the left, starting at the entrance, to Our Lady of Virtues, St Sebastian, the Blessed Sacrament and Our Lady of Life. The clerestory

The Basilica of Bom Jesus is on the World Monuments Fund's list of the world's 100 most endangered sites.

windows are protected by a shield crowned by a balustrade to keep out the sun. The main altar is superbly gilded and painted, with six further altars in the transept. The marble-top table in front of the main altar is where, since 1955, St Francis Xavier's remains have been held during their exposition. The main *reredos* has four panels illustrating the life of St Catherine. There is also an **art gallery** ⓘ *Mon-Thu, Sat 0900-1230, Sun 0900-1030, closed during services, Rs 5.*

Around the cathedral

Southwest of the cathedral's front door are the ruins of the **Palace of the Inquisition**, where over 16,000 cases were heard between 1561 and 1774. The Inquisition was finally suppressed in 1814. Beneath the hall were dungeons. In Old Goa's heyday this was the town centre.

There are two churches and a museum in the same complex as the Cathedral. The **Church** (and Convent) **of St Francis of Assisi** is a broad vault of a church with two octagonal towers. The floor is paved with tombstones and on either side of the baroque high altar are paintings on wood depicting scenes from St Francis' life while the walls above have frescoes with floral designs. The original **Holy Spirit Church** in the Portuguese gothic (manueline) style was begun by Franciscan friars in 1517; everything except the old doorway was replaced by the larger present structure in the 1660s (itself restored 1762-65). The convent now houses the **Archaeological Museum and Portrait Gallery** ⓘ *T0832-228 6133, 1000-1230, 1500-1830, Rs 5*, with sculptures pre-dating the Portuguese, many from the 12th-13th centuries when Goa was ruled by the Kadamba Dynasty. There are 'hero stones' commemorating naval battles, and 'sati stones' marking the practice of widow burning. There is also a rather fine collection of portraits of Portuguese governors upstairs that is revealing both for its charting of the evolution of court dress as well as the physical robustness of the governors inside. Some governors were remarkable for their sickly pallor, others for the sheer brevity of their tenure of office, which must have set the portrait painters something of a challenge.

The ASI booklet on the monuments, Old Goa, by S Rajagopalan, is available from the Archaeological Museum here, Rs 10.

To the west is **St Catherine's Chapel**. It was built at the gate of the old city on the orders of Albuquerque as an act of gratitude after the Portuguese defeat of the forces of Bijapur in 1510. The original mud and thatch church was soon replaced by a stone chapel which in 1534 became the cathedral (considerably renovated in 1952), remaining so until Sé Cathedral was built.

On the road towards the Mandovi, northeast from the cathedral compound, lies the **Arch of the Viceroys (Ribeira dos Viceroys)**, commemorating the centenary of Vasco da Gama's discovery of the sea route to India. It was built at the end of the 16th century by his great-grandson, Francisco da Gama, Goa's Viceroy from 1597 to 1600. Its laterite block structure is faced with green granite on the side approached from the river. This was the main gateway to the seat of power: on arrival by ship each new Viceroy would be handed the keys and enter through this ceremonial archway before taking office. The statue of Vasco da Gama above the arch was originally surmounted by a gilded statue of St Catherine, the patron saint of the city. Walking east towards the convent from the arch you pass **the Gate of the Fortress of the Adil Shahs**, probably built by Sabaji, the Maratha ruler of Goa before the Muslim conquest of 1471. The now-ruined palace was home to the Adil Shahi sultans of Bijapur who occupied Goa before the arrival of the Portuguese. It was the Palace of the Viceroys until 1554 after which it served as both the hall of trials for the Inquisition and to house prisoners.

A little further still stands the splendid, domed baroque **Convent and Church of St Cajetan (Caetano).** Pope Urban III dispatched a band of Italian friars of the Theatine order to spread the Gospel to the Deccani Muslim city of Golconda near Hyderabad but they got a frosty reception so headed back west to settle in Goa. They acquired land around 1661 to build this church, which is shaped like a Greek cross and is partly modelled on St Peter's in Rome. It is the last domed church in Goa.

The crypt below the main altar, where the Italian friars were buried, has some sealed lead caskets that are supposed to contain the embalmed bodies of senior Portuguese officials who never returned home. Next door is the beautiful former convent building which is now a pastoral foundation (closed to the public).

On a hill a good way further east is the modest **Chapel of Our Lady of the Mount**, dating from 1510, which gives you a good idea of how the other churches here must originally have looked. It is a peaceful spot with excellent panoramic views across Old Goa, evocative of the turbulent past when Albuquerque and Adil Shah vied for control of the surrounding area. The altar gilding inside has been beautifully restored. In front of the main altar lies the body of architect Antonio Pereira whose burial slab requests the visitor to say an Ave Maria for his soul.

Holy Hill

Between the domineering central monuments of Old Goa's broad tree-lined centre and Panjim stand the cluster of churches of Holy Hill. The first building you reach (on your left) as you leave the central plaza is the **Church and Convent of St John of God**, built in 1685 and abandoned in 1835. The **Museum of Christian Art** ⓘ *Sun-Thu 1000-1700, Rs 5*, is to the right, with 150 items gathered from Goa's churches, convents and Christian homes to give a rich cross section of Indo-Portuguese sacred craft in wood, ivory, silver and gold.

Next door sits the **Convent of St Monica** (1607-27), the first nunnery in India and the largest in Asia. A huge three-storey square building, with the church in the southern part, it was built around a sunken central courtyard containing a formal garden. At one time it was a Royal Monastery, but in 1964 it became a theological institute, the Mater Dei Institute for Nuns. It was here in 1936 that Bishop Dom Frei Miguel Rangel is believed to have had a vision of the Christ figure on the Miraculous Cross opening his eyes, his stigmata bleeding and his lips quivering as if to speak. The vision was repeated later that year in the presence of the Bishop, the Viceroy Dom Pedro de Silva and a large congregation.

It is well worth the effort of the hike, taking the left fork of the road, to reach the **Royal Chapel of St Anthony** (1543) – dedicated to Portugal's national saint and restored by its government in 1961 – and, opposite, the **tower of St Augustine**. The Augustinians came to Goa in 1572; the church they immediately began, bar the belfry, now lies in ruins. It once boasted eight chapels, a convent and an excellent library and was enlarged to become one of the finest in the kingdom. It was finally abandoned in 1835 because of religious persecution. The vault collapsed in 1842, burying the image; the façade and main tower followed in 1931 and 1938. Only one of the original four towers survives. The large bell now hangs in Panjim's Church of the Immaculate Conception. The Archaeological Survey of India is spearheading extensive repairs.

Behind is the **Chapel of Our Lady of the Rosary** (1526). Belonging to the earliest period of church building, it is called Manueline after Manuel I, the Portuguese king who oversaw a period of great prosperity that coincided with the country's conquest of Goa. The use of Hindu and Muslim craftsmen in building the chapel led to an architectural style that borrowed from Iberian decoration but also absorbed both local naturalistic motifs and Islamic elements (seen on the marble cenotaph). The church here has a two-storey entrance, a single tower and low flanking turrets. It was from here that Albuquerque directed the battle against the Adil Shahi forces in 1510.

Around Panjim » p376

Miramar and Gaspar Dias

Gaspar Dias Fortress was finished around 1606. The Panjim-Ribandar causeway, built in 1634, gave it direct land access to the capital at Old Goa and its significance grew accordingly. The walls, likely laterite blocks 1½ m thick and 5 m high, made space for 16 cannons. These saw repeated action against the Dutch until the middle of the 17th century, but the fortress' importance waned after the Maratha onslaught and it fell into disrepair under 15 years of occupation by a British garrison in the early 19th century. It was made new but the Portuguese army finally abandoned it in 1870 as a result of further damage sustained during the mutiny against the Prefect of 1835. For a while the military still stationed soldiers here to convalesce but by the 20th century it had crumbled beyond recognition. All that is left is one cannon at the Miramar circle that marks the possible site of the fort.

Miramar beach is a bit grubby but it's a pleasant drive with good views over the sea and, if you've got a little time to kill, it offers the best quick escape from the city.

Cabo Raj Niwas

The nearby fort Cabo Raj Niwas has fared little better: six cannons and some bits of wall crumbling in the gardens of Raj Bhavan, or the State Governor's House, are all that remain. It is closed to the public but you can get passes for Sunday mass at 0930 on the gate. The first small **Our Lady of Cabo shrine** was built in 1541. Documents from 1633 refer to both the chapel and a fort with four guns. A British troops garrison stationed here from 1799 during the Napoleonic Wars explains the overgrown graves in the nearby **British Cemetery**. Around 1844, after the religious orders were abolished, the Archbishop of Goa was given the convent, which he converted into an impressive residence. It was the official address of the governor-general of Goa in 1918. Its grand interior was left intact after the Portuguese left in 1961. The viewing platform near the entrance gives superb views over the sweep of the coastline across the Mandovi estuary to Fort Aguada.

Sleeping

Panjim has a wide choice of places to stay, while Old Goa has none. There are upmarket options south of Panjim in the beach resorts of Miramar and Dona Paula, but for character it's best to book into one of the guest houses in the atmospheric Fontainhas district. If you don't want to stay overnight you can pack the best of Panjim and Old Goa into a day. Guest houses have early checkout to make way for new arrivals on trains and buses.

Panjim *p365, maps p366 and p369*

A **Pousada Guest House**, Luis de Menezes Rd, T0832-561 8308. Pousada's basic rooms are higgledy-piggledy but have a/c, TV and fridge, and attached bath, from Rs 500.

A-B **Mandovi**, D B Marg, T0832-242 6270, www.hotelmandovigoa.com. Old building with hints of art deco, relaxing but lacks great character. 66 large a/c rooms (river facing more expensive); rates include breakfast. 1st floor **Riorico** restaurant, popular pastry shop, terrace bar, exchange.

B-C **Delmon**, C de Albuquerque Rd, T0832-222 6846, www.alcongoa.com. 50 clean rooms with TV and desk, some a/c, breakfast included. Modern, comfortable hotel with popular restaurant.

D **Manvins**, 4th floor, Souza Towers, Muncipal Gardens/Church Sq, T0832-222 4412, www.goamanvins.com. 45 acceptable rooms with TV, some sleep 4, stunning views over Municipal Gardens and Mandovi river, hot

For an explanation of the sleeping and eating price codes used in this guide, see inside the front cover. Other relevant information is found in Essentials pages 40-44.

water. Terrace has great views of Panjim. Unusual approach to interior design. Disco and pub. 4th floor site only accessed by lift.

D Palacio de Goa, Gama Pinto Rd, T0832-222 1785. Modern 6-storey building, 55 decent rooms with phone, TV, (good value 4- or 5-bed) a/c extra Rs 100, top floor best views, restaurant, far from bus stand.

D Rajdhani, Dr Atmaram Borkar Rd, T0832-222 5362. Modern business hotel with 35 smallish clean rooms with bath, some a/c (Rs 100 extra), pure vegetarian restaurant.

D-E Blessings, MG Rd, behind Bhatkar House, T0832-222 4770, hotelblessings@yahoo.com. 18 ordinary rooms, TV (extra Rs 50), 2 have huge terraces instead of balconies, restaurant, quiet tree-filled backyard.

D-E Panjim Residency (GTDC), overlooking the river, T0832-222 7103. Best views from top floor, 40 good-sized rooms with balcony, some a/c (overpriced at Rs 950), good open-air restaurant, often full.

D-E Virashree, opposite Mahalaxmi Temple, Dr Dada Vaidya Rd, T0832-222 6656, virashree @hotmail.com. 12 large, comfortable rooms with TV but lacking quality finish.

F Comfort Guest House, 31 January Rd, on the parallel road to **Pousada Guest House**, T0832-664 2250. The cheaper of its 12 basic rooms have shared bath.

F Frank's Inn, 83 Menezes Braganza Rd, T0832-222 6716. Shared bath in 10 clean rooms.

San Thome and Fontainhas *p370, map 366*

A The Panjim Peoples, opposite **Panjim Inn**, www.panjiminn.com. The latest heritage project from the Sukhija family behind the Panjim Inn, this one is genuinely top end with just 4 rooms, antique 4-poster beds and bathtubs, plus internet access.

C Panjim Inn, E212, 31 January Rd, T0832-222 6523, www.panjiminn.com. Goa's first heritage hotel is idiosyncratic, even in the context of the historic Fontainhas district. 14 rooms of varying size all fitted with 4-poster beds, a/c for an extra Rs 250.

C Panjim Pousada, up the road from **Panjim Inn**. Slightly cheaper sister hotel to the **Panjim Inn** with double rooms set around a permanent art gallery in a courtyard. It is an evocative, attractive renovation. Best rooms at the back overlook another courtyard. Recommended.

E Afonso, near San Sebastian Chapel, Fontainhas, T0832-2222359. A family-run guest house, obliging and friendly, 8 clean rooms with bath, shaded roof terrace for breakfast, reserve ahead. Recommended.

Around Panjim *p375*

All the below are in Miramar.

AL-A Goa Marriott Resort, Mandovi River, T0832-246 3333, www.marriott.com. 153 large rooms, good facilities, pool, close to public beach, best hotel in area. Weekend buffet lunches popular with Panjim locals.

B Swimsea Beach Resort, T0832-246 4481, swimsea@satyam.net.in. 28 a/c rooms with small balconies (in need of a makeover), sea facing best, pool, close to black sandy beach.

C Blue Bay, Caranzalem beach, T0832-246 4881, bluebay@sancharnet.in. 12 simple modern rooms, some a/c, well-kept grounds, friendly owner, quiet and isolated.

D Miramar Beach Resort, close to the beach, T0832-222 7754. Better (and cheaper) rooms in newer wing by shaded groves. 60 clean rooms, some a/c, good restaurant.

Eating

Panjim *p365, maps p366 and p369*

TT Horseshoe, Rua de Ourem, T0832-243 1788, Mon-Sat 1200-1430, 1900-1030. Low-key Portuguese/Goan restaurant set in 2 high-ceilinged rooms with exceptionally good service. Most meals are excellent value (Rs 60-80) but daily fish specials like red snapper are far more costly (from Rs 300). The house pudding, a cashew cake, Bolo San Rival (Rs 50), trumps all the great main courses. Recommended.

TT Quarterdeck, next to Betim ferry jetty, T0832-243 2905. Goan, Indian, Chinese. Riverside location is the best in Panjim, very pleasant in the evening when brightly lit cruise boats glide gaudily by. Live music.

TT Venite, 31 Janeiro Rd, T0832-222 5537, Mon-Sat 0800-2200, closes in the afternoon. The most charming of Panjim's eateries has 1st-floor balconies overlooking the Sao Thome street life and good music. Simple breakfasts and good Goan food, Rs 80 plus for main dishes, pricier lobsters. Beer.

TT Viva Panjim, house no 178, signposted from 31 Janeiro Rd, T0832-242 2405.

This family-run joint in the atmospheric Fontainhas quarter dishes up specials of Goan food like *xacuti* and *cafreal* along with seafood plus takeaway parcels of Indian, Chinese and continental.

Café Tato, off east side of Church Sq, closed evenings. Something of a local institution, tiny little Tato is packed at lunchtime when office workers descend for its limited range of Goan vegetarian food. Expect tiny platters of chickpea, tomato or mushroom bhaji served with fresh puffed puris or soft bread rolls, or vegetarian cutlets and thalis. Upstairs is a/c.

Kamat, south end of Municipal Gardens. Pure vegetarian canteen sloshing up huge servings of thalis, excellent paper dosas and puri bhajis. Very popular large central dining hall (quieter a/c upstairs).

Bakeries, cafés and fast food

A Pastelaria, Dr Dada Vaidya Rd. Good choice of cakes, pastries and breads. **Mandovi Hotel** has a branch too (side entrance).

Bars and clubs

Panjim *p365, maps p366 and p369*

You can't go 20 paces in Panjim without finding a bar: pokey little rooms with tables and chairs and some snacks being fried up in the corner. Many are clustered around Fontainhas. The *feni* (Goa's cashew- or coconut-extracted moonshine) comes delivered in jerry cans, making it cheaper than restaurants. Try **Café Moderna** near Cine National, food none too good, claustrophobic upstairs dining area, quality atmosphere.

Entertainment

Panjim *p365, maps p366 and p369*

Read the 'today's events' columns in the local papers for concerts and performances.

Astronomical Observatory, 7th floor, Junta House, 18th June Rd (entrance in Vivekananda Rd), open 14 Nov-31 May, 1900-2100, in clear weather. Rooftop 6-inch Newtonian reflector telescope and binoculars. Worth a visit on a moonless night, and for views over Panjim at sunset.

Kala Academy, D B Marg, Campal, T0832-222 3288. This modern and architecturally impressive centre designed by Charles Correa was set up to preserve and promote the cultural heritage of Goa. There are exhibition galleries, a library and comfortable indoor and outdoor auditoria. Art exhibitions, theatre and music programmes (from contemporary pop and jazz to Indian classical) are held, mostly during the winter months. There are also courses on music and dance.

MV Caravela, Fisheries dept building, D B Marg, Panjim, www.casinocity.com/in/panjim/caravela. India's first floating casino is docked on the Mandovi, 66 m of high-rupee-rolling catamaran casino, all plush wall-to-wall carpets, chandeliers and sari-wearing croupiers. The boat accommodates 300 people, has a sun deck, swimming pool and restaurant and the Rs 1200 entrance includes short eats and dinner and booze from 1730 till the morning.

Festivals and events

Panjim *p365, maps p366 and p369*

Feb/Mar: As well as the major festivals in Feb, the **Mardi Gras Carnival** (3 days preceding Lent in Feb/Mar) is a Mediterranean-style riot of merrymaking, marked by feasting, colourful processions and floats down streets: it kicks off near the Secretariat at midday. One of the best bits is the red-and-black dance held in the cordoned-off square outside the old world Clube Nacional on the evening of the last day: everyone dresses up (some cross-dressing), almost everyone knows each other, and there's lots of old-fashioned slow dancing to curiously Country and Western-infused live music. The red and black theme is strictly enforced.

Mar-Apr: **Shigmotsav** is a spring festival held at full moon (celebrated as Holi elsewhere in India); colourful float processions through the streets often display mythological scenes accompanied with plenty of music on drums and cymbals.

First Sun after Easter: **Feast of Jesus of Nazareth**. Procession of All Saints in Goa Velha, on the Mon of Holy Week.

Nov/Dec: **Fontainhas Festival of Arts**. Timed to coincide with the film festival (see below), 30 heritage homes open up as temporary art and artefact galleries in an event organized by Fundacao Oriente, Goa Heritage Action Group and the Entertainment Society of Goa.

International Film Festival of India, www.iffigoa.org. India's answer to Cannes: a 10-day film mart packed with screenings for the industry and general public alike, with its headquarters based around the Kala Academy and the Inox building on the banks of the Mandovi. Held in Goa since 2004.

Food and Culture Festival at Miramar beach.

Dec 8: Feast of Our Lady of the Immaculate Conception. A big fair is held in the streets around Church Sq and a firework display is put on in front of the church each night of the week before the feast (at 1930). After morning mass on the Sun, the Virgin is carried in a procession through the town centre.

Dec 24: Christmas Eve. Midnight mass at 140 churches in Goa; some of the best attended are the Church of the Immaculate Conception and Dom Bosco Church in Panjim and the Basilica of Bom Jesus in Old Goa.

Shopping

Panjim *p365, maps p366 and p369*

Books

Mandovi Hotel bookshop has a good range including American news magazines.

Utopia, Dr A Borkar Rd, near Dominos Pizza, 1000-2000. Goa tourism booklets and maps, books on Goan and Indian cuisine, helpful staff.

Varsha, near Azad Maidan, carries a wide stock in tiny premises, and is especially good for books on Goa. Obscure titles are not displayed but ask the knowledgeable staff.

Clothes and textiles

Goa Government handicrafts shops are at the tourist hotels and the Interstate Terminus. There are other emporia on RS Rd.

Carey Franklin, Church Sq, next to GOI Tourist Office. Smart a/c shops near Delhi Durbar restaurant have genuine stock of international brands including Adidas, Lacoste, Lee, Levi's (jeans Rs 1200-1600).

Government Emporia on RS Rd. Good value for fixed-rate clothes, fabric and handicrafts.

Khadi Showroom, Municipal (Communidade) Building, Church Sq, good value for fixed-rate clothes, fabric and handicrafts. Nehru jackets, Rs 250, plus perishables like honey and pickles.

Kohinoor, 14 Patto Plaza, Shiv Towers. For high-class pieces, beautifully displayed.

Madame Butterfly, opposite Azad Maidan. For carefully crafted designer wear for women plus accessories.

Sosa's, E 245 Rue De Ourem Panjim, T0832-222 8063. Clothes as well as jewellery in papier mâché and silver.

Velha Goa Galeria, 4/191 Rua De Ourem, Fontainhas, T0832-242 6628. Hand-painted ceramics, wall hangings and tabletops of tiles.

Wendell Rodricks Design Space, B5 Suryadarshan Colony, T0832-223 8177. Rodricks is probably Goa's most famous fashion designer who built his name making minimalist clothing. Here you'll find his luxury clothes and footwear.

Transport

Panjim *p365, maps p366 and p369*

Air

The airport is at Dabolim. From Dabolim airport, 29 km via the Zuari Bridge from Panjim, internal flights can be taken through **Air India to Mumbai** and **Thiruvananthapuram**. For pre-paid taxis, see Ins and outs, page 364.

Airline offices: **Air India**, 18th June Rd, T0832-243 1101. **Indian Airlines and Alliance Air**, Dempo House, D B Marg, T0832-223 7821, reservations 1000-1300, 1400-1600, airport T0832-254 0788, flights to **Bengaluru (Bangalore)**, **Delhi** and **Mumbai** daily (US$95), and **Chennai**. **British Airways**, 2 Excelsior Chambers, opposite Mangaldeep, MG Rd, T0832-222 4573. **Jet Airways**, Sesa Ghor, 7-9 Patto Plaza, T0832-243 1472, airport T0832-251 0354. Flights to **Mumbai** (US$103), and **Bengaluru (Bangalore)**. **Kuwait Airways**, 2 Jesuit House, Dr DR de Souza Rd, Municipal Garden Sq, T0832-222 4612. **Sahara**, Live-In Appt, Gen Bernard Guedes Rd, airport office, T0832-254 0043. To **Mumbai**, US$95, daily, and **Delhi**.

Auto-rickshaw

Easily available but agree a price beforehand (Rs 20-35), more after dark. Motorcycle taxis and private taxis are a little cheaper.

Bus

Local Crowded **Kadamba (KTC)** buses and private buses operate from the bus stand in Patto to the east of town, across Ourem Creek, T0832-222 2634. Booking 0800-1100, 1400-1630. The timetable is not accurate: buses leave when full. Frequent service to **Calangute** 35 mins, Rs 7; **Mapusa** 25 mins, Rs 5. Via

Cortalim (Zuari bridge) to **Margao** 1 hr, Rs 8; **Vasco** 1 hr, Rs 8. To **Old Goa** (every 10 mins) 20 mins, Rs 5, continues to **Ponda** 1 hr, Rs 8.

Long distance 'Luxury' buses and 'Sleepers' (bunks are shared). Private operators: **Laxmi Motors**, near Customs House, T0832-222 5745; company at Cardozo Building near KTC bus stand; **Paulo Tours**, Hotel Fidalgo, T0832-222 6291. State buses are run by **Kadamba TC, Karnataka RTC, Maharashtra RTC**. Check times and book in advance at Kadamba Bus Stand. Unlicensed operators use poorly maintained, overcrowded buses; check out beforehand.

Buses to **Bengaluru (Bangalore)**: 1530-1800 (13 hrs), Rs 300; **Belgaum**: 0630-1300 (5 hrs); **Gokarna** and **Hospet (Hampi)**: 0915-1030 (10 hrs), Rs 150 (Rs 350 sleeper); **Hubli**: many; **Londa**: 4 hrs, Rs 60; **Mangalore**: 0615-2030 (10 hrs), Rs 180; **Miraj**: 1030 (10 hrs); **Mumbai**: 1530-1700 (15 hrs+), Rs 550 (sleeper), others (some a/c) Rs 300-450; **Pune**: 0615-1900 (12 hrs), Rs 200, sleeper Rs 400.

Car hire

Sai Service, 36/1 Alto Porvorim, north of the Mandovi Bridge, T0832-241 7063, or at airport. **Hertz**, T0832-222 3998; **Joey's**, town centre opposite the Mandovi Hotel, T0832- 242 2050, Rs 700 per day (80 km) with driver. **Wheels**, T0832-222 4304, airport, T0832-251 2138.

Ferry

Flat-bottomed ferries charge a nominal fee to take passengers (and usually vehicles) when rivers are not bridged. **Panjim-Betim** (the Nehru bridge over the Mandovi supplements the ferry); **Old Goa-Diwar Island; Ribandar-Chorao** for Salim Ali Bird Sanctuary.

Taxi

Tourist taxis are white; hire from Goa Tourism, Trionora Apts, T0832-222 3396, about Rs 700 per day (80 km). Share-taxis run on certain routes; available near the the ferry wharves, main hotels and market places (up to 5). **Mapusa** from Panjim, around Rs 10 each. **Airport** about 40 mins; Rs 380.

Train

Some Konkan Railway trains stop at **Karmali**, T0832-228 6398, near Old Goa (20 mins taxi). **Rail Bookings**, Kadamba Bus Station, 1st floor, T0832-243 5054, 0930-1300 and 1430-1700. South Central Railway serves the Vasco-Londa/Belgaum line; for details see page 364, and Margao (Madgaon), page 421.

❶ Directory

Panjim *p365, maps p366 and p369*

Banks Many private agencies change TCs and cash. **Thomas Cook**, 8 Alcon Chambers, D B Marg, T0832-243 1732, Mon-Sat. Also for Thomas Cook drafts, money transfers; **Amex**, at Menezes Air Travel, Rua de Ourem, but does not cash TCs. Cash against certain credit cards from **Central Bank**, Nizari Bhavan; **Andhra Bank**, Dr Atmaram Borkar Rd, opposite EDC House, T0832-222 3513; **Bank of Baroda**, Azad Maidan; **HDFC**, 18 June Rd, T0832-242 1922, 24-hr ATM, most convienient way to obtain cash in Panjim. **High commissions and consulates** Germany, Hon Consul, c/o Cosme Matias Menezes Group, Rua de Ourem, T0832-222 3261; **Portugal**, LIC Bldg, Patto, T0832-222 4233; **UK**, room 302, 3rd floor, Manguirish Bldg, 18th June Rd, T0832-222 8571, bcagoa@goa1.dot.net. **Hospitals** **Goa Medical College**, Av PC Lopez, west end of town, T0832-222 3026, is very busy; newer College at Bambolim; **CMM Poly Clinic**, Altinho, T0832-222 5918. **Internet** Among many charging Rs 35-40 per hr: **little.dot.com cyber café**, 1st floor, Padmavati Towers, 18th June Rd, 0930-2300. Best in town: **Suraj Business Centre**, 5 terminals upstairs, excellent fast connection (128 kbps ISDN line), 0900-2300. **Post** Old Tobacco Exchange, St Thome, towards Old Patto Bridge, with Poste Restante on left as you enter, Mon-Sat 0930-1730, closed 1300-1400.

North Goa

While Baga and Calangute, the fishing villages first settled by the 'freaks', now stand as cautionary tales to all that's worse in mass tourism, Anjuna, a place synonymous with psychedelia, drugs and Goa trance parties, has managed to retain a village feel despite the existence of its unquestionably shady underbelly. The weekly flea market is a brilliant bazar – like Camden or Portobello but with sacred cows, sadhus, fakirs and snake charmers – and makes it onto every holidaymaker's itinerary, but if you stick around you'll find that the little stretch of shoreline from South Anjuna to the mouth of the Chapora river is beautifully desolate – rust-coloured rugged cliffs covered with scrub interrupt scrappy bays strewn with laterite boulders. Pretty cliff-backed Vagator stands just south of the romantic ruins of Chapora Fort, with its busy fishing jetty, where trawler landings are met by a welcoming committee of kites, gulls and herons wheeling hungrily on high, while further upstream young men wade through mangrove swamps to sift the muds for clams, mussels and oysters. Over the Chapora lies Arambol, a warm, hippy backpacker hamlet, and its beach satellites of Mandrem, Asvem and Keri and the wonderful wee Catholic enclave clustered around the ancient Tiracol Fort and its chapel. *» For Sleeping, Eating and other listings, see pages 384-390 for Baga to Candolim; 395-399 for Anjuna to Vagator and 402-405 for Morjim.*

Baga to Candolim » *pp384-390*

The faultless fawn shoreline of Bardez *taluka*, particularly Calangute, until 40 years ago lay at the feet of a string of fishing villages. Now it acts as sandpit to the bulk of Goa's travel trade. Chock full of accommodation, eateries, travel agents, money changers, beggars and under-dressed, over-sunned charter tourists, the roads snarl up with minivans, buses and bikes, and unchecked development has made for a largely concrete conurbation of breezeblock hotels and pile-em-high mini markets. For all that, squint hard, or come in monsoon, and you can still see what once made it such a hippy magnet: wonderful coconut-fringed sands backed by plump dunes occasionally broken by rocky headlands and coves. The main reason to head this way is for business, banks, or posh food and nightlife. To get out again, you can paddle in the waters of the Arabian Sea all the way between the forts of Aguada and Vagator.

Ins and outs

Getting there The NH17 acts as the main arterial road between all of Goa's coastal belt. From Panjim, the highway crosses the Mandovi Bridge to the area's main hub, Calangute (16 km from Panjim, 10 km from Mapusa). Buses from Mapusa (20 minutes) and Panjim (35 minutes) arrive at Calangute bus stand near the market; a few continue to Baga to the north from the crossroads. You can charter tourist minivans from places such as Panjim and Dabolim. The closest stop on the Konkan railway route between Mumbai and Mangalore is Tivim near Mapusa. On market days there are boats between Baga and Anjuna. There are buses from Mapusa and Panjim to Calangute, Anjuna, Chapora and Arambol.

Getting around There are taxis, motorcycle taxis, tourist vans and old Ambassador cabs, or cheap but slow public buses. Roads are fairly good for motorcycles and scooters; watch out for speed bumps. Accidents happen with grim regularity, but bikes give you unparalleled independence in zipping between pockets of sand.

Orientation and information There are 9 km of uninterrupted beach between Fort Aguada and the bridge over Baga river in the north, which takes you to Anjuna. These are split into four beaches: south to north Sinquerim, Candolim, Calangute and Baga. Each has its own stab at a high street, Calangute's being the most built up.

Background

The name Bardez may have come from the term *bara desh* (12 'divisions of land'), which refers to the 12 Brahmin villages that once dominated the region. Another explanation is that it refers to 12 *zagors* celebrated to ward off evil. Or it could be *bahir des*, meaning 'outside land' – ie, the land beyond the Mandovi river. It was occupied by the Portuguese as part of their original conquest, and so bears the greatest direct imprint of their Christianizing influence.

Mapusa → *Colour map 1a, A1.*

Standing in the nape of one of Goa's east-west ridges lies Bardez's administrative headquarters: a buzzy, unruly market town filled with 60s low-rise buildings set on former marshland on the banks of the Mapusa river; 'Maha apsa' means 'great swamps', a reference to Mapusa's watery past. Mapusa town won't find its way onto many tourist postcards, but it's friendly, small and messy, is an important transport hub and has an excellent daily **municipal market**, worth journeying inland for, especially on its busiest day, Friday. Open from early morning Monday to Saturday, it peters out from noon to three, then gathers steam again till night, and has giant rings of chourica sausage, tumbles of spices and rows upon rows of squatting fruit and vegetable hawkers.

Walk east for the small 16th-century **St Jerome's Church**, or 'Milagres', Our Lady of Miracles (1594), rebuilt first in 1674 then again in 1839 after a candle sparked a devastating fire. In 1961 the roof was badly damaged when the Portuguese blew up a nearby bridge in their struggle with the liberating Indian army. The church has a scrolled gable, balconied windows in the façade, a belfry at the rear and an interesting slatted wood ceiling. The main altar is to Our Lady, and on either side are St John and St Jerome: the *retables* (shelves behind the altar) were brought from Daugim. The church is sacred to Hindus as well as Catholics, not only because it stands near the site of the Shanteri Temple but also because 'Our Lady of Miracles'

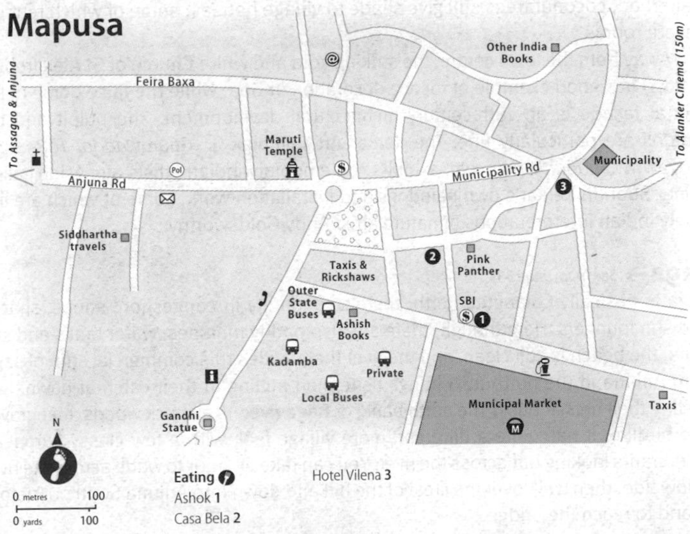

was one of seven Hindu sisters converted to Christianity. Her lotus pattern gold necklace (kept under lock and key) may also have been taken from a Hindu deity who preceded her.

The **Maruti temple** ⓘ *west of the market opposite the taxi stand*, was built on the site of a firecracker shop where Rama followers in the 1840s would gather in clandestine worship of first a picture, then a silver image, of monkey god Hanuman after the Portuguese destroyed the local Hindu temples.

Barely 5 km east of Mapusa lies **Moira**, deep in the belly of a rich agricultural district that was once the scene of Portuguese mass baptisms. The town is ancient – some say it was the site of a sixth or seventh century AD Mauryan settlement – and until the arrival of the Portuguese it must have been a Brahmin village. A total of seven important temples were destroyed during the Inquisition and six idols moved to Mulgaon in Bicholim district (immediately east).

Today the village is dominated by the unusual **Church of Our Lady of the Immaculate Conception**. Originally built of mud and thatch in 1619, it was rebuilt during the 19th century with square towers close to the false dome. The balustrades at the top of the first and second floors run the length of the building and the central doorways of the ground and first floors have Islamic-looking trefoil arches that contrast with the romanesque flanking arches. There is an interesting exterior pulpit. Inside, the image of the crucifixion is unusual in having its feet nailed apart instead of together. A Siva *lingam* recycled here as the base of the font after its temple was razed is now in the Archaeological Museum at Old Goa (see page 373). Moira's famous long red bananas (grown nearby) are not eaten raw but come cooked with sugar and coconuts as the cavity-speeding sweet *figada*.

Calangute ➔ *See map, page 383. Colour map 1a, A1.*

More than 25 years of package tourism has guaranteed that there is little left to draw you to Calangute, bar ATMs, some wonderful restaurants and a quirky hexagonal *barbeiria* (barber's shop) at the northern roundabout. In the 60s, the village was short-hand for the alternative life, but the main distinguishing feature of the streets today is their messy, Indian take on beach commercialism; shops peddle everything from cheap ethnic tat to extravagant precious gemstones. The shacks on the beach serve good food and cheap beer and most fly the St George's Cross in tribute to Calangute's charter coin. Between the busy beachfront and the grubby main road, coconut trees still give shade to village houses; some of which rent out private rooms.

Away from the town centre, the striking gold and white **Church of St Alex** (rebuilt in 1741) is a good example of rococo decoration in Goa, while the false dome of the central façade is an 18th-century architectural development. The pulpit and the *reredos* are particularly fine. The **Kerkar Art Complex** ⓘ *Gaurawaddo, T0832-227 6017, www.subodhkerkar.com*, exhibits contemporary Indian artists alongside gallery owner Subodh Kerkar's own paintings and installation work, some of which are like lovely Indian interpretations of nature artist Andy Goldsworthy.

Baga ➔ *See map, page 383.*

Baga is basically Calangute north: there's continuity in congestion, shops, shacks and sun loungers. Here though, there are also paddy marshes, water tanks and salt pans, the beach is still clean, and the river that divides this commercial strip of sand from Anjuna in the north also brings fishermen pulling in their catch at dawn, and casting their nets at dusk. The north bank, or **Baga river**, is all thick woods, mangroves and birdlife; it has quite a different, more village feel, with a few classy European restaurants looking out across the river. You can take an hour to wade across the river at low tide, then walk over the crest of the hill and down into Anjuna South, or detour inland to reach the bridge.

Candolim and Sinquerim beaches

The wide unsheltered stretch of beach here, backed by scrub-covered dunes, is more staid than Baga and Calangute to the north, chiefly because its restaurants and hotels are pricier and the average holidaymaker more senior. The beach at the foot of the Taj complex offers the full gamut of watersports – including jet skis, windsurfers, catamaran and dinghies are all for hire – making it a favourite of India's fun-loving domestic tourists.

Fort Aguada

The Portuguese colonizer's strongest coastal fort was built on this northern tip of the Mandovi estuary in 1612 with one goal: to stay the Dutch navy. Two hundred guns were stationed here along with two magazines, four barracks, several residences for officers and two prisons. It was against the Marathas, though, rather than the Dutch, that Aguada saw repeated action – Goans fleeing the onslaught at Bardez took refuge here – and its ramparts proved time and again impregnable. The main fortifications (laterite walls nearly 5 m high and 1.3 m thick) are still intact, and the buildings at sea level now house Goa's Central Jail, whose 142 male and 25 female inmates are incarcerated in what must be one of the world's prettiest lock-ups.

Baga & Calangute

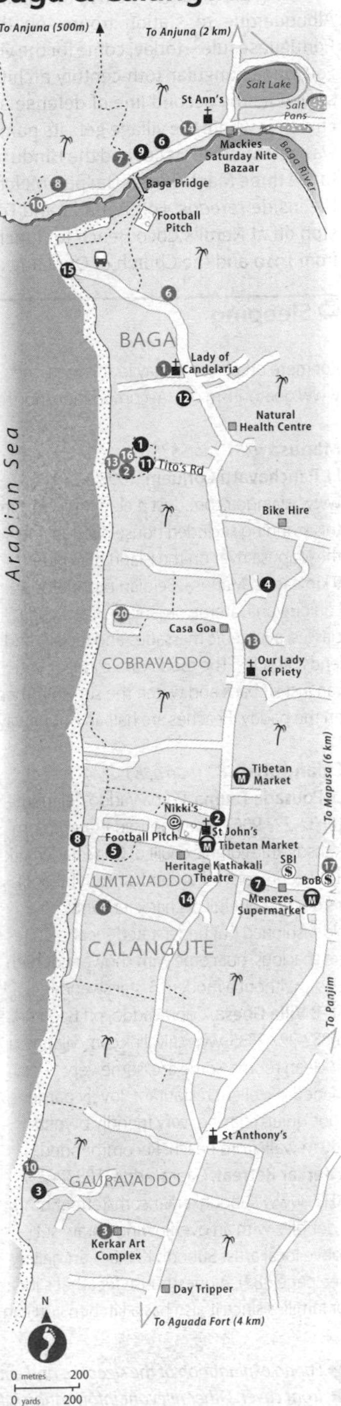

Sleeping
Alidia Beach Cottages 1
Baga Queen Beach Resort 2
Cavala 6
Coco Banana 4
Golden Eye 10
Kerkar Retreat 3
Lina's 7
Martin's Guest Rooms 13
Nani's & Rani's 8
Pousada Tauma 17
Villa Goesa 20
Villa Melnisha 14

Eating
A Reverie 3
Britto's 15
Casa Portuguesa 12
Citrus 11
Fiesta 1
Infanteria 2
J&A's Italiano House 6
Le Restaurant Français 4
Lila's Café 9
Oriental at Hotel Mira 14
Plantain Leaf 7
Souza Lobo 8
Tibetan Kitchen 5

Bars & clubs
Mambo's 13
Sunset 10
Tito's 16

Reis Magos, the Nerul river and Coco Beach

Reis Magos's position across the Mandovi river from Panjim made it imperative for Albuquerque to station troops on this shoulder of headland from day one of Portuguese rule – today, come for the views to the capital, and for the crumbling Royal Fort whose angular 16th-century architecture is now overrun with jungle. Its canons served as the second line of defense against the Dutch after Aguada. The next door church is where the village gets its name – this was where the first mass on Goan soil was celebrated in 1550, and the Hindu temple was promptly turned over into a church to the three Magi Kings – Gaspar, Melchior and Balthazar – whose stories are told on the inside *reredos*. Fort Aguada and Fort Reis Magos are divided by the Nerul river: stop off at Nerul's Coco Beach for lunch and a swim. The temple in the village dates from 1910 and the Church of Our Lady of Remedies from 1569.

Sleeping

For more on places to stay in this area, see www.goatourism.org/Accomodation/north.

Mapusa *p381, map p381*

LL Panchavatti Corjuem, T0982-258 0632, www.islaingoa.com. Just 4 elegant rooms in this stunning secluded house overlooking the Mapusa river on the island of Corjuem, 9 km east of Mapusa. Belgian proprietor Loulou Van Damme organizes Bihari yoga classes, ayurvedic massages and facials, and lends bicycles. The food is amazing, or you can just sit back and watch the sun shimmer on the paddy. Beaches are half an hour away.

Calangute *p382, map p383*

LL Pousada Tauma, Porba Vaddo Calangute T0832-227 9061, www.pousada-tauma.com. A shady little complex built of Goa's trademark rust laterite rock set around a beautiful pool. It's discreet but full of character, with old-fashioned but understated service. Suites are spacious, but come with shower not bath. Classy without a modern 5-star swagger.

AL-B Villa Goesa, Cobravaddo, off Baga Rd, T0832-227 7535, www.nivalink.com/vilagoesa. 57 clean rooms, some a/c, some very shaded, excellent restaurant, lovely gardens, pool, quiet, relaxing, very friendly owners, 300 m walk from beach. Recommended.

A Kerkar Retreat, Gauravaddo, T0832-227 6017, www.subodhkerkar.com/retreat.html. 5 doubles with an overflowing library set above local artist Subodh Kerkar's art gallery (see page 382). A guesthouse feel that's ideal for families since it also has a kitchen you can use. Somewhat sedate by Calangute's standards – but that's a compliment.

A-D Golden Eye, Philip's Cottages, Gauravaddo, T0832-227 7308, www.hotelgoldeneye.com. 25 roomy suites and clean rooms, all with balcony, a/c or non a/c, half-price singles, right on the beach (built before restrictions) with genuine sea views.

C-E Coco Banana, 5/139A Umtavaddo, back from Calangute beach, T/F0832-227 6478, www.cocobananagoa.com. One of the best local guest houses, Coco Banana has 6 spotless en suite bungalows set in a leafy garden. All rooms come with nets and fridges, some have TV and a/c, and the place is airy, light and comfortable. Swiss German owners are caring and helpful, also rent 2 apartments in **Casa Leyla** and have a whole house, Soledad, which has all mod cons and maid service. Highly recommended.

D Martin's Guest Rooms, Baga Rd, T0832-227 7306, martins@goatelecom.com. 5 rooms in family house, clean, attractive verandas, use of kitchen but on the busy main road.

Baga *p382, map p383*

Of the family guest houses on the northern side of Baga river, up towards Arpora, those to the left of the bridge (west or seaward) are quieter. Rooms in houses/cottages cost about Rs 300 but good discounts are possible for weekly or monthly rental. Standards vary so check room and security first. Try Wilson Fernandes at **Nani's & Rani's** or ask at **Four Seasons Restaurant** at Jack's Corner.

For an explanation of the sleeping and eating price codes used in this guide, see inside the front cover. Other relevant information is found in Essentials pages 40-44.

C-D Cavala, Sauntavaddo, top end of Baga village, T0832-227 6090, www.cavala.com. Sandwiched between Baga Road and a big field stretching towards the mountains, Cavala is traditional but very well maintained, with friendly and attentive management, and set in lovely gardens. The 30 rooms are big, with giant fridges and huge bathrooms, although only shower. Some have TV. Recommended.

D Alidia Beach Cottages Behind the Church, Sauntavaddo, T0832-227 9014, alidia@rediffmail.com. Weave around a few pot-plant covered Goan yards to reach this charming hotel in a series of two-storey cottages, run professionally but with the warmth of a guest house. Rooms are old-fashioned, with features including hand-made fitted wardrobes, and spotless with lots of privacy around the well-tended garden. New pool. One of the best of its kind so book ahead. Highly recommended.

E-F Nani's & Rani's, T0832-227 7014. 8 spartan rooms (shared or own bath), budget meals served in pleasant garden, bar, email, STD/ISD. One of the few local budget options with a sea view and a relaxing quiet location. Short walk across Baga Bridge for nightlife.

G Baga Queen Beach Resort, T0832-227 6880. Close to beach, better value than others nearby, 15 good-sized, clean rooms with bath.

G Lina's, north of Baga River, T0832-228 1142. Secluded guest house with 4 good-value rooms. Recommended.

G Villa Melnisha, T0832-227 7805. 4 simple, clean rooms with bath, kitchenette, good cheap thalis, owners live upstairs.

Candolim and Sinquerim beaches

p383

LL-AL Kamal Retreat, Dando, towards Aguada, T0832-247 9296, www.kamalretreat.com. 23 large, quality rooms (all a/c, suites and de luxe Atrium suite) on a spacious site with immaculate grounds, large pool, direct beach access, one of few Candolim hotels not to be hemmed in, nor will it be, charming owner ensures high standards. Recommended.

LL-AL Lemon Tree Amarante Beach Resort, Vadi, Candolim, T0832-398 8188, www.lemontreehotels.com. Try to get one of the 6 heritage rooms here, housed inside a grand century-old Portuguese mansion, but restored now, as the rest of the hotel, in mock 15th-century Portuguese style. Under new management from the former Costa Nicola, the complex now has Wi-Fi, kids' centre, pool, 2 onsite restaurants, a spa and all mod cons.

L Fort Aguada Beach Resort, Sinquerim, T0832-664 5858, www.tajhotels.com. The self-confessed sprawling Taj complex spreads over 36 ha. In descending order of cost, these are 17 hilltop family villas that make up the Aguada Hermitage, 130 rooms with sea views at the Fort Aguada Beach Resort, built in the fort's ruins, and scores of cottages for up to 8 on the beach in the Taj Holiday Village. The complex has many 5-star facilities including 2 freshwater pools, 9 restaurants, ayurvedic and other spa treatments, plus golf, tennis and a crèche.

A Marbella Tourist Home, left off the road to Taj Fort Aguada Beach Resort, T0832-247 9551, www.marbellagoa.com. Splendid mock-Portuguese period mansion with 6 lovingly decorated rooms. Its owners have scavenged bona fide antiques and furnishings like mosaic tiles from old villas to create this elegant and unpretentious homestay in a forest at the end of a dirt track. Lovely garden sit-out for meals. All rooms have a/c and cable TV.

G Ludovici Tourist Home, Dando, Sinquerim, T0832-237 9684. Just inland of the road leading to the fort sits this family home with 4 modest en suite doubles, all with fan. There's also a bar and restaurant and a lovely porch scattered with chairs that gives onto a spacious garden. Sedate and modest guesthouse with traditional charm.

Eating

Food is unlikely to be the highlight of a trip to Mapusa, but even its most ardent detractors will brave Calangute for its restaurants, some of which are world class. While costly by Indian standards a slap-up meal will cost you a fraction of its equivalent at European prices.

Mapusa *p381, map p381*

Ashok, opposite the market's entrance. Serves genuine South Indian breakfasts like uttapam and dosa.

Casa Bela, near Coscar Corner. Goan food.

Hotel Vilena has 2 restaurants, 1 on the rooftop and 1 a/c indoors serving some of the best food in town.

Ɏ **Mahalaxmi**, Anjuna Rd. A/c, South Indian vegetarian.

Calangute *p382, map p383*

ɎɎ **A Reverie**, next to **Hotel Goan Heritage**, Holiday St, T0832-317 4927, areverie@rediffmail.com. All white tableclothes and quiet garden, this is a splash-out venue. Pricey and out of the way, it is popular with expats.

ɎɎ **Le Restaurant Français**, Baga Rd, T0832-212 1712. Extremely pragmatically, the day-time dairy curd café the Milky Way gets a wave of a magic wand to become **Le Restaurant** by night. Sofas are wheeled in and huge paintings of French street scenes are erected as a backdrop to the authentic Gallic menu.

ɎɎ **Souza Lobo**, on the beach, excellent fresh seafood, lobster (Rs 550) and sizzlers served on a shaded terrace, well-known restaurant that has managed to retain a good reputation for years. Recommended.

Ɏ **Infanteria**, 'the breakfast place' to locals, has Rs 125 set breakfast, eggs, coffee, juice, toast. Bakery and confectionery includes butterscotch swiss rolls.

Ɏ **Oriental**, The Royal Thai Cuisine, Hotel Mira, Umtawaddo, T0832-329 2898, T982-212 1549, Henry.Pfeifer@gmx.com. Impeccable Thai food made by Chawee, the Thai wife of German proprietor Henry Pfeiffer, in new leafy location from longstanding address in Candolim. Home-made tofu daily, plus pasta, steaks, schnitzel, goulash, cakes and excellent espresso. Cookery courses Mon 1400-1700.

Ɏ **Plantain Leaf,** near petrol pump, Almita III. T0832-227 6861. Mean dosas, jumbo thalis, sizzlers and a range of curries; unbeatable for your pukka pure vegetarian Indian.

Ɏ **The Tibetan Kitchen**, 0900-1500, 1800-2230. This airy garden restaurant at the bottom of a track leading off Calangute Beach Rd is part tent, part wicker awning, part open to the skies. Tibet's answer to ravioli – *momos* – are good here, but more adventurous starters like prawns, mushrooms and tomatoes seeping onto wilting lettuce leaves are exceptional.

Baga *p382, map p383*

ɎɎ **Fiesta**, Tito's Lane, T0832-227 9894. Only open for dinner, closed Tue. One of Baga's destination eateries serving Mediterranean nosh in stylish surroundings, unusual Portuguese and Italian dishes (Rs 200), and great desserts. Tends to attract wealthy types en route to Tito's.

ɎɎ **J&A's Ristorante Italiano House**, 560 Baga river, T0832-228 2364, www.littleitalygoa.com. Jamshed and Ayesha Madon's operation – along with their pizzas and pastas – has earned them an evangelical following. Open for dinner Oct-Apr.

Ɏ **Britto's Bar and Restaurant**, Baga beach, T0832-227 7331. Cajie Britto's puddings are an institution and his staff (of 50) boast that in high season you'll be pushed to find an inch of table space from the restaurant's inside right out to the seashore. Seafood platters come for Rs 170, or plump for a breakfast of Heinz beans on toast for Rs 60. Good fish curry and rice too.

Ɏ **Casa Portuguesa**, Baga Rd, an institution of a restaurant run by German/Goan couple with live music in the gloriously overgrown jungle of a garden. Strongly recommended.

Ɏ **Citrus**, Tito's Lane. Impeccable vegetarian Med-style food in simple surroundings, prides itself on hygiene. European-run.

Ɏ **Lila's Café**, north bank of Baga River T0832-227 9843, lilacafe@sify.com. Slick German-run restaurant, good selection of European dishes, check blackboard for specials, smoked kingfish Rs 110. Home-made cheeses and jams, muesli and orange juice Rs 60, fresh bread, good coffee. Also serves beers. Shaded terrace overlooking the river. Closed evenings. Recommended.

Bars and clubs

Baga *p382, map p383*

Locals know which way their bread is buttered, and in this neighbourhood, it's beer up. Many bars here have a happy hour from 1700 to 1930 and show live Premier League football, in a bit of a home-from-home for many visitors. Along the beach, shacks also serve a wide range of drinks and cocktails to sip while watching the sunset.

Cavala, Sauntavaddo, top end of Baga village. A genuine bar, with friendly atmosphere, attentive staff, great cocktails, and occasional live music evenings.

Sunset, north of Baga river, a great place to watch the goings-on of Baga beach as dusk falls. Prime location but less hectic as it's north of the river bridge.

Tito's, Tito's Lane, T0832-227 5028, www.titosgoa.com. Tito's is an institution in Goa, and has adapted down the decades to reflect the state's changing tourist reality by going from a down-at-heel hippie playground in the 60s to a swish international dance club that's more popular with India's preening fashion, film and media set than crusty international travellers.

Further along Tito's Lane towards the beach is the Tito's spin-off, **Mambo's**. It's more laid back than the club and free to get in.

Candolim and Sinquerim beaches *p383*

Congo Lounge, 242 Souzavaddo (Fort Aguada Rd), T0832-564 4226. Snazzy super-modern venue serving breakfast, lunch and dinner. It's popular with the Mumbai/MTV crowd.

Rock Your Blues, south end of Candolim near Taj complex, open 2030. Playing retro music and selling sensibly priced drinks.

Entertainment

Calangute *p382, map p383*

Heritage Kathakali Theatre, at the Hotel Sunflower, opposite the football ground, Calangute Beach Rd, T0832-258 8059, daily in season, 1800-2000. The breathtakingly elaborate mimes of 17th-century Keralan mime dance drama take over 12 hrs to perform in the southern state. Here, however, it comes abbreviated for tourist attention spans: you watch the players apply their make-up, are spoon-fed a brief background of the dance, then shown a snatch of a classic dance-drama.

Festivals and events

Mapusa *p381, map p381*

Mon of the 3rd week after Easter: Feast of Our Lady of Miracles The *Nossa Senhora de Milagres* image is venerated by Christians as well as Hindus who join together to celebrate the feast day of the Saibin. Holy oil is carried from the church to Shanteri temple and a huge fair and a market are held.

Calangute *p382, map p383*

Mar: **Carnival** is best celebrated in villages or in the main district towns but Calangute has brought the party to the tourists.

May (2nd week): **The Youth Fête** attracts Goa's leading musicians and dancers.

Shopping

Mapusa *p381, map p381*

Municipal Mapusa Bazaar, on south edge of the fruit and veg market, has fixed-price basic food supplies like rice, spice, lentils and cereals: useful if you're here long term.

Other India Bookstore, 1st floor, St Britto's Apartment, above Mapusa clinic, T0832-226 3306, is unconventional and excellent. It is heavily eco conscious, has a large catalogue and will post worldwide.

Calangute *p382, map p383*

Mini markets like Menezes on Calangute Beach Rd or Lawande on Fort Aguada Rd for staples, plus adaptor plugs, water heating filaments, quince jam, wine, cashew *feni* in plastic bottles to take home, full range of sun lotion factors and brands, tampons etc and money change. For silver, head for either of the Tibetan covered handicraft markets where the Tibetan community in exile gently sell silver, which you can buy by weight.

Casa Goa, Cobravado, Baga Rd, T0832-228 1048, cezarpinto@hotmail.com. Cezar Pinto's shop is quite a razzy lifestyle store: beautifully restored reclining plantation chairs next to plates brought over by the Portuguese from Macau plus modern-day dress from local fashion designer Wendell Rodricks. Cool modern twists on old Goan shoes by local Edwin Pinto too.

Candolim and Sinquerim beaches *p383*

Acron Arcade, 283 Fort Aguada Rd, Candolim, T0832-564 3671, www.acronarcade.com. A posh mini-mall with well-stocked bookstore (yoga, ayurveda, Indian cookery, Indian flora and fauna, guidebooks, plus fiction and business books) and swish Indian lifestyle products (modestly ethnic cushions and throws and bedspreads, good stainless steel items) and fancy clothes.

Camelot, 139 Fondvem, Ribandar, T0832-223 4255. Classic countryside furniture.

Rust, 409A Fort, Aguada Rd, Candolim, T0832-247 9340. Everything from wrought-iron furniture to clothes.

Sangolda, Chogm Rd, opposite Mac de Deus Chapel, Sangolda, T0832-240 9309, sangolda @sancharnet.in, Mon-Sat 1000-1930. Lifestyle gallery and café run by the owners of **Nilaya Hermitage** selling handcrafted metalware, glass, ethnic furniture, bed and table linen, lacquerware, wooden objects.

▲ Activities and tours

Calangute *p382, map p383*

Body and soul

Holystamina Yoga Ashram, Naikavaddo, T0832-249 7400, www.cyrilyoga.com. 4 classes daily, 0830, 1000, 1530 and 1630, Rs 300 a class. Courses for all abilities. Inner healing yoga meditation, juice bar, yoga camps and good karma-promoting volunteer activities also on offer.

River cruises

Floating Palace, you can try a Kerala-style backwater cruise by staying overnight in this 4-cabin bamboo, straw and coir houseboat. You sail from Mandovi in the late afternoon, are fed a high tea then a feast of a continental dinner as you drift past the Chorao Island bird sanctuary. International standards of safety. Book through **Kennedy's Adventure Tours and Travels** (T0832-227 6493, T982-327 6520, kennedy@goatelecom .com, opposite Milky Way, Khobravaddo.

Tour operators

Many double as money changers, but there are **State Bank of India** and **ICICI** ATM on either sides of Beach Rd.

Day Tripper, Gauravaddo, T0832-227 6726, www.daytrippergoa.com. Offers tours all over Goa, best deals in the region: Palolem beach Rs 350, spice plantations Rs 700, backwaters Rs 1010 (combined £16), with pick-ups from your hotel. Also runs short tours out of state, for birdwatching or empty beaches in Karnataka. Recommended.

Baga *p382, map p383*

Boat trips and wildlife cruises

Mikes Marine, Fortune Travels, Sauntavaddo, by the bus stand at the top end of Baga, T0832-227 9782. Covered boat, dolphin trips, river cruises and birdwatching.

Body and soul

Ayurvedic Natural Health Centre, Baga-Calangute Rd, Villa 2, Beira Mar Complex, www.healthandayurveda.com. Also in Saligao. The ANHC is not for the faint-hearted; the centre was originally built for the local community that it continues to serve and hasn't made many concessions to Western sensibilities. Those checking into the 2-week *panchakarma* can expect almost every cavity to be flushed. They do offer smaller, less daunting packages, like 2½ hr rejuvenations (Rs 300), and have a herb garden where you can taste first-hand leaves that tingle your tongue (used to stop stuttering) or others that eliminate your sense of sweet taste.

Natural Health Centre, opposite Tito's Lane, offers alternative therapies including ayurvedic massage and yoga lessons.

Diving and snorkelling

Goa Dive Center, Tito's Lane, T0832-215 7094. Goa isn't really on the diving map, chiefly because it has only 2 dive sites, both of which have what's known as variable, ie less than great, visibility. However, this outfit offers inexpensive PADI courses. Options range from the half-day Discover Scuba programme (from aged 10 years, Rs 2700) to the 4-day Open Water Diver programme, Rs 14,500. Snorkelling tours also available.

Candolim and Sinquerim beaches *p383*

Body and soul

Amrita Kerala Ayurvedic, next to Lawande supermarket, Annavaddo, T0832-312 5668, 0730-2000. This massage centre, set inside an old Goan villa, is neatly geared up for the foreign tourist. Westerners are on hand to explain the philosophy behind the Indian life science. The centre teaches as well as gives massages. A basic course, with classes every morning, takes 7 days. Courses in *panchakarma* last 6 months (Rs 7500). Rs 750 for 75-min massage.

Dolphin watching

John's Boats, T0832-227 7780, promises 'guaranteed' dolphin watching, morning trips start around 0900, Rs 550 (includes meal and hotel pick-up). Also crocodile-spotting river trips with lunch.

Parasailing
Occasionally offered independently on Candolim beach, Rs 600-850 for a 5-min flight.

Fort Aguada *p383*
Taj Sports Complex, Fort Aguada Beach Resort. Excellent facilities that are open to non-residents at the **Taj Holiday Village**, and a separate access between Aguada Beach Resort and the Holiday Village. Rs 450 per day for the complex, Rs 350 for the pool. Tennis (Rs 450 per hr); squash and badminton (Rs 150 for 30 mins); mini golf (Rs 200). Yoga classes,scuba diving, sailing/ water skiing/windsurfing/rod fishing Rs 450-500 per hr; parasailing/jet ski Rs 900-950 per hr.

Transport

Mapusa *p381, map p381*
Bus
To **Calangute** (every 20-30 mins), some continue on to **Aguada** and **Baga**, some go towards **Candolim**; check before boarding or change at Calangute. Non-stop mini-buses to **Panjim**; buy tickets from booth at market entrance. Buses also go to **Vagator** and **Chapora** via **Anjuna** and towns near by. Buses to **Tivim** for Konkan Railway and trains to Mumbai, Rs 8 (allow 25 mins).

Long-distance buses line up opposite the taxi stand and offer similar routes and rates. To **Bengaluru (Bangalore)**: 1830, 12 hrs, Rs 250 (Luxury), Rs 450 (Sleeper). **Hospet** (for Hampi): 1800, 10 hrs, Rs 350 (Sleeper). **Mumbai** 1600, 14 hrs, Rs 300 (Luxury), Rs 500 (Sleeper).

Car hire
Pink Panther, T0832-226 3180.

Motorcycle hire
Peter & Friends Classic Adventures, Casa Tres Amigos, Socol Vado 425, Parra, Assagao, 5 km east (off the Anjuna Rd), T0832-225 4467, www.classic-bike-india.de, recommended for reliable bikes and tours of Southern India, Himachal and Nepal. Also has quality rooms.

Taxis
Often shared by up to 5. To **Panjim** Rs 70; **Calangute/Baga**, Rs 100; **Chapora/Siolim**, Rs 80. Auto to **Calangute**, Rs 50. Motorcycle taxi to **Anjuna** or **Calangute**, about Rs 40, open to bargaining.

Train
Tivim train station on the Konkan railway is convenient if you want to head straight to the **northern beaches** (Calangute, Baga, Anjuna and Vagator), avoiding Panjim and Margao. A local bus meets each train and usually runs as far as the Kadamba bus stand in Mapusa. From here you either continue on a local bus to the beach or share a tourist taxi (rates above). Enquiries and computerized tickets: T0832-229 8682.

To **Ernakulam** (for junction): *Mangalore Exp 2618*, 1952 (arr 1345), 18 hrs. To **Jaipur** (from Ernakulam): *Exp 2977*, 1138, Mon. . To **Margao**: *Mandovi Exp 0103*, 1650, 90 mins; *Konkan Kanya Exp 0111*, 0924, 90 mins. To **Mumbai (CST)**: *Mandovi Exp 0104*, 1113, 10 hrs; *Konkan Kanya Exp 0112*, 1846, 11 hrs (via Pernem). To **Mumbai Kurla (Tilak)** (from Trivandrum): *Netravati Exp 6346*, 0747, 11 hrs. To **Thiruvananthapuram (Trivandrum)**: *Netravati Exp 6345*, 2152, 19 hrs (via Margao and Canacona for Palolem beach).

Baga *p382, map p383*
The only place in Baga to hire bikes is 200 m down a small lane past the Hacienda, on the left. Rs 40 per day, a little extra to keep it overnight. As for scooters, almost every guest house owner or hotelier can rustle up a scooter at short notice – expect to pay Rs150 for one day or Rs100 per day for longer periods. Recycled water bottles of lurid orange liquid balanced in glass display boxes at roadsides denote your local gas station. Petrol is Rs 40 per litre.

Directory

Mapusa *p381, map p381*
Ambulance T0832-226 2372. **Banks** Bank of India, opposite Municipal Gardens, changes TCs, cash against Visa and Mastercard. Mon-Fri 1000-1400, Sat 1000-1200. Pink Panther Agency changes Visa and Mastercard, Mon-Fri 0900-1700, Sat 0900-1300. State Bank of India, exchanges cash and TCs, 15-20 mins. Foreign exchange on 1st floor, Mon-Fri 1000-1600, Sat 1000-1200. **Hospitals and medical services** Asilo Hospital, T0832-226 2211. Pharmacies: including Bardez Bazar; Drogaria, near the Swiss Chapel, open 24 hrs; Mapusa Clinic, T0832-226 2350.

Internet Several across town, well signposted. Most charge Rs 90 per hr. Best at LCC 3rd floor, Bhavani Apartments, daily 0700-2130, Rs 15 per 15 mins, 6 terminals. **Police** T0832-226 2231. **Post** Opposite the police station.

Calangute *p382, map p383*
Banks Bank of Baroda, Baga; State Bank of India, Baga. **Internet** I way, NetXcess Cyber Café, Shop No 1, Sunshine Complex, Baga Rd, T0832-228 1516, netxcess@mail.com. Broadband internet chain I way's branch is faster than most. Nikki's Internet Café, Calangute Tourist Resort Annexe, T0832-228 1950, 0900-2400, Rs 40 per hr, 8 terminals, café, forex, pool table. Useful during periods of frequent power cuts. **Police** T0832-227 8284. **Telephone** Look for the yellow STD ISD signs.

Candolim and Sinquerim beaches *p383*
Hospitals and medical services Health Centre, Main Rd; Bosto Hospital, Panjim Rd.

Anjuna and around

» *pp395-399.*

Colour map 1a, A1.

When the freaks waded across the Baga river after the squares got hip to Calangute, Anjuna was where they washed up. The village still plays host to a large alternative community: some from that first generation of hippies, but the latest influx of spiritual Westerners has brought both an enterprising spirit and often young families, meaning there's fresh pasta, gnocci, marinated tofu or chocolate brownies to be had, cool homespun threads to buy, great, creative childcare, amazing tattoo artists, alternative therapists and world-class yoga teachers. For the beautiful life lived cheap Anjuna is still hard to beat; the countryside here is hilly and lush and jungly, the beaches good for swimming and seldom crowded. A state crackdown in 2006/2007 has made for a hiatus in the parties for which Anjuna was once synonymous, but as you head south along the shore the beach shack soundtracks get progressively more hardcore, until Curlies, where you'll still find arm-thumping techno and trance till all hours.

Flea Market ⓘ *Dandovaddo, south Anjuna, Oct-Apr Wed 0800 till sunset, water taxis or shared taxis from anywhere in Goa*, is a brilliant hullabaloo with 2000 stalls hawking everything from Gujarati wooden printing blocks to Bhutanese silver and even Burberry-check pashminas. The trade is so lucrative by the subcontinent's standards that for six months a year several thousand Rajasthani, Gujaratis, Karnatakans and Tibetans decamp from their home states to tout their wares. The flea had very different origins, and was once an intra-community car boot-style bric-a-brac sale for the freaks. Anjuna's links with trade pre-date the hippies though – the port was an important Arab trading post in the 10th and 12th centuries.

Ingo's Night Bazaar ⓘ *Arpora Hill, 1630-2400*, is a more sanitized and less headlong version of the flea. There's no shortage of dazzling stall fronts draped with glittering saris and the beautiful Rajasthani fare, but while there are fewer stalls there's slightly more variety here; expats who've crafted everything from baby Maharaja outfits, designer mosquito nets and hand-made leather goods are more likely to pitch up here than at the Wednesday event. But there's no need to shop at all – the live music and huge range of food stalls make Ingo's the weekly social event for tourist and long-stayer alike – you'll find most of North Goa empties out for the evening, and most businesses shut up shop for the night as a result of the Bazaar's magnetic appeal. Bring cash and an appetite.

Anjuna and Assagao are also home to two of Goa's best contemporary yoga schools: Brahmani and Purple Valley. **Brahmani** ⓘ *www.brahmaniyoga.com*, housed in two airy shalas in the gardens of Hotel Bougainvillea, runs workshops and drop-in classes, from excellent ashtanga, Mysore-style, to more experimental forms of yoga,

The Divine Comedy

It's one of those funny ironies that yoga, now at the zenith of its international popularity, is given a resounding thumbs down by your average metropolitan Indian, who's much more likely to pull on Lycra to jog or pump iron down the gym than pursue the perfect trikonasana. They look with curiosity at the swarms of foreign yogis yearning to pick up extreme postures from the various guru-jis scattered about the sub-continent. "For them, it's the equivalent of having hoards of middle-class Indians rocking up in Yorkshire to study something we see as outmoded as morris dancing," admits Phil Dane, who runs a yoga-centric hotel, Yogamagic Canvas Ecotel, near Goa's foremost Western-style yoga school, Purple Valley.

While some Indians look askance at the vast numbers of *firangi* yogis, others are making the most of it. Devotees of Sri Pattabhi Jois, the venerated octogenarian who developed his own brand of the ashtanga vinyasa (dynamic) practice, note his growing penchant for items like Louis Vuitton luggage sets.

Devout though he and his disciples doubtless are, the popularity, and price, of the practice has prompted accusations of commercialization by those who see ashtanga yoga as the lowliest building block towards the greater endeavour of advanced Hindu consciousness. Asana CDs, featuring cameos from students like Sting, and clothing lines designed by the likes of Christy Turlington, only serve to irk these traditionalists.

India remains, nevertheless, one of the best places to study the ancient art, and many people who have embarked on yoga courses purely for its physical benefits do end up reaping some mental and emotional rewards too; this may not stretch to doing puja to Ganesh but is likely to include improved concentration, better posture and digestion.

The large alternative communities settled around Arambol and Anjuna in Goa make good starting points if you are looking for some ad hoc teaching, but if you are travelling to India specifically to practice it's worth doing your homework first. Brahmani Yoga in Anjuna and Purple Valley offer retreats (see page 390 and below). Purple Valley particularly attracts internationally acclaimed yoga teachers, such as Sharath Jois, John Scott and Gingi Lee; for these, you need to book far in advance, both for courses and flights.

Good books to start you off include BKS Iyengar's *Light On Yoga*, *Light On Life*, *Light on the Yogasutras of Patanjali*, *Practice Manual* by David Swenson and *Yoga Darshan*.

Four key schools of practice have their headquarters (ashram/shala) in Pune (BKS Iyengar), Mysore (Pattabhi Jois), Neyyar Dam (Sivananda) and Bihar (Paramahamsa Satyananda).

See under Activities and tours in the listings sections of individual towns for further information.

like Kundalini, dance yoga, and Scaravelli. Packages with unlimited yoga are offered, but accommodation is not onsite or specifically for yoga students.

The neighbouring ashtanga yoga centre, the **Purple Valley Yoga Retreat** ① *T0832-226 8364, www.yogagoa.com, US$600 per room per week including yoga and meals,* runs two-week retreats with leading teachers like Sharath Rangaswamy, grandson of Sri K Pattabhi Jois, David Swenson and Nancy Gilgoff, two of the first to introduce ashtanga to the West in the 70s. Lessons are held in a lovely shala in delightful gardens, food is vegetarian and the atmosphere collegiate.

Anjuna, Vagator & Chapora

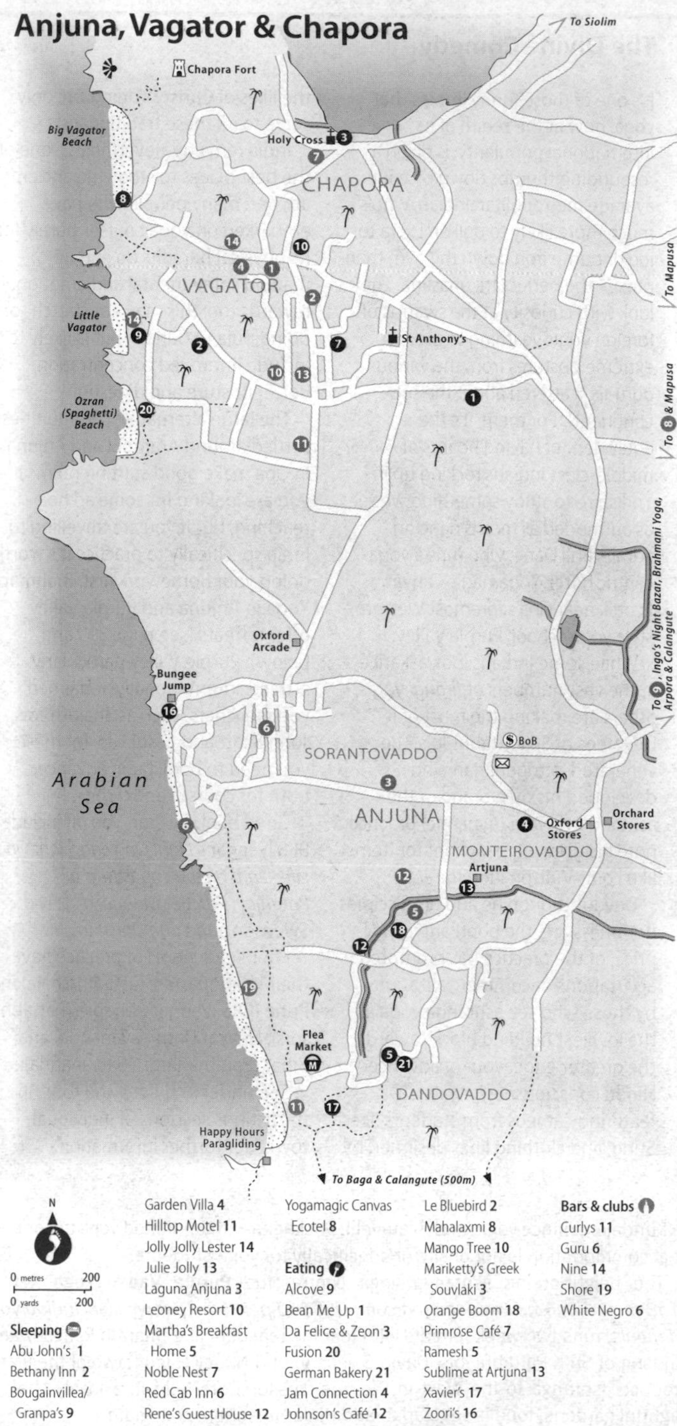

Sleeping
- Abu John's 1
- Bethany Inn 2
- Bougainvillea/ Granpa's 9
- Garden Villa 4
- Hilltop Motel 11
- Jolly Jolly Lester 14
- Julie Jolly 13
- Laguna Anjuna 3
- Leoney Resort 10
- Martha's Breakfast Home 5
- Noble Nest 7
- Red Cab Inn 6
- Rene's Guest House 12
- Yogamagic Canvas Ecotel 8

Eating
- Alcove 9
- Bean Me Up 1
- Da Felice & Zeon 3
- Fusion 20
- German Bakery 21
- Jam Connection 4
- Johnson's Café 12
- Le Bluebird 2
- Mahalaxmi 8
- Mango Tree 10
- Marikettys Greek Souvlaki 3
- Orange Boom 18
- Primrose Café 7
- Ramesh 5
- Sublime at Artjuna 13
- Xavier's 17
- Zoori's 16

Bars & clubs
- Curlys 11
- Guru 6
- Nine 14
- Shore 19
- White Negro 6

South Anjuna to Chapora Fort

There's a footpath just inland of the bungee jump in north Anjuna that takes you over the headland to Ozran (or 'Spaghetti beach', named by English settlers for its Italian community) in Vagator: thread your way down the gravelly terracing here and stroll along Spaghetti before climbing over the headland to the north to reach the wide sands of Big Vagator beach. Pause for a sundowner at trance stronghold Nine Bar or press on for the tranquil ruination around Chapora Fort, built by Adil Shah (hence the name: Shah pura). There's little left of the actual edifice, the crumbling blocks of black rock are overgrown with tawny grasses, but follow the ramparts to reach the jutting promontory for spectacular sunset views across the Chapora river mouth, where fishing boats edge slowly out of harbour and the sand spits level with Morjim are settled with flocks of birds.

Chapora village itself may be too feral for some tastes – at dusk the smoke from domestic fires spreads a haze through the jungle canopy between which Portuguese houses stand worn and derelict; at the river edge men lean to mend their fuzzy nets, boats nudge out to sea, while village boys saunter out to bat on threshed fields and the potholed roads hums with the engines of Enfields and Hondas bearing longstayers and Goan village folk home. Along the village's main street the shady bars are decked with fairy lights and the internationals who call Chapora both home and, in an affectionate nod to its less savoury side, 'the Bronx,' settle down to nurse their drinks.

The flat arc of the estuary here is perfect for cycling: the rim-side road will take you all the way out to the bridge at **Siolim** where you can loop back to take a look at the **Church of St Anthony**. Built in 1606, it replaced an earlier Franciscan church dating from 1568. Both Goa's Hindu and Catholic communities pray to St Anthony, Portugal's patron saint, in the hope of good fishing catches. The high, flat-ceilinged church has a narrow balustraded gallery and Belgian glass chandeliers, with statues of Jesus and St Anthony in the gabled west end.

Splendid Portuguese houses stand scattered about the village's shadows in varying degrees of disrepair; it's worth walking around to take in some of the facades. You can even stay in one which has been refurbished, the lovely **Siolim House**, see page 395.

Vagator

Vagator's beaches are possibly Goa's most dramatic: here, muddied sand bays upset by slabs of gray rock, quite different from the bubblings of porous laterite in Anjuna, fall at the bottom of terraced red cliffs planted with coconut trees that lean out towards the crashing waves, some of their trunks painted bright neon from past parties.

Big Vagator Beach is a long sweep of beach to the right of the main access road, behind which stands the profile of the wide outer rim of the ruined **Chapora Fort** against a stunning backdrop of India's western coastline, stretching beyond Goa's northern borders and beyond, into Maharashtra. The factory you can just pick out in the distance marks the border.

To your left, running inland, is **Little Vagator Beach**, its terracing lorded over by **Nine Bar**, a giant venue with an unswerving musical loyalty to trance (see page 398). Just out of sight is **Ozran Beach,** a scrappy, atmospheric bay (an excellent swimming spot) that ends with rocks and jungle.

Spaghetti, though dogged by persistent sarong sellers, is more sheltered, more scenic and more remote than the others. One of the shacks here has rooms. To get straight to Spaghetti follow the signposts to **Leoney Resorts**, then when you reach the headland turn off the tarmac road onto one of the gravel tracks towards the sign for **Shiva Place** shack.

The trance dance experience

The 'freaks' – beatniks with super nomadic genes, giant drug habits and names like Eight Finger Eddie – first shipped into Goa shortly after the Portuguese left. Some brought guitars on which, after soaking up a bit of Hindu spirituality on the way, they were charged with playing devotional songs at beach campfire parties.

By the end of the 60s, thousands of freaks were swarming into Goa, often spilling down from Freak HQ in Kathmandu, and word had got back to proper paid-up acid rock musicians about the scene. Some more substantial entertainment was called for. People started playing records after the Flea Market.

The first music to run through the speakers was rock and reggae. Led Zeppelin, The Who and George Harrison rocked up and played live, but the freaks' entertainment was mostly recorded: Santana, Stones and Marley. Kraftwerk and synth had filtered in by the late 70s but the shift to electronica only really came in the early 80s when musicians got bored of the lyrics and blanked out all the words on albums of industrial noise, rock and disco, using the fully lo-fi production method of taping between two cassette decks. Depeche Mode and New Order albums were stripped down for their drum and synth layers. Some of the rock faithful were angry with the change in the soundtrack to their lives; at those early 80s parties, when the psychedelic-meets-machine-drum sound that still defines Goa trance was first being pumped out, legend has it that the decks had to be flanked by bouncers.

The music, developing in tandem to German nosebleed techno and UK acid house, locked into a worldwide tapestry of druggy drumscapes, but the Goan climate created its own sound. As records would warp in India's high temperatures, music had to be put down on DATS rather than vinyl which in turn meant tracks were played out in full, unmixed. A track had to be interesting enough then, self-contained, so it could be played uninterrupted in full; producers had to pay more attention to intros, middles and outros – in short, the music had to have a story. It also meant there was less art to a set by a trance DJ in Goa than DJs in Manchester, Detroit and Paris, who could splice records together to make their own new hybrid sounds.

Many of the original makers of this music had absorbed a fair whack of psychedelia and had added the inevitable layer of sadhu thinking to this – superficially measured in incense, *oms*, dreads and the swirling dayglo mandalas that unmistakeably mark out a Goa trance party. The music reflected this: sitars noodled alongside sequencer music to make the Goan signature sound.

By the 90s, though, Ecstasy had arrived in Goa. The whole party scene opened right up, peopled by Spiral Tribe crusties as well as middle-class gap year lovelies and global party scenesters who came looking for an alternative to the more mainstream fare in Ibiza. Paul Oakenfold's Perfecto was a key label in fuelling the sound's popularity but there were more: Dragonfly, The Infinity Project, Return to the Source. Today the music comes from labels like Electrojump, Hux Flux, Errorhead, Color Drop, Wizzy Noise, Psycho+ Trolls, Droidsect, Parasense, Peace Data, In-R-Voice. Although much of it is from European or Japanese studios, there's the odd label that's more homegrown, like the resolutely Goan label Made In Chapora.

Sleeping

Anjuna and around *p390, map p392*

At the budget end, the best options in Anjuna, Vagator and Chapora tend to be unofficial, privately owned residences.

LL Nilaya Hermitage Bhati, T0832-227 6793, www.nilayahermitage.com. A luxury retreat in topaz on a hilltop over Anjuna. Elite accommodation in 10 unique bungalows and 4 tents in lush gardens set around a beautiful plunge pool. Ultra-chichi and fashion pack, with tennis, badminton, gym, yoga, jogging trail, DVD library and excellent restaurant, but some have found fault with the warmth of service and food.

L Laguna Anjuna, Sorantovaddo, T0832-227 4305, www.lagunaanjuna.com. A series of spacious cottages set less than1 km from the hullabaloo of the beach. Unassuming style, a little dog-eared, but a happening place; it has both a snooker table and a frangipani-fringed pool. Great staff, but soundproofing is negligible and soundtrack nonstop, so don't come if you need utter quiet.

A-D Hotel Bougainvillea/Granpa's, Gaumwadi, T0832-227 3270, www.goacom .org/hotels/granpas/. A billiard table stands off an airy reception hall and all rooms are set around a garden of some sort. TV, fridge and phone in most rooms. Open during monsoon season. More likely to attract TV crews and yogis than the party crowd.

B Yogamagic Canvas Ecotel, T0832-562 3796, www.yogamagic.net. A luxury campsite in a field of paddy and palms featuring 7 Rajasthani hunting tents, a naturally filtered pool, immaculate gardens of bougainvillea, lilies and lotus flowers, yoga and holistic therapies, delicious vegetarian South Indian food and environmentalism. There are also eco-lodges, teepees and the Maharani suite, a wing of the main house with its own veranda. Solar panels, compost loos, 5 mins' walk from Brahmani yoga centre (page 390), 2 km from Anjuna beach.

C The Tamarind, Kumar Vaddo, T0832-561 2399, www.thetamarind.com. 22 rooms with flagstone floors and balconies in stone-built Portuguese-style house set in landscaped gardens with pool, which some complain fails to catch sunlight. 3 km inland from Anjuna. Courtesy bus service to beaches.

C-F Martha's Breakfast Home, House no 907, Monteiro Vaddo Anjuna, T0832-227 3365, mpd8650@hotmail.com. Martha and Paul D'Souza let out 8 spic-and-span rooms, twin beds, small shower rooms (cold water only) with nice little balconies in the gardens of their house that give onto an orchard where pigs roam in the shade. Better though are the 2 villas with 2 doubles, little lounges with telly, and kitchenettes with gas stove, sink and fridge. Ask for the Sunset Villa which has incredible views. Basic but perfect.

D-E Red Cab Inn, De Mello Vaddo, T0832-227 4427, redcabinn@rediffmail.com. 5-min walk from Starco crossroads. 4 newly decorated rooms in old house, high ceilings, nice and cool, plus a room on the roof, good for long stay, plus a bright red cottage in the garden. Very clean and neat, own freshwater well, good evening restaurant. 15 mins' walk from the beach.

D-F Days Guest House, Mazal Vaddo, Anjuna, T0832-227 3289, days_guest_house @yahoo.com. Cable TV, toilet, rooms with fridges, doctor on call.

E Rene's Guest House, Monterio Waddo, Anjuna, T0832-227 3405, renesguesthouse goa@yahoo.co.in. A real gem: 14 rooms spread around colourful garden belonging to the family bungalow of John Baptiste, his wife Rene and their kids. Best are the 3 self-contained cottages, with 4-poster beds, good kitchens with gas stove, sinks and big fridges; these are meant for long lets (2 are designed for couples, the other sleeps 3). Individual rooms are decent too. US$366 a month.

South Anjuna to Chapora Fort *p393, map p392*

Chapora caters mainly for long-term budget travellers.

A Siolim House, Vaddy, opposite Vaddy Chapel, T0832-227 2138, www.siolimhouse. com. This beautiful, environmental restoration of a 2-storey 300-year-old house once owned by the governor of Macau has 7 huge proportioned, romantic suites –

For an explanation of the sleeping and eating price codes used in this guide, see inside the front cover. Other relevant information is found in Essentials pages 40-44.

4-poster beds, sprawling bathrooms. Good food, pool in diminutive garden, video library. Recommended.

F Noble Nest, opposite the Holy Cross Chapel, Chapora, T0832-227 4335. Basic but popular, 21 rooms, 2 with bath but ample facilities for sharing, exchange and internet.

Vagator *p393, map p392*

B Leoney Resort, T0832-227 3634, www.leoneyresort.com. 13 rooms, 3 cottages, a/c extra Rs 400. Clean, modern, family run, low-key, quiet, pool, 10-min walk from beach.

D Bethany Inn, opposite **Mango Tree**, T0832-227 3973, bethany@goatelecom.com. 7 clean, comfortable modern rooms (some 4 bedded) with bath, central village location.

E Abu John's, 6 small rooms with bath, good restaurant, garden, pleasant, quiet.

E Hilltop Motel, away from the beach, T0832-227 3665. Popular late-night venue, 14 small rooms, those with bath reasonable.

E-F Garden Villa, T0832-227 3571. 8 clean rooms, some with bath, restaurant with a decent choice.

F Hotel Jolly Goa, T0832-227 3357, www.hoteljollygoa .com. A/c and non a/c with hot showers, TV.

Eating

Anjuna *p390, map p392*

Aniket and **Joe Banana's** serve the best Goan food.

TTT **Xavier's**, Praias de San Miguel (follow signs from behind small chapel near flea market site, bring a torch at night), T0832-227 3402. One of the very first restaurants for foreigners has grown into a smart restaurant with 3 separate kitchens (Indian/Chinese/continental), excellent fresh seafood, tucked away under palm trees.

TT **Bean Me Up**, near the petrol pump. Closed Sat and 1600-1900 daily. Californian-owned Bean Me Up serves raw food, from the macrobiotic to the wholesome, in a big shady garden. Portions are giant – expect tofu salads, falafel in pita, tempeh gado gado with brown rice and every imaginable combination of vegetable and fruit juice. There's massage offered onsite, a good noticeboard on mind-body-spirit stuff, kids' area and a few simple, clean rooms for rent. Loyal following. Also does takeaway.

TT **Blue Tao**, on previous site of **Bean Me Up**, serves similar fare (including wheatgrass), also has a kids' area and puts on entertainment like belly dancing.

TT **The Johnson's Café**, Flea Market Rd, South Anjuna, T0988-467426. Scrupulously clean branch of the Manali institution close to the German Bakery, elegantly lit with fairy lights hanging through the carefully landscaped coconut garden. Fish is excellent here – kingfish, calamari and mussels – served with Goan rarities like zucchini and asparagus. Also thalis, lasagne, pizza, fried kidney and chicken liver, and tasty puddings like crème caramel and apple crumble. Immaculate service.

TT **Ramesh**. Traditional family restaurant that's been running as long as **Xavier's**; particularly good for fish.

TT **Sublime at Artjuna**, Flea Market Rd, T0982-248 4051. A limited menu done very well: ratatouille with penne, blue cheese vegetable gratin with rocket, rosemary lime marinated chicken leg and thigh, beef fillet with baby potatoes and vegetables and banana leaf-wrapped steamed fish fillet with wet coconut rice and asparagus spears, plus daily specials. Reassuring open kitchen. Lovely situation, just a few tables and chairs under trees, relocated from previous Calangute site. Not to be confused with restaurant set up under same name beside Baga River.

T **German Bakery**, south Anjuna, towards the Flea Market and Curlies. A little fiefdom of bohemian perfection: the German Bakery's sign is hung over a huge garden with an awning of thick tropical trees, where tatty mattresses pad out the sides of low-slung booths. There's a massage parlour, a tailor and clothes shop and a little shop onsite. The atmosphere alone is habit-forming, but the food is the real thing too: huge salads with every healthy thing under the sun – sprouts and avocado – plus good veggie burgers, Indian food and extreme juices.

T **The Jam Connection**, opposite Tin Tin In Tibet, South Anjuna. An unkempt leafy garden complete with tree house, slides, sandpits and baby teepee for little 'uns and day beds and hammocks for grown-ups makes this a family favourite. There are 21 types of home-made ice creams, chocolate fondue, éclairs and profiteroles, while mains are mostly Mediterranean and Middle Eastern like quiches, salads, gazpacho, humous and tahini plates. Proper coffee. Open 1100 till 1900 daily except Wednesday.

Ỵ Orange Boom, south Anjuna, Flea Market Rd. Daytime only. Efficient and spotlessly clean canteen – food is hyper-hygienic and meticulously made, with a menu offering the usual breakfast fare plus 100 ways with eggs (like poached eggs and French toast), most served with mushrooms and grilled tomatoes. Baked beans can be masala or Heinz (proper ketchup on the tables), also croque madame and sautéed avocado on toast.

Ỵ Zoori's, next to Paradiso, House no 652, Saint Anthony Praise, Anjuna Beach, T0832-227 3476. Goa may feel closer to Italy than the rest of the subcontinent, but good, strong coffee remains hard to come by, so having a choice between Illy and Lavazza blends makes this place a bit special. Set across 2 big balconies built around a tree high above the beach, this café has great views over Anjuna's rock pools and the headland towards Vagator. Food is good (humous, spaghetti bolognese, burgers, good meat and Mexican, baked cheesecake) and altogether a lovely place to hang out.

South Anjuna to Chapora Fort *p393, map p392*

Chapora village

ỴỴ Da Felice & Zeon, above Babba's, Chapora, 1800-2400. Just a handful of tables dancing with fairy lights and psychedelic art at this rooftop restaurant run by the Italian brothers Felice and Zeon. Felice is an Italian chef in London over monsoon, Zeon makes trance music and trance art. Carbonara, lasagna, prosciutto, spaghetti alla vongole all feature but meat is recommended.

Ỵ Mariketty's Greek Souvlaki (Kebab). Chapora Village, T0985-003 3537. Just a counter with an open griddle behind it, on which you can see grilled any one of only 3 dishes: chicken, lamb or vegetable kebabs, all brilliantly tender and stuffed inside hot bread and drizzled with garlic sauce, fresh chilli, marinated sliced tomatoes and onions. No plates, no cutlery, nowhere to sit, but brilliant all the same. Sit out on the porch or take away to one of Chapora's fairy lit bars. Also serves Greek salad.

Vagator *p393, map p392*

Several restaurants line the streets to the beach. Some serve good fresh fish including **Mahalaxmi**. **Primrose Café** serves tasty health foods and also hosts spontaneous parties.

ỴỴỴ Le Bluebird. A short and excellent menu matched by an amazing wine list (Chablis, Sauterne, Sancerre) and fine cheeses (Camembert and goat's cheese) in garden restaurant of long-standing reputation run by Goan/French couple. Entrecôte and fillet are cooked in a variety of ways and sauces, and there's ratatouille and bouillabaisse, king and tiger prawns and lobster. Not to be confused with the plain **Bluebird** recently established in the same village.

ỴỴ The Alcove, on the cliff above Little Vagator. Smartish, ideal position, excellent food, pleasant ambience in the evening, sometimes live music.

ỴỴ Mango Tree, in the village, offers a wide choice of continental favourites.

Ỵ Alcove Resorts, T0832-227 4491, www.alcovegoa.com. Restaurant, pub, swimming pool and rooms.

Ỵ Fusion. On the clifftop above Ozran beach is a sprawling tent strewn with cushions and low tables, offering beautiful sunset views through silhouettes of coconuts. Try spit-roasted chicken, humous, baba ghanoush, vegetable quiche, roast tatties or one of the dozens of salads (including beetroot, Caprese and carrot). More substantial stuff is mostly Italian: spaghetti, lasagne, meatballs, a great pizza list and for pudding, panacotta, tiramisu and profiteroles. Lemonade recommended.

Bars and clubs

Anjuna *p390, map p392*

Wed and Fri nights tend to be the main evenings, but there is usually something going on each night over the Christmas and New Year period; just ask around (taxi drivers invariably know where). Venues are often recognizable by illuminated trees and luminous wall hangings. A purpose-built set, Jungle Grove, has been created inland, south of Anjuna. It is best to walk there and back in a group. Politicians have tried to impose a ban or a curb on loud music after 2200.

Curlys, at the very far south of Anjuna, a kind of unofficial headquarters of the scene, playing techno and ambient music.

Guru, along the beach, popular, mops up after the flea market.
Paradiso, the biggest, looks like a wild Fred Flintstone flight of fancy. Although it advertises itself as a performance art space, it's dyed-in-the-wool techno.
Shore Bar, lovely raised beach bar with wide deckchairs padded out with thick cushions on the way to Anjuna south. There are pot plants and sarongs, bat and ball for loan, but it's the food that really sets it apart – great big trustily hygienic salads. Turkish coffee is also excellent here.

Vagator *p393, map p392*
Nine Bar, Ozran beach. A booming mud-packed bar with huge gargoyle adornments and a manic neon man carved out of the fountain. Great sound system and majestic sunset views.

Shopping

Anjuna *p390, map p392*
Artjuna, House no 972, Monteiro Vaddo, T0832-321 8468. Nicely Westernized takes on generic Indian lifestyle goods – chunky jewellery, swanky hammocks, blankets and quilts of pure silk and floaty dresses. Pricey.
Flea Market, Wed, attracts hordes of tourists from all over Goa. By mid-morning all approach roads are blocked with taxis, so arrive early.
Natural Health Food Store, Monteirovaddo.
Orchard Stores, Monteirovaddo. Amazing selection catering for Western cravings. Olive oil, pasta, fresh cheese, frozen meats etc.
Oxford Arcade, De Mellovaddo, next to Munche's. Good general store close to beach.
Oxford Stores, for groceries, foreign exchange and photo processing.

South Anjuna to Chapora Fort *p393, map p392*
Do your homework before you buy: prices in tourist shops are massively inflated, and goods are often worth less than a third of the asking. 92.5 silver should be sold by weight; prices are quoted on the international market and in 2004 a biscuit would go for Rs 11 per g; pay a little more for elaborate workmanship. The bigger Kashmiri shops, particularly, are notorious both for refusing to sell by weight, instead quoting by the 'piece', and for their commission tactic whereby rickshaw and taxi drivers get Rs 100 per tourist delivered to shops plus 10% commission on anything sold.
Narayan, Chapora. Book stall, sells local newspapers.

Activities and tours

Anjuna *p390, map p392*
Body and soul
Some excellent yoga teachers teach in Goa during the season, many of whom gravitate towards Anjuna: check the noticeboards at the **German Bakery**, **The Jam Connection** and **Bean Me Up** (see page 396). You'll also stumble on practitioners of all sorts of alternative therapies: reiki healers, acupuncturists, chakra and even vortex cleansing can all be bought.
Healing Here And Now, The Health Center, St Michael's Vaddo, T0832-227 3487, www.healinghereandnow.com. If you want an 'ultimate cleanse', sign up for a 5-day detox: fasting, detoxifying drinks and twice-daily enemas. Also offers parasite cleansing, kidney cleanse and wheat grass therapy.
Purple Valley Yoga Retreat (see page 391) has 2-week retreats with celebrities of the ashtanga vinyasa yoga circuit or drop in for all sorts of different styles of yoga and pranayama at **Brahmani** (see page 390).
Shri Dhanwantari's Ayur Sampada, church grounds, near Tamarind, T0832-226 8361, mayura_goa@sancharnet.in. Dr Laxmi Bharne has 4 years of experience in treating specific ailments, gives treatment only after check up, dietary advice, pure herbal treatments. Also full body massage, *shirodhara*, etc.

Bungee jumping
Offered by a Mumbai-based firm with US-trained staff, at Rs 500 a go. Safety is a priority, with harnesses, carabinas and air bags employed. There are pool tables, a bar, an auditorium for slide/film shows and beach volleyball. 1000-1230 and 1730 until late.

Paragliding
Happy Hours Café, south Anjuna beach, 1230-1400; Rs 500 (children welcome), or at the hilltop between Anjuna and Baga, or at Arambol.

Directory

There is no bank in Vagator or Chapora.

Anjuna *p390, map p392*
Banks Bank of Baroda, Sorranto Vaddo, Mon-Wed, Fri 0930-1330, Sat 0930-1130, accepts most TCs, Visa/Mastercard, 1% commission (minimum Rs 50); also provides Safe Custody Packets. Thomas Cook agent at Oxford Stores, central, quicker and more efficient. **Internet** Space Ride Internet, opposite St Anthony's Church, has high speed connections. **Pharmacy** St Michael's Pharmacy, Main Rd, Sorranto, open 24 hrs. **Police** T0832-227 3233. Poste Restante at post office, open Mon-Sat 1000-1600; efficient, parcels are also accepted without a fuss.

South Anjuna to Chapora Fort *p393, map p392*
Internet Sonya Travels, near Holy Cross. Offers foreign exchange, money transfers, ticketing and internet.

Arambol, Keri, Morjim, Asvem, Mandrem

» *pp402-405. Colour map 1a, A1.*

The long bridge that spans the Chapora River and joins Bardez to the last – and so most heavily Hindu – of the new conquests, hilly Pernem *taluka*, also acts as the gateway to a series of gently uncommercialized beaches that hug the coastal road in a nearly unbroken strip up to the Maharashtra border, where a tiny pocket of Catholicism squats in the shadow of the pretty pride of the district, Tiracol Church and Fort. Haphazard and hippy Arambol has a warm community feel and is rightly popular with open-minded travellers of all ages, who are drawn to its hippy scene, its live music, the dolphins that fin along its beaches and its famous saltwater lake. Mandrem and Asvem are much more chichi, and will suit those less prepared to compromise on their accommodation, something at which Arambol doesn't excel.

Ins and outs

All of Pernem *taluka* is within easy reach of the hotels in Panjim or Calangute, but you'd be doing yourself a disservice to visit these – arguably North Goa's loveliest – beaches just on a day trip. Better to set up camp in one from where you can explore the rest. If you are crossing the bridge at Siolim on a motorbike turn left off the new main road immediately after the bridge to use the smaller, more scenic coastal roads. There are also regular buses to the villages from Mapusa and from Chopdem. Each beach is about 10 minutes apart from the next.

History

The Bhonsles of Sawantwadi in modern Maharashtra were the last to rule Pernem before being ousted by the Portuguese in 1788, and Maratha influences here remain correspondingly strong.

Arambol (Harmal) → *Colour map 1a, A1.*

Arambol, which you reach when the plateau road noses down through paddy fields and cashew trees, is a beautiful long stretch of sand at the bottom of a bumpy dirt track that's fringed with stalls selling brightly coloured, heavily embroidered clothes – halternecks and pretty lungis flutter in the breeze – and has attracted longstayers wanting somewhere less frantic than Goa's central beaches. Because people have put down roots here, the village is abuzz with industriousness. Bits of A4 paper advertise *satsang* with smiling Western gurus: there's also tabla teaching, yoga teacher training, reiki and belly dancing. Arambol is also synonymous with live music, with everything from rock to reggae sessions, open mike, jamming or proper metal bands playing in rotation at the beach bars.

But you have to skirt the beach's northern cliff and tiny basalt rocky bays by foot to reach the real lure: a second bay cut off from the roads and **a natural 'sweet water' lake** that collects at the base of a jungle spring. The lagoon collects just metres from the high tide line where the lush forest crawls down to the water's edge. You can walk up the spring's path to reach a belt of natural mineral clay: an idyllic spot for self-service **mud baths**. Further into the jungle is the famous **banyan tree**, its branches straddling 50 m, which has long been a point of Hindu and hippy pilgrimage. Or clamber over the boulders at the north to join the scrappy dirt track over the headland for the half-hour walk it takes to reach the achingly lovely and reliably empty Keri beach.

Keri (Querim) and Tiracol Fort → *Colour map 1a, A1.*

Goa's northernmost beach is uniquely untouched. The drive towards Keri (Querim) along the banks of the Tiracol river from Pernem passes through some stunning rural areas untouched by any tourist development.

Walk across deep dunes to a casuarina thicket and out onto empty sand that stretches all the way from the mouth of the Tiracol river to the highland that splits it from Arambol. There's just one solitary shack at either end of the beach, both of which can arrange rooms with villagers from Rs 100.

Querim does get busy on weekends and is now host to the parties that have been forced on from Anjuna, but remains a lovely spot of sand. You can reach the beach from the north on foot from the Tiracol ferry terminal, or from the south by walking round the headland from Arambol. The Tiracol ferry runs half hourly from 0600 to 2130 taking 15 minutes. If you arrive outside these times you can charter a fishing boat for Rs 55.

Tiracol (Terekhol), at the northernmost tip of Goa, is a tiny enclave of just 350 Catholics on the Maharashtra border just 3½ km across where *feni* production is the biggest business. Its name probably comes from *tir-khol* (meaning steep river bank)

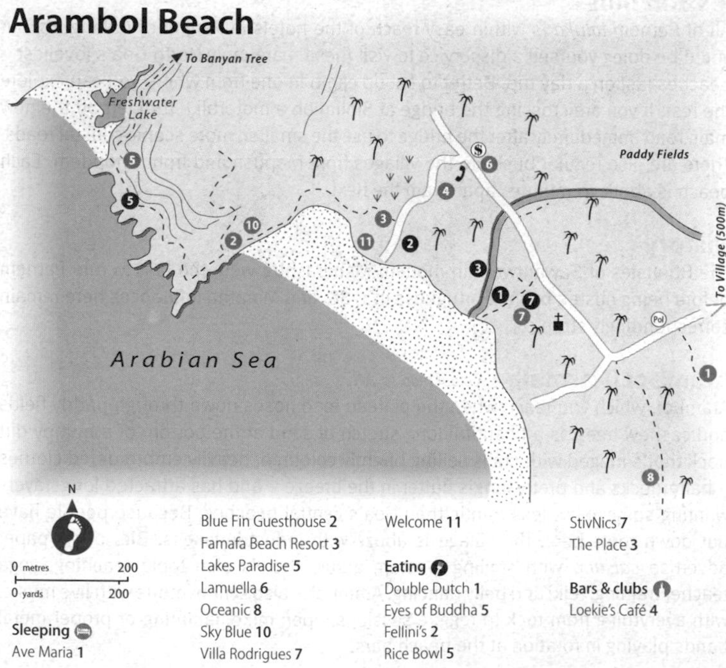

and it's a jungly little patch of land full of cashew trees, banyans, orange blossoms, black-faced monkeys and squirrels.

The small but strategic **fort** ⓘ *0900-1800, cross Tiracol river by ferry (half-hourly, 0600-2130) and walk the remaining 2 km. Ferries take cars and motorbikes*, stands above the village on the north side of the Tiracol river estuary on a rugged promontory with amazing views across the water. Its high battlement walls are clearly visible from the Arambol headland. Built by the Maharaja Khem Sawant Bhonsle in the 17th century, it is protected from attacks from the sea, while the walls on the land side rise from a dry moat. It was captured in 1746 by the Portuguese Viceroy Dom Pedro Miguel de Almeida (Marques de Alorna), who renamed it Holy Trinity and had a chapel built inside (now St Anthony's). You can explore the fort's battlements and tiny circular turrets that scarcely seem fit for slaying the enemy. The views south are magnificent. Steps lead down to a terrace on the south side while the north has an open plateau.

St Anthony's Church ⓘ *open on Wed and Sun for Mass at 1730*, inside the tiny fort, was built in the early 1750s soon after the Portuguese takeover. It has a classic Goan façade and is just large enough to cater for the small village. In the small courtyard, paved with laterite blocks, stands a modern statue of Christ. The Festival of St Anthony is held here at the beginning of May (usually on the second Tuesday) instead of on the conventional festival day of 13 June.

Morjim (Morji) to Asvem

Morjim, which stands on the opposite side of the estuary from Chapora, has two wide sweeping beaches that both sit at the bottom of separate dead end streets. This inaccessibility means that, development-wise, it has got away relatively unscathed. The southern, protected, turtle beach appears at the end of the narrow track that winds along the north bank of the Chapora river mouth. Loungers, which are mostly empty, are strewn haphazardly north of the official-looking **Turtle Nesting Control Room**.

The wide shoreline with its gentle incline (the water is hip height for about 100 m) washed by easy rolling breakers makes it one of North Goa's best swimming beaches. The northern beach, or **Little Morjim**, a left turn off the main coast road, is by comparison an established tourist hamlet with guest houses and beach huts. Plans for an upmarket hotel complex here with a private beach, which would deny local people free access to a section of the waterfront, have been dropped, so this fine stretch of beach should be safe for some time to come.

The road from Morjim cuts inland over the low wooded hills running parallel to the coast. After a few kilometres the road drops down to the coast and runs along the edge of northeast tilting **Asvem Beach**. (Morjim faces Chapora to the south and west.) The northern end of this peaceful palm-fringed beach is divided by a small river.

Mandrem

Mandrem creek forces the road to feed inland where it passes through a small commercial centre with a few shops and a bank. Mandrem village has the **Shri Bhumika Temple** housing an ancient image. In the **Shri Purchevo Ravalnatha Temple** there is a particularly striking medieval image of the half-eagle, half-human Garuda, who acts as the *vahana* (carrier) of Vishnu.

A little further on, a lane off to the left leads down towards the main beach and a secluded hamlet in a beautifully shaded setting. The **beach** is one of the least developed along this stretch of coast; for the moment it is managing to tread that fine line between having enough facilities for comfort and enough isolation to guarantee idyllic peace. Further north there is a lagoon fringed by palm trees and some simple rooms, virtually all with sea view. The beach has mercifully yet to draw hawkers, trinket sellers and tourist operators.

Sleeping

Arambol *p399, map 400*
Arambol is low budget. Pack a sleepsheet and a lock (few rooms are secure but many have lockers).

D **Famafa Beach Resort**, Beach Rd, Khalchawada, T0832-224 2516, famafa_in@yahoo.com. You don't head for Arambol for its swanky accommodation; this place, with 25 rooms in an unimaginative development on the right of the stall-studded track down to the beach, is top of the range here. No a/c, but as pukka a hotel as it gets for this price.

D **Villa Rodrigues**, T0832-651 4563, lamuella@gmail.com. In a hibiscus garden are 2 bungalows with 7 big rooms each painted in sunny colours with big beds. This is easily the nicest place to stay in Arambol – each room has hot water, a little fridge, a sink and counter so you can make your own simple food, and there's a shared stove outside. Managed by **Lamuella**.

D-E **Lamuella**, 292 Beach Rd, T0832-651 4563, lamuella@gmail.com. One floor of spotless and brilliantly maintained rooms sandwiched between the health food café ground floor and therapy treatment rooftop of Lamuella, which is on the approach road to Arambol's beach. Rooms are sweet and clean and have hot water. Well run. The rooftop offers reiki, full body massage, ayurvedic yoga massage, Thai massage, tarot readings and there's drop in yoga Mon-Fri and drum workshops on Sun.

E **Ave Maria**, inland, down track opposite police post, Modhlowado, T0832-229 7674, avemaria@satyam.net.in. One of the originals, offering some of the best accommodation. Simple but nevertheless recommended.

E **Luciano Guest Rooms**, Cliffside, T0982-218 0215. Family house with toilet and shower. Cliffside rooms get heavily booked up.

E **Oceanic**, inland at south end, T0832-229 2296. Secluded guest house with simple rooms, all hidden behind wall in mature gardens, no drugs, popular. Recommended.

E **Residensea Beach Huts**, Arambol Beach, T0832-229 2413, pkresidensea_37@hotmail.com. Basic bamboo shacks set around restaurant all have fans and secure locker facilities (outside toilets). German Shepherd keeps watch.

E **Welcome,** at end of road on seafront, T0832-229 7733. Clean rooms, bath with hot water, serves the best muesli, taxi hire.

F **Blue Fin Guesthouse**, north end of beach. T0832-224 2332, rferns_in@yahoo.com. 3 rooms tucked behind a shop, small courtyard, limited views but more privacy than others.

F **Lakes Paradise**. Tiny place that also serves Goan curry and rice.

F **Sky Blue**. 4 small rooms in a cottage, shared veranda, great beach view, usually taken by long-term visitors.

F **The Surf Shack**, T0985-055 4006, flyinfishbarbados@hotmail.com. 8 doubles with balcony, attached shower and Western loo above one of Arambol's live music venues, English proprietor. Shady gardens, international restaurant and bar with film nights, backgammon sets and pool tables. Hires sports equipment and runs tutorials.

F-G **God's Gift**, Arambol House No 411, Girkar Waddo, T0832-224 2391. Budget-friendly family guest house a little way from village, with hammocks hanging about its balconies. Western loos, balconies and kitchenettes.

Keri (Querim) and Tiracol fort *p400*
Around the Christmas and New Year period a handful of shacks appear at the south end of the beach. Simple snacks are available from kiosks by the ferry at the north end of the beach, or buy mineral water and provisions back in the village.

L **Fort Tiracol Heritage Hotel,** Tiracol, T0832-662 27631, nilaya@sancharnet.in. In 2003 the owners of **Nilaya** took over Fort Tiracol to create isolated, personalised luxury with unbroken views of the Arabian Sea. Just 7 exquisite rooms, all with giant en suite, set in the fort walls that surround the Catholic Church which is still used by the 350 villagers of the wholly Christian Tiracol for their mass. Goa's most romantic hotel.

Morjim to Asvem *p401*
A **Yoga Village**, New Wada, Morjim, T0832-320 6615, www.yogavillage.org.

For an explanation of the sleeping and eating price codes used in this guide, see inside the front cover. Other relevant information is found in Essentials pages 40-44.

Retreat centre set in jungle 500 m from Morjim beach, offering 2-week workshops in yoga and week-long courses in ayurveda led by Yogi Manmoyanand, who concentrates on mental elements of yoga, employing Vedic astrology and Yogic mysticism to explore karmic and spiritual details of people's past lives. 'The retreat marks the beginning 14 days in the life of a Yogi'. 2-week packages feature yoga, spirituality, cottage accommodation, all ayurvedic meals.

B Yab Yum Eco Resort, Asvem Beach, Mandrem, T0832-651 0392, www.yabyum resorts.com. 10 deluxe 'eco-domes' made of local materials – blue painted lava rocks make up the bases, woven palm leaves and mango wood the roofs, spread across a huge shady expanse of coconut and banana grove tucked behind a row of trees from the sand dunes of Asvem beach. The pods come in two sizes – family or single – but both have living areas, banquettes, en suite bathrooms with flushing loos and hot showers. It's classy, discreet and bohemian. There's a reading room over the sea, a yoga shala, and a children's teepee crammed with toys. The price includes breakfast and papers.

C Yoga Gypsys Asvem,T0932-613 0115, yogagypsys@yahoo.com. 5 terracotta bungalows and tree huts in a peaceful palm grove close to a Hindu temple the base for group yoga retreats. Apple Yoga (www.appleyoga.com) holds 10-day sivananda, ashtanga and vinyasa flow retreats, intensives from Scaravelli teachers Marc Woolford, www.yogawithmarc.co.uk) and Sophy Hoare (www.sophyhoare.co.uk).

C-D Montego Bay Beach Village, Vithaldas Wado, Morjim, T0832-298 2753, www.montegobaygoa.com. Rajasthani-style luxury tents pitched in the shade past beach shrubs at the southern end of the beach, plus log cabins, a/c rooms and a beach villa.

F-G Palm Grove, Asvem towards Morjim. 6 cottages, fan, in a discreet low-lying stone building with communal veranda (Rs 250), 5 well-built tree houses (Rs 450) close to the beach among casuarinas, plus 2 very basic huts. Communal wash facilities. Recommended for long stays.

Mandrem *p401*

LL Elsewhere's Beach House, T0832-373 8757, www.aseascape.com. 3 lovely bedrooms in the understated luxury of a redecorated 19th-century house on a sandy spit with the sea on one side and a saltwater creek the other. Living room, dining room and kitchen are sea facing; facilities include maid service, day and nightwatchman, stereo, extra for cook. Minimum rental period 1 week at US$2000-4000. Also runs the Priest's Houses, 3 similarly carefully restored villas nearby.

L Elsewhere Otter Creek Tents. Under same ownership as above, 3 luxury Rajasthani tents each with 4-poster beds, en suite hot showers, private jetties and sit-outs.

C-D Villa River Cat, Junasvaddo, T0832-224 7928, www.villarivercat.com. 13 rooms in a 3-tiered roundhouse overlooking the river and a wade over deep sand dunes from the beach. The whole place is ringed with a belt of shared balconies and comes with big central courtyards that are stuffed with swings, sofas, plantation chairs and daybeds. There's a mosaic spiral staircase and a cavalier approach to colour: it's downbeat creative and popular with musicians and actors – in the best possible way, the poor man's Nilaya. Strongly recommended; booking essential.

F Merryland Coco huts, T942-306 0311. Price includes breakfast.

Eating

Arambol *p399, map 400*

There are beach cafés all along the main beach and around the headland to the north. The **Chinese Garden** and **Little Tibet**, both on the Beach Rd, serve good value, great food. The former is recommended for soups, special salads with generous helpings of prawn, and does a mean beef and mutton omelette. Little Tibet is one of the best local options for Indian food. Standards at the 2 German Bakeries here fall short of the high ones set by the lovely restaurant in Anjuna.

TT Fellini's, Beach Rd, T0832-229 2278, arambolfellini95@yahoo.com. Daily 1000-2300 except Wed 1800-2300. Fellini's is an institution and rightly so. The pizzas and calzone are the genuine article, properly made with all the right raw materials like buffalo mozzarella, balsamic and proscuitto. There's a big salad and pasta menu (lasagne to gnocci) and meats, like chicken in white wine sauce or beef Milanese, but it's for the pizzas, only available from 1830, that the place gets packed out come nightfall.

The Place, T0985-094 1726, vitagoa@yahoo.com. Tucked away in the village by the creek is this relaxed little open-air Bulgarian bistro. The menu revolves around chicken, pork, veal and fish, which come with mash, not rice. Try the Shopski-style cheese, a big wedge of white cooked in a clay dish with tomato, onion and herbs, carrot and steamed with an egg on top. Heavy chocolate cake with mousse or biscuit cake for pud.

StivNics, follow signs to Police Outpost off Arambol Beach Rd, T0996-050 9007. Opens 1700. A kitchen manned by 2 professional chefs from Berlin guarantees you a stout menu of excellent meats with rich sauces and marvellous mash. Also Hungarian goulash with home-made egg noodles, beef marinated in red wine and spices, chicken stroganoff. Fish is fried, in white wine sauce, or try mussels in capsicum. Huge salads and kids' menu, plus good vegetarian options centred around those same rich noodles. Lovely location, on a rooftop overlooking the beach through a row of coconut trees.

Double Dutch, Beach Rd, T0832-652 5973, doubledutchgoa@yahoo.co.uk. 0700-2300. Lovely laid-back garden restaurant with sand underfoot and lots of leafy foliage around. Great brown breads served with home-made jams, peanut butter, mashed avocado, as well as prawn crackers, grilled mushrooms, quiches, salads, steaks, goulash and Indonesian and Thai dishes too. Arguably Arambol's best coffee shop. Excellent tea, coffee, good snacks through the day, imported journals.

Eyes Of Buddha, Cliffside, Arambol Beach. Long on Arambol's catering scene, this place has you well looked after with scrupulously clean avocado salads and an enviable cliffside position overlooking the Arabian Sea.

Rice Bowl, Cliffside, next door to **Eyes of Buddha**. Great views south across Arambol beach, with a billiard table. Simple restaurant that has been serving reliably good Chinese for years. All the usual chop suey, wontons, noodles and sweet and sours of calamari, pork, beef or fish, plus Japanese dishes like gyoza, sukiyaki, tempura and Tibetan momos. Apple pie and brownies for afters.

Morjim to Asvem *p401*

You're not spoiled for gastronomic choice in Morjim yet; shacks like **Hard Rock**, **Planet Hollywood** and **Harry Ramsden's** on turtle beach do decent, although average, fresh fish dishes. Big Morjim has more, but most are aimed at Russian tastebuds.

There are plenty of shacks catering to Asvem and Mandrem beaches. Some have free loungers, others charge up to Rs 100. **Sea View** is good for Indian food, **Pink Orange** is sweet, **Here and Now** is a bit more hippy.

La Plage, Asvem, T0832-212 1712. Prim tables and crisp service from waiters in crisp black dhoti uniforms marks La Plage out as somewhere a bit special. The food is excellent (if a bit pricey) and ambitious; tapas include beef carpaccio, chicken liver and fish ceviche, there's fish soup with aioli and quails braised with fresh green grapes or *ile flottante* for pudding. Vegetarians well catered for too, and the breakfasts are legendary. Nice wines and rare juices like cucumber mint lassi or Spanish-style gazpacho round off the menu, all just paces from the beach in a lovely sand and grass enclave with own loungers. Also has rooms.

Bars and clubs

Arambol *p399, map 400*

The southern end of Arambol's main beach is the only place to offer any real nightlife. The music rotates between the **Surf Club**, **Coco Loco**, **Loekie's**, the **Pyramid** and the **Arkan Bar**. At dusk there's normally drumming outside the **Dreamcatcher**. The following both wind down by 2300 to meet Goan laws curbing outdoor music.

Butterfly, plays house and techno. Entry fee (itself something of a shock here).

Surf Club, T0832-229 2484. Run by an English guy, with rock and live jamming sessions.

Keri (Querim) and Tiracol fort *p400*

Keri sometimes hosts trance parties.

Mandrem *p401*

The Prawn Factory has been turned into a dance venue.

Activities and tours

Arambol *p399, map 400*

Boat trips and dolphin watching

21 Coconuts Inn, 2nd restaurant on left after stepping on to the beach. For dolphin watching trips or boats to Anjuna, Rs 150 for each.

Body and soul

Himalaya Iyengar Yoga Centre, T01892-221312, www.hiyogacentre.com. Classes conducted on a hard floor shaded by a parachute with breezes from the sea. Tipis are provided for long-term students.

Paragliding can also be arranged from beach shacks.

Morjim to Asvem *p401*

Body and soul

Raso Vai, S No 162/2-A, Morjim-Aswem Rd (towards Mandrem from Morjim), Mardi Wada, Morjim, T0932-626 6633, www.rasovai.com. Runs training courses in various forms of ayurvedic massage (10 days, US$270, 4 days US$180), as well as offering treatments such as panchakarma, swedan, pizhichil, dhara and snehapanam, from a community oriented centre with meditation.

Tour operators

Speedy, near post office Mazalvaddo, T0832-227 3208, 0900-1830. Very helpful for all your onward travel arrangements; also changes money. Very helpful, comprehensive service.

Windsurfing

Boards are sometimes available for hire at the south end of the beach for Rs 100 per hr.

Transport

Arambol *p399, map 400*

Regular buses from **Mapusa** and a frequent service from **Chopdem**, 12 km along the main road (about 40 mins); the attractive coastal detour via Morjim is slightly longer. It's a 2-hr walk north through Morjim and Mandrem by the coast. **Delight and Tara**, in the village, exchange cash and TCs, good for train tickets (Rs 100 service charge); also sells bus tickets.

Keri (Querim) and Tiracol fort *p400*

From **Panjim** direct bus at 1700, arrives 1930, returns to Panjim 0700 next morning.

Mandrem *p401*

Buses towards **Siolem** pass along the main road at about 0930 and 1345. Direct services also to **Mapusa** and **Panjim**.

Directory

Arambol *p399, map 400*

Medical services Pharmacy, on the main road; Health centre, T0832-229 1249. **Police** T0832-229 7614. **Post** The small village post office is at the T junction, 1500 m from the beach.

Mandrem *p401*

Banks Canara Bank, on the main road accepts TCs. **Hospital** T0832-223 0081.

South Goa

The prosperous south is poster-paint green; lush coconut thickets that stretch along the coastline blend with broad swathes of iridescent paddy, broken by the piercingly bright white spears of splendid church steeples. Beneath the coastal coconut fronds sit the pretty villages of fishermen and agriculturalists: Salcete taluka is where the Portuguese were most deeply entrenched, and in the district's interior lie the beautiful fossilized remnants of centuries-old mansion estates built by the Goan colonial elite. Sprawling drawing rooms and ballrooms are stuffed with chandeliers and antiques and paved with splendid marble, every inch the fairy tale doll's house. ▸▸ *For Sleeping, Eating and other listings, see pages 415-423.*

Margao and coastal Salcete

▸▸ *pp415-423. Colour map 1a, B2.*

A wide belt of golden sand runs the length Salcete's coast in one glorious long lazy sweep; tucked inland lie Goa's most imposing and deluxe hotels. Some beaches, like Varca and Cavelossim, are little more than an empty stretch of dune beside an isolated fishing hamlet, whereas Colva's tall palms spill over the beach to shade restaurants and a mini village of hotels and shops. Inland, in varied states of decline, lie the stately homes of Goa's landowning classes, the worn cases of homes once fit for princes.

Ins and outs

Getting there and around The Konkan Railway connects Margao directly with Mumbai, Mangalore and Kerala. Madgaon/Margao station is 1½ km southeast of the bus stands, municipal gardens and market area (where you'll find most of the hotels and restaurants). Rickshaws charge Rs 15 to transfer or walk the 800 m along the railway line. Interstate buses and those running between here and North Goa use the New Kadamba (State) bus stand 2 km north of town. City buses take you to the town bus stands for destinations south of Margao. Colva and Benaulim buses leave from the local stand east of the gardens. There are plenty of auto-rickshaws and eight-seater van taxis for hire. ▸▸ *See Transport, page 420, for futher details.*

Margao (Madgaon) → *Colour map 1a, B2.*

Margao is a fetching, bustling market town which, as the capital of the state's historically richest and most fertile fertile *taluka*, Salcete, is a shop window for fans of grand old Portuguese domestic architecture and churches. Sadly, in their haste to get to the nearby beaches, few tourists explore this charming, busy provincial town.

The impressive baroque **Church of the Holy Spirit** with its classic Goan façade dominates the Old Market square, the Largo de Igreja. Originally built in 1564, it was sacked by Muslims in 1589 and rebuilt in 1675. A remarkable pulpit on the north wall has carvings of the Apostles. There are also some glass cabinets in the north aisle containing statues of St Anthony and of the Blessed Joseph Vaz. Vaz was a homegrown Catholic missionary who smuggled himself to Sri Lanka dressed as a porter when the Dutch occupation challenged the island's faith. The church's feast day is in June.

The real gem of Margao is the glut of run-down 18th-century houses especially in and around Abade Faria Road, of which the **Da Silva House** ⓘ *Da Silva's descendants still live in a small wing of the house but visits can be fixed up via the local tourist office at the GTDC Residency*, is a splendid example. Built around 1790 when Inacio da Silva stepped up to become Secretary to the Viceroy, it has a long façade whose roof was once divided into seven separate 'towers', hence its other name, **Seven Shoulders**;

only three of these have survived. The house's grandeur is also evident in its interiors, featuring lavishly carved dark rosewood furniture, gilded mirrors and some fine chandeliers.

The **municipal market** (Mercado de Afonso de Albuquerque) is a labyrinthine treat of flower garlands, silks and agricultural yield.

Chandor

→ *Colour map 1a, B2.*

By the late 18th century, an educated middle-class elite had emerged in the villages of the Old Conquests. With newly established rights to property, well-to-do Goans began to invest in large homes and very fine living. West of the Zuari River, the villages of Lutolim and Chandor are two of a number that saw the development of estates and houses built on this grand scale. Their houses were stuffed with tokens of their Europeanization and affluence, mixed with traditions appropriated from their native ancestry, installing personal chapels instead of *devachem kuds*, or Hindu prayer rooms.

Despite being something of a backwater today, the once-grand village of Chandor nonetheless boasts several fine Portuguese mansions. Foremost among them is the

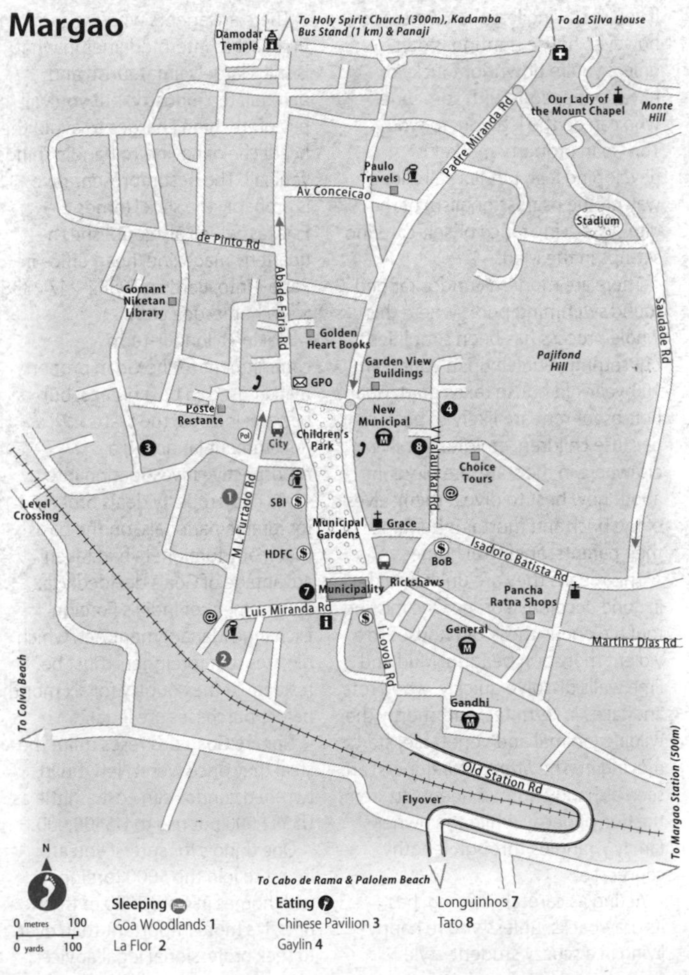

Living the dream?

The happy combination of easy living, tropical sun, cheap flights and the innumerable beautiful Portuguese-style houses – big porches, bright white lime walls, window panes of oyster shell and red tile roofs crumbling into disrepair – all across Goa has triggered many a foreigner's fantasy of getting their own tattered toehold in the state.

Renting is commonplace, and for US$300 a month you can snare yourself a six-bedroom place so romantically derelict you'd swoon. If you're staying less than the season, however, house hunting is daft, unless you're downright lucky or have connections with someone who can do the legwork for you. The Goan property market is developing fast, but it's still a long way off the professionalism of the gîte system in France or self-catering set-ups in the Med.

There are modern condos ranged round swimming pools where this whole process has been simplified, but setting yourself up in your own 100-year-old house takes graft. Goan houses for rent are likely to be vacant because children, emigrant or living elsewhere in the state, are bickering about how best to divest themselves of the brick and mortar inheritance of their parents' ancestral homes.

This means they are unlikely to be in good decorative order. One missing roof tile opens these old houses to a violent monsoon beating. Mud and lime walls dissolve quickly, wood rots and takes in termites, and shortly the wildlife (animal and vegetable) starts moving in. The *firangi* (foreigners) are seen as handy human agents to stem the tide of decay while the owner's family wrangles through lengthy court cases.

Acting as caretaker *firangi* has its drawbacks: unless you're happy living in a scuzzy student-style atmosphere, on your shopping list on day one will probably be a fridge, gas stove, pots and pans, beds, mattresses, sofas, water filter system and, importantly if you have possessions you'd worry about losing, some form of security. Landlords, fingers often burned, will ask for a steep deposit for things like telephones (up to Rs 5000), and you'll have to sign a short-term lease agreement. All of the above of course comes far cheaper than in England, Australia or America, but you could easily cough up US$2000 initially.

There are agents who are springing up to act as intermediaries in what is still a largely amateurish and deregulated industry, but you will pay pretty high charges to avoid the headache of having to handle things yourself. The best representative is probably the slick **Homes & Estates**, which also publishes a quarterly magazine, head office in Parra-Tinto, Bardez, T0832-247 2338, www.homesgoa.com.

Making a longer-term commitment to the Goan property market used to be a breeze, but beware. In 2006, the state government launched a retrospective investigation into some 445 property deals brokered for foreign nationals, on the basis that many foreigners had taken advantage of Goa's decidedly lax enforcement of India's Foreign Exchange Management Act, which dictates that foreigners must be resident in the country for six months before purchases are legal.

Nor are Goan des reses quite the steal they once were: New-build two-bed condos can cost as little as US$34,000 but rise to US400,000.

One thing's for sure: if you are intent to join the 5000 foreigners with homes in Goa, 3000 of them Brits, it's more important than ever to seek professional legal advice.

enormous **Menezes Braganza family house** ⓘ *13 km east of Margao, both wings are usually open 1000-1730 but it may be best to confirm by telephone. West Wing: T0832-278 4201, 1300-1400 or early evening after 1830. East Wing: T0832-278 4227. A donation of Rs 100 at the end of the tour will be greatly appreciated.* Luis de Menezes Braganza was an influential journalist and politician (1878-1938) who not only campaigned for freedom from colonial rule but also became a champion of the less privileged sections of Goan society. The late 16th-century two-storey mansion he inherited (extended in the 18th and 19th centuries), still complete with much of the family furniture and effects, shows the sheer opulence of the life enjoyed by those old Goan families who established great plantation estates. The two wings are occupied separately by members of the Braganza family who have inherited the property.

The **West Wing**, which is better maintained and has finer antiques, is owned by Aida de Menezes Braganza. The guided tour by this elderly member of the family – when she resides here – is fascinating. She has managed to restore the teak ceiling of the 250-year-old library gallery to its original state; the old *mareta* wood floor survived better since this native Goan timber can withstand water. There is much carved and inlaid antique furniture and very fine imported china and porcelain, some specially ordered, and bearing the family crest.

The faded **East Wing**, occupied by Sr Alvaro de Perreira-Braganza, partly mirrors the West Wing. It also has some excellent carved and inlaid furniture and a similar large salon with fine chandeliers. The baroque family chapel at the back now has a prized relic added to its collection, the bejewelled nail of St Francis Xavier, which had, until recently, been kept guarded away from public view.

The guide from the East Wing of the Braganza House can also show you the **Fernandes House** ⓘ *open daily, phone ahead T0832-278 4245, suggested donation Rs 100*, if he's not too busy. It's another example of a once-fine mansion just to the southeast of the village, on the Quepem road. This too has an impressive grand salon occupying the front of the house and a hidden inner courtyard. Recent excavations have unearthed an underground hiding place for when Christian families were under attack from Hindu raiders.

Back in Chandor village itself, the **Church of Our Lady of Bethlehem**, built in 1645, replaced the principal *Sapta Matrika* (Seven Mothers) temple, which was demolished in the previous century.

Chandor is closest to Margao but can also easily be visited from Panjim or the beaches in central Goa. It would be an arduous day trip from the northern beaches. Buses from Margao Kadamba bus stand (45 minutes) take you within walking distance of the sights but it is worth considering a taxi. Madgaon railway station, with connections to Mumbai and the Konkan coastal route as well as direct trains to Hospet, is close by.

Colva (Colwa) → *Colour map 1a, B2.*

Although it's just 6 km from the city and is the tourist hub of the southern beaches, sleepy Colva is a far cry from its overgrown northern equivalent Calangute. The village is a bit scruffy, but the beach ticks all the right boxes: powder puff white sands, gently swaying palms, blue waters and lines of local fishermen drawing their nets in hand over fist, dumping pounds of mackerel which are left to dry out in glistening silver heaps.

Margao's parasol-twirling elite, in their search for *mudanca* or a change of air, were the first to succumb to Colva's charms. They would commandeer the homes of local fisherfolk, who had decamped to their shacks for months leading up to the monsoon.

The large **Church of Our Lady of Mercy** (Nossa Senhora das Merces), dating from 1630 and rebuilt in the 18th century, has a relatively simple façade and a single tower on the south side that is so short as to be scarcely noticeable, and the strong horizontal lines normally given to Goan churches by three of four full storeys is broken by a narrow band of shallow semi-circular arches above the second floor. But the church is much less famous for its architecture than for the huge fair it hosts, thanks to its association with the miraculous **Menino Jesus**. Jesuit Father Bento Ferreira found the original image in the river Sena, Mozambique, en route to Goa, and brought it to Colva where he took up his position as rector in 1648. The image's miraculous healing powers secured it special veneration.

The **Fama of Menino Jesus festival** (Monday of 12-18 October) sees thousands of frantic devotees flock to kiss the statue in hope of a miracle. Near the church, specially blessed lengths of string are sold, as well as replicas of limbs, offered to the image in thanks for cures.

Betalbatim to Velsao

A short walk away is Betalbatim, named after the main Hindu temple to Betall which stood here before the deity was moved to Queula in Ponda for safety. This is a pleasant stretch with a mix of coconut palms and casuarinas on the low dunes. At low tide, when the firm sand is exposed, you can cycle for miles along the beach in either direction.

The four beaches north, **Velsao**, **Arossim**, **Utorda** and **Majorda** – broad, flat and open – are the emptiest: the odd fishing village or de luxe resort complex shelters under coconut thicket canopy.

Bogmalo is a small, palm-fringed and attractive beach that's very handy for the airport (only 4 km and a 10-minute drive away). **Hollant Beach**, 2 km further on, is a small rocky cove fringed with palm trees. From Bogmalo village you can get to **Santra Beach**, where fishermen will ferry you to two small islands for about Rs 350 per boat.

The quiet back lanes snaking between these drowsy villages make perfect bicycle terrain and Velsao boasts some particularly grand examples of old mansions.

Verna

The church at Verna (the 'place of fresh air'), inland from the northern Salcete beaches on the NH17, was initially built on the site of the Mahalsa Temple, which had housed the deity now in Mardol (see page 425) and featured exquisite carvings, but was

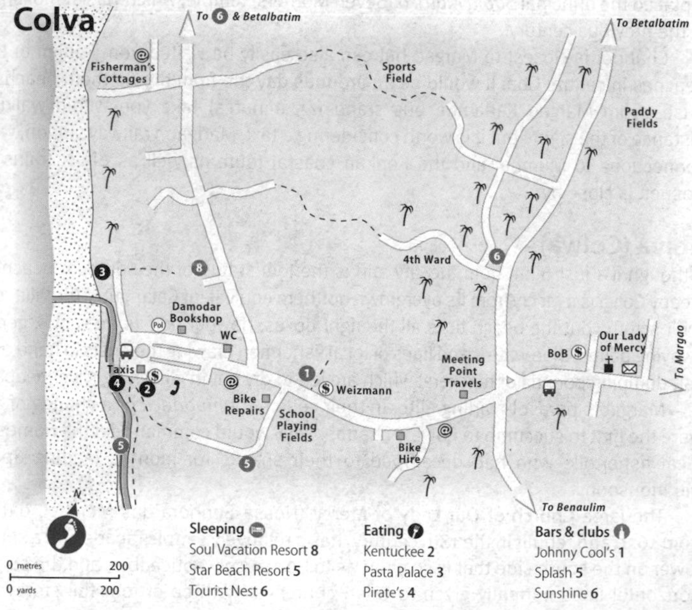

destroyed and marked by the cross to prevent it being re-used for Hindu worship. As a sanctuary for widows who did not commit *sati*, it was dubbed the Temple of Nuns.

Verna was also picked to house the ancient 2½ m **Mother Goddess figure** (fifth century BC) from Curdi (Kurdi) in Sanguem, which was under threat of being submerged by the Selaulim Dam project in 1988. Two megalithic sites were found in the area. It is surrounded by seven healing springs.

Just north towards Cortalim are the popular medicinal **Kersarval springs**.

Benaulim to Mobor → *Colour map 1a, B2. See also map, page 416.*

At Colva Beach's southern end lies tranquil **Benaulim**, which, according to the myth of Parasurama, is 'where the arrow fell' to make Goa. It is now a relaxed village set under palms, where business centres around toddy tapping and fishing. The hub of village activity is Maria Hall crossing, just over 1 km from the beach.

On a hill beyond the village is the diminutive **Church of St John the Baptist**, a fine piece of Goan Christian architecture rebuilt in 1596. Although the gable façade, with twin balustraded towers, is striking, the real treat is inside, in its sumptious altar *reredos* and wonderful rococo pulpit with its depiction of the Lamb of the Apocalypse from the Book of Revelation.

The picturesque lane south from Benaulim runs through small villages and past white-painted churches. Paddy gives way to palm, and tracks empty onto small seaside settlements and deserted beaches. Benaulim beach runs into **Varca**, and then Fatrade. **Cavelossim beach** is a short walk away, through scrub vegetation and dunes.

Farthest south, **Mobor**, about 8 km from Varca, lies on the narrow peninsula where the river Sal joins the sea. The Sal is a busy fishing route, but doubles as a lovely spot for boat rides.

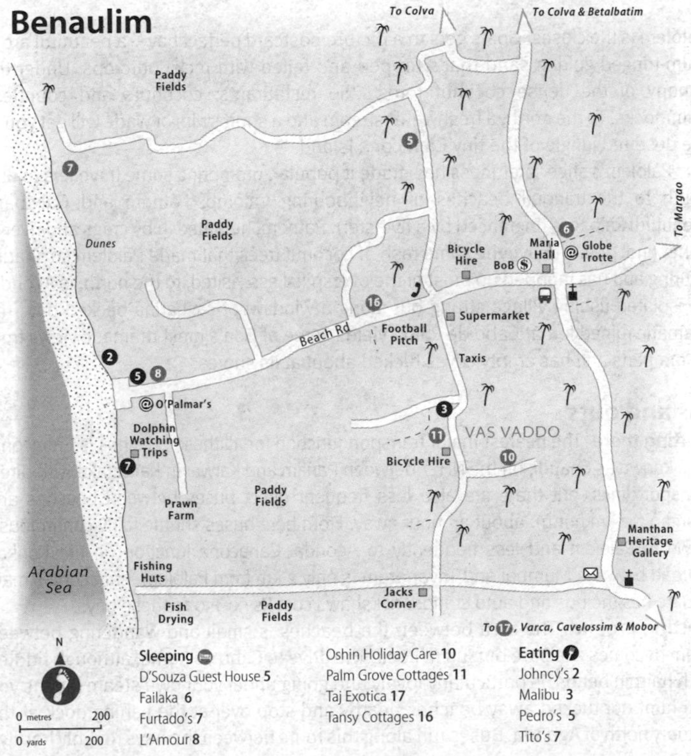

Betul → *See map, page 416.*

Idyllic Betul, which overlooks Mobor from the opposite bank of the Sal in Quepem *taluka*, is an important fishing and coir village shaded by coconut palms and jackfruit, papaya and banana trees. A sand bar traps the estuary into a wide and protected lagoon and the cool breezes from the sea temper even the hottest Goan high noon. Just after the bridge, which crosses the mouth of a small river, a narrow road off to the right by the shops zigzags through the village along the south side of the Sal.

From Cavelossim the shortest route to Betul is by taking the ferry across the Sal (signposted, just southeast) to Assolna; turn left off the ferry, then turn right in the village to join the main road towards Betul. From Margao, the NH17 forks right (6 km) towards Assolna at Chinchinim. A further 6 km on, there is a second turning in Cuncolim for Assolna. Buses from Margao to Betul can be very slow, but there is a fairly regular service stopping in all the settlements along the way (a couple of them continue as far as Cabo de Rama).

Cuncolim

The Jesuits razed Cuncolim's three principal Hindu temples (including the Shantadurga) and built churches and chapels in their stead.

Hindu 'rebels' killed five Jesuits and several converts in reprisal, triggering a manhunt which saw 15 men killed by the captain of Rachol Fort's soldiers. The relics of the Christian 'martyrs of Cuncolim' now lie in the Sé Cathedral in Old Goa (see page 372). The cathedral's golden bell, Goa's largest, was cast here in 1652.

Cabo de Rama, Palolem and the far south

» pp417-423. Colour map 1a, C2.

Palolem is the closest Goa's gets to a picture postcard perfect bay – a beautiful arc of palm-fringed golden sand that's topped and tailed with rocky outcrops. Under the canopy of the dense coconut forests lie restaurants, cocohuts and countless hammocks. To the north, a freshwater stream and a short swim or wade will get you to the deserted jungle of the tiny Canacona Island.

Palolem's sheer prettiness has made it popular, prompting some travellers to drift south to the tranquil beaches of neighbouring Calomb, Patnem and Galgibaga (beautiful Rajbag is ringfenced by a five-star). Patnem, hemmed in by crags and river at either end, doesn't have the same rash of coconut trees that made Palolem so shadily alluring and has mopped up most of the overspill. Less visited, to the north, is Agonda, an isolated fishing village strung out along a windswept casuarina-backed bay. The dramatic ruined fort at Cabo de Rama yields some of Goa's most dramatic views from its ramparts and has empty coves tucked about at its shores.

Ins and outs

Getting there The nearest major transport junction for all these beaches is Canacona, also known as Chaudi, on the NH17 between Panjim and Karwar in Karnataka with direct transport links, but there are also less frequent direct buses between beaches and Margao (37 km north), about an hour away. From here buses shuttle fairly continuously down to Palolem and less frequently to Agonda. Canacona Junction on the Konkan railroad between Mumbai and Trivandrum is only 2 km from Palolem. Canacona's main square has the bus and auto stands; rickshaws cost Rs 50-150 to these bays.

Getting around The area between the beaches is small and wandering between them becomes a leisure pursuit in itself. The drive to Cabo de Rama, although riddled with hairpin bends, is particularly lovely and going under your own steam means you can hunt out tucked away beaches nearby and stop over at the fishing dock at the estuary north of Agonda. Buses run along this route between the bays roughly hourly.

Cabo de Rama (Cape Rama) → *Colour map 1a, C2.*

Legend has it that the hero of the Hindu epic Ramayana lived in this desolate spot with his wife Sita during their exile from Ayodhya, and the fort predated the arrival of the Portuguese who seized it from its Hindu rulers in 1763. Its western edge, with its sheer drop to the Arabian Sea, gives you a stunning vista onto a secluded stretch of South Goa's coastline.

The main entrance seems far from impregnable, but the outer ramparts are excellently preserved with several cannons still scattered along their length. The gatehouse is only 20 m or so above the sea, and is also the source of the fort's water supply. A huge tank was excavated to a depth of about 10 m, which even today contains water right through the dry season. If a local herdsman is about ask him to direct you to the two springs, one of which gives out water through two spouts at different temperatures.

Agonda

Snake through forests and bright paddy south from Cabo De Rama towards Palolem to uncover artless Agonda, a windswept village backed by mountains of forestry full of acrobatic black-faced monkeys. Local political agitators thwarted plans for a five-star hotel and so have, temporarily at least, arrested the speed of their home's development as a tourist destination. Their success makes for a primitive holiday scene: a handful of internet points, less than a dozen restaurants and a small number of hotels and cocohuts are strewn out over the beach village's length. There's no house music, little throttling of Enfield engines and you need to be happy to make your own entertainment to stay here for any serious length of time. Less photogenic than Palolem, Agonda bay has pine-like casuarina trees lining the beach instead of coconuts and palms. The swimming is safe and the beach wonderfully calm. The northern end of the beach, close to the school and bus stop, has a small block of shops including the brilliantly chaotic and original **Fatima stores & restaurant** (Fatima Rodrigues, not one to be a jack of all trades, has limited her menu to just spaghetti and thali) and **St Annes bookstore**, a video library.

Palolem → *Colour map 1a, C2.*

For a short spell, when the police cracked down most severely on parties up north, Palolem looked like it might act as the Anjuna overflow. Today, **Neptune's Point** has permission to hold parties once every two weeks, but so far, Palolem's villagers are resisting the move to make the beach a mini-party destination and authorities are even stumping up the cash to pay for litter pickers. The demographic here is chiefly late-twenties and thirty-something couples, travellers and students. Canacona is the nearest settlement of any significant size and has shops and direct transport links – it is the southernmost stop on the Konkan Railway in Goa and is the crossroads on the NH17 between Panjim and the Karnataka port city of Karwar. The large church and high school of **St Tereza of Jesus** (1962) are on the northern edge of town.

Beaches further south

Over the rocky outcrops to the south you come to the sandy cove of **Calomb**. Wholly uncommercial, its trees are pocked with longstayers' little picket fences and stabs at growing banana plants, their earthy homesteads cheek by jowl with fishermen's huts. The only sound here is the rattle of coconut fronds and bird song. Although just a bay away, you could almost be on a different planet to Palolem.

At the end of the track through Calomb a collection of huts marks the start of the fine sweep of **Patnem Beach**. The 500 villagers here have both put a limit on the number of shacks and stopped outsiders from trading, and as a result the beach has conserved much of its unhurried charm. The deep sandbanks cushion volleyball players' falls and winds whip through kite flyers' sails: but fishing boats far outnumber sun loungers. A hit with old rockers, Israelis and long-stayers, there is no nightlife, no parties and, no coincidence, a healthy relationship between villagers and tourism.

Further south, wade across a stream (possible before the monsoon) to reach the dune- and casuarina-fringed **Rajbag Beach**, its southern waters a-bob with fishing boats. Although it's virtually unvisited and has perfect swimming, the luxury five-star that opened here in 2004 has provoked a storm of protest; allegations against the hotel include the limited access to the sea, the failure to meet local employment quotas, and the rebuilding of the ancient Shree Vita Rukmayee temple which villagers argue was tantamount to the hotel 'swallowing our God'. The isolated **Kindlebaga Beach** is east of Rajbag, 2 km from Canacona.

Hindu temples in Patnem have music most Fri and Sat with tabla, symbols and harmonica.

Galgibaga

Nip across the Talpona river by the ferry to reach a short strip of land jutting out to sea, where well-built houses lie among lucrative casuarina plantations. Like Morjim, Galgibaga beach is a favourite stopover for Olive Ridley turtles which travel vast distances to lay their eggs here each November. Shacks are mushrooming, to environmentalists' concern.

Partagali and Cotigao Wildlife Sanctuary → *Colour map 1a, C3.*

At a left turn-off the NH17, 7 km south of Canacona, to Partagali, a massive concrete gateway marks the way to the temple. If you go a little further, you reach a 2 km-long road that leads to the Cotigao Wildlife Sanctuary. Partagali's **Shri Sausthan Gokarn Partagali Jeevotam Math** is a centre for culture and learning on the banks of the river Kushavati. The *math* (religious establishment) was set up in AD 1475 at Margao when the followers, originally Saivites, were converted and became a Vaishnav sect. During the period of Portuguese Christianization (1560-68), the foundation was moved south to Bhatkal (in northern Karnataka). The sixth Swami returned the *math* to Partagali, and built its Rama, Lakshman, Sita and Hunuman temple. An ancient *Vatavriksha* (banyan tree) 65 m by 75 m, which represents this Vaishnav spiritual movement, is a sacred meditation site known as *Bramhasthan*. The tree and its *Ishwarlinga* (the *lingam* of the Lord, ie Siva) have drawn pilgrims for more than a millennium. The temple, which also has a typical tall Garuda pillar, celebrates its festival in March/April.

Cotigao Wildlife Sanctuary ⓘ *60 km south of Panjim, www.goaforest.com/wildlife mgmt/body_cotigao.htm, Rs 5, 2-wheelers Rs 10, cars Rs 50; camera Rs 25; video Rs 100, 0730-1730 all year (but may not be worthwhile during the monsoon)*, lies in one of the most densely forested areas of the state. The 86 sq km sanctuary is hilly to the south and east and has the Talpona river flowing through it. There is a nature interpretation centre with a small reference library and map of the park roads at the entrance. The vegetation is mostly moist deciduous with some semi-evergreen and evergreen forest cover. You may be very lucky and spot gazelles, panther, sloth bear, porcupine and hyena, and several reptiles, but only really expect wild boar, the odd deer and gaur and many monkeys; birdspotting is more rewarding. Rare birds include rufous woodpecker, Malabar crested lark and white-eyed eagle. You need your own vehicle to reach the treetop watchtowers and waterholes that are signposted, 3 km and 7 km off the main metalled road on a variable rough track. No guides but the forest paths are easy to follow – just make sure you have drinking water and petrol. The chances of seeing much wildlife, apart from monkeys, are slim, since by the opening time of 0730 animal activity has already died down to its daytime minimum.

The first tower by a waterhole is known as **Machan Vhutpal**, 400 m off the road, with great views of the forest canopy. The second tower is sturdier and the best place to spend a night (permission required).

Most visitors come for a day trip, but if you are keen on walking in the forest this is a great place to spend a day or two. You can either stay near the sanctuary office or spend a night in a watchtower deep in the forest. A short way beyond the sanctuary entrance the metalled road passes through a small hamlet where there is a kiosk for the villagers living within the reserve, which sells the usual array of basic provisions. If you are planning to spend a few days in the park it is best to bring your own fresh provisions and then let the staff prepare meals. Rudimentary facilities like snake proof campsites, with canvas tents available from the forest office. You'll also need written permission to stay in the forest resthouse or watchtower from the **Deputy Conservator Of Forests** ⓘ *3rd Floor, Junta House, Panaji,* as far in advance of a visit as possible.

The cheapest way to visit the park is to get a group together for a half day from Palolem. If you leave the beach just before 0700 you will be at the park gates when they open. Motorbikes are also allowed in the sanctuary.

Sleeping

Margao *p406, map p407*

D-E Goa Woodlands, ML Furtado Rd, opposite City Bus Stand, T0832-271 5521, woodland_goa@sancharnet.in. Good value, 35 rooms, 18 a/c, clean and spacious with bath, restaurant, bar, but has had mixed reports.

E La Flor, E Carvalho St, T0832-273 1402, laflor @sancharnet.in. 35 rooms with bath, half a/c, restaurant, clean, away from bustle of town.

Chandor *p407*

B The Big House, T0832-264 3477, www.ciarans.com. This is the renovated ancestral Portuguese/Goan home of John Coutinho, owner of Ciaran's Camp in Palolem (see page 417). It has high-beamed ceilings, stone walls and a terracotta tiled roof, large sitting room, fully fitted kitchen, hot water, a master bedroom with 4-poster and a twin, maid service, cable TV and DVD, phone and cooking available. Great for families, couples or groups of friends.

Colva *p409, map p410*

Most hotels are 6-8 km from Margao railway station. Prices rise on 1 Dec. Discounts are possible for stays of a week or more.

AL Soul Vacation Resort, 4th Ward, T0832-278 8144, www.nivalink.com/vistadecolva. 25 large a/c studio rooms, restaurant/bar with Goan specialities, large pool with chic loungers and daybeds, live entertainment, very comfortable. Formerly Vista De Colva.

C-D Star Beach Resort, just off Colva Beach Rd, T0832-273 4921, www.starbeachresort goa.com. 41 large rooms, TV, some a/c, good value from mid-Jan (Rs 600), clean pool, children's pool, best rooms 1st floor poolside have views across paddy fields, restaurant.

E Tourist Nest, 2 km from the sea, T0832-278 8624, touristnest@indiatimes.com. Old Portuguese house, 12 rooms in secure new block, fan, Rs 200 with bathroom, 2 small self-contained cottages, good restaurant. Old part of house recommended for atmospheric long stay (Rs 8000 per month for 2 bedrooms), spacious dining area, large lounge with antique furniture, private balcony, bathroom and cooking facilities.

F Maria Guest House, 4th Ward, near beach cafés. 7 rooms, some with bath, very friendly, helpful, car hire, popular with backpackers, good value. Recommended.

Betalbatim to Velsao *p410*

B Nanu Resort, near Betalbatim beach and paddy fields, T0832-288 0111, www.nivalink .com/nanu. 72 comfortable and spacious a/c rooms in 3-star, 2-storey chalet complex, refurbished restaurant arranged in a neat terrace with sea views. Imaginatively planned, good pool with great beach views, garden, beach beyond a narrow stream, tennis, badminton, secluded and peaceful. Very good value 1 May-30 Sep. Recommended.

D-E Manuelina Tourist House, behind Ray's. 5 spacious, clean rooms with bath, TV lounge, some food available, pleasant, secure, quiet. Recommended.

For an explanation of the sleeping and eating price codes used in this guide, see inside the front cover. Other relevant information is found in Essentials pages 40-44.

E Baptista, Beach Rd. 2 simple rooms with fan, 2 self-catering flats with gas stove, use of fridge and utensils (Rs 350), good for long stays, short walk from beach.

Benaulim to Mobor *p411, maps p411 and below*

Budget hotels can be found along Benaulim Beach Rd, and in the coconut groves on either side. Rooms in private houses and 'garden cottages' go for Rs 80-Rs 150; south along the beach from **Johncy's**, rooms just off the beach with bath, are Rs 80-Rs 100.

LL Taj Exotica, Calvaddo, towards Varca, T0832-277 1234, exoticabc.goa@tajhotels.com. 56 acres of greenery and views of virgin beaches from each of its 138 luxurious rooms. Good choice of restaurants, including Mediterranean, plus coffee shop, nightclub, excellent pool, golf course, floodlit tennis, kids' activities, jacuzzi, watersports, gym, jogging track, library and bike hire. Taamra Spa offers treatments like acupuncture, aromatherapy and Balinese massage.

L Club Mahindra, Varca Village, Varca, T0832-274 4555, www.clubmahindra.com. Top class, 51 spotless rooms with tubs, 5 suites, spacious public areas, excellent pool, gym, direct access to quiet beach, bit isolated.

C-D L'Amour, end of Beach Rd, Benaulim, T0832-277 0404. Close to sea, 20 rooms in a well-established hotel run by **Johncy's** beach shack. Good terrace restaurant, handy for exchange and booking rail and bus tickets.

D Failaka, Adsulim Nagar, near Maria Hall crossing, Benaulim, T0832-277 1270, hotel failaka@hotmail.com. 16 spotless, comfortable rooms, 4 with TV, quieter at rear, excellent restaurant, friendly family set-up. Recommended.

D Gaffino's, opposite Dona Sylvia, Mobor, 5 mins' walk from beach, T0832-287 1441, briangaffino@yahoo.com. 16 clean, simple rooms with bath on 4 floors, 2 a/c, balconies overlook river or sea (in the distance), B&B, personal service, package oriented, in the centre of all the action.

D Hippo Cool, next to Gaffino's, Mobor, T0832-287 1201. Only 5-min walk from the beach, 6 clean, very comfortable rooms with fan (a/c on request) and shower, restaurant. Recommended.

D-E Palm Grove Cottages, Vas Vaddo, Benaulim, T0832-277 0059, palmgrovecottages@yahoo.com. 14 clean spacious rooms. The newer block at rear with showers and balconies is better. Pleasant palm-shaded garden, good food, not on the beach but plenty of places to hire a bicycle just outside. Recommended.

E D'Souza Guest House, north of Beach Rd in Benaulim, T0832-277 0583. 5 very clean rooms, good food (see below), garden, friendly family. Recommended.

E Oshin Holiday Care, House no 126, Vas Vaddo, Benaulim, T0832-277 0069. You'll need a bicycle to get to the beach but the peaceful location overlooking ponds is well worth it. 14 good large rooms with bath on 3 floors (room 11 best, **D**), breakfast, dinner on request, friendly manager, superb well-kept grounds. Highly recommended.

E Tansy Cottages, Beach Rd, Benaulim, T0832-277 0574. Good value, 7 very clean,

large rooms with bath, 2 cottages, good restaurant (super breakfast), friendly. Recommended.

F Furtado's, T0832-274 5474. In the dunes just above the beach, 6 basic rooms set around a small garden with palms. Popular budget option. Shacks for meals nearby.

Agonda *p413*

E Casa Maria, T0832-264 7237. Sea views, but overlooks the back of Eldfra. 4 rooms with clean tiled bathroom, fan, veranda.

E-F Dercy Beach Resort, T0832-264 7503. 50-year-old family house developed to fit 12 clean rooms with bathrooms. Over the road on the beach are 12 basic bamboo huts with spotless shared wash block.

F Sun Set Bar, T0832-264 7381. This place has 7 simple cottages (with more planned) with great views, shared facilities. The restaurant perched high on the rocks has the prime location in Agonda. Recommended.

Palolem *p413*

Palolem's popularity has soared inordinately. Off season, bargain hard and ask around for rooms inside family houses. These can have very basic facilities (eg 'pig' toilets, raised on a platform where pigs do the necessary 'cleaning out' below), some are lovely though and let you use their kitchen and fridge, **F**.

B Ciaran's Camp, beach, T0832-264 3477, johnciaran@hotmail.com. Huts are spaced wide apart in palm-covered landscaped gardens. A library, lovely shop, table tennis and great restaurant plus promises of live jazz all make it the leader in Palolem cool.

B-C Bhakti Kutir, T0832-264 3469, www.bhaktikutir.com. On a hilltop in a coconut grove is this visionary home of unhurried eco-friendly charm. The German Goan owners have a family – children are generously catered for with special school classes and babysitters. The food is super-healthy. Accommodation is rustic ethno-eco-hippy: compost toilets, bucket baths, cabanas made of rice straw, bamboo and mud. Highly recommended.

D Dream Catcher, riverbank, North Palolem, T0832-264 4873, lalalandjackie7@yahoo.com. 11 lovely huts all with fan. Yoga, reiki courses, massage, jazz, funk soul, chill-out music policy. Great atmosphere.

E Cozy Nook, at northern end, T0832-264 3550. Plastered bamboo huts, fans, nets, shared toilets, in a good location between the sea and river, ayurvedic centre, art and crafts, friendly. Recommended.

F Palolem Beach Resort and south of Cocohuts, camping and parking for campers and travellers (Rs 15-20 per day).

Beaches further south *p413*

Demand and room rates rocket over the Christmas period in Patnem.

LL InterContinental, Rajbaga, T0832-264 4777, www.ichotelsgroup.com. 34 ha of 5-star hotel between the Talpone river and the Sahayadri mountain range. 255 sea-facing rooms, 9-hole golf course, 5 restaurants, health spa, watersports, even a luxury yacht.

B Oceanic Hotel, T0832-264 3059, www.hotel-oceanic.com. 9 good rooms, either large or small doubles (some with TV) swimming pool and hot water. Massage available, good cocktails and restaurant.

C-D Home Guesthouse, Patnem, T0832- 264 3916, homeispatnem@yahoo.com. Just 8 rooms with fan and French linen close to the beach. Aims to become a forum for local artists and has occasional live music.

D Solitude Dream Woods, Patnem, T0832-271 1186, ashper2002@yahoo.com. All-wood beach camp with pine and bamboo structures, one of the most advanced developments in Patnem.

Eating

Margao *p406, map p407*

TT Chinese Pavilion, M Menezes Rd (400 m west of Municipal Gardens). Chinese. Smart, a/c, good choice.

TT Gaylin, 1 V Valaulikar Rd. Chinese. Tasty, hot Szechuan, comfortable a/c.

TT Longuinhos, near the Municipality. Goan, North Indian. Open all day for meals and snacks, bar drinks and baked goodies.

TT Tato, G-5 Apna Bazaar, Complex, V Valaulikar Rd. Superb vegetarian, a/c upstairs.

TT Utsav, Nanutel Hotel. Pleasant, serving a large range of Goan dishes.

T Café Margao. Good South Indian snacks.

Colva *p409, map p410*

¥ **Joe Con's**, 4th Ward. Excellent fresh fish and Goan dishes, good value.

¥ **Kentuckee**, good seafood, select from fresh fish brought to table.

¥ **Pasta Palace**, overlooking the beach at the Colmar. Good Italian with bar.

¥ **Pirate's**, near the beach. Recommended for seafood.

Betalbatim to Velsao *p410*

¥¥¥ **Martin's Corner**, T0832-213 1676. Coming from the south, look for sign on left after village, 500 m down lane on right, opposite open ground. Holds over 200 undercover in front of an old house. Extensive menu, superb lobster Rs 1500, tiger prawns Rs 500-700, crab Rs 300-500. Recommended.

¥¥ **Roytanzil Garden Pub**, set back from the beach at the end of Majorda beach road past **Martin's Corner** (no sea views). Neat grounds, alfresco and small covered area. Seafood and Indian. One of the best restaurants on the south coast.

Benaulim to Mobor *p411, maps p411 and p416*

Beach shacks offer Goan dishes and seafood at reasonable prices. Around **Dona Sylvia**, several come alive in the evening.

¥¥¥ **Taj Exotica's**, Benaulim, restaurants are faultless; spread of Mediterranean, gourmet Goan or authentic Chinese.

¥¥ **Grill Room**, Fatrade Beach Rd. 1830-2230. Pleasant steakhouse with a simple menu. Tiger prawns Rs 400, steaks Rs 150.

¥¥ **La Afra**, Tamborin, Fatrade. Excellent steaks and fresh fish, sensibly priced. Boatmen ferry holidaymakers to **River Sal**, Betul.

¥¥ **Pedro's**, by the car park above the beach, Benaulim. Good seafood and tandoori. Imaginative menu, friendly.

¥¥ **River View**, Cavelossim. Tranquil, open-air location, overlooking river. International menu, wide choice, good ambience despite ugly hotel developments surrounding it. Cocktails Rs 100, sizzlers Rs 150-200, tiger prawns Rs 500.

¥¥ **Tito's**, Benaulim, on beach. English breakfast Rs 80.

¥ **D'Souza's**, Benaulim, good juices, lassis and fast food.

¥ **Goan Village**, lane opposite Dona Sylvia, Tamborim, south of Cavelossim. The best here for all cuisines.

¥ **Johncy's**, Benaulim, varied menu, good seafood, big portions, tandoori recommended (after 1830) but service can be erratic. Pleasant atmosphere though; backgammon, scrabble.

¥ **Malibu**, Benaulim, nice lush garden setting for spicy fish/meat kebabs.

Cabo de Rama *p412*

¥ **Pinto's Bar**, near the fort entrance. Meals and cool drinks on a sandy shaded terrace, may also have rooms. If there are few visitors about (most likely) ask here for a meal before exploring the fort to save time waiting later.

Palolem *p413*

¥¥ **Bhakti Kutir** serves excellent fresh fish dishes, homegrown organic produce and fresh juices. Name any number of obscure nutritious grains and they'll be here.

¥¥ **The Cheeky Chapatti**, sells kingfish wraps and tasty fusion food; the closest you'll get to a gastropub in Goa. Great veggie choices.

¥¥ **Cool Breeze**, Main Rd, T0942-206 0564, coolbreezegoa@hotmail.com. One of the perennial favourites like **Dropadi** that's probably got the best steaks in town.

¥¥ **Dropadi Beach Restaurant and Bar**. Routinely packed out. Lobster and lasagne and North Indian food are the specials.

¥¥ **Mamoo's**, on the corner where the road turns to meet the beach, T0832-264 4261, mamoosplace@rediffmail.com. A third long-standing favourite, famous for its grilled fish. Only comes alive in the evening.

¥¥ **Oceanic Hotel**, up on the hill north of the beach. Fresh soup on the menu every day and their chef spent last season moving through the Delia Smith recipe books. Great seafood and cocktails; popular in the evening.

¥ **Brown Bread and Health Food**, near Syndicate Bank, T0832-264 3604. Quite possibly the best breakfast in Palolem.

¥ **Tibet Bar and Restaurant**, Main Rd, T0982-214 2775. Super fresh ingredients in excellent Himalayan dishes. Small restaurant that's worth stepping back from the beach for.

Bars and clubs

Colva *p409, map p410*

Johnny Cool's, halfway up busy Beach Rd. Scruffy surroundings but popular for chilled beer and late-night drinks.

Splash, this is *the* place for music, dancing and late drinking, open all night, trendy, very busy on Sat (full after 2300 Mon-Fri in season), good cocktails, poor bar snacks. It may not appeal to all, especially unaccompanied women.
Sunshine, bar and restaurant, north end of beach. Popular evenings, hammocks overlooking beach, pool table, 60s music, small dance floor, gardens. Relaxed atmosphere.

Benaulim to Mobor *p411, maps p411 and p416*
Aqua, Leela Palace, Mobor, is a gaming room and cigar lounge which turns into a late-night disco after 2000.

Palolem *p413*
Bridge and Tunnel Pub Living Huts, in the rocks towards Calomb, T0832-263 3237, sera_goa@rediffmail.com. Pool for Rs 100 per hr and a laid-back beach pub/lounge area filled with rugs and cushions, but allegations centring on the development's proximity to the beach and methods of waste disposal have led some to boycott it.
Cuba Beach Cafe, behind Syndicate Bank, T0832-264 3449. Cool, upbeat bar for a sundowner. **Café Del Mar** next door does excellent fresh nosh too.
Neptune's Point Bar and Restaurant, T0982-258 4968. Wide dancefloor for a mellow daily chill-out from 1700-2200 with a proper party on a weekly basis.
Rock It Café, north end of beach. Coffee from Bodum filters, backgammon, and Sade often on the playlist; a stoner's paradise shack.

❁ Festivals and events

Chandor *p407*
Jan 6 Three Kings Festival Crowds gather on each year at Epiphany for the Three Kings Festival, which is similarly celebrated at Reis Magos, with a big fair, and at Cansaulim (Quelim) in southern Goa. The 3 villages of Chandor (Cavorim, Guirdolim and Chandor) come together to put on a grand show. Boys chosen from the villages dress up as the three kings and appear on horseback carrying gifts of gold, frankincense and myrrh. They process through the village before arriving at the church where a large congregation gathers.

Colva *p409, map p410*
Oct 12-18 (Mon that falls between these dates) **Fama of Menino Jesus** when thousands of pilgrims flock to see the statue in the **Church of our Lady of Mercy** in the hope of witnessing a miracle.

Benaulim to Mobor *p411, maps p411 and p416*
In Benaulim, **Jun 24 Feast of St John the Baptist** (*Sao Joao*) gives thanks for the arrival of the monsoon. Young men wearing crowns of leaves and fruits tour the area singing for gifts. They jump into wells (which are usually full) to commemorate the movement of St John in his mother's womb when she was visited by Mary, the mother of Jesus!

Palolem *p413*
Feb Rathasaptami The Shri Malikarjuna Temple 'car' festival attracts large crowds.
Apr Shigmo, also at the Shri Malikarjuna Temple, also very popular.

O Shopping

Margao *p406, map p407*
The Old Market was rehoused in the 'New' (Municipal) Market in town. The covered **market** (Mon-Sat, 0800-1300, 1600-2000) is fun to wander around. It is not at all touristy but holidaymakers come on their shopping trip to avoid paying inflated prices in the beach resorts. To catch a glimpse of the early morning arrivals at the **Fish Market** head south from the Municipal Building.

Books and CDs
Golden Heart, off Abbé Faria Rd, behind the GPO, closed 1300-1500. Bookshop.
Nanutel Hotel. Small bookshop.
Trevor's, 5 Luis Miranda Rd. Sells CDs.

Clothes
J Vaz, Martires Dias Rd, near Hari Mandir, T0832-272 0086. Good quality men's tailor.
MS Caro, Caro Corner. An extensive range including 'suiting', and will advise on tailors.

Benaulim to Mobor *p411, maps p411 and p416*
Khazana, Taj Exotica, Benaulim. A veritable treasure chest (books, crafts, clothes) culled from across India. Pricey.

Manthan Heritage Gallery, main road. Quality collection of art items.

Activities and tours

Colva *p409, map p410*

Tour operators

Meeting Point, T0832-272 3338, for a very efficient, reliable travel service, Mon-Sat 0830-1900 (sometimes opens later if busy).

Betalbatim to Velsao *p410*

Watersports

Goa Diving, Bogmalo. A morning office at Joet's, and based at Chapel Bhat, Chicalim, T0832-255 5117, goadiving@goatelecom.com. PADI certification from Open Water to Assistant Instructor.

Splash Watersports, Bogmalo, T0832-240 9886. Run by Derek, a famous Indian champion windsurfer. Operates from a shack on the beach just below **Joet's**, providing parasailing, windsurfing, waterskiing, trips to nearby islands; during the high season only.

Benaulim to Mobor *p411, maps p411 and p416*

Body and soul

At **Taj Exotica**, Benaulim, yoga indoors or on the lawn. Also aromatherapy, reflexology.

Dolphin watching

The trips are scenic and chances of seeing dolphin are high, but it gets very hot (take a hat, water and something comfy to sit on). Groups of dolphins here are usually seen swimming near the surface. Boats from **Café Dominick**, Benaulim, (signs on the beach) and several others charge about Rs 300. Most hotels arrange river trips and dolphin viewing, or call T0832-287 1455. River trips 1600-1730, dolphin trips 0800-1000 and sunset cruises depart at 1700. Expect to pay Rs 250.

Betty's Place, in a road opposite Holiday Inn, Mobor, arranges boat trips for fishing, dolphin viewing and trips up river Sal 1030-1630 (food included). Recommended.

Palolem *p413*

Boat hire and trips

You can hire boats to spend a night under the stars on the secluded Butterfly or Honeymoon beaches, and many offer dolphin watching and fishing trips. You can see the dolphins from dry land around Neptune's Point, or ask for rowing boats instead of motorboats if you want to reduce pollution. Mornings 0830-1230 are best. Arrange through **Palolem Beach Resort**, travel agents or a fisherman. 4 people for about Rs 600 for 1-hr trip, Rs 1500 for 3 hrs. Take sunscreen, shirt, hat and drinking water.

Ciaran's Camp, T0832-264 3477, runs 2-hr mountain bike tours or charter a yacht overnight through Ciaran's bar for Rs 8000.

Body and soul

Harmonic Healing and Music Centre, Colomb, T0982-251 2814, www.harmonicingoa.com. US$350 for a 2-week course.

A non-residential reiki, alternative medicine and Indian classical music healing retreat by the sea run by an English couple, Natalie Mathos and Marc Clayton. Accommodation options include **Green Park**, a lively place with pleasant huts on the shore and a good restaurant and bar, and **Laguna Vista**, which is a little more basic with bamboo huts and good Goan health food. Retreats generally run Nov-Mar. Transfers to the hotel of your choice from Dabolim airport for US$68.

Tour operators

Bliss Travels 118/1 near main gate, Palolem Beach, T0832-264 3456, bliss_travels@rediffmail.com. Air tickets (domestic and international), money change, bus services, speedy internet, ISD, plus package tours to nature reserves and retreat farm.

Rainbow Travels, T0832-264 3912. Efficient flight and train bookings, exchange, Western Union money transfer, safe deposit lockers (Rs 10 per day), good internet connection.

Transport

Margao *p406, map p407*

Bus

The local bus stand is by the municipal gardens. You can usually board buses near Kamat Hotel, southeast of the gardens. The Kadamba (new) bus stand is 2 km north of town (city buses to the centre, or motorcycle taxi Rs 8); buses arriving before 1000 and after 1900, proceed to the centre. To **Benaulim**, **Cabo da Rama** 0730 (2 hrs);

Canacona and Palolem, several; **Colva**: hourly; **Gokarna**, 1300 daily.

Non-stop KTC buses to **Panjim**: 1 hr. Buy tickets from booth at stand No 1.

Private buses (eg Paulo, Metropole Hotel, T0832-272 1516), Padre Miranda Rd: to **Bengalure (Bangalore)** (15 hrs); **Mangalore** 1800, 2130 (8-10 hrs), Rs 140; **Mumbai (Dadar/CST)** 1400, 1700 (16 hrs), Rs 600 (sleeper); **Pune** 1700 (13 hrs), Rs 450 (sleeper).

Car hire

Sai Service, T0832-273 5772. Rs 700-Rs 900 per day with driver.

Rickshaw

Auto-rickshaw to **Colva**, Rs 30; beach, Rs 50.

Train

Enquiries T0832-273 2255. The new station on the broad gauge network is 500 m south of the old station. The reservation office on the 1st floor of the new station is usually quick and efficient, with short queues. Mon- Sat 0800-1400, 1415-2000, Sun 0800-1400. Tickets for **Mumbai** and **Delhi** should be booked well ahead. Confirm Indrail Pass reservations in Vasco, Mumbai or Mangalore.

Konkan Kanya Express (night train) and Mandovi Express (day train) from **Mumbai** also stop at **Tivim** (for northern beaches; take the local bus into Mapusa and from there catch another bus or take a taxi) and **Karmali** (for Panjim and Dabolim airport) before terminating at **Margao**. Both are very slow and take nearly 12 hrs. From **Mumbai (CST)**: *Mandovi Exp 0103*, 0515 (arr 1815), (13 hrs, 2nd class 3-tier Rs 670), doesn't stop at Pernem; *Konkan Kanya Exp 0111*, 2250 (arr 1045).

Delhi (Nizamuddin): *Rajdhani Exp 2431*, 1145, Wed, Fri; *Goa Exp 2779*, 1427, 35 hrs. **Ernakulam (Jn)**: *Mangalore Exp 2618*, 2055, 17 hrs. **Hospet (for Hampi)**: *Vasco-da-Gama Vijayawada Exp 7228*, 0720, Wed, Sat, 8½ hrs. **Mumbai (CST)**: *Mandovi Exp 0104*, 1030, 11½ hrs (via Karmali, Tivim); *Konkan Kanya Exp 0112*, 1800, 12 hrs (via Karmali, Tivim, Pernem). **Mumbai Kurla (Tilak)**: *Netravati Exp 6346*, 0640, 12 hrs (via Karmali, Tivim). **Thiruvananthapuram (Trivandrum)**: *Rajdhani Exp 2432*, 1300, Mon, Wed, 18 hrs. *Netravati Exp 6345*, 2255, 18 hrs (via Canacona for Palolem beach).

The broad gauge line between **Vasco** and **Londa** in Karnataka runs through Margao and Dudhsagar Falls and connects stations on the line with **Belgaum**. There are services to **Bengaluru (Bangalore)** *Vasco Bangalore Exp 7310*, 2059, Mon, Thu.

The pre-paid taxi stand is to the right of the exit (charges are for 1 person with 1 piece of luggage); to **Margao centre** Rs 50, **Panjim** Rs 480 (45 mins), **Anjuna** Rs 670; **Calangute** Rs 600; **Colva** Rs 130, **Palolem** Rs 480; rates are clearly displayed outside the office. **Autos** to **Colva** Rs 100, to **Panjim** Rs 320. Avoid tourist taxis, they can be 5 times the price.

Colva *p409, map p410*

Air From the airport, taxis charge about Rs 280. If arriving by train at Margao, 6 km away, opt for a bus, auto-rickshaw or taxi for transfer. Buses pull in at the main crossroads and then continue to the beach 1 km away before returning. Auto-rickshaws have a Rs 30 'minimum charge' around Colva itself.

Bicycle hire Mostly through hotels, Rs 20-25 per day (discounts for long term). Motorbikes for hire through most hotels (see also Panjim), Rs 200 per day (less for long-term rental), more for Enfields, bargain hard.

Bus To **Anjuna** Wed for the Flea Market, tickets through travel agents, depart 0930, return 1730, Rs 90-100; to **Margao** half-hourly, take 30 mins, Rs 3 (last bus 1915, last return, 2000).

Taxi Also to **Margao**, motorcycle taxi, Rs 20-25 (bargain hard); auto-rickshaw, Rs 30-40.

Betalbatim to Velsao *p410*

Bus

Buses from Margao (12 km), motorcycle taxis charge Rs 35. The **Margao-Vasco** bus service passes through the Cansaulim centre.

Taxi

Taxis to/from **airport**, 20 mins (Rs 300); **Margao** 15 mins (Rs 200). From **Nanu Resort**, Panjim Rs 500, Anjuna Rs 750, or Rs 700 for 8 hrs, 80 km.

Train

Cansaulim station on the Vasco-Margao line is handy for **Velsao** and **Arossim** beaches and Majorda station for **Utorda** and **Majorda** beaches. Auto-rickshaws meet trains.

From Cansaulim there are 3 trains a day to **Vasco** (Rs 6) via **Dabolim** for the airport; 0746, 1411, 1818. For **Kulem** (Dudhsagar Falls) (Rs 12) via Margao (Rs 6), 0730, 1330, 1750.

From Majorda there are 3 trains a day to **Vasco** (Rs 5) 0741, 1406, 1813. For **Kulem** (Dudhsagar Falls) (Rs 10) via Margao (Rs 5), 0737, 1337, 1757.

Benaulim to Mobor *p411, maps p411 and p416*

Buses from all directions arrive at Maria Hall crossing, Benaulim. Taxis and autos from the beach esplanade near Pedro's and at Maria Hall crossing. To/from **Margao**: taxis Rs 100; autos Rs 80; bus Rs 5. **Anjuna** Wed flea market bus 0930, return 1530, Rs 95, 2 hrs.

From Margao to **Cavelossim**, the bus is uncomfortably slow (18 km); autos transfer from bus stand to resorts. From **Margao** taxis charge around Rs 200, and from **Dabolim airport**, takes under 1 hr. It crosses the river Sal, southeast of Cavelossim and **Assolna**, which sells petrol, and the lane from the river joins the main road, NH17.

Rocks, outside Dona Sylvia, cycles Rs 10 per hr, Rs 150 a day; scooters Rs 300 a day without petrol, Rs 500 with 7 litres of fuel. In Benaulim, bikes and scooters for hire, Rs 35 and Rs 150 per day.

Agonda *p413*

From Palolem/Chaudi Junc, auto-rickshaws charge Rs 120-150; turn off the road by Niki bar and restaurant. **Dunhills Hotel**, Agonda, hires out scooters, motorbikes and cars.

Bus

First direct bus for **Margao** leaves between 0600-0630, last at 1000, takes about 1 hr. Alternatively, arrange a lift to the main road and flag down the next bus (last bus for Margao passes by at around 2000, but it is advisable to complete your journey before dark). Hourly buses between **Betul** and **Palolem** call at Agonda (and Cabo de Rama). Easy to visit for the day by taxi, motorbike or bicycle from Palolem beach.

Palolem *p413*

Bus

There are 6 daily direct buses run between Margao and **Canacona** (40 km via Cuncolim), Rs 9, on their way to **Karwar**. From Canacona, taxis and auto-rickshaws charge Rs 40-60 to **Palolem** beach only 2 km away. From Palolem, direct buses for Margao leave at around 0615, 0730, 0930, 1415, 1515, 1630 and take 1 hr. At other times of the day take a taxi or rickshaw to the main road, and flag down the next private bus. Frequent private services run to Palolem and Margao as well as south into **Karnataka**.

Train

From Canacona Junction station, 2 km away from Palolem beach. The booking office opens 1 hr before trains depart. Inside the station there is a phone booth and a small chai stall. A few auto-rickshaws and taxis meet all trains. If none is available walk down the approach road and turn left under the railway bridge. At the next corner, known locally as Chaurasta, you will find an auto-rickshaw to take you to **Palolem** beach (Rs 50) or **Agonda** beach; expect to pay double for a taxi.

To **Ernakulam Junction**, *Netravati Exp 6345*, 2325, 15 hrs, sleeper Rs 280, 3 tier a/c Rs 790, and on to **Thiruvananthapuram** (20 hrs); **Mangalore**, *Matsyagandha Exp 2619*, 0105, 6 hrs, Rs 49; **Margao**, 2 passenger trains a day, *KAM 2up*, 0630, *KAR 2up*, 1237, 45 mins, Rs 11; **Mumbai (Tilak)**, *Netravati Exp 6346*, 0548, 13 hrs, 2nd Cl sleeper Rs 300, 3 tier a/c Rs 800; via Margao 45 mins; **Mumbai (Thane)**, *Matsyagandha Exp 2620*, 1910, 12 hrs; via Margao 45 mins.

Beaches further south *p413*

For **Canacona**, buses run to Palolem and Margao and also to Karnataka.
You can hire a bicycle for Rs 4 per hr or Rs 35 per day. Direct buses for Margao leave at around 0615, 0730, 0930, 1415, 1515, 1630 and take an hour. Alternatively, take a taxi or rickshaw to the main road and flag down the next private bus. Palolem is 3 km from Canacona Junction station, which is now on the Konkan line (*Netravati Express*).

Directory

Margao *p406, map p407*

Banks Bank of Baroda, behind Grace Church; also in Market, Station Rd; **Bank of India**, exchanges cash, TCs, Visa and Mastercard; **HDFC**, 24 hr ATM for MasterCard. **State Bank of India**, west of the Municipal Gardens. Get exchange before visiting beaches to the south where it is more difficult. International money transfer is possible through **Weizmann**, 650 Costa Dias Building, NH 17 (Mon-Sat 1000-1800). There is also a branch in Colva. **Fire** T0832-272 0168. **Hospital** Ambulance T0832-272 2722; **JJ Costa Hospital**, Fatorda, T0832-272 2586; **Hospicio**, T0832-272 2164; **Holy Spirit Pharmacy**, 24 hrs. **Internet** **Cyber Inn**, 105 Karnika Chambers, V Valauliker Rd, 0900-2000, Rs 30 per hr; **Cyber Link**, Shop 9, Rangavi Complex. **Police** T0832-272 2175. **Post office** North of children's park; **Poste Restante**, near the telegraph office, down lane west of park, 0830-1030 and 1500-1700 Mon-Sat.

Benaulim to Mobor *p411, maps p411 and p416*

In Benaulim: **Bank** **Bank of Baroda**, near Maria Hall, best rates (better than at travel agents and STD booths). **Bank of Baroda**, near the church in Cavelossim, Mon-Wed, Fri, Sat 0930-1330, accepts Visa, Mastercard, Tcs and has very helpful staff. **Internet** **GK Communications**, Beach Rd. 24 hr phone, money exchange and internet with 4 terminals, book ahead when very busy, Rs 100 per hr. **Pharmacy** Late night near the main crossroads.

Palolem *p413*

Banks Several exchanges along the beach approach road issue cash against credit cards, usual commission, 3-5%. **Internet** Widely available throughout the village, rates approximately Rs 60 per hr. **Post** Nearest in Canacona. **Useful services** Petrol Aryadurga HP station 1 km north of the Palolem turning, towards Margao.

Ponda and interior Sanguem

There is enough spirituality and architecture in the neighbouring districts of Ponda and Salcete to reverse even the most cynical notions of Goa as a state rich in beach but weak on culture. Once you've had your fill of basking on the sand you'll find that delving into this geographically small area will open up a whole new, and richly rewarding, Goa.

Just over the water lies Salcete and the villages of Goa's most sophisticated and urbane elite, steeped in the very staunchest Catholicism. Here you can see the most eloquent symbols of the graceful living enjoyed by this aristocracy in the shape of palatial private homes, the fruits of their collusion with the colonizers in faith. Ironically, one of the finest – Braganza House in Chandor – is also the ancestral home of one of the state's most vaunted freedom fighters, Luis de Menezes-Braganza. ▸▸ *For Sleeping, Eating and other listings, see pages 430-430.*

Ponda and around

▸▸ *pp430-430. Colour map 1a, B2.*

Ponda, once a centre of culture, music, drama and poetry, is Goa's smallest *taluka*. It is also the richest in Goan Hindu religious architecture. A stone's throw from the Portuguese capital of Old Goa and within 5 km of the district's traffic-snarled and fume-filled town centre are some of Goa's most important temples including the Shri Shantadurga at Queula and the Nagesh Temple near Bandora. Ponda is also a pastoral haven full of spice gardens and scenic views from low hills over sweeping rivers. The Bondla Sanctuary in the east of the *taluka*, though small and underwhelming in terms of wildlife, is a vestige of the forest that once cloaked the foothills of the Western Ghats.

Ins and outs

Getting there Ponda town is an important transport intersection where the main road from Margao via Borlim meets the east-west National Highway, NH4A. Buses to Panjim and Bondla via Tisk run along the NH4A, which passes through the centre of town. ▸▸ *See Transport details, page 430, for further details.*

Getting around The temples are spread out so it's best to have your own transport: take a bike or charter an auto-rickshaw or taxi; you'll find these around the bus stand.

History

The Zuari river represented the stormy boundary between the Christianized Old Conquests and the Hindu east for two centuries. St Francis Xavier found a dissolute band of European degenerates in the first settlers when he arrived in the headquarters of Luso-India and recommended the formation of an Inquisition. Although founded – in 1560 – to redress the failings within their own community, the Portuguese panel's remit quickly broadened as they found that their earliest Goan converts were also clinging clandestinely to their former faith. So the inquisitors set about weeding out these 'furtive Hindus', too, seeking to impose a Catholic orthodoxy and holding great show trials every few years with the public executions of infidels. Outside those dates set aside for putting people to death, intimidation was slightly more subtle: shrines were desecrated, temple tanks polluted and landowners threatened with confiscation of their holdings to encourage defection. Those unwilling to switch religion instead had to look for places to flee, carrying their idols in their hands.

When the Conquistadores – or *descubridores* – took to sacking shrines and desecrating temple images, building churches in their place, the keepers of the Hindu faith fled for the broad river's banks and the Cumbarjua creek to its west, crossing it to build new homes for their gods.

Ponda

Ponda wasn't always the poster-boy for Goa's Hindu identity that it is today. The **Safa Mosque** (Shahouri Masjid), the largest of 26 mosques in Goa, was built by Ibrahim 'Ali' Adil Shah in 1560. It has a simple rectangular chamber on a low plinth, with a pointed pitched roof, very much in the local architectural style, but the arches are distinctly Bijapuri. Because it was built of laterite the lower tier has been quite badly eroded. On the south side is a tank with *meherab* designs for ritual cleansing. Large gardens and fountains here were destroyed under the Portuguese, today the mosque's backdrop is all natural instead – it's set off by low rising forest-covered hills.

Khandepar

Meanwhile, for a picture of Goa's Buddhist history, travel 4 km east from Ponda on the NH4A to Khandepar to visit Goa's best-preserved cave site. Believed to be Buddhist, it dates from the 10th or 11th century. The first three of the four laterite caves have an outer and an inner cell, possibly used as monks' living quarters. Much more refined than others discovered in Goa, they show clear evidence of schist frames for doors to the inner cells, sockets on which wooden doors would have been hung, pegs carved out of the walls for hanging clothing, and niches for storage and for placing lamps. The site is hidden on the edge of a wooded area near a tributary of the Mandovi: turn left off the main road from Ponda, look for green and red archaeological survey sign, just before the bridge over the river. Right after the football pitch then walk down the track off to the right by the electric substation.

Farmagudi

On the left as you approach Farmagudi from Ponda is a **Ganesh Temple** built by Goa's first Chief Minister, Shri D Bandodkar, back in the 1960s. It is an amalgam of ancient and modern styles. Opposite is a statue of Sivaji commemorating the Maratha leader's association with **Ponda's fort**. The fort was built by the Adil Shahis of Bijapur and destroyed by the Portuguese in 1549. It lay in ruins for over a century before Sivaji conquered the town in 1675 and rebuilt it. The Portuguese Viceroy attempted to re-take it in October 1683 but quickly withdrew, afraid to take on the Maratha King Sambhaji, who suddenly appeared with his vast army.

Velinga

Lakshmi-Narasimha Temple ⓘ *from the north take a right immediately after crossing a small river bridge*, Goa's only temple to Vishnu's fourth avatar, the Lakshmi-Narasimha or Lakshmi-Narayana, is just north of Farmagudi at Velinga. The small half-man, half-lion image at this 18th-century temple was whisked away from the torches of Captain Diogo Rodrigues in 1567 Salcete. Its tower and dome over the sanctuary are markedly Islamic. Inside there are well-carved wooden pillars in the *mandapa* and elaborate silverwork on the screen and shrine.

Priol

The Shri Mangesh Temple ⓘ *to the northwest of Ponda set on a wooded hill at Priol on the NH4A leading to Old Goa*, is an 18th-century temple to Siva's incarnation as the benevolent Mangesh is one of the most important Hindu temples in Goa. Its Mangesh *lingam* originally belonged to an ancient temple in Kushatali (modern day Cortalim) across the river. The complex is typical of Goan Hindu temple architecture and the surrounding estate on which the temple depends provides a beautiful setting. Note the attractive tank on the left as you approach which is one of the oldest parts of the site. The complex, with its *agrashalas* (pilgrims' hostel), administrative offices and other rooms set aside for religious ceremonies, is a good representative of Goan Hindu temple worship: the temple is supported by a large resident community who serve its various functions. **Jatra** is 25 February.

Mardol

Two kilometres on from Shri Mangesh, the early 16th-century **Mahalsa Narayani Temple** is dedicated to Mahalsa, a Goan form of Vishnu's consort Lakshmi or, according to some, the god himself in female form *Mohini* (from the story of the battle between the *devas* and *asuras*). The deity was rescued from what was once a fabulous temple in Verna at around the same time as the Mangesh Sivalinga was brought to Priol. The entrance to the temple complex is through the arch under the *nagarkhana* (drum room). There is a seven-storeyed *deepstambha* and a tall brass Garuda pillar which rests on the back of a turtle, acting as an impressive second lamp tower. The half-human half-eagle *Garuda*, Vishnu's vehicle, sits on top. A stone 'cosmic pillar' with rings, next to it, signifies the axis along which the temple is aligned. The new *mandapa* (columned assembly hall) is made of concrete, but is hidden somewhat under the red tiling, finely carved columns and a series of brightly painted carvings of the 10 *avatars*, or incarnations, of Vishnu. The unusual dome above the sanctuary is particularly elegant. A decorative arched gate at the back leads to the peace and cool of the palm-fringed temple tank. A palanquin procession with the deity marks the February Mardol Jatra, Mahasivaratri is observed in February-March and Kojagiri Purnima celebrated at the August-September full moon.

Bandora

A narrow winding lane dips down to this tiny hamlet and its **temple** ⓘ *head 4 km west of Ponda towards Farmagudi on the NH4A, look for a fork signposted to Bandora*, to Siva as Nagesh (God of Serpents). The temple's origin is put at 1413 by an inscribed tablet here, though the temple was refurbished in the 18th century. The temple tank, which is well stocked with carp, is enclosed by a white-outlined laterite block wall and surrounded by shady palms. The five-storey lamp tower near the temple has brightly coloured deities painted in niches just above the base, the main *mandapa* (assembly hall) has interesting painted woodcarvings illustrating stories from the epics *Ramayana* and *Mahabharata* below the ceiling line, as well as the *Ashtadikpalas*, the eight Directional Guardians (Indra, Agni, Yama, Nirritti, Varuna, Vayu, Kubera and Ishana). The principal deity has the usual *Nandi* and in addition there are shrines to Ganesh and Lakshmi-Narayan and subsidiary shrines with *lingams*, in the courtyard. The Nagesh Jatra, normally in November, is celebrated at full moon to commemorate Siva's victory.

In a valley south of the Nagesh Temple lies the **Mahalakshmi Temple**, thought to be the original form of the deity of the Shakti cult. Mahalakshmi was worshipped by the Silaharas (chieftains of the Rashtrakutas, AD 750-1030) and the early Kadamba kings. The sanctuary has an octagonal tower and dome, while the side entrances have shallow domes. The stone slab with the Marathi inscription dating from 1413 on the front of the Nagesh Temple refers to a temple to Mahalakshmi at Bandora. The *sabhamandap* has an impressive gallery of 18 wooden images of Vishnu. Mahalakshmi is special in that she wears a *lingam* in her headdress and is believed to be a peaceful, 'Satvik', form of Devi; the first temple the Portuguese allowed at Panjim is also dedicated to her.

Queula (Kavale)

Just 3 km southwest from Ponda's town centre bus stand is one of the largest and most famous of Goa's temples; dedicated to **Shantadurga** (1738), the wife of Siva as the Goddess of Peace. She earns the Shanti (Sanskrit for peace) prefix here because, at the request of Brahma, she mediated in a great quarrel between her husband and Vishnu, and restored peace in the universe. In the sanctuary here she stands symbolically between the two bickering gods. The temple, which stands in a forest clearing, was built by Shahu, the grandson of the mighty Maratha ruler Sivaji, but the deity was taken from Quelossim well before then, back in the 16th century. It is neo-classical in design: its two-storey octagonal drum, topped by a dome with a lantern, is a classic example of the strong impact church architecture made on Goan temple design. The interior of polished marble is lit by several chandeliers. Steps lead up to the temple complex which has a very large tank cut into the hillside and a spacious courtyard surrounded by the usual pilgrim hostels and administration offices.

Shri Sausthan Goud Padacharya Kavale Math, named after the historic seer and exponent of the Advaita system of Vedanta, was founded between Cortalim and Quelossim. This Hindu seminary was destroyed during the Inquisition in the 1560s and was temporarily transferred to Golvan and Chinar outside Goa. After 77 years, in the early 17th century, the Math regrouped here in Queula, the village where the Shantadurga deity (also originating in Quelossim) had been reinstalled. There is a temple to Vittala at the Math. The foundation has another Math at Sanquelim.

Goa Ponda & interior Sanguem

North of Ponda

» *pp429-430. Colour map 1a, B2.*

The Spice Hills

There are a number of spice plantations in the foothills around northeast Ponda that have open their gates to offer in-depth tours on medicinal and food uses of plants during a walk through cultivated forests. These are surprisingly informative and fun. Of these, Savoi Spice Plantation is probably the most popular and the guide is excellent.

Savoi Spice Plantation ⓘ *T0832-234 0243, www.savoiplantation.com, 0800-1800, guided tour Rs 300, 1 hr, awkward to reach by public transport, ask buses from Ponda or Banastari heading for Volvoi for the plantation*, 6 km from Savoi, now over 200 years old, covers 40 ha focused around a large irrigation tank. Half the area is wetland and the other half on a hillside, making it possible for a large variety of plants and trees to grow. The plantation was founded by Mr Shetye and is now in the hands of the fourth generation of his family, who regularly donate funds to local community projects such as the school and temple. All plants are grown according to traditional Goan methods of organic farming. The tour includes drinks and snacks on arrival, and concludes with the chance to buy packets of spices (good gifts to take home) and a tot of *feni* to 'give strength' for the return journey to your resort. You will even be offered several cheap, natural alternatives to Viagra, whether you need them or not!

Pascoal Spice Plantation ⓘ *near Khandepar between Ponda and Tisk, T0832-234 4268, 0800-1800, tours Rs 300, signposted 1½ km off the NH4A*, grows a wide variety of spices and exotic fruit and is pleasantly located by a river. A guided tour takes you through a beautiful and fascinating setting. Spices are sold.

Sahakari Spice Farm ⓘ *on the Ponda-Khandepar road, Curti, T0832-231 1394*, is also open to the public. The spice tour includes an authentic banana-leaf lunch.

Tropical Spice Plantation ⓘ *Keri, T0832-234 0329, tours Rs 300, boats for hire Rs 100, clearly signposted off the NH4A, just south of the Sri Mangesh temple*, is a pleasant plantation located in a picturesque valley in Keri. It has well-informed guides and friendly staff. It specializes in medicinal uses for the spices, the majority of which seem to be good for the skin. At the end of the tour an areca nut picker will demonstrate the art of harvesting by shinning up a tall palm with his feet tied together in a circle of rope. The demonstration ends with the equally impressive art of descent, a rapid slide down the trunk like a fireman. After the tour a delicious lunch is served in the shade overlooking a lake, with boats for hire – good for early morning birdwatching.

> *Taxis from the coastal resorts cost around Rs 700 return from Candolim, but it's better value to ask a travel agent as many offer competitive rates including entrance fees.*

Bondla Wildlife Sanctuary

ⓘ *Mid-Sep to mid-Jun, Fri-Wed 0930-1730. Rs 5, camera Rs 25, video Rs 100, 2-wheelers Rs 10, cars Rs 50. Buses from Ponda via Tisk and Usgaon stop near the sanctuary where you can get taxis and motorcycle taxis. KTC buses sometimes run weekends from Panjim. During the season the Forest Department minibus should do 2 daily trips (except Thu) between Bondla and Tisk: from Bondla, 0815, 1745; from Tisk, 1100 (Sun 1030) and 1900. Check at the tourist office first. If you are on a motorbike make sure you fill up with petrol; the nearest pumps are at Ponda and Tisk. Bondla is well signposted from the NH4A east of Ponda (5 km beyond Usgaon, a fork to the right leads to the park up a winding steep road).*

Bondla, 20 km northeast of Ponda, is the most popular of Goa's three sanctuaries because it is relatively easily accessible. The small, 8 sq km sanctuary is situated in the foothills of the Western Ghats; sambar, wild boar, gaur (Indian bison) and monkeys live alongside a few migratory elephants that wander in from Karnataka during the summer. The mini-zoo here guarantees sightings of 'Goa's wildlife in natural surroundings', although whether the porcupine and African lion are examples of indigenous species is another matter. Thankfully, the number of animals in the zoo has decreased in recent years and those that remain seem to have adequate space compared to other zoos in India. The small and basic Nature Education Centre has the facility to show wildlife videos, but is rarely used. Five-minute elephant rides are available 1100-1200 and 1600-1700. A deer safari (minimum eight people), 1600-1730, costs Rs 10. The park also has an attractive picnic area in a botanical garden setting and a 2.4 km nature trail with waterholes, lake and treetop observation tower.

Central and southern interior » pp430-430.

Colour map 1a, B2/3.

Sanguem, Goa's largest *taluka*, covers the state's eastern hill borderland with Karnataka. The still-forested hills, populated until recently by tribal peoples practising shifting cultivation, rise to Goa's highest points. Just on the Goan side of the border with Karnataka are the Dudhsagar falls, some of India's highest waterfalls, where the river, which flows into the Mandovi, cascades dramatically down the hillside. Both Bhagwan Mahaveer Sanctuary and the beautiful, small Tambdi Surla Temple can be reached in a day from the coast (about two hours from Panaji).

Ins and outs

Getting there Buses running along the NH4A between Panjim, Ponda or Margao and Belgaum or Bengaluru (Bangalore) in Karnataka stop at Molem, in the north of the *taluka*. Much of the southeastern part of Sanguem remains inaccessible. Trains towards Karnataka stop at Kulem (Colem) and Dudhsagar stations. Jeeps wait at Kulem to transfer tourists to the waterfalls. If you are traveling to Tambdi Surla or the falls from north or central Goa, then the best and most direct route is the NH4A via Ponda. By going to or from the southern beaches of Salcete or Canacona you can travel through an interesting cluster of villages, only really accessible if you have your own transport, to see the sites of rock-cut caves and prehistoric cave art. ➡ *See Transport, page 430.*

Getting around There is no direct public transport between Molem and the sites, but the town is the start of hikes and treks in December and January.

Bhagwan Mahaveer Sanctuary → *Colour map 1a, B3.*

ⓘ *T0832-4260 0231. 0830-1730 except public holidays. Rs 5, 2-wheelers Rs 10, cars Rs 500. Tickets at the Nature Interpretation Centre, 100 m from the police check post, Molem. Entrance to the Molem National Park, within the sanctuary, 100 m east of the Tourist Complex, is clearly signed but the 14 km of tracks in the park are not mapped.*

Goa's largest wildlife sanctuary holds 240 sq km of lush moist deciduous to evergreen forest types and a herd of gaur (*bos gaurus*, aka Indian bison). The **Molem National Park**, in the central section of the sanctuary, occupies about half the area with the **Dudhsagar Falls** located in its southeast corner; the remote **Tambdi Surla Temple** is hidden in the dense forest at the northern end of the sanctuary. Forest department jeeps are available for viewing within the sanctuary; contact the Range Forest Officer (Wildlife), Molem. Motorbikes, but not scooters, can manage the rough track outside the monsoon period. In theory it is possible to reach Devil's Canyon and Dudhsagar Falls via the road next to the Nature Interpretation Centre (from where entrance tickets are sold), although the road is very rough and it may require a guide. Make sure you have a full tank of petrol if attempting a long journey into the forest.

Sambar, barking deer, monkeys and rich birdlife are occasionally joined by elephants that wander in from neighbouring Karnataka during the summer months, but these are rarely spotted. Birds include the striking golden oriole, emerald dove, paradise flycatcher, malabar hornbill and trogon and crested serpent eagle.

Dudhsagar Falls

The spectacular Dudhsagar Falls on the border between Goa and Karnataka are the highest in India and measure a total drop of about 600 m. The name, meaning 'the sea of milk', is derived from the white foam that the force of the water creates as it drops in stages, forming pools along the way. They are best seen just after the monsoon, between October and December, but right up to April there is enough water to make a visit worthwhile. You need to be fit and athletic to visit the falls.

Until quite recently it was possible to visit Dudhsagar by rail as the line runs across about the mid-point of the vertical drop of the cascades, and the small **Dudhsagar railway station** ⓘ *at present the trains run twice a week (Tue and Sat from Margao), but there are no return trains on these days*, allowed you to step down and then walk back to the opening between the two train tunnels, offering a route to the beautiful pools. As the road route described below is in some ways tougher and less attractive than visiting by train we have retained the following description in case the station re-opens in the near future. When arriving by train, a rough, steep path takes you down to a viewing area which allows you a better appreciation of the falls' grandeur, and to a beautifully fresh pool which is lovely for a swim (take your costume and towel). There are further pools below but you need to be sure-footed. The final section of the journey is a scramble on foot across stream beds with boulders; it is a difficult task for anyone but the most athletic. For the really fit and adventurous the arduous climb up to the head of the falls with a guide, is well worth the effort. Allow three hours, plus some time to rest at the top.

By road, motorbikes, but not scooters, can get to the start of the trail to the falls from Molem crossroads by taking the road south towards Kulem. From there it is 17 km of rough track with at least two river crossings, so is not recommended after a long period of heavy rain. The ride through the forest is attractive and the reward at the end spectacular, even in the dry season. A swim in the pool at the falls is refreshing after a hot and dusty ride. Guides are available but the track is easy to follow even without one.

Tambdi Surla

ⓘ *A taxi from Panjim takes about 2½ hrs for the 69 km. There is no public transport to Tambdi Surla but it is possible to hike from Molem. From the crossroads at Molem on the NH4A, the road north goes through dense forest to Tambdi Surla. 4 km from the crossroads you reach a fork. Take the right fork and after a further 3 km take a right turn at Barabhumi village (there is a sign). The temple is a further 8 km, just after Shanti Nature Resort. Make sure you have enough petrol before leaving Molem. It is also possible to reach the site along minor roads from Valpoi. The entrance to the temple is a short walk from the car park.*

This **Mahadeva (Siva) Temple** is a beautifully preserved miniature example of early Hindu temple architecture from the Kadamba-Yadava period. Tucked into the forested foothills, the place is often deserted, although the compound is well maintained by the Archaeology Department. The temple is the only major remaining example of pre-Portuguese Hindu architecture in Goa; it may well have been saved from destruction by its very remoteness.

Sleeping

Ponda *p424*
Ponda is within easy reach of any of Goa's beach resorts and Panjim.
C-D **Menino**, 100 m east of Bus Stand junction, 1st floor, T0832-231 3148. Good value, impressive modern hotel, 20 rooms, some a/c, pleasant, comfortable, good restaurant serves generous main courses.
E **Padmavi**, Gaunekar House, 100 m north of bus stand on NH4A, T0832-231 2144. Some of the 20 large clean rooms, have bath and TV.
E **President**, 1 km east of bus stand, supermarket complex, T0832-231 2287. 11 rooms, basic but clean and reasonable.

Farmagudi *p424*
C-D **Atish**, just below Ganesh Temple on NH4A, T0832-233 5124, www.hotelatish.com. 40 comfortable rooms, some a/c, restaurant, large pool in open surrounds, gym, modern hotel, many pilgrim groups, friendly staff.
E **Farmagudi Resort**, attractively located though too close to NH4A, T0832-233 5122. 39 clean rooms, some a/c, dorm (Rs 80), adequate restaurant (eat at Atish).

The Spice Hills *p426*
B **Savoi Farmhouse**, T0832-234 0243. An idyllic traditional Goan-style farmhouse built from mud with 2 adjoining en suite double rooms each with private veranda. Electricity and hot water; rates are for full board and include plantation tour. A night in the forest is memorable, highly recomm ended. Ideally, stay 2 nights exploring deep into the forested hills, good for birdwatching.

Bondla Wildlife Sanctuary *p427*
F **Eco-Cottages**, reserve ahead at Deputy Conservator of Forests, Wildlife Division, 4th floor, Junta House, 18th June Rd, Panjim, T0832-222 9701, although a room

or bed is often available to anyone turning up. 8 basic rooms with attached bath, newer ones better. Also 1 km inside park entrance (which may be better for seeing wildlife at night) are 2 dorms of 12 beds each (Rs 30).

Bhagwan Mahaveer Sanctuary *p428*
There is no accommodation inside the sanctuary; carry provisions. The nearest GTDC accommodation is the Tourist Complex in Molem, east along the NH4A from the Molem National Park entrance.
E Tourist Resort (GTDC), 300 m east of police check post, about 500 m from the temple, Molem, T0832-260 0238.
23 simple but well-maintained, clean rooms, some a/c, dorm, check-out 1200, giving time for a morning visit to Tambdi Surla, uninspired restaurant with limited menu serving north Indian food and beer.
F Molem Forest Resthouse. Book via the Conservator's Office, 3rd floor, Junta House, 18th June Rd, Panjim, T0832-222 4747.

Tambdi Surla *p429*
C Shanti Nature Resort, 500 m from temple. Contact in advance **Passive Active Tourism** (Freedom Holidays), Hotel Four Pillars, Panjim, T0832-222 2986. Emphasis on rest, ayurvedic treatment and meditation, 9 large mud huts with palm-thatched roofs, electricity and running water in natural forest setting. Restaurant, spice garden visits, birdwatching, hikes, trips to Dudhsagar etc, arranged (2 nights, US$120). Highly recommended for location and eco-friendly approach.

Eating

Ponda *p424*
Amigos, 2 km east of centre on Belgaum rd.
Spoon Age, Upper Bazaar, T0832-2316191. Garden restaurant, Goan meals for locals, friendly set-up. Occasional live music Sat-Sun.

The Spice Hills *p426*
Glade Bar and Restaurant, Pascoal Spice Plantation. 1130-1800. Good but pricey. **Tropical Spice Plantation** also serves delicious lunches.

Bondla Wildlife Sanctuary *p427*
The Den Bar and Restaurant near the entrance, serves chicken, vegetables or fish with rice. A small café, inside park near mini-zoo, sells snacks and cold drinks.

Activities and tours

Bhagwan Mahaveer Sanctuary *p428*
Popular hiking routes lead to Dudhsagar (17 km), the sanctuary and Atoll Gad (12 km), Matkonda Hill (10 km) and Tambdi Surla (12 km). Contact the **Hiking Association**, 6 Anand Niwas, Swami Vivekananda Rd, Panjim.

Transport

Ponda *p424*
Bus To **Panjim** and **Bondla** via Tisk, but it is best to have your own transport.

Bhagwan Mahaveer Sanctuary *p428*
Road
If coming from the south, travel via Sanguem. The road from Sanvordem to the NH17 passes through mining country and is therefore badly pot-holed and has heavy lorry traffic. From Kulem, jeeps do the rough trip to **Dudhsagar** (Rs 300 per head, Rs 1800 per jeep). This is a very tough and tiring journey at the best of times. From Molem, a road to the south off the NH4A leads through the forested hills of Sanguem *taluka* to **Kulem** and **Calem** railway stations and then south to **Sanguem**. From there, a minor road northwest goes to **Sanvordem** and then turns west to **Chandor**.

Buses between **Panjim**, **Ponda** or **Margao**, and **Belgaum/Bengaluru (Bangalore)**, stop at Molem for visiting the Bhagwan Mahaveer Sanctuary and Dudhsagar Falls.

Train
From the southern beaches, you can get the Vasco-Colem Passenger from Vasco at 0710, or more conveniently Margao (Madgaon) at 0800, arriving at **Kulem** (Colem) at 0930. Return trains at 1640, arriving **Margao** at 1810; leave plenty of time to enjoy the falls. Jeep hire is available from Kulem Station.

Directory

Ponda *p423*
Internet Fun World.Com, Viradh Building, T0832-231 6717. **Useful contacts** Deputy Conservator of Forests (North) T0832-231 2095. Community Health Centre, T0832-231 2115.

Mumbai (Bombay)

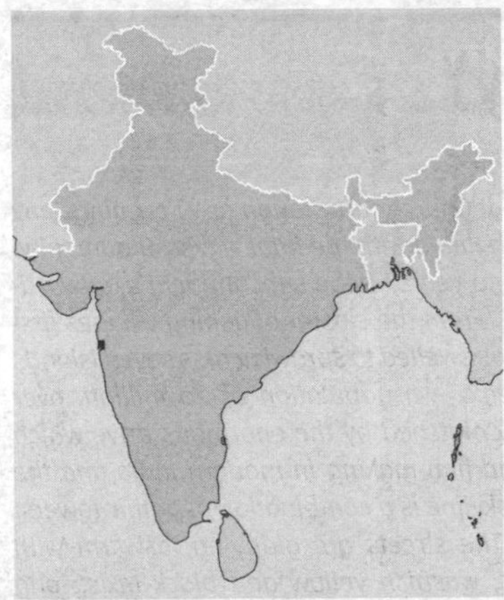

Footprint features

Mumbai (Bombay)

➔ *Phone code: 022. Colour map 1, grid B3.*

You are always in a crowd in this city. Stand at Churchgate station or VT terminus any time after 0600 on a weekday and be overwhelmed with the tidal waves of humanity. Mumbai, India's economic capital for over 150 years, is the subcontinent's outward-looking commercial face and its melting pot. From the cluster of fishing villages first linked by the British East India Company, it has swelled to sprawl across seven islands joined into an artificial isthmus. Its problems – a population of 20 million, over two-thirds of whom live in slums – are only matched by the enormous drive which makes it the centre of business, fashion and film-making in modern India and the great repository for the country's hopes. Its skyline is a combination of gothic towers, skyscrapers, mill chimneys and shanties. The streets are giddying, aswarm with panel-beaten English double-decker buses, waspish yellow and black taxis, long wooden carts stacked with hessian-stitched blocks of cargo and mangoes carried in pyramids on plates. ▸▸ *For Sleeping, Eating and other listings, see page 442-454.*

Ins and outs

Getting there Chhatrapati Sivaji International air terminal is 30 km from Nariman Point, the business heart of the city. The domestic terminals at Santa Cruz are 5 km closer. Pre-paid taxis to the city centre are good value and take between 40 minutes and 1½ hours, but there are also cheaper but slower buses. If you arrive late at night without a hotel booking it is best to stay at one of the hotels near the domestic terminal before going into town early in the morning. ▸▸ *See Transport, page 451, for further details.*

Getting around The sights are spread out and you need transport. Taxis are metered and generally good value. There are frequent buses on major routes, and the two suburban railway lines are useful out of peak hours on some routes, but get horrendously crowded. Auto-rickshaws are only allowed in the suburbs.

Tourist information **Government of India** ⓘ *123 M Karve Rd, opposite Churchgate, T022-2209 3229, Mon-Sat 0830-1730 (closed 2nd Sat of month from 1230); counters open 24 hrs at both airports; Taj Mahal Hotel, Mon-Sat 0830-1530 (closed 2nd Sat from 1230)*. Helpful staff who can also issue liquor permits (essential for Gujarat). **Maharashtra Tourist Development Corporation** ⓘ *www.maharashtratourism.gov.in, CDO Hutments, Express Towers, 9th floor, Nariman Pt, T022-2202 4482; Madam Cama Rd, T022-2202 6713; Koh-i-Noor Rd, near Pritam Hotel, Dadar T022-2414 3200; CST Railway Station, T022-2262 2859; Gateway of India, T022-2284 1877*. Information and booking counters at international and domestic terminals.

History

Hinduism made its mark on Mumbai long before the Portuguese and then the British transformed it into one of India's great cities. The caves on the island of Elephanta were excavated under the Kalachuris (AD 500-600). Yet, only 350 years ago, the area occupied by this great metropolis comprised seven islands inhabited by Koli fishermen. The British acquired these marshy and malarial islands as part of the marriage dowry paid by the Portuguese when Catherine of Braganza married Charles II in 1661. Four years later, the British took possession of the remaining islands and neighbouring mainland area and in 1668 the East India Company leased the whole area from the crown for £10 a year, which was paid for nearly 50 years. The East India Company shifted its headquarters to Mumbai in 1672. Until the

Bombay, named after the Portuguese for good harbour (bom bahia), was rechristened Mumbai after Mumba Devi, a Koli goddess, following fierce lobbying from Shiv Sena.

Mumbai

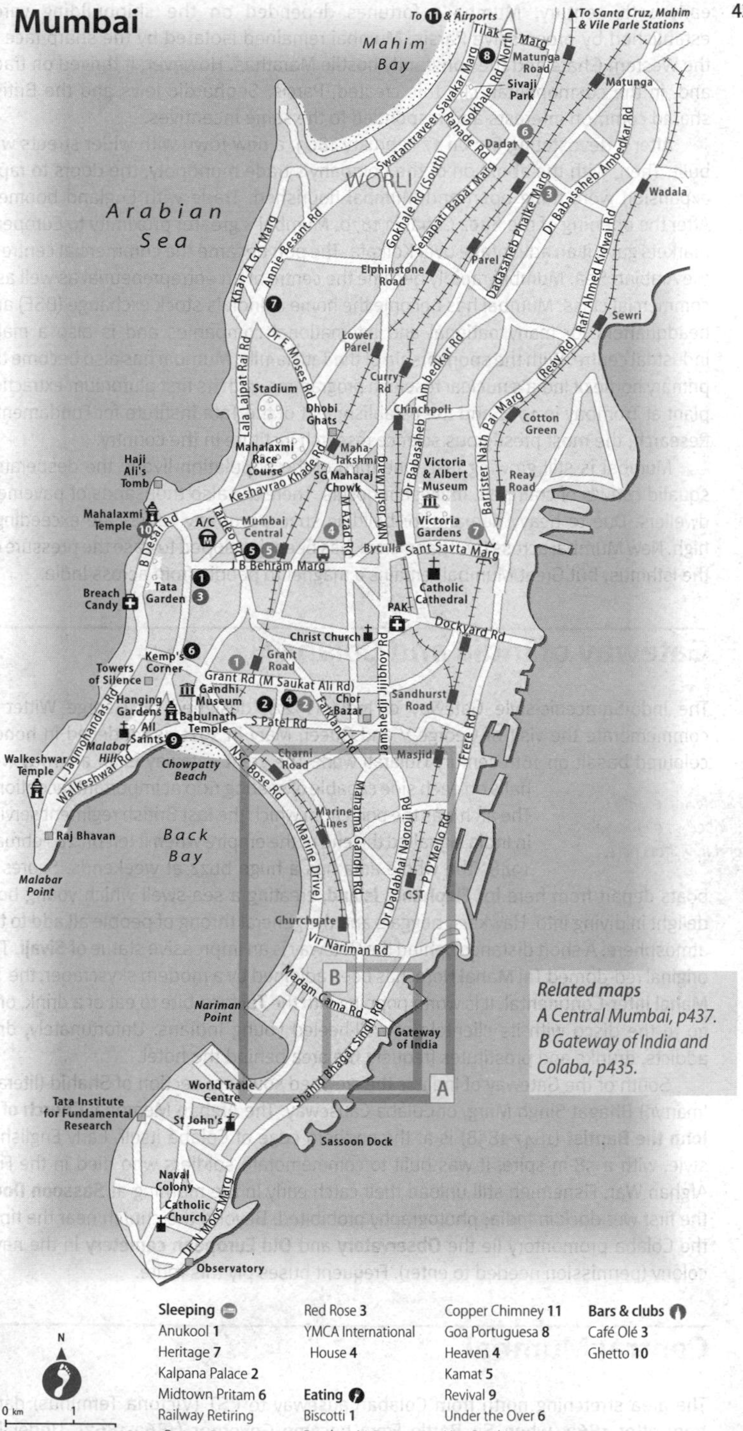

Related maps
A Central Mumbai, p437.
B Gateway of India and Colaba, p435.

Sleeping
Anukool **1**
Heritage **7**
Kalpana Palace **2**
Midtown Pritam **6**
Railway Retiring Rooms **5**
Red Rose **3**
YMCA International House **4**

Eating
Biscotti **1**
Bombay A1 **2**
Copper Chimney **11**
Goa Portuguesa **8**
Heaven **4**
Kamat **5**
Revival **9**
Under the Over **6**
Viva Paschim **7**

Bars & clubs
Café Olé **3**
Ghetto **10**

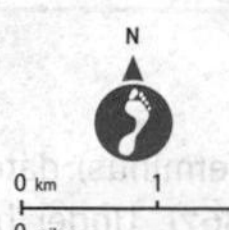

early 19th century, Mumbai's fortunes depended on the shipbuilding yards established by progressive Parsis. Mumbai remained isolated by the sharp face of the Western Ghats and the constantly hostile Marathas. However, it thrived on trade and, in the cosmopolitan city this created, Parsis, Sephardic Jews and the British shared common interests and responded to the same incentives.

After a devastating fire on 17 February 1803, a new town with wider streets was built. Then, with the abolition of the Company's trade monopoly, the doors to rapid expansion were flung open and Mumbai flourished. Trade with England boomed. After the opening of the Suez Canal in 1870, Mumbai's greater proximity to European markets gave it an advantage over Kolkata. The port became the commercial centre of the Arabian Sea. Mumbai rapidly became the centre of an entrepreneurial as well as a commercial class. Mumbai has become the home of India's stock exchange (BSE) and headquarters for many national and international companies and is also a major industrial centre. With the sponsorship of the Tata family, Mumbai has also become the primary home of India's nuclear research programme, with its first plutonium extraction plant at Trombay in 1961 and the establishment of the Tata Institute for Fundamental Research, the most prestigious science research institute in the country.

Mumbai is still growing fast. One third of the population live in the desperately squalid *chawls* of cramped, makeshift hovels. There are also thousands of pavement dwellers. Due to heavy demand for building space, property values are exceedingly high. New Mumbai across the Thane Creek has been developed to ease the pressure on the isthmus, but Great Mumbai remains a magnet to people from across India.

Gateway of India and Colaba

The Indo-Saracenic-style Gateway of India (1927), designed by George Wittet to commemorate the visit of George V and Queen Mary in 1911, is modelled in honey-coloured basalt on 16th-century Gujarati work. The great gateway is an archway with halls on each side capable of seating 600 at important receptions. The arch was the point from which the last British regiment serving in India signalled the end of the empire when it left on 28 February 1948. The whole area has a huge buzz at weekends. Scores of boats depart from here for **Elephanta Island,** creating a sea-swell which young boys delight in diving into. Hawkers, beggars and the general throng of people all add to the atmosphere. A short distance behind the Gateway is an impressive statue of **Sivaji**. The original red-domed **Taj Mahal Hotel** has been adjoined by a modern skyscraper, the **Taj Mahal Inter-Continental**. It is worth popping into the **Taj** for a bite to eat or a drink, or to go to the disco with its clientele of well-heeled young Indians. Unfortunately, drug addicts, drunks and prostitutes frequent the area behind the hotel.

Sadly, increasing numbers of beggars target foreign visitors here.

South of the Gateway of India is the crowded southern section of Shahid (literally 'martyr') Bhagat Singh Marg, or Colaba Causeway. The Afghan Memorial **Church of St John the Baptist** (1847-1858) is at the northern edge of Colaba itself. Early English in style, with a 58-m spire, it was built to commemorate soldiers who died in the First Afghan War. Fishermen still unload their catch early in the morning at **Sassoon Dock**, the first wet dock in India; photography prohibited. Beyond the church near the tip of the Colaba promontory lie the **Observatory** and **Old European cemetery** in the naval colony (permission needed to enter). Frequent buses ply this route.

Central Mumbai

The area stretching north from Colaba Causeway to CST (Victoria Terminus) dates from after 1862, when Sir Bartle Frere became Governor (1862-1867). Under his

Gateway of India & Colaba

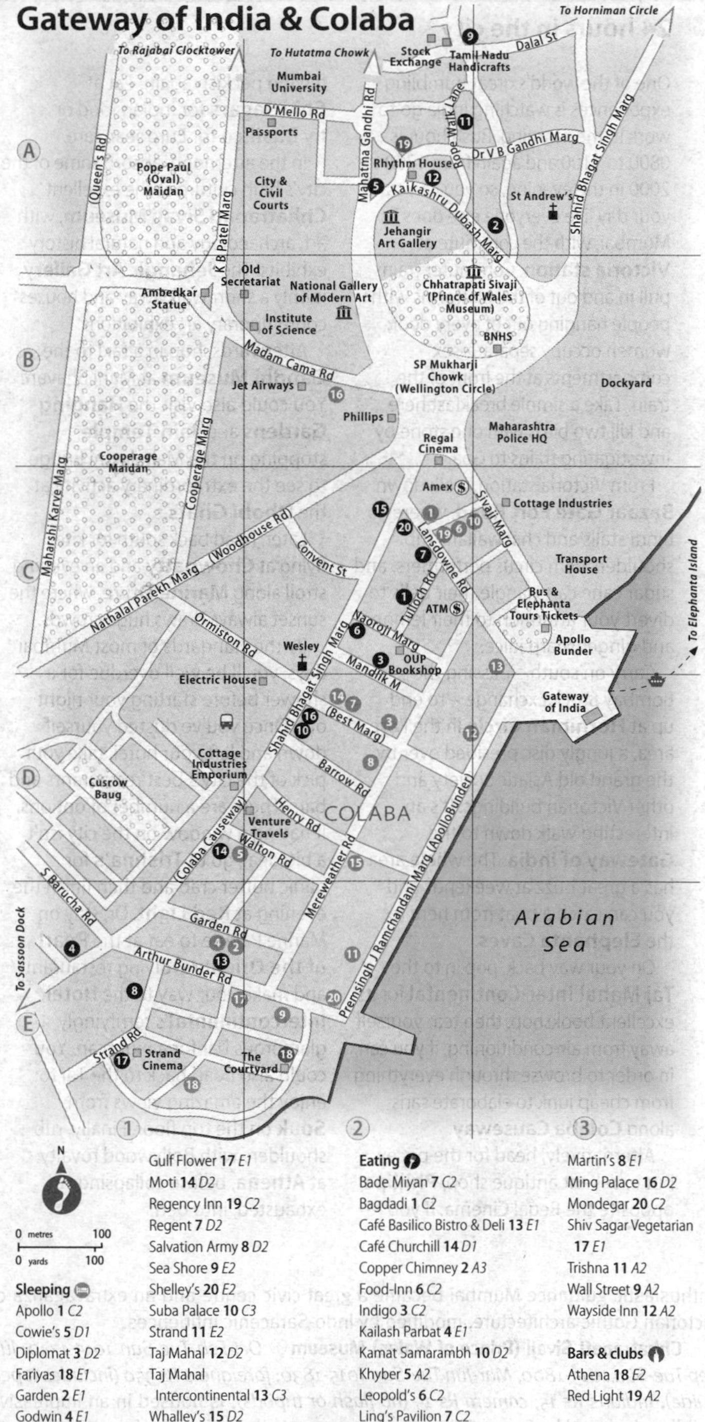

Sleeping
Apollo 1 *C2*
Cowie's 5 *D1*
Diplomat 3 *D2*
Fariyas 18 *E1*
Garden 2 *E1*
Godwin 4 *E1*
Gordon House 6 *C2*
Gulf Flower 17 *E1*
Moti 14 *D2*
Regency Inn 19 *C2*
Regent 7 *D2*
Salvation Army 8 *D2*
Sea Shore 9 *E2*
Shelley's 20 *E2*
Suba Palace 10 *C3*
Strand 11 *E2*
Taj Mahal 12 *D2*
Taj Mahal Intercontinental 13 *C3*
Whalley's 15 *D2*
YWCA International Centre 16 *B2*

Eating
Bade Miyan 7 *C2*
Bagdadi 1 *C2*
Café Basilico Bistro & Deli 13 *E1*
Café Churchill 14 *D1*
Copper Chimney 2 *A3*
Food-Inn 6 *C2*
Indigo 3 *C2*
Kailash Parbat 4 *E1*
Kamat Samarambh 10 *D2*
Khyber 5 *A2*
Leopold's 6 *C2*
Ling's Pavilion 7 *C2*
Majestic Hotel 15 *C2*
Martin's 8 *E1*
Ming Palace 16 *D2*
Mondegar 20 *C2*
Shiv Sagar Vegetarian 17 *E1*
Trishna 11 *A2*
Wall Street 9 *A2*
Wayside Inn 12 *A2*

Bars & clubs
Athena 18 *E2*
Red Light 19 *A2*

24 hours in the city

One of the world's great humbling experiences is watching India go to work in the morning. Rush hour is 0800 to 1100 and again from 1700 to 2000 in the evening, so you can start your day like everyone else does in Mumbai: with the commute at **Victoria station**. Commuter trains pull in and out of the platforms with people hanging out of every door; women occupy separate-sex compartments at the front of the train. Take a simple breakfast here, and kill two birds with one stone by investigating trains to Goa.

From Victoria station, walk down **Bazaar Gate Fort Road**, where bindi stalls and chai wallahs rub shoulders with circus performers, and sugar cane carts jangle their bells to divert your attention to their lemon and ginger sharp juice.

Carry on south – passing the Bombay Stock Exchange – to end up at **Horniman Circle** in the Fort area, a jungly disc presided over by the grand old Asiatic Society and other Victorian buildings. It's an interesting walk down to the **Gateway of India**. The whole area has a great buzz at weekends and you can catch a boat from here to the **Elephanta Caves**.

On your way back, pop in to the **Taj Mahal Inter-Continental** for its excellent bookshop, then tear yourself away from air-conditioning, if you can, in order to browse through everything from cheap junk to elaborate saris along **Colaba Causeway**.

Alternatively, head for the pricey but excellent antique shop, **Phillips**, opposite the Regal Cinema. If you're feeling peckish again, eat at **Shiv Sagars** for Indian food or try **Basilico** for European fare.

In the afternoon, absorb some of the city's high culture at the excellent **Chhatrapati Sivaji Museum**, with art, archaeology and natural history exhibits. The **Jehangir Art Gallery** is only a short walk away and houses contemporary art exhibitions.

Afterwards, hop in a taxi to the **Gandhi Museum** at Mani Bhavan. You could also visit the **Hanging Gardens** and **Jain Temple**, stopping on the Mahalaxmi Bridge to see the extraordinary activity at the **Dhobi Ghats**.

Later, head back south for kite-flying at **Chowpatty** and an evening stroll along **Marine Drive**, where the sunset always draws huge crowds.

By the standards of most Mumbai days, you'll be well overdue for a shower before starting your night out. Once you've dusted yourself down and left your hotel, take your pick of the city's best restaurants and bars. There are a number of options. If having a window on the city isn't a big deal, go to **Trishna's** for garlic butter crab and then finish the evening at **Red Light**. Or, stay on Marine Parade to eat at the **Pearl of the Orient** revolving restaurant and make your way to the **Hotel Intercontinental**'s terrifyingly glamorous bar for a nightcap. You could also head back to the Taj to enjoy the amazing views from **Souk** on the top floor. Finally, rub shoulders with Bollywood royalty at **Athena**, before collapsing, exhausted, into bed.

enthusiastic guidance Mumbai became a great civic centre and an extravaganza of Victorian Gothic architecture, modified by Indo-Saracenic influences.

Chhatrapati Sivaji (Prince of Wales) Museum ⓘ *Oct-Feb Tue-Sun 1015-1730, Jul-Sep Tue-Sun 1015-1800, Mar-Jun Tue-Sun 1015-1830; foreigners Rs 350 (includes taped guide), Indians Rs 15, camera Rs 15 (no flash or tripods)*, is housed in an impressive building designed by George Wittet to commemorate the visit of the Prince of Wales to

Central Mumbai

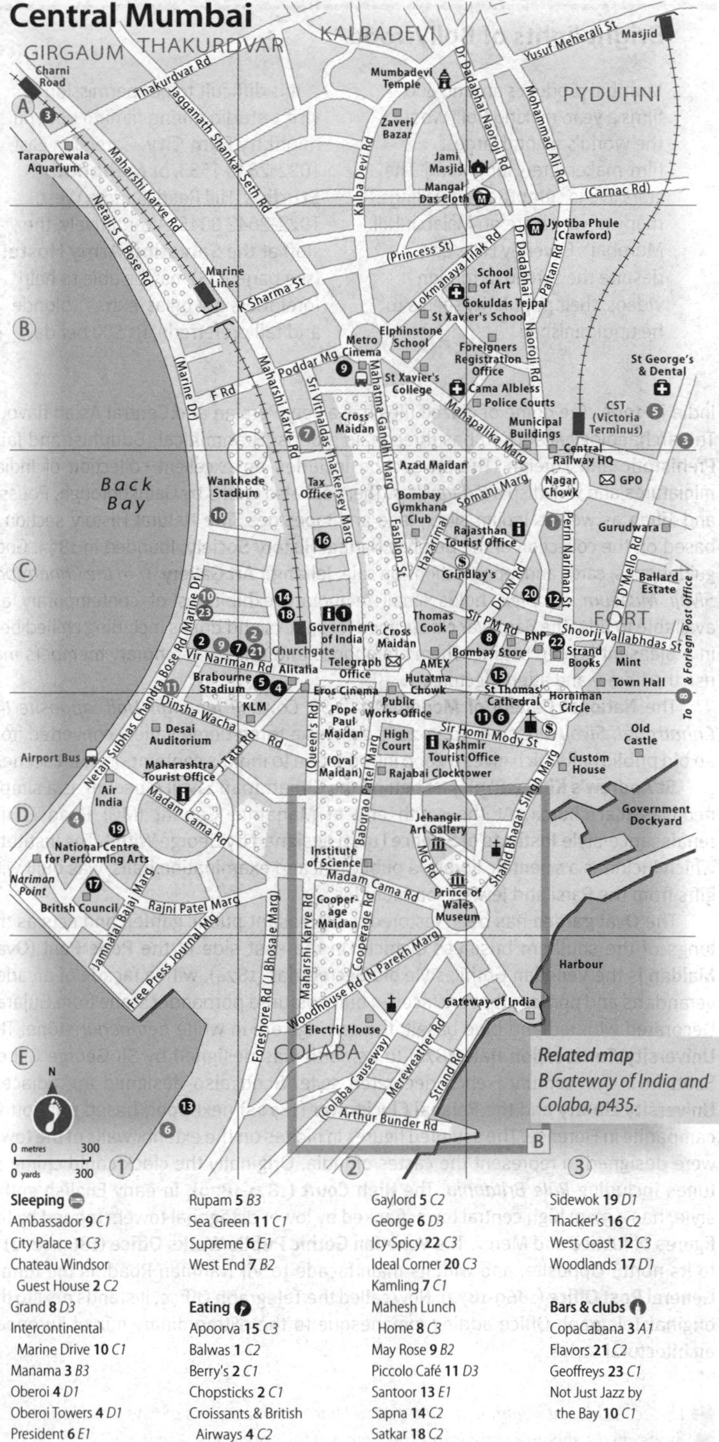

Sleeping
Ambassador **9** *C1*
City Palace **1** *C3*
Chateau Windsor Guest House **2** *C2*
Grand **8** *D3*
Intercontinental Marine Drive **10** *C1*
Manama **3** *B3*
Oberoi **4** *D1*
Oberoi Towers **4** *D1*
President **6** *E1*
Rupam **5** *B3*
Sea Green **11** *C1*
Supreme **6** *E1*
West End **7** *B2*

Eating
Apoorva **15** *C3*
Balwas **1** *C2*
Berry's **2** *C1*
Chopsticks **2** *C1*
Croissants & British Airways **4** *C2*
Gaylord **5** *C2*
George **6** *D3*
Icy Spicy **22** *C3*
Ideal Corner **20** *C3*
Kamling **7** *C1*
Mahesh Lunch Home **8** *C3*
May Rose **9** *B2*
Piccolo Café **11** *D3*
Santoor **13** *E1*
Sapna **14** *C2*
Satkar **18** *C2*
Sidewok **19** *D1*
Thacker's **16** *C2*
West Coast **12** *C3*
Woodlands **17** *D1*

Bars & clubs
CopaCabana **3** *A1*
Flavors **21** *C2*
Geoffreys **23** *C1*
Not Just Jazz by the Bay **10** *C1*

Bright lights of Bollywood

Mumbai produces around 860 films a year, making Bollywood the world's second largest film-maker after Hong Kong. The stars live in sumptuous dwellings, many of which are on Malabar Hill, Mumbai's Beverley Hills, and despite the spread of foreign videos, their popularity seems to be undiminished.

It is difficult to get permission to visit a studio during filming but you might try **Film City**, Goregaon East, T022-2840 1533, or **Mehboob Studios**, Hill Road, Bandra West, T022-2642 8045. Alternatively, the staff at the **Salvation Army Hostel** (see page 443) may be able to help foreigners get on as 'extras' (blonde and tall preferred!); Rs 500 per day.

India in 1905. The dome of glazed tiles has a very Persian and Central Asian flavour. The archaeological section has three main groups: Brahminical; Buddhist and Jain; Prehistoric and Foreign. The art section includes an excellent collection of Indian miniatures and well displayed *tankhas*. There are also works by Gainsborough, Poussin and Titian as well as Indian silver, jade and tapestries. The Natural History section is based on the collection of the **Bombay Natural History Society**, founded in 1833. Good guidebooks, cards and reproductions on sale. **Jehangir Art Gallery** ⓘ *in the Chhatrapati Sivaji Museum complex*, holds small temporary exhibitions of contemporary art, available to buy. The **Samovar café** is good for snacks and drinks including chilled beer in a pleasant garden setting. There are phones and toilets. Temporary members may use the library and attend lectures.

The **National Gallery of Modern Art** ⓘ *Sir Cowasji Jehangir Hall, opposite the Chhatrapati Sivaji Museum, T022-2285 2457*, is a three-tiered gallery converted from an old public hall which gives a good introduction to India's contemporary art scene.

St Andrew's Kirk, (1819), just behind the Chhatrapati Sivaji Museum, is a simple neo-classical church. At the south end of Mahatma Gandhi (MG) Road is the renaissance-style **Institute of Science** (1911) designed by George Wittet. The Institute, which includes a scientific library, a public hall and examination halls, was built with gifts from the Parsi and Jewish communities.

The **Oval garden** has been restored to a pleasant public garden and acts as the lungs of the southern business district. On the east side of the **Pope Paul (Oval) Maidan** is the Venetian Gothic-style **old Secretariat** (1874), with a façade of arcaded verandahs and porticos that are faced in buff-coloured porbander stone from Gujarat. Decorated with red and blue basalt, the carvings are in white *hemnagar* stone. The **University Convocation Hall** (1874) to its north was designed by Sir George Gilbert Scott in a 15th-century French decorated style. Scott also designed the adjacent **University Library** and the **Rajabai Clocktower** (1870s) next door, based on Giotto's campanile in Florence. The sculpted figures in niches on the exterior walls of the tower were designed to represent the castes of India. Originally the clock could chime 12 tunes including *Rule Britannia*. The **High Court** (1871-1879), in early English gothic style, has a 57-m high central tower flanked by lower octagonal towers topped by the figures of Justice and Mercy. The **Venetian Gothic Public Works Office** (1869-1872) is to its north. Opposite, and with its main façade to Vir Nariman Road, is the former **General Post Office** (1869-1872). Now called the Telegraph Office, it stands next to the original Telegraph Office adding romanesque to the extraordinary mix of European architectural styles.

The acquisition of wealth is nothing new to Mumbai. The city has always worshipped money in the shape of Mahalaxmi, the temple to the goddess of wealth.

Fort area

Horniman Circle was laid out in 1860. On the west edge are the Venetian Gothic **Elphinstone Buildings** (1870) in brown sandstone. **Cathedral Church of St Thomas** was begun in 1672, opened in 1718, and subject to a number of later additions. Inside are a number of monuments forming a heroic 'Who's Who of India'. The **Custom House** is believed to incorporate a Portuguese barrack block of 1665. Over the entrance is the crest of the East India Company. Parts of the old Portuguese fort's walls can be seen and many Malabar teak 'East Indiamen' ships were built here. **The Mint** (1824-1829), built on the Fort rubbish dump, has ionic columns and a water tank in front of it. The **Town Hall** (1820-1823) has been widely admired as one of the best neo-classical buildings in India. The original idea of paired columns was abandoned as being too monumental, and half the columns – imported from Britain – were used at Christ Church, Byculla. The Corinthian interior houses the **Assembly Rooms** and the **Bombay Asiatic Society**. From the imposing Horniman Circle, Vir Nariman Road leads to Flora (or Frere) Fountain (1869), now known as **Hutatma Chowk**.

The fort area is worth visiting after 1900, when the old buildings are floodlit.

Around the CST (VT)

Chhatrapati Sivaji Terminus, formerly Victoria Terminus or VT (1878-1887), the most remarkable example of Victorian Gothic architecture in India, was opened during Queen Victoria's Golden Jubilee year. The first train in India left from this terminus for Thane in April 1853. Now known as CST, over 500,000 commuters use the station daily.

The station was built at a time when fierce debate was taking place among British architects working in India as to the most appropriate style to develop to meet the demands of the late 19th-century boom. One view held that the British should restrict themselves to models derived from the best in western tradition. Others argued that architects should draw on Indian models, trying to bring out the best of Indian tradition and encourage its development. By and large, the former were dominant, but the introduction of gothic allowed a blending of western traditions with Indian (often Islamic Indian) motifs, which became known as the Indo-Saracenic style. The giant caterpillar-like walkway with perspex awnings looks incongruous against the gothic structure of 'VT'. The frontage is symmetrical with a large central dome flanked by two wings, capped by a 4-m high statue of Progress. The booking hall with its arcades, stained glass and glazed tiles was inspired by London's St Pancras station.

Opposite the CST station are the grand **Municipal Buildings** (1893), built by Stevens. In Mahapalika Marg (Cruickshank Road) are the **Police Courts** (1888), **Cama Albless Hospital**, which has interesting gothic windows with conical iron hoods to provide shade, **St Xavier's College** founded in 1867, and **Elphinstone High School** (1872). On the opposite side of the road is the **Azad Maidan**.

St Xavier's School and **Gokuldas Tejpal Hospital** (1877), built by Parsi benefactors, are in Lokmanya Tilak Marg (Camac Road). On the southeast and southwest faces are medallions by Rudyard Kipling's father Lockwood Kipling. **Crawford Market**, Mumbai (1865-1871), now **Jyotiba Phule Market**, was designed by Emerson in the 12th-century French gothic style. Over the entrance is more of Lockwood Kipling's work; the paving stones are from Caithness. The market is divided into sections for fruit, vegetables, fish, mutton and poultry.

Between Crawford Market and Mumbai Central Railway Station is **Falkland Road**, the centre of Mumbai's red-light district. Prostitutes stand behind barred windows,

Bollywood churns out 860 films each year; of those 854 fail.

giving the area its other name 'The Cages' – many of the girls are sold or abducted from various parts of India and Nepal. Medical reports suggest that AIDS is very widespread.

Marine Drive, Malabar Hill and around

You can do an interesting half-day trip from Churchgate Station, along Marine Drive to the **Taraporewala Aquarium**, **Mani Bhavan** (Gandhi Museum), the **Babulnath Temple**, past the **Parsi Towers of Silence** to **Kamla Nehru Park**, the **Hanging Gardens** and the **Jain Temple**. You can go further towards Malabar Point to glimpse **Raj Bhavan** and the **Walkeshwar Temple**, before returning via the **Mahalaxmi Temple** and **Haji Ali's tomb**.

Churchgate Station (1894-1896) was designed by FW Stevens for the Mumbai, Baroda and Central India Railway. Stevens was a great protagonist of the indo-saracenic style. With its domes and façades, Churchgate Station is byzantine in flavour. The statue on the western gable shows a figure holding a locomotive and wheel, symbols of technological progress.

Chowpatty Beach, a long stretch of white sand, looks attractive from a distance, but is polluted. Swimming here is not recommended but there is a lot of interesting beach activity in the evening. Chowpatty was the scene of a number of important 'Quit India' rallies during the Independence Movement. At important festivals like *Ganesh Chaturthi* and *Dasara* (see Festivals, page 448), it is thronged with jubilant Hindu devotees. Netaji Subhash Road, better known as Marine Drive, runs round Back Bay along Chowpatty from just below the Hanging Gardens on Malabar Hill to **Nariman Point.** At night, lined with lights, it is a very attractive sight from Malabar Hill.

Mahatma Gandhi Museum (Mani Bhavan) ⓘ *west of Grant Rd, 19 Laburnum Rd, 0930-1800, Rs 3, allow 1 hr*, is further north towards Nana Chowk, at Mani Bhavan. This private house, where Mahatma Gandhi used to stay on visits to Mumbai, is now a memorial museum and research library with 20,000 volumes. There is a diorama depicting important scenes from Gandhi's life; slides without a mount are available, Rs 100. The display of photos and letters on the first floor is more interesting, and includes letters Gandhi wrote to Hitler in 1939 asking him not to go to war, and those to Roosevelt and Tolstoy; there are also letters from Einstein and Tolstoy.

Join the crowds at sunset for an entertaining walk: hawkers and sand sculptors mingle with joggers and Mumbai's high society walking their dogs.

In the heart of the Muslim quarter where agate minarets mingle with the upper storeys of 1960s residential towers lies **Chor Bazaar**. The atmosphere here is totally different from the crumbling colonial architectural glory of the Colaba and Fort area, and at sunset the ramshackle roads hum with yellow and black taxis, adolescent boys wielding wooden carts through traffic at a run, and Muslim women at a stroll. The jumble of the bazar is a brilliant place to poke around in, there are tonnes of dealers in old watches, film posters, Belgian – or Indian-made temple lamps, enamel tiles and door knobs. The area around Mutton Street is popular with film prop-buyers and foreign and domestic bric-a-brac hunters. Further out the produce is more local: tarpaulins and tools, Mecca paintings, and burqas with gold geometric embroidery. Balconies come bedecked with fairy lights on faded apartment blocks and wooden shutters lie over grilling, pollution stains streaked over the pastel buildings.

The **Towers of Silence**, Mumbai (Parsi 'temple') are in secluded gardens 500 m west of Mani Bhavan. This very private place is not accessible to tourists but it can be glimpsed from the road. Sir Jamshetji Jeejeebhoy gave a large area of land around the towers, thus affording them privacy and allowing the creation of a tranquil garden. Parsis believe that the elements of water, fire and earth must not be polluted by the dead, so they lay their 'vestments of flesh and bone' out on the top of the towers to be picked clean by vultures. The apparent decline in vulture numbers is a cause for concern.

Dabbawallahs

If you go inside Churchgate station at mid-morning or after lunch, you will see the dabbawallahs, members of the Bombay Union of Tiffin Box Carriers. Each morning, the 2500 dabbawallahs call on suburban housewives who pack freshly cooked lunch into small circular stainless steel containers – *dabbas*. Three or four are stacked one on the other and held together by a clip with a handle. Typically the dabbawallah will collect 30-40 tiffin boxes, range them out on a long pole and cycle to the nearest station. Here he will hand them over to a fellow dabbawallah who will transport them into the city for delivery to the consumer.

Over 100,000 lunches of maybe *sabze* (vegetable curry), chappatis, dahl and pickle make their way daily across town to the breadwinner. The service, which costs a few rupees a day, is a good example of the fine division of labour in India, reliable and efficient, for the dabbawallahs pride themselves on never losing a lunch. He makes sure that the carefully prepared pukka (proper) food has not in any way been defiled.

The **Hanging Gardens (Pherozeshah Mehta Gardens)** immediately south of the Towers of Silence, on top of a low hill, are so named since they are located on top of a series of tanks that supply water to Mumbai. The gardens are well kept with lots of topiary animals and there are good views over the city from the children's park across the road. Snake charmers operate from the roadside. It's worth a visit.

Nearby is the Church of North India **All Saints' Church** (1882). Across the road from the Hanging Gardens is the **Kamla Nehru Park**, laid out in 1952 and named after the wife of India's first prime minister. The **Jain Temple** (1904) was built of marble and dedicated to the first Jain Tirthankar. Much of the decoration depicts the lives of the Tirthankars. Visitors can watch various rituals being performed. Jains play a prominent part in Mumbai's banking and commerce and are one of the city's wealthiest communities.

One of the oldest buildings in Mumbai, the **Walkeshwar Temple** ('Lord of Sand') was built about AD 1000. In legend this was a resting point for Rama on his journey from Ayodhya to Lanka to free Sita from the demon king Ravana. One day Rama's brother Lakshman failed to return from Varanasi at the usual time with a *lingam* which he fetched daily for Rama's worship. Rama then made a *lingam* from the sand to worship Siva.

On Bhulabhai Desai Road, Cumballa Hill are the **Mahalakshmi temples**, the oldest in Mumbai and dedicated to three goddesses whose images were found in the sea. **Haji Ali's Tomb** and the mosque here are devoted to a Muslim saint who drowned here. They are reached by a causeway only at low tide. The money changers exchange 1 rupee coins into smaller coins, enabling pilgrims to make several individual gifts to beggars rather than one larger one, thereby reputedly increasing the merit of the gift.

From Haji Ali's Tomb go along Keshavrao Khade Road to **SG Maharaj Chowk (Jacob's Circle)**. From the Mahalakshmi Bridge there is a view of the astonishing Municipal dhobi ghats. Go down Maulana Azad Road then turn left into Clare Road. On your right is **Christ Church**, Byculla (1835), which incorporated half the pillars originally intended for the Town Hall. Clare Road leads down the side of the **Victoria Gardens**.They are very attractive – marked as Jijamata Udyan on some maps.

North of Byculla Station is the **Victoria and Albert Museum (Bhav Daji Laud Museum)** ⓘ *Mon and Tue, Thu-Sat 1030-1700, Sun 0830-1645*. Inspired by the V&A in London and financed by public subscription, it was built in 1872 in a palladian style. The collection covers the history of Mumbai and contains prints, maps and models.

Sleeping

There's no low-season when it comes to accommodation in Mumbai: whenever possible make reservations in advance. If you have not, arrive as early in the day as you can. Most hotels are concentrated in the central area (Marine Drive, Nariman Point, Apollo Bunder and Colaba).

There are stacks of moderately priced hotels immediately behind the Taj Mahal Hotel. Backpackers usually head for the Colaba area to the south. The alternative is to look around CST and Dadar railway stations. On Arthur Bunder Rd, Colaba, there are several, often on upper floors, usually shared facilities, cold water only, some windowless rooms; arrive early and inspect room first. There are several 5-star hotels on Juhu beach and close to the airports. For paying guest accommodation contact India Tourist Office, 123 M Karve Rd, T022-2203 2932.

Gateway of India and Colaba

p434, map p435

Rooms with sea view are more expensive. There are few budget hotels left in the area charging under Rs 400 though you may get a dormitory bed for Rs 250.

LL Gordon House Hotel, 5 Battery St, Apollo Bunder, Colaba, T022-2287 1122, www.ghhotel.com. Amazingly, a spruce boutique hotel in the run-down Colaba district, on 3 themed floors that really do leave India outside: yellow Med-style walls, quilts in the country cottage rooms and all blonde wood on the Scandinavian floor.

LL Taj Mahal Apollo Bunder, T022-6665 3366, www.tajhotels.com. The grand dame of Mumbai lodging, over a century old, with 294 rooms on the Gateway to India and 306 in the **Taj Mahal Intercontinental**, its newer wing. So good, even the corridors look like art galleries. 9 restaurants and bars, plus fitness centre and even a yacht on call.

L-AL Fariyas, off Arthur Bunder Rd, Colaba, T022-2204 2911, www.fariyas.com. Obliging service, 80 upgraded rooms, good restaurants, pub, roof garden, pool (open to non-residents).

A Diplomat, 24-26 BK Boman Behram Marg, behind **Taj**, T022-2202 1661, www.hoteldiplomat-bombay.com. 52 a/c rooms, restaurant, quiet, friendly, relaxed atmosphere, good value. Very simple furnishings, small beds. Recommended.

A Godwin, 41 Garden Rd, T022-2287 2050, www.hotelgodwin@mail.com. 48 large, clean, renovated, a/c rooms (upper floors have better views), good rooftop restaurant (full of wealthy Mumbaiites on Fri and Sat night), very helpful management. Recommended.

A Regent, 8 Ormiston Rd (Best Marg), T022-2287 1854. Modern hotel that's popular with sheiks, hence the camels and pastels theme. 50 well-furnished a/c rooms, no restaurant but good room service.

A Suba Palace, Apollo Bunder, T022-2220 2063, hotelsubapalace.com. Clean, modern, well run. Recommended.

B Apollo, 22 Lansdowne Rd, Colaba, behind **Taj**, T022-2202 0223, hotelapollogh@hotmail.com. 39 rooms, some a/c, some amazing sea views. Tatty linen and walls, but friendly staff.

B Garden Hotel, 42 Garden Rd, T022-2284 1476, gardenhotel@mail.com. Efficient sister hotel to the Godwin next door, with similar facilities. All rooms have bath tubs.

B Gulf Flower, Kamal Mansions, Arthur Bunder Rd, T022-2283 3742. Off-putting exterior but modern and clean rooms inside.

B Hotel Cowie's, 15 Walton Rd, near Electric House, Colaba T022-2284 0232. 20 rooms, all with central a/c, bathroom en suite, television and phone, in old-world hotel on one of the tree-lined residential streets off Colaba Causeway. Excellent value.

B Regency Inn, 18 Landsdowne Rd behind Regal Cinema, Colaba, T022-2202 0292. Spacious a/c rooms, fridge, good value.

B YWCA International Centre, 2nd floor, 18 Madam Cama Rd (entrance on side), Fort, T022-2202 0122, www.ywca bombay.com. For both sexes, 34 clean, pleasant rooms with bath, breakfast and dinner included, essential to write in advance with Rs 1300 deposit. Recommended.

B-C Strand, 25 PJ Ramchandani Marg, T022-2288 2222, www.hotelstrand.com.

For an explanation of the sleeping and eating price codes used in this guide, see inside the front cover. Other relevant information is found in Essentials pages 40-44.

Friendly, clean, decent rooms, some with bath and sea view.

C Moti Hotel, 10 Best Marg, opposite Electric House, Colaba, T022-2202 5714. In a mansion block, 8 a/c rooms with slatted wood doors, yellow walls made of plywood, original mosaic flooring. Extremely narrow bathrooms with plastic mirrors, 24-hr hot water, TV.

C-D Whalley's, 41 Mereweather Rd, T022-2283 4206. Old fashioned, 25 rooms (inspect first), some good, a/c with balcony and bath, includes breakfast, accepts TCs.

D India Guest House, 1/49 Kamal Mansion, Arthur Bunder Rd. 20 rooms along long corridor, white partitions that you could, at a push, jump over. Fan, no toilet or shower. The corner room has a neat panorama over the bay. Sound will travel.

D Sea Shore, top floor, 1/49 Kamal Mansion, Arthur Bunder Rd, T022-2287 4238. Kitsch as you like, 15 bright gloss-pink rooms and purple corridors with plastic flowers, shower in room but no sink, 7 with window and TV and fan, 8 without. Sea view room has 4 beds. 2 rooms come with toilet, TV and hot water.

E-G The Salvation Army, Red Shield House, 30 Mereweather Rd, T022-2284 1824, redshield@vsnl.net. A/c (more expensive), includes all meals. Dormitory **F** rate includes breakfast only. Mostly dorm Rs 130 including breakfast, Rs 200 including meals), some doubles (Rs 450, all meals), lockers Rs 30 per item 0800-2200, showers, checkout 0900, book in advance or arrive early, bus ticketing (eg Goa) at reception. Recommended as convenient, friendly, best value but could be cleaner.

Around the CST (VT) *p439, map p437*

B Grand, 17 Sprott Rd, Ballard Estate, T022-6658 0500, www.grandhotelbombay.com. Old-fashioned, built around a central courtyard, 73 a/c rooms, exchange, book counter, helpful service, very relaxing.

B-C City Palace, 121 City Terrace (Nagar Chowk), opposite CST Main Gate, T022-2261 5515. Tiny though clean, functional rooms (some no windows), with bath (Indian WC), some a/c, helpful staff, convenient location. Recommended.

D Popular Place, 104-106 Mint Rd, near GPO, Fort Market, T022-2269 5506. Clean rooms with bath (hot water), some a/c, helpful staff, good value.

D-E Manama , 221 P D'Mello Rd, T022-2261 3412. Decent rooms, some with bath and a/c, popular.

D-E Rupam , 239 P D'Mello Rd, T022-2261 8298. Some of the 37 rooms have a/c with phone, clean, friendly, comfortable beds.

Marine Drive, Malabar Hill and around *p440, map p437*

LL Intercontinental Marine Drive, 135 Marine Drive, T022-3987 9999, www.mumbai.intercontinental.com. 59 rooms in boutique hotel overlooking Marine Drive. Bose stereo, plasma TV screens, Bulgari toiletries, personal butler service and beautiful rooftop pool.

LL-AL The Oberoi, Nariman Pt, T022-2232 5757, www.oberoimumbai.com. The newer Oberoi combining modern technology with period furniture, 350 large rooms, excellent restaurants.

LL-AL Oberoi Towers, Nariman Pt, T022-2232 4343. Superb views from the higher floors, 650 rooms, good buffets, garden and swimming pool, excellent shopping complex. Recommended.

LL-AL President, 90 Cuffe Pde, T022-2215 0808. Informal but lacks character, poor value, 317 rooms, business facilities, good service.

L-AL Ambassador, Churchgate Extn, Vir Nariman Rd, T022-2204 1131, www.ambassadorindia.com. 127 rooms, revolving restaurant and pastry shop, slightly run-down feel.

AL Nataraj, 135 Marine Drive, T022-2204 4161. 83 rooms, some with views over bay, food and live music in restaurant, good but a bit noisy and overpriced.

A West End, 45 New Marine Lines, T022-2203 9121, www.westendhotelmumbai.com. 80 small, pleasant suites but in need of refurbishment. Good restaurant, excellent service, efficient front desk, well located, good value. Recommended.

B Astoria, 4 J Tata Rd, Churchgate, T022-2285 2626. 75 a/c rooms, restaurant, bar.

B Sea Green, 145 Marine Dr, T/F022-2282 2294, www.seagreenhotel.com. 34 rooms, 22 a/c, pleasant breezy informal sitting area.

B-C Chateau Windsor Guest House, 86 Vir Nariman Rd, T022-2204 3376, www.chateauwindsor.com. 36 rooms (some a/c) vary,

some very small and dark, room service for light snacks and drinks, friendly, clean, good value. Recommended. Cash only.
C-D Supreme, 4 Pandey Rd, near President, T022-2218 5623. Clean rooms with bath, good service but can be a little noisy.

Other areas

Dadar, Mumbai Central Station and Grant Road area *map p437*

Dadar is a good option, with many restaurants and good trains to Churchgate and CST.
A-B Midtown Pritam, 20-B Pritam Estates, Senapati Bapat Marg, 2 mins to Dadar station, T022-2414 5555. Terrace garden, 63 rooms.
C Sagar, Nagpada Junction (Bellasin Rd/JB Behram Marg corner), Byculla, T022-2309 2727. Very clean rooms, good restaurant, friendly. Recommended.
C-D Red Rose, Gokuldas Pasta Rd, Dadar East, T022-2413 7843. Some a/c in the 31 rooms, mostly shared but clean baths. Flexible checkout, friendly. Recommended.
D Anukool, 292-8 Maulana Saukat Ali Rd, T022-3081 4013, hotelanukool@hotmail.com. 23 rooms, some a/c, friendly, helpful, good value, but inspect room first.
D Heritage, Sant Savta Marg, Byculla, T022-2371 4891. A/c in the 84 rooms, restaurant (good Parsi), bar.
D Kalpana Palace, 181 P Bapurao Marg, opposite Daulat Cinema, Grant Rd, T022-2300 0846. Some of the 30 decent rooms have a/c.
D Railway Retiring Rooms, Mumbai Central, T022-2307 7292. Some a/c with bath.
D-E YMCA International House, 18 YMCA Rd, near Mumbai Central, T022-2309 1191. Decent rooms, shared bath, meals included, temp membership Rs 60, deposit Rs 1300, good value, book 3 months ahead.

Juhu Beach and Bandra *p441*

The listings below are in Juhu Beach.
LL Sun-n-Sand, 39 Juhu Beach, T022-2620 1811, www.sunnsandhotelcom. 118 rooms, best refurbished, comfortable, though cramped poolside, good restaurant.
L-AL Holiday Inn, Balraj Sahani Marg, T022-2620 4444. Reliable, 190 rooms, 2 pools, courtesy coach to town.
A Citizen, 960 Juhu Tara Rd, T022-2611 7273, citizen@bom2.vsnl.net.in. Unexciting exterior, 45 smallish but well appointed rooms, suites, efficient airport transfer. Recommended.
B Juhu Hotel, Juhu Tara Rd, T022-2618 4014. Spacious comfortable cottage-style rooms, sea-facing lawns, good restaurant (try the seafood and Mughlai dishes), soundproofed disco.
B Sands, 39/2 Juhu Beach, T022-2620 4511. 40 rooms, excellent restaurant. Recommended.

Airport

Most airport hotels offer free transfer. Tourist information at the airport will help to book.
LL-L Leela Palace, near International Terminal, T022-5691 1234, www.theleela.com. 460 modern rooms, excellent restaurants, pricey but excellent, bar (closed to non residents after 2300).
L Renaissance, near Chinmayanand Ashram, Powai, 9 km from international airport, T022- 2692 8888, www.renaissancehotels.com. 286 stylish rooms, superb restaurants, pleasant green setting, large pool, relaxing.
L-AL Orchid, 70C Nehru Rd, Vile Parle (east), 5 mins' walk from domestic terminal, T022-2610 0707, www.orchidhotelcom. Totally refurbished, attractive rooms, eco friendly. Boulevard restaurant boasts a good midnight buffet and '15-min lightning' buffet. Recommended.
A Transit, off Nehru Rd, Vile Parle (east), T022-2610 5812. Modern, 54 rooms, reasonable overnight halt for airport, excellent restaurant (draught beer), airport transfer.
B Metro Palace, Hill Rd, near Bandra station (W), T022-2642 7311. Convenient, close to domestic airport and shops, good restaurant.
B Pali Hills, 14 Union Park, Pali Hill, Bandra, T022-2649 2995. Quiet location, near market, continental restaurant (see below).
B-C Atithi, 77A Nehru Rd, 7 mins' walk from domestic terminal, T022-2611 6124. 47 rooms, functional, clean, 3 star, set meals included, good value, efficient desk, popular.
B-C Residency, Suren Rd, T022-2692 3000, www.residencymumbai.com. New hotel 3 km from the airport, request free pickup. 72 a/c smallish rooms, good restaurant, quiet back street, friendly staff. Recommended.
D Airport Rest Rooms, old Domestic Terminal, Santa Cruz. For passengers with connecting flights within 24 hrs of arrival, comfortable, clean, but often full.

Eating

Gateway of India and Colaba

p434, map p435

TTT **All Stir Fry**, **Gordon House Hotel**, oriental nosh served up in *Wagamama*-style at long shared benches. DIY food too.

TTT **Copper Chimney**, 18 K Dubash Marg, T022-2204 1661. Indian. Subdued lighting and quietly tasteful, excellent North Indian dishes, must reserve.

TTT **Indigo**, 4 Mandlik Rd, behind **Taj Hotel**, T022-2285 6316. Excellent Mediterranean in smart new restaurant, good atmosphere, additional seating on rooftop.

TTT **Khyber**, 145 MG Rd, Kala Ghoda, Fort, T022-2263 2174. North Indian. For an enjoyable evening in beautiful surroundings, outstanding food, especially lobster and *reshmi* chicken kebabs, try *paya* soup (goats' trotters).

TTT **Ling's Pavilion**, 19/21 KC College Hostel Building, off Colaba Causeway (behind Taj and Regal Cinema), T022-2285 0023. Stylish decor, good atmosphere and delightful service, colourful menu, seafood specials, generous helpings. Recommended.

TTT **Souk**, Taj Mahal Apollo Bunder, T022-5665 3366, www.tajhotels.com. Taj's top floor is now home to a North African themed restaurant. Open from 1900, great views. You can just have a drink but a glass of imported red wine, excellent though it may be, costs Rs 500 before tax.

TTT **Tides**, **Gordon House Hotel**, seafood restaurant, bar, wines and coffee shop with submarine theme.

TTT **Trishna**, Sai Baba Marg, next to Commerce House, Fort T022-2261 4991, behind Kala Ghoda, by Old Synagogue. Indian. Good coastline cuisine, seafood, excellent butter garlic crab. Recommended.

TT **Café Basilico Bistro & Deli**, Sentinel House, Arthur Bunder Rd, T022-5634 5670, www.cafebasilico.com. Very chichi, European-style café with waffles from Rs 85, soups, salads, pastas and smoothies.

TT **Ming Place**, Apsara Building, Colaba Causeway, T022-2287 2820. Chinese. Big a/c place with cosmic murals and heavy wooden chairs. Try the Shanghai potatoes.

T **Bade Miyan**, behind Ling's Pavilion. Streetside Kebab corner but very clean. Try *baida roti*, *shammi* and *boti* kebabs.

T **Bagdadi**, Tullock Rd (behind **Taj Hotel**), T022-2202 8027. Mughlai. One of the cheapest, first-class food, fragrant biryani, delicious chicken, crowded but clean. Recommended.

T **Café Churchill**, T022-2284 4689, 1000- 2400. A tiny little caff with 7 tables crammed with people basking in a/c, towered over by a cake counter and a Winston Churchill portrait. Great breakfasts, club sandwiches, seafood, fish and chips, lasagne and irish stew.

T **Kamat Samarambh**, opposite Electric House, SB Singh Marg. Indian vegetarian. Very good thalis and snacks, try *chola battura* (puri topped with spiced chickpeas).

T **Majestic Hotel.** Bustling, cheap columned and boothed canteen doing a fast business in thalis and the old South Indian favourites like iddli and sambar.

T **Martin's**, near Strand Cinema. Goan. Simple, authentic Goan food, excellent seafood and pork *sorpotel*.

T **Paradise**, Sindh Chambers, Colaba Causeway, Tue-Sun. Parsi and others. Spotless, excellent dhansak; try *sali boti* (mutton and 'chips'), not a/c.

T **Shiv Sagar Vegetarian Restaurant**, mouth of Colaba Market, Mistry Chambers, opposite Telephone Bhawan, Colaba, T022-2281 1550. Excellent very simple vegetarian restaurant, hygienic and clean that does South Indian snacks outside normal restaurant mealtimes.

Cafés and fast food

Many serve chilled beer and waiters care too much for large tips from tourist groups:

Food-Inn, 50 m from **Leopold's**. Mainly Indian (some Western) snacks. Pleasant (a/c upstairs), reasonably priced, friendly. Recommended.

Kailash Parbat, 1st Pasta La, Colaba. Excellent snacks and chats. In an old-style eatery serving Punjabi thalis, tooth-rotting sweets from the counter.

Leopold's, Colaba, T022-2283 0585. An institution among Colaba backpackers and Mumbai shoppers, good Western food and drink (limited Indian vegetarian), but pricey. Similar cafés nearby are far better value.

Mondegar, near Regal Cinema, T022-2281 2549. Similar, but a little cheaper and with a loud rock soundtrack.

Wayside Inn, 38 K Dubash Marg, T022-2284 4324. Quaint country inn-style place, good breakfast menu, average continental but perfect for an afternoon beer in heart of the city. Breezy, laid back and leisurely, moderately priced.

Around the CST (VT) *p439, map p437*

ŦŦ **Apoorva**, near Horniman Circle, Fort, T022-2288 1457. Very good seafood, especially crabs and prawns (downstairs is a cheaper menu).

ŦŦ **Bharat**, 317 SB Singh Marg, opposite Fort Market, T022-2261 8991. Excellent seafood and crab as well as naans and rotis: or try fried, stuffed Bombay Duck.

ŦŦ **George**, 20 Apollo St, near Horniman Circle. Pleasant quiet atmosphere, colonial feel, good service, lunchtime biriyanis and thalis.

ŦŦ **Sadanand**, opposite Crawford Market. Excellent thalis and vegetarian food, popular with Indian families.

ŦŦ **Wall Street**, 68 Hamam St, behind Stock Exchange. Coastal cuisine, excellent seafood, try spicy Malabari prawns, squid green garlic, fish *patta*.

Ŧ **Icy Spicy**, off PM Rd, next to Fort Central Restaurant. Great vegetarian snack bar.

Ŧ **Ideal Corner**, Hornby View, Gunbow St, Fort, CST. Lunchtime Parsi food and snacks in café.

Ŧ **Mahesh Lunch Home**, Sir PM Rd, Fort. Excellent for Mangalorean, Goan and tandoori seafood, a/c, bar, very popular.

Ŧ **West Coast**, Rustom Sidhwa Rd, off Sir Perin Nariman Rd. Very good meals. On MG Rd (north end), you can have a traditional breakfast, often served as early as 0600.

Marine Drive, Malabar Hill and around *p440, map p437*

ŦŦŦ **Gaylord**, Vir Nariman Rd, T022-2282 1231. Indian. Good food (huge portions) and service, tables inside and out, barbecue, pleasant, good bar, tempting pastry counter.

ŦŦŦ **Indian Summer**, 80 Vir Nariman Rd, T022-2283 5445. Indian. Excellent food, tasty kebabs, interesting modern glass decor, smart dress, reserve.

ŦŦŦ **Pearl of the Orient**, Ambassador Hotel, T022-2204 1131. Excellent Chinese, Japanese and Thai. The revolving restaurant offers stunning views especially at night. For a less expensive stationary view try the bar on the floor above which does simple meals.

ŦŦŦ **RG's Kitchen**, Intercontinental, Marine Drive, T022-5639 9999. Features 3 open kitchens: Indian, Oriental and Western. Where Mumbai's posh socialites eat.

ŦŦŦ **Santoor**, Maker Arcade, Cuffe Parade, near **President Hotel**, T022-2218 2262. North Indian. Small place, Mughlai and Kashmiri specialities: creamy chicken *malai* chop, *chana*, Peshawari (puri with chickpeas), Kashmiri soda made with salt and pepper.

ŦŦŦ **Sidewok**, next to NCPA theatre, T022-2281 8132. Interesting southeast Asian/fusion cuisine. Innovative menu, imaginative cocktails (try non-alcoholic too), surprise entertainment by staff, a special, fun dining experience. Reserve in advance.

ŦŦ **Berry's**, Vir Nariman Rd, near Churchgate Station, T022-2287 5691. North Indian. Tandoori specialities, good kulfi.

ŦŦ **Chopsticks**, 90A Vir Nariman Rd, Churchgate, T022-2283 2308. Chinese, good, hot and spicy. Offering unusual dishes (*taro* nest, date pancakes, toffee bananas).

ŦŦ **Kamling**, 82 Vir Nariman Rd, T022-2204 2618. Genuine Cantonese. Simple surroundings, but excellent preparations, try seafood, often busy.

ŦŦ **May Rose**, Cinema Rd (next to Metro), T022-2208 1104. Chinese. Clean a/c, very good food.

ŦŦ **Sapna**, Vir Nariman Rd. Indian, very traditional Mughlai delicacies, bar, some tables outside, attentive service, good value.

ŦŦ **Satkar**, Indian Express Building, opposite Churchgate station, T022-2204 3259. Indian. Delicious vegetarian, fruit juices and shakes; a/c section more expensive.

Ŧ **Balwas**, Maker Bhavan, 3 Sir V Thackersey Marg. Inexpensive, well-prepared food.

Ŧ **Piccolo Café**, 11A Sir Homi Mody St. Parsi. 0900-1800, closed Sat afternoon and Sun. Profits to charity, homely, clean, good dhansak.

Ŧ **Purohit's**, Vir Nariman Rd. Indian. Excellent vegetarian thalis, also Parsi.

Ŧ **Thacker's**, corner Maharshi Karve Rd and 1st Marine St. Indian. Good thalis.

Ŧ **Woodlands**, Mittal Chambers, Nariman Pt, Mon-Sat. South Indian. Excellent iddli and dosa and good thalis, busy at lunchtime.

Cafés and fast food

Croissants, Vir Nariman Rd, opposite Eros Cinema. Burgers, sandwiches, hot croissants with fillings, ice cream, lively atmosphere.

Fountain, MG Rd. For sizzlers and apple pie in a café atmosphere.

Other areas

Dadar, Mumbai Central Station and Grant Road area *map p437*

TTT Biscotti, Crossroads, Haji Ali, T022-2495 5055. Excellent Italian. Wholesome, leisurely dining, try batter-fried calamari, giant prawns in liqueur, flavoured sugar-free soda, zabaglioni, bistro-style complete with fiddler.
TTT Goa Portuguesa, THK Rd, Mahim. Goan. Authentic dishes, taverna-style with guitarist, try *sungto* (prawn) served between *papads*, *kalwa* (oyster), *teesryo* (shell) and clams, lobsters cooked with tomatoes, onions and spices and *bebinca* to end the meal.
TTT Revival, Chowpatty Sea Face, near footbridge. Classy, good Indian/continental buffets and desserts.
TT Bombay A1, 7 Vadilal A Patel Marg (Grant Rd Junction). Parsi. Cheerful, varied menu, try Patrani *machli*.
TT Copper Chimney, Dr AB Rd, Worli, T022-2492 4488. Indian. Window into kitchen, excellent food from extensive menu, reasonable prices, undiscovered by tourists.
TT Under the Over, 36 Altamount Rd (by flyover). Bistro-like, for Mexican, Creole dishes, sizzlers and rich desserts, reasonably priced, no alcohol.
TT The Village, Poonam Intercontinental, near Mahalaxmi racecourse. Gujarati. 'Village' setting, sea views, good authentic food.
TT Viva Paschim, City View, Dr AB Rd, Worli, T022-2498 3636. Quality coastal Maharashtrian. Sunday lunch buffet great value (Rs 225), folk dances at dinner often.
T Heaven, corner of Grant Rd/P Bapurao Marg. Very cheap, friendly (*egaloo matar* Rs 10).
T Kamat, Navrose Mansion, Tardeo Rd. Indian. Very inexpensive thalis and vegetarian snacks.

Juhu Beach and Bandra *p441*

TT Gazalee, Kadambari Complex, Hanuman Rd, Vile Parle (E), T022-2838 8093. Finest coastal cuisine, try stuffed Bombay Duck and shellfish.
TT Just around the Corner, 24th-30th road junction, TPS III, Bandra (W). Bright casual American-style diner. Long breakfast menu (0800-1100). Lots of combination options, excellent salads, low calorie.
TT Olive Bar & Kitchen, Pali Hill Tourist Hotel, 14 Union Park Khar (W), T022-2605 8228, www.olivebarandkitchen.com. Olive caters to an ultra-chic Bollywood Bombay crowd. This also means that they do not encourage male gawpers, so men need to be escorted by women to get in.
TT Out of the Blue, at Pali Hills. Steak and fondue, great sizzlers, unusual combinations, flavoured ice teas, flambéed desserts, UV lit inside or outside smoke-free.
TT Trim with Taste, 500 Sant Kutir, Linking Rd, Bandra (lane behind KBN store). Small, spotless, serving unusual health food. Try stuffed iddlis, peach and yoghurt smoothies.
T Crunchy Munchy, Agarwal Market, next to Vile Parle (E) station. Open-air café serving vegetarian Indian and Mexican mini-meals. Very clean, good service and portions.
T Kanchi, Mittal Industrial Estate, Andheri-Kurla Rd, Marol, Andheri (E). Excellent South Indian vegetarian, unusual daily specials. Recommended.
T Lucky, 9 SV Rd (Hill Rd junction), Bandra (W). Good mughlai especially chicken biriyani and tandooris.

Bars and clubs

All major hotels and restaurants have bars, others may only serve beer. Many pubs expect couples Fri-Sun. Most pubs charge Rs 175-250 for a 'pitcher' (bottle); cocktails Rs 75-150. Pick up *Mumbai This Fortnight*, an informative free booklet on everything that is hot in the city, free from larger bookshops and stores.

Gateway of India and Colaba *p434, map p435*

Athena, 41/44 Minoo Desai Marg, Colaba, T022-2202 8699, www.athenaontheweb.com, 1930-0130, food till 2345. At Chateau Indage, champagne cigar lounge and restaurant. A slick celeb-festooned hangout, 300 capacity joint. Rs1000 per couple (Rs 300 entry then Rs 700 redeemed against drinks). Slick lounge with drapes and white leatherette and pearly pink lounge beds. Lounge music.
Insomnia, Taj. Snazzy.
Polly Esther, Gordon House Hotel. A reggae, pop, rock disco, retro-themed club.
Provogue Lounge, Phoenix Mills, Lower Parel. By day a boutique for natty fashion brand, by night they clad the clothes rails

with white wood and the sales tills turn to ringing out tequilas. Very in-crowd Mumbai. **Red Light**, Khala Gowda, sleazy as they come, see behaviour from Mumbaikars that would shock the hell out of you if you saw it on your local high-street disco, but brilliant all the same – proper bhangra and Hindi pop plus Western dance music.

Central Mumbai *p434, map p437*

Flavors, a bright 24-hr coffee shop-resto-bar. Chic, interesting cocktails and starters (PSP prawns, corn and spinach toast), barbecue buffet lunch (Rs 300-800), happy hour (1800-2000), try Graveyard (huge) or Flavothon (a shooter race), big screen, DJ (weekends). Fun at a price.

Café Olé, Ground floor, Cross Rds, Haji Ali, T022-2495 5123. Classic sports bar, chrome and glass, interesting menu (some Indianized), try Cactus Passion or Red Ginger (non-alcoholic), mini dance floor, DJ at weekends, fun place, affordable drinks.

Copa Cabana, Dariya Vihar, 39/D Girgaum, Chowpatty, T022-2368 0274. Small, playing 70s hits and Latino music, packed at weekends so little space for dancing.

Geoffreys, **Hotel Marine Plaza**, Marine Drive, T022-2285 1212. Soft music, relaxing for a drink and a bite, no dancing.

Ghetto, B Desai Rd (100 m from Mahalakshmi Temple). Western pop from 60s, 70s, 80s, free entry (couples only), neon graffiti.

Juhu Paparazzi, opposite Juhu Bus Depot, Juhu Beach Rd, T022-2660 2199, Tue-Sun. Small, cosy disco bar, packed after 2300, drinks and snacks.

Razzberry Rhinoceros, **Juhu Hotel**, Juhu Tara Rd, T022-2618 4012. Disco, nightclub. Lots of space for dancing, pool tables, live acts.

Marine Drive, Malabar Hill and around *p440, map p437*

Intercontinental, 135 Marine Drive, T022-5639 9999, www.intercontinental.com. Extremely expensive, and trendy, nightclub that comes alive with house music on Fri and Sat night. For beautiful people.

Not Just Jazz by the Bay, 143 Marine Drive, T022-2285 1876. Modern chrome and glass, live music (varied), karaoke, good food menu (great starters, desserts), generous portions, wide selection of drinks, very lively, a fun place.

Entertainment

Cinema

Bollywood films are screened in dozens of cinemas: try **Eros** opposite Churchgate station or **Metro**, on MG Rd, northwest corner of Azad Maidan.

English language films are shown at many, including **Regal**, Colaba Causeway, **New Empire** and **Sterling**, Marzaban Rd, southwest of CST station. It is best for women to get seats in the circle.

Theatres

Plays are performed in English, Hindi, Marathi and Gujarati, usually beginning at 1815-1900. Check *Mumbai This Fortnight* for details. See a modern Hindi play at **Privthi Theatre** to sample local culture; cool café for drinks and snacks outside.

Festivals and events

In addition to the national Hindu and Muslim festivals there are the following:

First weekend in Jan **Banganga Classical Music Festival** at Walkeshwar Temple. Magical atmosphere around temple tank with fine musicians taking part; tickets Rs 50-150 (much in demand).

Feb **Elephanta Cultural Festival** at the caves. Great ambience. Contact MTDC, T022-2202 6713, for tickets Rs 150-200 including launch at 1800. **Kala Ghoda Arts Festival.** New annual showcase of all forms of fine arts. T022-2284 2520; also weekend festival, mid-Dec to mid-Jan includes food and handicrafts at Rampart Row, Fort.

Mar **Jamshed Navroz.** This is New Year's Day for the Parsi followers of the Fasli calendar. The celebrations which include offering prayers at temples, exchanging greetings, alms-giving and feasting at home, date back to Jamshed, the legendary King of Persia.

Jul-Aug **Janmashtami** celebrates the birth of Lord Krishna. Boys and young men form human pyramids and break pots of curd hung up high between buildings.

Aug **Coconut Day.** The angry monsoon seas are propitiated by devotees throwing coconuts into the ocean.

Aug-Sep **Ganesh Chaturthi.** Massive figures of Ganesh are worshipped and immersed in the sea on several days following the festival.

Sep **Mount Mary's Feast**, celebrated at St Mary's Church, Bandra. A fair is also held.

Sep-Oct **Dasara**. During this nationwide festival, in Mumbai there are group dances by Gujarati women in all the auditoria. There are also Ramlila celebrations at Chowpatty Beach. **Diwali** (The Festival of Lights) is particularly popular in mercantile Mumbai when the business community celebrate their New Year and open new account books.

25 Dec **Christmas**. Christians across Mumbai celebrate the birth of Christ. A pontifical High Mass is held at midnight in the open air at the Cooperage Grounds.

Shopping

Most shops are open 1000-1900 (closed Sun), the bazars sometimes staying open as late as 2100. Mumbai prices are often higher than in other Indian cities, and hotel arcades tend to be very pricey but carry good quality select items. Best buys are textiles, particularly tie-and-dye from Gujarat, hand-block printed cottons, Aurangabad and 'Patola' silks, gold bordered saris from Surat and Khambat, handicrafts, jewellery and leather goods. **Crossroads** and **Pyramid**, Haji Ali, are modern shopping centres.

Antiques

It is illegal to take anything over 100 years old out of the country.

Natesan in Jehangir Gallery basement and in Taj Hotel. For fine antiques and copies.

Phillips, Madame Cama Rd. An Aladdin's cave of bric-a-brac and curios.

Bazars

Crawford Market, Ambedkar Rd (fun for bargain hunting) and **Mangaldas Market**. Other shopping streets are South Bhagat Singh Marg, M Karve Rd and Linking Rd, Bandra. For a different experience try **Chor (Thieves') Bazaar**, on Maulana Shaukat Ali Rd in central Mumbai, full of finds from Raj left-overs to precious jewellery. Make time to stop at the **Mini Market**, 33-31 Mutton St, T022-2347 24257 (closed Fri), minimarket@rediffmail.com and nose through the Bollywood posters, lobby cards, and photo-stills. On Fri, 'junk' carts sell less expensive 'antiques' and fakes.

Books

There are lines of 2nd hand stalls along Churchgate St and near the University. An annual book fair takes place at the Cross Maidan near Churchgate each Dec.

Crossword, 22 B Desai Rd, near Mahalakshmi Temple, smart, spacious, good selection.

Danai, 14th Khar Danda Rd. Books and music.

Dial-a-book, T022-2649 5618. Quick delivery.

Nalanda, Taj Mahal Hotel, excellent art books, Western newspapers/magazines.

Strand Books, off Sir PM Rd near HMV, T022-2206 1994. Excellent selection, best deals, shipping (reliable).

Clothes

Benzer, B Desai Rd, Breach Candy (open Sun), good saris and Indian garments.

The Courtyard, 41/44 Minoo Desai Marg, Colaba. Very new, very elite and fashionable mini-mall includes boutiques full of stunning heavy deluxe designs (Swarovski crystal-studded saris, anyone?) by **Rohit Bal**, www.balance.ws. **Rabani & Rakha** (Rs 17,000 for a sari) but probably most suitable to the Western eye is textile designer Neeru Kumar's **Tulsi** label, a cotton textiles designer from Delhi. Beautiful linen/silk stoles and fine *kantha* thread work. There's also a store from Indian designer **Pratap**, spelt à la Prada.

Ensemble, 130-132 South Bhagat Singh Marg, T022-2287 2882. Superb craftsmanship and service for women's clothes – Indian and 'East meets West'.

Fabindia, 66 Pali Hill, Bandra (W), handloom kurtas etc, Bamboo earthenware and jute home furnishings, *khadi* and *mulmul* cloth.

Melange, 33 Altamount Rd, T022-2385 4492. Western-tailored, Indian embroidery clothes. Stocks designs from great labels.

Michele Boutique, shop No 21, Shah House, Mandlik Rd, T022-2288 5312. 25 tailors, 24-hr turnaround, fabric onsite includes linen, raw silk and cashmere.

Crafts and textiles

Government emporia from many states sell good handicrafts and textiles; several at **World Trade Centre**, Cuffe Parade. In

Colaba, a street **Craft Market** is held on Sun (Nov-Jan) in K Dubash Marg.

Anokhi, 4B August Kranti Marg, opposite Kumbala Hill Hospital. Good gifts.

Bombay Store, Western India House, 1st floor, PM Rd, Fort. Spacious, ethnic lifestyle, gifts (open Sun), value for money.

Contemporary Arts and Crafts, 19 Napeansea Rd, T022-2363 1979. Handicrafts, weaves and crockery, ethnic, traditional or modern.

Cottage Industries Emporium, Apollo Bunder. A nationwide selection, especially Kashmiri embroidery, South Indian handicrafts and Rajasthani textiles. Colaba Causeway, next to **BEST**, for ethnic ware, handicrafts and fabrics.

Curio Cottage, 19 Mahakavi Bhushan Rd, near the Regal Cinema, T022-2202 2607. Silver jewellery and antiques.

Good Earth, 104 Kemp's Corner. Smart, trendy, pottery, glass and handmade paper stationery.

Sadak Ali, behind **Taj Hotel**. Good range of carpets, but bargain hard.

Yamini, President House, Wodehouse Rd, Colaba, especially for vibrant textiles.

Jewellery

Le Bijou Mahavir Bhuvansh, 37 Hill Rd, Bandra, T022-2644 3473. Trinkets, junk jewels.

Popli Suleman Chambers, Battery St, Apollo Bunder, T022-2285 4757. Semi-precious stones, gems, garnets and pearls.

Music

Groove, West Wing, 1st floor, Eros Cinema, Churchgate. Has café.

Hiro, SP Mehta St. Good Indian classical CDs.

Planet M, opposite CST station. Also has book/poetry readings, gigs.

Rhythm House, north of Jehangir Gallery. Excellent selection of jazz and classical CDs.

Musical instruments on VB Patel Rd, RS Mayeka at No 386, **Haribhai Vishwanath** at No 419 and **Ram Singh** at Bharati Sadan.

Photography

Heera Panna Shopping Arcade, Haji Ali, T022-2494 6318. All things electrical: mini-disc gadgets, camera, phone accessories etc.

Kodak Express,1B East and West Court, Colaba Causeway (near Churchill café).

Mazda at 231, T022-2300 4001. Hasselblad, Metz, Nikon, offers free pick up/delivery.

Remedios, opposite Khadi Bhandar, between CST and Flora Fountain, reliable repairs. Best buy cameras from DN Rd.

Silks and saris

Many including **Kala Niketan**, MG Rd and **Juhu Reclamation**.

Sheetal, Tirupati Apartments, B Desai Rd, saris from all over India; fair prices.

Vama, in Kanchenjunga (next to Kemp's Corner), tailoring possible.

Activities and tours

Adventure tourism

Maharashtra Tourism actively encourages adventure tourism (including jungle safaris and watersports) by introducing 'rent-a-tent' and hiring out trekking gear. Prices range from US$35-150 per day/weekend depending on season and activity. Some provide electricity, linen, bathrooms and authentic cuisine. It has also set up 27 holiday resorts providing cheap accommodation at hill stations, beaches, archaeological sites and scenic spots. Details from tourist offices.

Body and soul

Iyengar Yogashraya Mumbai, Elmac House, 126 Senapati Bapat Marg, Lower Parel 91, T022-2494 8416, info@bksiyengar.com. Iyengar drop-in centre.

Kaivalyadahama, next to Taraporewala Aquarium, Marine Drive.

The Yoga Institute, Praghat Colony, Santa Cruz (E).

Yoga Training Centre, 51 Jai Hind Club, Juhu Scheme.

Yoga Vidhya Niketan, Sane Guruji Marg, Dadar, T022-2430 6258.

Horse racing

Mahalaxmi Race Course, opposite Haji Ali. Season Nov-Mar, Sun and holidays, 1400-1700. Many of India's top races are held at the delightful course (1878), including the Derby in Feb/Mar.

Swimming

Breech Candy Club, B Desai Rd, T022-2361 2543. For the select set, 2 clean pools including a large one; non-members Rs 250.

Tours

If you wish to sightsee independently with a guide, ask at the tourist office. See page 432.

Ajanta and Ellora MTDC 4-day tour to the famous caves at Ajanta and Ellora.

City sightseeing Approved guides from the **India tourist office**, T022-2203 6854. City tour usually includes visits to The Gateway of India, the Chhatrapati Sivaji (Prince of Wales) Museum, Jain temple, Hanging Gardens, Kamla Nehru Park and Mani Bhavan (Gandhi Museum). Suburban tour includes Juhu Beach, Kanheri Caves and Lion Safari Park.

MTDC Madam Cama Rd, opposite LIC Building, T022-2202 6713. City tour daily except Mon, 0900-1300 and 1400-1800, Rs 100. Suburban tour 0915 (from Dadar 1015-1815. Fort walk is a heritage walk around CST and Fort area with the Kala Ghoda Association, Army & Navy Building, T022-2285 2520, www.artindia.co.in. Elephanta tours from Gateway of India. Boat, 0900-1415, Rs 70 return; reserve at Apollo Bunder, T022-2202 6364.

Transport

Air

International Departure Tax, Rs 500 (Rs 250 within south Asia) is often included in the price of your ticket. Look for 'FT' in the tax column.

Chhatrapati Sivaji International airport, T022-2632 9090. Left luggage counter, across the drive from end of departure terminal, Rs 35-45 per item per day. The tourist office counter helps to book rooms in upmarket hotels. There is an Indian Railways reservations and car hire desks inside, and domestic airlines' counters just outside the exit. The new domestic terminal (1A), exclusively for Indian Airlines, is 400 m from the old terminal (1B), used by others. Enquiries: T140, 143.

Touts are very pushy at both terminals but the hotels they recommend are often appalling. It is worth making your own telephone call to hotels of your choice from the airport. The rest rooms in the old domestic terminal are clean, comfortable (rooms Rs 500, dorm Rs 200); available for those flying within 24 hrs, but are often full; apply to the Airport Manager.

Transport to and from the airport

Pre-paid taxis into town, from counter at the exit at the Chhatrapati Sivaji International terminal (ignore taxi touts near the baggage hall). Give the exact area or hotel, and the number of pieces of luggage. Hand the receipt to the driver at the end of the journey. There is no need to tip. To **Nariman Point** or **Gateway of India**, about Rs 260, 1 hr. During 'rush hour' it can take 2 hrs. Late at night, taxis take about ½ hr – hair-raising! To **Juhu Beach** Rs 150. From Santa Cruz: metered taxis should charge around the same. Dispatchers at the airport claim that each taxi can take only 3 passengers. Stand firm as this law is totally disregarded elsewhere. The red BEST buses connect both terminals with the city. No buses at present to New Mumbai.

Airline offices

Domestic Air India to **Chennai**, **Delhi**, **Hyderabad**, **Kolkata**, **Thiruvanantha-puram**. **Indian Airlines**, Nariman Pt, T022-2202 3031, to all major cities. **Jet Airways**, B1 Amarchand Mansions, Madam Cama Rd, T022-2285 5788, airport, T022-2615 6666, www.jetairways.com. To 23 destinations. **Sahara**, Tulsani Chambers, Nariman Pt, T022-2288 2718, airport T022-2613 4159. To **Bengaluru (Bangalore)**, **Bhopal**, **Delhi**, **Goa**, **Indore**, **Jaipur**, **Kolkata**, **Lucknow**, **Patna**, **Varanasi**.

International Air India, 1st floor, Nariman Pt (Counters also at Taj Mahal Hotel, Centaur Hotel and Santa Cruz), T022-2202 4142, Airport T022-2836 6767.

Aeroflot, Tulsani Chambers, Nariman Pt, T022-2287 1942. **Air Canada**, Amarchand Mansions, Madam Cama Rd, T022-2202 7632, Airport T022-2604 5653. **Air France**, Maker Chamber VI, Nariman Pt, T022-2202 5021, Airport T022-2832 8070. **Alitalia**, Industrial Assur Building, Vir Nariman Rd, Churchgate, T022-2204 5023, airport T022-2837 9657. **Biman**, 199 J Tata Rd, Churchgate, T022-2282 4659. **British Airways**, 202-B Vulcan Ins Building, Vir Nariman Rd, T022-2282 0888, Mon-Fri 0800-1300, 1345-1800. Sat 0900-1300, airport T022-2832 9061. **Canadian**, Taj Intercontinental, T022-2202 9112, Airport T022-2836 6205. **Delta**, Taj Mahal Hotel, T022-2288 5660, Airport T022-2834 9890. **Emirates**, Mittal Chamber, Nariman Pt, T022-2287 1649. **Gulf Air**, Maker

Chambers, 5 Nariman Pt, T022-2202 1626. **Japan**, Raheja Centre, Nariman Pt, T022-2287 4940. **KLM**, 198 J Tata Rd, T022-2288 6973. **Kuwait**, 2A Stadium House, 86 Vir Nariman Rd, Churchgate, T022-2204 5351. **Lufthansa**, Express Towers, Nariman Pt, T022-2202 3430. **PIA**, Mittal Towers, Nariman Pt, T022-2202 1455. **Qantas**, 42 Sakhar Bhavan, Nariman Pt, T022-2202 0343. **Royal Jordanian**, 199 J Tata Rd, T022-2282 3065. **Saudia**, Express Tower, Nariman Pt, T022-2202 0199. **Singapore Airlines**, Taj Inter- continental, T022-2202 2747. **Sri Lanka**, Raheja Centre, Nariman Pt, T022-2284 4148, Airport T022-2832 7050. **Thai Airways**, 15 World Trade Centre, Cuffe Parade, T022-2218 6502.

Bus

Red **BEST** (Bombay Electrical Supply Co) buses are available in most parts of Greater Mumbai, T022-2412 8725. Within the Central Business District, buses are marked 'CBD'.

Maharashtra RTC operates bus services to all the major centres and District HQs in the state as well as to **Ahmadabad**, **Bengaluru (Bangalore)**, **Goa**, **Mangalore**, **Indore**, **Vadodara** and **Hyderabad** in other states. Information on services from **MSRTC**, central bus stand, Mumbai Central, T022-2307 6622.

Private buses also travel long-distance routes. Some long-distance buses also leave from Dadar which has many travel agents. Information and tickets from **Dadar Tourist Centre**, outside Dadar station, T022-2411 3398.

Car

For 8 hrs or 80 km: Luxury a/c cars Rs 1500; Maruti/Ambassador, a/c Rs 1000, non a/c Rs 800. **Auto Hirers**, 7 Commerce Centre, Tardeo, T022-2494 2006. **Blaze**, Colaba, T022-2202 0073. **Budget**, T022-2494 2644, and **Sai**, Phoenix Mill Compound, Senapati Bapat Marg, Lower Parel, T022-2494 2644. Recommended. **Wheels**, T022-2282 2874. Holiday caravans with driver, T022-2202 4627.

Rickshaw

Not available in central Mumbai (south of Mahim). Metered; about Rs 8 per km, revised tariff card held by the driver (x8, in suburbs) 25% extra at night (2400-0500). Some rickshaw drivers show the revised tariff card for taxis! It's worth buying a card for a couple of rupees from hawkers at traffic junctions.

Victorias (horse-drawn carriages), available at Mumbai Central, Chowpatty and Gateway of India. Rates negotiable.

Taxi

Metered yellow-top or blue a/c: easily available. Rs 12 for first km and Rs 12 for each Re 1 on meter. Revised tariff card held by drivers. Taxis called by hotel doormen often arrive with meter registering Rs 12. Always get a prepaid taxi at the airport.

Train

Suburban electric trains are economical. They start from Churchgate for the west suburbs and CST (VT) for the east suburbs but are often desperately crowded (stay near the door or you may miss your stop!); there are 'Ladies' cars. Trains leaving Mumbai Central often have seats at the terminus but soon fill up. Avoid peak hours (southbound 0700-1100, northbound 1700-2000), and keep a tight hold on valuables. The difference between 1st and 2nd class is not always obvious although 1st class is 10 times as expensive. Inspectors fine people for travelling in the wrong class or without a ticket.

Times for trains are published each Sat in the *Indian Express* paper. To book trains foreign tourists must have foreign currency or an encashment certificate and passport.

Mumbai is the HQ of the **Central and Western Railways**, enquiries, T134/135; reservations, T022-2265 9512, 0800-1230, 1300-1630 (Foreigners' Counter opens 0900; best time to go). **Western Railway**, Churchgate, and Mumbai Central, 0800-1345, 1445-2000. All for 1st class bookings and Indrail Passes.

Foreign tourists Tourist Quota counter on mezzanine floor above tourist office opposite Churchgate Station for Northern Railways. Otherwise, queue downstairs at reservations. For **Southern Railways**, at CST, the tourist counter is on the ground floor (towards the left), credit cards upstairs. **Railway Tourist Guides** at CST and Churchgate, bus 138 goes between them.

The following depart from CST unless specified by these abbreviations: Bandra (B), Central (C), Dadar (D), Lokmanya Tilak (LT): **Ahmadabad** (all from Mumbai Central): *Shatabdi Exp 2009*, 0625, except Fri, 7 hrs; *Karnavati Exp 2933*,1340, except Wed, 7¾ hrs;

Saurashtra Mail 9005, 2025, 9 hrs; *Gujarat Mail 2901*, 2150, 9 hrs. **Allahabad**: *Howrah Mail 3004*, 2110, 23½ hrs; *Mahanagari Exp 1093*, 2355, 24¼ hrs. **Agra Cantonment**: *Punjab Mail 2137*, 1910, 21½ hrs. **Aurangabad** (for **Ajanta** and **Ellora**): *Tapovan Exp 7617*, 0610, 7½ hrs; *Devgiri Exp 1003*, 2120, 7½ hrs. **Bengaluru (Bangalore)**: *Udyan Exp 6529*, 0755, 24¾ hrs; *Coimbatore Exp 1013*, 2220 (LT), 23¾ hrs. **Bhopal**: *Pushpak Exp 2133*, 0810, 14 hrs; *Punjab Mail, 2137*, 1910, 14 hrs. **Chennai**: *Dadar Chennai Exp 1063*, 2020 (D), 23¾ hrs; *Chennai Exp 6011*, 1400, 26¾ hrs.

Ernakulam (for **Kochi**): *Netravati Exp 6345*, 2300 (LT), 29½ hrs. **Guntakal** (for **Hospet/ Hampi**): *Dadar Chennai Exp 1063*, 2020 (D), 15 hrs; *Udyan Exp 6529*, 0755, 16¾ hrs; *Coimbatore Exp 1013*, 2220 (LT), 16¼ hrs; *Kanniyakumari Exp 1081*, 1535, 17¾ hrs. **Gwalior**: *Punjab Mail 2137*, 1910, 19¾ hrs. **Hyderabad**: *Hussainsagar Exp 7001*, 2155, 15¼ hrs; *Hyderabad Exp 7031*, 1235, 17½ hrs. **Kolkata** (**Howrah**): *Gitanjali Exp 2859*, 0600, 33 hrs; *Howrah Mail 8001*, 2015, 35½ hrs. **Lucknow**: *Pushpak Exp 2133*, 0810, 25½ hrs.

Madgaon (for **Goa**): The day train is a good option, the night service is heavily booked. Special trains during the winter. *Mandavi Exp 0103*, 0515, 11 hrs; *Konkan Kanya Exp 0111*, 2240, 12 hrs; *Netravati Exp 6635*, 1640, 13½ hrs (LT). **New Delhi**: *Rajdhani Exp 2951*, 1655 (C), 17 hrs; *Golden Temple Mail 2903*, 2130 (C), 21½ hrs; *August Kranti Rajdhani Exp 2953*, 1740 (C), 17¼ hrs (to Hazrat Nizamuddin). **Pune**: deluxe trains *Shatabdi Exp 2027*, 0640, 3½ hrs; *Deccan Queen Exp 2123*, 1710, 3½ hrs, among many. **Thiruvananthapuram**: *Netravati Exp 6345*, 2300 (LT), 35 hrs. **Ujjain**: *Avantika Exp 2961*, 1925 (C), 12½ hrs. **Varanasi**: *Lokmanya Tilak Varanasi Exp 2165*, 0520 (LT), Mon, Thu, Sat, 26 hrs; *Muzaffarpur/ Darbanga Exp 5217/5219*, 1125 (LT), 27¼ hrs.

Directory

Ambulance T102. **Banks** Most are open 1000-1400, Mon-Fri, 1000-1200, Sat. Closed on Sun, holidays, 30 Jun, 31 Dec. Best to change money at the airport, or at Bureau de Change (upstairs) in Air India Building, Nariman Pt or at **Thomas Cook**, 324 Dr DN Rd, T022-2204 8556; also at 102B Maker Tower, 10th floor, F Block, Cuffe Pde; TCI, Chander Mukhi, Nariman Pt; A/2 Silver Arch, JB Nagar, Andheri; and at International Airport. **American Express**, Regal Cinema Building, Colaba. ATMs for Visa card holders using their usual PIN at **British Bank of the Middle East**, 16 Vir Nariman Rd; **Citibank**, Air India Building, Nariman Pt, 293 Dr DN Rd; **Hongkong Bank**, 52/60 MG Rd, Fort; Standard Chartered, 81 Ismaili Building, Dr DN Rd, 264 Annie Besant Rd and elsewhere. **Credit cards** American **Express**, Lawrence and Mayo Building, Dr DN Rd; **Diners Club**, Raheja Chambers, 213 Nariman Pt; **Mastercard**, C Wing, Mittal Tower, Nariman Pt; **Visa**, Standard Chartered Grindlays Bank, 90 MG Rd. Usually open 1000-1700. Sahar Airport 24 hrs. Post offices all over the city and most 5-star hotels. **Embassies and consulates** Australia, Maker Tower East, 16th floor, Cuffe Pde, T022-2218 1071. **Austria**, Maker Chambers VI, Nariman Pt, T022-2285 1066. **France**, Datta Prasad, NG Cross Rd, T022-2495 0918. **Germany**, 10th floor, Hoechst House, Nariman Pt, T022-2283 2422. **Indonesia**, 19 Altamount Rd, T022-2386 8678. **Israel**, 50 Deshmukh Marg, Kailas, T022-2386 2794. **Italy**, Kanchenjunga, 72G Deshmukh Marg, T022-2380 4071. **Japan**, 1 ML Dahanukar Marg, T022-2493 4310. **Malaysia**, Rahimtoola House, Homji St, T022-2266 0056. **Netherlands**, 1 Marine Lines Cross Rd, Churchgate, T022-2201 6750. **Philippines** , Sekhar Bhavan, Nariman Pt, T022-2281 4103. **Spain**, 6 K Dubash Marg, T022-2287 4797. **Sri Lanka**, 34 Homi Modi St, T022-2204 5861. **Sweden**, 85 Sayani Rd, Prabhadevi, T022-2421 2681. **Thailand**, 43 B Desai Rd, T022-2363 1404. **UK**, Maker Chamber IV, Nariman Pt, T022-2283 0517. **USA**, Lincoln House, B Desai Rd, T022-2368 5483. **Fire** T101. **Internet** Among many: **British Council**, A Wing, 1st floor, Mittal Tower, Nariman Pt, T022-2282 3560, Tue-Sat 1000-1745; **Cybercafé**, Waterfield, Bandra; **Infotek** , Express Towers, ground floor, Nariman Pt, I-way, Barrow Rd junction with Colaba Causeway and branches across Mumbai. Easily the fastest access in this 2nd floor shop with many terminals. You must first register as a member but it's well worth it. **Medical services** The larger hotels usually have a house doctor, the others invariably have a doctor on call. Ask hotel staff for prompt action. The telephone directory lists hospitals and GPs. Admission to private hospitals may not be allowed without a large cash advance (eg Rs 50,000). Insurers' guarantees may not be sufficient. **Prince Aly Khan Hospital**, Nesbit Rd near the harbour, T022-2375 4343, has been recommended. Several chemists are open 24 hours especially opposite Bombay Hospital. **Wordell**, Stadium House, Churchgate; **New Royal Chemist**, New Marine Lines. **Police** Emergency T100. **Post** Nagar Chowk, Mon- Sat, 0900-2000 (**Poste Restante** facilities 0900-1800) and Sun 1000-1730; parcels from 1st floor, rear of building, 1000-1700 (Mon- Sat); cheap 'parcelling' service on pavement outside; **Central telegraph office**, Hutatma Chowk, Churchgate PO, 'A' Rd, Colaba PO, Colaba Bus Station and also at Mandlik Rd, behind Taj Mahal Hotel. Foreign PO, Ballard Pier.

Counter at Santa Cruz. **Travel agents** Cox and Kings, 270-271 Dr DN Rd, T022-2207 3066; **Everett**, 1 Regent Chambers, Nariman Pt, T022-2284 5339; **Mercury**, 70VB Gandhi Rd, T022-2202 4785; **Space Travels**, 4th floor, Sir PM Rd, T022- 2286 4773, for discounted flights and special student offers, Mon-Fri, 1000-1700, Sat 1030- 1500; **TCI**, Chandermukhi, Nariman Pt, T022- 2202 1881; **Thomas Cook**, Cooks Building, Dr DN Rd, T022- 2281 3454; **Venture**, ground floor, Abubakar Mansion, South Bhagat Singh Marg, T022-2202 1304, efficient, helpful. **Useful addresses Foreigners' Regional Registration Office**, Annexe 2, Police Commissioner's Office, Dr DN Rd, near Phule Market. **Passport office**, T022-2493 1731.

Background

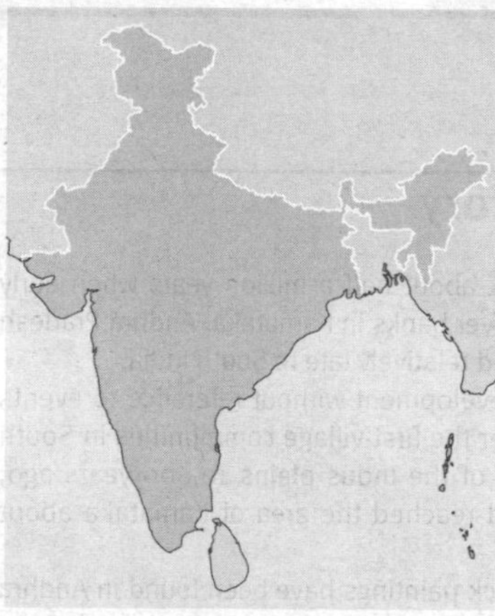

Footprint features

History

Settlement and early history

South India's earliest settlements go back about half a million years when early Palaeolithic villages were scattered along river banks in Karnataka, Andhra Pradesh and Tamil Nadu. However, cultivation arrived relatively late to South India.

It is impossible to understand this development without reference to events elsewhere in the Indian subcontinent. After the first village communities in South Asia grew up on the arid western fringes of the Indus plains 10,000 years ago, farming spread gradually southwards and reached the area of Karnataka about 3000 BC.

A series of developments followed. Rock paintings have been found in Andhra Pradesh dating from 2000 BC, and by 1650 BC copper began to be widely used. Gram and millet cultivation was introduced, and cattle, sheep and goats became widespread as domesticated animals. South India's first Iron Age site, Hallur in Karnataka, dates from around 1200 BC and from 1000 BC the use of iron was common across the whole peninsula.

All these developments appear to have lagged behind their earlier introduction in northwestern India. In the Baluchistan hills of southern Pakistan there is evidence of agricultural settlement as early as 8500 BC. By 3500 BC agriculture had spread throughout the Indus plains and in the thousand years following there were independent settled villages well to the east of the Indus. At its height the Indus Valley civilization covered as great an area as Egypt or Mesopotamia. However, the culture that developed was distinctively South Asian. The language, which is still untranslated, may well have been an early form of the Dravidian languages which today are found largely in South India.

India from 2000 BC to the Mauryas

In about 2000 BC Mohenjo Daro, widely presumed to be the capital of the Indus Valley civilization, became deserted and within the next 250 years the entire civilization disintegrated. Whatever the causes, some features of Indus Valley culture were carried on by succeeding generations.

BC	Northern South Asia	Peninsular India	External events	BC
900,000 500,000	Lower Palaeolithic sites from NW to the Peninsula; Pre-Soan stone industries in NW.	Earliest Palaeolithic sites - Narmada Valley; Karnataka; Tamil Nadu and Andhra.	Earliest hominids in West Asia First occupation of N China. Origin of *homo sapiens* in Africa. *Homo sapiens* in East Asia. First human settlement in Americas (Brazil).	450,000 150,000 100,000 30,000
10,000	Beginning of Mesolithic period.	Continuous occupation of caves and riverside sites.	Earliest known pottery - Kukui, Japan. Ice Age retreats - Hunter gatherers in Europe.	10,500 8300
8000	First wheat and barley grown in Indus plains.	Mesolithic.	First domesticated wheat, barley in fertile crescent; first burials in North America.	8000
7500	Pottery at Mehrgarh; development of villages.	Increase in range of cereals in Rajasthan.	Agriculture begins in New Guinea.	7000
6500	Humped Indian cattle domesticated, farming develops.	Cultivation extends south.	Britain separated from Continental Europe by sea level.	6500

From 1500 BC northern India entered the Vedic period. Aryan settlers moved southeast towards the Ganga valley. Classes of rulers *(rajas)* and priests *(brahmins)* began to emerge. Grouped into tribes, conflict was common. In one battle of this period a confederacy of tribes known as the Bharatas defeated another grouping of 10 tribes. They gave their name to the region to the east of the Indus which is the official name for India today – Bharat.

The centre of population and of culture shifted east from the banks of the Indus to the land between the rivers Yamuna and Ganga, the *doab* (pronounced *doe-ahb*, literally 'two waters'). This region became the heart of emerging Aryan culture, which, from 1500 BC onwards, laid the literary and religious foundations of what ultimately became Hinduism, spreading to embrace the whole of India.

The Vedas The first fruit of this development was the Rig Veda, the first of four Vedas, composed, collected and passed on orally by Brahmin priests from 1300 BC to about 1000 BC. In the later Vedic period, from about 1000 BC to 600 BC, the Sama, Yajur and Artha Vedas show that the Indo-Aryans developed a clear sense of the Ganga-Yamuna *doab* as 'their' territory. Modern Delhi lies just to the west of this region, central both to the development of history and myth in South Asia. Later texts extended the core region from the Himalaya to the Vindhyans and to the Bay of Bengal in the east. Beyond lay the lands, first of mixed peoples and then of barbarians, outside the pale of Aryan society.

From the sixth to the third centuries BC the region from the foothills of the Himalaya across the Ganga plains to the edge of the Peninsula was governed by a variety of kingdoms or *Mahajanapadhas* – 'great states'. Trade gave rise to the birth of towns in the Ganga plains themselves, many of which have remained occupied to the present. Varanasi (Benaras) is perhaps the most famous example, but a trade route was established that ran from Taxila (20 km from modern Islamabad in Pakistan) to Rajgir 1500 km away in what is now Bihar. It was into these kingdoms of the Himalayan foothills and north plains that both Mahavir, founder of Jainism and the Buddha, were born.

The Mauryas

Alexander the Great Political developments in the north often left an imprint on South India.

Within a year of the retreat of Alexander the Great's invading army in 326BC, **Chandragupta Maurya** established the first indigenous empire to exercise control

BC	Northern South Asia	Peninsular India	External events	BC
3,500	Potter's wheel in use. Long distance trade.		Sumeria, Mesopotamia: first urban civilization.	3500
3,000	Incipient urbanization in the Indus plains.	First neolithic settlements in south Deccan (Karnataka). Ash mounds, cattle herding.	First Egyptian state; Egyptian hieroglyphics; walled citadels in Mediterranean Europe.	3100
2500	Indus valley civilization cities of Moenjo Daro, Harappa and many others.	Chalcolithic ('copper' age) in Rajasthan; Neolithic continues in south.	Great Pyramid of Khufu China: walled settlements; European Bronze Age begins: hybridization of maize in South America.	2530 2500
2000	Occupation of Moenjo Daro ends.	Chalcolithic in Malwa Plateau, Neolithic ends in south; in Karnataka and Andhra - rock paintings.	Earliest ceramics in Peru. Collapse of Old Kingdom in Egypt. Stonehenge in Britain. Minoan Crete.	2300 2150
1750	Indus Valley civilization ends.	Hill-top sites in south India.	Joseph sold into Egypt - Genesis.	1750

Indo-Aryans and Dravidians

Recent genetic research suggests that homo sapiens originated in Africa less than 150,000 years ago. Southern and northern Indian types developed distinct genetic characteristics less than 40,000 years ago as they moved out of their central Asian homeland, first into West Asia and then into India, disproving all ideas of racial purity. Early Mediterranean groups form the main component of the Dravidian speakers of the four South Indian states. Later Mediterranean types also seem to have come from the northwest and down the Indus Valley, but more important were the Indo-Aryans, who migrated from the steppes of Central Asia from around 2000 BC.

over much of the subcontinent. Under his successors that control was extended to all but the extreme south of peninsular India.

The centre of political power had shifted steadily east into wetter, more densely forested, but also more fertile regions. The Mauryans had their base in the region known as Magadh (now Bihar) and their capital at Pataliputra, near modern Patna. Their power was based on massive military force and a highly efficient, centralized administration. Chandragupta's army may have had as many as 9000 elephants, 30,000 cavalry and 600,000 infantry. Chandragupta is believed to have been cremated on Chandragiri, a small hillock in southern Karnataka. Bindusara, his successor, extended the empire south as far as Mysore.

Asoka The greatest of the Mauryan emperors, Asoka took power in 272 BC. He inherited a full-blown empire, but extended it further by defeating the Kalingans in modern Orissa, before turning his back on war and preaching the virtues of Buddhist pacifism. Asoka's empire stretched from Afghanistan to Assam and from the Himalaya to Mysore. He inherited a structure of government set out by Chandragupta's Prime Minister, **Kautilya,** in a book on the principles of government, the *Arthashastra*. The state maintained itself by raising revenue from taxation – on everything from agriculture to gambling and prostitution. He decreed that 'no waste land should be occupied and not a tree cut down' without permission, not out of a modern 'green' concern for protecting the forests, but because all were potential sources of revenue for the state. The *sudras* (lowest of Hindu castes) were used as free labour for clearing forest and cultivating new land.

BC	Northern South Asia	Peninsular India	External events	BC
1750 1500	Successors to Indus Valley. Aryans invade in successive waves. Development of Indo-Aryan language.	Copper Age spreads, Neolithic continues. Gram and millet cultivation. Hill terracing. Cattle, goats and sheep.	Anatolia: Hittite Empire. New Kingdom in Egypt. First metal working in Peru. First inscriptions in China; Linear B script in Greece, 1650.	1650 1570 1500 1400
1400	Indo-Aryan spread east and south to Ganga – Yamuna doab.	Horses introduced into south. Cave paintings, burials.	Tutankhamun buried in Valley of Kings.	1337
1200	Composition of Rig Veda begins?	Iron age sites at Hallur, Karnataka.	Middle America: first urban civilization in Olmec; collapse of Hittite Empire, 1200.	1200
1000	Earliest Painted Grey Ware in Upper Ganga Valley; Brahmanas begin to be written.	Iron Age becomes more widespread across Peninsula.	Australia: large stone-built villages; David King of Israel, Kingdom of Kush in Africa.	

Asoka (described on the edicts as 'the Beloved of the Gods, of Gracious Countenance') left a series of inscriptions on pillars and rocks across the subcontinent. Over most of India these inscriptions were written in *Prakrit*, using the *Brahmi* script. They were unintelligible for over 2000 years after the decline of the empire until James Prinsep deciphered the Brahmi script in 1837.

Through the edicts Asoka urged all people to follow the code of **dharma** or *dhamma* – translated by the Indian historian Romila Thapar as 'morality, piety, virtue and social order'. He established a special force of *dharma* officers to try to enforce the code, which encouraged toleration, non-violence, respect for priests and those in authority and for human dignity.

However, Romila Thapar suggests that the failure to develop any sense of national consciousness, coupled with the massive demands of a highly paid bureaucracy and army, proved beyond the abilities of Asoka's successors to sustain. Within 50 years of Asoka's death in 232 BC the Mauryan Empire had disintegrated and with it the whole structure and spirit of its government.

A period of fragmentation: 185 BC-300 AD

Beyond the Mauryan Empire other kingdoms had survived in South India. The Satavahanas dominated the central Deccan for over 300 years from about 50 BC. Further south in what is now Tamil Nadu, the early kingdoms of the Cholas and the Pandiyas gave a glimpse of both power and cultural development that was to flower over 1000 years later. In the centuries following the break-up of the Mauryan Empire these kingdoms were in the forefront of developing overseas trade, especially with Greece and Rome. Internal trade also flourished and South Indian traders carried goods to China and Southeast Asia.

The classical period – the Gupta Empire: 319-467 AD

Although the political power of Chandra Gupta and his successors never approached that of his unrelated namesake nearly 650 years before him, the Gupta Empire which was established with his coronation in AD 319 produced developments in every field of Indian culture. Even though their political power was restricted to North India, their influence has been felt profoundly across South Asia to the present.

Geographically the Guptas originated in the same Magadhan region that had given rise to the Mauryan Empire. Extending their power by strategic marriage alliances, Chandra Gupta's empire of Magadh was extended across North India by his son, Samudra Gupta, who took power in AD 335. He also marched as far south as Kanchipuram in modern Tamil Nadu, but the heartland of the Gupta Empire remained the plains of the Ganga.

BC	Northern South Asia	Peninsular India	External events	BC
800	Mahabharata war – Bhagavad Gita; Aryan invaders reach Bengal. Rise of city states in Ganga plains, based on rice cultivation.		First settlement at Rome. Celtic Iron Age begins in north and east of Alps.	850 800
750		Megalithic grave sites.	Greek city states.	750
700	Upanishads begin to be written; concept of transmigration of souls develops; Panini's Sanskrit grammar.		Iliad composed.	700
600	Northern Black Pottery.		First Latin script; first Greek coins.	600
599	Mahavir born – founder of Jainism.		First iron production in China; Zoroastrianism becomes official religion in Persia.	550
563	Gautama Buddha born.			

Chandra Gupta II reigned for 39 years from AD 376 and was a great patron of the arts. Political power was much less centralized than under the Mauryans and as Thapar points out, collection of land revenue was deputed to officers who were entitled to keep a share of the revenue, rather than to highly paid bureaucrats. Trade with Southeast Asia, Arabia and China all added to royal wealth.

That wealth was distributed to the arts on a previously unheard of scale, but Hindu institutions also benefited and some of the most important features of modern Hinduism date from this time. The sacrifices of Vedic worship were given up in favour of personal devotional worship, known as *bhakti*. Tantrism, both in its Buddhist and Hindu forms, with its emphasis on the female life force and worship of the Mother Goddess, developed. The focus of worship was increasingly towards a personalized and monotheistic deity, represented in the form of either Siva or Vishnu. The myths of Vishnu's incarnations also arose at this period.

The Brahmins The priestly caste who were in the key position to mediate change, reformed earlier literature to give focus to the emerging religious philosophy. In their hands the Mahabharata and the Ramayana were transformed from secular epics to religious stories. The excellence of contemporary sculpture both reflected and contributed to an increase in image worship and the growing role of temples as centres of devotion.

Regional kingdoms and cultures

The collapse of Gupta power in the north opened the way for successive smaller kingdoms to assert themselves. In doing so the main outlines of the modern regional geography of South Asia began to take clear shape. Regional kingdoms developed, often around comparatively small natural regions.

The southern Deccan was dominated by the Chalukyas from the sixth century up to 750 AD and again in the 11th and 12th centuries. To their south the Pandiyas, Cholas and Pallavas controlled the Dravidian lands of what is now Kerala, Tamil Nadu and coastal Andhra Pradesh. The Pallavas, responsible for building the temples at Mahabalipuram, just south of modern Chennai, flourished in the seventh century. They warded off attacks both from the Rashtrakutas to their north and from the Pandiyas, who controlled the southern deltas of the Vaigai and Tamraparni rivers, with Madurai as their capital.

In the eighth century Kerala began to develop its own regional identity with the rise of the **Kulashekharas** in the Periyar Valley. Caste was a dominating feature of the kingdom's social organization, but with the distinctive twist that the **Nayars**, the most aristocratic of castes, developed a matrilineal system of descent.

BC	Northern South Asia	Peninsular India	External events	BC
500	Upanishads finished; Taxila and Charsadda become important towns and trade centres.	Aryans colonize Sri Lanka. Irrigation practised in Sri Lanka.	Wet rice cultivation introduced to Japan.	500
326 321	Alexander at Indus. Chandragupta establishes Mauryan Dynasty.	Megalithic cultures.	Crossbow invented in China.	350
300 297	Sarnath and Sanchi stupas. Mauryan power extends to Mysore.	First Ajanta caves in original form.	Mayan writing and ceremonial centres established.	300
272- 250 232	Asoka's Empire. Brahmi script. Death of Asoka.	Chola Pandiya, Chera kingdoms: earliest Tamil inscriptions.	Ptolemy. First towns in Southeast Asia. Rome captures Spain.	285 250 206
185	Shunga Dynasty, centred on Ujjain.	Megalithic cultures in hills of south.	Romans destroy Greek states.	146

It was the **Cholas** who came to dominate the south from the eighth century. Overthrowing the Pallavas, they controlled most of Tamil Nadu, south Karnataka and southern Andhra Pradesh from 850 AD to 1278 AD. They often held the Kerala kings under their control. Under their kings **Rajaraja I** (984-1014) and **Rajendra** (1014-1044) the Cholas also controlled north Sri Lanka, sent naval expeditions to Southeast Asia and successful military campaigns north to the Ganga plains. They lavished endowments on temples and also extended the gifts of land to Brahmins instituted by the Pallavas and Pandiyas. Many thousands of Brahmin priests were brought south to serve in major temples such as those in Chidambaram and Rajendra wished to be remembered above all as the king who brought water from the holy Ganga all the way to his kingdom.

The spread of Islamic power

The Delhi Sultanate From about 1000 AD the external attacks which inflicted most damage on Rajput wealth and power in northern India came increasingly from the Arabs and Turks. Mahmud of Ghazni raided the Punjab virtually every year between 1000 and 1026, attracted both by the agricultural surpluses and the wealth of India's temples. By launching annual raids during the harvest season, Mahmud financed his struggles in Central Asia and his attacks on the profitable trade conducted along the Silk Road between China and the Mediterranean. The enormous wealth in cash, golden images and jewellery of North India's temples drew him back every year and his greed for gold, used to remonetize the economy of the remarkable Ghaznavid Sultanate of Afghanistan, was insatiable. He sacked the wealthy centres of Mathura (UP) in 1017, Thanesar (Haryana) in 1011, Somnath (Gujarat) in 1024 and Kannauj (UP) 1018. He died in 1030, to the Hindus just another *mlechchha* ('impure' or sullied one), as had been the Huns and the Sakas before him. Such raids were never taken seriously as a long term threat by kings further east or south and as the Rajputs continually feuded among themselves the northwest plains became an attractive prey.

Muslim political power was heralded by the raids of Mu'izzu'd Din from 1192 onwards inflicting crushing defeats on Hindu opponents from Gwalior to Benaras. The foundations were then laid for the first extended period of Muslim power, which came under the Delhi sultans.

The Delhi Sultanate never achieved the dominating power of earlier empires or of its successor, the Mughal Empire. It exercised political control through crushing military raids, some of which reached deep into the south, and the exaction of tribute from defeated kings, but there was no real attempt to impose central administration.

BC	Northern South Asia	Peninsular India	External events	BC
100	Kharavela King of Kalingans in Orissa. Final composition of Ramayana.	South Indian trade with Indonesia and Rome. Roman pottery and coins in South India.	Indian religions spread to Southeast Asia. Discovery of monsoon winds Introduction of Julian calendar.	100

Power depended on maintaining vital lines of communication and trade routes, keeping fortified strongholds and making regional alliances. In the Peninsula to the south, the Deccan, regional powers contested for survival, power and expansion. The Bahmanis were the forerunners of a succession of Muslim dynasties, who sometimes competed with each other and sometimes jointly collaborated against a mutual external enemy.

The Vijayanagar Empire Across West and South India today are the remains of the only major medieval Hindu empire to resist effectively the Muslim advance. The ruins at Hampi in modern Karnataka demonstrate the power of a Hindu coalition that rose to power in the south Deccan in the first half of the 14th century, only to be defeated by its Muslim neighbours in 1565, see page 475.

For over 200 years Vijayanagar the kings of (*'City of Victory'*) fought to establish supremacy. It was an empire that, in the words of one Indian historian, made it 'the nearest approach to a war state ever made by a Hindu kingdom'. At times its power reached from Orissa in the northeast to Sri Lanka. In 1390 King Harihara II claimed to have planted a victory pillar in Sri Lanka. Much of modern Tamil Nadu and Andhra Pradesh were added to the core region of Karnataka in the area under Vijayanagar control.

The Mughal Empire

Despite the ability of the Vijayanagar Empire to hold out against local Muslim powers, all regional kingdoms in the south were ultimately brought however fleetingly under Muslim influence through the power of the Mughal Empire.The descendants of conquerors, with the blood of both Tamburlaine (Timur) and Genghis Khan in their veins, the Mughals came to dominate Indian politics from Babur's victory near Delhi in 1526 to Aurangzeb's death in 1707. Their legacy was not only some of the most magnificent architecture in the world, but a profound impact on the culture, society and future politics of South Asia.

Babur (the tiger) Founder of the Mughal Dynasty, Babur was born in Russian Turkestan on 15 February 1483, the fifth direct descendant on the male side of Timur and 13th on the female side from Genghis Khan. He established the Mughal Empire in 1526. Though when he died four years later, the Empire was still far from secured, he had not only laid the foundations of political and military power but had also begun to establish courtly traditions of poetry, literature and art which became the hallmark of subsequent Mughal rulers.

Within two generations the Mughals had become fully at home in their Indian environment and brought some radical changes. Babur was charismatic. He ruled by

AD	North India	Peninsular India	External events	AD
		Satavahanas control much of Peninsula up to 300 AD. Thomas brings Christianity to South India. *Tamil Sangram*.	Rome population of 1 mn. Pyramid of the sun at City of Teotihuacan, Mexico.	50
78	Kushan rulers in Northwest followed by Scythians.			
		Arikamedu – trade with Rome.		68
100	Vaishnavism spreads to north and northwest.		Buddhism reaches China. Paper introduced in China; first metal work in Southeast Asia.	100
	Lawbook of Manu Gandharan art.	Mahayana Buddhism spreads. Nagarjunakonda major centre in Andhra Pradesh. First cities on Deccan plateau.	Hadrian's wall in Britain.	125
200	Hinayana/Mahayana Buddhist split.			

keeping the loyalty of his military chiefs, giving them control of large areas of territory. However, his son Humayun was forced to flee Delhi, only returning to power a year before his death.

Akbar Akbar, who was to become one of the greatest of India's emperors, was only 13 when he took the throne in 1556. The next 44 years were one of the most remarkable periods of South Asian history, paralleled by the Elizabethan period in England, where Queen Elizabeth I ruled from 1558 to 1603. Although Akbar inherited the throne, it was he who really created the empire. He also gave it many of its distinguishing features.

Through his marriage to a Hindu princess he ensured that Hindus were given honoured positions in government and respect for their religious beliefs and practices. He sustained a passionate interest in art and literature, matched by a determination to create monuments to his empire's political power and he laid the foundations for an artistic and architectural tradition which developed a totally distinctive Indian style. This emerged from the separate elements of Iranian and Indian traditions by a constant process of blending and originality of which he was the chief patron.

But these achievements were only possible because of his political and military gifts. From 1556 until his 18th birthday in 1560 Akbar was served by a prince regent, Bairam Khan. However, already at the age of 15 he had conquered Ajmer and large areas of Central India. He brought Kabul back under Mughal control in the 1580s and established a presence from Kashmir, Sind and Baluchistan in the north and west to the Godavari River on the border of modern Andhra Pradesh in the south.

It was Akbar who created the administrative structure employed by successive Mughal emperors to sustain their power. Revenue was raised using detailed surveying methods. Rents were fixed according to the quality of the soil in a move which was carried through into British revenue raising systems. Akbar introduced a new standard measure of length and calculated the assessment of tax due on the basis of a 10 year average of production. Each year the oldest record was dropped out of the calculation, while the average produce for the current year was added. The government's share of the produce was fixed at one quarter.

Akbar deliberately widened his power base by incorporating Rajput princes into the administrative structure and giving them extensive rights in the revenue from land. He abolished the hated tax on non-Muslims *(jizya)* – ultimately reinstated by his strictly orthodox great-grandson Aurangzeb – ceased levying taxes on Hindus who went on pilgrimage and ended the practice of forcible conversion to Islam.

Akbar was a patron not just of art but of an extraordinary range of literature. His library contained books on 'biography, theology, comparative religion, science, mathematics, history, astrology, medicine, zoology and anthropology'. Almost

AD	North India	Peninsular India	External events	AD
300		Rise of Pallavas.	Classic period of Mayan civilization.	300
319	Chandra Gupta founds Gupta Dynasty (Samudra 335, Chandra II 376, Kumara 415).		Constantinople founded.	330
454	Skanda Gupta, the last imperial Gupta, takes power. Dies 467.		End of Roman Empire.	476
			Teotihuacan, Mexico, population 200,000.	500
540	Gupta rule ends.		Saint Sophia, Constantinople.	532
550		First Chalukya Dynasty,	Buddhism arrives in Japan.	550
578		Badami cave temple; last Ajanta paintings.		
600	Period of small Indian states.	Bhakti movement. Chalukyan Dynasty in west		
629	Hiuen Tsang travels India.	and central Deccan.	Death of Mohammad.	632
630		Pallavas in Tamil Nadu.		

 hyperactive throughout his life, he required very little sleep, using moments of rest to commission books and works of art.

The influence of his father Humayun's Iranian artists is still clearly evident in the earlier of these works, but the works were not just those of unidentified 'schools' of artists, but of brilliant individuals such as **Basawan** and **Miskin**, unparalleled in their ability to capture animal life. Examples of their work can be seen not just in India, but at major museums in Europe and the United States.

Artistic treasures abound from Akbar's court – paintings, jewellery, weapons – often bringing together material and skills from across the known world. Emeralds were particularly popular, with the religious significance which attaches to the colour green in mystic Islam adding to their attraction. Some came from as far afield as Colombia. Akbar's intellectual interests were extraordinarily Catholic. He met the Portuguese Jesuits in 1572 and welcomed them to his court, along with Buddhists, Hindus and Zoroastrians, every year between 1575 and 1582.

Akbar's eclecticism had a purpose, for he was trying to build a focus of loyalty beyond that of caste, social group, region or religion. Like Roman emperors before him, he deliberately cultivated a new religion in which the emperor himself attained divinity, hoping thereby to give the empire a legitimacy which would last. While his religion disappeared with his death, the legitimacy of the Mughals survived another 200 years, long after their real power had almost disappeared.

Jahangir Akbar died of a stomach illness in 1605. He was succeeded by his son, Prince Salim, who inherited the throne as Emperor Jahangir ('World Seizer'). He added little to the territory of the empire, consolidating the Mughals' hold on the Himalayan foothills and parts of central India but restricting his innovative energies to pushing back frontiers of art rather than of land. By 1622 his Persian wife Nur Jahan effectively controlled the empire but despite her power she was unable to prevent the accession of her least favoured son, Prince Khurram to the throne in 1628. He took the title by which he is now known around the world, Shah Jahan (Ruler of the World) and in the following 30 years his reign represented the height of Mughal power.

Shah Jahan The Mughal Empire was under attack in the Deccan and the northwest when Shah Jahan became Emperor. He tried to re-establish and extend Mughal authority in both regions by a combination of military campaigns and skilled diplomacy. He was much more successful in pushing south than he was in consolidating the Mughal hold in Afghanistan and most of the Deccan was brought firmly under Mughal control.

AD	North India	Peninsular India	External events	AD
			Buddhism reaches Tibet.	645
670	Rajputs become powerful force in northwest.	Mahabalipuram shore temples.		
712	Arabs arrive in Sind.	Nandivarman II in Tamil Nadu. Pandiyas in Madurai.	Muslim invasions of Spain.	711
757		Rashtrakutas dominate central Peninsula.		
775		Kailasanath Temple, Ellora.	Charlemagne crowned.	800
		Rise of Cholas.	Settlement of New Zealand.	850
			Cyrillic script developed.	863
950	Khajuraho temples started.	Rajendra Chola.		
			Sung Dynasty in China.	979
984		Rajaraja 1st.		

But he too commissioned art, literature and, above all, architectural monuments, on an unparalleled scale. The Taj Mahal may be the most famous of these, but a succession of brilliant achievements can be attributed to his reign.

Aurangzeb The need to expand the area under Mughal control was felt even more strongly by Aurangzeb ('The Jewel in the Throne'), than by his predecessors. He had shown his intellectual gifts in his grandfather's court when held hostage to guarantee Shah Jahan's good behaviour, learning Arabic, Persian, Turkish and Hindi. When he seized power at the age of 40, he needed all his political and military skills to hold on to an unwieldy empire that was in permanent danger of collapse from its own size.

If the empire was to survive, Aurangzeb realized that the resources of the territory he inherited from his father were not enough and thus through a series of campaigns he pushed south, while maintaining his hold on the east and north. For the last 39 years of his reign he was forced to push ever further south, strugging continuously to sustain his power.

The East India Company and the rise of British power

The British were unique among the foreign rulers of India in coming by sea rather than overland from the northwest and in coming first for trade rather than for military conquest. Some of the great battles that established British power in India were fought in South India, but trade was even more important than military conquest.The ports that they established – Madras (now Chennai), Bombay (Mumbai) and Calcutta (Kolkata) – became completely new centres of political, economic and social activity. Before them Indian empires had controlled their territories from the land. The British dictated the emerging shape of the economy by controlling sea-borne trade. From the middle of the 19th century railways transformed the economic and political structure of South Asia and it was those three centres of British political control, along with the late addition of Delhi, which became the foci of economic development and political change.

The East India Company in Madras

In its first 90 years of contact with South Asia after the Company set up its first trading post at **Masulipatnam**, on the east coast of India in modern Andhra Pradesh, it had depended almost entirely on trade for its profits. However, in 1701, only 11 years after a British settlement was first established at Calcutta, the Company was given rights to land revenue in Bengal.

The Company was accepted and sometimes welcomed, partly because it offered to bolster the inadequate revenues of the Mughals by exchanging silver bullion for the cloth it bought. However, in the south the Company moved further and faster

AD	North India	Peninsular India	External events	AD
1001	Mahmud of Ghazni raids Indus plains. Rajput dynasties grow.	Chola kings – navies sent to Southeast Asia: Chola bronzes.	Easter Island stone carvings.	1000
1050	Sufism in North India. Rajput dynasties in northwest.		Norman conquest of England.	1066
			First European universities.	1100
1110		Rise of Hoysalas.		
1118	Senas in Bengal.			
			Angkor Wat, Cambodia; paper making spreads from Muslim world.	1150
1192	Rajputs defeated by Mu'izzu'd Din.		Srivijaya Kingdom at its height in Java; Angkor Empire at greatest.	1170

 towards consolidating its political base. Wars between South India's regional factions gave the Company the opportunity to extend their influence by making alliances and offering support to some of these factions in their struggles, which were complicated by the extension to Indian soil of the European contest for power between the French and the British.

Robert Clive The British established effective control over both Bengal and Southeast India in the middle of the 17th century. Robert Clive, who started his East India Company life in Madras with a victory over the French at Arcot, defeated the new Nawab of Bengal, the 20-year-old Siraj-ud-Daula, in June 1757 at **Plassey** (Palashi), about 100 km north of Calcutta.

In 1773 Calcutta had already been put in charge of Bombay and Madras. The essential features of British control were mapped out in the next quarter of a century through the work of **Warren Hastings**, Governor-General from 1774 until 1785 and **Lord Cornwallis** who succeeded and remained in charge until 1793. Cornwallis was responsible for putting Europeans in charge of all the higher levels of revenue collection and administration and for introducing government by the rule of law, making even government officers subject to the courts.

The decline of Muslim power

The extension of East India Company power in the Mughal periphery of India's south and east took place against a background of weakening Mughal power at the centre in Delhi and on the Peninsula. Some of the Muslim kingdoms of the Deccan refused to pay the tribute to the Mughal Empire that had been forced on them after defeats in 1656. This refusal, and their alliance with the rising power of Sivaji and his Marathas, had led Aurangzeb to attack the Shi'i-ruled states of Bijapur (1686) and Golconda (1687), in an attempt to reimpose Mughal supremacy.

Sivaji Sivaji was the son of a Hindu who had served as a small-scale chief in the Muslim ruled state of Bijapur. The weakness of Bijapur encouraged Sivaji to extend his father's area of control and he led a rebellion. The Bijapur general Afzal Khan, sent to put it down, agreed to meet Sivaji in private to reach a settlement. In an act which is still remembered by both Muslims and Marathas, Sivaji embraced him with steel claws attached to his fingers and tore him apart. It was the start of a campaign which took Maratha power as far south as Madurai and to the doors of Delhi and Calcutta.

Sivaji had taken the fratricidal struggle for the succession which brought Aurangzeb to power as the signal and the opportunity for launching a series of attacks

AD	North India	Peninsular India	External events	AD
1198	First mosque built in Delhi; Qutb Minar Delhi.		Rise of Hausa city states in West Africa.	1200
1206	Delhi Sultanate established.		Mongols begin conquest of Asia under Genghis Khan.	1206
1206	Turkish 'slave dynasty'.	Pandiyas rise.		
			First Thai kingdom.	1220
1222	Iltutmish Sultan of Delhi.			
1230		Konark, Sun Temple, Orissa		
			Marco Polo reaches China.	1275
1290	Khaljis in Delhi; Jalal ud Din Khalji.			
1320-24	Ghiyas ud Din Tughluq.		Black Death spreads from Asia to Europe.	1348
1324-51	Mohammad bin Tughluq.			

against the Mughals. This in turn brought a riposte from Aurangzeb, once his hold on the centre was secure. However, despite the apparent expansion of his power the seeds of decay were already germinating. Although Sivaji himself died in 1680, Aurangzeb never fully came to terms with the rising power of the Marathas, though he did end their ambitions to form an empire of their own.

Nor was Aurangzeb able to create any wide sense of identity with the Mughals as a legitimate popular power. Instead, under the influence of Sunni Muslim theologians, he retreated into insistence on Islamic purity. He imposed Islamic law, the *sharia*, promoted only Muslims to positions of power and authority, tried to replace Hindu administrators and revenue collectors with Muslims and reimposed the *jizya* tax on all non-Muslims. By the time of his death in 1707 the empire no longer had either the broadness of spirit or the physical means to survive.

Bahadur Shah The decline was postponed briefly by the five-year reign of Aurangzeb's son. Sixty-three when he acceded to the throne, Bahadur Shah restored some of its faded fortunes. He made agreements with the Marathas and the Rajputs and defeated the Sikhs in Punjab before taking the last Sikh guru into his service.

The decay of the Mughal Empire has been likened to 'a magnificent flower slowly wilting and occasionally dropping a petal, its brilliance fading, its stalk bending ever lower'. Nine emperors succeeded Aurangzeb between his death and the exile of the last Mughal ruler in 1858. It was no accident that it was in that year that the British ended the rule of its East India Company and decreed India to be its Indian empire.

Successive Mughal rulers saw their political control diminish and their territory shrink. **Nasir ud Din Mohammad Shah**, known as Rangila ('the Pleasure-loving'), who reigned between 1719 and 1748, presided over a continued flowering of art and music, but a disintegration of political power. Hyderabad, Bengal and Oudh (the region to the east of Delhi) became effectively independent states; the Marathas dominated large tracts of Central India, the Jats captured Agra, the Sikhs controlled Punjab.

Mohammad Shah remained in his capital of Delhi, resigning himself to enjoying what Carey Welch has called "the conventional triad of joys: the wine was excellent, as were the women and for him the song was especially rewarding". The idyll was rudely shattered by the invasion of **Nadir Shah** in 1739, an Iranian marauder who slaughtered thousands in Delhi and carried off priceless Mughal treasures, including the Peacock Throne.

The Maratha confederacy

Nadir Shah's invasion was a flash in the pan. Of far greater substance was the development through the 18th century of the power of the Maratha confederacy.

AD	North India	Peninsular India	External events	AD
1336		Vijayanagar Empire established, Harihara I.		
1347		Ala-ud-Din sets up Bahmani dynasty, independent of Delhi, in Gulbarga.		
1351-88	Firoz Shah Tughluq.		Ming dynasty in China established.	1368
			Peking the largest city in the world.	1400
1398	Timur sacks Delhi.		Ming sea-going expeditions to Africa.	1405
1412	End of Tughlaq Dynasty.			
1414	Sayyid Dynasty.	Bidar/Bahmani Kingdom in Deccan.		1428
1440	Mystic Kabir born in Benaras.		Aztecs defeat Atzcapatzalco. Incas centralize power.	1438
1451	Afghan Lodi Dynasty established under Bahlul.		Byzantine Empire falls to Ottomans.	1453
1469	Guru Nanak born in Punjab.			
1482		Fall of Bahmanis.	Columbus reaches the Americas; Arabs and Jews expelled from Spain.	1492

They were unique in India in uniting different castes and classes in a nationalist fervour for the region of Maharashtra. As Spear has pointed out, when the Mughals ceded the central district of Malwa, the Marathas were able to pour through the gap created between the Nizam of Hyderabad's territories in the south and the area remaining under Mughal control in the north. They rapidly occupied Orissa in the east and raided Bengal.

By 1750 they had reached the gates of Delhi. When Delhi collapsed to Afghan invaders in 1756-1757 the Mughal minister called on the Marathas for help. Yet again Panipat proved to be a decisive battlefield, the Marathas being heavily defeated by the Afghan forces on 13 January 1761. However Ahmad Shah left a power vacuum when he was forced to retreat to Afghanistan by his own rebellious troops demanding two years arrears of pay.

The Maratha confederacy dissolved into five independent powers, with whom the incoming British were able to deal separately. The door to the north was open.

The East India Company's push for power

Alliances In the 150 years that followed the death of Aurangzeb, the British East India Company extended its economic and political influence into the heart of India. As the Mughal Empire lost its power India fell into many smaller states. The Company undertook to protect the rulers of several of these states from external attack by stationing British troops in their territory. In exchange for this service the rulers paid subsidies to the Company. As the British historian Christopher Bayly has pointed out, the cure was usually worse than the disease and the cost of the payments to the Company crippled the local ruler. The British extended their territory through the 18th century as successive regional powers were annexed and brought under direct Company rule.

Progress to direct British control was uneven and often opposed. The Sikhs in Punjab, the Marathas in the west and the Mysore sultans in the south fiercely contested British advances. **Haidar Ali** and **Tipu Sultan**, who had built a wealthy kingdom in the Mysore region, resisted attempts to incorporate them. Tipu was finally killed in 1799 at the battle of Srirangapatnam, an island fort in the Kaveri River just north of Mysore, where Arthur Wellesley, later the Duke of Wellington, began to make his military reputation.

The Marathas were not defeated until the war of 1816-1818, a defeat which had to wait until Napoleon was defeated in Europe and the British could turn their wholehearted attention once again to the Indian scene. Even then the defeat owed as much to internal faction-fighting as to the power of the British-led army. Only the northwest of the subcontinent remained beyond British control until well into the 19th century.

In 1818 India's economy was in ruins and its political structures destroyed. Irrigation works and road systems had fallen into decay and gangs terrorized the

AD	North India	Peninsular India	External events	AD
		Vasco da Gama reaches India.	Inca Empire at its height.	1498
1500			Spanish claim Brazil; Safavid Empire founded in Persia.	1500
1506	Sikander Lodi founds Agra.	Vijayanagar dominates South India; Krishnadevraya rules 1509-30.		
		Albuquerque seizes Goa; Nizamshahis establish independent Ahmadnagar sultanate.		1510
1526	Babur defeats Ibrahim Lodi to establish Mughal power in Delhi.		Ottomans capture Syria, Egypt and Arabia.	1516
		Dutch, French, Portuguese and Danish traders.	Spaniards overthrow Aztecs in Mexico.	1519
			Potato introduced to Europe from South America.	1525
1540	Sher Shah forces Humayun into exile.			

countryside. The peace and stability of the Mughal period had long since passed. Between 1818 and 1857 there was a succession of local and uncoordinated revolts in different parts of India. Some rebels were bought off, some put down by military force.

A period of reforms

While existing political systems were collapsing, the first half of the 19th century was also a period of radical social change in the territories governed by the East India Company. **Lord William Bentinck** became Governor-General at a time when England was entering a period of major reform. In 1828 he banned the burning of widows on the funeral pyres of their husbands (**sati**) and then moved to suppress **thuggee** (the ritual murder and robbery carried out in the name of the goddess Kali). But his most far-reaching change was to introduce education in English.

The resolution of 7 March 1835 stated that "the great objects of the British government ought to be the promotion of European literature and science" promising funds to impart "to the native population the knowledge of English literature and science through the medium of the English language". Out of this concern were born new educational institutions such as the Calcutta Medical College. From the late 1830s massive new engineering projects began to spring up; first canals, then railways.

The innovations stimulated change and change contributed to the growing unease with the British presence, particularly under the Governor-Generalship of the Marquess of Dalhousie (1848-1856). The development of the telegraph, railways and new roads, three universities and the extension of massive new canal irrigation projects in North India seemed to threaten traditional society, a risk increased by the annexation of Indian states to bring them under direct British rule. The most important of these was Oudh.

The Rebellion

Out of the growing discontent and widespread economic difficulties came the Rebellion or 'Mutiny' of 1857 (now widely known as the First War of Independence). Appalling scenes of butchery and reprisals marked the struggle, which was only put down by troops from outside. None of the major Indian princes took the side of the rebels, and South India was almost entirely unaffected.

The Period of Empire

The 1857 rebellion marked the end not only of the Mughal Empire but also of the East India Company, for the British government in London took overall control in 1858. Yet within 30 years a movement for self-government had begun and there were the first signs of a demand among the new western educated elite that political rights be awarded to match the sense of Indian national identity.

AD	North India	Peninsular India	External events	AD
1542		St Francis Xavier reaches Goa.		
1555	Humayun re-conquers Delhi.			
1556	Akbar Emperor.			
1565		Vijayanagar defeated.	William Shakespeare born.	1564
		First printing press in Goa.		1566
			Dutch East India Co set up.	1602
1603	Guru Granth Sahib compiled.		Tokugawa Shogunate in Japan.	1603
1605	Jahangir Emperor.		First permanent English settlement in America.	1607
1608		East India Co base at Surat.		
			Telescope invented in Holland.	1609

The Indian National Congress The movement for independence went through a series of steps. The creation of the Indian National Congress in 1885 was the first all-India political institution and was to become the key vehicle of demands for independence. However, the educated Muslim elite of what is now Uttar Pradesh saw a threat to Muslim rights, power and identity in the emergence of democratic institutions which gave Hindus, with their built-in natural majority, significant advantages. Sir Sayyid Ahmad Khan, who had founded a Muslim university at Aligarh in 1877, advised Muslims against joining the Congress, seeing it as a vehicle for Hindu and especially Bengali, nationalism.

The Muslim League The educated Muslim community of North India remained deeply suspicious of the Congress, making up less than 8% of those attending its conferences between 1900-1920. Muslims from UP created the All-India Muslim League in 1906. However, the demands of the Muslim League were not always opposed to those of the Congress. In 1916 it concluded the Lucknow Pact with the Congress, in which the Congress won Muslim support for self-government, in exchange for the recognition that there would be separate constituencies for Muslims. The nature of the future Independent India was still far from clear, however. The British conceded the principle of self-government in 1918, but however radical the reforms would have seemed five years earlier they already fell far short of heightened Indian expectations.

Mahatma Gandhi Into a tense atmosphere Mohandas Karamchand Gandhi returned to India in 1915 after 20 years practising as a lawyer in South Africa. On his return the Bengali Nobel Laureate poet, Rabindranath Tagore, had dubbed him 'Mahatma' – Great Soul. The name became his. He arrived as the government of India was being given new powers by the British parliament to try political cases without a jury and to give provincial governments the right to imprison politicians without trial. In opposition to this legislation Gandhi proposed to call a *hartal*, when all activity would cease for a day, a form of protest still in widespread use. Protests took place across India, often accompanied by riots.

On 13 April 1919 a huge gathering took place in the enclosed space of Jallianwala Bagh in Amritsar. It had been prohibited by the government and General Dyer ordered troops to fire on the people without warning, killing 379 and injuring at least a further 1200. It marked the turning point in relations with Britain and the rise of Gandhi to the key position of leadership in the struggle for complete independence.

The thrust for Independence Through the 1920s Gandhi developed concepts and political programmes that were to become the hallmark of India's Independence struggle. Rejecting the 1919 reforms, Gandhi preached the doctrine of *swaraj*, or self

AD	North India	Peninsular India	External events	AD
1628	Shah Jahan Emperor.		Masjid-i-Shah Mosque in Isfahan.	1616
1632-53	Taj Mahal built.			
		Fort St George, Madras, founded by East India Co.		1639
			Manchus found Ch'ing Dynasty.	1644
			Tasman 'discovers' New Zealand.	1645
1658	Aurangzeb Emperor.			
			Louis XIV of France - the 'Sun King'.	1653-1715

rule, developing an idea he first published in a leaflet in 1909. He saw swaraj not just as political independence from a foreign ruler but, in Judith Brown's words, as made up of three elements: "It was a state of being that had to be created from the roots upwards, by the regeneration of individuals and their realization of their true spiritual being ... unity among all religions; the eradication of Untouchability; and the practice of *swadeshi*." Swadeshi was not simply dependence on Indian products rather than foreign imports, but a deliberate move to a simple life style, hence his emphasis on hand spinning as a daily routine.

Ultimately political Independence was to be achieved not by violent rebellion but by *satyagraha* – a "truth force" which implied a willingness to suffer through non-violent resistance to injustice. This gave birth to Gandhi's advocacy of "non-cooperation" as a key political weapon and brought together Gandhi's commitment to matching political goals with moral means. Although the political achievements of Gandhi's programme continues to be strongly debated, the struggles of the 1920s established his position as a key figure in the Independence movement.

In 1930 the Congress declared that 26 January would be Independence day – still celebrated as Republic Day in India today. The Leader of the Muslim League, Mohammad Iqbal, took the opportunity of his address to the League in the same year to suggest the formation of a Muslim state within an Indian Federation. Also in 1930 a Muslim student in Cambridge, **Chaudhuri Rahmat Ali**, coined a name for the new Muslim state – **PAKISTAN.** The letters were to stand 'P' for Punjab, 'A' for Afghania, 'K' for Kashmir, 'S' for Sind with the suffix '*stan*', Persian for country. The idea still had little real shape however and waited on developments of the late 1930s and 1940s to bear fruit.

By the end of second world war the positions of the Muslim League, now under the leadership of **Mohammad Ali Jinnah** and the Congress led by Jawaharlal Nehru, were irreconcilable. While major questions of the definition of separate territories for a Muslim and non-Muslim state remained to be answered, it was clear to General Wavell, the British Viceroy through the last years of the War, that there was no alternative but to accept that independence would have to be given on the basis of separate states.

Independence and Partition

One of the main difficulties for the Muslims was that they made up only a fifth of the total population. Although there were regions both in the northwest and the east where they formed the majority, Muslims were also scattered throughout India. It was therefore impossible to define a simple territorial division which would provide a state to match Jinnah's claim of a **'two-nation theory'**. On 20 February 1947, the British Labour government announced its decision to replace Lord Wavell as Viceroy with Lord Mountbatten, who was to oversee the transfer of power to new independent governments. It set a deadline of June 1948 for British withdrawal. The announcement

AD	North India	Peninsular India	External events	AD
1677		**Shivaji** and Marathas.	Pennsylvania founded.	1681
1690	Calcutta founded.			
1699	Guru Gobind Singh forms Sikh Khalsa.	Regional powers dominate through 18th century:	Chinese occupy Outer Mongolia.	1697
1703	Nawabs of Bengal.	Nawabs of Arcot (1707);	Foundation of St Petersburg, capital of Russian Empire.	1703
1707	Death of Aurangzeb; Mughal rulers continue to rule from Delhi until 1858 Nawabs of Avadh.	Maratha Peshwas (1714); Nizams of Hyderabad (1724).		
1739	The Persian Nadir Shah captures Delhi and massacres thousands.			
1757	Battle of Plassey; British power extended from East India.	East India Co strengthens trade and political power through 18th century.	US War of Independence.	1775-8

Mahatma Gandhi

Mohandas Karamchand Ghandi, a westernized, English-educated lawyer, had lived outside India from his youth to middle age. He preached the general acceptance of some of the doctrines he had grown to respect in his childhood, which stemmed from deep Indian traditions – notably ahimsa, or non-violence. On his return the Bengali Nobel Laureate poet, Rabindranath Tagore, had dubbed him 'Mahatma' – Great Soul. From 1921 he gave up his Western style of dress and adopted the hand-spun dhoti worn by poor Indian villagers. Yet, he was also fiercely critical of many aspects of traditional Hindu society. He preached against the discrimination of the caste system which still dominated life for the overwhelming majority of Hindus. Often despised by the British in India, his death at the hands of an extreme Hindu chauvinist in January 1948 was a final testimony to the ambiguity of his achievements: successful in contributing so much to achieving India's Independence, yet failing to resolve some of the bitter communal legacies which he gave his life to overcome.

of a firm date made the Indian politicians even less willing to compromise and the resulting division satisfied no one.

When Independence arrived – on 15 August for India and the 14 August for Pakistan, because Indian astrologers deemed the 15th to be the most auspicious moment – many questions remained unanswered. Several key princely states had still not decided firmly to which country they would accede. Kashmir was the most important of these, with results that have lasted to the present day. Yet 40 million Muslims, including many in South India, retained their Indian nationality, part of a Mulsim community that now totals about 120 million.

Tamil Nadu

Tamil Nadu's cultural identity has been shaped by the Dravidians, who have inhabited the south since at least the fourth millennium BC. Tamil, India's oldest living language, developed from the earlier languages of people who were probably displaced from the north by Aryan-based culture from 2000 BC to 1500 BC.

By the fourth century BC Tamil Nadu was under the rule of three dynasties. The **Cholas** occupied the coastal area east of Thanjavur and inland to the head of the Kaveri Delta at Tiruchi. The south – Madurai, Tirunelveli and a part of southern Kerala were under the **Pandiyas** while the **Cheras** controlled much of what is now Kerala on the west coast of the peninsula.

The **Pandiyas** returned to power in the Tamil area after the decline of the Cholas and ruled from 1175 to 1300. In the 13th century, international trade flourished under their control and was only superseded by the rise of Vijayanagar (Hampi, see page 300.

The **Pallavas** of Kanchi came to power in the fourth century AD and were dominant between AD 550-869. Possibly of northern origin, under their control Mahabalipuram (Mamallapuram) became an important port in the seventh century.

The **Cholas** returned to power in 850 and were a dominant political force until 1173. During the 11th-century, Rajendra Chola (1013-1044) extended Chola power to the River Ganga in Bengal. His naval expeditions to the Malayan Peninsula resulted in Chola domination over the trade routes of the Indian Ocean to Java, Sumatra and China until the resumption of Pandiya power for a further century.

The defeat of the great Vijayanagar Empire by a confederacy of Muslim states in 1565 forced their leaders south. As the Nayaka kings they continued to rule from as far south as Madurai well into the 17th century. Ultimately when Muslim political control finally reached Tamil Nadu it was as brief as it was tenuous.

It was more than 150 years after their founding of Fort St George at Madras in 1639 before the **East India Company** could claim political supremacy in South India. Haidar Ali, who mounted the throne of Mysore in 1761, and his son Tipu Sultan, allied with the French, won many battles against the English. The Treaty of Versailles in 1783 brought the French and English together and Tipu was forced to make peace. The English took Malabar in 1792, and in 1801 Lord Wellesley brought together most of the south under the Madras Presidency.

Kerala

The name Kerala is often widely explained today as meaning 'land of coconuts', derived from the Malayalam word 'kera' or coconut palm. However this is not its origin. '*Keralaputra*' – land of the sons of the Cheras – *putra*, son – was referred to in **Asoka's** edicts dating from between 273-236 BC, over a thousand years before the Malayalam language of contemporary Kerala took shape. To the Tamils the region was known for centuries as *Seranadu*, again meaning land of the Cheras.

Periodically the region had been under Tamil control. The Cheras, who established themselves in the Kuttanad region around Alappuzha as the first Kerala power, continued to use Tamil as the state language up to the seventh century. Two hundred years separated the ending of the first Chera Dynasty and the emergence of the powerful and prosperous second empire.

The Cheras developed a wide network of trade links in which both the long-established Christian community and the Jewish community participated fully. Mahodayapuram (modern Kodangallur) traded from Cordoba in the west to Sumatra in the east. However, the neighbouring Cholas launched several successful attacks against Chera power from AD 985 onwards. When Chola power itself disintegrated at the end of the 11th century, minor principalities emerged, dominated by a new group, the Nambudiri Brahmans, and contested for control of the region's vital trade in spices – pepper, ginger, cardamom and cinnamon.

Calicut gradually became dominant under the **Zamorin** (literally *Lord of the Sea*), who had well-established contacts with the Arab world. By some accounts he was the wealthiest ruler in contemporary India. He was unable to use these advantages to unite Kerala, and during the 16th century the Portuguese exploited the rivalry of the Raja of Kolattiri with the Zamorin of Calicut, being granted permission to trade from Kochi in 1499. Over the following century there was fierce competition and sometimes open warfare between the Portuguese, bent on eliminating Arab trading competition, and the Zamorin, whose prosperity depended on that Arab trade. The competition was encouraged by the rulers of Kochi, in the hope that by keeping the hands of both tied in conflict their own independence would be strengthened.

After a century of hostility, the **Dutch** arrived on the west coast. The Zamorin seized the opportunity of gaining external support, and on 11 November 1614 concluded a Treaty giving the Dutch full trading rights. In 1615 the British East India Company was also given the right to trade by the Zamorin. By 1633 the Dutch had captured all the Portuguese forts of Kollam, Kodungallur, Purakkad, Kochi and Kannur. The ruler of Kochi rapidly made friends with the Dutch, in exchange having the new Mattancherry Palace built for him, and inevitably facing renewed conflict with Calicut as a result.

In the decade after 1740 Raja Marthanda Varma succeeded in uniting a number of petty states around Thiruvananthapuram and led them to a crushing victory over the Dutch in the Battle of Kolachel in 1741. By 1758 the Zamorin of Calicut was forced to withdraw from Kochi, but the **Travancore** ruler's reign was brief. In 1766 Haidar Ali had led his cavalry troops down onto the western coastal plain, and he and his son Tipu Sultan pushed further and further south with a violence that is still bitterly remembered. In 1789, as Tipu was preparing to launch a final assault on the south of Travancore, the British attacked him from the east. He withdrew his army from Kerala and the Zamorin and other Kerala leaders looked to the British to take control of the forts previously held by Tipu's officers. Tipu Sultan's first defeat at the hands of Lord Cornwallis led to the Treaty of Seringapatam in 1792, under which Tipu surrendered all his captured territory in the northern part of Kerala, to direct British rule. Travancore and Kochi became princely states under ultimate British authority.

Karnataka

The region between the Tungabhadra and the Krishna rivers, was home to some of the earliest settlements in peninsular India, over 500,000 years ago. By the Middle Stone Age there was already a regional division appearing between the black cotton soil area of the north and the granite-quartzite plateau of the south. The division appears between the Krishna and Tungabhadra rivers in the modern districts of Raichur and Bellary. In the north hunters used pebbles of jasper taken from river beds while quartz tools were developed to the south. The first agricultural communities of the peninsula have also been identified from what is now northern Karnataka. Radiocarbon datings put the earliest of these settlements at about 3000 BC, and millet and gram were already widely grown by the first millennium BC. They have remained staple crops ever since.

Tradition in Karnataka states that Chandragupta Maurya, India's first emperor, became a Jain, renounced all worldly possessions and retired to Sravanabelagola. Dynasties, rising both from within the region and outside it, exercised varying degrees of control. The Western Gangas, from the third to 11th centuries, and the Banas (under the Pallavas), from fourth to ninth centuries, controlled large parts of modern Karnataka. The Chalukyas of central Karnataka took some of the lands between the Tungabhadra and Krishna rivers in the sixth century and built great temples in Badami. They and the Rashtrakutas tried to unite the plateau and the coastal areas while there were Tamil incursions in the south and east. The break-up of the Tamil Chola Empire allowed new powers in the neighbouring regions to take control. In Karnataka the Hoysalas (11th-14th centuries) took advantage of the opportunity, and built the magnificent temples at Belur, Halebid and Somnathpur, symbolizing both their power and their religious authority. Then came the Sangama and Tuluva kings of the Vijayanagara Empire, which reached its peak in the mid-16th century.

Muhammad bin Tughlaq had attacked northern Karnataka in the 13th century. Even during the Vijayanagar period the **Muslim sultanates** to the north were extending their influence. The Bidar period (1422-1526) of Bahmani rule was marked by wars with Gujarat and Malwa, continued campaigns against Vijayanagara, and expeditions against Orissa. **Mahmud Gawan**, the Wazir of the Bahmani sultanate, seized Karnataka between 1466 and 1481, and also took Goa, formerly guarded by Vijayanagar kings. By 1530 the kingdom had split into five independent sultanates: **Adil Shahis** of Bijapur, the **Qutb Shahi** of Golconda, the **Imad Shahi** of Ahmadnagar, the **Barid Shahi** of Bidar, and the **Imad Shahi** of Berar. From time to time they still came together to defend common interests, and in 1565 they cooperated to oust the Vijayanagar Raja, but Bijapur and Golconda gathered the lion's share of the spoils and the Muslim sultanates were rapidly succeeded by the Mughals and then the British. The south experienced a different succession of powers. While the Mughals were preoccupied fighting off the Marathas, the **Wodeyar** rulers of Mysore took Srirangapatnam and then Bangalore (now Bengaluru). They lost control to **Haidar Ali** in 1761, the opportunist commander-in-chief who with French help extended control and made Srirangapatnam his capital. The Mysore Wars followed and with the deaths, first of Haidar Ali and then his son Tipu Sultan's, the **British** re-established rule of the Wodeyars in 1799. The Hindu royal family was still administering Mysore up to the reorganization of the states in the 1950s when the Maharaja was appointed state governor.

Andhra Pradesh

The first historical evidence of a people called the 'Andhras' came from Emperor Asoka. The first known Andhra power, the **Satavahanas** encouraged various religious groups including Buddhists. Their capital at Amaravati shows evidence of the great skill of early Andhra artists and builders. Around AD 150 there was also a fine university at Nagarjunakonda.

In 1323 Warangal, just to the northeast of the present city of Hyderabad, was captured by the armies of Muhammad bin Tughlaq. Muslim expansion further south was prevented for two centuries by the rise of the **Vijayanagar Empire**, itself crushed at the Battle of Talikota in 1565 by a short-lived federation of Muslim States, and the cultural life it supported had to seek fresh soil.

From then on **Muslim rulers** dominated the politics of central Andhra, Telangana. The Bahmani Kingdoms in the region around modern Hyderabad controlled central Telangana in the 16th century. They were even able to keep the Mughals at bay until Aurangzeb finally forced them into submission at the end of the 17th century. **Hyderabad** was the most important centre of Muslim power in central and South India from the 17th to the 19th centuries. It was founded by the fifth in line of an earlier Muslim Dynasty, **Mohammad Quli Qutb Shah**, in 1591. Through his successors Hyderabad became the capital of a princely state the size of France, ruled by a succession of Muslim Nizams from 1724 till after India's Independence in 1947.

Through the 18th century **British and French traders** were spreading their influence up the coast. Increasingly they came into conflict and looked for alliances with regional powers. At the end of the 18th century the British reached an agreement with the **Nizam of Hyderabad** whereby he accepted British support in exchange for recognition of British rights to trade and political control of the coastal districts. Thus Hyderabad retained a measure of independence until 1947 while accepting British suzerainty.

There was doubt as to whether the Princely State would accede to India after Partition. The Nizam of Hyderabad would have liked to join fellow Muslims in the newly created Muslim State of Pakistan. However, political disturbances in 1949 gave the Indian government the excuse to take direct control, and the state was incorporated into the Indian Union.

Goa

Some identify Goa in the *Mahabharata* (the Sanskrit epic) as Gomant, where Vishnu, reincarnated as Parasurama, shot an arrow from the Western Ghats into the Arabian Sea and with the help of the god of the sea reclaimed the beautiful land of Gomant.

Arab geographers knew Goa as Sindabur. Ruled by the Kadamba Dynasty from the second century AD to 1312 and by Muslim invaders from 1312 to 1367, it was then annexed by the Hindu Kingdom of Vijayanagar and later conquered by the Bahmani Dynasty of Bidar in North Karnataka, who founded Old Goa in 1440. When the Portuguese arrived, Yusuf Adil Shah, the Muslim King of Bijapur, was the ruler. At this time Goa was an important starting point for Mecca-bound pilgrims, as well as continuing to be a centre importing Arab horses.

The Portuguese were intent on setting up a string of coastal stations to the Far East in order to control the lucrative spice trade. Goa was the first Portuguese possession in Asia and was taken by **Alfonso de Albuquerque** in March 1510, the city surrendering without a struggle. Three months later Yusuf Adil Shah blockaded it with 60,000 men. In November Albuquerque returned with reinforcements, recaptured the city after a bloody struggle, massacred all the Muslims and appointed a Hindu as Governor. At first they employed Hindus as officials and troops. Mutual hostility towards Muslims encouraged links between Goa and the Hindu Kingdom of Vijayanagar. Religion only became an issue when missionary activity in India increased. Franciscans, Dominicans and Jesuits arrived, carrying with them both religious zeal and intolerance. The Inquisition was introduced in 1540 and all evidence of earlier Hindu temples and worship was eradicated from the territories of the "Old Conquests".

Goa became the capital of the Portuguese Empire in the east and was granted the same civic privileges as Lisbon. It reached its greatest splendour between 1575 and 1600, the age of 'Golden Goa', but when the Dutch began to control trade in the Indian Ocean it declined. The fall of the Vijayanagar Empire in 1565 caused the lucrative trade between Goa and the Hindu state to dry up. Between 1695 and 1775 the population of Old Goa dwindled from 20,000 to 1600 and by the mid-19th century only a few priests and nuns remained.

Albuquerque's original conquest was of the island of Tiswadi (then called Ilhas), where Old Goa is situated, plus the neighbouring areas – Bardez, Ponda, Mormugao and Salcete. The coastal provinces formed the heart of the Portuguese territory and are known as the **Old Conquests**. The **New Conquests** cover the remaining peripheral areas which came into Portuguese possession considerably later, either by conquest or treaty. Initially they provided a refuge for not only the peoples driven from the Old Conquest but also their faith. By the time they were absorbed, the full intolerant force of the Inquisition had passed. Consequently, the New Conquests did not suffer as much cultural and spiritual devastation.

The Portuguese came under increasing pressure in 1948 and 1949 to cede Goa, Daman and Diu to India. The problem festered until 1961 when the Indian Army, supported by a naval blockade, marched in and brought to an end 450 years of Portuguese rule. Originally Goa became a Union Territory together with the old Portuguese enclaves of Daman and Diu, but on 30 May 1987 it became a full state of the Indian Union.

Modern India

India, with an estimated 1.13 billion people in 2001, is the second most populous country in the world after China. That population size reflects the long history of human occupation and the fact that an astonishingly high proportion of India's land is relatively fertile. Some 60% of India's surface area is cultivated today, compared with about 10% in China and 20% in the United States, and although it occupies only 2.4% of the world's land area, it supports over 15% of the world's population.

The birth rate has fallen steadily over the last 40 years, but death rates initially fell faster and the rate of population increase has continued to be nearly 2% – or 18 million – a year. Today over 320 million of the population lives in towns and cities: in 1971, the urbanized population stood at 109 million, by 1999 this figure had swollen to 300 million. South India has seen particularly rapid progress compared with the north in both health and education. In both Kerala and Tamil Nadu birth rates have fallen to match death rates so that population stability has been reached, and Kerala claims 100% literacy. According to the 2001 census, Andhra is the most populous state in the South, with over 76 million people, then Tamil Nadu

The Indian flag

In 1921, the All Indian Congress considered a red and green flag to represent the two dominant religious groups (Hindu and Muslim); Gandhi suggested white be added to represent the other communities, as well as the chakra (spinning wheel) symbolizing the Swadeshi movement, now centred in the party flag.

In 1931, the Indian National Congress adopted the tricolor as the national flag. This was intended to have no communal significance. The top band of deep saffron denoted 'Courage and Sacrifice', the middle white band 'Truth and Peace' and the dark green bottom band 'Faith and Chivalry'. On the white stripe, the Dharma chakra represented the Buddhist Wheel of Law from Asoka's Lion capital at Sarnath.

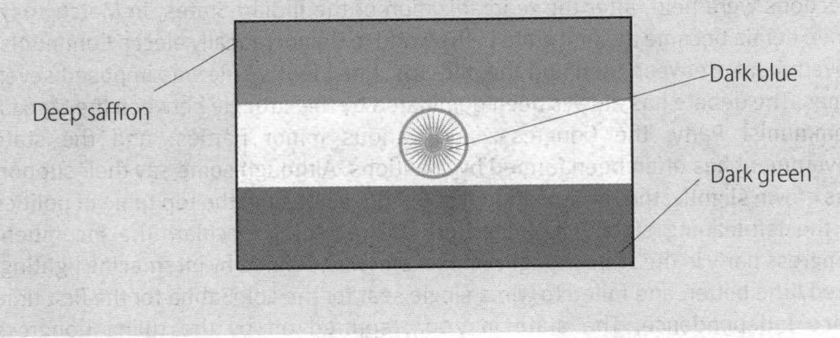

with 62 million, Karnataka has 52 million, Kerala 32 million and Goa holds just over one million.

Tamil Nadu

Tamil Nadu took its present form as a result of the States Reorganization Act of 1956. Until 1967 the Assembly was dominated by the Indian National Congress, but after an attempt by the central government to impose Hindi as the national language the Congress Party was routed in 1967 by a regional party, the **Dravida Munnetra Kazhagam (the DMK)** under its leader CN Annadurai. After his death the party split and since then either the DMK, or the splinter party, the **All India Anna DMK**, has been in power in the State. Neither party has any constituency beyond Tamil Nadu and thus at the all India level each has been forced to seek alliances with national parties. From the late 1960s the **AIADMK**, which controlled the State Assembly for most of the time, has been led by two film stars. The first, **MG Ramachandran** remained the chief minister until his death (even after suffering a stroke which left him paralysed). The record of **Jayalalitha**, his successor, one-time lover and fellow film star, has been less consistent, and her rule dogged by scandal. She and her party were ousted by the DMK in the May 1996 elections and she was temporarily jailed until, cleared of a wide range of criminal charges, she re-entered the Legislative Assembly in March 2002, taking over once more as Chief Minister after winning the state elections with an 80% margin (her administration then arrested the previous chief minister, senescent 83-year-old Karunanidhi, in a corruption case that some say was motivated by revenge). In the May 2004 national elections, though, the party, allied to the BJP and vocal in its opposition to Sonia Gandhi's foreign origin, failed to win a single seat. A coalition of opposition parties, arguing that she had lost her political mandate, demanded Jayalalitha's resignation, but she hung on to office, albeit swiftly reversing a raft of controversial policies – such as scrapping free electricity schemes, reducing rice rations, banning animal sacrifices – introduced during the earlier years of power. Karunanidhi, though, DMK co-founder in 1949, got the last laugh and became CM for the fifth time in the elections of May 2006.

The situation of the Tamil population, and the activities of the liberation movement the LTTE, in neighbouring Sri Lanka play a role in the politics of the state. While Karunanidhi has been a vocal advocate for Tamil rights, Jayalalitha suggests that the LTTE have been using Tamil Nadu as a sanctuary for their continuing struggle against the Sinhalese majority rule on the island.

Kerala

The reorganization of the Indian States in 1956 brought together the Malayalam language area of Kerala into one political unit. With the exception of some of the Kanniyakumari districts now in Tamil Nadu, it comprises all of Travancore, Kochi, Malabar and a part of South Kanara District from Karnataka.

Kerala politics have often been unstable – even turbulent – since the first elections were held, after the reorganization of the Indian States, in March 1957, when Kerala became the first state in the world to democratically elect a Communist government. Between then and the mid-80s, President's Rule was imposed seven times. The debate has always been dominated by the struggle between the Marxist Communist Party, the Congress, and various minor parties: and the state government has often been formed by coalitions. Although some say their support has grown slightly, the Hindu nationalist BJP does not sit at the top table of politics in the left-leaning state – politics here are resolutely secular. The incumbent Congress party in the state though, whose term was defined by internecine fighting, fared little better, and failed to win a single seat for the Lok Sabha for the first time since Independence. The state in 2004, spurred on by the ruling Congress government's poor handling of one of the worst droughts in the state's history in the run-up to the elections, voted instead to be represented at the Center by the Communist Party of India (Marxist) and the Left Democratic Front.

Karnataka

The 19 districts are grouped into four divisions – Bengaluru (Bangalore), Mysore, Belgaum and Gulbarga. Caste rivalry between Vokkaligas and Lingayats remains a powerful factor in the state's politics and faction fighting within the parties has been a recurrent theme. In 2004, Congress suffered a swingeing backlash against its liberal economic policies that had fuelled the rise of Bengaluru (Bangalore) to become the darling of the IT and biotechnology industries. The BJP became the largest single party in the Assembly with 79 seats, the Congress's 65 and the Janata Dal's 58. The result produced a coalition government, first with Dharam Singh of the BJP as chief minister, followed by HD Kumaraswamy of the Janata Dal (Secular). Opponents have seized on the apparent opportunism of a party with 'secular' in its title joining forces with the avowedly Hindu nationalist BJP. The coalition has witnessed major tensions and some question whether it will last the full term.

Andhra Pradesh

In 1953 Andhra Pradesh was created on the basis of the Telugu-speaking districts of Madras Presidency. This was not enough for those who were demanding statehood for a united Telugu-speaking region. One political leader, Potti Sreeramulu, starved himself to death in protest at the government's refusal to grant the demand. In 1956, Andhra Pradesh took its present form; all Telugu-speaking areas were grouped together in the new state of Andhra Pradesh.

Andhra Pradesh was regarded as a stronghold of the Congress Party until 1983 when a regional party, the Telugu Desam, won a crushing victory in the State Assembly elections. The Assembly elections on 5 October 1999 saw a repeat performance, with the highly regarded modernizing Chief Minister N Chandrababu Naidu being swept back to power in the State Assembly with nearly a two-thirds majority. Allied with the BJP in the governing coalition in New Delhi, the Telugu Desam had a reputation for pushing ahead with rapid economic modernization, particularly visible in Hyderabad, but Naidu, who borrowed heavily from the World Bank and took China, Singapore and Malaysia as his business models, won only 47 of the 295 seats in the State Assembly elections in 2004.

The Congress and its newly formed regional party ally, the Telangana Rashtra Samiti, with 226 seats, reclaimed power. The Congress Chief Minister YS Rajasekhara Reddy (known as YSR) took charge of a state with high debts to the World Bank and where poverty remains endemic in many rural areas and suicide had become a major problem among poor farmers. The Congress-led government offered to resolve the long standing terrorist activities of the Peoples War Group and the Naxalites by offering a peace settlement. However, talks broke down in 2004, and operating in some of the remotest areas of northwestern Andhra Pradesh, they continue to carry out murder, bombing and kidnapping, and the execution of summary penalties through 'people's courts'.

Goa

The Goa Legislative Assembly has 40 elected members while the state elects three members to the Lok Sabha, India's central government. Political life is strongly influenced by the regional issue of the relationship with neighbouring Maharashtra, with the Congress Party's 2005 coalition partner the Maharashtrawadi Gomantak Party (which held office between 1963 and 1979) campaigning for Marathi to replace Konkani as the state language. Communal identity also plays a part in elections, with the Congress largely securing the Catholic vote and the BJP winning the support of a significant part of the Hindu population. There is also a strong environmental lobby, in which the Catholic Church plays a role. Goa has had a series of unstable governments with periods of governor's imposed by the central government to try and override failures of the democratic process. The state assembly elections in 2007 saw the Congress win 16 and the BJP 14 of the total of 40 seats, and a Congress administration resumed office under the Chief Ministership of Digambar Kamat, who took office on 8 June 2007.

Politics and institutions

South Indian politics has always marched to its own music. Regional movements have played a major part in state level government, especially in Tamil Nadu and Andhra Pradesh, where national parties like the Congress have struggled to form working partnerships with regional parties to help form a majority in India's central Parliament, or Lok Sabha.

In the years since Independence, striking political achievements have been made. With the two year exception of 1975-1977, when Mrs Gandhi imposed a state of emergency in which all political activity was banned, India has sustained a democratic system in the face of tremendous pressures. The General Elections of May 2004 saw the Congress Party return as the largest single party with 220 of the 540 Lok Sabha seats. They managed to forge alliances with some of the smaller parties and thus formed the new United Progressive Alliance government under the prime ministership not of the Congress party's leader, Sonia Gandhi, but of ex-finance minister, Manmohan Singh.

The constitution

Establishing itself as a sovereign democratic republic, the Indian Parliament accepted Nehru's advocacy of a secular constitution. The President is formally vested with all executive powers exercised under the authority of the Prime Minister.

Effective power under the constitution lies with the Prime Minister and Cabinet, following the British model. In practice there have been long periods when the Prime Minister has been completely dominant. In principle, Parliament chooses the Prime Minister. The Parliament has a lower house (the *Lok Sabha*, or 'house of the people') and an upper house (the *Rajya Sabha* – Council of States). The former is made up of directly elected representatives from the 543 parliamentary constituencies (plus two nominated members from the Anglo-Indian community), the latter of a mixture of members elected by an electoral college and of nominated members. Constitutional amendments require a two-thirds majority in both houses.

India's federal constitution devolves certain powers to elected state assemblies. Each state has a Governor who acts as its official head. Many states also have two chambers, the upper generally called the Rajya Sabha and the lower (often called the Vidhan Sabha) being of directly elected representatives. In practice many of the state assemblies have had a totally different political complexion from that of the Lok Sabha. Regional parties have played a more prominent role, though in many states central government has dictated both the leadership and policy of state assemblies.

States and Union Territories Union Territories are administered by the President "acting to such an extent as he thinks fit". In practice Union territories have varying forms of self-government. Pondicherry has a legislative Assembly and Council of

Prime ministers and presidents since 1947

Date	Prime Minister	Date	President
1947-64	Jawaharlal Nehru	1948-50	C Rajagopalachari
1964-66	Lal Bahadur Shastri	1950-62	Rajendra Prasad
1966-77	Indira Gandhi	1962-67	S Radhakrishnan
1977-79	Morarji Desai	1967-69	Zakir Hussain
1979-80	Charan Singh	1969-74	V V Giri
1980-84	Indira Gandhi	1974-77	Fakhruddin Ali Ahmed
1984-89	Rajiv Gandhi	1977-82	Neelam Sanjiva Reddy
1989-90	VP Singh	1982-87	Giani Zail Singh
1990-91	S Chandrasekhar	1987-92	R Venkataraman
1991- 96	PV Narasimha Rao	1992-97	Shankar Dayal Sharma
1996 (May)	Atal Behari Vaypayee	1997	K R Narayanan
1996-97 (May)	H D Deve Gowda		
1997-98 (May)	Inder Kumar Gujral		
1998-04	Atal Bihari Vajpayee		
2004	Manmohan Singh	2002	Abdul Kalam

Ministers. The 69th Amendment to the Constitution in 1991 provided for a legislative assembly and council of Ministers for Delhi, elections for which were held in December 1993. The Assemblies of Union Territories have more restricted powers of legislation than full states. Some Union Territories, such as Andaman and Nicobar Islands and Lakshadweep, have elected bodies known as Pradesh Councils. These councils have the right to discuss and make recommendations on matters relating to their territories.

Secularism One of the key features of India's constitution is its secular principle. This is not based on the absence of religious belief, but on the commitment to guarantee freedom of religious belief and practice to all groups in Indian society. Some see the commitment to a secular constitution as having been under increasing challenge from the Hindu nationalism of the Bharatiya Janata Party, the BJP. The BJP persuaded a number of regional parties to join it in government after the 1998 and 1999 elections, appearing to move away from its narrowly defined conception of a Hindu state. The BJP is torn between the fundamental Hindu beliefs of its core support and the electoral demands of an enormously varied population.

The judiciary India's Supreme Court has similar but somewhat weaker powers to those of the United States. The judiciary has remained effectively independent of the government except under the Emergency between 1975-1977.

The civil service India continued to use the small but highly professional administrative service inherited from the British period. Renamed the Indian Administrative Service (IAS), it continues to exercise remarkable influence across the country. The administration of many aspects of central and regional government is in the hands of this elite, who act largely by the constitutional rules which bind them as servants of the state. Many Indians accept the continuing efficiency and high calibre of the top ranking officers in the administration while believing that the bureaucratic system as a whole has been overtaken by widespread corruption.

The police India's police service is divided into a series of groups, numbering nearly one million. While the top ranks of the Indian Police Service are comparable to the IAS, lower levels are extremely poorly trained and very badly paid. In addition to the domestic police force there are special groups among them the Border Security Force and the Central Reserve Police. They may be armed with modern weapons and are called in for special duties.

The armed forces Unlike its immediate neighbours Pakistan and Bangladesh, India has never had military rule. It has approximately one million men in the army – one of the largest armed forces in the world. Although they have remained out of politics, the armed services have been used increasingly frequently to put down civil unrest especially in Kashmir.

The Congress Party For over forty years Indian national politics was dominated by the Congress Party. Its strength in the Lok Sabha often overstated the volume of its support in the country, however and state governments have frequently been formed by parties – and interests – only weakly represented at the centre.

The Congress won overall majorities in seven of the ten general elections held before the 1996 election, although in no election did the Congress obtain more than 50% of the popular vote. It was defeated only in 1977 and in 1989 when the Opposition parties united against it. In the latter election it still gained the largest number of seats, though not enough to form a government on its own and it was unable to find allies.

The Congress had built its broad-based support partly by championing the causes of the poor, the backward castes and the minorities. It regained power in mid-1991 in the wake of Rajiv Gandhi's assassination at Sriperumbudur in Tamil Nadu, and under the leadership of Narasimha Rao, who came from Andhra Pradesh, it succeeded in governing for its full five-year term, introducing the most radical economic reform programme since Independence. In 1998 it lost support across India, and its power base in the South weakened.

The Non-Congress Parties Political activity outside the Congress can seem bewilderingly complex. There are no genuinely national parties. The only alternative governments to the Congress have been formed by coalitions of regional and ideologically-based parties. Parties of the left – Communist and Socialist – have never broken out of their narrow regional bases. The **Communist Party of India** split into two factions in 1964, with the Communist Party of India Marxist **(CPM)** ultimately taking power in West Bengal and Kerala.

At the right of the political spectrum, the **Jan Sangh** was seen as a party of right wing Hindu nationalism but was almost entirely a north Indian party. The most organized political force outside the Congress, the Jan Sangh merged with the **Janata Party** for the elections of 1977. After the collapse of that government it re-formed itself as the **Bharatiya Janata Party** (BJP). In 1990-1991 it developed a powerful campaign focusing on reviving Hindu identity against the minorities. The elections of 1991 showed it to be the most powerful single challenger to the Congress in North India. In the decade that followed it became the most powerful opponent of the Congress across northern India and established a series of footholds and alliances in the South, enabling it to become the most important national alternative to the Congress through the 1990s.

Elsewhere a succession of regional parties dominated politics in several key states. The most important were Tamil Nadu and Andhra Pradesh in the south. In Tamil Nadu power has alternated since 1967 between the **Dravida Munnetra Kazhagam** (the DMK) and a faction which split from it, the All India Anna DMK, named after one of the earliest leaders of the Dravidian political movement, CN Annadurai ('Anna'). In Andhra Pradesh, the **Telugu Desam**, currently under the leadership of the cyber whizz-kid of South India, Chandrababu Naidu, offered a similar regional alternative to Congress rule.

Recent developments The early 1998 national elections saw the BJP return as the largest single party in India, though without an overall majority, and still with a sparse representation in most of South India. This time however they were able to forge some previously impossible alliances with regional parties and formed the new government with Atal Behari Vajpayee as Prime Minister. The Congress party was in trouble, and coaxed Italian-born widow Sonia Gandhi into taking to the stage as their figurehead in the Assembly elections. Her subsequent election as Party President suggested that the Nehru-Gandhi dynasty still carried political legitimacy, but autumn 1999 confirmed the BJP government in power at the head of a broad coalition, the National Democratic Alliance (NDA) steered again by Vajpayee. It gave him a mandate of political stability and economic reforms that built into the 'feel-good factor' of the early 21st-century India. The upset came in the May 2004 elections, when the 675 million-strong Indian electorate took to their electronic voting machines. Despite a showy subcontinent-wide campaign from the BJP declaring that 'India [was] Shining', Vajpayee and his saffron-clad cronies hadn't reckoned on the ruffled feathers of the often illiterate rural poor, who saw little change in their everyday circumstances and instead felt alienated from this hyped-up boom-time happening in the cities. Far from shining, most of these people still don't even have an electricity supply with which to power a lamp. Gandhi, alongside her daughter Priyanka and son Rahul, took to the dusty sandbowls of these seats, and led Congress to victory, contrary to all expectations. Sonia's prime ministership looked certain, but the Mumbai Stock Exchange crashed so fast on the election results that trading was suspended, the world markets held their breath and the Hindu nationalists circled around her foreign origin and faltering Hindi. Eventually she ceded the post to economic reformer Manmohan Singh.

State level politics in South India is dominated by the affairs of the State Legislative Assemblies. With a wide range of powers, these reflect the social and historic traditions of the different major linguistic regions. Politics and films get mixed up as the stars of one medium have traded places with those of the other. Film stars have been leading politicians right across the south, charismatic stars such as the late chief minister MG Ramachandran in Tamil Nadu or NT Rama Rao in Andhra Pradesh enjoyed a massive following of worshipping fans. Jayalalitha, herself a former film star and MGR's one-time girlfriend, is current chief minister of Tamil Nadu, see page 477.

Economy

India's economic growth has been headline news for the past few years in the international business press – it has been expanding at an average of above 6% from the early 90s. But for all the talk of software, biotechnology and call centre outsourcing – the country has been quick to employ its 'human capital' of excellent English-speaking, low-cost graduates – the economy's performance is still very much harnessed to the ox's yoke: food grain production, and that all depends on the monsoon, so the country's economic circumstance is still unpredictable to say the least. According to Goldman Sachs, though, the Indian economy is set to be the third biggest in the world by 2032, trailing only the USA and China.

Tamil Nadu

Since Independence in 1947 Tamil Nadu has become one of India's leading industrial states. With a quarter of India's spinning capacity, textiles are tremendously important and the state is famous both for handloom cottons and silks and for factory-made textiles. Leather and fabrics have also long been a vital export industry, but in recent years a range of new industries have developed using locally available raw materials like iron ore, bauxite and magnesite. Chennai has become home to the Ford car factory and the city also makes lorries, buses and trains.

Kerala

Traditionally Kerala's economy has depended heavily on agriculture. Estate crops, especially tea and rubber, make a major contribution to exports, while coconut and coconut products like coir, the coarse fibre used for matting and string and rope production, or copra, the oil-rich flesh of the coconut, continue to be vital to the state. Newer cash crops like pineapples have also begun to establish a national and international market. Rice production has been in long term decline, and between 1990 and 2000 production fell by 25% as farmers converted paddy land to other more profitable uses, stimulated by the rise of Kerala as a remittance economy, with large flows of money being repatriated by Malayali workers in the Gulf to invest in land, housing and small scale industries.

60% of India's labour force is engaged in agriculture, 23% in services and 17% in industry.

Karnataka

Karnataka is now widely known as one of India's most rapidly modernizing states. Along with Hyderabad in Andhra Pradesh, Bengaluru (Bangalore) is an undisputed leader in IT skills and industrial activity. Based on its early development of aeronautics and high precision machine tools, Bengaluru (Bangalore) has become a world centre for the computer industry, receiving a much-quoted seal of approval from Bill Gates. Outside the cities agriculture and forestry remain important. Demand for irrigation is growing rapidly, causing tension with neighbouring states like Tamil Nadu and Andhra Pradesh. Major food crops are rice, sorghum, millet and oil seeds.

Andhra Pradesh

The last decade has seen a great surge in Hyderabad's focus on IT and computing, but the city already had a significant industrial base. From pharmaceuticals to aerospace electronics, and fertilizers to glass and watches, the city's industrial base has expanded rapidly. However, apart from coal mining in northern Andhra and the extraction of some copper, manganese and mica, the state's economy continues to depend heavily on agriculture which still employs nearly 70% of the population. Rice is by far the most important crop, especially in the fertile coastal districts where good soils also benefit from intensive irrigation. The much drier interior has a quite different range of crops, jowar and millet being dominant. Sugar cane, cotton and tobacco are particularly important cash crops, and forest products also contribute significantly to the state's income.

Goa

In common with much of the west coast of India, Goa's rural economy depends on rice as the main food crop, cash crops being dominated by coconut, cashewnut and areca nut. Mangos, pineapples and bananas are also important, and forests still give some produce. Seasonal water shortages have prompted the development of irrigation projects, the latest of which was the interstate Tillari Project in Pernem Taluka, completed with the government of Maharashtra. Iron ore and bauxite have been two of the state's major exports but heavy industrial development has remained relatively limited. Tourism remains one of the state's biggest earners.

Agriculture

Although agriculture now accounts for less than 30% of India's GDP, it remains the most important single economic activity. More than half of India's people depend directly on agriculture, and its success has a crucial effect on the remainder of the economy.

South Indian agriculture is enormously varied, reflecting the widely different conditions of climate, soil and relief. Cereal farming dominates most areas. Rice is by far India's most important single foodgrain, concentrated in the wetter regions of the east and south. Production has more than doubled in the last 20 years.

Other cereal crops – sorghum and the millets – predominate in the drier areas, though both are grown under irrigated conditions in South India. In addition to its cereals and a range of pulses, South India produces important crops of tea, cotton and sugar cane. All have seen significant growth, tea and cotton manufacturers making important contributions to export earnings.

Between Independence and the late 1960s most of the increase in India's agricultural output came from extending the cultivated area. About 60% of India's total area is now cultivated. In the last 20 years increasingly intensive use of land through greater irrigation and use of fertilizer, pesticides and high yielding varieties of seeds (HYVs) has allowed growth to continue. The area under irrigation has risen to over 35% in 2002, while fertilizer use has increased 25 times since 1961. Indian agriculture is dominated by smallholdings. Only 20% of the land is farmed in units of more than 10 ha (compared with 31 20 years ago), while nearly 60% of farms are less than 1 ha. While the Green Revolution – the package of practices designed to increase farm output – has had its opponents, it has now transformed the agricultural productivity of many regions of India, allowing a population twice the size of that thirty years ago to be fed without recourse to imports or aid. Much of this has been achieved as the result of seed breeding and agricultural research in India's own agricultural research institutions.

Resources and industry

South India has extensive resources of iron ore, lignite, and some other minerals. Very limited oil and gas reserves have been discovered off the South Indian coast, and the South also has one nuclear power station just south of Chennai.

India's Five Year Plans

In the early 1950s India embarked on a programme of planned industrial development. Borrowing planning concepts from the Soviet Union, the government tried to stimulate development through massive investment in the public sector, imposing a system of tight controls on foreign ownership of capital in India and playing a highly interventionist role in all aspects of economic policy. The private sector was allowed to continue to operate in agriculture and in a wide range of 'non-essential' industrial sectors.

Although significant achievements were made in the first two Five Year Plans (1951-1956, 1956-1961), the Third Five Year Plan failed catastrophically. Agriculture was particularly hard hit by three poor monsoons. After a period of dependence on foreign aid at the end of the 1960s, the economy started moving forward again. The 'Green Revolution' enabled Indian agriculture to increase production faster than demand and through the 1980s it was producing surplus foodgrains, enabling it to build up reserves.

Industrial development continued to lag behind expectations, however. Although India returned to the programme of Five Year Plans (in 2000 it was nearing the end of the Ninth Plan), central control has been progressively loosened.

Achievements and problems

South India today has a far more diversified industrial base than seemed imaginable at Independence. It produces goods, from aeroplanes and rockets to watches and computers, from industrial and transport machinery to textiles and consumer goods. South India is particularly noted for the speed of its development of computer-based technologies. Hyderabad and Bengaluru (Bangalore) have attracted visits from both Bill Gates and Bill Clinton, and South India's computer industries now have world reach. According to the London Financial Times, since the early 1990s India has become one of the world's leading centres for software development. With 21.1 million Indians on the net in 2007, India is rapidly transforming itself into a computer-based society. Yet despite the economic successes, many in India claim that the weaknesses remain profound. Perhaps half of the population continues to live in absolute poverty and despite surplus grain production many still lack an adequate diet.

While India's industrial economy is producing a range of modern products, many are still uncompetitive on world markets. Furthermore, critics within India increasingly argue that goods are made in factories that often fail to observe basic safety and health rules and that emit enormous pollution into the environment. On top of that, the industrial expansion barely seems to have touched the problems of unemployment.

Culture

People

Tamil Nadu

The great majority of Tamilians are Dravidians with Mediterranean ethnic origins. They have been settled in Tamil Nadu for several thousand years. Tamil, the main language of the state, is spoken by over 85% of the population and over 5% are Christian, a group especially strong in the south where Roman Catholic and Protestant missions have been active for over 500 years. There are a small but significant minorities of Muslims, Jains and Parsis.

Kerala

The distinctiveness of Kerala's cultural identity is reflected in the Brahmin myths of its origin. As Robin Jeffrey has put it, Parasurama, the sixth incarnation of Vishnu, having been banished from India, was given permission by Varuna, the Lord of the Sea, to reclaim all the land within the throw of his axe. When Parasaruma threw the axe it fell from Kanniyakumari to Gokarnam, and as the sea withdrew Kerala was formed. However, the new land had to be settled, so Parasurama introduced a special race of Brahmins, the **Nambudris**, to whom he gave all the land and unique customs. He then brought in Nairs – to act as servants and bodyguards for the Nambudris. "He gave them the matrilineal system of family, and stated that they should have no formal marriage, and that Nair women should always be available to satisfy the desires of Nambudri men."

Matriarchy may have originated in the 10th-century conflict with the Cholas, when the Nairs' vital role as soldiers allowed them to rise in status. The immigrant Nambudri Brahmins had far fewer women than men, so while the eldest sons married Nambudri women other sons married Kshatriya or Nair girls. Krishna Chaitanya suggests that as many Nair and Kshatriya men were slaughtered in the Chola wars there was a surplus of women in all three communities, encouraging the development of a **matrilineal system** in which women controlled family property. Nairs became numerically and politically the dominant force. In the mid-19th century the system was still dominant, as was slavery which was a widespread feature both socially and economically. From 1855, when European missionary pressure encouraged the Travancore government to abolish slavery, Nair dominance weakened. Education spread rapidly, contributing to the belief that qualifications rather than inherited status should determine economic opportunity, and by the beginning of the 20th century literacy in the towns was already higher than in Calcutta and there were over 20 daily newspapers.

Kerala is the first state in India to claim 100% **literacy** in some districts and women enjoy a high social status. The 2001 Census shows that overall literacy has reached 91%, and uniquely in India there are more women than men in the population.

The majority of the **population** is Hindu, but as much as a quarter of the population is Christian and there is also a large Muslim population. Religious communities have often lived amicably together. There is no conflict between the varying Hindu sects, and most temples have shrines to each of the major Hindu divinities. Christianity, which is thought to have been brought by St Thomas the Apostle to the coast of Kerala at Kodungallur in AD 52, has its own very long tradition. The equally large Muslim community traces its origins back to the spread of Islam across the Indian Ocean with Arab traders from the seventh century.

Karnataka

While the **Lingayats** are the dominant caste group in northern Karnataka, a peasant caste, the **Vokkaligas**, is dominant in the south. Their rivalry still runs through Karnataka politics. Karnataka has its share of tribal people. The nomadic Lambanis in the north and west, are among several tribal peoples in the hill regions.

Most people speak the Dravidian **language** *Kannada* (Kanarese) although in the north there has been a lot of intermixture with speakers of Indo-Aryan languages. Kannada has the second oldest Dravidian **literary tradition**. The earliest classic known is *Kavirajamarga* which dates from the ninth century. A treatise on the writing of poetry, it refers to several earlier works which suggests that the language had been in existence for some centuries. Kannada inscriptions dating from fifth and sixth centuries support this view. Early writings in both Telugu and Kannada owe a lot to Jain influence. Kannada made a distinctive contribution in its very early development of prose writing. From the 10th to the 12th centuries a mixed poetry and prose form was developed by the writers **Pampa**, **Ponna** and **Ranna** – the 'three gems of Kannada literature'. Towards the end of the 12th century the Saivite saint **Basavanna** started a new Hindu renaissance and founded Virosivism. He disliked Brahmins and didn't believe in transmigration of souls; he didn't support child marriages or the veto on widow-remarriage. His sect, the reforming Lingayats, used simple rhythmic prose, the vachanas, to spread its teaching. The Hindu-Sanskrit tradition was greatly strengthened by the rise of the Vijayanagar Empire. One of their greatest kings, **Krishna Deva Raya** (ruled 1509-1529), was also a poet in Telugu and Sanskrit. Later, Muslim power encouraged Hindu art forms almost to go underground, and expressions of Hindu devotion and faith became associated with song and dance for popular entertainment – the Yakshagana in Kannada, and the remarkable *Kathakali* in Kerala, see page 175.

Andhra Pradesh

Most of Andhra Pradesh's 78 million people are Dravidians. Over 85% of the **population** speak Telugu. However, there are important minorities. Tamil is widely spoken in the extreme south, and on the border of Karnataka there are pockets of Kanarese speakers. In Hyderabad there are large numbers of Urdu speakers who make up 7% of the state's population.

Hyderabad, the capital of modern Andhra Pradesh, was the seat of government of the Muslim Nizams. Under their rule many Muslims came to work in the court, from North India and abroad. The Nizam's capital was a highly cosmopolitan centre, drawing extensively on Islamic contacts in North India and in west Asia – notably Persia. Its links with the Islamic world and the long tradition of political power that the Nizams had enjoyed encouraged them to hope that they might gain complete independence from India in 1947. That option was foreclosed by the Indian government's decision to remove the Nizam by force in 1948 after a half-hearted insurrection.

Goa

While in the area of the Old Conquests tens of thousands of people were converted to Christianity, the Zuari River represents a great divide between Christian and predominantly Hindu Goa. Today about 70% of the state's population is Hindu, and there is also a small but significant Muslim minority.

Portuguese used to be much more widely spoken in Goa than was English in most of the rest of India, but local **languages** remained important. The two most significant were Marathi, the language of the politically dominant majority of the neighbouring state to the north, and Konkani, the language commonly spoken on the coastal districts further south. Goa's official language now. English and Hindi are understood in the parts visited by travellers but in rural areas, Konkani predominates.

Architecture

Hindu Temple Buildings

The principles of religious building were laid down by priests in the Sastras. Every aspect of Hindu, Jain and Buddhist religious building is identified with conceptions of the structure of the universe. This applies as much to the process of building – the timing of which must be undertaken at astrologically propitious times – as to the formal layout of the buildings. The cardinal directions of north, south, east and west are the basic fix on which buildings are planned. George Michell suggests that in addition to the cardinal directions, number is also critical to the design of the religious building. The key to the building's final scale is derived from the measurements of the sanctuary at its heart.

Indian temples were nearly always built to a clear and universal design, which had built into it philosophical understandings of the universe. This cosmology, of an infinite number of universes, isolated from each other in space, proceeds by imagining various possibilities as to its nature. Its centre is seen as dominated by Mt Meru which keeps earth and heaven apart. The concept of separation is crucial to Hindu thought and social practice. Continents, rivers and oceans occupy concentric rings around the mountain, while the stars encircle the mountain in another plane. Humans live on the continent of Jambudvipa, characterized by the roseapple tree (*jambu*).

Mandalas The Sastras show plans of this continent, organized in concentric rings and entered at the cardinal points. This type of diagram was known as a mandala. Such a geometric scheme could be subdivided into almost limitless small compartments, each of which could be designated as having special properties or be devoted to a particular deity. The centre of the mandala would be the seat of the major god. Mandalas provided the ground rules for the building of stupas and temples across India and gave the key to the symbolic meaning attached to every aspect of religious buildings.

Temple design The focal point of the temple, its sanctuary, was the home of the presiding deity, the 'womb-chamber' (*garbhagriha*). A series of doorways, in large temples leading through a succession of buildings, allowed the worshipper to move towards the final encounter with the deity to obtain *darshan* – a sight of the god. Both Buddhist and Hindu worship encourage the worshipper to walk clockwise around the shrine, performing *pradakshina*.

The elevations are symbolic representations of the home of the gods. Mountain peaks such as Kailasa are common names for the most prominent of the towers. In north and East Indian temples the tallest of these towers rises above the *garbagriha* itself, symbolizing the meeting of earth and heaven in the person of the enshrined deity. In later South Indian temples the gateways to the temple come to overpower the central tower. In both, the basic structure is embellished with sculpture. When first built this would usually have been plastered and painted and often covered in gems. In contrast to the extraordinary profusion of colour and life on the outside, the interior is dark and cramped but here it is believed, lies the true centre of divine power.

Temple development Buddhist and Hindu architecture probably began with wooden building, for the rock carving and cave-excavated temples show clear evidence of copying styles which must have been developed first in wooden buildings. The third to second century BC caves of the Buddhists were followed in the seventh and eighth centuries AD by free standing but rock-cut temples such as those at Mahabalipuram (see page 87). They were subsequently replaced by temples built entirely out of assembled material, usually stone. By the 13th century AD most of India's most remarkable Hindu temples had been built, from the Chola temples of the south to the Khajuraho temples of the north peninsula. Only the flowering of Vijayanagar architecture in South India produced continuing development, culminating in the Meenakshi Temple in Madurai (see page 153).

Muslim religious architecture

Although the Muslims adapted many Hindu features, they also brought totally new forms. Their most outstanding contribution, dominating the architecture of many North Indian cities, are the mosques and tomb complexes (*dargah*). The use of brickwork was widespread and they brought with them from Persia the principle of constructing the true arch. Muslim architects succeeded in producing a variety of domed structures, often incorporating distinctively Hindu features such as the surmounting finial. By the end of the great period of Muslim building in 1707, the Muslims had added magnificent forts and palaces to their religious structures, a statement of power as well as of aesthetic taste.

European buildings

Nearly two centuries of architectural stagnation and decline followed the demise of Mughal power. The Portuguese built a series of remarkable churches in Goa that owed nothing to local traditions and everything to Baroque developments in Europe. Not until the end of the Victorian period, when British imperial ambitions were at their height, did the British colonial impact on public rather than domestic architecture begin to be felt. Fierce arguments divided British architects as to the merits of indigenous design. The ultimate plan for New Delhi was carried out by men who had little time for Hindu architecture and believed themselves to be on a civilizing mission. Others at the end of the 19th century wanted to recapture and enhance a tradition for which they had great respect. They have left a series of buildings, both in formerly British-ruled territory and in the Princely States, which illustrate this concern through the development of what became known as the Indo-Saracenic style.

Art and architecture Karnataka's role as a border territory was illustrated in the magnificent architecture of the Chalukyan Dynasty from AD 450 to 650. Here, notably in **Aihole**, were the first stirrings of **Brahman** temple design. A mixture of Jain temples illustrates the contact with the north of India which continued to influence the development of the Dravidian temples which grew alongside them. In Pattadakal alone it is possible to see examples of four temples built on North Indian '*Nagari*' principles and six built on South Indian '*Dravida*' lines. That contact was developed through the Hoysalas four centuries later. In **Belur**, **Halebid** and **Somnathpur**, the star-shaped plan of the base and the shrine, with the bell-shaped tower above and exquisitely crafted exterior and interior surfaces became a hallmark of their temples, a distinctive combination of the two traditions. The Vijayanagara kings advanced temple architecture to blend in with the rocky, boulder-ridden landscape at **Hampi**. Flat-roofed pavilions and intricately carved pillars characterized their style. **Bijapur** has some of the finest Muslim monuments on the Deccan, from the austere style of the Turkish rulers to the refinement in some of the pavilions and the world's second largest dome at the Gol Gumbaz.

Arts and crafts

Kerala

Temples and palaces have excellent carving, and rosewood is still inlaid with other woods, bone or plastics (to replace the traditional ivory). Wooden boxes with brass binding where plain or patterned strips of brass are used for decoration are also made, as are carved models of the 'snake boats'. Kerala produces astonishing **masks** and **theatrical ornaments**, particularly the Krishnattam masks which resemble the mask-like make up of the *Kathakali* dancers. Conch shells, which are also available in great numbers, are carved out in relief.

Martial arts **Kalaripayattu**, possibly developed as a form of military training during the 11th-century wars with the Cholas, is still practised in *kalaris* or gymnasia. The four disciplines give training in self-defence and attack. *Kalaripayattu* underlay the development of *Kathakali* and of other Kerala dance forms. The folk dance *Valekali*, common during temple festivals, and the Christian *Chavittu-Natakam*, in which dramatic pounding of the feet is a major feature, both derive from the martial arts.

Andhra Pradesh

Andhra's **bidriware** uses dark matt gunmetal (a zinc and copper alloy) with silver damascening in beautiful flowing floral and arabesque patterns and illustrates the Persian influence on Indian motifs. The articles vary from large vases and boxes, jewellery and plates to tiny buttons and cuff links. The name is derived from Bidar in Karnataka and dates back to the Bahmani rulers.

Miniature wooden figures, animals, fruit, vegetables and birds are common subjects of *Kondapalli* **toys** which are known for their bright colours. *Nirmal* toys look more natural and are finished with a herbal extract which gives them a golden sheen, *Tirupati* toys are in a red wood while *Ethikoppaka* toys are finished in coloured lacquer. Andhra also produces fine figurines of deities in sandalwood.

Hyderabadi **jewellers** work in gold and precious stones which are often uncut. The craftsmen can often be seen working in the lanes around the Char Minar with shops selling the typical local bangles set with glass to the west. Hyderabadi cultured pearls and silver filigree ware from Karimnagar are another speciality.

The state is famous for **himru shawls** and **fabrics** produced in cotton/silk mixes with rich woven patterns on a special handloom. Silver or gold threads produce even richer 'brocade' cloth. A young boy often sits with the weavers, 'calling out' the intricate pattern. The art of weaving special **ikat** fabrics has been revived through the efforts of the All India Handicrafts Board in the villages of Pochampalli, Chirala, Puttapaka and Koyyalagudem among others. The practice of dyeing the warp and weft threads before weaving in such a way as to produce a pattern, additionally used oil in the process when it was woven into pieces of cloth *teli rumal* (literally oil kerchief) to be used as garments. Other towns produce their own special weaves.

Kalamkari paintings (*kalam* refers to the pen used) produced in Kalahasti in the extreme south of Andhra, have a distinctive style using indigo and vegetable dyes extracted from turmeric, pomegranate skin etc, on cloth. Fabric is patterned with dyes, then glued. The blues stand out markedly from the otherwise dullish ochre colours. Originally designed to tell stories from mythology (Mahabharata and Ramayana), they make good wall hangings. Pallakollu and Masulipatam were particularly famous for printing and painting of floral designs. In addition hand-block printed textiles are also produced.

Carpets produced in Warangal and Eluru are known as 'Deccan rugs' with designs that reflect a Persian influence.

Literature

Sanskrit was the first all-India language. Its literature has had a fundamental influence on the religious, social and political life of the entire region. Its early literature was memorized and recited. The hymns of the Rig Veda probably did not reach its final form until about the sixth century BC, but its earliest parts may go back as far as 1300 BC – approximately the period of the fall of Mycenean Greece in Europe.

The Vedas

The Rig Veda is a collection of 1,028 hymns, not all directly religious. Its main function was to provide orders of worship for priests responsible for the sacrifices which were central to the religion of the Indo-Aryans. Two later texts, the Yajurveda and the Samaveda, served the same purpose. A fourth, the Atharvaveda, is largely a collection of magic spells.

The Brahmanas Central to the Vedic literature was a belief in the importance of sacrifice. At some time after 1000 BC a second category of Vedic literature, the Brahmanas, began to take shape. Story telling developed as a means to interpret the significance of sacrifice. The most famous and the most important of these were the Upanishads, probably written at some time between the seventh and fifth centuries BC.

The Mahabharata The Brahmanas gave their name to the religion emerging between the eighth and sixth centuries BC, Brahmanism, the ancestor of Hinduism. Two of its texts remain the best known and most widely revered epic compositions in South Asia, the Mahabharata and the Ramayana.

Dating the Mahabharata

The details of the great battle recounted in the Mahabharata are unclear. Tradition puts its date at precisely 3102 BC, the start of the present era and names the author of the poem as a sage, Vyasa. Evidence suggests however that the battle was fought around 800 BC, at **Kurukshetra**. It was another 400 years before priests began to write the stories down, a process which was not complete until 400 AD. The Mahabharata was probably an attempt by the warrior class, the Kshatriyas, to merge their brand of popular religion with the ideas of Brahmanism. The original version was about 3000 stanzas long, but it now contains over 100,000 – eight times as long as Homer's Iliad and the Odyssey put together.

Good and evil The battle was seen as a war of the forces of good and evil, the **Pandavas** being interpreted as gods and the **Kauravas** as devils. The arguments were elaborated and expanded until about the fourth century AD by which time, as Shackle says, "Brahmanism had absorbed and set its own mark on the religious ideas of the epic and Hinduism had come into being". A comparatively late addition to the Mahabharata, the Bhagavad-Gita is the most widely read and revered text among Hindus in South Asia today.

The Ramayana

Valmiki is thought of in India as the author of the second great Indian epic, the Ramayana, though no more is known of his identity than is known of Homer's. Like the Mahabharata, it underwent several stages of development before it reached its final version of 48,000 lines.

Sanskrit Literature

Sanskrit was always the language of the court and the elite. Other languages replaced it in common speech by the third century BC, but it remained in restricted use for over 1,000 years after that period. The remarkable Sanskrit grammar of Panini helped to establish grammar as one of the six disciplines essential to understanding the Vedas properly and to conducting Vedic rituals. The other five were phonetics, etymology, metre, ritual practice and astronomy. Sanskrit literature continued to be written in the courts until the Muslims replaced it with Persian, long after it had ceased to be a language of spoken communication. One of India's greatest poets, **Kalidasa**, contributed to the development of Sanskrit as the language of learning and the arts.

The story of Rama

Under Brahmin influence, Rama was transformed from the human prince of the early versions into the divine figure of the final story. Rama, the 'jewel of the solar kings', became deified as an incarnation of Vishnu. The story tells how Rama was banished from his father's kingdom. In a journey that took him as far as Sri Lanka, accompanied by his wife Sita and helper and friend Hanuman (the monkey-faced God depicted in many Indian temples, shrines and posters), Rama finally fought the king **Ravana**, again changed in later versions into a demon. Rama's rescue of Sita was interpreted as the Aryan triumph over the barbarians. The epic is widely seen as South Asia's first literary poem and is known and recited in all Hindu communities.

Ravana, demon king of Lanka

Vatsyana's Kamasutra not only explores the diversity of physical love but sheds light on social customs. In architecture the Nagara and Dravida styles were first developed. The Brahmins also produced theses on philosophy and on the structure of society, but these had the negative effect of contributing to the extreme rigidity of the caste system which became apparent from this period onwards.

Literally 'stories of ancient times', the Puranas are about Brahma, Vishnu and Siva. Although some of the stories may relate to real events that occurred as early as 1500 BC, they were not compiled until the fifth century AD. Margaret and James Stutley record the belief that "during the destruction of the world at the end of the age, Hayagriva is said to have saved the Puranas. A summary of the original work is now preserved in Heaven!"

The stories are often the only source of information about the period immediately following the early Vedas. Each Purana was intended to deal with five themes: "the creation of the world (sarga); its destruction and recreation (pratisarga); the genealogy of gods and patriarchs (vamsa); the reigns and periods of the Manus (manvantaras); and the history of the solar and lunar dynasties".

The Muslim influence

Persian In the first three decades of the 10th century AD Mahmud of Ghazni carried Muslim power into India. For considerable periods until the 18th century, Persian became the language of the courts. Classical Persian was the dominant influence, with Iran as its country of origin and Shiraz its main cultural centre, but India developed its own Persian-based style. Two poets stood out at the end of the 13th century AD, when Muslim rulers had established a sultanate in Delhi, Amir Khusrau, who lived from 1253 to 1325 and the mystic Amir Hasan, who died about AD 1328.

Turki The most notable of the Mughal sponsors of literature, Akbar (1556-1605) was himself illiterate. Babur left one of the most remarkable political autobiographies of any generation, the Babur-nama (History of Babur), written in Turki and translated into Persian. His grandson Akbar commissioned a biography, the Akbar-nama, which reflected his interest in all the world's religions. His son Jahangir left his memoirs, the Tuzuk-i Jahangiri, in Persian. They have been described as intimate and spontaneous and showing an insatiable interest in things, events and people.

The Colonial Period

Persian was already in decline during the reign of the last great Muslim Emperor, **Aurangzeb** and as the British extended their political power so the role of English grew. There is now a very wide Indian literature accessible in English, which has thus become the latest of the languages to be used across the whole of South Asia.

In the 19th century English became a vehicle for developing nationalist ideals. However, notably in the work of **Rabindranath Tagore**, it became a medium for religious and philosophical prose and for a developing poetry. Tagore himself won the Nobel Prize for Literature in 1913 for his translation into English of his own work, Gitanjali. Leading South Asian philosophers of the 20th century have written major works in English, including not only MK Gandhi and Jawaharlal Nehru, the two leading figures in India's Independence movement, but S Radhakrishnan, Aurobindo Ghose and Sarojini Naidu, who all added to the depth of Indian literature in English.

Some suggestions for reading are listed on page 537. In addition, several South Asian regional languages have their own long traditions of both religious and secular literature which are discussed in the relevant sections of this handbook.

Language

The graffiti written on the walls of any Indian city bear witness to the number of major languages spoken across the country, many with their own distinct scripts. In all the South India states a Dravidian language predominates, in contrast to North and West India where Indo-Aryan languages – the easternmost group of the Indo-European family – are most common. Sir William Jones, the great 19th-century scholar, discovered close links between Sanskrit (the basis of nearly all North Indian languages) German and Greek. He showed that they all must have originated in the common heartland of Central Asia, being carried by the nomadic tribes who shaped so much of the history of both Europe and Asia. Sanskrit has left its mark on all major Indian laguages, though recently there have been efforts to eradicate it from the Tamil language.

Malayalam

Malayalam, the state language, is the most recent of the Dravidian languages, developing from the 13th century with its origin in Sanskrit and the Proto-Dravidian language which also gave rise to Tamil.

Sanskrit

As the pastoralists from Central Asia moved into South Asia from 2000 BC onwards, their Indo-Aryan languages were gradually modified. **Sanskrit** developed from this process, emerging as the dominant classical language of India by the sixth century BC, when it was classified in the grammar of **Panini**. It remained the language of the educated until AD 1000, though it had ceased to be in common use several centuries earlier. The Muslims brought Persian into South Asia as the language of the rulers, where it became the language of the numerically tiny but politically powerful elite.

Hindi and Urdu

The most striking example of Muslim influence on the earlier Indo-European languages is that of the two most important languages of India and Pakistan, Hindi and Urdu respectively. Hindi is increasingly commonly used as a lingua franca in many parts of India, though it is very rarely heard in Tamil Nadu. Urdu, written from right to left in the flowing Perso-Arabic script, is widely spoken among the Muslim population of towns and cities in the South.

The Dravidian languages

One of the major language families of South Asia today, Dravidian, has been in India since before the arrival of the Indo-Aryans. Four of South Asia's major living languages belong to this family group – Tamil, Telugu, Kannada and Malayalam, spoken in Tamil Nadu (and northern Sri Lanka) Andhra Pradesh, Karnataka and Kerala respectively.

Each has its own script. All the Dravidian languages were influenced by the prevalence of Sanskrit as the language of the ruling and educated elite. There have been recent attempts to rid Tamil of its Sanskrit elements and to recapture the supposed purity of a literature that stretches back to the early centuries BC. Kannada and Telugu were clearly established by AD 1000, while Malayalam, which started as a dialect of Tamil, did not develop its fully distinct form until the 13th century. Today the four main Dravidian languages are spoken by nearly 200 million people.

Scripts

It is impossible to spend even a short time in India or the other countries of South Asia without coming across several of the different scripts that are used. The earliest ancestor of scripts in use today was **Brahmi**, in which Asoka's famous inscriptions were written in the third century BC. Written from left to right, a separate symbol represented each different sound. The Muslim rulers developed a right to left script based on Persian and Arabic.

Dravidian scripts The Dravidian languages were written originally on leaves of the palmyra palm. Cutting the letters on the hard palm leaf made particular demands which had their impact on the forms of the letters adopted. The letters became rounded because they were carved with a stylus. This was held stationary while the leaf was turned. The southern scripts were carried overseas, contributing to the form of the non-Dravidian languages of Thai, Burmese and Cambodian.

Devanagari For about a thousand years the major script of northern India has been the Nagari or Devanagari, which means literally the script of the 'city of the gods'. Hindi, Nepali and Marathi join Sanskrit in their use of Devanagari. Hindi is used for place names on sign boards right across India

Numerals Many of the Indian alphabets have their own notation for numerals. This is not without irony, for what in the western world are called 'Arabic' numerals are in fact of Indian origin. In some parts of South Asia local numerical symbols are still in use, but by and large you will find that the Arabic number symbols familiar in Europe and the West are common.

The role of English

English now plays an important role across India. It is widely spoken in towns and cities and even in quite remote villages it is usually not difficult to find someone who speaks at least a little English. Other European languages are almost completely unknown. The accent in which English is spoken is often affected strongly by the mother tongue of the speaker and there have been changes in common grammar which sometimes make it sound unusual. Many of these changes have become standard Indian English usage, as valid as any other varieties of English used around the world.

Music and dance

Kerala

The special dance form of Kerala, *Kathakali*, has its origins in the *Theyyam*, a ritual tribal dance of North Kerala, and *Kalaripayattu*, the martial arts practised by the high-caste Nayars, going back 1000 years. In its present form of dance-drama, *Kathakali* has evolved over the last 400 years. The performance is usually out of doors, the stage is bare but for a large bronze oil-lamp, with the drummers on one side and the singers with cymbal and gong, who act as narrators, on the other. The art of mime reaches its peak in these highly stylized performances which always used to last through the night; now they often take just three to four hours. *Kathakali* is no longer strictly the preserve of the male dancer.

Putting on the elaborate make-up and costumes is very time consuming. The costume consists of a large, billowing skirt, a padded jacket, heavy ornaments and headgear. The make-up is all-important: *Thecha* (painted make-up) – *Pacha* (green) characterizing the Good and *Kathi* (knife, shape of a painted 'moustache'), the Villain; *Thadi* (bearded) – white for superhuman *hanumans*, black for the hunter and red for evil and fierce demons; *Kari* (black) signifying demonesses; *Minukku* (shining) 'simple' make-up representing the Gentle and Spiritual. The paints are natural pigments while the stiff 'mask' is created with rice paste and lime. The final application of a flower seed in the lower eyelid results in the red eyes you will see on stage.

This classical dance requires lengthy and hard training to make the body supple, the eyes expressive. The 24 *mudras* express the nine emotions of serenity, wonder, kindness, love, valour, fear, contempt, loathing and anger. The gods and mortals play out their roles amid the chaos brought about by human ambition, but the dance ends in peace and harmony restored by the gods.

Every 12 years the North Malabar village communities of Kannur and Kasaragod organize a *Theyyam* festival. The term itself is a corruption of *deivam*, or God. A combination of music and dance, the festival brings together all castes and religions, but is a development of a pre-Hindu cult. Many folk gods and goddesses continue to hold a place in the festival. Initial rituals invoke the deity while the drum beats, flaming torches and music and dance create a surreal atmosphere for the performance which is believed to ward off evil and bring prosperity.

The sensuous *Mohiniyattam*, performed by women, is known as the dance of the charmer or temptress. It evolved through the influence of Tamil dancers who brought Bharata Natyam to the Kerala royal courts. It is performed solo as in Bharata Natyam with a similar core repertoire and musical accompaniments but with the addition of *idakkai*, a percussion instrument. *Tullal*, again peculiar to Kerala, is another classical solo dance form which comes closer to contemporary life, and is marked for its simplicity, wit and humour.

Karnataka

Open-air folk theatre or *Bayalata* of Karnataka has developed from religious ritual and is performed in honour of the local deity. The plays evolve and are improvised by the actors on an informal stage. The performances usually start at night and often last into the early hours. The famous *Yakshagana* or *Parijata* usually has a single narrator while the other forms of Bayalata have four or five, assisted by a jester. The plots of the *Dasarata* which enacts several stories and *Sannata* which elaborates one theme, are taken loosely from mythology but sometimes highlight real-life incidents and are performed by a company of actors and actresses. There is at least one star singer and dancer in each company and a troupe of dancers who perform in these dance-dramas and are also asked to perform at religious festivals and family celebrations.

The *Doddata* is less refined than the Yakshagana but both have much in common, beginning with a prayer to the god Ganesh, using verse and prose and drawing from the stories of the epics Ramayana and Mahabharata. The costumes are very elaborate with fantastic stage effects, loud noises and war cries and vigorous dances. It all amounts to a memorable experience but requires stamina as they continue all night!

Music Indian music can trace its origins to the metrical hymns and chants of the Vedas, in which the production of sound according to strict rules was understood to be vital to the continuing order of the Universe. Through more than 3000 years of development and a range of regional schools, India's musical tradition has been handed on almost entirely by ear. The chants of the **Rig Veda** developed into songs in the **Sama Veda** and music found expression in every sphere of life, reflecting the cycle of seasons and the rhythm of work.

Over the centuries the original three notes, which were sung strictly in descending order, were extended to five and then seven and developed to allow freedom to move up and down the scale. The scale increased to 12 with the addition of flats and sharps and finally to 22 with the further subdivision of semitones. Books of musical rules go back at least as far as the third century AD. Classical music was totally intertwined with dance and drama, an interweaving reflected in the term *sangita*.

At some point after the Muslim influence made itself felt in the north. North and South Indian styles diverged, to become Carnatic (Karnatak) music in the south and Hindustani music in the north. However, they still share important common features: *svara* (pitch), *raga* (the melodic structure) and *tala* or *talam* (metre).

Changes constantly occurred in different schools of music within the basic framework of **raga-tala-prabandha** which was well established by the seventh century. From the 13th century the division between the *Hindustani* or the northern system (which included the western and eastern regions as well) and the *Carnatic* or the southern system, became pronounced. The southern school has a more scale-based structure of *raga* whereas the northern school has greater flexibility and thus continued to develop through the centuries. The *tala* too is much more precise. It is also nearly always devotional or didactic whereas the northern system also includes non-religious, everyday themes which are sometimes sensuous. The language that lends itself naturally to the southern system is Telugu and the only bowed instrument that is used to accompany vocal music is the violin, imported from the West but played rather differently.

The essential structure of a melody is known as a **raga** which usually has five to seven notes and can have as many as nine (or even 12 in mixed ragas). The music is improvised by the performer within certain governing rules and although theoretically thousands of ragas are possible, only around a hundred are commonly performed. Ragas have become associated with particular moods and specific times of the day. Music festivals often include all night sessions to allow performers a wider choice of repertoire.

Carnatic (Karnatak) music

Contemporary South Indian music is traced back to Tyagaraja (1759-1847), Svami Shastri (1763-1827) and Dikshitar (1775-1835), three musicians who lived and worked in Thanjavur. They are still referred to as 'the Trinity'. Their music placed more emphasis on extended compositions than Hindustani music.

Perhaps the best known South Indian instrument is the stringed *vina*, the flute being commonly used for accompaniment along with the violin. An oboe-like instrument called the *nagasvaram* has a wooden mouthpiece and evolved from the snake charmer's *pangi* with two bamboo or metal pipes which have holes. In addition to the drums, *tavil*, there is the unusual *ghatam*, a round clay pot which has the open neck pressed against the player's stomach while he strikes and taps with his hands, wrists and fingers.

Dance and music festivals

Many cities hold annual festivals, particularly during winter months. See page 46. Some important ones are: **January**: *Thyagaraja Festival,* Tiruvayyaru, near Thanjavur; *Siddheswara Temple Festival*, Bijapur; *Nrutytsava*, Pattadakal. **January-February**: *Mamallapuram Nritya Utsav,* Mahabalipuram. **February-March**: *Sivaratri Natyanjali Utsav,* Chidambaram. **October-November**: *Hampi Utsav of Vijaynagar,* Hampi; *Shanmukhananda*, Mumbai. **October-March**: *Nishagandhi Nritya Utsav,* Thiruvananthapuram. **November**: *Sangeet Sanmelan,* Chennai; *Sur-Singar Festival*, Mumbai. **December**: *Music Academy Festival and Tamil Isa Sangam*, Chennai.

Dance

The rules for classical dance were laid down in the Natya shastra in the second century BC, which is still one of the bases for modern dance forms. The most common sources for Indian dance are the epics, but there are three essential aspects of the dance itself, Nritta (pure dance), Nrittya (emotional expression) and Natya (drama). The religious influence in dance was exemplified by the tradition of temple dancers, *devadasis*, girls and women who were dedicated to the deity in major temples. In South India there were thousands of *devadasis* associated with temple worship, though the practice fell into disrepute and was banned in independent India. Various dance forms (for example *Bharat Natyam, Kathakali, Mohinyattam*) developed in the southern states.

There are specific folk dance traditions which are widely performed during festivals.

Cuisine

Kerala

Kerala's cuisine reflects its diverse religious traditions, its seaboard location and the ubiquitous presence of the coconut. Uniquely in India, for example, beef is widely eaten, although seafood is far more common. *Fish Moilee* is prepared with coconut milk and spices while for *Pollichathu* the fish is baked with chilli paste, curry leaves and spices. Coconut-based dishes such as *thoran*, a dry dish of mixed vegetables chopped very small, herbs and a variety of curry leaves, with *avial*, similar to thoran but cooked in a sauce, are widely eaten. *Erisseri* is a thick curry of banana or yam and *kichadi* is beetroot or cucumber in coconut-curd paste. You can try these with the soft centred, lacy pancake *appam* or the soft noodle rice cakes *iddiappam*. Jack fruit, pineapples, custard apples and a seemingly endless variety of bananas also play a vital part in many dishes. Rice is the staple cereal, around which in the typical Kerala *thali* will be a range of vegetables, served with *pappadum*, *rasam* (a thin clear pepper water or soup), spicy *sambar* made with lentils and vegetables, and curd. For dessert, you might get milk *payasam,* made with rice or vermicelli.

Karnataka

Try a typical Udupi meal which follows the pattern of a south Indian vegetarian thali, and is traditionally served on a green plantain leaf or on a stainless steel plate. The vegetable curries which accompany the rice may differ a little from those served in Tamil Nadu but are just as satisfying.

Andhra Pradesh

Andhra food stands out as distinct because of its northern influence and larger number of non-vegetarians. The rule of the Muslim Nawabs for centuries is reflected in the rich, spicy local dishes, especially in the area around the capital. Try *haleem* (spiced pounded wheat with mutton), *paya* (soup) or *baghara baigan* (stuffed aubergines). Rice and meat *biryani*, *nahari*, *kulcha*, egg *paratha*, and *kababs* have a lot in common with the northern Mughlai cuisine. Vegetarian biryani replaces meat with cashew nuts and sultanas. The growing of hot chillies has led to its liberal use in food preparation. Good quality locally-grown grapes (especially *anab-e-shahi*) or *khobani* (puréed apricots) provide a welcome neutralizing effect.

Science

The science of early India By about 500 BC Indian texts illustrated the calculation of the **calendar**, although the system itself almost certainly goes back to the eighth or ninth century BC. The year was divided into 27 *nakshatras*, or fortnights, years being calculated on a mixture of lunar and solar counting.

Views of the universe Early Indian views of the universe were based on the square and the cube. The earth was seen as a square, one corner pointing south, rising like a pyramid in a series of square terraces with its peak, the mythical Mount Meru. The sun moved round the top of Mount Meru in a square orbit and the square orbits of the planets were at successive planes above the orbit of the sun. These were seen therefore as forming a second pyramid of planetary movement. Mount Meru was central to all early Indian schools of thought, Hindu, Buddhist and Jain.

However, about 200 BC the Jains transformed the view of the universe by replacing the idea of square orbits with that of the circle. The earth was shown as a circular disc, with Mount Meru rising from its centre and the Pole Star directly above it.

Technology The only copy of Kautiliya's treatise on government (which was only discovered in 1909) dates from about 100 BC. It describes the **weapons** technology of catapults, incendiary missiles and the use of elephants, but it is also evident that gunpowder was unknown. Large scale **irrigation** works were developed, though the earliest examples of large tanks may be those of the Sri Lankan King Panduwasa at Anuradhapura, built in 504 BC. During the Gupta period dramatic progress was made in **metallurgy**, evidenced in the extraordinarily pure iron pillar which can be seen in the Qutb Minar in Delhi.

Mathematics Conceptions of the universe and the mathematical and geometrical ideas that accompanied them were comparatively advanced in South Asia by the time of the Mauryan Empire and were put to use in the rules developed for building temple altars. Indians were using the concept of zero and decimal points in the Gupta period. Furthermore in AD 499, just after the demise of the Gupta Empire, the astronomer Aryabhatta calculated Pi as 3.1416 and the length of the solar year as 365.358 days. He also postulated that the earth was a sphere rotating on its own axis and revolving around the sun and that the earth's shadow falling on the moon caused lunar eclipses.

The development of science in India was not restricted to the Gupta court. In South India, Tamil kings developed extensive contact with Roman and Greek thinkers during the first four centuries of the Christian era. Babylonian methods used for astronomy in Greece remained current in Tamil Nadu until very recent times. The basic texts of astronomy (the Surya Siddhanta) were completed by AD 400.

Religion

It is impossible to write briefly about religion in India without greatly over-simplifying. Over 80% of Indians are Hindu, but there are significant minorities. Muslims number about 120 million and there are over 23 million Christians, 18 million Sikhs, six million Buddhists and a number of other religious groups. In the south the balance is rather different, for while there are only tiny numbers of Sikhs or Buddhists, Christianity is relatively strong, especially in Kerala and some districts of Tamil Nadu. One of the most persistent features of Indian religious and social life is the caste system. This has undergone substantial changes since Independence, especially in towns and cities, but most people in India are still clearly identified as a member of a particular caste group. The government has introduced measures to help the backward, or 'scheduled' castes, though in recent years this has produced a major political backlash.

Hinduism

It has always been easier to define Hinduism by what it is not than by what it is. Indeed, the name 'Hindu' was given by foreigners to the peoples of the subcontinent who did not profess to adhering to one of the other major faiths, such as Islam or Christianity. The beliefs and practices of modern Hinduism began to take shape in the centuries on either side of the birth of Christ. But while some aspects of modern Hinduism can be traced back more than 2000 years before that, other features are recent. Hinduism has undergone major changes both in belief and practice, originating from outside as well as from within. As early as the sixth century BC the Buddhists and Jains had tried to reform the religion of Vedism (or Brahmanism) which had been dominant in some parts of South Asia for 500 years.

Key ideas

A number of ideas run like a thread through Hinduism. According to the great Indian philosopher and former President of India, S Radhakrishnan, religion for the Hindu "is not an idea but a power, not an intellectual proposition but a life conviction. Religion is consciousness of ultimate reality, not a theory about God".

Some Hindu scholars and philosophers talk of Hinduism as one religious and cultural tradition, in which the enormous variety of belief and practice can ultimately be interpreted as interwoven in a common view of the world. Yet there is no Hindu organization, like a church, with the authority to define belief or establish official practice. There are spiritual leaders and philosophers who are widely revered and there is an enormous range of literature that is treated as sacred. Not all Hindu groups believe in a single supreme God. In view of these characteristics, many authorities argue that it is misleading to think of Hinduism as a religion at all.

Be that as it may, the evidence of the living importance of Hinduism is visible across India. Hindu philosophy and practice has also touched many of those who belong to other religious traditions, particularly in terms of social institutions such as caste.

Darshan One of Hinduism's recurring themes is 'vision', 'sight' or 'view' – **darshan**. Applied to the different philosophical systems themselves, such as *yoga* or *vedanta*, 'darshan' is also used to describe the sight of the deity that worshippers hope to gain when they visit a temple or shrine hoping for the sight of a *guru* (teacher). Equally it may apply to the religious insight gained through meditation or prayer.

The four stages of life

Popular Hindu belief holds that an ideal life has four stages: that of the student, the householder, the forest dweller and the wandering dependent or beggar (*sannyasi*). These stages represent the phases through which an individual learns of life's goals and of the means of achieving them.

One of the most striking sights today is that of the saffron-clad *sannyasi* (sadhu) seeking gifts of food and money to support himself in the final stage of his life. There may have been sadhus even before the Aryans arrived. Today, most of these have given up material possessions, carrying only a strip of cloth, a *danda* (staff), a crutch to support the chin during *achal* (meditation), prayer beads, a fan to ward off evil spirits, a water pot, a drinking vessel, which may be a human skull and a begging bowl. You may well see one, almost naked, covered only in ashes, on a city street.

The four human goals Many Hindus also accept that there are four major human goals; material prosperity (*artha*), the satisfaction of desires (*kama*) and performing the duties laid down according to your position in life (*dharma*). Beyond those is the goal of achieving liberation from the endless cycle of rebirths into which everyone is locked (*moksha*). It is to the search for liberation that the major schools of Indian philosophy have devoted most attention. Together with dharma, it is basic to Hindu thought.

The Mahabharata lists ten embodiments of **dharma**: good name, truth, self-control, cleanness of mind and body, simplicity, endurance, resoluteness of character, giving and sharing, austerities and continence. In dharmic thinking these are inseparable from five patterns of behaviour: non-violence, an attitude of equality, peace and tranquillity, lack of aggression and cruelty and absence of envy. Dharma, an essentially secular concept, represents the order inherent in human life.

Karma The idea of *karma*, 'the effect of former actions', is central to achieving liberation. As C Rajagopalachari put it: "Every act has its appointed effect, whether the act be thought, word or deed. The cause holds the effect, so to say, in its womb. If we reflect deeply and objectively, the entire world will be found to obey unalterable laws. That is the doctrine of karma". See also box opposite.

Rebirth The belief in the transmigration of souls (*samsara*) in a never-ending cycle of rebirth has been Hinduism's most distinctive and important contribution to Indian culture. The earliest reference to the belief is found in one of the Upanishads, around the seventh century BC, at about the same time as the doctrine of karma made its first appearance. By the late Upanishads it was universally accepted and in Buddhism and Jainism it is never questioned.

Ahimsa AL Basham pointed out that belief in transmigration must have encouraged a further distinctive doctrine, that of non-violence or non-injury – *ahimsa*. The belief in rebirth meant that all living things and creatures of the spirit – people, devils, gods, animals, even worms – possessed the same essential soul. One inscription threatens that anyone who interferes with the rights of Brahmins to land given to them by the king will 'suffer rebirth for 80,000 years as a worm in dung'. Belief in the cycle of rebirth was essential to give such a threat any weight!

Karma – an eye to the future

According to the doctrine of karma, every person, animal or god has a being or 'self' which has existed without beginning. Every action, except those that are done without any consideration of the results, leaves an indelible mark on that 'self', carried forward into the next life.

The overall character of the imprint on each person's 'self' determines three features of the next life: the nature of his next birth (animal, human or god), the kind of family he will be born into if human and the length of the next life. Finally, it controls the good or bad experiences that the self will experience. However, it does not imply a fatalistic belief that the nature of action in this life is unimportant. Rather, it suggests that the path followed by the individual in the present life is vital to the nature of its next life and ultimately to the chance of gaining release from this world.

Schools of philosophy

It is common now to talk of six major schools of Hindu philosophy. *Nyaya*, *Vaisheshika*, *Sankhya*, *Yoga*, *Purvamimansa* and *Vedanta*.

Yoga Yoga can be traced back to at least the third century AD. It seeks a synthesis of the spirit, the soul and the flesh and is concerned with systems of meditation and self denial that lead to the realization of the Divine within oneself and can ultimately release one from the cycle of rebirth.

Vedanta These are literally the final parts of the Vedic literature, the Upanishads. The basic texts also include the Brahmasutra of Badrayana, written about the first century AD and the most important of all, the Bhagavad-Gita, which is a part of the epic the Mahabharata. There are many interpretations of these basic texts. Three are given here.

Advaita Vedanta This holds that there is no division between the cosmic force or principle, *Brahman* and the individual Self, *atman* (also referred to as 'soul'). The fact that we appear to see different and separate individuals is simply a result of ignorance. This is termed *maya* (illusion), but Vedanta philosophy does not suggest that the world in which we live is an illusion. *Jnana* (knowledge) is held as the key to understanding the full and real unity of Self and Brahman. Shankaracharya, born at Kalady in modern Kerala, in the seventh century AD, is the best known Advaitin Hindu philosopher. He argued that there was no individual Self or soul separate from the creative force of the universe, or Brahman, and that it was impossible to achieve liberation (*moksha*), through meditation and devotional worship, which he saw as signs of remaining on a lower level and of being unprepared for true liberation.

Vishishtadvaita The 12th-century philosopher, Ramanuja, repudiated such ideas. He transformed the idea of God from an impersonal force to a personal God and viewed both the Self and the World as real but only as part of the whole. In contrast to Shankaracharya's view, Ramanuja saw *bhakti* (devotion) as of central importance to achieving liberation and service to the Lord as the highest goal of life.

Dvaita Vedanta The 14th-century philosopher Madhva believed that Brahman, the Self and the World are completely distinct. Worship of God is a key means of achieving liberation.

Worship

As S Radhakrishnan puts it, for millions of Hindus: "It does not matter what conception of God we adopt so long as we keep up a perpetual search after truth".

Puja For most Hindus today worship ('performing *puja*') is an integral part of their faith. The great majority of Hindu homes will have a shrine to one of the gods of the Hindu pantheon. Individuals and families will often visit shrines or temples and on special occasions will travel long distances to particularly holy places such as Benaras or Puri. Such sites may have temples dedicated to a major deity but will always have numerous other shrines in the vicinity dedicated to other favourite gods.

Acts of devotion are often aimed at the granting of favours and the meeting of urgent needs for this life – good health, finding a suitable wife or husband, the birth of a son, prosperity and good fortune. In this respect the popular devotion of simple pilgrims of all faiths in South Asia is remarkably similar when they visit shrines, whether Hindu, Buddhist or Jain temples, the tombs of Muslim saints or even churches such as Bom Jesus in Goa, where St Francis Xavier lies entombed.

Puja involves making an offering to God and darshan (having a view of the deity). Hindu worship is generally, though not always, an act performed by individuals. Thus Hindu temples may be little more than a shrine in the middle of the street, tended by a priest and visited at special times when a darshan of the resident God can be obtained. When it has been consecrated, the **image**, if exactly made, becomes the channel for the godhead to work. According to KM Sen "in popular Hinduism, God is worshipped in different forms" showing "a particular attachment to a particular figure in Hindu mythology". Images are, Françoise Bernier quotes "something before the eyes that fixes the mind".

Holy places Certain rivers and towns are particularly sacred to Hindus. Thus there are seven holy rivers – the Ganga, Yamuna, Indus and mythical Sarasvati in the north and the Narmada, Godavari and Kaveri in the Peninsula. There are also seven holy places – Haridwar, Mathura, Ayodhya and Varanasi, again in the north, Ujjain, Dwarka and Kanchipuram to the south. In addition to these seven holy places there are four holy abodes: Badrinath, Puri and Ramesvaram, with Dwarka in modern Gujarat having the unique distinction of being both a holy abode and a holy place.

Rituals and festivals The temple rituals often follow through the cycle of day and night, as well as yearly lifecycles. The priests may wake the deity from sleep, bathe, clothe and feed it. Worshippers will be invited to share in this process by bringing offerings of clothes and food. Gifts of money will usually be made and in some temples there is a charge levied for taking up positions in front of the deity in order to obtain a darshan at the appropriate times.

Every temple has its special festivals. At festival times you can see villagers walking in small groups, brightly dressed and often high spirited, sometimes as far as 80-100 km.

Kerala's festivals Useful website www.keralatourism.org, or pick up their annual 'Fairs and Festivals of Kerala'.

March-April (Meenam) and **October-November (Thulam)**: **Arattu** is the closing festival of the 10-day celebrations of the Padmanabhasvami Temple in Thiruvananthapuram in which the deity is processed around the temple inside the fort, and then down to the sea.

April-May: **Vishukani** celebrates the start of the rainy season. The fire crackers exploded to ward off evil spirits can be quite terrifyingly loud.

August-September: The biggest and most important festival is **Thiruvonam (Onam)**, a harvest festival, celebrated throughout Kerala. **Onam Tourist Week** is a cultural feast of art and folk presentations at 20 venues in Thiruvananthapuram and other major Kerala towns. The four-day festival is marked with elephant processions, *Kathakali* dances, fireworks, water carnivals and **vallam kalli**, the famous snake boat races, at Aranmula, Alappuzha, Kottayam, Kochi and Payipad; early September. **Nehru Trophy Boat Race** at Punnamadakayal, Alappuzha; 9 August 2008, 8 August 2009: a ceremonial water procession followed by the famed snake-boat race.

December-January: **Tiruvathira** is exclusively a festival for women, generally unmarried, and is associated with Kamadeva, the god of love. Swings are improvised from trees especially for the day.

Hindu Deities

Today three Gods are widely seen as all-powerful: Brahma, Vishnu and Siva. Their functions and character are not readily separated. While Brahma is regarded as the ultimate source of creation, Siva also has a creative role alongside his function as destroyer. Vishnu in contrast is seen as the preserver or protector of the universe. Vishnu and Siva are widely represented (where Brahma is not) and have come to be seen as the most powerful and important. Their followers are referred to as Vaishnavite and Shaivites respectively and numerically they form the two largest sects in India.

Brahma Popularly Brahma is interpreted as the Creator in a trinity, alongside Vishnu as Preserver and Siva as Destroyer. In the literal sense the name Brahma is the masculine and personalized form of the neuter word *Brahman*.

In the early Vedic writing, Brahman represented the universal and impersonal principle which governed the Universe. Gradually, as Vedic philosophy moved towards a monotheistic interpretation of the universe and its origins, this impersonal power was increasingly personalized. In the Upanishads, Brahman was seen as a universal and elemental creative spirit. Brahma, described in early myths as having been born from a golden egg and then to have created the Earth, assumed the identity of the earlier Vedic deity Prajapati and became identified as the creator.

Some of the early Brahma myths were later taken over by the Vishnu cult. For example in one story Brahma was believed to have rescued the earth from a flood by taking the form of a fish or a tortoise and in another he became a boar, raising the Earth above the flood waters on his tusks. All these images were later associated with Vishnu.

By the fourth and fifth centuries AD, the height of the classical period of Hinduism, Brahma was seen as one of the trinity of Gods – *Trimurti* – in which Vishnu, Siva and Brahma represented three forms of the unmanifested supreme being. It is from Brahma that Hindu cosmology takes its structure. The basic cycle through which the whole cosmos passes is described as one day in the life of Brahma – the *kalpa*. It equals 4320 million years, with an equally long night. One year of Brahma's life – a cosmic year – lasts 360 days and nights. The universe is expected to last for 100 years of Brahma's life, who is currently believed to be 51 years old.

By the sixth century AD Brahma worship had effectively ceased (before the great period of temple building), which accounts for the fact that there are remarkably few temples dedicated to Brahma. Nonetheless images of Brahma are found in most temples. Characteristically he is shown with four faces, a fifth having been destroyed by the fire from Siva's third eye. In his four arms he usually holds a copy of the Vedas, a sceptre and a water jug or a bow. He is accompanied by the goose, symbolizing knowledge.

How Sarasvati turned Brahma's head

Masson-Oursel recounts one myth that explains how Brahma came to have five heads. "Brahma first formed woman from his own immaculate substance and she was known as Sarasvati, Savitri, Gayatri or Brahmani. When he saw this lovely girl emerge from his own body Brahma fell in love with her. Sarasvati moved to his right to avoid his gaze, but a head immediately sprang up from the god. And when Sarasvati turned to the left and then behind him, two new heads emerged. She darted towards heaven and a fifth head was formed. Brahma then said to his daughter, 'Let us beget all kinds of living things, men, Suras and Asuras'. Hearing these words Sarasvati returned to earth, Brahma wedded her and they retired to a secret place where they remained together for a hundred (divine) years".

Sarasvati Seen by some Hindus as the 'active power' of Brahma, popularly thought of as his consort, Sarasvati has survived into the modern Hindu world as a far more important figure than Brahma himself. In popular worship Sarasvati represents the goddess of education and learning, worshipped in schools and colleges with gifts of fruit, flowers and incense. She represents 'the word' itself, which began to be deified as part of the process of the writing of the Vedas, which ascribed magical power to words. The development of her identity represented the rebirth of the concept of a mother goddess, which had been strong in the Indus Valley Civilization over 1000 years before and which may have been continued in popular ideas through the worship of female spirits.

In addition to her role as Brahma's wife, Sarasvati is also variously seen as the wife of Vishnu and Manu or as Daksha's daughter, among other interpretations. Normally white coloured, riding on a swan and carrying a book, she is often shown playing a vina. She may have many arms and heads, representing her role as patron of all the sciences and arts. See also box above.

Vishnu Vishnu is seen as the God with the human face. From the second century a new and passionate devotional worship of Vishnu's incarnation as Krishna developed in the South. By 1000 AD Vaishnavism had spread across South India and it became closely associated with the devotional form of Hinduism preached by **Ramanuja,** whose followers spread the worship of Vishnu and his 10 successive incarnations in animal and human form. For Vaishnavites, God took these different forms in order to save the world from impending disaster. AL Basham has summarized the 10 incarnations (see table opposite).

Rama and Krishna By far the most influential incarnations of Vishnu are those in which he was believed to take recognizable human form, especially as Rama (twice) and Krishna. As the Prince of Ayodhya, history and myth blend, for Rama was probably a chief who lived in the eighth or seventh century BC.

Although Rama is now seen as an earlier incarnation of Vishnu than Krishna, he came to be regarded as divine very late, probably after the Muslim invasions of the 12th century AD. The story has become part of the cultures of Southeast Asia.

Rama (or Ram – pronounced to rhyme with *calm*) is a powerful figure in contemporary India. His supposed birthplace at Ayodhya became the focus of fierce disputes between Hindus and Muslims in the early 1990s.

Krishna is worshipped extremely widely as perhaps the most human of the gods. His advice on the battlefield of the Mahabharata is one of the major sources of guidance for the rules of daily living for many Hindus today.

Lakshmi Commonly represented as Vishnu's wife, Lakshmi is widely worshipped as the goddess of wealth. Earlier representations of Vishnu's consorts portrayed her as Sridevi, often shown in statues on Vishnu's right, while Bhudevi, also known as Prithvi, who represented the earth, was on his left. Lakshmi is popularly shown in her own right as standing on a lotus flower, although eight forms of Lakshmi are recognized.

Hanuman The Ramayana tells how Hanuman, Rama's faithful servant, went across India and finally into the demon Ravana's forest home of Lanka at the head of his monkey army in search of the abducted Sita. He used his powers to jump the sea channel separating India from Sri Lanka and managed after a series of heroic and magical feats to find and rescue his master's wife. Whatever form he is shown in, he remains almost instantly recognizable.

Vishnu's ten incarnations

Name	Form	Story
1 *Matsya*	Fish	Vishnu took the form of a fish to rescue Manu (the first man), his family and the Vedas from a flood.
2 *Kurma*	Tortoise	Vishnu became a tortoise to rescue all the treasures lost in the flood, including the divine nectar (Amrita) with which the gods preserved their youth. The gods put Mount Kailasa on the tortoise's back and when he reached the bottom of the ocean they twisted the divine snake round the mountain. They then churned the ocean with the mountain by pulling the snake.
3 *Varaha*	Boar	Vishnu appeared again to raise the earth from the ocean's floor where it had been thrown by a demon, Hiranyaksa. The story probably developed from a non-Aryan cult of a sacred pig.
4 *Narasimha*	Half-man, half lion	Having persuaded Brahma to promise that he could not be killed either by day or night, by god, man or beast, the demon Hiranyakasipu then terrorized everybody. When the gods pleaded for help, Vishnu appeared at sunset, when it was neither day nor night, in the form of a half man and half lion and killed the demon.
5 *Vamana*	A dwarf	Bali, a demon, achieved supernatural power by asceticism. To protect the world Vishnu appeared before him in the form of a dwarf and asked him a favour. Bali granted Vishnu as much land as he could cover in three strides. Vishnu then became a giant, covering the earth in three strides. He left only hell to the demon.
6 *Parasurama*	Rama with the axe	Vishnu was incarnated as the son of a Brahmin, Jamadagni as Parasurama and killed the wicked king for robbing his father. The king's sons then killed Jamadagni and in revenge Parasurama destroyed all male kshatriyas, 21 times in succession.
7 *Rama*	The Prince of Ayodhya	As told in the Ramayana, Vishnu came in the form of Rama to rescue the world from the dark demon, Ravana. His wife Sita is the model of patient faithfulness while Hanuman, is the monkey-faced god and Rama's helper.
8 *Krishna*	Charioteer of Arjuma Many forms	Krishna meets almost every human need, from the mischievous child, the playful boy, the amorous youth to the Divine.
9 The *Buddha*		Probably incorporated into the Hindu pantheon in order to discredit the Buddhists, dominant in some parts of India until the 6th century AD. An early Hindu interpretation suggests that Vishnu took incarnation as Buddha to show compassion for animals and to end sacrifice.
10 *Kalki*	Riding on a horse	Vishnu's arrival will accompany the final destruction of this present age, Kaliyuga, judging the wicked and rewarding the good.

Siva Professor Wendy Doniger O'Flaherty argues that "Siva is in many ways the most uniquely Indian god of them all". She argues that the key to the myths through which his character is understood, lies in the explicit ambiguity of Siva as the great ascetic and at the same time as the erotic force of the universe.

Siva is interpreted as both creator and destroyer, the power through whom the universe evolves. He lives on Mount Kailasa with his wife **Parvati** (also known as **Uma, Sati, Kali** and **Durga**) and two sons, the elephant-headed Ganesh and the six-headed Karttikeya, known in South India as Subrahmanya. To many contemporary Hindus they form a model of sorts for family life. In sculptural representations Siva is normally accompanied by his 'vehicle', the bull (*Nandi* or *Nandin*).

Siva is also represented in Shaivite temples throughout India by the lingam, literally meaning 'sign' or 'mark', but referring in this context to the sign of gender or phallus and *yoni*, the female gender. On the one hand a symbol of energy, fertility and potency, as Siva's symbol it also represents the yogic power of sexual abstinence and penance. The lingam has become the most important symbol of the cult of Siva. O'Flaherty suggests that the worship of the lingam of Siva can be traced back to the pre-Vedic societies of the Indus Valley civilization (circa 2000 BC), but that it first appears in Hindu iconography in the second century BC.

From that time a wide variety of myths appeared to explain the origin of lingam worship. The myths surrounding the 12 **jyotirlinga** (lingam of light) found at centres like Ujjain go back to the second century BC and were developed in order to explain and justify lingam worship.

Siva's alternative names Although Siva is not seen as having a series of rebirths, like Vishnu, he none the less appears in very many forms representing different aspects of his varied powers. Some of the more common are:

Chandrasekhara The moon (*chandra*) symbolizes the powers of creation and destruction.

Mahadeva The representation of Siva as the god of supreme power, which came relatively late into Hindu thought, shown as the lingam in combination with the *yoni*.

Nataraja, the Lord of the Cosmic Dance. The story is based on a legend in which Siva and Vishnu went to the forest to overcome 10,000 heretics. In their anger the heretics attacked Siva first by sending a tiger, then a snake and thirdly a fierce black dwarf with a club. Siva killed the tiger, tamed the snake and wore it like a garland and then put his foot on the dwarf and performed a dance of such power that the dwarf and the heretics acknowledged Siva as the Lord.

Rudra Siva's early prototype, who may date back to the Indus Valley Civilization.

Virabhadra Siva created Virabhadra to avenge himself on his wife Sati's father, Daksha, who had insulted Siva by not inviting him to a special sacrifice. Sati attended the ceremony against Siva's wishes and when she heard her father grossly abusing Siva she committed suicide by jumping into the sacrificial fire. This act gave rise to the term *sati* (*suttee*, a word which simply means a good or virtuous woman). Recorded in the Vedas, the self-immolation of a woman on her husband's funeral pyre probably did not become accepted practice until the early centuries BC. Even then it was mainly restricted to those of the kshatriya caste.

Nandi Siva's vehicle, the bull, is one of the most widespread of sacred symbols of the ancient world and may represent a link with Rudra, who was sometimes represented as a bull in pre-Hindu India. Strength and virility are key attributes and pilgrims to Siva temples will often touch the *Nandi*'s testicles on their way into the shrine.

Ganesh Ganesh is one of Hinduism's most popular gods. He is seen as the great clearer of obstacles. Shown at gateways and on door lintels with his elephant head and pot belly, his image is revered across India. Meetings, functions and special

Worship of Siva's lingam

Worship of Siva's lingam – the phallic symbol of fertility, power and creativeness – is universal across India. Its origins lie in the creation myths of the Hindu trinity and in the struggle for supremacy between the different Hindu sects. Shaivite myths illustrate the supreme power of Siva and the variety of ways in which Brahma and Vishnu were compelled to acknowledge his supreme power.

One such story tells how Siva, Vishnu and Brahma emerged from the ocean, whereupon Vishnu and Brahma begged him to perform creation. Siva agreed – but then to their consternation disappeared for 1000 celestial years. They became so worried by the lack of creation that Vishnu told Brahma to create, so he produced everything that could lead to happiness. However, no sooner had Brahma filled the universe with beings than Siva reappeared. Incensed by the usurping of his power by Brahma. Siva decided to destroy everything with a flame from his mouth so that he could create afresh.

As the fire threatened to consume everything Brahma acknowledged Siva's total power and pleaded with him to spare the creation that Brahma had brought forth. "But what shall I do with all my excess power?" "Send it to the sun", replied Brahma, "for as you are the lord of the sun we may all live together in the sun's energy."

Siva agreed, but said to Brahma "What use is this lingam if I cannot use it to create?" So he broke off his lingam and threw it to the ground. The lingam broke through the earth and went right into the sky. Vishnu looked for the end of it below and Brahma for the top, but neither could find the end. Then a voice from the sky said "If the lingam of the god with braided hair is worshipped, it will grant all desires that are longed for in the heart." When Brahma and Vishnu heard this, they and all the divinities worshipped the lingam with devotion."

family gatherings will often start with prayers to Ganesh and any new venture, from the opening of a building to inaugurating a company, will not be deemed complete without a Ganesh puja.

Shakti, The Mother Goddess Shakti is a female divinity often worshipped in the form of Siva's wife Durga or Kali. As Durga she agreed to do battle with Mahish, an *asura* (demon) who threatened to dethrone the gods. Many sculptures and paintings illustrate the story in which, during the terrifying struggle which ensued, the demon changed into a buffalo, an elephant and a giant with 1000 arms. Durga, clutching weapons in each of her ten hands, eventually emerges victorious. As Kali ('black') the mother goddess takes on her most fearsome form and character. Fighting with the chief of the demons, she was forced to use every weapon in her armoury, but every drop of blood that she drew became 1000 new giants just as strong. The only way she could win was by drinking the blood of all her enemies. Having succeeded she was so elated that her dance of triumph threatened the earth. Ignoring the pleas of the gods to stop, she even threw her husband Siva to the ground and trampled over him, until she realized to her shame what she had done. She is always shown with a sword in one hand, the severed head of the giant in another, two corpses for earrings and a necklace of human skulls. She is often shown standing with one foot on the body and the other on the leg of Siva.

The worship of female goddesses developed into the widely practised form of devotional worship called Tantrism. Goddesses such as Kali became the focus of

Hindu deities

Deity	Association	Relationship
Brahma	Creator	One of Trinity
Sarasvati	Education and culture, "the word"	Wife of Brahma
Siva	Creator/destroyer	One of Trinity
Bhairava	Fierce aspect of Siva	
Parvati (Uma)	Benevolent aspect of female divine power	Consort of Siva, mother of Ganesh
Kali	The energy that destroys evil	Consort of Siva
Durga	In fighting attitude	Consort of Siva
Ganesh/ Ganapati	God of good beginnings, clearer of obstacles	Son of Siva
Skanda (Karttikkeya, Murugan, Subrahmanya)	God of War/bringer of disease	Son of Siva and Ganga
Vishnu	Preserver	One of Trinity
Prithvi/ Bhudevi	Goddess of Earth	Wife of Vishnu
Lakshmi	Goddess of Wealth	Wife of Vishnu
Agni	God of Fire	
Indra	Rain, lightning and thunder	
Ravana	King of the demons	

worship which often involved practices that flew in the face of wider Hindu moral and legal codes. Animal and even human sacrifices and ritual sexual intercourse were part of Tantric belief and practice, the evidence for which may still be seen in the art and sculpture of some major temples. Tantric practice affected both Hinduism and Buddhism from the eighth century AD; its influence is shown vividly in the sculptures of Khajuraho and Konarak and in the distinctive Hindu and Buddhist practices of the Kathmandu Valley in Nepal.

Skanda The God of War, Skanda (known as Murugan in Tamil Nadu and by other regional names) became known as the son of Siva and Parvati. One legend suggests that he was conceived by the Goddess Ganga from Siva's seed.

Gods of the warrior caste Modern Hinduism has brought into its pantheon (over many generations) gods who were worshipped by the earlier pre-Hindu Aryan civilizations. The most important is **Indra**, often shown as the god of rain, thunder and lightning. To the early Aryans, Indra destroyed demons in battle, the most important being his victory over Vritra, 'the Obstructor'. By this victory Indra released waters from the clouds, allowing the earth to become fertile. To the early Vedic writers the clouds of the southwest monsoon were seen as hostile, determined to keep their precious treasure of water to themselves and only releasing it when forced to by a greater power. Indra, carrying a bow in one hand, a thunderbolt in another and lances in the others and riding on his vehicle Airavata, the elephant, is thus the Lord of Heaven. His wife is the relatively insignificant **Indrani**.

Attributes	Vehicle
4 heads, 4 arms, upper left holds water pot and rosary or sacrificial spoon, sacred thread across left shoulder	Hamsa (goose/swan)
Two or more arms, vina, lotus, plam leaves, rosary	Hamsa
Linga; Rudra, matted hair, 3 eyes, drum, fire, deer, trident; Nataraja, Lord of the Dance	Bull - Nandi
Trident, sword, noose, naked, snakes, garland of skulls, dishevelled hair, carrying destructive weapons	Dog
2 arms when shown with Siva, 4 when on her own, blue lily in right hand, left hand hangs down	Lion
Trident, noose, human skulls, sword, shield, black colour	Lion
4 arms, conch, disc, bow, arrow, bell, sword, shield	Lion or tiger
Goad, noose, broken tusk, fruits	Rat/ mouse/ shrew
6 heads, 12 arms, spear, arrow, sword, discus, noose cock, bow, shield, conch and plough	Peacock
4 arms, high crown, discus and conch in upper arms, club and sword (or lotus) in lower	Garuda - mythical eagle
Right hand in abhaya gesture, left holds pomegranate, left leg on treasure pot	
Seated/standing on red lotus, 4 hands, lotuses, vessel, fruit	Lotus
Sacred thread, axe, wood, bellows, torch, sacrificial spoon	2-headed ram
Bow, thunderbolt, lances	
10 heads, 20 arms, bow and arrow	

Mitra and **Varuna** have the power both of gods and demons. Their role is to sustain order, Mitra taking responsibility for friendship and Varuna for oaths, and as they have to keep watch for 24 hours a day Mitra has become the god of the day or the sun, Varuna the god of the moon.

Agni, the god of fire, is a god whose origins lie with the priestly caste rather than with the kshatriyas, or warriors. He was seen in the Vedas as being born from the rubbing together of two pieces of dead wood and as Masson-Oursel writes "the poets marvel at the sight of a being so alive leaping from dry dead wood. His very growth is miraculous". Riding on a ram, wearing a sacred thread, he is often shown with flames leaping from his mouth and he carries an axe, wood, bellows or a fan, a torch and a sacrificial spoon, for he is the god of ritual fire.

Soma The juice of the soma plant, the nectar of the gods guaranteeing eternal life, Soma is also a deity taking many forms. Born from the churning of the ocean of milk, in later stories Soma was identified with the moon. The golden haired and golden skinned god **Savitri** is an intermediary with the great power to forgive sin and as king of heaven he gives the gods their immortality. **Surya**, the god of the sun, fittingly of overpowering splendour is often described as being dark red, sitting on a red lotus or riding a chariot pulled by the seven horses of the dawn (representing the days of the week). **Usha**, sometimes referred to as Surya's wife, is the goddess of the dawn, daughter of Heaven and sister of the night. She rides in a chariot drawn by cows or horses.

Devas and Asuras In Hindu popular mythology the world is also populated by innumerable gods and demons, with a somewhat uncertain dividing line between them. Both have great power and there are frequent conflicts and battles between them.

The **Rakshasas** form another category of semi-divine beings devoted to performing magic. Although they are not themselves evil, they are destined to cause havoc and evil in the real world.

The **Nagas** and **Naginis** The multiple-hooded cobra head often seen in sculptures represents the fabulous snake gods the Nagas, though they may often be shown in other forms, even human. In South India it is particularly common to find statues of divine Nagas being worshipped. They are usually placed on uncultivated ground under trees in the hope and belief, as Masson-Oursel puts it, that "if the snakes have their own domain left to them they are more likely to spare human beings". The Nagas and their wives, the Naginis, are often the agents of death in mythical stories.

Hindu society

Dharma This is seen as the most important of the objectives of individual and social life. But what were the obligations imposed by dharma? Hindu law givers, such as those who compiled the code of Manu (AD 100-300), laid down rules of family conduct and social obligations related to the institutions of caste and *jati* which were beginning to take shape at the same time.

Caste Although the word caste was given by the Portuguese in the 15th century AD, the main feature of the system emerged at the end of the Vedic period. Two terms – varna and jati – are used in India itself and have come to be used interchangeably and confusingly with the word caste.

Varna Literally meaning colour, varna had a fourfold division. By 600 BC this had become a standard means of classifying the population. The fair-skinned Aryans distinguished themselves from the darker-skinned earlier inhabitants. The priestly varna, the Brahmins, were seen as coming from the mouth of Brahma; the Kshatriyas (or Rajputs as they are commonly called in Northwest India) were warriors, coming from Brahma's arms; the Vaishyas, a trading community, came from Brahma's thighs and the Sudras, classified as agriculturalists, from his feet. Relegated beyond the pale of civilized Hindu society were the untouchables or outcastes, who were left with the jobs which were regarded as impure, usually associated with dealing with the dead (human or animal) or with excrement.

Jati Many Brahmins and Rajputs are conscious of their varna status, but the majority of Indians do not put themselves into one of the four varna categories, but into a jati group. There are thousands of different jatis across the country. None of the groups see themselves as equal in status to any other, but all are part of local or regional hierarchies. These are not organized in any institutional sense and traditionally there was no formal record of caste status. While individuals found it impossible to change caste or to move up the social scale, groups would sometimes try to gain recognition as higher caste by adopting practices of the Brahmins such as becoming vegetarians. Many used to be identified with particular activities and occupations used to be hereditary. Caste membership is decided simply by birth. Although you can be evicted from your caste by fellow members, usually for disobedience to caste rules such as over marriage, you cannot join another caste and technically you become an outcaste.

Right up until Independence in 1947 such punishment was a drastic penalty for disobeying one's dharmic duty. In many areas all avenues into normal life could be blocked, families would disregard outcaste members and it could even be impossible for the outcaste to continue to work within the local community.

The Dalits Gandhi spearheaded his campaign for independence from British colonial rule with a powerful campaign to abolish the disabilities imposed by the

Auspicious signs

Some of Hinduism's sacred symbols are thought to have originated in the Aryan religion of the Vedic period.

Om The primordial sound of the universe, 'Om' (or more correctly the three-in-one 'Aum') is the supreme syllable. It is the opening, and sometimes closing, chant for Hindu prayers. Some attribute the three constituents to the Hindu triad of Brahma, Vishnu and Siva. It is believed to be the cosmic sound of Creation which encompasses all states from wakefulness to deep sleep and though it is the essence of all sound; it is outside our hearing.

Svastika Representing the Sun and its energy, the svastika usually appears on doors or walls of temples, in red, the colour associated with good fortune and luck. The term, derived from the Sanskrit 'svasti', is repeated in Hindu chants. The arms of the symbol point in the cardina' directions which may reflect the ancient practice of lighting fire sticks in the four directions. When the svastika appears to rotate clockwise it symbolizes the positive creative energy of the sun; the anti-clockwise svastika, symbolizing the autumn/winter sun, is considered unlucky.

Six-pointed star The intersecting triangles in the 'Star of David' symbol represents Spirit and Matter held in balance. A central dot signifies a particle of divinity. The star is incorporated as a decorative element in some Muslim buildings such as Humayun's tomb in Delhi.

Lotus The 'padma' or 'kamal' flower with its many petals appears not only in art and architecture but also in association with gods and goddesses. Some deities are seen holding one, others are portrayed seated or standing on the flower, or as with Padmanabha it appears from Vishnu's navel. The lotus represents purity, peace and beauty, a symbol also shared by Buddhists and Jains and as in nature stands away and above the impure, murky water from which it emerges. In architecture, the lotus motif occurs frequently.

Om

Svastika

Six-pointed star

Lotus

caste system. Coining the term *Harijan* (meaning 'person of God'), which he gave to all former outcastes, Gandhi demanded that discrimination on the grounds of caste be outlawed. Lists – or 'schedules' – of backward castes were drawn up during the early part of this century in order to provide positive help to such groups. The term itself has now been widely rejected by many former outcastes as paternalistic and as implying an adherence to Hindu beliefs which some explicitly reject and today many argue passionately for the use of the secular term 'dalits' – the 'oppressed'.

Affirmative action Since 1947 the Indian government has extended its positive discrimination (a form of affirmative action) to scheduled castes and scheduled tribes, particularly through reserving up to 30% of jobs in government-run institutions and in further education, leading to professional qualifications for these groups and members of the scheduled castes are now found in important positions throughout the economy. Furthermore, most of the obvious forms of social discrimination, particularly rules which prohibit eating or drinking with members of lower castes, or

The sacred thread

The highest three varnas were classified as "twice born" and could wear the sacred thread symbolizing their status. The age at which the initiation ceremony (upanayana) for the upper caste child was carried out, varied according to caste – eight for a Brahmin, 11 for a Kshatriya and 12 for a Vaishya.

The boy, dressed like an ascetic and holding a staff in his hand, would have the sacred thread (yajnopavita) placed over his right shoulder and under his left arm. A cord of three threads, each of nine twisted strands, it was made of cotton for Brahmans, hemp for Kshatriyas or wool for Vaishyas. It was – and is – regarded as a great sin to remove it.

The Brahmin who officiated would whisper a verse from the Rig Veda in the boy's ear, the Gayatri mantra. Addressed to the old solar god Savitri, the holiest of holy passages, the Gayatri can only be spoken by the three higher classes. AL Basham translated it as: "Let us think on the lovely splendour of the god Savitri, that he may inspire our minds".

from plates and cups that have been touched by them, have disappeared. Yet caste remains an extremely important aspect of India's social structures.

Marriage Still generally arranged by members of all religious communities, marriage continues to be dictated almost entirely by caste and clan rules. Even in cities, where traditional means of arranging marriages have often broken down and where many people resort to advertising for marriage partners in the columns of the Sunday newspapers, caste is frequently stated as a requirement. Marriage is generally seen as an alliance between two families. Great efforts are made to match caste, social status and economic position, although the rules which govern eligibility vary from region to region. In some groups marriage between even first cousins is common, while among others marriage between any branch of the same clan is strictly prohibited.

Caste also remains an explosive political issue. Attempts to improve the social and economic position of harijans and what are termed 'other backward castes' (OBCs) continues to cause sometimes violent conflict.

Hindu reform movements

Hinduism today is a more self-conscious religious and political force than it was even at Independence in 1947. Reform movements of modern Hinduism can be traced back at least to the early years of the 19th century. These movements were unique in Hinduism's history in putting the importance of political ideas on the same level as strictly religious thinking and in interrelating them.

In the 19th century, English education and European literature and modern scientific thought, alongside the religious ideas of Christian missionaries, all became powerful influences on the newly emerging western-educated Hindu opinion. That opinion was challenged to re-examine inherited Hindu beliefs and practice.

Some reform movements have had regional importance. Two of these originated, like the **Brahmo Samaj**, in Bengal. The **Ramakrishna Mission** was named after a temple priest in the Kali temple in Kolkata, Ramakrishna (1834-1886), who was a great mystic, preaching the basic doctrine that 'all religions are true'. He believed that the best religion for any individual was that into which he or she was born. One of his followers, **Vivekenanda**, became the founder of the Ramakrishna Mission, which has been an important vehicle of social and religious reform, notably in Bengal.

From liberal reform to a new fundamentalism

The first major reform movement was launched by the Bengali Brahmin, Ram Mohan Roy (1772-1833). He founded the **Brahmo Samaj**, the Society of God, in 1828, "to teach and to practise the worship of the one God". Services were modelled closely on those of the Unitarian Church, but he never broke with orthodox Hinduism. The Brahmo Samaj became very influential, particularly in Bengal, even though it divided and its numbers remained tiny.

In North India reform was carried out under the leadership of what one writer has called "the Luther of modern Hinduism", Dayananda Saraswati (1824-83). Rejecting idolatry and many of the social evils associated with mid-19th century Hinduism, Dayananda Saraswati established the **Arya Samaj** (the Aryan Society). In the early 19th century the Arya Samaj launched a major attack on the caste system, through recruiting low caste Hindus and investing them with high caste status. At the same time they encouraged a movement for the reconversion of Christians and Muslims (the suddhi movement). By 1931 the Arya Samaj claimed about one million members. With a strongly Hindu nationalist political line, its programme underlay the rise in post-Independence India of the Jana Sangh Party and the present day BJP.

Aurobindo Ghose (1872-1950) links the great reformers from the 19th century with the post-Independence period. Educated in English – and for 14 years in England itself – he developed the idea of India as 'the Mother', a concept linked with the pre-Hindu idea of Shakti, or the Mother Goddess. For him 'nationalism was religion'. After imprisonment in 1908 he retired to Pondicherry, where his ashram became a focus of an Indian and international movement (see page 107).

The Hindu calendar While for its secular life India follows the Gregorian calendar, for Hindus, much of religious and personal life follows the Hindu calendar (see also Festivals). This is based on the lunar cycle of 29 days, but the clever bit comes in the way it is synchronized with the 365-day Gregorian solar calendar of the west by the addition of an 'extra month' (*adhik maas*), every two to three years.

Hindus follow two distinct eras. The *Vikrama Samvat* which began in 57 BC (and is followed in Goa), and the *Salivahan Saka* which dates from 78 AD and has been the official Indian calendar since 1957. The *Saka* new year starts on 22 March and has the same length as the Gregorian calendar. In most of South India (except Tamil Nadu) the New Year is celebrated in the first month, *Chaitra* (corresponding to March to April). In North India (and Tamil Nadu) it is celebrated in the second month of *Vaisakh*.

The year itself is divided into two, the first six solar months being when the sun 'moves' north, known as the *Makar Sankranti* (which is marked by special festivals), and the second half when it moves south, the *Karka Sankranti*. The first begins in January and the second in June.

The 29 day lunar month with its 'dark' (*Krishna*) and 'bright' (*Shukla*) halves based on the new (*Amavasya*) and full moons (*Purnima*), are named after the 12 constellations, and total a 354-day year. The day itself is divided into eight *praharas* of three hours each and the year into six seasons: *Vasant* (spring), *Grishha* (summer), *Varsha* (rains), *Sharat* (early autumn), *Hemanta* (late autumn), *Shishir* (winter).

Hindu and corresponding Gregorian calendar months

Chaitra	March-April	*Ashwin*	September-October
Vaishakh	April-May	*Kartik*	October-November
Jyeshtha	May-June	*Margashirsha*	November-December
Aashadh	June-July	*Poush*	December-January
Shravan	July-August	*Magh*	January-February
Bhadra	August-September	*Phalgun*	February-March

Islam

Islam is a highly visible presence in India today. Even after partition in 1947 over 40 million Muslims remained in India and today there are just over 120 million. It is the most recent of imported religions. Islamic contact with India was first made around 636 AD and then by the navies of the Arab Mohammad al Qasim in 710-712 AD. These conquerors of Sindh made very few converts, although they did have to develop a legal recognition for the status of non-Muslims in a Muslim-ruled state. From the creation of the Delhi Sultanate in 1206, by Turkish rather than Arab power, Islam became a permanent living religion in India.

The victory of the Turkish ruler of Ghazni over the Rajputs in AD 1192 established a 500-year period of Muslim power in India. The contact between the courts of the new rulers and the indigenous Hindu populations produced innovative developments in art and architecture, language and literature. Hindus and Hindu culture were profoundly affected by the spread and exercise of Muslim political power, but Islam too underwent major modifications in response to the new social and religious context in which the Muslim rulers found themselves.

The early Muslim rulers looked to the Turkish ruling class and to the Arab caliphs for their legitimacy and to the Turkish elite for their cultural authority. From the middle of the 13th century, when the Mongols crushed the Arab caliphate, the Delhi sultans were left on their own to exercise Islamic authority in India. From then onwards the main external influences were from Persia. Small numbers of migrants, mainly the skilled and the educated, continued to flow into the Indian courts. Periodically their numbers were augmented by refugees from Mongol repression in the regions to India's northwest as the Delhi Sultanate provided a refuge for craftsmen and artists from the territories the Mongols had conquered from Lahore westwards.

Muslim populations Muslims only became a majority of the South Asian population in the plains of the Indus and west Punjab and in parts of Bengal. Elsewhere they formed important minorities, and where there was already a densely populated, Hindu region, little attempt was made to achieve converts.

In some areas Muslim society shared many of the characteristic features of the Hindu society from which the majority of them came. Many of the Muslim migrants from Iran or Turkey, the elite **Ashraf** communities, continued to identify with the Islamic elites from which they traced their descent. They held high military and civil posts in imperial service. In sharp contrast, many of the non-Ashraf Muslim communities in the towns and cities were organized in social groups very much like the jatis of their neighbouring Hindu communities. While the elites followed Islamic practices close to those based on the Qur'an as interpreted by scholars, the poorer, less literate communities followed devotional and pietistic forms of Islam. The distinction is still very clear today and the importance of veneration of the saints can be seen at tombs and shrines across Pakistan, India and Bangladesh.

Muslim beliefs The beliefs of Islam (which means 'submission to God') could apparently scarcely be more different from those of Hinduism. Islam, often described

Islamic patronage

The spread of Islam across India was achieved less by forcible conversion than by the patronage offered by the new rulers to Muslim saints and teachers. These were particularly influential in achieving mass conversions among the lower castes of Hindus.

Islam underwent important modifications as it became entrenched in India. From the outset the Muslim invaders had to come to terms with the Hindu majority population. If they had treated them as idolators they would have been forced, under Qur'anic law, to give them the choice of conversion or death. The political impossibility of governing as a tiny minority on those terms encouraged them to give Indian subjects the status of 'protected peoples'.

as having "five pillars" of faith (see box, page 516) has a fundamental creed: 'There is no God but God; and Mohammad is the Prophet of God' (*La Illaha illa 'llah Mohammad Rasulu 'llah*). One book, the Qur'an, is the supreme authority on Islamic teaching and faith. Islam preaches the belief in bodily resurrection after death and in the reality of heaven and hell.

The idea of heaven as paradise is pre-Islamic. Alexander the Great is believed to have brought the word into Greek from Persia, where he used it to describe the walled Persian gardens that were found even three centuries before the birth of Christ. For Muslims, Paradise is believed to be filled with sensuous delights and pleasures, while hell is a place of eternal terror and torture, which is the certain fate of all who deny the unity of God.

Islam has no priesthood. The authority of Imams derives from social custom and from their authority to interpret the scriptures, rather than from a defined status within the Islamic community. Islam also prohibits any distinction on the basis of race or colour and most Muslims believe it is wrong to represent the human figure. It is often thought, inaccurately, that this ban stems from the Qur'an itself. In fact it probably has its origins in the belief of Mohammad that images were likely to be turned into idols.

Muslim sects During the first century after Mohammad's death Islam split into two sects which were divided on political and religious grounds, the Shi'is and Sunnis. The religious basis for the division lay in the interpretation of verses in the Qur'an and of traditional sayings of Mohammad, the *Hadis*. Both sects venerate the Qur'an but have different *Hadis*. They also have different views as to Mohammad's successor.

The Sunnis – always the majority in South Asia – believe that Mohammad did not appoint a successor and that Abu Bak'r, Omar and Othman were the first three caliphs (or vice-regents) after Mohammad's death. Ali, whom the Sunni count as the fourth caliph, is regarded as the first legitimate caliph by the Shi'is, who consider Abu Bak'r and Omar to be usurpers. While the Sunni believe in the principle of election of caliphs, Shi'is believe that although Mohammad is the last prophet there is a continuing need for intermediaries between God and man. Such intermediaries are termed Imams and they base both their law and religious practice on the teaching of the Imams.

The two major divisions are marked by further sub-divisions. The Sunni Muslims in India have followers of the Hanafi, Shafei, Maliki and Hanbali groups, named after their leaders. Numerically one of the smallest groups in South Asia is that of the Ismailis, who regard their leader, the Aga Khan, as their spiritual head.

From the Mughal emperors, who enjoyed an unparalleled degree of political power, down to the poorest peasant farmers of Bengal, Muslims in India have found

The five pillars of Islam

In addition to the belief that there is one God and that Mohammad is his prophet, there are four obligatory requirements imposed on Muslims. Daily prayers are prescribed at daybreak, noon, afternoon, sunset and nightfall. Muslims must give alms to the poor. They must observe a strict fast during the month of Ramadan. They must not eat or drink between sunrise and sunset. Lastly, they should attempt the pilgrimage to the Ka'aba in Mecca, known as the Hajj. Those who have done so are entitled to the prefix Hajji before their name.

Islamic rules differ from Hindu practice in several other aspects of daily life. Muslims are strictly forbidden to drink alcohol (though some suggest that this prohibition is restricted to the use of fermented grape juice, that is wine, it is commonly accepted to apply to all alcohol). Eating pork, or any meat from an animal not killed by draining its blood while alive, is also prohibited. Meat prepared in the appropriate way is called Halal. Finally, usury (charging interest on loans) and games of chance are forbidden.

different ways of adjusting to their Hindu environment. Some have reacted by accepting or even incorporating features of Hindu belief and practice in their own. Akbar, the most eclectic of Mughal emperors, went as far as banning activities like cow slaughter which were offensive to Hindus and celebrated Hindu festivals in court.

In contrast, the later Mughal Emperor, Aurangzeb, pursued a far more hostile approach to Hindus and Hinduism, trying to point up the distinctiveness of Islam and denying the validity of Hindu religious beliefs. That attitude generally became stronger in the 20th century, related to the growing sense of the Muslim minority position within South Asia and the fear of being subjected to Hindu rule. It was a fear that led to the creation of the separate Muslim majority state of Pakistan in 1947 and which still permeates political as well as religious attitudes across South Asia.

The Islamic Calendar

The calendar begins on 16 July 622 AD, the date of the Prophet's migration from Mecca to Medina, the Hijra, hence AH (Anno Hejirae). *Murray's Handbook for Travellers in India* gives a wonderfully precise method of calculating the current date in the Christian year from the AH date: "To correlate the Hijra year with the Christian year, express the former in years and decimals of a year, multiply by .970225, add 621.54 and the total will correspond exactly with the Christian year".

The Muslim year is divided into 12 lunar months, totalling 354 or 355 days, hence Islamic festivals usually move 11 days earlier each year according to the solar (Gregorian) calendar. The first month of the year is *Moharram,* followed by *Safar, Rabi-ul-Awwal, Rabi-ul-Sani, Jumada-ul-Awwal, Jumada-ul-Sani, Rajab, Shaban, Ramadan, Shawwal, Ziquad* and *Zilhaj*.

Buddhism

India was the home of Buddhism, which had its roots in the early Hinduism, or Brahmanism, of its time. Today it is practised only on the margins of the subcontinent, from Ladakh, Nepal and Bhutan in the north to Sri Lanka in the south, where it is the religion of the majority Sinhalese community.

The Buddha's Four Noble Truths

The Buddha preached Four Noble Truths: that life is painful; that suffering is caused by ignorance and desire; that beyond the suffering of life there is a state which cannot be described but which he termed nirvana; and that nirvana can be reached by following an eightfold path.

The concept of nirvana is often understood in the west in an entirely negative sense – that of 'non-being'. The word has the rough meaning of 'blow out' or 'extinguish', meaning to blow out the fires of greed, lust and desire. In a more positive sense it has been described by one Buddhist scholar as "the state of absolute illumination, supreme bliss, infinite love and compassion, unshakeable serenity and unrestricted spiritual freedom". The essential elements of the eightfold path are the perfection of wisdom, morality and meditation.

India's Buddhist significance is now mainly as the home for the extraordinarily beautiful artistic and architectural remnants of what was for several centuries the region's dominant religion.

India has sites of great significance for Buddhists around the world. Some say that the Buddha himself spoke of the four places his followers should visit. **Lumbini,** the Buddha's birthplace, is in the Nepali foothills, near the present border with India. **Bodh Gaya,** where he attained what Buddhists term his 'supreme enlightenment', is about 80 km south of the modern Indian city of Patna; the Deer Park at **Sarnath,** near Benaras, where he preached his first sermon and set in motion the Wheel of the Law, is just outside Varanasi; and **Kushinagara,** where he died at the age of 80, is 50 km east of Gorakhpur. There were four other sacred places of pilgrimage – **Rajgir,** where he tamed a wild elephant; **Vaishali,** where a monkey offered him honey; **Sravasti,** associated with his great miracle; and **Sankasya,** where he descended from heaven. The eight significant events associated with the holy places are repeatedly represented in Buddhist art.

The Buddha's Life Siddharta Gautama, who came to be given the title of the Buddha – the Enlightened One – was born a prince into the warrior caste in about 563 BC. He was married at the age of 16 and his wife had a son. When he reached the age of 29 he left home and wandered as a beggar and ascetic. After about six years he spent some time in Bodh Gaya. Sitting under the Bo tree, meditating, he was tempted by the demon Mara with all the desires of the world. Resisting these temptations, he received enlightenment. These scenes are common motifs of Buddhist art.

The next landmark was the preaching of his first sermon on 'The Foundation of Righteousness' in the Deer Park in Sarnath. By the time he died the Buddha had established a small band of monks and nuns known as the *Sangha* and had followers across North India. His body was cremated and the ashes, regarded as precious relics, were divided among the peoples to whom he had preached.

After the Buddha's death From the Buddha's death, or *parinirvana*, to the destruction of Nalanda (the last Buddhist stronghold in India) in 1197 AD, Buddhism in India divided into three forms. These are often referred to as Hinayana, Mahayana and Vajrayana, though they were not mutually exclusive, being followed simultaneously in different regions.

Hinayana The Hinayana or Lesser Way insists on a monastic way of life as the only path to the personal goal of *nirvana* (see box above) achieved through an austere life. Divided into many schools, the only surviving Hinayana tradition is the **Theravada** Buddhism, which was taken to Sri Lanka by the Emperor Asoka's son Mahinda, where it became the state religion.

Mahayana In contrast to the Hinayana schools, the followers of the Mahayana school (the Great Way) believed in the possibility of salvation for all. They practised a far more devotional form of meditation and new figures came to play a prominent part in their beliefs and their worship – the **Bodhisattvas**, saints who were predestined to reach the state of enlightenment through thousands of rebirths. They aspired to Buddhahood, however, not for their own sake but for the sake of all living things. The Buddha is believed to have passed through numerous existences in preparation for his final mission. Mahayana Buddhism became dominant over most of South Asia and its influence is evidenced in Buddhist art from Gandhara in north Pakistan to Ajanta in Central India and Sigiriya in Sri Lanka.

Vajrayana The Diamond Way resembles magic and yoga in some of its beliefs. The ideal of Vajrayana Buddhists is to be 'so fully in harmony with the cosmos as to be able to manipulate the cosmic forces within and outside himself'. It had developed in the north of India by the seventh century AD, matching the parallel growth of Hindu Tantrism.

Buddhism's decline The decline of Buddhism in India probably stemmed as much from the growing similarity in the practice of Hinduism and Buddhism as from direct attacks. Mahayana Buddhism, with its reverence for Bodhisattvas and its devotional character, was more and more difficult to distinguish from the revivalist Hinduism characteristic of several parts of North India from the seventh to the 12th centuries AD. The Muslim conquest dealt the final death blow, being accompanied by the large-scale slaughter of monks and the destruction of monasteries. Without their institutional support Buddhism faded away.

Jainism

Like Buddhism, Jainism started as a reform movement of the Brahmanic religious beliefs of the sixth century BC. Its founder was a widely revered saint and ascetic, Vardhamma, who became known as **Mahavir** – 'great hero'. Mahavir was born in the same border region of India and Nepal as the Buddha, just 50 km north of modern Patna, probably in 599 BC. Thus he was about 35 years older than the Buddha. His family, also royal, were followers of an ascetic saint, Parsvanatha, who according to Jain tradition had lived 200 years previously.

Mahavir's life story is embellished with legends, but there is no doubt that he left his royal home for a life of the strict ascetic. He is believed to have received enlightenment after 12 years of rigorous hardship, penance and meditation. Afterwards he travelled and preached for 30 years, stopping only in the rainy season. He died aged 72 in 527 BC. His death was commemorated by a special lamp festival in the region of Bihar, which Jains claim is the basis of the now common Hindu festival of lights, *Diwali*.

Unlike Buddhism, Jainism never spread beyond India, but it has survived continuously into modern India, claiming 4 million adherents. In part this may be because Jain beliefs have much in common with puritanical forms of Hinduism and are greatly respected and admired. Some Jain ideas, such as vegetarianism and reverence for all life, are widely recognized by Hindus as highly commendable, even by those who do not share other Jain beliefs. The value Jains place on non-violence has contributed to their importance in business and commerce, as they regard nearly

The Jain spiritual journey

The two Jain sects differ chiefly on the nature of proper ascetic practices. The Svetambara monks wear white robes and carry a staff, some wooden pots and a woollen mop for sweeping the path in front of them, wool being the softest material available and the least likely to hurt any living thing swept away. The highest level of Digambara monks will go completely naked, although the lower levels will wear a covering over their genitalia. They carry a waterpot made of a gourd and peacock feathers to sweep the ground before they sit.

Jains believe that the spiritual journey of the soul is divided into 14 stages, moving from bondage and ignorance to the final destruction of all karma and the complete fulfilment of the soul. The object throughout is to prevent the addition of new karma to the soul, which comes mainly through passion and attachment to the world. Bearing the pains of the world cheerfully contributes to the destruction of karma.

all occupations except banking and commerce as violent. The 18-m high free-standing statue of Gommateshvara at Sravana Belgola near Mysore (built about 983 AD) is just one outstanding example of the contribution of Jain art to India's heritage.

Jain beliefs Jains (from the word Jina, literally meaning 'descendants of conquerors') believe that there are two fundamental principles, the living (*jiva*) and the non-living (*ajiva*). The essence of Jain belief is that all life is sacred and that every living entity, even the smallest insect, has within it an indestructible and immortal soul. Jains developed the view of ahimsa – often translated as 'non-violence', but better perhaps as 'non-harming'. Ahimsa was the basis for the entire scheme of Jain values and ethics and alternative codes of practice were defined for householders and for ascetics.

The five vows may be taken both by monks and by lay people: not to harm any living beings (Jains must practise strict vegetarianism—and even some vegetables, such as potatoes and onions, are believed to have microscopic souls); to speak the truth; not to steal; to give up sexual relations and practice complete chastity; to give up all possessions—for the *Digambara* sect that includes clothes.

Celibacy is necessary to combat physical desire. Jains also regard the manner of dying as extremely important. Although suicide is deeply opposed, vows of fasting to death voluntarily may be regarded as earning merit in the proper context. Mahavir himself is believed to have died of self-starvation, near Rajgir in modern Bihar.

In principle the objectives for both lay and ascetic Jains is the same and many lay Jains pass through the stage of being a householder and then accept the stricter practices of the monks. The essence of all the rules is to avoid intentional injury, which is the worst of all sins. Like Hindus, the Jains believe in *karma*, by which the evil effects of earlier deeds leave an indelible impurity on the soul. This impurity will remain through endless rebirths unless burned off by extreme penances.

Jain sects Jains have two main sects, whose origins can be traced back to the fourth century BC. The more numerous **Svetambaras** – the 'white clad' – concentrated more in eastern and western India, separated from the **Digambaras** – or 'sky-clad'– who often go naked. The Digambaras may well have been forced to move south by drought and famine in the northern region of the Deccan and they are now concentrated in the south of India.

Unlike Buddhists, Jains accept the idea of God, but not as a creator of the universe. They see him in the lives of the 24 **Tirthankaras** (prophets, or literally 'makers of fords' – a reference to their role in building crossing points for the spiritual journey over the river of life), or leaders of Jainism, whose lives are recounted in the Kalpsutra – the third century BC book of ritual for the Svetambaras. Mahavir is regarded as the last of these great spiritual leaders. Much Jain art details stories from these accounts and the Tirthankaras play a similar role for Jains as the Bodhisattvas do for Mahayana Buddhists.

Sikhism

Guru Nanak, the founder of the religion was born just west of Lahore and grew up in what is now the Pakistani town of Sultanpur. His followers, the Sikhs, (derived from the Sanskrit word for 'disciples') form perhaps one of India's most recognizable groups. Beards and turbans give them a very distinctive presence and although they represent less than 2% of the population they are both politically and economically significant. See also table opposite.

Christianity

There are about 23 million Christians in India. Christianity ranks third in terms of religious affiliation after Hinduism and Islam and there are Christian congregations in all the major towns of India.

The great majority of the Protestant Christians in India are now members of the Church of South India, formed from the major Protestant denominations in 1947. Together they account for approximately half the total number of Christians. Roman Catholics make up the majority of the rest. Many of the church congregations, both in towns and villages, are active centres of Christian worship.

Origins Some of the churches owe their origin either to the modern missionary movement of the late 18th century onwards, or to the colonial presence of the European powers. However, Christians probably arrived in India during the first century after the birth of Christ. There is evidence that one of Christ's Apostles, **Thomas**, reached India in 52 AD, only 20 years after Christ was crucified. He settled in Malabar and then expanded his missionary work to China. It is widely believed that he was martyred in Tamil Nadu on his return to India in 72 AD and is buried in Mylapore, in the suburbs of modern Madras. St Thomas' Mount, a small rocky hill just north of Madras airport, takes its name from him. Today there is still a church of Thomas Christians in Kerala.

The Syrian church Kerala was linked directly with the Middle East, when Syrian Christians embarked on a major missionary movement in the sixth century AD. The Thomas Christians have forms of worship that show very strong influence of the Syrian church and they still retain a Syriac order of service. They remained a close-knit community, coming to terms with the prevailing caste system by maintaining strict social rules very similar to those of the surrounding upper caste Hindus. They lived in an area restricted to what is now Kerala, where trade with the Middle East, which some centuries later was to bring Muslims to the same region, remained active.

Roman Catholicism The third major development took place with the arrival of the Portuguese. The Jesuit St Francis Xavier landed in Goa in 1542 and in 1557 Goa was made an Archbishopric. Goa today bears rich testimony to the Portuguese influence on community life and on church building. They set up the first printing press in India in 1566 and began to print books in Tamil and other Dravidian languages by the end of the 16th century.

Northern missions The nature and the influence of Christian missionary activity in North India were different. There are far fewer Christians in North India than in the south, but Protestant missions in Bengal from the end of the 18th century had a profound influence on cultural and religious development. On 9 November 1793 the Baptist missionary **William Carey** reached the Hugli River. Although he went to India to preach, he had wide-ranging interests, notably in languages and education and the work of 19th-century missions rapidly widened to cover educational and medical

Sikhism's Gurus

Guru	Teachings and practice	Developments and events	External powers
1 *Nanak* 1469-1539	The life stories (**janam-sakhis**) of Guru Nanak, written between 50 and 80 years after his death, recorded wide travels, including Bengal and Mecca, studying different faiths.	Devotional and mystic tradition established by Guru Nanak, similar to that of Kabir.	Delhi sultanates
2 *Angad* 1504-1538	Special ceremonies and festivals began to augment individual devotions.		
3 *Amar Das* 1509-1574	Introduction of worship in Gurudwaras.		Portuguese make contact with India.
4 *Ram Das* 1534-1581	Built first lake temple in Amritsar; the first hereditary guru. Widening of congregational worship.	Tolerance for religious experiment.	Akbar
5 *Arjan Dev* 1563-1606	In 1603-4 collected hymns and sayings of the first 3 Gurus, of Sikh mystics and of his father's and his own in a single volume the Adi Granth (the Guru Granth Sahib). Started the Golden Temple at Amritsar.	The Adi Granth comprises nearly 6,000 hymns, 974 attributed to Guru Nanak. Written in Gurumukhi script, developed from Punjabi by the second Guru.	Akbar and Jahangir. Arjan Dev executed by Jahangir at Lahore
6 *Har Gobind* 1595-1645	Jat caste becomes dominant influence. Sikhs began to take up arms, largely to protect themselves against Mughal attacks. Har Gobind decided to withdraw to the Siwalik Hills.	The next 4 Gurus all spent much of their time outside Punjab in the Siwalik Hills, where they developed new martial traditions.	Jahangir and Shah Jahan
7 *Har Rai* 1630-1661			Shah Jahan
8 *Har Krishna* 1656-1664		Died at Delhi.	Aurangzeb
9 *Tegh Bahadur* 1622-1675		Executed by Aurangzeb.	Aurangzeb
10 *Gobind Singh* 1666-1708	Reformed Sikh government introduced the features now universally associated with Sikhism today. Assassinated at Nanded in Maharashtra.	The Khalsa was open to both men and women, who replaced their caste names with the names Singh (lion) and Kaur ('lioness' or 'princess') respectively.	Aurangzeb

 work as well. The influence of Christian missions in education and medical work was greater than in proselytizing. Education in Christian schools stimulated reformist movements in Hinduism itself and mission hospitals supplemented government-run hospitals, particularly in remote rural areas. Some of these Christian-run hospitals, such as that at Vellore, continue to provide high class medical care alongside Government-run and private medical services.

Christian beliefs Christian theology had its roots in Judaism, with its belief in one God, the eternal Creator of the universe. Judaism saw the Jewish people as the vehicle for God's salvation, the 'chosen people of God' and pointed to a time when God would send his Saviour, or Messiah. Jesus, whom Christians believe was 'the Christ' or Messiah, was born in the village of Bethlehem, some 20 km south of Jerusalem. Very little is known of his early life except that he was brought up in a devout Jewish family. At the age of 29 or 30 he gathered a small group of followers and began to preach in the region between the Dead Sea and the Sea of Galilee. Three years later he was crucified in Jerusalem by the authorities on the charge of blasphemy – that he claimed to be the son of God.

Christians believe that all people live in a state of sin, in the sense that they are separated from God and fail to do his will. They believe that God is personal, 'like a father'. As God's son, Jesus accepted the cost of that separation and sinfulness himself through his death on the cross. Christians believe that Jesus was raised from the dead on the third day after he was crucified and that he appeared to his closest followers. They believe that his spirit continues to live today and that he makes it possible for people to come back to God.

The New Testament of the Bible, which, alongside the Old Testament, is the text to which Christians refer as the ultimate scriptural authority, consists of four 'Gospels' (meaning 'good news') and a series of letters by several early Christians referring to the nature of the Christian life.

Christian worship Although Christians are encouraged to worship individually as well as together, most forms of Christian worship centre on the gathering of the church congregation for praise, prayer and the preaching of God's word, which usually takes verses from the Bible as its starting point. Different denominations place varying emphases on the main elements of worship, but in most church services today the congregation will take part in singing hymns (songs of praise), prayers will be led by the minister, priest or a member of the congregation, readings from the Bible will be given and a sermon preached. For many Christians the most important service is the act of Holy Communion (Protestant) or Mass (Catholic) which celebrates the death and resurrection of Jesus in sharing bread and wine, which are held to represent Christ's body and blood given to save people from their sin. Although Christian services may be held daily in some churches most Christian congregations in India meet for worship on Sunday, and services are held in all the local languages. In most cities some churches also have services in English. They are open to all.

Denominations Between the second and the fourth centuries AD there were numerous debates about the interpretation of Christian doctrine, sometimes resulting in the formation of specific groups focusing on particular interpretations of faith. One such group was that of the Nestorian Christians, who played a major part in the theology of the Syrian Church in Kerala. They regarded the Syrian patriarch of the East their spiritual head and followed the Nestorian tradition that there were two distinct natures in Christ, the divine and human. The Roman Catholic church believes that Christ declared that his disciple Peter should be the first spiritual head of the Church and that his successors should lead the Church on earth. Modern Catholic churches still recognize the spiritual authority of the Pope and cardinals.

The reformation which took place in Europe from the 16th century onwards resulted in the creation of the Protestant churches, which became dominant in several European countries. They reasserted the authority of the Bible over that of the church. A number of new denominations were created. The reunification of the church which has taken significant steps since 1947 has progressed faster in South Asia than in most other parts of the world.

Zoroastrianism

The first Zoroastrians arrived on the west coast of India in the mid-eighth century AD, forced out from their native Iran by persecution of the invading Islamic Arabs. Until 1477 they lost all contact with Iran and then for nearly 300 years maintained contact with Persian Zoroastrians through a continuous exchange of letters. They became known by their now much more familiar name, the **Parsis** (or Persians).

Although they are a tiny minority (approximately 100,000), even in the cities where they are concentrated, they have been a prominent economic and social influence, especially in West India. Parsis adopted westernized customs and dress and took to the new economic opportunities that came with colonial industrialization. Families in West India such as the Tatas continue to be among India's leading industrialists, part of a community that in recent generations has spread to Europe and north America.

Origins Zoroastrians trace their beliefs to the prophet Zarathustra, who lived in Northeast Iran around the seventh or sixth century BC. His place and even date of birth are uncertain, but he almost certainly enjoyed the patronage of the father of Darius the Great. The passage of Alexander the Great through Iran severely weakened support for Zoroastrianism, but between the sixth century BC and the seventh century AD it was the major religion of peoples living from North India to central Turkey. The spread of Islam reduced the number of Zoroastrians dramatically and forced those who did not retreat to the desert to emigrate.

Land and environment

Geography

The origins of India's landscapes

Only 100 million years ago the Indian Peninsula of which South India is a part was still attached to the great land mass of what geologists call 'Pangaea' alongside South Africa, Australia and Antarctica. Then as the great plates on which the earth's southern continents stood broke up, the Indian Plate started its dramatic shift northwards, eventually colliding with the Asian plate. As the Indian Plate continues to get pushed under the Tibetan Plateau so the Himalaya continue to rise.

The crystalline rocks of the Peninsula are some of the oldest in the world, the **Charnockites** – named after Job Charnock the founder of Kolkata and an enthusiastic amateur geologist – being over 3100 million years old. Over 60 million years ago a mass of volcanic lava welled up through cracks in the earth's surface and covered some 500,000 sq km including northern Karnataka.

The fault line which severed India from Africa was marked by a north-south ridge of mountains, known today as the Western Ghats, set back from the sea by a coastal plain which is never more than 80 km wide. In the south, the Nilgiris and Palanis are over 2500 m high.

From the crest line of the **Western Ghats**, the Peninsula slopes generally eastwards, interrupted on its eastern edge by the much more broken groups of hills sometimes referred to as the **Eastern Ghats**. The east flowing rivers have created flat alluvial deltas which have been the basis of successive peninsular kingdoms.

Kerala

Stretching from some of the highest mountains of the Western Ghats to the lush coastal plain, Kerala encapsulates the rich diversity of western India's coastal landscapes. Its narrow coastal fringe has been raised from the sea in the last million years. Immediately inland are low, rolling hills of laterite, followed by the ancient rocks which form the backbone of the Western Ghats.

Dotted along the edge of the ghats from Ponmudi in the south to Sulthan Bathery in the north, Kerala's hill stations experience the full force of the southwest and northeast monsoons from May to November, but out of the monsoon season the hills offer lovely country for walks and treks.

The state's palm-fringed backwaters along the coastline are a special attraction. The Silent Valley National Park in the Western Ghats (restricted entry) has the only substantial area of tropical evergreen rain forest in the country. As forested land is increasingly under threat from soaring land values and growing population the government has legislated to make all ecologically sensitive areas in Kerala the direct responsibility of the state.

Andhra Pradesh

The land For much of the year the interior of Andhra looks hot, dry and desolate although the great delta of the Krishna and Godavari rivers retains its lush greenness due to irrigation. Water is the state's lifeblood, and the great peninsular rivers have a sanctity which reflects their importance. The **Godavari**, rising less than 200 km north of Mumbai, is the largest of the peninsular rivers. The **Krishna** rises near **Mahabaleshwar** at an altitude of 1360 m. After the Ganga these two rivers have the largest watersheds in India, and between them they irrigate nearly six million ha of farmland.

Climate

South India lies well to the south of the Tropic of Cancer. Although much of South India has a climate which ranges from very warm to hot it is much cooler in the hills. There are also huge contrasts in rainfall, largely reflecting the influence of the Western Ghats, which lie astride the thrust of the monsoon winds.

The monsoon

→ *Monsoon is an Arabic word meaning 'season'.*

The term monsoon refers to the wind reversal which replaces the dry northeasterlies characteristic of winter and spring, with the very warm and wet southwesterlies of the summer. Many myths surround the onset of the monsoon. In fact its arrival is as variable as is the amount of rain which it brings. What makes the Indian monsoon quite exceptional is not its regularity but the depth of moist air which passes over the subcontinent. Over South India, for example, the highly unstable moist airflow is over 6000 m thick compared with only 2000 m over Japan, giving rise to the bursts of torrential rain which mark out the wet season.

Winter

In winter high pressure builds up over Central Asia. Most of India is protected from the resulting cold northeast monsoon winds by the massive bulk of the Himalaya

Water wars

India's economy, for all the lofty hyperbole about feel-good factors, software booms and call centre outsourcing, is still harnessed to the state of its agriculture. And that means rain. The interiors of Karnataka, Andhra Pradesh, Tamil Nadu and even Kerala, traditionally the wettest of the southern states, have all been routinely devastated by drought. Low rainfall leads to an annual exodus from thirsty villages to towns and cities, as whole families empty out of their homes to do menial graft (some say for as little as Rs 30 a day).

For many farmers the only way out they've seen from their debts has been death. According to a study published in June 2007 by the National Social Watch Coalition, the southern states record some of India's highest suicide rates. Nearly 6000 farmers in Karnataka – where 29,000 farmers are in debt – have committed suicide since 2001, while in Andhra Pradesh, with nearly 50,000 indebted farmers, this figure is 2400.

The water issue is, naturally, at the forefront of political minds and is the subject of fierce battles between chief ministers of the southern states which often end up in court. Both Andhra Pradesh and Tamil Nadu lay claim to water from Karnataka's Krishna and Cauvery rivers.

The century-old dispute over water sharing in the Cauvery Delta has provoked some of the most virulent protests, principally between Tamil Nadu and Karnataka, although Kerala is also affected. In early 2007, after 16 years of hearings, a tribunal announced its verdict for each state, with Tamil Nadu qualifying for 12 km^3 of Cauvery waters, Karnataka 7.6 km^3, Kerala 0.85 km^3 and Pondicherry 0.2 km^3.

As a result of the decision, Tamils were targeted in Bengaluru (Bangalore) in Karnataka, while schools were closed and buses between Tamil Nadu and Karnataka were suspended as authorities anticipated the backlash against Tamils. A 1991 ruling had led to riots against the minority Tamil population in Bengaluru, leaving 18 dead and causing thousands to flee the city.

In a state known for social agitation, the Kerala branches of the multinational soft drink giants have been high-profile targets of farm workers' unrest. The Coca-Cola plant in Palakkad was closed in 2004 following demonstrations by the local population. Coca-Cola had been found to be drawing water from boreholes to use groundwater for the production of its fizzy pop, severely affecting the water table.

and daytime temperatures rise sharply in the sun. To the south the winter temperatures have a minimum of around 20°C. The winter is a dry season through nearly all of India.

Summer

From March onwards as the sun passes overhead much of South India on the plains is almost unbearably hot. Temperatures are generally over 40°C though it never gets as hot as in North India. It is a time of year to get up to the hills. At the end of May the upper air westerly jet stream, which controls the atmospheric system over the Indo-Gangetic plains through the winter, suddenly breaks down. It re-forms to the north of Tibet, thus allowing very moist southwesterlies to sweep across South India and the Bay of Bengal.

The wet seasons

The monsoon seasons in South India differ from the rest of India. In Kerala, Karnataka and much of inland Andhra Pradesh the main rainy season comes between June and September, as in the rest of India, However in coastal Tamil Nadu and Andhra Pradesh it is the season of the so-called retreating monsoon, between October and December, which brings the heaviest rainfall. The wet seaon brings an enveloping dampness which makes it very difficult to keep things dry. If you are travelling in the wetter parts of India during the monsoon you need to be prepared for extended periods of torrential rain. However, many parts of India receive a total of under 1000 mm a year, mainly in the form of heavy isolated showers.

Storms

Some regions of India suffer major storms. Cyclones may hit the east coast causing enormous damage and loss of life, the risk being greatest between the end of October and early December.

Humidity

The coastal regions have humidity levels above 70% for most of the year which can be very uncomfortable. However, sea breezes often bring some relief on the coast itself. Moving north and inland, between December-May humidity drops sharply, often falling as low as 20% during the daytime.

Flora

Vegetation

India's tropical location and its position astride the wet monsoonal winds ensured that 16 different forest types were represented in India. The most widespread was tropical dry deciduous forest. Areas with more than 1700 mm of rainfall had tropical moist deciduous, semi-evergreen or wet evergreen forest, while much of the remainder had types ranging from tropical dry deciduous woodland to dry alpine scrub, found at high altitudes. However, today forest cover has been reduced to about 13% of the surface area, mainly the result of the great demand for wood as a fuel.

Deciduous forest Two types of deciduous tree remain particularly important, **sal** (*Shorea robusta*), now found mainly in eastern India and **teak** (*Tectona grandis*). Most teak today has been planted. Both are resistant to burning, which helped to protect them where man used fire as a means of clearing the forest.

Tropical rainforest In wetter areas, particularly along the Western Ghats, you can still find **tropical wet evergreen forest,** but even these are now extensively managed. Across the drier areas of the peninsula heavy grazing has reduced the forest cover to little more than thorn scrub.

Mountain forests and grassland At between 1000-2000 m in the eastern hill ranges of India and in Bhutan, wet hill forest includes evergreen oaks and chestnuts. Further west in the Himalayan foothills are belts of subtropical pine at roughly the same altitudes. Deodars (*Cedrus deodarus*) form large stands and moist temperate forest, with pines, cedars and spruce, is dominant, giving many valleys a beautifully fresh, alpine feel.

Between 3000-4000 m alpine forest predominates. Rhododendrons are often mixed with other forest types. Birch, juniper, poplars and pine are widespread.

There are several varieties of coarse grassland along the southern edge of the Terai and alpine grasses are important for grazing above altitudes of 2000 m. A totally distinctive grassland is the bamboo (*Dendo calamus*) region of the eastern Himalaya.

Trees

Flowering trees Many Indian trees are planted along roadsides to provide shade and they often also produce beautiful flowers. The **Silk cotton tree** (*Bombax ceiba*), up to 25 m in height, is one of the most dramatic. The pale greyish bark of this buttressed tree usually bears conical spines. It has wide spreading branches and keeps its leaves for most of the year. The flowers, which appear when the tree is leafless, are cup-shaped, with curling, rather fleshy red petals up to 12 cm long while the fruit produces the fine, silky cotton which gives it its name.

Other common trees with red or orange flowers include the Dhak (also called the 'Flame of the forest' or *Palas*), the Gulmohur, the Indian coral tree and the Tulip tree. The smallish (6 m) deciduous **Dhak** (*Butea monosperma*), has light grey bark and a gnarled, twisted trunk and thick, leathery leaves. The large, bright orange and sweet pea-shaped flowers appear on leafless branches. The 8-9 m high umbrella-shaped **Gulmohur** (*Delonix regia*), a native of Madagascar, is grown as a shade tree in towns. The fiery-coloured flowers make a magnificent display after the tree has shed its feathery leaves. The scarlet flowers of the **Indian coral tree** (*Erythrina indica*) also appear when its branches with thorny bark are leafless. The tall **Tulip tree** (*Spathodea campanulata*) (not to be confused with the North American one) has a straight, darkish brown, slender trunk. It is usually evergreen except in the drier parts of India. The scarlet, bell-shaped, tulip-like, flowers grow in profusion at the ends of the branches from November to March.

Often seen along roadsides the **Jacaranda** (*Jacaranda mimosaefolia*), has attractive feathery foliage and purple-blue thimble-shaped flowers up to 40 mm long. When not in flower it resembles a Gulmohur, but differs in its general shape. The valuable **Tamarind** (*Tamarindus indica*), with a short straight trunk and a spreading crown, often grows along the roadside. An evergreen with feathery leaves, it bears small clusters of yellow and red flowers. The noticeable fruit pods are long, curved and swollen at intervals. In parts of India, the rights to the fruit are auctioned off annually for up to Rs 4000 (US$100) per tree.

Of these trees the Silk cotton, the Dhak and the Indian coral are native to India. Others were introduced mostly during the last century: the Tulip tree from East Africa, the Jacaranda from Brazil and the Tamarind, possibly, from Africa.

Fruit trees The familiar apple, plum, apricot and cherry grow in the cool upland areas of India. In the warmer plains tropical fruits flourish. The large, spreading **Mango** (*Mangifera indica*) bears the delicious, distinctively shaped fruit that comes in hundreds of varieties. The evergreen **Jackfruit** (*Artocarpus heterophyllus*) has dark green leathery leaves. The huge fruit (up to 90 cm long and 40 cm thick), growing from a short stem directly off the trunk and branches, has a rough, almost prickly, skin and is almost sickly sweet. The **Banana** plant (*Musa*), actually a gigantic herb (up to 5 m high) arising from an underground stem, has large leaves which grow directly off the trunk. Each purplish flower produces bunches of up to 100 bananas. The **Papaya** (*Carica papaya*) grows to about 4 m with the large hand-shaped leaves clustered near the top. Only the female tree bears the fruit, which hang close to the trunk just below the leaves.

Palm trees **Coconut Palms** (*Cocos nucifera*) are extremely common all round the coast of India. They have tall (15-25 m), slender, unbranched trunks, feathery leaves and large green or golden fruit with soft white flesh filled with milky water, so different from the brown fibre-covered inner nut which makes its way to Europe. The 10-15 m high **Palmyra palms** (*Borassus flabellifer*), indigenous to South and East India, have very distinctive fan-like leaves, as much as 150 cm across. The fruit, which is smaller than a coconut, is round, almost black and very shiny. The **Betel Nut palm** (*Areca catechu*) resembles the coconut palm, its slender trunk bearing ring marks left by fallen leaf stems. The smooth, round nuts, only about 3 cm across, grow in large hanging bunches. **Wild Date palms** (*Phoenix sylvestris*) originally came from North Africa. About 20-25 m tall, the trunks are also marked with the ring bases of the leaves which drop off. The distinctive leaflets which stick out from the central vein give the leaf a spiky appearance. Bunches of dates are only borne by the female tree.

All these palm trees are of considerable **commercial importance.** From the fruit alone the coconut palm produces coir from the outer husk, copra from the fleshy kernel from which coconut oil or coconut butter is extracted, in addition to the desiccated coconut and coconut milk. The sap is fermented to become a drink called toddy. A similar drink is produced from the sap of the Wild Date and the Palmyra palms which are also important for sugar production. The fruit of the Betel Nut palm is wrapped in a special leaf and chewed. The trunks and leaves of all the palms are widely used in building and thatching.

Other trees Of all Indian trees the **Banyan** (*Ficus benghalensis*) is probably the best known. It is planted by temples, in villages and along roads. The seeds often germinate in the cracks of old walls, the growing roots splitting the wall apart. If it grows in the bark of another tree, it sends down roots towards the ground. As it grows, more roots appear from the branches, until the original host tree is surrounded by a 'cage' which eventually strangles it.

Related to the banyan, the **Pipal** or Peepul (*Ficus religiosa*), also cracks open walls and strangles other trees with its roots. With a smooth grey bark, it too is commonly found near temples and shrines. You can distinguish it from the banyan by the absence of aerial roots and its large, heart shaped leaf with a point tapering into a pronounced 'tail'. It bears abundant 'figs' of a purplish tinge about 1 cm across.

The **Ashok** or **Mast** (*Polyalthia longifolia*) is a tall evergreen which can reach 15 m or more in height. One variety, often seen in avenues, is trimmed and tapers towards the top. The leaves are long, slender and shiny and narrow to a long point.

Acacia trees with their feathery leaves are fairly common in the drier parts of India. The best known is the **Babul** (*Acacia arabica*) with a rough, dark bark. The leaves have long silvery white thorns at the base and consist of many leaflets while the flowers grow in golden balls about 1 cm across.

The **Eucalyptus** or **Gum tree** (*Eucalyptus grandis*), introduced from Australia in the 19th century, is now widespread and is planted near villages to provide both shade and firewood. There are various forms but all may be readily recognized by their height, their characteristic long, thin leaves which have a pleasant fresh smell and the colourful peeling bark.

The wispy **Casuarina** (*Casuarina*) grows in poor sandy soil, especially on the coast and on village wasteland. It has the typical leaves of a pine tree and the cones are small and prickly to walk on. It is said to attract lightning during a thunder storm.

Bamboo (*Bambusa*) strictly speaking is a grass which can vary in size from small ornamental clumps to the enormous wild plant whose stems are so strong and thick that they are used for construction and for scaffolding and as pipes in rural irrigation schemes.

Flowering plants

Common in the Himalaya is the beautiful flowering shrub or tree, which can be as tall as 12 m, the **Rhododendron** which is indigenous to this region. In the wild the commonest colour of the flowers is crimson, but other colours, such as pale purple occur too. From March to May the flowers are very noticeable on the hill sides. Another common wild flowering shrub is **Lantana**. This is a fairly small untidy-looking bush with rough, toothed oval leaves, which grow in pairs on the square and prickly stem. The flowers grow together in a flattened head, the ones near the middle being usually yellowish, while those at the rim are pink, pale purple or orange. The fruit is a shiny black berry.

Many other flowering plants are cultivated in parks, gardens and roadside verges. The attractive **Frangipani** (*Plumeria acutifolia*) has a rather crooked trunk and stubby branches, which if broken give out a white milky juice which can be irritating to the skin. The big, leathery leaves taper to a point at each end and have noticeable parallel veins. The sweetly scented waxy flowers are white, pale yellow or pink. The **Bougainvillea** grows as a dense bush or climber with small oval leaves and rather long thorns. The brightly-coloured part (which can be pinkish-purple, crimson, orange, yellow etc) which appears like a flower is not formed of petals, which are quite small and undistinguished, but by large papery bracts.

The trumpet-like flower or the unusually-shaped **Hibiscus** is as much as 7 or 8 cm across, has a very long 'tongue' growing out from the centre and varies in colour from scarlet to yellow or white. The leaves are somewhat oval or heart shaped with jagged edges. In municipal flowerbeds the commonest planted flower is probably the **Canna lily**. It has large leaves which are either green or bronzed and lots of large bright red or yellow flowers. The plant can be more than 1 m high.

On many ponds and tanks the floating plants of the **Lotus** (*Nelumbo nucifera*) and the **Water hyacinth** (*eichornia crassipes*) are seen. Lotus flowers, which rise on stalks above the water, can be white, pink or a deep red and up to 25 cm across. The very large leaves either float on the surface or rise above the water. Many dwarf varieties are cultivated. The rather fleshy leaves and lilac flowers of the Water hyacinth float to form a dense carpet, often clogging the waterways.

Crops

Of India's enormous variety, the single most widespread crop is **rice** (commonly *Orysa indica*). This forms the most important staple in South and East India, though other cereals and some root crops are also important elsewhere. The rice plant grows in flooded fields called *paddies* and virtually all planting or harvesting is done by hand. Millets are favoured in drier areas inland, while wheat is the most important crop in the northwest.

There are many different sorts of millet, but the ones most often seen are finger millet, pearl millet (bajra) and sorghum (jowar). **Finger millet**, commonly known as ragi (*Eleusine corocana*), is so-called because the ear has several spikes which radiate out, a bit like the fingers of a hand. Usually less than 1 m high, it is grown extensively in the south. Both **pearl millet** (*Pennisetum typhoideum*, known as *bajra* in the north and *cumbu* in Tamil Nadu) and **sorghum** (*Sorghum vulgare*, known as *jowar* in the north and *cholam* in the south) and look superficially similar to the more familiar maize though each can be easily distinguished when the seed heads appear. Pearl millet, mainly grown in the north, has a tall single spike which gives it its other name of bulrush millet. The sorghum bears an open ear at the top of the plant.

Another staple grown fairly widely is **cassava** or **tapioca** (*Manihot esculenta*). This is a straight-stemmed bush some 2 m high with dark green leaves divided into thin 'fingers'. The part that is eaten is the root. Cassava is traditionally a famine or reserve crop, because the root can stay in the ground a long time without spoiling and be harvested when needed – a sort of living larder.

To some people India is the home of **tea** (*Camellia sinensis*) which is a very important cash crop. It is grown on a commercial scale in tea gardens in areas of high rainfall, often in highland regions. Over 90 comes from Assam and West Bengal in the Northeast and Tamil Nadu and Kerala in the South. Left to itself tea grows into a tree 10 m tall. In the tea gardens it is pruned to waist height for the convenience of the tea pluckers and forms flat-topped bushes, with shiny bright green oval leaves.

Coffee (*Coffea*) is not as widely grown as tea, but high quality arabica is an important crop in parts of South India. Coffee is also a bush, with fairly long, shiny dark green leaves. The white, sweet smelling flowers, which yield the coffee berry, grow in groups along the stems. The coffee berries start off green and turn red when ripe.

Sugar cane (*Saccharum*) is another commercially important crop. This looks like a large grass which stands up to 3 m tall. The crude brown sugar is sold as jaggery and has a flavour of molasses.

Pineapples (*Ananas comosus*) are often grown under trees, for example under coconut palms on the coast. The pineapple fruit grows out of the middle of a rosette of long, spiky leaves.

Of the many spices grown in India, the two climbers pepper and vanilla and the grass-like cardamom are the ones most often seen. The **pepper** vine (*Piper nigrum*) is indigenous to India where it grows in the warm moist regions. As it is a vine it needs support such as a trellis or a tree. It is frequently planted up against the betel nut palm and appears as a leafy vine with almost heart-shaped leaves. The peppercorns cluster along hanging spikes and are red when ripe. Both black and white pepper is produced from the same plant, the difference being in the processing.

Vanilla (*Vanilla planifolium*), which belongs to the orchid family, also grows up trees for support and attaches itself to the bark by small roots. It is native to South America, but grows well in India in areas of high rainfall. It is a rather fleshy-looking plant, with white flowers and long slender pods.

Cardamom (*Elettaria cardomomum*) is another spice native to India and is planted usually under shade. It grows well in highland areas such as Sikkim and the Western Ghats. It is a herbaceous plant looking rather like a big clump of grass, with long leafy shoots springing out of the ground as much as 2-3 m in height. The white flowers grow on separate shoots which can be upright, but usually sprawl on the ground. It is from these flowers that the seed-bearing capsules grow.

The **cashew nut** tree (*Anacardium occidentale*) was introduced into India, but now grows wild as well as being cultivated. It is a medium sized tree with bright green, shiny, rounded leaves. The nut grows on a fleshy fruit called a cashew apple and hangs down below this.

Cotton (*Gossypium*) is important in parts of the west and south. The cotton bush is a small knee-high bush and the cotton boll appears after the flower has withered. This splits when ripe to show the white cotton lint inside.

The **castor oil** plant (*Ricinus communis*) is cultivated as a cash crop and is planted in smallholdings among other crops and along roads and paths. It is a handsome plant up to about 2 m in height, with very large leaves which are divided into some 12 'fingers'. The young stems are reddish and shiny. The well known castor oil is extracted from the bean which is a mottled brown in colour.

Fauna

India has an extremely rich and varied wildlife, though many species only survive in very restricted environments.

Conservation

Alarmed by the rapid loss of wildlife habitat the Indian government established the first conservation measures in 1972, followed by the setting up of national parks and reserves. Some 25,000 sq km were set aside in 1973 for Project Tiger. Now tigers are reported to be increasing steadily in several of the game reserves. The same is true of other, less well known species. Their natural habitat has been destroyed both by

Room at the park...

Booking accommodation in national parks can be very frustrating for independent travellers. In many parks it is essential to book in advance. Offices outside may tell you that it is fully-booked, even when outgoing tourists say that the accommodation is empty. This is because cancellation information is not relayed to all offices. The only way in is patient, friendly persistence, asking for just one day inside. This can then be extended once in. Be prepared for a lot of frustration, especially in Ramnagar (Corbett National Park). Where possible go to the park itself and book. You may prefer to try a specialist travel agent in one of the main towns in the region.

people and by domesticated animals (there are some 250 million cattle and 50 million sheep and goats). There are now nearly 70 national parks across India as a whole and 330 sanctuaries in addition to programmes of afforestation and coastline preservation. Most parks and sanctuaries are open from October-March; those in the northeast are closed from April-September.

The animals

The big cats Of the three Indian big cats the Asiatic lion is virtually confined to a single reserve. The other two, the tiger and leopard, occasionally occur outside. The **tiger** (*Panthera tigris*), which prefers to live in fairly dense cover, is most likely to be glimpsed as it lies in long grass or in dappled shadow. The **leopard** or **panther** as it is often called in India (*Panthera pardus*), is far more numerous than the tiger, but is even more elusive. The all black form is not uncommon in areas of higher rainfall such as the Western Ghats and Northeast India, though the typical form is seen more often.

Elephant and rhino The **Indian elephant** (*Elephas maximus*) has been domesticated for centuries and today it is still used as a beast of burden. In the wild it inhabits hilly country with forest and bamboo, where it lives in herds which can number as many as 50 or more individuals. They are adaptable animals and can live in all sorts of forest, except those in the dry areas.Wild elephants are mainly confined to reserves, but occasionally move out into cultivation, where they cause great damage. See also box, page 532.

Deer, antelope, oxen and their relatives Once widespread, these animals are now largely confined to the reserves. The male deer (stags) carry antlers which are branched, each 'spike' on the antler being called a tine. Antelopes and oxen, on the other hand, have horns which are not branched.

Deer There are several deer species in India, mainly confined to very restricted ranges. Three species are quite common. The largest and one of the most widespread, is the magnificent **sambar** (*Cervus unicolor*) which can be up to 150 cm at the shoulder. It has a noticeably shaggy coat, which varies in colour from brown with a yellowish or grey tinge through to dark, almost black, in the older stags. The sambar is often found on wooded hillsides and lives in groups of up to 10 or so, though solitary individuals are also seen.

The much smaller **chital** or **spotted deer** (*Axis axis*), only about 90 cm tall, are seen in herds of 20 or so, in grassy areas. The bright rufous coat spotted with white is unmistakable; the stags carry antlers with three tines.

Elephants

The Indian elephant (Elephas maximas), smaller than the African, is the world's second largest land mammal. Unlike the African elephant, the male rarely reaches a height of over 3 m; it also has smaller ears. Other distinguishing features include the high domed forehead, the rounded shape of the back and the smooth trunk with a single 'finger' at the end. Also the female is often tuskless or bears small ones called tushes and even the male is sometimes tuskless (makhnas). The Indian elephant has five nails on its front feet and four on the back (compared to the African's four and three respectively). There are approximately 6500 elephants living in the wild in northern West Bengal, Assam and Bhutan. There are a further 2000 in Central India and 6000 in the three South Indian states of Kerala, Tamil Nadu and Karnataka.

The loss of habitat has made wild elephants an increasing danger to humans and about 300 people are killed every year by wild elephants, mainly in the northeast. The tribal people have developed skilled techniques for capturing and training wild elephants, which have been domesticated in India for about 5000 years. They need a lot of feeding – about 18 hours a day. Working elephants are fed on a special diet, by hand straight into the mouth, and they eat between 100 and 300 kg per day.

The **nilgai** or **blue bull** (*Boselaphus tragocamelus*) is about 140 cm at the shoulder and is rather horse-like, with a sloping back. The male has a dark grey coat, while the female is sandy coloured. Both sexes have two white marks on the cheek, white throats and a white ring just above each hoof. The male carries short, forward-curving horns and has a tuft of long black hairs on the front of the neck. They occur in small herds on grassy plains and scrub land.

Oxen The commonest member of the oxen group is the **Asiatic wild buffalo** or water buffalo (*Bubalus bubalis*). About 170 cm at the shoulder, the wild buffalo, which can be aggressive, occurs in herds on grassy plains and swamps near rivers and lakes. The black coat and widespreading curved horns, which are carried by both sexes, are distinctive.

The **Indian bison** or **gaur** (*Bos gaurus*) can be up to 200 cm at the shoulder with a heavy muscular ridge across it. Both sexes carry curved horns. The young gaur is a light sandy colour, which darkens with age, the old bulls being nearly black with pale sandy coloured 'socks' and a pale forehead. Basically hill animals, they live in forests and bamboo clumps and emerge from the trees to graze.

Others The **wild boar** (*Sus scrofa*) has mainly black body and a pig-like head; the hairs thicken down the spine to form a sort of mane. A mature male stands 90 cm at the shoulder and, unlike the female, bears tusks. The young are striped. Quite widespread, they often cause great destruction among crops.

One of the most important scavengers of the open countryside, the **striped hyena** (*Hyena hyena*) usually comes out at night. It is about 90 cm at the shoulder with a large head with a noticeable crest of hairs along its sloping back.

The **common giant flying squirrel** is frequently found in the larger forests of India, except in the northeast (*Petaurista petaurista*). The body can be 45 cm long and the tail another 50 cm. They glide from tree to tree using a membrane stretching from front leg to back leg which acts like a parachute.

In towns and villages The **common langur** (*Presbytis entellus*), 75 cm, is a long-tailed monkey with a distinctive black face, hands and feet. Usually a forest dweller, it is found almost throughout India. The Nilgiri langur (Presbytis johni) is slightly taller at 80 cm, with glossy black hair and a yellowish brown head. Females have a clearly visible patch of white hair on the inside of their thighs. The Nilgiri langur has made the dense evergreen sholas its major habitat, but the beauty of its fur has sadly made it prized by hunters. The **lion tailed macaque** (*Macaca mulatta*), 50-60 cm, has a striking mane of grey hair, a glossy black coat and a tufted tail – hence its name. It lives in the higher hills in herds of up to 20,and the male's voice is said to sound almost human, but it is yet another endangered species.

Palm squirrels are very common. The **five-striped** (*Funambulus pennanti*) and the **three-striped palm squirrel** (*Funambulus palmarum*), are both about the same size (30 cm long, about half of which is tail). The five-striped is usually seen in towns.

The two bats most commonly seen in towns differ enormously in size. The larger so-called **flying fox** (*Pteropus giganteus*) has a wing span of 120 cm. These fruit-eating bats, found throughout, except in the driest areas, roost in large noisy colonies where they look like folded umbrellas hanging from the trees. In the evening they can be seen leaving the roost with slow measured wing beats. The much smaller **Indian pipistrelle** (*Pipistrellus coromandra*), with a wing span of about 15 cm, is an insect eater. It comes into houses at dawn, roosting under eaves and has a fast, erratic flight.

The **jackal** (*Canis aureus*), a lone scavenger in towns and villages, looks like a cross between a dog and a fox and varies in colour from shades of brown through to black. The bushy tail has a dark tip.

The **common mongoose** (*Herpestes edwardsi*) lives in scrub and open jungle. It kills snakes, but will also take rats, mice and chickens. Tawny coloured with a grey grizzled tinge, it is about 90 cm in length, of which half is pale-tipped tail.

The **sloth bear** (*Melursus ursinus*), about 75 cm at the shoulder, lives in broken forest, but may be seen on a lead accompanying a street entertainer who makes it 'dance' to music as a part of an act. They have a long snout, a pendulous lower lip and a shaggy black coat with a yellowish V-shaped mark on the chest.

If you take a boat trip look out for the **common dolphin** (Delphinus delphis) as they comes to the surface to breathe.

Birds

Town and village birds Some birds perform a useful function scavenging and clearing refuse. One of the most widespread is the brown **pariah kite** (*Milvus migrans*, 65 cm). The more handsome chestnut and white **brahminy kite** (*Haliastur indus*, 48 cm) is largely confined to the waterside. The common brown **white-backed vulture** (*Gyps bengalensis*, 90 cm) looks ungainly and has a bare and scrawny head and neck. The smaller **scavenger vulture** (*Neophron percnopterus*, 65 cm) is mainly white, but often has dirty looking plumage and the bare head and neck of all vultures. In flight its wedge-shaped tail and black and white colouring are characteristic.

The **house crow** (*Corvus splendens*, 45 cm) on the other hand is a very smart looking bird with a grey body and black tail, wings, face and throat. It occurs in almost every town and village in India. The **jungle crow** (*Corvus macrorhynchos*, 50 cm) originally a bird of the countryside has started to move into populated areas and in the hill stations tends to replace the house crow. Unlike the house crow it is a glossy black all over and has a much deeper, hoarser caw.

The **feral pigeon**, or **blue rock dove** (*Columba livia*, 32 cm), found throughout the world, is generally a slaty grey in colour. It invariably has two dark bars on the wing and a white rump. The **little brown dove** (*Streptopelia senegalensis*, 25 cm) is bluey grey and brown above, with a pink head and underparts and a speckled pattern on the neck. The **collared dove** (*Streptopelia decaocto*, 30 cm) with a distinct half collar on the back of its neck, is common, especially in the drier parts of India.

Bulbuls are common in gardens and parks. The **red-vented bulbul** (*Pycnonotus cafer*, 20 cm), a mainly brown bird, can be identified by the slight crest and a bright red patch under the tail. The **house sparrow** (*Passer domesticus*, 15 cm) can be seen in towns throughout the mainland. The ubiquitous **common myna** (*Acridotheres tristis*, 22 cm), feeds on lawns, especially after rain or watering. Look for the white under the tail and the bare yellow skin around the eye, yellow bill and legs and in flight the large white wing patch.

A less common, but more striking bird also seen feeding in open spaces, is the **hoopoe** (*Upupa epops*, 30 cm), easily identified by its sandy plumage with black and white stripes and long thin curved bill. The marvellous fan-shaped crest is sometimes raised. Finally there is a member of the cuckoo family which is heard more often than seen. The **koel** (*Eudynamys scolopacea*, 42 cm), is commonly heard during the hot weather – kuoo-kuoo-kuoo, the double note starts off low and flute-like, rises in pitch and intensity, then suddenly stops, only to start all over again. The male is all black with a greenish bill and a red eye; the female streaked and barred.

Water and waterside birds The *jheels* (marshes or swamps) of India form one of the richest bird habitats in the world. Cormorants abound; the commonest, the **little cormorant** (*Phalacrocorax niger*, 50 cm) is found on most inland waters. An almost entirely black bird with just a little white on the throat, it has a long tail and a hooked bill. The **coot** (*Fulica atra*, 40 cm), another common black bird, seen especially in winter has a noticeable white shield on the forehead.

The magnificent **sarus crane** (*Grus antigone*, 150 cm) is one of India's tallest birds. It is widespread all year round across northern India, almost invariably in pairs. The bare red head and long red legs combined with its height and grey plumage make it easy to identify. The commonest migrant crane is probably the **common crane** (*Grus grus*, 120 cm), present only in winter, often in large flocks. It has mainly grey plumage with a black head and neck. There is a white streak running down the side of the neck and above the eye is a tuft of red feathers.

The **openbill stork** (*Anastomus oscitans*, 80 cm) and the **painted stork** (*Ibis leucocephalus*, 100 cm) are common too and are spotted breeding in large colonies. The former is white with black wing feathers and a curiously shaped bill. The latter, mainly white, has a pinkish tinge on the back and dark marks on the wings and a broken black band on the lower chest. The bare yellow face and yellow down-curved bill are conspicuous.

By almost every swamp, ditch or rice paddy up to about 1,200 m you will see the **paddy bird** (*Ardeola grayii*, 45 cm). An inconspicuous, buff-coloured bird, it is easily overlooked as it stands hunched up by the waterside. As soon as it takes off, its white wings and rump make it very noticeable. The **bronze-winged jacana** (*Metopidius indicus*, 27 cm) has very long toes which enable it to walk on the floating leaves of water-lilies and there is a noticeable white streak over and above the eye. Village ponds often have their resident bird.

The commonest and most widespread of the Indian kingfishers is the jewel-like **common kingfisher** (*Alcedo atthis*, 18 cm). With its brilliant blue upperparts and orange breast it is usually seen perched on a twig or a reed beside the water.

Open grassland, light woodland and cultivated land The **cattle egret** (*Bubulcus ibis*, 50 cm), a small white heron, is usually seen near herds of cattle, frequently perched on the backs of animals. Equal in height to the sarus crane is the impressive, but ugly **adjutant stork** (*Leptopilos dubius*, 150 cm). This often dishevelled bird is a scavenger and is thus seen near rubbish dumps and carcasses. It has a naked red head and neck, a huge bill and a large fleshy pouch which hangs down the front of the neck.

The **rose-ringed parakeet** (*Psittacula krameri*, 40 cm) is found throughout India up to about 1500 m while the **pied myna** (*Sturnus contra*, 23 cm) is restricted to northern and central India. The rose-ringed parakeet often forms huge flocks, an impressive sight coming in to roost. The long tail is noticeable both in flight and when the bird is perched. They can be very destructive to crops, but are attractive birds which are frequently kept as pets. The pied myna, with its smart black and white plumage is conspicuous, usually in small flocks in grazing land or cultivation. It feeds on the ground and on village rubbish dumps. The all black **drongo** (*Dicrurus adsimilis*, 30 cm) is almost invariably seen perched on telegraph wires or bare branches. Its distinctively forked tail makes it easy to identify.

Weaver birds are a family of mainly yellow birds, all remarkable for the intricate nests they build. The most widespread is the **baya weaver** (*Ploceus philippinus*, 15cm) which nest in large colonies, often near villages. The male in the breeding season combines a black face and throat with a contrasting yellow top of the head and the yellow breast band. In the non-breeding season both sexes are brownish sparrow-like birds.

Hill birds Land above about 1500 m supports a distinct range of species, although some birds, such as the ubiquitous **common myna**, are found in the highlands as well as in the lower lying terrain.

The highland equivalent of the red-vented bulbul is the **white-cheeked bulbul** (*Pycnonotus leucogenys*, 20 cm) which is found in gardens and woodland in the Himalaya up to about 2500 m and as far south as Mumbai. It has white underparts with a yellow patch under the tail. The black head and white cheek patches are distinctive. The crest varies in length and is most prominent in birds found in Kashmir, where it is very common in gardens. The **red-whiskered bulbul** (*Pycnonotus jocosus*, 20 cm) is widespread in the Himalaya and the hills of South India up to about 2500 m. Its pronounced pointed crest, which is sometimes so long that it flops forward towards the bill, white underparts and red and white 'whiskers' serve to distinguish it. It has a red patch under the tail.

In the summer the delightful **verditer flycatcher** (*Muscicapa thalassina*, 15 cm) is a common breeding bird in the Himalaya up to about 3000 m. It is tame and confiding, often builds its nest on verandahs and is seen perching on telegraph wires. In winter it is much more widely distributed throughout the country. It is an active little bird which flicks its tail up and down in a characteristic manner. The male is all bright blue-green with somewhat darker wings and a black patch in front of the eyes. The female is similar, but duller.

Another species associated with man is the **white wagtail** (*Motacilla alba*, 21 cm), very common in the Himalayan summer up to about 3000 m. It is always found near water, by streams and lakes, on floating vegetation and among the house boats in Kashmir. Its black and white plumage and constantly wagging tail make it easy to identify.

Yet another species common in Kashmir and in other Himalayan hill stations is the **red-billed blue magpie** (*Urocissa erythrorhyncha*, 65 cm). With a long tail and pale blue plumage, contrasting with its black head, it is usually seen in small flocks as it flies from tree to tree. This is not so much a garden bird, but prefers tea gardens, open woodland and cultivation.

Jungle fowl and pheasants The highlands of India, especially the Himalaya, are the home of the ancestors of domestic hens and also of numerous beautiful pheasants. These are mainly forest dwellers and are not easy to see as they tend to be shy and wary of man.

Last but not least, mention must be made of India's national bird, the magnificent and well-known **peafowl** (*Pavo cristatus*, male 210 cm, female 100 cm), which is more commonly known as the peacock. Semi-domesticated birds are commonly seen and heard around towns and villages, especially in the northwest of India. In the wild it favours hilly jungles and dense scrub.

Reptiles and amphibians

India is famous for its reptiles, especially its snakes which feature in many stories and legends. In reality, snakes keep out of the way of people. One of the most common is the **Indian rock python** (*Python molurus*) a 'constrictor' which kills it's prey by suffocation. Usually about 4 m in length, they can be much longer. Their docile nature make them favourites of snake handlers.

The other large snakes favoured by street entertainers are cobras. The various species all have a hood which is spread when the snake draws itself up to strike. They are all highly venomous and the snake charmers prudently de-fang them to render them harmless. The best known is probably the **spectacled cobra** (*Naja naja*), which has a mark like a pair of spectacles on the back of its hood. The largest venomous snake in the world is the **king cobra** (*Ophiophagus hannah*) which is 5 m in length. It is usually brown, but can vary from cream to black and lacks the spectacle marks of the other. In their natural state cobras are generally inhabitants of forest regions.

Equally venomous, but much smaller, the **common krait** *(Bungarus caeruleus)* is just over 1 m in length. The slender, shiny, blue-black snake has thin white bands which can sometimes be almost indiscernible. They are found all over the country except in the northeast where the canniballistic **banded krait** with bold yellowish and black bands has virtually eradicated them.

In houses everywhere you cannot fail to see the **gecko** (*Hemidactylus*). This small harmless, primitive lizard is active after dark. It lives in houses behind pictures and curtain rails and at night emerges to run across the walls and ceilings to hunt the night-flying insects which form its main prey. It is not usually more than about 14 cm long, with a curiously transparent, pale yellowish brown body. At the other end of the scale is the **monitor lizard** (*Varanus*), which can grow to 2 m in length. They can vary from a colourful black and yellow, to plain or speckled brown. They live in different habitats from cultivation and scrub to waterside places and desert.

The most widespread crocodile is the freshwater **mugger** or Marsh crocodile (*Crocodilus palustrus*) which grows to 3-4 m in length. The only similar fresh water species is the **gharial** (*Gavialis gangeticus*) which lives in large, fast flowing rivers. Twice the length of the mugger, it is a fish-eating crocodile with a long thin snout with, in the case of the male, an extraordinary bulbous growth on the end. The enormous, aggressive **estuarine** or **saltwater crocodile** (*Crocodilus porosus*) is now restricted to the brackish waters of the Sundarbans, on the east coast and in the Andaman and Nicobar Islands. It grows to 7 m in length and is much sleeker looking than the rather docile mugger.

Books

The literature on India is as huge and varied as the subcontinent itself. India is a good place to buy English language books as foreign books are often much cheaper than the published price. There are also cheap Indian editions and occasionally reprints of out-of-print books. There are excellent bookshops in all the major Indian cities. Below are a few suggestions.

Art and architecture

Burton, T Richard *Hindu Art*. A well-illustrated paperback; a broad view of art and religion.
Cooper, Ilay and Dawson,Barry *Traditional Buildings of India*. (Thames & Hudson)
Dwivedi, Sharada *Bombay: the Cities Within*. Takes architecture as a starting point for telling the story of the development of this mega 'metro'.
Lovegrove, Keith *Graphicswallah: Graphics in India*. Beefy coffee table book of commercial graphic design in Mumbai and Chennai.
Michell, George *The Hindu Temple*. (University of Chicago Press, 1988.) An authoritative account of Hindu architectural development.
Pandit, Heta *Hidden Hands Master Builders of Goa*. For the architecture-obsessed

Non-fiction

Arundhati, Roy *The Algebra of Infinite Justice*. A collection of Roy's provocative political writings – often first published in *Outlook* magazine.
Aurora Couto, Maria *Goa: A Daughter's Story*. A painstaking and moving account of and mourning for Goa's past.
Dalrymple, William *The Age of Kali*. Wide-ranging travelogue includes masterly reconjuring of Hyderabad, Madurai and Portugese Goa plus a profile of Mumbai's first lady of porn and glimpses of the anti-globalization movement of Bengaluru (Bangalore).
Dalrymple, William *White Mughals*. Masterly conjuring of the personalities at the centre of the 18th-century court of the Nizam of Hyderabad, shot through with a classic love story across caste, religious, racial and national lines.
Hall, Richard *Empires of the Monsoon*. An all-too vivid record of life on the Indian Ocean rim as tussled over by waves of Portugese, Dutch, British and Arab traders (Hall's bias is for Africa finally, but there is good detail on India too).
Iyengar, BKS *Light on Yoga*. The manual for Iyengar yogis and good grounding for postures for ashtanga practice too.
Jack, Ian (ed) *India: The Golden Jubilee: Granta issue 57*. Bitingly incisive essays from the best of India's domestic and foreign commentators including an essay on Southern wildlife.
Logan, William *Malabar Manual*. An employee of the British Madras Presidency, Scotsman Logan earned a place in the Keralite heart, and history books, with this 2-volume chronicle of North Keralite customs and mores.
Naipaul, VS *India: A Wounded Civilization*. Written contemporaneously to Indira Gandhi's declaration of Emergency in 1975, Naipaul takes a scalpel to the subcontinent through the skin of its literary history. Fascinating detail on Hampi.
Also see *An Area of Darkness* and *India: A Million Mutinies Now*. The continuation of the trilogy.
Narayan, RK *The Emerald Route*. Hardly Narayan at full throttle, but a nice account of a rove around Karnataka by one of the state's most illustrious sons.
Odzer, Cleo *Goa Freaks: My Hippie Years in India*. Often frustratingly narcissistic but a good window on the shift in the freak scene of the 70s and 80s: Odzer charts its members' gradation from smack to coke and back.
Price, Frederick *Ootacamund: A History*. The paperback reprint of this 1908 documentary of the Madras Presidency's

favourite hill station is a brilliant guide to the development of the Britisher's summer residency.

Theroux, Paul *The Great Railway Bazaar*. Travel writing master takes to the railroads of Asia – not restricted to India but a brilliant companion to a train-based itinerary round the South.

Tully, Mark *India in Slow Motion*. Collection of essays from former BBC South Asia correspondent includes incisive interview with then chief minister of Andhra Pradesh

Fiction

Kunzru, Hari *The Impressionist*. First novel charts the shifting identity of the bastard child of an expat Englishman and Indian mother.

Mascarenhas, Margaret *Skin*. Goa's heritage and much mixed ancestry explored through fiction.

Mistry, Rohinton *A Fine Balance*. The many layers of Mumbai society teased apart. Memorable, too, for 'beggar-mastery' explained.

Narayan, RK *Malgudi Omnibus*. The South Indian equivalent of Our Town from Karnataka-born Narayan.

Roy, Arundhati *The God of Small Things*. Excellent, poetic novel of family turmoil in a Syrian Christian pickle-making family near Kottayam in Kerala.

Yoga and spirituality

Dr Lad, Vasant *Ayurveda, The Science of Self-Healing*. Illustrated book of ancient medicine.

Scott, John *Ashtanga Yoga: The Definitive Step-by-Step Guide to Dynamic Yoga*. Well respected teacher breaks dynamic yoga down into sequence.

Silva, Mira, Shyam Mehta *Yoga: The Iyengar Way*. A beginner's introduction to Iyengar yoga, with photographs

Vyasa (translated by NK Narayan) *Mahabharata and the Bhagavad Gita*. Hinduism's great epics distilled into brilliant, vivid prose by one of India's greatest contemporary novelists.

Footnotes

Language

Hindi words and phrases

Pronunciation

'a' as in ah | 'i' as in bee | nasalized vowels are shown as an 'un'
'o' as in oh | 'u' as oo in book

Basics

Hello, good morning, goodbye	*namaste*
Thank you/no thank you	*dhanyavad or shukriya/nahin shukriya*
Excuse me, sorry	*maf kijiye*
Yes/no	*ji han/ji nahin*
Never mind/that's all right	*koi bat nahin*

Questions

What is your name?	*apka nam kya hai?*
My name is...	*mera nam... Hai*
Pardon?	*phir bataiye?*
How are you?	*kya hal hai?*
I am well, thanks, and you?	*main thik hun, aur ap?*
Not very well	*main thik nahin hun*
Where is the?	*kahan hai?*
Who is?	*kaun hai?*
What is this?	*yeh kya hai?*

Shopping

How much?	*Kitna?*
That makes (20) rupees	*(bis) rupaye*
That is very expensive!	*bahut mahanga hai!*
Make it a bit cheaper!	*thora kam kijiye!*

The hotel

What is the room charge?	*kiraya kitna hai?*
Please show the room	*kamra dikhaiye*
Is there an airconditioned room?	*kya a/c kamra hai?*
Is there hot water?	*garam pani hai?*
... a bathroom/fan/mosquito net	*... bathroom/pankha/machhar dani*
Is there a large room?	*bara kamra hai?*
Please clean it	*saf karwa dijiye*
Are there clean sheets/blanket?	*saf chadaren/kambal hain?*
Bill please	*bill dijiye*

Travel

Where's the railway station?	*railway station kahan hai?*
How much is the ticket to Agra?	*Agra ka ticket kitne ka hai?*
When does the Agra bus leave?	*Agra bus kab jaegi?*
How much?	*Kitna?*
left/right	*baien/dahina*
go straight on	*sidha chaliye*
nearby	*nazdik*

Please wait here	*yahan thahariye*
Please come at 8	*ath bajai ana*
quickly	*jaldi*
stop	*rukiye*

Time and days

right now	*abhi*	month	*mahina*
morning	*suba*	year	*sal*
afternoon	*dopahar*	Sunday	*ravivar*
evening	*sham*	Monday	*somvar*
night	*rat*	Tuesday	*mangalvar*
today	*aj*	Wednesday	*budhvar*
tomorrow/yesterday	*kal/kal*	Thursday	*virvar*
day	*din*	Friday	*shukravar*
week	*hafta*	Saturday	*shanivar*

Numbers

1	*ek*	13	*terah*
2	*do*	14	*chaudah*
3	*tin*	15	*pandrah*
4	*char*	16	*solah*
5	*panch*	17	*satrah*
6	*chhai*	18	*atharah*
7	*sat*	19	*unnis*
8	*ath*	20	*bis*
9	*nau*	100/200	*sau/do sau*
10	*das*	1000/2000	*hazar/do hazar*
11	*gyara*	100,000	*lakh*
12	*barah*		

Tamil words and phrases

Basics

Hello, good morning, goodbye	*Vanakkam*
Thank you/no thank you	*Nandri*
Excuse me, sorry/pardon	*Mannikkavum*
Yes/no	*am/illai*
Never mind/that's all right	*paruvai illai*

Questions

What is your name?	*Ungaludaya peyr enna?*
My name is...	*Ennudaya peyr*
How are you?	*Ningal eppadi irukkirirgal?*
I am well, thanks	*Nan nantraga irrukkirain*
Not very well	*paruvayillai*

Shopping

How much?	*Ithan vilai enna?*
That makes (20) rupees	*athan vilai irupatha rupa*
Make it a bit cheaper!	*Thayavu seithu konjam kuraikavuam!*

The hotel

What is the room charge?	*Arayin vilai enna?*
May I see the room please?	*thayavu seithu arayai parka mudiyama?*
Is there an a/c room?	*Kulir sathana arai irrukkatha?*
Is there hot water?	*Sudu thanir irukkuma?*
... a bathroom	*...oru kuliyal arai*
...a fan	*...katotra sathanam*
... mosquito net	*...kosu valai*
Please clean the room	*thayavu seithu arayai suththap paduthava*
Bill please	*bill tharavum*

Travel

Where's the railway station?	*station enge?*
How much is it to Chennai?	*Chennai poga evalavu?*
When does the Chennai bus leave?	*Eppa Chennai bus pogum?*
left/right	*idathu/valathu*
go straight on	*naerakapogavum*
nearby	*aruqil*
Please wait here	*thayavu seithu ingu nitkavum*
Please come at 8	*thayavu seithu ingu ettu*
stop	*nivuthu*

Time and days

right now	*ippoh*	month	*maatham*
morning	*kalai*	Sunday	*gnatruk kilamai*
afternoon	*pitpagal*	Monday	*thinkat kilamai*
evening	*malai*	Tuesday	*sevai kilamai*
night	*iravu*	Wednesday	*puthan kilamai*
today	*indru*	Thursday	*viyalak kilamai*
tomorrow/yesterday	*nalai/naetru*	Friday	*velli kilamai*
day	*thinam*	Saturday	*sanik kilamai*
week	*vaaram*		

Numbers

1	*ontru*	7	*arlu*
2	*erantru*	8	*ettu*
3	*moontru*	9	*onparthu*
4	*nangu*	10	*pattu*
5	*ainthu*	20	*erupathu*
6	*aru*	100/200	*nooru/irunooru*

Food and drink

Eating out is normally cheap and safe but menus can often be dauntingly long and full of unfamiliar names. Here are some Hindi words to help you. Pronunciation is explained on page 540.

Meat and fish

gosht, mas	meat	*jhinga*	prawns
Macchli	fish	*murgh*	chicken

Vegetables (*sabzi*)

aloo	potato	*khumbhi*	mushroom
baingan	aubergine	*matar*	peas
band gobi	cabbage	*piaz*	onion
bhindi	okra, ladies' fingers	*phool gobi*	cauliflower
gajar	carrots	*sag*	spinach

Styles of cooking

bhoona in a thick, fairly spicy sauce
chops minced meat, fish or vegetables, covered with mashed potato, crumbed and fried
cutlet minced meat, fish, vegetables formed into flat rounds or ovals, crumbed and fried (eg prawn cutlet, flattened king prawn)
do piaza with onions (added twice during cooking)
dumphuk steam baked
jhal frazi spicy, hot sauce with tomatoes and chillies
jhol thin gravy (Bengali)
Kashmiri cooked with mild spices, ground almonds and yoghurt, often with fruit
kebab skewered (or minced and shaped) meat or fish; a dry spicy dish cooked on a fire
kima minced meat (usually 'mutton')
kofta minced meat or vegetable balls
korma in fairly mild rich sauce using cream/yoghurt
masala marinated in spices (fairly hot)
Madras hot
makhani in butter rich sauce
moli South Indian dishes cooked in coconut milk and green chilli sauce
Mughlai rich North Indian style
Nargisi dish using boiled eggs
navratan curry ('9 jewels') colourful mixed vegetables and fruit in mild sauce
Peshwari rich with dried fruit and nuts (Northwest Indian)
tandoori baked in a tandoor (special clay oven) or one imitating it
tikka marinated meat pieces, baked quite dry
vindaloo hot and sour Goan meat dish using vinegar

Typical dishes

aloo gosht potato and mutton stew
aloo gobi dry potato and cauliflower with cumin
aloo, matar, kumbhi potato, peas, mushrooms in a dryish mildly spicy sauce
bhindi bhaji lady's fingers fried with onions and mild spices
boti kebab marinated pieces of meat, skewered and cooked over a fire
dal makhani lentils cooked with butter
dum aloo potato curry with a spicy yoghurt, tomato and onion sauce
matar panir curd cheese cubes with peas and spices (and often tomatoes)

murgh massallam chicken in creamy marinade of yoghurt, spices and herbs with nuts
nargisi kofta boiled eggs covered in minced lamb, cooked in a thick sauce
rogan josh rich, mutton/beef pieces in creamy, red sauce
sag panir drained curd (*panir*) sautéed with chopped spinach in mild spices
sarson-ke-sag and **makkai-ki-roti** mustard leaf cooked dry with spices served with maize four roti from Punjab
shabdeg a special Mughlai mutton dish with vegetables
yakhni lamb stew

Rice

bhat/sada chawal plain boiled rice
biriyani partially cooked rice layered over meat and baked with saffron
khichari rice and lentils cooked with turmeric and other spices
pulao/pilau fried rice cooked with spices (cloves, cardamom, cinnamon) with dried fruit, nuts or vegetables. Sometimes cooked with meat, like a biriyani

Roti – breads

chapati (roti) thin, plain, wholemeal unleavened bread cooked on a tawa (griddle), usually made from ata (wheat flour). Makkaikiroti is with maize flour.
nan oven baked (traditionally in a tandoor) white flour leavened bread often large and triangular; sometimes stuffed with almonds and dried fruit
paratha fried bread layered with *ghi* (sometimes cooked with egg or with potatoes)
poori thin deep-fried, puffed rounds of flour

Sweets

These are often made with reduced/thickened milk, drained curd cheese or powdered lentils and nuts. They are sometimes covered with a flimsy sheet of decorative, edible silver leaf.
barfi fudge-like rectangles/diamonds
gulab jamun dark fried spongy balls, soaked in syrup
halwa rich sweet made from cereal, fruit, vegetable, nuts and sugar
khir, payasam, paesh thickened milk rice/vermicelli pudding
kulfi cone-shaped Indian ice cream with pistachios/almonds, uneven in texture
jalebi spirals of fried batter soaked in syrup
laddoo lentil based batter 'grains' shaped into rounds
rasgulla (roshgulla) balls of curd in clear syrup
sandesh dry sweet made of curd cheese

Snacks

bhaji, pakora vegetable fritters (onions, potatoes, cauliflower etc) deep-fried in batter
chat sweet and sour fruit and vegetables flavoured with tama rind paste and chillis
chana choor, chioora ('Bombay mix') lentil and flattened rice snacks mixed with nuts and dried fruit
dosa South Indian pancake made with rice and lentil flour; served with a mild potato and onion filling (*masala dosa*) or without (*ravai* or plain *dosa*)
idli steamed South Indian rice cakes, a bland breakfast given flavour by spiced accompaniments
kachori fried pastry rounds stuffed with spiced lentil/peas/potato filling
samosa cooked vegetable or meat wrapped in pastry triangles and deep fried
utthappam thick South Indian rice and lentil flour pancake cooked with spices/ onions/tomatoes
vadai deep fried, small savoury lentil 'doughnut' rings. **Dahi vada** are similar in yoghurt

Glossary

Words in italics are common elements of words, often making up part of a place name.

A

aarti (arati) Hindu worship with lamps
abacus square or rectangular table resting on top of a pillar
abad peopled
acanthus thick-leaved plant, common decoration on pillars, esp Greek
achalam hill (Tamil)
acharya religious teacher
Adi Granth Guru Granth Sahib, holy book of the Sikhs
Adinatha first of the 24 Tirthankaras, distinguished by his bull mount
agarbathi incense
Agastya legendary sage who brought the Vedas to South India
Agni Vedic fire divinity, intermediary between gods and men, guardian of the Southeast
ahimsa non-harming, non-violence
akhand path unbroken reading of the Guru Granth Sahib
alinda verandah
amalaka See amla
ambulatory processional path
amla (amalaka) circular ribbed pattern (based on a gourd) at the top of a temple tower
amrita ambrosia; drink of immortality
ana See anna
ananda joy
Ananda the Buddha's chief disciple
Ananta a huge snake on whose coils Vishnu rests
anda literally 'egg', spherical part of the stupa
Andhaka demon killed by Siva
anicut irrigation channel (Tamil)
anna (ana) one sixteenth of a rupee (still occasionally referred to)
Annapurna Goddess of abundance; one aspect of Devi
antarala vestibule, chamber in front of shrine or cella
antechamber chamber in front of the sanctuary
apsara celestial nymph
apse semi-circular plan
arabesque ornamental decoration with intertwining lines
aram pleasure garden
arati See aarti
architrave horizontal beam across posts or gateways
ardha mandapam chamber in front of main hall of temple
Ardhanarisvara Siva represented as half-male and half-female
Arjuna hero of the Mahabharata, to whom Krishna delivered the Bhagavad Gita
arrack alcoholic spirit fermented from potatoes or grain
aru river (Tamil)
Aruna charioteer of Surya, Sun God; Red
Aryans literally 'noble' (Sanskrit); prehistoric peoples who settled in Persia and North India
asana a seat or throne (Buddha's) pose
ashram hermitage or retreat
Ashta Matrikas The eight mother goddesses who attended on Siva or Skanda
astanah threshold
atman philosophical concept of universal soul or spirit
atrium court open to the sky in the centre. In modern architecture, enclosed in glass
aus summer rice crop (Apr-Aug) Bengal
Avalokiteshwara Lord who looks down; Bodhisattva, the Compassionate
avatara 'descent'; incarnation of a divinity
ayacut irrigation command area (Tamil)
ayah nursemaid, especially for children

B

babu clerk
bada cubical portion of a temple up to the roof or spire
badgir rooftop structure to channel cool breeze into the house
badlands eroded landscape
bagh garden
bahadur title, meaning 'the brave'
baksheesh tip 'bribe'
Balabhadra Balarama, elder brother of Krishna
baluster balustrade, a small column supporting a handrail
bandh a strike
bandhani tie dyeing
Bangla (Bangaldar) curved roof, based on thatched roofs in Bengal
bania merchant caste
banian vest
baoli or vav rectangular well surrounded by steps
baradari literally '12-pillared', a pavilion with columns
barrel-vault semi-cylindrical shaped roof or ceiling
bas-relief carving of low projection
basement lower part of walls, usually with decorated mouldings
basti Jain temple
batter slope of a wall, especially in a fort
bazar market
bedi (vedi) altar/platform for reading holy texts
beedi See bidi
begum Muslim princess/woman's courtesy title
beki circular stone below the *amla* in the finial of a roof
belvedere summer house; small room on a house roof
bhadra flat face of the sikhara (tower)
Bhadrakali Tantric goddess and consort of Bhairav
Bhagavad-Gita Song of the Lord; section of the Mahabharata
Bhagiratha the king who prayed to Ganga to descend to earth
bhai brother
Bhairava Siva, the Fearful
bhakti adoration of a deity
bhang Indian hemp
Bharata half-brother of Rama

bhavan building or house
bhikku Buddhist monk
Bhima Pandava hero of the Mahabharata, famous for his strength
Bhimsen Deity worshipped for his strength and courage
bhisti a water-carrier
bhogamandapa the refectory hall of a temple
bhumi literally earth; a horizontal moulding of a sikhara
bidi (beedi) Indian cigarette, tobacco wrapped in tendu leaves
bigha measure of land – normally about one-third of an acre
Bo-tree (or Bodhi) *Ficus religiosa*, pipal tree associated with the Buddha
Bodhisattva Enlightened One, destined to become Buddha
bodi tuft of hair on back of the shaven head (also *tikki*)
Brahma Universal self-existing power; Creator in the Hindu Triad.
Brahmachari religious student, accepting rigorous discipline (eg chastity)
Brahman (Brahmin) highest Hindu (and Jain) caste of priests
Brahmanism ancient Indian religion, precursor of modern Hinduism
Buddha The Enlightened One; founder of Buddhism
bund an embankment
bundh (literally closed) a strike
burj tower or bastion
burqa (burkha) over-dress worn by Muslim women observing purdah
bustee slum

C

cantonment planned military or civil area in town
capital upper part of a column
caryatid sculptured human female figure used as a support for columns
catamaran log raft, logs (*maram*) tied (*kattu*) together (Tamil)
cave temple rock-cut shrine or monastery
cella small chamber, compartment for the image of a deity
cenotaph commemorative monument, usually an open-domed pavilion
chaam Himalayan Buddhist masked dance
chadar sheet worn as clothing
chai tea
chaitya large arched opening in the façade of a hall or Buddhist temple
chajja overhanging cornice or eaves
chakra sacred Buddhist wheel of the law; also Vishnu's discus
chala Bengali curved roof
Chamunda terrifying form of the goddess Durga
Chandra Moon; a planetary deity
chankramana place of the promenade of the Buddha at Bodh Gaya
chapati unleavened Indian bread cooked on a griddle
chaprassi messenger or orderly usually wearing a badge
char sand-bank or island in a river
char bagh formal Mughal garden, divided into quarters
char bangla (char-chala) 'four temples' in Bengal, built like huts
charan footprint
charka spinning wheel
charpai 'four legs' – wooden frame string bed
chatt(r)a ceremonial umbrella on stupa (Buddhist)
chauk See chowk
chauki recessed space between pillars: entrance
chaukidar (chowkidar) night-watchman; guard
chaultri (choultry) travellers' rest house (Telugu)
chaumukha Jain sanctuary with a quadruple image, approached through four doorways
chauri fly-whisk, symbol for royalty
chauth 25% tax raised for revenue by Marathas
cheri outcaste settlement; slum (Tamil Nadu)
chhang strong mountain beer of fermented barley maize rye or millet or rice
chhatri umbrella shaped dome or pavilion
chhetri (kshatriya) Hindu warrior caste
chit sabha hall of wisdom (Tamil)
chitrakar picture maker
chlorite soft greenish stone that hardens on exposure
choli blouse
choultry See chaultri
chowk (chauk) a block; open place in a city where the market is held
chowkidar See chaukidar
chunam lime plaster or stucco made from burnt seashells
circumambulation clockwise movement around a shrine
clerestory upper section of the walls of a building which allows light in
cloister passage usually around an open square
coir fibre from coconut husk
corbel horizontal block supporting a vertical structure or covering an opening
cornice horizontal band at the top of a wall
crewel work chain stitching
crore 10 million
cupola small dome
curvilinear gently curving shape, generally of a tower
cusp, cusped projecting point between small sections of an arch
cutcha See kutcha

D

daal lentils, pulses
dacoit bandit
dada (dadu) grandfather; elder brother
dado part of a pedestal between its base and cornice
dahi yoghurt
dais raised platform
dak bungalow rest house for officials
dak post
dakini sorceress
Dakshineshvara Lord of the South; name of Siva
dan gift
dandi wooden 'seat' carried by bearers
darbar (durbar) a royal gathering

dargah a Muslim tomb complex
darshan (darshana) viewing of a deity or spiritual leader
darwaza gateway, door
Dasara (dassara/dussehra/dassehra) 10-day festival in Sep-Oct
Dasaratha King of Ayodhya and father of Rama
Dattatraya syncretistic deity; an incarnation of Vishnu, a teacher of Siva, or a cousin of the Buddha
daulat khana treasury
dentil small block used as part of a cornice
dervish member of Muslim brotherhood, committed to poverty
deval memorial pavilion built to mark royal funeral pyre
devala temple or shrine (Buddhist or Hindu)
devasthanam temple trust
Devi Goddess; later, the Supreme Goddess
dhaba roadside restaurant, truck drivers' stop
dharamshala (dharamsala) pilgrims' rest-house
dharma moral and religious duty
dharmachakra wheel of 'moral' law (Buddhist)
dhobi washerman
dhol drums
dhooli swinging chair on a pole, carried by bearers
dhoti loose loincloth worn by Indian men
dhurrie See durrie
dhyana meditation
digambara literally 'sky-clad' Jain sect in which the monks go naked
dikka raised platform around ablution tank
dikpala guardian of one of the cardinal directions mostly appearing in a group of eight
dikshitar person who makes oblations or offerings
dipdan lamp pillar
divan (diwan) smoking-room; also a chief minister
Diwali festival of lights (Oct-Nov)
diwan See divan
diwan-i-am hall of public audience
diwan-i-khas hall of private audience
diwan chief financial minister
doab interfluve, land between two rivers
dokra tribal name for lost wax metal casting (cire perdu)
dosa (dosai) thin pancake
double dome composed of an inner and outer shell of masonry
Draupadi wife-in-common of the five Pandava brothers in the Mahabharata
drug *(durg)* fort (Tamil, Telugu)
dry masonry stones laid without mortar
duar (dwar) door, gateway
dun valley
durbar See darbar
durg See drug
Durga principal goddess of the Shakti cult
durrie (dhurrie) thick handloom rug
durwan watchman
Dussehra See dasara
dvarpala doorkeeper
dvipa lamp-column, generally of stone or brass-covered wood
dwar See duar

E

eave overhang that shelters a porch or verandah
ek the number 1, a symbol of unity
ekka one-horse carriage
epigraph carved inscription
eri tank (Tamil)

F

faience coloured tilework, earthenware or porcelain
fakir Muslim religious mendicant
fan-light fan-shaped window over door
fenestration the use of windows or openings
filigree ornamental work or delicate tracery
finial emblem at the summit of a stupa, tower, dome, or at the end of a parapet
firman edict or grant issued by a sovereign

G

gable end of an angled roof
gaddi throne
gadi/gari car, cart, train
gali (galli) lane, alley
gana child figures in art
Ganapati See Ganesh
Gandharva semi-divine flying figure; celestial musician
Ganesh (Ganapati) elephant-headed son of Siva and Parvati
Ganga goddess personifying the Ganges
ganj market
ganja Indian hemp
gaon village
garbhagriha literally 'womb-chamber'; a temple sanctuary
garh fort
Garuda Mythical eagle, half-human Vishnu's vehicle
Gauri 'Fair One'; Parvati
Gaurishankara Siva with Parvati
ghagra (ghongra) long flared skirt
ghanta bell
ghat hill range, hill road; landing place; steps on the river bank
ghazal Urdu lyric poetry/love songs, often erotic
ghee clarified butter for cooking
gherao industrial action, surrounding home or office of politician or industrial manager
ghongra See ghagra
giri hill
Gita Govinda Jayadeva's poem of the Krishnalila
godown warehouse
gola conical-shaped storehouse
Gopala (Govinda) cowherd; a name of Krishna
Gopis cowherd girls; milk maids who played with Krishna
gopuram towered gateway in South Indian temples
Gorakhnath historically, an 11th-century yogi who founded a Saivite cult; an incarnation of Siva
gosain monk or devotee (Hindi)
Govinda See Gopala
gram chick pea, pulse
gram village; gramadan, gift of village
gudi temple (Karnataka)

gumbaz (gumbad) dome
gumpha monastery, cave temple
gur palm sugar
guru teacher; spiritual leader, Sikh religious leader

H

Haj (Hajj) annual Muslim pilgrimage to Mecca
haat See hat
hakim judge; a physician (usually Muslim)
halwa a special sweet meat
hammam Turkish bath
Hanuman Monkey devotee of Rama; bringer of success to armies
Hara (Hara Siddhi) Siva
harem women's quarters (Muslim), from 'haram', Arabic for 'forbidden by law'
Hari Vishnu Harihara, Vishnu-Siva as a single divinity
Hariti goddess of prosperity and patroness of children, consort of Kubera
harmika the finial of a stupa in the form of a pedestal where the shaft of the honorific umbrella was set
hartal general strike
Hasan the murdered eldest son of Ali, commemorated at Muharram
hat (haat) market
hathi pol elephant gate
hathi (hati) elephant
hauz tank or reservoir
haveli a merchant's house usually in Rajasthan
havildar army sergeant
hawa mahal palace of the winds
Hidimba Devi Durga worshipped at Manali
hindola swing
hippogryph fabulous griffin-like creature with body of a horse
Hiranyakashipu Demon king killed by Narasimha
hiti a water channel; a bath or tank with water spouts
Holi spring festival (Feb-Mar)
hookah 'hubble bubble' or smoking vase
howdah seat on elephant's back, sometimes canopied
hundi temple offering
Hussain the second murdered son of Ali, commemorated at Muharram
huzra a Muslim tomb chamber
hypostyle hall with pillars

I

Iat pillar, column
icon statue or image of worship
Id principal Muslim festivals
Idgah open space for the Id prayers
idli steamed rice cake (Tamil)
ikat 'resist-dyed' woven fabric
imam Muslim religious leader
imambara tomb of a Shiite Muslim holy man; focus of Muharram procession
Indra King of the gods; God of rain; guardian of the East
Ishana Guardian of the North East
Ishvara Lord; Siva
iwan main arch in mosque

J

jadu magic
Jagadambi literally Mother of the World, Parvati
Jagannath literally Lord of the World, particularly Krishna worshipped at Puri
jagati railed parapet
jaggery brown sugar, made from palm sap
jahaz ship, building in form of ship
jali literally 'net'; any lattice or perforated pattern
jama See jami
jamb vertical side slab of doorway
Jambudvipa Continent of the Rose-Apple Tree; the earth
jami masjid (Jama, Jumma) Friday mosque, for congregational worship
Jamuna Hindu goddess who rides a tortoise; river
Janaka Father of Sita
jangha broad band of sculpture on the outside of the temple wall
jarokha balcony
jataka stories accounts of the previous lives of the Buddha
jauhar mass suicide by fire of women, to avoid capture
jawab literally 'answer,' a building which duplicates another to provide symmetry
jawan army recruit, soldier
jaya stambha victory tower
jee See ji
jheel (jhil) lake; a marsh; a swamp
jhilmil projecting canopy over a window or door opening
ji (jee) honorific suffix added to names out of reverence and/or politeness; also abbreviated 'yes' (Hindi/Urdu)
jihad striving in the way of god; holy war by Muslims against non-believers
Jina literally 'victor'; spiritual conqueror or Tirthankara, after whom Jainism is named
Jogini mystical goddess
Jyotirlinga luminous energy of Siva manifested at 12 holy places, miraculously formed lingams

K

kabalai (kavalai) well irrigation using bullock power (Tamil Nadu)
kabigan folk debate in verse
kacha See kutcha
kachcha man's 'under-shorts' (one of five Sikh symbols)
kacheri (kutchery) a court; an office for public business
kadal wooden bridge (Kashmir)
kadu forest (Tamil)
Kailasa mountain home of Siva
kalamkari special painted cotton hanging from Andhra
kalasha pot-like finial of a tower
Kali literally 'black'; terrifying form of the goddess Durga, wearing a necklace of skulls/heads
Kalki future incarnation of Vishnu on horseback
kalyanamandapa marriage hall
kameez women's shirt
kanga comb (one of five Sikh symbols)
kankar limestone pieces, used for road making

kapok the silk cotton tree
kara steel bracelet (one of five Sikh symbols)
karma impurity resulting from past misdeeds
Kartikkeya (Kartik) Son of Siva, God of war
kashi-work special kind of glazed tiling, probably derived from Kashan in Persia
kati-roll Muslim snack of meat rolled in a 'paratha' bread
kavalai See kabalai
keep tower of a fort, stronghold
kere tank (Kanarese)
keystone central wedge-shaped block in a masonry arch
khadi woven cotton cloth made from home-spun cotton (or silk) yarn
khal creek, canal
khana suffix for room/office/place; also food or meal
khanqah Muslim (Sufi) hospice
kharif monsoon season crop
khave khana tea shop
kheda enclosure in which wild elephants are caught; elephant depot
khet field
khola river or stream in Nepal
khondalite crudely grained basalt
khukri traditional curved Gurkha weapon
kirpan sabre, dagger (one of five Sikh symbols)
kirti-stambha 'pillar of fame,' free standing pillar in front of temple
kohl antimony, used as eye shadow
koil See kovil
konda hill (Telugu)
kos minars Mughal 'mile' stones
kot (kota/kottai/kotte) fort
kothi house
kotla citadel
kovil (koil) temple (Tamil)
Krishna Eighth incarnation of Vishnu
kritis South Indian devotional music
kshatriya See chhetri
Kubera Chief yaksha; keeper of the treasures of the earth, Guardian of the North
kulam tank or pond (Tamil)
kumar a young man. See also kumhar
Kumari Virgin, Durga
kumbha a vase-like motif, pot
Kumbhayog auspicious time for bathing to wash away sins
kumhar (kumar) potter
kund lake, well or pool
kuppam hamlet (Tamil)
kurti-kanchali small blouse
kutcha (cutcha/kacha) raw, crude, unpaved, built with sun-dried bricks
kutchery See kacheri
kwabgah bedroom; literally 'palace of dreams'

L

lakh 100,000
Lakshmana younger brother of Rama
Lakshmi Goddess of wealth and good fortune, consort of Vishnu
Lakulisha founder of the Pashupata sect, believed to be an incarnation of Siva
lama Buddhist priest in Tibet
lassi iced yoghurt drink
lath monolithic pillar
lathi bamboo stick with metal bindings, used by police
lena cave, usually a rock-cut sanctuary
lingam (linga) Siva as the phallic emblem
Lingaraja Siva worshipped at Bhubaneswar
liwan cloisters of a mosque
Lokeshwar 'Lord of the World', Avalokiteshwara to Buddhists and form of Siva to Hindus
lunette semicircular window opening
lungi wrapped-around loin cloth, normally checked

M

madrassa Islamic theological school or college
mahamandapam large enclosed hall in front of main shrine
maha great
Mahabharata Sanskrit epic about the battle between the Pandavas and Kauravas
Mahabodhi Great Enlightenment of Buddha
Mahadeva literally 'Great Lord'; Siva
mahal palace, grand building
mahalla (mohulla) division of a town, quarter, ward
mahant head of a monastery
maharaja great king
maharana Rajput clan head
maharani great queen
Maharishi (Maharshi) literally 'great teacher'
Mahavira literally 'Great Hero', last of the 24 Tirthankaras, founder of Jainism
Mahayana The Greater Vehicle; form of Buddhism practised in East Asia, Tibet and Nepal
Mahesha (Maheshvara) Great Lord, Siva
Mahisha Buffalo demon killed by Durga
mahout elephant driver/keeper
mahseer large freshwater fish found especially in Himalayan rivers
maidan large open grassy area in a town
Maitreya the future Buddha
makara crocodile-shaped mythical creature symbolizing the river Ganga
makhan butter
malai hill (Tamil)
mali gardener
Manasa Snake goddess; Sakti
manastambha free-standing pillar in front of temple
mandala geometric diagram symbolizing the structure of the Universe
mandalam region, tract of country (Tamil)
Mandapa (mukha) columned hall preceding the temple sanctuary
mandi market
mandir temple
mani (mani wall) stones with sacred inscriptions at Buddhist sites
mantra chant for meditation by Hindus and Buddhists
maqbara chamber of a Muslim tomb
Mara Tempter, who sent his daughters (and soldiers) to disturb the Buddha's meditation

marg wide roadway
masjid literally 'place of prostration'; mosque
mata mother
math Hindu or Jain monastery
maulana scholar (Muslim)
maulvi religious teacher (Muslim)
maund measure of weight about 20 kilos
mausoleum large tomb building
maya illusion
medallion circle or part-circle framing a figure or decorative motif
meena enamel work
Meenakshi literally 'fish-eyed'; Parvati
mela festival or fair, usually Hindu
memsahib married European woman, term used mainly before Independence
Meru mountain supporting the heavens
mihrab niche in the western wall of a mosque
mimbar pulpit in mosque
minar (minaret) slender tower of a mosque
mitthai Indian sweets
mithuna couple in sexual embrace
mofussil the country as distinct from the town
Mohammad 'the praised', The Prophet, founder of Islam
mohulla See mahalla
moksha salvation, enlightenment; literally 'release'
moonstone the semi circular stone step before a shrine (also *chandrasila*)
mouza (mowza) village, a parcel of land having a separate name in the revenue records
mridangam barrel-shaped drum (musical)
muballigh second prayer leader
mudra symbolic hand gesture
muezzin mosque official who calls the faithful to prayer
Muharram period of mourning in remembrance of Hasan and Hussain, two murdered sons of Ali
mukha See mandapa
mullah religious teacher (Muslim)
mund Toda village
muqarna Muslim stalactite design
mural wall decoration
musalla prayer mat
muta limited duration marriage (Leh)
muthi measure equal to 'a handful'

N

nadi river
nadu region, country (Tamil)
Naga (nagi/nagini) Snake deity; associated with fertility and protection
nagara city, sometimes capital
nakkar khana (naggar or naubat khana) drum house, arched structure or gateway for musicians
nal mandapa porch over a staircase
nallah (nullah) ditch, channel
namaaz Muslim prayers, worship
namaste common Hindu greeting (with joined palms) translated as: 'I salute all divine qualities in you'
namda rug
Nandi a bull, Siva's vehicle and a symbol of fertility
nara durg large fort built on a flat plain
Narayana Vishnu as the creator of life
nata mandapa (nat-mandir; nritya sala) dancing hall in a temple
Nataraja Siva, Lord of the cosmic dance
nath literally 'place' eg Amarnath
natya the art of dance
nautch display by dancing girls
navagraha nine planets, represented usually on the lintel or architrave of the front door of a temple
navaranga central hall of temple
navaratri literally '9 nights'; name of the Dasara festival
nawab prince, wealthy Muslim, sometimes used as a title
niche wall recess containing a sculpted image or emblem, mostly framed by a pair of pilasters
Nihang literally 'crocodile': followers of Guru Gobind Singh (Sikh)
nirvana enlightenment; literally 'extinguished'
niwas small palace
nritya pure dance
nullah See nallah

P

pada foot or base
padam dance which tells a story
padma lotus flower, Padmasana, lotus seat; posture of meditating figures
paga projecting pilaster-like surface of an Orissan temple
pagoda tall structure in several stories
pahar hill
paisa (poisa) one hundredth of a rupee
palanquin covered litter for one, carried on poles
palayam minor kingdom (Tamil)
pali language of Buddhist scriptures
palli village
pan leaf of the betel vine; sliced areca nut, lime and other ingredients wrapped in leaf for chewing
panchayat a 'council of five'; a government system of elected councils
pandal marquee made of bamboo and cloth
pandas temple priests
pandit teacher or wise man, a Sanskrit scholar
pankah (punkha) fan, formerly pulled by a cord
parabdis special feeding place for birds
parapet wall extending above the roof
pargana sub-division of a district usually comprising many villages, a fiscal unit
Parinirvana the Buddha's state prior to nirvana, shown usually as a reclining figure
parishads political division of group of villages
Parsi (Parsee) Zoroastrians who fled from Iran to West India in the eighth century to avoid persecution
parterre level space in a garden occupied by flowerbeds
Parvati daughter of the Mountain. Siva's consort
pashmina fine wool from a mountain goat
Pashupati literally Lord of the Beasts, Siva
pata painted hanging scroll
patan town or city (Sanskrit)
patel village headman

patha See pradakshina
patina green film that covers materials exposed to air
pattachitra specially painted cloth
pau measure for vegetables and fruit equal to 250g
paya soup
pediment mouldings, often in a triangular formation above an opening or niche
pendant hanging, a motif depicted upside down
peon servant, messenger (from Portuguese *peao*)
peristyle range of columns surrounding a court or temple
Persian wheel well irrigation system using bucket lift
pettah suburbs, outskirts of town (Tamil: *pettai*)
pice (old form) one 100th of a rupee
picottah water lift using horizontal pole pivoted on vertical pole (Tamil Nadu)
pida (pitha) basement
pietra dura inlaid mosaic of hard, semi-precious stones
pilaster ornamental small column, with capital and bracket
pinjra lattice work
pinjrapol animal hospital (Jain)
pipal *Ficus religiosa*, the Bodhi tree
pir Muslim holy man
pitha base, pedestal. See pida
pithasthana place of pilgrimage
podium stone bench; low pedestal wall
poisa See paisa
pokana bathing tank (Sri Lanka)
pol fortified gateway
porch covered entrance to a shrine or hall, generally open and with columns
portico space enclosed between columns
pradakshina (patha) processional passage
prakaram open courtyard
pralaya the end of the world
prasadam consecrated temple food
prayag confluence considered sacred by Hindus
puja ritual offerings to the gods; worship (Hindu)
pujari worshipper; one who performs puja (Hindu)
pukka literally 'ripe' or 'finished'; reliable; solidly built
punkha See pankah
punya merit earned through actions and religious devotion (Buddhist)
Puranas literally 'the old' Sanskrit sacred poems
purdah literally curtains, seclusion of Muslim women from public view
pushkarani sacred pool or tank

Q

qabr Muslim grave
qibla direction for Muslim prayer
qila fort
Quran holy Muslim scriptures
qutb axis or pivot

R

rabi winter/spring season crop
Radha Krishna's favourite consort
raiyat See ryot
raj rule or government
raja (rao, rawal) king, ruler
rajbari palaces of a small kingdom
Rajput dynasties of western and central India
Rakshakas Earth spirits
Rama Seventh incarnation of Vishnu
Ramayana Sanskrit epic – the story of Rama
Ramazan (Ramadan) Muslim month of fasting
rangamandapa painted hall or theatre
rani queen
rao See raja
rath chariot or temple car
Ravana Demon king of Lanka; kidnapper of Sita
rawal head priest. See also raja
rayat See ryot
rekha curvilinear portion of a spire or sikhara (rekha deul, sanctuary, curved tower of an Orissan temple)
reredos screen behind an altar
rickshaw 3-wheeled bicycle-powered (or 2-wheeled hand-powered) vehicle
Rig (Rg) Veda oldest and most sacred of the Vedas
rishi 'seer'; inspired poet, philosopher
rupee unit of currency in India
ryot (rayat/raiyat) a subject, a cultivator, a farmer

S

sabha columned hall (*sabha mandapa*, assembly hall)
sabzi vegetables, vegetable curry
sadar (sadr/saddar) chief, main especially Sikh
sadhu ascetic, religious mendicant, holy man
sagar lake, reservoir
sahib title of address, like 'sir'
sahn open courtyard of a mosque
Saiva (Shaiva) the cult of Siva
sal a hall
salaam literally 'peace'; greeting (Muslim)
salwar (shalwar) loose trousers (Punjab)
samadh(i) literally concentrated thought, meditation, a funerary memorial
sambar lentil and vegetable soup dish, accompanying main meal (Tamil)
samsara transmigration of the soul
samudra large tank or inland sea
sangam junction of rivers
sangarama monastery
sangha ascetic order founded by Buddha
sangrahalaya rest-house for Jain pilgrims
sankha (shankha) the conch shell (symbolically held by Vishnu), the shell bangle worn by Bengali women
sanyasi wandering ascetic, final stage in the ideal life of a man
sarai caravansarai, halting place
saranghi small four-stringed viola shaped from a single piece of wood
Saraswati wife of Brahma and goddess of knowledge
sarkar the government, the state, a writer, an accountant
sarod Indian stringed musical instrument
sarvodaya uplift, improvement of all
sati (suttee) a virtuous woman, act of self-immolation on a husband's funeral pyre
Sati wife of Siva who destroyed herself by fire
satyagraha 'truth force', passive resistance

sayid title (Muslim)
schist grey or green finely grained stone
seer (ser) weight (about 1 kg)
sepoy (sepai) Indian soldier, private
Sesha See Shesha
seth merchant, businessman
seva voluntary service
shahnai See shehnai
shahtush very fine wool from the Tibetan antelope
Shaiva See Saiva
Shakti Energy, female divinity often associated with Siva
shala barrel-vaulted roof
shalagrama stone containing fossils worshipped as a form of Vishnu
shalwar See salwar
shaman doctor/priest, using magic, an exorcist
shamiana cloth canopy
Shankara Siva
shankha See sankha
sharia corpus of Muslim theological law
shastras ancient texts defining temple architecture
shastri religious title (Hindu)
sheesh mahal palace apartment with mirror work
shehnai (shahnai) Indian oboe-like wind instrument
sherwani knee-length coat for men
Shesha (Sesha) serpent who supports Vishnu
shikar hunting
shisham a valuable building timber
Shiva See Siva
sikhara curved temple tower or spire
shloka (sloka) Sanskrit sacred verse
shola patch of forest or wood (Tamil)
shri See sri
sileh khana armoury
sindur vermilion powder used in temple ritual, married women mark their hair parting with it
singh (sinha) lion, Rajput caste name adopted by Sikhs
sinha stambha lion pillar. See also Singh
sirdar a guide who leads trekking groups
Sita Rama's wife, heroine of the Ramayana epic
sitar classical stringed musical instrument with a gourd for soundbox
Siva (Shiva) The Destroyer in the Hindu triad of Gods
Sivaratri literally 'Siva's night', a festival in Feb-Mar
Skanda the Hindu god of war, Kartikkeya
sloka See shloka
soma sacred drink mentioned in the Vedas
spandrel triangular space between the curve of an arch and the square enclosing it
squinch arch across an interior angle
sri (shri, sree) honorific title, often used for 'Mr', repeated as sign of great respect
sridhara pillar with octagonal shaft and square base
stalactite system of vaulting, remotely resembling stalactite formations in a cave
stambha free-standing column or pillar, often for a lamp or figure
steatite finely grained grey mineral
stele upright, inscribed slab used as a gravestone
sthan place (suffix)
stupa hemispheric Buddhist funerary mound
stylobate base on which a colonnade is placed
Subahdar (subedar) the governor of a province, viceroy under the Mughals
Subrahmanya Skanda, one of Siva's sons; Kartikkeya in South India
sudra lowest of the Hindu castes
sufi Muslim mystic
sufism Muslim mystic worship
sultan Muslim prince (sultana, wife of sultan)
Surya Sun, Sun God
suttee See sati
svami (swami) holy man, a suffix for temple deities
svastika (swastika) auspicious Hindu/Buddhist cross-like sign
swadeshi home made goods
swaraj home rule
swatantra freedom

T

tabla a pair of drums
tahr wild goat
tahsildar revenue collector
taikhana underground apartments
takht throne
talao (*tal*, talar) water tank
taluk administrative subdivision of a district
tamasha spectacle, festive celebration
tandava (dance) of Siva
tank lake dug for irrigation, a masonry-lined temple pool with stepped sides
tapas (tapasya) ascetic meditative self-denial
Tara literally 'star', a goddess
tatties cane or grass screens used for shade
Teej Hindu festival
tempera distemper, method of mural painting by means of a 'body', such as white pigment
tempo three-wheeler vehicle
teri soil formed from wind-blown sand (Tamil Nadu)
thali South and West Indian vegetarian meal
thana a police jurisdiction, police station
thangka (thankha) cloth (often silk) painted with a Tibetan Mahayana deity
thug professional robber/murderer (Central India)
tiffin snack, light meal
tika (tilak) vermilion powder, auspicious mark on the forehead, often decorative
tikka tender pieces of meat, marinated and barbecued
tilak See tika
tillana abstract dance
tirtha ford, bathing place, holy spot (Sanskrit)
Tirthankara literally 'ford-maker', title given to 24 religious 'teachers', worshipped by Jains
tonga two-wheeled horse carriage
topi (topee) pith helmet
torana gateway, two posts with an architrave
tottam garden (Tamil)
tribhanga triple-bended pose for standing figures
Trimurti the Hindu Triad, Brahma, Vishnu and Siva
tripolia triple gateway
trisul the trident chief symbol of the god Siva
triveni triple-braided

tsampa ground, roasted barley, eaten dry or mixed with milk, tea or water (Himalayan)
tuk fortified enclosure containing Jain shrines
tulsi sacred basil plant
tympanum triangular space within cornices

U

Uma Siva's consort in one of her many forms
untouchable 'outcastes', with whom contact of any kind was believed by high caste Hindus to be defiling
Upanishads ancient Sanskrit philosophical texts, part of the Vedas
ur village (Tamil)
usta painted camel leather goods
ustad master
uttarayana northwards

V

vahana 'vehicle' of the deity
vaisya 'middle-class' caste of merchants and farmers
Valmiki sage, author of the Ramayana epic
Vamana dwarf incarnation of Vishñu
vana grove, forest
Varaha boar incarnation of Vishnu
varam village (Tamil)
varna 'colour'; social division of Hindus into Brahmin, Kshatriya, Vaishya and Sudra
Varuna Guardian of the West, accompanied by Makara (see above)
vav See wav
Vayu Wind god; Guardian of the North-West
Veda (Vedic) oldest known Hindu religious texts
vedi (bedi) altar, also a wall or screen
Vedic See Veda
verandah enlarged porch in front of a hall
vihara Buddhist or Jain monastery with cells around a courtyard
vilas house or pleasure palace
vimana towered sanctuary containing the cell in which the deity is enshrined
vina plucked stringed instrument, relative of sitar
Vishnu a principal Hindu deity, the Preserver (and Creator)
vyala (yali) leogryph, mythical lion-like sculpture

W

wallah suffix often used with a occupational name, eg rickshaw-wallah
wav (vav) step-well, particularly in Gujarat and western India (*baoli*)
wazir chief minister of a raja (from Turkish 'vizier')

Y

yagya (yajna) major ceremonial sacrifice
Yaksha (Yakshi) a demi-god, associated with nature
yali see vyala
Yama God of death, judge of the living
yantra magical diagram used in meditation, instrument
yatra pilgrimage
Yellow Hat Gelugpa Sect of Tibetan Buddhism – monks wear yellow headdress
yoga school of philosophy stressing mental and physical disciplines
yogi teacher of yoga
yoni a hole symbolizing female sexuality, vagina

Z

zamindar a landlord granted income under the Mughals
zari silver and gold thread used in weaving or embroidery
zarih cenotaph in a Muslim tomb
zenana segregated women's apartments
ziarat holy Muslim tomb
zilla (zillah) district

Index

→ *Entries in bold refer to maps.*

Abbreviations used for state references: AP = Andhra Pradesh; Goa = Goa; Kar = Karnataka; Ke = Kerala; Lak = Lakshadweep Islands; TN = Tamil Nad

Footnotes Index

U

V

W

Y

Z

Advertisers' index

South India

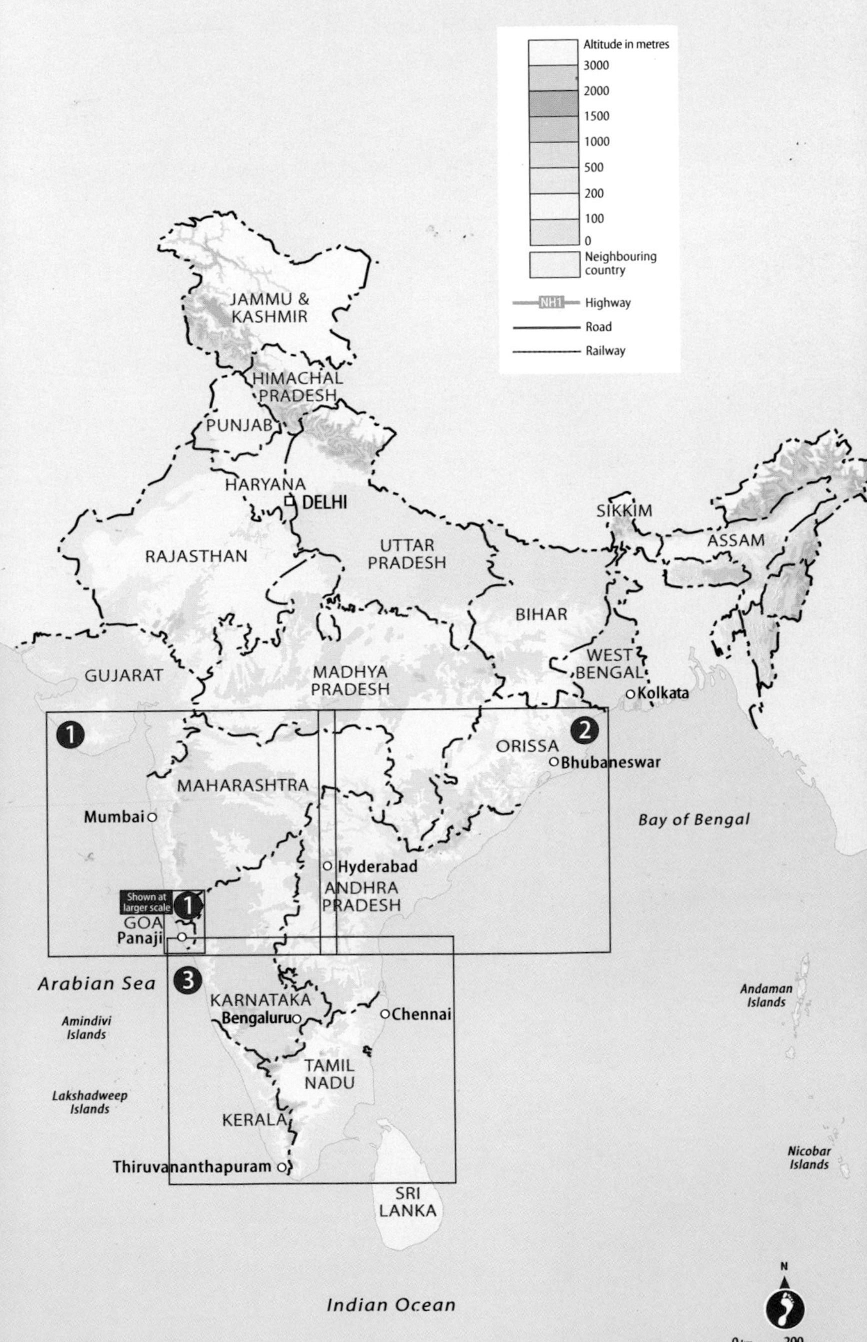

Altitude in metres
3000
2000
1500
1000
500
200
100
0
Neighbouring country
NH1 Highway
Road
Railway
JAMMU & KASHMIR
HIMACHAL PRADESH
PUNJAB
HARYANA
DELHI
RAJASTHAN
UTTAR PRADESH
SIKKIM
ASSAM
BIHAR
WEST BENGAL
Kolkata
GUJARAT
MADHYA PRADESH
1
2
ORISSA
Bhubaneswar
MAHARASHTRA
Mumbai
Bay of Bengal
Hyderabad
ANDHRA PRADESH
Shown at larger scale
1
GOA
Panaji
Arabian Sea
3
KARNATAKA
Bengaluru
Chennai
Andaman Islands
Amindivi Islands
TAMIL NADU
Lakshadweep Islands
KERALA
Thiruvananthapuram
Nicobar Islands
SRI LANKA
Indian Ocean
N
0 km 200
0 miles 200
The Government of India state that "the external boundaries of India are neither correct nor authenticated"

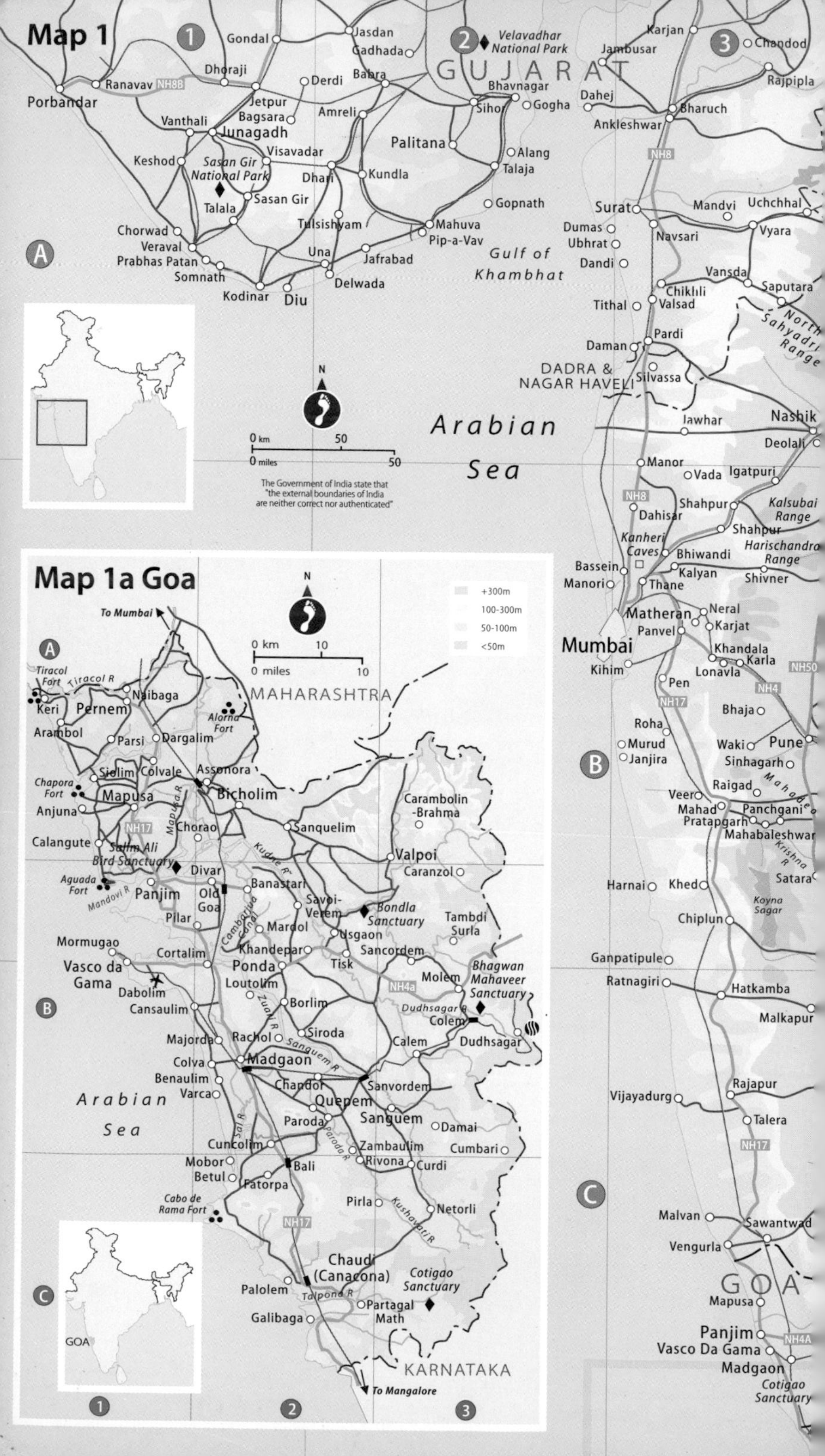
Map 1
Map 1a Goa
Arabian Sea
Gulf of Khambhat
GUJARAT
DADRA & NAGAR HAVELI
MAHARASHTRA
KARNATAKA
GOA
Porbandar
Ranavav
Gondal
Jasdan
Gadhada
Dhoraji
Derdi
Babra
Jetpur
Bagsara
Amreli
Bhavnagar
Sihor
Gogha
Vanthali
Junagadh
Visavadar
Palitana
Alang
Talaja
Keshod
Sasan Gir National Park
Dhari
Kundla
Sasan Gir
Talala
Gopnath
Tulsishyam
Mahuva
Pip-a-Vav
Chorwad
Veraval
Prabhas Patan
Somnath
Una
Jafrabad
Delwada
Kodinar
Diu
Velavadhar National Park
Karjan
Jambusar
Chandod
Rajpipla
Dahej
Bharuch
Ankleshwar
Surat
Mandvi
Uchchhal
Vyara
Dumas
Ubhrat
Dandi
Navsari
Vansda
Saputara
Chiklili
Valsad
Tithal
North Sahyadri Range
Pardi
Daman
Silvassa
Jawhar
Nashik
Deolali
Manor
Vada
Igatpuri
Shahpur
Kalsubai Range
Dahisar
Kanheri Caves
Bhiwandi
Harischandra Range
Bassein
Manori
Kalyan
Thane
Shivner
Matheran
Neral
Panvel
Karjat
Mumbai
Khandala
Kihim
Lonavla
Karla
Pen
Bhaja
Roha
Murud
Janjira
Waki
Pune
Sinhagarh
Raigad
Veer
Mahad
Panchgani
Pratapgarh
Mahabaleshwar
Krishna R
Satara
Harnai
Khed
Koyna Sagar
Chiplun
Ganpatipule
Ratnagiri
Hatkamba
Malkapur
Rajapur
Vijayadurg
Talera
Malvan
Sawantwad
Vengurla
Mapusa
Panjim
Vasco Da Gama
Madgaon
Cotigao Sanctuary
NH8B
NH8
NH17
NH4
NH50
NH4A
0 km 50
0 miles 50
The Government of India state that "the external boundaries of India are neither correct nor authenticated"
To Mumbai
0 km 10
0 miles 10
+300m
100-300m
50-100m
<50m
Tiracol Fort
Tiracol R
Keri
Naibaga
Pernem
Alorna Fort
Arambol
Parsi
Dargalim
Siolim
Colvale
Assonora
Chapora Fort
Mapusa
Bicholim
Anjuna
Chorao
Sanquelim
Carambolin -Brahma
Calangute
Salim Ali Bird Sanctuary
Valpoi
Aguada Fort
Divar
Caranzol
Mandovi R
Panjim
Old Goa
Banastari
Savoi-Verem
Bondla Sanctuary
Tambdi Surla
Pilar
Mardol
Usgaon
Mormugao
Cortalim
Khandepar
Sancordem
Vasco da Gama
Ponda
Tisk
Bhagwan Mahaveer Sanctuary
Dabolim
Loutolim
Molem
Cansaulim
Borlim
Dudhsagar R
Colem
Majorda
Rachol
Siroda
Calem
Dudhsagar
Colva
Madgaon
Benaulim
Chandor
Sanvordem
Varca
Quepem
Paroda
Sanguem
Damai
Cuncolim
Zambaulim
Cumbari
Mobor
Rivona
Curdi
Betul
Bali
Fatorpa
Cabo de Rama Fort
Pirla
Netorli
Kushavati R
NH17
NH4a
Chaudi (Canacona)
Cotigao Sanctuary
Palolem
Talpona R
Partagal Math
Galibaga
To Mangalore
GOA

MADHYA PRADESH
MAHARASHTRA
KARNATAKA
ANDHRA PRADESH
Narmada R
Narmada Gorge
Sanawad
Mandhatta Gorge
Purnasa L
Navdatoli
Julwania
Khandwa
Betul
Amla
Multai
Chiklhaldara
Melghat WLS
Gawilgarh Hills
Achalpur
Nandurbar
Burhanpur
Akot
Tapti R
NH3
NH6
Map 2
Sakri
Dhule
Jalgaon
Bhusawal
Jamner
Malkapur
Murtajapur
Amravati
Wardha
Badnera
Sevagram
Akola
Fardapur
Ajanta
Buldana
Girna R
Malegaon
Chandor
Chalisgaon
Shilod
Manmad
Ellora
Washim
Daulatabad
Lonar
Pandharkawada
Aurangabad
Jalna
Mahur
Ellora Hills
Hingol Hills
Hingol
Adilabad
Pandu Leni
Sangamner
Shrirampur
Kinwat WLS
Shirdi
Nirmal
NH50
Paithan
Junnar
Godavari R
Basmath
Parbhani
Nanded
Ahmadnagar
Agargaon Range
Bid
Purna
Pali
Godavari R
Balaghat Range
Armur
Jalgaon
Nizamabad
Bodham
Manjira R
Veshdi
Latur
Barsi
Udgir
Yellareddi
NH9
Dhond
Osmanabad
Kurduvadi
Kamareddi
Indapur
Medak
Deura
Baramati
Vadgaon
Mohol
Bidar
Pandharpur
Zahirabad
Solapur
Hotgi
Sangreddi
Homanabad
Aland
Morangpalli
Secunderabad
Golconda
Karad
Gulbarga
Vikarabad
Hyderabad
Sedam
Tandur
Ibrahimpatnam
Indi
NH4
Bhima R
Wadi
Panhala
Miraj
Mahbubnagar
Badepalli
Bijapur
Kolhapur
Athni
Yadgir
Bagevadi
Jamkhandi
Nidgundi
Shorapur
Krishna R
Talikota
Hunsigi
Mudhol
Muddebihal
Raichur
Gadwal
Linsugur
Bagalk
Gokak
Hungund
Krishna
Aihole
Alampur
Atmakur
Amboli
Belgaum
Ramdurg
Badami
Pattadakal
Tungabhadra
Kurnool
Mahakuta
NH13
Nargund
Kushtagi
Adoni
Nandyal
Alnavar
Dharwad
Gadag
Gangawati
Londa
Koppal
Hampi
Map 3
Hubli
Dambal
Lakkundi
Hospet
Ahobilam
Tungabhadra Dam
Bellary
Allagadda
Dandeli NP
Guntakal
Gooty
Shiggaon
Itiki
Swamihalli
Yellapur
Mundgod
Haveri
A
B
C
4
5
6

Map 3

Dandeli NP
Mundgod
Shiggaon
Yellapur
Karwar
Ankola
Gokarna
Haveri
Kudligi
Swamihalli
Bellary
Map 1
Molakalmuru
Kalyandr
Sirsi
Ranibennur
Jagalur
Kumta
Harihar
Siddapur
Davangere
Challakere
Honavar
Talguppa
Jog Falls
Tunga R
Bhadra R
Chitradurga
Manki
Sagar
Holalkere
Hiriyur
Pavagada
NH4
Bhatkal
Arasalu
Shimoga
Hosdurga
Hasangara
Bhadrav
Sira
Mandagaddi
Tarikere
Tirthahalli
Lakavalli
Bhadra
KARNATAKA
Kundapura
Sibi
Agumbe
Kemmannagundi
Kadur
Koratagere
NH17
Sringeri
Tumkur
Udupi
Malpe
Manipal
Chikmagalur
Ariskere
Dobbspet
Karkala
Mudigere
Halebid
Tiptur
Sivaganga
Belur
Mudabidri
Kunigal
Sakleshpur
Hassan
Nelligere
NH48
Beltangadi
Yediyur
Mangalore
Bantval
Sravanbelgaola
Ramanagara
Nagamangala
Channapatna
Holenarsipur
COORG (KODAGU)
Puttur
Maddur
Kasargod
Mandya
Halag
Kaveri
Madikeri
Kushalnagar
Malavalli
Bekal
Krishnarajasagar
Sivasamudra
Kanhangad
Talacauvery
Srirangapatnam
Hunsur
Mysore
Kollegal
Ezhimala
Virajendrapet
Nagarhole National Park
Somnathpur
Nanjangud
Chemrajnag
Karapur
Kannur
Gundlupet
Bandipur National Park
Thalassery
Manandavady
Mahe
Sulthan Bathery
Bhava Saga
Mudumalai WLS
Arabian Sea
Kalpetta
Gudal
Udhagamandalam (Ooty)
Vyttiri
Satyamangala
Kappad
Mettupalaya
Kozhikode
KERALA
Coonoor
Beypore
Nilanbur
Avanas
Malappuram
Silent Valley National Park
Tiruppur
NH17
Perintalmanna
Coimbatore
Shornur Jn
Kunnamkulam
Palakkad
Pollach
Alathur
Guruvayur
Peechi
Thrissur
Udumalpettai
Peruvanum
Parambikulam
Angamali
Kodungallur
Kalady
Eravikulam National Park
Aluva
Munnar
Nedumbassery
Ernakulam
Devikulam
Bodinayak
Kochi
Muvattapuzha
Chinnamanu
Iduki
Kamban
Vaikom
Ettumanoor
NH47
Periyar WLS
Gudalur
Lakshadweep Sea
Kumarakom
Kanjirapalli
Thekkady
Alappuzha
Kottayam
Peermade
Ambalapuzha
Changanacherry
Kaviyur
Sabarimala
Thiruvalla
Chengannur
Puliangu
Chavara
Kayankulam
Vadckkeula
Shenkott
Tenmalai
Kollam
Kuttalam Fa
Tenka
Ponmudi
Varkala
Nedumangad
Anjengo
Neyyar Dam
Thiruvananthapuram
Kovalam
Padmanabhapuram
A
B
C
1
2
3
N
0 km
50
0 miles
50
The Government of India state that "the external boundaries of India are neither correct nor authenticated"

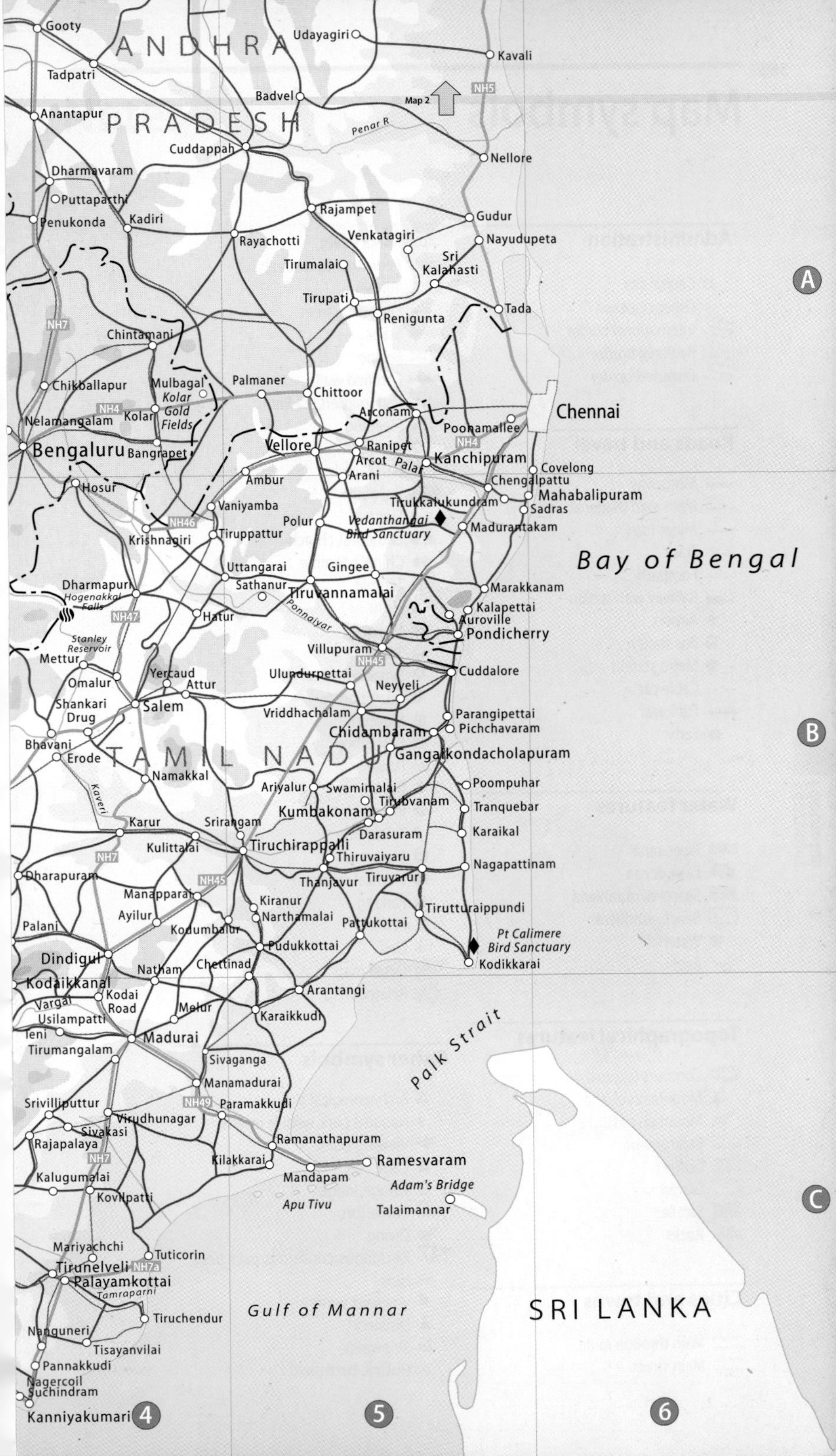

Gooty
ANDHRA
PRADESH
Udayagiri
Kavali
Tadpatri
NH5
Badvel
Map 2
Anantapur
Penar R
Cuddappah
Nellore
Dharmavaram
Puttaparthi
Rajampet
Penukonda
Kadiri
Gudur
Rayachotti
Venkatagiri
Nayudupeta
Tirumalai
Sri Kalahasti
A
Tirupati
Tada
Renigunta
NH7
Chintamani
Chikballapur
Mulbagal
Palmaner
Chittoor
Kolar Gold Fields
NH4
Kolar
Arconam
Chennai
Nelamangalam
Poonamallee
NH4
Bengaluru
Bangrapet
Vellore
Ranipet
Arcot
Palar
Kanchipuram
Covelong
Ambur
Arani
Chengalpattu
Hosur
Mahabalipuram
Tirukkalukundram
Vaniyamba
Sadras
NH46
Polur
Vedanthangai Bird Sanctuary
Madurantakam
Krishnagiri
Tiruppattur
Bay of Bengal
Uttangarai
Gingee
Dharmapuri
Sathanur
Tiruvannamalai
Marakkanam
Hogenakkal Falls
Kalapettai
NH47
Hatur
Ponnaiyar
Auroville
Pondicherry
Stanley Reservoir
Mettur
Villupuram
NH45
Cuddalore
Yercaud
Ulundurpettai
Omalur
Attur
Neyveli
Salem
Shankari Drug
Vriddhachalam
Parangipettai
Pichchavaram
Chidambaram
B
Bhavani
TAMIL NADU
Gangaikondacholapuram
Erode
Namakkal
Poompuhar
Ariyalur
Swamimalai
Kaveri
Tiruvanam
Tranquebar
Kumbakonam
Srirangam
Karur
Karaikal
Darasuram
Kulittalai
Tiruchirappalli
NH7
Thiruvaiyaru
Nagapattinam
Dharapuram
NH45
Thanjavur
Tiruvarur
Manapparai
Kiranur
Tirutturaippundi
Ayilur
Narthamalai
Pattukottai
Palani
Kodumbalur
Pt Calimere Bird Sanctuary
Pudukkottai
Dindigul
Chettinad
Kodikkarai
Natham
Kodaikkanal
Arantangi
Kodai Road
Vargai
Melur
Usilampatti
Karaikkudi
Teni
Madurai
Tirumangalam
Palk Strait
Sivaganga
Manamadurai
NH49
Srivilliputtur
Paramakkudi
Virudhunagar
Sivakasi
Rajapalaya
Ramanathapuram
NH7
Kilakkarai
Ramesvaram
Kalugumalai
Mandapam
Adam's Bridge
Kovilpatti
C
Apu Tivu
Talaimannar
Mariyachchi
Tuticorin
Tirunelveli
NH7a
Palayamkottai
Tamraparni
Gulf of Mannar
SRI LANKA
Tiruchendur
Nanguneri
Tisayanvilai
Pannakkudi
Nagercoil
Suchindram
Kanniyakumari
4
5
6

Complete title listing

Footprint publishes travel guides to over 150 destinations worldwide. Each guide is packed with practical, concise and colourful information for anyone from first-time travellers to travel aficionados. The list is growing fast and current titles are noted below. Available from all good bookshops and online www.footprintbooks.com

(P) denotes pocket guide

Latin America & Caribbean
Antigua & Leeward Islands (P)
Argentina
Barbados (P)
Bolivia
Brazil
Caribbean Islands
Chile
Costa Rica
Cuba
Cuzco & the Inca Heartland
Dominican Republic (P)
Ecuador & Galápagos
Mexico & Central America
Nicaragua
Patagonia
Peru
Peru, Bolivia & Ecuador
South American Handbook

North America
Vancouver (P)
Western Canada

Australasia
Australia
East Coast Australia
New Zealand
Sydney (P)
West Coast Australia

Africa
Cape Town (P)
Egypt
Kenya
Namibia
South Africa
Tanzania

Europe
Andalucía
Antwerp & Ghent (P)
Barcelona (P)
Bilbao (P)
Cardiff (P)
Copenhagen (P)
Costa de la Luz (P)
Croatia
Dublin (P)
Lisbon (P)
London
London (P)
Madrid (P)
Naples (P)
Northern Spain
Reykjavik (P)
Scotland Highlands & Islands
Seville (P)
Siena (P)
Tallinn (P)
Turin (P)
Valencia (P)
Verona (P)

Middle East
Dubai (P)

Asia
Borneo
Cambodia
India
Laos
Malaysia & Singapore
Northeast India
Rajasthan
South India
Sri Lanka
Thailand
Vietnam
Vietnam, Cambodia & Laos

Activity guides
Diving the World
Snowboarding the World
Surfing Britain
Surfing Europe
Surfing the World

Lifestyle guides
Body & Soul Escapes
European City Breaks
Travel with Kids
Travellers Handbook
Wine Travel Guide World

The Footprint Story

It was 1921

Ireland had just been partitioned, the British miners were striking for more pay and the federation of British industry had an idea. Exports were booming in South America – how about a Handbook for businessmen trading in that far away continent? The *Anglo-South American Handbook* was born that year, written by W Koebel, the most prolific writer on Latin America of his day.

1924

Two editions later the book was 'privatized' and in 1924, in the hands of Royal Mail, the steamship company for South America, became *The South American Handbook*, subtitled 'South America in a nutshell'. This annual publication became the 'bible' for generations of travellers to South America and remains so to this day. In the early days travel was by sea and the Handbook gave all the details needed for the long voyage from Europe. What to wear for dinner; how to arrange a cricket match with the Cable & Wireless staff on the Cape Verde Islands and a full account of the journey from Liverpool up the Amazon to Manaus: 5898 miles without changing cabin!

1939

As the continent opened up, *The South American Handbook* reported the new Pan Am flying boat services, and the fortnightly airship service from Rio to Europe on the Graf Zeppelin. For reasons still unclear but with extraordinary determination, the annual editions continued through the Second World War.

1970s

From the 1970s, jet aircraft transformed travel. Many more people discovered South America and the backpacking trail started to develop. All the while the Handbook was gathering fans, including literary vagabonds such as Paul Theroux and Graham Greene (who once sent some updates addressed to **"The publishers of the best travel guide in the world, Bath, England"**.)

1990s

During the 1990s Patrick and James Dawson, the publishers of *The South American Handbook* set about developing a new travel guide series using this legendary title as the flagship. By 1997 there were over a dozen guides in the series and the Footprint imprint was launched.

2000s

In 2003, Footprint launched a new series of pocket guides focusing on short-break European cities. The series grew quickly and there were soon over 100 Footprint travel guides covering more than 150 destinations. In January 2004, *The South American Handbook* reached another milestone as it celebrated its 80th birthday. Later that year, Footprint launched its first Activity guide: *Surfing Europe*, packed with colour photographs, maps and charts. This was followed by further Activity guides such as *Surfing Britain*, *Surfing the World*, *Diving the World*, *Snowboarding the World*, *Body & Soul Escapes* and *Wine Travel Guide to the World*.

The future

There are many more guides in the pipeline. To keep up-to-date with new releases check out the Footprint website for all the latest news and information, **www.footprintbooks.com**

Notes

Goa → Hampi ⇓ Bangalore → Ooty – Fort Kochi